Ethical Theory and Business

Ethical Theory and Business

SIXTH EDITION

Edited by

Tom L. Beauchamp
Georgetown University

Norman E. Bowie
University of Minnesota

Upper Saddle River, New Jersey 07458

Library of Congress Cataloging-in-Publication Data

Ethical theory and business / edited by Tom L. Beauchamp, Norman E.
   Bowie.—6th ed.
       p. cm.
     Includes bibliographical references.
     ISBN 0–13–083144–1
       1. Business ethics—United States. 2. Business ethics—United
States—Case studies. 3. Industries—Social aspects—United States.
4. Industries—Social aspects—United States—Case studies.
5. Commercial crimes—United States—Cases. 6. Consumer protection—
Law and legislation—United States—Cases. I. Beauchamp, Tom L.
II. Bowie, Norman E.
HF5387.E82 2001
174′.4—dc21   00–033643
                                                                        CIP

This book was set in 10/12 Baskerville by Pine Tree Composition, Inc.,
and was printed and bound by R R Donnelley & Sons Company.
The cover was printed by Phoenix Color Corp.

Editorial director: *Charlyce Jones Owen*
Managing editor: *Jan Stephan*
Acquisitions editor: *Katie Janssen*
Production liaison: *Fran Russello*
Editorial/production supervision
   and interior design: *Bruce Hobart (Pine Tree Composition)*
Marketing manager: *Don Allmon*
Cover art director: *Jayne Conte*
Cover design: *Kiwi Design*
Prepress and manufacturing buyer: *Sherry Lewis*

© 2001, 1997, 1993, 1988, 1983, 1979 by Prentice-Hall, Inc.
A Division of Pearson Education
Upper Saddle River, New Jersey 07458

Printed in the United States of America

10 9 8 7 6 5 4 3 2 1

ISBN 0-13-083144-1

Prentice-Hall International (UK) Limited, *London*
Prentice-Hall of Australia Pty. Limited, *Sydney*
Prentice-Hall Canada Inc., *Toronto*
Prentice-Hall Hispanoamericana, S.A., *Mexico*
Prentice-Hall of India Private Limited, *New Delhi*
Prentice-Hall of Japan, Inc., *Tokyo*
Pearson Education Asia Pte. Ltd., *Singapore*
Editora Prentice-Hall do Brasil, Ltda., *Rio de Janeiro*

Contents

LEGAL PERSPECTIVES

CASES

Chapter Six
HIRING, FIRING, AND DISCRIMINATING   369

INTRODUCTION

AFFIRMATIVE ACTION AND REVERSE DISCRIMINATION

PAY EQUITY AND COMPARABLE WORTH

SEXUAL HARASSMENT

LEGAL PERSPECTIVES

CASES

Chapter Seven
MARKETING AND DISCLOSURE   455

INTRODUCTION

MARKETING, TRUTH, AND TRUST

ADVERTISING

SALES

BLUFFING

LEGAL PERSPECTIVES

CASES

Chapter Eight
ETHICAL ISSUES IN INTERNATIONAL BUSINESS   527

INTRODUCTION

WHEN IN ROME, SHOULD YOU DO AS THE ROMANS DO?

BRIBERY

CAPITALISM IN THE THIRD WORLD

LEGAL PERSPECTIVES

Chapter Nine
SOCIAL AND ECONOMIC JUSTICE   641

INTRODUCTION

THEORIES OF SOCIAL JUSTICE

INTERNATIONAL ECONOMIC JUSTICE

LEGAL PERSPECTIVES

CASES

Preface

We are delighted that *Ethical Theory and Business* has continued into the new millennium. The continued good fortune of this book is made possible by the many comments and suggestions that loyal readers have given us over more than a quarter of a century.

As the field of business ethics has matured, there has been an increased stability in the topics discussed. Nonetheless, the field is moving forward and we try to select readings that reflect those changes. Several changes simply update the discussion of topics in earlier editions. We do note that philosophers are taking empirical work in the field more seriously and that turn of events is reflected in some of the readings that we have chosen. Two of the areas where change is most noticeable are in the areas of employee rights and international business ethics. Advances in technology have increased the pressures on business to use that technology to improve the bottom line even if it comes at the cost of violating privacy. We have added an article on the electronic surveillance of employees and another article on the use of genetic testing in hiring decisions. In the international arena, discussions of bribery are not limited to the implications of the Foreign Corrupt Practices Act. In addition the alleged sweatshop conditions in factories that supply the developed world with cheap textiles and other goods have become a concern on college campuses and in the business press. Thoughtful people are also asking whether the western industrialized version of capitalism will work everywhere, and some even wonder if capitalism has a contribution to make in the less developed countries. These issues are introduced in the chapter on international business ethics.

As we enter a new decade, we are not sure which topics in business ethics will receive the most attention. We might speculate that the present concern about genetically altered foods in Europe might become a concern in the U.S. as well. However, as the field develops, we pledge that we will continue to reflect those changes in future editions.

As in the past, several persons deserve special recognition for their assistance in preparing this edition. Three anonymous reviewers provided Prentice Hall and us with valuable suggestions for updating the book. In addition we are thankful for the comments of Denis Arnold, Thomas Carson, Michael DeWilde, Mark W. Matthews, and Barbara McGraw.

In this edition, we have been ably assisted by Padma Shah, Mark Gaspers, and Michael Hammer—three student research assistants who exceeded their duties in searching data bases, locating new materials, and suggesting many changes to make the book useful for students. Special thanks go to Scott Reynolds, a doctoral candidate in business ethics at the University of Minnesota, who has provided library research, editorial assistance, and obtained permission to reprint many of the articles in this edition. Permission for the other articles was obtained by Moheba Hanif, who worked on manuscript preparation from the beginning of the project and made manuscript corrections for five of the nine chapters.

Tom L. Beauchamp
Norman E. Bowie

Chapter One

Ethical Theory and Business Practice

C AN LARGE BUSINESS ORGANIZATIONS be just? Should the chief obligation of business be to look out for the bottom line? Is nonvoluntary employee drug testing immoral? How far should business go to protect and preserve the environment? These are some of the many questions that permeate discussions of the role of ethics in business.

The essays and cases in this book provide an opportunity to discuss these questions by reading and reflecting on influential arguments that have been made on these subjects. The goal of this first chapter is to provide a foundation in ethical theory sufficient for reading and critically evaluating the material in the ensuing chapters. The first part of this chapter introduces basic and recurring distinctions, definitions, and issues. The second part examines influential and relevant types of normative ethical theory. The third part discusses "the case method" as an exercise in moral reflection.

FUNDAMENTAL CONCEPTS AND PROBLEMS

Morality and Ethical Theory

A distinction between morality and ethical theory runs throughout this volume. Attention to this distinction is important because in classroom discussions of business ethics, the various participants may use these terms in incompatible ways. The term *morality* refers to the principles or rules of moral conduct. Thus, the term *morality* has a broad meaning that extends beyond the rules in professional codes of conduct adopted by corporations and professional associations. Morality is concerned with social practices defining right and wrong. These practices, together with other kinds of customs, rules, and mores, are transmitted within cultures and institutions from generation to generation. Similar to political constitutions and natural languages, morality exists prior to the acceptance (or rejection) of its standards by particular individuals. In this respect morality cannot be purely a personal policy or code.

In contrast to *morality,* the terms *ethical theory* and *moral philosophy* suggest reflection on the nature and justification of right actions. These words refer to attempts to introduce clarity, substance, and precision of argument into the domain of morality. Although many people go through life with an understanding of morality dictated by their culture, other persons are not satisfied simply to conform to the morality of society. They want difficult questions answered: Is what our society forbids wrong? Are social values the best values? What is the purpose of morality? Does religion have anything to do with morality? Do the moral rules of society fit together in a unified whole? If there are conflicts and inconsistencies in our practices and beliefs, how should they be resolved? What should people do when facing a moral problem for which society has, as yet, provided no instruction?

Moral philosophers seek to answer such questions and to put moral beliefs and social practices of morality into a unified and defensible shape. Sometimes this task involves challenging traditional moral beliefs by assessing the quality of moral arguments and suggesting modifications in existing beliefs. Morality, we might say, consists of what persons ought to do in order to conform to society's norms of behavior, whereas ethical theory concerns the philosophical reasons for and against aspects of the morality stipulated by society. Usually the latter effort centers on *justification:* Philosophers seek to justify a system of standards or some moral point of view on the basis of carefully analyzed and defended concepts and principles such as respect for autonomy, distributive justice, equal treatment, human rights, beneficence, and truthfulness.

Most moral principles are already embedded in public morality, but usually in a vague and underanalyzed form. Justice is a good example. Recurrent topics in the pages of the *Wall Street Journal, Fortune, Business Week,* and other leading business journals often discuss the justice of the present system of corporate and individual taxation as well as the salaries paid to chief executive officers. However, an extended or detailed analysis of principles of justice is virtually never provided in the media. Such matters are left at an intuitive level, where the correctness of a moral point of view is assumed, without argumentation. Yet the failure to provide anything more than a superficial justification, in terms of intuitive principles learned from parents or peers, leaves people unable to defend their principles when challenged. In a society with many diverse views of morality, one can be fairly sure that one's principles will be challenged.

Thus, the terms *ethical theory, philosophical ethics,* and even *moral philosophy* are reserved for philosophical theories that include reflection on and criticism of social morality. Although many people distinguish *ethics* and *morality,* philosophers tend to use *ethics* as a general term referring to both moral beliefs and ethical theories. This practice is followed in this book.

Morality and Prudence

Many students do not encounter moral philosophy as a topic of study until college or graduate school. Morality, however, is learned by virtually every young child as part of the acculturation process. The first step in this process is learning to distinguish moral rules from rules of prudence (self-interest). This task can be difficult, because the two kinds of rules are taught simultaneously, without being distinguished by the children's teachers. For example, people are constantly reminded in their early years to observe rules such as, "Don't touch the hot stove," "Don't cross the street without looking both ways," "Brush your teeth after meals," and "Eat your vegetables." Most of these oughts and ought nots are instructions in self-interest; that is, they are instructions in prudence. At the same time, however, people are given oughts or ought-nots of a moral kind. Parents, teachers, and peers teach that certain things *ought not* to be done because they are "wrong" and that certain things *ought* to be done because they are "right." "Don't pull your sister's hair." "Don't take money from your mother's pocketbook." "Share your toys." "Write a thank-you note to Grandma." These moral instructions seek to control actions that affect the interests of other people. As people mature, they learn what society expects of them in terms of taking into account the interests of other people.

One of the most common observations in business is that self-interest and good ethics generally coincide, because it is usually in one's interest to act morally. This fact makes evaluating another's conduct difficult and may tend to confuse moral reasoning with prudential reasoning. A simple example of moral and prudential reasoning run together in business is found in the decision of the Marriott Corporation to make a concerted effort to hire persons who had been on welfare. These individuals had often been considered high-risk as employees, but changes in the U.S. welfare system in the late 1990s forced many welfare recipients to seek work. Marriott was one of the few major companies to take the initiative to hire them in large numbers. Such behavior might be considered an example of moral goodwill and ethical altruism. Although corporate officials at Marriott clearly believed that their decision was ethically sound and promoted the public good, they also believed that their initiative to hire former welfare recipients was good business and that the hiring was done for that purpose. J. W. Marriott Jr. said, "We're getting good employees for the long term, but we're also helping these communities. If we don't step up in these inner cities and provide work, they'll never pull out of it. But it makes bottom line sense. If it didn't, we wouldn't do it."[1]

The mixture of moral language with the language of prudence is often harmless. Many people are more concerned about the *actions* businesses take than with their *motivations* to perform those actions. These people will be indifferent as to whether businesses use the language of prudence or the language of morality to justify what they do. This distinction between motives and actions is very important to philosophers, however, because a business practice that might be prudentially justified may lack moral merit and may even be morally wrong. History has shown how some actions that were long accepted or at least condoned in the business community were eventually condemned as immoral, for example, the discharge of pollution into the air and water, plant relocation purely for economic gain, and large political contributions to people of influence.

Businesspeople often reflect on the morality of their actions not because it is prudent to do so but because it is right to do so. For example, Elo TouchSystems, Inc., a subsidiary of Raychem Corporation that manufactures computer and other monitors, decided to relocate the company from Oak Ridge, Tennessee, to

Freemont, California. As a matter of fidelity to its 300 employees, the company attempted to find new jobs for them in the Oak Ridge area by placing advertisements, sponsoring job fairs, and the like. It also offered generous bonuses for those who would relocate to California. In light of the pool of talent known to the company to be available in California, none of this activity in Tennessee seemed in the company's prudential interest. It simply seemed the morally appropriate policy.

It is widely believed that acting morally is in the interest of business, and thus prudence seems to be a strong motive for acting ethically. However, throughout this text we will repeatedly see that prudence often dictates a different business decision than does morality.

Morality and Law

Business ethics in the United States is currently involved in an entangled, complex, and mutually stimulating relationship with law, as is illustrated in the legal cases reprinted near the end of the following chapters. Morality and law share concerns over matters of basic social importance and often have in common certain principles, obligations, and criteria of evidence. Law is the public's agency for translating morality into explicit social guidelines and practices and for stipulating punishments for offenses. Chapter selections mention both case law (judge-made law expressed in court decisions) and statutory law (federal and state statutes and their accompanying administrative regulations). In these forms law has forced vital issues before the public. Case law, in particular, has established influential precedents that provide material for reflection on both legal and moral questions.

Some have said that corporate concern about business ethics can be reduced or eliminated by turning problems over to the legal department. The operative idea is, "Let the lawyers decide; if it's legal, it's moral." Although this tactic would simplify matters, moral evaluation needs to be distinguished from legal evaluation. Despite an intersection between morals and law, the law is not the repository of a society's moral standards and values, even when the law is directly concerned with moral problems. A law-abiding person is not necessarily morally sensitive or virtuous, and the fact that something is legally acceptable does not imply that it is morally acceptable. For example, the doctrine of employment at will permits employers to fire employees for unjust reasons and is (within certain limits) legal, yet such firings are often morally unacceptable. Again, questions are raised in later chapters about the morality of business actions, such as plant relocation and mergers that cause unemployment, even though such actions are not illegal.

A typical example is the following: It was perfectly legal when Houston financier Charles E. Hurwitz doubled the rate of tree cutting in the nation's largest privately owned virgin redwood forest. He did so to reduce the debt he incurred when his company, the Maxxam Group, borrowed money to complete successfully a hostile takeover of Pacific Lumber Company, which owned the redwoods. Before the takeover, Pacific Lumber had followed a conservative cutting policy but nonetheless had consistently operated at a profit. Despite the legality of the new clear-cutting policy initiated by the new owner, it has been criticized as immoral.[2]

A related problem involves the belief that a person found guilty under law is therefore morally guilty. Such judgments are not necessarily correct but rather depend on the moral acceptability of the law on which the judgment has been reached. For example, before the Foreign Corrupt Practices Act was signed into law by President Jimmy Carter, slush funds, bribes, and the like had not been illegal for U.S. corporations dealing with foreign governments. Ever since the new legislation was enacted, an intense and still ongoing debate has surrounded the act's implications. It served to frustrate many businesses whose now illegal practices were deemed not only acceptable but also necessary to the conduct of business in various foreign cultures. Many businesspeople believe that the act put U.S. business firms at a competitive disadvantage, because other industrialized countries have no such laws. Many people today still believe there is nothing unethical or morally corrupt in these illegal acts. The real problem, they contend, is a shortsightedness in the legislation.

Furthermore, the courts have often been accused, with some justification, of causing moral inequities through court judgments rendered against corporations. Here are some examples:[3] (1) Monsanto Chemical was successfully sued for $200 million, although the presiding judge asserted that there was no credible evidence linking Monsanto's Agent Orange to the severe harms that had been described in the case. (2) Chevron Oil was successfully sued for mislabeling its cans of paraquat, although the offending label conformed exactly to federal regulations, which permitted no other form of label to be used. (3) Although whooping cough vaccine indisputably reduces the risk of this disease for children who receive the vaccine, almost no manufacturer will produce it for fear of costly suits brought under product liability laws.

In each of these instances it is easy to understand why critics have considered as morally unjustified various regulations, legislation, and case-law decisions. Taken together, these considerations lead to the following conclusion: If something is legal, it is not necessarily moral; if something is illegal, it is not necessarily immoral. Certainly to discharge one's legal responsibilities is not necessarily to discharge one's moral responsibilities.

The Rule of Conscience

The slogan "Let your conscience be your guide" has long been, for many, what morality is all about. Yet, despite their admiration for persons of conscience, philosophers have typically judged appeals to conscience as alone insufficient and untrustworthy for ethical judgment. Consciences vary radically from person to person and time to time; moreover, they are often altered by circumstance, religious belief, childhood, and training. One example is found in Stanley Kresge, the son of the founder of S. S. Kresge Company — now known as the Kmart Corporation — who is a teetotaler for religious reasons. When the company started selling beer and wine, Kresge sold all his stock. His conscience, he said, would not let him make a profit on alcohol. The company, though, dismissed his objection as "his own business" and said that it sees nothing wrong with earning profits on alcohol.[4] A second example is found in many individuals who believe that business has been conducted in ways that damage the environment. These feelings are particularly strong in the Pacific Northwest where the lumber industry has allegedly threatened endangered species such as the spotted owl. The consciences of members of Earth First have been so aroused that they have engaged in acts of eco-terrorism such as putting large spikes in trees that can injure loggers who are cutting them. The members of Earth First believe that they are acting as required by conscience. But whether their acts are morally acceptable is seriously in doubt.

The reliability of conscience, then, is not self-certifying. Moral justification must be based on a source external to conscience itself. This external source is often the common morality or ethical theory, as we shall see.

Approaches to the Study of Morality

Morality and ethical theory can be studied and developed by a variety of methods, but three general approaches have dominated the literature. Two of these approaches describe and analyze morality, presumably without taking moral positions. The other approach takes a moral position and appeals to morality or ethical theory to underwrite judgments. These three approaches can be outlined as follows:

> Descriptive approaches
> Conceptual approaches
> Prescriptive (normative) approaches

These categories do not express rigid and always clearly distinguishable approaches. Nonetheless, when understood as broad, polar, and contrasting positions, they can serve as models of inquiry and as valuable distinctions.

Social scientists often refer to the *descriptive approach* as the *scientific study* of ethics. Factual description and explanation of moral behavior and beliefs, as performed by anthropologists, sociologists, and historians, are typical of this approach. Moral attitudes, codes, and beliefs that are described include corporate policies on sexual harassment and codes of ethics in trade associations. Examples of this approach can be found in *Harvard Business Review* articles and *Forbes* magazine polls that report what business executives believe is morally acceptable and unacceptable.

The second approach involves the *conceptual study* of ethics. Here, the meanings of central terms in ethics such as *right, obligation, justice, good, virtue,* and *responsibility* are analyzed. Crucial terms in business ethics such as *liability* and *deception* can be given this same kind of careful conceptual attention. The proper analysis of the term *morality* (as defined at the beginning of this chapter) and the distinction between the moral and the nonmoral are typical examples of these conceptual problems.

The third approach, *prescriptive or normative ethics,* is a prescriptive study attempting to formulate and defend basic moral norms. Normative moral philosophy aims at determining what *ought* to be done, which needs to be distinguished from what *is,* in fact, practiced. Ideally, an ethical theory provides reasons for adopting a whole system of moral principles or virtues. *Utilitarianism* and *Kantianism* are widely discussed theories, but they are not the only such theories. Utilitarians argue that there is but a single fundamental principle determining right action, which can be roughly stated as follows: "An action is morally right if and only if it produces at least as great a balance of value over disvalue as any available alternative action." Kantians, by contrast, have argued for principles that specify duties rather than a balance of value. For example, one of Kant's best known principles of obligation is "Never treat another person merely as a means to your own goals," even if doing so creates a net balance of positive value. Both forms of these theories, together with other dimensions of ethical theory, are examined in the second part of this chapter.

Principles of normative ethics are commonly used to treat specific moral problems such as abortion, famine, conflict of interest, mistreatment of animals, and racial and sexual discrimination. This use of ethical theory is often referred to, somewhat misleadingly, as *applied ethics.* Philosophical treatment of medical ethics, engineering ethics, journalistic ethics, jurisprudence, and business ethics involves distinct areas that employ general ethical principles to attempt to resolve moral problems that commonly arise in the professions.

Substantially the same general ethical principles apply to the problems across professional fields and in areas beyond professional ethics as well. One might appeal to principles of justice, for example, to illuminate and resolve issues of taxation, health care distribution, environmental responsibility, criminal punishment, and racial discrimination. Similarly, principles of veracity (truthfulness) apply to debates about secrecy and deception in international politics, misleading advertisements in business ethics, balanced reporting in journalistic ethics, and disclosure of illness to a patient in medical ethics. Increased clarity about the general conditions under which truth must be told and when it may be withheld would presumably enhance understanding of moral requirements in each of these areas.

The exercise of sound judgment in business practice together with appeals to ethical theory are central in the essays and cases in this volume. Rarely is there a straightforward "application" of principles that mechanically resolves problems. Principles are more commonly *specified,* that is, made more concrete for the context, than applied. Much of the best work in contemporary business ethics involves arguments for how to specify principles to handle particular problems.

Relativism and Objectivity of Belief

Some writers have contended that moral views simply express the ways in which a culture accommodates the desires of its people. Cultural relativists note that moral standards vary from place to place. In the early part of the twentieth century, defenders of relativism used the discoveries of anthropologists in the South Sea Islands, Africa, and South America as evidence of a diversity of moral practices throughout the world. Their empirical discoveries about what is the case led them to the conclusion that rightness is contingent on cultural beliefs and that the concepts of rightness and wrongness are meaningless apart from the specific contexts in which they arise. The claim is that patterns of culture can only be understood as unique wholes and that moral beliefs about normal behavior are closely connected in a culture.

These descriptive claims about what is the case in cultures have often been used to justify a *normative* position known as ethical relativism. Ethical relativism asserts that whatever a culture thinks is right or wrong really is right or wrong for the members of that culture. Thus, if the Swedish tradition allows abortion, then abortion really is morally permissible in Sweden. If the Irish tradition forbids abortion, then abortion really is wrong in Ireland. If ethical relativism is correct, then there is no criterion independent of one's culture for determining whether a practice really is right or wrong.

Ethical relativism provides a theoretical basis for those who challenge what they consider to be the imposition of Western values on the rest of the world. Specifically, some spokespersons in Asia have criticized what they regard as the attempts of westerners to impose their values on Asian societies. Despite the influence of relativism and multiculturalism, there have been many recent attempts by both government agencies and multinational corporations to promulgate international codes of business conduct that surmount relativism (see Chapter 8). Moreover, moral philosophers have tended to reject relativism, and it is important to understand why. First they ask, what does the argument from the fact of cultural diversity reveal? When early anthropologists probed beneath surface "moral" disagreements, they often discovered agreement at deeper levels on more basic values.

For example, one anthropologist discovered a tribe in which parents, after raising their children and when still in a relatively healthy state, would climb a high tree. Their children would then shake the tree until the parents fell to the ground and died. This cultural practice seems vastly different from Western practices. The anthropologist discovered, however, that the tribe believed that people went into the afterlife in the same bodily state in which they left this life. Their children, who wanted them to enter the afterlife in a healthy state, were no less concerned about their parents than are children in Western cultures. Although cultural disagreement exists concerning the afterlife, there is no ultimate moral disagreement over the moral principles determining how children should treat their parents.

Thus, despite differing practices and beliefs, people often actually agree about ultimate moral standards. For example, both Germany and the United States have laws to protect consumers from the adverse affects of new drugs and to bring drugs to the market as quickly as possible so that lives are saved. Yet Germany and the United States have different standards for making the tradeoff between protecting from side effects and saving lives as soon as possible. This suggests that two cultures may agree about basic principles of morality (which is a solid basis for rejecting at least descriptive relativism), yet disagree about how to live by those principles in particular situations.

This analysis implies that a fundamental conflict between cultural values could occur only if cultural disagreements about proper principles or rules exist at the deepest level of moral rules. It does not follow that underlying moral standards differ even if beliefs, judgments, and actions differ. People may differ only because they have different factual beliefs. For instance, individuals often differ over appropriate actions to protect the environment, not because they have different sets of standards about environmental ethics but because they hold different factual views about how certain discharges of chemicals and airborne particles will or will not harm the environment. Identical sets of normative standards might be invoked in their arguments about environmental protection, yet different policies and actions might be recommended.

It is therefore important to distinguish *relativism of judgments* from *relativism of standards*. This distinction rests on the fact that many different particular judgments call upon the same general standards for their justification. Moreover, relativism of judgment is so pervasive in human social life that it would be foolish to deny it. However, when people differ about whether to buy one brand of telephone over another, it does not follow that they have different standards for telephones. Perhaps one person has had success with AT&T products in the past, whereas another person has not. Similarly in ethics, people may differ about whether one policy for keeping hospital information confidential is more acceptable than another, but it does not follow that they have different moral standards of confidentiality. The people may hold the same moral standard on protecting confidentiality but differ over how to implement that standard.

However, these observations do not decide whether a relativism of standards provides the most adequate account of morality. If moral conflict did turn out to be fundamental, such conflict could not be removed even if there were perfect agreement about the facts, concepts, and background beliefs of a case.

Suppose, then, that disagreement exists at the deepest level of moral thinking, that is, suppose that two cultures disagree on basic or fundamental norms. It still does not follow from this relativity of standards that there is no ultimate norm or set of norms in which everyone *ought* to believe. Consider the following analogy to religious disagreement: From the fact that people have incompatible religious or atheistic beliefs, it does not follow that there is no single correct set of religious or atheistic propositions. Nothing more than skepticism seems justified by the facts about religion that are adduced by anthropology; and nothing more than this skepticism would be justified if fundamental conflicts of belief were discovered in ethics.

A Pragmatic Argument Against Cultural Relativism. If ethical relativism were accepted, serious reflection on, and resolution of, moral problems would be impossible. Yet, in circumstances of disagreement, moral reflection is in order whether or not ethical relativism is true. When two parties argue about some serious, divisive, and contested moral issue — for example, conflicts of interest in business —

people tend to think that some fair and justified compromise may be reached. People seldom infer from the mere fact of a conflict between beliefs that there is no way to judge one view as correct or as better argued than the other. The more absurd the position advanced by one party, the more convinced others become that some views are mistaken or require supplementation. People seldom conclude that there is no correct ethical perspective or reasonable negotiation.

Moreover, it seems that there is a set of basic moral principles that every culture must adopt. There would be no culture unless the members of the group adopted these moral principles. Consider an anthropologist who arrives on a populated island: How many tribes are on the island? To answer that question, the anthropologist tries to determine whether people on some parts of the island are permitted to kill, commit acts of violence against, or steal from persons on other parts of the island. If such behavior is not permitted, that prohibition counts as a reason for saying that there is only one tribe. The underlying assumption is that a set of moral principles exists that must be followed if there is to be a culture at all.

Moral Disagreements

Even if ethical relativism is unacceptable, we still must confront the indisputable fact of moral disagreement. In any pluralistic culture many conflicts of value exist. In this volume several controversies and dilemmas are examined, such as withholding pertinent information in business deals, whistleblowing in industry, advertising on children's television, practicing preferential hiring policies, and the like. Although some disagreements seem overwhelming, there are ways to resolve them or at least to reduce the level of disagreement. Several methods have been employed in the past to deal constructively with moral disagreements, each of which deserves recognition as a method of easing disagreement and conflict.

Obtaining Objective Information. Many moral disagreements can be at least partially resolved by obtaining additional factual information on which moral controversies turn. Earlier it was shown how useful such information can be in trying to ascertain whether cultural variations in belief are fundamental. Unfortunately, it has often been assumed that moral disputes are by definition produced solely by differences over moral principles or their application and not by a lack of scientific or factual information. This assumption is misleading, inasmuch as moral disputes — that is, disputes over what morally ought or ought not to be done — often have nonmoral elements as their main ingredients. For example, debates over the allocation of tax dollars to prevent accidents or disease in the workplace often become bogged down in factual issues of whether particular measures such as the use of masks or lower levels of toxic chemicals actually function best to prevent death and disease.

Yet another example is provided by the dispute between Greenpeace and Royal Dutch Shell. After considerable investigation, Royal Dutch Shell proposed to sink a loading and storage buoy for oil in the North Sea (off England). Despite some evidence that such an operation posed no environmental danger, Greenpeace conducted protests and even used an armada of small boats to thwart the attempt. Royal Dutch Shell yielded to its critics, and the buoy was cut up and made into a quay in Norway. Later, however, even Greenpeace was forced to admit that new facts indicated that there had never been any serious environmental danger.

Controversial issues such as the use of new sweeteners in diet sodas; the presence of toxic substances in the workplace; the fluoridation of public waters; and the manufacture, dissemination, and advertisement of vaccines for medical use are laced with issues of both values and facts. The arguments used by disagreeing parties may turn on a dispute about liberty or justice and therefore may be primarily moral; but they may also rest on factual disagreements over, for example, the efficacy of a product. Information may thus have only a limited bearing on the resolution of some controversies, yet it may have a direct and almost overpowering influence in others.

Definitional Clarity. Sometimes controversies have been settled by reaching conceptual or definitional agreement over the language used by disputing parties. Controversies discussed in Chapter 6 over the morality of affirmative action, reverse discrimination, and comparable worth, for example, are often needlessly complicated because different senses of these expressions are employed, and yet disputing parties may have much invested in their particular definitions. If there is no common point of contention in such cases, parties will be addressing entirely separate issues through their conceptual assumptions. Often these parties will not have a bona fide moral disagreement.

Although conceptual agreement provides no guarantee that a dispute will be settled, it will facilitate direct discussion of the outstanding issues. For this reason, many essays in this volume dwell at some length on problems of conceptual clarity.

Example–Counterexample. Resolution of moral controversies can also be aided by posing examples and opposed counterexamples, that is, by bringing forward cases or examples that are favorable to one point of view and counterexamples that are in opposition. For instance, in a famous case against AT&T a dispute over discriminatory hiring and promotion between the company and the Equal Employment Opportunities Commission (EEOC) was handled through the citation of statistics and examples that (allegedly) documented the claims made by each side. AT&T showed that 55 percent of the employees on its payroll were women and that 33 percent of all management positions were held by women. To sharpen its allegation of discriminatory practices in the face of this evidence, the EEOC countered by citing a government study demonstrating that 99 percent of all telephone operators were female, whereas only 1 percent of craft workers were female. Such use of example and counterexample serves to weigh the strength of conflicting considerations.

Analysis of Arguments and Positions. Finally, a serviceable method of philosophical inquiry is that of exposing the inadequacies in and unexpected consequences of arguments and positions. A moral argument that leads to conclusions that a proponent is not prepared to defend and did not previously anticipate will have to be changed, and the distance between those who disagree will perhaps be reduced by this process. Inconsistencies not only in reasoning but also in organizational schemes or pronouncements can be uncovered. However, in a context of controversy, sharp attacks or critiques are unlikely to eventuate in an agreement unless a climate of reason prevails. A fundamental axiom of successful negotiation is "reason and be open to reason." The axiom holds for moral discussion as well as any other disagreement.

No contention is made here that moral disagreements can always be resolved or that every reasonable person must accept the same method for approaching such problems. Many moral disagreements may not be resolvable by any of the four methods that have been discussed. A single ethical theory or method may never be developed to resolve all disagreements adequately, and the pluralism of cultural beliefs often presents a considerable barrier to the resolution of issues. Given the possibility of continual disagreement, the resolution of crosscultural conflicts such as those faced by multinational corporations may prove especially elusive. However, if something is to be done about these problems, a resolution seems more likely to occur if the methods outlined in this section are used.

The Problem of Egoism

Attitudes in business have often been deemed fundamentally egoistic. Executives and corporations are said to act from prudence — that is, each business is out to promote solely its own interest. Some people say that the corporation has no other interest, because its goal is to be as successful in competition as possible.

The philosophical theory called *egoism* has familiar origins. Each person has been confronted, for example, with occasions on which a choice must be made between spending money on oneself or on some worthy charitable enterprise. When one elects to purchase new clothes for oneself rather than contribute to a university scholarship fund for poor students, self-interest is being given priority over the interests of others. Egoism generalizes beyond these occasions to all human choices. The egoist contends that all choices either involve or should involve self-promotion as their sole objective. Thus, a person's or a corporation's goal and perhaps only obligation is self-promotion. No sacrifices or obligations are owed to others.

Psychological Egoism. There are two main varieties of egoism: psychological egoism and ethical egoism. Psychological egoism is the view that everyone is always motivated to act in his or her perceived self-interest. This factual theory regarding human motivation offers an explanation of human conduct, in contrast to a justification of human conduct. It claims that people always do what pleases them or what is in their interest. Popular ways of expressing this viewpoint include the following: "People are at heart selfish, even if they appear to be unselfish"; "People look out for Number One first"; "In the long run, everybody does what he or she wants to do"; and "No matter what a person says, he or she acts for the sake of personal satisfaction."

Psychological egoism presents a serious challenge to moral philosophy. If this theory is correct, there may be no purely altruistic moral motivation. Normative ethics (with the exception of ethical egoism) presupposes that people ought to behave in accordance with certain moral principles, whether or not such behavior promotes their own interests. If people *must act* in their own interest, to ask them to do otherwise would be absurd. Accordingly, if psychological egoism is true, the whole enterprise of normative ethics is futile.

Those who accept psychological egoism are convinced by their observation of themselves and others that people are entirely self-centered in their motivation. Conversely, those who reject the theory do so not only because they see many examples of altruistic behavior in the lives of friends, saints, heroes, and public servants, but also because contemporary anthropology, psychology, and biology offer many compelling studies of sacrificial behavior. Even if it is conceded that people are basically selfish, critics of egoism maintain that there are at least some outstanding examples of preeminently unselfish actions such as when corporations cut profits in order to provide public services (see Chapter 2) and when employees "blow the whistle" on unsafe or otherwise improper business practices even though they could lose their jobs and suffer social ostracism (see Chapter 5).

The defender of psychological egoism is not impressed by the exemplary lives of saints and heroes or by social practices of corporate sacrifice. The psychological egoist maintains that all those persons who expend effort to help others, to promote fairness in competition, to promote the general welfare, or to risk their lives for the welfare of others are really acting to promote themselves. By sacrificing for their children, parents receive satisfaction in their children's promise or achievements. By following society's moral and legal codes, people avoid both the police and social ostracism.

Egoists maintain that no matter how self-sacrificing a person's behavior may at times seem, the desire behind the action is self-regarding. One is ultimately out for oneself, whether in the long or the short run, and whether one realizes it or not. Egoists view egoistic actions as perfectly compatible with behavior that others categorize as altruistic. For example, many corporations have adopted "enlightened self-interest" policies through which they are responsive to community needs and promote worker satisfaction to promote their corporate image and ultimately their earnings. The clever person or corporation can appear to be unselfish, but the action's true character depends on the *motivation* behind the appearance. Apparently altruistic agents may simply believe that an unselfish appearance best promotes their long-range interests. From the egoist's point of view, the fact that some (pseudo?) sacrifices may be necessary in the short run does not count against egoism.

Consider a typical example. In mid-1985 Illinois Bell argued before the Illinois Commerce Commission that its competitors should be allowed full access to markets and that there should be no regulation to protect Illinois Bell from its competitors. Illinois Bell had long been protected by such regulation, under which it had grown to be a successful $2.7 billion company. Why, then, was it now arguing that a complete free market would be the fairest business arrangement? *Forbes* magazine asked, "Is this 'altruism' or is it 'enlightened self-interest'?" *Forbes* editors answered that, despite the appearance of altruism, what Illinois Bell wanted was "to get the state regulators off their backs" so that the company would be able to compete more successfully with fewer constraints and to avoid losing business to large companies that could set up their own telephone systems. Self-interest, not fairness, was, according to *Forbes*, the proper explanation of Illinois Bell's behavior.[5]

Even if Illinois Bell's behavior is best explained as motivated by self-interest, it need not follow that all human behavior can best be explained as motivated by self-interest. The question remains, is psychological egoism correct? At one level this question can be answered only by empirical data — by looking at the facts. Significantly, there is a large body of evidence both from observations of daily practice and from experiments in psychological laboratories that counts against the universality of egoistic motivation.[6] The evidence from daily practice is not limited to heroic action but includes such mundane practices as voting and leaving tips in restaurants and hotels where a person does not expect to return and has nothing to gain.

When confronted with such conflicting empirical data, the dispute often is raised from the empirical level to the conceptual. It is tempting for the psychological egoist to make the theory *necessarily true* because of the difficulties in proving it to be *empirically* true. When confronted with what look like altruistic acts, egoists may appeal to unconscious motives of self-interest or claim that every act is based on some desire of the person performing the act and that acting on that desire is what is meant by *self-interest.*

The latter explanation seems to be a conceptual or verbal trick: The egoist has changed the meaning of *self-interest.* At first, *self-interest* meant "acting exclusively on behalf of one's own self-serving interest." Now the word has been redefined to mean "acting on any interest one has." Yet the central questions remain unresolved: Are there different kinds of human motives? Do people sometimes have an interest in acting for themselves and at other times on behalf of others, or do people act only for themselves? Philosophy and psychology have yet to establish that people never act contrary to perceived self-interest; for this reason psychological egoism remains a speculative hypothesis.

Ethical Egoism. Ethical egoism is a theory stating that the only valid standard of conduct is the obligation to promote one's well-being above everyone else's. Whereas psychological egoism is a descriptive psychological theory about human motivation, ethical egoism is a normative theory about what people ought to do. According to psychological egoism, people always *do* act on the basis of perceived self-interest. According to ethical egoism, people always *ought* to act on the basis of perceived self-interest.

Ethical egoism is dramatically different from common morality. Consider maxims such as, "You're a sucker if you don't put yourself first and others second." This maxim is unacceptable by the norms of common morality, which require that people return a lost wallet to a known owner and that they correct a bank loan officer's errors in their favor. Nevertheless, questions about why people should look out for the interests of others on such occasions have troubled many reflective persons. Some have concluded that acting against one's interest is contrary to reason. These thinkers, who regard conventional morality as tinged with irrational sentiment and indefensible constraints on the individual, are the supporters of ethical egoism. It is not their view that one should always ignore the interests of others, but rather that one should consider the interests of others only when it suits one's own interests.

What would society be like if ethical egoism were the conventional, prevailing theory of proper conduct? Some philosophers and political theorists have argued that anarchism and chaos would result unless preventive measures were adopted. A classic statement of this position was made by the philosopher Thomas Hobbes. Imagine a world with limited resources, he said, where persons are approximately equal in their ability to harm one another and where everyone acts exclusively in his or her interest. Hobbes argued that in such a world everyone would be at everyone else's throat and society would be plagued by anxiety, violence, and constant danger. As Hobbes declared, life would be "solitary, poor, nasty, brutish, and short."[7] However, Hobbes also assumed that human beings are sufficiently rational to recognize their interests. To avoid the war of all against all, he urged his readers to form a powerful state to protect themselves.

Egoists accept Hobbes's view in the following form: Any clever person will realize that she or he has no moral obligations to others besides those obligations she or he voluntarily assumes. Each person should accept moral rules and assume specific obligations only when doing so promotes one's self-interest. Even if agreeing to live under a set of laws of the state that are binding on everyone, one should obey rules and laws only to protect oneself and to create a situation of communal living that is personally advantageous. One should also back out of an obligation whenever it becomes clear that it is to one's long-range disadvantage to fulfill the obligation. When confronted by a social revolution, the questionable trustworthiness of a colleague, or an incompetent administration at one's place of employment, no one is under an obligation to obey the law, fulfill contracts, or tell the truth. These obligations exist only because one assumes them, and one ought to assume them only as long as doing so promotes one's own interest.

An arrangement whereby everyone acts on more or less fixed rules such as those found in conventional moral and legal systems would produce the most desirable state of affairs from an egoistic point of view. The reason is that such rules arbitrate conflicts and make social life more agreeable. These rules would include, for example, familiar moral and legal principles of justice that are intended to make everyone's situation more secure and stable.

Only an unduly narrow conception of self-interest, the egoist might argue, leads critics to conclude that the egoist would not willingly observe conventional rules of justice. If society can be structured to resolve personal conflicts through courts and other peaceful means, egoists will view it as in their interest to accept those binding social arrangements, just as they will perceive it as prudent to treat other individuals favorably in personal contacts. Notice that the egoist is not saying that his or her interests are served by promoting the good of others but rather is claiming that his or her personal interests are served by observing impartial rules irrespective of the outcome for others. Egoists do not care about the welfare of others unless it affects their welfare, and this desire for personal well-being alone motivates acceptance of the conventional rules of morality.

Egoistic Business Practices and Utilitarian Results. A different view from that of Hobbes, and one that has been extremely influential in the philosophy of the business community, is found in Adam Smith's economic and moral writings. Smith believed that the public good evolves out of a suitably restrained clash of competing individual interests. As individuals pursue their self-interest, the interactive process is guided by an "invisible hand," ensuring that the public interest is achieved. Ironically, according to Smith, egoism in commercial transactions leads not to the war of all against all, but rather to a utilitarian outcome; that is, the largest number of benefits for the largest number of persons. The free market is, Smith thought, a better method of achieving the public good than the highly visible and authoritarian hand of Hobbes's all-powerful sovereign state.

Smith believed that government should be limited in order to protect individual freedom. At the same time, he recognized that concern with freedom and self-interest could get out of control. Hence, he proposed that minimal state regulatory activity is needed to provide and enforce the rules of the competitive game. Smith's picture of a restrained egoistic world has captivated many people in the business and economic community. They, like Smith, do not picture themselves as selfish and indifferent to the interests of others, and they recognize that a certain element of cooperation is essential if their interests are to flourish. These people recognize that when their interests conflict with the interests of others, they should pursue their interests within the established rules of the competitive game. Within the rules of business practice, they understand ethics as the maxims of a suitably restrained egoist. Their view is egoistic because it is based on the active pursuit of personal interest. It is restrained because self-interest is kept within the bounds of the prevailing rules of business for the sake of the common good.

Many people in the business community have actively supported the view that a restrained egoism leads to commendable utilitarian outcomes. This is a major defense of a free market economy; competition advances the good of corporations, and competition among individual firms advances the good of society as a whole. Hence, a popular view of business ethics might be captured by the phrase "Ethical egoism leads to utilitarian outcomes." As Smith said, corporations and individuals pursuing their individual interests also thereby promote the public good, so long as they abide by the rules that protect the public.

A controversial figure who defends his actions through this line of argument is T. Boone Pickens, chairman of Mesa Petroleum Company. Pickens is a corporate "raider," who works to spot undervalued corporations and then threatens to take them over. Using speculative stock purchases and hostile tender offers, raiders such as Pickens strike fear in the hearts of corporate managers, who sometimes modify their growth plans to defend the corporation from the takeover attempt. Pickens believes that he is simply drawing attention to undervalued companies whose true value comes to light through his activities, benefiting the stockholders (the only owners of public corporations in his view), whose stock suddenly increases in monetary value. Pickens's immediate ambition seems clearly to be his self-interest in gaining profit for himself and his company, but he claims that the public is a large benefactor of his efforts to improve his own financial position.

Many corporate managers vigorously disagree with Pickens, and many also disagree with the confident optimism underlying Adam Smith's more general perspective. Furthermore, they reject all forms of egoism. We can begin to understand their reservations by turning at this point to the study of ethical theory, and to utilitarian ethical theories in particular.

NORMATIVE ETHICAL THEORY

The central question discussed in this section is What constitutes an acceptable ethical standard for business practice, and by what authority is the standard acceptable? One time-honored answer is that the acceptability of a moral standard is determined by prevailing practices in business or by authoritative, profession-generated documents such as codes. Many businesspersons find this viewpoint congenial and therefore do not see the need for revisions in practices that they find comfortable and adequate.

Professional standards do play a role in business ethics and will be discussed in some detail. Ultimately, however, these standards need to be justified in terms of independent ethical standards, just as the moral norms of a culture need to be justified by more than an appeal to those norms themselves. For this reason, the later parts in this section are devoted to a discussion of widely discussed theories and analyses of morality in the history of philosophy.

Utilitarian Theories

Utilitarian theories hold that the moral worth of actions or practices is determined solely by their consequences. An action or practice is right if it leads to the best possible balance of good consequences over bad consequences for all the parties affected. In taking this perspective, utilitarians believe that the purpose or function of morality is to promote human welfare by minimizing harms and maximizing benefits.

The first developed utilitarian philosophical writings were those of David Hume (1711–1776), Jeremy Bentham (1748–1832), and John Stuart Mill (1806–1873). Mill's *Utilitarianism* (1863) is still today considered the major theoretical exposition. Mill discusses two foundations or sources of utilitarian thinking: a *normative* foundation in the principle of utility and a *psychological* foundation in human nature. He proposes the principle of utility — the "greatest happiness principle" —

as the foundation of normative ethical theory. Actions are right, Mill says, in proportion to their tendency to promote happiness or absence of pain, and wrong insofar as they tend to produce pain or displeasure. According to Mill, pleasure and freedom from pain are alone desirable as ends. All desirable things (which are numerous) are desirable either for the pleasure inherent in them or as means to promote pleasure and prevent pain.

Mill's second foundation derives from his belief that most persons, and perhaps all, have a basic desire for unity and harmony with their fellow human beings. Just as people feel horror at crimes, he says, they have a basic moral sensitivity to the needs of others. Mill sees the purpose of morality as tapping natural human sympathies to benefit others, while controlling unsympathetic attitudes that cause harm to others. The principle of utility is conceived as the best means to these basic human goals.

Essential Features of Utilitarianism.

Several essential features of utilitarianism can be extracted from the reasoning of Mill and other utilitarians. First, utilitarianism is committed to the maximization of the good and the minimization of harm and evil. It asserts that society ought always to produce the greatest possible balance of positive value or the minimum balance of disvalue for all persons affected. The means to maximization is efficiency, a goal that persons in business find congenial, because it is highly prized throughout the economic sector. Efficiency is a means to higher profits and lower prices, and the struggle to be maximally profitable seeks to obtain maximum production from limited economic resources. The utilitarian commitment to the principle of optimal productivity through efficiency is an essential part of the traditional business conception of society and a standard part of business practice.

Many businesses, as well as government agencies, have adopted specific tools such as cost-benefit analysis, risk assessment, or management by objectives — all of which are strongly influenced by a utilitarian philosophy. Many other businesses do not employ such specific tools, but make utililitarian judgments about the benefits and costs of layoffs, scrapping advertising campaigns, and reducing discretionary spending. Though unpopular in the short-term, these adjustments are often welcomed because they are directed at long-term financial improvement and job security. In this respect business harbors a fundamentally utilitarian conception of the goals of its enterprise.

The need both to minimize harm and to balance risks against benefits has been a perennial concern of the business community. For example, executives in the petroleum industry know that oil and gas operations exist tenuously with wetlands areas, waterfowl, and fish. However, if the demands of U.S. consumers are to be met, corporate and public policies must balance possible environmental harms against the benefits of industrial productivity. Similarly, those in the nuclear power industry know that U.S. power plants are built with heavy containment structures to withstand internal failures; but they also recognize the possibility of major disasters such as those at Chernobyl, in the former USSR, in 1986 and in Japan in 1999. Planning for such structures requires that the planners balance public benefits, probability of failure, and the magnitude of harm in the event of failure. The utilitarian believes that such examples from public policy exhibit a general truth about the moral life.

However, utilitarianism involves more than valuing efficiency, reducing evil, and maximizing positive outcomes in the tradeoff situation. A second essential feature of the utilitarian theory is a *theory of the good*. Efficiency itself is simply an instrumental good; that is, it is valuable strictly as a means to something else. In the corporation, efficiency is valuable as a means to growth and to profit maximization. Within the free enterprise system of competing firms, efficiency is valuable as a means toward maximizing the production of goods and services. Within utilitarian ethical theory, efficiency is the means for maximizing human good.

But what is "good" according to the utilitarian? An answer to this question can be formed by considering the working of the New York stock market. Daily results on Wall Street are not intrinsically good. They are extrinsically good as a means to other ends, such as financial security and happiness. Utilitarians believe that people ought to seek certain experiences and conditions that are good in themselves without reference to further consequences, and that all values are ultimately to be gauged in terms of these intrinsic goods. Health, friendship, and freedom from pain are among such values. An intrinsic value is simply a value in life that people wish to possess and enjoy just for its sake and not as a means to something else.

However, utilitarians disagree concerning what constitutes the complete range of things or states that are good. Bentham and Mill are hedonists. They believe that only pleasure or happiness (synonymous for the purposes of this discussion) can be intrinsically good. Everything besides pleasure is instrumentally good to the end of pleasure. *Hedonistic* utilitarians, then, believe that any act or practice that maximizes pleasure (when compared with any alternative act or practice) is right. Later utilitarian philosophers, however, have argued that other values besides pleasure possess intrinsic worth, for example, friendship, knowledge, courage, health, and beauty. Utilitarians who believe in multiple intrinsic values are referred to as *pluralistic* utilitarians.

In recent philosophy, economics, and psychology, neither the approach of the hedonists nor that of the pluralists has prevailed. Both approaches have seemed relatively useless for purposes of objectively aggregating widely different interests. Another approach appeals to individual preferences. From this perspective, the concept of utility is understood, not in terms of states of affairs such as happiness, but in terms of the satisfaction of individual preferences, as determined by a person's behavior. In the language of business, utility is measured by a person's purchases or pursuits. To maximize a person's utility is to provide that which he or she has chosen or would choose from among the available alternatives. To maximize the utility of all persons affected by an action or a policy is to maximize the utility of the aggregate group.

Although the preference-based utilitarian approach to value has been viewed by many as superior to its predecessors, it is not trouble-free as an ethical theory. A major problem arises over morally unacceptable preferences. For example, an airline pilot may prefer to have a few beers before going to work, or an employment officer may prefer to discriminate against women, yet such preferences are morally intolerable. Utilitarianism based purely on subjective preferences is satisfactory, then, only if a range of acceptable preferences can be formulated. This latter task has proved difficult in theory, and it may be inconsistent with a pure preference approach. Should products like cigarettes, fireworks, and semiautomatic rifles be legally prohibited because they cause such harm, even though many people would prefer to purchase them? How could a preference utilitarian answer this question?

One possible utilitarian response is to ask whether society is better off as a whole when these preferences are prohibited and when the choices of those desiring them are frustrated. If these products work against the larger objectives of utilitarianism (maximal public welfare) by creating unhappiness, the utilitarian could argue that preferences for these products should not be counted in the calculus of preferences. Preferences that serve to frustrate the preferences of others would then be ruled out by the goal of utilitarianism. As Mill argued, the cultivation of certain kinds of desires and the exclusion of antithetical desires are built into the ideal of utilitarianism.

A third essential feature of utilitarianism is its commitment to the measurement and comparison of goods. With the hedonistic view, people must be able to measure pleasurable and painful states and be able to compare one person's pleasures with another's to decide which is greater. Bentham, for example, worked out a measurement device that he called the *hedonic calculus*. He thought he could add the quantitative units of individual happiness, subtract the units of individual unhappiness, and thereby arrive at a total measure of happiness. By the use of this system it is allegedly possible to determine the act or practice that will provide the greatest happiness to the greatest number of people.

Act and Rule Utilitarianism. Utilitarian moral philosophers are conventionally divided into two types — act utilitarians and rule utilitarians. An *act utilitarian* argues that in all situations, one ought to perform the act that leads to the greatest good for the greatest number. The act utilitarian regards rules such as "You ought to tell the truth in making contracts" and "You ought not to manipulate persons through advertising" as useful guidelines, but also as expendable in business and other relationships. An act utilitarian would not hesitate to break a moral rule if breaking it would lead to the greatest good for the greatest number in a particular case. *Rule utilitarians*, however, reserve a more significant place for rules, which they do not regard as expendable on grounds that utility is maximized in the circumstances.

There are many applications of both types of utilitarianism in business ethics.[8] Consider the following case in which U.S. business practices and standards run up against the quite different practices of the Italian business community. The case involves the tax problems encountered by the Italian subsidiary of a major U.S. bank. In Italy the practices of corporate taxation typically involve elaborate negotiations among hired company representatives and the Italian tax service, and the tax statement initially submitted by a corporation is regarded as a dramatically understated bid intended only as a starting point for the negotiating process. In the case in question, the U.S. manager of the Italian banking subsidiary decided, against the advice of locally experienced lawyers and tax consultants, to ignore the native Italian practices and file a conventional U.S.-style tax statement (that is, one in which the subsidiary's profits for the year were not dramatically understated). His reasons for this decision included his belief that the local customs violated the moral rule of truth telling.[9]

An act utilitarian might well take exception to this conclusion. Admittedly, to file an Italian-style tax statement would be to violate a moral rule of truth telling; but the act utilitarian would argue that such a rule is only a guideline and can justifiably be violated to produce the greatest good. In the present case, the greatest good would evidently be done by following the local consultants' advice and conforming to the Italian practices. Only by following those practices will the appropriate amount of tax be paid. This conclusion is strengthened by the ultimate outcome of the present case: The Italian authorities forced the bank to enter into the customary negotiations, a process in which the original, truthful tax statement was treated as an understated opening bid, and a dramatically excessive tax payment was consequently exacted.

In contrast to the position of act utilitarians, rule utilitarians hold that rules have a central position in morality that cannot be compromised by the demands of particular situations. Such compromise threatens the general effectiveness of the rules, the observance of which maximizes social utility. An example of rule utilitarian reasoning is found in a case involving John Zaccaro, the husband of 1984 vice-presidential candidate Geraldine A. Ferraro. In late 1982, Zaccaro was appointed the guardian of an elderly woman's estate. For his business purposes, Zaccaro borrowed $175,000 from the estate to be repaid at 12 percent interest. The propriety of Zacarro's actions was questioned in court, where it was determined that he had not acted dishonestly or with malicious intent and may well have earned larger dividends for the woman than she would have reaped through more conservative investing. In effect, the court found that Zaccaro may have maximized the utility of everyone who was directly affected.

Nonetheless, Zaccaro had placed himself in a position of conflict of interest, and the court found that "the rule is inflexible that a trustee shall not place himself in a position where his interest is or may be in conflict with his obligation." For his part, Zaccaro maintained that he acted in good faith and benefited the woman as best he could, but said, "I understand and accept the decision of the court that general principles of law must nevertheless be applied rigidly to guide the actions of other conservators."[10] In effect, both the judge and Zaccaro agreed that rule utilitarianism takes precedence over act utilitarianism. Even if Zaccaro had maximized everyone's utility in the circumstance, his act violated a basic, inflexible rule that had to take precedence.

For the rule utilitarian, then, actions are justified by appeal to abstract rules such as "Don't kill," "Don't bribe," and "Don't break promises." These rules, in turn, are justified by an appeal to the principle of utility. The rule utilitarian believes this position can escape the objections to act utilitarianism, because rules are not subject to change by the demands of individual circumstances. Utilitarian rules are in theory firm and protective of all classes of individuals, just as human rights are rigidly protective of all individuals regardless of social convenience and momentary need.

Act utilitarians, however, have a reply to these criticisms. They argue that there is a third option beyond ignoring rules and strictly obeying them, which is that the rules should be obeyed only sometimes. An example of this act utilitarian form of reasoning is found in the defense offered by A. Carl Kotchian, former president of Lockheed Corporation, of $12 million of "grease payments" made to high Japanese officials to facilitate sales of Lockheed's TriStar plane. Kotchian recognized that "extortion," as he called it, was involved and that U.S. rules of business ethics forbid such payments. Kotchian advanced these two arguments in defense of the payments: (1) "Such disbursements did not [at the time] violate American laws"; and (2) "the TriStar payments . . . would provide Lockheed workers with jobs and thus redounded to the benefit of their dependents, their communities, and stockholders of the corporation." Kotchian went on to argue that the financial consequences of "commercial success" and the public interest in both Japan and the United States were sufficient to override "a purely ethical and moral standpoint."[11] This is precisely the form of reasoning that rule utilitarians have generally rejected but act utilitarians have defended as at least meriting serious consideration. In the end, the act utilitarian view seems to invoke a prediction that society will be improved if people sometimes obey but sometimes disobey rules, because this kind of conduct will not fundamentally erode either moral rules or the general respect for morality.

However, it is appropriate to ask whether rule utilitarians can escape the very criticisms they level at act utilitarians. Rules often conflict. For example, rules of confidentiality conflict with rules protecting individual welfare. This issue surfaces in discussions of implementing genetic and drug-screening policies in the workplace. If the moral life were so ordered that everyone always knew which rules and rights should receive priority, there would be no serious problem for ethical theory. Yet such a ranking of rules is impossible. Mill, who briefly considered this problem, held that the principle of utility should itself decide in any given circumstance which rule is to take priority. However, if this solution is accepted by rule utilitarians, their theory must, on some occasions, rely on the principle of utility to decide *directly* which actions are preferable to which alternatives in the absence of a governing rule. This view resembles those views associated with act reasoning rather than rule reasoning.

Criticisms of Utilitarianism. A major problem for utilitarianism is whether units of happiness or some other utilitarian value can be measured and compared in order to determine the best action among the alternatives. In deciding whether to open a pristine national wildlife preserve to oil exploration and drilling, for example, how does one compare the combined value of an increase in the oil supply, jobs, and consumer purchasing power with the value of wildlife preservation and environmental protection? How does a corporate public affairs officer decide how to distribute limited funds allocated for charitable contributions? If a corporate social audit (an evaluation of the company's acts of social responsibility) were attempted, how could the auditor measure and compare a corporation's ethical assets and liabilities?

Utilitarians have also encountered other problems with measurement. Economists, for example, either appropriated the word *utility* to denote the experience of satisfaction of preference or abandoned the word *utility* and talked about "preference ordering" instead. Many still doubt that construing utility in these ways resolves problems of measuring utilities. Suppose Jim prefers to spend his $0.97 on milk, and Sally prefers to spend her $0.97 on bread. Then suppose that Sally and Jim have only $1.30 to distribute between them. What can utilitarianism advise when utility is limited to preference orderings? It seems that no advice is possible unless some inferences are made that enable people to go from known preferences to other considerations of welfare and happiness.

The utilitarian reply to these criticisms is that the alleged problem is either a pseudoproblem or a problem that affects all ethical theories. People make crude, rough-and-ready comparisons of values every day, including those of pleasures and dislikes. For example, workers decide to go as a group to a bar rather than have an office party, because they think the bar function will satisfy more members of the group. Utilitarians acknowledge that accurate measurements of others' goods or preferences can seldom be provided because of limited knowledge and time. In everyday affairs such as purchasing supplies, administering business, or making legislative decisions, severely limited knowledge regarding the consequences of one's actions is often all that is available. It is crucial, from the utilitarian perspective, that a person conscientiously attempts to determine the most desirable action and then with equal seriousness attempts to perform that action.

Utilitarianism has also been criticized on the grounds that it ignores nonutilitarian factors that are needed to make moral decisions. Much of the remainder of this chapter considers these alleged sins of omission. The most prominent omission cited is a consideration of justice: The action that produces the greatest balance of value for the greatest number of people may bring about unjustified treatment of a minority. Suppose society decides that the public interest is served by denying health insurance of any sort to those testing positive for the AIDS virus. Moreover, in the interest of efficiency, suppose insurance companies are allowed to use as selective data lifestyle characteristics that are statistically associated with an enhanced risk of AIDS. Finally, suppose such policies would serve the larger public's financial interest. Utilitarianism seems to *require* that public law and insurance companies deny coverage to these AIDS victims. If so, would not this denial be unjust to those who have AIDS or are at high risk for contracting AIDS?

In the last opinion he wrote for the U.S. Supreme Court, former Chief Justice Warren Burger noted, "The fact that a given law or procedure is efficient, convenient and useful in facilitating functions of government, standing alone, will not save it if it is contrary to the Constitution. Convenience and efficiency are not the primary objectives, or the hallmarks, of democratic government."[12] Burger's criticism captures the essence of what many have argued against utilitarianism, namely, that it fails to account for basic principles in documents such as the Bill of Rights in the U.S. Constitution that morally and legally cannot be modified in the name of efficiency, productivity, and convenience.

Utilitarians insist against such criticisms that all entailed costs and benefits of an action or practice must be weighed, including, for example, the costs that would occur from modifying a constitution or statement of basic rights. In a decision that affects employee and consumer safety, for example, the costs often include protests from labor and consumer groups, public criticism from the press, further alienation of employees from executives, the loss of customers to competitors, and the like. Also, rule utilitarians emphatically deny that narrow cost-benefit determinations are acceptable. Instead, they argue that general rules of justice (which are themselves justified by broad considerations of utility) ought to constrain particular actions or uses of cost-benefit calculations in all cases. Rule utilitarians maintain that the criticisms of utilitarianism previously noted are short-sighted because they focus on injustices that might be caused through a superficial or short-term application of the principle of utility. In a long-range view, utilitarians argue, promoting utility does not eventuate in overall unjust outcomes.

Kantian Ethics

Consider now a case involving the Plasma International Company.[13] After an earthquake in Nicaragua produced a sudden need for fresh blood, Plasma International supplied the blood from underdeveloped West African countries, paying the donors as little as 15 cents per pint. Because of the shortage in Nicaragua, Plasma sold the blood at a premium price. The transaction ultimately yielded the firm nearly a quarter of a million dollars in profits. What is it about Plasma International's conduct that provokes moral outrage?

Immanuel Kant's (1724–1804) ethical theory may help clarify the basis of this outrage. It is likely that Kant would argue that Plasma International treated human beings as though they were merely machines or capital and seemed to deny people the respect appropriate to their dignity as rational human beings. Kant's respect-for-persons principle says that persons should be treated as ends and never purely as means. Failure to respect persons is to treat them as a means in accordance with one's *own* ends, and thus as if they were not independent agents. To exhibit a lack of respect for a person is either to reject the person's considered judgments, to ignore the person's concerns and needs, or to deny the person the liberty to act on those judgments. For example, manipulative advertising that attempts to make sales by interfering with the potential buyer's reflective choice violates the principle of respect for persons.

In Kantian theories respect for the human being is said to be necessary — not just as an option or at one's discretion — because human beings possess a moral dignity and therefore should be treated as if they had merely the conditional value possessed by machinery, industrial plants, robots, and capital. This idea of "respect for persons" has sometimes been expressed in corporate contexts as "respect for the individual." An example is found in Hewlett-Packard, a U.S. firm that has been praised for its employee relationships. Because Hewlett-Packard does not fire employees (instead, it uses partial-hour layoffs and similar strategies) and attempts to make the corporate setting as pleasant as possible for workers, its employees tend to be tenaciously loyal and highly productive. Hewlett-Packard has thereby gained a reputation as a corporation that respects rather than exploits the individual.

Some have interpreted Kant to hold categorically that people can never treat other persons as a means to their ends. This interpretation, however, is a misrepresentation. Kant did not categorically prohibit the use of persons as means to the ends of other people. He argued only that people must not treat another *exclusively* as a means to their ends. When employees are ordered to perform odious tasks, they are being treated as a means to an employer's or a supervisor's ends, but the employees are not exclusively used for others' purposes because they are not mere servants or objects. In an economic exchange suppose that Jones is using Smith to achieve her end, but similarly Smith is using Jones to achieve her end. So long as the exchange is freely entered into without coercion or deception by either party, neither party has used the other merely for her end. A person is used as a means merely when he or she is manipulated to act in a way that benefits the manipulator without rationally and freely assenting. Thus even in a hierarchical organization an employer can be the boss without exploiting the employee, so long as the employee freely entered in that relationship. The key to not using others merely as a means is to respect their autonomy. Kant's principle demands only that such persons be treated with the respect and moral dignity to which every person is entitled, including those times when they are used primarily as a means to the ends of others.

Kant's principle finds *motives* for actions morally important, in that it expects persons to make the right decisions *for the right reasons.* If persons are honest only because they believe that honesty pays, their "honesty" is cheapened. Indeed, it seems like no honesty at all, only an action that appears to be honest. For example, when corporate executives announce that the reason they made the morally correct decision was because it was good for their business, this reason seems to have nothing to do with morality. According to Kantian thinking, if a corporation does the right thing only when (and for the reason that) it is profitable or when it will enjoy good publicity, its decision is prudential, not moral.

Consider the following three examples of three people making personal sacrifices for a sick relative. Fred makes the sacrifices only because he fears the social criticism that would result if he failed to do so. He hates doing it and secretly resents being involved. Sam, by contrast, derives no personal satisfaction from taking care of his sick relative. He would rather be doing other things and makes the sacrifice purely from a sense of obligation. Bill, by contrast, is a kind-hearted person. He does not view his actions as a sacrifice and is motivated by the satisfaction that comes from helping others. Assume in these three cases that the consequences of all the sacrificial actions are equally good and that the sick relatives are adequately cared for, as each agent intends. The question to consider is which persons are behaving in a morally praiseworthy manner. If utilitarian theory is used, this question may be hard to answer, especially if act utilitarianism is the theory in question, because the good consequences in each case are identical. The Kantian believes, however, that motives — in particular, motives of moral obligation — count substantially in moral evaluation.

It appears that Fred's motives are not moral motives but motives of prudence that spring from fear, although his actions have good consequences. Fred does not, however, deserve any moral credit for his acts because they are not morally motivated. To recognize the prudential basis of an action does not detract from its good consequences. Given the purpose or function of the business enterprise, a motive of self-interest may be the most appropriate motive to ensure good consequences. The point, however, is that a business executive derives no special moral credit for acting in the corporate self-interest, even if society is benefited by and pleased by the action.

If Fred's motive is not moral, what about Bill's and Sam's? Here moral philosophers disagree. Kant maintained that moral action must be motivated by obligation alone. From this perspective, Sam is the only individual whose actions may be appropriately described as moral. Bill deserves no more credit than Fred, because Bill is motivated by sympathy and compassion, not by obligation. Bill is naturally kind-hearted and has been well socialized by his family, but this motivation merits no moral praise from a Kantian, who believes that actions motivated by self-interest alone or compassion alone cannot be morally praiseworthy. To be deserving of moral praise, a person must act from obligation.

Kant insisted that all persons must act not only *in accordance with* obligation, but for the *sake* of obligation; that is, the person's motive for action must be a recognition of the duty to act. Kant tried to establish the ultimate basis for the validity of rules of obligation in pure reason, not in intuition, conscience, utility, or compassion. Morality provides a rational framework of principles and rules that constrain and guide all people, independent of their personal goals and preferences. He believed that all considerations of utility and self-interest are secondary, because the moral worth of an agent's action depends exclusively on the moral acceptability of the rule according to which the person is acting, or, as Kant preferred to say, moral acceptability depends on the rule that determines the agent's will.

An action has moral worth only if performed by an agent who possesses what Kant called a "good will." A person has a good will only if the sole motive for action is moral obligation, as determined by a universal rule. Kant developed this notion into a fundamental moral law: "I ought never to act except in such a way that I can also will that my maxim should become a universal law." Kant called this principle the *categorical imperative*. It is categorical because it admits of no exceptions and is absolutely binding. It is imperative because it gives instruction about how one must act. He gave several controversial examples of imperative moral maxims: "Do not lie," "Help others in distress," "Do not commit suicide," and "Work to develop your abilities."

Kant's strategy was to show that the acceptance of certain kinds of action is self-defeating, because *universal* participation in such behavior undermines the action. Some of the clearest cases involve persons who make a unique exception for themselves for purely selfish reasons. Suppose a person considers breaking a promise that would be inconvenient to keep. According to Kant, the person must first formulate her or his reason as a universal rule. The rule would say, "Everyone should break a promise whenever keeping it is inconvenient." Such a rule is contradictory, Kant held, because if it were consistently recommended that all individuals should break their promises when it was convenient for them to do so, the practice of making promises would be senseless. Given the nature of a promise, a rule allowing people to break promises when it becomes convenient makes the institution of promise-making unintelligible. A rule that allows cheating on an exam similarly negates the purpose of testing. For Kant, one does not keep promises because it pays or because one has a natural disposition to do so, but rather from respect for moral law that requires the obligation of promise keeping.

Kant's belief is that the conduct stipulated in these rules could not be made universal without some form of contradiction emerging. If a corporation kites checks to reap a profit in the way E. F. Hutton Brokerage did in a scandal that led to the end of the firm, the corporation makes itself an exception to the system of monetary transfer, thereby cheating the system, which is established by certain rules. This conduct, if carried out consistently by other corporations, violates the rules presupposed by the system, thereby rendering the system inconsistent. Kant's view is that actions involving invasion of privacy, theft, line cutting, cheating, kickbacks, and bribes are contradictory in that they are not consistent with the institutions or practices they presuppose.

Despite Kant's contributions to moral philosophy, his theories have been criticized as narrow and inadequate to handle various problems in the moral life. He has no place for moral emotions or sentiments such as sympathy and caring. Neither does Kant have much to say about moral character and virtue other than his comments on the motive of obligation.

Some people also think that Kant emphasized universal obligations (obligations common to all people) at the expense of particular obligations (obligations that fall only on those in particular relationships or who occupy certain roles such as those of a business manager). Whereas the obligation to keep a promise is a universal obligation, the obligation to grade students fairly falls only on teachers. Many managerial obligations result from special roles played in business. For example, businesspersons tend to treat each customer according to the history of their relationship. If a person is a regular customer and the merchandise being sold is in short supply, the regular customer will be given preferential treatment because a relationship of commitment and trust has already been established. Japanese business practice has extended this notion to relations with suppliers and employees. At many firms, after a trial period, the regular employee has a job for life. Also, the bidding system is used infrequently in Japan. Once a supplier has a history with a firm, the firm is loyal to its supplier, and each trusts the other not to exploit the relationship.

However, considerations of particular obligations and special relationships may not be inconsistent with Kantianism because they may be formulated as universal. For example, the rule "Quality control inspectors have special obligations for customer safety" can be made into a "universal" law for all quality control inspectors. Although Kant wrote little about such particular duties, he would no doubt agree that a complete explanation of moral agency in terms of duty requires an account of *both* universal *and* particular duties.

A related aspect of Kant's ethical theory that has been scrutinized by philosophers is his view that moral motivation involves *impartial* principles. Impartial motivation may be distinguished from the motivation that a person might have for treating a second person in a certain way because the first person has a particular interest in the well-being of the second person (a spouse or good friend, for example). A conventional interpretation of Kant's work suggests that if conflicts arise between one's obligation and other motivations — such as friendship, reciprocation, or love — the motive of obligation should always prevail. Arguing against this moral view, some critics maintain that persons appropriately show favoritism to their loved ones and that they are entitled to do so. This criticism suggests that Kantianism (and utilitarianism as well) does not adequately account for those parts of the moral life involving intimate and special relationships.

Special relationships with a unique history are often recognized in business. For instance, the Unocal Corporation sharply criticized its principal bank, Security Pacific Corporation, for knowingly making loans of $185 million to a group that intended to use the money to buy shares in Unocal for a hostile takeover. Fred Hartley, chairman and president of Unocal, argued that the banks and investment bankers were "playing both sides of the game." Hartley said that Security Pacific had promised him that it would not finance such takeover attempts three months before doing so and that it had acted under conditions "in which the bank [has] continually received [for the last 40 years] confidential financial, geological, and engineering information from the company."[14] A forty-year history in which the bank has stockpiled confidential information should not simply be cast aside for larger goals. Security Pacific had violated a special relationship it had with Unocal.

Nonetheless, impartiality seems at some level an irreplaceable moral concept, and ethical theory should recognize its centrality for many business relationships. For example, a major scandal occurred for some U.S. banks in 1991, because they were caught lending money to bank insiders.[15] The essence of federal rules is that banks can lend money to insiders if and only if insiders are treated exactly as outsiders are treated. Here the rule of impartiality is an essential moral constraint.

In concluding this section on Kantian ethics, it should be observed that almost no moral philosopher today finds Kant's system fully satisfactory. His defenders tend to say only that Kant provides the elements that are essential for a sound moral position. However, by using Kantian elements as a basis, some philosophers have attempted to construct a more encompassing theory. They use the Kantian notion of respect for persons, for example, as a ground for providing ethical theories of justice and rights. Considerable controversy persists as to whether Kantian theories are adequate to this task and whether they have been more successful than utilitarian theories.

Contemporary Challenges to the Dominant Theories

Thus far utilitarian and Kantian theories have been examined. Both meld a wide variety of moral considerations into a surprisingly systematized framework, centered around a single major principle. There is much that is attractive in these theories, which have been the dominant models in ethical theory throughout much of the twentieth century. In fact, they have sometimes been presented as the only types of ethical theory, as if there were no available alternatives to choose from. However, much recent philosophical writing has focused on defects in these theories and on ways in which the two theories actually affirm a similar conception of the moral life oriented around universal principles and rules.

These critics promote alternatives to the utilitarian and Kantian models. They believe that the contrast between the two types of theory has been overestimated and that they do not merit the attention they have received and the lofty position they have occupied. Four popular replacements for, or perhaps supplements to, Kantian and utilitarian theories are (1) common morality theories (which are generally obligation-based), (2) rights theories (which are based on human rights), (3) virtue theories (which are based on character traits), and (4) feminist theories and the ethics of care (which are disposition-based). These theories are the topics of the next four sections.

Each of these four types of theory has treated some problems well and has supplied insights not found in utilitarian and Kantian theories. Although it may seem as if there is an endless array of disagreements across the theories, these theories are not in all respects competitive, and in many ways they are complementary. The convergent insights in these theories are valuable and we stand to learn from each.

Common Morality Theories

One set of theories builds on the idea that there is a common morality that all people share by virtue of communal life. A straightforward example of this type of theory is found in Alan Donagan's *The Theory of Morality*, in which he locates the "philosophical core" of the common morality in the Hebrew-Christian tradition, whose morality he interprets in secular rather than religious terms. His identification of the fundamental principle of this tradition is that "It is impermissible not to respect every human being, oneself or any other, as a rational creature."[16] Donagan believes that all other moral rules in the common morality are derived from this fundamental rule.

There are many versions of a common morality approach, but W. D. Ross's theory has had a particularly imposing influence. He argues that there are several basic rules of moral obligation and that they do not derive from either the principle of utility or Kant's categorical imperative. Some of Ross's basic rules are as follows: "Promises create obligations of fidelity." "Wrongful actions create obligations of reparation." "The generous gifts of friends create obligations of gratitude." Ross defends several additional obligations, such as obligations of self-improvement, nonmaleficence, beneficence, and justice.

Unlike Kant's system and the utilitarian system, Ross's list of obligations is not based on a single overarching principle. Ross defends his principles on the grounds of their faithfulness to the ordinary moral beliefs and judgments. He argues that to determine one's obligation, the greatest obligation in any given circumstance must be found on the basis of the greatest balance of right over wrong in that particular context. To determine this balance, Ross introduces an influential distinction between *prima facie* obligations and *actual* obligations. *Prima facie* refers to an obligation that must be acted upon unless it conflicts on a particular occasion with an equal or stronger obligation. Such an obligation is right and binding, all other things being equal. A prima facie obligation becomes an obligation to be acted on in particular circumstances if it is not overridden or outweighed by some competing moral demand. One's actual obligation is determined by an examination of the respective weights of the competing prima facie obligations. Although prima facie obligations are not absolute, they are binding in a way that mere guidelines are not.

For example, Ross considers promise keeping a prima facie obligation. Does this consideration mean that a person must, under all circumstances, keep a promise, as if promise keeping were a categorical imperative? No, there are situations in which breaking a promise is justified. To call promise breaking "prima facie wrong" means that promise breaking is always wrong *unless* some more weighty moral consideration in the circumstances is overriding. If the obligation to keep promises conflicts with the obligation to protect innocent persons, for example, then the actual obligation is to protect innocent persons (overriding the prima facie obligation of promise keeping).

The idea that moral principles are absolute has had a long but troubled history. Both utilitarians and Kantians have defended their basic rule (the principle of utility and the categorical imperative) as absolute, but the claim that any rule or principle is absolute has been widely challenged. For Ross's reasons, among others, many moral philosophers have come to regard obligations and rights not as inflexible standards, but rather as strong prima facie moral demands that may be validly overridden in circumstances of competition with other moral claims. The idea of an exception-free hierarchy of rules and principles has vanished, as has the claim that moral principles can be arranged in a hierarchical order that avoids conflict. This position seems to entail that in cases of conflict there may not be a single right action, because two or more morally acceptable actions may be unavoidably in conflict and may prove to be of equal weight in the circumstances.

Rights Theories

Terms from moral discourse such as *value, goal,* and *obligation* have thus far in this chapter dominated the discussion. *Principles* and *rules* in Kantian, utilitarian, and common morality theories have been understood as statements of obligation. Yet many assertions that will be encountered throughout this volume are claims to have rights, and public policy issues often concern rights or attempts to secure rights. Many current controversies in professional ethics, business, and public policy involve the rights to property, work, privacy, a healthy environment, and the like. This section will show that rights have a distinctive character in ethical theory and yet are connected to the obligations that have previously been examined.

In the twentieth century, public discussion about moral protections for persons vulnerable to abuse, enslavement, or neglect have typically been stated in terms of human rights. Many believe these and other rights transcend national boundaries and particular governments. For example, the ongoing controversies over exploitive labor conditions in factories (so-called sweatshop conditions) that make products for Nike, Reebok, Adidas, Levi Strauss, Liz Claiborne, L. L. Bean, and many other companies is fundamentally a discussion about the human rights of hundreds of thousands of workers around the globe. Under discussion are the rights of workers to appropriate working conditions and open-factory inspections, irrespective of the location of the plant, the illiteracy rate among workers, and the status under law of collective bargaining agreements. As this book was going to press, the Chairman and CEO of Reebok International, Paul Fireman, called upon all companies that purchase from these factories to disclose the factories they use, to ensure the rights of all workers, and to accept monitoring programs that will ensure that these rights are observed.[17]

Unlike legal rights, human rights are held independently of membership in a state or other social organization. Historically, human rights evolved from the notion of natural rights. As formulated by Locke and others in early modern philosophy, natural rights are claims that individuals have against the state. If the state does not honor these rights, its legitimacy is in question. Natural rights were thought to consist primarily of rights to be free of interference, or liberty rights. Proclamations of rights to life, liberty, property, a speedy trial, and the pursuit of happiness subsequently formed the core of major Western political and legal documents. These rights came to be understood as powerful assertions demanding respect and status.

A number of influential philosophers have maintained that ethical theory or some part of it must be "rights-based."[18] They seek to ground ethical theory in an account of rights that is not reducible to a theory of obligations or virtues. Consider a theory to be discussed in Chapter 9 that takes liberty rights to be basic. One representative of this theory, Robert Nozick, refers to his social philosophy as an "entitlement theory." The appropriateness of that description is apparent from this provocative line with which his book begins: "Individuals have rights, and there are things no person or group may do to them (without violating their rights)." Starting from this assumption, Nozick builds a political theory in which government action is justified only if it protects the fundamental rights of its citizens.

This political theory is also an ethical theory. Nozick takes the following moral rule to be basic: All persons have a right to be left free to do as they choose. The moral obligation not to interfere with a person follows from this right. That the obligation *follows* from the right is a clear indication of the priority of rights over obligations; that is, in this theory the obligation is derived from the right, not the other way around. A related rights-based conception uses *benefit* rights rather than *liberty* rights, as Alan Gewirth has proposed:

> Rights are to obligations as benefits are to burdens. For rights are justified claims to certain benefits, the support of certain interests of the subject or right-holder. Obligations, on the other hand, are justified burdens on the part of the respondent or obligation-bearer; they restrict his freedom by requiring that he conduct himself in ways that directly benefit not himself but rather the right-holder. But burdens are for the sake of benefits, and not vice versa. Hence obligations, which are burdens, are for the sake of rights, whose objects are benefits. . . .
>
> Respondents have correlative obligations *because* subjects have certain rights.[19]

These rights-based theories hold that rights form the justifying basis of obligations because they best express the purpose of morality, which is the securing of liberties or other benefits for a right-holder. Some might object that obligations are not necessarily burdens and that they may be welcomed as expressions of human rationality or as a basic form of human activity. However, rights theorists insist that obligations are essentially what Mill and Kant said they are — namely, moral constraints on autonomous choice — and, hence, burdens placed on autonomous action. Obligations restrict in a way that rights do not, and the purpose of morality is to benefit, not burden.

Theories of moral rights have not traditionally been a major focus of business ethics, but this situation seems at present to be changing. For example, employees traditionally could be fired for what superiors considered disloyal conduct, and employees have had no internal right to "blow the whistle" on corporate misconduct. When members of minority groups complain about discriminatory hiring practices that violate their human dignity and self-respect, one plausible interpretation of these complaints is that those who register them believe that their moral rights are being infringed. Current theories of employee, consumer, and stockholder rights all provide frameworks for contemporary debates within business ethics.

The language of moral rights is greeted by some with skepticism because of the apparently absurd proliferation of rights and the conflict among diverse claims to rights (especially in recent political debates). For example, some parties claim that a pregnant woman has a right to have an abortion, whereas others claim that fetuses have a right to life that precludes the right to have an abortion. As we shall see throughout this volume, rights language has been extended to include such controversial rights as the right to financial privacy, rights of workers to obtain information, the right to work in a pollution-free environment, the right to hold a job, and the right to health care.

Clashes between rights are often between what philosophers have distinguished as positive and negative rights. For instance, the right to well-being — that is, to receive goods and services when in need — is a positive right, whereas the right to liberty — the right not to be interfered with — is a negative right. The right to liberty is negative because no one has to act to honor it; presumably, all that must be done is to leave people alone. The same is not true regarding positive rights; in order to honor these rights, someone has to provide something. For example, if a starving person has a human right to well-being, someone has an obligation to provide that person with food.

The main difficulty is that positive rights place an obligation to provide something on others, who can respond that this requirement interferes with their property right to use their resources for their chosen ends. The distinction between positive and negative rights has often led those who would include various rights to well-being (to food, housing, health care, etc.) on the list of human rights to argue that the obligation to provide for positive rights falls on the political state. This distinction has intuitive appeal to many businesspersons, because they wish to limit both the responsibilities of their firms and the number of rights conflicts they must address.

A conflict involving negative rights is illustrated by the debate surrounding attempts by employers to control the lifestyle of their employees. Some employers will not accept employees who smoke. Some will not permit employees to engage in dangerous activities such as skydiving, auto racing, or mountain climbing. By making these rules, one can argue that employers are violating the liberty rights of the employees as well as the employees' right to privacy. On the other hand, the employer can argue that he or she has a right to run the business as he or she sees fit. Thus, both sides invoke negative rights to make moral case.

Many writers in ethics now agree that a person can legitimately exercise a right to something only if sufficient justification exists — that is, when a right has an overriding status. Rights such as a right to equal economic opportunity, a right to do with one's property as one wishes, and a right to be saved from starvation may have to compete with other rights. The fact that rights theorists have failed to provide a hierarchy for rights claims that has won even minimal acceptance may indicate that rights, like obligations, are prima facie claims, not absolute moral demands that cannot be overridden in particular circumstances by more stringent competing moral claims.

Virtue Ethics

Our discussion of utilitarian, Kantian, common morality, and rights-based theories has looked chiefly at obligations and rights. These theories do not typically emphasize the agents or actors who perform actions, have motives, and follow principles. Yet people commonly make judgments about good and evil persons, their traits of character, and their willingness to perform actions. In recent years, several philosophers have proposed that ethics should redirect its preoccupation with principles of obligation, directive rules, and judgments of right and wrong and should look to decision making by persons of good character, that is, virtuous persons.

Virtue ethics, as it is called here, descends from the classical Hellenistic tradition represented by Plato and Aristotle, in which the cultivation of virtuous traits of character is viewed as morality's primary function. Aristotle held that virtue is neither a feeling nor an innate capacity but is rather a disposition bred from an innate capacity properly trained and exercised. People acquire virtues much as they do skills such as carpentry, playing a musical instrument, or cooking. They become just by performing just actions and become temperate by performing temperate actions. Virtuous character, says Aristotle, is neither natural nor unnatural; it is cultivated and made a part of the individual, much like a language or tradition.

But an ethics of virtue is more than habitual training. This approach relies even more than does Kant's theory on the importance of having a correct *motivational structure*. A just person, for example, has not only a disposition to act fairly but also a morally appropriate desire to do so. The person characteristically has a moral concern and reservation about acting in a way that would be unfair. Having only the motive to act in accordance with a rule of obligation, as Kant demands, is not morally sufficient for virtue. Imagine a Kantian who always performs his or her obligation because it is an obligation but who intensely dislikes having to allow the interests of others to be taken into account. Such a person does not cherish, feel congenial toward, or think fondly of others, and this person respects others only because obligation requires it. This person can, nonetheless, on a theory of moral obligation such as Kant's or Mill's, perform a morally right action, have an ingrained disposition to perform that action, and act with obligation as the foremost motive. If the desire is not right, though, a necessary condition of virtue seems to be lacking, at least from the perspective of virtue ethics.

Consider an encounter with a tire salesperson. You tell the salesperson that safety is most important and that you want to be sure to get an all-weather tire. He listens carefully and then sells you exactly what you want, because he has been well trained by his manager to see his primary obligation as that of meeting the customer's needs. Acting in this way has deeply ingrained in this salesperson by his manager's training. There is no more typical encounter in the world of retail sales than this one. However, going behind the salesperson's behavior to his underlying motives and desires reveals that this man detests his job and hates having to spend time with every customer who comes through the door. He cares not at all about being of service to people or creating a better environment in the office. All he wants to do is watch the television set in the waiting lounge and pick up his paycheck. Although this man meets his moral obligations, something in his character is morally defective.

When people engage in business or take jobs simply for the profit or wages that will result, they may meet their obligations and yet not be engaged in their work in a morally appropriate manner. On the other hand, if persons start a business because they believe in a quality product — a new, healthier yogurt, for example — and deeply desire to sell that product, their character is more in tune with our moral expectations. The practice of business is morally better if it is sustained by persons whose character manifests truthfulness, justice, compassion, respectfulness, and patience.

Some interesting discussions in business ethics now center on the appropriate virtues of managers, employees, and other participants in business activity, as will be seen many times in this book. Among the virtues that have received considerable discussion are integrity, courage, and compassion. However, some alleged "virtues" of business life have been sharply contested in recent years. Competitiveness and toughness are two examples. *Fortune* has long published a list of the toughest bosses to work for. For many years before he was fired as CEO of Sunbeam, Al Dunlap was perennially on the list. He had earned the nickname "Chainsaw Al" for his propensity to fire people and shut down plants even when they were marginally profitable. Dunlap was notorious for making stock price and profitability the only worthy goals of a business enterprise. Many would argue that in this particular case business toughness was a vice. This example simply suggests that what some in business allege as a virtue is subject to critical moral scrutiny.

But what about near-opposite character traits to toughness, such as generosity and kindness? Could they possibly qualify as virtues in a rough-and-tumble competitive environment? Are these traits ever to be admired in a CEO? An example to suggest that they have a solid place in the ethics of business is found in John Chambers, the Chairman of Cisco Systems (the fifth most valuable company in North America). He has been called the "the high priest of good management" and "the best boss in the country" because of his generosity to his workers and denial of privileges to himself and his executives. By design, Chambers creates generous salaries and bonuses for his workers, the most favorable benefits packages, and no-layoff policies. Forty percent of the stock options awarded each year go to regular staff; and approximately one-eighth of those who receive stock options are already millionaires as a result. Yet Chambers and his executives work in tiny offices and never fly first-class (they must pay for upgrades themselves). Each worker celebrating a birthday — from janitor to vice-president — is invited for breakfast with Chambers. There they are invited to ask tough questions to the boss about company operations. Apparently Chambers has found that the softer virtues can be as admirable in business as elsewhere.

There is a final reason why virtue ethics may be important for business ethics. A morally good person with the right desires or motivations is more likely to understand what should be done, more likely to be motivated to perform required acts, and more likely to form and act on moral ideals than would a morally bad person. A person who is ordinarily trusted is one who has an ingrained motivation and desire to perform right actions and who characteristically cares about morally appropriate responses. A person who simply follows rules of obligation and who otherwise exhibits no special moral character may not be trustworthy. It is not the rule follower, then, but the person disposed by *character* to be generous, caring, compassionate, sympathetic, and fair who should be the one recommended, admired, praised, and held up as a moral model. Many experienced businesspersons say that such trust is the moral cement of the business world.

Feminist Theories and the Ethics of Care

Related to virtue ethics in some respects is a body of moral reflection that has come to be known as the "ethics of care." This theory develops some of the themes found in virtue ethics about the centrality of character, but the ethics of care focuses on a set of character traits that are deeply valued in close personal relationships — sympathy, compassion, fidelity, love, friendship, and the like. Noticeably absent are universal moral rules and impartial utilitarian calculations such as those espoused by Kant and Mill.

The ideas behind an ethics of care has grown out of the eloquent work of a group of recent philosophers who have contributed to or are indebted to feminist theory. Feminist approaches to ethics may be characterized by at least two presuppositions. First, the subordination of women is as wrong as it is common. Second, the experiences of women are worthy of respect and should be taken seriously. Although these may seem entirely noncontroversial assumptions, feminists argue that if these suppositions were acted upon, the theory and practice of ethics in business and elsewhere would be radically transformed.[20] Feminist scholars are committed to pinpointing and excising male bias and to reformulating ethical theory in a manner that does not subordinate the interests of women. However, there is disagreement among feminists about how best to accomplish this task. The issues are complex, and feminists take different perspectives on matters such as equality, diversity, impartiality, community, autonomy, and the objectivity of moral knowledge.

Nonetheless, several central components of feminist ethical thinking may be delineated. Feminist philosophers point out that rationality in modern ethical theory, in particular in Kantian and utilitarian theories, has most often been understood in terms of the formulation and impartial application of universally binding moral principles. Many feminist philosophers now argue that universal principles are inadequate guides to action and that abstract formulations of hypothetical moral situations separate moral agents from the particularities of their individual lives and inappropriately separate moral problems from social and historical facts. Further, they have criticized the autonomous, unified, rational beings that typify both the Kantian and the utilitarian conception of the moral self.

Feminist philosophers generally agree that Kantian and utilitarian impartiality fails to recognize the moral importance of valuing the well-being of another for her or his own sake. Furthermore, they point out that although impartiality has historically been associated with respect for the individual, impartiality can actually undermine this very respect because it treats individuals impersonally, as anonymous and interchangeable moral agents without distinctive needs and abilities. In addition, impartial moral evaluations often pave over important differences in social, political, and economic power that are crucial to assessing the morally correct course of action in particular situations. For example, a statistical evaluation indicating that 50 percent of a telecommunication company's workforce consists of women would suggest that the company is morally praiseworthy in this respect. However, a different assessment may be appropriate if 90 percent of the women are employed as telephone operators and clerical staff. Similarly, in evaluating a waste disposal company's competitive contract bid, feminist philosophers would urge management to look beyond the bottom line if, for example, 80 percent of the company's toxic waste disposal sites are located in poor, minority neighborhoods.

Kantian and utilitarian theories have been criticized by contemporary feminist philosophers for advocating a conception of morality that leaves little room for virtues such as empathy, compassion, fidelity, love, and friendship. An understanding of the context of a situation is particularly important when taking into account the distinctive "voice" that many psychologists, philosophers, and management theorists have associated with women. This distinctive moral stance was first articulated by psychologist Carol Gilligan in her influential work *In a Different Voice*.[21] The voice is one of care and compassion, and although most feminist scholars do not associate this voice or perspective with women exclusively, they argue that it does represent an important contrast to the voice of rights and justice that Gilligan associated with men.

This distinct moral perspective is characterized by a concern with relationships — especially responsiveness to the particular needs of others — and by a commitment to others' well-being. The ideas Gilligan advanced on the basis of her psychological studies have been developed by those who find the same different voice in contemporary philosophy. Contractarian models of ethics, with their emphasis on justice and rights, are firmly rejected because they omit integral virtues and place a premium on *autonomous choice* among *free* and *equal* agents. Here the ethics of care offers a fundamental rethinking of the moral universe: The terms of social cooperation, especially in families and in communal decision making, are *unchosen, intimate,* and among *unequals.* The contractarian model fails to appreciate that parents and service-oriented professionals, for example, do not perceive their responsibilities to their children and customers in terms of contracts or universal rules but see them rather in terms of care, needs, and long-term attachment. Only if every form of human relation were modeled on an exchange could these forms of caring be reduced to contract or moral law.[22]

There are additional reasons for thinking that a morality centered on virtues of care and concern cannot be squeezed into a morality of rules. Both of their frameworks are fundamentally dissimilar. Human warmth, friendliness, and trust in responding to others cannot be brought under rules of behavior. For example, although a lawyer may follow all the rules of good legal practice in attending to the affairs of a bankrupt businessperson, the lawyer still does not display the sensitivity and warmth that this heartsick person needs; yet such virtues of a good lawyer may be the most important part of the encounter.

Crucial to the ethics of care is a willingness to listen to distinct and previously unacknowledged perspectives. For example, a manager considering the implementation of a mandatory drug-testing program might come to an impasse because employers, employees, and customers have legitimate rights. Many feminists and management experts would urge the manager to help employees to feel concern for the customers while also striving to make the workplace experience one in which the worker is less alienated and hence less likely to take drugs. Employees must feel that they can trust their managers, and managers must be willing to listen and respond to their employees.

This moral theory has the potential to transform business practice to exhibit more of the characteristics of a moral community. Traditional metaphors for business practice are often drawn from competitive arenas; they are war-oriented and sports-oriented. Family metaphors seem out of place, as does the language of cooperation and compassion. Yet such language is undeniably central to morality, and if some contemporary management theorists are correct, such language is central to success in business as well. Cooperation among managers and employers is no less important for success than product quality.

This aspect of business has traditionally been ignored as "soft" and less important than a strong bottom line. Perhaps business will in the future be more open to the contributions of the ethics of care, resulting in an improvement in both corporate morality and corporate productivity.

A Prologue to Theories of Justice

Many rules and principles form the terms of cooperation in society. Society is laced with implicit and explicit arrangements and agreements under which individuals are obligated to cooperate or abstain from interfering with others. Philosophers are interested in the justice of these terms of cooperation. They pose questions such as these: What gives one person or group of people the right to expect cooperation from another person or group of people in some societal interchange (especially an economic one) if the former benefit and the latter do not? Is it just for some citizens to have more property than others? Is it fair for one person to gain an economic advantage over another, if both abide strictly by existing societal rules?

In their attempts to answer such questions, some philosophers believe that diverse human judgments and beliefs about justice can be brought into systematic unity through a general theory of justice. Justice has been analyzed differently, however, in rival and often incompatible theories. These general theories of justice are treated in Chapter 9. Here we need note only that in the literature on justice there exists a key distinction between just *procedures* and just *results*.

Ideally, it is preferable to have both, but this is not always possible. For example, a person might achieve a just result in redistributing wealth but might use an unjust procedure to achieve that result, such as undeserved taxation of certain groups. By contrast, just procedures sometimes eventuate in unjust results, as when a fair trial finds an innocent person guilty. Some writers in business ethics are concerned with issues of procedural justice when they discuss such concerns as the use of ombudsmen, grievance procedures, peer review, and arbitration procedures.

Many problems of justice that a cooperative society must handle involve some system or set of procedures that foster, but do not ensure, just outcomes. Once there is agreement on appropriate procedures, the outcome must be accepted as just, even if it produces inequalities that seem unjust by other standards. If procedural justice is the best that can be attained — as, for example, is claimed in the criminal justice system — society should accept the results of its system with a certain amount of humility and perhaps make allowances for inevitable inequalities and even inequities and misfortunes.

ANALYSIS OF CASES

Every subsequent chapter of this volume contains judicial opinions ("case law") and cases involving business activities. Although these materials are not derived from ethical theory, they merit moral analysis. The *case method,* as it is often called, has long been used in law and business for such purposes. However, only recently has philosophical ethics drawn attention to the importance of case studies and the case method, and their use is still controversial and unsettled.

The Case Method in Law

Case law establishes precedents of evidence and justification. The earliest developments in the law's use of the case method occurred around 1870, when Christopher Columbus Langdell revolutionized academic standards and teaching techniques by introducing this system at the Harvard Law School.[23] Langdell's textbooks contained cases selected and arranged to reveal the pervasive meaning of legal terms and the rules and principles of law. He envisioned a dialectical or Socratic manner of argument to show students how concepts, rules, and principles are found in the legal reasoning of the judges who wrote the opinions. A teacher or legal scholar was to extract fundamental principles, much in the way a skillful biographer might extract the principles of a person's reasoning by studying his or her considered judgments.

However, Langdell's "principles" did not prove to be as invariant or as consistently applied across courts, contexts, or times as Langdell had thought they would. It turned out that incompatible and rival theories or approaches by judges tended to control in many precedent cases. Nevertheless, the case method ultimately prevailed in U.S. law schools, and still today it offers teachers and students a powerful tool for generalizing from cases. In the thrust-and-parry classroom setting, teacher and student alike reach conclusions about a case's rights and wrongs.

The Case Method in Business

When the Harvard Business School was opened in 1908, its first dean, Edwin F. Gay, adopted the Law School curriculum as a prototype for courses on commercial law and eventually as a model throughout the business school. By 1919 the method had taken hold, and eventually it came to dominate business schools that emphasize deliberation and decision making, weighing competing considerations, and reaching a decision in complex and difficult circumstances.[24] Judgment, rather than doctrine, principle, or fact, was taught. Cases involving puzzles and dilemmas that have no definitive solution by reference to principles or precedents were preferred for instructional purposes over those failing to present a difficult dilemma.

Cases, in this method, are typically developed to recreate a managerial situation in which dilemmas are confronted. Cases are not primarily used to illustrate principles or rules, because the latter abstractions are invariably inadequate for final resolutions in real-world business situations. The objective is to develop a capacity to grasp problems and to find novel solutions that work in this context: *Knowing how* to think and act is more prized than *knowing that* something is the case or that a principle applies.

This use of the case method in business schools springs from an ideal of education that puts the student in the decision-making role after an initial immersion into the facts of a complex situation. Theories and generalizations are downplayed, and the skills of thinking and acting in complex and uncertain environments are upgraded. The essence of the case method is to present a situation replete with the facts, opinions, and prejudices an executive might encounter (often in an actual case) and to lead the student in making decisions in such an environment.

This method makes no assumption that there is a *right* answer to any problem but maintains only that there are more or less successful ways of handling problems. Understanding argument and analysis (as outlined in the first section of this chapter) is more important than understanding substantive theories (as presented in the second section). These forms of understanding need not be antagonistic or competitive, but the case method in business schools has placed the premium on problem-based analysis rather than on analysis by appeal to theory. This method also avoids the authority-based method relied on in law schools, where judges and the body of law are overriding authorities.

The Case Method in Ethics

The term *casuistry* is now commonly used in ethics to refer to a method of using cases to analyze and propose solutions for moral problems. Casuists see ethics as based on seasoned experience in resolving hard cases.[25] The casuistical method is to start with *paradigm* cases whose conclusions on ethical matters are settled and then to compare and contrast the central features in the paradigm (morally clear and settled) cases with the features of cases in need of a decision.

To illustrate this point, consider a comparison to case law and the doctrine of precedent. Judicial decisions have the potential to become authoritative for other judges confronting similar cases in similar circumstances. Contemporary casuistry places a similar premium on case authority, together with a strong preference for analogical reasoning over ethical theory and abstract principles. It is analogical reasoning that links one case to the next. Moral reasoning occurs by appeal to analogies, models, classification schemes, and even immediate intuition and discerning insight about particulars.

Casuists also maintain that principles and rules are typically too indeterminate to yield specific moral judgments. It is therefore impossible, casuists insist, that there be a unidirectional movement of thought from principles to cases — what has often been called the "application" of a principle to a case. Moreover, from a casuists' perspective, principles are merely summaries of peoples' experience in reflecting on cases, not independent norms.

There is much in these casuistical arguments that is revealing and worth serious consideration, but casuists sometimes write as though cases lead to moral paradigms or judgments entirely by their facts alone. This thesis seems mistaken. The properties that people observe to be of moral importance in cases are selected by the values that they have already accepted as being morally important or have come to appreciate while examining the case. No matter how many salient facts are assembled, there will still need to be some *value* premises in order to reach a moral conclusion.

Appeals to "paradigm cases" can easily conceal this fact. These "cases" might just as well be called "cases that contain a norm." Paradigm cases gain status as paradigms because of some commitment to central values that are preserved from one case to the next case. For someone to move constructively from case to case, one or more values must connect the cases. Even to recognize a case as a paradigm case is to accept whatever principles or values allow the paradigms to be extended to other cases. Whatever can be learned from a case and then exported to another case cannot be entirely specific to the first case; only some form of general norm can lead to the next case.

In difficult cases, several possibilities for moral action emerge from the analysis of the case since the maxims derived from the case give competing advice. The casuist's job is to determine which maxim is to rule in the case and how powerfully the maxim is to rule. From this perspective, casuistry is a morality of cases that is complementary to the use of principles in ethics, though their exact relationship still needs to be worked out in moral philosophy.

Ethical Theory and Case Analysis

There are dangers in transferring the case methods in law and business to business ethics. Not much is drearier than a tedious and unrewarding exposure to the moral opinions of those ignorant of the kinds of material outlined in the first and second parts of this chapter. Studying cases in business ethics is facilitated by a knowledge of the history of ethics and types of ethical theory. Theory and history, however, also should not remain isolated from modification by case study. Several reasons support this judgment.

First, it seems mistaken to say that ethical theory is not extracted from the examination of cases but only applied to or specified in cases. Cases not only provide data for theory but also act as the testing ground for theories. Illuminating cases lead to modification and refinements of theoretical commitments, especially by pointing to limitations of theories. In thinking through the possible role of case analysis in ethics, it is useful to consider John Rawls's celebrated account of "reflective equilibrium." In developing an ethical theory, he argues, it is appropriate to start with the broadest possible set of considered moral judgments and to erect a provisional set of principles that reflects them. Reflective equilibrium views ethics as a reflective testing of moral beliefs to make them as coherent as possible. Starting with paradigms of what is morally proper or morally improper, one then searches for principles that are consistent with these paradigms. Widely accepted principles of right action and considered judgments are taken, as Rawls puts it, "provisionally as fixed points" but also as "liable to revision."

Considered judgments is a technical term referring to "judgments in which our moral capacities are most likely to be displayed without distortion." Examples are judgments about the wrongness of racial discrimination, religious intolerance, and political conflict of interest. By contrast, judgments in which one's confidence level is low or in which one is influenced by the possibility of personal gain are excluded. The goal is to match and prune considered judgments and principles in an attempt to make them coherent.[26]

Traditional ethical theory, from this perspective, has as much to learn from practical decision-making contexts as the other way around. Ethical theory can profit from a close scrutiny of a wide variety of moral phenomena, and an understanding of right action could be constructed by generalizing from what is discovered. This strategy should prevent theoreticians from overly streamlining the complexity of the moral life. From this perspective, moral thinking is similar to other forms of theorizing: Hypotheses must be tested, buried, or modified through experimental thinking. Principles can be justified, modified, or refuted, and new insights gained, by examination of cases that function as experimental data. Similarly, one's principles allow one to interpret cases and arrive at moral judgments in a reflective manner.

In conclusion, we can recall the previous discussions in the first part of the chapter of relativism and moral disagreement. Often when discussing difficult cases, many points of view are bounced around the classroom, and the controversies may seem intractable and not subject to a persuasive form of analysis transcending personal opinion. Far from viewing their class as an environment of learning, students may perceive the class as a bulletin board upon which scores of opinions are tacked. It would be a mistake, however, to conclude that such discussion eventuates only in opinion and monologue. Many apparent dilemmas do turn out to be partially resolvable, and often a consensus position emerges through dialogue, even if no one entirely agrees on the best reasons for defending the position.

In case analysis, disagreements should not be avoided or minimized, but there should also be an attempt to surmount them. A study of cases to determine how management might avoid problems can be profitable, as can reflection on procedures that deflect or defuse problems. Cases should be examined in terms of alternative strategies and actions. Invariably, many alternatives will be proposed, but just as invariably they will not all be equally good. Even if intractable disagreement does occur, learning how to spot problems and help alleviate or deflect them may turn out to be as important as the substantive issues themselves.

One temptation should be avoided, however. Those who study the facts of cases invariably desire more facts, viewing a solution as dependent on knowing more than is given in the write-up of the case. If additional data can be discovered, they think, the problems can be handled and the dilemmas disentangled. A related temptation is to doctor the known facts, thereby presenting a hypothetical case or a new case, rather than the actual cases. Both of these temptations should be avoided. Cases are interesting in part because only limited information is available. Discussants are called upon to treat problems under real-life conditions of information scarcity. Businesses function under such conditions day in and day out, and business people well know that a case must be addressed as it actually is and not as it might be in some possible world.

NOTES

1. Dana Milbank, "Hiring Welfare People, Hotel Chain Finds, Is Tough But Rewarding," *Wall Street Journal* (October 31, 1996).

2. Robert Lindsey, "Ancient Redwood Trees Fall to a Wall Street Takeover," *New York Times* (March 2, 1988), pp. A16–17.

3. Taken from Peter Huber, "The Press Gets Off Easy in Tort Law," *Wall Street Journal* (July 24, 1985), editorial page.

4. "Principle Sale," *Wall Street Journal* (May 22, 1985), p. 35.

5. "Bowing to the Inevitable," *Forbes* (August 12, 1985), p. 66.

6. See, for example, Werner Guth, Rolf Schmittberger, and Bernd Schwarze, "An Experimental Analysis of Ultimatum Bargaining," *Journal of Economic Behavior and Organization* 3 (1982): 367–388.

7. Thomas Hobbes, *Leviathan*, Part I, Chap. 13, Par. 9.

8. For an act-utilitarian example in business ethics, see R. M. Hare, "Commentary on Beauchamp's Manipulative Advertising," *Business and Professional Ethics Journal* 3 (1984): 23–28; for a rule-utilitarian example, see Robert Almeder, "In Defense of Sharks: Moral Issues in Hostile Liquidating Takeovers," *Journal of Business Ethics* 10 (1991): 471–484.

9. Tom L. Beauchamp, ed., *Case Studies in Business, Society, and Ethics*, 4th ed. (Upper Saddle River, NJ: Prentice Hall, 1996), Chap. 6.

10. As quoted in Charles R. Babcock, "Zaccaro Ousted as Guardian of Elderly Woman's Estate," *Washington Post* (August 31, 1984), sec. A, pp. 1, 8.

11. A. Carl Kotchian, *Saturday Review* (July 9, 1977).

12. See Al Kamen, "Budget Law Rejected by High Court," *Washington Post* (July 8, 1986), p. 1.

13. T. W. Zimmerer and P. L. Preston, "Plasma International," in R. D. Hay, and others, *Business and Society* (Cincinnati, OH: South-Western Publishing, 1976).

14. See Jennifer Hull, "Unocal Sues Bank," *Wall Street Journal* (March 13, 1985), p. 22; and Charles McCoy, "Mesa Petroleum Alleges Unocal Coerced Banks," *Wall Street Journal* (March 22, 1985), p. 6.

15. David S. Hilzenrath, "Taking Aim at Insider Bank Deals," *Washington Post* (September 30, 1991), Washington Business sec., p. 1.

16. See Alan Donagan, *The Theory of Morality* (Chicago: University of Chicago Press, 1977), p. 66.

17. Steven Greenhouse, "Students Urge Colleges to Join a New Anti-Sweatshop Group," *New York Times* (Oct. 20, 1999), p. 23; and Gregg Krupa, "The Battle Cry against Sweatshops Resounds Across College Campuses," *Boston Globe* (April 18, 1999), p. F1; Steven Greenhouse, "Nike Identifies Plants Abroad Making Goods for Universities," *New York Times* (Oct. 8, 1999), p. C1.

18. Ronald Dworkin argues that *political* morality is rights-based in *Taking Rights Seriously* (London: Duckworth, 1977), p. 171. John Mackie has applied this thesis to *morality generally* in "Can There Be a Right-Based Moral Theory?" *Midwest Studies in Philosophy* 3 (1978): esp. p. 350.

19. Alan Gewirth, "Why Rights Are Indispensable," *Mind* 95 (1986): 333.

20. For examples of the kind of transformation envisaged, see Ramona L. Paetzold and Bill Shaw, "A Postmodern Feminist View of 'Reasonableness' in Hostile Environment Sexual Harassment," *Journal of Business Ethics* 13 (September 1994): 681–691; Joan E. van Tol, "Eros Gone Awry: Liability Under Title VII for Workplace Sexual Favoritism," *Industrial Relations Law Journal* 13 (1991): 153–182; and Liz Armstrong, "The Fight for Equality," *Canadian Insurance* 91 (December 1986): 24, 31.

21. Carol Gilligan, *In a Different Voice* (Cambridge, MA: Harvard University Press, 1982).

22. Annette Baier, *Moral Prejudices* (Cambridge, MA: Harvard University Press, 1994), Chapter 4; and *Postures of the Mind* (Minneapolis: University of Minnesota Press, 1985), pp. 210–219.

23. Christopher Columbus Langdell's first casebook on *Contracts* is treated in Lawrence M. Friedman, *A History of American Law* (New York: Simon and Schuster, 1973), pp. 531f. The general account of the case method in this section is indebted to this source, and also to G. Edward White, *Tort Law in America: An Intellectual History* (New York: Oxford University Press, 1980).

24. See M. P. McNair, ed., *The Case Method at the Harvard Business School* (New York: McGraw-Hill, 1954).

25. See Albert Jonsen and Stephen Toulmin, *Abuse of Casuistry* (Berkeley: University of California Press, 1988), pp. 11–19, 66–67, 251–254, 296–299; John Arras, "Principles and Particularity," *Indiana Law Journal* 69 (1994).

26. John Rawls, *A Theory of Justice* (Cambridge, MA: Harvard University Press, 1971), pp. 20ff, 46–48.

Chapter Two

The Purpose
of the Corporation

THIS CHAPTER FOCUSES on corporate social responsibility. The socially respon-sible corporation is the good corporation. Over two thousand years ago the Greeks thought they could answer questions about the goodness of things by know-ing about the purpose of things. These Greek philosophers provided a functional analysis of good. For example, if one determines what a good racehorse is by know-ing the purpose of racehorses (to win races) and the characteristics — for instance, speed, agility, and discipline — horses must have to win races, then a good race-horse is speedy, agile, and disciplined. To adapt the Greeks' method of reasoning, one determines what a good (socially responsible) corporation is by investigating the purpose corporations should serve in society.

STOCKHOLDER MANAGEMENT
VERSUS STAKEHOLDER MANAGEMENT

For many, the view that the purpose of the corporation is to make a profit for stockholders is beyond debate and is accepted as a matter of fact. The classical U.S. view that a corporation's primary and perhaps sole purpose is to maximize profits for stockholders is most often associated with the Nobel Prize-winning economist Milton Friedman. This chapter presents arguments for and against the Friedman-ite view that the purpose of a corporation is to maximize stockholder profits.

Friedman has two main arguments for his position. First, stockholders are the *owners* of the corporation, and hence corporate profits *belong* to the stockholders. Managers are agents of the stockholders and have a moral obligation to manage the firm in the interest of the stockholders, that is, to maximize shareholder wealth. If the management of a firm donates some of the firm's income to charita-ble organizations, it is seen as an illegitimate use of stockholders' money. If individ-ual stockholders wish to donate their dividends to charity, they are free to do so since the money is theirs. But managers have no right to donate corporate funds to charity. If society decides that private charity is insufficient to meet the needs of the poor, to maintain art museums, and to finance research for curing diseases, it is the responsibility of government to raise the necessary money through taxation. It should not come from managers purportedly acting on behalf of the corporation.

Second, stockholders are entitled to their profits as a result of a contract among the corporate stakeholders. A product or service is the result of the productive efforts of a number of parties — employees, managers, customers, suppliers, the local community, and the stockholders. Each of these stakeholder groups has a contractual relationship with the firm. In return for their services, the managers and employees are paid in the form of wages; the local community is paid in the form of taxes; and suppliers, under the constraints of supply and demand, negotiate the return for their products directly with the firm. Funds remaining after these payments have been made represent profit, and by agreement the profit belongs to the stockholders. The stockholders bear the risk when they supply the capital, and profit is the contractual return they receive for risk taking. Thus each party in the manufacture and sale of a product receives the remuneration it has freely agreed to.

Friedman believes that these voluntary contractual arrangements maximize economic freedom and that economic freedom is a necessary condition for political freedom. Political rights gain efficacy in a capitalist system. For example, private employers are forced by competitive pressures to be concerned primarily with a prospective employee's ability to produce rather than with that person's political views. Opposing voices are heard in books, in the press, or on television so long as there is a profit to be made. Finally, the existence of capitalist markets limits the number of politically based decisions and thus increases freedom. Even political decisions reached democratically coerce the opposing minority. Once society votes on how much to spend for defense or for city streets, the minority must go along. In the market, each consumer can decide how much of a product or service he or she is willing to purchase. Thus Friedman entitled his book defending the classical view of the purpose of the firm *Capitalism and Freedom.*

The classical view that a corporation's primary responsibility is to maximize the stockholder profit is embodied in the legal opinion *Dodge v. Ford Motor Company* included in this chapter. The Court ruled that the benefits of higher salaries for Ford workers and the benefits of lower auto prices to consumers must not take priority over stockholder interests. According to *Dodge,* the interests of the stockholder are supreme.

Some have criticized Friedman on the grounds that his view justifies anything that will lead to the maximization of profits including acting immorally or illegally if the manager can get away with it. We think that criticism of Friedman is unfair. In his classic article reprinted in this chapter Friedman says:

> In such a society, "there is one and only one social responsibility of business — to use its resources and engage in activities designed to increase its profit so long as it stays within the rules of the game, which is to say, engages in open and free competition without deception or fraud." (1970, p. 126)

Thus the manager may not do anything to maximize profits. Unfortunately, Friedman has never fully elaborated on what rules of the game in a capitalist economy are. And some of his followers have argued for tactics that strike many as unethical. For example, Theodore Levitt has argued in defense of deceptive advertising[1] and in favor of strong industry lobbying to have the government pass laws that are favorable to business and to reject laws that are unfavorable.[2] And Albert Carr has argued that business is like the game of poker and thus, just as in poker, behavior that is unethical in everyday life is justified in business.[3] (Carr does admit that just as in poker there are some moral norms for business.)

Others have criticized Friedman on the grounds that the manager should use employees, customers, and suppliers if by doing so it can generate profit. Thus if wages can be cut to generate profit, they should be cut. Theoretically, that may indeed follow from Friedman's view and some managers and CEOs even behave that way. But as a practical matter, the manager usually can only generate profits if she treats employees, customers, and suppliers well — thus the expression "close to the customer" and books such as Jeffery Pfeiffer's *Competitive Advantage Through People* and Frederick F. Reichheld's book *The Loyalty Effect*. In 1953, the legal system acknowleged the connection between corporate philanthropy and goodwill. In the case of *A.P. Smith Manufacturing v. Barlow et al.* a charitable contribution to Princeton University was deemed to be a legitimate exercise of management authority. In the appeals case reprinted in this chapter, Judge Jacobs recognizes that an act that supports the public welfare can also be in the best interest of the corporation itself. The implication of this discussion is that in terms of behavior there may be no discernible difference between an "enlightened" Friedmanite and a manager who holds to the view that the purpose of the corporation involves more than the maximization of profit. The difference, to put it in a Kantian context, is in the motive. The enlightened Friedmanite treats employees well in order to generate profit. The non–Friedmanite treats employees well because that is one of the things a corporation is supposed to do.

Nearly all business ethicists concur with the general public that one of the purposes of a publicly held firm is to make a profit and thus making a profit is an obligation of the firm. Although many people also believe that the managers of publicly held corporations are legally required to maximize the profits for stockholders, this is not strictly true. Even in the most traditional interpretation managers have a fiduciary obligation to the corporation, which is then interpreted as a fiduciary obligation to stockholder interests. But during the merger and acquisition craze of the 1980s, several states passed laws permitting the managers to take into account the needs of the other stakeholders. Indiana was one of the first states to do so and many other states have followed. Other countries are even less enamored with the Friedman model. The London Stock Exchange has endorsed the Turnbull Committee report and as a result all companies listed on the London Stock Exchange will have to take into account "environment, reputation, business probity issues" when implementing internal controls.[4]

Although managers may not be obligated to maximize profits, they certainly do have an obligation to avoid conflicts of interest where it appears that they benefit at the expense of the stockholders. Many groups that defend stockholder rights are legitimately concerned with serious issues of corporate governance. Such issues as excessive executive pay, especially when it is not linked to performance, overly generous stock options, and golden parachutes in case of a hostile takeover or even friendly merger have all legitimately come under scrutiny. And stockholders need to be concerned about more than conflicts of interest. Managers like to keep information secret as well. Even if a case can be made for charitable contributions on the part of corporations, it would seem that stockholders have a right to know which charities receive corporate funds. But corporations have opposed a law that would require disclosing such information to shareholders.[5] TIAA-CREF, one of the largest pension funds in the world, has adopted a policy statement on corporate governance that is included in this chapter. And the interest in corporate governance is not confined to the United States. The Cadbury Commission in the United Kingdom has also issued a set of guidelines of corporate governance.

An alternative way to understand the purpose of the corporation is to consider those affected by business decisions, which are referred to as corporate stakeholders. From the stakeholders' perspective, the classical view is problematic in that all emphasis is placed on one stakeholder — the stockholder. The interests of the other stakeholders are unfairly subordinated to the stockholders' interests. Although any person or group affected by corporate decisions is a stakeholder, most stakeholder analysis has focused on a special group of stakeholders: namely, members of groups whose existence was necessary for the firm's survival. Traditionally, six stakeholder groups have been identified: stockholders, employees, customers, managers, suppliers, and the local community. Managers who manage from the stakeholder perspective see their task as harmonizing the legitimate interests of the primary corporate stakeholders. In describing stakeholder management, R. Edward Freeman proposes a set of principles that could make this kind of harmonizing possible.

Both in corporate and academic circles, stakeholder terminology has become very fashionable. For example, many corporate codes of conduct are organized around stakeholder principles as is the Caux Roundtable Principle for Business, which is reprinted in Chapter 8.

However, many theoretical problems remain. Stakeholder theory is still in its early developmental stage. Much has been said of the obligations of managers to the other corporate stakeholders, but little has been said about the obligations of the other stakeholders, for instance, the community or employees, to the corporation. Do members of a community have an obligation to consider the moral reputation of a company when they make their purchasing decisions? Do employees have an obligation to stay with a company that has invested in their training even if they could get a slightly better salary by moving to another corporation?

Perhaps the most pressing problems for stakeholder theory is to specify in more detail the rights and responsibilities that each stakeholder group has and to suggest how the conflicting rights and responsibilities among the stakeholder groups can be resolved.

Which Perspective Is Better?

Is the Friedmanite view that the purpose of the firm is to maximize profits or the stakeholder view that the firm is to be managed in the interests of the various stakeholders more adequate? In the two articles that conclude the chapter, Ken Goodpaster criticizes Freeman's stakeholder theory, while John Boatright presents additional difficulties for the Friedmanite position.

Ken Goodpaster's main complaint with Freeman's stakeholder analysis is that it seems to treat all stakeholder interests as equal. But that is a mistake, Goodpaster contends, because managers have special obligations to the stockholders that they do not have to any other stakeholder group. Managers have fiduciary duties to stockholders but only nonfiduciary duties to other stakeholders. These fiduciary duties are established in law and are characterized as the duties that agents have to principals. In a principal-agent relationship, the agent is to act in the best interest of the principal.

That an agent is always to act in the interest of the principal implies that whenever the interests of the stockholders conflict with the interests of another stakeholder group, the manager is obligated to honor the interests of the stockholders. If this view is justifiable, isn't Goodpaster really defending the classical Friedmanite position? Goodpaster thinks not, because even in a fiduciary relationship the principal cannot demand that the agent do something in her or his behalf that violates the basic moral principles of the community. But Friedman himself states something similar to this view when he concludes his article by saying, "There is one and only one social responsibility of business — to use its resources and engage in activities designed to increase its profits so long as it stays within the rules of the game, which is to say, engages in open and free competition without deception or fraud." If free competition without deception or fraud represents the community's view of business morality, little difference seems to exist between the views of Friedman and Goodpaster. On the other hand, if Goodpaster has a broader notion of the "basic moral principles of the community," he must say more about resolving conflicts concerning fiduciary duties to stockholders and nonfiduciary duties to other stakeholders.

Whereas Goodpaster seeks to show that there is a special relationship between managers and stockholders, John Boatright asks provocatively, "What's so special about shareholders?" Boatright's point is that the rights of shareholders are sufficiently protected without an appeal to the special fiduciary duties Goodpaster supports. Moreover, he argues that Friedman and his followers are mistaken in their view that a firm is a nexus of contracts and that managers are mere agents of the stockholders. As Boatright points out, managers are denied some of the powers of genuine agents in the legal sense. Simultaneously, the managers are not significantly under the control of the stockholders — a view that has been argued for over fifty years and is often expressed by corporate raiders who desire to take over a firm. Boatright concludes by showing that stockholders have been given special attention because public policy believed it was in the public interest to do so.

What is one to conclude with respect to this dispute? It seems that stockholders are in a special relationship with respect to profits but the relationship is not so special as has been traditionally thought. Moreover, it may not even be in the public interest to retain the traditional idea about the preeminence of the stockholder. Critics have argued that American managers are forced to manage to please Wall Street, which means they are forced to manage for the short term. And these critics have gone on to argue that the focus on the short term has led to inordinate cutbacks in employees and frayed relationships with top managers of corporations and the rank and file. In a time of near-record stock prices, these critics have a harder time being heard.

However, if a shift is made to consider long-term profitability, then there is a greater likelihood that in terms of managerial behavior, the stockholder theory and the stakeholder theory will coincide. Thus it can be argued that as a practical matter there may not be a great difference between the two perspectives. Even charitable giving and the attempt by corporations to solve social problems can be defended on Friedmanite grounds. In the twin cities of Minneapolis/St. Paul, it is believed that Target maintains a competitive advantage over Wal-Mart because of the former's reputation for charitable activities. What distinguishes a Friedmanite from a stakeholder theorist is the motivation a manager has for considering stakeholder interests. The Friedmanite treats stakeholders well in order to make a profit, while the stakeholder theorist treats stakeholders well because it is the right thing to do. Paradoxically, treating stakeholders well because it is right may end up being more profitable. In 1987 the Dayton Hudson Corporation was able to avoid a hostile takeover by the Hafts because the Minnesota legislature intervened to protect a good corporate citizen.

NOTES

1. Theodore Levitt, "The Morality (?) of Advertising," *Harvard Business Review* (July–August, 1970), pp. 84–92.
2. Theodore Levitt, "The Dangers of Social Responsibility," *Harvard Business Review* (September–October, 1958), pp. 41–50.
3. Albert Z. Carr, "Is Business Bluffing Ethical?" *Harvard Business Review* (January–February, 1968), pp. 143–153.
4. *Ethical Performance*, 1 (1999).
5. Adam Bryant, "Companies Oppose Idea of Disclosing Charitable Giving," *New York Times* (April 3, 1998).

The Social Responsibility of Business Is to Increase Its Profits

Milton Friedman

When I hear businessmen speak eloquently about the "social responsibilities of business in a free-enterprise system," I am reminded of the wonderful line about the Frenchman who discovered at the age of 70 that he had been speaking prose all his life. The businessmen believe that they are defending free enterprise when they declaim that business is not concerned "merely" with profit but also with promoting desirable "social" ends; that business has a "social conscience" and takes seriously its responsibilities for providing employment, eliminating discrimination, avoiding pollution and whatever else may be the catchwords of the contemporary crop of reformers. In fact they are — or would be if they or anyone else took them seriously — preaching pure and unadulterated socialism. Businessmen who talk this way are unwitting puppets of the intellectual forces that have been undermining the basis of a free society these past decades.

The discussions of the "social responsibilities of business" are notable for their analytical looseness and lack of rigor. What does it mean to say that "business" has responsibilities? Only people can have responsibilities. A corporation is an artificial person and in this sense may have artificial responsibilities, but "business" as a whole cannot be said to have responsibilities, even in this vague sense. The first step toward clarity in examining the doctrine of the social responsibility of business is to ask precisely what it implies for whom.

Presumably, the individuals who are to be responsible are businessmen, which means individual proprietors or corporate executives. Most of the discussion of social responsibility is directed at corporations, so in what follows I shall mostly neglect the individual proprietors and speak of corporate executives.

In a free-enterprise, private-property system, a corporate executive is an employee of the owners of the business. He has direct responsibility to his employers. That responsibility is to conduct the business in accordance with their desires, which generally will be to make as much money as possible while conforming to the basic rules of the society, both those embodied in law and those embodied in ethical custom. Of course, in some cases his employers may have a different objective. A group of persons might establish a corporation for an eleemosynary purpose — for example, a hospital or a school. The manager of such a corporation will not have money profit as his objective but the rendering of certain services.

In either case, the key point is that, in his capacity as a corporate executive, the manager is the agent of the individuals who own the corporation or establish the eleemosynary institution, and his primary responsibility is to them.

Needless to say, this does not mean that it is easy to judge how well he is performing his task. But at least the criterion of performance is straightforward, and the persons among whom a voluntary contractual arrangement exists are clearly defined.

Of course, the corporate executive is also a person in his own right. As a person, he may have many other responsibilities that he recognizes or assumes voluntarily — to his family, his conscience, his feelings of charity, his church, his clubs, his city, his country. He may feel impelled by these responsibilities to devote part of his income to causes he regards as worthy, to refuse to work for particular corporations, even to leave his job, for example, to join his country's armed forces. If we wish, we may refer to some of these responsibilities as "social responsibilities." But in these respects he is acting as a principal, not an agent; he is spending his own money or time or energy, not the money of his employers or the time or energy he has contracted to devote to their purposes. If these are "social responsibilities," they are the social responsibilities of individuals, not of business.

What does it mean to say that the corporate executive has a "social responsibility" in his capacity as businessman? If this statement is not pure rhetoric, it must mean that he is to act in some way that is not in the interest of his employers. For example, that he is to refrain from increasing the price of the product in order to contribute to the social objective of preventing inflation, even though a price increase would be in the best interests of the corporation. Or that he is to make expenditures on reducing pollution beyond the amount that is in the best interests of the corporation or that is required by law in order to contribute to the social objective of improving the environment. Or that, at the expense of corporate profits, he is to hire "hardcore" unemployed instead of better qualified available workmen to contribute to the social objective of reducing poverty.

In each of these cases, the corporate executive would be spending someone else's money for a general social interest. Insofar as his actions in accord with his "social responsibility" reduce returns to stockholders, he is spending their money. Insofar as his actions raise the price to customers, he is spending the customers' money. Insofar as his actions lower the wages of some employees, he is spending their money.

The stockholders or the customers or the employees could separately spend their own money on the particular action if they wished to do so. The executive is exercising a distinct "social responsibility," rather than serving as an agent of the stockholders or the customers or the employees, only if he spends the money in a different way than they would have spent it.

But if he does this, he is in effect imposing taxes, on the one hand, and deciding how the tax proceeds shall be spent, on the other.

This process raises political questions on two levels: principle and consequences. On the level of political principle, the imposition of taxes and the expenditure of tax proceeds are governmental functions. We have established elaborate constitutional, parliamentary, and judicial provisions to control these functions, to assure that taxes are imposed so far as possible in accordance with the preferences and desires of the public — after all, "taxation without representation" was one of the battle cries of the American Revolution. We have a system of checks and balances to separate the legislative function of imposing taxes and enacting expenditures from the executive function of collecting taxes and administering expenditure programs and from the judicial function of mediating disputes and interpreting the law.

Here the businessman — self-selected or appointed directly or indirectly by stockholders — is to be simultaneously legislator, executive, and jurist. He is to decide whom to tax by how much and for what purpose, and he is to spend the proceeds — all this guided only by general exhortations from on high to restrain inflation, improve the environment, fight poverty and so on and on.

The whole justification for permitting the corporate executive to be selected by the stockholders is that the executive is an agent serving the interests of his principal. This justification disappears when the corporate executive imposes taxes and spends the proceeds for "social" purposes. He becomes in effect a public employee, a civil servant, even though he remains in name an employee of a private enterprise. On grounds of political principle, it is intolerable that such civil servants — insofar as their actions in the name of social responsibility are real and not just window-dressing — should be selected as they are now. If they are to be civil servants, then they must be elected through a political process. If they are to impose taxes and make expenditures to foster "social" objectives, then political machinery must be set up to make the assessment of taxes and to determine through a political process the objectives to be served.

This is the basic reason why the doctrine of "social responsibility" involves the acceptance of the socialist view that political mechanisms, not market mechanisms, are the appropriate way to determine the allocation of scarce resources to alternative uses.

On the grounds of consequences, can the corporate executive in fact discharge his alleged "social responsibilities?" On the other hand, suppose he could get away with spending the stockholders' or customers' or employees' money. How is he to know how to spend it? He is told that he must contribute to fighting inflation. How is he to know what action of his will contribute to that end? He is presumably an expert in running his company — in producing a product or selling it or financing it. But nothing about his selection makes him an expert on inflation. Will his holding down the price of his product reduce inflationary pressure? Or, by leaving more spending power in the hands of his customers, simply divert it elsewhere? Or, by

forcing him to produce less because of the lower price, will it simply contribute to shortages? Even if he could answer these questions, how much cost is he justified in imposing on his stockholders, customers, and employees for this social purpose? What is his appropriate share and what is the appropriate share of others?

And, whether he wants to or not, can he get away with spending his stockholders', customers' or employees' money? Will not the stockholders fire him? (Either the present ones or those who take over when his actions in the name of social responsibility have reduced the corporation's profits and the price of its stock.) His customers and his employees can desert him for other producers and employers less scrupulous in exercising their social responsibilities.

This facet of "social responsibility" doctrine is brought into sharp relief when the doctrine is used to justify wage restraint by trade unions. The conflict of interest is naked and clear when union officials are asked to subordinate the interest of their members to some more general purpose. If the union officials try to enforce wage restraint, the consequence is likely to be wildcat strikes, rank-and-file revolts, and the emergence of strong competitors for their jobs. We thus have the ironic phenomenon that union leaders — at least in the U.S. — have objected to Government interference with the market far more consistently and courageously than have business leaders.

The difficulty of exercising "social responsibility" illustrates, of course, the great virtue of private competitive enterprise — it forces people to be responsible for their own actions and makes it difficult for them to "exploit" other people for either selfish or unselfish purposes. They can do good — but only at their own expense.

Many a reader who has followed the argument this far may be tempted to remonstrate that it is all well and good to speak of Government's having the responsibility to impose taxes and determine expenditures for such "social" purposes as controlling pollution or training the hard-core unemployed, but that the problems are too urgent to wait on the slow course of political processes, that the exercise of social responsibility by businessmen is a quicker and surer way to solve pressing current problems.

Aside from the question of fact — I share Adam Smith's skepticism about the benefits that can be expected from "those who affected to trade for the public good" — this argument must be rejected on grounds of principle. What it amounts to is an assertion that those who favor the taxes and expenditures in question have failed to persuade a majority of their fellow citizens to be of like mind and that they are seeking to attain by undemocratic procedures what they cannot attain by democratic procedures. In a free society, it is hard for "evil" people to do "evil," especially since one man's good is another's evil.

I have, for simplicity, concentrated on the special case of the corporate executive, except only for the brief digression on trade unions. But precisely the same argument applies to the newer phenomenon of calling upon stockholders to require corporations to exercise social responsibility (the recent G.M. crusade for example). In most of these cases, what is in effect involved is some stockholders trying to get other stockholders (or customers or employees) to contribute against their will to "social" causes favored by the activists. Insofar as they succeed, they are again imposing taxes and spending the proceeds.

The situation of the individual proprietor is somewhat different. If he acts to reduce the returns of his enterprise in order to exercise his "social responsibility," he is spending his own money, not someone else's. If he wishes to spend his money on such purposes, that is

his right, and I cannot see that there is any objection to his doing so. In the process, he, too, may impose costs on employees and customers. However, because he is far less likely than a large corporation or union to have monopolistic power, any such side effects will tend to be minor.

Of course, in practice, the doctrine of social responsibility is frequently a cloak for actions that are justified on other grounds rather than a reason for those actions.

To illustrate, it may well be in the long-run interest of a corporation that is a major employer in a small community to devote resources to providing amenities to that community or to improving its government. That may make it easier to attract desirable employees, it may reduce the wage bill or lessen losses from pilferage and sabotage or have other worthwhile effects. Or it may be that, given the laws about the deductibility of corporate charitable contributions, the stockholders can contribute more to charities they favor by having the corporation make the gift than by doing it themselves, since they can in that way contribute an amount that would otherwise have been paid as corporate taxes.

In each of these — and many similar — cases, there is a strong temptation to rationalize these actions as an exercise of "social responsibility." In the present climate of opinion, with its wide-spread aversion to "capitalism," "profits," the "soulless corporation," and so on, this is one way for a corporation to generate goodwill as a by-product of expenditures that are entirely justified in its own self-interest.

It would be inconsistent of me to call on corporate executives to refrain from this hypocritical window-dressing because it harms the foundations of a free society. That would be to call on them to exercise a "social responsibility"! If our institutions, and the attitudes of the public make it in their self-interest to cloak their actions in this way, I cannot summon much indignation to denounce them. At the same time, I can express admiration for those individual proprietors or owners of closely held corporations or stockholders of more broadly held corporations who disdain such tactics as approaching fraud.

Whether blameworthy or not, the use of the cloak of social responsibility, and the nonsense spoken in its name by influential and prestigious businessmen, does clearly harm the foundations of a free society. I have been impressed time and again by the schizophrenic character of many businessmen. They are capable of being extremely farsighted and clear-headed in matters that are internal to their businesses. They are incredibly short-sighted and muddle-headed in matters that are outside their businesses but affect the possible survival of business in general. This short-sightedness is strikingly exemplified in the calls from many businessmen for wage and price guidelines or controls or income policies. There is nothing that could do more in a brief period to destroy a market system and replace it by a centrally controlled system than effective governmental control of prices and wages.

The short-sightedness is also exemplified in speeches by businessmen on social responsibility. This may gain them kudos in the short run. But it helps to strengthen the already too prevalent view that the pursuit of profits is wicked and immoral and must be curbed and controlled by external forces. Once this view is adopted, the external forces that curb the market will not be the social consciences, however highly developed, of the pontificating executives; it will be the iron fist of Government bureaucrats. Here, as with price and wage controls, businessmen seem to me to reveal a suicidal impulse.

The political principle that underlies the market mechanism is unanimity. In an ideal free market resting on private property, no individual can coerce any other, all cooperation is voluntary, all parties to such cooperation benefit or they need not participate. There are no values, no "social" responsibilities in any sense other than the shared values and responsibilities of individuals. Society is a collection of individuals and of the various groups they voluntarily form.

The political principle that underlies the political mechanism is conformity. The individual must serve a more general social interest — whether that be determined by a church or a dictator or a majority. The individual may have a vote and say in what is to be done, but if he is overruled, he must conform. It is appropriate for some to require others to contribute to a general social purpose whether they wish to or not.

Unfortunately, unanimity is not always feasible. There are some respects in which conformity appears unavoidable, so I do not see how one can avoid the use of the political mechanism altogether.

But the doctrine of "social responsibility" taken seriously would extend the scope of the political mechanism to every human activity. It does not differ in philosophy from the most explicitly collectivist doctrine. It differs only by professing to believe that collectivist ends can be attained without collectivist means. That is why, in my book *Capitalism and Freedom,* I have called it a "fundamentally subversive doctrine" in a free society, and have said that in such a society, "there is one and only one social responsibility of business — to use its resources and engage in activities designed to increase its profits so long as it stays within the rules of the game, which is to say, engages in open and free competition without deception or fraud."

A Stakeholder Theory
of the Modern Corporation

R. Edward Freeman

INTRODUCTION

Corporations have ceased to be merely legal devices through which the private business transactions of individuals may be carried on. Though still much used for this purpose, the corporate form has acquired a larger significance. The corporation has, in fact, become both a method of property tenure and a means of organizing economic life. Grown to tremendous proportions, there may be said to have evolved a "corporate system" — which has attracted to itself a combination of attributes and powers, and has attained a degree of prominence entitling it to be dealt with as a major social institution.[1]

Despite these prophetic words of Berle and Means (1932), scholars and managers alike continue to hold sacred the view that managers bear a special relationship to the stockholders in the firm. Since stockholders own shares in the firm, they have certain rights and privileges, which must be granted to them by management, as well as by others. Sanctions, in the form of "the law of corporations," and other protective mechanisms in the form of social custom, accepted management practice, myth, and ritual, are thought to reinforce the assumption of the primacy of the stockholder.

The purpose of this paper is to pose several challenges to this assumption, from within the framework of managerial capitalism, and to suggest the bare bones of an alternative theory, *a stakeholder theory of the modern corporation*. I do not seek the demise of the modern corporation, either intellectually or in fact. Rather, I seek its transformation. In the words of Neurath, we shall attempt to "rebuild the ship, plank by plank, while it remains afloat."[2]

My thesis is that I can revitalize the concept of managerial capitalism by replacing the notion that managers have a duty to stockholders with the concept that managers bear a fiduciary relationship to stakeholders. Stakeholders are those groups who have a stake in or claim on the firm. Specifically I include suppliers, customers, employees, stockholders, and the local community, as well as management in its role as agent for these groups. I argue that the legal, economic, political, and moral challenges to the currently received theory of the firm, as a nexus of contracts among the owners of the factors of production and customers, require us to revise this concept. That is, each of these stakeholder groups has a right not to be treated as a means to some end, and therefore must participate in determining the future direction of the firm in which they have a stake.

The crux of my argument is that we must reconceptualize the firm around the following question: For whose benefit and at whose expense should the firm be managed? I shall set forth such a reconceptualization in the form of a *stakeholder theory of the firm*. I shall

Portions of this essay are contained in William E. Evan and R. Edward Freeman, "A Stakeholder Theory of the Modern Corporation: Kantian Capitalism" published in the third (1988) and fourth (1993) edition of this anthology and in R. Edward Freeman, "The Politics of Stakeholder Theory," *Business Ethics Quarterly*, 4 (1994), pp. 409–21. I am grateful to the editors of this volume for their editing of these two works. Used by permission.

then critically examine the stakeholder view and its implications for the future of the capitalist system.

THE ATTACK ON MANAGERIAL CAPITALISM

The Legal Argument

The basic idea of managerial capitalism is that in return for controlling the firm, management vigorously pursues the interests of stockholders. Central to the managerial view of the firm is the idea that management can pursue market transactions with suppliers and customers in an unconstrained manner.

The law of corporations gives a less clearcut answer to the question: In whose interest and for whose benefit should the modern corporation be governed? While it says that the corporations should be run primarily in the interests of the stockholders in the firm, it says further that the corporation exists "in contemplation of the law" and has personality as a "legal person," limited liability for its actions, and immortality, since its existence transcends that of its members. Therefore, directors and other officers of the firm have a fiduciary obligation to stockholders in the sense that the "affairs of the corporation" must be conducted in the interest of the stockholders. And stockholders can theoretically bring suit against those directors and managers for doing otherwise. But since the corporation is a legal person, existing in contemplation of the law, managers of the corporation are constrained by law.

Until recently, this was no constraint at all. In this century, however, the law has evolved to effectively constrain the pursuit of stockholder interests at the expense of other claimants on the firm. It has, in effect, required that the claims of customers, suppliers, local communities, and employees be taken into consideration, though in general they are subordinated to the claims of stockholders.

For instance, the doctrine of "privity of contract," as articulated in *Winterbottom v. Wright* in 1842, has been eroded by recent developments in products liability law. Indeed, *Greenman v. Yuba Power* gives the manufacturer strict liability for damage caused by its products, even though the seller has exercised all possible care in the preparation and sale of the product and the consumer has not bought the product from nor entered into any contractual arrangement with the manufacturer. Caveat emptor has been replaced, in large part, with caveat venditor.[3] The Consumer Product Safety Commission has the power to enact product recalls, and in 1980 one U.S. automobile company recalled more cars than it built. Some industries are required to provide information to customers about a product's ingredients, whether or not the customers want and are willing to pay for this information.[4]

The same argument is applicable to management's dealings with employees. The National Labor Relations Act gave employees the right to unionize and to bargain in good faith. It set up the National Labor Relations Board to enforce these rights with management. The Equal Pay Act of 1963 and Title VII of the Civil Rights Act of 1964 constrain management from discrimination in hiring practices; these have been followed with the Age Discrimination in Employment Act of 1967.[5] The emergence of a body of administrative case law arising from labor-management disputes and the historic settling of discrimination claims with large employers such as AT&T have caused the emergence of a body of practice in the corporation that is consistent with the legal guarantee of the rights of the employees. The law has protected the due process rights of those employees who enter into collective bargaining agreements with management. As of the present, however, only 30 percent of the labor force are participating in such agreements; this has prompted one labor law scholar to propose a statutory law prohibiting dismissals of the 70 percent of the work force not protected.[6]

The law has also protected the interests of local communities. The Clean Air Act and Clean Water Act have constrained management from "spoiling the commons." In an historic case, *Marsh v. Alabama,* the Supreme Court ruled that a company-owned town was subject to the provisions of the U.S. Constitution, thereby guaranteeing the rights of local citizens and negating the "property rights" of the firm. Some states and municipalities have gone further and passed laws preventing firms from moving plants or limiting when and how plants can be closed. In sum, there is much current legal activity in this area to constrain management's pursuit of stockholders' interests at the expense of the local communities in which the firm operates.

I have argued that the result of such changes in the legal system can be viewed as giving some rights to those groups that have a claim on the firm, for example, customers, suppliers, employees, local communities, stockholders, and management. It raises the question, at the core of a theory of the firm: In whose interest and for whose benefit should the firm be managed? The answer proposed by managerial capitalism is clearly "the stockholders," but I have argued that the law has been progressively circumscribing this answer.

The Economic Argument

In its pure ideological form managerial capitalism seeks to maximize the interests of stockholders. In its perennial criticism of government regulation, management espouses the "invisible hand" doctrine. It contends that it creates the greatest good for the greatest number, and therefore government need not intervene. However, we know that externalities, moral hazards, and monopoly power exist in fact, whether or not they exist in theory. Further, some of the legal apparatus mentioned above has evolved to deal with just these issues.

The problem of the "tragedy of the commons" or the free-rider problem pervades the concept of public goods such as water and air. No one has an incentive to incur the cost of clean-up or the cost of nonpollution, since the marginal gain of one firm's action is small. Every firm reasons this way, and the result is pollution of water and air. Since the industrial revolution, firms have sought to internalize the benefits and externalize the costs of their actions. The cost must be borne by all, through taxation and regulation; hence we have the emergence of the environmental regulations of the 1970s.

Similarly, moral hazards arise when the purchaser of a good or service can pass along the cost of that good. There is no incentive to economize, on the part of either the producer or the consumer, and there is excessive use of the resources involved. The institutionalized practice of third-party payment in health care is a prime example.

Finally, we see the avoidance of competitive behavior on the part of firms, each seeking to monopolize a small portion of the market and not compete with one another. In a number of industries, oligopolies have emerged, and while there is questionable evidence that oligopolies are not the most efficient corporate form in some industries, suffice it to say that the potential for abuse of market power has again led to regulation of managerial activity. In the classic case, AT&T, arguably one of the great technological and managerial achievements of the century, was broken up into eight separate companies to prevent its abuse of monopoly power.

Externalities, moral hazards, and monopoly power have led to more external control on managerial capitalism. There are de facto constraints, due to these economic facts of life, on the ability of management to act in the interests of stockholders.

A STAKEHOLDER THEORY OF THE FIRM

The Stakeholder Concept

Corporations have stakeholders, that is, groups and individuals who benefit from or are harmed by, and whose rights are violated or respected by, corporate actions. The concept of stakeholders is a generalization of the notion of stockholders, who themselves have some special claim on the firm. Just as stockholders have a right to demand certain actions by management, so do other stakeholders have a right to make claims. The exact nature of these claims is a difficult question that I shall address, but the logic is identical to that of the stockholder theory. Stakes require action of a certain sort, and conflicting stakes require methods of resolution.

Freeman and Reed (1983)[7] distinguish two senses of *stakeholder*. The "narrow definition" includes those groups who are vital to the survival and success of the corporation. The "wide-definition" includes any group or individual who can affect or is affected by the corporation. I shall begin with a modest aim: to articulate a stakeholder theory using the narrow definition.

Stakeholders in the Modern Corporation

Figure 1 depicts the stakeholders in a typical large corporation. The stakes of each are reciprocal, since each can affect the other in terms of harms and benefits as well as rights and duties. The stakes of each are not univocal and would vary by particular corporation. I merely set forth some general notions that seem to be common to many large firms.

Owners have financial stake in the corporation in the form of stocks, bonds, and so on, and they expect some kind of financial return from them. Either they have given money directly to the firm, or they have some historical claim made through a series of morally justified exchanges. The firm affects their livelihood or, if a substantial portion of their retirement income is in stocks or bonds, their ability to care for themselves when they can no longer work. Of course, the stakes of owners will differ by type of owner, preferences for money, moral preferences, and so on, as well as by type of firm. The owners of AT&T are quite different from the

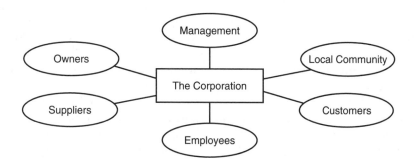

FIGURE 1.   A Stakeholder Model of the Corporation.

owners of Ford Motor Company, with stock of the former company being widely dispersed among 3 million stockholders and that of the latter being held by a small family group as well as by a large group of public stockholders.

Employees have their jobs and usually their livelihood at stake; they often have specialized skills for which there is usually no perfectly elastic market. In return for their labor, they expect security, wages, benefits, and meaningful work. In return for their loyalty, the corporation is expected to provide for them and carry them through difficult times. Employees are expected to follow the instructions of management most of the time, to speak favorably about the company, and to be responsible citizens in the local communities in which the company operates. Where they are used as means to an end, they must participate in decisions affecting such use. The evidence that such policies and values as described here lead to productive company-employee relationships is compelling. It is equally compelling to realize that the opportunities for "bad faith" on the part of both management and employees are enormous. "Mock participation" in quality circles, singing the company song, and wearing the company uniform solely to please management all lead to distrust and unproductive work.

Suppliers, interpreted in a stakeholder sense, are vital to the success of the firm, for raw materials will determine the final product's quality and price. In turn the firm is a customer of the supplier and is therefore vital to the success and survival of the supplier. When the firm treats the supplier as a valued member of the stakeholder network, rather than simply as a source of materials, the supplier will respond when the firm is in need. Chrysler traditionally had very close ties to its suppliers, even to the extent that led some to suspect the transfer of illegal pay-

ments. And when Chrysler was on the brink of disaster, the suppliers responded with price cuts, accepting late payments, financing, and so on. Supplier and company can rise and fall together. Of course, again, the particular supplier relationships will depend on a number of variables such as the number of suppliers and whether the supplies are finished goods or raw materials.

Customers exchange resources for the products of the firm and in return receive the benefits of the products. Customers provide the lifeblood of the firm in the form of revenue. Given the level of reinvestment of earnings in large corporations, customers indirectly pay for the development of new products and services. Peters and Waterman (1982)[8] have argued that being close to the customer leads to success with other stakeholders and that a distinguishing characteristic of some companies that have performed well is their emphasis on the customer. By paying attention to customers' needs, management automatically addresses the needs of suppliers and owners. Moreover, it seems that the ethic of customer service carries over to the community. Almost without fail the "excellent companies" in Peters and Waterman's study have good reputations in the community. I would argue that Peters and Waterman have found multiple applications of Kant's dictum, "Treat persons as ends unto themselves," and it should come as no surprise that persons respond to such respectful treatment, be they customers, suppliers, owners, employees, or members of the local community. The real surprise is the novelty of the application of Kant's rule in a theory of good management practice.

The local community grants the firm the right to build facilities and, in turn, it benefits from the tax base and economic and social contributions of the firm. In return for the provision of local services, the firm is expected to be a good citizen, as is any person, either "natural or artificial." The firm cannot expose the community to unreasonable hazards in the form of pollution, toxic waste, and so on. If for some reason the firm must leave a community, it is expected to work with local leaders to make the transition as smoothly as possible. Of course, the firm does not have perfect knowledge, but when it discovers some danger or runs afoul of new competition, it is expected to inform the local community and to work with the community to overcome any problem. When the firm mismanages its relationship with the local community, it is in the same position as a citizen who commits a crime. It has violated the implicit social contract with the community and should expect to be distrusted and ostracized. It should not be surprised when punitive measures are invoked.

I have not included "competitors" as stakeholders in the narrow sense, since strictly speaking they are not necessary for the survival and success of the firm; the stakeholder theory works equally well in monopoly contexts. However, competitors and government would be the first to be included in an extension of this basic theory. It is simply not true that the interests of competitors in an industry are always in conflict. There is no reason why trade associations and other multi-organizational groups cannot band together to solve common problems that have little to do with how to restrain trade. Implementation of stakeholder management principles, in the long run, mitigates the need for industrial policy and an increasing role for government intervention and regulation.

The Role of Management

Management plays a special role, for it too has a stake in the modern corporation. On the one hand, management's stake is like that of employees, with some kind of explicit or implicit employment contract. But, on the other hand, management has a duty of safeguarding the welfare of the abstract entity that is the corporation. In short, management, especially top management, must look after the health of the corporation, and this involves balancing the multiple claims of conflicting stakeholders. Owners want higher financial returns, while customers want more money spent on research and development. Employees want higher wages and better benefits, while the local community wants better parks and day-care facilities.

The task of management in today's corporation is akin to that of King Solomon. The stakeholder theory does not give primacy to one stakeholder group over another, though there will surely be times when one group will benefit at the expense of others. In general, however, management must keep the relationships among stakeholders in balance. When these relationships become imbalanced, the survival of the firm is in jeopardy.

When wages are too high and product quality is too low, customers leave, suppliers suffer, and owners sell their stocks and bonds, depressing the stock price and making it difficult to raise new capital at favorable rates. Note, however, that the reason for paying returns to owners is not that they "own" the firm, but that their support is necessary for the survival of the firm, and that they have a legitimate claim on the firm. Similar reasoning applies in turn to each stakeholder group.

A stakeholder theory of the firm must redefine the purpose of the firm. The stockholder theory claims that the purpose of the firm is to maximize the welfare of the stockholders, perhaps subject to some moral or social constraints, either because such maximization leads to the greatest good or because of property rights. The purpose of the firm is quite different in my view.

"The stakeholder theory" can be unpacked into a number of stakeholder theories, each of which has a "normative core," inextricably linked to the way that corporations should be governed and the way that managers should act. So, attempts to more fully define, or more carefully define, a stakeholder theory are misguided. Following Donaldson and Preston, I want to insist that the normative, descriptive, instrumental, and metaphorical (my addition to their framework) uses of 'stakeholder' are tied together in particular political constructions to yield a number of possible "stakeholder theories." "Stakeholder theory" is thus a genre of stories about how we could live. Let me be more specific.

A "normative core" of a theory is a set of sentences that includes among others, sentences like:

(1) Corporations ought to be governed . . .
(2) Managers ought to act to . . .

where we need arguments or further narratives which include business and moral terms to fill in the blanks. This normative core is not always reducible to a fundamental ground like the theory of property, but certain normative cores are consistent with modern understandings of property. Certain elaborations of the theory of private property plus the other institutions of political liberalism give rise to particular normative cores. But there are other institutions, other political conceptions of how society ought to be structured, so that there are different possible normative cores.

So, one normative core of a stakeholder theory might be a feminist standpoint one, rethinking how we would restructure "value-creating activity" along principles of caring and connection.[9] Another would be an ecological (or several ecological) normative cores. Mark Starik has argued that the very idea of a stakeholder theory of the *firm* ignores certain ecological necessities.[10] Exhibit 1 is suggestive of how these theories could be developed.

In the next section I shall sketch the normative core based on pragmatic liberalism. But, any normative core must address the questions in columns A or B, or explain why these questions may be irrelevant, as in the ecological view. In addition, each "theory," and I use the word hesitantly, must place the normative core within a more full-fledged

EXHIBIT 1.   A Reasonable Pluralism

	A. Corporations ought to be governed . . .	*B.* Managers ought to act . . .	*C.* The background disciplines of "value creation" are . . .
Doctrine of Fair Contracts	. . . in accordance with the six principles.	. . . in the interests of stakeholders.	— business theories — theories that explain stakeholder behavior
Feminist Standpoint Theory	. . . in accordance with the principles of caring/connection and relationships.	. . . to maintain and care for relationships and networks of stakeholders.	— business theories — feminist theory — social science understanding of networks
Ecological Principles	. . . in accordance with the principle of caring for the earth.	. . . to care for the earth.	— business theories — ecology — other

account of how we could understand value-creating activity differently (column C). The only way to get on with this task is to see the stakeholder idea as a metaphor. The attempt to prescribe one and only one "normative core" and construct "a stakeholder theory" is at best a disguised attempt to smuggle a normative core past the unsophisticated noses of other unsuspecting academics who are just happy to see the end of the stockholder orthodoxy.

If we begin with the view that we can understand value-creation activity as a contractual process among those parties affected, and if for simplicity's sake we initially designate those parties as financiers, customers, suppliers, employees, and communities, then we can construct a normative core that reflects the liberal notions of autonomy, solidarity, and fairness as articulated by John Rawls, Richard Rorty, and others.[11] Notice that building these moral notions into the foundations of how we understand value creation and contracting requires that we eschew separating the "business" part of the process from the "ethical" part, and that we start with the presumption of equality among the contractors, rather than the presumption in favor of financier rights.

The normative core for this redesigned contractual theory will capture the liberal idea of fairness if it ensures a basic equality among stakeholders in terms of their moral rights as these are realized in the firm, and if it recognizes that inequalities among stakeholders are justified if they raise the level of the least well-off stakeholder. The liberal ideal of autonomy is captured by the realization that each stakeholder must be free to enter agreements that create value for themselves, and solidarity is realized by the recognition of the mutuality of stakeholder interests.

One way to understand fairness in this context is to claim *a la* Rawls that a contract is fair if parties to the contract would agree to it in ignorance of their actual stakes. Thus, a contract is like a fair bet, if each party is willing to turn the tables and accept the other side. What would a fair contract among corporate stakeholders look like? If we can articulate this ideal, a sort of corporate constitution, we could then ask whether actual corporations measure up to this standard, and we also begin to design corporate structures which are consistent with this Doctrine of Fair Contracts.

Imagine if you will, representative stakeholders trying to decide on "the rules of the game." Each is rational in a straightforward sense, looking out for its own self-interest. At least *ex ante,* stakeholders are the relevant parties since they will be materially affected. Stakeholders know how economic activity is organized and could be organized. They know general facts about the way the corporate world works. They know that in the real world there are or could be transaction costs, externalities, and positive costs of contracting. Suppose they are uncertain about what other social institutions exist, but they know the range of those institutions. They do not know if government exists to pick up the tab for any externalities, or if they will exist in the nightwatchman state of libertarian theory. They know success and failure stories of businesses around the world. In short, they are behind a Rawls-like veil of ignorance, and they do not know what stake each will have when the veil is lifted. What groundrules would they choose to guide them?

The first groundrule is "The Principle of Entry and Exit." Any contract that is the corporation must have clearly defined entry, exit, and renegotiation conditions, or at least it must have methods or processes for so defining these conditions. The logic is straightforward: each stakeholder must be able to determine when an agreement exists and has a chance of fulfillment. This is not to imply that contracts cannot contain contingent claims or other methods for resolving uncertainty, but rather that it must contain methods for determining whether or not it is valid.

The second groundrule I shall call "The Principle of Governance," and it says that the procedure for changing the rules of the game must be agreed upon by unanimous consent. Think about the consequences of a majority of stakeholders systematically "selling out" a minority. Each stakeholder, in ignorance of its actual role, would seek to avoid such a situation. In reality this principle translates into each stakeholder never giving up its right to participate in the governance of the corporation, or perhaps into the existence of stakeholder governing boards.

The third groundrule I shall call "The Principle of Externalities," and it says that if a contract between A and B imposes a cost on C, then C has the option to become a party to the contract, and the terms are renegotiated. Once again the rationality of this condition is clear. Each stakeholder will want insurance that it does not become C.

The fourth groundrule is "The Principle of Contracting Costs," and it says that all parties to the contract must share in the cost of contracting. Once again the logic is straightforward. Any one stakeholder can get stuck.

A fifth groundrule is "The Agency Principle" that says that any agent must serve the interests of all stakeholders. It must adjudicate conflicts within the bounds of the other principals. Once again the logic is clear. Agents for any one group would have a privileged place.

A sixth and final groundrule we might call, "The Principle of Limited Immortality." The corporation shall be managed as if it can continue to serve the interests of stakeholders through time. Stakeholders are uncertain about the future but, subject to exit conditions, they realize that the continued existence of the corporation is in their interest. Therefore, it would be rational to hire managers who are fiduciaries to their interest and the interest of the collective. If it turns out the "collective interest" is the empty set, then this principle simply collapses into the Agency Principle.

Thus, the Doctrine of Fair Contracts consists of these six groundrules or principles:

(1) The Principle of Entry and Exit
(2) The Principle of Governance
(3) The Principle of Externalities
(4) The Principle of Contracting Costs
(5) The Agency Principle
(6) The Principle of Limited Immortality

Think of these groundrules as a doctrine which would guide actual stakeholders in devising a corporate constitution or charter. Think of management as having the duty to act in accordance with some specific constitution or charter.

Obviously, if the Doctrine of Fair Contracts and its accompanying background narratives are to effect real change, there must be requisite changes in the enabling laws of the land. I propose the following three principles to serve as constitutive elements of attempts to reform the law of corporations.

The Stakeholder Enabling Principle

Corporations shall be managed in the interests of its stakeholders, defined as employees, financiers, customers, employees, and communities.

The Principle of Director Responsibility

Directors of the corporation shall have a duty of care to use reasonable judgment to define and direct the affairs of the corporation in accordance with the Stakeholder Enabling Principle.

The Principle of Stakeholder Recourse

Stakeholders may bring an action against the directors for failure to perform the required duty of care.

Obviously, there is more work to be done to spell out these principles in terms of model legislation. As they stand, they try to capture the intuitions that drive the liberal ideals. It is equally plain that corporate constitutions which meet a test like the doctrine of fair contracts are meant to enable directors and executives to manage the corporation in conjunction with these same liberal ideals.[12]

Notes

1. Cf. A. Berle and G. Means, *The Modern Corporation and Private Property* (New York: Commerce Clearing House, 1932), 1. For a reassessment of Berle and Means' argument after 50 years, see *Journal of Law and Economics* 26 (June 1983), especially G. Stigler and C. Friedland, "The Literature of Economics: The Case of Berle and Means," 237–68; D. North, "Comment on Stigler and Friedland," 269–72; and G. Means, "Corporate Power in the Marketplace," 467–85.

2. The metaphor of rebuilding the ship while afloat is attributed to Neurath by W. Quine, *Word and Object* (Cambridge: Harvard University Press, 1960), and W. Quine and J. Ullian, *The Web of Belief* (New York: Random House, 1978). The point is that to keep the ship afloat during repairs we must replace a plank with one that will do a better job. Our argument is that stakeholder capitalism can so replace the current version of managerial capitalism.

3. See R. Charan and E. Freeman, "Planning for the Business Environment of the 1980s," *The Journal of Business Strategy* 1 (1980): 9–19, especially p. 15 for a brief account of the major developments in products liability law.

4. See S. Breyer, *Regulation and Its Reform* (Cambridge: Harvard University Press, 1983), 133, for an analysis of food additives.

5. See I. Millstein and S. Katsh, *The Limits of Corporate Power* (New York: Macmillan, 1981), Chapter 4.

6. Cf. C. Summers, "Protecting All Employees Against Unjust Dismissal," *Harvard Business Review* 58 (1980): 136, for a careful statement of the argument.

7. See E. Freeman and D. Reed, "Stockholders and Stakeholders: A New Perspective on Corporate Governance," in C. Huizinga, ed., *Corporate Governance: A Definitive Exploration of the Issues* (Los Angeles: UCLA Extension Press, 1983).

8. See T. Peters and R. Waterman, *In Search of Excellence* (New York: Harper and Row, 1982).

9. See, for instance, A. Wicks, D. Gilbert, and E. Freeman, "A Feminist Reinterpretation of the Stakeholder Concept," *Business Ethics Quarterly*, Vol. 4, No. 4, October 1994; and E. Freeman and J. Liedtka, "Corporate Social Responsibility: A Critical Approach," *Business Horizons*, Vol. 34, No. 4, July–August 1991, pp. 92–98.

10. At the Toronto workshop Mark Starik sketched how a theory would look if we took the environment to be a stakeholder. This fruitful line of work is one example of my main point about pluralism.

11. J. Rawls, *Political Liberalism*, New York: Columbia University Press, 1993; and R. Rorty, "The Priority of Democracy to Philosophy" in *Reading Rorty: Critical Responses to Philosophy and the Mirror of Nature (and Beyond)*, ed. Alan R. Malachowski, Cambridge, MA: Blackwell, 1990.

WHICH VIEW IS RIGHT?

Business Ethics
and Stakeholder Analysis

Kenneth E. Goodpaster

So we must think through what management should be accountable for; and how and through whom its accountability can be discharged. The stockholders' interest, both short- and long-term, is one of the areas. But it is only one.*

What is ethically responsible management? How can a corporation, given its economic mission, be managed with appropriate attention to ethical concerns? These are central questions in the field of business ethics. One approach to answering such questions that has become popular during the last two decades is loosely referred to as "stakeholder analysis." Ethically responsible management, it is often suggested, is management that includes careful attention not only to stockholders *but to stakeholders generally* in the decision-making process.

This suggestion about the ethical importance of stakeholder analysis contains an important kernel of truth, but it can also be misleading. Comparing the ethical relationship between managers and stockholders with their relationship to other stakeholders is, I will argue, almost as problematic as ignoring stakeholders (ethically) altogether — presenting us with something of a "stakeholder paradox."

---

*Peter Drucker, 1988. *Harvard Business Review.*

DEFINITION

The term "stakeholder" appears to have been invented in the early '60s as a deliberate play on the word "stockholder" to signify that there are other parties having a "stake" in the decision making of the modern, publicly held corporation in addition to those holding equity positions. Professor R. Edward Freeman, in his book *Strategic Management: A Stakeholder Approach* (Pitman, 1984), defines the term as follows:

> A stakeholder in an organization is (by definition) any group or individual who can affect or is affected by the achievement of the organization's objectives. (46)

Examples of stakeholder groups (beyond stockholders) are employees, suppliers, customers, creditors, competitors, governments, and communities. . . .

Another metaphor with which the term "stakeholder" is associated is that of a "player" in a game like poker. One with a "stake" in the game is one who plays and puts some economic value at risk.

Much of what makes responsible decision making difficult is understanding how there can be an ethical relationship between management and stakeholders that avoids being too weak (making stakeholders mere means to stockholders' ends) or too strong (making

---

From Kenneth E. Goodpaster, "Business Ethics and Stakeholder Analysis," *Business Ethics Quarterly*, 1 (January 1991), pp. 53–73. Reprinted by permission.

stakeholders quasistockholders in their own right). To give these issues life, a case example will help. So let us consider the case of General Motors and Poletown.

THE POLETOWN CASE

In 1980, GM was facing a net loss in income, the first since 1921, due to intense foreign competition. Management realized that major capital expenditures would be required for the company to regain its competitive position and profitability. A $40 billion five-year capital spending program was announced that included new, state-of-the-art assembly techniques aimed at smaller, fuel-efficient automobiles demanded by the market. Two aging assembly plants in Detroit were among the ones to be replaced. Their closure would eliminate 500 jobs. Detroit in 1980 was a city with a black majority, an unemployment rate of 18% overall and 30% for blacks, a rising public debt and a chronic budget deficit, despite high tax rates.

The site requirements for a new assembly plant included 500 acres, access to long-haul railroad and freeways, and proximity to suppliers for "just-in-time" inventory management. It needed to be ready to produce 1983 model year cars beginning in September 1982. The only site in Detroit meeting GM's requirements was heavily settled, covering a section of the Detroit neighborhood of Poletown. Of the 3,500 residents, half were black. The whites were mostly of Polish descent, retired or nearing retirement. An alternative "green field" site was available in another midwestern state.

Using the power of eminent domain, the Poletown area could be acquired and cleared for a new plant within the company's timetable, and the city government was eager to cooperate. Because of job retention in Detroit, the leadership of the United Auto

Workers was also in favor of the idea. The Poletown Neighborhood Council strongly opposed the plan, but was willing to work with the city and GM.

The new plant would employ 6,150 workers and would cost GM $500 million wherever it was built. Obtaining and preparing the Poletown site would cost an additional $200 million, whereas alternative sites in the midwest were available for $65 to $80 million.

The interested parties were many — stockholders, customers, employees, suppliers, the Detroit community, the midwestern alternative, the Poletown neighborhood. The decision was difficult. GM management needed to consider its competitive situation, the extra costs of remaining in Detroit, the consequences to the city of leaving for another part of the midwest, and the implications for the residents of choosing the Poletown site if the decision was made to stay. The decision about whom to talk to and *how* was as puzzling as the decision about *what* to do and *why*.

STAKEHOLDER ANALYSIS AND STAKEHOLDER SYNTHESIS

Ethical values enter management decision making, it is often suggested, through the gate of stakeholder analysis. But the suggestion that introducing "stakeholder analysis" into business decisions is the same as introducing ethics into those decisions is questionable. To make this plain, let me first distinguish between two importantly different ideas: stakeholder analysis and stakeholder synthesis. I will then examine alternative kinds of stakeholder synthesis with attention to ethical content.

The decision-making process of an individual or a company can be seen in terms of a sequence of six steps to be followed after an issue or problem presents itself for resolution. For ease of reference and recall, I will name the sequence PASCAL, after the six letters in the name of the French philosopher-mathematician Blaise Pascal (1623–1662), who once remarked in reference to ethical decision making that "the heart has reasons the reason knows not of."

1. PERCEPTION or fact gathering about the options available and their short- and long-term implications;
2. ANALYSIS of these implications with specific attention to affected parties and to the decision-maker's goals, objectives, values, responsibilities, etc.;
3. SYNTHESIS of this structured information according to whatever fundamental priorities obtain in the mindset of the decision-maker;
4. CHOICE among the available options based on the synthesis;
5. ACTION or implementation of the chosen option through a series of specific requests to specific individuals or groups, resource allocation, incentives, controls, and feedback;
6. LEARNING from the outcome of the decision, resulting in either reinforcement or modification (for future decisions) of the way in which the above steps have been taken.

We might simplify this analysis, of course, to something like "input," "decision," and "output," but distinguishing interim steps can often be helpful. The main point is that the path from the presentation of a problem to its resolution must somehow involve gathering, processing, and acting on relevant information.

Now, by *stakeholder analysis* I simply mean a process that does not go beyond the first two steps mentioned above. That is, the affected parties caught up in each available option are identified and the positive and negative impacts on each stakeholder are determined. But questions having to do with processing this information into a decision and implementing it are *left unanswered*. These steps are not part of the *analysis* but of the *synthesis*, *choice*, and *action*.

Stakeholder analysis may give the initial appearance of a decision-making process, but in fact it is only a *segment* of a decision-making process. It represents the preparatory or opening phase that awaits the crucial application of the moral (or nonmoral) values of the decision-maker. So, to be informed that an individual or an institution regularly makes stakeholder analysis part of decision making or takes a "stakeholder approach" to management is to learn little or nothing about the ethical character of that individual or institution. It is to learn only that stakeholders are regularly identified — *not why and for what purpose*. To be told that stakeholders are or must be "taken into account" is, so far, to be told very little. Stakeholder analysis is, as a practical matter, morally *neutral*. It is therefore a mistake to see it as a substitute for normative ethical thinking.

What I shall call "stakeholder synthesis" goes further into the sequence of decision-making steps mentioned above to include actual decision-making and implementation (S,C,A). The critical point is that stakeholder synthesis offers *a pattern or channel by which to move from stakeholder identification to a practical response or resolution*. Here we begin to join stakeholder analysis to questions of substance. But we must now ask: What kind of substance? And how does it relate to *ethics*? The stakeholder idea, remember, is typically offered as a way of integrating *ethical* values into management decision making. When and how does substance become *ethical* substance?

STRATEGIC STAKEHOLDER SYNTHESIS

We can imagine decision-makers doing "stakeholder analysis" for different underlying reasons, not always having to do with ethics. A management team, for example, might be careful to take positive and (especially) negative stakeholder effects into account for no other reason than that offended stakeholders might resist or retaliate (e.g., through political action or opposition to necessary regulatory clearances). It might not be *ethical* concern for the stakeholders that motivates and guides such analysis, so much as concern about potential impediments to the achievement of strategic objectives. Thus positive and negative effects on relatively powerless stakeholders may be ignored or discounted in the synthesis, choice, and action phases of the decision process.

In the Poletown case, General Motors might have done a stakeholder analysis using the following reasoning: our stockholders are the central stakeholders here, but other key stakeholders include our suppliers, old and new plant employees, the City of Detroit, and the residents of Poletown. These other stakeholders are not our direct concern as a corporation with an economic mission, but since they can influence our short- or long-term strategic interests, they must be taken into account. Public relation's costs and benefits, for example, or concerns about union contracts or litigation might well have influenced the choice between staying in Detroit and going elsewhere.

I refer to this kind of stakeholder synthesis as "strategic" since stakeholders outside the stockholder group are viewed instrumentally, as factors potentially affecting the overarching goal of optimizing stockholder interests. They are taken into account in the decision-making process, but as external environmental forces, as potential sources of either good will or retaliation. "We" are the economic principals and management; "they" are significant players whose attitudes and future actions might affect our short-term or long-term success. We must respect them in the way one "respects" the weather — as a set of forces to be reckoned with.

It should be emphasized that managers who adopt the strategic stakeholder approach are not necessarily *personally* indifferent to the plight of stakeholders who are "strategically unimportant." The point is that *in their role as managers,* with a fiduciary relationship that binds them as agents to principals, their basic outlook subordinates other stakeholder concerns to those of stockholders. . . . During the Poletown controversy, GM managers as individuals may have cared deeply about the potential lost jobs in Detroit, or about the potential dislocation of Poletown residents. But in their role as agents for the owners (stockholders) they could only allow such considerations to "count" if they served GM's strategic interests (or perhaps as legal constraints on the decision).

The essence of a strategic view of stakeholders is not that stakeholders are ignored, but that all but a special group (stockholders) are considered on the basis of their actual or potential influence on management's central mission. The basic normative principle is fiduciary responsibility (organizational prudence), supplemented by legal compliance.

IS THE SUBSTANCE ETHICAL?

The question we must ask in thinking about a strategic approach to stakeholder synthesis is this: Is it really an adequate rendering of the *ethical* component in managerial judgment? Unlike mere stakeholder *analysis,* this kind of synthesis does go beyond simply *identifying* stakeholders. It integrates the stakeholder information by using a single interest group (stockholders) as its basic normative touchstone. If this were formulated as an explicit rule or principle, it would have two parts and would read something like this: (1) Maximize the benefits and minimize the costs to the stockholder group, short- and long-term, and (2) Pay close attention to the interests of other stakeholder groups that might potentially influence the achievement of (1). But while expanding the list of stakeholders may be a way of "enlightening" self-interest for the organization, is it really a way of introducing ethical values into business decision making?

There are really two possible replies here. The first is that as an account of how ethics enters the managerial mind-set, the strategic stakeholder approach fails not because it is *im*moral; but because it is *non*moral. By most accounts of the nature of ethics, a strategic stakeholder synthesis would not qualify as an ethical synthesis, even though it does represent a substantive view. The point is simply that while there is nothing necessarily *wrong* with strategic reasoning about the consequences of one's actions for others, the kind of concern exhibited should not be confused with what most people regard as *moral* concern. Moral concern would avoid injury or unfairness to those affected by one's actions because it is wrong, regardless of the retaliatory potential of the aggrieved parties.

The second reply does question the morality (*vs.* immorality) of strategic reasoning as the ultimate principle behind stakeholder analysis. It acknowledges that strategy, when placed in a highly effective legal and regulatory environment and given a time-horizon that is relatively longterm, may well avoid significant forms of anti-social behavior. But it asserts that as an operating principle for managers under time pressure in an imperfect legal and regulatory environment, strategic analysis is insufficient. In the Poletown case, certain stakeholders (e.g., the citizens of Detroit or the residents of Poletown) may have merited more *ethical* consideration than the strategic approach would have allowed. Some critics charged that GM only considered these stakeholders *to the extent that* serving their interests also served GM's interests, and that as a result, their interests were undermined.

Many, most notably Nobel Laureate Milton Friedman, believe that market and legal forces are adequate to translate or transmute ethical concerns into straightforward strategic concerns for management. He believes that in our economic and political system (democratic capitalism), direct concern for stakeholders (what Kant might have called "categorical" concern) is unnecessary, redundant, and inefficient, not to mention dishonest:

> In many cases, there is a strong temptation to rationalize actions as an exercise of "social responsibility." In the present climate of opinion, with its widespread aversion to "capitalism," "profits," the "soulless corporation" and so on, this is one way for a corporation to generate good will as a by-product of expenditures that are entirely justified in its own self-interest. If our institutions, and the attitudes of the public make it in their self-interest to cloak their actions in this way, I cannot summon much indignation to denounce them. At the same time, I can express admiration for those individual proprietors or owners of closely held corporations or stockholders of more broadly held corporations who disdain such tactics as approaching fraud.

Critics respond, however, that absent a pre-established harmony or linkage between organizational success and ethical success, some stakeholders, some of the time, will be affected a lot but will be able to affect in only a minor way the interests of the corporation. They add that in an increasingly global business environment, even the protections of law are fragmented by multiple jurisdictions.

At issue then is (1) defining ethical behavior partly in terms of the (nonstrategic) decision-making values *behind* it, (2) recognizing that too much optimism about the correlation between strategic success and virtue runs the risk of tailoring the latter to suit the former.

Thus the move toward substance (from analysis to synthesis) in discussions of the stakeholder concept is not necessarily a move toward ethics. And it is natural to think that the reason for this has to do with the instrumental status accorded to stakeholder groups other than stockholders. If we were to treat all stakeholders by strict analogy with stockholders, would we have arrived at a more ethically satisfactory form of stakeholder synthesis? Let us now look at this alternative, what I shall call a "multi-fiduciary" approach.

MULTI-FIDUCIARY STAKEHOLDER SYNTHESIS

In contrast to a strategic view of stakeholders, one can imagine a management team processing stakeholder information by giving the same care to the interests of, say, employees, customers, and local communities as to the economic interests of stockholders. This kind of substantive commitment to stakeholders might involve trading off the economic advantages of one group against those of another, e.g., in a plant closing decision. I shall refer to this way of integrating stakeholder analysis with decision making as "multi-fiduciary" since all stakeholders are treated by management as having equally important interests, deserving joint "maximization" (or what Herbert Simon might call "satisficing").

Professor Freeman, quoted earlier, contemplates what I am calling the multi-fiduciary view at the end of his 1984 book under the heading *The Manager As Fiduciary to Stakeholders:*

> Perhaps the most important area of future research is the issue of whether or not a theory of management can be constructed that uses the stakeholder concept to enrich "managerial capitalism," that is, can the notion that managers bear a fiduciary relationship to stockholders or the owners of the firm, be replaced by a con-

cept of management whereby the manager *must* act in the interests of the stakeholders in the organization? (249)

As we have seen, the strategic approach pays attention to stakeholders as factors that might affect economic interests and as market forces to which companies must pay attention for competitive reasons. They become actual or potential legal challenges to the company's exercise of economic rationality. The multi-fiduciary approach, on the other hand, views stakeholders apart from their instrumental, economic, or legal clout. On this view, the word "stakeholder" carries with it, by the deliberate modification of a single phoneme, a dramatic shift in managerial outlook.

In 1954, famed management theorist Adolf Berle conceded a long-standing debate with Harvard law professor E. Merrick Dodd that looks in retrospect very much like a debate between what we are calling strategic and multi-fiduciary interpretations of stakeholder synthesis. Berle wrote:

> Twenty years ago, [I held] that corporate powers were powers in trust for shareholders while Professor Dodd argued that these powers were held in trust for the entire community. The argument has been settled (at least for the time being) squarely in favor of Professor Dodd's contention.

The intuitive idea behind Dodd's view, and behind more recent formulations of it in terms of "multiple constituencies" and "stakeholders, not just stockholders" is that by expanding the list of those in whose trust corporate management must manage, we thereby introduce ethical responsibility into business decision making.

In the context of the Poletown case, a multi-fiduciary approach by GM management might have identified the same stakeholders. But it would have considered the interests of employees, the city of Detroit, and the Poletown residents *alongside* stockholder interests, not solely in terms of how they might *influence* stockholder interests. This may or may not have entailed a different outcome. But it probably would have meant a different approach to the decision-making process in relation to the residents of Poletown (talking with them, for example).

We must now ask, as we did of the strategic approach: How satisfactory is multi-fiduciary stakeholder synthesis as a way of giving ethical substance to management decision making? On the face of it, and in stark contrast to the strategic approach, it may seem that we have at last arrived at a truly moral view. But we should be cautious. For no sooner do we think we have found the proper interpretation of ethics in management than a major objection presents itself. And, yes, it appears to be a *moral* objection!

It can be argued that multi-fiduciary stakeholder analysis is simply incompatible with widely-held moral convictions about the special fiduciary obligations owed by management to stockholders. At the center of the objection is the belief that the obligations of agents to principals are stronger or different in kind from those of agents to third parties.

THE STAKEHOLDER PARADOX

Managers who would pursue a multi-fiduciary stakeholder orientation for their companies must face resistance from those who believe that a strategic orientation is the only *legitimate* one for business to adopt, given the economic mission and legal constitution of the modern corporation. This may be disorienting since the word "illegitimate" has clear negative ethical connotations, and yet the multi-fiduciary approach is often defended on ethical grounds. I will refer to this anomalous situation as the *Stakeholder Paradox:*

It seems essential, yet in some ways illegitimate, to orient corporate decisions by ethical values that go beyond strategic stakeholder considerations to multi-fiduciary ones.

I call this a paradox because it says there is an ethical problem whichever approach management takes. Ethics seems both to forbid and to demand a strategic, profit-maximizing mind-set. The argument behind the paradox focuses on management's *fiduciary* duty to the stockholder, essentially the duty to keep a profit-maximizing promise, and a concern that the "impartiality" of the multi-fiduciary approach simply cuts management loose from certain well-defined bonds of stockholder accountability. On this view, impartiality is thought to be a *betrayal of trust.*

TOWARD A NEW STAKEHOLDER SYNTHESIS

We all remember the story of the well-intentioned Doctor Frankenstein. He sought to improve the human condition by designing a powerful, intelligent force for good in the community. Alas, when he flipped the switch, his creation turned out to be a monster rather than a marvel! Is the concept of the ethical corporation like a Frankenstein monster?

Taking business ethics seriously need not mean that management bears *additional* fiduciary relationships to third parties (nonstockholder constituencies) as multi-fiduciary stakeholder synthesis suggests. It may mean that there are morally significant *nonfiduciary* obligations to third parties surrounding any fiduciary relationship (See *Figure 1.*) Such moral obligations may be owed by private individuals as well as private-sector organizations to those whose freedom and well-being is affected by their economic behavior. It is these very obligations in fact (the duty not to

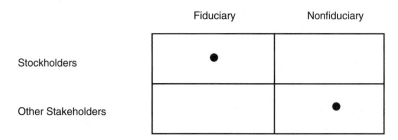

FIGURE 1.   Direct Managerial Obligations.

harm or coerce and duties not to lie, cheat, or steal) that are cited in regulatory, legislative, and judicial arguments for constraining profit-driven business activities. These obligations are not "hypothetical" or contingent or indirect, as they would be on the strategic model, wherein they are only subject to the corporation's interests being met. They are "categorical" or direct. They are not rooted in the *fiduciary* relationship, but in other relationships at least as deep.

It must be admitted . . . that the jargon of "stakeholders" in discussions of business ethics can seem to threaten the notion of what corporate law refers to as the "undivided and unselfish loyalty" owed by managers and directors to stockholders. For this way of speaking can suggest a multiplication of management duties *of the same kind* as the duty to stockholders. What we must understand is that the responsibilities of management toward stockholders are of a piece with the obligations that *stockholders themselves* would be expected to honor in their own right. As an old Latin proverb has it, *nemo dat quod non habet,* which literally means "nobody gives what he doesn't have." Freely translating in this context we can say: No one can expect of an *agent* behavior that is ethically less responsible than what he would expect of himself. I cannot (ethically) *hire* to have done on my behalf something that I would not (ethically) *do* myself. We might refer to this as

the "Nemo Dat Principle" (NDP) and consider it a formal requirement of consistency in business ethics (and professional ethics generally):

(NDP)   Investors cannot expect of managers (more generally, principals cannot expect of their agents) behavior that would be inconsistent with the reasonable ethical expectations of the community.

The NDP does not, of course, resolve in advance the many ethical challenges that managers must face. It only indicates that these challenges are of a piece with those that face us all. It offers a different kind of test (and so a different kind of stakeholder synthesis) that management (and institutional investors) might apply to policies and decisions.

The foundation of ethics in management — and the way out of the stakeholder paradox — lies in understanding that the conscience of the corporation is a logical and moral extension of the consciences of its principals. It is *not* an expansion of the *list* of principals, but a gloss on the principal-agent relationship itself. Whatever the structure of the principal-agent relationship, neither principal nor agent can ever claim that an agent has "moral immunity" from the basic obligations that would apply to any human being toward other members of the community.

Indeed, the introduction of moral reasoning (distinguished from multi-fiduciary stakeholder reasoning) into the framework of management thinking may *protect* rather than threaten private sector legitimacy. The conscientious corporation can maintain its private economic mission, but in the context of fundamental moral obligations owed by any member of society to others affected by that member's actions. Recognizing such obligations does *not* mean that an institution is a public institution. Private institutions, like private individuals, can be and are bound to respect moral obligations in the pursuit of private purposes.

Conceptually, then, we can make room for a moral posture toward stakeholders that is both *partial* (respecting the fiduciary relationship between managers and stockholders) and *impartial* (respecting the equally important nonfiduciary relationships between management and other stakeholders). . . .

Whether this conceptual room can be used *effectively* in the face of enormous pressures on contemporary managers and directors is another story, of course. For it is one thing to say that "giving standing to stakeholders" in managerial reasoning is conceptually coherent. It is something else to say that it is practically coherent.

Yet most of us, I submit, believe it. Most of us believe that management at General Motors *owed* it to the people of Detroit and to the people of Poletown to take their (nonfiduciary) interests very seriously, to seek creative solutions to the conflict, to do more than use or manipulate them in accordance with GM's needs only. We understand that managers and directors have a special obligation to provide a financial return to the stockholders, but we also understand that the word "special" in this context needs to be tempered by an appreciation of certain fundamental community norms that go beyond the demands of both laws and markets.

There are certain class-action suits that stockholders ought not to win. For there is sometimes a moral defense.

CONCLUSION

The relationship between management and stockholders is ethically different in kind from the relationship between management and other parties (like employees, suppliers, customers, etc.), a fact that seems to go unnoticed by the multi-fiduciary approach. If it were not, the corporation would cease to be a private sector institution — and what is now called business ethics would become a more radical critique of our economic system than is typically thought. On this point, Milton Friedman must be given a fair and serious hearing.

This does not mean, however, that "stakeholders" lack a morally significant relationship to management, as the strategic approach implies. It means only that the relationship in question is different from a fiduciary one. Management may never have promised customers, employees, suppliers, etc. a "return on investment," but management is nevertheless obliged to take seriously its extra-legal obligations not to injure, lie to, or cheat these stakeholders *quite apart from* whether it is in the stockholders' interests.

As we think through the *proper* relationship of management to stakeholders, fundamental features of business life must undoubtedly be recognized: that corporations have a principally economic mission and competence; that fiduciary obligations to investors and general obligations to comply with the law cannot be set aside; and that abuses of economic power and disregard of corporate stewardship in the name of business ethics are possible.

But these things must be recognized as well: that corporations are not solely financial institutions; that fiduciary obligations go beyond short-term profit and are in any case subject to moral criteria in their execution; and that mere compliance with the law can be unduly limited and even unjust.

The *Stakeholder Paradox* can be avoided by a more thoughtful understanding of the nature of moral obligation and the limits it imposes on the principal-agent relationship. Once we understand that there is a practical "space" for identifying the ethical values shared by a corporation and its stockholders — a space that goes beyond strategic self-interest but stops short of impartiality — the hard work of filling that space can proceed.

Fiduciary Duties and the Shareholder-Management Relation: Or, What's So Special About Shareholders?

John R. Boatright

INTRODUCTION

It is well-established in law that officers and directors of corporations are fiduciaries. Much of the debate on corporate social responsibility from the 1930s to the present has focused on the questions: For whom are managers fiduciaries? And what are their specific fiduciary duties? The common-law view is that officers and directors are fiduciaries primarily for shareholders, who are legally the owners of a corporation, and their main fiduciary duty is to operate the corporation in the interests of the shareholders. As a result, the social responsibility of corporations is sharply restricted. In the words of Milton Friedman, "there is one and only one social responsibility of business," and that is to make as much money for the shareholders as possible.[1]

Those who argue for an expanded view of social responsibility offer a different answer to the question, for whom are managers fiduciaries? Merrick Dodd contended in 1932 that the powers of management are held in trust for the whole community. The modern corporation, he maintained, "has a social service as well as a profit-making function," and managers ought to take the interests of many different constituencies into account.[2] More recently, R. Edward Freeman has popularized the stakeholder approach, in which every group with a stake in a corporation has claims that rival those of stockholders.[3] Consequently, the fiduciary duties of management include serving the interests of employees, customers, suppliers, and the local community in addition to the traditional duties to shareholders.

A prominent critic of both Dodd and Freeman is Kenneth E. Goodpaster, who cautions that a multi-fiduciary stakeholder approach overlooks an important point: that the "relationship between management and stockholders is ethically different in kind from the

From John R. Boatright, "Fiduciary Duties and the Shareholder Management Relation: Or, What's So Special About Shareholders?", *Business Ethics Quarterly*, 4 (1994). Reprinted by permission.

relationship between management and other parties (like employees, suppliers, customers, etc.)."[4] Goodpaster contends that managers have many *nonfiduciary* duties to various stakeholders, but the shareholder-management relation is unique in that managers have *fiduciary* duties to shareholders alone. Whether the relation between managers and shareholders is "ethically different," as Goodpaster claims, is a question that requires some understanding of the ethical basis of the duties of management to different constituencies. The stakeholder approach focuses largely on the basis of the duties of management to constituencies other than shareholders, which is to say, duties to employees, suppliers, customers, and the like. Another procedure, however, is to look more closely at the ethical basis of the fiduciary duties of officers and directors of corporations to shareholders. Since the common-law view is that shareholders are special in that managers have a fiduciary duty to run the corporation in their interests alone, we need to ask, what entitles them to this status? In short, what's so special about shareholders?

SHAREHOLDERS AS OWNERS

There is no question but that the fiduciary duties of management have been based, historically, on the assumption that shareholders are the owners of a corporation. In *The Modern Corporation and Private Property*, Berle and Means observed that our thinking about the shareholder-management relation derives, in part, from the notion of equity in the treatment of property owners, dating from the time when business ventures were undertaken by individuals with their own assets. About the origin of the fiduciary relation they wrote:

Taking this doctrine back into the womb of equity, whence it sprang, the foundation becomes plain. Wherever one man or a group of men entrusted another man or group with the management of property, the second group became fiduciaries. As such they were obliged to act conscionably, which meant in fidelity to the interests of the persons whose wealth they had undertaken to handle.[5]

Ownership of a corporation is different, of course, from the ownership of personal assets. Most notably, shareholders do not have a right to possess and use corporate assets as they would their own; instead, they create a fictitious person to conduct business, with the shareholders as the beneficiaries. To the extent that shareholders do not manage a corporation but leave control to others, there is a problem of ensuring that the hired managers run the corporation in the interests of the shareholders.

The law of corporate governance has addressed this problem by creating a set of shareholder rights along with a set of legal duties for corporate officers and directors. The most important rights of shareholders are to elect the board of directors and to receive the earnings of a corporation in the form of dividends. A main duty of officers and directors is to act as fiduciaries in the management of the corporation's assets. Since these various rights and duties are legally enforceable, they provide a relatively effective solution to the problem of accountability.

Now, even if it is granted that shareholders are the owners of a corporation in the sense of possessing these rights, it does not follow that officers and directors have a fiduciary duty to run the corporation in the interests of shareholders. It is entirely consistent to hold that shareholders are the owners of a corporation and that the managers have a fiduciary duty to run the corporation in the interests of other constituencies. There is a logical gap, in other words, between the property rights of shareholders and the fiduciary duties of management. This does not mean that ownership is irrelevant to fiduciary duties. J. A. C. Hetherington has described ownership as "the formal legal substructure on which the fiduciary duty of management rests."[6] The point is, rather, that some further premises are needed for the argument to go through.

The most common argument for the fiduciary duties of officers and directors is that the property interests which holders have in a corporation can be protected only by a stringent set of duties to act in the interests of shareholders. Shareholders, as equity suppliers, are different from bondholders and others who provide debt — and they are different, as well, from suppliers, employees, customers, and others who have dealings with a corporation. The difference, as explained by Oliver E. Williamson, is: "The whole of their investment in the firm is potentially placed at hazard."[7] Bondholders, suppliers, and so on, are protected by contracts and other safeguards, leaving shareholders, as the owners of a corporation, to bear the preponderance of risk. The various rights of shareholders are thus important means for protecting the shareholders' investment.

Williamson observes that shareholders are unique in several other respects. He writes:

> They are the only voluntary constituency whose relation with the corporation does not come up for periodic renewal. . . . Labor, suppliers . . . debt-holders, and consumers all have opportunities to renegotiate terms when contracts are renewed. Stockholders, by contrast, invest for the life of the firm. . . . [8]

Shareholders are also unique in that "their investments are not associated with particular assets." This feature makes it more difficult to devise contracts and other safeguards like those which protect other constituencies, who can generally withdraw what they have provided. A shareholder, who has only a residual claim, can be protected only by assurance that the corporation will continue to prosper.

This argument — let us call it the equity argument — is an important justification for shareholder rights. Since shareholders are different in certain respects, and since their investment ought to be protected, it is necessary to create a governance structure which assigns them a significant role. The argument does not succeed, however, in supporting the strong claim that managers have fiduciary duties to shareholders and to shareholders alone.

First, if the only justification for fiduciary duties is the need to protect the shareholders' investment, then it is unclear why this end is not achieved by existing shareholder rights and, hence, why fiduciary duties are also necessary. That is, the rights of shareholders to elect the board of directors, vote on shareholder resolutions, and so on, constitute a kind of protection which other constituencies lack and which would seem to be adequate. Some of the fiduciary duties of management, especially those which prohibit self-dealing, may also be important safeguards, but the protection of shareholders can be achieved without a strong profit-maximizing imperative which imposes a fiduciary duty to act solely in the interests of shareholders. This more stringent fiduciary duty needs some further justification.

Second, shareholders have another important source of protection that is denied to other constituencies. Through the stock market, a shareholder can, with little effort or cost, dispose of a disappointing stock.[9] Banks, by contrast, are often stuck with bad loans; employees can change employers only with great difficulty; and communities must be content with the businesses located in their midst. The stock market also provides protection in the form of *ex ante* compensation, since stockholders have the opportunity to purchase stock that may increase in value.

Investors are compensated for their risk by the opportunity to reap great rewards, and usually the greater the risk, the greater the potential rewards. Further, the stock market allows for diversification, so that a properly diversified investor should face little risk. Indeed, managers and employees of firms generally have far more at stake in the success of a corporation than do the shareholders.

For these reasons, then, the equity argument does not justify the view that officers and directors have a fiduciary duty to run a corporation in the interests of the shareholders. Insofar as shareholders are owners, they have property interests which ought to be protected, but doing so does fully account for the special status that common law gives to shareholders. Indeed, the argument treats shareholders as one class of investors among many, albeit an especially vulnerable class. Some observers have even suggested that shareholders are not properly the "owners" of the corporation at all. Just as bondholders own their bonds, so shareholders, they claim, are merely the owners of their stock.[10]

CONTRACTS AND AGENCY

Another possible basis for fiduciary duties is provided by the supposition of a contract between shareholders and management and, in particular, of an agency relation whereby the managers of a corporation agree specifically to act as agents of shareholders in the latter's pursuit of wealth. This basis is logically independent of ownership, but if we ask what enables shareholders to contract with management or act as a principal, one answer is their status as owners. Thus, the logical gap between ownership and fiduciary duties might be bridged by the idea that owners hire other persons by means of a contract to become the managers of their property.

In his rejection of a multi-fiduciary approach, Goodpaster clearly assumes that the shareholder-management relation is based on a contract or an agency relation. He writes:

> It can be argued that multi-fiduciary stakeholder analysis is simply incompatible with widely-held moral convictions about the special fiduciary obligations owed by management to stockholders. At the center of the objection is the belief that the obligations of agents to principals are stronger or different in kind from those of agents to third parties.[11]

In another passage Goodpaster explains how the duties of management to third parties can be "morally significant" yet different from the duties owed to shareholders by observing that "management may never have *promised* customers, employees, suppliers, etc. a 'return on investment,' but management is nevertheless obliged to take seriously its extra-legal obligations" to these stakeholders.[12] The suggestion is that management has made a promise to shareholders to act in their interests and that the obligation created by this promise is a legal obligation. The obligations to other constituencies, in contrast, are based on something other than a promise and are nonlegal in character.

Further, Goodpaster claims that what he calls the stakeholder paradox "can be avoided by a more thoughtful understanding of the nature of moral obligation and the limits it imposes on the principal-agent relationship."[13] The stakeholder paradox, according to Goodpaster, is that:

> It seems essential, yet in some ways illegitimate, to orient corporate decisions by ethical values that go beyond strategic stakeholder considerations to multi-fiduciary ones.[14]

The resolution of this paradox, in Goodpaster's view, lies in recognizing that just as shareholders themselves are constrained in the pursuit of their self-interest by the ethical expectations of society, managers are constrained by these same ethical expectations in their service as the agents of the shareholders. Goodpaster writes:

> The foundation of ethics in management — and the way out of the stakeholder paradox — lies in understanding that the conscience of the corporation is a logical and moral extension of the consciences of its principals. It is *not* an expansion of the list of principals, but a gloss on the principal-agent relationship itself. Whatever the structure of the principal-agent relationship, neither principal nor agent can ever claim that an agent has "moral immunity" from the basic obligations that would apply to any human being toward other members of the community.[15]

In order to base the fiduciary duties of management to shareholders on a contract between management and shareholders — and, in particular, to argue that the relation is a principal-agent relationship — it is necessary, obviously, to show that some kind of contract exists.[16] There is, of course, no *express* contract between the two parties that spells out in writing the terms of the relation, but a defender of the argument might contend that there is still an *implied* contract, which is a kind recognized in law. The courts have frequently found implied contracts to exist in the relations between buyers and sellers and between employers and employees. Why not between shareholders and management?

The case for an implied contract is not very promising. In most cases, a shareholder buys shares of a corporation from previous owners, not from the corporation itself, and even in the case of original purchases of stock, there is no agreement beyond the prospectus. The available evidence suggests that shareholders buy stock with roughly the same expectations as those who make any other financial investment. The conclusion of one study is that "shareholders expect to be treated as 'investors,' much like bondholders, for example, and expect corporate managers to consider a wide constituency when making corporate decisions."[17] Moreover, the lack of any face-to-face dealings between the two parties and the lack of any specific representations by management to individual shareholders further mitigate against any presumption that an implied contract exists. In short, the standard legal conditions for an implied contract are absent in the shareholder-management relation.

Even if there is no legal contract, it is still possible to argue that the idea of a contract provides the best means for understanding the moral features of the shareholder-management relation. The classical social contract theories of Hobbes, Locke, and others provide a means for establishing political obligations, and recently some philosophers have made use of a social contract to provide a framework for the responsibility of corporations to society. Although social contract theory may be a useful normative model in some contexts, it is not easily applied to the shareholder-management relation.

First, the idea of a contract is most at home in situations in which two parties are able to negotiate a set of mutual obligations which governs specific interactions. In the case of shareholders and management, however, there is virtually no opportunity for the two parties to negotiate the terms of their relation. (As noted earlier, Williamson considers the fact that the relation never comes up for periodic renewal to be a reason for regarding shareholders as owners and not ordinary investors.) Also, the "terms" of any supposed contract are set largely by the laws of corporate governance, which have been created by legislatures and courts for reasons unrelated to any contract between shareholders and the management of a corporation. While employers and employees are free to negotiate on specific details, such as wages and working conditions, shareholders are offered shares of stock on a "take it or leave it" basis.

Second, and more important, there is relatively little interaction between shareholders and the managers with whom they are supposed to be related by means of a contract, and most of the obligations which are placed on managers are not related directly to shareholders, as the contractual model suggests. The fiduciary duties of management, for example, cover a wide variety of matters which make no reference to shareholders. . . .

THE AGENCY RELATION

Just as the shareholder-management relation does not meet the conditions for an implied contract, so too does it not fit the conditions for agency. As a matter of law, officers are agents, but they are agents of the corporation, not the shareholders; and directors, who in a sense are the corporation, are not agents at all. Furthermore, many of the fiduciary duties of management involve activities which are, for the most part, unrelated to shareholders, . . . Thus, the claim that managers are agents for shareholders, even if true, could not account for all of the fiduciary duties of management.

That corporate managers are not agents of the shareholders follows from the standard legal definition given by the second *Restatement of Agency*, Section 1 (1), which reads: "Agency is the fiduciary relation which results from the manifestation of consent by one person to another that the other shall act on his behalf and subject to his control, and consent by the other so to act." The crucial elements in this definition are: (1) consent to the relation, (2) the power to act on another's behalf, and (3) the element of

control. None of these is present in the shareholder-management relation.

First, directors and officers, upon assuming their positions, agree to abide by a set of duties, which are largely those prescribed by the laws of a state concerning corporate governance. It is unrealistic to suppose that these managers do anything that can be described as "manifesting consent" to serve the shareholders' interests. Further, none of the fine distinctions used by the courts to decide when an agency relation has been created or terminated ("actual" versus "implied" agency, for example) or to distinguish among kinds of agency (such as "special" and "universal" agency) is usefully applied to the relation between shareholders and management.

Second, officers and directors have no power to act on behalf of the shareholders insofar as this is understood in the legal sense of changing a legal relation of the principal with regard to a third party. In fact, all decisions which change the legal relation of shareholders with regard to third parties (merging with another company, for example, or changing the bylaws of the corporation) must be approved by shareholders; management is barred by law from making decisions of this kind on its own authority. If managers were agents of the shareholders, they ought to have a right to make some decisions of this kind.

Third, management is in no significant sense under the control of the shareholders. Day-to-day operations of a corporation, along with long-term strategic planning, are the province of the officers and directors. Shareholders have no right to intervene, and even shareholder suits over mistaken decisions are generally blocked by the business judgment rule. As long as their fiduciary duties are met, management can enter into new lines of business and abandon old lines, undertake rapid expansion or cut back, and, in short, make virtually all ordinary business decisions without regard for the desires of shareholders. . . .

The inescapable conclusion is that officers and directors of corporations are not, legally, in a contractual or an agency relation with shareholders and that, moreover, there are no good ethical reasons for regarding them as being in such a relation. As a result, Goodpaster's claim — that the shareholder-management relation is fiduciary in character because of a contract or agency relation — is untenable. This cannot be the basis for the fiduciary duties of management and hence for the claim that such duties are owed to shareholders alone.

PUBLIC POLICY AS A BASIS

Even if Goodpaster is mistaken about the ethical basis for fiduciary duties, it is still possible for him to hold that the shareholder-management relation is "ethically different" because of its fiduciary character. There is an important distinction between fiduciary and nonfiduciary duties, which the stakeholder approach tends to disregard. Thus, Freeman argues for the stakeholder approach by citing the many legal obligations which management owes to various constituencies. Goodpaster willingly concedes that corporations have these obligations and that they are "morally significant," but he insists that a crucial difference remains: the obligations of corporations to other constituencies are not fiduciary duties but duties of another kind. On this point Goodpaster is correct.

It is necessary, however, to find some basis for fiduciary duties, if they are to exist at all. And if fiduciary duties are confined to the shareholder-management relation, then a basis must be found which singles out shareholders as a special constituency. That is, there must be something special about shareholders which makes them, and no other constituency, the object of the fiduciary duties of management. . . . [It could be argued]

that the value of maintaining the private, profit-making nature of the corporation comes from considerations of public policy. Put simply, the argument is that institutions in which management is accountable primarily to shareholders provides the most socially beneficial system of economic organization.

One exponent of this view was A. A. Berle, who conducted a debate with Merrick Dodd in the 1930s over a version of the stakeholder approach. Both Dodd and Berle recognized that the assumption that shareholders are the owners of a corporation no longer serves as a basis for the fiduciary duties of management. With the separation of ownership and control, the "traditional logic of property" became outmoded, with the result that shareholders lost any special status based on property rights. According to Berle and Means:

> . . . [T]he owners of passive property, by surrendering control and responsibility over the active property, have surrendered the right that the corporation should be operated in their sole interest, — they have released the community from the obligation to protect them to the full extent implied in the doctrine of strict property rights.[18]

But by taking control away from the owners, managers have not thereby conferred upon themselves the right to run the corporation for their benefit.

> The control groups have, rather, cleared the way for the claims of a group far wider than either the owners or the control. They have placed the community in a position to demand that the modern corporation serve not alone the owners or the control but all society.[19]

Dodd's position (and Freeman's, as well) is that the fiduciary duties of management should be extended now to include all other constituencies. Berle rejected this alternative, however, because he feared that extending the range of constituencies would result, not in benefits to these constituencies but in absolute power for management. In his response to Dodd, Berle wrote, "When the fiduciary obligation of the corporate management and 'control' to stockholders is weakened or eliminated, the management and 'control' become for all practical purposes absolute."[20] Thus, it would be dangerous to the community and harmful to business to remove the strong fiduciary duties which the law imposes on managers. He wrote:

> Unchecked by present legal balances, a social-economic absolutism of corporate administrators, even if benevolent, might be unsafe; and in any case it hardly affords the soundest base on which to construct the economic commonwealth which industrialism seems to require. Meanwhile . . . we had best be protecting the interests we know, being no less swift to provide for the new interests as they successively appear.[21]

Ultimately, Berle's argument is that corporations ought to be run for the benefit of shareholders, not because they "own" the corporation, or because of some contract or agency relation, but because all other constituencies are better off as a result. The underlying assumption is that the fiduciary duties of management are and ought to be determined by considerations of public policy. The present state of corporate governance is not ideal, but it is a workable arrangement that had been fashioned by historical forces. Any reform, therefore, should be incremental, so as to avoid unwanted disruptions.

Courts and legislatures in the United States have largely followed Berle's advice and have been very reluctant to weaken the strict profit-maximizing imperative that the law of fiduciary duties imposes on management. Managers, by law, must consider primarily the interests of shareholders in certain matters, and shareholders may bring suit against officers and directors for failing to do so.

The fiduciary duties of management have been weakened to some extent by so-called "other constituency" statutes, which permit (but do not require) officers and directors to consider the impact of their decisions on constituencies besides shareholders.[22] This is an exception that proves the rule, however, since these statutes have been enacted mainly to protect management from shareholder suits in the adoption of anti-takeover measures in the belief that the interests of the public are best served by allowing a wider range of considerations in defending against hostile takeovers. . . .

These considerations tend to support the Berle view that the basis for the fiduciary duties of management is public policy. If this is so, then the shareholder-management relation is not "ethically different" for any reason that is unique to that relation. Consequently, there is no reason in principle why the distinction between fiduciary and nonfiduciary duties and the distinction between shareholders and other constituencies should cut as neatly as Goodpaster suggests. And, indeed, we find that Goodpaster's identification of fiduciary duties with shareholders and nonfiduciary duties with other constituencies is not wholly accurate. Many of the fiduciary duties of officers and directors are owed not to shareholders but to the corporation as an entity with interests of its own, which can, on occasion, conflict with those of shareholders. Further, corporations have some fiduciary duties to other constituencies, such as creditors (to remain solvent so as to repay debts) and to employees (in the management of a pension fund, for example).

THE STAKEHOLDER PARADOX REVISITED

For Goodpaster, the distinction between fiduciary and nonfiduciary duties is at the heart of the stakeholder paradox. The reason why "[i]t seems essential to orient corporate decisions by ethical values that go beyond strategic stakeholder considerations to multi-fiduciary ones" is that other constituencies have interests which are the subject of many obligations that are nonfiduciary in character. The reason why orienting corporate decisions by multi-fiduciary ethical values seems illegitimate is that the fiduciary duties are concerned primarily with maintaining the profit-maximizing function of the corporation. It is the existence of both fiduciary and nonfiduciary duties, then, that makes what seems to be the same thing both "essential" and "illegitimate."

Goodpaster's solution to the paradox — that shareholders cannot expect managers as their agents to act in ways which are inconsistent with the ethical standards of the community — does not work, however, if managers are not agents of the shareholders. However, if public policy is accepted as the basis for fiduciary duties, then a rather different solution to the stakeholder paradox becomes possible.

In corporate law, a fairly sharp distinction is made between the fiduciary duties of officers and directors, for which they can be held personally liable, and their other obligations and responsibilities for which they are not personally liable. Traditionally, the fiduciary duties of management are those of obedience and diligence, which require that they act within the scope of their authority and exercise ordinary care and prudence. These duties constitute a minimal level of oversight for which managers are held to a high degree of personal accountability. As long as they fulfill these fiduciary duties and act in ways which they believe to be in the best interests of the corporation, officers and directors are shielded from personal liability for any losses that occur. Losses that occur because of honest mistakes of judgment are covered, instead, by the business judgment rule, which

prevents the courts from "second-guessing" the judgment of management.

As a result of this distinction, the obligations of management to shareholders are themselves divisible into fiduciary and nonfiduciary. The shareholder-management relation is not a single relation that is fiduciary in character; rather, it is a manifold relation in which management has some obligations to shareholders which are fiduciary duties and other obligations which are nonfiduciary duties. The fiduciary duties of officers and directors in the corporation are limited, moreover, to the most general matters of organization and strategy, so that in the ordinary conduct of business, where the business judgment rule applies, the interests of other constituencies may be taken into account without the possibility of a successful shareholder suit for the breach of any fiduciary duty.

An alternative solution to the stakeholder paradox, then, is to distinguish between the decisions of management which bear on their fiduciary duties and those that do not. A statement of the stakeholder paradox which includes this distinction might read as follows:

> It is illegitimate to orient corporate decisions that bear on the fiduciary duties of management by ethical values that go beyond strategic stakeholder considerations to include the interests of other constituencies, but it is essential to orient other corporate decisions by these values.

So stated, there is no longer any paradox, and we have an explanation of why "[e]thics seems both to forbid and to demand a strategic, profit-maximizing mind-set."[23]

The explanation is to be found, not in making the conscience of the corporation "a logical and moral extension of the consciences of its principals," as Goodpaster claims, but in the public policy considerations which have led to a distinction in law between fiduciary and nonfiduciary duties. On questions about the nature and structure of the corporation, with which fiduciary duties are largely concerned, courts and legislatures have held, for reasons of public policy, that the profit-making function of corporations and accountability to shareholders ought to be preserved. On questions of ordinary business operation, however, public policy dictates that corporations be allowed to take the interests of many constituencies besides shareholders into account.

CONCLUSION

This account of the relation between shareholders and management constitutes a third position, somewhere between Goodpaster's view and the stakeholder approach. On all three positions, fiduciary duties play a prominent but different role, and each involves a different ethical basis for the fiduciary duties of management. In the account presented here, shareholders are special to the extent that public policy considerations support the continuation of the corporation as a private, profit-making institution, with strong accountability to shareholders. . . .

Whether shareholders should continue to occupy the status that they do is also a matter to be decided by considerations of public policy. Since the 1930s, there has been a steady erosion in shareholder power, largely as a result of the increasing separation of ownership and control and the rise of large institutional investors. This has not occasioned much concern, since market forces and government regulation, along with a limited role for shareholders, have been regarded as sufficient checks on the power of management to ensure that corporate activity is generally beneficial. In recent years, there has been a movement to increase the influence of shareholders in major corporate decisions, but the main arguments have come from economists who believe that shareholder activism would force corporations to be more efficient.

The strongest force for change at the present time comes from once passive institutional investors who, in their role as fiduciaries for their own investors, have objected to anti-takeover measures, high executive compensation, and other matters that advance the interests of incumbent management over those of shareholders. Some of the largest pension funds have also taken an active role in major restructurings and the selection of CEOs. Pressure is also being placed on the SEC to change the interpretation of Rule 14a-8 to allow shareholder resolutions on a broader range of issues.

The current debate over the role of shareholders suggests that the delicate balance of shareholder power, market forces, and government regulation has not fully succeeded in achieving maximum efficiency or in preventing some management abuses. Whether the answer lies in increasing shareholder power, changing the conditions of competition, or imposing more government regulation — or in some combination of the three — remains to be decided. What is clear is that the current debate is being conducted, not on the basis of ownership or of a contract or an agency relation, but in terms of public policy. Thus, to answer the question posed in the title: except for the useful role they play in corporate governance, there is nothing special about shareholders.

NOTES

1. Milton Friedman, *Capitalism and Freedom* (Chicago: University of Chicago Press, 1962), 133; and "The Social Responsibility of Business Is to Increase Its Profits," *The New York Times Magazine*, September 13, 1970, p. 33.
2. E. Merrick Dodd, Jr., "For Whom Are Corporate Managers Trustees?" *Harvard Law Review*, 45 (1932), 1148.

3. R. Edward Freeman, *Strategic Management: A Stakeholder Approach* (Boston: Pitman, 1984). See also, R. Edward Freeman and Daniel R. Gilbert, Jr., *Corporate Strategy and the Search for Ethics* (Englewood Cliffs, NJ: Prentice Hall, 1988), and William M. Evan and R. Edward Freeman, "A Stakeholder Theory of the Modern Corporation: Kantian Capitalism," in Tom L. Beauchamp and Norman E. Bowie, eds., *Ethical Theory and Business,* 4th ed. (Englewood Cliffs, NJ: Prentice Hall, 1993), 75–84.

4. Kenneth E. Goodpaster, "Business Ethics and Stakeholder Analysis," *Business Ethics Quarterly,* 1 (1991), 69.

5. A. A. Berle, Jr., and Gardiner C. Means, *The Modern Corporation and Private Property* (New York: Macmillan, 1932), 336.

6. J. A. C. Hetherington, "Fact and Legal Theory: Shareholders, Managers, and Corporate Social Responsibility," *Stanford Law Review,* 21 (1969), 256.

7. Oliver E. Williamson, *The Economic Institutions of Capitalism* (New York: The Free Press, 1985), 304.

8. Williamson, *The Economic Institutions of Capitalism,* 304–5.

9. Williamson replies that although individual investors can protect themselves by selling stock, shareholders as a class cannot. Williamson, *The Economic Institutions of Capitalism,* 304.

10. See Bayless Manning, review of *The American Stockholder* by J. A. Livingston, *Yale Law Journal,* 67 (1958), 1492.

11. Goodpaster, "Business Ethics and Stakeholder Analysis," 63.

12. Goodpaster, "Business Ethics and Stakeholder Analysis," 69–70 (emphasis added).

13. Goodpaster, "Business Ethics and Stakeholder Analysis," 70.

14. Goodpaster, "Business Ethics and Stakeholder Analysis," 63. By "strategic stakeholder considerations" Goodpaster means considering the interests of stakeholders as a means to the end of serving the interests of the shareholders. A multi-fiduciary stakeholder approach makes the interests of all stakeholder groups the end of corporate activity.

15. Goodpaster, "Business Ethics and Stakeholder Analysis," 68.

16. The idea that corporations are a "nexus" of contracting relations among individuals is familiar from the work of agency theorists. See, for example, Michael C. Jensen and William H. Meckling. "Theory of the Firm: Managerial Behavior, Agency Costs and Ownership Structure," *Journal of Financial Economics,* 3 (1976), 310. Agency theory does not suppose that the relations in question are contracts that create obligations, however; it asks us, rather, to think of the relation involving shareholders, along with those of all other constituencies, *as though they were a multitude of contracts* for explanatory purposes only. On this point, see Robert C. Clark, "Agency Costs *versus* Fiduciary Duties," in John W. Pratt and Richard J. Zeckhauser, eds., *Principles and Agents: The Structure of Business* (Boston: Harvard Business School Press, 1985), 59–62.

17. Larry D. Sonderquist and Robert P. Vecchio, "Reconciling Shareholders' Rights and Corporate Responsibility: New Guidelines for Management," *Duke Law Journal,* 1978, p. 840.

18. Berle and Means, *The Modern Corporation and Private Property,* 355.

19. Berle and Means, *The Modern Corporation and Private Property,* 355–56.

20. A. A. Berle, Jr., "For Whom Corporate Managers Are Trustees: A Note," *Harvard Law Review,* 45 (1932), 1367.

21. Berle, "For Whom Corporate Managers Are Trustees," 1372.

22. At least 28 states have adopted other constituency statutes. In some states this has been accomplished by legislative enactments; in others, by court decisions interpreting state law. For an overview, see Charles Hansen, "Other Constituency Statutes: A Search for Perspective," *The Business Lawyer,* 46 (1991), 1355–75. A penetrating analysis that criticizes Hansen is Eric W. Orts, "Beyond Shareholders: Interpreting Corporate Constituency Statutes," *The George Washington Law Review,* 61 (1992), 14–135.

23. Goodpaster, "Business Ethics and Stakeholder Analysis," 63.

LEGAL PERSPECTIVES

Dodge v. Ford Motor Co.

Michigan Supreme Court

. . . When plaintiffs made their complaint and demand for further dividends, the Ford Motor Company had concluded its most prosperous year of business. The demand for its cars at the price of the preceding year continued. It could make and could market in the year beginning August 1, 1916, more than 500,000 cars. Sales of parts and repairs would necessarily increase. The cost of materials was likely to advance, and perhaps the price of labor; but it reasonably might have expected a profit for the year of upwards of $60,000,000. . . . Considering only these facts, a refusal to declare and pay further dividends appears to be not an exercise of discretion on the part of the directors, but an arbitrary refusal to do what the circumstances required to be done. These facts and others call upon the directors to justify their action, or failure or refusal to act. In justification, the defendants have offered testimony tending to prove and which does prove, the following facts: It had been the policy of the corporation for a considerable time to annually reduce the selling price of cars, while keeping up, or improving, their quality. As early as in June, 1915, a general plan for the expansion of the productive capacity of the concern by a practical duplication of its plant had been talked over by the executive officers and directors and agreed upon; not all of the details having been settled, and no formal action of directors having been taken. The erection of a smelter was considered, and engineering and other data in connection therewith secured. In consequence, it was determined not to reduce the selling price of

cars for the year beginning August 1, 1915, but to maintain the price to accumulate a large surplus to pay for the proposed expansion of plant and equipment, and perhaps to build a plant for smelting ore. It is hoped, by Mr. Ford, that eventually 1,000,000 cars will be annually produced. The contemplated changes will permit the increased output.

The plan, as affecting the profits of the business for the year beginning August 1, 1916, and thereafter, calls for a reduction in the selling price of the cars. . . . In short, the plan does not call for and is not intended to produce immediately a more profitable business, but a less profitable one; not only less profitable than formerly, but less profitable than it is admitted it might be made. The apparent immediate effect will be to diminish the value of shares and the returns to shareholders.

It is the contention of plaintiffs that the apparent effect of the plan is intended to be the continued and continuing effect of it, and that it is deliberately proposed, not of record and not by official corporate declaration, but nevertheless proposed, to continue the corporation henceforth as a semi-eleemosynary institution and not as a business institution. In support of this contention, they point to the attitude and to the expressions of Mr. Henry Ford. . . .

"My ambition," said Mr. Ford, "is to employ still more men, to spread the benefits of this industrial system to the greatest possible number, to help them build up their lives and their homes. To do this we are putting the greatest share of our profits back in the business."

---

204 Mich. 459, 170 N.W. 668, 3 A.L.R. 413 (1919). Majority opinion by Justice J. Ostrander.

"With regard to dividends, the company paid sixty per cent, on its capitalization of two million dollars, or $1,200,000, leaving $58,000,000 to reinvest for the growth of the company. This is Mr. Ford's policy at present, and it is understood that the other stockholders cheerfully accede to this plan."

He had made up his mind in the summer of 1916 that no dividends other than the regular dividends should be paid, "for the present."

"Q. For how long? Had you fixed in your mind any time in the future, when you were going to pay — A. No."
"Q. That was indefinite in the future? A. That was indefinite; yes, sir."

The record, and especially the testimony of Mr. Ford, convinces that he has to some extent the attitude towards shareholders of one who has dispensed and distributed to them large gains and that they should be content to take what he chooses to give. His testimony creates the impression, also, that he thinks the Ford Motor Company has made too much money, has had too large profits, and that, although large profits might be still earned, a sharing of them with the public, by reducing the price of the output of the company, ought to be undertaken. We have no doubt that certain sentiments, philanthropic and altruistic, creditable to Mr. Ford, had large influence in determining the policy to be pursued by the Ford Motor Company — the policy which has been herein referred to. It is said by his counsel that —

"Although a manufacturing corporation cannot engage in humanitarian works as its principal business, the fact that it is organized for profit does not prevent the existence of implied powers to carry on with humanitarian motives such charitable works as are incidental to the main business of the corporation." ...

In discussing this proposition counsel have referred to decisions [citations omitted]. These cases, after all, like all others in which the subject is treated, turn finally upon the point, the question, whether it appears that the directors were not acting for the best interests of the corporation. We do not draw in question, nor do counsel for the plaintiffs do so, the validity of the general proposition stated by counsel nor the soundness of the opinions delivered in the cases cited. The case presented here is not like any of them. The difference between an incidental humanitarian expenditure of corporate funds for the benefit of the employees, like the building of a hospital for their use and the employment of agencies for the betterment of their condition, and a general purpose and plan to benefit mankind at the expense of others, is obvious. There should be no confusion (of which there is evidence) of the duties which Mr. Ford conceives that he and the stockholders owe to the general public and the duties which in law he and his codirectors owe to protesting, minority stockholders. A business corporation is organized and carried on primarily for the profit of the stockholders. The powers of the directors are to be employed for that end. The discretion of directors is to be exercised in the choice of means to attain that end, and does not extend to a change in the end itself, to the reduction of profits, or to the nondistribution of profits among stockholders in order to devote them to other purposes. . . . As we have pointed out, and the proposition does not require argument to sustain it, it is not within the lawful powers of a board of directors to shape and conduct the affairs of a corporation for the merely incidental benefit of shareholders and for the primary purpose of benefiting others, and no one will contend that, if the avowed purpose of the defendant directors was to sacrifice the interests of shareholders, it would not be the duty of the courts to interfere. . . . It is obvious that an annual dividend of 60 per cent, upon $2,000,000, or $1,200,000, is the equivalent of a very small dividend upon $100,000,000, or more.

The decree of the court below fixing and determining the specific amount to be distributed to stockholders is affirmed. . . .

A. P. Smith Manufacturing Co. v. Barlow

Supreme Court of New Jersey

The Chancery Division, in a well-reasoned opinion by Judge Stein, determined that a donation by the plaintiff The A. P. Smith Manufacturing Company to Princeton University was *intra vires*. Because of the public importance of the issues presented, the appeal duly taken to the Appellate Division has been certified directly to this court under Rule 1:5–1(a).

The company was incorporated in 1896 and is engaged in the manufacture and sale of valves, fire hydrants, and special equipment, mainly for water and gas industries. Its plant is located in East Orange and Bloomfield and it has approximately 300 employees. Over the years the company has contributed regularly to the local community chest and on occasions to Upsala College in East Orange and Newark University, now part of Rutgers, the State University. On July 24, 1951 the board of directors adopted a resolution which set forth that it was in the corporation's best interests to join with others in the 1951 Annual Giving to Princeton University, and appropriated the sum of $1,500 to be transferred by the corporation's treasurer to the university as a contribution towards its maintenance. When this action was questioned by stockholders the corporation instituted a declaratory judgment action in the Chancery Division and trial was had in due course.

Mr. Hubert F. O'Brien, the president of the company, testified that he considered the contribution to be a sound investment, that the public expects corporations to aid philanthropic and benevolent institutions, that they obtain good will in the community by so doing, and that their charitable donations create favorable environment for their business operations. In addition, he expressed the thought that in contributing to liberal arts institutions, corporations were furthering their self-interest in assuring the free flow of properly trained personnel for administrative and other corporate employment. Mr. Frank W. Abrams, chairman of the board of the Standard Oil Company of New Jersey, testified that corporations are expected to acknowledge their public responsibilities in support of the essential elements of our free enterprise system. He indicated that it was not "good business" to disappoint "this reasonable and justified public expectation," nor was it good business for corporations "to take substantial benefits from their membership in the economic community while avoiding the normally accepted obligations of citizenship in the social community." Mr. Irving S. Olds, former chairman of the board of the United States Steel Corporation, pointed out that corporations have a self-interest in the maintenance of liberal education as the bulwark of good government. He stated that "Capitalism and free enterprise owe their survival in no small degree to the existence of our private, independent universities" and that if American business does not aid in their maintenance it is not "properly protecting the long-range interest of its stockholders, its employees, and its customers." Similarly, Dr. Harold W. Dodds, President of Princeton University, suggested that if private institutions of higher learning were replaced by governmental institutions our society would be vastly different and private

98 A 2d 581 (1953). Opinion by Judge J. Jacobs.

enterprise in other fields would fade out rather promptly. Further on he stated that "democratic society will not long endure if it does not nourish within itself strong centers of non-governmental fountains of knowledge, opinions of all sorts not governmentally or politically originated. If the time comes when all these centers are absorbed into government, then freedom as we know it, I submit, is at an end." . . .

When the wealth of the nation was primarily in the hands of individuals they discharged their responsibilities as citizens by donating freely for charitable purposes. With the transfer of most of the wealth to corporate hands and the imposition of heavy burdens of individual taxation, they have been unable to keep pace with increased philanthropic needs. They have therefore, with justification, turned to corporations to assume the modern obligations of good citizenship in the same manner as humans do. Congress and state legislatures have enacted laws which encourage corporate contributions, and much has recently been written to indicate the crying need and adequate legal basis therefor[e]. . . .

During the first world war corporations loaned their personnel and contributed substantial corporate funds in order to insure survival; during the depression of the '30s they made contributions to alleviate the desperate hardships of the millions of unemployed; and during the second world war they again contributed to insure survival. They now recognize that we are faced with other, though nonetheless vicious, threats from abroad which must be withstood without impairing the vigor of our democratic institutions at home and that otherwise victory will be pyrrhic indeed. More and more they have come to recognize that their salvation rests upon sound economic and social environment which in turn rests in no insignificant part upon free and vigorous nongovernmental institutions of learning. It seems to us that just as the conditions prevailing when corporations were originally created required that they serve public as well as private interests, modern conditions require that corporations acknowledge and discharge social as well as private responsibilities as members of the communities within which they operate. Within this broad concept there is no difficulty in sustaining, as incidental to their proper objects and in aid of the public welfare, the power of corporations to contribute corporate funds within reasonable limits in support of academic institutions. But even if we confine ourselves to the terms of the common-law rule in its application to current conditions, such expenditures may likewise readily be justified as being for the benefit of the corporation; indeed, if need be the matter may be viewed strictly in terms of actual survival of the corporation in a free enterprise system. The genius of our common law has been its capacity for growth and its adaptability to the needs of the times. Generally courts have accomplished the desired result indirectly through the molding of old forms. Occasionally they have done it directly through frank rejection of the old and recognition of the new. But whichever path the common law has taken it has not been found wanting as the proper tool for the advancement of the general good. . . .

In the light of all of the foregoing we have no hesitancy in sustaining the validity of the donation by the plaintiff. There is no suggestion that it was made indiscriminately or to a pet charity of the corporate directors in furtherance of personal rather than corporate ends. On the contrary, it was made to a preeminent institution of higher learning, was modest in amount and well within the limitations imposed by the statutory enactments, and was voluntarily made in the reasonable belief that it would aid the public welfare and advance the interests of the plaintiff as a private corporation and as part of the community in which it operates. We find that it was a lawful exercise of the corporation's implied and incidental powers under common-law principles and that it came within the express authority of the pertinent state legislation. As has been indicated, there is now widespread belief throughout the nation that free and vigorous non-governmental institutions of learning are vital to our democracy and the system of free enterprise and that withdrawal of corporate authority to make such contributions within reasonable limits would seriously threaten their continuance. Corporations have come to recognize this and with their enlightenment have sought in varying measures, as has the plaintiff by its contribution, to insure and strengthen the society which gives them existence and the means of aiding themselves and their fellow citizens. Clearly then, the appellants, as individual stockholders whose private interests rest entirely upon the well-being of the plaintiff corporation, ought not be permitted to close their eyes to present-day realities and thwart the long-visioned corporate action in recognizing and voluntarily discharging its high obligations as a constituent of our modern social structure.

The judgment entered in the Chancery Division is in all respects Affirmed.

Policy Statement on Corporate Governance

TIAA-CREF

Teachers Insurance and Annuity Association-College Retirement Equities Fund, as responsible long-term investors, recognize the overriding interest that our economy and our society have in the long-term development and vitality of our public corporations. We acknowledge that even an ideal system of corporate governance does not guarantee superior performance. Conversely, superior performance can be achieved despite a governance system that is less than perfect. Nevertheless, TIAA-CREF believes that certain principles are the hallmark of an equitable and efficient corporate governance structure. Good corporate governance must be expected to maintain an appropriate balance between the rights of shareholders — the owners of the corporation — and the need of management and the board to direct the corporation's affairs free from distracting short-term pressures. TIAA-CREF acknowledges a responsibility to be an advocate for improved corporate governance and performance discipline. This statement, based on a process of our boards' Corporate Governance and Social Responsibility Committees, is offered as a basis for dialogue with senior corporate management and boards of directors with the objective of improving corporate governance practices. It represents the TIAA-CREF perspective on what we believe are important elements of good corporate governance, and it identifies our voting guidelines on certain proxy issues.

BOARD OF DIRECTORS

It is recognized that the primary responsibility of the board of directors is to foster the long-term success of the corporation consistent with its fiduciary responsibility to the shareholders. TIAA-CREF supports the primary authority of the board in such areas as the selection of the chief executive officer, review of the corporation's long-term strategy, and selection of nominees for election to the board. However, in order to sharpen the accountability of directors to shareholders, we believe:

- The board should be composed of a substantial majority of independent directors. The board committee structure should include audit, compensation and nominating committees consisting entirely of independent directors. For this purpose independence means no present or former employment by the company or any significant financial or personal tie to the company or its management which could interfere with the director's loyalty to the shareholders. To us, an independent board is one that excludes people who regularly perform services for the company, if a disinterested observer would consider the relationship material. It does not matter if the service is performed individually or as a representative of an organization that is a professional adviser, consultant, or legal counsel to the company. However, we might consider a director independent if the person was involved in commercial transactions that were carried out at arm's length in the ordinary course of business, as long as the relationship didn't interfere with the individual's ability to exercise independent judgment. All monetary arrangements with directors for services outside normal board activities should be approved by a committee of the board that is composed of independent directors and should be reported in the proxy statement.

- The board should establish a fixed retirement policy for directors, and a requirement that all directors should own common shares in the company. A reasonable minimum ownership interest could be defined as stock holdings equal to approximately one-half of the amount of the director's annual retainer fee.

- The board should be composed of qualified individuals who reflect diversity of experience, gender, race and age. Each director should be able and prepared to devote sufficient time and effort to his or her duties as a director. Each director should represent all shareholders; therefore, TIAA-CREF opposes the nomination of specific representational directors, and the practice of cumulative voting in the election of directors.

- TIAA-CREF recognizes the responsibility of the board to organize its functions and conduct its business in the manner it deems most efficient, consistent with these or similar good guidelines. Therefore, in the absence of special circumstances, ordinarily we would not support shareholder resolutions concerning separation of the positions of CEO and Chairman, the formation of shareholder advisory committees, the requirement that candidates for the board be nominated by shareholders, shareholder mandated election of directors on an annual basis, or a requirement that directors must attend a specific percentage of board meetings, unless the board supports such measures. We are also against restricting the date of the annual meeting since it is management's prerogative to set the meeting date. The corporation should be free to indemnify directors for legal expenses and judgments in connection with their service as directors and eliminate the directors' liability for ordinary negligence. Directors should be held liable to the corporation for violations of their fiduciary duty involving gross or sustained and repeated negligence.

- The board should have a mechanism to evaluate its performance and that of individual directors. At a minimum, there should be an annual review of performance by the board that measures results against appropriate criteria defined by the board.

- The board should hold periodic executive sessions. Also, in those companies that do not separate the positions of the Chairman and the CEO of the company, the board should consider the selection of one or more independent directors as lead directors.

- While TIAA-CREF normally votes for the board's nominees, we vote for alternative candidates when our analysis indicates that those candidates will better represent shareholder interests. We may withhold our vote from unopposed candidates when their record indicates that their election to the board would not be in the interest of shareholders, or when we have requested a meeting with independent directors and have been refused. We may also withhold our vote from unopposed directors when the composition of the board as a whole raises serious concerns about board independence.

SHAREHOLDERS RIGHTS AND PROXY VOTING

Unlike other groups that have dealings with the corporation — customers, suppliers, lenders and labor — common shareholders do not have contractual protection of their interests. They must rely on the board of directors — whom they elect — and on their right to vote on proposals the corporation is required to submit for shareholder approval. The proxy vote is thus the key mechanism by which shareholders play a role in the governance of the corporation.

TIAA-CREF takes the position that, in exercising its votes, the corporation should adhere to the following principles:

- The board should adopt confidential voting for the election of directors and all other matters voted on by shareholders. This procedure protects the importance of the proxy vote and eliminates even the appearance of impropriety or unfairness.
- The board should adhere to the principle that each share of common stock has one vote. It should therefore not create multiple classes of common stock with disparate voting rights.
- The board should not issue any previously authorized shares — with voting rights to be determined by the board — unless it has prior shareholder approval for the specific intended use.
- The board should adopt equal financial treatment for all shareholders. TIAA-CREF supports "fair price" provisions and measures to limit the corporation's ability to buy back shares from a particular shareholder at higher-than-market prices. TIAA-CREF also supports proposals that eliminate preemptive rights, except where our analysis indicates that such rights have value to shareholders.
- The board should submit for prior shareholder approval any action that alters the fundamental relationship between shareholders and the board. This includes "anti-takeover" measures.
- The board should oppose any action to adopt "super-majority" requirements that interfere with a shareholder's right to elect directors and ratify corporate actions.

- The board should propose a change in the corporation's domicile only for valid business reasons, and not to obtain protection against unfriendly takeovers.
- The board should opt out of coverage, where possible, under state laws mandating anti-takeover protection.
- The board should not eliminate or reduce the shareholders' right to demand independent appraisal of the value of holdings. This includes any attempt to make changes in the by-laws or in the state of incorporation.
- The board should not combine disparate issues and present them for a single vote. Normally, TIAA-CREF votes against an entire package if it opposes any of the constituent parts.
- The board should request an increase in the authorized number of common shares only if they are intended for a valid corporate purpose and are not to be used in a manner inconsistent with shareholder interests — for example, an excessively generous stock option plan. TIAA-CREF does not oppose an increase in the authorized number of preferred shares unless they can be used without further shareholder approval as part of an anti-takeover program. For example, they should not fund a "poison pill" plan that has not been approved by shareholders or confer "super-voting" rights on particular shareholders friendly to management.
- TIAA-CREF supports equal access for large shareholders to a company's proxy statements to comment on management proposals, unless such access would impose undue costs or other burdens on the corporation.
- The board should state in its charter or by-laws that, when tallying shareholder votes, abstentions will not be counted as votes present, if state law allows. (If state law already makes this provision, the board need not include it.) But the board may still count abstentions for purposes of establishing a quorum.

EXECUTIVE COMPENSATION

TIAA-CREF believes a board and its compensation committee should set executive compensation levels adequate to attract and retain qualified executives. These executives should be rewarded in direct relationship to the contribution they make in maximizing shareholder wealth. A "pay for performance" system is needed to ensure equitable treatment between the shareholders and corporate management.

The three key issues are:

- Determining what constitutes "excessive" executive compensation.
- Evaluating the soundness and reasonableness of the policies, standards, and processes for setting compensation levels.
- Deciding what constitutes adequate disclosure of executive compensation to shareholders and the public.

With the number of firms in a large institutional investor's portfolio, it is difficult for an investor to determine what constitutes "excessive" compensation without thoroughly evaluating a whole range of topics and data, to which the investor does not have ready access. Therefore, it seems more prudent for an investor to recommend policies, standards and processes for setting executive compensation levels. These include:

- Compensation should include salary and performance components.
- Salary should have a defined relationship to salaries in industry peer groups.
- Total compensation should be adequate to attract, motivate and retain quality talent.
- Performance measures should relate to key characteristics accepted within the particular industry to measure success. Performance should be measured over time periods adequate to assess and link actual performance with responsibilities.
- Compensation should be appropriate in light of the current financial rewards to shareholders and employees.
- Compensation should be determined by the compensation committee of a board and care should be taken to avoid interlocking compensation committee memberships with other boards.

- Stock options and restricted stock awards should be integrated with other elements of compensation to formulate a competitive package.
- The board should fairly set forth annually in the proxy statement the criteria used to evaluate performance of the chief executive officer and other senior management. TIAA-CREF supports the spirit of the SEC rules on enhanced executive compensation disclosure and compensation committee reports to shareholders.
- TIAA-CREF opposes any outright ban on "golden parachute" severance agreements. We abstain on resolutions calling for prior shareholder ratification of golden parachute severance agreements, but TIAA-CREF supports resolutions that call for shareholder approval of golden parachutes which exceed IRS guidelines.
- Public companies should provide full and clear disclosure of all significant compensation arrangements with senior management in a form such that shareholders can evaluate the reasonableness of the entire compensation package. Full and clear disclosure is particularly important for specific elements of deferred compensation such as supplemental executive retirement plans ("SERPS"), which may be significant and which may impose a liability on the company for many years after an executive's retirement. Additionally, contractual arrangements granting significant other benefits to executives, including payment of certain non-business expenses, should be disclosed.
- Stock options, stock purchase, stock appreciation rights, savings, pensions, bonus and management incentive award proposals are scrutinized closely by TIAA-CREF. Consideration should be given to the need of the company to attract, motivate and reward people. This must be balanced against the concerns of shareholders. TIAA-CREF guidelines for voting proxies on these issues are in the appendix to this statement.

CEO PERFORMANCE EVALUATION

The evaluation of a corporation's chief executive officer is a critical board responsibility. A clear understanding between the board and the CEO regarding the corporation's expected performance and how that performance will be measured is very important. We believe:

- A high standard of performance accountability and ethical behavior should be set at the top of the corporation.
- The board should establish a specific set of performance objectives for the CEO annually. These should include concerns of shareholders, other investors, employees, customers and the community in which the company is located. Performance objectives should include both annual and multi-year time periods.
- The board should establish an annual review process that would permit it to evaluate CEO performance in executive session. A subsequent dialogue with the CEO is encouraged.

STRATEGIC PLANNING

Every company needs a strategic plan to ensure future economic success. The strategic allocation of corporate resources to each of the company's businesses is critical to its future success and to increased shareholder value needed for efficient capital formation. The board should discuss the strategic plan of each of the company's businesses at least annually. The strategic plan can be expected to include many of the following components, though TIAA-CREF recognizes that each company will need to fashion its own specific blend:

- An assessment of customers, markets and products for each business segment.
- A review of the competitive strengths of the business and its position in the marketplace.
- A review of human resource management issues.
- A review of the technological leadership, product attributes and costs of production and/or providing the service necessary to maintain a competitive advantage.
- An evaluation of the marketing and distribution channels for price and competitive superiority.

- A review of the information processing technology required to provide competitive leadership.
- A projection of the capital formation and financial implications of the plan.

FIDUCIARY OVERSIGHT

The board has a primary duty to exercise its fiduciary responsibility in the best interests of the corporation and its shareholders. This would include periodic reviews to ensure that corporate resources are used only for appropriate business purposes. To address some of the most important areas of fiduciary responsibility, the board should:

- Foster and encourage a corporate environment of strong internal controls, fiscal accountability, high ethical standards and compliance with applicable laws and regulations. Develop appropriate procedures to assure the board is advised of alleged or suspected violations of corporate standards or of non-compliance and management's resolution thereof, on a timely basis. (For example, by regular reports from the general counsel to the full board or a committee thereof.)
- Appoint an audit committee composed exclusively of outside independent directors. The audit committee has the primary responsibility to select independent audit firms to conduct an annual audit of the company's books and records.
- Install a mechanism to review corporate policies and practices (e.g., travel and entertainment policy, executive perquisites, etc.) to ensure proper use of corporate resources.
- Provide an explicit mechanism for major shareholders to communicate directly with the board (e.g., designating a non-executive chairman, a lead director, or a committee of independent directors).

SOCIAL RESPONSIBILITY ISSUES

TIAA-CREF believes building long-term shareholder value is consistent with directors giving careful consideration to social responsibility issues and the common good of the community. The board should develop policies and practices to address the following issues:

- The environmental impact of the corporation's operations and products.
- Equal employment opportunities for all segments of our population.

- Open channels of communication permitting employees, customers, suppliers and the community to freely express their concerns.
- Effective employee training and development.
- Evaluation of corporate actions that can negatively affect the common good of the community and its residents.
- To prohibit deliberate and knowing exploitation of any of the non-shareholder constituencies, both domestically and internationally. . . .

CASES

CASE 1. *Shutdown at Eastland*

When Speedy Motors Company closed its assembly plant in Eastland, Michigan, lobbyists for organized labor cited the case as one more reason why the Federal government should pass a law regulating plant closings. With less than a month's notice, the company laid off nearly 2,000 workers and permanently shut down the facility, which had been in operation more than 20 years. The local union president called the action "a callous and heartless treatment of the workers and of the community."

Company executives defended the decision as inevitable in view of the harsh competitive realities of the automotive industry. "Purchases of the Speedy model produced at Eastland have fallen to almost nothing and there is nothing we can do about changes in consumer preferences," a company spokesman said.

Labor lobbyists insist that instances such as this show the need for a Federal law which would require companies to give as much as two years' notice before closing a major fac-

tory, unless they can demonstrate that an emergency exists. The proposed legislation would also require the employer to provide special benefits to workers and the community affected by the shutdown.

"Closing plants needlessly and without warning is an antisocial, criminal act," a union leader said. "Giant corporations don't give a thought to the hardships they are imposing on long-time employees and communities that depend on their jobs. The only thing they consider is their profit."

Opponents of the legislation maintain that the proposed law would strike at the heart of the free enterprise system. "Companies must be free to do business wherever they choose without being penalized," a corporate spokesman argued. "Plant closing legislation would constitute unjustified interference in private decision making. Laws which restrict the ability of management to operate a business in the most efficient manner are counterproductive and in direct conflict with the theory of free enterprise."

Adapted from a case by John P. Kavanagh, Emeritus Assistant Professor of Philosophy, Center for the Study of Values, University of Delaware. Reprinted by permission.

Questions

1. Does the closing of a plant when it ceases to be profitable violate the "moral minimum"?
2. Who are the affected stakeholders, and how should their interests be considered?

3. Who should take primary responsibility for those laid off or terminated because of a plant closing?

CASE 2.   *The NYSEG Corporate Responsibility Program*

We are responsible to the communities in which we live and work and to the world community as well. We must be good citizens and support good works and charities. . . . We must encourage civic improvements and better health and education.[1]

Many large corporations currently operate consumer responsibility or social responsibility programs, which aim to return something to the consumer or to the community in which the company does business. New York State Electric and Gas (NYSEG) is one company that has created a program to discharge what its officers consider to be the company's responsibility to its public.

NYSEG is a New York Stock Exchange-traded public utility with approximately 60,500 shareholders. It supplies gas and electricity to New York State. NYSEG currently earns 89 percent of its revenues from electricity and 11 percent from gas sales. The company is generally ranked as having solid but not excellent financial strength. Earnings per share have declined in recent years because

of the regulatory climate and the company's write-offs for its Nine Mile Point #2 nuclear unit. In order to finance the unit, the company at one point had to absorb delay costs of several million dollars per month. The setback reduced shareholders' dividends for the first time in many years. NYSEG's financial base is now less secure than in the past because of the lowered earnings per share and the increased plant costs.

The company's corporate responsibility program has been in effect throughout this period of financial reversal. NYSEG designed the program to aid customers who are unable to pay their utility bills for various reasons. The program does not simply help customers pay their bills to the company. Rather, NYSEG hopes the program will find people in the community in unfortunate or desperate circumstances and alleviate their predicament. The two objectives often coincide.

NYSEG has created a system of consumer representatives, social workers trained to deal with customers and their problems. Since the program's 1978 inception, NYSEG has maintained a staff of 13 consumer representatives. Each handles approximately 40 cases a month, over half of which result in successful

---

[1]"The Johnson and Johnson Way" (from the Johnson and Johnson Company credo), 1986, p. 26.

This case was prepared by Kelley MacDougall and Tom L. Beauchamp and revised by John Cuddihy. Not to be duplicated without permission of the holder of the copyright, © 1991 Tom L. Beauchamp. This case is indebted to Cathy Hughto-Delzer, NYSEG Consumer Assistance Program Supervisor. Used by permission.

financial assistance. The remaining cases are referred to other organizations for further assistance.[2]

The process works as follows: When the company's credit department believes a special investigation should be made into a customer's situation, the employee refers the case to the consumer representative. Referrals also come from human service agencies and from customers directly. Examples of appropriate referrals include unemployed household heads; paying customers who suffer serious injury, lengthy illness, or death; and low-income senior citizens or those on fixed incomes who cannot deal with rising costs of living. To qualify for assistance, NYSEG requires only that the customers must be suffering from hardships they are willing to work to resolve.

Consumer representatives are primarily concerned with preventing the shutoff of service to these customers. They employ an assortment of resources to put them back on their feet, including programs offered by the New York State Department of Social Services and the federal Home Energy Assistance Program (HEAP), which awards annual grants of varying amounts to qualified families. In addition the consumer representatives provide financial counseling and help customers with their medical bills and education planning. They arrange assistance from churches and social services, provide food stamps, and help arrange VA benefits.

NYSEG also created a direct financial assistance program called Project Share, which enables paying customers who are not in financial difficulty to make charitable donations through their bills. They are asked voluntarily to add to their bill each month one, two, or five extra dollars, which are placed in a special fund overseen by the American Red Cross. This special Fuel Fund is intended to help those 60 years and older on fixed incomes who have no other means of paying their bills. Help is also provided for the handicapped and blind who likewise have few sources of funds. Many Project Share recipients do not qualify for government-funded assistance programs but nonetheless face energy problems. Through December 1990 Project Share had raised over $1.5 million and had successfully assisted more than 8,000 people.

The rationale or justification of this corporate responsibility program is rooted in the history of public utilities and rising energy costs in North America. Originally public utilities provided a relatively inexpensive product. NYSEG and the entire industry considered its public responsibility limited to the business function of providing energy at the lowest possible costs and returning dividends to investors. NYSEG did not concern itself with its customers' financial troubles. The customer or the social welfare system handled all problems of unpaid bills.

However, the skyrocketing energy costs in the 1970s changed customer resources and NYSEG's perspective. The energy crisis caused many long-term customers to encounter difficulty in paying their bills, and the likelihood of power shutoffs increased as a result. NYSEG then accepted a responsibility to assist these valued customers by creating the Consumer Representative system.

NYSEG believes its contribution is especially important now because recent reductions in federal assistance programs have shifted the burden of addressing these problems to the private sector. Project Share is viewed as "a logical extension of the President's call for in-

---

[2]Consumer representatives are viewed as liaisons between NYSEG and human services agencies. All of these representatives have extensive training and experience in human services, including four to six years of college with a degree in social work or social science. They must also have a minimum of four years of work experience in human services so that they are adequately qualified to deal with the problems facing customers.

creased volunteerism at the local level."[3] NYSEG chose the American Red Cross to cosponsor Project Share because of its experience in providing emergency assistance.

The costs of NYSEG's involvement in the program are regarded by company officers as low. NYSEG has few additional costs beyond the consumer representatives' salaries and benefits, which total $462,625 annually and are treated as operating expenses. To augment Project Share's financial support, NYSEG shareholders give the program an annual, need-based grant. In the past, shareholder grants have ranged from $40,000 to $100,000. NYSEG also pays for some personnel and printing costs through consumer rate increases, despite a recent ruling by the New York State Supreme Court that forbids utilities from raising consumer rates to obtain funds for charitable contributions (*Cahill v. Public Service Commission*). The company has also strongly supported Project Share by giving $490,000 over a seven-year period. The company's annual revenues are in the range of $1.5 billion, and the company's total debt also runs to approximately $1.5 billion.

The company views some of the money expended for the corporate responsibility program

as recovered because of customers retained and bills paid through the program. NYSEG assumes that these charges would, under normal circumstances, have remained unpaid and would eventually have been written off as a loss. NYSEG's bad-debt level is 20 percent lower than that of the average U.S. utility company. The company believes that its corporate responsibility policy is *both* altruistic *and* good business, despite the program's maintenance costs, which seem to slightly exceed recovered revenue.

Questions

1. Do you agree that NYSEG's Project Share is both altruistic and good business? Why or why not?
2. Would Ken Goodpaster or John Boatright believe that Project Share is consistent with NYSEG's fiduciary responsibility to its shareholders?
3. To what extent, if any, is Project Share an example of stakeholder management principles?
4. Could adherents to a stockholder theory of corporate responsibility and adherents to a stakeholder theory both endorse Project Share as socially responsible? Why or why not?

---

[3]NYSEG, Project Share Procedures Manual, 1988, p. 2.

CASE 3.   *H. B. Fuller in Honduras: Street Children and Substance Abuse*

Normally a marketing manager's dream is to have the name of a product it manufactures become the name for the generic product. Many companies beside Xerox make copiers

but nearly everyone refers to all copy machines as *xerox machines*. At H. B. Fuller the marketing manager's dream had become a nightmare. Kativo Chemical Industries, a

---

This case is based on a much longer case with the same name authored by Norman E. Bowie and Stefanie Lenway. The full "H. B. Fuller in Honduras: Street Children and Substance Abuse" was the Case award winner in the Columbia University Graduate School of Business Ethics in Business Program.

wholly owned foreign subsidiary of H. B. Fuller, sells a solvent-based adhesive (glue) in several countries in Latin America. The brand name of the glue is Resistol. In 1985 it came to H. B. Fuller's attention that large numbers of street children in the Central American country of Honduras were sniffing glue and that Resistol was among the glues being abused. Indeed all these children who sniff glue are being referred to as *Resistoleros*.

That the name of a Fuller product should be identified with a social problem was a matter of great concern to the H. B. Fuller Company. H. B. Fuller was widely known as a socially responsible corporation. Among its achievements were an enlightened employee relations policy that included giving each employee a day off on his or her birthday and, on the 10th anniversary of employment, bonus vacation time and a substantial check so that employees could travel and see the world. H. B. Fuller contributes 5 percent of its pretax profits to charity and continually wins awards for its responsibility to the environment. A portion of its corporate mission statement reads as follows:

> H. B. Fuller Company is committed to its responsibilities, in order of priority, to its customers, employees and shareholders. H. B. Fuller will conduct business legally and ethically, support the activities of its employees in their communities, and be a responsible corporate citizen.

The issue of the abuse of glue by Honduran street children received attention in the Honduran press as early as 1983. Initial responses to the problem were handled by officials at Kativo. These responses included requests to the press not to use "Resistolero" as a synonym for a street child glue sniffer and attempts to persuade the Honduran legislature not to require the addition of oil of mustard to its glue. Evidence indicated that oil of mustard was a carcinogen and hence was potentially dangerous to employees and consumers. Kativo officials believed that glue sniffing was a social problem and that Kativo was limited in what it could do about the problem. The solution was education.

From 1985 through 1989, officials at H. B. Fuller headquarters in St. Paul, Minnesota, were only dimly aware of the problem. While some of these officials assisted their Kativo subsidiary by providing information on the dangers of oil of mustard, the traditional policy of H. B. Fuller was to give great autonomy to foreign-owned subsidiaries. However, on June 7, 1989, Vice President for Corporate Relations Dick Johnson received a call from a stockholder whose daughter was in the Peace Corps in Honduras. The stockholder's question was how can a company like H. B. Fuller claim to have a social conscience and continue to sell Resistol which is "literally burning out the brains" of children in Latin America. Johnson knew that headquarters should become actively involved in addressing the problem. But given the nature of the problem and H. B. Fuller's policy of local responsibility, what should headquarters do?

Questions

1. To what extent can Honduran street children who obtain an H. B. Fuller product illegitimately be considered stakeholders? If they are stakeholders, how can their interests be represented?

2. What obligations does a company have to solve social problems?

3. Where does the responsibility for solving this problem rest — with the local subsidiary Kativo or with H. B. Fuller headquarters?

4. To what extent should officials at H. B. Fuller headquarters be concerned about potential criticisms that they are meddling in a problem where they don't understand the culture?

CASE 4.   *The Wall Street Effect*

First Interstate Bancorp of Los Angeles had been ailing for years. The bank — which has more than 500 branches in thirteen states, most of them in California — had failed to see the high-tech future of the industry, priding itself instead on old-fashioned teller service. So last October 18, when Wells Fargo & Co., a San Francisco-based banking company beloved by Wall Street for replacing traditional branches with supermarket ATM sites, announced a hostile takeover of First Interstate, the move was seen by many financiers as a logical step in the evolution of banking.

But First Interstate chairman William Siart and the rest of the bank's executives spurned Wells Fargo's first offer — $10.1 billion in Wells Fargo stock—and began searching for a "white knight" — another bank whose bid might be more palatable, even if somewhat lower. They found one in the Minneapolis-based First Bank System Inc., which offered $9.9 billion worth of its stock for First Interstate. Although Wells Fargo promptly upped its offer to $10.7 billion, First Interstate executives announced that they preferred to merge with First Bank and signed a "poison pill" pledge that would force First Interstate to pay First Bank a $200 million penalty if First Interstate merged with Wells Fargo.

First Interstate's shareholders were considering two very different deals. One offered instant gratification; the other, a long-term commitment. Wells Fargo's plan for First Interstate was to save $700 million a year by firing up to 10,000 people (mostly First Interstate employees in California) and closing more than 350 branches. Shareholders' profits would be substantial and immediate.

First Bank, on the other hand, proposed a more long-term approach. To produce $500 million in annual savings, 6,000 jobs would be eliminated. But since the two banks had overlapping operations only in Colorado, Montana, and Wyoming, few of their combined 1,500 branches would be closed, cuts would be thinly spread across twenty-one states, and many of the cuts could be accomplished through attrition.

The CEOs of First Interstate and First Bank began to crisscross the country, making their pitch to shareholders that although Wells Fargo was offering more per share, the First Bank merger would be the best opportunity for growth. They also pointed out that fewer jobs would be lost.

That turned out to be a tactical error. Although concern over jobs buoyed the plan's favor with California politicians — Los Angeles mayor Richard Riordan had denounced the proposed Wells Fargo merger as a "job killer" and a "disaster for lower-income communities" where branches would close — it angered stockholders. "First Interstate shareholders are not at all happy," analyst Thomas Brown noted at the time. "I have talked to four of the five largest holders, and the reaction ranges from modestly negative to violently negative. The shareholders are saying that they have no obligation to the state of California." Some shareholders went so far as to sue First Interstate's directors, accusing them of a breach of fiduciary responsibility by spurning Wells Fargo's offer.

More than 80 percent of First Interstate's shares were held by fifty large financial institutions — mutual funds, pension funds, and investment partnerships such as Kohlberg, Kravis, Roberts & Co. The pressure on fund managers is to maximize investor returns — now. Their responsibility is, out of necessity, to the bottom line. First Interstate's institutional shareholders were not concerned by the prospect of layoffs; they wanted the bank's stock price boosted quickly. In fact, many managers favored the Wells deal precisely *because* of the proposed layoffs and branch closings. Those moves would guarantee profit, at least in the short term.

In hearings before the Federal Reserve, California politicians and community activists made their case against the Wells Fargo deal, arguing that poor neighborhoods in L.A. need more, not less, access to banking services, and that promises of techno-banking nodes in supermarkets were of little consolation to communities that didn't have supermarkets. They also pointed out that Wells Fargo had recently stopped offering home mortgages and was the only major regional bank that had not provided financial support to the Southern California Business Development Corporation.

Wall Street investors made their feelings known in their own, more convincing way. They signaled their enthusiasm for the Wells Fargo deal by trading up its stock dramatically. The increase in the price of Wells stock automatically increased the value of its offer to First Interstate's investors. By January 15 the gap between the two deals was almost $1.5 billion. Ten days later, First Interstate executives announced that Wells Fargo's merger offer had been accepted.

Layoffs were expected to begin in April. Terminated First Interstate employees will get four weeks' pay for every year of service. Thirty-nine First Interstate executives fared better; they will receive golden parachutes worth a total of about $29 million. The top five will receive at least $2 million each. Chairman Siart will get $4.57 million.

Questions

1. How would you assess the decision of First Interstate stockholders to accept the takeover offer from Wells Fargo? How would the stockholders actions be defended morally?

2. Are the actions of Wells Fargo immoral from the stakeholder perspective? If no, explain. If yes, indicate why the rights of the stockholders should be overridden in this case.

3. Can you think of a way that Wells Fargo management might have done better at satisfying both the rights of the stockholders and the needs of the other stakeholders?

CASE 5. *The Health Business*[1]

In August 1992, Christy deMeurers, a 32-year-old Los Angeles school teacher and the happily married mother of two small children, discovered a lump in her breast. It was cancer. Two months earlier she had signed up to become a member of Health Net, a health maintenance organization (HMO) that provides medical care for its members and that was one of the medical insurance plans offered by the school where she taught. Health

From *Business Ethics: Concepts and Cases,* 4th edition by Manuel Valasquez, © 1993. Reprinted by permission of Prentice Hall, Inc., Upper Saddle River, NJ.

Net paid for a radical mastectomy as well as for radiation therapy and chemotherapy treatments. In May 1993, however, a bone scan revealed that her cancer had recurred and spread into her bone marrow. Her doctor, Dr. Gupta, now suggested she consider a bone-marrow transplant and arranged for her to see Dr. McMillan, a specialist who would evaluate whether she was a suitable candidate for a transplant, a treatment that probably would cost at least $100,000. When Christy and her family visited Dr. McMillan, however, he declined even to describe what was involved in a bone-marrow transplant, saying she would first have to undergo preliminary drug treatments to determine whether her tumor would respond to the drugs used in a bone-marrow transplant.

Suspicious that Health Net, which paid both Dr. Gupta and Dr. McMillan, might be unduly influencing their decisions in order not to have to pay for the transplant, Christy and her family flew to Denver the next day to consult Dr. Roy B. Jones, a leading bone-marrow transplant specialist. On June 8, 1993, Dr. Jones recommended a transplant indicating that the research showed that "its efficacy in breast cancer is at least equivalent to many other procedures that we do every day." That same day, however, back in Los Angeles, Health Net determined it would not pay for a transplant for Christy because it had decided to classify such transplants as "investigational" or experimental, and Health Net was not contractually required to pay for "investigational" procedures. When the deMeurers returned to Los Angeles, they found Dr. Gupta now unwilling to recommend a transplant.

Health Net was founded as an independent company in 1979 by Blue Cross of Southern California. The new company made $17,000 its first year, and $17 million the second. Health Net operated as an independent company until 1994 when it was sold to another HMO named QualMed. As an HMO, Health Net collects monthly premiums from employers in return for providing their employees with medical care. In 1995 Health Net collected a total of $2 billion from employers. The HMO enters contracts with doctors and hospitals whom it pays to provide the actual care. Each patient is assigned to a hospital as well as to a "primary care" doctor whom the patient regularly visits and who must approve any medical services the patient receives. Any specialists seen by the patient must be approved by the primary care doctor and must have a contract with the HMO. In order to keep costs low, the HMOs use a system called "capitation."

In a capitation system an HMO pays doctors, specialists, groups of doctors, and hospitals a fixed monthly fee for each patient assigned to them. If the doctor, specialist, doctors' group, or hospital spends less than the capitation fee for medical services for the patient, they can keep the difference; if they spend more than the capitation fee, they must cover the loss themselves. The capitation system thus provides an economic incentive to provide reduced levels of medical care. As one former Health Net doctor commented: "Understand, every time a patient comes into the doctor's office, it's a liability, not an asset — because he's on a fixed income."

The capitation system is, in fact, partly responsible for putting a brake on medical costs that had skyrocketed during the 1980s and that had in turn made medical insurance premiums rise astronomically. Rising medical costs had precipitated a crisis as companies increasingly found they could no longer afford insurance for their employees, and as growing numbers of people found they could no longer afford medical care for serious illnesses. HMOs and the capitation system brought the crisis under control. A survey of HMOs, for example, found that HMO premiums had actually declined between 1994 and

1995, and that the number of days HMO patients spent in the hospital declined from 315 per 1000 patients, to 275.

By using the capitation system and by introducing other kinds of cost controls from the world of business into the world of medicine, HMOs had been turned into very profitable businesses. Consider Dr. Malik M. Hasan, for example, the founder of Qual-Med, a for-profit company that owns several HMOs and that acquired Health Net in 1994. When he founded QualMed, he found that by imposing tight cost controls and corporate management systems designed to force doctors and hospitals to become economically efficient, he could take over failing HMOs and turn them into lucrative profit centers. When QualMed went public, for example, his stock in the company was suddenly worth $150 million, and, he commented, "We all got very rich."

In December 1995 Health Net was accredited by the National Committee for Quality Assurance (NCQA), an industry group that provides accreditation to HMOs that meet certain standards. The NCQA also publishes comparative surveys of HMOs. According to a survey report issued by NCQA, Health Net spent less than the others on medical care, and more than the others on marketing, salaries, and other administrative expenses.

When Dr. Gupta refused to recommend a transplant for her, Christy petitioned to see another cancer specialist, Dr. Schinke, who was also a Health Net doctor. Dr. Schinke examined Christy and agreed that a transplant should be considered and he recommended she be evaluated for a transplant at the UCLA Medical Center. Dr. Schinke, however, later received a telephone call from a Health Net administrator and, he later said, "I didn't understand an administrator calling up and in an abrupt tone saying, 'Why in the world, what was your thinking, why are you recommending this patient consider such an op-

tion?'" Nevertheless, Dr. Schinke did not withdraw his recommendation. The UCLA Medical Center to which Dr. Schinke sent Christy was one of the hospitals with which Health Net had a contract.

Extremely distrustful now, Christy did not reveal that she was a Health Net patient when she visited Dr. John Glaspy, a cancer specialist at UCLA Medical Center on June 25, 1993. Unaware that Christy was a Health Net member, Dr. Glaspy agreed that a transplant was "on the rational list" of options for her. He, too, said, however, that she would have to undergo an initial drug treatment to test the responsiveness of her cancer to the drugs. Two months later, when tests showed that she was responding favorably to the drugs, Christy and her family signed an agreement promising to pay the hospital $92,000 from their own pockets for the full costs of the transplant.

Christy and her family appealed to Health Net to reconsider its policy of classifying transplants as investigatory and so refusing to pay for them. In 1990, in fact, Health Net's chief medical officer had commissioned a study to evaluate the status of transplants, and the study had concluded that 3 out of 4 insurers paid for such transplants and that by 1991 such transplants would become "prevailing practice among practitioners, providers, and payers." However, Dr. Ossorio, a Health Net administrator, again refused to allow payment for the transplant. Then, according to the findings of an arbitration panel that eventually reviewed the case, Dr. Ossorio called the head of the UCLA Medical Clinic's cancer unit and in a statement made to "influence or intimidate" the hospital, demanded why UCLA was allowing a transplant to deMeurers in violation of Health Net guidelines. Shaken, the head of the cancer unit said he was unfamiliar with the case, but would look into it. Under the terms of its contract, Health Net could terminate its contract with the hospital with 90 days warning, a move that could create a substantial financial crisis for UCLA since a large fraction of its money comes from Health Net. A week later UCLA Medical Center notified Health Net that it would swallow the costs of the expensive treatment since it had already been approved.

On September 23, 1993 Christy finally began her treatment in UCLA hospital. By now she hardly had enough strength to walk from one room to another. A few weeks after her release from the hospital, she felt healthy enough to mow the lawn. She remained cancer-free for four more months, then discovered in Spring 1994 that the cancer had recurred. That summer she and her family went on a camping trip across the United States. Her family has fond memories of that period and the subsequent Christmas. On Friday March 10, 1995 she died.

Questions

1. Should medical care be subjected to the competitive forces of the free market? Should the provision of medical care be turned into a business? Explain your answer.

2. In your judgment, is it morally appropriate for an HMO to use a capitation system that provides economic incentives to increase efficiency in the delivery of medical care? Explain your answer.

3. Evaluate the ethics of the activities of the various individuals involved in this case.

NOTE

1. The information for this case is drawn from Erik Larson, "The Soul of an HMO," *Time*, 22 January, 1996, vol. 147, no. 4, pp. 44–52.

Suggested Supplementary Readings

BOATRIGHT, JOHN, R. *Ethics in Finance*, Malden, MA: Blackwell Publishers, 1999.

CARSON, THOMAS. "Friedman's Theory of Corporate Social Responsibility." *Business and Professional Ethics Journal* 12 (Spring 1993): 3–32.

CLARKSON, MAX B. E. "A Stakeholder Framework for Analyzing and Evaluating Corporate Social Performance." *The Academy of Management Review* 20 (January 1995): 92–117.

DONALDSON, THOMAS, and LEE E. PRESTON. "The Stakeholder Theory of the Corporation: Concepts, Evidence, and Implications." *Academy of Management Review* 20 (January 1995): 65–91.

FORT, TIMOTHY L. "Business as Mediating Institution," *Business Ethics Quarterly* 6: 149–164.

FRANK, ROBERT H. "Can Socially Responsible Firms Survive in a Competitive Environment." In *Codes of Conduct: Behavioral Research into Business Ehics*, David Messick and Ann Tenbrunsel (eds.). New York: Russell Sage Foundation, 1996, 86–103.

FREDERICK, WILLIAM C. "Toward CSR3: Why Ethical Analysis Is Indispensable and Unavoidable in Corporate Affairs." *California Management Review* 28 (Winter 1986): 126–41.

FREEMAN, R. EDWARD. *Strategic Management: A Stakeholder Approach.* Boston: Pitman, 1984.

FREEMAN, R. EDWARD, and DANIEL R. GILBERT, JR. *Corporate Strategy and the Search for Ethics.* Englewood Cliffs, NJ: Prentice Hall, 1988.

FRIEDMAN, MILTON. *Capitalism and Freedom.* Chicago University Press, 1962.

GOODPASTER, KENNETH E., and THOMAS R. HOLLORAN. "In Defense of a Paradox." *Business Ethics Quarterly* 4 (October 1994): 423–29.

JONES, THOMAS M. "Instrumental Stakeholder Theory: A Synthesis of Ethics and Economics." *The Academy of Management Review* 20 (April 1995): 404–37.

JONES, THOMAS M. and ANDREW C. WICKS. "Convergent Stakeholder Theory." *Academy of Management Review* 24 (April 1999): 191–221. Commentaries by Linda Klebe Trevino and Gary R. Weaver, Dennis Gioia, R. Edward Freeman, and Thomas Donaldson follow in the same volume.

LANGTRY, BRUCE. "Stakeholders and the Moral Responsibilities of Business." *Business Ethics Quarterly* 4 (October 1994): 431–43.

LEVITT, THEODORE. "The Dangers of Social Responsibility." *Harvard Business Review* 36 (September–October 1958): 41–50.

MAITLAND, IAN. "The Morality of the Corporation: An Empirical or Normative Disagreement?" *Business Ethics Quarterly* 4 (October 1994): 445–58.

MINTZBERG, HENRY. "The Case for Corporate Social Responsibility." *Journal of Business Strategy* 4 (Fall 1983): 3–15.

SCHLOSSBERGER, EUGENE. "A New Model of Business: Dual Investor Theory." *Business Ethics Quarterly* 4 (October 1994): 459–74.

WICKS, ANDREW C., DANIEL R. GILBERT, JR., and R. EDWARD FREEMAN. "A Feminist Reinterpretation of the Stakeholder Concept." *Business Ethics Quarterly* 4 (October 1994) 475–97.

Chapter Three

The Regulation of Business: Accountability and Responsibility

INTRODUCTION

CHAPTER TWO ADDRESSED the general problem of corporate responsibility. This chapter explores some of the issues surrounding how society can make businesses and those who manage them behave responsibly. In developing this chapter we focus on making firms accountable for their actions. Some argue that accountability can be achieved through self-regulation by the businesses themselves. Others argue that accountability can only be achieved through law and associated stiff penalties for misconduct. In order to determine accountability, we need to ask questions of responsibility. Who is responsible and should be held accountable? Some have argued that individuals too often hide behind the shield of a large corporation and as a result escape punishment when they have committed a misdeed. The corporation provides a bit of anonymity. Others argue that the search for individuals is often misguided and counterproductive. Many corporate misdeeds or untoward events are the result of corporate structures and incentive systems. To avoid future errors, some of which could result in catastrophes, the focus should be on organizational structures and technological fixes rather than on the search for responsible individuals to punish. This chapter considers these issues in depth.

Accountability: Government Regulation Versus Self-Regulation

One way to ensure good behavior is to make bad behavior punishable by law. This is the approach that has been adopted by the U.S. government and thus, with the passage of the Federal Sentencing Guidelines, implicitly by society. The Federal Sentencing Guidelines may mark the apex of society's attempt to regulate corporate behavior. It is somewhat ironic that the Federal Sentencing Guidelines were enacted in 1991, just at the end of twelve years of Republican domination of the White House and at the end of a period that was known for the deregulation of corporations. To understand the significance of this new law, a brief review of regulatory history is in order.

Until the 1980s, the government regulation of business in the United States had increased steadily. In many respects that history of increased regulation is understandable. Just before and after the beginning of the twentieth century, regulation was aimed at controlling large corporations and thus at protecting competition. This was the era of monopoly-busting legislation. The next wave of regulation in the 1930s, which occurred during the Great Depression, was designed to protect stockholders, employees, and customers from the failures of capitalism. Protection was given to employees who formed unions, but protection from fraud was also given to consumers and stockholders. In the 1960s the regulation of business was expanded to achieve social goals, especially to end discrimination in the workplace and to protect the environment.

But government regulation brought burdens as well as benefits. Among the most common criticisms is that government regulation is expensive, inflexible, and unfair. As an example of unfairness, property owners are held responsible for cleaning up discovered environmentally hazardous material even if they were not responsible for its being there and even if they were not the owners of the property at the time the damage occurred. A *Newsweek* op. ed. piece described a daughter's lament as her elderly mother nearly lost everything as a result of hazardous waste being discovered on her property.[1] In 1952 her mother, a widow at 38 with two small children to raise, used $1500 from death benefits to construct a small commercial building. One of the inhabitants was a small dry cleaner. The dry cleaner had disposed of chemicals according to the standard practice of the time. However, in 1995 the chemicals deposited on the property twenty years earlier were judged to be the likely cause of the contamination of city park well water. The state of Oregon was holding her responsible for the cleanup conservatively estimated to cost $200,000. Her mother's financial security, the small building, was worth $70,000. To bankrupt her mother for contamination caused by another and caused by following standard practice seemed unfair. During the 1980s these objections began to turn the tide toward less regulation.

Although regulation in many areas of business has certainly declined, the Federal Sentencing Guidelines, which are described in detail in the article by O. C. Ferrell et al., have greatly increased the regulatory burden of businesses large and small. In effect, they require that business firms adopt comprehensive systems of self-regulation. These systems are called *compliance systems,* and the attempt to make business behave ethically through specific laws with appropriate penalties is called the *compliance approach to business ethics.* Should a business firm fail to have compliance systems in place and should the firm or someone acting in the name of the firm commit a federal tort, the fines that could be levied are severe enough to put the firm out of business. Even if they are not that draconian, the fines could do serious damage to the bottom line. At first many in business and academe were skeptical that the significant fines under the law would ever be imposed. All that changed in 1996 when Daiwa Bank was fined $340 million under the guidelines. At that time that was the largest criminal fine in U.S. history. And it resulted from the actions of a Bank employee, Toshihide Iguchi, who had lost $1.1 billion in concealed securities trading. Daiwa Bank had investigated Iguchi's confession and replaced the lost pension account funds with its own money. But it did not disclose these crimes to the public or to the U.S. government until it could do so as part of its regularly scheduled reporting. That delay put Daiwa Bank in violation of a U.S. law that requires that a "Criminal Referral Form" be filed within thirty days of learning of an employee's offense. The delay also meant that Daiwa Bank needed to falsify certain records and thus compounded its offenses. Moreover, Daiwa Bank had no compliance system in place. And this omission cost Daiwa Bank. At the sentencing, Assistant U.S. Attorney Reid Figel told the court,

> It is virtually impossible for any financial institution to protect itself against every potential criminal act by its employees, particularly given the highly specialized nature and complexity of the securities now traded in the world's capital markets. It is precisely because of this complexity, however, that it is essential that corporations institute and insist upon a corporate culture of absolute compliance with the rules and regulations of the marketplace. One of the most important ways to do this is to establish and enforce a system of checks and balances that are designed to protect against the criminal acts of corporate employees.[2]

More recently, pharmaceutical giant Hoffman-LaRoche, Ltd. was fined $500 million, the largest fine ever imposed under the federal sentencing guidelines, following their conviction for antitrust conspiracy in the vitamin market. The penalties could have been much worse, as the company was in fact liable for a fine of as high as $1.3 billion under the guidelines.[3]

This *compliance-based approach* to business ethics should be contrasted with what Linda Trevino et al. in their article call a *values-based approach*. In a compliance-based approach, a business acts ethically because it is afraid of the legal consequences if it does not. In a values-based approach a business acts ethically because it believes it is the right thing to do. Ethical behavior is a natural part of its corporate culture. A corporation with a values-based approach will focus on self-regulation and the various means to promote good corporate conduct through self-regulation.

Trevino et al. consider the advantages and disadvantages of compliance-based systems and values-based systems. On the basis of an extensive survey, they argue that the values-based approach works best. The survey results would cheer Kantians who argue that a person should do what is right because it is right rather than simply because it is what the law requires and one is afraid of the punishment if one should get caught. The survey results also would cheer utilitarians who argue that a person or firm should adopt policies that bring good results.

Codes of Ethics

Among the most common means to this end of self-regulation is the business code of ethics. There are several advantages to such codes: First, they provide guidance in ethically ambiguous situations. This process is done in a number of ways. Codes provide more stable guides to right or wrong than do human personalities or continual ad hoc decisions. Codes of ethics are particularly important in dealing with supervisors since they can act as at least some check on autocratic power. In theory, at least, a business code of ethics can provide an independent ground of appeal when one is urged by a supervisor to commit an unethical act. "I'm sorry, but company policy strictly forbids it" is a gracious and relatively safe way of ending a conversation about a "shady" deal. Finally, codes of conduct help specify the social responsibilities of business itself by defining policy concerning such issues as conflict of interest, receipt of gift and gratuities, and comprehension of questionable payment.

For example, with respect to insider information, IBM gives the following directives to its employees.[4]

> If IBM is about to announce a new product or make a purchasing decision and the news could affect the stock of a competitor or supplier, you must not trade in the stock of those companies.
> If IBM is about to make an announcement that could affect the price of its stock, you must not trade in IBM stock.
> If IBM is about to build a new facility, you must not invest in land or business near the new site.

And with respect to tips, gifts, and entertainment, IBM says,

> No IBM employee, or any member of his or her immediate family, can accept gratuities or gifts of money from a supplier, customer, or anyone in a business relationship. Nor can they accept a gift or consideration that could be perceived as having been offered because of the business relationship. "Perceived" simply means this: If you read about it in the local newspaper, would you wonder whether the gift just might have had something to do with a business relationship?
> No IBM employee can give money or a gift of significant value to a customer, supplier, or anyone if it could reasonably be viewed as being done to gain a business advantage.

A second advantage of a code of ethics is that it enables a company to do the morally responsible act that it wants to do but, because of competitive pressures, would otherwise be unable to do. In other words, sometimes the competitive nature of business makes it impossible for an individual corporation to do the morally appropriate act and survive. Suppose, for example, that textile company A is polluting a river and that expensive technology is now available to enable company A to reduce pollution. Since that pollution is causing an avoidable harm, it seems that company A ought to install the pollution control device. However, suppose that company A can show that all other textile companies are similarly polluting rivers. If company A installs the pollution control devices and the other textile companies do not, company A's product will rise in price and hence will run the risk of becoming noncompetitive. Eventually company A may be forced out of business. The competitive situation thus makes it unfair and, from an economic perspective, impossible for company A to do the morally appropriate thing. Only a rule that requires all textile companies to install pollution control devices will be fair and effective. It is often maintained that in situations paralleling this textile pollution case, government regulation is the only viable answer.

Kenneth Arrow argues that the textile pollution case can potentially be adequately handled by an industry-wide code of ethics and that at least some evidence exists that industry-wide codes can work. Not all moral problems of personal conflict in society need to be resolved in courts by law or by regulatory agencies. Some are suitably handled by society's general moral codes or even by formal committee decisions. Indeed, if moral codes and practices were not widely efficacious, the courts and the regulatory systems would be overwhelmed.

Of course, codes of ethics by themselves are mere window dressing if they are not enforced and if they are not buttressed by a commitment by top management to ethical conduct. In other words, a code of ethics is not sufficient by itself. It needs to be part of a corporate culture that promotes ethical conduct. This is especially true given the fact that codes of ethics have certain inherent weaknesses. For example, no matter how specifically a code of conduct is written, there is always a certain amount of vagueness and ambiguity. That is why even a well-written code needs to be interpreted and enforced by ethical people.

Determining Responsibility

Many of the most dramatic cases in business ethics are cases that involve accidents or other catastrophic events. Airline crashes, the Challenger explosion, and the Chernobyl nuclear power accident are perfect examples. But some of the accidents do not make the news headlines, although they are just as tragic for the individuals involved. Medical mistakes when people are misdiagnosed, given the wrong medicine, or given the wrong amount of medicine are illustrations. When events like this occur, there is a natural tendency to want to find who was responsible and often to punish them. However, philosophers know that assigning responsibility is a difficult task — both factually and conceptually. The task can be difficult factually because the facts are hard to determine. The task can be difficult conceptually because an event can have multiple causes and it can be extremely difficult to parse out the responsibility among the multiple causes. The assignment of responsibility becomes particularly difficult when the problem results from the way an organization is structured or the way the organization has arranged the incentives that indicate success within the organization. For example, in October 1999, there was a terrible train accident outside Paddington Station in London. Many were killed. Subsequent investigation showed that one engineer ran a red light, but the investigation also showed that the red lights were often placed in positions that were obscure and hard to see. How much of the responsibility for the accident rests with the engineer who perished and how much with those who designed the placement of the lights?

Some believe that the organizational structure is so important that when an accident happens, the organization and society should often not try to find who is individually responsible and thereby put all the blame and often the punishment on them. An early example of this kind of thinking occurred with 1979 crash of Air New Zealand TE-901 into Mt. Erebus in Antarctica. The Royal Commission that investigated the crash identified the essential cause as the failure of the airline to inform Captain Collins of the change of the coordinates in the aircraft's internal computer system. Further investigation indicated that this communication failure was not simply the oversight of one individual. Rather the communications gap resulted from general flaws in management procedure. To avoid another disaster, the management needed to improve the means of communication so that pilots were given complete information concerning the coordinates placed into the aircraft's computer. In her article, "How Can We Save the Next Victim?," Lisa Belkin investigates a particularly poignant tragedy in which a young child was given ten times the dose of medication as was prescribed and died as a result. Her recommendation on the basis of this study is that often we should seek organizational or technical solutions rather than search for a person to blame.

On the other hand, some feel it is too easy for irresponsible individuals to avoid responsibility for their actions by invoking organizational structures, managerial practices and incentive systems. In the article by Russell Boisjoly et al., the authors are critical of the Rogers Commission that investigated the Challenger disaster on just such grounds. The Rogers Commission had concluded that the problem was with management systems and that decisions became collective rather than individual. However, Boisjoly et al. argue that there were individuals who could have stopped the launch and the responsibility for the accident rests on them.

Reflection indicates that we should strike a balance between these two positions. Some accidents are clearly the responsibility of an easily identified individual or set of individuals. Others result from a combination of perverse incentives, management practices and organizational structures. Some, like the train crash in London, result from both factors. The ethical corporation needs both supportive organizational structures and responsible individuals if accidents like those discussed are to be minimized.

NOTES

1. Carolyn Scott Kortge, "Taken to The Cleaners," *Newsweek* (October 23, 1995), p. 16.
2. Jeffrey M. Kaplan, "Why Daiwa Bank Will Pay $340 Million Under the Sentencing Guidelines," *Ethikos* 9 (May/June 1996): 1–3, 11.
3. Kaplan, Jeff, "Legal Update." *EOA News* (Summer/Fall, 1999), p. 12.
4. IBM Business Code of Conduct Guidelines (internal document), pp. 11–12.

COMPLIANCE THEORY AND SELF-REGULATION

Business Codes and Economic Efficiency

Kenneth J. Arrow

This paper makes some observations on the widespread notion that the individual has some responsibility to others in the conduct of his economic affairs. It is held that there are a number of circumstances under which the economic agent should forgo profit or other benefits to himself in order to achieve some social goal, especially to avoid a disservice to other individuals. For the purpose of keeping the discussion within bounds, I shall confine my attention to the obligations that might be imposed on business firms. . . . Is it reasonable to expect that ethical codes will arise or be created? . . . This may seem to be a strange possibility for an economist to raise. But when there is a wide difference in knowledge between the two sides of the market, recognized ethical codes can be, as has already been suggested, a great contribution to economic efficiency. Actually we do have examples of this in our everyday lives, but in very limited areas. The case of medical ethics is the most striking. By its very nature there is a very large difference in knowledge between the buyer and the seller. One is, in fact, buying precisely the service of someone with much more knowledge than you have. To make this relationship a viable one, ethical codes have grown up over the centuries, both to avoid the possibility of exploitation by the physician and to assure the buyer of medical services that he is not being exploited. I am not suggesting that these are universally obeyed, but there is a strong presumption that the doctor is going to perform to a large extent with your welfare in mind. Unnecessary medical ex-penses or other abuses are perceived as violations of ethics. There is a powerful ethical background against which we make this judgment. Behavior that we would regard as highly reprehensible in a physician is judged less harshly when found among businesspersons. The medical profession is typical of professions in general. All professions involve a situation in which knowledge is unequal on two sides of the market by the very definition of the profession, and therefore there have grown up ethical principles that afford some protection to the client. Notice there is a mutual benefit in this. The fact is that if you had sufficient distrust of a doctor's services, you wouldn't buy them. Therefore the physician wants an ethical code to act as assurance to the buyer, and he certainly wants his competitors to obey this same code, partly because any violation may put him at a disadvantage but more especially because the violation will reflect on him, since the buyer of the medical services may not be able to distinguish one doctor from another. A close look reveals that a great deal of economic life depends for its viability on a certain limited degree of ethical commitment. Purely selfish behavior of individuals is really incompatible with any kind of settled economic life. There is almost invariably some element of trust and confidence. Much business is done on the basis of verbal assurance. It would be too elaborate to try to get written commitments on every possible point. Every contract depends for its observance on a mass of unspecified conditions which suggest that the perfor-

From Kenneth J. Arrow, "Social Responsibility and Economic Efficiency," *Public Policy* 21 (Summer 1973). Copyright © 1973 by the President and Fellows of Harvard College.

mance will be carried out in good faith without insistence on sticking literally to its wording. To put the matter in its simplest form, in almost every economic transaction, in any exchange of goods for money, somebody gives up his valuable asset before he gets the other's; either the goods are given before the money or the money is given before the goods. Moreover there is a general confidence that there won't be any violation of the implicit agreement. Another example in daily life of this kind of ethics is the observance of queue discipline. People line up; there are people who try to break in ahead of you, but there is an ethic which holds that this is bad. It is clearly an ethic which is in everybody's interest to preserve; one waits at the end of the line this time, and one is protected against somebody's coming in ahead of him.

In the context of product safety, efficiency would be greatly enhanced by accepted ethical rules. Sometimes it may be enough to have an ethical compulsion to reveal all the information available and let the buyer choose. This is not necessarily always the best. It can be argued that under some circumstances setting minimum safety standards and simply not putting out products that do not meet them would be desirable and should be felt by the businessperson to be an obligation.

Now I've said that ethical codes are desirable. It doesn't follow from that that they will come about. An ethical code is useful only if it is widely accepted. Its implications for specific behavior must be moderately clear, and above all it must be clearly perceived that the acceptance of these ethical obligations by everybody does involve mutual gain. Ethical codes that lack the latter property are unlikely to be viable. How do such codes develop? They may develop as a consensus out of lengthy public discussion of obligations, discussion which will take place in legislatures, lecture halls, business journals, and other public forums. The codes are commu-

nicated by the very process of coming to an agreement. A more formal alternative would be to have some highly prestigious group discuss ethical codes for safety standards. In either case to become and to remain a part of the economic environment, the codes have to be accepted by the significant operating institutions and transmitted from one generation of executives to the next through standard operating procedures, through education in business schools, and through indoctrination of one kind or another. If we seriously expect such codes to develop and to be maintained, we might ask how the agreements develop and above all, how the codes remain stable. After all, an ethical code, however much it may be in the interest of all, is, as we remarked earlier, not in the interest of any one firm. The code may be of value to the running of the system as a whole, it may be of value to all firms if all firms maintain it, and yet it will be to the advantage of any one firm to cheat — in fact the more so, the more other firms are sticking to it. But there are some reasons for thinking that ethical codes can develop and be stable. These codes will not develop completely without institutional support. That is to say, there will be need for focal organizations, such as government agencies, trade associations, and consumer defense groups, or all combined to make the codes explicit, to iterate their doctrine and to make their presence felt. Given that help, I think the emergence of ethical codes on matters such as safety, at least, is possible. One positive factor here is something that is a negative factor in other contexts, namely that our economic organization is to such a large extent composed of large firms. The corporation is no longer a single individual; it is a social organization with internal social ties and internal pressures for acceptability and esteem. The individual members of the corporation are not only parts of the corporation but also members of a larger society whose esteem is desired. Power in a large corporation is necessarily diffused; not many individuals in such organizations feel so thoroughly identified with the corporation that other kinds of social pressures become irrelevant. Furthermore, in a large, complex firm where many people have to participate in any decision, there are likely to be some who are motivated to call attention to violations of the code. This kind of check has been conspicuous in government in recent years. The Pentagon Papers are an outstanding illustration of the fact that within the organization there are those who recognize moral guilt and take occasion to blow the whistle. I expect the same sort of behavior to occur in any large organization when there are well-defined ethical rules whose violation can be observed.

One can still ask if the codes are likely to be stable. Since it may well be possible and profitable for a minority to cheat, will it not be true that the whole system may break down? In fact, however, some of the pressures work in the other direction. It is clearly in the interest of those who are obeying the codes to enforce them, to call attention to violations, to use the ethical and social pressures of the society at large against their less scrupulous rivals. At the same time the value of maintaining the system may well be apparent to all, and no doubt ways will be found to use the assurance of quality generated by the system as a positive asset in attracting consumers and workers.

One must not expect miraculous transformations in human behavior. Ethical codes, if they are to be viable, should be limited in their scope. They are not a universal substitute for the weapons mentioned earlier, the institutions, taxes, regulations, and legal remedies. Further, we should expect the codes to apply in situations where the firm has superior knowledge of the situation. I would not want the firm to act in accordance with some ethical principles in regard to matters of which it has little knowledge. For example, with quality standards which consumers can observe, it may not be desirable that the firm decide for itself, at least on ethical grounds, because it is depriving the consumer of the freedom of choice between high-quality, high-cost and low-quality, low-cost products. It is in areas where someone is typically misinformed or imperfectly informed that ethical codes can contribute to economic efficiency.

The Federal Sentencing Guidelines for Organizations: A Framework for Ethical Compliance

O. C. Ferrell
Debbie Thorne LeClair
Linda Ferrell

Ethical and legal issues continue to be at the forefront of organizational concerns as managers and employees face increasingly complex decisions. . . . An organizational ethics program establishes formal accountability and responsibility for appropriate

From O. C. Ferrell, Debbie Thorne LeClair and Linda Ferrell, "The Federal Sentencing Guidelines for Organizations: A Framework for Ethical Compliance," *Journal of Business Ethics* 17:353–363 (1998). Reprinted with permission from Kluwer Academic Publishers.

business conduct with top management. An effective ethics program has the potential to encourage all employees to understand the values of the business and comply with policies and codes of conduct that create the ethical climate of the business. It takes into account company values and legal requirements, helping an organization develop trust and prevent misconduct. Examples of issues in the development of an organizational ethics program include the establishment of a code of conduct, organizational responsibility for ethics programs, ethics training, employee control mechanisms, and procedures for feedback on, and improvement of, the ethical compliance program. . . .

The government's response to deterring white-collar crime is the Federal Sentencing Guidelines (FSG), and its goal is to reward organizations for establishing a legal/ethical compliance program. The guidelines are so powerful and explicit that "expectations for reasonable business conduct will never be the same." The effectiveness of a compliance program is determined by its success in preventing misconduct by focusing on the risk associated with a particular area of business. It should be emphasized that it is impossible to take a strict legalistic approach in developing an ethical compliance program. Failing to incorporate the program within the corporate culture will result in greater culpability and increased penalties.

The purpose of this article is to provide a framework for understanding the legal and ethical ramifications of the Federal Sentencing Guidelines of 1991. First, we delineate the nature of the guidelines and the process by which organizations are penalized for employee misconduct. Second, we examine the guidelines' impact on business ethics programs. The government's requirements for compliance programs are discussed in the context of ethics training and organizational culture. . . .

THE FEDERAL SENTENCING GUIDELINES

The Federal Sentencing Guidelines were developed because of an increase in white-collar crime and the government's determination to place the responsibility for such crime with organizations, not just individual decision makers. A wide range of organizations can be held accountable under the Federal Sentencing Guidelines for Organizations, including corporations, associations, unions, governments, unincorporated organizations and non-profit organizations. The guidelines were developed by the U.S. Sentencing Commission and became effective November 1, 1991. These guidelines provide guidance to organizations and encourage internal control systems by mandating punishment and possible restitution if the organization's internal systems fail.

The Sentencing Reform Act of 1984 authorized the U.S. Sentencing Commission to create categories of offense behavior (i.e., bribing government officials with over $25,000) and offender characteristics (i.e., first or second offense) that are used to develop appropriate sentence and fine levels. The court must choose a sentence from these guidelines, which differentiates among similar crimes and similar offenders. The FSG are designed to enhance the ability of the justice system to fight crime with an effective and fair sentencing system.

Under this mandate, an organization is held accountable and responsible and may be indicted if a federal crime is committed by one or more of its employees. Both federal and state governments are moving toward organizational accountability for crime occurring within organizations and will act on it accordingly. In the past, laws limited the enforcement action to those employees directly responsible for an offense. Due to the lengthy litigation process, by 1995 approximately 280 cases had been prosecuted based on the 1991 FSG. A large number of cases based on the FSG will probably be produced over the next few years.

The government has placed the responsibility for controlling and preventing illegal and unethical activities squarely on the shoulders of top management. Managers are responsible for their own actions and those of individuals they supervise. The guidelines include the principle of vicarious liability which means managers must demonstrate due diligence in attempting to prevent misconduct. Historically, companies have incorporated for limited liability, but the principle of vicarious liability means that now organizations can be held liable if they have not followed the minimum requirements of the Federal Sentencing Guidelines for organizations.

To demonstrate due diligence, a company has to create and document an effective internal compliance program to ensure an ethical corporate culture. Moreover, ethical and legal standards must be communicated to the entire organization. The objective is for an ethics compliance program to act as a buffer so that legal violations do not occur. When violations occur, management must prove that a proactive compliance program was in effect.

One of the main reasons for ethics program ineffectiveness is the failure to develop an ethical climate. . . . If the corporate culture provides rewards or the opportunity to engage in unethical behavior through decentralization, weak internal control systems, or a lack of managerial concern, then the firm is in danger of high penalties based on the FSG. On a more positive note, many companies attempt to set standards much higher than legal compliance. Corporations such as Lockheed Martin, NYNEX, General Motors, Waste Management, Teledyne, and Dun & Bradstreet have codes of ethics, ethics training, compliance programs, and depending on the issue, use various punishments to impede employees' misconduct as defined by company standards. Still all of these firms have both legal and ethical misconduct issues to resolve. Dow Corning had a vaunted ethics program that was a model for corporate America. This program did not prevent the controversy of silicone breast implants from pushing the company into bankruptcy.

The Purpose of the FSG

The main objectives of the Federal Sentencing Guidelines are to self-monitor and police, aggressively work to deter unethical acts, and punish those organizational members or stakeholders who engage in unethical behavior. The sentencing of organizations is accomplished with four considerations in mind. First, the court will order the organization to remedy any harm caused by the offense. Second, if the organization operated primarily for criminal purpose, fines will be set sufficiently high to divest the firm of all assets. Third, fines levied against the organization are based on the seriousness of the offense and the culpability of the organization. Fourth, probation is an appropriate sentence for an organizational defendant when it will ensure that the firm will take actions to reduce future criminal conduct. The guidelines require federal judges to increase fines for organizations that tolerate misconduct and reduce fines for firms with extensive ethics and compliance activities. The main thrust for an organization is to avoid the mandatory restitution, monetary fines, and affirmative action steps which result from violations. . . .

Offenses and Resulting Penalties Under the FSG

The offenses under the FSG include all federal felony and Class A misdemeanor offenses. Major offenses governed by the FSG include bid rigging, fraud, customs violations, theft, embezzlement, extortion, drug offenses, civil rights violations, antitrust violations, conflict of interest, invasion of privacy, forgery, racketeering, tax fraud, transportation of hazardous materials, copyright infringements, and environmental crimes (U.S. Sentencing Commission, 1994).

Penalties. The penalties for these offenses are based on two premises, the seriousness of the offense and the culpability of the organization. Seriousness is measured in terms of the monetary gains or losses suffered as a result of the wrongful conduct. An organization's culpability is determined by the organization's efforts to prevent and detect criminal conduct and the organization's involvement in or tolerance of the conduct by high level personnel or those with substantial authority. The final consideration in determining culpability is the actions of the organization after an offense has been committed.

Severe mandatory penalties are required by the guidelines, with base fines ranging from $5,000 to $72,500,000 (see Table I). In the past, U.S. district judges had much discretion in imposing fines and sentences. Under the new guidelines, judges utilize a formula to determine the fine ranges from which they choose the final fine. Since the government does not have the resources to regulate compliance, federal judges were given the power to impose fines on an organization based on the seriousness of the offense and the culpability of the organization. Management's lack of knowledge or association with the crime is not an adequate mitigating defense.

Measures that can be imposed upon the organization, outside of the base fines, include restitution or compensation to return affected individuals to the status quo, a probationary period, a defined term of commu-

TABLE I. Base Offense Level Fines

Offense Level	Amount
6 or less	$ 5,000
10	$ 20,000
15	$ 125,000
20	$ 650,000
25	$ 2,800,000
30	$10,500,000
35	$36,000,000
38 or more	$72,500,000

Source: Federal Sentencing Guidelines for Organizations, October 1991.

nity service, and/or a notification to all victims of the organizational activity. These measures of restitution can virtually "delimit" the amount of financial obligation imposed upon the organization since there are no fine tables for these remedial measures.

Seriousness of the Offense. The fine that can be levied against an organization committing an offense is based on the greatest of either pecuniary gain, pecuniary loss, or the base offense level indicated in Table I. Pecuniary gain is the before-tax profit gained by the organization as a result of the offense. A pecuniary loss is the monetary loss caused by the knowing, intentional or reckless acts of the organization. Finally, the base fine may be determined by the number and type of offenses that the organization has previously committed. As the offense level increases, so does the base fine that must be assessed under the sentencing guidelines.

Each federal offense has been assigned a corresponding base level (i.e., 1 to 38 or more). For instance, the commercial bribery of federal, state or local government officials carries a base offense level of 10. However, this level increases if the bribe exceeds $2,000. Price-fixing and market-allocation (i.e., collusion) agreements among competitors carry a base offense level of 10 but increase as the volume of commerce exceeds $400,000.

Culpability of the Organization. As a general rule, the base fine measures the seriousness of the offense. However, in order to determine the final fine ranges, a culpability score must also be assessed. Culpability is based on three interrelated principles. First, organizations become more culpable when high-ranking individuals participate, condone, or willfully ignore criminal conduct. This can be evidenced by looking at the prior history of the organization — how long has it been since a previous offense has occurred (10 years: +1; 5 years: +2). Second, in larger and more professional organizations, criminal conduct by high-level employees is increasingly a breach of trust and abuse of position. The culpability score gradually increases based on the size of the organization (10 employees: +1; 5,000 employees: +5). Third, culpability increases in organizations where management's tolerance of offenses is pervasive. Other factors directly affecting the culpability score include violations of a judicial order and obstruction of justice. Factors which can mitigate or lessen the culpability level include an effective program to detect violations of the law, self-reporting, cooperation, and acceptance of responsibility.

The base fine depends on the organization's efforts to prevent the offense as shown by the offense level. The above fine table can be further adjusted based on severity of the offense (resulting in death or bodily injury), the potential threat to national security, the potential threat to the environment, the potential threat to a market, if the organization is a public entity, and/or if the remedial costs exceed the gains achieved by the organization.

FSG REQUIREMENTS FOR THE COMPLIANCE PROCESS

The Federal Sentencing Guidelines require organizations to develop a compliance program that can prevent, detect, and deter employees from engaging in misconduct. The ethics component acts as a buffer keeping firms away from the thin line separating unethical and illegal conduct. To be considered effective, compliance programs must disclose any wrongdoing, cooperate with the government, and accept the responsibility for misconduct. Codes of ethical conduct, employee training, hotline phone numbers, compliance officers, newsletters, brochures, monitoring employee conduct, and an enforcement system are typical components of a compliance program. The risk of severe penalties can be reduced under the guidelines if the organization has established an effective compliance program. The cornerstone of an effective program is that companies must exercise due diligence in seeking to prevent and detect criminal conduct by employees.

Although criminal conduct may be defined by law, the interpretation of ethical versus unethical behavior is often a judgment even when there is a program to curb unethical behavior. Most organizations with compliance programs still have ethics violations as defined by their standards of conduct. A recent Ethics Resource Center business ethics survey of employees revealed that 55% never or only occasionally found their company's standards of conduct useful in guiding their business decisions and actions. An additional 8% had never read the standards, and 45% found ethics training to be ineffective. Organizational ethics programs have yet to reach a level of effectiveness and usefulness desired through the Federal Sentencing Guidelines.

An effective compliance program is more a commitment and process than an exact blueprint for conduct. There are three major components of the process. First, larger organizations are required to develop and review formal written standards and procedures for conduct. A code of ethics by itself is not enough to ensure ethical behavior within an organization or profession. On the other hand, it is possible for an effective code of ethics to provide specific guidelines to address major areas of risk within an entire industry. For example, the Water Quality Association has developed a detailed code of ethics that provides specific guidelines within the water treatment industry worldwide. Second, organizations must establish and continuously revise guidelines for specific offenses that are most likely to occur due to the nature of its business. For instance, if the organization gives salespeople great flexibility in setting prices, then it must have standards to detect and prevent price-fixing and bid rigging. Price discrimination and human resource issues such as privacy and conflict of interest must be closely monitored by all managers. Finally, the prior history of the organization may indicate offenses for which preventive action should be taken. The recurrence of similar offenses casts doubt on an organization's effort to prevent misconduct.

The Ethical Compliance Program

An effective program is a process of continuous activities that are designed, implemented, and enforced to prevent and detect misconduct. The FSG suggest a compliance program, with the organization exercising due diligence by performing the following steps (U.S. Sentencing Commission, 1994):

1. Codes of conduct must be developed that are capable of reducing misconduct.
2. Specific high level personnel must be responsible for the compliance program (i.e., compliance officers) and support the ethics/compliance program (i.e., top management).

3. Substantial discretionary authority in the organization must not be given to persons with a propensity to engage in illegal conduct.
4. Standards and procedures must be communicated to employees, other agents (such as advertising agencies), and independent contractors (or consultants) through training programs and formal communication systems. (All relevant stakeholders should be exposed to the company code of conduct).
5. The organization must take reasonable steps to achieve compliance with its standards, by using monitoring and internal auditing systems to detect misconduct. A reporting system must allow employees and agents to report misconduct without fear (i.e., anonymous ethics hotlines).
6. Standards and punishment must be enforced consistently in an organization, and the organization must create a process to prevent further offenses.
7. A plan to review and modify the compliance program is necessary to demonstrate a continuous improvement process in self-monitoring.

These seven steps represent the minimum an organization can do to demonstrate due diligence. The end result of the process is compliance and ethics programs that reduce the opportunity for employees to engage in misconduct. Further, the program requires high-ranking personnel to be responsible for compliance. An effective compliance and ethics program can reduce both employee misconduct and an organization's penalties if crimes are committed. Thus, the reduction of fines is an incentive for firms to implement compliance programs. Table II shows the potential mitigating effect an effective compliance program can have on fines. A high culpability score has a significant impact on increasing fine levels. . . .

Cases Tried Under the FSG

Approximately 280 cases have now been tried under the FSG (Davidson, 1995). The most frequent offenses include fraud, antitrust

TABLE II.   FSG Ranges Based on Various Culpability Scores

Offense Level	Culpability	Fine Minimum	Maximum
25	10	$5.6 M	$11.2 M
25	7	$3.92 M	$7.84 M
25	2	$1.12 M	$2.24 M

offenses, environmental and tax violations. The fastest growing violation prosecuted under the FSG is the evasion of import/export duties (Apel, 1995). Some of the early results are due to implications of the point system. "The guidelines have a point system for assigning penalties and fines. And since its implementation, 91 percent of organizations plead guilty because points are subtracted for this" (Apel, 1995). But of those who plead guilty, thus far, 65% of the organizations were placed on probation (Apel, 1995). Probation may mean significant cost to a firm because consultants may be required by the court to improve conduct or monitor activities. The highest fine issued was $7.5 million, and the longest probationary period established was 60 months which was not an uncommon probationary period (Apel, 1995).

A majority (93%) of the organizations sentenced under the FSG have been private organizations, although publicly held organizations may be sentenced more in the future. Small business is a major offender with 79% of all organizations sentenced having less than 50 employees. Organizations with less than 20 employees represent 56% of the cases through June 30, 1995 (U.S. Sentencing Commission, 1995). Scalia (1995) indicates that large, publicly traded firms are not being seen in current cases or have not been sentenced as much as smaller companies because of the complexity and length of the cases and prosecutors' tendencies to pursue these cases in civil, not criminal court.

CONCLUSIONS

Most crimes and unethical actions are not committed by individuals who want to advance themselves and destroy their organizations. Instead they occur because of two organizational factors: opportunity and the actions of peers and supervisors. . . .

After years of debate over the importance of business ethics in organizations, the federal government has decided to institutionalize ethics as a required buffer to prevent legal violations in organizations. This is the incentive that organizations need to show greater initiative in the ethics area. If the guidelines do not get the attention of top management, one mid-level fine for a Federal Sentencing Guidelines violation should. The goal is that companies will see the opportunity to improve their ethical climate and reduce the need for excessive regulation by becoming a "good citizen" in society.

REFERENCES

Apel, A. "Ethics Violations: A Change in Guilt?", *Business Ethics* (January/February 1995); 14.

Davidson, J. "Corporate Sentencing Guidelines Have Snagged Mostly Small Firms," *The Wall Street Journal* (August 28, 1995), p. B4.

Scalia, J. Jr. "Cases Sentenced Under the Guidelines," in *Corporate Crime in America: Strengthening the "Good Citizenship" Corporation* (United States Sentencing Commission: Washington, D.C., 1995), pp. 253–268.

United States Sentencing Commission. *Federal Sentencing Guidelines Manual* (West Publishing, St. Paul, MN, 1994).

Managing Ethics and Legal Compliance: What Works and What Hurts

Linda Klebe Treviño
Gary R. Weaver
David G. Gibson
Barbara Ley Toffler

Ten years ago, a Business Roundtable report titled Corporate Ethics: A Prime Business Asset suggested that "there are no precise ways to measure the end results of the widespread and intensive efforts to develop effective corporate ethics programs."[1] Despite this difficulty in measuring their accomplishments, corporate ethics and legal compliance programs have become even more widespread over the last decade. Companies are investing millions of dollars on ethics and compliance management. A recent survey of *Fortune 1000* firms found that 98% of responding firms address ethics or conduct issues in formal documents. Of those firms, 78% have a separate code of ethics, and most distribute these policies widely within the organization. Many employees also receive ethics training and have access to a telephone line for reporting problems or seeking advice. Much of this activity has been attributed to the 1991 U.S. Sentencing Commission's Guidelines for organizational defendants. The Guidelines prescribe more lenient sentences and fines to companies that have taken measures to prevent employee misconduct.

What do these ethics and legal compliance programs actually accomplish? A firm's approach to ethics and legal compliance management has an enormous impact on employees' attitudes and behaviors. In this study, we found that specific characteristics of the formal ethics or compliance program matter less than broader perceptions of the program's orientation toward values and ethical aspirations. What helps the most are consistency between policies and actions as well as dimensions of the organization's ethical culture such as ethical leadership, fair treatment of employees, and open discussion of ethics in the organization. On the other hand, what hurts the most is an ethical culture that emphasizes self-interest and unquestioning obedience to authority, and the perception that the ethics or compliance program exists only to protect top management from blame.

In order to investigate what works and what hurts in ethics and compliance management, we administered a survey to over 10,000 randomly selected employees at all levels in six large American companies from a variety of industries. The companies varied in their ethics/compliance program approaches. Because we were relying on employees' perceptions, we had to be concerned about socially desirable responses — having employees tell us what they thought we wanted to hear rather than the truth. We took a number of steps to guard against such biased responding. Surveys were completely anonymous, they were sent to employees' homes, and they were returned directly to the researchers for analysis.

In designing the survey, we first had to identify meaningful outcomes of ethics/

compliance programs. Second, we wanted to understand how different approaches to ethics/compliance management would affect these outcomes. For example, a program can punish rule violators after the fact or it can focus on prevention. Programs can emphasize deterrence of illegal conduct or encouragement of ethical conduct. . . .

WHAT CAN EFFECTIVE ETHICS/COMPLIANCE PROGRAMS ACCOMPLISH?

We began by asking: "What should we look for to determine whether an ethics/compliance program is effective?" . . . We identified seven outcomes relevant to effective ethics/compliance management.

Unethical/Illegal Behavior

The bottom line for ethics/compliance management is the extent of unethical/illegal behavior in the organization. Effective ethics/compliance management should be associated with less unethical and illegal behavior. Employees know the most about the misconduct that exists, so we asked them to report on the extent to which they had observed (from never to very frequently) 32 specific unethical or illegal behaviors over the preceding year (e.g., lying to customers, padding an expense account, falsifying financial reports, giving kickbacks, stealing from the company, misusing insider information, violating environmental laws/regulations). Asking employees about "observed" misconduct in the firm is also less prone to produce socially desirable responses. Employees are more likely to report that they saw others engaged in misconduct than they are to report their own misdeeds. The scale we developed was adapted from past research on business ethics.

Employee Awareness of Ethical/Legal Issues That Arise at Work

Norm Augustine, Chairman of the Board of Lockheed Martin, has stated, "We don't teach ethics, we teach ethics awareness." Many experienced managers of ethics and legal compliance consider raising employees' awareness of ethical and legal issues to be their primary challenge. No matter how strong their values, employees cannot be expected to be naturally familiar with all of the laws and regulations that pertain to their work. Nor can they be expected to be automatically aware of the ethical ambiguities that they might face in a particular industry or position. However, if employees are aware of relevant ethical and legal issues, they will more likely ask the right questions and ultimately do the right thing when faced with a dilemma. Many people do the wrong thing simply because they are unaware — they don't know that they should be concerned or ask for help. Effective ethics/compliance management should increase employees' ethics awareness.

Looking for Ethics/Compliance Advice Within the Company

Once an employee is aware that she or he is facing an ethics or legal compliance issue, effective ethics/compliance management should make it more likely that the employee would ask for help and guidance within the firm. Many ethics offices spend much of their time responding to questions about company policy and the law (e.g., questions regarding gift giving or receiving, conflicts of interest, or human resources problems). Getting good advice early can nip problems in the bud and provide employees with accurate guidance on company policies and the law. It can also provide the ethics officer with input that can be used to plan future training needs or ethics code revisions. Essentially, employees' willingness to ask for advice within the company may be key to keeping the ethics/compliance program dynamic and responsive to employees' needs. In an effective ethics/compliance management program, employees are more willing to look for ethical/legal advice within the company.

Delivering Bad News to Management

Many ethics/compliance managers believe that part of their job is to assure an environment of candor and safety in the organization. Unless employees believe they can deliver "bad news" to management without fear of repercussions, they may be unwilling to inform management of developing ethical risks or problems until it is too late. For example, one of Badaracco and Webb's interviewees noted that "no one wants to report bad news up. What [management] should be hearing gets filtered."[2]

As a result of this reticence to report bad news to their supervisors, ethical and legal risks can escalate quickly if managers make decisions based upon half-truths or untruths that are passed up the management line. Effective ethics/compliance management should increase employees' willingness to report bad news to management.

Ethics/Compliance Violations Are Reported in the Organization

Employees are the organization's first line of defense against ethical or legal problems because they are most likely to know about violations of the law or of ethical guidelines. One of the key components of most ethics/compliance programs is a reporting system (often a telephone "hotline") that employees can use to report ethical or legal violations that they observe. An ethics or compliance program cannot be effective unless employees are willing to report violations to management. These violations can then be followed up and acted upon. Yet, employees may fail to report violations for many reasons. They may not care enough about the organization to go to the trouble or take the personal risk. They may fear retaliation especially if they don't trust that their identity will be protected. Or, they may believe that nothing will come of their efforts. Finally, if employees are uncomfortable reporting violations inside the company, they may be more likely to report violations outside, to the government or media organizations. Accordingly, effective ethics/compliance management should influence employees to be willing to report violations to management.

Better Decision Making in the Company Because of the Ethics/Compliance Program

Many organizations have the formal components of an ethics/compliance program: a code, training, and a reporting hotline. However, are these program elements infused into everyday decision making, contributing to better decisions? Sometimes, employees view ethics/compliance programs as mere window dressing, implemented to respond to external pressure while leaving decision processes unchanged. Unless these programs have an impact on every day decision-making effectiveness, they are not a good use of resources. An effective ethics/compliance program will be perceived by employees as contributing to better decision making in the organization.

Employee Commitment to the Organization

Employee commitment is a general concept that is influenced by many management actions. Previous research has shown that a key dimension of organizational commitment has to do with value congruence — the extent to which employees feel a sense of belonging and connection to the organization. Commitment also has to do with how employees represent the organization to outsiders. Do they represent it as a good place to work and do they defend it when it's criticized? Further, previous research has suggested that employee commitment is higher in organizations with certain ethical culture characteristics. Finally, management is clearly interested in employee commitment, especially in an economy in which companies are competing for the best employees.

WHAT INFLUENCES ETHICS/COMPLIANCE PROGRAM EFFECTIVENESS?

There are several key organizational and program design factors that are associated with ethics/compliance management effectiveness. . . .

Program Orientation

Ethics/compliance programs can be designed with very different goals and orientations. Previous research has referred to two types of approaches, a compliance-based approach and an integrity or values-based approach. According to Paine, a compliance approach focuses primarily on preventing, detecting, and punishing violations of the law, while a values-based approach aims to define organizational values and encourage employee commitment to ethical aspirations.[3] She asserts that the values-based approach should be more effective than a compliance-based approach because a values-based approach is rooted in personal self-governance and is more likely to motivate employees to behave in accordance with

shared values. She argues that compliance approaches can be counterproductive because they emphasize avoiding punishment instead of self-governance. They define ethics in terms of legal compliance rather than ethical aspirations, and they implicitly endorse a "code of moral mediocrity."

A recent study of *Fortune 1000* firms was conducted in part to determine the orientations of their ethics/compliance management efforts. The survey found that the compliance and values-based approaches are not mutually exclusive. Rather, most firms' approaches to ethics/compliance management combine these orientations in some way. Nevertheless, the compliance approach predominated over the values-based approach in over half of the firms. The U.S. Sentencing Guidelines (implemented in late 1991) contribute to the development of compliance approaches because fines and sanctions for companies convicted of crimes very dramatically depending upon management's cooperation and whether the firm has a legal compliance program in place.

Given that a compliance-based approach predominates in most firms, our study needed to test the contention that a values-based approach is "better" (achieves more positive outcomes) than a compliance-based approach. Also, many companies hope to maintain or improve their public image and relationships with external stakeholders by adopting an ethics/compliance program. Therefore, we identified an orientation toward satisfying external stakeholders (customers, the community, suppliers) as a third approach in our study. Alternatively, employees sometimes suspect that an ethics/compliance program is introduced in part to protect top management from blame for ethical failures or legal problems. In fact, Paine associated this suspicion with a compliance-based program, suggesting that skeptical employees may see a compliance-oriented program as "nothing more than liability insurance for senior management."[4] Another of Badaracco and Webb's interviewees put it this way: "I'm cynical. To me, corporate codes of conduct exist to cover the potential problems companies may have. It provides deniability. It gives the employers an excuse. . . . The top officers can say, 'These employees messed up. They violated our way of doing business.'"[5] Therefore, we also assessed the impact of a "protect top management from blame" orientation.

A Values Orientation Is the Most Effective Single Orientation

Across the six firms in this study, employees perceived the presence of each of the four orientations (compliance-based, values-based, external stakeholder, and protect top management) to varying degrees, and all of them were important in influencing outcomes. However, it is clearly most important to have a program that employees perceive to be values-based. In these six companies, if employees perceived a values-based program, each of the seven outcomes studied was significantly more positive and the relationships were quite strong. Unethical/illegal behavior was lower, awareness of ethical/legal issues was higher, and employees were more likely to look for advice within the firm, to be willing to deliver bad news to management, and to report ethical violations. They also were more committed to the organization and more likely to believe that decision making was better because of the ethics/compliance program.

Compliance and External Orientations Are Also Helpful

Outcomes were also more positive if employees perceived a compliance or an external stakeholder orientation. Contrary to Paine's argument, if employees perceived a compliance-based program, all of the outcomes were significantly more positive. However, the relationships were not as strong as with the values orientation. If employees perceived an external stakeholder orientation, once again the same outcomes were significantly more positive. However, the relationships were even weaker than those for compliance orientation.

Combining These Orientations May Be Effective

The data also supported the idea that these orientations are not mutually exclusive. . . . So, it is clearly possible to design a program that combines these different orientations, while also emphasizing a values-based approach. A values orientation can be backed up with accountability systems and discipline for violators. Values can include a concern for customers, suppliers, and the community as well as shareholders and internal stakeholders such as employees. The ideal mix of orientations likely depends on specific organizational circumstances, such as the organization's culture, product, and industry.

"Protect Top Management" Is Clearly a Harmful Approach

Not surprisingly, where employees perceived that the ethics/compliance program was oriented toward protecting top management from blame, all of the important outcomes were significantly more negative. These relationships were particularly strong and negative for commitment to the organization, for the perception that it's okay to deliver bad news to management, and that employees would report ethical/legal violations to management. In addition, unethical/illegal behavior was higher, employees were less aware of ethical issues, and they were less likely to seek advice about ethical concerns. Furthermore, they did not believe that decision making was better because of the ethics/compliance program.

Summary of Program Orientation Findings

A key finding of this study is the importance of designing an ethics program that is perceived by employees to be first and foremost about shared organizational values and about guiding employees to act on their ethical aspirations. Such programs motivate employees to be aware of ethical or legal issues, report bad news to management, report ethical or legal violations, and refrain from engaging in unethical or illegal conduct. In addition, unethical/illegal behavior is reduced, employee commitment is higher, and employees believe that decision making in the organization is better because of the ethics program.

This values-based approach can be supplemented with an orientation toward legal compliance and satisfying external stakeholders. Valuing external stakeholders such as customers and the community has a positive impact on all outcomes, as does holding employees accountable for their behavior through monitoring and disciplinary systems. Discipline for rule violators serves an important symbolic role in organizations — it reinforces standards, upholds the value of conformity to shared norms, and maintains the perception that the organization is a just place where wrongdoers are held accountable for their actions.

Finally, a program must avoid conveying the message to employees that it exists to protect top management from blame. Having a program that is perceived in this way by employees may be worse than having no program at all. Recall Paine's proposal that employees were likely to associate a compliance approach with this "protect top management from blame" orientation. Our data did not support this contention. There was little association between employees' perceptions of the program as compliance-oriented and their perceptions of the program as being oriented toward protecting top management from blame. However, this protect top management orientation

was even less likely to be associated with a program that employees perceived to be values-based. Perhaps the most important message to executives is that this protect top management perception is real. Employees judge top management's *motives* in implementing an ethics/compliance program. Also, it is important that they perceive it to be a sincere attempt to have all employees do what's right rather than just an attempt to create legal "cover" for executives in case of a legal mishap. . . .

What Do the Study Results Imply for Public Policy?

In 1991, the U.S. Sentencing Commission articulated seven requirements for corporations wishing to demonstrate due diligence and an effective legal compliance program. These requirements have had a profound impact on compliance management because many corporations have focused intently on them. However, this study has found that a narrow focus on the formal structures and processes addressed in the requirements (e.g., establishment of codes, training, hotlines) does not lead to an effective legal compliance program.

If the Sentencing Commission wishes to reduce illegal/unethical behavior in the workplace, it must focus its attention beyond these superficial program characteristics. We found that the most important influential factors have to do with program follow-through and the broader ethical culture of the firm. The Commission could influence the effectiveness of corporate legal compliance efforts by incorporating these key factors in future guidelines and requirements. For example, the importance of policy/action consistency suggests that employees often see policies as just "window dressing." Therefore, the Commission should be looking for evidence of follow-through. Do employees perceive that the company will follow up on reports of violations? Do employees perceive that the firm's actions are consistent with its policies? Employees' perceptions of how rewards are distributed are even more important than their perceptions of the distribution of punishments (that violators are detected and punished). Currently, the guidelines focus more on detection and discipline. Leadership has also been ignored by the guidelines. Although they require specific high-level individuals to be assigned responsibility to oversee compliance standards, they do not require that these high-level individuals actually interact with the top management team or that other leaders be involved in ethics/compliance management. In fact, previous research has suggested that most ethics/compliance officers have little contact with their CEOs. The Commission could require that line managers at all levels be involved in ethics/compliance management. Employee fair treatment is another neglected issue. Its powerful impact on outcomes means that the Commission should consider it in their evaluation of program effectiveness.

We recognize that it is easier to look for evidence that a policy exists than it is to evaluate the deeper commitments that are key to compliance program effectiveness. However, if the Commission wishes to influence the development of "effective" programs, it must delve deeper into corporate ethical culture than it has in the past. This study demonstrates that it is possible to survey randomly selected employees and learn a great deal about the factors that are most important for program effectiveness. . . .

Notes

1. The Business Roundtable, *Corporate Ethics: A Prime Business Asset* (New York: The Business Roundtable, 1988), p. 9.
2. J.J. Badaracco and A.P. Webb, "Business Ethics: A View from the Trenches" *California Management Review* 37/2 (Winter 1995) p. 16.
3. L.S. Paine, "Managing for Organizational Integrity" *Harvard Business Review* 72/2 (March/April, 1994.)
4. Paine, op. cit., p. 111.
5. Badaracco and Webb, op. cit., p. 15.

DETERMINING RESPONSIBILITY

Roger Boisjoly and the *Challenger* Disaster: The Ethical Dimensions

Russell P. Boisjoly
Ellen Foster Curtis
Eugene Mellican

INTRODUCTION

On January 28, 1986, the space shuttle *Challenger* exploded 73 seconds into its flight, killing the seven astronauts aboard. As the nation mourned the tragic loss of the crew members, the Rogers Commission was formed to investigate the causes of the disas-

From Russell P. Boisjoly, Ellen Foster Curtis, and Eugene Mellican, "Roger Boisjoly and the *Challenger* Disaster: The Ethical Dimensions," *Journal of Business Ethics* 8 (April 1989). Copyright © 1989 by Kluwer Academic Publishers. Reprinted by permission of Kluwer Academic Publishers.

ter. The Commission concluded that the explosion occurred due to seal failure in one of the solid rocket booster joints. Testimony given by Roger Boisjoly, Senior Scientist and acknowledged rocket seal expert, indicated that top management at NASA and Morton Thiokol had been aware of problems with the O-ring seals, but agreed to launch against the recommendation of Boisjoly and other engineers. Boisjoly had alerted management to problems with the O-rings as early as January 1985, yet several shuttle launches prior to the *Challenger* had been approved without correcting the hazards. This suggests that the management practice of NASA and Morton Thiokol had created an environment which altered the framework for decision making, leading to a breakdown in communication between technical experts and their supervisors, and top level management, and to the acceptance of risks that both organizations had historically viewed as unacceptable. With human lives and the national interest at stake, serious ethical concerns are embedded in this dramatic change in management practice.

In fact, one of the most important aspects of the *Challenger* disaster — both in terms of the causal sequence that led to it and the lessons to be learned from it — is its ethical dimension. Ethical issues are woven throughout the tangled web of decisions, events, practices, and organizational structures that resulted in the loss of the *Challenger* and its seven astronauts. Therefore, an ethical analysis of this tragedy is essential for a full understanding of the event itself and for the implications it has for any endeavor where public policy, corporate practice, and individual decisions intersect.

The significance of an ethical analysis of the *Challenger* disaster is indicated by the fact that it immediately presents one of the most urgent, but difficult, issues in the examination of corporate and individual behavior

today, i.e., whether existing ethical theories adequately address the problems posed by new technologies, new forms of organization, and evolving social systems. At the heart of this issue is the concept of responsibility. No ethical concept has been more affected by the impact of these changing realities. Modern technology has so transformed the context and scale of human action that not only do the traditional parameters of responsibility seem inadequate to contain the full range of human acts and their consequences, but even more fundamentally, it is no longer the individual that is the primary locus of power and responsibility, but public and private institutions. Thus, it would seem, it is no longer the character and virtues of individuals that determine the standards of moral conduct, it is the policies and structures of the institutional settings within which they live and work.

Many moral conflicts facing individuals within institutional settings do arise from matters pertaining to organizational structures or questions of public policy. As such, they are resolvable only at a level above the responsibilities of the individual. Therefore, some writers argue that the ethical responsibilities of the engineer or manager in a large corporation have as much to do with the organization as with the individual. Instead of expecting individual engineers or managers to be moral heroes, emphasis should be on the creation of organizational structures conducive to ethical behavior among all agents under their aegis. It would be futile to attempt to establish a sense of ethical responsibility in engineers and management personnel and ignore the fact that such persons work within a sociotechnical environment which increasingly undermines the notion of individual, responsible moral agency (Boling and Dempsey, 1981; De George, 1981).

Yet, others argue that precisely because of these organizational realities individual accountability must be re-emphasized to counteract the diffusion of responsibility within large organizations and to prevent its evasion under the rubric of collective responsibility. Undoubtedly institutions do take on a kind of collective life of their own, but they do not exist, or act, independently of the individuals that constitute them, whatever the theoretical and practical complexities of delineating the precise relationships involved. Far from diminishing individuals' obligations, the reality of organizational life increases them because the consequences of decisions and acts are extended and amplified through the reach and power of that reality. Since there are pervasive and inexorable connections between ethical standards and behavior of individuals within an organization and its structure and operation, "the sensitizing of professionals to ethical considerations should be increased so that institutional structures will reflect enhanced ethical sensitivities as trained professionals move up the organizational ladder to positions of leadership" (Mankin, 1981, p. 17).

By reason of the courageous activities and testimony of individuals like Roger Boisjoly, the *Challenger* disaster provides a fascinating illustration of the dynamic tension between organizational and individual responsibility. By focusing on this central issue, this article seeks to accomplish two objectives: first, to demonstrate the extent to which the *Challenger* disaster not only gives concrete expression to the ethical ambiguity that permeates the relationship between organizational and individual responsibility, but also, in fact, is a result of it; second, to reclaim the meaning and importance of individual responsibility within the diluting context of large organizations.

In meeting these objectives, the article is divided into two parts: a case study of Roger Boisjoly's efforts to galvanize management support for effectively correcting the high risk O-ring problems, his attempt to prevent the launch, the scenario which resulted in the launch decision, and Boisjoly's quest to set the record straight despite enormous personal and professional consequences; and an ethical analysis of these events.

PREVIEW FOR DISASTER

On January 24, 1985, Roger Boisjoly, Senior Scientist at Morton Thiokol, watched the launch of Flight 51-C of the space shuttle program. He was at Cape Canaveral to inspect the solid rocket boosters from Flight 51-C following their recovery in the Atlantic Ocean and to conduct a training session at Kennedy Space Center (KSC) on the proper methods of inspecting the booster joints. While watching the launch, he noted that the temperature that day was much cooler than recorded at other launches, but was still much warmer than the 18 degree temperature encountered three days earlier when he arrived in Orlando. The unseasonably cold weather of the past several days had produced the worst citrus crop failures in Florida history.

When he inspected the solid rocket boosters several days later, Boisjoly discovered evidence that the primary O-ring seals on two field joints had been compromised by hot combustion gases (i.e., hot gas blow-by had occurred) which had also eroded part of the primary O-ring. This was the first time that a primary seal on a field joint had been penetrated. When he discovered the large amount of blackened grease between the primary and secondary seals, his concern heightened. The blackened grease was discovered over 80 degree and 110 degree arcs, respectively, on two of the seals, with the larger arc indicating greater hot gas blow-by. Post-flight calculations indicated that the ambient temperature of the field joints at launch time was 53 degrees. This evidence, coupled with his recollection of the low temperature the day of the launch and the citrus crop damage caused by the cold spell, led to his conclusion that the severe hot gas blow-by may have been caused by, and related to, low temperature. After reporting these findings to his superiors. Boisjoly presented them to engineers and management at NASA's Marshall Space Flight Center (MSFC). As a result of his presentation at MSFC, Roger Boisjoly was asked to participate in the Flight Readiness Review (FRR) on February 12, 1985 for Flight 51-E which was scheduled for launch in April, 1985. This FRR represents the first association of low temperature with blow-by on a field joint, a condition that was considered an "acceptable risk" by Larry Mulloy, NASA's Manager for the Booster Project, and other NASA officials.

Roger Boisjoly had twenty-five years of experience as an engineer in the aerospace industry. Among his many notable assignments were the performance of stress and deflection analysis on the flight control equipment of the Advanced Minuteman Missile at Autonetics, and serving as a lead engineer on the lunar module of Apollo at Hamilton Standard. He moved to Utah in 1980 to take a position in the Applied Mechanics Department as a Staff Engineer at the Wasatch Division of Morton Thiokol. He was considered the leading expert in the United States on O-rings and rocket joint seals and received plaudits for his work on the joint seal problems from Joe C. Kilminster, Vice President of Space Booster Programs, Morton Thiokol (Kilminster, July, 1985). His commitment to the company and the community was further demonstrated by his service as Mayor of Willard, Utah from 1982 to 1983.

The tough questioning he received at the February 12th FRR convinced Boisjoly of the need for further evidence linking low temperature and hot gas blow-by. He worked closely with Arnie Thompson, Supervisor of Rocket Motor Cases, who conducted subscale laboratory tests in March, 1985, to further test the effects of temperature on O-ring resiliency. The bench tests that were performed provided powerful evidence to support Boisjoly's and Thompson's theory: Low temperatures greatly and adversely affected the ability of O-rings to create a seal on solid rocket booster joints. If the temperature was too low (and they did not know what the threshold temperature would be), it was possible that neither the primary or secondary O-rings would seal!

One month later the post-flight inspection of Flight 51-B revealed that the primary seal of a booster nozzle joint did not make contact during its two minute flight. If this damage had occurred in a field joint, the secondary O-ring may have failed to seal, causing the loss of the flight. As a result, Boisjoly and his colleagues became increasingly concerned about shuttle safety. This evidence from the inspection of Flight 51-B was presented at the FRR for Flight 51-F on July 1, 1985; the key engineers and managers at NASA and Morton Thiokol were now aware of the critical O-ring problems and the influence of low temperature on the performance of the joint seals.

During July, 1985, Boisjoly and his associates voiced their desire to devote more effort and resources to solving the problems of O-ring erosion. In his activity reports dated July 22 and 29, 1985, Boisjoly expressed considerable frustration with the lack of progress in this area, despite the fact that a Seal Erosion Task Force had been informally appointed on July 19th. Finally, Boisjoly wrote the following memo, labelled "Company Private," to R. K. (Bob) Lund, Vice President of Engineering for Morton Thiokol, to express the extreme urgency of his concerns. Here are some excerpts from that memo:

This letter is written to insure that management is fully aware of the seriousness of the current O-ring erosion problem. . . . The mistakenly accepted position on the joint problem was to fly without fear of failure . . . is now drastically changed as a result of the SRM 16A nozzle joint erosion which eroded a secondary O-ring with the primary O-ring never sealing. If the same scenario should occur in a field joint (and it could), then it is a jump ball as to the success or failure of the joint. . . . The result would be a catastrophe of the highest order — loss of human life. . . .

It is my honest and real fear that if we do not take immediate action to dedicate a team to solve the problem, with the field joint having the number one priority, then we stand in jeopardy of losing a flight along with all the launch pad facilities (Boisjoly, July, 1985a).

On August 20, 1985, R. K. Lund formally announced the formation of the Seal Erosion Task Team. The team consisted of only five full-time engineers from the 2500 employed by Morton Thiokol on the Space Shuttle Program. The events of the next five months would demonstrate that management had not provided the resources necessary to carry out the enormous task of solving the seal erosion problem.

On October 3, 1985, the Seal Erosion Task Force met with Joe Kilminster to discuss the problems they were having in gaining organizational support necessary to solve the O-ring problems. Boisjoly later stated that Kilminster summarized the meeting as a "good bullshit session." Once again frustrated by bureaucratic inertia, Boisjoly wrote in his activity report dated October 4th:

> . . . NASA is sending an engineering representative to stay with us starting Oct. 14th. We feel that this is a direct result of their feeling that we (MTI) are not responding quickly enough to the seal problem . . . upper management apparently feels that the SRM program is ours for sure and the customer be damned (Boisjoly, October, 1985b).

Boisjoly was not alone in his expression of frustration. Bob Ebeling, Department Manager, Solid Rocket Motor Igniter and Final Assembly, and a member of the Seal Erosion Task Force, wrote in a memo to Allan McDonald, Manager of the Solid Rocket Motor Project, "HELP! The seal task force is constantly being delayed by every possible means. . . . We wish we could get action by verbal request, but such is not the case. This is a red flag" (McConnell, 1987).

At the Society of Automotive Engineers (SAE) conference on October 7, 1985, Boisjoly presented a six-page overview of the joints and the seal configuration to approximately 130 technical experts in hope of soliciting suggestions for remedying the O-ring problems. Although MSFC had requested the presentation, NASA gave strict instructions not to express the critical urgency of fixing the joints, but merely to ask for suggestions for improvement. Although no help was forthcoming, the conference was a milestone in that it was the first time that NASA allowed information on the O-ring difficulties to be expressed in a public forum. That NASA also recognized that the O-ring problems were not receiving appropriate attention and manpower considerations from Morton Thiokol management is further evidenced by Boisjoly's October 24 log entry, ". . . Jerry Peoples (NASA) has informed his people that our group needs more authority and people to do the job. Jim Smith (NASA) will corner Al McDonald today to attempt to implement this direction."

The October 30 launch of Flight 61-A of the *Challenger* provided the most convincing, and yet to some the most contestable, evidence to date that low temperature was directly related to hot gas blow-by. The left booster experienced hot gas blow-by in the center and aft field joints without any seal erosion. The ambient temperature of the field joints was estimated to be 75 degrees at launch time based on post-flight calculations. Inspection of the booster joints revealed that the blow-by was less severe than that found on Flight 51-C because the seal grease was a grayish black color, rather than the jet black hue of Flight 51-C. The evidence was now consistent with the bench tests for joint resiliency conducted in March. That is, at 75 degrees the O-ring lost contact with its sealing surface for 2.4 seconds, whereas at 50 degrees the O-ring lost contact for 10 minutes. The actual flight data revealed greater hot gas blow-by for the O-rings on Flight 51-C which had an ambient temperature of 53 degrees than for Flight 61-A which had an ambient temperature of 75 degrees. Those who rejected this line of reasoning concluded that temperature must be irrelevant since hot gas blow-by had occurred even at room temperature (75 degrees). This difference in interpretation would receive further attention on January 27, 1986.

During the next two and one-half months, little progress was made in obtaining a solution to the O-ring problems. Roger Boisjoly made the following entry into his log on January 13, 1986, "O-ring resiliency tests that were requested on September 24, 1985 are now scheduled for January 15, 1986."

THE DAY BEFORE THE DISASTER

At 10 a.m. on January 27, 1986, Arnie Thompson received a phone call from Boyd Brinton, Thiokol's Manager of Project Engineering at MSFC, relaying the concerns of NASA's Larry Wear, also at MSFC, about the 18 degree temperature forecast for the launch of flight 51-L, the *Challenger*, scheduled for the next day. This phone call precipitated a series of meetings within Morton Thiokol, at the Marshall Space Flight Center; and at the Kennedy Space Center that culminated in a three-way telecon involving three teams of engineers and managers, that began at 8:15 p.m. E.S.T.

Joe Kilminster, Vice President, Space Booster Programs, of Morton Thiokol began the telecon by turning the presentation of the engineering charts over to Roger Boisjoly and Arnie Thompson. They presented thirteen charts which resulted in a recommendation against the launch of the *Challenger*. Boisjoly demonstrated their concerns with the performance of the O-rings in the field joints during the initial phases of *Challenger*'s flight with charts showing the effects of primary O-ring erosion, and its timing, on the ability to maintain a reliable secondary seal. The tremendous pressure and release of power from the rocket boosters create rotation in the joint such that the metal moves away from the O-rings so that they cannot maintain contact with the metal surfaces. If, at the same time, erosion occurs in the primary O-ring for any reason, then there is a reduced probability of maintaining a secondary seal. It is highly probable that as the ambient temperature drops, the primary O-ring will not seat, that there will be hot gas blow-by and erosion of the primary O-ring, and that a catastrophe will occur when the secondary O-ring fails to seal.

Bob Lund presented the final chart that included the Morton Thiokol recommendations that the ambient temperature including wind must be such that the seal temperature would be greater than 53 degrees to proceed with the launch. Since the overnight low was predicted to be 18 degrees, Bob Lund recommended against launch on January 28, 1986, or until the seal temperature exceeded 53 degrees.

NASA's Larry Mulloy bypassed Bob Lund and directly asked Joe Kilminster for his reaction. Kilminster stated that he supported the position of his engineers and he would not recommend launch below 53 degrees.

George Hardy, Deputy Director of Science and Engineering at MSFC, said he was "appalled at that recommendation," according to Allan McDonald's testimony before the Rogers Commission. Nevertheless, Hardy would not recommend to launch if the contractor was against it. After Hardy's reaction, Stanley Reinartz, Manager of Shuttle Project Office at MSFC, objected by pointing out that the solid rocket motors were qualified to operate between 40 and 90 degrees Fahrenheit.

Larry Mulloy, citing the data from Flight 61-A which indicated to him that temperature was not a factor, strenuously objected to Morton Thiokol's recommendation. He suggested that Thiokol was attempting to establish new Launch Commit Criteria at 53 degrees and that they couldn't do that the night before a launch. In exasperation Mulloy asked, "My God, Thiokol, when do you want me to launch? Next April?" (McConnell, 1987). Although other NASA officials also objected to the association of temperature with O-ring erosion and hot gas blow-by, Roger Boisjoly was able to hold his ground and demonstrate with the use of his charts and pictures that there was indeed a relationship: The lower the temperature the higher the probability of erosion and blow-by and the greater the likelihood of an accident. Finally, Joe Kilminster asked for a five-minute caucus off-net.

According to Boisjoly's testimony before the Rogers Commission, Jerry Mason, Senior Vice President of Wasatch Operations, began the caucus by saying that "a management decision was necessary." Sensing that an attempt would be made to overturn the no-launch decision, Boisjoly and Thompson attempted to re-review the material previously presented to NASA for the executives in the room. Thompson took a pad of paper and tried to sketch out the problem with the joint, while Boisjoly laid out the photos of the compromised joints from Flights 51-C and 61-A. When they became convinced that no one was listening, they ceased their efforts. As Boisjoly would later testify, "There was not

one positive pro-launch statement ever made by anybody" (Report of the Presidential Commission, 1986, IV, p. 792, hereafter abbreviated as R.C.).

According to Boisjoly, after he and Thompson made their last attempts to stop the launch, Jerry Mason asked rhetorically, "Am I the only one who wants to fly?" Mason turned to Bob Lund and asked him to "take off his engineering hat and put on his management hat." The four managers held a brief discussion and voted unanimously to recommend *Challenger's* launch.

Exhibit I shows the revised recommendations that were presented that evening by Joe Kilminster after the caucus to support management's decision to launch. Only one of the rationales presented that evening supported the launch (demonstrated erosion sealing threshold is three times greater than 0.038″ erosion experienced on SRM-15). Even so, the issue at hand was sealability at low temperature, not erosion. While one other rationale could be considered a neutral statement of engineering fact (O-ring pressure leak check places secondary seal in outboard position which minimizes sealing time), the other seven rationales are negative, anti-launch, statements. After hearing Kilminster's presentation, which was accepted without a single probing question, George Hardy asked him to sign the chart and telefax it to Kennedy Space Center and Marshall Space Flight Center. At 11 p.m. E.S.T. the teleconference ended.

Aside from the four senior Morton Thiokol executives present at the teleconference, all others were excluded from the final decision. The process represented a radical shift from previous NASA policy. Until that moment, the burden of proof had always been on the engineers to prove beyond a doubt that it was safe to launch. NASA, with their objections to the original Thiokol recommendation against the launch, and

EXHIBIT I.   MTI Assessment of Temperature Concern on SRM-25 (51L) Launch

---

- CALCULATIONS SHOW THAT SRM-25 O-RINGS WILL BE 20° COLDER THAN SRM-15 O-RINGS
- TEMPERATURE DATA NOT CONCLUSIVE ON PREDICTING PRIMARY O-RING BLOW-BY
- ENGINEERING ASSESSMENT IS THAT:
  - COLDER O-RINGS WILL HAVE INCREASED EFFECTIVE DUROMETER ("HARDER")
  - "HARDER" O-RINGS WILL TAKE LONGER TO "SEAT"
  - MORE GAS MAY PASS PRIMARY O-RING BEFORE THE PRIMARY SEAL SEATS (RELATIVE TO SRM-15)
  - DEMONSTRATED SEALING THRESHOLD IS 3 TIMES GREATER THAN 0.038″ EROSION EXPERIENCED ON SRM-15
  - IF THE PRIMARY SEAL DOES NOT SEAT, THE SECONDARY SEAL WILL SEAT
  - PRESSURE WILL GET TO SECONDARY SEAL BEFORE THE METAL PARTS ROTATE
  - O-RING PRESSURE LEAK CHECK PLACES SECONDARY SEAL IN OUTBOARD POSITION WHICH MINIMIZES SEALING TIME
- MTI RECOMMENDS STS-51L LAUNCH PROCEED ON 28 JANUARY 1986
- SRM-25 WILL NOT BE SIGNIFICANTLY DIFFERENT FROM SRM-15

Joe C. Kilminster, Vice President Space Booster Programs.

Mason, with his request for a "management decision," shifted the burden of proof in the opposite direction. Morton Thiokol was expected to prove that launching *Challenger* would not be safe (R.C., IV, p. 793).

The change in the decision so deeply upset Boisjoly that he returned to his office and made the following journal entry:

> I sincerely hope this launch does not result in a catastrophe. I personally do not agree with some of the statements made by Joe Kilminster's written summary stating that SRM-25 is okay to fly (Boisjoly, 1987).

THE DISASTER AND ITS AFTERMATH

On January 28, 1986, a reluctant Roger Boisjoly watched the launch of the *Challenger*. As the vehicle cleared the tower, Bob Ebeling whispered, "We've just dodged a bullet." (The engineers who opposed the launch assumed that O-ring failure would result in an explosion almost immediately after engine ignition.) To continue in Boisjoly's words, "At approximately T+60 seconds Bob told me he had just completed a prayer of thanks to the Lord for a successful launch. Just thirteen seconds later we both saw the horror of the destruction as the vehicle exploded" (Boisjoly, 1987).

Morton Thiokol formed a failure investigation team on January 31, 1986, to study the *Challenger* explosion. Roger Boisjoly and Arnie Thompson were part of the team that was sent to MSFC in Huntsville, Alabama. Boisjoly's first inkling of a division between himself and management came on February 13 when he was informed at the last minute that he was to testify before the Rogers Commission the next day. He had very little time to prepare for his testimony. Five days later, two Commission members held a closed session with Kilminster, Boisjoly, and Thompson. During the interview Boisjoly gave his memos and activity reports to the Commissioners. After that meeting, Kilminster chastised Thompson and Boisjoly for correcting his interpretation of the technical data. Their response was that they would continue to correct his version if it was technically incorrect.

Boisjoly's February 25th testimony before the Commission, rebutting the general manager's statement that the initial decision against the launch was not unanimous, drove a wedge further between him and Morton Thiokol management. Boisjoly was flown to MSFC before he could hear the NASA testimony about the pre-flight telecon. The next day, he was removed from the failure investigation team and returned to Utah.

Beginning in April, Boisjoly began to believe that for the previous month he had been used solely for public relations purposes. Although given the title of Seal Coordinator for the redesign effort, he was isolated from NASA and the seal redesign effort. His design information had been changed without his knowledge and presented without his feedback. On May 1, 1986, in a briefing preceding closed sessions before the Rogers Commission, Ed Garrison, President of Aerospace Operations for Morton Thiokol, chastised Boisjoly for "airing the company's dirty laundry" with the memos he had given the Commission. The next day, Boisjoly testified about the change in his job assignment. Commission Chairman Rogers criticized Thiokol management, "... if it appears that you're punishing the two people or at least two of the people who are right about the decision and objected to the launch which ultimately resulted in criticism of Thiokol and then they're demoted or feel that they are being retaliated against, that is a very serious matter. It would seem to me, just speaking for myself, they should be promoted, not demoted or pushed aside" (R.C., V, p. 1586).

Boisjoly now sensed a major rift developing within the corporation. Some co-workers perceived that his testimony was damaging the company image. In an effort to clear the air, he and McDonald requested a private meeting with the company's three top executives, which was held on May 16, 1986. According to Boisjoly, management was unreceptive throughout the meeting. The CEO told McDonald and Boisjoly that the company "was doing just fine until Al and I testified about our job reassignments" (Boisjoly, 1987). McDonald and Boisjoly were nominally restored to their former assignments, but Boisjoly's position became untenable as time passed. On July 21, 1986, Roger Boisjoly requested an extended sick leave from Morton Thiokol.

ETHICAL ANALYSIS

It is clear from this case study that Roger Boisjoly's experiences before and after the *Challenger* disaster raise numerous ethical questions that are integral to any explanation of the disaster and applicable to other management situations, especially those involving highly complex technologies. The difficulties and uncertainties involved in the management of these technologies exacerbate the kind of bureaucratic syndromes that generate ethical conflicts in the first place. In fact, Boisjoly's experiences could well serve as a paradigmatic case study for such ethical problems, ranging from accountability to corporate loyalty and whistleblowing. Underlying all these issues, however, is the problematic relationship between individual and organizational responsibility. Boisjoly's experiences graphically portray the tensions inherent in this relationship in a manner that discloses its importance in the causal sequence leading to the *Challenger* disaster. The following analysis explicates this and the implications it has for other organizational settings.

By focusing on the problematic relationship between individual and organizational responsibility, this analysis reveals that the organizational structure governing the space shuttle program became the locus of responsibility in such a way that not only did it undermine the responsibilities of individual decision makers within the process, but it also became a means of avoiding real, effective responsibility throughout the entire management system. The first clue to this was clearly articulated as early as 1973 by the board of inquiry that was formed to investigate the accident which occurred during the launch of *Skylab 1*:

> The management system developed by NASA for manned space flight places large emphasis on rigor, detail, and thoroughness. In hand with this emphasis comes formalism, extensive documentation, and visibility in detail to senior management. While nearly perfect, such a system can submerge the concerned individual and depress the role of the intuitive engineer or analyst. It may not allow full play for the intuitive judgment or past experience of the individual. An emphasis on management systems can, in itself, serve to separate the people engaged in the program from the real world of hardware (Quoted in Christiansen, 1987, p. 23).

To examine this prescient statement in ethical terms is to see at another level the serious consequences inherent in the situation it describes. For example, it points to a dual meaning of responsibility. One meaning emphasizes carrying out an authoritatively prescribed review process, while the second stresses the cognitive independence and input of every individual down the entire chain of authority. The first sense of responsibility shifts the ethical center of gravity precipitously away from individual moral agency onto the review process in such a way that what was originally set up to guarantee flight readiness with the professional and personal integrity of the responsible individuals, instead becomes a means of evading personal responsibility for decisions made in the review process.

A crucial, and telling, example of this involves the important question asked by the Rogers Commission as to why the concerns raised by the Morton Thiokol engineers about the effects of cold weather on the O-rings during the teleconference the night before the launch were not passed up from Level III to Levels II or I in the preflight review process. The NASA launch procedure clearly demands that decisions and objections methodically follow a prescribed path up all levels. Yet, Lawrence Mulloy, operating at Level III as the Solid Rocket Booster Project Manager at MSFC, did not transmit the Morton Thiokol concerns upward (through his immediate superior, Stanley Reinartz) to Level II. When asked by Chairman Rogers to explain why, Mr. Mulloy testified:

> At that time, and I still consider today, that was a Level III issue, Level III being a SRB element or an external tank element or Space Shuttle main engine element or an Orbiter. There was no violation of Launch Commit Criteria. There was no waiver required in my judgment at that time and still today (R.C., I, p. 98).

In examining this response in terms of shifting responsibility onto the review process itself, there are two things that are particularly striking in Mr. Mulloy's statement. The first is his emphasis that this was a "Level III issue." In a formal sense, Mr. Mulloy is correct. However, those on Level III also had the authority — and, one would think, especially in this instance given the heated discussion on the effects of cold on the O-rings, the motivation — to pass objections and concerns on to Levels II and I. But here the second important point in Mr. Mulloy's testimony comes into play when he states, "there was no violation of Launch Commit Criteria." In other words, since there was no Launch Commit Criteria for joint temperature, concerns about joint temperature did not officially fall under the purview of the review process.

Therefore, the ultimate justification for Mr. Mulloy's position rests on the formal process itself. He was just following the rules by staying within the already established scope of the review process.

This underscores the moral imperative executives must exercise by creating and maintaining organizational systems that do not separate the authority of decision makers from the responsibility they bear for decisions, or insulate them from the consequences of their actions or omissions.

Certainly, there can be no more vivid example than the shuttle program to verify that, in fact, "an emphasis on management systems can, in itself, serve to separate the people engaged in the program from the real world of hardware." Time and time again the lack of communication that lay at the heart of the Rogers Commission finding that "there was a serious flaw in the decision making process leading up to the launch of flight 51-L" (R.C., I, p. 104) was explained by the NASA officials or managers at Morton Thiokol with such statements as, "that is not my reporting channel," or "he is not in the launch decision chain," or "I didn't meet with Mr. Boisjoly, I met with Don Ketner, who is the task team leader" (R.C., IV, p. 821, testimony of Mr. Lund). Even those managers who had direct responsibility for line engineers and workmen depended on formalized memo writing procedures for communication to the point that some "never talked to them directly" (Feynman, 1988, p. 33).

Within the atmosphere of such an ambiguity of responsibility, when a life-threatening conflict arose within the management system and individuals (such as Roger Boisjoly and his engineering associates at Morton Thiokol) tried to reassert the full weight of their individual judgments and attendant responsibilities, the very purpose of the flight readiness review process, i.e., to arrive at the "technical" truth of the situation, which includes the recognition of the uncertainties involved as much as the findings, became subverted into an adversary confrontation in which "adversary" truth, with its suppression of uncertainties, became operative (Wilmotte, 1970).

What is particularly significant in this radical transformation of the review process, in which the Morton Thiokol engineers were forced into "the position of having to prove that it was unsafe instead of the other way around" (R.C., IV, p. 822; see also p. 793), is that what made the suppression of technical uncertainties possible is precisely that mode of thinking which, in being challenged by independent professional judgments, gave rise to the adversarial setting in the first place: groupthink. No more accurate description for what transpired the night before the launch of the *Challenger* can be given than the definition of groupthink as:

> . . . a mode of thinking that people engage in when they are deeply involved in a cohesive in-group, when the members' strivings for unanimity override their motivation to realistically appraise alternative courses of action. . . . Groupthink refers to the deterioration of mental efficiency, reality testing, and moral judgment that results from in-group pressures (Janis, 1972, p. 9).

From this perspective, the full import of Mr. Mason's telling Mr. Lund to "take off his engineering hat and put on his management hat" is revealed. He did not want another technical, reality-based judgment of an independent professional engineer. As he had already implied when he opened the caucus by stating "a management decision was necessary," he wanted a group decision, specifically one that would, in the words of the Rogers Commission, "accommodate a major customer" (R.C., I, p. 104). With a group decision the objections of the engineers could be mitigated, the risks shared, fears allayed, and the attendant responsibility diffused.

This analysis is not meant to imply that groupthink was a pervasive or continuous mode of thinking at either NASA or Morton Thiokol. What is suggested is a causal relationship between this instance of groupthink and the ambiguity of responsibility found within the space shuttle program. Whenever a management system such as NASA's generates "a mindset of 'collective responsibility'" by leading "individuals to defer to the anonymity of the process and not focus closely enough on their individual responsibilities in the decision chain" (N.R.C. Report, 1988, p. 68), and there is a confluence of the kind of pressures that came to bear on the decision making process the night before the launch, the conditions are in place for groupthink to prevail.

A disturbing feature of so many of the analyses and commentaries on the *Challenger* disaster is the reinforcement, and implicit acceptance, of this shift away from individual moral agency with an almost exclusive focus on the flaws in the management system, organizational structures and/or decision making process. Beginning with the findings of the Rogers Commission investigation, one could practically conclude that no one had any responsibility whatsoever for the disaster. The Commission concluded that "there was a serious flaw in the decision making process leading up to the launch of flight 51-L. A well structured and managed system emphasizing safety would have flagged the rising doubts about the Solid Rocket Booster joint seal." Then the Commission report immediately states, "Had these matters been clearly stated and emphasized in the flight readiness process in terms reflecting the views of most of the Thiokol engineers and at least some of the Marshall engineers, it seems likely that the launch of 51-L might not have occurred when it did" (R.C., I, p. 104). But the gathering and passing on of such information was the responsibility of specifically designated individuals, known by name and position in the highly structured review process. Throughout this process there had been required "a series of formal, legally binding certifications, the equivalent of airworthiness inspections in the aviation industry. In effect the myriad contractor and NASA personnel involved were guaranteeing *Challenger's* flight readiness with their professional and personal integrity" (McConnell, 1987, p. 17).

When the Commission states in its next finding that "waiving of launch constraints appears to have been at the expense of flight safety," the immediate and obvious question would seem to be: Who approved the waivers and assumed this enormous risk? And why? This is a serious matter! A launch constraint is only issued because there is a safety problem serious enough to justify a decision not to launch. However, the Commission again deflects the problem onto the system by stating, "There was no system which made it imperative that launch constraints and waivers of launch constraints be considered by all levels of management" (R.C., 1986, I, p. 104).

There are two puzzling aspects to this Commission finding. First, the formal system already contained the requirement that project offices inform at least Level II of launch constraints. The Commission addressed the explicit violation of this requirement in the case of a July 1985 launch constraint that had been imposed on the Solid Rocket Booster because of O-ring erosion on the nozzle:

> NASA Levels I and II apparently did not realize Marshall had assigned a launch constraint within the Problem Assessment System. This communication failure was contrary to the requirement, contained in the NASA Problem Reporting and Corrective Action Requirements System, that launch constraints were to be taken to Level II (R.C., 1986, I, pp. 138–139; see also p. 159).

Second, the Commission clearly established that the individual at Marshall who both imposed and waived the launch constraint was Lawrence Mulloy, SRB Project Manager. Then why blame the management system, especially in such a crucial area as that of launch constraints, when procedures of that system were not followed? Is that approach going to increase the accountability of individuals within the system for future flights?

Even such an independent-minded and probing Commission member as Richard Feynman, in an interview a year after the disaster, agreed with the avoidance of determining individual accountability for specific actions and decisions. He is quoted as saying, "I don't think it's correct to try to find out which particular guy happened to do what particular thing. It's the question of how the atmosphere could get to such a circumstance that such things were possible without anybody catching on." Yet, at the same time Feynman admitted that he was not confident that any restructuring of the management system will ensure that the kinds of problems that resulted in the *Challenger* disaster — "danger signs not seen and warnings not heeded" — do not recur. He said, "I'm really not sure that any kind of simple mechanism can cure stupidity and dullness. You can make up all the rules about how things should be, and they'll go wrong if the spirit is different, if the attitudes are different over time and as personnel change" (Chandler, 1987, p. 50).

The approach of the Rogers Commission and that of most of the analyses of the *Challenger* disaster is consistent with the growing tendency to deny any specific responsibility to individual persons within corporate or other institutional settings when things go wrong. Although there are obviously many social changes in modern life that justify the shift in focus from individuals to organizational structures as bearers of responsibility, this shift is reinforced and exaggerated by the way people think about and accept those changes. One of the most pernicious problems of modern times is the almost universally held belief that the individual is powerless, especially within the context of large organizations where one may perceive oneself, and be viewed, as a very small, and replaceable, cog. It is in the very nature of this situation that responsibility may seem to become so diffused that no one person IS responsible. As the National Research Council committee, in following up on the Rogers Commission, concluded about the space shuttle program:

> Given the pervasive reliance on teams and boards to consider the key questions affecting safety, 'group democracy' can easily prevail . . . in the end all decisions become collective ones . . . (N.R.C. Report, pp. 68 and 70).

The problem with this emphasis on management systems and collective responsibility is that it fosters a vicious circle that further and further erodes and obscures individual responsibility. This leads to a paradoxical — and untenable — situation (such as in the space shuttle program) in which decisions are made and actions are performed by individuals or groups of individuals but not attributed to them. It thus reinforces the tendency to avoid accountability for what anyone does by attributing the consequences to the organization or decision making process. Again, shared, rather than individual, risktaking and responsibility became operative. The end result can be a cancerous attitude that so permeates an organization or management system that it metastasizes into decisions and acts of life-threatening irresponsibility.

In sharp contrast to this prevalent emphasis on organizational structures, one of the most fascinating aspects of the extensive and exhaustive investigations into the *Challenger* disaster is that they provide a rare opportunity to re-affirm the sense and importance of individual responsibility. With the inside look into the space shuttle program these investigations detail, one can identify many instances where personal responsibility, carefully interpreted, can properly be imputed to NASA officials and to its contractors. By so doing, one can preserve, if only in a fragmentary way, the essentials of the traditional concept of individual responsibility within the diluting context of organizational life. This effort is intended to make explicit the kind of causal links that are operative between the actions of individuals and the structures of organizations.

The criteria commonly employed for holding individuals responsible for an outcome are two: (1) their acts or omissions are in some way a cause of it; and (2) these acts or omissions are not done in ignorance or under coercion (Thompson, 1987, p. 47). Although there are difficult theoretical and practical questions associated with both criteria, especially within organizational settings, nevertheless, even a general application of them to the sequence of events leading up to the *Challenger* disaster reveals those places where the principle of individual responsibility must be factored in if our understanding of it is to be complete, its lessons learned, and its repetition avoided.

The Rogers Commission has been criticized — and rightly so — for looking at the disaster "from the bottom up but not from the top down," with the result that it gives a clearer picture of what transpired at the lower levels of the *Challenger's* flight review process than at its upper levels (Cook, 1986). Nevertheless, in doing so, the Commission report provides powerful testimony that however elaborately structured and far reaching an undertaking such as the space shuttle program may be, individuals at the bottom of the organizational structure can still play a crucial, if not deciding, role in the outcome. For in the final analysis, whatever the defects in the *Challenger's* launch decision chain were that kept the upper levels from being duly informed about the objections of the engineers at Morton Thiokol, the fact remains that the strenuous objections of these engineers so forced the decision process at their level that the four middle managers at Morton Thiokol had the full responsibility for the launch in their hands. This is made clear in the startling testimony of Mr. Mason, when Chairman Rogers asked him: "Did you realize, and particularly in view of Mr. Hardy's (Deputy Director of Science and Engineering at MSFC) point that they wouldn't launch unless you agreed, did you fully realize that in effect, you were making a decision to launch, you and your colleagues?" Mr. Mason replied, "Yes, sir" (R.C., 1986, IV, p. 770).

If these four men had just said no, the launch of the *Challenger* would not have taken place the next day. . . .

Although fragmentary and tentative in its formulation, this set of considerations points toward the conclusion that however complex and sophisticated an organization may be, and no matter how large and remote the institutional network needed to manage it may be, an active and creative tension of responsibility must be maintained at every level of the operation. Given the size and complexity of such endeavors, the only way to ensure that tension of attentive and effective responsibility is to give the primacy of responsibility to that ultimate principle of all moral conduct: the human individual — even if this does necessitate, in too many instances under present circumstances, that individuals such as Roger Boisjoly, when they attempt to exercise their responsibility, must step forward as moral heroes. In so doing, these individuals do not just bear witness to the desperate need for a system of full accountability in the face of the immense power and reach of modern technology and institutions. They also give expression to the very essence of what constitutes the moral life. As Roger Boisjoly has stated in reflecting on his own experience, "I have been asked by some if I would testify again if I knew in advance of the potential consequences to me and my career. My answer is always an immediate 'yes'. I couldn't live with any self-respect if I tailored my actions based upon the personal consequences . . ." (Boisjoly, 1987).

REFERENCES

Boisjoly, Roger M.: 1985a, Applied Mechanics Memorandum to Robert K. Lund, Vice President, Engineering, Wasatch Division, Morton Thiokol, Inc., July 31.

Boisjoly, Roger M.: 1985b, Activity Report, SRM Seal Erosion Task Team Status, October 4.

Boisjoly, Roger M.: 1987, Ethical Decisions: Morton Thiokol and the Shuttle Disaster. Speech given at Massachusetts Institute of Technology, January 7.

Boling, T. Edwin and Dempsey, John: 1981, "Ethical dilemmas in government: Designing an organizational response," *Public Personnel Management Journal* 10, 11–18.

Chandler, David: 1987. "Astronauts gain clout in 'revitalized' NASA," *Boston Globe* 1 (January 26):50.

Christiansen, Donald: 1987, "A system gone awry," *IEEE Spectrum* 24(3):23.

Cook, Richard C.: 1986, "The Rogers commission failed," *The Washington Monthly* 18 (9), 13–21.

De George, Richard T.: 1981, "Ethical responsibilities of engineers in large organizations: The Pinto Case," *Business and Professional Ethics Journal* 1, 1–14.

Feynman, Richard P.: 1988, "An outsider's view of the Challenger inquiry," *Physics Today* 41 (2):26–37.

Janis, Irving L.: 1972, *Victims of Groupthink*, Boston, MA: Houghton Mifflin Company.

Kilminster, J. C.: 1985, Memorandum (E000-FY86–003) to Robert Lund, Vice President, Engineering, Wasatch Division, Morton Thiokol, Inc., July 5.

Mankin, Hart T.: 1981, "Commentary on 'Ethical responsibilities of engineers in large organizations: The Pinto Case,'" *Business and Professional Ethics Journal* 1, 15–17.

McConnell, Malcolm: 1987, *Challenger, A Major Malfunction: A True Story of Politics, Greed, and the Wrong Stuff*, Garden City, N.J.: Doubleday and Company, Inc.

National Research Council: 1988, *Post-Challenger Evaluation of Space Shuttle Risk Assessment and Management*, Washington, D.C.: National Academy Press.

Report of the Presidential Commission on the Space Shuttle Challenger Accident: 1986, Washington, D.C.: U.S. Government Printing Office.

Thompson, Dennis F.: 1987, *Political Ethics and Public Office*, Cambridge, MA: Harvard University Press.

Wilmotte, Raymond M.: 1970, "Engineering truth in competitive environments," *IEEE Spectrum* 7 (5):45–49.

How Can We Save the Next Victim?

Lisa Belkin

On a Friday afternoon last summer, tiny Jose Eric Martinez was brought to the outpatient clinic of Hermann Hospital in Houston for a checkup. The 2-month-old looked healthy to his parents, and he was growing well, so they were rattled by the news that the infant had a ventricular septal defect, best described as a hole between the pumping chambers of his heart.

He was showing the early signs of congestive heart failure, the doctors said, and those symptoms would need to be brought under control by a drug, Digoxin, which would be given intravenously during a several-day stay. The child's long-term prognosis was good, the doctors explained. Time would most likely close the hole, and if it did not, routine surgery in a year or so would fix things. The Digoxin was a bridge between here and there. There was nothing to worry about.

The lesson of what happened next is not one of finger-pointing or blame. In fact, the message of this story is quite the opposite: that finger-pointing does not provide answers, and that often no one — no *one* — is to blame.

No single person caused the death of that child in the pediatric special care unit of Hermann Hospital on Aug. 2, 1996. No isolated error led his heart to slow and then stop, suddenly and irreversibly, while his mother, Maria, was cuddling him and coaxing him to suck on a bottle. No one person was responsible, because it is virtually impossible for one mistake to kill a patient in the highly mechanized and backstopped world of a modern hospital. A cascade of unthinkable things must happen, meaning catastrophic errors are rarely a failure of a single person, and almost always a failure of a system. It seems an obvious point, one long understood in other potentially deadly industries like aviation, aerospace, nuclear power. In those realms, a finding of human error is likely to be the *start* of an investigation, not its conclusion.

"If a pilot taxis out and takes off with the flaps up, yes, it's human error," says John Nance, an airline pilot and aviation analyst who has spent much of his time this past year as an adviser to the health care industry. "But the next question is, 'What caused the error?' It's not because the folks in the cockpit say, 'O.K., guys, we can go take off with the flaps up and die, or we can put them down and make it home for dinner.'

"Were they confused? Tired? Misinformed? That's still not an answer. What caused them to be confused or tired or misinformed? That's where you learn something useful." This systems approach to errors has been slow in coming to the health care industry. Perhaps it is because operating room slips are far less obvious and dramatic than plane crashes, and to discuss error as an integral part of medicine is to shine a light on how many errors there actually are. Or maybe it is because we accept that machines are in charge of the space shuttle, but still want to believe that human beings are in charge of our health. Possibly it is because doctors have long been trained to think that they can be — must be — perfect, and patients have been conditioned to accept no less.

Whatever the reason, medicine continues to focus on *who* while other fields try to focus on *why*.

From Lisa Belkin, "How Can We Save the Next Victim?" *New York Times Magazine,* June 15, 1997. Reprinted with Permission.

"The mentality has always been: 'Who's the person? Who do I blame? Give me a name,'" says James Conway, who became chief operating officer of the Dana-Farber Cancer Institute in Boston in 1995 during the restructuring after the death of a patient and the injury of another from a medication error. "But that 'going for the jugular' approach hides problems in the system, problems you don't see if you don't look at it as a system error.

"People don't make errors because they want to, or because they're bad people. Everybody makes errors. Every human being. What we need to focus on is how to best design our systems so that those efforts are caught before they reach the patient."

Slowly, tentatively and very recently, health care started to shift that focus. Patient safety is coming to be recognized as a systems problem, for a chain of reasons — the death at Dana-Farber, the tort reform movement in Congress, fears that quality is suffering under managed care.

That awareness is growing throughout medicine — at the American Medical Association, at several major malpractice insurers, in the offices of academic researchers and at dozens of medical centers nationwide. Soon it will be everywhere, because the organization that accredits hospitals has announced that systemic evaluation of errors will be required at all hospitals that report a serious mistake.

One of the newly converted is Hermann Hospital, which stumbled into this burgeoning revolution by accident and as a result of an accident. The significance of the death of one baby, therefore, lies not only in how he died, but also in what happened at the hospital after he died.

"The entire organization was mobilized to go back and look at this from a systemic point of view," says Lynn Walts, Hermann's chief operating officer. The internal investigation found that six separate people had noticed,

or had a chance to notice, that the infant was being given 10 times the appropriate dose of Digoxin. As a result, nearly every procedure at Hermann is now being looked at anew.

These changes in philosophy and procedure, Walts knows, will not undo the damage already done. They will not ease the anguish of the Martinez family nor soothe the psyches of their baby's doctors and nurses. Nor will the new approach absolve the hospital of liability for its mistake. But what it can do — indeed, is already doing — is to keep mistakes like that from happening again. And it can replace a paralyzing atmosphere of blame with the healing sense of moving forward, toward a goal.

"If we had looked at things differently five years ago," Walts says, "maybe this mistake wouldn't have happened. We can't change it, but we can make sure we don't look back with the same regret five years from now."

The night Jose Martinez died, Hermann Hospital was two weeks away from a visit from the Joint Commission on the Accreditation of Healthcare Organizations, a body with the power to take away a hospital's economic lifeblood by making it ineligible for payments from H.M.O.'s and other health care organizations.

The commission, sanctioned by organizations like the A.M.A. and the American Hospital Association, is an example of an industry's governing itself. It has its share of critics, who call it a watchdog with no teeth; in fact, the joint commission rarely removes hospital accreditations. But whatever teeth it has, they are sharp enough to cause great stress at hospitals preparing for a joint commission inspection. At Hermann, those preparations had been under way for a year, and in the final weeks employees were given lists of possible questions, with the proper answers. Administrators walked around conducting mock reviews: What do you do in case of a fire? What is your job? How does it fit into the hospital system?

When word spread about the overdose given to Jose Martinez, therefore, the first question asked on the executive floors at Hermann was, "How did this happen?" The question asked immediately after that was, "Should we tell the joint commission?"

"They don't directly ask you, 'Did you have a sentinel event?'" Walts says, using the commission's term for a major mishap. "And it was so recent that they probably wouldn't have discovered it in our paper trail."

It was soon decided, she says, that full confession would serve the hospital best. Joanne Turnbull, chief quality and utilization officer, was assigned the task of figuring out what happened and explaining it to the visitors.

Turnbull, a take-charge woman who is a social worker and psychologist by training, spoke with each of the central figures in the case, and each interview seemed to widen the circle. Within a few days, in time for the all-important meeting, she had a sense of the scenario that had caused Jose Martinez to die.

On the Friday afternoon that the boy was admitted, she says, the attending doctor discussed the Digoxin order in detail with the resident. First, the appropriate dose was determined in micrograms, based on the baby's weight, then the micrograms were converted to milligrams. They did those calculations together, double-checked them and determined that the correct dose was .09 milligrams, to be injected into an intravenous line.

They went on to discuss a number of tests that also needed to be done, and the resident left to write the resulting list of orders on the baby's chart. With a slip of the pen that would prove fatal, the resident ordered 0.9 milligrams of Digoxin rather than .09.

The list complete, the resident went back to the attending doctor and asked, "Is there anything else I need to add on here?" The attending scanned the list, and said no, there was nothing to add. The error went unnoticed.

A copy of the order was faxed to the pharmacy, and a follow-up original copy was sent by messenger. The pharmacist on duty read the fax and thought that the amount of Digoxin was too high. The pharmacist paged the resident, and then put the order on top of the pharmacy's coffeepot, site of the unofficial "important" pile. What the pharmacist did not know was that the resident had left for the day and did not receive the page.

Sometime later, the backup copy of the as-yet-unfilled order arrived at the pharmacy. This time a technician looked at it and filled a vial with 0.9 milligrams of Digoxin. The technician then set the order and the vial together on the counter so that the pharmacist could double-check the work.

The pharmacist verified that the dosage on the prescription matched the dosage in the vial, and did not remember questioning the dosage in the first place. The order of the Digoxin was sent up to the pediatric floor.

A nurse there took the vial, read its dosage and worried that it was wrong. She approached a resident who was on call but had not personally gone over the drug calculation with the attending.

"Would you check this order," she asked. Or maybe she said, "Is this what you want me to give?"

The resident took out a calculator, redid the math and came up with .09, the correct dose. Looking from the calculator to the vial, the resident saw a "0" and a "9" on both and did not notice the difference in the decimal point.

There was one remaining step. Following procedure, the first nurse asked a second nurse to verify that the order in the chart was the same as the label on the vial. She did, and it was.

At 9:35 P.M., a troubled nurse gave Jose Martinez a dose of Digoxin that was 10 times what was intended. It took 20 minutes for the entire dose to drip through his IV tube. At

10 P.M., the baby began to vomit while drinking a bottle, the first sign of a drug overdose.

Digoxin works by changing the flux of ions in the heart, altering the cell membranes. Too much allows the heart to flood with calcium, so it cannot contract. There is an antidote, called Digibind, and the nurse, her fears confirmed, called for it immediately. But even immediately was too late.

"They killed my son," the boy's father, Jose Leonel Martinez, sobbed on the local TV news. "Those people who work there are not professional and they shouldn't be there." A restaurant worker who had moved his family from Mexico a few years earlier, Martinez was shocked that the world's best health care system could make such a mistake.

"When I asked the doctor if the medicine they were going to put in him was strong, the doctor said no, that it was normal," he said through an interpreter. "That it was just so the child would function better."

The residents and the nurse were "given some time off" during the investigation, Walts says; no one was fired. "It sobered us to realize that we've always dealt with errors as a discipline problem, yet we're not eliminating errors by firing people," she adds.

All those in the chain of error are back at work, and all are still haunted by the death of Jose Martinez. When the system fails, the patient is not the only victim. "It was an absolutely devastating thing," the attending doctor says. "The loss to the parents was indescribable. There are no words. . . . The only thing that made it possible for me to struggle through was my concern for these young people" — meaning the two residents. "I had to make them understand that this did not mean they were bad doctors."

After hearing Turnbull's account, the joint commission placed Hermann on "accreditation watch," a category so new that the hospital was in the first group to receive the designation. It required that Hermann analyze the root cause of the error — not only what went wrong, but also why it went wrong — and develop a plan to fix it.

The change of approach at Hermann, the change of approach throughout medicine, all of it had its start those frightening, disorienting, reorienting months in 1995. That was the year, says Dr. Dennis S. O'Leary, the joint commission's president, that "medicine went to hell in a handbasket."

It is impossible to tell whether errors increased significantly in 1995 and, if so, whether the increasing complexity of medicine and the concomitant cost-cutting of managed care were to blame. What is clear is that it seemed as if error was everywhere, as if the system was out of control.

The year began with the news that Betsy Lehman, 39, a health columnist for The Boston Globe, had died not of breast cancer but of a fourfold miscalculation in the amount of Cytoxan she was being given at Dana-Farber to battle her breast cancer. It happened because the total dose to be given over four days was instead given on *each* of the four days, an error that was not corrected by doctors, nurses or pharmacists.

At about the same time, a vascular surgeon at University Community Hospital, in Tampa, Fla., was accused of amputating the wrong leg. Then came reports that the wrong side of a brain had been operated on at Memorial Sloan-Kettering Cancer Center in New York. In an echo of the Dana-Farber error, a patient at the University of Chicago Hospitals died of a huge overdose of chemotherapy medication, also because the wrong dose was written down and the error wasn't noticed until the drug was administered.

The joint commission had recently visited and accredited all those hospitals. That fact alone was reason for concern at the commission's headquarters in Oakbrook Terrace, Illinois, and the immediate response was to conduct some surprise reinspections. The accreditation of the Tampa hospital was temporarily lifted, and Dana-Farber was placed on probation.

The longer-term response was to create the category of "accreditation watch." It was intended to replace the punishment of probation with a more collaborative, problem-solving approach. "The policy should not focus on what happened from an action standpoint, because you can't undo what's been done," O'Leary says. "What can be done is to reduce the likelihood of this happening in the future."

While the public feared more mistakes, and the joint commission feared overlooking mistakes, doctors began to fear something else entirely. What sobered and stunned organized medicine was not only the enormity of these errors, but also how quickly they became infamous single-sentence sound bites. The stories took on lives of their own, told and retold with no room for nuance, no blame for anyone but the bungling idiot of a doctor.

The wrong side of the brain incident at Sloan-Kettering, for instance, was quickly abbreviated into a description of a doctor who could not tell his left from right. In reality, the case was never that simple. When the surgeon stood at the operating table and cut into the wrong side of a patient's brain, it was because he was being guided by a CAT scan and an M.R.I. showing a large tumor on the same side of the brain as he cut into. The wrong set of films, those belonging to another patient, was brought into the operating room. The surgeon was fired. Now the policy at Sloan-Kettering requires a more comprehensive preoperation check, including matching X-rays with the patient's ID bracelet.

The case of the wrong leg, in Tampa, was similarly simplified into a story of a doctor who could not tell the difference between a diseased leg and a healthy one. To the contrary, the patient had two seriously diseased legs, a result of diabetes. The circulation in both was so poor that there was no pulse present in either leg and both feet were cold to the touch. A mistake on the surgical schedule said that the left leg was to be amputated. The error was noticed, but only one copy of the schedule was corrected.

When the surgeon scrubbed for the actual operation, therefore, he did so staring at an O.R. schedule saying that the left leg should be amputated. He then walked into the operating room, past a blackboard at the control desk, when also indicated that the left leg was to be amputated. The schedule inside the O.R. said the same thing. When the surgeon approached the operating table, he found his patient already completely draped, save for his ulcerated and swollen left leg, which had been prepped by the nurse for amputation. The surgeon was placed on probation for two years (but his license was reinstated after six months), and he was fined $10,000. The hospital has changed its policy so that corrections on one copy of the schedule must appear on all copies of the schedule.

For decades, the American Medical Association's approach to error has been to describe it as an aberration in a system that is basically safe. For instance, when researchers at Harvard University released a 1993 study estimating that one million preventable injuries and 120,000 preventable deaths occurred in American hospitals in a single year, the A.M.A. dismissed the study's methods as unsound and its conclusions as alarmist.

"We were very defensive on the Harvard study," says Martin J. Hatlie, executive director of the National Patient Safety Foundation at the A.M.A. "We found ourselves in a position of denying it had any validity at all," a position that sounded hollow and disingenuous, even to those within the A.M.A.

But in 1995, when everything seemed to go wrong, the denials stopped. Not directly because of the errors, but because of the fallout from the errors. Things were bad enough for medicine when doctors were seen merely as arrogant and insensitive. Now a new popular caricature was taking shape, portraying doctors as inept, if not downright murderous.

Hatlie marks the moment of change as an afternoon when the new, 104th Congress began a debate long at the center of the A.M.A.'s agenda — limits on the amount patients can be awarded in malpractice suits. Hatlie remembers losing all hope for that provision when Representative Greg Ganske, a Republican from Iowa who is also a doctor, tried to speak in favor of the bill and was interrupted by a fellow Republican, Ed Bryant of California.

"Last week a member of the gentleman's profession did some surgery down in Florida," Bryant drawled. "I heard on the radio, he was supposed to cut off a person's foot. He amputated it, and when the person woke up, they had cut off the wrong foot."

Ganske, flustered, did not respond eloquently: "It is inevitable that mistakes are going to be made."

That was when insiders at the A.M.A. stopped quibbling over how many mistakes doctors make and decided to be seen as trying to do something about those mistakes. It is when they stopped arguing about the methodology of the Harvard study and instead turned for help to Dr. Lucien Leape, the report's primary author, who was a surgeon for 20 years and now studies medical errors. That two-year-old partnership has become the basis of some tangible, structured efforts. The National Patient Safety Foundation, for instance, was designed to root out and reduce error in the way that a similar organization, the Anesthesia Patient Safety Foundation, revolutionized that segment of the industry in the 1980's. Similarly, the U.S. Pharmacopeia Convention established the National Coordinating Council for Medication Reporting and Prevention to track medication errors. And the Institute for Healthcare Improvement began a project to reduce adverse drug events.

There are also less tangible but equally important results. Specifically, all these separate efforts add up to a growing recognition that the health of health care may lie in its ability to admit and to prevent its mistakes.

"In hockey," says Nancy W. Dickey, a Texas family practitioner and chairman of the A.M.A. board of trustees, "you don't go where the puck is. You go where the puck is going to be. We're trying to go where the puck is going to be."

Human factors experts are a patient group. They sit in their laboratories and huddle over their research papers, waiting until whole industries are ready — really ready — to hear what they have to say. Skeptics turn into believers, they know, during times of confusion and remorse.

The human factors field first began in the 1940s, when psychologists and engineers came together to prevent assembly-line errors that were threatening the war effort. The 1970s brought another burst of interest, with the Three Mile Island nuclear accident and a series of plane crashes. In 1986 came the Challenger explosion.

Now it seems to be medicine's turn, and human factors researchers have been expecting the call. Even before anyone asked for their help, they had spent a lot of time analyzing that industry. From where they sat, health care was the pinnacle of challenges, the most complex of industries, the ultimate test of systems theory.

"Health care is really interesting from our point of view because it straddles the entire span, the spectrum of accidents," says James Reason, a psychology professor at the University of Manchester and one of the first human factors researchers.

In other industries, the relationships are between operators and equipment — pilots and their airplanes, nuclear plant personnel and their walls of confusing displays and dials. In medicine, the relationships involve operators, equipment and patients — patients who, by definition, are not in perfect working order, creating infinitely more ways for things to go wrong.

It was inevitable, human factors experts agree, that medicine would eventually shed its resistance to being seen as a system in which human beings were but one fallible component. That it took a string of tragedies to spur that realization is probably also inevitable. The first step, researchers are telling clinicians, is to accept that perfect human performance is not an attainable goal. People are not perfect outside a hospital. Half asleep, they spray deodorant on their heads and hair spray under their arms. Distracted, they write the wrong dates on checks. On autopilot, they leave their phone numbers when they mean to leave their fax numbers.

They are equally imperfect inside a hospital. They write the cumulative chemotherapy dose instead of the daily dose. They write "left leg" when they mean "right leg."

Admitting to imperfection is a first step for medicine, because many in the profession seem to believe that they can be perfect, says Robert L. Helmreich, a human factors expert at the University of Texas at Austin who spent years helping airlines teach pilots that they were fallible. "They think they're bulletproof," Helmreich says.

He cites a 1988 survey of pilots in which 42 percent agreed with the statement, "Even when I am fatigued, I perform effectively." He was amazed by that until 1996, when he gave the same survey to surgeons, anesthesiologists and nurses and found that 60 percent agreed with the statement.

The central problem with the belief in perfection is that hospital systems are designed around it. They rely on concentration — that the nurse, for instance, will connect the nutrition bag to the nutrition line and not to the dialysis line. But things should be designed, human factors experts would argue, so that the connective port on the nutrition bag fits only into the connective port on the nutrition line.

Systems based on perfection also deny the possibility of confusion — trusting that a nurse will always double-check whether she is dispensing the right drug and not a similarly packaged or a similarly named one. And they depend on memory — on a resident remembering to write down the correct dose of Digoxin, rather than on a computer system devised so that it won't accept a prescription with an erroneous dose of Digoxin.

The possible remedies for this dependence are many, and they vary with the problems of each hospital, which leads to perhaps the most important message of human factors research. "You cannot solve your problems," says David Woods, a professor of cognitive systems engineering at Ohio State University, "until you know what they are. And you will not know what they are unless you create an environment where people feel free to tell you."

Every industry that has substantially reduced error, experts say, has created a blame-free environment for reporting errors. And that includes not only actual errors, but also near misses, which have traditionally been seen as evidence of the strength of the system, but are more likely examples of errors waiting to happen.

For instance, an airline pilot must carry a form as part of the Aviation Safety Reporting System. When he makes or sees a major foulup, Helmreich says, he fills out that form — including his name — and sends it to NASA. The agency has a week to contact the pilot for amplification or clarification. Then the information is put in a computer, but without the pilot's name.

While the thorough and honest reporting of error is a central message of the experts, it is the trickiest for medicine to hear. Some hospitals are trying: James Conway at Dana-Farber, for one, has sent thank-you notes to staff members who report errors. But this zealous honesty does not come easily to a profession trained to understand that anything written down is discoverable evidence in a malpractice suit; it doesn't help that many states have chosen to confront error by publishing lists of doctors who have been disciplined or sued. In fact, no one is more interested in these latest changes by doctors than malpractice lawyers.

"On the surface, it does sound intriguing," says Judith A. Livingston, a personal injury lawyer at Kramer, Dillof, Tessel, Duffy & Moore in Manhattan. "But of course I'm skeptical." She does not see health care workers the same way human factors researchers do, and worries that this is merely a way for doctors to avoid blame. Yes, she says, the system often fails, but that does not mean that the individuals in that system are not responsible for their contributory actions.

"You can't just say, 'Everyone makes mistakes,'" she says. "If a reporter makes a mistake in a magazine article, you can run a correction," but when health care workers make a mistake, "someone dies. The gravity is so much greater. The responsibility should be greater, too."

It is too early to tell, malpractice lawyers say, what the effects of this systems approach will be on medical malpractice suits. If the new thinking does in fact reduce errors, it follows that it will reduce lawsuits. But the very methods used to root out error — admitting it, measuring it, discussing it — have the side effect of providing evidence of error, evidence that plaintiffs' lawyers are eager to see.

In most states the results of internal surveys would be protected by laws of privilege. But Thomas Demetrio of the Chicago personal injury firm Corboy & Demetrio believes public pressure might cause that to change.

If hospitals begin legitimate investigations of their error rate, "the consumer is entitled to know the findings," he says. "If the numbers are there, and they are solid, they'll come out."

To hospitals, anything that intrigues malpractice lawyers is unsettling, which is the major stumbling block for those who would like to see a human factors takeover of health care. When the joint commission created the category of accreditation watch, for instance, the agency saw it as a nonpunitive way to monitor hospital error. The hospitals saw it as something else entirely.

"It was supposed to be a neutral, nonjudgmental designation," says O'Leary, of the joint commission. "We thought we were saying, 'You tell us about your sentinel events, and we'll work together on the solutions.'"

Turnbull, of Hermann Hospital, responds: "They say, 'Report, report, report,' and then when you report, they punish you. They give the information to the newspapers."

O'Leary admits that "the policy is a work in progress — I would not be surprised to see us come back with a further iteration this fall."

Ben Kolb was scared when he arrived at Martin Memorial Hospital, in Stuart, Fla., in December 1995. This was to be the third ear operation on the 7-year-old Ben. His doctor wanted to remove scar tissue that was left from the prior surgeries, at ages 2 and 5.

So his mother, Tammy, spent the time before surgery joking with her son, talking about soccer (he was the captain of his team) and Christmas (when he would be singing in the yearly pageant at school). By the time an orderly came to take the boy into surgery, he was calm.

"Give your mom a kiss," the nurse said, and he did. "Have fun," his mother said, waving as he left.

Ben was given general anesthesia, and about 20 minutes later it took full effect. His surgeon was handed what everyone thought was a syringe of lidocaine, a local anesthetic, which reduces bleeding. He injected it inside and behind Ben's ear. Moments later, for no apparent reason, Ben's heart rate and blood pressure increased alarmingly. Dr. George McLain, an anesthesiologist on standby for emergencies, was summoned. McLain helped to stabilize the child, but a short time later Ben's heart rate and blood pressure dropped precipitously. For an hour and 40 minutes, frantic doctors performed CPR on the boy, knowing it was futile.

More than a year later, the memories are fresh, and McLain sits at lunch, crying as he speaks. The other diners stare, but he makes no attempt to hide the tears.

How long would he have kept up the CPR?

"If it was my kid, I would want them to keep trying," he says. "I think we were never going to stop."

Ben's heart did begin to beat again, and he was transferred to Martin Memorial's intensive-care unit. The surgeon, who had known Ben since he was a baby, went with McLain to talk to Tammy Kolb. "There has been a serious problem with your son," McLain remembers telling the woman. "His heart stopped. We had to restart his heart. He is extremely critical, in a comalike state."

He winces at the memory: "You don't know how strong to be to get your point across. You want her to understand, but you can't stick a knife in her."

At first, Tammy Kolb did not seem to understand. "I know he's going to wake up just fine," she said.

"I don't —," McLain said.

"I've seen this on TV. As soon as he wakes up I have a Christmas present for him. I brought it for him early."

Ben remained in a coma for nearly 24 hours. His parents and older sister remained at his bedside as their fog of denial slowly lifted. The next day they agreed that his ventilator should be removed, and he was de-

clared brain dead. As with the death of Jose Martinez, a lot can be learned by what happened after Ben Kolb died.

First, the hospital's risk manager, Doni Haas, had all the syringes and vials used on Ben locked away, then sent to an independent laboratory for analysis. Second, Haas promised Ben's parents that she "was going to find them an answer, if there was one."

There was. Tests showed that there had been a mixup, a mistake, a human error in a system that made that error more likely. Ben Kolb, lab reports showed, was never injected with lidocaine at all. The syringe that was supposed to contain lidocaine actually contained adrenaline, a highly concentrated strength that was intended only for external use.

Procedure in the Martin Memorial operating room at the time was for topical adrenaline to be poured into one cup, made of plastic, and lidocaine to be poured into a cup nearby, made of metal. The lidocaine syringe was then filled by placing it in the metal cup. It is a procedure used all over the country, a way of getting a drug from container to operating table. According to Richmond Harman, the hospital's C.E.O., "It has probably been done 100,000 times in our facility without error."

But it is a flawed procedure, the hospital learned. It allows for the possibility that the solution can be poured into or drawn out of the wrong cup. Instead, a cap, called a spike, could be put on the vial of lidocaine, allowing the drug to be drawn directly out of the labeled bottle and into a labeled syringe. The elimination of one step eliminates one opportunity for the human factor to get in the way.

Haas received the lab results three weeks after Ben died. The family had hired an attorney by then, and Haas and McLain drove two hours and met with the Kolbs at Krupnick, Campbell, Malone, Roselli, Buser, Slama & Hancock.

"It was very unusual," says Richard J. Roselli, one of Florida's most successful malpractice lawyers and the president of the Academy of Florida Trial Lawyers. "This is the first occasion where I ever had a hospital step forward, admitting their responsibility and seeking to do everything they can to help the family."

A financial settlement was reached by nightfall, but neither side will confirm the amount paid to the Kolbs.

After the papers were signed, the family asked for a chance to talk with the doctors at the hospital. The first thing Ben's father, Tim, did when he entered the emotion-filled room was to hug his son's surgeon. Then came the torrent of questions, questions that had kept the Kolbs awake at night, questions they might never have been able to ask had the case spent years in court.

Was Ben scared when his heart rate started dropping? Was he in pain? How much did he suffer?

The doctors explained what the Kolbs did not know, that Ben had been put under general anesthesia long before anything went wrong.

"The decisions I made for him were the same I would have made if it were my child," McLain said.

Just before the family left, they asked if it would be O.K. for them to continue to use Martin Memorial for their medical care.

"Of course," Haas said, grateful and amazed.

Would the hospital promise to spread the word about how Ben died, so that the procedure in question could be changed in other places?

Haas promised.

With that, the Kolb case was closed, but it wasn't over. Tom Kolb still coaches his son's soccer team. The family still grieves.

The doctors in the operating room that day still have nightmares of their own. "I let that child's life slip through my fingers," McLain says. "They tell me there was nothing I could do. I know there was nothing I could

do. But it's like I was a lifeguard and he died on my watch. There must have been something."

And the lawyers at Krupnick, Campbell are still searching, too.

"We're not done with this yet," Roselli says. Why, he asks, was it possible to mix up the lidocaine and the adrenaline? Did the two bottles look alike? "We're still investigating the product liability aspect of it," he says. "The questions of packaging and labeling."

Joanne Turnbull did not fully realize she was part of a sea change until she was in a Palm Springs auditorium last October — two months after the death of Jose Martinez, nearly two years after the death of Betsy Lehman, one day after what would have been Ben Kolb's eighth birthday — and marveled at what was going on around her.

At the front of the room were representatives from Martin Memorial Hospital. Keeping their promise to the Kolb family, the group spent nearly two hours retelling the story of how and why the boy died. In the audience, fighting tears as they took notes, were more than 300 doctors, nurses, pharmacists and administrators, each of whom had been given a smiling photograph of the child at the three-day conference on "Examining Errors in Health Care."

"Five years ago if we'd held this conference, very few people would have come," Leape, of Harvard, said at the operating session. But the list of sponsors included not only the A.M.A. and the joint commission, but also four medical insurance organizations, three pharmaceutical groups and the American Hospital Association.

"This is a miracle that this is happening," Turnbull remembers thinking as the session concluded. "Everyone's telling the truth."

In the months since Jose Martinez died, Turnbull has become an expert herself on the world of human factors research. She has done her root-cause analysis for the joint commission and learned a lot more about what went wrong that night: that the hospital's pharmacy was short one technician because someone called in sick and that policies there require that the phone be answered in four rings and visitors greeted within five seconds of their arrival; that the nurse who questioned the order was trained in a country where women rarely confront men and nurses rarely confront doctors; that the first resident was distracted by personal problems. Turnbull has made changes, too, ones she hopes will be strong enough to make such human imperfections matter less. Hermann Hospital's computer now flags questionable orders for the most dangerous drugs, including Digoxin. The hospital is looking into a paging system that alerts a caller when the person being paged has his beeper turned off. Double copies of a prescription are no longer sent to the pharmacy unless it is a prescription that must be filled within 15 minutes.

Administrators even asked the joint commission to schedule its accreditation review for April, not August, to ease the stress during the hospital's busiest month. Two research experiments are being planned to increase error reporting.

As a result of Turnbull's analysis, and the accompanying changes, Hermann Hospital is no longer under "accreditation watch." On Dec. 27, 1996, it was given full accreditation, with commendation, the highest designation given by the joint commission.

That brings satisfaction, she says, but mostly she feels sadness for the little boy and his family and concern for the staff members who are also still burdened by the event. She is wary, too, because everything she has learned tells her that no institution can ever be certain that something like this will not happen again. And she feels a sense of responsibility, an understanding that this moment and movement might well be seen as a crossroads for medicine. "We've become part of something," she says. "We want to make sure it is something that's done right."

LEGAL PERSPECTIVES

Federal Sentencing Guidelines — Sentencing of Organizations

INTRODUCTORY COMMENTARY

The guidelines and policy statements in this chapter apply when the convicted defendant is an organization. Organizations can act only through agents and, under federal criminal law, generally are vicariously liable for offenses committed by their agents. At the same time, individual agents are responsible for their own criminal conduct. Federal prosecutions of organizations therefore frequently involve individ-

ual and organizational co-defendants. Convicted individual agents of organizations are sentenced in accordance with the guidelines and policy statements in the preceding chapters. This chapter is designed so that the sanctions imposed upon organizations and their agents, taken together, will provide just punishment, adequate deterrence, and incentives for organizations to maintain internal mechanisms for preventing, detecting, and reporting criminal conduct.

Reprinted with permission from *The United States Law Week*, Vol. 50 pp. 4226–29 (March 26, 1991). Published by The Bureau of National Affairs, Inc. (800-372-1033)

This chapter reflects the following general principles: First, the court must, whenever practicable, order the organization to remedy any harm caused by the offense. The resources expended to remedy the harm should not be viewed as punishment, but rather as a means of making victims whole for the harm caused. Second, if the organization operated primarily for a criminal purpose or primarily by criminal means, the fine should be set sufficiently high to divest the organization of all its assets. Third, the fine range for any other organization should be based on the seriousness of the offense and the culpability of the organization. The seriousness of the offense generally will be reflected by the highest of the pecuniary gain, the pecuniary loss, or the amount in a guideline offense level fine table. Culpability generally will be determined by the steps taken by the organization prior to the offense to prevent and detect criminal conduct, the level and extent of involvement in or tolerance of the offense by certain personnel, and the organization's actions after an offense has been committed. Fourth, probation is an appropriate sentence for an organizational defendant when needed to ensure that another sanction will be fully implemented, or to ensure that steps will be taken within the organization to reduce the likelihood of future criminal conduct.

PART A — GENERAL APPLICATION PRINCIPLES

§8A1.1. Applicability of Chapter Eight

This chapter applies to the sentencing of all organizations for felony and Class A misdemeanor offenses.

Commentary

Application Notes:
1. "Organization" means "a person other than an individual." 18 U.S.C. § 18. The term in-

cludes corporations, partnerships, associations, joint-stock companies, unions, trusts, pension funds, unincorporated organizations, governments and political subdivisions thereof, and non-profit organizations. . . .
3. The following are definitions of terms used frequently in this chapter:

* * *

(k) An "effective program to prevent and detect violations of law" means a program that has been reasonably designed, implemented, and enforced so that it generally will be effective in preventing and detecting criminal conduct. Failure to prevent or detect the instant offense, by itself, does not mean that the program was not effective. The hallmark of an effective program to prevent and detect violations of law is that the organization exercised due diligence in seeking to prevent and detect criminal conduct by its employees and other agents. Due diligence requires at a minimum that the organization must have taken the following types of steps:

 (1) The organization must have established compliance standards and procedures to be followed by its employees and other agents that are reasonably capable of reducing the prospect of criminal conduct.
 (2) Specific individual(s) within high-level personnel of the organization must have been assigned overall responsibility to oversee compliance with such standards and procedures.
 (3) The organization must have used due care not to delegate substantial discretionary authority to individuals whom the organization knew, or should have known through the exercise of due diligence, had a propensity to engage in illegal activities.
 (4) The organization must have taken steps to communicate effectively its standards and procedures to all employees and other agents, e.g., by requiring participation in training programs or by disseminating publications that explain in a practical manner what is required.

(5) The organization must have taken reasonable steps to achieve compliance with its standards, e.g., by utilizing monitoring and auditing systems reasonably designed to detect criminal conduct by its employees and other agents and by having in place and publicizing a reporting system whereby employees and other agents could report criminal conduct by others within the organization without fear of retribution.

(6) The standards must have been consistently enforced through appropriate disciplinary mechanisms, including, as appropriate, discipline of individuals responsible for the failure to detect an offense. Adequate discipline of individuals responsible for an offense is a necessary component of enforcement; however, the form of discipline that will be appropriate will be case specific.

(7) After an offense has been detected, the organization must have taken all reasonable steps to respond appropriately to the offense and to prevent further similar offenses — including any necessary modifications to its program to prevent and detect violations of law.

The precise actions necessary for an effective program to prevent and detect violations of law will depend upon a number of factors. Among the relevant factors are:

(i) Size of the organization — The requisite degree of formality of a program to prevent and detect violations of law will vary with the size of the organization: the larger the organization, the more formal the program typically should be. A larger organization generally should have established written policies defining the standards and procedures to be followed by its employees and other agents.

(ii) Likelihood that certain offenses may occur because of the nature of its business — If because of the nature of an organization's business there is a substantial risk that certain types of offenses may occur, management must have taken steps to prevent and detect those types of offenses. For example, if an or-

ganization handles toxic substances, it must have established standards and procedures designed to ensure that those substances are properly handled at all times. If an organization employs sales personnel who have flexibility in setting prices, it must have established standards and procedures designed to prevent and detect price-fixing. If an organization employs sales personnel who have flexibility to represent the material characteristics of a product, it must have established standards and procedures designed to prevent fraud.

(iii) Prior history of the organization — An organization's prior history may indicate types of offenses that it should have taken actions to prevent. Recurrence of misconduct similar to that which an organization has previously committed casts doubt on whether it took all reasonable steps to prevent such misconduct.

An organization's failure to incorporate and follow applicable industry practice or the standards called for by any applicable governmental regulation weighs against a finding of an effective program to prevent and detect violations of law.

PART B — REMEDYING HARM FROM CRIMINAL CONDUCT

Introductory Commentary

As a general principle, the court should require that the organization take all appropriate steps to provide compensation to victims and otherwise remedy the harm caused or threatened by the offense. A restitution order or an order of probation requiring restitution can be used to compensate identifiable victims of the offense. A remedial order or an order of probation requiring community service can be used to reduce or eliminate the harm threatened, or to repair the harm caused by the offense, when that harm or threatened harm would otherwise not be remedied. An order of notice to victims can be used to notify unidentified victims of the offense. . . .

* * *

2. Determining the Fine — Other Organizations

* * *

§8C2.4. Base Fine

(a) The base fine is the greatest of:
- (1) the amount from the table in subsection (d) below corresponding to the offense level determined under §8C2.3 (Offense Level); or
- (2) the pecuniary gain to the organization from the offense; or
- (3) the pecuniary loss from the offense caused by the organization, to the extent the loss was caused intentionally, knowingly, or recklessly.

(b) *Provided,* that if the applicable offense guideline in Chapter Two includes a special instruction for organizational fines, that special instruction shall be applied, as appropriate.

(c) *Provided, further,* that to the extent the calculation of either pecuniary gain or pecuniary loss would unduly complicate or prolong the sentencing process, that amount, *i.e.,* gain or loss as appropriate, shall not be used for the determination of the base fine.

(d)   Offense Level Fine Table

Offense Level	Amount
6 or less	$5,000
7	$7,500
8	$10,000
9	$15,000
10	$20,000
11	$30,000
12	$40,000
13	$60,000
14	$85,000
15	$125,000
16	$175,000
17	$250,000
18	$350,000
19	$500,000
20	$650,000
21	$910,000
22	$1,200,000
23	$1,600,000
24	$2,100,000
25	$2,800,000
26	$3,700,000
27	$4,800,000
28	$6,300,000
29	$8,100,000
30	$10,500,000
31	$13,500,000
32	$17,500,000
33	$22,000,000
34	$28,500,000
35	$36,000,000
36	$45,500,000
37	$57,500,000
38 or more	$72,500,000

* * *

§8C2.5. Culpability Score

(a) Start with 5 points and apply subsections (b) through (g) below.

(b) Involvement in or Tolerance of Criminal Activity

If more than one applies, use the greatest:
- (1) If —
  - (A) the organization had 5,000 or more employees and
    - (i) an individual within high-level personnel of the organization participated in, condoned, or was willfully ignorant of the offense; or
    - (ii) tolerance of the offense by substantial authority personnel was pervasive throughout the organization; or
  - (B) the unit of the organization within which the offense was committed had 5,000 or more employees and
    - (i) an individual within high-level personnel of the unit participated in, condoned, or was willfully ignorant of the offense; or
    - (ii) tolerance of the offense by substantial authority personnel was pervasive throughout such unit,
  add 5 points; or
- (2) If —
  - (A) the organization had 1,000 or more employees and
    - (i) an individual within high-level personnel of the organization participated in, condoned, or was willfully ignorant of the offense; or

(ii) tolerance of the offense by substantial authority personnel was pervasive throughout the organization; or

(B) the unit of the organization within which the offense was committed had 1,000 or more employees and

  (i) an individual within high-level personnel of the unit participated in, condoned, or was willfully ignorant of the offense; or

  (ii) tolerance of the offense by substantial authority personnel was pervasive throughout such unit,

add 4 points; or

(3) If —

(A) the organization had 200 or more employees and

  (i) an individual within high-level personnel of the organization participated in, condoned, or was willfully ignorant of the offense; or

  (ii) tolerance of the offense by substantial authority personnel was pervasive throughout the organization; or

(B) the unit of the organization within which the offense was committed had 200 or more employees and

  (i) an individual within high-level personnel of the unit participated in, condoned, or was willfully ignorant of the offense; or

  (ii) tolerance of the offense by substantial authority personnel was pervasive throughout such unit,

add 3 points; or

(4) If the organization had 50 or more employees and an individual within substantial authority personnel participated in, condoned, or was willfully ignorant of the offense, add 2 points; or

(5) If the organization had 10 or more employees and an individual within substantial authority personnel participated in, condoned, or was willfully ignorant of the offense, add 1 point.

(c) Prior History

If more than one applies, use the greater:

(1) If the organization (or separately managed line of business) committed any part of the instant offense less than 10 years after (A) a criminal adjudication based on similar misconduct; or (B) civil or administrative adjudication(s) based on two or more separate instances of similar misconduct, add 1 point; or

(2) If the organization (or separately managed line of business) committed any part of the instant offense less than 5 years after (A) a criminal adjudication based on similar misconduct; or (B) civil or administrative adjudication(s) based on two or more separate instances of similar misconduct, add 2 points.

(d) Violation of an Order

If more than one applies, use the greater:

(1) (A) If the commission of the instant offense violated a judicial order or injunction, other than a violation of a condition of probation; or (B) if the organization (or separately managed line of business) violated a condition of probation by engaging in similar misconduct, *i.e.,* misconduct similar to that for which it was placed on probation, add 2 points; or

(2) If the commission of the instant offense violated a condition of probation, add 1 point.

(e) Obstruction of Justice

If the organization willfully obstructed or impeded, attempted to obstruct or impede, or aided, abetted, or encouraged obstruction of justice during the investigation, prosecution, or sentencing of the instant offense, or, with knowledge thereof, failed to take reasonable steps to prevent such obstruction or impedance or attempted obstruction or impedance, add 3 points.

(f) Effective Program to Prevent and Detect Violations of Law

If the offense occurred despite an effective program to prevent and detect violations of law, subtract 3 points.

Provided, that this subsection does not apply if an individual within high-level personnel of the organization, a person within high-level personnel of the unit of the organization within which the offense was committed where the unit had 200 or more employees, or an individual responsible for the administration or enforcement of a program to prevent and detect violations of law participated in, condoned, or was willfully ignorant of the offense. Participation of an individual within substantial authority personnel in an offense results in a rebuttable presumption that the organization did not have an effective program to prevent and detect violations of law.

Provided, further, that this subsection does not apply if, after becoming aware of an offense, the organization unreasonably delayed reporting the offense to appropriate governmental authorities.

(g) Self-Reporting, Cooperation, and Acceptance of Responsibility

If more than one applies, use the greatest:

(1) If the organization (A) prior to an imminent threat of disclosure or government investigation; and (B) within a reasonably prompt time after becoming aware of the offense, reported the offense to appropriate governmental authorities, fully cooperated in the investigation, and clearly demonstrated recognition and affirmative acceptance of responsibility for its criminal conduct, subtract 5 points; or

(2) If the organization fully cooperated in the investigated and clearly demonstrated recognition and affirmative acceptance of responsibility for its criminal conduct, subtract 2 points; or

(3) If the organization clearly demonstrated recognition and affirmative acceptance of responsibility for its criminal conduct, subtract 1 point. . . .

§8C.2.6. Minimum and Maximum Multipliers

Using the culpability score from §8C2.5 (Culpability Score) and applying any applicable special instruction for fines in Chapter Two, determine the applicable minimum and maximum fine multipliers from the table below.

Culpability Score	Minimum Multiplier	Maximum Multiplier
10 or more	2.00	4.00
9	1.80	3.60
8	1.60	3.20
7	1.40	2.80
6	1.20	2.40
5	1.00	2.00
4	0.80	1.60
3	0.60	1.20
2	0.40	0.80
1	0.20	0.40
0 or less	0.05	0.20

* * *

§8C2.8. Determining the Fine Within the Range (Policy Statement)

(a) In determining the amount of the fine within the applicable guideline range, the court should consider:

(1) the need for the sentence to reflect the seriousness of the offense, promote respect for the law, provide just punishment, afford adequate deterrence, and protect the public from further crimes of the organization;

(2) the organization's role in the offense;

(3) any collateral consequences of conviction, including civil obligations arising from the organization's conduct;

(4) any nonpecuniary loss caused or threatened by the offense;

(5) whether the offense involved a vulnerable victim;

(6) any prior criminal record of an individual within high-level personnel of the organization or high-level personnel of a unit of the organization who participated in, condoned, or was willfully ignorant of the criminal conduct;

(7) any prior civil or criminal misconduct by the organization other than that counted under §8C2.5(c);

(8) any culpability score under §8C2.5 (Culpability Score) higher than 10 or lower than 0;

(9) partial but incomplete satisfaction of the conditions for one or more of the mitigating or aggravating factors set forth in §8C2.5 (Culpability Score); and

(10) any factor listed in 18 U.S.C. § 3572(a).

(b) In addition, the court may consider the relative importance of any factor used to determine the range, including the pecuniary loss caused by the offense, the pecuniary gain from the offense, any specific offense characteristic used to determine the offense level, and any aggravating or mitigating factor used to determine the culpability score.

Excerpts from V-Chip Legislation U.S. Congress Telecommunications Act of 1996

I FINDINGS

The Congress makes the following findings:

(1) Television influences children's perception of the values and behavior that are common and acceptable in society.

(2) Television station operators, cable television system operators, and video programmers should follow practices in connection with video programming that take into consideration that television broadcast and cable programming has established a uniquely pervasive presence in the lives of American children.

(3) The average American child is exposed to 25 hours of television each week and some children are exposed to as much as 11 hours of television a day.

(4) Studies have shown that children exposed to violent video programming at a young age have a higher tendency for violent and aggressive behavior later in life than children not so exposed, and that children exposed to violent video programming are prone to assume that acts of violence are acceptable behavior.

(5) Children in the United States are, on average, exposed to an estimated 8,000 murders and 100,000 acts of violence on television by the time the child completes elementary school.

(6) Studies indicate that children are affected by the pervasiveness and casual treatment of sexual material on television, eroding the ability of parents to develop responsible attitudes and behavior in their children.

(7) Parents express grave concern over violent and sexual video programming and strongly support technology that would give them greater control to block video programming in the home that they consider harmful to their children.

(8) There is a compelling governmental interest in empowering parents to limit the negative influences of video programming that is harmful to children.

(9) Providing parents with timely information about the nature of upcoming video programming and with the technological tools that allow them easily to block violent, sexual, or other programming that they believe harmful to their children is a nonintrusive and narrowly tailored means of achieving that compelling governmental interest.

II RATINGS

(b) Establishment of Television Rating Code

(1) AMENDMENT

Section 303 (47 U.S.C. 303) is amended by adding at the end the following:

"(w) Prescribe —

(1) on the basis of recommendations from an advisory committee established by the Commission in accordance with section 551(b)(2) of the Telecommunications Act of 1996, guidelines and recommended procedures for the identification and rating of video programming that contains sexual, violent, or other indecent material about which parents should be informed before it is displayed to children: Provided, That nothing in this paragraph shall be construed to authorize any rating of video programming on the basis of its political or religious content; and

(2) with respect to any video programming that has been rated, and in consultation with the television industry, rules requiring distributors of such video programming to transmit such rating to permit parents to block the display of video programming that they have determined is inappropriate for their children."

Public Law 104-104, section 551.

(2) ADVISORY COMMITTEE REQUIRE-MENTS — In establishing an advisory committee for purposes of the amendment made by paragraph (1) of this subsection, the Commissions shall —

(A) ensure that such committee is composed of parents, television broadcasters, television programming producers, cable operators, appropriate public interest groups, and other interested individuals from the private sector and is fairly balanced in terms of political affiliation, the points of view represented, and the functions to be performed by the committee;

(B) provide to the committee such staff and resources as may be necessary to permit it to perform its functions efficiently and promptly; and

(C) require the committee to submit a final report of its recommendations within one year after the date of the appointment of the initial members.

III V-CHIP

(c) Requirement for Manufacture of Televisions that Block Programs

Section 303 (47 U.S.C. 303), as amended by subsection (a), is further amended by adding at the end the following:

"(x) Require, in the case of an apparatus designed to receive television signals that are shipped in interstate commerce or manufactured in the United States and that have a picture screen 13 inches or greater in size (measured diagonally), that such apparatus be equipped with a feature designed to enable viewers to block display of all programs with a common rating, except as otherwise permitted by regulations pursuant to section 330(c)(4)."

THE TV PARENTAL GUIDELINES

For Programs Designed Solely for Children

TV-Y (All Children — This program is designed to be appropriate for all children.) Whether animated or live-action, the themes and elements in this program are specifically designed for a very young audience, including children from ages 2–6. This program is not expected to frighten younger children.

TV-Y7 (Directed to Older Children — This program is designed for children age 7 and above.) It may be more appropriate for children who have acquired the developmental skills needed to distinguish between make-believe and reality. Themes and elements in this program may include mild fantasy or comedic violence, or may frighten children under the age of 7. Therefore, parents may wish to consider the suitability of this program for their very young children. Note: For those programs where fantasy violence may be more intense or more combative than other programs in this category, such programs will be designated TV-Y7-FV. For programs designed for the entire audience, the general categories are:

TV-G (General Audience — Most parents would find this program suitable for all ages.) Although this rating does not signify a program designed specifically for children, most parents may let younger children watch this program unattended. It contains little or no violence, no strong language and little or no sexual dialogue or situations.

TV-PG (Parental Guidance Suggested — This program contains material that parents may find unsuitable for younger children.) Many parents may want to watch it with their younger children. The theme itself may call for parental guidance and/or the program contains one or more of the following: moderate violence (V), some sexual situations (S), infrequent coarse language (L), or some suggestive dialogue (D).

TV-14 (Parents Strongly Cautioned — This program contains some material that many parents would find unsuitable for children under 14 years of age.) Parents are strongly urged to exercise greater care in monitoring this program and are cautioned against letting children under the age of 14 watch unattended. This program contains one or more of the following: intense violence (V), intense sexual situations (S), strong coarse language (L), or intensely suggestive dialogue (D).

TV-MA (Mature Audience Only — This program is specifically designed to be viewed by adults and therefore may be unsuitable for children under 17.) This program contains one or more of the following: graphic violence (V), explicit sexual activity (S), or crude indecent language (L).

Johnson & Johnson: Our Credo

We believe our first responsibility is to the doctors, nurses and patients, to mothers and fathers and all others who use our products and services.

In meeting their needs everything we do must be of high quality.

We must constantly strive to reduce our costs in order to maintain reasonable prices.

Customers' orders must be serviced promptly and accurately.

Our suppliers and distributors must have an opportunity to make a fair profit.

We are responsible to our employees, the men and women who work with us throughout the world.

Everyone must be considered as an individual.

We must respect their dignity and recognize their merit.

They must have a sense of security in their jobs.

Compensation must be fair and adequate, and working conditions clean, orderly and safe.

We must be mindful of ways to help our employees fulfill their family responsibilities.

Employees must feel free to make suggestions and complaints.

There must be equal opportunity for employment, development and advancement for those qualified.

We must provide competent management, and their actions must be just and ethical.

We are responsible to the communities in which we live and work and to the world community as well.

We must be good citizens — support good works and charities and bear our fair share of taxes.

We must encourage civic improvements and better health and education.

We must maintain in good order the property we are privileged to use, protecting the environment and natural resources.

Our final responsibility is to our stockholders.

Business must make a sound profit.

We must experiment with new ideas.

Research must be carried on, innovative programs developed and mistakes paid for.

New equipment must be purchased, new facilities provided and new products launched.

Reserves must be created to provide for adverse times.

When we operate according to these principles, the stockholders should realize a fair return.

Courtesy of Johnson & Johnson.

CASES

CASE 1. *Retailers and Weapons: Self-Imposed Bans*

In October 1993, a court ordered Kmart Corporation to pay $12.5 million to Deborah Kitchen, who was left a quadriplegic after her boyfriend, Thomas Knapp, shot her point-blank in the neck with a rifle he purchased at Kmart. The trial records show he was so drunk at the time of purchase that he could not legibly complete the federal firearms forms, so a clerk did it for him. The family of a couple slain by their schizophrenic son with a .38 caliber handgun he had purchased at Wal-Mart sued Wal-Mart in December 1993.

By the end of 1993, both Wal-Mart and Kmart announced they would no longer sell any guns at their retail stores. Firearm sales for the two discounters totaled $158 million. A Wal-Mart spokesman said, "A majority of our customers tell us they would prefer not to shop in a retail store that sells handguns."

Both retailers were the last to stop selling guns. Montgomery Ward and Sears, Roebuck stopped in 1981; Ward's felt the sales were too problematic, and Sears cited burdensome paperwork.

In September 1994, a thirteen-year-old boy was fatally shot by a police officer in the stairwell of a New York City housing project because he was carrying a toy gun the officer assumed to be real. A similar incident occurred when another officer shot and wounded a 16-year-old youth who was also carrying just a toy gun.

By October 1994, both Kay-Bee Toy Stores and Toys 'R' Us announced that they would no longer carry realistic-looking military- or police-style weapons. They would sell only brightly colored, oversized toy guns or those with logos or decals that clearly distinguish them from real weapons.

Said Ann Iverson, president and CEO of Kay-Bee, which has a chain of 1,100 stores nationwide, "This step is just a part of Kay-Bee's strategy to re-evaluate our merchandise mix and address what families need today in terms of fun, safe, and developmentally sound toys." Toy guns represent 2 percent of Kay-Bee's inventory.

CEO Michael Goldstein of Toys 'R' Us has led an industry initiative to eliminate the realistic-looking guns. He said, "The issue is the potential harm that these products pose to children and others. We believe that by taking this step we can help raise awareness and encourage manufacturers and other retailers to join us in this effort."

A Toys 'R' Us shopper commented, "If it saves a couple kids' lives, I think it's a good thing. Actually, it's a courageous move. They're going to lose business."

Questions

1. Are the Kmart and Wal-Mart decisions on gun sales rooted in ethics or potential liability?
2. Do retailers have a potential liability in selling toy guns?
3. Did the ban on realistic toy weapons earn publicity for the toy store chains? Do you believe that was partially their motivation? Consider the following comment by a spokeswoman for Target, which has never carried the realistic-looking guns: "The only guns we have are neon plastic

From *Business Ethics: Case Studies and Selected Readings,* 3rd edition, by M.M. Jennings. © 1999. Reprinted with permission of South-Western College Publishing, a division of Thomson Learning. Fax 800 730-2215 toy guns. We cater to the family, and we don't really consider realistic toy guns to be a family toy."

4. If you were a toy retailer, would you carry realistic-looking toy guns?

5. If you were a retailer, would you sell guns? If no retailers sell guns, have consumers lost a fundamental constitutional right?

CASE 2.   *Rock Music Warning Labels*

In the summer of 1985, Tipper Gore, the wife of then-Senator Albert Gore of Tennessee, and Susan Baker, the wife of former U.S. Treasury Secretary James Baker, formed a citizens' group called the Parents Resource Music Center (PMRC). The group's concern was that rock music advocates "aggressive and hostile rebellion, the abuse of drugs and alcohol, irresponsible sexuality, sexual perversions, violence and involvement in the occult." Gore began the group after she listened to the song "Darling Nikki" from her eleven-year-old daughter's *Purple Rain* album by Prince. The song is about a girl masturbating as she looks at a magazine. Gore then discovered Sheena Easton singing about "genital arousal," Judas Priest singing about oral sex at gunpoint, and the following lyrics in Motley Crue's top-selling *Shout at the Devil* album: "\ . . . now I'm killing you. . . . Watch your face turning blue."

PMRC's strategy was to work with record companies to reach a mutually agreeable solution to the problem. PMRC met with the Recording Industry Association of America to request a ratings system for records, similar to that used for movies, and a requirement that printed lyrics be included with all records so that disc jockeys would know what they are sending out over the airwaves. In the first month after PMRC was organized, it received over 10,000 letters of support and inquiry. PMRC maintains a database with the following information:

Teenagers listen to their music four to six hours per day for a total of 10,000 hours between grades seven and twelve.

Of all violent crimes, 70 percent are committed by youths under the age of seventeen.

Teenage suicide has increased by 300 percent since 1955.

U.S. teenage pregnancy rates are the highest in the world.

When PMRC failed to reach an agreement with the record industry, congressional hearings were held on a proposed bill to require labeling on records. Susan Baker and Tipper Gore testified, as did musicians Frank Zappa, former member of the Mothers of Invention, and Dee Snider of Twisted Sister. Zappa stated, "Putting labels on albums is the equivalent of treating dandruff by decapitation."

Though nothing came of the hearings, by 1990, bills were pending in thirty-five state legislatures to require labeling of records. PMRC backed state groups lobbying for the legislation. In Arizona, a reporter for *New Times* asked a sponsor of a labeling bill, Senator Jan Brewer, to read some of the objectionable lyrics. The reporter recorded the read-

From *Business Ethics: Case Studies and Selected Readings*, 3rd edition, by M.M. Jennings. © 1999. Reprinted with permission of South-Western College Publishing, a division of Thomson Learning. Fax 800 730-2215

ing, set it to music, and played the tape over the speakers in the Capitol.

In May 1990, with the state legislative debates on the label requirements still in progress, the Recording Industry Association of America introduced a uniform label for albums with explicit lyrics and expressed hope that its voluntary use by industry members would halt the passage of legislation. The black-and-white label appears in the lower right-hand corner of the album and reads: "Parental Advisory — Explicit Lyrics." The label is to be used on albums with lyrics relating to sex, violence, suicide, drug abuse, bigotry, or satanic worship. Use of the label is the decision of the record company and the artist.

The PMRC and the National Parent and Teacher Association endorsed the warning system and asked state legislators to consider dropping proposed label legislation.

Controversy continued to surround rock music lyrics. In the summer of 1990, parents of a teenager who committed suicide sued the rock group Judas Priest, alleging that its lyrics resulted in murderous mind control and the death of their son. Their subliminal persuasion argument was unsuccessful.

By 1995, the record industry's then 10-year-old warning label program was reviewed with the conclusion that parents don't know what the explicit-lyrics stickers are. A meeting between the Recording Industry Association of America and the National Association of Recording Merchandisers resulted in new plans to help the system work better. The provisions include:

- Display signs in stores explaining the "Parental Advisory Explicit Lyrics" logo.
- Ensure that record companies use the correct size (1-inch by ½-inch) and placement (lower right) on the record's permanent packaging.

- Alert reviewers of each record's sticker status.
- Encourage inclusion of a record's warning label in ads and promotional materials.

The attention to gangsta rap music also resulted in increased attention to lyrics. Recording company MCA was targeted in 1996 for marketing "death and degradation." MCA refused to make changes other than complying with warning labels and called Mr. William Bennett, a former secretary of Education and author, a "warden of morality." Wal-Mart continued to refuse to stock explicit lyric music.

In late November 1997, the Senate began exploring the effects of music on children. One parent testified that his 15-year-old son committed suicide after listening to the Marilyn Manson album, "Antichrist Superstar." The Senate is considering warning labels on albums for violence, death and drugs.

Questions

1. What are the ethical issues in the production of songs with explicit lyrics?
2. Will voluntary regulation work for the recording industry?
3. If you were a record producer, would your company sign artists who sing explicit lyrics?
4. If you were a record producer, would you feel an obligation to do more than put a warning label on albums with explicit lyrics?
5. You have just been informed that a teenager committed suicide while listening to the music of one of the artists your company produces. The music suggested suicide as an alternative to unhappiness. Would you feel morally responsible for the suicide? Should the artist feel morally responsible?

CASE 3. *An Auditor's Dilemma*

Sorting through a stack of invoices, Alison Lloyd's attention was drawn to one from Ace Glass Company. Her responsibility as the new internal auditor for Gem Packing is to verify all expenditures, and she knew that Ace had already been paid for the June delivery of the jars that are used for Gem's jams and jellies. On closer inspection, she noticed that the invoice was for deliveries in July and August that had not yet been made. Today was only June 10. Alison recalled approving several other invoices lately that seemed to be misdated, but the amounts were small compared with the $130,000 that Gem spends each month for glass jars. I had better check this out with purchasing, she thought.

Over lunch, Greg Berg, the head of purchasing, explains the system to her. The jam and jelly division operates under an incentive plan whereby the division manager and the heads of the four main units — sales, production, distribution, and purchasing — receive substantial bonuses for meeting their quota in pre-tax profits for the fiscal year, which ends on June 30. The bonuses are about one-half of annual salary and constitute one-third of the managers' total compensation. In addition, meeting quota is weighted heavily in evaluations, and missing even once is considered to be a death blow to the career of an aspiring executive at Gem. So the pressure on these managers is intense. On the other hand, there is nothing to be gained from exceeding a quota. An exceptionally good year is likely to be rewarded with an even higher quota the next year, since quotas are generally set at corporate headquarters by adding 5 percent to the previous year's results.

Greg continues to explain that several years ago, after the quota had been safely met, the jam and jelly division began prepaying as many expenses as possible — not only for glass jars but for advertising costs, trucking charges, and some commodities, such as sugar. The practice has continued to grow, and sales also helps out by delaying orders until the next fiscal year or by falsifying delivery dates when a shipment has already gone out. "Regular suppliers like Ace Glass know how we work," Greg says, "and they sent the invoices for July and August at my request." He predicts that Alison will begin seeing more irregular invoices as the fiscal year winds down. "Making quota gets easier each year," Greg observes, "because the division gets an ever increasing head start, but the problem of finding ways to avoid going too far over quota has become a real nightmare." Greg is not sure, but he thinks that other divisions are doing the same thing. "I don't think corporate has caught on yet," he says. "But they created the system, and they've been happy with the results so far. If they're too dumb to figure out how we're achieving them, that's their problem."

Alison recalls that upon becoming a member of the Institute of Internal Auditors, she agreed to abide by the IIA code of ethics. This code requires members to exercise "honesty, objectivity, and diligence" in the performance of their duties, but also to be loyal to the employer. However, loyalty does not include being a party to any "illegal or improper activity." As an internal auditor, she is also responsible for evaluating the adequacy and effectiveness of the company's

---

From *Ethics and the Conduct of Business*, 2nd edition by John R. Boatright, © 1993. Reprinted by permission of Prentice Hall, Inc., Upper Saddle River, NJ.

system of financial control. But what is the harm of shuffling a little paper around? she thinks. Nobody is getting hurt, and it all works out in the end.

Questions

1. Is the IAA code of ethics really helpful in resolving Alison's dilemma? Why or why not?

2. Greg blames the incentive system for the dilemma. Is he right?

3. Could Gem Packing be subject to prosecution under the Federal Sentencing Guidelines, and if so would Gem Packing be subject to increased fines?

4. What should Alison do?

CASE 4.   *Beech-Nut Corporation*

Beech-Nut Corporation was the second-largest baby food company in the United States. It was founded in 1891 and was incorporated in the state of Pennsylvania. The company primarily produced and distributed baby food and dietetic specialty products. Over the years, Beech-Nut had built a reputation on purity, high-quality products, and natural ingredients. Because of competition and other difficulties, however, Beech-Nut was eventually forced to reduce its product line to a single product, which was baby food. This product line, unfortunately, had almost never turned a profit.[1] Its market share in 1977 was only 15 percent compared with a 70 percent market share attained by the Gerber company, its major competitor. By 1978, Beech-Nut, burdened with losses, owed millions of dollars to suppliers and was under great financial pressure.[2]

To cope with the threat of insolvency, Beech-Nut executives switched to a supplier that offered apple juice concentrate at a price 20 percent below market. At that time, rumors of apple juice adulteration had already spread in the industry, and therefore the purchase of concentrate at 20 percent

below market raised suspicions among the employees in Beech-Nut's Research and Development Department.[3] In 1977, tests by a company-hired laboratory suggested that the cheap apple concentrate that Beech-Nut bought from Universal Juice Company might be adulterated. The company, however, continued to claim that its products contained no artificial ingredients.

In 1981, Jerome J. LiCari, director of research and development at Beech-Nut, mounted a major drive to improve adulteration testing. He found that the apple juice concentrate Beech-Nut was buying to use in its juice and other products was a blend of beet sugar, cane syrup, and other synthetic ingredients. With this fresh evidence, LiCari informed Niels Hoyvald and John Lavery, then president and vice-president of Beech-Nut, respectively, that the concentrate was bogus, and he suggested getting another concentrate supplier. He believed that continuing to deal with Universal could jeopardize the productline restructuring that Beech-Nut was planning, which would emphasize nutritional values and the absence of artificial ingredients in its products.[4] Despite LiCari's

This case was prepared by Rogene Buchholz of Loyola University, New Orleans, and reprinted from *Business Environment and Public Policy,* Prentice Hall, 1992.

efforts, Hoyvald and Lavery took no action, and the company continued to produce and distribute adulterated apple juice under the label "100% fruit juice."

In 1982, federal and state agencies started investigations and established that Universal's concentrate was bogus. Beech-Nut immediately canceled its apple concentrate contracts, but it continued to distribute millions of bottles of "fake" apple juice at deep discounts in the U.S. market as well as other parts of the world. Despite warnings from the Food and Drug Administration and the New York State Agriculture Department, Beech-Nut did not issue a national apple juice recall until late October of the year and continued to unload its $3.5 million of inventory of adulterated apple juice. This behavior gave the prosecutors reason to believe that the company's main concern was making money even if it meant selling a phony product.[5]

NOTES

1. Chris Welles, "What Led Beech-Nut Down the Road to Disgrace." *Business Week* (February 22, 1988), p. 125.

2. Ibid.
3. Ibid.
4. Ibid., p. 125.
5. Leonard Burder, "Two Former Executives of Beech-Nut Guilty in Phony Juice Case," *Wall Street Journal* (February 18, 1988), p. D-3.

Questions

1. After reporting his findings to Hoyvald and Lavery, did LiCari have any additional moral responsibility to expose the distribution of the adulterated apple juice?
2. In what ways is LiCari's position as director of research and development at Beech-Nut similar to Boisjoly's at Morton Thiokol?
3. Who is responsible for distribution of the adulterated apple juice in 1977? In 1981?
4. Evaluate the options available to LiCari after he reported his findings to Beech-Nut's senior management.

CASE 5. *Grantman Piedman*

Grantman Piedman[1] originally instituted its ethics program in the 1980s as a part of the company's compliance program in order to correct real and perceived abuses in its defense contracting business with the government. The ethics program consists of legal compliance standards, in addition to a general ethics code requiring respect of persons (employees, customers, suppliers, etc.), fairness, truthfulness, and the like.

Before the adoption of the ethics program, Grantman Piedman had operated in much the same manner as the companies described by Robert Jackall in *Moral Mazes: The*

---

[1]"Grantman Piedman" is a pseudonym. This case is based on a confidential report to senior management at the company that was the result of an interview project that Barbara A. McGraw conducted in 1997, pursuant to a grant provided through the University of Southern California by the company. The interviews were conducted in a manner that maintained the anonymity of the interviewees, so that they were able to speak freely.

Case prepared by Barbara A. McGraw. Reprinted by permission. ©1999 Barbara A. McGraw.

World of Corporate Managers. There were layers of fairly insular groups that were governed by managers who, because of this structure, were permitted to develop these groups as small independent units. Rather than being concerned, for example, whether the product being produced was of the best quality and was delivered on time to the customer, the concern was whether one's unit appeared successful in reports to very senior management. As one middle manager reported:

> Grantman was [like] a bunch of little companies that really felt they could win or lose by themselves. They didn't have to worry about the other functions succeeding. As a matter of fact, they seemed to take delight if the other functions were having a tough time. It made them look superior. . . . [For example,] as long as tooling was on schedule and [they] were meeting [their] budgets, [they] really didn't care whether fabrication or assembly — whether they were doing it. As a matter of fact, [they] took great delight if [fabrication or assembly] were struggling.

As a consequence, the company was not functioning as a whole toward consistent goals.

This phenomena was coupled with a "heavy handed" management style of "absolute control," where such management treated their independent units as little "fiefdoms" within the overall corporate structure. There, adherence to the "chain-of-command" was the main ethic and reporting an ethics violation in that context would have been unthinkable. Instead of being viewed as a positive effort to help keep the company out of trouble, an ethics violation report was viewed by senior management with this "fiefdom" mentality as a violation of group loyalty. As one manager put it:

> They [the old-style managers] weren't necessarily promoted [so much] for management skills as they were promoted for their ability to get results. And so, if someone was able to achieve,

no one really went and walked his . . . line to see how he was able to achieve. So, had they done that, they probably would have come out terrified in some camps . . . how they actually made it happen. There were sheer reigns of terror. The guy who took the high road and tried to do it right had a much more difficult journey. It was easier for the guy that just was a brutal tyrant and threatened everybody.

Another said:

> We have had leadership . . . who managed by intimidation. . . . When you manage by intimidation, you run a high risk of people making wrong decisions for the wrong reasons.

Furthermore, under this sort of system people were treated not as respected human beings contributing to the well-being of the company, but as functional beings, in effect, replacement parts.

When the ethics program initially was instituted in this fiefdom context, the program was experienced as insincere — merely something required by the government to stay in business. One manager said, "The way the program was introduced made me seriously wonder: Was this window dressing for our customer to say Grantman has values?" As time went on, however, the ethics program came to be more integrated into the fabric of the company's culture. This was accomplished primarily because there was a real commitment to integrity from the very top where the CEO, himself, championed the ethics program.

This overall commitment to the ethics program was, then, cultivated by new management who were hired to institute a different management style. Some managers expressed the view that the change in management style resulted directly from the change in the ethical context of the company. It was felt that an authoritative management style undermines relationships and trust and leads to a situation that limits the ability of the employees to participate fully in the company. And so the new commitment to the ethics program, in particular its emphasis on respect of persons, necessitated a more respectful, team-oriented management style.

As more were hired who exemplified the new management style, and the ethics program was integrated into the fabric of the corporate culture, morale was improved and employees began to feel more valued and "empowered" to take responsibility. It was clear from one manager's comments that morale and job satisfaction are intimately linked with the ability to operate out of one's personal sense of morals without conflict in the job, particularly for those who feel they have a clear and strong "moral compass," which they prefer not to have to leave at home when they go to work.

One specific aspect of the ethics program that appeared to have the most impact in empowering employees to promote the values expressed in the ethics program was the "Challenge Up" program. The Grantman Piedman ethics program encouraged employees to "challenge up" the corporate hierarchy, to the very top, if necessary, when they believed they had reason to suspect ethics program principles were not being followed. The "Challenge Up" program was especially effective in overriding the old "chain-of-command" rule when ethics violations were at issue. Again, there was a commitment to the "Challenge Up" program by the very top management at the company. Several managers commented that this commitment from the top to the "Challenge Up" program was critical to the success of the ethics program at Grantman Piedman overall. Otherwise, those on the lower levels of the corporate hierarchy would be required to risk their livelihood if they raised ethics concerns that had an impact on managers above them on the corporate ladder.

"Challenge up" was something that you primarily didn't do [under the old system]. It was kind of like the military. If you were a private, you didn't go around questioning the drill sergeant as to why he would make you do that. The environment has changed from that standpoint. It now has that open-door, challenge up — encouragement actually.

It was noted by managers that when empowered as individuals to make moral choices, managers and other employees are likely to give more of themselves to the company than they would have under the old authoritative, fiefdom system.

One thing you really miss [under an authoritative management style] and that's the human spirit. In that kind of environment, people are waiting to be told what to do and they're not going to tell *you* anything. They won't share anything with you at all. If something goes wrong, you got to go find it out. What they're going to tell you: "If you're so damn smart and you're responsible for everything, then you figure it out."

You cannot have any authoritative measure that will ever get down to the heart of an individual. When you get down to that real root of productivity — I'm talking about the potential of an individual — they have to give that up willingly. Now why would they do that? Only because there's an environment and a relationship within a team, within a group, that says I want to do that because that's what I want to do.

In other words, the human spirit thrives more in a context where people are making decisions with integrity and where people are valued. Not only does this boost morale and empower employees to make moral choices, but it promotes the freedom of employees to contribute to the company in other ways as well.

Grantman Piedman came along and there's significant change. I mean very significant ... Grantman Piedman is, I mean, right there in their values, they tell you that we value you. We value Grantman Piedman people. And says we treat one another with respect. Take pride in the contributions of the company. The diversity of individuals and ideas. And if we're going to continue to be successful, we got to continue to do that. To help things grow. That's what they tell you. . . . Grantman Piedman put two things in our values that was we act with integrity in all we do and we value people — which I thought was significant.

Moreover, managers at Grantman Piedman were of the firm belief that this commitment to ethics ultimately serves the long-term profitability of the company.

I think . . . you never have to worry about ethics getting in the way of making money. Because it seems to me like the more ethically the businesses run themselves, the more prosperous they are. And, if any lesson needs to be taught to people, that message probably ought to come through the loudest and the clearest. Ethics doesn't stand in the way of businesses making money. They just help you make money. Nobody wants to deal with cheats, liars, scoundrels . . . unethical people. . . . You may win on that basis one time but not over the long haul.

Questions

1. Did Grantman Piedman make a good business decision to establish a compliance program?
2. Based on the information in the case, would the compliance program established by Grantman Piedman be adequate as an ethics program that could mitigate any fines under the Federal Sentencing Guidelines?
3. Did the compliance program at Grantman Piedman evolve into a genuine values-based ethics program?
4. How can one account for the change in culture at Grantman Piedman? Do you believe the change is genuine and that it will be long lasting?

Suggested Supplementary Readings

BROOKS, LEONARD, J. "Corporate Codes of Conduct." *Journal of Business Ethics* 8 (February–March, 1989): 117–29.

CONDREN, CONAL. "Code Types: Functions and Failings and Organizational Diversity." *Business and Professional Ethics Journal* 14 (1995) 69–87.

CORLETT, J. ANGELO. "Corporate Responsibility and Punishment." *Public Affairs Quarterly* 2 (January, 1988): 1–16.

DAVIS, MICHAEL. "Technical Decisions: Time to Rethink the Engineer's Responsibilities?" 11 (Fall–Winter, 1992): 41–55.

DE GEORGE, RICHARD T. "GM and Corporate Responsibility." *Journal of Business Ethics* 5 (June, 1986): 177–79.

GAWANDE, ATUL. "When Doctors Make Mistakes." *The New Yorker* (February 1, 1999), p. 40–55.

GETZ, KATHLEEN A. International Codes of Conduct: An Analysis of Ethical Reasoning." *Journal of Business Ethics* 9 (July, 1990): 567–77.

GRUNDER, RICHARD S. "Just Punishment and Adequate Deterrence for Organizational Misconduct: Scaling Economic Penalties Under the New Corporate Sentencing Guidelines." *Southern California Law Review* 66 (1993): 225–88.

HOFFMAN, W. MICHAEL, JENNIFER MILLS MOORE, and DAVID FEDO, eds. *Corporate Governance and Institutionalizing Ethics.* Lexington, MA: Lexington Books, 1984.

HUMMELS, HARRY. "Safety and Aircraft Maintenance: A Moral Evaluation." *International Journal of Value-Based Management* 10 (2) (1997).

JAMAL, KARIM, and NORMAN E. BOWIE. "Theoretical Considerations for a Meaningful Code of Professional Ethics." *Journal of Business Ethics* 14 (September, 1995): 703–14.

MARTIN, MIKE W. "Whistleblowing: Professionalism, Personal Life and Shared Responsibility for Safety in Engineering." *Business and Professional Ethics Journal* 12 (1992) 21–40.

MATHEWS, M. C. "Codes of Ethics: Organizational Behaviour and Misbehaviour." *Research in Corporate Social Performance* 9 (1987): 107–30.

MITNICK, BARRY M. *The Political Economy of Regulation.* New York: Columbia University Press, 1980.

MOORE, JENNIFER. "Corporate Culpability Under the Federal Sentencing Guidelines." *Arizona Law Review,* 34 (1992): 743–798.

MURPHY, PATRICK E. *Eighty Exemplary Ethics Statements*. Notre Dame, IN: University of Notre Dame Press, 1998.

MURPHY, PATRICK E. "Corporate Ethics Statements: Current Status and Future Prospects." *Journal of Business Ethics* 14 (September, 1995): 727–40.

NAGEL, ILENE H., and WINTHROP W. SWENSON. "The Federal Sentencing Guidelines For Corporations: Their Development, Theoretical Underpinnings, and Some Thoughts About Their Future." *Washington University Law Quarterly* 71 (1993): 205–59.

NIELSEN, RICHARD P. "What Can Managers Do About Unethical Management?" *Journal of Business Ethics* 6 (May, 1987): 309–20.

PHILLIPS, MICHAEL J. "Corporate Moral Responsibility." *Business Ethics Quarterly* 5 (July, 1995): 555–76.

SANDERS, JOHN T. "Assessing Responsibility: Fixing Blame versus Fixing Problems." *Business and Professional Ethics Journal* 12 (1993) 73–86.

STONE, CHRISTOPHER D. *Where the Law Ends: The Social Control of Corporate Behavior*. New York: Harper and Row, 1975.

WERHANE, PATRICIA H. "Engineers and Management: The Challenge of the *Challenger* Incident." *Journal of Business Ethics* 10 (August, 1991): 605–16.

Chapter Four

Acceptable Risk

INTRODUCTION

GOVERNMENT IS CONSTITUTED to protect citizens from risk to the environment, risk from external invasion, risk to health, risk from crime, risk from fire, risk of highway accidents, and similar risks. A natural extension of this idea is that the social contract obligates government to protect citizens against risks to health, bodily safety, financial security, and the environment. However, society has not yet decided on the extent to which government should restrain business activities in order to protect health, safety, financial security, and environmental interests.

Corporate activities present several types of risk of harm. This chapter concentrates on judgments of acceptable risk for consumers, workers, investors, and the environment. We focus more on the responsibilities of business and methods for reducing risk and less on the nature and types of harm caused. These risk-reduction methods include disclosure of information about risks as well as risk-reduction techniques.

Nature and Types of Risk

The Nature of Harm. Competing conceptions of harm exist, but Joel Feinberg has supplied this useful working definition:

> [Interests] can be blocked or defeated by events in impersonal nature or by plain bad luck. But they can only be "invaded" by human beings, . . . singly, or in groups and organizations. . . . One person harms another in the present sense, then, by invading, and thereby thwarting or setting back, his interest. The test . . . of whether such an invasion has in fact set back an interest is whether that interest is in a worse condition than it would otherwise have been in had the invasion not occurred at all. . . . Not all invasions of interest are wrongs, since some actions invade another's interests excusably or justifiably, or invade interests that the other has no right to have respected.[1]

Causing a setback to interests in health, financial goals, or the environment can constitute a harm without necessarily being an unjustifiable harm. Almost everyone would agree that harming another person's interests is blameworthy if the harm results in little compensating benefit and if the damage could easily be avoided. But people rarely, if ever, experience such a clear and uncomplicated scenario. Benefits that offset risk usually exist, and the risk of harm is often expensive to eliminate or control. Some heated debates over products that appeared to be harmful — for example, presweetened children's cereals — have shown that they also create benefits. In the workplace it has become increasingly difficult simply to banish dangerous chemicals that provide major social benefits. In each case their risks must be weighed against their benefits.

Kinds of Risk.   Different kinds of risk raise distinct issues. For example, risks of psychological harm, physical harm, legal harm, and economic harm require different analyses and different remedies. Some representative risks pertinent to the material in this chapter are the following:

Risks to Consumers (and Their Families)
Prepared foods (increased fat and sugar)
Drugs (side effects such as gastrointestinal bleeding)
Cigarettes (lung cancer)

Risks to Workers (and Their Families)
Benzene (leukemia)
Asbestos (asbestosis)
Lead (impairment of reproductive capacities)

Risks to the Public and the Environment
Coal-dust emissions (respiratory complications)
Carbon and other fuel emissions (respiratory complications)
Toxic chemicals (genetic defects)

Risks to Investors
Savings accounts (decline in the rate of return)
Stocks (decline of principal)
Real estate (loss of liquidity)

Problems of Risk Assessment.   It is difficult for society to adequately grasp the extent of the risks inherent in thousands of toxic chemicals, foods, drugs, energy sources, machines, and environmental emissions. Some conditions have serious, irreversible consequences; others do not. Moreover, the *probability* of exposure to a risk may be known with some precision, whereas virtually nothing may be known about the harm's *magnitude,* or the magnitude may be precisely expressible, whereas the probability remains too indefinite to be calculated accurately. "Wild guess" sometimes best describes the accuracy with which physical and chemical risks may be determined, for example, for a worker who constantly changes locations, who works with multiple toxic substances, and whose physical problems can be attributed in part to factors independent of the workplace, such as smoking.

Product Safety and Risk to Consumers

We all consume products that carry minor, significant, or unknown risks. No household is complete without several dozen potentially hazardous products, including ovens, electrical lines, furniture cleaners, spray paints, insecticides, medicines, and video display terminals. Millions of people in North America are the victims of household and office accidents involving these products every year, and more of our young people die from failures and accidents involving products than from disease. Thousands of lawsuits are filed by businesses against other businesses each year because of product failure, hazard, and harm, and there are related problems about deceptive marketing practices and inadequate warranties.

Some responsibility for the occurrence of these harms rests primarily on the consumer, who may carelessly use products or fail to read clearly written instructions. However, some risks can be described as inherent in the product: a cautious and reasonable judgment of acceptable risk has been made that the product cannot be made less risky without unduly increasing cost or limiting use. Still other problems of risk derive from use of cheap materials, careless design, poor construction, or new discovery about risk in an already marketed product.

Disclosure of Risk Information.   A consumer presumably controls what to purchase, because the seller must satisfy consumers or fail to sell the product and be driven from the market; yet serious questions exist about whether the information supplied to the consumer is adequate for making an informed and free choice. For example, is a customer told how a kerosene heater should be cleaned and stored and how often new filters should be installed? Are the side effects of a drug disclosed when a prescription is filled? Sellers may list only a minimal set of facts about known hazards, especially regarding technologically advanced products, because a seller attempts to sell in the most cost-effective manner. Disclosure of risk information costs money and adversely affects sales. Thus, the seller has an economic incentive to keep disclosure to a selective minimum.

These topics of disclosure and understanding have been under intense discussion in recent years. By the late 1970s a major right-to-know movement had taken hold in consumer affairs and in the U.S. workplace. Numerous laws were passed, notably the Consumer Product Safety Act of 1972, to protect consumers by setting safety standards, examining consumer product marketing, providing more adequate risk information, and upgrading the quality of warranty statements.

Product Safety and Quality Control.   Quality control supplements disclosure of risk information as a strategy to protect consumers. Corporations such as Johns Manville (asbestos), A. H. Robins (the Dalkon Shield), and Dow-Corning (silicone breast implants) have faced massive product liability judgments. Although higher standards of quality control would presumably protect manufacturers as well as customers, both theoretical and practical problems exist in establishing and enforcing such standards. Consumer protection methods incur significant costs that increase product price and frequently force companies to abandon the market. For example, some lawn mower prices almost doubled after the introduction of new safety requirements, with the result that several companies floundered. Liberty issues are also at stake. For instance, the freedom to put a new "junk food" on the market might be jeopardized (in theory, the freedom to produce junk foods would be eliminated), and the freedom to buy cheap, substandard products would be lost (because they could not be marketed).

These quality control controversies raise questions about liability and manufacturer warranties, discussed in this chapter in *Henningsen* v. *Bloomfield Motors and Chrysler Corporation*. In this case, the court held both Chrysler and the car dealer liable for an injury caused by a defective steering gear, without finding any evidence of negligence. The court argued that an implied warranty of suitability for use is owed the purchaser and contended that a major assumption behind free-market "contracting" or bargaining among equals can be questioned when products prove to be defective. Because the *Henningsen* case cast doubt on the efficacy of disclaimers by manufacturers, it quickly came to be applied to many products, including glass doors, guns, and stoves.

Manuel G. Velasquez considers in his essay how to differentiate between the obligations of consumers to themselves and the obligations of manufacturers to consumers. He distinguishes three theories of business obligations, showing that each strikes a different balance between consumer and manufacturer obligations. The first theory rests on an account of the social contract between consumers and business (under which Velasquez cites *Henningsen* as a classic example), and the second provides a theory of due care. The third theory presents an account of strict liability, a discussion of which follows.

Liability for Harm.   Two tests affecting liability are that professionals should conform to the minimally acceptable professional standards and that they should perform any actions that a reasonably prudent person would perform in the circumstances. Sometimes, even when the utmost care has been exercised, an accident, lack of information, or lack of documents might still cause harm. However, if due care has been exercised to make a product safe (and affected parties have been apprised of known risks), it would appear that a business is not at fault for any harm caused, even if the business helped bring about the harm.

This rule suggests that a manufacturer can be held liable for unsafe or inefficacious products or unsafe workplaces only if the manufacturer knew or *should have known* about the risks involved. However, difficulties arise regarding what an employer or manufacturer "should have known." A product or technique may be so thoroughly researched and thus delayed that the time involved will ensure a manufacturer's loss rather than profit. Should businesses be held to this kind of economic risk? If so, how can it be determined that enough research and development had been carried out? Can the problem be handled through adequate insurance? Or is a modified conception of liability needed?

Some argue that manufacturers should be held liable not only to a standard of prudent behavior but also to a stronger standard: liability for injuries caused to parties by defects in the manufacturing process, even if the manufacturer exercised due diligence and still could not have reasonably foreseen the problem. This principle is referred to as *strict product liability*, that is, liability without fault. Here questions of good faith, negligence, and absence of knowledge are not pertinent to a determination of liability. The advocates of this no-fault principle use primarily utilitarian arguments. They maintain that manufacturers are in the best position to pay and recover the costs of injury because they can pass the costs on through the product's price and, moreover, will have the added benefit of increasing manufacturers' objectivity, diligence, and prudence before marketing a product. This argument constitutes a shift from the traditional doctrine of "let the buyer beware" (*caveat emptor*) to "let the seller beware."

This utilitarian justification is controversial and is assessed in this chapter by George G. Brenkert, who thinks it more important to ask whether strict liability conforms to principles of justice, and in particular, whether it is just to ask manufacturers to bear the cost of injury merely because they are in the best position to do so. Brenkert maintains that in a free market society it is just to use strict liability because it is essential to maintain a consumer's equal opportunity to function.

Protecting Investors Against Risk

Many of the problems regarding risk of economic harm to consumers apply equally well to investors. At issue is a complex set of relationships encompassing problems of conflict of interest as well as problems of deception and manipulation through improper disclosures. Brokerage houses, money managers, and investment counselors demand as much freedom as possible to deal with their clients. The time spent making disclosures to customers is uncompensated and restricted by business requirements. Brokers with a large client base often do not adequately grasp the risk attached to the financial instruments they sell. Monitoring systems are usually loose, and direct supervisors do not closely track how investments are sold or which, if any, disclosures are made to clients. For example, Paine Webber, Inc., was fined $900,000 by the New York Stock Exchange in early 1992 for ignoring these problems and allowing its brokers to make hundreds of overly risky recommendations to customers.

Small investors who use brokerage houses and banks usually do not have the same access to relevant information that is available to professional investors. Amateur investors, not having such information, can only hope that their brokers are well informed or that the market price already reflects the relevant information. Even if brokers are sufficiently informed, the house policy may be more aggressive and thus may introduce more risk than the average customer wishes. For example, the firm may be primarily interested in limited partnerships in real estate, fully margined common stock, futures and commodities, and oil and gas drilling partnerships, rather than the more mundane unit investment trusts, certificates of deposit, and municipal bonds that a particular customer needs.

A broker has little incentive to match client needs with investments aside from the desire to maintain a business relationship. Although brokerage firms often advertise a full range of products and free financial planning by experts, brokers dislike financial planning per se, because it requires a heavy investment of time and carries no commission. They also dislike pedestrian forms of investing such as certificates of deposit and no-load mutual funds. Riskier investments generally carry higher commissions, and brokerage houses typically give brokers complete discretion to recommend a range of investments to their clients. At the same time, brokers are skillfully taught to be salespersons, to avoid lengthy phone calls, and to flatter clients who pride themselves on making their own decisions. In some firms brokers are taught to make recommendations to clients based primarily on the commission. Consequently, brokers are motivated to sell risky and complicated forms of investment to unsuspecting clients.

An inherent conflict of interest troubles many industry critics. The broker has a fiduciary responsibility to make recommendations based on the client's financial best interest, but the broker is also a salesperson who makes a living by selling securities and who is obligated to maximize profits for the brokerage house. The more trades that are made, the better it is for the broker, but this rule seldom works to the client's advantage. Commissions are an ever-present temptation influencing a recommendation, and the structure of incentives drives up the risk for the client.

The law requires securities firms to disclose commissions to clients. However, statistics on the full range of fees involved in many instruments are rarely mentioned to clients. When available, the figures are often buried beneath a pile of information in a thick prospectus that clients do not read prior to a purchase. Most clients do not obtain the prospectus until after the purchase, which often places no dollar figure on the commission. Brokers are not required to disclose commissions in advance of a sale to clients, nor are they required to disclose that they are given additional, expensive free vacations for selling large numbers of certain mutual funds. Moreover, clients rarely ask about the commission amount or the range of fees, not because of lack of interest, but because they fear that the inquiry might harm their relationship with the broker.

The U.S. Securities and Exchange Commission (SEC) was created by the Securities Exchange Act of 1933 to regulate a wide variety of manipulative stock practices. Although sensitive to issues such as insider trading, the SEC does not set ceilings on commissions and does not require brokers to receive written consent from clients prior to purchase. The SEC occasionally determines that a brokerage house's markup is so high that the commission amounts to fraud, but these cases are rare.

In recent years ethical brokerage houses have increasingly realized that tighter SEC control and a more developed sense of moral responsibility may serve their best interest. Ethical lapses are so common to the financial markets that the whole industry has been tarred with the brush of greed. Many reformers who lack an adequate understanding of the industry have introduced new legislation in order to control the industry more tightly. Although significant reforms are beginning to emerge, their outline is not yet clear.

One proposal for protecting investors, which is seriously considered in this chapter's essay by Robert E. Frederick and W. Michael Hoffman, is that the at-risk investor be denied access to securities markets to safeguard the investor from financial harm. They argue that restricting access to markets is justified only in cases in which the right not to be harmed by exposure to excessive risk is being protected. In a second article, Robert F. Bruner and Lynn Sharp Paine argue that the managers' fiduciary obligations to shareholders are jeopardized in a circumstance of management buyouts. These managers have an obligation to maximize the shareholders' interest by keeping the price high, but they have a strong incentive to negotiate a low price on their own behalf, thereby minimizing shareholders' interests. Buyouts place investors at the risk of having managers who might take advantage of shareholders through their superior knowledge and control over information and by an intentional understatement of the stock's value. The authors note that the management buyout functions to undermine shareholder trust in corporate leadership, and yet buyouts often present shareholders with a rich opportunity to protect their investments and sell at the highest possible price. Bruner and Paine argue for standards whereby a buyout offer should at least equal the value shareholders could achieve on their own. Such standards, they maintain, protect the at-risk investor and satisfy management's fiduciary obligations to shareholders.

Worker Safety, Occupational Risk, and the Right to Know

Critics of business and government have long contended that uninformed workers are routinely, and often knowingly, exposed to dangerous conditions. For example, employers did not tell asbestos workers for many years of the known dangers of contracting asbestosis. Although little is currently understood about the knowledge and comprehension of workers, evidence from at least some industries shows that ignorance is a causal factor in occupational illness or injury. The simplest solution is to ban hazardous products from use, but to do so would be to shut down a large segment of industrial manufacturing. Hundreds of products still contain asbestos either because no functional substitute is available or replacement is not cost efficient.

The implications of worker ignorance are chillingly present in the following worker's testimony before an Occupational Safety and Health Administration (OSHA) hearing on the toxic agent DBCP:

> We had no warning that DBCP exposure might cause sterility, testicular atrophy, and perhaps cancer. If we had known that these fumes could possibly cause the damage that we have found out it probably does cause, we would have worn equipment to protect ourselves. As it was, we didn't have enough knowledge to give us the proper respect for DBCP.[2]

The regulation of workplace risks has consistently sought to determine an objective level of acceptable risk and then to ban or limit exposure above that level. However, the goal of safety is not the primary justification for disclosures of risk. Individuals need the information upon which the objective standard is based to determine whether the risk it declares acceptable is *acceptable to them*. Here a subjective standard of acceptable risk seems more appropriate than an objective standard established by "experts." Choosing to risk testicular atrophy seems rightly a worker's personal choice, one not fully decidable by health and safety standards established for groups of workers. Even given objective standards, substantial ambiguity prevails when the experts are uncertain about the risks and dangerous dose levels cannot be established.

Problems also surface about both the strategy of information disclosure and the strategy of protective schemes if either is used in isolation. Often there are no meaningful figures to define the relationship between acceptable risk and the ease with which the risk can be eliminated or controlled. There also may be no consensus about which levels of probability of serious harm, such as death, constitute risks sufficiently high to require that steps be taken to reduce or eliminate the risk or to provide information to those affected.

Both the employer's responsibility to inform employees and the employee's right to refuse hazardous job assignments are the concern of the essay by Ruth Faden and Tom L. Beauchamp. They support a standard of information disclosure and consider three possible standards for determining the justifiability of a refusal to work or of a safety walkout. In a second essay in this section, Thomas O. McGarity focuses on the worker's right to receive information from employers and the effectiveness of the current system. He maintains that the right to know is actually an agglomeration of several rights, which impose correlative duties on employers. Also included in the legal perspectives section of this chapter is the case of *Automobile Workers v. Johnson Controls, Inc.*, which determined that employers cannot legally adopt "fetal protection policies" that exclude women of childbearing age from a hazardous workplace, because such policies involve illegal sex discrimination. However, the Supreme Court decision was, in some respects, narrow; it left U.S. corporations in uncertainty over an acceptable policy for protecting fetuses from reproductive hazards.

Risk to the Environment and Health

Controversy over protecting the environment and preventing the depletion of natural resources has mushroomed in the last four decades, a period that has caught business, government, and the general public unprepared to handle environmental problems. In the 1960s and 1970s, the government first instituted regulatory programs, and ever since the public has become increasingly concerned about the environmental impact of chemical dumping, supersonic transport, burning coal, nuclear power, oil spills, and the like. In this debate, environmental deterioration is often linked to corporate actions, and thus corporate responsibility has become a major issue.

Environmental issues have traditionally been conceived in free-market terms: Natural resources are available to entrepreneurs who are free to purchase and use them. Markets transfer resources and rules of private property and free choice allow use of the environment to maximize profits. Conflicts were handled by relatively simple procedures that balanced conflicting interests. Those who polluted, for example, could be prosecuted and fined. People assumed that the environment, once properly tended to, was sufficiently resilient to return to its former state.

Recently, this optimistic outlook has been vigorously challenged. First, it became apparent that a market conception of resource use did not fit the environment, because air, water, and much of the land environment is owned in common, and their value is not determined by prices in the market. Also, new technology and increased production now appear to have damaged the environment to a point at which unrectifiable and uncontrollable global imbalances may emerge. Yet, corporations still "externalize" rather than internalize costs by passing on the costs of pollution to the public. Attempts to bring market "externalities" such as pollution into standard pricing mechanisms — by, for instance, taxing effluents — have generally proved to be inadequate in handling environmental problems.

Some writers depict the environment as analogous to a common rangeland where competing cattle ranchers graze so many cattle in search of profits (as it is economically rational for each cattle rancher to do) that eventually the common land is overgrazed and can no longer support animal life. As businesspersons pursue their economic interests, collectively they work toward the ruin of all humanity. This analysis has been disputed by those who see environmental problems as involving tradeoffs that need not do irreversible damage to "the commons." However, society acknowledges that some tradeoffs will require additional tradeoffs that may only mortgage the future. For example, air-pollution scrubbers used in industry to remove sulfur dioxide from flue gas produce three to six tons of sludge for every ton of sulfur dioxide they remove. The sludge is then buried in landfills, creating a risk of water pollution. Efforts to clean the air thereby risk polluting the water.

Classic conflicts between public and private interests have emerged in these environmental debates. For example, there have been attempts to show that fluorocarbons in aerosol spray cans so badly damage the earth's ozone shield that serious repercussions may occur from continued use — for example, melting the polar ice caps, flooding the cities along the world's coasts, and producing radioactive contamination. Critics have charged that the food industry rapes the land by its failure to balance high-level methods of food production with the land's lower-level production capacity. Environmentalists have accused the timber industry of deforestation without replenishment. Responsibility for various forms of pollution has been attributed to bottle and can industries, plastics industries, smelters, chemical industries, and the oil industry. In recent years industrial disposal of hazardous wastes, including mercury, benzene, and dioxin, has been condemned because of the contamination of groundwater, landfills, and even waste recovery plants.

Those who promote a new environmental ethic argue that western culture has a special problem because of entrenched attitudes about the use of nature for human enjoyment and betterment. Within this conception, humans live not as part of the ecosystem but as external dwellers. Others argue, however, that people should view the environment in a different way only to the extent that doing so would improve the quality of life and continued existence. They maintain that environmental concerns are valid only if they improve the human situation and not because animals, plants, or ecosystems have rights. This approach emphasizes the freedom of businesses to use the environment unless their activities harm other individuals in society.

Many now believe that only severe curbs on industry and severe judicial penalties will protect the environment, whereas others believe that environmental impact statements and various now-standard practices are sufficient. The core of the environmental problem is how to balance the liberty rights of those who want to use the environment in typical free-market style with the rights of those who want safe workplaces, safe products, and the right to a contamination-free environment.

Three readings in this chapter examine these problems of environmental risk and protection. The article by Richard T. De George deals with the complexities present in cases of corporate pollution. He explores a range of issues about environmental responsibility and the conflicting principles at work. In the end, he offers three practical and "justified" approaches to "ethically handling" corporate pollution. In the ensuing article, R. Edward Freeman, Jessica Pierce, and Richard Dodd are concerned with moral problems centering on how corporations can protect the environment and still make money. They are interested in a framework for thinking about environmental harm that allows both goals to "work together." They argue that businesses can, in their core values and commitments, stand for more than profits. Some of these values, they maintain, can be based on "green principles."

Finally, the Supreme Court of the United States, in the 1998 case of *U.S. v. Bestfoods et al.*, deals with the issue of whether a parent corporation may be held liable for the polluting activities of one of its subsidiaries. The court maintains that liability depends on the level of active participation and control by the corporation, especially where wrongful purposes are involved (most notably fraud). This opinion explores several levels of corporate responsibility to avoid disposal of hazardous materials. The court notes that the language of the laws is plain about corporate responsibility, but "the difficulty comes in defining actions sufficient to constitute direct parental 'operation'."

NOTES

1. Joel Feinberg, *Harm to Others* (New York: Oxford University Press, 1984), pp. 34–35.
2. Occupational Safety and Health Administration, "Access to Employee Exposure and Medical Records — Final Rules," *Federal Register* (May 23, 1980), p. 35222.

CONSUMER RISK

The Ethics of Consumer Production

Manuel G. Velasquez

Where . . . do the consumer's duties to protect his or her own interests end, and where does the manufacturer's duty to protect consumers' interests begin? Three different theories on the ethical duties of manufacturers have been developed, each one of which strikes a different balance between the consumer's duty to himself or herself and the manufacturer's duty to the consumer: the contract view, the "due care" view, and the social costs view. The contract view would place the greater responsibility on the consumer, while the "due care" and social costs views place the larger measure of responsibility on the manufacturer. We will examine each of these views.

THE CONTRACT VIEW OF BUSINESS'S DUTIES TO CONSUMERS

According to the contract view of the business firm's duties to its customers, the relationship between a business firm and its customers is essentially a contractual relationship, and the firm's moral duties to the customer are those created by this contractual relationship.[1] When a consumer buys a product, this view holds, the consumer voluntarily enters into a "sales contract" with the business firm. The firm freely and knowingly agrees to give the consumer a product with certain characteristics and the consumer in turn freely and knowingly agrees to pay a certain sum of money to the firm for the product. In virtue of having voluntarily entered this agreement, the firm then has a duty to provide a product with those characteristics, and the consumer has a correlative right to get a product with those characteristics. . . .

Traditional moralists have argued that the act of entering into a contract is subject to several secondary moral constraints:

1. Both of the parties to the contract must have full knowledge of the nature of the agreement they are entering.
2. Neither party to a contract must intentionally misrepresent the facts of the contractual situation to the other party.
3. Neither party to a contract must be forced to enter the contract under duress or undue influence.

These secondary constraints can be justified by the same sorts of arguments that Kant and Rawls use to justify the basic duty to perform one's contracts. Kant, for example, easily shows that misrepresentation in the making of a contract cannot be universalized, and Rawls argues that if misrepresentation were not prohibited, fear of deception would make members of a society feel less free to enter contracts. But these secondary constraints can also be justified on the grounds that a contract cannot exist unless these constraints are fulfilled. For a contract is essentially a *free agreement* stuck between two parties. Since an agreement cannot exist unless both parties know what they are agreeing to, contracts require full knowledge and the absence of misrepresentation. And since freedom implies the absence of coercion, contracts must be made without duress or undue influence.

The contractual theory of business's duties to consumers, then, claims that a business has four main moral duties: The basic duty of (1) complying with the terms of the sales contract, and the secondary duties of (2) disclosing the nature of the product, (3) avoiding misrepresentation, and (4) avoiding the use of duress and undue influence. By acting in accordance with these duties, a business respects the right of consumers to be treated as free and equal persons, that is, in accordance with their right to be treated only as they have freely consented to be treated.

The Duty to Comply

The most basic moral duty that a business firm owes its customers, according to the contract view, is the duty to provide consumers with a product that lives up to those claims that the firm expressly made about the product, which led the customer to enter the contract freely, and which formed the customer's understanding concerning what he or she was agreeing to buy. In the early 1970s, for example, Winthrop Laboratories marketed a pain-killer that the firm advertised as "nonaddictive." Subsequently, a patient using the painkiller became addicted to it and shortly thereafter died from an overdose. A court in 1974 found Winthrop Laboratories liable for the patient's death because, although it had expressly stated that the drug was nonaddictive, Winthrop Laboratories had failed to live up to its duty to comply with this express contractual claim.[2]

As the above example suggests, our legal system has incorporated the moral view that firms have a duty to live up to the express claims they make about their products. The Uniform Commercial Code, for example, states in Section 2-314:

> Any affirmation of fact or promise made by the seller to the buyer that related to the goods and becomes part of the basis of the bargain creates an express warranty that the goods shall conform to the affirmation or promise.

In addition to the duties that result from the *express* claim a seller makes about the product, the contract view also holds that the seller has a duty to carry through on any *implied* claims he or she knowingly makes about the product. The seller, for example, has the moral duty to provide a product that can be used safely for the ordinary and special purposes for which the customer, relying on the seller's judgment, has been led to believe it can be used. . . .

The express or implied claims that a seller might make about the qualities possessed by the product range over a variety of areas and are affected by a number of factors. Frederick Sturdivant classifies these areas in terms of four variables: "The definition of product quality used here is: the degree to which product performance meets predetermined expectation with respect to (1) reliability, (2) service life, (3) maintainability, and (4) safety."[3]

Reliability. Claims of reliability refer to the probability that a product will function as the consumer is led to expect that it will function. If a product incorporates a number of interdependent components, then the probability that it will function properly is equal to the result of multiplying together each component's probability of proper functioning.[4] As the number of components in a product multiplies, therefore, the manufacturer has a corresponding duty to ensure that each component functions in such a manner that the total product is as reliable as he or she implicitly or expressly claims it will be. This is especially the case when malfunction poses health or safety hazards. The U.S. Consumer Product Safety Commission lists hundreds of examples of hazards from product malfunctions in its yearly report.[5]

Service Life.   Claims concerning the life of a product refer to the period of time during which the product will function as effectively as the consumer is led to expect it to function. Generally, the consumer implicitly understands that service life will depend on the amount of wear and tear to which one subjects the product. In addition, consumers also base some of their expectations of service life on the explicit guarantees the manufacturer attaches to the product.

A more subtle factor that influences service life is the factor of obsolescence.[6] Technological advances may render some products obsolete when a new product appears that carries out the same functions more efficiently. Or purely stylistic changes may make last year's product appear dated and less desirable. The contract view implies that a seller who knows that a certain product will become obsolete has a duty to correct any mistaken beliefs he or she knows buyers will form concerning the service life they may expect from the product.

Maintainability.   Claims of maintainability are claims concerning the ease with which the product can be repaired and kept in operating condition. Claims of maintainability are often made in the form of an express warranty. Whirlpool Corporation, for example, appended this express warranty on one of its products:

> During your first year of ownership, all parts of the appliance (except the light bulbs) that we find are defective in materials or workmanship

will be repaired or replaced by Whirlpool free of charge, and we will pay all labor charges. During the second year, we will continue to assume the same responsibility as stated above except you pay any labor charges.[7]

But sellers often also imply that a product may be easily repaired even after the expiration date of an express warranty. In fact, however, product repairs may be costly, or even impossible, due to the unavailability of parts.

Product Safety.   Implied and express claims of product safety refer to the degree of risk associated with using a product. Since the use of virtually any product involves some degree of risk, questions of safety are essentially questions of *acceptable known levels* of risk. That is, a product is safe if its attendant risks are known and judged to be "acceptable" or "reasonable" by the *buyer* in view of the benefits the buyer expects to derive from using the product. This implies that the seller complies with his or her part of a free agreement if the seller provides a product that involves only those risks he or she says it involves, and the buyer purchases it with that understanding. The National Commission on Product Safety, for example, characterized "reasonable risk" in these terms:

> Risks of bodily harm to users are not unreasonable when consumers understand that risks exist, can appraise their probability and severity, know how to cope with them, and voluntarily accept them to get benefits they could not obtain in less risky ways. When there is a risk of this character, consumers have reasonable opportunity to protect themselves; and public authorities should hesitate to substitute their value judgments about the desirability of the risk for those of the consumers who choose to incur it. But preventable risk is not reasonable (a) when consumers do not know that it exists; or (b) when, though aware of it, consumers are unable to estimate its frequency and severity; or (c) when consumers do not know how to cope with it, and hence are likely to incur harm

unnecessarily; or (d) when risk is unnecessary in that it could be reduced or eliminated at a cost in money or in the performance of the product that consumers would willingly incur if they knew the facts and were given the choice.[8]

Thus the seller of a product (according to the contractual theory) has a moral duty to provide a product whose use involves *no greater risks* than those the seller *expressly* communicates to the buyer or those the seller *implicitly* communicates by the implicit claims made when marketing the product for a use whose normal risk level is well known. . . .

The Duty of Disclosure

An agreement cannot bind unless both parties to the agreement know what they are doing and freely choose to do it. This implies that the seller who intends to enter a contract with a customer has a duty to disclose exactly what the customer is buying and what the terms of the sale are. At a minimum, this means the seller has a duty to inform the buyer of any facts about the product that would affect the customer's decision to purchase the product. For example, if the product the consumer is buying possesses a defect that poses a risk to the user's health or safety, the consumer should be so informed. Some have argued that sellers should also disclose a product's components or ingredients, its performance characteristics, costs of operation, product ratings, and any other applicable standards.[9]

Behind the claim that entry into a sales contract requires full disclosure is the idea that an agreement is free only to the extent that one knows what alternatives are available: Freedom depends on knowledge. The more the buyer knows about the various products available on the market and the more comparisons the buyer is able to make

among them, the more one can say that the buyer's agreement is voluntary. . . . [10]

Since entry into a contract requires *freely* given consent, the seller has a duty to refrain from exploiting emotional states that may induce the buyer to act irrationally against his or her own best interests. For similar reasons, the seller also has the duty not to take advantage of gullibility, immaturity, ignorance, or any other factors that reduce or eliminate the buyer's ability to make free rational choices.

Problems with the Contractual Theory

The main objections to the contract theory focus on the unreality of the assumptions on which the theory is based. First, critics argue, the theory unrealistically assumes that manufacturers make direct agreements with consumers. Nothing could be farther from the truth. Normally, a series of wholesalers and retailers stand between the manufacturer and the ultimate consumer. The manufacturer sells the product to the wholesaler, who sells it to the retailer, who finally sells it to the consumer. The manufacturer never enters into any direct contract with the consumer. How then can one say that manufacturers have contractual duties to the consumer?

Advocates of the contract view of manufacturers' duties have tried to respond to this criticism by arguing that manufacturers enter into "indirect" agreements with consumers. Manufacturers promote their products through their own advertising campaigns. These advertisements supply the promises that lead people to purchase products from retailers who merely function as "conduits" for the manufacturer's product. Consequently, through these advertisements, the manufacturer forges an indirect contractual relationship not only with the immediate retailers who purchase the manufacturer's product but also with the ultimate consumers of the product. The most famous application of this doctrine of broadened indirect contractual relationships is to be found in a 1960 court opinion, *Henningsen v. Bloomfield Motors.*[11]. . .

A second objection to the contract theory focuses on the fact that a contract is a double-edged sword. If a consumer can freely agree to buy a product *with* certain qualities, the consumer can also freely agree to buy a product *without* those qualities. That is, freedom of contract allows a manufacturer to be released from his or her contractual obligations by explicitly *disclaiming* that the product is reliable, serviceable, safe, etc. Many manufacturers fix such disclaimers on their products. . . . The contract view, then, implies that if the consumer has ample opportunity to examine the product and the disclaimers and voluntarily consents to buy it anyway, he or she assumes the responsibility for the defects disclaimed by the manufacturer, as well as for any defects the customer may carelessly have overlooked. Disclaimers can effectively nullify all contractual duties of the manufacturer.

A third objection to the contract theory criticizes the assumption that buyer and seller meet each other as equals in the sales agreement. The contractual theory assumes that buyers and sellers are equally skilled at evaluating the quality of a product and that buyers are able to adequately protect their interests against the seller. . . . In practice, this laissez faire ideology gave birth to the doctrine of "caveat emptor": let the buyer take care of himself.

In fact, sellers and buyers do not exhibit the equality these doctrines assume. A consumer who must purchase hundreds of different kinds of commodities cannot hope to be as knowledgeable as a manufacturer who specializes in producing a single product. Consumers have neither the expertise nor the time to acquire and process the information on which they must base their purchase decisions. Consumers, as a consequence, must usually rely on the judgment of the seller in making their purchase decisions, and are particularly vulnerable to being harmed by the seller. Equality, far from being the rule, as the contract theory assumes, is usually the exception.

THE DUE CARE THEORY

The "due care" theory of the manufacturer's duties to consumers is based on the idea that consumers and sellers do not meet as equals and that the consumer's interests are particularly vulnerable to being harmed by the manufacturer who has a knowledge and an expertise that the consumer does not have. Because manufacturers are in a more advantaged position, they have a duty to take special "care" to ensure that consumers' interests are not harmed by the products that they offer them. The doctrine of "caveat emptor" is here replaced with a weak version of the doctrine of "caveat vendor": let the seller take care. . . .

The "due care" view holds, then, that because consumers must depend upon the greater expertise of the manufacturer, the manufacturer not only has a duty to deliver a product that lives up to the express and implied claims about it, but in addition the manufacturer has a duty to exercise due care to prevent others from being injured by the product, *even if the manufacturer explicitly disclaims such responsibility and the buyer agrees to the disclaimer.* The manufacturer violates this duty and is "negligent" when there is a failure to exercise the care that a reasonable person could have foreseen would be necessary to prevent others from being harmed by use of the product. Due care must enter into the design of the product, into the choice of reliable materials for constructing the product, into the manufacturing processes involved in putting the product together, into the quality control used to test and monitor production, and into the warnings, labels, and instructions attached to the product. In each of these areas, according to the due care view, the manufacturer, in virtue of a greater expertise and knowledge, has a positive duty to take whatever steps are necessary to ensure that when the product leaves the plant it is as safe as possible, and the customer has a right to such assurance. Failure to take such steps is a breach of the moral duty to exercise due care and a violation of the injured person's right to expect such care, a right that rests on the consumer's need to rely on the manufacturer's expertise. . . .

The Duty to Exercise Due Care

According to the due care theory, manufacturers exercise sufficient care when they take adequate steps to prevent whatever injurious effects they can foresee that the use of their product may have on consumers after having conducted inquiries into the way the product will be used and after having attempted to anticipate any possible misuses of the product. A manufacturer, then, is *not* morally negligent when others are harmed by a product and the harm was not one that the manufacturer could possibly have foreseen or prevented. Nor is a manufacturer morally negligent after having taken all reasonable steps to protect the consumer and to ensure that the consumer is informed of any irremovable risks that might still attend the use of the product. A car manufacturer, for example, cannot be said to be negligent from a moral point of view when people carelessly misuse the cars the manufacturer produces. A car manufacturer would be morally negligent only if the manufacturer had allowed unreasonable dangers to remain in the design of the car that consumers cannot

be expected to know about or that they cannot guard against by taking their own precautionary measures.

What specific responsibilities does the duty to exercise due care impose on the producer? In general, the producer's responsibilities would extend to three areas:

Design. The manufacturer should ascertain whether the design of an article conceals any dangers, whether it incorporates all feasible safety devices, and whether it uses materials that are adequate for the purposes the product is intended to serve. The manufacturer is responsible for being thoroughly acquainted with the design of the item, and to conduct research and tests extensive enough to uncover any risks that may be involved in employing the article under various conditions of use. . . .

Production. The production manager should control the manufacturing processes to eliminate any defective items, to identify any weaknesses that become apparent during production, and to ensure that short-cuts, substitution of weaker materials, or other economizing measures are not taken during manufacture that would compromise the safety of the final product. To ensure this, there should be adequate quality controls over materials that are to be used in the manufacture of the product and over the various stages of manufacture.

Information. The manufacturer should fix labels, notices, or instructions on the product that will warn the user of all dangers involved in using or misusing the item and that will enable the user to adequately guard himself or herself against harm or injury. These instructions should be clear and simple, and warnings of any hazards involved in using or misusing the product should also be clear, simple, and prominent. . . .

Problems with "Due Care"

The basic difficulty raised by the "due care" theory is that there is no clear method for determining when one has exercised enough "due care." That is, there is no hard and fast rule for determining how far a firm must go to ensure the safety of its product. Some authors have proposed the general utilitarian rule that the greater the probability of harm and the larger the population that might be harmed, the more the firm is obligated to do. But this fails to resolve some important issues. Every product involves at least some small risk of injury. If the manufacturer should try to eliminate even low-level risks, this would require that the manufacturer invest so much in each product that the product would be priced out of the reach of most consumers. Moreover, even *attempting* to balance higher risks against added costs involves measurement problems: How does one quantify risks to health and life?

A second difficulty raised by the "due care" theory is that it assumes that the manufacturer can discover the risks that attend the use of a product before the consumer buys and uses it. In fact, in a technologically innovative society new products whose defects cannot emerge until years or decades have passed will continually be introduced into the market. Only years after thousands of people were using and being exposed to asbestos, for example, did a correlation emerge between the incidence of cancer and exposure to asbestos. Although manufacturers may have greater expertise than consumers, their expertise does not make them omniscient. Who, then, is to bear the costs of injuries sustained from products whose defects neither the manufacturer nor the consumer could have uncovered beforehand?

Thirdly, the due care view appears to some to be paternalistic for it assumes that the *manufacturer* should be the one who makes the important decisions for the consumer, at least

with respect to the levels of risks that are proper for consumers to bear. But one may wonder whether such decisions should not be left up to the free choice of consumers who can decide for themselves whether or not they want to pay for additional risk reduction.

THE SOCIAL COSTS VIEW OF THE MANUFACTURER'S DUTIES

A third theory on the duties of the manufacturer would extend the manufacturer's duties beyond those imposed by contractual relationships and beyond those imposed by the duty to exercise due care in preventing injury or harm. This third theory holds that a manufacturer should pay the costs of any injuries sustained through any defects in the product, *even when the manufacturer exercised all due care in the design and manufacture of the product and has taken all reasonable precautions to warn users of every foreseen danger.* According to this third theory a manufacturer has a duty to assume the risks of even those injuries that arise out of defects in the product that no one could reasonably have foreseen or eliminated. The theory is a very strong version of the doctrine of "caveat vendor": let the seller take care.

This third theory, which has formed the basis of the legal doctrine of "strict liability," is founded on utilitarian arguments. The utilitarian arguments for this third theory hold that the "external" costs of injuries resulting from unavoidable defects in the design of an artifact constitute part of the costs society must pay for producing and using an artifact. By having the manufacturer bear the external costs that result from these injuries as well as the ordinary internal costs of design and manufacture, all costs will be internalized and added on as part of the price of the product. Internalizing all costs in this way, according to proponents of this theory, will lead to a more efficient use of society's resources. First, since the price will reflect *all* the costs of producing and using the artifact, market forces will ensure that the product is not overproduced, and that resources are not wasted on it. (Whereas if some costs were not included in the price, then manufacturers would tend to produce more than is needed.) Second, since manufacturers have to pay the costs of injuries, they will be motivated to exercise greater care and to thereby reduce the number of accidents. Manufacturers will therefore strive to cut down the social costs of injuries, and this means a more efficient care for our human resources. In order to produce the maximum benefits possible from our limited resources, therefore, the social costs of injuries from defective products should be internalized by passing them on to the manufacturer, even when the manufacturer has done all that could be done to eliminate such defects. And third, internalizing the costs of injury in this way enables the manufacturer to distribute losses among all the users of a product instead of allowing losses to fall on individuals who may not be able to sustain the loss by themselves.

Underlying this third theory on the duties of the manufacturer are the standard utilitarian assumptions about the values of efficiency. The theory assumes that an efficient use of resources is so important for society that social costs should be allocated in whatever way will lead to a more efficient use and care of our resources. On this basis, the theory argues that a manufacturer should bear the social costs for injuries caused by defects in a product, even when no negligence was involved and no contractual relationship existed between the manufacturer and the user.

Problems with the Social Costs View

The major criticism of the social costs view of the manufacturer's duties is that it is unfair.[12] It is unfair, the critics charge, because it violates the basic canons of compensatory justice. Compensatory justice implies that a person should be forced to compensate an injured party only if the person could foresee and could have prevented the injury. By forcing manufacturers to pay for injuries that they could neither foresee nor prevent, the social costs theory (and the legal theory of 'strict liability' that flows from it) treats manufacturers unfairly. Moreover, insofar as the social costs theory encourages passing the costs of injuries on to all consumers (in the form of higher prices), consumers are also being treated unfairly.

A second criticism of the social costs theory attacks the assumption that passing the costs of all injuries on to manufacturers will reduce the number of accidents.[13] On the contrary, critics claim, by relieving consumers of the responsibility of paying for their own injuries, the social costs theory will encourage carelessness in consumers. And an increase in consumer carelessness will lead to an increase in consumer injuries.

A third argument against the social costs theory focuses on the financial burdens the theory imposes on manufacturers and insurance carriers. Critics claim that a growing number of consumers successfully sue manufacturers for compensation for any injuries sustained while using a product, even when the manufacturer took all due care to ensure that the product was safe.[14] Not only have the number of "strict liability" suits increased, critics claim, but the amounts awarded to injured consumers have also escalated. Moreover, they continue, the rising costs of the many liability suits that the theory of "strict liability" has created have precipitated a crisis in the insurance industry because insurance companies end up paying the liability suits brought against manufacturers. . . .

The arguments for and against the social costs theory deserve much more discussion than we can give them here. The theory is essentially an attempt to come to grips with the problem of allocating the costs of injuries between two morally innocent parties: The manufacturer who could not foresee or prevent a product-related injury, and the consumer who could not guard himself or herself against the injury because the hazard was unknown. This allocation problem will arise in any society that, like ours, has come to rely upon a technology whose effects do not become evident until years after the technology is introduced. Unfortunately, it is also a problem that may have no "fair" solution.

NOTES

1. See Thomas Garrett and Richard J. Klonoski, *Business Ethics,* 2nd ed. (Englewood Cliffs, NJ: Prentice Hall, 1986), p. 88.

2. *Crocker v. Winthrop Laboratories, Division of Sterling Drug, Inc.,* 514 Southwestern 2d 429 (1974).

3. Frederick D. Sturdivant, *Business and Society,* 3rd ed. (Homewood, IL: Richard D. Irwin, Inc., 1985), p. 392.

4. Ibid., p. 393.

5. U.S. Consumer Products Safety Commission, *1979 Annual Report* (Washington, DC: U.S. Government Printing Office, 1979), pp. 81–101.

6. A somewhat dated but still incisive discussion of this issue is found in Vance Packard, *The Wastemakers* (New York: David McKay Co., Inc., 1960).

7. Quoted in address by S. E. Upton (vice-president of Whirlpool Corporation) to the American Marketing Association in Cleveland, OH: 11 December 1969.

8. National Commission on Product Safety, *Final Report,* quoted in William W. Lowrance, *Of Acceptable Risk* (Los Altos, CA: William Kaufmann, Inc., 1976), p. 80.

9. See Louis Stern, "Consumer Protection via Increased Information," *Journal of Marketing,* 31, no. 2 (April 1967).

10. Lawrence E. Hicks, *Coping with Packaging Laws* (New York: AMACOM, 1972), p. 17.

11. *Henningsen v. Bloomfield Motors, Inc.,* 32 New Jersey 358, 161 Atlantic 2d 69 (1960).

12. George P. Fletcher, "Fairness and Utility in Tort Theory," *Harvard Law Review,* 85, no. 3 (January 1972): 537–73.

13. Posner, *Economic Analysis of Law,* 2nd ed. (Boston: Little, Brown and Co., 1977), pp. 139–42.

14. See "Unsafe Products: The Great Debate Over Blame and Punishment," *Business Week,* 30 April 1984; Stuart Taylor, "Product Liability: the New Morass," *New York Times,* 10 March 1985; "The Product Liability Debate," *Newsweek,* 10 September 1984.

Strict Products Liability and Compensatory Justice

George G. Brenkert

I

Strict products liability is the doctrine that the seller of a product has legal responsibilities to compensate the user of that product for injuries suffered because of a defective aspect of the product, even when the seller has not been negligent in permitting that defect to occur.[1] Thus, even though a manufacturer, for example, has reasonably applied the existing techniques of manufacture and has anticipated and cared for nonintended uses of the product, he may still be held liable for injuries a product user suffers if it can be shown that the product was defective when it left the manufacturer's hands.

To say that there is a crisis today concerning this doctrine would be to utter a commonplace which few in the business community would deny. The development of the doctrine of strict products liability, according to most business people, threatens many businesses financially. Furthermore, strict products liability is said to be a morally questionable doctrine, since the manufacturer or seller has not been negligent in permitting the injury-causing defect to occur. On the other hand, victims of defective products complain that they deserve full compensation for injuries sustained in using a defective product whether or not the seller is at fault. Medical expenses and time lost from one's job are costs no individual should have to bear by himself. It is only fair that the seller share such burdens.

In general, discussions of this crisis focus on the limits to which a business ought to be held responsible. Much less frequently, discussions of strict products liability consider the underlying question of whether the doctrine of strict products liability is rationally justifiable. But unless this question is answered it would seem premature to seek to determine the limits to which businesses ought to be held liable in such cases. In the following paper I discuss this underlying philosophical question and argue that there is a rational justification for strict products liability which links it to the very nature of the free enterprise system.

II

. . . To begin with, it is crucial to remember that what we have to consider is the relationship between an entity doing business and an individual. The strict liability attributed to business would not be attributed to an individual who happened to sell some product he had made to his neighbor or a stranger. If Peter sold an article he had made to Paul and Paul hurt himself because the article had a defect which occurred through no negligence of Peter's, we would not normally hold Peter morally responsible to pay for Paul's injuries. . . .

It is different for businesses. They have been held to be legally and morally obliged to pay the victim for his injuries. Why? What is the difference? The difference is that when Paul is hurt by a defective product from corporation X, he is hurt by something produced in a socioeconomic system purportedly embodying free enterprise. In other words, among other things:

1. Each business and/or corporation produces articles or services it sells for profit.
2. Each member of this system competes with other members of the system in trying to do as well as it can for itself not simply in each exchange, but through each exchange for its other values and desires.
3. Competition is to be "open and free, without deception or fraud."
4. Exchanges are voluntary and undertaken when each party believes it can benefit thereby. One party provides the means for another party's ends if the other party will provide the first party the means to its ends.
5. The acquisition and disposition of ownership rights — that is, of private property — is permitted in such exchanges.
6. No market or series of markets constitutes the whole of a society.
7. Law, morality, and government play a role in setting acceptable limits to the nature and kinds of exchange in which people may engage.

What is it about such a system which would justify claims of strict products liability against businesses? . . . In the free enterprise system, each person and/or business is obligated to follow the rules and understandings which define this socioeconomic system. Following the rules is expected to channel competition among individuals and businesses to socially positive results. In providing the means to fulfill the ends of others, one's own ends also get fulfilled.

Though this does not happen in every case, it is supposed to happen most of the time. Those who fail in their competition with others may be the object of charity, but not of other duties. Those who succeed, qua members of this socioeconomic system, do not have moral duties to aid those who fail. Analogously, the team which loses the game may receive our sympathy but the winning team is not obligated to help it to win the next game or even to play it better. Those who violate the rules, however, may be punished or penalized, whether or not the violation was intentional and whether or not it redounded to the benefit of the violator. Thus, a team may be assessed a penalty for something that a team member did unintentionally to a member of the other team but which injured the other team's chances of competition in the game by violating the rules.

This point may be emphasized by another instance involving a game that brings us close to strict products liability. Imagine that you are playing table tennis with another person in his newly constructed table tennis room. You are both avid table tennis players and the game means a lot to both of you. Suppose that after play has begun, you are suddenly and quite obviously blinded by the light over the table — the light shade has a hole in it which, when it turned in your direction, sent a shaft of light unexpectedly into your eyes. You lose a crucial point as a result. Surely it would be unfair of your opponent to seek to maintain his point because he was faultless — after all, he had not intended to blind you

when he installed that light shade. You would correctly object that he had gained the point unfairly, that you should not have to give up the point lost, and that the light shade should be modified so that the game can continue on a fair basis. It is only fair that the point be played over.

Businesses and their customers in a free enterprise system are also engaged in competition with each other. The competition here, however, is multifaceted as each tries to gain the best agreement he can from the other with regard to the buying and selling of raw materials, products, services, and labor. Such agreements must be voluntary. The competition which leads to them cannot involve coercion. In addition, such competition must be fair and ultimately result in the benefit of the entire society through the operation of the proverbial invisible hand.

Crucial to the notion of fairness of competition are not simply the demands that the competition be open, free, and honest, but also that each person in a society be given an equal opportunity to participate in the system in order to fulfill his or her own particular ends. . . .

Equality of opportunity requires that one not be prevented by arbitrary obstacles from participating (by engaging in a productive role of some kind or other) in the system of free enterprise, competition, and so on in order to fulfill one's own ends ("reap the benefits"). Accordingly, monopolies are restricted, discriminatory hiring policies have been condemned, and price collusion is forbidden.

However, each person participates in the system of free enterprise *both* as a worker/producer *and* as a consumer. The two roles interact; if the person could not consume he would not be able to work, and if there were no consumers there would be no work to be done. Even if a particular individual is only (what is ordinarily considered) a consumer, he or she plays a theoretically significant role in the competitive free enterprise system. The fairness of the system depends upon what access he or she has to information about goods and services on the market, the lack of coercion imposed on that person to buy goods, and the lack of arbitrary restrictions imposed by the market and/or government on his or her behavior.

In short, equality of opportunity is a doctrine with two sides which applies both to producers and to consumers. If, then, a person as a consumer or a producer is injured by a defective product — which is one way his activities might arbitrarily be restricted by the action of (one of the members of) the market system — surely his free and voluntary participation in the system of free enterprise will be seriously affected. Specifically, his equal opportunity to participate in the system in order to fulfill his own ends will be diminished.

Here is where strict products liability enters the picture. In cases of strict liability the manufacturer does not intend for a certain aspect of his product to injure someone. Nevertheless, the person is injured. As a result, he is at a disadvantage both as a consumer and as a producer. He cannot continue to play either role as he might wish. Therefore, he is denied that equality of opportunity which is basic to the economic system in question just as surely as he would be if he were excluded from employment by various unintended consequences of the economic system which nevertheless had racially or sexually prejudicial implications. Accordingly, it is fair for the manufacturer to compensate the person for his losses before proceeding with business as usual. That is, the user of a manufacturer's product may justifiably demand compensation from the manufacturer when its product can be shown to be defective and has injured him and harmed his chances of participation in the system of free enterprise.

Hence, strict liability finds a basis in the notion of equality of opportunity which plays a central role in the notion of a free enterprise system. That is why a business which does *not* have to pay for the injuries an individual suffers in the use of a defective article made by that business is felt to be unfair to its customers. Its situation is analogous to that of a player's unintentional violation of a game rule which is intended to foster equality of competitive opportunity.

A soccer player, for example, may unintentionally trip an opposing player. He did not mean to do it; perhaps he himself had stumbled. Still, he has to be penalized. If the referee looked the other way, the tripped player would rightfully object that he had been treated unfairly. Similarly, the manufacturer of a product may be held strictly liable for a product of his which injures a person who uses that product. Even if he is faultless, a consequence of his activities is to render the user of his product less capable of equal participation in the socioeconomic system. The manufacturer should be penalized by way of compensating the victim. Thus, the basis upon which manufacturers are held strictly liable is compensatory justice.

In a society which refuses to resort to paternalism or to central direction of the economy and which turns, instead, to competition in order to allocate scarce positions and resources, compensatory justice requires that the competition be fair and losers be protected.[2] Specifically, no one who loses should be left so destitute that he cannot reenter the competition. Furthermore, those who suffer injuries traceable to defective merchandise or services which restrict their participation in the competitive system should also be compensated.

Compensatory justice does not presuppose negligence or evil intentions on the part of those to whom the injuries might ultimately be traced. It is not perplexed or incapacitated by the relative innocence of all parties involved.

Rather, it is concerned with correcting the disadvantaged situation an individual experiences due to accidents or failures which occur in the normal working of that competitive system. It is on this basis that other compensatory programs which alleviate the disabilities of various minority groups are founded. Strict products liability is also founded on compensatory justice.

An implication of the preceding argument is that business is not morally obliged to pay, as such, for the physical injury a person suffers. Rather, it must pay for the loss of equal competitive opportunity — even though it usually is the case that it is because of a (physical) injury that there is a loss of equal opportunity. Actual legal cases in which the injury which prevents a person from going about his or her daily activities is emotional or mental, as well as physical, support this thesis. If a person were neither mentally nor physically harmed, but still rendered less capable of participating competitively because of a defective aspect of a product, there would still be grounds for holding the company liable.

For example, suppose I purchased and used a cosmetic product guaranteed to last a month. When used by most people it is odorless. On me, however, it has a terrible smell. I can stand the smell, but my co-workers and most other people find it intolerable. My employer sends me home from work until it wears off. The product has not harmed me physically or mentally. Still, on the above argument, I would have reason to hold the manufacturer liable. Any cosmetic product with this result is defective. As a consequence my opportunity to participate in the socioeconomic system is curbed. I should be compensated.

III

There is another way of arriving at the same conclusion about the basis of strict products liability. To speak of business or the free enterprise system, it was noted above, is to speak of the voluntary exchanges between producer and customer which take place when each party believes he has an opportunity to benefit. Surely customers and producers may miscalculate their benefits; something they voluntarily agreed to buy or sell may turn out not to be to their benefit. The successful person does not have any moral responsibilities to the unsuccessful person — at least as a member of this economic system. If, however, fraud is the reason one person does not benefit, the system is, in principle, undermined. If such fraud were universalized, the system would collapse. Accordingly, the person committing the fraud does have a responsibility to make reparations to the one mistreated.

Consider once again the instance of a person who is harmed by a product he bought or used, a product that can reasonably be said to be defective. Has the nature of the free enterprise system also been undermined or corrupted in this instance? Producer and consumer have exchanged the product but it has not been to their mutual benefit; the manufacturer may have benefited, but the customer has suffered because of the defect. Furthermore, if such exchanges were universalized, the system would also be undone.

Suppose that whenever people bought products from manufacturers the products turned out to be defective and the customers were always injured, even though the manufacturers could not be held negligent. Though one party to such exchanges might benefit, the other party always suffered. If the rationale for this economic system — the reason it was adopted and is defended — were that in the end both parties share the equal opportunity to gain, surely it would collapse with the above consequences. Consequently, as with fraud, an economic system of free enterprise requires that injuries which result from defective products be compensated. The question is: Who is to pay for the compensation?

There are three possibilities. The injured party could pay for his own injuries. However, this is implausible since what is called for is compensation and not merely payment for injuries. If the injured party had simply injured himself, if he had been negligent or careless, then it is plausible that he should pay for his own injuries. No compensation is at stake here. But in the present case the injury stems from the actions of a particular manufacturer who, albeit unwittingly, placed the defective product on the market and stands to gain through its sale.

The rationale of the free enterprise system would be undermined, we have seen, if such actions were universalized, for then the product user's equal opportunity to benefit from the system would be denied. Accordingly, since the rationale and motivation for an individual to be part of this socioeconomic system is his opportunity to gain from participation in it, justice requires that the injured product user receive compensation for his injuries. Since the individual can hardly compensate himself, he must receive compensation from some other source.

Second, some third party — such as government — could compensate the injured person. This is not wholly implausible if one is prepared to modify the structure of the free enterprise system. And, indeed, in the long run this may be the most plausible course of action. However, if one accepts the structure of the free enterprise system, this alternative must be rejected because it permits the interference of government into individual affairs.

Third, we are left with the manufacturer. Suppose a manufacturer's product, even though the manufacturer wasn't negligent, always turned out to be defective and injured those using his products. We might sympathize with his plight, but he would either have to stop manufacturing altogether (no one would buy such products) or else compensate the victims for their losses. (Some people

might buy and use his products under these conditions.) If he forced people to buy and use his products he would corrupt the free enterprise system. If he did not compensate the injured users, they would not buy and he would not be able to sell his products. Hence, he could partake of the free enterprise system — that is, sell his products — only if he compensated his user/victims. Accordingly, the sale of this hypothetical line of defective products would be voluntarily accepted as just or fair only if compensation were paid the user/victims of such products by the manufacturer.

The same conclusion follows even if we consider a single defective product. The manufacturer put the defective product on the market. Because of his actions others who seek the opportunity to participate on an equal basis in this system in order to benefit therefrom are unable to do so. Thus, a result of his actions, even though unintended, is to undermine the system's character and integrity. Accordingly, when a person is injured in his attempt to participate in this system, he is owed compensation by the manufacturer. The seller of the defective article must not jeopardize the equal opportunity of the product user to benefit from the system. The seller need not guarantee that the buyer/user will benefit from the purchase of the product; after all, the buyer may miscalculate or be careless in the use of a nondefective product. But if he is not careless or has not miscalculated, his opportunity to benefit from the system is illegitimately harmed if he is injured in its use because of the product's defectiveness. He deserves compensation.

It follows from the arguments in this and the preceding section that strict products liability is not only compatible with the system of free enterprise but that if it were not attributed to the manufacturer the system itself would be morally defective. And the justification for requiring manufacturers to pay compensation when people are injured by defective products is that the demands of compensatory justice are met.[3]

NOTES

1. This characterization of strict products liability is adapted from Alvin S. Weinstein et al., *Products Liability and the Reasonably Safe Product* (New York: John Wiley & Sons, 1978), ch. 1. I understand the seller to include the manufacturer, the retailer, distributors, and wholesalers. For the sake of convenience, I will generally refer simply to the manufacturer.

2. I have drawn heavily, in this paragraph, on the fine article by Bernard Boxhill, "The Morality of Reparation," reprinted in *Reverse Discrimination,* ed. Barry R. Gross (Buffalo, New York: Prometheus Books, 1977), pp. 270–278.

3. I would like to thank the following for providing helpful comments on earlier versions of this paper: Betsy Postow, Jerry Phillips, Bruce Fisher, John Hardwig, and Sheldon Cohen.

OCCUPATIONAL RISK

The Right to Risk Information and the Right to Refuse Workplace Hazards

Ruth R. Faden
Tom L. Beauchamp

In recent years, the right of employees to be informed about health hazards in the workplace has become a major issue in occupational health policy. We focus on several philosophical and policy-oriented problems concerning the right to know and correlative obligations to disclose relevant information. Related rights are also addressed, including the right to refuse hazardous work and the right of workers to contribute to workplace safety standards.

I

A government and industry consensus has gradually evolved that workers have a right to know about occupational risks, and correlatively that there is a moral and a legal obligation to disclose relevant information to workers.[1] The National Institute for Occupational Safety and Health (NIOSH) and other U.S. federal agencies informed the U.S. Senate as early as July, 1977 that "workers have the right to know whether or not they are exposed to hazardous chemical and physical agents regulated by the Federal Government."[2] The Occupational Safety and Health Administration (OSHA) implemented regulations in 1980 guaranteeing workers access to medical and exposure records,[3] and then developed regulations in 1983, 1986, and 1988 regarding the right to know about hazardous chemicals and requiring right-to-know training programs in many industries.[4] Numerous states and municipalities have passed additional legislation.[5]

Although some form of right to risk information is now well established in law and ethics, no consensus exists about the nature and extent of an employer's obligation to disclose such information. Considerable ambiguity also attends the nature and scope of the right — that is, which protections and actions the right entails, to whom these rights apply, and when notification should occur. For example, corporations and workers usually do not distinguish between the obligation to disclose currently available information, to seek information through literature searches, to generate information through new research, and to communicate hazards through educational or other training programs. The relevant literature also does not discuss whether corporations owe workers information that exceeds federal and state requirements.

II

A diverse set of recent U.S. laws and federal regulations reflect the belief that citizens in general, and workers in particular, have a right to learn about significant risks. These include The Freedom of Information Act, The Federal Insecticide, Fungicide, and Rodenticide Amendments and Regulations, The Motor Vehicle and School Bus Safety Amendments, The Truth-in-Lending Act, The Pension Reform Act, The Real Estate Settlement Procedures Act, The Federal Food, Drug, and Cosmetic Act, The Consumer Product Safety Act, and The Toxic Substances Control Act. Taken together, this legislation communicates the message that manufacturers and other businesses have a moral (and often a legal) obligation to disclose information needed by individuals to decide about their participation, employment, or enrollment.

Recent developments in the right to know in the workplace have consistently held to this general trend towards disclosure and have included an expanded notion of corporate responsibility to provide adequate information to workers. These developments could revolutionize corporate workplace practices. Until the 1983 OSHA Hazard Communication Standard (HCS) went into effect in 1986 for the manufacturing sector and in 1988 for the non-manufacturing sector,[6] workers did not routinely receive extensive information from many employers.

Today, by contrast, some corporations have established model programs. For example, the Monsanto Company has a right-to-know program in which it distributes information on hazardous chemicals to its employees and both notifies and monitors past and current employees exposed to carcinogenic and toxic chemicals. Hercules Inc. has videotape training sessions that incorporate frank discussions of workers' anxieties. The tapes depict workplace dangers and on-the-job accidents. Those employees who have seen the Hercules film are then taught how to read safety data and how to protect themselves.[7]

Job-training programs, safety data sheets, proper labels, and a written program are all now HCS-mandated. According to the present standards, all employers must "establish hazard-communication programs to transmit information on the hazards of chemicals to their employees." The training of new employees must occur before they are exposed to hazardous substances, and each time a new hazard is introduced. Each employee must sign a written acknowledgment of training, and OSHA inspectors may interview employees to check on the effectiveness of the training sessions.[8]

The sobering statistics on worker exposure and injury and on dangerous chemicals in the workplace make such corporate programs essential. The annual Registry of Toxic Effects of Chemical Substances lists over 25,000 hazardous chemicals, at least 8,000 of which are present in the workplace. As OSHA mentioned in the preamble to its Hazard Communication Standard, an estimated 25 million largely uninformed workers in North America (1 in 4 workers) are exposed to toxic substances regulated by the federal government. Approximately 6,000 U.S. workers die from workplace injuries each year, and perhaps as many as 100,000 deaths annually are caused to some degree by workplace exposure and consequent disease. One percent of the labor force is exposed to known carcinogens, and over 44,000 U.S. workers are exposed full time to OSHA-regulated carcinogens.[9]

Despite OSHA's HCS regulations, compliance problems persist. By March, 1989, OSHA had recorded over 49,000 HCS violations in the workplace. The agency described the non-compliance rate as "incredible."[10] Part of the problem stems from ignorance both about the dangers and current OSHA requirements.

III

The most developed models of general disclosure obligations and the right to know are presently found in the extensive literature on informed consent, which also deals with informed refusal. Physicians have broadly recognized moral and legal obligations to disclose known risks (and benefits) that are associated with a proposed treatment or form of research. No parallel obligation has traditionally been recognized in relationships between management and workers. Workmen's compensation laws originally designed for problems of accident in instances of immediately assessable damage handled risks in this environment. Obligations to warn or to disclose were irrelevant under the "no-fault" conception in workmen's compensation.

However, needs for information in the workplace have gradually become associated with occupational disease. In particular, knowledge is needed about the serious long-term risks of injury, disease, and death from exposure to toxic substances. These risks to health carry increased need for information on the basis of which a person may wish to take various actions, including choosing to forego employment completely, to refuse certain work environments within a place of employment, to request improved protective devices, and to request lowered levels of exposure. Notification of workers should provide benefits of early disease diagnosis and prevention and promote needed lifestyle as well as occupational changes. Information should also improve workers' opportunities for appropriate compensation.[11]

Employee-employer relationships — unlike physician-patient relationships — are often confrontational and present to workers a constant danger of undisclosed or underdisclosed risk. This danger and the relative powerlessness of employees may not be sufficient to justify employer disclosure obligations in all circumstances, but placing relevant information in the workers' hands seems morally required in all hazardous conditions. By what criteria, then, shall such disclosure obligations be determined?

One plausible argument is the following: Because large employers, unions, and government agencies must deal with multiple employees and complicated causal conditions, no standard should be more demanding than the so-called reasonable person standard. This standard is what a fair and informed member of the relevant community believes is needed. Under this standard, no employer, union, or other party should be held responsible for disclosing information beyond that needed to make an informed choice about the adequacy of safety precautions, industrial hygiene, long-term hazards, and the like, as determined by what the reasonable person in the community would judge to be the worker's need for information material to a decision about employment or working conditions.

However, this reasonable person standard of disclosure is not adequate for all disclosures. In the case of serious hazards — such as those involved in short-term, concentrated doses of radiation — a standard tied to individual persons may be more appropriate. When disclosures to individual workers may be expected to have a subjective impact that varies with each individual, the reasonable person standard should be supplemented by a standard that addresses each worker's personal informational needs.

Perhaps the best solution to the problem of a general standard is a compromise between a reasonable-person and a subjective standard: Whatever a reasonable person would judge material to the decision-making process should be disclosed, and in addition any remaining information that is material to an individual worker should be provided through a process of asking whether he or she has any additional or special concerns. This standard should avoid a narrow focus on the employer's obligation to disclose information and should seek to ensure the quality of a worker's understanding and consent. These problems center on communication rather than on legal standards of disclosure. The key to effective communication is to invite participation by workers in a dialogue. Asking questions, eliciting concerns, and establishing a climate that encourages questions may be more meaningful than the full corpus of disclosed information. Different levels of education, linguistic ability, and sophistication about the issues need to be accommodated.

We need also to consider which groups of workers will be included. The majority of the nation's workplaces are presently exempted from OSHA regulations, leaving these workers largely uninformed. Even in workplaces that are covered, former workers often have as much of a need for the information as do presently employed workers. The federal government has the names of approximately 250,000 former workers whose risk of cancer, heart disease, and lung disease has been increased by exposure to asbestos, polyvinyl chloride, benzene, arsenic, beta-naphthalamine, and dozens of other chemicals. Employers have the names of several million such workers.

The U.S. Congress has passed a bill to notify those workers at greatest risk, so that checkups and diagnosis of disease can be made before a disease's advanced stage.[12] But at this writing, neither industry nor the government has developed a systematic program. They claim that the expense of notification would be prohibitive, that many workers would be unduly alarmed, and that existing screening and surveillance programs should prove adequate in monitoring and treating disease. Critics rightly charge, however, that existing programs are inadequate and that workers have a right to know in order to investigate potential problems at their initiative.[13]

IV

Despite the apparent consensus on the desirability of having some form of right to know in the workplace, hurdles exist that will make it difficult to implement this right. Complicated questions arise about the kinds of information to be disclosed, by whom, to whom, under what conditions, and with what warrant in ambiguous or uncertain circumstances. Trade secrets have also been a long-standing thorn in the side of progress,[14] because companies resist disclosing information about an ingredient or process claimed as a trade secret. They insist that they should never be required to reveal their substances or processes if their competitors could then obtain the information. For this reason, OSHA has been required to balance the protection of workers through disclosure against the protection of corporate interests in nondisclosure. Also, economic and related social constraints sometimes inhibit workers from exercising their full range of workplace options. For example, in industries in which ten people apply for every available position, bargaining for increased protection is an unlikely event.

However, we must set these problems aside in order to consider perhaps the most perplexing difficulty about the right to know in the workplace: the right to refuse hazardous work assignments and to have effective mechanisms for workers to reduce the risks they face. Shortly after the Hazard Communication Standard went into effect, labor saw that the right to know was often of little practical use unless some parallel method were in place to modify hazardous working conditions. U.S. law has generally made unsafe working conditions a punishable offense, and the United States Occupational Safety and Health Act of 1970 (OSH Act)[15] limited rights to refuse to work when there is good evidence of life-threatening conditions. Specifically, the OSH Act grants workers the right to request an OSHA inspection if they believe an OSHA standard has been violated or an imminent hazard exists. Under the Act, employees also have the right to "walk around," i.e., to participate in OSHA inspections of the worksite and to consult freely with the inspection officer. Most importantly, the OSH Act expressly protects employees who request an inspection or otherwise exercise their rights under the OSH Act from discharge or any discriminatory treatment in retaliation for legitimate safety and health complaints.[16]

While these worker rights under the OSH Act are essential, they are not sufficiently strong to assure that all workers have effective mechanisms for initiating inspections of suspected health hazards. The OSH Act does not cover small businesses (those employing fewer than ten workers) or federal, state, and municipal employees. Questions also remain about OSHA's ability to enforce these provisions of the OSH Act. But if workers are to effectively use disclosed information on health hazards, they must have access to a workable and efficient regulatory system. The OSH Act is also written to protect the rights of individuals, not groups. It has no provisions for collective action by workers and does not mandate workplace health and safety committees, as does legislation in some countries.

Workers still need an adequately protected right to refuse unsafe work and a right to refuse an employer's request that they sign OSHA-mandated forms acknowledging that they have been trained about hazardous chemicals. One cannot easily determine the current extent to which these rights are protected.[17] Although the OSH Act does not grant a general right to refuse unsafe work, provisions to this effect exist in some state occupational safety laws. In addition, former Secretary of Labor Ray Marshall issued a regulation that interprets the OSH Act as including a limited right to refuse unsafe work, a right upheld by the U.S. Supreme Court in 1980.[18] The Labor-Management Relations Act (LMRA) also provides a limited right of refusal, which is also included implicitly in the National Labor Relations Act (NLRA).[19]

These statutory protections have not established uniform conditions granting to workers a right to refuse. For example, OSHA regulations allow workers to walk off the job if there is a "real danger of death or serious injury," while the LMRA permits refusals only under "abnormally dangerous conditions."[20] Under the LMRA, the nature of the occupation determines the extent of danger justifying refusal, while under OSHA the character of the threat, or so-called "imminent danger," determines worker action. By contrast, under the NLRA a walk-out by two or more workers may be justified for even minimal safety problems, so long as the action can be construed as a "concerted activity" for mutual aid and protection and a no-strike clause does not exist in any collective bargaining agreements. While the NLRA appears to provide the broadest protection to workers, employees refusing to work under the NLRA can lose the right to be reinstated in their positions if permanent replacements can be hired.

The relative merits of the different statutes are further confused by questions of overlapping authority, called "preemption." It is not always clear (1) whether a worker is eligible to claim protection under a given law, (2) which law affords a worker maximum protections or remedies in a particular circumstance, and (3) whether or under what conditions a worker can seek relief under another law or through the courts, once a claim under a given law has been rejected or invalidated.

The current legal situation concerning the right to refuse hazardous work also fails to resolve other questions. Consider, for example, whether a meaningful right to refuse hazardous work entails an obligation to continue to pay nonworking employees, or to award the employees back pay if the issue is resolved in their favor. On the one hand, workers without union strike benefits or other income protections would be unable to exercise their right to refuse unsafe work due to economic pressures. On the other hand, to permit such workers to draw a paycheck is to legitimize strike with pay, a practice traditionally considered unacceptable by management and by Congress.

The situation does not resolve whether the right to refuse unsafe work should be restricted to cases of obvious, imminent, and serious risks to health or life (the current OSHA and LMRA position) or should be expanded to include lesser risks and uncertain risks — for example, exposure to suspected toxic or carcinogenic substances that although not immediate threats, may prove more dangerous over time. In order for "the right to know" to lead to meaningful worker action, workers must be able to remove themselves from exposure to suspected hazards, as well as obvious or known hazards.

The question of the proper standard for determining whether a safety walkout is justified is connected to this issue. At least three different standards have been applied in the past: a good-faith subjective standard, which requires only that the worker honestly believe that a health hazard exists; a reasonable person standard, which requires that the belief be reasonable under the circumstances as well as sincerely held; and an objective standard, which requires evidence — commonly established by expert witnesses — that the threat exists. Although the possibility of worker abuse of the right to refuse has been a major factor in a current trend to reject the good faith standard, recent commentary has argued that this trend raises serious equity issues in the proper balancing of this concern with the needs of workers confronted with basic self-preservation issues.[21]

No less important is whether the right to refuse hazardous work should be protected only until a formal review of the situation is initiated (at which time the worker must return to the job) or whether the walk-out should be permitted until the alleged hazard is at least temporarily removed. Requirements that workers continue to be exposed while OSHA or the NLRB conduct investigations is certain to prove unacceptable to workers when the magnitude of potential harm is significant. However, compelling employers to remove suspected hazards during the evaluation period may also result in intolerable economic burdens. This situation is worsened by the fact that workers are often not in a position to act on information about health hazards by seeking alternative employment elsewhere.

We need, then, to delineate the conditions under which workers may be compelled to return to work during an alleged hazard investigation and the conditions that can compel employers to remove alleged hazards.

V

Legal rights will prove useless if workers remain ignorant of their options. Despite recent requirements that employers initiate training programs, it remains doubtful that many workers, particularly nonunion workers and those in small businesses, are aware that they have a legally protected right to refuse hazardous work, let alone that at least three statutory provisions protect that right. Even if workers were to learn of such a right, they could probably not weave their way through the maze of legal options unaided. OSHA officials have acknowledged that both employers and workers are puzzled about proper strategies of education and compliance.[22] But if the workplace is to have a meaningful right to know, workers must have an adequate program to educate them not only about hazards but about their rights and how to exercise them. In general, they attempt to regulate the workplace rather than to empower workers in the workplace — two very different strategies.

Although the interests in health and safety of business are sometimes in sharp conflict with the interests of workers and society employers and managers have an obligation to explain the right to notification and the right (at least temporarily) to refuse work under unduly hazardous conditions. Such programs

of information and training in hazards are as important for employers and managers as for workers. In several recent court cases corporate executives have been tried — and in some cases convicted — for murder and manslaughter, because they negligently caused worker deaths by failing to notify of hazards. In Los Angeles and Chicago occupational deaths are investigated as possible homicides.[23] An improved system of corporate disclosures of risk and the rights of workers will therefore benefit everyone.

NOTES

1. See, for example, International Commission on Occupational Health, "Occupational Health Code of Ethics," *Bulletin of Medical Ethics,* 82 (October, 1992): 7–11.

2. NIOSH et al., "The Right to Know: Practical Problems and Policy Issues Arising from Exposures to Hazardous Chemical and Physical Agents in the Workplace" (Washington, DC: July, 1977), pp. 1 and 5; see also Ilise L. Feitshans, "Hazardous Substances in the Workplace: How Much Does the Employee have the Right to Know?" *Detroit Law Review* 3 (1985).

3. Occupational Safety and Health Administration, "Access to Employee Exposure and Medical Records—Final Rules," *Federal Register,* May 23, 1980, pp. 35212–77.

4. OSHA, Regulations 29 CFR 1910.1200 et seq; printed in 48 FR 53, 278 (1983) and (1986). See also *United Steelworkers v. Auchter,* No 83-3554 et al; 763 F.2d 728 (3rd Cir., 1985).

5. See Deborah Shalowitz, "OSHA to Ease State Right-to-Know Burdens," *Business Insurance* 22 (Jan. 11, 1988): 17.

6. 29 CFR 1910.1200; 48 FR 53, 280 (1983); and see Linda D. McGill, "OSHA's Hazard Communication Standards: Guidelines for Compliance," *Employment Relations Today* 16 (Autumn 1989): 181–87.

7. Laurie Hays, "New Rules on Workplace Hazards Prompt Intensified on the Job Training Programs," *The Wall Street Journal* (July 8, 1986), p. 31; Cathy Trost, "Plans to Alert

Workers," *The Wall Street Journal,* (March 28, 1986), p. 15.

8. "Hazard Communication," *Federal Register,* August 24, 1987; and see William J. Rothwell, "Complying with OSHA," *Training & Development Journal* 43 (May, 1989): 53–54; McGill, "OSHA's Hazard Communication Standards: Guidelines for Compliance," p. 184.

9. See 48 CFR 53, 282 (1983); Office of Technology Assessment, *Preventing Illness and Injury in the Workplace* (Washington: U.S. Government Printing Office, 1985). See also Sheldon W. Samuels, "The Ethics of Choice in the Struggle Against Industrial Disease," *American Journal of Industrial Medicine* 23(1993): 43–52, and David Rosner and Gerald E. Markowitz, eds. *Dying for Work: Workers' Safety and Health in Twentieth-Century America* (Bloomington: University of Indiana Press, 1987).

10. Current Reports, *O.S.H. Reporter* (March 15, 1989), p. 1747, as quoted in McGill, "OSHA's Hazard Communication Standard," p. 181.

11. See the articles by Gregory Bond, Leon Gordis, John Higgenson and Flora Chu, Albert Jonsen, and Paul A. Schulte in *Industrial Epidemiology Forum's Conference on Ethics in Epidemiology,* ed. William E. Fayerweather, John Higgenson, and Tom L. Beauchamp (New York: Pergamon Press, 1991).

12. High Risk Occupational Disease Notification and Prevention Act, HR 1309.

13. See Cathy Trost, "Plans to Alert Workers to Health Risks Stir Fears of Lawsuits and High Costs," *The Wall Street Journal* (March 28, 1986), p. 15; Peter Perl, "Workers Unwarned," *The Washington Post* (January 14, 1985), pp. A1, A6.

14. Under current standards, an employer is not required to disclose the name or any information about a hazardous chemical that would require disclosure of a bona fide trade secret; but in a medical emergency the company must disclose this information to physicians or nurses as long as confidentiality is assured.

15. 29 U.S.C. §651–658 (1970).

16. OSH Act 29 U.S.C. 661(c). If the health or safety complaint is not determined to be legitimate, there are no worker protections.

17. The right to refuse an employer's request to sign a training acknowledgment form is upheld in *Beam Distilling Co. v. Distillery and Allied Workers' International,* 90 Lab. Arb. 740 (1988). See also Ronald Bayer, ed. *The Health and Safety of Workers* (New York: Oxford University Press, 1988); James C. Robinson, *Toil and Toxics: Workplace Struggles and Political Strategies for Occupational Health* (Berkeley: University of California Press, 1991).

18. *Whirlpool v. Marshall* 445 US 1 (1980).

19. See the exposition in Susan Preston, "A Right Under OSHA to Refuse Unsafe Work or A Hobson's Choice of Safety or Job?," *University of Baltimore Law Review* 8 (Spring, 1979): 519–550.

20. 29 U.S.C. §143 (1976), and 29 CFR §1977.12 (1979).

21. James C. Robinson, "Labor Union Involvement in Occupational Safety and Health, 1957–1987," *Journal of Health Politics, Policy, and Law* 13 (Fall, 1988): p. 463; Nancy K. Frank, "A Question of Equity: Workers' Right to Refuse' Under OSHA Compared to the Criminal Necessity Defense," *Labor Law Journal* 31 (October 1980): 617–626.

22. McGill, "OSHA's Hazard Communication Standard," p. 181.

23. See *Illinois v. Chicago Magnet Wire Corporation,* No. 86-114, *Amicus Curiae* for The American Federation of Labor and Congress of Industrial Organizations; R. Henry Moore, "OSHA: What's Ahead for the 1990s," *Personnel* 67 (June, 1990): 69

The Nature of the Worker's Right to Know

Thomas O. McGarity

The "hazard communication" standard, issued by the Occupational Safety and Health Administration . . . is a series of rules that . . . grant employees, their unions, or OSHA access to medical and exposure records that are kept by an employer. They require manufacturers to label and to post a "Material Safety Data Sheet" (MSDS) for each hazardous chemical; and they place on the employer the duty to disclose information regarding the use of specific hazardous substances. Existing state laws also provide access and disclosure rules, as well as enforcement procedures and trade secret protection. Although these laws vary from state to state, many are more stringent and protective of the workers' "right to know" than are the OSHA rules. Thus it is a matter of concern that federal preemption of state laws is now a possibility.

Although the OSHA rules may prove useful to workers and their unions seeking chemical identification and compensation claims, their effectiveness depends upon the initiative of workers, voluntary record keeping by employers, and the limitations imposed by trade secret restrictions. What are the ethical principles undergirding the rules, and what guidance do they offer in grappling with the obligations and rights of employers and employees?

Modern ethical thinking has almost universally concluded that a patient has a right to make an informed consent to a doctor's therapeutic recommendation. Moreover, when society as a whole can benefit from a person's voluntary assumption of a risk as in the case of human experimentation, the ethical mandate that the subject's consent be informed is especially stringent. Although the ethical principles underlying informed consent would seem to translate readily into the context of the workplace, employers do not always acknowledge the "right" of workers to be informed about the substances to which they are exposed. The "worker's right to know" is at approximately the same stage of development as was informed consent in the 1960s.

Employers often maintain that their reluctance to inform employees about toxic workplace risks springs from the same considerations that motivated doctors—a paternalistic concern for the well-being of individuals and a corresponding belief that they lack the education or training to put the information to good use. This solicitude is even more suspect in the workplace than in the doctor's office, because the employer derives a direct financial benefit from the worker's ignorance. Informed workers may demand higher wages (risk premiums) or safer working conditions. It is unlikely that employers will concede that extracting risk premiums constitutes a "good use" for health and safety information. Were paternalism the only ethical consideration justifying the employers' stance, the ethical analysis of the issue would be straightforward—the worker should have a right to know. The issue, however, is complicated by three considerations that do not relate directly to the doctor-patient question.

First, the right of employees to know is an agglomeration of rights that requires

From *The Hastings Center Report,* by Thomas O. McGarity, August, 1984.

increasingly burdensome responses from employers or from society in general. Indeed, it may be more accurate to define the right to know by reference to the four categories of correlative duties that it imposes on employers: (1) the duty to *reveal* information already possessed; (2) the duty to *communicate* information about hazards through labeling, written communications, and training programs; (3) the duty to *seek out* existing information from the scientific literature and other sources; (4) the duty to *produce* new information (for example, through animal testing) relevant to employee health. General assertions of broad workers' right to know often do not distinguish among these four separate duties. The doctor–patient relationship gives rise to, at most, the first three duties, but proponents of a worker's right to know would impose the third and fourth duties on employers, thus obliging the corporation to do something that it would not otherwise do, solely for the benefit of its employees.

A second distinction between the workers' right to know and informed consent is the nature of the relationship between the information user and the information provider. The doctor–patient relationship is a joint enterprise whose acknowledged goal is the welfare of the patient. The employer–employee relationship is more adversarial. The more employees know about workplace hazards, the less happy they are likely to be about their jobs. An employee may demand more money or may quit, in which case the employer may have to replace the worker at a higher wage. Similarly, informed employees who later become ill may use their knowledge about workplace risks to support workers' compensation claims. The employer, therefore, has a direct financial incentive not to communicate workplace hazard information to employees.

To be sure, an employer has an interest in the health and well-being of employees. A great deal of money may be spent on employee training and education, which will be wasted if employees become diseased or are injured. In the no-fault workers' compensation scheme that is currently in effect in most states, only by keeping the workers healthy can the employer avoid paying benefits. This gives the employer some incentive to communicate information about hazards to workers, but it applies almost exclusively to acute safety hazards that are easily avoided by well-informed workers. Since there is not much an employee can do to reduce chronic health hazards (short of wearing uncomfortable and often ineffective respirators), the employer has little incentive to communicate information about chronic and latent disease hazards.

All of the duties associated with the right to know are thus affirmative obligations that require employers to expend resources without much corresponding gain. Making existing information available to employees requires only the cost of maintaining and updating files. But affirmative communication of hazards to workers requires that pipes, vessels, walls, barrels, and other containers be clearly labeled. According to some versions of the right to know, the employer is further obliged to conduct training programs to ensure that employees are informed of chronic risks and how best to reduce them. If the substances in the workplace change frequently, the employer must endure the increased cost of changing the labels and additional training. Imposing the still more burdensome requirement of searching out existing literature for evidence of potential hazards requires employers to absorb the cost of making the literature accessible and providing a technically proficient staff. Finally, an employer can easily spend millions of dollars testing substances for toxicity, if that duty is also imposed.

A third distinction between the doctor–patient and the employer–employee relationships is the larger stake that society may have in the confidentiality of "trade secret" information. An employer's reluctance to convey information to employees may stem from fear that disloyal employees will reveal confidential information to competitors, who can thereby avoid the research and development costs of a new manufacturing process. . . .

Because of the adversarial nature of the employer–employee relationship, it is probably best to set the rights-oriented model aside and begin to search for a new model to guide decisions in this area. As important social interests permeate both sides of the adversarial relationship, the balancing paradigm may be more appropriate.

COMPETING MORAL AND PRACTICAL CONSIDERATIONS

Autonomy

Our society highly values individual autonomy. Yet free choices require information. When those who have information about risks convey it to those who are subject to those risks, autonomy is enhanced and society is the better for it. Considerations of autonomy would therefore seem to support a general moral duty on everyone with knowledge of risks to convey that knowledge to persons who are exposed to those risks.

Yet this process is rarely cost-free. To the extent that a duty to convey risks would require a person to do something that he would not otherwise do, its imposition restricts that person's autonomy. Hence, the law, for example, does not impose a general duty on an individual to warn another of his or her peril.

Requiring an employer to warn employees of workplace hazards can impinge heavily on the employer's autonomy. Merely requiring the corporation to open up its health and safety files to employees and their representatives, although not imposing large direct costs, can risk the unlawful appropriation of valuable trade secrets. Trade secrets have been called "property" by some courts and commentators. Causing an employer to risk sacrificing a valuable property interest could be a significant intrusion on corporate autonomy. Imposing any of the other three aforementioned duties add increasingly burdensome direct financial outlays on employers. Clearly, a government requirement that one person expend resources for the benefit of another reduces that person's autonomy.

Autonomy considerations alone are not especially helpful in resolving the clash of interests. An attractive solution might be a bargain between the employer and employee, where each party voluntarily sacrifices some autonomy in order to gain some autonomy. Because acquiring information costs money, employees desiring information about workplace risks should be willing to pay the employer (in reduced wages) or someone else to produce or gather the relevant information. A straightforward economic analysis would suggest that employees would be willing to pay for health and safety information up to the point at which the value in wage negotiations of the last piece of information purchased equaled the cost of that additional information.

While the bargaining approach seems appropriate in theory, it suffers considerably in practice, for employees cannot know in advance what the value of information will be in wage negotiations. For example, an expensive study that concludes that a particular workplace is relatively safe will have no value to employees in wage negotiations. A second practical drawback is the familiar "transaction cost" and "free rider" problems that plague any economic analysis of collective action. It costs money to bring employees together to decide how much money to spend on information, and a free rider can have the benefits of the collective action without contributing to its costs, thus reducing the incentive of every individual to participate in the collective action. Finally, since the employer is likely to be the source of most information on workplace risks, there can be no real market in workplace risk information. The employer is a monopolist and will not part with this information without charging something in excess of what the employees are willing to pay; that is, the amount they hope to gain in wage negotiations by using the information.

The bargaining model has failed in practice; most information on chronic risks is now conveyed to workers not voluntarily by employers but by virtue of governmental requirements. Yet it is virtually impossible for an external agency to measure in an unbiased way a reduction in one person's autonomy against a different sort of reduction in the autonomy of a corporation. Unless one is willing to afford corporate entities no autonomy interests at all, the comparison is probably futile. Unfortunately, not only is this subjective comparison necessary to a thorough analysis of the issue, but the net autonomy balance must also be weighed against other incommensurable values.

Fairness

Just as our society values autonomy, it also values fairness. Indeed, autonomy must yield to fairness when the circumstances call for it. The no-duty-to-warn rule of the common law, for example, has an important exception for cases in which the person who failed to warn also played a role in placing the injured person in peril. It is unfair to allow a person to assert that his autonomy should supersede another's when the risk is attributable in part to him.

In the workplace context, fairness considerations help sway the balance in favor of an employee's right to know. The employer is not merely a passive gatherer of information, but the source of the risk. The activities that bring profit to the employer also impose risks on employees. Employers should not be allowed to profit from an employee's unnecessary ignorance. Considerations of basic fairness, therefore, argue strongly in favor of requiring employers to warn employees about risks of which the employers are aware, and the common law (prior to the enactment of workers' compensation statutes) imposed such a duty to warn upon employers.

Fairness, however, offers little help when the issue is whether employers have a duty to expend resources on labeling, training, information gathering, and data production. When the employer, too, is unaware of the risks, fairness does not as strongly dictate a result. It may be unfair to require employers to ferret out information on risks to employees when such information can only cause employers economic harm. In response, it could be argued that employers can usually write at least some of the costs of data gathering into the prices of the products that they sell, thereby channeling part of the cost to the consumer. This may be fairer than allowing consumers to pay less for products at the employee's expense. Even so, fairness alone cannot effectively dictate *how many* resources should be devoted to information production, gathering, and processing.

Utility/Efficiency

The utilitarian would argue that the employer–employee conflict over workplace risks should be resolved in the way that provides the greatest good for the greatest number of people. The primary difficulty with this goal is valuation. What is the value of a one-in-a-thousand risk that a worker will be killed? How many resources should be expended in reducing this risk from one in a thousand to one in a million? Most economists would answer these questions by letting the employers and employees themselves decide in the bargaining process.

According to economists, in the labor market an employee's wage is determined to a large extent by his or her knowledge, skills, credentials, and so on, and the existing demand for those resources. Health and safety risks can also play a role, and the wage for jobs requiring exposure to health and safety risks will be determined in part by the price at which employees are willing to accept additional risks. The employer may either pay the risk premium to those willing to accept it or make capital expenditures aimed at reducing risks. The employer will "clean up the workplace" to the point at which the last dollar spent on health and safety controls equals the increased wage premiums (and perhaps added workers' compensation expenditures) that would result from the failure to do so. The remaining risks are willingly accepted by the employees. Some economists, in fact, argue that as long as the labor market functions efficiently, there is no need for governmental intervention by agencies like OSHA: The market will ensure that society achieves the mix of production technologies and health and safety controls that maximizes overall welfare.

A crucial component of the free market model of wage and risk determination is its assumption that workers are fully informed about the risks that they face as they bargain over wages. To the extent that risks are unknown to employees, they will undervalue overall workplace risks in wage negotiations. The result will be lower wages and an inadequate incentive to employers to install health and safety devices. In addition, to the extent that employees can avoid risks by taking preventive action, uninformed employees will fail to do so. Society will then underinvest in wages and risk prevention, and overall societal wealth will decline. Moreover, a humane society is not likely to require diseased or injured workers to suffer without proper medical attention. In many cases, society will pick up the tab through Medicare, Medicaid, and welfare payments.

The foregoing argument would support a governmental requirement that employers make existing risk information available to employees in all cases. The analysis is less compelling in the real world where producing, gathering, and conveying information is expensive. The market paradigm can be corrected by erecting a surrogate market in which information itself is purchased and sold. Under this approach, society would produce, gather, and convey information to employees up to the point at which the benefits of the next additional piece of information equals the cost of its production. It is difficult, however, to put a value on an intangible like information; most economists would probably argue that despite the difficulty of determination, its value should be measured by the employee's willingness to pay.

In the interests of efficiency at least some resources should probably be spent on producing, gathering, and conveying information about workplace risks beyond what employers will voluntarily expend. Note, however, that the utilitarian criterion is neutral as to *who* should expend these resources, whether it be employees, employers and their consumers, or the Treasury. The economist would probably argue that the cost should be imposed on the party that faces the lowest "transaction" costs, in this case, the employer or the Treasury, which do not encounter the "coming together" and "free rider" problems that employees face in attempting to collect resources.

Innovation

The free market paradigm contains a fundamental tension between competition and innovation. A properly functioning competitive market should ensure that a product is sold at the optimal price. If a firm is charging more than this price, its competitors will manufacture and sell the same product for less, forcing the first manufacturer to reduce its price or lose the entire market. The key to this price mechanism is the ability of a competitor to produce the same product at the same cost, which assumes knowledge of the precise makeup of the product and the production process. If, however, competitors have immediate access to this information, a strong incentive to develop a new product or process is lost. The cost of research and development can be very high, and a firm will not undertake these efforts without some assurance that they will be reflected in the price of the new product. At best, the original developer will have a brief lead time to include its costs in the price of its product if its competitors can enter the market at once with products whose prices do not have to reflect research and development costs. Under these circumstances innovation suffers. Consumers may be better off in the short run because they pay lower prices for existing products, but society is worse off without better products and processes. In the long run, manufacturers in countries that protect research and development incentives may ultimately take whole markets away from domestic producers.

Virtually all societies have resolved this tension between competition and innovation by protecting innovative efforts to some degree. Typically, the government grants the innovator a monopoly — a patent — for a fixed period of time, during which research and development costs may be recouped. As a quid pro quo, the government requires the developer to reveal to the world the identity of its patented product and explain how its innovative processes work. . . .

An entirely separate route to market protection is the state common law of trade secrets. State law generally provides a remedy to the holder of a trade secret against anyone who unlawfully appropriates that secret. For a product, process, or other information to be a "trade secret" it must be of commercial value to the holder and it must be kept secret from the rest of the world. The basic purpose of the common law of trade secrets is to punish faithless employees and unscrupulous competitors who engage in industrial espionage and other tactics aimed at eliminating the holder's competitive advantage. A subsidiary purpose, not often alluded to in common law cases, is to foster innovation.

The trade secret alternative is often more attractive to innovators, because the developer does not have to reveal product and process information, and because a trade secret has no explicitly limited duration. In addition, the holder of a trade secret, unlike a patent holder, is not generally required to demonstrate that the innovation is novel and unusual. Not surprisingly, developers often elect the trade secret route, rather than the patent route, to market protection. But society may never learn the nature of important inventions if the trade secret route is commonly used. Indeed, the entire state common law of trade secrets barely escaped being abolished in the Supreme Court case of *Kewanee Oil Co. v. Bicron Corp.* The Court by a five-to-four majority rejected the argument that state trade secret law was preempted by the federal patent laws.

In the workplace context, employers claim that if they are forced to reveal information about risks to employees, the employees, in turn, will channel the information to competitors, with resulting harm to the employers' competitive position. This two-pronged argument depends, first, upon the validity of the assumption that risk information could be of commercial value to competitors; and second, that federal patent law and state trade secret laws are inadequate to protect research and development incentives.

The first assumption is probably not true. If employees were willing to trust employers (or some independent governmental agency such as OSHA) to characterize workplace risks, the nature of virtually all risks could be communicated without reducing research and development incentives even slightly. Workers, however, are not especially trusting of employers and they are disinclined to place complete faith in an agency that can become the captive of powerful trade associations. The two sides inevitably come to loggerheads over the question of whether the identity of chemicals to which employees are exposed must be revealed to them.

Employees contend that knowledge of chemical identity is essential to an independent evaluation of workplace risks; it is the key to the scientific literature; it is important for a doctor's diagnosis of many occupational diseases. Without this knowledge it is impossible to perform epidemiological studies across industries or to make an independent determination of what further health and safety studies should be performed. In sum, employees argue, chemical identity is essential to an independent assessment of workplace risks.

Employers, on the other hand, contend that the identity of some chemicals is a commercially valuable thing in and of itself. The identity of chemicals in most commercial products cannot always be ascertained by a good analytical chemist; some chemicals, such as catalysts, that are essential to the manufacturing process do not find their way into the marketed product. If those identities are made available to employees, employers argue, this commercially valuable information will inevitably leak out to competitors.

There are at least two rejoinders to the employers' arguments. First, the innovator/employer can nearly always secure a patent. Second, even if the innovator/employer elects to forego the protection afforded by a patent, employees who reveal trade secrets to competitors and competitors who solicit those secrets can be sued under state common law and, in most states, prosecuted under state criminal law. Should employers argue that federal patent law and state trade secret laws afford such flimsy protections that requiring disclosure will reduce research and development incentives, the debate is likely to turn upon the locus of the burden of proof.

Paternalism

It was earlier suggested that paternalism may account for much of the reluctance of employers to inform employees of workplace risks. Management typically takes the position that its health and safety specialists know what is best for employees, and it is not necessary to concern employees with these matters. Occasionally, management representatives will argue that workers will not fully comprehend information on chemical identities and toxological effects and may use it irrationally. Confused employees will attempt to bid wages up too high and society will either spend too much on wages or be forced to endure industrial strife.

Coming from employers, these arguments are self-serving and entirely unpersuasive. Still, there is a kernel of truth in the proposition that employees will not know how to evaluate the information with which they are provided. It might be more desirable from the employee's point of view to adopt a system of symbols that identifies hazards in broad functional categories. The symbols could vary with increasing risk, thus informing employees in a rough way about the nature of the risk they face. Additionally, the employer's trade secrets could be preserved. Several systems of symbols have been suggested and some are currently in existence, but since they are not standardized, the same or similar symbols can mean different things in different companies.

The primary problem with the symbol solution is again one of trust. Employees are generally unwilling to allow employers or an independent agency, such as OSHA, to characterize risks for purposes of adapting a symbolic warning system to the workplace. Employees will probably want to characterize risks for themselves or allow someone of their own choosing to do so. . . .

ENVIRONMENTAL RISK

Safety, Risk, and Environmental Protection

Richard T. DeGeorge

ENVIRONMENTAL HARM

Who should decide how clean our air and water should be? Since these are common goods, the decisions should be made by all those affected. Since it is a public policy question, the population in general should make it through the political process. Yet voters are often given little information about the trade-offs they as a society are actually making. Americans have typically left it up to government to determine what degree of pollution is dangerous, to decide what degree is acceptable, and to come up with regulations that will punish violations beyond that level. The public has rarely voted on alternatives or been told just what the alternatives are or what it is trading off against what. In some states voters have been asked to vote on specific issues — for instance, whether they want to construct nuclear power plants or establish toxic waste centers. Generally speaking, the public has voted on no comprehensive environmental package. Guidelines determined by various parts of government have been prescribed piecemeal. The claim might be made that the subject is technical and best left to the technicians, but we have seen that any choice of levels involves value judgments and there is little reason to assume that technicians represent or hold the same values as even the majority of the society. Many plausibly claim that, as rational agents, people have a right to decide issues that directly concern and affect them.

The blame for the deterioration of the environment frequently falls squarely on business. Factories pollute; manufacturers pour toxic substances into rivers and streams and bury noxious substances, often without regard to public safety; greedy entrepreneurs denude forests, strip-mine the land, and heedlessly eliminate increasing numbers of species. Business has had a serious and often deleterious effect on the environment. Yet the fact that, with respect to the degradation of their environment, socialist countries have fared no better, and often worse, than free-enterprise countries indicates that the harm may be due more to modern technology and its abuse than to business greed alone.

With the development of modern chemistry and increasing industrialization, a great

From *Business Ethics* by Richard T. DeGeorge, 5th edition, 1999.

many possibilities have been created and realized without adequate concern for their side effects and for the sometimes hidden costs of their production. For instance, pesticides and herbicides have been a boon for farmers, increasing crop yield and ridding food products of the pests that have plagued farmers for centuries. But pesticides and herbicides can also have deleterious effects. They can seep into the ground and eventually pollute ground water and wells. They can wend their way into streams and rivers, killing fish, or contaminating them. Eventually, they find their way through the food chain to humans, causing cancer, birth deformities, and other ills. The price of introducing new products often involves a certain amount of risk. In many instances the harm done was, at least at first, not intentional and was unknown. It was only after the incidence of disease and birth defects increased that scientists sought the causes and identified the chemical culprits. Can pesticides and herbicides be developed that do not eventually and indirectly harm people? The answer seems to be yes; and promoting their development is one purpose of governmental controls. Knowing there are safer and equally effective alternatives makes it unreasonable to accept the greater risks and actual harm produced by the outlawed products.

A similar analysis can be given of other activities. Strip-mining and denuding the land of forests are both short-sighted activities. We know that cutting down forests without replanting the trees leads to loss of topsoil and to flooding, both of which cause harm, and both of which can be prevented. Yet in underdeveloped countries the local timber often provides the only source of fuel and of housing material for the local people. They have no resources for reforestation and are concerned with present survival rather than with the long-term impact of their deeds. Large paper mills have less excuse for deforestation, but even they provide some good by

their activities — namely, the goods they produce and are able to provide for less cost than they could otherwise.

The issues of pollution raise serious concerns about harm. Other environmental issues are less clear. Treatment of animals is of very great concern to some people and of considerably less to others, and what is proper treatment is debated. Questions such as whether the redwood forests of the U.S. West coast should be opened to lumber companies, and whether and how much land should be preserved as wilderness and kept from commercial development are issues on which there is no consensus. Similarly, how much harm is done by industrial processes and development that lead in one way or another to the elimination of animal species is a debated issue. While some argue in terms of the rights of those species, others claim that only human beings properly speaking have rights. The ground then often switches to whether harm can be demonstrated to human beings by felling the redwoods; or acting so as to endanger different animal, insect, or plant species; or treating animals with hormones and other drugs, and keeping them in crowded pens in which they can barely move.

In many instances of environmental harm, the harm done is not wanton and produces some good. From a utilitarian point of view we must ask whether more good is done than harm, looking at all those affected, not only immediately but in the long run as well. From a deontological perspective we need to ask whether the activities violate people's rights. From either perspective we must remember that though harming the environment is bad, at least to the extent that it directly or indirectly harms people, the actions that cause the harm frequently have positive effects as well, as in the case of pesticides, which can be of great help in keeping people alive because of higher crop yields than would otherwise be possible.

In dealing with environmental harm, therefore, the task is to minimize the harm done while maximizing the benefits made available by increased scientific knowledge and technological advances, and while respecting the rights of all those affected.

There is no need to belabor the point that direct, intentional, preventable harm is morally wrong. Manufacturers who knowingly dump harmful by-products and chemicals into streams or onto the ground are guilty of willfully harming others. Those involved in the production of radioactive waste know full well the damage such products can cause and the care they must take in disposing of these products. If they fail to take the appropriate measures, they are knowingly causing harm to others. The same is true with respect to farmers who knowingly misuse pesticides and herbicides, to foresters who do not plant trees to replace those they cut, and to strip-miners who do not heal the land they scar.

The problem of environmental harm and pollution is much more complex than this, however. Although the problems of pollution are only one aspect of the ethical problems involved with the environment, pollution raises a number of issues that illustrate an approach to dealing with environmental problems.

POLLUTION AND ITS CONTROL

We can distinguish intentional from unintentional pollution, and major from minor polluters. In all cases, what we mean by *pollution* is crucial, and defining it is no easy task. As far as nature is concerned, there is no strict sense of pollution. When the volcano Mount St. Helens, in the State of Washington, erupted in May 1980, it damaged 220,000 acres of timberland; befouled the Touttle, Cowlitz, and Columbia rivers; emitted enormous amounts of sulfur; and spread its emissions in measurable amounts across the United States. In one sense the eruption polluted the air. But the eruption was natural, and the larger amount of sulfur in the air was no more unnatural than the smaller amount in the air prior to the eruption. In a literal sense, nature did not care about the amount of sulfur in the air. Human beings did, because they were adversely affected. What we often mean by *pollution* is the contamination of air, water, and land with substances that harm us or our interests, and in pollution control we are primarily concerned with preventing harm that can be avoided and that results from human activity. That is the only kind of activity that we can classify as moral or immoral.

Pollution, moreover, is sometimes a relative term. Certain gases and chemicals are not dangerous in very small amounts but are dangerous in large amounts. When present in small amounts, they are not usually considered pollutants; they become pollutants only when they reach a certain, dangerous level. Other substances are noxious in even minute amounts and are considered pollutants in whatever amounts they are present. What is considered to be a pollutant in drinking water may not be considered a pollutant in river water.

Since pollution is linked with harm, we wish to prevent the type of pollution that causes harm. For many years people used a variety of materials that either because of their small use did not in fact cause harm or because of ignorance were not known to cause harm. Thus, asbestos for a long while was used both as a fire retardant and as an insulator, with no knowledge that asbestos could cause cancer. When it was determined that asbestos could cause cancer, it became a pollutant to be withdrawn from the human living environment to the extent possible. Those who built with asbestos materials and had no knowledge of its harmful effects had no intention of harming others. (At what point they began to have suspicions, and then knowledge, and what they did thereafter, are questions with moral import.) Similarly, many manufacturers used rivers as dumps for their wastes, and in many instances the ratio of waste to the water into which it was dumped was sufficiently low that no harm was done. The ecosystem was able to dispose of the waste through natural means. In like manner, early motorists were few enough in number that the exhausts that their cars emitted were not dangerous and were carried away by the wind.

Pollution became a major issue when the free use of land, water, and air as means of waste disposal started to cause known harmful effects on others. This happened because of the increasing toxicity of the wastes, the better knowledge of the links between waste and human disease, and the growing number of sources of contamination. The sulfur emitted by one car might be harmless; but the sulfur emitted by millions of cars in a large city can produce harm. There is a threshold above which certain substances become harmful. Determining that level is the job of scientists. The aim of society is to keep such substances below their harmful level. And those who willfully produce those substances in such a way as to create harm are morally guilty of harming others.

One question is how much of given substances is necessary to cause harm. This level is sometimes disputed, and scientists as well as nations may vary in what they consider safe. Once a level is determined, the next step is to try to prevent crossing the harm threshold. The problem here is that very often there is no one person or firm that produces the harmful level. If the harm is caused by the wastes of a single firm, then the solution is relatively simple — namely, to preclude that firm from polluting. Determining how to do that may be a difficult problem both technically and politically, but the situation is exacerbated when multiple sources produce the harmful pollution.

Because pollution can involve harm to others, it has a moral dimension, but because it can be controlled or handled in a number of ways, it has a social dimension that may vary from city to city, state to state, and nation to nation.

Consider the following case. Jason City, a community of 150,000 people, has five factories in an industrially zoned section on the east side of the city. One of the factories is much older than the others and emits three times more sulfur into the atmosphere than the newer plants, each of which emits about the same amount of sulfur as the others. The atmosphere can absorb a certain amount of pollution and carry it away without ill effects to either people or property. Therefore, the city has had no need to do anything about the emissions from the factories, and the factories have not invested in any pollution control equipment. A sixth factory is built. It emits the same amount of sulfur as the other four new factories, but it adds just enough so that now a possibly dangerous level of sulfur is discharged into the air. The pollution may now cause harm. We have said that corporations have a moral obligation not to cause harm to people or property. Who is morally responsible to do what? The oldest factory claims that it was in the town first, and although it produces the most pollution, it caused no harm until the sixth factory arrived. The other four claim that they are minor polluters and would cause no harm if either the sixth factory had not opened or if the first factory lowered its sulfur emissions to the same level as the other factories. The sixth plant claims that it has as much right to emit sulfur into the atmosphere as the other plants, and therefore should not bear any special burden. By itself, it claims, it does no harm.

Clearly, the six plants together cause the harm, even though each one by itself would not cause harm. The moral obligation not to cause harm implies that collectively the plants must reduce and limit the total sulfur they emit. But this does not tell us what each plant should do. Ethics alone will not tell us that, because there are many ethical ways of reducing the pollution to an acceptable level. Let us consider a few.

Jason City might decide that the pollution is small enough, the harm done to residents and property slight, and the benefits to the city from having six plants great enough that nothing need be done about it. The city might decide that if anyone claims damage from the pollution, that individual should sue one or all the plants for compensation. The city could impose a limit on the amount of sulfur any plant can emit. It could prevent the construction of any more plants. It could allow future plants to be built only if they emit no sulfur whatsoever, keeping the emission level at its present rate. The city might even take it upon itself to supply emission control devices to the plants, thereby controlling pollution at the source, at city expense. It might also tell the six companies that they are causing the pollution, and that they must lower the level or face a series of fines, thus leaving it up to the plants to arrange among themselves how to lower the sulfur to an acceptable level.

There is no one right and best way for Jason City to solve the problem of sulfur pollution, but there are many ways of approaching the problem. It is appropriate, however, that the plants emitting the sulfur control their emissions because the sulfur belongs to them. They have been allowed to use the air to get rid of their wastes when doing so injured no one, but when such a procedure threatens to harm others, then the action can be rightfully curtailed. The claim that because the air belongs to all of us, any of us can discharge what we want into it cannot be successfully defended.

Wastes belong to those who produce them. Just because people do not want their wastes does not release them (or firms) of the responsibility of disposing of their wastes in a way that does not harm others. The principle is recognized with respect to garbage. Individual households in some cities pay to have their garbage disposed of; in other cities this is a service provided through tax funds; and in rural communities people are sometimes allowed to dispose of it by burning it or carrying it themselves to the town dump. Air and water pollutants are industrial wastes, which belong to the plants that produce them as truly as a household's garbage belongs to the household. The method of disposal of such wastes varies with communities. But the principle that the wastes belong to the producer and that producers have no right to harm others by their wastes is a sound moral basis for imposing limits on what pollutants are admissible, in what amounts, and how the rest are to be controlled or disposed of.

Jason City exemplifies some dimensions of the problem of pollution. But the problem has many other facets and dimensions; it is often extremely complicated, and it involves conflicting principles. There is also much uncertainty about facts, the dangers posed, and the probable effects of proposed solutions.

Pollutants produced by many chemical and manufacturing processes are highly noxious. Such chemical byproducts can clearly cause harm. Those who produce these substances have the moral obligation to dispose of them in safe ways; otherwise, they are morally guilty of the harm they produce. Their obligation to dispose of them properly and safely was a moral obligation even prior to government regulation of such waste disposal. After a number of widely publicized reports about improper disposal and the sad effects thereof, the federal government passed a law requiring a "paper trace" that covered the handling of such wastes from the producing plant through the final disposition in a proper facility. Just before the law went into effect, a number of companies — both originators of the waste and haulers — dumped toxic wastes along open roads, to save the cost of hauling the waste to the proper disposal locations. Clearly, such acts threatened the health and safety of people who would be affected by the runoff and seepage into their drinking water supplies. The action was immoral — a blot on the record of the firms involved.

Pollution, we noted, can be ethically handled in many ways. One way is for those who produce harm to reimburse those harmed for the harm done. In this way compensatory justice is brought into play after the fact. When the harm done is both serious and preventable, such pollution is not usually ethically justifiable, even though reimbursing those harmed is preferable to not reimbursing them. In some cases, however, the harm done is not serious and recompense is a satisfactory remedy. The involved parties may even agree, prior to the harm, to a fee that is to be paid those who will be damaged. This is a form of licensing the harm done by compensating those harmed. This might be the procedure, for instance, in dealing with noise pollution produced by airport traffic as it affects those living near the field. The owners of the airport might buy from the neighbors affected the right to produce the noise. (Property values decrease, and the residents suffer from the disturbance of noisy airplanes flying overhead.) One approach to pollution, as these examples show, is to allow it, but to compensate, either before or after the fact, those who are adversely affected.

A second approach allows a firm to pollute but attempts to eliminate the pollution or clean it up before it damages anyone. The cleaning up might be done by the firm that produces it, the firm might hire someone else to handle the cleanup process, or the cleanup might be carried out by some governmental agency or body. In the last-named case, the cleanup might be done at public expense (in which case the taxpayers subsidize the polluting industry) or at the expense of the polluting firms.

A third approach to pollution is to prevent it at the source. This means that the pollution will not be allowed to develop. Government might mandate this, or firms might decide on their own that preventing the damage is preferable to paying for it afterward. If government mandates the prevention of pollution, it may either specify the means to be taken to prevent the pollution or simply require that there be no effluents of a certain type produced and allow the firms involved to take whatever measures they wish to achieve the mandated end. Many firms prefer the latter approach, claiming it offers them greater incentives to find cost-effective means of preventing pollution. Government-mandated procedures are usually not individually tailored to particular needs and so are not cost effective. A variant of this approach is to set certain limits on the pollution to be tolerated, requiring that it be kept at or below a certain threshold level. . . .

The problem of pollution is complex and open to a variety of solutions. There is controversy about acceptable levels of pollution, the necessity for producing certain kinds of wastes, the relative benefits involved with producing nuclear wastes for which there are no agreed-upon disposal procedures, and so on. These issues involve corporate, social, and ethical responsibility. But the issues are not always as easy to solve as some who attack corporate policy claim. In dealing with pollution, as in dealing with other issues of social responsibility, it would be helpful to distinguish what is ethically mandatory, what is desirable but not mandatory, what is to be decided by the political process, and how goals are to be achieved. A moral audit — or a social audit, of which a moral audit is a clear part — can be constructed to include an evaluation of corporate actions with respect to pollution. We would all benefit if such instruments helped make clear what the problem is, what the variety of solutions are, and which companies are fulfilling their ethical, legal, and social responsibilities in this area.

Shades of Green: Business, Ethics, and the Environment

R. Edward Freeman,
Jessica Pierce,
and Richard Dodd

THE CHALLENGE OF BUSINESS LEADERSHIP TODAY

It is possible for business leaders to make money, do the right thing, and participate in saving the earth. It is possible to fit these ideas together, but it is not easy. We have to warn you here and now that we don't have any quick solutions, magic bullets, or foolproof formulas for success. The issues are too difficult and messy for any such nonsense. Instead we are going to suggest how to begin to understand the concepts of business, ethics, and the environment so that they can work together.

This is an exercise about possibilities. Instead of showing the myriad ways that business, ethics, and the environment conflict and lead to impossible choices, we are going to ask the question, "How is it possible to put these ideas together?" In today's world and the one we are creating for our children, all three are necessary. Our businesses must continue to create value for their financiers and other stakeholders. In an interconnected global economy, we can no longer afford the ethical excesses that many see as characteristic of the last several decades. And, if we are to leave a livable world for our children and their children, we simply must pay attention to environmental matters.

Most of the methods, concepts, ideas, theories, and techniques that we use in business do not put business, ethics, and the environment together. From discounted cash flow to human resources planning, neither ethics nor the environment are central to the way we think about business.

Everyone shares the joke about the very idea of "business ethics" as an oxymoron, two words whose definitions are contradictory. Much of business language is oriented toward seeing a conflict between business and ethics. We routinely juxtapose profits with ethics, as if making an ethical decision costs profits. We sometimes qualify difficult choices that distribute harms and benefits to communities and employees as "business decisions," signaling that business and ethics are not compatible.

R. Edward Freeman, Jessica Pierce, and Richard Dodd, "Shades of Green: Business, Ethics, and the Environment," pp. 339–48, 352, Rowman & Littlefield Publishers, Inc. Reprinted by permission.

The environment fares no better. It is seen as a necessary evil, a cost to be minimized or a regulation with which to comply. We almost never think about the environment as central to the main metaphors of business, its strategic and people management systems, unless, of course, there is some regulation that constrains business strategy, a mess to be cleaned up or a public issue that pits executives against environmentalists. Historically, business people have been neither encouraged nor discouraged to get involved with environmental concerns. Our models and theories of business have traditionally been simply *silent* on the subject of the environment. The world of the 1990s, however, is beginning to make a great deal of noise.

More and more citizens see themselves as environmentalists. Governments are increasing their cooperative actions to address global environmental concerns such as global warming and biodiversity. And interest groups are beginning to propose solutions to problems that involve business decision making outside of and beyond government regulation.

So, what we desperately need are some new ideas, concepts, and theories that allow us to think about business, ethics, and the environment in one full breath. We need to see these issues as going together rather than in conflict. Today's challenge to business leadership is sustaining profitability, doing the right thing, and being green.

THE ENVIRONMENT: IT'S EVERYWHERE

Early on the morning of March 24, 1989, the super tanker Exxon *Valdez* ran aground on Bligh Reef in Prince William Sound off the coast of Alaska. In the days following the accident, every action or inaction by Exxon executives, government officials and environ-mentalists was subjected to an unprecedented public scrutiny.

In addition to the damage caused by the release of millions of gallons of oil into the ecosystem, the *Valdez* incident symbolizes an important milestone in business history. The environment is an issue that has come to stay. It is not a fad, passing fancy, or the issue of the day.

There is not a single aspect of our world today that can escape the scrutiny of environmental analysis. Pollution of air, water, and land; the production and disposal of hazardous wastes; solid waste disposal; chemical and nuclear spills and accidents; global warming and the greenhouse effect; ozone depletion; deforestation and desertification; biodiversity; and overpopulation are a few of the issues that today's executive needs to understand to be environmentally literate.

We are treated to daily doom and gloom press reports about the state of the earth. Scientists have "discovered" that global warming is or is not a problem, is or is not caused by solar storms, is or is not related to the emission of greenhouse gases, and so forth. We want to know the answer, the whole truth, "just the facts," about the environment, and we get disturbed by so many conflicting reports.

The truth is this: There is no one truth about the environment. The truth is also this: We have not lived in a way that respects the environment and preserves it for our children's children.

OUR CHILDREN'S FUTURE: A WAGER

Let's assume an optimistic scenario that implies that the gloomy forecasts are all wrong. Maybe there is enough land for landfills for generations to come. Global warming may be elusive. Many chemicals may well be harmless. The destruction of forests may be insignificant and worth the benefits of development. Clean and healthful water may someday be plentiful. And it may be that we can invent the technology we need to compensate for whatever damage we actually have done to the earth.

Are you willing to bet the future of your children on this optimistic scenario? If it is wrong, or even partially wrong, with respect to, say, global warming, then there will be no inhabitable world left for our children. . . . We are going to assume that it is reasonable to bet that there is, in fact, an environmental crisis. The consequences of being wrong are too great to bet otherwise.

Yet the great majority of responses to the environmental crisis have been at best ineffective. The main response mode has been to marshal the public policy process to legislate that the air and water be cleaner, and to assign the costs of doing so to states, localities, and businesses. Twenty-plus years of environmental regulation in the United States has led to "environmental gridlock." There is disagreement and contention at several important levels.

First of all, as we stated earlier, there isn't any one truth about the state of the environment. Many (but not all) individual scientific "facts" are disputable. There is widespread disagreement about the scientific answers to environmental questions, even about how the questions should be stated.

Second, among those who agree about the science around a particular issue, there is still disagreement about the appropriate public policy. Even if we agree that greenhouse gases lead to global warming, we may well disagree that limiting carbon dioxide emissions to 1990 levels will solve the problem.

Third, there is disagreement about the underlying values. How should we live? By exploiting the earth's resources? By conserving the earth's resources? By living with nature? Should we be vegetarians to improve the ability of advanced societies to feed the hungry and use land efficiently? Should we recycle or should we consume green products or should we build an ethic of "anti-consumption," of saving the earth rather than consuming it?

These three levels of disagreement lead to gridlock, especially in a public policy process that purports to base policy on facts rather than values. Overlay these three levels of disagreement on a litigious system of finding, blaming, and punishing pollutes of the past and the result is a conversation about the environment that goes nowhere fast.

We believe that this public policy process needs to change, that we need to have a better conversation about the environment and the role of governments, but we are not willing to wait for these changes to take place. Instead we want to suggest another mode of response to the environmental crisis: business strategy. If we can come to see how business activity can take place, systematically, in environmentally friendly ways, then we can respond to the environmental crisis in lasting and effective ways.

THE BASICS OF BUSINESS: WHAT DO YOU STAND FOR?

At the thousands of McDonald's franchises around the world one thing is the same: McDonald's values. "QVC" means Quality, Value, and Cleanliness, and the very idea of McDonald's is built around realizing these values. This is why at any McDonald's anywhere you get good quality, fast-food, a clean restaurant, and a good comparative price. The very meaning of McDonald's encompasses these values, and everyone, from CEO to fry cook, has to understand his or her job in terms of these values.

Strangely enough, a tiny company, only a fraction of the size of McDonald's, works the same way. The company is called Johnsonville

Sausage in Johnsonville and Sheboygan, Wisconsin. It is highly profitable, fast growing, and is based on different values from McDonald's. At Johnsonville Sausage the operating philosophy is self-improvement. The company exists in order for the individuals in it to realize their goals and to continue to improve themselves.

There is a revolution afoot in business today. And it is a revolution with values at its core. Sparked by Tom Peters and Bob Waterman's best-selling book, *In Search of Excellence,* the rediscovery of Edward Demming's ideas on the productive workplace and the role of values and quality, and the countless programs for individual and organizational change that have been ignited by an increasingly competitive global marketplace, business today is turning to values.

At one level, this emphasis on values cuts against the traditions of business. It has always been assumed that business promotes only one primary value — profits. Both the academic research and the how-to books on business are full of ideas on how to become more profitable. And profits are important as they are the lifeblood of business. But surely the purpose of life is not simply to breathe or to have our hearts go on beating. As important as these activities are, we humans are capable of more, of standing for some principles, or caring for others, or creating value for ourselves and others. Even those few people who care only for themselves still must be good enough citizens to avoid trampling on the rights and projects of others.

Organizations are no different. Profits are important, necessary — add any words you want — but there is more. Businesses can, and often do, stand for something more than profitability. Some, like IBM, stand for creating value for customers, employees, and shareholders. Others, like Merck, stand for the alleviation of human suffering. Still others, like Mesa Petroleum, may well stand for

creating value for shareholders only, but even those companies must do so within the confines of the law and public expectations that could be turned into law.

This concern for values can be summarized in the idea of enterprise strategy, or asking the question, "What do you stand for?" The typical strategy process in a company asks someone to think about these questions: (1) What businesses are we in? (2) What is our competitive advantage in these businesses? (3) How can we sustain competitive advantage? What product/market focus should we take? What needs to change in order to be successful?

Some set of these questions goes into every company architecture of its portfolio of businesses. Even small businesses have to have some business plan, perhaps in the mind of the entrepreneur, which articulates how that small business creates, captures, and sustains value.

But, if this values revolution in business is meaningful, there is a prior question, the question of enterprise strategy: "What do you stand for?" By articulating an answer to this question, thereby setting forth a statement of the core values of the organization, the strategy questions mentioned earlier will have some context in which they can be answered. For instance, if you stand for human dignity and some basic idea of human rights for all, then there are probably some markets that you will not serve, and some products and services that you will not provide. If you stand for quality, cleanliness, and value, then there are certain business opportunities that you will forego because you cannot produce the quality service, or do it in a clean environment, or provide it at a price that gives good value.

Now all of this may sound rather fanciful, but the basic point is that businesses have discovered that articulating some bedrock, some foundation, some basic values has enormous benefits. The business becomes focused around these values. People, from executives to mail clerks, begin to believe in them or are attracted to the firm because of these values. In short, business strategy just makes more sense in the context of values.

It is easy to see how thinking about the environment and about ethics is compatible with the values revolution. By clearly stating and understanding the core beliefs that an organization has or wants to adopt about ethical issues such as honesty, integrity, dignity of individuals, caring about others, and so on, policies that are straightforward and easily implementable can be designed. By clearly thinking through a position on the environment — whether it is just complying with the law or trying to leave the earth better than we found it — we can begin to marshal resources to realize these basic beliefs.

Executives can begin to meet the challenge of leadership we articulated earlier — being profitable, doing the right thing, and helping to save the earth — by understanding and articulating an enterprise strategy, an answer to the question, "What do we stand for?" From huge DuPont to little Ben and Jerry's, from oil and chemical companies to retail boutiques, articulating what you stand for on the environment is step one to a greener world, one that we can pass along to our children.

IT'S NOT EASY BEING GREEN

There are many ways that businesses can adopt strategies that are more friendly toward the environment. None of them are simple. In the words of that great philosopher, Kermit the Frog, "It's not easy being green."

We want to suggest that there are four primary "shades of green," and each has its own logic, and each has many interpretations.

Let's call these shades: (1) light green; (2) market green; (3) stakeholder green; and (4) dark green. You can think of these shades as phases of development of a company's strategy, moving from light green to dark green, but keep in mind that each shade has its own logic. It isn't necessary to move from one shade to the next. And each shade offers its own way to create and sustain value, so that business, ethics, and the environment go together. Here's a brief thumbnail sketch of the logic of each shade of green.

Light Green, or Legal Green, is a shade with which most companies are familiar. Being Light Green involves complying with the following principle:

Light Green Principle

Create and sustain competitive advantage by ensuring that your company is in compliance with the law.

The logic of Light Green relies on the public policy process to drive its strategy. But, it is a mistake to think that no competitive advantage is possible for every company that has to obey the law — a mistake on two counts.

First, as Michael Porter and his colleagues have argued, countries with strict environmental standards seem to gain an edge in global marketplaces — they become more efficient and have better technology. Secondly, within an industry, companies actively can pursue public policies that fit with their special competitive advantage. By innovating with technology and know-how, a company gains an advantage over a competitor who cannot comply as efficiently. Light Green thinking thus creates the possibility for competitive advantage.

Market Green logic is different. Rather than focus on the public policy process, Market Green logic focuses on customers. The following principle is at work:

Market Green Principle

Create and sustain competitive advantage by paying attention to the environmental preferences of customers.

Market Green strategies are based on the greening of the customer, a fast-growing yet controversial phenomenon. Today's customer-focused, market-driven company cannot afford to miss the fact that customers prefer environmentally friendly products — and without added costs. Again it is easy to see that creating and sustaining competitive advantage is a matter of "better, cheaper, faster." Companies that can meet these environmental needs will be the winners. Customer perceptions about the shade of green of the company will be crucial, but most importantly the products and services have to perform.

McDonald's decision to ban Styrofoam cartons was driven in part by customers' perceptions that polystyrene was bad for the environment. But if the new containers made from treated paper cannot be recycled or biodegraded, customer needs will not have been met, and someone else will produce a more environmentally friendly burger.

Market Green logic just applies good old-fashioned "smell the customer" thinking to the environment. Note that this may or may not be in conjunction with Legal Green. Market Green logic roots competitive advantage in customer needs and the ability of the customer-driven company to deliver on these needs. There is nothing unusual except giving up the costly belief that environmentally friendly products always entail higher costs and competitive disadvantages. Notice that Market Green logic can apply to the indus-

trial sector as well as the consumer sector and to services as well as products.

Stakeholder Green is a shade darker than Market Green. It applies Market Green logic to key stakeholder groups such as customers, suppliers, employees, communities, shareholders, and other financiers. There are many different ways to slice the stakeholder pie. Companies can seek to maximize the benefits of one group, or they can seek to harmonize the interests of all groups. The point is that Stakeholder Green gets its color from responding to the needs of some or all stakeholder groups. It obeys the following principle:

Stakeholder Green Principle

Create and sustain competitive advantage by responding to the environmental preferences of stakeholders.

Stakeholder Green strategies are based on a more thoroughgoing adoption of environmental principles among all aspects of a company's operations. Many companies have adopted a version of Stakeholder Green by requiring suppliers to meet environmental requirements and by setting strict standards for the manufacturing process. Paying attention to recyclable material in consumer packaging, educating employees on environmental issues, participating in community efforts to clean up the environment, and appealing to investors who want to invest in green companies are all a part of Stakeholder Green. This shade is different because it does not require one action or a focused set of actions; rather, it requires anticipating and responding to a whole set of issues regarding the environment. As such it is more complicated than the earlier shades. The logic of Stakeholder Green is similar to the logic of quality processes. Unless quality processes permeate a company at all levels, they are doomed to fail. There are different levels of commitment to Stakeholder Green, just as there are different levels of commitment to quality, but any effective commitment must be pervasive.

Dark Green is a shade for which few companies strive. Being Dark Green commits a company to being a leader in making environmental principles a fundamental basis for doing business. Dark Green suggests the following principle:

Dark Green Principle

Create and sustain value in a way that sustains and cares for the earth.

To most business people this principle will sound pretty idealistic or fanciful. Their skepticism only points out how much we have ignored the environment in our ways of thinking about business. Indigenous people know that this principle must be obeyed. We teach our children to care for their things and the things — such as our homes and land — that we share. It is not a large stretch of the imagination to expect that the same values are possible in business.

Dark Green logic is not antibusiness, though many people will believe it is. Humans create value for each other, and *business* is the name we have given that process. Dark Green logic just says that we must respect and care for the earth in this process of value creation.

There are more than four shades of green. Look at these four as anchors that can define what is possible for your company. Dark Green is not for everyone, while Light Green may be more universal. Indeed Dark Green raises more questions than it answers. It reminds us that the very idea of "living with the earth" or "treating the earth with respect" are difficult issues that bring forth deep philosophical questions.

Our argument is not that we should find the optimal shade for everyone, but that variation is good. That is, imagine a world in which there are thousands of enterprises each trying to realize competitive advantage through environmental means. Undoubtedly, many of these innovations will fail, but some will succeed, and many will lead to other, more important innovations. It is only through a large-scale process of many small innovations that real, lasting change can occur. Perhaps while such innovation is emerging, someone, somewhere, will invent a revolutionary "pollution machine" that will cure all of our environmental ills, or some official will "discover" the perfect set of regulations. All well and good if that happens, but we are suggesting a more modest and, we believe, more workable approach.

TOUGH QUESTIONS

Ultimately how we run our companies reflects our commitment to how we want to live. Our values are lived through our behavior. Someone who espouses green values but who does nothing to realize those values lives in bad faith or self-deception. Bad faith means that we say one thing and do another, and self-deception means we are not honest with ourselves about what we truly believe and how we really want to live. Ethics, in life and in business, starts with an assumption of good faith and self-awareness, or at least an acknowledgment of the difficulties involved in being authentic to our true beliefs.

Nowhere do we see these issues more plainly than in environmental values. Talk is cheap, and its price is related to a shared history and culture of not living in a way that guarantees our children a future. We believe there are many ways to live — indeed many ways to live in an environmentally sustainable way — but we also know that our values have not always led us in any sustainable direction.

The point is that we do depend on the natural world and, especially today, the natural world depends on us for its survival. Humans have the capability to destroy life on earth, and such a capability implies a responsibility to live ethically. We argue that any shade of green that you adopt raises important questions about our responsibility to live ethically. We explore three of these philosophical challenges here. Briefly they are conservation, social justice, and ecology.

The conservation challenge tells us to conserve the earth's resources for the future and is a minimal response to Our Children's Future Wager.

The social justice challenge tells us that there are many ways to improve the institutions that we have created. It focuses on those who have been mistreated by those institutions — women, minorities, indigenous peoples — and traces a connection between their mistreatment and the way we view the environment.

The ecological challenge comes in many forms, but it asks us to view the Earth as a living organism and to find a way to talk about the Earth and its creatures in our human-centered moral discourse. We should live in a way that is sustainable and self-renewing, rather than destructive of current resources.

Each of these three philosophies challenges our ways of doing business. It is easiest to integrate conservation with the normal ways we think about business, but we argue that what is necessary to meet Our Children's Future is a conversation that takes all three philosophies into account. We need to understand how we redefine business and make it consistent with each of these three views. . . .

SUMMARY

We have chosen a difficult project — we want to engage you in a conversation about how to think about business, ethics, and the environment together rather than separately. We are optimistic that the fruits of such a conversation can make a difference, to us and to our children. If you are confident that your children have a safe and secure future then you don't need to wrestle with the questions that this conversation raises, and you don't need to examine your values and behavior to see if there needs to be change, but we do not share your confidence.

We do not have confidence that the future is secure, nor do we have confidence that our current institutions, as well meaning as they may be, are doing all that is necessary. We are confident that if we can begin to think about business in environmentally sound ways, we can make real progress.

INVESTMENT RISK

The Individual Investor in Securities Markets: An Ethical Analysis

Robert E. Frederick
and W. Michael Hoffman

Securities markets are full of pitfalls for individual investors. Examples of fraud and regulatory violations in the markets are common. For instance, a recent *Business Week* cover story reports that investors are being duped out of hundreds of millions a year in penny stock scams in spite of SEC regulations.[1] A report in the *Wall Street Journal* on the Chicago futures trading fraud highlights the "danger of being ripped off in futures markets" by unscrupulous floor brokers filling customers' "market orders" — a type of order that "individual investors should avoid using."[2]

But securities markets present risks to individual investors that go beyond clear violations of regulations and fraud. The above *Wall Street Journal* story, for example, also issued a more general warning to investors:

> Futures are fast moving, risky investment vehicles that are unsuitable for anyone who can't afford to lose and who doesn't have time to pay close attention to trading positions?[3]

Furthermore, it is not only the high risk futures and commodities markets that are perilous for investors. For example, the North American Securities Administration reports that "the securities industry isn't responding well to the problems of small investors in the wake of the stock market crash," problems such as poor execution of trades and being misled by brokers.[4] Even the bond markets,

which in the past at least gave the outside appearance of stability, are in increasing turmoil. For instance, the SEC is now investigating the possibility that securities firms dumped billions of dollars of risky municipal bonds on individual investors because they were unable to sell them to institutions.[5] And MetLife is suing RJR-Nabisco on the grounds that individual investors were unjustifiably harmed when the A rated corporate bonds they purchased lost millions in value due to the junk bond financing of the RJR-Nabisco leveraged buyout.[6]

In light of these and many other examples that could be given, suppose the SEC announced that individual investors, for their own protection, no longer have access to securities markets. They are no longer permitted to buy stocks, bonds, or commodities or futures options. If this were to happen there surely would be a public outcry of protest, even moral outrage. The reasons for such outrage probably would revolve around the belief that some fundamental right had been violated, perhaps the presumed right that markets should be free and open so that everyone has an opportunity to better his or her position and enjoy the goods and services of society.

A quick look, however, reveals that not all markets have unrestricted access. Nor is there a generally accepted belief that any rights are being unjustifiably violated in such cases. In

Journal of Business Ethics 9 (1990): 579–89. © 1990 Kluwer Academic Publishers. Reprinted by permission of Kluwer Academic Publishers.

consumer markets, for example, individuals under a certain age are prohibited from voting, buying alcoholic beverages, and seeing certain movies. Regardless of age, not just anyone can buy a fully automatic rifle or order a few dozen hand grenades. In fact, not just anyone can drive a car; one must pass a test and be licensed to do that. Furthermore, even after being allowed to drive, this privilege can be revoked if it is abused. And, of course, none of our citizens is legally permitted to participate in certain drug markets, such as cocaine.

But it will be argued that there is good reason for these and other such restrictions. We are attempting to prevent people, the argument goes, from harming themselves or causing harm to others. This is what makes it morally permissible, or even obligatory, to restrict access to certain kinds of consumer products. The ethical principle here is that, when possible, persons ought to be protected from undue harm. Hence, the restrictions in question are justified.

Yet might not this be exactly the rationale behind a possible SEC ban against individual investors entering securities markets? Just as unrestricted access to some drugs is thought to present unacceptable risks to consumers, trading in today's securities markets may present unacceptable risks to many investors, resulting in great financial rather than physical harm. And since we feel justified in prohibiting consumers from buying what we take to be highly dangerous drugs or other consumer products, shouldn't we, by analogy, be justified in prohibiting certain investors from buying highly risky financial instruments? . . .

EXACTLY WHAT KIND OF INVESTOR ARE WE TALKING ABOUT?

The type of investor we will be concerned with, and the type we take to be the most likely candidate for the SEC prohibition mentioned earlier, is one that (a) is at relatively *high risk*, where risk is a function of the probability of a certain market event occurring and the degree of harm the investor would suffer were the event to occur, and (b) an investor who is relatively *unsophisticated* about the functioning of the market and hence unappreciative of the degree of risk he or she faces. For example, suppose Jones invests his life savings in high yield bonds issued to finance an LBO, and suppose a few months later the company that issued the bonds suddenly announces that it is going into Chapter 11 bankruptcy. The value of the bonds drops precipitously and, for all practical purposes, in a matter of hours Jones' savings are wiped out. If Jones did not realize that the high return he was initially receiving was a reflection of the risky nature of the bonds, then he would fall within the category of investors with which we are concerned even assuming he had several million dollars invested. . . .

DO AT-RISK INVESTORS HAVE A RIGHT TO PARTICIPATE IN SECURITIES MARKETS?

Obviously at-risk investors are legally permitted to invest in securities markets, but do they have a right to do so? And if they do, what kind of right is it? These questions are important since how they are answered will determine in large part what kind of justification will be required to restrict or suspend investments by at-risk investors, or whether a justification is possible at all.

Since the word "right" is used in many different senses, we will give rough definitions of the sense in which we will use "right" and associated terms. A "claim right," as we will understand it, is a right established within a system of rules. To have such a right is to have a valid or justified claim for action or forbearance against some person or institution. The notion of a "liberty" is weaker than that of a right. To have a liberty is not to have a duty or obligation to act toward a person or institution in a certain way. Rights imply liberties, but one may have a liberty without an associated right. A still weaker notion is that of a "privilege." To have a privilege is to have revocable permission to act in a certain way.[7]

Claim rights, liberties, and privileges can be either legal or moral depending on whether the rules in question are established by legislative action or follow from a system of morality. It is important to see that legal rights and moral rights need not be the same. A moral right may not be recognized by law, and one may have a legal right to engage in an immoral action.

If at-risk investors have claim rights to invest in the market, then the government has a corresponding duty not to interfere with their activity. On the other hand, if they have a liberty to invest, they have no duty not to invest. If they have a privilege, then they are permitted to invest but such permission can be withdrawn. Now, if at-risk investors have a claim right to invest, as opposed to a weaker liberty or an even weaker privilege to invest, then the justification required for infringing on that right will be very different from that required if they have a liberty or privilege. Hence, it is important to decide, as best we can, exactly which they have.

We believe a strong case can be made that at-risk investors have a moral claim right to invest in the market, and that this right follows from the classic "right to freedom" that is so much a part of the American tradition. . . .

It follows from the right to freedom that it is morally permissible for persons to choose to invest in any way they deem appropriate within the bounds of law and a proper regard for the wrongful effects their actions may have on the lives of others.

If this is correct, then any interference with this right, whether by some individual or government agency, is prima facie unjustified. There are, however, several objections that could be raised. One of them is that persons simply have no such moral right because they have no rights at all other than those granted by law. Thus, no moral right is violated if the legal right to invest is altered or eliminated. Another is that although persons have moral rights, they do not have the right to freedom that we have attributed to them. . . .

There is one other objection to the right of freedom that we proposed. It is that even if all competent persons have an equal right to freedom, it still does not follow that they have the right to make any choice within the sphere of choices that do not wrongfully harm others. It does not follow, for example, that they have the right to make choices that seriously harm themselves. Intervention in such cases may be justified to prevent harm.

But is it? In order to decide, we must consider the possible justifications for interfering with the choices of others.

WHAT SORT OF JUSTIFICATION MIGHT BE OFFERED FOR RESTRICTING THE INVESTMENTS OF AT-RISK INVESTORS?

One kind of justification that might be proposed is paternalistic. By paternalism we roughly mean interfering with a person's actions or preferences by restricting their freedom of action or the range of choices normally available to them for the reason that such a restriction promotes or preserves their good, welfare, happiness, or interests. A paternalistic justification for restricting at risk investors would be that exposure to risk for many investors is too great to permit them to continue without some sort of protection that reduces the risk to an acceptable degree. For certain investors an acceptable degree may be no risk at all. For others some risk may be permissible.

In either case, the argument goes, as long as the intent of intervention is to protect or promote the good of at risk investors, and as long as it does not wrong other persons, then intervention is at least permissible and may be obligatory. It is only in this way that harm to many investors can be prevented.

The standard objection to paternalistic justifications is something like this: If people choose to run the risk to gain what they believe will be the rewards, who are we to interfere? From where do we derive a special dispensation to overrule their choices and interfere with their lives?

Although there is a kernel of truth in this objection, it is much too facile. Some paternalistic acts are clearly justified. Paternalistic reasoning is commonly used to justify restricting the choices of children and people judged incompetent or otherwise unable rationally to consider the consequences of their acts. Moreover, paternalistic justifications are not obviously unreasonable even in cases where the competence of the person is not in question. It is at least initially credible that some consumer products, such as prescription drugs, are not in unrestricted circulation precisely because of paternalistic reasons.

Let us confine our discussion to those persons ordinarily taken to be competent and rational. We still do not believe that paternalism *per se* justifies restricting at-risk investors that fall within this category. One reason is that it may be impossible to find out just what the good or welfare of an individual investor is. Not only is there the thorny problem of trying to reach a common and precise understanding of the vague idea of the "good" of a person, there are immense practical difficulties in discovering whether a certain individual's good is served by restricting his or her access to the market. There may be situations where an individual's good is not served, and intervention in those cases would be a wrongful violation of his or her rights.

But suppose regulators do know the good of some individuals. Would paternalism then justify intervening to preserve or promote their good? We believe not in cases where regulators and the person in question have differing conceptions of that person's good. Even if regulators happen to know a person's "true" good better than he or she does themselves, imposing on that person a conception of his or her good they do not accept is not justified. Regulators may attempt to persuade at-risk investors to take a different course or provide them with information that they need to make an informed decision, but it is not permissible to deny them the right to direct their lives. . . .

Although paternalism as characterized thus far does not justify interference with the choices of at-risk investors, there are circumstances in which intervention is justified. This can best be explained by using an example not related to investing. Suppose Jones mistakenly believes the food he is about to eat is wholesome but we have good reason to think it is contaminated with botulism. As he raises the fork to his mouth, we only have time to strike it away. At first he is angry, but after we explain the reason for our action he is grateful. The act of striking the fork away is an example of paternalistic intervention since it is done for Jones' good but against his wishes. It seems obvious, however, that we acted properly. Intervention in this case is justified since if Jones were fully aware of the circumstances he would act differently or would agree to have us intervene on his behalf. He would consent to our action. Hence, intervention here respects his right to freedom since it is compatible with his goals and does not force upon him some version of his good he would not accept.

Note that it is not merely our superior knowledge of the situation that justifies interference, but also our judgment that Jones would agree that our actions preserve or promote his good. The case would be different were Jones attempting suicide instead of trying to have a decent meal. Paternalistic intervention may not be justified when a person voluntarily undertakes an action harmful to him- or herself, provided that person has a reasonably complete understanding of his or her circumstances and the consequences of the action. But it is at least prima facie justified, we suggest, when an action is based on incomplete information and thus is, in one sense, less than fully voluntary.

Now suppose there are compelling grounds to believe that some otherwise competent investors are unappreciative of the high degree of risk they face, and that if they were presented with information about those risks they would act either to reduce or eliminate them, or would consent to having restrictions placed on the kinds of investments they could make. Since they would consent to intervention or act differently were they fully aware of the circumstances, intervention on their behalf is justified just as it was justified for Jones. Their rights are not violated since nothing is imposed on them that they would not consent to were they fully aware of the dangers they faced.

A major difference between the Jones case and at-risk investors is that we dealt with Jones as an individual, but a regulatory or legislative body would have to deal with at-risk investors as a group. There simply is no way to reach them all individually. Furthermore, although such bodies may be able to make reasonable assumptions about the kinds of risks acceptable to most at-risk investors, and about the kinds of restrictions to which most of them would agree, it seems inevitable that there will be some investors who would not consent to restrictions because, for example, they have an unusual conception of their good or welfare, or because they find the restrictions highly offensive. For these people restrictions on investing will impose a foreign conception of their good on them and thus is not compatible with their right to direct their lives. . . .

If the *reason* given for intervening is promoting the good of at-risk investors as a group, then, as we have tried to argue, it is not justified. Suppose, however, the reason is not only that the good of some investors is promoted, but that there is a duty to intervene to protect certain *rights,* in particular, the right of investors not to be harmed. The argument would go something like this: There is good reason to believe that some at-risk investors would consent to having restrictions placed on them to protect their financial position and prevent them from suffering financial harm. Since it is a basic function of government to protect its citizens from harm, there is a duty to protect these investors. Hence, placing restrictions on their investment activities is justified even though such restrictions may violate the right of other investors to direct their lives as they see fit.

If this argument is plausible, then there is a conflict of rights between two groups of at-risk investors. This is a genuine moral dilemma that can only be resolved by deciding whose rights are to prevail. We believe it should be the right not to be harmed. An analogy with prescription drugs may be helpful here. One reason there are restrictions on access to drugs is to prevent harm to persons who do not know how to use them correctly. These restrictions are justified, in our view, even supposing there are some individuals willing to take the risk. The right to freedom of this latter group should be and should remain a serious consideration in devising restrictions on drugs, but it does not override the right of others not to be exposed to excessive risk and possible serious harm.

The same holds true of at-risk investors. The right of some of them not to be exposed to excessive risk and possible serious financial harm overrides the right of others to invest without restrictions. We emphasize, however, that the right to freedom cannot be lightly dismissed, and must be given due consideration when formulating policies and regulations governing the markets. . . .

IF SOME INVESTORS ARE RESTRICTED, HOW SHOULD IT BE DONE?

Since we are not experts in the regulation of securities markets, the best we can do here is make a few suggestions that seem to us worthy of additional investigation. It is a basic premise, essential for any just system of regulation and law, that relevantly different classes of persons be treated in relevantly different ways. Hence, it clearly would be unjust to restrict the activities of all investors to protect some of them. It also follows from this basic premise that distinctions must be drawn within the class of at-risk investors. It may turn out in the end that there is no workable method of protecting some at-risk investors while preserving the rights of all of them, but it would be a mistake to begin with this assumption.

In light of this it might be suggested that the only plausible course of action is to make sure that at-risk investors have all the information they need to make investment decisions. This has at least three advantages. The first is that providing information does not seriously infringe any rights. And establishing stringent policies to ensure that the information is received also may be reasonable. For example, suppose that to demonstrate a minimum level of competence persons must pass an examination before investing, just as they have to pass a driving exam before driving. Different kinds of exams could be given for different kinds of investments. Would such a procedure violate any rights? It certainly would be costly and inconvenient, but we doubt that it is an inordinate restriction on the right to freedom.

A second advantage is that providing information is already one function of the Securities and Exchange Commission. According to the Commission's pamphlet "Consumers' Financial Guide" the three main responsibilities of the Commission are:

1. To require that companies that offer their securities for sale in "interstate commerce" register with the Commission and make available to investors complete and accurate information.
2. To protect investors against misrepresentation and fraud in the issuance and sale of securities.
3. To oversee the securities markets to ensure they operate in a fair and orderly manner.

Although the pamphlet goes on to advise investors that "whatever the choice of investment, make sure that you have complete and accurate information before investing to ensure that you use your funds wisely," it also emphasizes that the SEC does not see itself as the guarantor of investments:

> Registration . . . does not insure investors against loss of their investments, but serves rather to provide information upon which investors may base an informed and realistic evaluation of the worth of a security.

Thus, providing information to at-risk investors is consistent with the mission of the SEC and would not require massive restructuring of the Commission.

The third advantage is that providing information would be the most direct way to discover whether investors would consent to restrictions. Earlier we argued that restrictions on some at-risk investors are justified because they would consent to intervention if they were fully aware of the risk they faced. But instead of imposing regulations based on what investors *would* do were they to have all the relevant information, it is preferable to give them the information whenever possible and see what they *actually* do. This would avoid the danger of imposing on them a conception of their good that they do not accept.

We agree that providing information to at-risk investors is a good idea, and propose that methods be initiated that ensure that investors receive the information, rather than just having it available for those that seek it out. However, this may not be enough to eliminate unacceptable risks for at-risk investors. Consider the prescription drug market again, and assume that the FDA made strenuous efforts to provide consumers with complete information about drugs. Supposing for a moment that it is legally permissible for consumers to buy drugs, as it is in some countries, this might be enough to eliminate unacceptable risk of harm from drugs for the few that had the time, energy, and expertise to use the information. But for most people it would be an overwhelming blizzard of paper that would be of no real use. As Steven Kelman has argued, the cost of organizing and understanding the information may be so high that the most sensible course of action for most people would be to assign their right to select drugs to some individual or institution with special expertise, provided the choice was made with their best interests in mind.[8] Merely providing information about drugs does not protect persons from harm unless the information is understood. When it appears unlikely that a large class of people will devote the time needed to understand it, then it is appropriate, we believe, to place legal restrictions on their choices. This protects them from harm, but is not an intolerable limitation of freedom.

The same reasoning applies in the securities markets. So much information is available and it is so complex that for many investors beyond a certain point it would be too costly to make the investment in time required to assimilate it all. Having "complete and accurate information," as the SEC suggests, is not enough. Leaving aside the issue of how one determines whether it is complete and accurate (note that not even the SEC does that), there remains the problem of understanding it well enough to make a wise investment decision. Perhaps it could be done, but would it be done by most at-risk investors? We are inclined to think not. So we suggest that, just as with prescription drugs, at-risk investors be required by law to engage the services of an expert. This would go a long way toward eliminating unacceptable risks for them, and given the significant possibility of harm many investors face, we do not feel it would be an excessive restriction on their freedom. Exceptions would have to be made for those investors willing to become expert in the markets (since they would no longer meet the definition of an at-risk investor), and some system of qualifications would need to be established to identify investment counselors capable of advising the other investors. . . .

NOTES

1. "The Penny Stock Scandal," *Business Week*, 23 (Jan. 1989), pp. 74–82.
2. "Investors Can Take a Bite Out of Fraud," *Wall Street Journal*, (Jan. 24, 1989), p. C1.
3. *Wall Street Journal*, (Jan. 24, 1989), p. C1.
4. "Many Crash Complaints Unresolved," *Wall Street Journal*, (Oct. 10, 1988), p. C1. For additional information on problems faced by individual investors, see John L. Casey, *Ethics in the Financial Marketplace* (Scudder, Stevens & Clark, New York, 1988).
5. "SEC Studies Municipals in Trusts," *Wall Street Journal*, (Oct. 11, 1988), p. C1.
6. "Bondholders Are Mad as Hell — And No Wonder," *Business Week*, (Dec. 5, 1988), p. 28.
7. Joel Feinberg, *Social Philosophy* (Prentice Hall, Englewood Cliffs, NJ, 1973), pp. 55–56. These definitions are based on the ones given by Feinberg.
8. Steven Kelman, "Regulation and Paternalism," in *Ethical Theory and Business*, eds. T. L. Beauchamp and N. E. Bowie (Prentice Hall, Englewood Cliffs, NJ, 1988), p. 153.

Management Buyouts and Managerial Ethics

Robert F. Bruner
and Lynn Sharp Paine

Because of their unusual terms, size, and number, management buyouts (MBOs) have emerged as one of the more arresting features in the corporate landscape. W. T. Grimm and Company estimated that in 1979 the value of firms going private was $636 million.[1] By 1986, *Mergers and Acquisitions* estimated the value of firms going private to be $40.9 billion.[2] As the volume of management buyouts rises, so does the volume of criticism. There are several avenues of attack. For instance, many critics doubt the social value of these transactions. They argue that MBOs threaten the financial stability of the American economy and are only financial rearrangements having no effect on the utilization of real assets.[3]

The attack most interesting from the standpoints of directors, senior managers, and shareholders rests on the claim that buyouts are unethical because of management's conflict of interest. In a buyout, managers' personal interests are pitted against their fiduciary duties to shareholders. Critics ask whether stockholders are getting the managerial loyalty to which they are entitled.[4] . . .

THE PROBLEM WITH BUYOUTS

In recent years, management buyouts have offered shareholders attractive returns. The cash flow gains from increased leverage and depreciation have permitted buyers to pay a premium over market price and at the same time to earn supernormal rates of return. On average, it appears that sellers receive almost a 30 percent premium for their equity claim. On the buyers' side, detailed case analyses suggest substantial internal rates of return on investment ranging from 25 to 50 percent. Superficially at least, it appears that both sides of the transaction win. Why, then, has management's role in buyouts been so heavily criticized?

The criticism is about fairness for the public shareholders. Management's position on both sides of the bargaining table may make buyout prices suspect even when shareholders are bought out at premiums. Critics find it difficult to see how management members of the buyout team can serve effectively as fiduciaries of selling shareholders and at the same time negotiate on their own behalf as buyers. As fiduciary, management's objective should be to obtain the highest price possible. As members of the buyout team, however, it would be natural for management to try to push the price as low as possible. A low price makes the purchase more attractive and enhances the potential future gains from going public again.

The risk is that management may take advantage of shareholders; but even if the buyout team offers shareholders a fair deal — one that satisfies its fiduciary obligations — the deal may not be perceived as fair by those who are aware of management's conflict of interest. The bevy of shareholder derivative lawsuits that have followed recent buyouts, even those at premium prices, and the criticisms produced by academics and policy makers indicate that shareholders lack confidence in the fairness of the prices they are offered.

Management's conflicting objectives are one source of concern about buyouts, but other issues are also involved. Management's superior knowledge exacerbates the problem of conflicting objectives. As insiders, managers have privileged access to information, sometimes secret, about the firm's prospects, and they have a unique feel for the company's value which comes from experience in handling its day-to-day affairs. Their knowledge of the firm and their special appreciation for its value give managers a decided advantage vis-à-vis shareholders and potential competitors when proposing a buyout price. A price which appears fair in light of publicly available information may be unfair when undisclosed plans, discoveries, and inventions are taken into account.

Management also has the ability to affect the company's stock price by controlling the flow of information, by its choice of accounting procedures, and by timing its strategic decisions. Opportunities to manipulate share price in conjunction with a buyout bid are significant. Quite apart from any deliberate efforts to manipulate stock prices, however, management has a unique ability to choose the most opportune time to propose a buyout.

Presumably, management proposes or participates in a buyout only if it is advantageous to management to do so. If management believes the share price is significantly below what could be obtained by releveraging or liquidating the company, it makes sense for management to buy the company and take steps to redeploy its assets. Under these circumstances shareholders may justifiably wonder whether management is taking for itself some opportunity that properly belongs to the corporation. Traditionally, under the corporate opportunity doctrine, the law has prohibited officers, directors, and senior managers from taking personal advantage of opportunities that come to them in their official capacities and are of potential benefit to the corporation.[5] If corporate leaders exploit corporate opportunities for themselves, the law permits shareholders to impose a trust on the profits earned. Couldn't management relever or liquidate directly to benefit shareholders rather than first taking the company private? On the face of it, the MBO appears to be a mechanism for transferring value from shareholders to management.

MANAGEMENT'S FIDUCIARY OBLIGATIONS

The concerns about conflicting interests, insider advantages, and misappropriation of corporate opportunities reflect management's special obligations to the corporation and its shareholders. In contrast to the arm's-length relationship that normally obtains between buyers and sellers in the marketplace, managers have a fiduciary responsibility toward the corporation and shareholders for whom they work.

According to the orthodox theory of the corporation, shareholders own — or at least invest in — the firm, while management runs it. In order for this arrangement to work, shareholders must be able to trust that the management will devote adequate attention to corporate business and run the business competently in a way that promotes the shareholders' interests. This trust is in part promoted through the board of directors, whose job it is to monitor management's performance on behalf of shareholders. But it depends more fundamentally on the continuing good faith performance by men and women in management positions.

The classic legal statement of the responsibility of corporate fiduciaries is found in the well-known case of *Guth v. Luft* decided by the Supreme Court of Delaware in 1939:

> A public policy, existing through the years, and derived from a profound knowledge of human characteristics and motives . . . demands of a corporate officer or director . . . the most scrupulous observance of his duty, not only affirmatively to protect the interests of the corporation committed to his charge, but also to refrain from doing anything that would work injury to the corporation, or to deprive it of profit or advantage which his skill and ability might properly bring to it, or to enable it to make in the reasonable and lawful exercise of its powers.[6]

The central element of this ideal is that management be dedicated to advancing the interests of the corporation, but most especially that management should not advance its own interests at the expense of the corporation.

The separation of ownership and control which underlies the modern public corporation is possible only if shareholders trust corporate leadership. In the absence of trust, monitoring management's performance becomes very costly. Without some fundamental assurance that their interests will be protected, equity investors would have little incentive to put their capital in the hands of professional managers. The benefits of corporate enterprise that flow to consumers, employees, suppliers, communities, and the general public — as well as to shareholders — are in jeopardy if management loses sight of its fiduciary obligations.

AN ETHICAL PERSPECTIVE ON MANAGEMENT BUYOUTS

Management buyouts threaten to undermine shareholder trust in corporate leadership if they are seen as or used as techniques for shrewd managers to benefit at shareholders' expense. Management's personal interest in buyouts, coupled with the absence of any generally accepted standard of fairness for evaluating buyout bids, make them especially potent threats to investor confidence. If there were no potential benefits for shareholders in these arrangements, there would be every reason to prohibit them. But, as noted earlier, buyouts sometimes offer shareholders the best alternative for protecting their investment or realizing its value. For example, management may be able, because of its position and superior knowledge, to see potential where outsiders do not, and thus be willing to take a seemingly moribund company private and rejuvenate it.[7] Management may, because of its position, be able to take a company private to ward off a hostile takeover bid offering a lower price.[8] Even in the absence of threatening conditions, a buyout may offer shareholders the best opportunity to realize the value of their investment because of the tax advantages and leveraging opportunities available as a result of going private. Any discussion of buyouts must recognize that sometimes they may be in shareholders' best interests.

From the perspective of managerial ethics, the practical challenge, then, is both to specify the conditions under which going private is consistent with management's fiduciary obligations and to motivate managers to propose only buyouts which satisfy those conditions.

MANAGEMENT'S CONFLICT OF INTEREST

Some observers consider buyouts inherently inconsistent with management's fiduciary obligations because of management's conflicting personal interests. These observers and many others apparently take the position that it is unethical to place oneself in a position in which personal interest may conflict with obligation. The appeal of such a position is obvious. In conflict of interest situations, there is always the possibility that personal interest will overwhelm obligation, that an abuse of trust will occur. However, the principle may be criticized on two grounds.

First, it is based on a misconception of conflicts of interest, one which sees potential conflict as characteristic of discrete, identifiable situations — which can be easily marked off from the normal state of affairs.

In fact, whenever a person is charged to act for the benefit of another — as corporate fiduciary, as parent, as employee — a conflict between personal interest and obligation to promote the interests of the other can erupt. The conflict may arise in connection with almost any type of decision or activity. An employee's decision not to search more widely for a competitive supplier, for example, may involve such a conflict. Potential conflict is not limited to exchanges between the agent and principal. Recognition that the potential for conflict exists continuously in every agency relationship renders the principle requiring avoidance of potential conflict totally unworkable. It is impossible to eliminate all potential conflicts without eliminating the relationships that give rise to them, and that would be too great a price to pay. Practical judgment is required to identify situations in which the potential gain to the agent or loss to the principle is great enough to warrant steps to monitor or restrain the agent's behavior.

The principle requiring avoidance of all potential conflict situations may also be criticized because it sometimes penalizes the very party it is meant to protect. If, for example, corporate directors were flatly prohibited from doing business with the corporations they serve, some opportunities advantageous to the corporation would have to be fore-

gone. Courts and state legislatures have long recognized the possibility that a flat prohibition on dealing between a corporation and its directors can in some circumstances work to the detriment of the corporation.

Conflicts of interest are problematic not because they are themselves unethical, but because they may lead to conduct that is unethical. It may be difficult to do what obligation requires when important personal interests seem to point in a different direction. More commonly, personal interest may threaten the objectivity or integrity of professional judgment. When personal interests loom large, the decision maker may have difficulty determining where his firm's interests lie. There is a very natural tendency to want to see the interests of the firm and self-interest as aligned, even if, from a more objective perspective, they are not.

While there is little reason to recommend avoiding all situations in which personal interest may conflict with fiduciary obligation, there is good reason for looking more closely at situations in which a conflict creates a risk of significant losses to the principal or benefits to the agent. A buyout is just such a situation. . . .

FAIR PRICE

Who is entitled to the gains from management buyouts? Selling shareholders may believe that the gains from the buyout should be theirs. The value created derives from unused debt capacity and a depreciable asset base. Shareholders own both of these before the transaction. Buyers, no doubt, believe that their ability to leverage the company beyond the level normally available to a public corporation entitles them to the gains. In a normal arm's-length transaction, buyers and sellers negotiate from these different perceptions to reach a mutually acceptable price.

Should the situation be any different in a management buyout? Should the normal arm's-length standard for fair price apply in the buyout context? Sometimes it is assumed that if buyouts give shareholders a premium over market price, then there should be no complaints. Shareholders should gladly accept the premium and be grateful to management for having taken the initiative to unlock some added value. This position, however, fails to take into account management's fiduciary obligation and the foundation upon which it rests.

A buyout proposal is, in effect, a proposal to convert a fiduciary relationship into an arm's-length relationship. Whether the buyout group should be held to a fiduciary standard under these circumstances is central to the analysis of fair price. Our discussion of disclosure and review was based on the view that management's fiduciary obligations continue even after a buyout is proposed. Permitting management unilaterally to divest itself of its responsibilities to the firm by making a buyout proposal and then permitting the buyout group to negotiate on the basis of information and resources management acquired in its capacity as fiduciary would seriously undermine shareholder confidence. From the time a buyout is proposed until it is consummated or the proposal dropped, management should be held to a fiduciary standard. Unlike the approach which says that anything over market price is fair, our approach to fair price takes management's fiduciary responsibility into account.

As stated earlier, at the heart of management's fiduciary responsibility is the obligation to promote the corporation's interests. But most especially, management must not benefit at the expense of shareholders. Sometimes it is easy to see when corporate fiduciaries are benefiting at the expense of shareholders. When they misappropriate corporate assets for themselves, for example, the harm to shareholders and the corresponding benefit to the fiduciaries is simply measured by the value of the assets taken. Determining the harm to shareholders in a buyout case is more difficult. While shareholders may benefit to the extent that the price exceeds market value, they may be harmed to the extent that the price is less than it ought to be by some other standard. For example, a buyout bid might be higher than market price, but still not as high as the price the shares would bring if management took certain initiatives such as relevering the company to improve share price.

Moreover, when a fiduciary steals from the corporation, there is no uncertainty about entitlements: The assets belong to the corporation and no reasonable person can claim to have any entitlement to them by virtue of his status in the corporation. However, where the question is the appropriate division of newly created wealth, particularly wealth created through the combined efforts of many people, entitlements are ambiguous. In order to determine whether one party is benefiting at the expense of another, there must be some benchmark or standard for the appropriate division of the gains. In the buyout situation, if shareholders get too little, then the buyout group benefits at their expense. Part of the problem of identifying buyouts which satisfy managements' fiduciary obligations is to specify a standard for determining whether the price is appropriate or fair.

Perhaps the most obvious standard is the firm's stock price before the buyout. Under the theory of capital market efficiency, the firm's value in the open market is fair in the sense that it reflects all public information about the company. One defect of this standard for evaluating buyout bids is that it is vulnerable to the asymmetry of information between insiders (i.e., managers) and outsiders (i.e., public shareholders). Asymmetries can arise because of differences in technical expertise between managers and the public, the possibly high cost of information gathering, and the size and complexity of the firm. A second defect of this standard is that it fails to distinguish between management's existing policies and those that might prevail if the firm were restructured or the management incentive scheme changed. To the extent that stock price before a buyout reflects managers' failure to utilize all their skills and abilities to maximize shareholder wealth, using it as a standard of fair price endorses managerial inefficiency.

A second standard is the price the firm would fetch if sold in an open auction. This standard explicitly controls for the fact that the buyout bid is not derived from arm's-length bidding. Certainly any bid lower than what an open market auction would bring is too low and may indicate that management is seeking to take advantage of shareholders. But the open market rule has the limitation that competing arm's-length bids are rarely available unless solicited, and even then may not be forthcoming. Nevertheless, this is an important standard because competing open market bidders have been known to intervene in instances of apparently low management bids.[9] Some commentators advocate a rule of open bidding once a management buyout is proposed. Such a rule has much to be said for it, but in the absence of actual interested bidders, it fails to give much guidance for assessing buyout bids.

A third and more useful standard of comparison is the value shareholders could obtain if they synthesized the buyout on their own: borrowed heavily, repurchased a large percentage of shares, and increased the shareholdings of managers (by sale or outright gift). Even the value created by depreci-

ation tax shields can be synthesized by selling plant and equipment and then leasing them back. This standard is not only more useful, since it does not depend on the presence of competing bidders, but it is also more consistent with management's duty of loyalty to shareholders. Management's fiduciary duty requires that it put forth its best efforts on shareholders' behalf. . . .

NOTES

1. News release, Doremus & Company, Chicago, January 12, 1984, p. 2.
2. "1987 Profile," *Mergers & Acquisitions* (May/June 1986): 71.
3. Louis Lowenstein, "No More Cozy Management Buyouts," *Harvard Business Review* (January/February 1986): 147–156.
4. Benjamin J. Stein, "Going Private Is Unethical," *Fortune* (November 11, 1985), p. 169.
5. For instance, *Durfee v. Durfee & Canning, Inc.*, 323 Mass. 187 (1948). See generally, Victor Brudney and Robert Charles Clark, "A New Look at Corporate Opportunities," *Harvard Law Review* 94 (1981): 997–1062.
6. *Guth v. Loft*, 5A.2d 503, 510 (Del. Supr. 1939).
7. For instance, employees at Weirton Steel saved it from imminent closing, then took a 19 percent pay cut, and raised $300 million to buy the assets in 1983. Since then, Weirton has embarked on a significant modernization program.
8. For instance, in April 1987, Dart Group, Inc., made an unsolicited takeover bid for Supermarkets General Corporation for $1.75 billion. Two weeks later, management offered to take the company private for $1.8 billion.
9. For example, competitive bidders intervened in response to J. B. Fuqua's 1981 attempt to buy out Fuqua Industries and in response to Chairman David Mahoney's 1983 proposal to take Norton Simon, Inc., private.

LEGAL PERSPECTIVES

Henningsen v. Bloomfield Motors, Inc. and Chrysler Corporation

Supreme Court of New Jersey

Claus H. Henningsen purchased a Plymouth automobile, manufactured by defendant Chrysler Corporation, from defendant Bloomfield Motors, Inc. His wife, plaintiff Helen Henningsen, was injured while driving it and instituted suit against both defendants to recover damages on account of her injuries. Her husband joined in the action seeking compensation for his consequential losses. The complaint was predicated upon breach of express and implied warranties and upon negligence. At the trial the negligence counts were dismissed by the court and the case was submitted to the jury for determination solely on the issues of implied warranty of merchantability.* Verdicts were returned against both defendants and in favor of the plaintiffs. Defendants appealed and plaintiffs cross-appealed from the dismissal of their negligence claim. . . .

. . . The particular car selected was described as a 1955 Plymouth, Plaza "6," Club Sedan. The type used in the printed parts of the [purchase order] form became smaller in size, different in style, and less readable toward the bottom where the line for the purchaser's signature was placed. The smallest type on the page appears in the two paragraphs, one of two and one-quarter lines and the second of one and one-half lines, on which great stress is laid by the defense in the case. These two paragraphs are the least legible and the most difficult to read in the instrument, but they are most important in the evaluation of the rights of the contesting parties. They do not attract attention and there is nothing about the format which would draw the reader's eye to them. In fact, a studied and concentrated effort would have to be made to read them. De-emphasis seems the motive rather than emphasis. . . . The two paragraphs are:

"The front and back of this Order comprise the entire agreement affecting this purchase and no other agreement or understanding of any nature concerning same has been made or entered into, or will be recognized. I hereby certify that no credit has been extended to me for the purchase of this motor vehicle except as appears in writing on the face of this agreement.

"I have read the matter printed on the back hereof and agree to it as a part of this order the same as if it were printed above my signature. . . ."

The testimony of Claus Henningsen justifies the conclusion that he did not read the two fine print paragraphs referring to the back of the purchase contract. And it is uncontradicted that no one made any reference to them, or called them to his attention. With respect to the matter appearing on the back, it is likewise uncontradicted that he did not read it and that no one called it to his attention.

---

*["Merchantability": The articles shall be of the kind described and be fit for the purpose for which they were sold. Fitness is impliedly warranted if an item is merchantable. Ed.]

Atlantic Reporter 161 A2d 69, pp. 73–75, 78–81, 83–87, 93–96, 102. This opinion was written by Justice John J. Francis.

. . . The warranty, which is the focal point of the case, is set forth [on the reverse side of the page]. It is as follows:

"7. It is expressly agreed that there are no warranties, express or implied, *made* by either the dealer or the manufacturer on the motor vehicle, chassis, or parts furnished hereunder except as follows.

"The manufacturer warrants each new motor vehicle (including original equipment placed thereon by the manufacturer except tires), chassis or parts manufactured by it to be free from defects in material or workmanship under normal use and service. Its obligation under this warranty being limited to making good at its factory any part or parts thereof which shall, within ninety (90) days after delivery of such vehicle *to the original purchaser* or before such vehicle has been driven 4,000 miles, whichever event shall first occur, be returned to it with transportation charges prepaid and which its examination shall disclose to its satisfaction to have been thus defective: *This warranty being expressly in lieu of all other warranties expressed or implied, and all other obligations or liabilities on its part,* and it neither assumes nor authorizes any other person to assume for it any other liability in connection with the sale of its vehicles. . . ." [Emphasis added] . . .

The new Plymouth was turned over to the Henningsens on May 9, 1955. No proof was adduced by the dealer to show precisely what was done in the way of mechanical or road testing beyond testimony that the manufacturer's instructions were probably followed. Mr. Henningsen drove it from the dealer's place of business in Bloomfield to their home in Keansburg. On the trip nothing unusual appeared in the way in which it operated. Thereafter, it was used for short trips on paved streets about the town. It had no servicing and no mishaps of any kind before the event of May 19. That day, Mrs. Henningsen drove to Asbury Park [New Jersey]. On the way down and in returning the car per-

formed in normal fashion until the accident occurred. She was proceeding north on Route 36 in Highlands, New Jersey, at 20–22 miles per hour. The highway was paved and smooth, and contained two lanes for northbound travel. She was riding in the right-hand lane. Suddenly she heard a loud noise "from the bottom, by the hood." It "felt as if something cracked." The steering wheel spun in her hands; the car veered sharply to the right and crashed into a highway sign and a brick wall. No other vehicle was in any way involved. A bus operator driving in the left-hand lane testified that he observed plaintiff's car approaching in normal fashion in the opposite direction; "all of a sudden [it] veered at 90 degrees . . . and right into this wall." As a result of the impact, the front of the car was so badly damaged that it was impossible to determine if any of the parts of the steering wheel mechanism or workmanship or assembly were defective or improper prior to the accident. The condition was such that the collision insurance carrier, after inspection, declared the vehicle a total loss. It had 468 miles on the speedometer at the time. . . .

The terms of the warranty are a sad commentary upon the automobile manufacturers' marketing practices. Warranties developed in the law in the interest of and to protect the ordinary consumer who cannot be expected to have the knowledge or capacity or even the opportunity to make adequate inspection of mechanical instrumentalities, like automobiles, and to decide for himself whether they are reasonably fit for the designed purpose. . . . But the ingenuity of the Automobile Manufacturers Association, by means of its standardized form, has metamorphosed the warranty into a device to limit the maker's liability. To call it an "equivocal" agreement, as the Minnesota Supreme Court did, is the least that can be said in criticism of it.

The manufacturer agrees to replace defective parts for 90 days after the sale or until the car has been driven 4,000 miles, whichever is first to occur, *if the part is sent to the factory, transportation charges prepaid, and if examination discloses to its satisfaction that the part is defective.* . . .

Chrysler points out that an implied warranty of merchantability is an incident of a contract of sale. It concedes, of course, the making of the original sale to Bloomfield Motors, Inc., but maintains that this transaction marked the terminal point of its contractual connection with the car. Then Chrysler urges that since it was not a party to the sale by the dealer to Henningsen, there is no privity of contract* between it and the plaintiffs, and the absence of this privity eliminates any such implied warranty.

There is no doubt that under early common-law concepts of contractual liability only those persons who were parties to the bargain could sue for a breach of it. In more recent times a noticeable disposition has appeared in a number of jurisdictions to break through the narrow barrier of privity when dealing with sales of goods in order to give realistic recognition to a universally accepted fact. The fact is that the dealer and the ordinary buyer do not, and are not expected to, buy goods, whether they be foodstuffs or automobiles, exclusively for their own consumption or use. Makers and manufacturers know this and advertise and market their products on that assumption; witness the "family" car, the baby foods, etc. The limitations of privity in contracts for the sale of goods developed their place in the law when marketing conditions were simple, when maker and buyer frequently met face to face on an equal bargaining plane and when many of the products were relatively uncomplicated

*["Privity of contract": A contractual relation existing between parties that is sufficiently close to confer a legal claim or right. Ed.]

and conducive to inspection by a buyer competent to evaluate their quality. With the advent of mass marketing, the manufacturer became remote from the purchaser, sales were accomplished through intermediaries, and the demand for the product was created by advertising media. In such an economy it became obvious that the consumer was the person being cultivated. Manifestly, the connotation of "consumer" was broader than that of "buyer." He signified such a person who, in the reasonable contemplation of the parties to the sale, might be expected to use the product. Thus, where the commodities sold are such that if defectively manufactured they will be dangerous to life or limb, then society's interests can only be protected by eliminating the requirement of privity between the maker and his dealers and the reasonably expected ultimate consumer. In that way the burden of losses consequent upon use of defective articles is borne by those who are in a position to either control the danger or make an equitable distribution of the losses when they do occur. . . .

Under modern conditions the ordinary layman, on responding to the importuning of colorful advertising, has neither the opportunity nor the capacity to inspect or to determine the fitness of an automobile for use; he must rely on the manufacturer who has control of its construction, and to some degree on the dealer who, to the limited extent called for by the manufacturer's instructions, inspects and services it before delivery. In such a marketing milieu his remedies and those of persons who properly claim through him should not depend "upon the intricacies of the law of sales. The obligation of the manufacturer should not be based alone on privity of contract. It should rest, as was once said, upon 'the demands of social justice.'" . . .

In a society such as ours, where the automobile is a common and necessary adjunct of daily life, and where its use is so fraught with danger to the driver, passengers, and the public, the manufacturer is under a special obligation in connection with the construction, promotion, and sale of his cars. Consequently, the courts must examine purchase agreements closely to see if consumer and public interests are treated fairly. . . .

What influence should these circumstances have on the restrictive effect of Chrysler's express warranty in the framework of the purchase contract? As we have said, warranties originated in the law to safeguard the buyer and not to limit the liability of the seller or manufacturer. It seems obvious in this instance that the motive was to avoid the warranty obligations which are normally incidental to such sales. The language gave little and withdrew much. In return for the delusive remedy of replacement of defective parts at the factory, the buyer is said to have accepted the exclusion of the maker's liability for personal injuries arising from the breach of the warranty, and to have agreed to the elimination of any other express or implied warranty. An instinctively felt sense of justice cries out against such a sharp bargain. But does the doctrine that a person is bound by his signed agreement, in the absence of fraud, stand in the way of any relief? . . .

The warranty before us is a standardized form designed for mass use. It is imposed upon the automobile consumer. He takes it or leaves it, and he must take it to buy an automobile. No bargaining is engaged in with respect to it. In fact, the dealer through whom it comes to the buyer is without authority to alter it; his function is ministerial — simply to deliver it. The form warranty is not only standard with Chrysler but, as mentioned above, it is the uniform warranty of the Automobile Manufacturers Association. . . . Of these companies, the "Big Three" (General Motors, Ford, and Chrysler) represented 93.5% of the passenger-car production for 1958 and the independents 6.5%.[1] And for the same year the "Big Three"

had 86.72% of the total passenger vehicle registrations. . . .

In the context of this warranty, only the abandonment of all sense of justice would permit us to hold that, as a matter of law, the phrase "its obligation under this warranty being limited to making good at its factory any part or parts thereof" signifies to an ordinary reasonable person that he is relinquishing any personal injury claim that might flow from the use of a defective automobile. Such claims are nowhere mentioned. . . .

In the matter of warranties on the sale of their products, the Automobile Manufacturers Association has enabled them to present a united front. From the standpoint of the purchaser, there can be no arm's-length negotiating on the subject. Because his capacity for bargaining is so grossly unequal, the inexorable conclusion which follows is that he is not permitted to bargain at all. He must take or leave the automobile on the warranty terms dictated by the maker. He cannot turn to a competitor for better security.

Public policy is a term not easily defined. Its significance varies as the habits and needs of a people may vary. It is not static and the field of application is an ever increasing one. A contract, or a particular provision therein, valid in one era may be wholly opposed to the public policy of another. Courts keep in mind the principle that the best interests of society demand that persons should not be unnecessarily restricted in their freedom to contract. But they do not hesitate to declare void as against public policy contractual provisions which clearly tend to the injury of the public in some way. . . .

In the framework of this case, illuminated as it is by the facts and the many decisions noted, we are of the opinion that Chrysler's attempted disclaimer of an implied warranty of the merchantability and of the obligations arising therefrom is so inimical to the public good as to compel an adjudication of its invalidity. . . .

The principles that have been expounded as to the obligation of the manufacturer apply with equal force to the separate express warranty of the dealer. This is so, irrespective of the absence of the relationship of principle and agent between these defendants, because the manufacturer and the Association establish the warranty policy for the industry. The bargaining position of the dealer is inextricably bound by practice to that of the maker and the purchaser must take or leave the automobile, accompanied and encumbered as it is by the uniform warranty. . . .

Under all of the circumstances outlined above, the judgments in favor of the plaintiffs and against the defendants are affirmed.

NOTES

1. Standard and Poor (Industrial Surveys, Autos, Basic Analysis, June 25, 1959), p. 4109.

Automobile Workers v. Johnson Controls, Inc.

Supreme Court of the United States

In this case we are concerned with an employer's gender-based fetal-protection policy. May an employer exclude a fertile female employee from certain jobs because of its concern for the health of the fetus the woman might conceive?

I

Respondent Johnson Controls, Inc., manufactures batteries. In the manufacturing process, the element lead is a primary ingredient. Occupational exposure to lead entails health risks, including the risk of harm to any fetus carried by a female employee.

Before the Civil Rights Act of 1964, 78 Stat. 241, became law, Johnson Controls did not employ any woman in a battery-manufacturing job. In June 1977, however, it announced its first official policy concerning its employment of women in lead-exposure work. . . .

Johnson Controls "stopped short of excluding women capable of bearing children from lead exposure," *id.,* at 138, but emphasized that a woman who expected to have a child should not choose a job in which she would have such exposure. The company also required a woman who wished to be considered for employment to sign a statement that she had been advised of the risk of having a child while she was exposed to lead. . . .

Five years later, in 1982, Johnson Controls shifted from a policy of warning to a policy of exclusion. Between 1979 and 1983, eight employees became pregnant while maintaining blood lead levels in excess of 30 micrograms per deciliter. Tr. of Oral Arg. 25, 34. This appeared to be the critical level noted by the Occupational Health and Safety Administration (OSHA) for a worker who was planning to have a family. See 29 CFR § 1910.1025 (1989). The company responded by announcing a broad exclusion of woman from jobs that exposed them to lead:

89 U.S. 1215 (1991). Opinion delivered by Justice Blackmun.

"... [I]t is [Johnson Controls'] policy that women who are pregnant or who are capable of bearing children will not be placed into jobs involving lead exposure or which could expose them to lead through the exercise of job bidding, bumping, transfer or promotion rights." App. 85–86.

The policy defined "women ... capable of bearing children" as "[a]ll women except those whose inability to bear children is medically documented." *Id.,* at 81. It further stated that an unacceptable work station was one where, "over the past year," an employee had recorded a blood lead level of more than 30 micrograms per deciliter or the work site had yielded an air sample containing a lead level in excess of 30 micrograms per cubic meter. *Ibid.*

II

In April 1984, petitioners filed in the United States District Court for the Eastern District of Wisconsin a class action challenging Johnson Controls' fetal-protection policy as sex discrimination that violated Title VII of the Civil Rights Act of 1964, as amended, 42 U.S. C. §2000e *et seq.* Among the individual plaintiffs were petitioners [such as] Mary Craig, who had chosen to be sterilized in order to avoid losing her job. . . .

III

The bias in Johnson Controls' policy is obvious. Fertile men, but not fertile women, are given a choice as to whether they wish to risk their reproductive health for a particular job. Section 703(a) of the Civil Rights Act of 1964, 78 Stat. 255, as amended, 42 U.S.C. §2000e-2(a), prohibits sex-based classifications in terms and conditions of employment, in hiring and discharging decisions, and in other employment decisions that adversely affect an employee's status. Respondent's fetal-protection policy explicitly discriminates against women on the basis of their sex. The policy excludes women with childbearing capacity from lead-exposed jobs and so creates a facial classification based on gender. Respondent assumes as much in its brief before this Court. Brief for Respondent 17, n. 24.

Nevertheless, the Court of Appeals assumed, as did the two appellate courts who already had confronted the issue, that sex-specific fetal-protection policies do not involve facial discrimination. . . . The court assumed that because the asserted reason for the sex-based exclusion (protecting women's unconceived offspring) was ostensibly benign, the policy was not sex-based discrimination. That assumption, however, was incorrect.

First, Johnson Controls' policy classifies on the basis of gender and childbearing capacity, rather than fertility alone. Respondent does not seek to protect the unconceived children of all its employees. Despite evidence in the record about the debilitating effect of lead exposure on the male reproductive system, Johnson Controls is concerned only with the harms that may befall the unborn offspring of its female employees. . . . Johnson Controls' policy is facially discriminatory because it requires only a female employee to produce proof that she is not capable of reproducing.

Our conclusion is bolstered by the Pregnancy Discrimination Act of 1978 (PDA), 92 Stat. 2076, 42 U.S.C. §2000e(k), in which Congress explicitly provided that, for purposes of Title VII, discrimination "on the basis of sex" includes discrimination "because of or on the basis of pregnancy, childbirth, or related medical conditions." "The Pregnancy Discrimination Act has now made clear that, for all Title VII purposes, discrimination based on a woman's pregnancy is, on its face, discrimination because of her sex." *Newport News Shipbuilding & Dry Dock Co. v. EEOC*, 462 U.S. 669, 684 (1983). In its use of the words "capable of bearing children" in the 1982 policy statement as the criterion for exclusion, Johnson Controls explicitly classifies on the basis of potential for pregnancy. Under the PDA, such a classification must be regarded, for Title VII purposes, in the same light as explicit sex discrimination. Respondent has chosen to treat all its female employees as potentially pregnant; that choice evinces discrimination on the basis of sex. . . .

The beneficence of an employer's purpose does not undermine the conclusion that an explicit gender-based policy is sex discrimination under § 703(a) and thus may be defended only as a BFOQ [bona fide occupational qualification].

The enforcement policy of the Equal Employment Opportunity Commission accords with this conclusion. On January 24, 1990, the EEOC issued a Policy Guidance in the light of the Seventh Circuit's decision in the present case. . . .

In sum, Johnson Controls' policy "does not pass the simple test of whether the evidence shows 'treatment of a person in a manner which but for that person's sex would be different.'" . . .

IV

Under § 703(e)(1) of Title VII, an employer may discriminate on the basis of "religion, sex, or national origin in those certain instances where religion, sex, or national origin is a bona fide occupational qualification reasonably necessary to the normal operation of that particular business or enterprise." 42 U.S.C. §2000e-2(e)(1). We therefore turn to the question whether Johnson Controls' fetal-protection policy is one of those "certain instances" that come within the BFOQ exception. . . .

The PDA's amendment to Title VII contains a BFOQ standard of its own: Unless pregnancy employees differ from others "in their ability or inability to work," they must be "treated the same" as other employees "for all employment-related purposes." 42 U.S.C. §2000e(k). This language clearly sets forth Congress' remedy for discrimination on the basis of pregnancy and potential pregnancy. Women who are either pregnant or potentially pregnant must be treated like others "similar in their ability . . . to work." *Ibid.* In other words, women as capable of doing their jobs as their male counterparts may not be forced to choose between having a child and having a job. . . .

V

We have no difficulty concluding that Johnson Controls cannot establish a BFOQ. Fertile women, as far as appears in the record, participate in the manufacture of batteries as efficiently as anyone else. Johnson Controls' professed moral and ethical concerns about the welfare of the next generation do not suffice to establish a BFOQ of female sterility. Decisions about the welfare of future children must be left to the parents who conceive, bear, support, and raise them rather than to the employers who hire those parents. Congress has mandated this choice through Title VII, as amended by the Pregnancy Discrimination Act. Johnson Controls has attempted to exclude women because of their reproductive capacity. Title VII and the PDA simply do not allow a woman's dismissal because of her failure to submit to sterilization.

Nor can concerns about the welfare of the next generation be considered a part of the "essence" of Johnson Controls' business. . . .

Johnson Controls argues that it must exclude all fertile women because it is impossible to tell which women will become pregnant while working with lead. This argument is somewhat academic in light of our conclusion that the company may not exclude fertile women at all; it perhaps is worth noting, however, that Johnson Controls has shown no "factual basis for believing that all or substantially all women would be unable to perform safely and efficiently the duties of the job involved." *Weeks v. Southern Bell Tel. & Tel. Co.,* 408 F. 2d 228, 235 (CA5 1969), quoted with approval in *Dothard,* 433 U.S., at 333. Even on this sparse record, it is apparent that Johnson Controls is concerned about only a small minority of women. Of the eight pregnancies reported among the female employees, it has not been shown that any of the babies have birth defects or other abnormalities. The record does not reveal the birth rate for Johnson Controls' female workers but national statistics show that approximately nine percent of all fertile women become pregnant each year. The birthrate drops to two percent for blue collar workers over age 30. See Becker, 53 U. Chi. L. Rev., at 1233. Johnson Controls' fear of prenatal injury, no matter how sincere, does not begin to show that substantially all of its fertile women employees are incapable of doing their jobs. . . .

It is no more appropriate for the courts than it is for individual employers to decide whether a woman's reproductive role is more important to herself and her family than her economic role. Congress has left this choice to the woman as hers to make.

The judgment of the Court of Appeals is reversed and the case is remanded for further proceedings consistent with this opinion.

United States, Petitioner v. Bestfoods et al.

Supreme Court of the United States

JUSTICE SOUTER delivered the opinion of the Court.

The United States brought this action for the costs of cleaning up industrial waste generated by a chemical plant. The issue before us, under the Comprehensive Environmental Response, Compensation, and Liability Act of 1980 (CERCLA), 94 Stat. 2767, as amended, 42 U. S. C. §9601 *et seq.,* is whether a parent corporation that actively participated in, and exercised control over, the operations of a subsidiary may, without more, be held liable as an operator of a polluting facility owned or operated by the subsidiary. We answer no, unless the corporate veil may be pierced. But a corporate parent that actively participated in, and exercised control over, the operations of the facility itself may be held directly liable in its own right as an operator of the facility.

I

In 1980, CERCLA was enacted in response to the serious environmental and health risks posed by industrial pollution. See *Exxon Corp. v. Hunt,* 475 U.S. 355, 358–359 (1986). "As its name implies, CERCLA is a comprehensive statute that grants the President broad power to command government agencies and private parties to clean up hazardous waste sites" *Key Tronic Corp. v. United States,* 511 U.S. 809, 814 (1994). If it satisfies certain statutory conditions, the United States may, for instance, use the "Hazardous Substance Superfund" to finance cleanup efforts, see 42 U. S. C. §§9601(11), 9604; 26 U. S. C. §9507, which it may then replenish by suits brought under §107 of the Act against, among others, "any person who at the time of disposal of any hazardous substance owned or operated any facility." 42 U. S. C. §9607(a)(2). So, those actually "responsible for any damage, environmental harm, or injury from chemical poisons [may be tagged with] the cost of their actions," S. Rep. No. 96–848, p. 13 (1980). The term "person" is defined in CERCLA to include corporations and other business organizations, see 42 U. S. C. § 9601(21), and the term "facility" enjoys a broad and detailed definition as well, see §9601(9). The phrase "owner or operator" is defined only by tautology, however, as "any person owning or operating" a facility, §9601(20)(A)(ii), and it is this bit of circularity that prompts our review. Cf. *Exxon Corp. v. Hunt, supra,* at 363 (CERCLA, "unfortunately, is not a model of legislative draftsmanship").

* * *

II

It is a general principle of corporate law deeply "ingrained in our economic and legal systems" that a parent corporation (so-called because of control through ownership of another corporation's stock) is not liable for the acts of its subsidiaries. Douglas & Shanks, Insulation from Liability Through Subsidiary Corporations, 39 Yale L. J. 193 (1929) (hereinafter Douglas) . . . Thus it is hornbook law that "the exercise of the 'control' which stock ownership gives to the stockholders . . . will not create liability beyond the assets of the subsidiary. That 'control' includes the elec-

tion of directors, the making of by-laws . . . and the doing of all other acts incident to the legal status of stockholders. Nor will a duplication of some or all of the directors or executive officers be fatal." Douglas 196 (footnotes omitted). Although this respect for corporate distinctions when the subsidiary is a polluter has been severely criticized in the literature, see, *e.g.,* Note, Liability of Parent Corporations for Hazardous Waste Cleanup and Damages, 99 Harv. L. Rev. 986 (1986), nothing in CERCLA purports to reject this bedrock principle, and against this venerable common-law backdrop, the congressional silence is audible. Cf. *Edmonds v. Compagnie Generale Transatlantique,* 443 U.S. 256, 266–267 (1979) ("silence is most eloquent, for such reticence while contemplating an important and controversial change in existing law is unlikely"). The Government has indeed made no claim that a corporate parent is liable as an owner or an operator under §107 simply because its subsidiary is subject to liability for owning or operating a polluting facility.

But there is an equally fundamental principle of corporate law, applicable to the parent-subsidiary relationship as well as generally, that the corporate veil may be pierced and the shareholder held liable for the corporation's conduct when, *inter alia,* the corporate form would otherwise be misused to accomplish certain wrongful purposes, most notably fraud, on the shareholder's behalf. . . . Nothing in CERCLA purports to rewrite this well-settled rule, either. CERCLA is thus like many another congressional enactment in giving no indication "that the entire corpus of state corporation law is to be replaced simply because a plaintiff's cause of action is based upon a federal statute," *Burks v. Lasker,* 441 U.S. 471, 478 (1979), and the failure of the statute to speak to a matter as fundamental as the liability implications of corporate ownership demands application of the rule that "[i]n order to abrogate a common-law principle, the statute must speak directly to the question addressed by the common law," *United States v. Texas,* 507 U.S. 529, 534 (1993) (internal quotation marks omitted). The Court of Appeals [for the Sixth Circuit] was accordingly correct in holding that when (but only when) the corporate veil may be pierced, may a parent corporation be charged with derivative CERCLA liability for its subsidiary's actions.

III

A

If the act rested liability entirely on ownership of a polluting facility, this opinion might end here; but CERCLA liability may turn on operation as well as ownership, and nothing in the statute's terms bars a parent corporation from direct liability for its own actions in operating a facility owned by its subsidiary. As Justice (then-Professor) Douglas noted almost 70 years ago, derivative liability cases are to be distinguished from those in which "the alleged wrong can seemingly be traced to the parent through the conduit of its own personnel and management" and "the parent is directly a participant in the wrong complained of." Douglas 207, 208. In such instances, the parent is directly liable for its own actions. . . . The fact that a corporate subsidiary happens to own a polluting facility operated by its parent does nothing, then, to displace the rule that the parent "corporation is [itself] responsible for the wrongs committed by its agents in the course of its business," *Mine Workers v. Coronado Coal Co.,* 259 U.S. 344, 395 (1922), and whereas the rules of veil-piercing limit derivative liability for the actions of another corporation, CERCLA's "operator" provision is concerned primarily with direct liability for one's own actions. See,

e.g., *Sidney S. Arst Co. v. Pipefitters Welfare Ed. Fund,* 25 F. 3d 417, 420 (CA7 1994) ("the direct, personal liability provided by CERCLA is distinct from the derivative liability that results from piercing the corporate veil") (internal quotation marks omitted). It is this direct liability that is properly seen as being at issue here.

Under the plain language of the statute, any person who operates a polluting facility is directly liable for the costs of cleaning up the pollution. See 42 U.S. C. §9607(a)(2). This is so regardless of whether that person is the facility's owner, the owner's parent corporation or business partner, or even a saboteur who sneaks into the facility at night to discharge its poisons out of malice. If any such act of operating a corporate subsidiary's facility is done on behalf of a parent corporation, the existence of the parent-subsidiary relationship under state corporate law is simply irrelevant to the issue of direct liability. See *Riverside Market Dev. Corp. v. International Bldg. Prods., Inc.,* 931 F. 2d 327, 330 (CA5) ("CERCLA prevents individuals from hiding behind the corporate shield when, as 'operators,' they themselves actually participate in the wrongful conduct prohibited by the Act"), cert. denied, 502 U.S. 1004 (1991); *United States v. Kayser-Roth Corp.,* 910 F. 2d 24, 26 (CA1 1990) ("a person who is an operator of a facility is not protected from liability by the legal structure of ownership").

This much is easy to say; the difficulty comes in defining actions sufficient to constitute direct parental "operation." Here of course we may again rue the uselessness of CERCLA's definition of a facility's "operator" as "any person . . . operating" the facility, 42 U.S. C. §9601(20)(A)(ii), which leaves us to do the best we can to give the term its "ordinary or natural meaning." *Bailey v. United States,* 516 U.S. 137, 145 (1995) (internal quotation marks omitted). In a mechanical sense, to "operate" ordinarily means "[t]o control the functioning of; run: *operate a sewing machine.*" American Heritage Dictionary 1268 (3d ed. 1992); see also Webster's New International Dictionary 1707 (2d ed. 1958) ("to work; as, to *operate* a machine"). And in the organizational sense more obviously intended by CERCLA, the word ordinarily means "[t]o conduct the affairs of; manage: *operate a business.*" *American Heritage Dictionary,* supra, at 1268; see also Webster's New International Dictionary, supra, at 1707 ("to manage"). So, under CERCLA, an operator is simply someone who directs the workings of, manages, or conducts the affairs of a facility. To sharpen the definition for purposes of CERCLA's concern with environmental contamination, an operator must manage, direct, or conduct operations specifically related to pollution, that is, operations having to do with the leakage or disposal of hazardous waste, or decisions about compliance with environmental regulations.

B

*   *   *

In our enquiry into the meaning Congress presumably had in mind when it used the verb "to operate," we recognized that the statute obviously meant something more than mere mechanical activation of pumps and valves, and must be read to contemplate "operation" as including the exercise of direction over the facility's activities. . . . The Court of Appeals recognized this by indicat-

ing that a parent can be held directly liable when the parent operates the facility in the stead of its subsidiary or alongside the subsidiary in some sort of a joint venture. See 113 F. 3d, at 579. We anticipated a further possibility . . . that a dual officer or director might depart so far from the norms of parental influence exercised through dual officeholding as to serve the parent, even when ostensibly acting on behalf of the subsidiary in operating the facility. . . . Yet another possibility, suggested by the facts of this case, is that an agent of the parent with no hat to wear but the parent's hat might manage or direct activities at the facility.

Identifying such an occurrence calls for line drawing yet again, since the acts of direct operation that give rise to parental liability must necessarily be distinguished from the interference that stems from a normal relationship between parent and subsidiary. Again norms of corporate behavior (undisturbed by any CERCLA provision) are crucial reference points. Just as we may look to such norms in identifying the limits of the presumption that a dual officeholder acts in his ostensible capacity, so here we may refer to them in distinguishing a parental officer's oversight of a subsidiary from such an officer's control over the operation of the subsidiary's facility. . . . The critical question is whether, in degree and detail, actions directed to the facility by an agent of the parent alone are eccentric under accepted norms of parental oversight of a subsidiary's facility.

CASES

CASE 1.   *Protecting Consumers Against Tobacco*

The dangers of smoking cigarettes are now generally conceded by almost everyone except certain tobacco companies. Far less clear is how to protect the consumer and the potential consumer of cigarettes. A major source of marketing is newspaper advertising. At the same time, newspapers are a major source of information transmitted to the public about the dangers of smoking cigarettes. Thus, newspapers have not only an interest in revenue from cigarette advertising but also an interest in informing the public about the dangers of what they advertise.

The American Newspaper Publishers Association and the Magazine Publishers Association have appealed to First Amendment protections of the right to advertise and to present the facts as newspapers see fit in order to justify their view that this matter should be left up to each individual newspaper.

The New Republic commissioned reporter David Owen to write an article on cancer and the cigarette lobby. He wrote a piece so blunt in stating the issues and laying blame that *The New Republic*'s editors killed it. According to *USA Today*, "In the candid (and no doubt regretted) words of Leon Wieseltier, the editor who assigned it, the threat of 'massive losses of advertising revenue' did it in." Although the editors of *The New Republic* had been willing to report on the dangers of smoking and on the pressures brought by lobbyists, they were not willing to support the forcefulness with which Owen stated his case. Owen later published his piece in the *Washington Monthly*, where he wrote that "The transcendent achievement of the cigarette lobby has been to establish the cancer issue as a 'controversy' or a 'debate' rather than as the clear-cut scientific case that it is." Owen portrayed an industry that intentionally uses newspapers and magazines to enhance its appeal by depicting the young smoker as healthy and sexy.

According to research by Kenneth E. Warner, rejection of Owens's article is one of many cases in which the American news media refused to report on smoking hazards for fear of loss of advertising revenue. This general problem prompted *Washington Post* ombudsman Sam Zagoria to chide newspapers for a failure to see the issues as moral rather than legal:

> Couldn't the newspapers of the country agree — voluntarily and collectively — to refuse cigarette advertising? Couldn't they do what is right rather than only what is not prohibited by law? Most papers take great pride in the service they render to their communities, not only in providing information but also in philanthropic activities that provide scholarships and underwrite athletic tournaments. Is not helping some youngster avert the tortures of life-shortening lung cancer even a greater gift? . . . Is there any media group for social responsibility?

This case was prepared by Tom L. Beauchamp. The case is based on the following sources: Charles Trueheart, "The Tobacco Industry's Advertising Smoke Screen," *USA Today* (March 15, 1985), p. 3D; Kenneth E. Warner, "Cigarette Advertising and Media Coverage of Smoking and Health," *New England Journal of Medicine* 312 (6), (February 7, 1985):384–88; Sam Zagoria, "Smoking and the Media's Responsibility," *Washington Post* (December 18, 1985), p. A26; Elizabeth Whelan, "Second Thoughts on a Cigarette-Ad Ban," *Wall Street Journal* (December 18, 1985), p. 28; Sam Zagoria, "Consumer Watchdogs," *Washington Post* (April 24, 1985), p. A24; Robert J. Samuelson, "Pacifying Media Hype," *Washington Post* (October 9, 1985), pp. F1, F12.

Only 6 out of 1,700 daily American newspapers, Zagoria noted (using statistics taken from the *New York State Journal of Medicine*), attempt wholeheartedly to report on the dangers of smoking.

Zagoria later wrote another column in which he took the position that the press has a "watchdog" role to play not only in government but in consumer safety as well. Few journalists disagree with Zagoria's judgment that this role is legitimate or that a newspaper can validly choose to emphasize reporting on the risks of smoking without introducing a bias. However, Zagoria's contentions that the press has an *obligation* to promote the interests of consumers has met a hostile reaction in newspaper front offices.

Questions

1. Has Zagoria confused the industry's responsibility and the government's responsibility to protect the public with that of the media's responsibilities, as many managers at newspapers believe?
2. Does anyone's obligation to protect consumers stretch as far as Zagoria suggests?
3. Are stiff warnings on packages of cigarettes adequate to protect consumers? Potential consumers?

CASE 2.   *Exposing Workers to Plutonium*

In August 1999 it was learned that several thousand uranium workers in a 750-acre plant in Paducah, Kentucky had also been exposed to plutonium and other radioactive materials. The exposures occurred at the Paducah Gaseous Diffusion Plant, which is owned by the Department of Energy of the U.S. government and is still in operation today. The 1,800 workers in the plant once labored to produce material for bombs from uranium dust. The radioactive contaminants that caused the exposure also spilled into ditches and eventually were carried into wildlife areas and private water wells. Some of the material had been deliberately dumped into landfills and nearby fields. In the last few years the enriched uranium produced at the plant has been sold to commercial nuclear power plants.

Many records on plutonium contamination were kept in archives, but workers were never told of potential risks to health, and there has never been a study of the medical histories of workers, as of this writing. Workers have traditionally been told that there were insignificant amounts of plutonium, but workers were not monitored to determine actual levels of exposure. High levels of radiation have been discovered in and around the plant as recently as 1996. Groundwater cleanups have been underway since 1988, when the serious levels of pollution in wells was discovered.

Union Carbide managed the plant for a 32-year period, when most of the pollution occurred. Lockheed Martin and Martin Marietta managed the plant during the 1980s and 1990s. The federal government for decades took the position that the amounts of exposure were too small to amount to a threat to health. However, internal documents show that Martin Marietta was very concerned about significant environmental damage that had occurred. The current plant operator is

This case was prepared by Tom Beauchamp, based on reports by Joby Warrick in *The Washington Post* of August 8, 1999 (p. A1); August 29, 1999 (p. A1); and September 16, 1999 (p. A1).

U.S. Enrichment Corp., which concedes that there were pollution problems under previous managers. A lawsuit has been filed against the federal government, but no corporation has as yet been named in the suit. Workers have maintained that even if the exposure should turn out not to constitute a threat to the health of workers, issues about not disclosing levels of pollution and not monitoring health records would remain.

In September 1999 the Clinton administration announced that it would spend several million dollars to compensate workers believed to have been harmed by exposures at the Paducah Gaseous Diffusion Plant. The Department of Energy announced that it would allot $21.8 million in new spending for environmental cleanup in the region.

Questions

1. Should management in the plant make a full disclosure of known risks, even when the risks are believed to be insignificant?

2. Does the government or any former and present manager have a responsibility to pay the workers for the risks they were asked to undertake, even if they turn out to have been insignificant?

3. In failing to make a full disclosure, are the plant owner and managers guilty of a punishable moral violation? What is the moral violation, and what form of punishment would be in order?

CASE 3.   *The McDonald's Polystyrene Case*

Environmental consciousness has increased dramatically in the United States in the past fifteen years. More and more people are conscious of toxic wastes, of pollution, of the mountains of garbage that pour into landfills, of the depletion of forests. McDonald's, the largest restaurant chain in the world, presents a notable environmental case study.

For years McDonald's, like most other quick-food chains, used polystyrene containers — the famous Big Mac clamshell — for its hamburgers. This container was lightweight, did not absorb grease, and kept the hamburgers warm. McDonald's had chosen polystyrene over paperboard for these projects and had joined with others in a $16 million project to build seven polystyrene-recycling plants around the country. But by the end of 1990 it

was to change its mind.[1] Because of its size and dominant position, McDonald's became the target of the Environmental Defense Fund, which claimed that making polystyrene packaging created toxic fumes, that it took up too much landfill, and that it took too long to biodegrade. In addition, a lobby called the Pro-Environment Packaging Council, funded by paper companies, started targeting schools with a campaign about the adverse impact of polystyrene products. McDonald's was soon faced with what *Forbes Magazine* called a "children's crusade," which involved a Send-It-Back campaign, letters written by classes of chil-

---

[1]Details of the case come from the sources noted below, as well as from *New York Times*, November 1, 1990, p. A1; November 2, 1990, p. A1; December 31, 1990, p. A3; and April 17, 1991, p. A14.

This case was written by Richard T. DeGeorge, *Business Ethics* (Prentice-Hall, 5th ed., 1999).

dren, and a threatened boycott.[2] On November 2, 1990, McDonald's announced that within sixty days it would phase out its polystyrene clams and replace them with coated paperboard.

The announcement was hailed as a victory for environmentalists and as a demonstration of the power of public opinion. Newspaper editorials across the country congratulated McDonald's for taking the leadership in environmental issues and put pressure on other chains to follow McDonald's lead.

Although no one spoke against the importance of environmental concern, several voices were raised, but scarcely heard, that questioned the soundness of McDonald's decision. Edward H. Rensi, head of McDonald's U.S. operations, who had long defended the clamshell boxes, said, "Although some scientific studies indicate that foam packaging is environmentally sound, our customers just don't feel good about it."[3] Jay Beyea, a scientist at the National Audubon Society, noted that the change would result in using a lot more paper and that "using a lot more paper means a lot more pollution."[4] It also means cutting a lot more trees. A study by the Stanford Research Institute concluded that there was no sound basis for claiming that using

paper products was environmentally superior to using polystyrene or other such plastic-based materials.[5] Nor would the change affect the landfill problems, since such material accounts for only one-third of 1 percent of landfill waste by volume. Lynn Scarlett, vice-president of research at Reason Foundation, pointed out that manufacturing polystyrene clamshells used 30 percent less energy than paperboard and produced 40 percent less air pollution and 42 percent less water pollution.[6]

Questions

1. In the end, environmentalists had won— or had a certain wing, together with large paper interests, won? Public opinion had had its way. But who informed grade school children of the facts that led to their uncharacteristic assertiveness on this issue, and did they get the whole story?

2. McDonald's move to paper products was probably a good business decision, given the circumstances and the pressure it was under. Was it the best environmental decision? Was it morally obliged to take the action it did?

[2]"McDonald's Caves In," *Forbes*, (February 4, 1991): 73–74.

[3]*Fortune* (June 3, 1991), p. 92.

[4]John Holusha, "Packaging and Public Image: McDonald's Fills a Big Order," *New York Times*, (November 2, 1990), p. A1.

[5]Benjamin Zycher, "Self-Flagellation Among the Capitalists," *Regulation* 14 (Winter 1991): 25–26.

[6]Lynn Scarlett, "Make Your Environment Dirtier—Recycle," *Wall Street Journal* (January 14, 1991), p. A12.

CASE 4.   *Virazole and Investor Risk*

On October 7, 1991, the U.S. Securities and Exchange Commission (SEC) filed suit against two pharmaceutical firms in a District of Columbia federal District Court, charging that the companies had falsely and misleadingly presented to investors a product's promise for combating the AIDS virus. The suit grew out of a four-year SEC investigation of ICN Pharmaceuticals and its Costa Mesa, California-based subsidiary, Viratek, Inc. The U.S. Food and Drug Administration (FDA) had approved the companies to market the drug ribavirin under the trade name Virazole, for hospital use in treating respiratory syncytial virus. In a January 1987 press conference, the companies announced that ribavirin had, in addition, proved effective in delaying the onset of AIDS symptoms in HIV-infected patients. Shortly after this announcement Viratek stock climbed from $14.00 a share to $70.00 a share. On the date the SEC filed suit, the stock declined to $5.12 a share.

The company provided a summary of its scientific findings, but AIDS advocacy groups maintained that ICN and Viratek had supplied few hard facts and test results to substantiate the conclusions announced. The SEC lawsuit alleged that corporate officials in 1987 deliberately made untrue claims regarding Virazole's effectiveness. According to SEC officials, in the placebo-controlled clinical trials, the patients who received placebos had exhibited severely weakened immune systems before the trial and so were certain to fare worse than the patients receiving the drug being tested. The placebo patients also showed an unusually rapid progression toward acute AIDS symptoms. Consequently, the ribavirin patients appeared to benefit from treatment only because their AIDS symptoms developed more slowly in comparison with their placebo counterparts. In April 1987, the FDA declined to approve ribavirin for AIDS treatment, based on its analysis of the clinical trials. When ICN and Viratek subsequently neglected to inform investors of the results of clinical trials, the SEC launched its investigation.

After the SEC filed its lawsuit, ICN and Viratek officials signed a consent order that did not address corporate culpability but that did stipulate that the corporations involved would take precautions not to make potentially "misleading statements to investors" in the future. At the same time, company spokespersons denied any wrongdoing in the ribavirin controversy. They held that the consent order was signed only because it was the fastest way to resolve the affair. According to Viratek's CEO, "We have always operated our business with integrity, and as good citizens we will continue to do so." The company claimed that it had a different view of the scientific evidence than the SEC did and that it had no moral or legal obligation to make disclosures to investors of the sort proposed by the SEC. Investors did not file suit in the case.

Questions

1. What should Viratek have told stockholders and potential stockholders? Should any information disclosure include a full, conservatively stated estimate of the scientific evidence?

2. Did Viratek officials manipulate potential investors into buying the stock through an incomplete disclosure?

3. Assuming trade secrets are involved, is the scientific evidence proprietary to the company and also confidential? If so, could hard facts and test results be disclosed without damage to the company?

This case was prepared by John Cuddihy, based in part on a report by Tracy Thompson in *The Washington Post*, "Drug Maker Settles SEC Suit over Notification of Investors" (October 8, 1991), D3.

CASE 5. *OSHA Noncompliance and Security*

TMW Corporation produces three-quarters of the world's micro-synchronizers, an integral part of apartment vacuum systems. This corporation has plants mostly in the Midwest, although a few are scattered on both the east and west coasts. The plants in the Midwest employ Electronic Worker's Union members under a contract that became effective last August and is in force for three years. This union is strong and the employees will do anything to preserve and maintain the strong union benefits that have been won.

Last year an OSHA official visited the St. Louis plant and discovered several discrepancies with the standards established by the OSH Act, including the absence of safety goggles on employees who weld tiny wires together and also an automatic shutoff switch on the wire-splicing machine. OSHA issued warnings to TMW for the noncompliance and informed company officials that it would impose drastic fines if they did not correct them.

The company immediately proceeded to correct the problems. They had to shut parts of the Midwest plants down on a rotating basis to alter the wire-splicing machines. These measures upset the union members, because the employer laid off older employees, not the new trainees on the machines. They threatened a walkout.

The safety goggles presented the company with another OSHA compliance hurdle. When told of the need to wear their goggles, the welders refused, saying they could not see as well. The welders said they would take responsibility for not wearing the goggles. The unions backed the welders in their refusal.

Questions

1. Was the TMW Corporation wrong in laying off the senior employees?

2. Should the company force the welders to comply with the safety goggle requirements? Since the welders refused to comply and assumed responsibility, is the company released of all responsibility in the event of an accident?

3. Should OSHA intervene and fine those responsible for any violations of OSHA standards? Is this case too minor for such intervention?

Suggested Supplementary Readings

Consumer Protection

BROBECK, STEPHEN. *The Modern Consumer Movement.* Boston: G. K. Hall & Co., 1990.

CAVANILLAS MUGICA, SANTIAGO. "Protection of the Weak Consumer Under Product Liability Rules." *Journal of Consumer Policy* 13 (1990).

OWEN, DAVID G. "Rethinking the Policies of Strict Products Liability." *Vanderbilt Law Review* 33 (1980).

PROSSER, WILLIAM L. "The Assault Upon the Citadel (Strict Liability to the Consumer)." *Yale Law Journal* 69 (1960).

SAXE, DIANNE. "The Fiduciary Duty of Corporate Directors to Protect the Environment for Future Generations." *Environmental Values* 1 (Autumn 1992): 243–52.

SORELL, TOM. "The Customer Is Not Always Right." *Journal of Business Ethics* 13 (November 1994): 913–18.

VISCUSI, W. KIP. "Toward a Proper Role for Hazard Warnings in Products Liability Cases." *Journal of Products Liability* 13 (1991).

This case was prepared by Professor Kenneth A. Kovach. Printed with permission.

WARNE, COLSTON E. *The Consumer Movement,* edited by Richard L. D. Morse. Manhattan, KS: Family Economics Trust Press, 1993.

Worker Protection

ANDERSON, ELIZABETH. "Values, Risks and Market Norms." *Philosophy and Public Affairs* 17 (1988): 54-65.

BEAUCHAMP, TOM L. *Case Studies in Business, Society, and Ethics.* 4th ed. Englewood Cliffs, NJ: Prentice Hall, 1997, Chaps. 1, 5.

BERITIC, T. "Workers at High Risk: The Right to Know." *Lancet* 341 (April 10, 1993): 933–34.

BRUENING, JOHN. "Risk Communication." *Occupational Hazards* 52 (October 1990).

EZORSKY, GERTRUDE, ed. *Moral Rights in the Workplace.* Albany: State University of New York Press, 1987.

GIBSON, MARY. *Workers' Rights.* Totowa, NJ: Rowman and Littlefield, 1983.

GOLDSMITH, WILLIS. "The Expanding Scope of Employers' Duties Under the Hazard Communication Standard and State and Local Right-to-Know Laws." *Employee Relations Law Journal* 12 (Spring 1987).

HIMMELSTEIN, JAY S., and HOWARD FRUMKIN. "The Right to Know About Toxic Exposures: Implications for Physicians." *New England Journal of Medicine* 312 (March 14, 1985): 687–90.

LURIE, SUE GENA. "Ethical Dilemmas and Professional Roles in Occupational Medicine." *Social Science and Medicine* 38 (May 1994): 1367–74.

ROSNER, DAVID, and GERALD MARKOWITZ. "Workers, Industry, and the Control of Information: Silicosis and the Industrial Hygiene Foundation." *Journal of Public Health Policy* 16 (1995): 29–58.

SASS, ROBERT. "The Worker's Right to Know, Participate, and Refuse Hazardous Work: A Manifesto Right." *Journal of Business Ethics* 5 (April 1986).

U.S. CONGRESS. OFFICE OF TECHNOLOGY ASSESSMENT. *Reproductive Hazards in the Workplace. Contractor Documents, Volume 1: Selected Ethical Issues in the Management of Reproductive Health Hazards in the Workplace.* [Set of six papers]. Washington: U.S. Office of Technology Assessment, January 1986.

WALTERS, VIVIENNE, AND MARGARET DENTON. "Workers' Knowledge of Their Legal Rights and Resistance to Hazardous Work." *Industrial Relations* 45 (Summer 1990).

WOKUTCH, RICHARD E. *Worker Protection, Japanese Style.* Ithaca, NY: ILR Press, 1992.

Environmental Protection

ATTFIELD, ROBIN. *The Ethics of Environmental Concern.* New York: Columbia University Press, 1983.

BLACKSTONE, WILLIAM T., ed. *Philosophy and Environmental Crisis.* Athens: University of Georgia Press, 1974.

DES JARDINS, JOSEPH R. *Environmental Ethics: An Introduction to Environmental Philosophy.* Belmont, CA: Wadsworth, 1993.

ENGEL, J. RONALD, and JOAN GIBB ENGEL, eds. *Ethics of Environment and Development.* Tucson: University of Arizona Press, 1991.

Environmental Ethics. "An Interdisciplinary Journal Dedicated to the Philosophical Aspects of Environmental Problems."

GIBSON, MARY. *To Breathe Freely: Risk, Consent, and Air.* Totowa, NJ: Rowman and Littlefield, 1985.

GOODIN, ROBERT E. "Property Rights and Preservationist Duties." *Inquiry* 33 (1991).

GUERRETTE, R. H.: "Environmental Integrity and Corporate Responsibility." *Journal of Business Ethics* 5 (1986): 409–15.

HARRIS, CHRISTOPHER, and others. "Criminal Liability of Federal Hazardous Waste Law: The 'Knowledge' of Corporations and their Executives." *Wake Forest Law Review* 23 (1988).

HOCH, DAVID, AND ROBERT A. GIACALONE. "On the Lumber Industry: Ethical Concerns as the Other Side of Profits." *Journal of Business Ethics* 13 (May, 1994): 357–67.

HOFFMAN, W. MICHAEL, and others, eds. *Business, Ethics, and the Environment: The Public Policy Debate.* New York: Quorum Books, 1990.

———, eds. *The Corporation, Ethics, and the Environment.* New York: Quorum Books, 1990.

LEDGERWOOD, GRANT. *Environment Ethics and the Corporation.* Basingstoke: Macmillan, 1999.

LUDWIG, DEAN C., and JUDITH A. LUDWIG. "The Regulation of Green Marketing: Learning Lessons from the Regulation of Health and Nutrition Claims." *Business and Professional Ethics Journal* 11 (Fall-Winter 1992): 73–91.

MILLER, ALAN S. *Gaia Connections: An Introduction to Ecology, Ecoethics, and Economics.* Totowa, NJ: Rowman and Littlefield, 1991.

NAESS, ARNE. *Ecology, Community, and Lifestyle,* trans. by D. Rothenberg. New York: Cambridge University Press, 1990.

NEWTON, LISA H. "The Chainsaws of Greed: The Case of Pacific Lumber." *Business and Professional Ethics Journal* 8 (Fall 1989): 29–61.

REGAN, TOM, ed. *Earthbound: New Introductory Essays in Environmental Ethics.* New York: Random House, 1984.

ROLSTON, HOLMES, III. *Environmental Ethics: Duties to and Values in the Natural World.* Philadelphia: Temple University Press, 1988.

———. *Philosophy Gone Wild: Environmental Ethics.* Buffalo, NY: Prometheus Books, 1991.

———. "Just Environmental Business." In *Just Business,* edited by Tom Regan. Philadelphia: Temple University Press, 1983.

ROSENTHAL, SANDRA B., and ROGEN A. BUCHHOLZ. "Bridging Environmental and Business Ethics: A Pragmatic Framework." *Environmental Ethics* 20 (1998): 393–408.

SAGOFF, MARK. *The Economy of the Earth.* New York: Cambridge University Press, 1990.

SAXE, DIANNE. "The Fiduciary Duty of Corporate Directors to Protect the Environment for Future Generations." *Environmental Values* 1 (Fall 1992): 243–52.

SINGH, JANG B., and EMILY F. CARASCO. "Business Ethics, Economic Development and Protection of the Environment in the New World Order." *Journal of Business Ethics* 15 (1996): 297–307.

SINGH, JANG B., and V. C. LAKHAN. "Business Ethics and the International Trade in Hazardous Wastes." *Journal of Business Ethics* 8 (1989): 889–899.

SKORPEN, ERLING. "Images of the Environment in Corporate America." *Journal of Business Ethics* 10 (1991).

SMITH, DENIS, ed. *Business and the Environment: Implications of the New Environmentalism.* New York: St. Martin's Press, 1993.

STARIK, MARK. "Should Trees Have Managerial Standing? Toward Stakeholder Status for Non-Human Nature." *Journal of Business Ethics* 14 (March 1995): 207–17.

VANDEVEER, DONALD, and CHRISTINE PIERCE. *Environmental Ethics and Policy Book: Philosophy, Ecology and Economics.* Belmont, CA: Wadsworth Publishing Co., 1994.

Investor Protection

ALMEDER, ROBERT F., and MILTON SNOEYENBOS. "Churning: Ethical and Legal Issues." *Business and Professional Ethics Journal* 6 (Spring 1987).

ALMEDER, ROBERT F., and DAVID CAREY. "In Defense of Sharks: Moral Issues in Hostile Liquidating Takeovers." *Journal of Business Ethics* 10 (1991): 471–84.

BROWN, DONNA. "Environmental Investing: Let the Buyer Beware." *Management Review* 79 (June 1990).

DAMM, RICHARD E. "A Question of Bias." *Best's Review* 86 (December 1985).

EASTERWOOD, JOHN C., RONALD F. SINGER, and ANJU SETH. "Controlling the Conflict of Interest in Management Buyouts." *The Review of Economics and Statistics* 76 (August 1994): 512–22.

FRANKS, JULIAN, and COLIN MAYER. *Risk, Regulation, and Investor Protection: The Case of Investment Management.* Oxford: Clarendon Press, 1989.

HEACOCK, MARIAN, and others. "Churning: An Ethical Issue in Finance." *Business and Professional Ethics Journal* 6 (Spring 1987).

HOFFMAN, W. MICHAEL, and RALPH J., MCQUADE. "A Matter of Ethics." *Financial Strategies and Concepts* 4 (1986).

JONES, THOMAS M., and REED O. HUNT. "The Ethics of Leveraged Management Buyouts Revisited." *Journal of Business Ethics* 10 (November 1991): 833–40.

KESTER, W. C., and T. A. LUEHRMAN. "Rehabilitating the Leveraged Buyout." *Harvard Business Review* 73 (May-June 1995): 119–30.

MOORE, JENNIFER. "What Is Really Unethical About Insider Trading?" *Journal of Business Ethics* 9 (March 1990).

"Note: Recent Trends in the Organization and Regulation of Securities Markets." *Financial Market Trends* 46 (May 1990).

SCHADLER, F. P., and J. E. KARNS. "The Unethical Exploitation of Shareholders in Management Buyout Transactions." *Journal of Business Ethics* 9 (July 1990): 595–602.

SCHIFRIN, MATTHEW. "Sellers Beware." *Forbes* 147 (January 21, 1991): 36–38.

WILLIAMS, OLIVER, and others. *Ethics and the Investment Industry.* Savage, MD: Rowman and Littlefield, 1989.

Chapter Five

Rights and Obligations of Employers and Employees

INTRODUCTION

T RADITIONALLY, BUSINESS FIRMS are organized hierarchically, with production line employees at the bottom and the CEO at the top. Also the interests of the stockholders are given priority over the interests of the other stakeholders. However, much recent literature presents a challenge to these arrangements, especially to underlying classical economic assumptions whereby labor is treated as analogous to land, capital, and machinery, that is, as replaceable and as a means to profit. Employees primarily want to be treated as persons who are genuine partners in the business enterprise. They want decent salaries and job security, as well as appreciation from supervisors, a sense of accomplishment, and fair opportunities to display their talents. Many employees are also interested in participating in planning the future directions of the company, defining the public responsibilities of the corporation, evaluating the role and quality of management, and — most especially — helping to set the tasks assigned to their jobs. These new developments in labor relations are all to the good, but they must be understood in light of a very different tradition whereby an employee is clearly subordinate to the employer, is legally obligated to obey the employer's orders, and has few rights except the right to quit.

Status and Scope of Employee Rights

In the traditional view, the freedom of the employee to quit, the freedom of the employer to fire, and the right of the employer to order the employee to do his or her bidding define the essence of the employment contract. The legal principle behind the traditional view is called the *employment-at-will principle*. This principle says that in the absence of a specific contract or law, an employer may hire, fire, demote, or promote an employee whenever the employer wishes. Moreover, the employer may act with justification, with inadequate justification, or with no justification at all. In the selection that opens this chapter, Patricia Werhane and Tara

Radin consider several arguments for the employment-at-will doctrine and find them wanting.

Over the years this master–servant relationship, which is at the core of the employment-at-will doctrine, has been legally constrained. Once unions were given legal protection, collective bargaining produced contracts that constrained the right of employers to fire at will. Employees who were protected by union contracts usually could be fired only for cause and then only after a lengthy grievance process. During the height of the union movement, the chief protection against an unjust firing was the union-negotiated contract. However, during the 1980s and early 1990s the percentage of the U.S. workforce belonging to unions fell into the teens, and as a result the protection offered by the union-negotiated contract covers millions fewer workers.

Some might argue that the decline in the number of U.S. workers who belong to unions has not significantly increased the number of employees who are at risk of an unjust dismissal. These people argue that a large number of enlightened companies have adopted policies that provide the same type of protection against unjust dismissal as was previously found in union-negotiated contracts. Moreover, where such policies exist they have the force of law. For example, on May 9, 1985, the New Jersey Supreme Court held that Hoffman-LaRoche Inc. was bound by job security assurances that were implied in an employee manual. The manual seemed to pledge that employees could be fired only for just cause and then only if certain procedures were followed. Hoffman-LaRoche argued that although the company manual gave company policy, adherence to it was voluntary and not legally enforceable. The court, however, said employers cannot have it both ways without acting unfairly and so illegally. Hoffman-LaRoche had to reinstate an employee who had been fired on grounds that his supervisor had lost confidence in his work.

In response to this and similar rulings, a number of corporations have taken steps to make it more difficult for employees to use company manuals and policy statements to protect their jobs. Some are simply eliminating the manuals and dismantling their grievance procedure apparatus. Sears Roebuck and other employers have their employees sign a form declaring that they can be fired "with or without just cause." Finally, several companies have developed internal procedures that examine every dismissal case as though it were a specific contract with a just-cause-for-firing provision in it.[1]

Others point out that during the 1980s and early 1990s, certain grounds for firing employees have been made illegal by federal or state law. Antidiscrimination statutes protect workers from being fired because of their race or sex, because they are handicapped, or because of age. Federal law also protects workers from being fired because they resist sexual advances from their bosses or refuse to date them. The protection given employees from this and other forms of sexual harassment is discussed in Chapter Six.

Although such laws are needed to curb past abuses, they are not always clear nor always effective. In the recession of 1991 and the subsequent downsizing that has occurred, many highly qualified white-collar middle-management employees who were over forty and laid off found it virtually impossible to find similar employment elsewhere. Rightly or wrongly, many of these people thought their age was a factor in their inability to obtain similar employment.

Yet another important development is the evolution of a common law protection to one's job if an employee disobeys an employer on the grounds that the employer ordered him or her to do something illegal or immoral. The notion that employees should not lose their jobs because they refuse to behave illegally or immorally might seem obvious, but as the two recent New Jersey cases included in this chapter show, the situation is more complex than it might appear. On some issues there is near unanimity that a course of action is right or wrong. But on other matters there is considerable difference of opinion. As we saw in the discussions of the *Challenger* in Chapter Three, conflicts concerning what is morally appropriate often occur between managers and engineers. As a practical matter, a large corporation cannot allow employees to refuse to abide by a corporate decision whenever it conflicts with a personal moral position. On the other hand, the public must support employees who refuse to obey an order or accept a decision that threatens the public with serious harm. *Potter v. Village Bank of New Jersey* and *Warthen v. Toms River Community Memorial Hospital* illustrate how the courts try to balance the public interest and legitimate business concerns on this issue.

Even more important, these laws do not provide sufficient protection for what many employees consider their most important workplace right — the right to a job. From the perspective of most employees, the most important contribution of capitalism is providing work. Job security is often ranked higher than increased pay in terms of what employees most want from employers. The desire for job security is captured in employee demands that workers have a right to a job and that this right deserves protection. The claim that a person has a right to a job has two components. First, workers believe they have a right to a job in the first place. Second, as employees continue to work at a job, they believe they have a right to retain that job. Provision of the right to a job in the first place is usually considered to be the responsibility of government and is not discussed here. However, the notion that employees gain rights to a job that they have been holding is a new idea. In an era in which downsizing has destroyed even the traditional social contract, the idea that a person can come to hold a right to one's job is not widely held.

Indeed, some scholars, especially from the law and economics school, have continued to support the traditional employment-at-will doctrine. For example, Richard A. Epstein has argued, in the article reprinted in this chapter, that employment-at-will is both fair and efficient. Spokespersons from the law and economics school take efficiency concerns very seriously, and Epstein spends considerable time developing some of these concerns.

The Right to Privacy

Although a right to one's job may be the workplace right that employees most value and want honored, they believe they have other rights that should be honored as well. Many people believe that the rights guaranteed by the Bill of Rights in the Constitution are rights that each U.S. citizen has in all aspects of his or her life. But this is not the case. Americans are protected against government infringements of the Bill of Rights, but they are not protected against corporate infringement of these rights. The Bill of Rights does not apply within the corporation. Thus there is no right to free speech within the corporation. Many believe that such a gap in the protection of the Constitution for individual citizens seems unjustified. They argue that since business activity takes place within U.S. society, business activity should be conducted consistent with the Bill of Rights. Others argue, however, that applying the Bill of Rights in the corporate setting would create great inefficiencies because discipline would break down. Besides, there are many companies in the United States for which a person can work, but there is only one U.S. government. Therefore, it is more important to have a Bill of Rights to protect individuals from government than to have a Bill of Rights to protect individuals from their boss.

The right to privacy is not explicitly listed as a right protected by the Constitution. Supreme Court Justice Louis Brandeis argued that right to privacy can be inferred from a number of other rights that are protected by the Constitution. He and Samuel Warren in a famous article defined privacy as "the right to be left alone." Philosophers have criticized this definition and few today find it satisfactory. Most philosophers argue that the right to privacy should be understood as a right that one must have to exercise personal autonomy. Without zones of privacy, we could not be fully autonomous persons.

Debates regarding the extent and scope of privacy rights are commonplace in U.S. business. Theft by employees and customers is a huge problem, accounting for billions of dollars in losses every year. Until recently a common technique for deterring theft was to subject employees to polygraph (lie detector) tests. However, doubts about their accuracy and arguments that the tests invaded the privacy of employees led to a legal prohibition of their use, enacted initially by some states and then by the federal government. In 1988 Congress passed the Employee Polygraph Protection Act (EPPA) that banned polygraphs, voice-stress analyzers, and other physiological tests. Exceptions are made for pharmaceutical firms, security guards, and the government. Now employers are turning to honesty tests that are based on statistical correlations between the answers to certain questions on the honesty test and the likelihood that an employee will commit theft.[2] The same issues of accuracy and invasion of privacy that confronted the use of polygraphs confront the use of honesty tests. However, the American Psychological Association has certified the validity of some tests, and the tests have escaped serious legal challenge up to the present time.[3]

Not all invasions of privacy can be justified as a means for protecting a company from the wrongful acts of others. Some invasions of privacy are justified because such acts increase profits.

Your financial information is not safe. Consider the case of U.S. Bancorp, which sold the telemarketer MemberWorks customer data such as names, phone numbers, bank account and credit card numbers, Social Security numbers, and account balances and credit limits. MemberWorks then used this information to call people and attempt to sell them everything from dental plans to video games. Often the sales pitch was couched as a free trial with 30 days to cancel. Consumers who did not cancel were stuck; the charges were put against their credit cards or bank balances. U.S.

Bancorp received a share of the revenues. The state of Minnesota brought suit and U.S. Bancorp abandoned the practice. Two other large banks followed suit. But there are no federal laws to prevent banks from selling the details of your account to telemarketers. There is no law against selling social security numbers, even though people often steal social security numbers to establish an identity that then allows them to behave criminally in the name of the person who really has that social security number. Your activity on the internet is similarly not protected.[4]

As computer technology matures, the number of concerns about privacy issues grows. Computer technology makes the invasion of privacy easier. Companies can build databases on individuals by monitoring purchases offline and databases online. They can then target ads to individuals. This practice is called *profiling*. In 1999, the online music distributor RealNetworks Inc., was roundly criticized for its surreptitious collection of the listening habits of those who visited its site. The information included the format a person stores his or her music in, the number of songs on a person's hard disk and the person's favorite type of music, among other things. RealNetworks has 13.5 million registered users. When the invasion of privacy was discovered, the information was put on the internet. Twenty-four hours later RealNetworks halted the practice and admitted that it had made a mistake.[5]

One of the more controversial policies of certain companies are rules that govern the dating of employees. Wal-Mart has been struggling with this issue. Wal-Mart had a policy that prohibited fraternization. Laurel Allen and Samuel Johnson were both sales associates at the Wal-Mart store in Johnstown, New York. Allen was separated and Johnson was single. The Wal-Mart policy stated: "Wal-Mart strongly believes in and supports the 'family unit.' A dating relationship between a married associate and another associate is prohibited." Both Allen and Johnson were fired. In 1992 the New York Attorney General filed suit claiming that Wal-Mart's policy was in violation of a New York law that prohibited employers from firing workers who engage in legal recreational activities. In 1995 a New York court found in favor of Wal-Mart on the grounds that dating was not a recreational activity protected by the statute. Nonetheless, Wal-Mart has now amended it policy so that it covers improper conduct at work. Improper conduct would include open displays of affection and other activity that would make the workplace uncomfortable. In 1995 a federal judge decided in another case that dating was a recreational activity protected by the New York law. These two important cases are reprinted in this chapter.

Another serious problem facing corporate America is the rising cost of health insurance. In order to reduce their insurance premiums, many corporations are taking a great interest in the personal habits of their employees. Some will not hire people who smoke.[6] Ford Meter Box of Wabash, Indiana is one of those companies who will not hire smokers and who will fire those who do smoke. Indiana has now passed a law that forbids companies from firing employees who smoke. However, companies are still permitted to charge higher health insurance premiums to persons who smoke.[7] Other companies will insist that employees lose weight, exercise, and abstain from risky activities off the job.[8] Rules that prohibit an employee from smoking tobacco violate both an employee's right to liberty and an employee's right to privacy. Employers argue that such violations are necessary with respect to tobacco in order to keep the cost of health insurance under control.

A concern with health insurance has also sparked an interest in genetic testing. In a 1996 University of Illinois study, more than one-third of Fortune 500 firms that responded admitted to using the medical records of employees in making job-related decisions.[9] Pre-hiring medical screening has already begun and has already generated legal disputes. Rockwell International Corporation screens potential hires to make sure they can perform certain jobs. In 1993 William Cowie was subjected to a test where electrodes were attached to his fingers, hands, and wrists, and he was given painful electric shocks. The purpose of the test was to measure nerve-ending conduction. Cowie was not hired on the basis of that test, which showed that he had a potential to develop carpal tunnel syndrome. In 1998 Cowie was one of 80 workers represented by the EEOC, which is charging Rockwell International with violating anti-discrimination laws. The alleged discrimination would be behavior in violation of The Americans With Disabilities Act.

Given the potential of genetic testing for identifying the propensity for a certain illness, genetic testing only increases the temptation for business firms to sacrifice privacy. Some employees already report that companies are testing for genetic markers that indicate a potential to develop breast cancer, colon cancer, and Huntington's disease.[10] In a series called 21 Ideas for the 21st Century, *Business Week* referred to genetic testing as the idea that the risk of disease will be treated as a disease. The moral implications of this "idea" are huge. None other than Nobel Prize Laureate in Economics Kenneth Arrow has addressed the epistemological and ethical issues. The dilemma occurs because a person with a genetic predisposition to a disease may not be hired because the employer would not want his of her health care premiums to go up. In theory, there is an economic solution to this dilemma. Assuming the person could afford it, he or she could purchase insurance to protect him or her from an unfavorable diagnosis. However, Arrow goes on to argue that such insurance does not make economic sense, and as a result, the proper ethical stance is that information obtained in prognostic tests should be disregarded in the setting of insurance premiums.[11]

These issues are discussed in two articles, one by Brockett and Tankersley that focuses on the insurance aspect of genetic testing and the other by Joseph Kupfer that points out some of the epistemological and ethical issues surrounding genetic testing. For example, Kupfer shows that even though a genetic marker may show a disposition for a disease, nonetheless relatively few people who have the marker contract the disease — even though a greater percentage may contract the disease than in the population at large. Brockett and Tankersley are cognizant of these issues and thus attempt to formulate guidelines for management with respect to genetic testing.

One of the most common invasions of privacy is presented by drug testing. Many corporations now give drug tests to prospective employees. If they fail, they are not hired. Many companies are also giving drug tests to persons they already employ. If any of these employees fail, companies take different actions. Some fire the employee outright; some retest the employee after a period of supposed abstinence and fire the employee if he or she tests positive again; still others insist that employees enroll in a drug treatment program. However, there is a common thread to all these approaches: The use of drugs even off the job will not be tolerated.

Despite the fact that the vast majority of companies do some drug testing and the fact that well-constructed drug-testing programs are legal, a few companies still do not test for drugs. One of the most remarkable is the Drexelbrook Engineering Company, a 300-employee company in Horsham, Pennsylvania that designs and manufactures electronic systems that measure and control levels of hazardous chemicals. Drexelbrook's vice president and general counsel, Lewis Maltby, admits that one of its employees on drugs could cause a disaster as tragic as the one that occurred in Bhopal, India, but despite the huge potential legal liability, Drexelbrook still won't test its employees for drugs. According to Maltby, the fundamental flaw with drug testing is that it tests the wrong thing. "A realistic program to detect workers whose condition puts the company or other people at risk would test for the condition that actually creates the danger. . . . A serious program would recognize that the real problem is worker's impairment and test for that."[12] A philosophical defense of Maltby's position is provided by the article by Joseph DesJardins and Ronald Duska.

Although the notion of testing for job impairment rather than drug use is appealing from the ethical point of view, there are certainly some occupations — teaching and law, for example — in which tests for impairment would be difficult to devise. In other situations testing for job impairment might be inordinately expensive. How much would it cost a school district to test its school bus drivers every school day? Thus the outlook for employee rights is mixed. Current trends indicate that a larger number of employee rights will be recognized and that some that are currently recognized will be expanded. On the other hand, the pressure on corporations to control cost will continue and, as a result, so will the pressures to avoid expenditures for honoring rights. Michael Cranford argues that a well-crafted drug testing program sufficiently balances the right to privacy against the protection of the public.

Yet another privacy issue involves the electronic monitoring of employees. New technology makes it easier to monitor employee behavior. Surely everyone has received the message "this call may be monitored for quality performance" when calling a company or civil agency. The number of keystrokes per minute is easily monitored when a person is working on a computer. The United Parcel Service has developed monitoring into a fine art. Each day the UPS worker picks up a personal box at the depot that contains the day's itinerary timed to the minute. As tasks are completed, that information is entered. Supervisors can, at any point, tell if the driver is on schedule. Each night all the day's information is entered into a computer that can be checked by a supervisor. Overnight the next day's itinerary is programmed into the box. And the UPS delivery person's freedom to make decisions on his or her own is seriously curtailed. The black box contains management's view of what is to be done and how it is to be done, right down to the precise routes the delivery person should follow, the number of pickups and deliveries, and the exact amount of time to be spent on each.[13]

And professionals are not immune from this kind of monitoring. Accountants, bank officers, insurance underwriters, personnel managers, and health maintenance organization (HMO) employees are subject to similar monitoring. HMOs tend to limit doctor-to-doctor conversations because they tend to talk too long. Rather, doctors are to consult the HMO database. HMO executives claim that such databases are superior to conversations with other doctors because the system has an extensive memory and huge calculating power that, the executives say, provides rules for dealing with practically every conceivable situation. The doctors are supposed to follow the system's recommendations. If a doctor deviates from the proscribed rule, he or she has some serious explaining to do.[14] In cases such as these, privacy issues interact with issues of employee freedom and empowerment. As management increases its ability to monitor, it also increases its power to limit employee discretion as well.

The article by G. Stoney Alder shows how teleological considerations lead us to accept electronic monitoring whereas Kantian considerations lead us to reject it. Alder concludes by attempting to develop constraints on electronic monitoring that would allow it to be both efficient and ethical.

Despite the concerns about loss of privacy, there are those who say that we have too much privacy and that the right to privacy must be balanced against other rights and social goals. Let us return to expert systems in medicine. At LDS hospital in Salt Lake City, Utah, 5,000 interlinked microcomputers instantaneously transmit medical data from 25 different clinical areas and feed it into electronic patient charts. An artificial intelligence system then scans this "real-time" data for potential medical missteps. The computers can override incorrect prescriptions and change intravenous drip rates. Recall the terrible accident discussed in Chapter Three. This system would have prevented that accident. In addition, the system automatically pages nurses if it encounters anomalous lab results. Physicians can log on at every bedside and order tests or view x-rays. Who could oppose such a system? Privacy advocates. The Department of Health and Human Services is thinking of taking the LDS Hospital idea national. It is considering a medical identifier for every citizen, much like a social security number, that would enable health professionals to obtain data from a variety of databases. As Dr. David Bates has said, "Confidentiality and safety are competing interests."[15] The idea of a national identifier is still very much alive as this book goes to press.

We also readily surrender privacy in more mundane cases. Many of us have received a call from our credit card companies asking us to verify certain purchases. The credit card companies have people monitoring our purchases to see if there are deviations from the pattern that might indicate fraudulent behavior. Most of us feel relief rather than indignation at this "invasion" of privacy. We also accept screening at airports and cameras on subway platforms and in public parking garages. In Europe the police photograph every car that passes a certain spot to see if there has been a violation such as running a red light. As Jonathan Franzen has said:

> When Americans do genuinely sacrifice privacy, moreover, they do so for tangible gains in health or safety or efficiency. Most legalized infringements — H.I.V. notification, airport X-rays, Megan's Law, Breathalyzer roadblocks, the drug testing of student athletes, . . . remote monitoring of automobile emissions, county-jail strip searches, . . . — are essentially public health measures.[16]

WHISTLEBLOWING AND THE DUTY OF LOYALTY

To suggest that the moral problems in employee–employer relationships are all about employee rights would, of course, be one-sided. No less important are employee obligations. Employees have moral obligations to respect the property of the corporation, to abide by employment contracts, and to operate within the bounds of the company's procedural rules. Indeed, it is legally established that an employer has a right to loyalty. This right is captured in the so-called law of agency. For example, Section 387 of the Restatement of Agency (1958) expresses the general principle that "an agent is subject to his principal to act solely for the benefit of the principal in all matters connected with his agency."[17] Specifically, the "agent is also under a duty not to act or speak disloyally," and the agent is to keep confidential any information acquired by him as an employee that might damage the agent or his business.[18]

Even if an employer is legally entitled to loyalty, is she or he morally entitled to loyalty? Ronald Duska has argued that loyalty can apply only in a relationship that transcends self-interest and must be based on a stable relationship of trust and confidence. The relationship of an employee to the corporation is not that kind of relationship, in his view, because it is a relationship of mutual self-interest. In this form of relationship, the employee does not have an obligation of loyalty to the employer.

If a corporation takes the position advocated by Milton Friedman in Chapter Two, then Duska's argument seems persuasive and indeed Friedman himself would probably accept it. In Friedman's view the only concern of the firm is to manage its assets in order to obtain profits for the stockholders, and the only concern of the workers is to get the best working conditions they can. Loyalty simply isn't in the picture. But if a broader stakeholder theory like R. Edward Freeman's is adopted, the corporation does have genuine obligations to employees. In a stakeholder-managed firm, the relationship between the employer and the employee is more likely to be characterized as a relationship of trust and confidence that transcends self-interest. If Duska accepted this characterization of the stakeholder account, these firms would be morally entitled to loyalty.

However, the duty of loyalty is not absolute. That an employee should be loyal is a *prima facie* duty. The object of the employee's duty must be deserving if the duty is genuine and overriding rather than *prima facie*. The virtue of loyalty does not require that the employee accept blindly the boss or corporate cause to which he or she is loyal. Nor does it require that when loyalty to the employer conflicts with other duties — such as protecting the public from harm — the duty to the employer is always overriding. Indeed, when a corporation is engaged in activity that is seriously wrong, employees may have a higher obligation to be disloyal to their employer and blow the whistle.

Well-publicized cases of whistleblowing bring public acclaim to the whistleblower but little else. The whistleblower finds it nearly impossible to get an equivalent job in the same industry and difficult enough to get another job at all. Many corporate executives share the sentiments of the former president of General Motors James M. Roche:

Some of the enemies of business now encourage an employee to be disloyal to the enterprise. They want to create suspicion and disharmony, and pry into the proprietary interests of the business. However this is labelled — industrial espionage, whistleblowing, or professional responsibility — it is another tactic for spreading disunity and creating conflict.[19]

Although Roche illegitimately confuses industrial espionage and whistleblowing, the attitude expressed by his remarks explains why it is so difficult for the whistleblower to find another job. Roche's point may seem extreme but, as Daryl Koehn points out in her article, whistleblowing does undermine trust and it should not be undertaken lightly. Both the whistleblower and the corporation have responsibilities toward a wide range of stakeholders. Although not much has changed in the United States concerning the fate of whistleblowers, progress has been made in other countries where there is less of a commitment to employment at will. For example, in 1999 the United Kingdom adopted the Public Interest Disclosure Act that provides financial compensation for whistleblowers who act in the public interest.

In conclusion, many of the moral grounds for employee loyalty have been destroyed. Commentators refer to the collapse of the social contract between a company and its employees. Each day seems to bring another announcement of a corporate downsizing. Yet there are some minimum requirements of loyalty based in law. Even today the most disgruntled employees usually treat others who whistleblow negatively; for them whistleblowing seems to violate a moral obligation to loyalty. Thus it is important pragmatically as well as ethically that whistleblowing be justifiable.

NOTES

1. See "Fear of Firing," *Forbes* (December 2, 1985), p. 90; and John Hoerr, and others, "Beyond Unions: A Revolution in Employee Rights in the Making," *Business Week* (July 8, 1985), p. 72.

2. Peggy Schmidt, "Lie-Detector Tests in a New Guise," *New York Times* (October 1, 1989), pp. 29, 31.

3. Gilbert Fuchsberg, "Prominent Psychologists Group Gives Qualified Support to Integrity Tests," *Wall Street Journal* (March 2, 1991).

4. Jane Bryant Quinn, "The Spies in Your Pocket," *Newsweek* (August 16, 1999).

5. The information on this incident was taken from "The Privacy Lobby Is Starting to Sting," *Business Week* (November 15, 1999), p. 57 and "A Few RealProblems for Real-Networks," *Newsweek* (November 15, 1999), p. 71.

6. "If You Light Up on Sunday, Don't Come in on Monday," *Business Week* (August 26, 1991), pp. 68–72.

7. Ellen Alderman and Caroline Kennedy, "Privacy," *Across the Board* (March 1996), pp. 43–45.

8. "Privacy," *Business Week* (March 28, 1988), pp. 61–68.

9. Cited in Maggie Scarf, "Brave New World," *The New Republic* (July 1999): p. 17.

10. Kirsten Downey Grimsley, "Pre-Hiring Medical Screening Put to Test," *The Washington Post* (October 27, 1998), C 1-2.

11. Kenneth J. Arrow, "The Use of Genetic and Other Medical Information: Ethical and Market Dilemmas," delivered as The George Seltzer Distinguished Lecture, The University of Minnesota, 1995.

12. Lewis Maltby, "Why Drug Testing Is a Bad Idea," *Inc.* (June 1987), p. 153.

13. Simon Head, "Big Brother in a Black Box," *Civilization* (August/September 1999): 53–55.

14. Ibid.

15. Katherine Eban Finkelstein, "The Computer Cure," in *The New Republic* (September 14 & 21, 1998), p. 30. All the facts regarding this case are taken from this article.

16. Jonathan Frazen, "Imperial Bedoom," *The New Yorker* (October 12, 1998).

17. Quoted from Phillip I. Blumberg, "Corporate Responsibility and the Employee's Duty of Loyalty and Obedience," in *Ethical Theory and Business,* edited by Thomas Beauchamp and Norman E. Bowie (Englewood Cliffs, NJ: Prentice Hall, 1979), 307.

18. Ibid., pp. 308, 307.

19. James M. Roche, "The Competitive System, to Work, to Preserve, and to Protect," *Vital Speeches of the Day* (May 1971), p. 445.

ETHICAL ISSUES SURROUNDING THE HIRING AND FIRING OF EMPLOYEES

Employment at Will and Due Process

Patricia H. Werhane
and Tara J. Radin

In 1980, Howard Smith III was hired by the American Greetings Corporation as a materials handler at the plant in Osceola, Arkansas. He was promoted to forklift driver and held that job until 1989, when he became involved in a dispute with his shift leader. According to Smith, he had a dispute with his shift leader at work. After work he tried to discuss the matter, but according to Smith, the shift leader hit him. The next day Smith was fired.

Smith was an "at-will" employee. He did not belong to, nor was he protected by, any union or union agreement. He did not have any special legal protection, for there was no apparent question of age, gender, race, or handicap discrimi-

nation. And he was not alleging any type of problem with worker safety on the job. The American Greetings Employee Handbook stated that "We believe in working and thinking and planning to provide a stable and growing business, to give such service to our customers that we may provide maximum job security for our employees." It did not state that employees could not be fired without due process or reasonable cause. According to the common law principle of Employment at Will (EAW), Smith's job at American Greetings could, therefore, legitimately be terminated at any time without cause, by either Smith or his employer, as long as that termination did not violate any law, agreement, or public policy.

Smith challenged his firing in the Arkansas court system as a "tort of outrage." A "tort of outrage" occurs when employer engages in "extreme or outrageous conduct" or intentionally inflicts terrible emotional stress. If such a tort is found to have occurred, the action, in this case, the dismissal, can be overturned.

Smith's case went to the Supreme Court of Arkansas in 1991. In court the management of American Greetings argued that Smith was fired for provoking management into a fight. The Court held that the firing was not in violation of law or a public policy, that the employee handbook did not specify restrictions on at-will terminations, and that the alleged altercation between Smith and his shift leader "did not come close to meeting" criteria for a tort of outrage. Howard Smith lost his case and his job.[1]

The principle of EAW is a common-law doctrine that states that, in the absence of law or contract, employers have the right to hire, promote, demote, and fire whomever and whenever they please. In 1887, the principle was stated explicitly in a document by H. G. Wood entitled *Master and Servant*. According to Wood, "A general or indefinite hiring is prima facie a hiring at will."[2] Although the term "master–servant," a medieval expression, was once used to characterize employment relationships, it has been dropped from most of the recent literature on employment.[3]

In the United States, EAW has been interpreted as the rule that, when employees are not specifically covered by union agreement, legal statute, public policy, or contract, employers "may dismiss their employees at will . . . for good cause, for no cause, *or even for causes morally wrong,* without being thereby guilty of legal wrong."[4] At the same time, "at will" employees enjoy rights parallel to employer prerogatives, because employees may quit their jobs for any reason whatsoever (or no reason) without having to give any notice to their employers. "At will" employees range from part-time contract workers to CEOs, including all those workers and managers in the

private sector of the economy not covered by agreements, statutes, or contracts. Today at least 60 percent of all employees in the private sector in the United States are "at-will" employees. These employees have no rights to due process or to appeal employment decisions, and the employer does not have any obligation to give reasons for demotions, transfers, or dismissals. Interestingly, while employees in the *private* sector of the economy tend to be regarded as "at-will" employees, *public*-sector employees have guaranteed rights, including due process, and are protected from demotion, transfer, or firing without cause.

Due process is a means by which a person can appeal a decision in order to get an explanation of that action and an opportunity to argue against it. Procedural due process is the right to a hearing, trial, grievance procedure, or appeal when a decision is made concerning oneself. Due process is also substantive. It is the demand for rationality and fairness: for good reasons for decisions. EAW has been widely interpreted as allowing employees to be demoted, transferred or dismissed without due process, that is, without having a hearing and without requirement of good reasons or "cause" for the employment decision. This is not to say that employers do not have reasons, usually good reasons, for their decisions. But there is no moral or legal obligation to state or defend them. EAW thus sidesteps the requirement of procedural and substantive due process in the workplace, but it does not preclude the institution of such procedures or the existence of good reasons for employment decisions.

EAW is still upheld in the state and federal courts of this country, as the Howard Smith case illustrates, although exceptions are made when violations of public policy and law are at issue. According to the *Wall Street Journal*, the court has decided in favor of the employees in 67 percent of the wrongful discharge suits that have taken place during the past three years. These suits were won not on the basis of a rejection of the principle of EAW but, rather, on the basis of breach of contract, lack of just cause for dismissal when a company policy was in place, or violations of public policy. The court has carved out the "public policy" exception so as not to encourage fraudulent or wrongful behavior on the part of employers, such as in cases where employees are asked to break a law or to violate state public policies, and in cases where employees are not allowed to exercise fundamental rights, such as the rights to vote, to serve on a jury, and to collect worker compensation. For example, in one case, the court reinstated an employee who was fired for reporting theft at his plant on the grounds that criminal conduct requires such reporting.[5] In another case, the court reinstated a physician who was fired from the Ortho Pharmaceutical Corporation for refusing to seek approval to test a certain drug on human subjects. The court held that safety clearly lies in the interest of public welfare, and employees are not to be fired for refusing to jeopardize public safety.[6]

During the last ten years, a number of positive trends have become apparent in employment practices and in state and federal court adjudications of employment disputes. Shortages of skilled managers, fear of legal repercussions, and a more genuine interest in employee rights claims and reciprocal obligations have resulted in a more careful spelling out of employment contracts, the development of elaborate grievance procedures, and in general less arbitrariness in employee treatment.[7] While there has not been a universal revolution in thinking about employee rights, an increasing number of companies have qualified their EAW prerogatives with restrictions in firing without cause. Many companies have developed grievance procedures and other means for employee complaint and redress.

Interestingly, substantive due process, the notion that employers should give good reasons for their employment actions, previously dismissed as legal and philosophical nonsense, has also recently developed positive advocates. Some courts have found that it is a breach of contract to fire a long-term employee when there is not sufficient cause — under normal economic conditions even when the implied contract is only a verbal one. In California, for example, 50 percent of the implied contract cases (and there have been over 200) during the last five years have been decided in favor of the employee, again, without challenging EAW.[8] In light of this recognition of implicit contractual obligations between employees and employers, in some unprecedented court cases *employees* have been held liable for good faith breaches of contract, particularly in cases of quitting without notice in the middle of a project and/or taking technology or other ideas to another job.[9]

These are all positive developments. At the same time, there has been neither an across-the-board institution of due process procedures in all corporations nor any direct challenges to the *principle* (although there have been challenges to the practice) of EAW as a justifiable and legitimate approach to employment practices. Moreover, as a result of mergers, downsizing, and restructuring, hundreds of thousands of employees have been laid off summarily without being able to appeal those decisions.

"At-will" employees, then, have no rights to demand an appeal to such employment decisions except through the court system. In addition, no form of due process is a requirement preceding any of these actions. Moreover, unless public policy is violated, the law has traditionally protected employers from employee retaliation in such actions. It is true that the scope of what is defined as "public policy" has been enlarged so that "at-will" dismissals without good reason are greatly reduced. It is also true that many companies have grievance procedures in place for "at will" employees. But such procedures are voluntary, procedural due process is not *required,* and companies need not give any reasons for their employment decisions.

In what follows we shall present a series of arguments defending the claim that the right to procedural and substantive due process should be extended to all employees in the private sector of the economy. We will defend the claim partly on the basis of human rights. We shall also argue that the public/private distinction that precludes the application of constitutional guarantees in the private sector has sufficiently broken down so that the absence of a due process requirement in the workplace is an anomaly.

EMPLOYMENT AT WILL

EAW is often justified for one or more of the following reasons:

1. The proprietary rights of employers guarantee that they may employ or dismiss whomever and whenever they wish.
2. EAW defends employee and employer rights equally, in particular the right to freedom of contract, because an employee voluntarily contracts to be hired and can quit at any time.
3. In choosing to take a job, an employee voluntarily commits herself to certain responsibilities and company loyalty, including the knowledge that she is an "at-will" employee.
4. Extending due process rights in the workplace often interferes with the efficiency and productivity of the business organization.
5. Legislation and/or regulation of employment relationships further undermine an already overregulated economy.

Let us examine each of these arguments in more detail. The principle of EAW is sometimes maintained purely on the basis of proprietary rights of employers and corporations. In dismissing or demoting employees,

the employer is not denying rights to *persons.* Rather, the employer is simply excluding that person's *labor* from the organization.

This is not a bad argument. Nevertheless, accepting it necessitates consideration of the proprietary rights of employees as well. To understand what is meant by "proprietary rights of employees" it is useful to consider first what is meant by the term "labor." "Labor" is sometimes used collectively to refer to the workforce as a whole. It also refers to the activity of working. Other times it refers to the productivity or "fruits" of that activity. Productivity, labor in the third sense, might be thought of as a form of property or at least as something convertible into property, because the productivity of working is what is traded for remuneration in employee-employer work agreements. For example, suppose an advertising agency hires an expert known for her creativity in developing new commercials. This person trades her ideas, the product of her work (thinking), for pay. The ideas are not literally property, but they are tradable items because, when presented on paper or on television, they are sellable by their creator and generate income. But the activity of working (thinking in this case) cannot be sold or transferred.

Caution is necessary, though, in relating productivity to tangible property, because there is an obvious difference between productivity and material property. Productivity requires the past or present activity of working, and thus the presence of the person performing this activity. Person, property, labor, and productivity are all different in this important sense. A person can be distinguished from his possessions, a distinction that allows for the creation of legally fictional persons such as corporations or trusts that can "own" property. Persons cannot, however, be distinguished from their working, and this activity is necessary for creating productivity, a tradable product of one's working.

In dismissing an employee, a well-intentioned employer aims to rid the corporation of the costs of generating that employee's work products. In ordinary employment situations, however, terminating that cost entails terminating that employee. In those cases the justification for the "at-will" firing is presumably proprietary. But treating an employee "at will" is analogous to considering her a piece of property at the disposal of the employer or corporation. Arbitrary firings treat people as things. When I "fire" a robot, I do not have to give reasons, because a robot is not a rational being. It has no use for reasons. On the other hand, if I fire a person arbitrarily, I am making the assumption that she does not need reasons either. If I have hired people, then, in firing them, I should treat them as such, with respect, throughout the termination process. This does not preclude firing. It merely asks employers to give reasons for their actions, because reasons are appropriate when people are dealing with other people.

This reasoning leads to a second defense and critique of EAW. It is contended that EAW defends employee and employer rights equally. An employer's right to hire and fire "at will" is balanced by a worker's right to accept or reject employment. The institution of any employee right that restricts "at-will" hiring and firing would be unfair unless this restriction were balanced by a similar restriction controlling employee job choice in the workplace. Either program would do irreparable damage by preventing both employees and employers from continuing in voluntary employment arrangements. These arrangements are guaranteed by "freedom of contract," the right of persons or organizations to enter into any voluntary agreement with which all parties of the agreement are in accord.[10] Limiting EAW practices or requiring due process would negatively affect freedom of contract. Both are thus clearly coercive, because in either case persons and organizations are forced to accept behavioral restraints that place unnecessary constraints on voluntary employment agreements.[11]

This second line of reasoning defending EAW, like the first, presents some solid arguments. A basic presupposition upon which EAW is grounded is that of protecting equal freedoms of both employees and employers. The purpose of EAW is to provide a guaranteed balance of these freedoms. But arbitrary treatment of employees extends prerogatives to managers that are not equally available to employees, and such treatment may unduly interfere with a fired employee's prospects for future employment if that employee has no avenue for defense or appeal. This is also sometimes true when an employee quits without notice or good reason. Arbitrary treatment of employees *or* employers therefore violates the spirit of EAW — that of protecting the freedoms of both the employees and employers.

The third justification of EAW defends the voluntariness of employment contracts. If these are agreements between moral agents, however, such agreements imply reciprocal obligations between the parties in question for which both are accountable. It is obvious that, in an employment contract, people are rewarded for their performance. What is seldom noticed is that, if part of the employment contract is an expectation of loyalty, trust, and respect on the part of an employee, the employer must, in return, treat the employee with respect as well. The obligations required by employment agreements, if these are free and noncoercive agreements, must be equally obligatory and mutually restrictive on both parties. Otherwise one party cannot expect — morally expect — loyalty, trust, or respect from the other.

EAW is most often defended on practical grounds. From a utilitarian perspective, hiring and firing "at will" is deemed necessary in productive organizations to ensure maximum efficiency and productivity, the goals of such organizations. In the absence of EAW unproductive employees, workers who are no longer needed, and even troublemakers, would be able to keep their jobs. Even if a business *could* rid itself of undesirable employees, the lengthy procedure of due process required by an extension of employee rights would be costly and time-consuming, and would likely prove distracting to other employees. This would likely slow production and, more likely than not, prove harmful to the morale of other employees.

This argument is defended by Ian Maitland, who contends,

> [I]f employers were generally to heed business ethicists and institute workplace due process in cases of dismissals and take the increased costs or reduced efficiency out of workers' paychecks — then they would expose themselves to the pirating of their workers by other employers who would give workers what they wanted instead of respecting their rights in the workplace. . . . In short, there is good reason for concluding that the prevalence of EAW does accurately reflect workers' preferences for wages over contractually guaranteed protections against unfair dismissal.[12]

Such an argument assumes (a) that due process increases costs and reduces efficiency, a contention that is not documented by the many corporations that have grievance procedures, and (b) that workers will generally give up some basic rights for other benefits, such as money. The latter is certainly sometimes true, but not always so, particularly when there are questions of unfair dismissals or job security. Maitland also assumes that an employee is on the same level and possesses the same power as her manager, so that an employee can choose her benefit package in which grievance procedures, whistleblowing protections, or other rights are included. Maitland implies that employers might include in that package of benefits

their rights to practice the policy of unfair dismissals in return for increased pay. He also at least implicitly suggests that due process precludes dismissals and layoffs. But this is not true. Procedural due process demands a means of appeal, and substantive due process demands good reasons, both of which are requirements for other managerial decisions and judgments. Neither demands benevolence, lifetime employment, or prevents dismissals. In fact, having good reasons gives an employer a justification for getting rid of poor employees.

In summary, arbitrariness, although not prohibited by EAW, violates the managerial ideal of rationality and consistency. These are independent grounds for not abusing EAW. Even if EAW itself is justifiable, the practice of EAW, when interpreted as condoning arbitrary employment decisions, is not justifiable. Both procedural and substantive due process are consistent with, and a moral requirement of, EAW. The former is part of recognizing obligations implied by freedom of contract, and the latter, substantive due process, conforms with the ideal of managerial rationality that is implied by a consistent application of this common law principle.

EMPLOYMENT AT WILL, DUE PROCESS, AND THE PUBLIC/PRIVATE DISTINCTION

The strongest reasons for allowing abuses of EAW and for not instituting a full set of employee rights in the workplace, at least in the private sector of the economy, have to do with the nature of business in a free society. Businesses are privately owned voluntary organizations of all sizes from small entrepreneurships to large corporations. As such, they are not subject to the restrictions governing public and political institutions. Political procedures such as due process, needed to safeguard the public against the arbitrary exercise of power by the state, do not apply to private organizations. Guaranteeing such rights in the workplace would require restrictive legislation and regulation. Voluntary market arrangements, so vital to free enterprise and guaranteed by freedom of contract, would be sacrificed for the alleged public interest of employee claims.

In the law, courts traditionally have recognized the right of corporations to due process, although they have not required due process for employees in the private sector of the economy. The justification put forward for this is that since corporations are public entities acting in the public interest, they, like people, should be afforded the right to due process.

Due process is also guaranteed for permanent full-time workers in the public sector of the economy, that is, for workers in local, state and national government positions. The Fifth and Fourteenth Amendments protect liberty and property rights such that any alleged violations or deprivation of those rights may be challenged by some form of due process. According to recent Supreme Court decisions, when a state worker is a permanent employee, he has a property interest in his employment. Because a person's productivity contributes to the place of employment, a public worker is entitled to his job unless there is good reason to question it, such as poor work habits, habitual absences, and the like. Moreover, if a discharge would prevent him from obtaining other employment, which often is the case with state employees who, if fired, cannot find further government employment, that employee has a right to due process before being terminated.[13]

This justification for extending due process protections to public employees is grounded in the public employee's proprietary interest in his job. If that argument makes sense, it is curious that private employees do not have similar rights. The basis for this distinction stems from a tradition in Western thinking that distinguishes between the public and private spheres of life. The public sphere contains that part of a person's life that lies within the bounds of government regulation, whereas the private sphere contains that part of a person's life that lies outside those bounds. The argument is that the portion of a person's life that influences only that person should remain private and outside the purview of law and regulation, while the portion that influences the public welfare should be subject to the authority of the law.

Although interpersonal relationships on any level — personal, family, social, or employee-employer — are protected by statutes and common law, they are not constitutionally protected unless there is a violation of some citizen claim against the state. Because entrepreneurships and corporations are privately owned, and since employees are free to make or break employment contracts of their choice, employee-employer relationships, like family relationships, are treated as "private." In a family, even if there are no due process procedures, the state does not interfere, except when there is obvious harm or abuse. Similarly, employment relationships are considered private relationships contracted between free adults, and so long as no gross violations occur, positive constitutional guarantees such as due process are not enforceable.

The public/private distinction was originally developed to distinguish individuals from the state and to protect individuals and private property from public — i.e., governmental — intrusion. The distinction, however, has been extended to distinguish not merely between the individual or the family and the state, but also between universal rights claims and national sovereignty, public and private ownership, free enterprise and public policy, publicly and privately held corporations, and even between public and private employees. Indeed, this distinction plays a role in national and international affairs. Boutros Boutros-Ghali, the head of the United Nations, recently confronted a dilemma in deciding whether to go into Somalia without an invitation. His initial reaction was to stay out and to respect Somalia's right to "private" national sovereignty. It was only when he decided that Somalia had fallen apart as an independent state that he approved U.N. intervention. His dilemma parallels that of a state, which must decide whether to intervene in a family quarrel, the alleged abuse of a spouse or child, the inoculation of a Christian Scientist, or the blood transfusion for a Seventh-Day Adventist.

There are some questions, however, with the justification of the absence of due process with regard to the public/private distinction. Our economic system is allegedly based on private property, but it is unclear where "private" property and ownership end and "public" property and ownership begin. In the workplace, ownership and control is often divided. Corporate assets are held by an ever-changing group of individual and institutional shareholders. It is no longer true that owners exercise any real sense of control over their property and its management. Some do, but many do not. Moreover, such complex property relationships are spelled out and guaranteed by the state. This has prompted at least one thinker to argue that "private property" should be defined as "certain patterns of human interaction underwritten by public power."[14]

This fuzziness about the "privacy" of property becomes exacerbated by the way we use the term "public" in analyzing the status of businesses and in particular corporations. For example, we distinguish between privately owned business corporations and government-owned or -controlled public institutions. Among those companies that are not government owned, we distinguish between regulated "public" utilities

whose stock is owned by private individuals and institutions; "publicly held" corporations whose stock is traded publicly, who are governed by special SEC regulations, and whose financial statements are public knowledge; and privately held corporations and entrepreneurships, companies and smaller businesses that are owned by an individual or group of individuals and not available for public stock purchase.

There are similarities between government-owned, public institutions and privately owned organizations. When the air controllers went on strike in the 1980s, Ronald Reagan fired them, and declared that, as public employees, they could not strike because it jeopardized the public safety. Nevertheless, both private and public institutions run transportation, control banks, and own property. While the goals of private and public institutions differ in that public institutions are allegedly supposed to place the public good ahead of profitability, the simultaneous call for businesses to become socially responsible and the demand for governmental organizations to become efficient and accountable further question the dichotomy between "public" and "private."

Many business situations reinforce the view that the traditional public/private dichotomy has been eroded, if not entirely, at least in large part. For example, in 1981, General Motors (GM) wanted to expand by building a plant in what is called the "Poletown" area of Detroit. Poletown is an old Detroit Polish neighborhood. The site was favorable because it was near transportation facilities and there was a good supply of labor. To build the plant, however, GM had to displace residents in a nine-block area. The Poletown Neighborhood Council objected, but the Supreme Court of Michigan decided in favor of GM and held that the state could condemn property for private use, with proper compensation to owners, when it was in the public good. What is particularly interesting about this case is that GM is not a government-owned corporation; its primary goal is *profitability*, not the common good. The Supreme Court nevertheless decided that it was in the *public* interest for Detroit to use its authority to allow a company to take over property despite the protesting of the property owners. In this case the public/private distinction was thoroughly scrambled.

The overlap between private enterprise and public interests is such that at least one legal scholar argues that "developments in the twentieth century have significantly undermined the 'privateness' of the modern business corporations, with the result that the traditional bases for distinguishing them from public corporations have largely disappeared."[15] Nevertheless, despite the blurring of the public and private in terms of property rights and the status and functions of corporations, the subject of employee rights appears to remain immune from conflation.

The expansion of employee protections to what we would consider just claims to due process gives to the state and the courts more opportunity to interfere with the private economy and might thus further skew what is seen by some as a precarious but delicate balance between the private economic sector and public policy. We agree. But if the distinction between public and private institutions is no longer clear-cut, and the traditional separation of the public and private spheres is no longer in place, might it not then be better to recognize and extend constitutional guarantees so as to protect all citizens equally? If due process is crucial to political relationships between the individual and the state, why is it not central in relationships between employees and corporations since at least some of the companies in question are as large and powerful as small nations? Is it not in fact inconsistent with our democratic tradition *not* to mandate such rights?

The philosopher T. M. Scanlon summarizes our institutions about due process. Scanlon says,

The requirement of due process is one of the conditions of the moral acceptability of those institutions that give some people power to control or intervene in the lives of others.[16]

The institution of due process in the workplace is a moral requirement consistent with rationality and consistency expected in management decision-making. It is not precluded by EAW, and it is compatible with the overlap between the public and private sectors of the economy. Convincing business of the moral necessity of due process, however, is a task yet to be completed.

NOTES

1. *Howard Smith III* v. *American Greetings Corporation*, 304 Ark. 596; 804 S.W.2d 683.

2. H. G. Wood, *A Treatise on the Law of Master and Servant* (Albany, NY: John D. Parsons, Jr., 1877), p. 134.

3. Until the end of 1980 the *Index of Legal Periodicals* indexed employee-employer relationships under this rubric.

4. Lawrence E. Blades, "Employment at Will versus Individual Freedom: On Limiting the Abusive Exercise of Employer Power," *Columbia Law Review*, 67 (1967), p. 1405, quoted from *Payne* v. *Western*, 81 Tenn. 507 (1884), and *Hutton* v. *Watters*, 132 Tenn. 527, S.W. 134 (1915).

5. *Palmateer* v. *International Harvester Corporation*, 85 Ill. App. 2d 124 (1981).

6. *Pierce* v. *Ortho Pharmaceutical Corporation* 845 NJ 58 (NJ 1980), 417 A.2d 505. See also Brian Heshizer, "The New Common Law of Employment: Changes in the Concept of Employment at Will," *Labor Law Journal*, 36 (1985), pp. 95–107.

7. See David Ewing, *Justice on the Job: Resolving Grievances in the Nonunion Workplace* (Boston: Harvard Business School Press, 1989).

8. See R. M. Bastress, "A Synthesis and a Proposal for Reform of the Employment at Will Doctrine," *West Virginia Law Review*, 90 (1988), pp. 319–51.

9. See "Employees' Good Faith Duties," *Hastings Law Journal*, 39 (198). See also *Hudson* v. *Moore Business Forms,* 609 Supp. 467 (N.D. Cal. 1985).

10. See *Lockner* v. *New York*, 198 U.S. (1905), and Adina Schwartz, "Autonomy in the Workplace," in Tom Regan, ed., *Just Business* (New York: Random House, 1984), pp. 129–40.

11. Eric Mack, "Natural and Contractual Rights," *Ethics*, 87 (1977), pp. 153–59.

12. Ian Maitland, "Rights in the Workplace: A Nozickian Argument," in Lisa Newton and Maureen Ford, eds., *Taking Sides* (Guilford, CT: Dushkin Publishing Group), 1990, pp. 34–35.

13. Richard Wallace, "Union Waiver of Public Employees' Due Process Rights," *Industrial Relations Law Journal*, 8 (1986), pp. 583–87.

14. Morris Cohen, "Dialogue on Private Property," *Rutgers Law Review* 9 (1954), pp. 357. See also *Law and the Social Order* (1933) and Robert Hale, "Coercion and Distribution in a Supposedly Non-Coercive State," *Political Science Quarterly*, 38 (1923), pp. 470; John Brest, "State Action and Liberal Theory," *University of Pennsylvania Law Review* (1982), 1296–1329.

15. Gerald Frug, "The City As a Legal Concept," *Harvard Law Review*, 93 (1980), p. 1129.

16. T. M. Scanlon, "Due Process," in J. Roland Pennock and John W. Chapman, eds., *Nomos XVIII: Due Process* (New York: New York University Press, 1977), p. 94.

In Defense of the Contract at Will

Richard A. Epstein

The persistent tension between private ordering and government regulation exists in virtually every area known to the law, and in none has that tension been more pronounced than in the law of employer and employee relations. During the last fifty years, the balance of power has shifted heavily in favor of direct public regulation, which has been thought strictly necessary to redress the perceived imbalance between the individual and the firm. In particular the employment relationship has been the subject of at least two major statutory revolutions. The first, which culminated in the passage of the National Labor Relations Act in 1935, set the basic structure for collective bargaining that persists to the current time. The second, which is embodied in Title VII of the Civil Rights Act of 1964, offers extensive protection to all individuals against discrimination on the basis of race, sex, religion, or national origin. The effect of these two statutes is so pervasive that it is easy to forget that, even after their passage, large portions of the employment relation remain subject to the traditional common law rules, which when all was said and done set their face in support of freedom of contract and the system of voluntary exchange. One manifestation of that position was the prominent place that the common law, especially as it developed in the nineteenth century, gave to the contract at will. The basic position was sell set out in an oft-quoted passage from *Payne v. Western & Atlantic Railroad:*

> [M]en must be left, without interference to buy and sell where they please, and to discharge or retain employees at will for good cause or for

From: Richard A. Epstein, "In Defense of the Contract at Will," *University of Chicago Law Review* 34 (1984). Reprinted by permission of the University of Chicago Law Review.

no cause, or even for bad cause without thereby being guilty of an unlawful act *per se.* It is a right which an employee may exercise in the same way, to the same extent, for the same cause or want of cause as the employer.[1]

* * *

In the remainder of this paper, I examine the arguments that can be made for and against the contract at will. I hope to show that it is adopted not because it allows the employer to exploit the employee, but rather because over a very broad range of circumstances it works to the mutual benefit of both parties, where the benefits are measured, as ever, at the time of the contract's formation and not at the time of dispute. To justify this result, I examine the contract in light of the three dominant standards that have emerged as the test of the soundness of any legal doctrine: intrinsic fairness, effects upon utility or wealth, and distributional consequences. I conclude that the first two tests point strongly to the maintenance of the at-will rule, while the third, if it offers any guidance at all, points in the same direction.

I. THE FAIRNESS OF THE CONTRACT AT WILL

The first way to argue for the contract at will is to insist upon the importance of freedom of contract as an end in itself. Freedom of contract is an aspect of individual liberty, every bit as much as freedom of speech, or freedom in the selection of marriage partners or in the adoption of religious beliefs or affiliations. Just as it is regarded as prima facie unjust to abridge these liberties, so too is it presumptively unjust to abridge the economic liberties of individuals. The desire to make one's own choices about employment may be as strong as it is with respect to marriage or participation in religious activities, and it is doubtless more pervasive than the desire to participate in political activity. Indeed for most people, their own health and comfort, and that of their families, depend critically upon their ability to earn a living by entering the employment market. If government regulation is inappropriate for personal, religious, or political activities, then what makes it intrinsically desirable for employment relations?

It is one thing to set aside the occasional transaction that reflects only the momentary aberrations of particular parties who are overwhelmed by major personal and social dislocations. It is quite another to announce that a rule to which vast numbers of individuals adhere is so fundamentally corrupt that it does not deserve the minimum respect of the law. With employment contracts we are not dealing with the widow who has sold her inheritance for a song to a man with a thin mustache. Instead we are dealing with the routine stuff of ordinary life; people who are competent enough to marry, vote, and pray are not unable to protect themselves in their day-to-day business transactions.

Courts and legislatures have intervened so often in private contractual relations that it may seem almost quixotic to insist that they bear a heavy burden of justification every time they wish to substitute their own judgment for that of the immediate parties to the transactions. Yet it is hardly likely that remote public bodies have better information about individual preferences than the parties who hold them. This basic principle of autonomy, moreover, is not limited to some areas of individual conduct and wholly inapplicable to others. It covers all these activities as a piece and admits no ad hoc exceptions, but only principled limitations.

This general proposition applies to the particular contract term in question. Any attack on the contract at will in the name of individual freedom is fundamentally misguided. As the Tennessee Supreme Court rightly stressed in *Payne,* the contract at will is sought by both persons.[2] Any limitation upon the freedom to enter into such contracts limits the power of workers as well as employers and must therefore be justified before it can be accepted. In this context the appeal is often to an image of employer coercion. To be sure, freedom of contract is not an absolute in the employment context, any more than it is elsewhere. Thus the principle must be understood against a backdrop that prohibits the use of private contracts to trench upon third-party rights, including uses that interfere with some clear mandate of public policy, as in cases of contracts to commit murder or perjury.

In addition, the principle of freedom of contract also rules out the use of force or fraud in obtaining advantages during contractual negotiations; and it limits taking advantage of the young, the feeble-minded, and the insane. But the recent wrongful discharge cases do not purport to deal with the delicate situations where contracts have been formed by improper means or where individual defects of capacity or will are involved. Fraud is not a frequent occurrence in employment contracts, especially where workers and employers engage in repeat transactions. Nor is there any reason to believe that such contracts are marred by misapprehensions, since employers and employees know the footing on which they have contracted: the phrase "at will" is two words long and has the convenient virtue of meaning just what it says, no more and no less.

An employee who knows that he can quit at will understands what it means to be fired at will, even though he may not like it after the fact. So long as it is accepted that the employer is the full owner of his capital and the employee is the full owner of his labor, the two are free to exchange on whatever terms and conditions they see fit, within the limited constraints just noted. If the arrangement

turns out to be disastrous to one side, that is his problem; and once cautioned, he probably will not make the same mistake a second time. More to the point, employers and employees are unlikely to make the same mistake once. It is hardly plausible that contracts at will could be so pervasive in all businesses and at all levels if they did not serve the interests of employees as well as employers. The argument from fairness then is very simple, but not for that reason unpersuasive.

II. THE UTILITY OF THE CONTRACT AT WILL

The strong fairness argument in favor of freedom of contract makes short work of the various for-cause and good-faith restrictions upon private contracts. Yet the argument is incomplete in several respects. In particular, it does not explain why the presumption in the case of silence should be in favor of the contract at will. Nor does it give a descriptive account of *why* the contract at will is so commonly found in all trades and professions. Nor does the argument meet on their own terms the concerns voiced most frequently by the critics of the contract at will. Thus, the commonplace belief today (at least outside the actual world of business) is that the contract at will is so unfair and one-sided that it cannot be the outcome of a rational set of bargaining processes any more than, to take the extreme case, a contract for total slavery. While we may not, the criticism continues, be able to observe them, defects in capacity at contract formation nonetheless must be present: the ban upon the contract at will is an effective way to reach abuses that are pervasive but difficult to detect, so that modest government interference only strengthens the operation of market forces.

In order to rebut this charge, it is necessary to do more than insist that individuals as a general matter know how to govern their own lives. It is also necessary to display the structural strengths of the contract at will that explain why rational people would enter into such a contract, if not all the time, then at least most of it. The implicit assumption in this argument is that contracts are typically for the mutual benefit of both parties. Yet it is hard to see what other assumption makes any sense in analyzing institutional arrangements (arguably in contradistinction to idiosyncratic, nonrepetitive transactions). To be sure, there are occasional cases of regret after the fact, especially after an infrequent, but costly, contingency comes to pass. There will be cases in which parties are naive, befuddled, or worse. Yet in framing either a rule of policy or a rule of construction, the focus cannot be on that biased set of cases in which the contract aborts and litigation ensues. Instead, attention must be directed to standard repetitive transactions, where the centralizing tendency powerfully promotes expected mutual gain. It is simply incredible to postulate that either employers or employees, motivated as they are by self-interest, would enter routinely into a transaction that leaves them worse off than they were before, or even worse off than their next best alternative.

From this perspective, then, the task is to explain how and why the at-will contracting arrangement (in sharp contrast to slavery) typically works to the mutual advantage of the parties. Here, as is common in economic matters, it does not matter that the parties themselves often cannot articulate the reasons that render their judgment sound and breathe life into legal arrangements that are fragile in form but durable in practice. The inquiry into mutual benefit in turn requires an examination of the full range of costs and benefits that arise from collaborative ventures. It is just at this point that the nineteenth-century view is superior to the emerging modern conception. The modern view tends to lay heavy emphasis on the need to control employer abuse. Yet, as the passage from *Payne* indicates, the rights under the contract at will are fully bilateral, so that the employee can use the contract as a means to control the firm, just as the firm uses it to control the worker.

The issue for the parties, properly framed, is not how to minimize employer abuse, but rather how to maximize the gain from the relationship, which in part depends upon minimizing the sum of employer and employee abuse. Viewed in this way the private-contracting problem is far more complex. How does each party create incentives for the proper behavior of the other? How does each side insure against certain risks? How do both sides minimize the administrative costs of their contracting practices? . . .

1. *Monitoring Behavior.* The shift in the internal structure of the firm from a partnership to an employment relation eliminates neither bilateral opportunism nor the conflicts of interest between employer and employee. Begin for the moment with the fears of the firm, for it is the firm's right to maintain at-will power that is now being called into question. In all too many cases, the firm must contend with the recurrent problem of employee theft and with the related problems of unauthorized use of firm equipment and employee kickback arrangements. . . . [The] proper concerns of the firm are not limited to obvious forms of criminal misconduct. The employee on a fixed wage can, at the margin, capture only a portion of the gain from his labor, and therefore has a tendency to reduce output. The employee who receives a commission equal to half the firm's profit attributable to his labor may work hard, but probably not quite as hard as he would if he received the entire profit from the completed sale, an arrangement that would solve the agency-cost problem only by undoing the firm. . . .

The problem of management then is to identify the forms of social control that are best able to minimize these agency costs. . . . One obvious form of control is the force of law. The state can be brought in to punish cases of embezzlement or fraud. But this mode of control requires extensive cooperation with public officials and may well be frustrated by the need to prove the criminal offense (including mens rea) beyond a reasonable doubt, so that vast amounts of abuse will go unchecked. Private litigation instituted by the firm may well be used in cases of major grievances, either to recover the property that has been misappropriated or to prevent the individual employee from further diverting firm business to his own account. But private litigation, like public prosecution, is too blunt an instrument to counter employee shirking or the minor but persistent use of firm assets for private business. . . .

Internal auditors may help control some forms of abuse, and simple observation by coworkers may well monitor employee activities. (There are some very subtle tradeoffs to be considered when the firm decides whether to use partitions or separate offices for its employees.) Promotions, bonuses, and wages are also critical in shaping the level of employee performance. But the carrot cannot be used to the exclusion of the stick. In order to maintain internal discipline, the firm may have to resort to sanctions against individual employees. It is far easier to use those powers that can be unilaterally exercised: to fire, to demote, to withhold wages, or to reprimand. These devices can visit very powerful losses upon individual employees without the need to resort to legal action, and they permit the firm to monitor employee performance continually in order to identify both strong and weak workers and to compensate them accordingly. The principles here are constant, whether we speak of senior officials or lowly subordinates, and it is for just this reason that

the contract at will is found at all levels in private markets. . . .

In addition, within the employment context firing does not require a disruption of firm operations, much less an expensive division of its assets. It is instead a clean break with consequences that are immediately clear to both sides. The lower cost of both firing and quitting, therefore, helps account for the very widespread popularity of employment-at-will contracts. There is no need to resort to any theory of economic domination or inequality of bargaining power to explain at-will contracting, which appears with the same tenacity in relations between economic equals and subordinates and is found in many complex commercial arrangements, including franchise agreements, except where limited by statutes.

Thus far, the analysis generally has focused on the position of the employer. Yet for the contract at will to be adopted ex ante, it must work for the benefit of workers as well. And indeed it does, for the contract at will also contains powerful limitations on employers' abuses of power. To see the importance of the contract at will to the employee, it is useful to distinguish between two cases. In the first, the employer pays a fixed sum of money to the worker and is then free to demand of the employee whatever services he wants for some fixed period of time. In the second case, there is no fixed period of employment. The employer is free to demand whatever he wants of the employee, who in turn is free to withdraw for good reason, bad reason, or no reason at all.

The first arrangement invites abuse by the employer, who can now make enormous demands upon the worker without having to take into account either the worker's disutility during the period of service or the value of the worker's labor at contract termination. A fixed-period contract that leaves the worker's obligations unspecified thereby creates a sharp tension between the parties, since the employer receives all the marginal benefits and the employee bears all the marginal costs.

Matters are very different where the employer makes increased demands under a contract at will. Now the worker can quit whenever the net value of the employment contract turns negative. As with the employer's power to fire or demote, the threat to quit (or at a lower level to come late or leave early) is one that can be exercised without resort to litigation. Furthermore, that threat turns out to be most effective when the employer's opportunistic behavior is the greatest because the situation is one in which the worker has least to lose. To be sure, the worker will not necessarily make a threat whenever the employer insists that the worker accept a less favorable set of contractual terms, for sometimes the changes may be accepted as an uneventful adjustment in the total compensation level attributable to a change in the market price of labor. This point counts, however, only as an additional strength of the contract at will, which allows for small adjustments *in both directions* in ongoing contractual arrangements with a minimum of bother and confusion. . . .

2. *Reputational Losses.* Another reason why employees are often willing to enter into at-will employment contracts stems from the asymmetry of reputational losses. Any party who cheats may well obtain a bad reputation that will induce others to avoid dealing with him. The size of these losses tends to differ systematically between employers and employees — to the advantage of the employee. Thus in the usual situation there are many workers and a single employer. The disparity in number is apt to be greatest in large industrial concerns, where the at-will contract is commonly, if mistakenly, thought to be most unsatisfactory because of the supposed inequality of bargaining power. The employer who decides to act for bad reason or no reason at all may not face any legal liability under the classical common law rule. But he faces very powerful adverse economic consequences. If coworkers perceive the dismissal as arbitrary, they will take fresh stock of their own prospects, for they can no longer be certain that their faithful performance will ensure their security and advancement. The uncertain prospects created by arbitrary employer behavior is functionally indistinguishable from a reduction in wages unilaterally imposed by the employer. At the margin some workers will look elsewhere, and typically the best workers will have the greatest opportunities. By the same token the large employer has more to gain if he dismisses undesirable employees, for this ordinarily acts as an implicit increase in wages to the other employees, who are no longer burdened with uncooperative or obtuse coworkers.

The existence of both positive and negative reputational effects is thus brought back to bear on the employer. The law may tolerate arbitrary behavior, but private pressures effectively limit its scope. Inferior employers will be at a perpetual competitive disadvantage with enlightened ones and will continue to lose in market share and hence in relative social importance. The lack of legal protection to the employees is therefore in part explained by the increased informal protections that they obtain by working in large concerns.

3. *Risk Diversification and Imperfect Information.* The contract at will also helps workers deal with the problem of risk diversification. . . . Ordinarily, employees cannot work more than one, or perhaps two, jobs at the same time. Thereafter the level of performance falls dramatically, so that diversification brings in its wake a low return on labor. The contract at will is designed in part to offset the concentration of individual investment in a single job by allowing diversification among employers *over time*. The

employee is not locked into an unfortunate contract if he finds better opportunities elsewhere or if he detects some weakness in the internal structure of the firm. A similar analysis applies on the employer's side where he is a sole proprietor, though ordinary diversification is possible when ownership of the firm is widely held in publicly traded shares.

The contract at will is also a sensible private adaptation to the problem of imperfect information over time. In sharp contrast to the purchase of standard goods, an inspection of the job before acceptance is far less likely to guarantee its quality thereafter. The future is not clearly known. More important, employees, like employers, *know what they do not know.* They are not faced with a bolt from the blue, with an "unknown unknown." Rather they face a known unknown for which they can plan. The at-will contract is an essential part of that planning because it allows both sides to take a wait-and-see attitude to their relationship so that new and more accurate choices can be made on the strength of improved information. ("You can start Tuesday and we'll see how the job works out" is a highly intelligent response to uncertainty.) To be sure, employment relationships are more personal and hence often stormier than those that exist in financial markets, but that is no warrant for replacing the contract at will with a for-cause contract provision. The proper question is: will the shift in methods of control work a change for the benefit of both parties, or will it only make a difficult situation worse?

4. *Administrative Costs.* There is one last way in which the contract at will has an enormous advantage over its rivals. It is very cheap to administer. Any effort to use a for-cause rule will in principle allow all, or at least a substantial fraction of, dismissals to generate litigation. Because motive will be a critical element in these cases, the chances of either side obtaining summary judgment will be negligible.

Similarly, the broad modern rules of discovery will allow exploration into every aspect of the employment relation. Indeed, a little imagination will allow the plaintiff's lawyer to delve into the general employment policies of the firm, the treatment of similar cases, and a review of the individual file. The employer for his part will be able to examine every aspect of the employee's performance and personal life in order to bolster the case for dismissal. . . .

III. DISTRIBUTIONAL CONCERNS

Enough has been said to show that there is no principled reason of fairness or utility to disturb the common law's longstanding presumption in favor of the contract at will. It remains to be asked whether there are some hitherto unmentioned distributional consequences sufficient to throw that conclusion into doubt. . . .

The proposed reforms in the at-will doctrine cannot hope to transfer wealth systematically from rich to poor on the model of comprehensive systems of taxation or welfare benefits. Indeed it is very difficult to identify in advance any deserving group of recipients that stands to gain unambiguously from the universal abrogation of the at-will contract. The proposed rules cover the whole range from senior executives to manual labor. At every wage level, there is presumably some differential in workers' output. Those who tend to slack off seem on balance to be most vulnerable to dismissal under the at-will rule; yet it is very hard to imagine why some special concession should be made in their favor at the expense of their more diligent fellow workers.

The distributional issues, moreover, become further clouded once it is recognized that any individual employee will have interests on both sides of the employment relation. Individual workers participate heavily in pension plans, where the value of the holdings depends in part upon the efficiency of the legal rules that govern the companies in which they own shares. If the regulation of the contract at will diminishes the overall level of wealth, the losses are apt to be spread far and wide, which makes it doubtful that there are any gains to the worst off in society that justify somewhat greater losses to those who are better off. The usual concern with maldistribution gives us situations in which one person has one hundred while each of one hundred has one and asks us to compare that distribution with an even distribution of, say, two per person. But the stark form of the numerical example does not explain how the skewed distribution is tied to the concrete choice between different rules governing employment relations. Set in this concrete context, the choices about the proposed new regulation of the employment contract do not set the one against the many but set the many against each other, all in the context of a shrinking overall pie. The possible gains from redistribution, even on the most favorable of assumptions about the diminishing marginal utility of money, are simply not present.

If this is the case, one puzzle still remains: who should be in favor of the proposed legislation? One possibility is that support for the change in common law rules rests largely on ideological and political grounds, so that the legislation has the public support of persons who may well be hurt by it in their private capacities. Another possible explanation could identify the hand of interest-group politics in some subtle form. For example, the lawyers and government officials called upon to administer the new legislation may expect to obtain increased income and power, although this explanation seems insufficient to account for the current pressure. A more uncertain line of inquiry could ask whether labor unions stand to benefit from the creation of a cause of action for wrongful discharge. Unions, after all, have some skill in working with for-cause contracts under the labor statutes that prohibit firing for union activities, and they might be able to promote their own growth by selling their services to the presently nonunionized sector. In addition, the for-cause rule might give employers one less reason to resist unionization, since they would be unable to retain the absolute power to hire and fire in any event. Yet, by the same token, it is possible that workers would be less inclined to pay the costs of union membership if they received some purported benefit by the force of law without unionization. The ultimate weight of these considerations is an empirical question to which no easy answers appear. What is clear, however, is that even if one could show that the shift in the rule either benefits or hurts unions and their members, the answer would not justify the rule, for it would not explain why the legal system should try to skew the balance one way or the other. The bottom line therefore remains unchanged. The case for a legal requirement that renders employment contracts terminable only for cause is as weak after distributional considerations are taken into account as before. . . .

CONCLUSION

The recent trend toward expanding the legal remedies for wrongful discharge has been greeted with wide approval in judicial, academic, and popular circles. In this paper, I have argued that the modern trend rests in large measure upon a misunderstanding of the contractual processes and the ends served by the contract at will. No system of regulation can hope to match the benefits that the contract at will affords in employment relations. The flexibility afforded by the contract at will permits the ceaseless marginal adjustments that are necessary in any ongoing productive activity conducted, as all activities are, in conditions of technological and business change. The strength of the contract at will should not be judged by the occasional cases in which it is said to produce unfortunate results, but rather by the vast run of cases where it provides a sensible private response to the many and varied problems in labor contracting. All too often the case for a wrongful discharge doctrine rests upon the identification of possible employer abuses, as if they were all that mattered. But the proper goal is to find the set of comprehensive arrangements that will minimize the frequency and severity of abuses by employers and employees alike. Any effort to drive employer abuses to zero can only increase the difficulties inherent in the employ-ment relation. Here, a full analysis of the relevant costs and benefits shows why the constant minor imperfections of the market, far from being a reason to oust private agreements, offer the most powerful reason for respecting them. The doctrine of wrongful discharge is the problem and not the solution. This is one of the many situations in which courts and legislatures should leave well enough alone.

NOTES

1. *Payne v. Western & Atl. R.R.*, 81 Tenn. 507, 518–19 (1884), overruled on other grounds, *Hutton v. Watters*, 132 Tenn. 527, 544, 179 S.W. 134, 138 (1915)....
2. Ibid.

PRIVACY

Drug Testing in Employment

Joseph DesJardins
and Ronald Duska

According to one survey, nearly one-half of all *Fortune* 500 companies were planning to administer drug tests to employees and prospective employees by the end of 1987.[1] Counter to what seems to be the current trend in favor of drug testing, we will argue that it is rarely legitimate to override an employee's or applicant's right to privacy by using such tests or procedures.

OPENING STIPULATIONS

We take privacy to be an "employee right" by which we mean a presumptive moral entitlement to receive certain goods or be protected from certain harms in the workplace.[2] Such a right creates a *prima facie* obligation on the part of the employer to provide the relevant goods or, as in this case, refrain from

From Joseph DesJardins and Ronald Duska, "Drug Testing in Employment," *Business & Professional Ethics Journal* 6 (1987). Reprinted by permission of the authors.

the relevant harmful treatment. These rights prevent employees from being placed in the fundamentally coercive position where they must choose between their job and other basic human goods.

Further, we view the employer–employee relationship as essentially contractual. The employer–employee relationship is an economic one and, unlike relationships such as those between a government and its citizens or a parent and a child, exists primarily as a means for satisfying the economic interests of the contracting parties. The obligations that each party incurs are only those that it voluntarily takes on. Given such a contractual relationship, certain areas of the employee's life remain their own private concern and no employer has a right to invade them. On these presumptions we maintain that certain information about an employee is rightfully private, i.e., the employee has a right to privacy.

THE RIGHT TO PRIVACY

According to George Brenkert, a right to privacy involves a three-place relation between a person A, some information X, and another person B. The right to privacy is violated only when B deliberately comes to possess information X about A, and no relationship between A and B exists which would justify B's coming to know X about A.[3] Thus, for example, the relationship one has with a mortgage company would justify that company's coming to know about one's salary, but the relationship one has with a neighbor does not justify the neighbor's coming to know that information. Hence, an employee's right to privacy is violated whenever personal information is requested, collected and/or used by an employer in a way or for any purpose that is *irrelevant to* or *in violation of* the contractual relationship that exists between *employer and employee.*

Since drug testing is a means for obtaining information, the information sought must be relevant to the contract in order for the drug testing not to violate privacy. Hence, we must first decide if knowledge of drug use obtained by drug testing is job-relevant. In cases where the knowledge of drug use is *not* relevant, there appears to be no justification for subjecting employees to drug tests. In cases where information of drug use is job-relevant, we need to consider if, when, and under what conditions using a means such as drug testing to obtain that knowledge is justified.

IS KNOWLEDGE OF DRUG USE JOB RELEVANT INFORMATION?

There seem to be two arguments used to establish that knowledge of drug use is job relevant information. The first argument claims that drug use adversely affects job performance thereby leading to lower productivity, higher costs, and consequently lower profits. Drug testing is seen as a way of avoiding these adverse effects. According to some estimates $25 billion ($25,000,000,000) are lost each year in the United States because of drug use.[4] This occurs because of loss in productivity, increase in costs due to theft, increased rates in health and liability insurance, and such. Since employers are contracting with an employee for the performance of specific tasks, employers seem to have a legitimate claim upon whatever personal information is relevant to an employee's ability to do the job.

The second argument claims that drug use has been and can be responsible for considerable harm to the employee him or herself, fellow employees, the employer, and/or third parties, including consumers. In this case drug testing is defended because it is seen as a way of preventing possible harm. Further, since employers can be held liable for harms done both to third parties, e.g., customers, and to the employee or his or her fellow employees, knowledge of employee drug use will allow employers to gain information that can protect themselves from risks such as liability. But how good are these arguments? We turn to examine the arguments more closely.

THE FIRST ARGUMENT: JOB PERFORMANCE AND KNOWLEDGE OF DRUG USE

The first argument holds that drug use leads to lower productivity and consequently implies that a knowledge of drug use obtained through drug testing will allow an employer to increase productivity. It is generally assumed that people using certain drugs have their performances affected by such use. Since enhancing productivity is something any employer desires, any use of drugs that reduces productivity affects the employer in an undesirable way, and that use is, then, job-relevant. If such production losses can be eliminated by knowledge of the drug use, then knowledge of that drug use is job-relevant information. On the surface this argument seems reasonable. Obviously some drug use in lowering the level of performance can decrease productivity. Since the employer is entitled to a certain level of performance and drug use adversely affects performance, knowledge of that use seems job-relevant.

But this formulation of the argument leaves an important question unanswered. To what level of performance are employers entitled? Optimal performance, or some lower level? If some lower level, what? Employers have a valid claim upon some *certain level* of performance, such that a failure to perform up to this level would give the employer a justification for disciplining, firing or at least finding fault with the employee. But that does not necessarily mean that the employer has a right to a maximum or optimal level of performance, a level above and beyond a certain level of acceptability. It might be nice if the employee gives an employer a maximum effort or optimal performance, but that is above and beyond the call of the employee's duty and the employer can hardly claim a right at all times to the highest level of performance of which an employee is capable.

That there are limits on required levels of performance and productivity becomes clear if we recognize that job performance is person related. It is person-related because one person's best efforts at a particular task might produce results well below the norm, while another person's minimal efforts might produce results abnormally high when compared to the norm. For example a professional baseball player's performance on a ball field will be much higher than the average person's since the average person is unskilled at baseball. We have all encountered people who work hard with little or no results, as well as people who work little with phenomenal results. Drug use by very talented people might diminish their performance or productivity, but that performance would still be better than the performance of the average person or someone totally lacking in the skills required. That being said, the important question now is whether the employer is entitled to an employee's maximum effort and best results, or merely to an effort sufficient to perform the task expected.

If the relevant consideration is whether the employee is producing as expected (according to the normal demands of the position and contract) not whether he or she is producing as much as possible, then knowledge of drug use is irrelevant or unnecessary. Let's see why.

If the person is producing what is expected, knowledge of drug use on the grounds of production is irrelevant since, *ex hypothesi* the production is satisfactory. If, on the other hand, the performance suffers, then, to the extent that it slips below the level justifiably expected, the employer has *prima facie* grounds for warning, disciplining or releasing the employee. But the justification for this is the person's unsatisfactory performance, not the person's use of drugs. Accordingly, drug use information is either unnecessary or irrelevant and consequently there are not sufficient grounds to override the right of privacy. Thus, unless we can argue that an employer is entitled to optimal performance, the argument fails.

This counterargument should make it clear that the information which is job-relevant, and consequently which is not rightfully private, is information about an employee's level of performance and not information about the underlying causes of that level. The fallacy of the argument which promotes drug testing in the name of increased productivity is the assumption that each employee is obliged to perform at an optimal, or at least quite high, level. But this is required under few, if any, contracts. What is required contractually is meeting the normally expected levels of production or performing the tasks in the job-description adequately (not optimally). If one can do that under the influence of drugs, then on the grounds of job-performance at least, drug use is rightfully private. If one cannot perform the task adequately, then the employee is not fulfilling the contract, and knowledge of the cause of the failure to perform is irrelevant on the contractual model.

Of course, if the employer suspects drug use or abuse as the cause of the unsatisfactory performance, then she might choose to help the person with counseling or rehabilitation. However, this does not seem to be something morally required of the employer. Rather, in the case of unsatisfactory performance, the employer has a *prima facie* justification for dismissing or disciplining the employee.

Before turning to the second argument which attempts to justify drug testing, we should mention a factor about drug use that is usually ignored in talk of productivity. The entire productivity argument is irrelevant for those cases in which employees use performance enhancing drugs. Amphetamines and steroids, for example, can actually enhance some performances. This points to the need for care when tying drug testing to job-performance. In the case of some drugs used by athletes, for example, drug testing is done because the drug-influenced performance is too good and therefore unfair, not because it leads to inadequate job-performance. In such a case, where the testing is done to ensure fair competition, the testing may be justified. But drug testing in sports is an entirely different matter than drug testing in business.

To summarize our argument so far. Drug use may affect performances, but as long as the performance is at an acceptable level, the knowledge of drug use is irrelevant. If the performance is unacceptable, then that is sufficient cause for action to be taken. In this case an employee's failure to fulfill his or her end of a contract makes knowledge of the drug use unnecessary.

THE SECOND ARGUMENT: HARM AND THE KNOWLEDGE OF DRUG USE TO PREVENT HARM

Even though the performance argument is inadequate, there is an argument that seems somewhat stronger. This is an argument based on the potential for drug use to cause harm. . . . One could argue that drug testing might be justified if such testing led to knowledge that would enable an employer to prevent harm. Drug use certainly can lead to harming others. Consequently, if knowledge of such drug use can prevent harm, then, knowing whether or not one's employee uses drugs might be a legitimate concern of an employer in certain circumstances. This second argument claims that knowledge of the employee's drug use is job-relevant because employees who are under the influence of drugs can pose a threat to the health and safety of themselves and others, and an employer who knows of that drug use and the harm it can cause has a responsibility to prevent it. Employers have both a general duty to prevent harm and the specific responsibility for harms done by their employees. Such responsibilities are sufficient reason for an employer to claim that information about an employee's drug use is relevant if that knowledge can prevent harm by giving the employer grounds for dismissing the employee or not allowing him/her to perform potentially harmful tasks. Employers might even claim a right to reduce unreasonable risks, in this case the risks involving legal and economic liability for harms caused by employees under the influence of drugs, as further justification for knowing about employee drug use.

This second argument differs from the first in which only a lowered job performance was relevant information. In this case, even to allow the performance is problematic, for the performance itself, more than being inadequate, can hurt people. We cannot be as sanguine about the prevention of harm as we can about inadequate production. Where drug use can cause serious harms, knowledge of that use becomes relevant if the knowledge of such use can lead to the prevention of harm and drug testing becomes justified as a means for obtaining that knowledge.

As we noted, we will begin initially by accepting this argument . . . where restrictions on liberty are allowed in order to prevent harm to others. . . . In such a case an employer's obligation to prevent harm may over-ride the obligation to respect an employee's privacy.

But let us examine this more closely. Upon examination, certain problems arise, so that even if there is a possibility of justifying drug testing to prevent harm, some caveats have to be observed and some limits set out.

JOBS WITH POTENTIAL TO CAUSE HARM

To say that employers can use drug-testing where that can prevent harm is not to say that every employer has the right to know about the drug use of every employee. Not every job poses a serious enough threat to justify an employer coming to know this information.

In deciding which jobs pose serious enough threats certain guidelines should be followed. First, the potential for harm should be *clear* and *present*. Perhaps all jobs in some extended way pose potential threats to human well-being. We suppose an accountant's error could pose a threat of harm to someone somewhere. But some jobs like those of airline pilots, school bus drivers, public transit drivers and surgeons, are jobs in which unsatisfactory performance poses a clear and present danger to others. It would be much harder to make an argument that job performances by auditors, secretaries, executive vice-presidents for public relations, college teachers, professional athletes, and the like, could cause harm if those performances were carried on under the influence of drugs. They would cause harm only in exceptional cases.

NOT EVERY PERSON IS TO BE TESTED

But, even if we can make a case that a particular job involves a clear and present danger for causing harm if performed under the influence of drugs, it is not appropriate to treat everyone holding such a job the same. Not every job-holder is equally threatening. There is less reason to investigate an airline pilot for drug use if that pilot has a twenty-year record of exceptional service than there is to investigate a pilot whose behavior has become erratic and unreliable recently, or than one who reports to work smelling of alcohol and slurring his words. Presuming that every airline pilot is equally threatening is to deny individuals the respect that they deserve as autonomous, rational agents. It is to ignore previous history and significant differences. It is also probably inefficient and leads to the lowering of morale. It is the likelihood of causing harm, and not the fact of being an airline pilot *per se*, that is relevant in deciding which employees in critical jobs to test.

So, even if knowledge of drug use is justifiable to prevent harm, we must be careful to limit this justification to a range of jobs and people where the potential for harm is clear and present. The jobs must be jobs that clearly can cause harm, and the specific employee should not be someone who is reliable with a history of such reliability. Finally, the drugs being tested should be those drugs, the use of which in those jobs is really potentially harmful.

LIMITATIONS ON DRUG TESTING POLICIES

Even when we identify those jobs and individuals where knowledge of drug use would be job relevant information, we still need to examine whether some procedural limitations should not be placed upon the employer's testing for drugs. We have said that in cases where a real threat of harm exists and where evidence exists suggesting that a particular employee poses such a threat, an employer could be justified in knowing about drug use in order to prevent the potential harm. But we need to recognize that as long as the employer has the discretion for deciding when

the potential for harm is clear and present, and for deciding which employees pose the threat of harm, the possibility of abuse is great. Thus, some policy limiting the employer's power is called for.

Just as criminal law places numerous restrictions protecting individual dignity and liberty on the state's pursuit of its goals, so we should expect that some restrictions be placed on an employer in order to protect innocent employees from harm (including loss of job and damage to one's personal and professional reputation). Thus, some system of checks upon an employer's discretion in these matters seems advisable. Workers covered by collective bargaining agreements or individual contracts might be protected by clauses in those agreements that specify which jobs pose a real threat of harm (e.g., pilots but not cabin attendants) and what constitutes a just cause for investigating drug use. Local, state, and federal legislatures might do the same for workers not covered by employment contracts. What needs to be set up is a just employment relationship — one in which an employee's expectations and responsibilities are specified in advance and in which an employer's discretionary authority to discipline or dismiss an employee is limited.

Beyond that, any policy should accord with the nature of the employment relationship. Since that relationship is a contractual one, it should meet the condition of a morally valid contract, which is informed consent. Thus, in general, we would argue that only methods that have received the informed consent of employees can be used in acquiring information about drug use.[5]

A drug-testing policy that requires all employees to submit to a drug test or to jeopardize their job would seem coercive and therefore unacceptable. Being placed in such a fundamentally coercive position of having to choose between one's job and one's privacy does not provide the conditions for a truly free consent. Policies that are unilaterally established by employers would likewise be unacceptable. Working with employees to develop company policy seems the only way to insure that the policy will be fair to both parties. Prior notice of testing would also be required in order to give employees the option of freely refraining from drug use. It is morally preferable to prevent drug use than to punish users after the fact, since this approach treats employees as capable of making rational and informed decisions.

Further procedural limitations seem advisable as well. Employees should be notified of the results of the test, they should be entitled to appeal the results (perhaps through further tests by an independent laboratory) and the information obtained through tests ought to be kept confidential. In summary, limitations upon employer discretion for administering drug tests can be derived from the nature of the employment contract and from the recognition that drug testing is justified by the desire to prevent harm, not the desire to punish wrong doing.

EFFECTIVENESS OF DRUG TESTING

Having declared that the employer might have a right to test for drug use in order to prevent harm, we still need to examine the second argument a little more closely. One must keep in mind that the justification of drug testing is the justification of a means to an end, the end of preventing harm, and that the means are a means which intrude into one's privacy. In this case, before one allows drug testing as a means, one should be clear that there are not more effective means available.

If the employer has a legitimate right, perhaps duty, to ascertain knowledge of drug use to prevent harm, it is important to examine exactly how effectively, and in what situations, the *knowledge* of the drug use will prevent the harm. So far we have just assumed that the *knowledge* will prevent the harm. But how?

Let us take an example to pinpoint the difficulty. Suppose a transit driver, shortly before work, took some cocaine which, in giving him a feeling of invulnerability, leads him to take undue risks in his driving. How exactly is drug-testing going to contribute to the knowledge which will prevent the potential accident?

It is important to keep in mind that; (1) if the knowledge doesn't help prevent the harm, the testing is not justified on prevention grounds; (2) if the testing doesn't provide the relevant knowledge it is not justified either; and finally, (3) even if it was justified, it would be undesirable if a more effective means for preventing harm were discovered.

Upon examination, the links between drug testing, knowledge of drug use, and prevention of harm are not as clear as they are presumed to be. As we investigate, it begins to seem that the knowledge of the drug use even though relevant in some instances is not the most effective means to prevent harm.

Let us turn to this last consideration first. Is drug testing the most effective means for preventing harm caused by drug use?

Consider. If someone exhibits obviously drugged or drunken behavior, then this behavior itself is grounds for preventing the person from continuing in the job. Administering urine or blood tests, sending the specimens out for testing and waiting for a response, will not prevent harm in this instance. Such drug testing because of the time lapse involved, is equally superfluous in those cases where an employee is in fact under the influence of drugs, but exhibits no or only subtley impaired behavior.

Thus, even if one grants that drug testing somehow prevents harm an argument can be made that there might be much more effective methods of preventing potential harm such as administering dexterity tests of the type employed by police in possible drunk-driving cases, or requiring suspect pilots to pass flight simulator tests.[6] Eye-hand coordination, balance, reflexes, and reasoning ability can all be tested with less intrusive, more easily administered, reliable technologies which give instant results. Certainly if an employer has just cause for believing that a specific employee presently poses a real threat of causing harm, such methods are just more effective in all ways than are urinalysis and blood testing.

Even were it possible to refine drug tests so that accurate results were immediately available, that knowledge would only be job relevant if the drug use was clearly the cause of impaired job performance that could harm people. Hence, testing behavior still seems more direct and effective in preventing harm than testing for the presence of drugs *per se*.

In some cases, drug use might be connected with potential harms not by being causally connected to motor-function impairment, but by causing personality disorders (e.g., paranoia, delusions, etc.) that affect judgmental ability. Even though in such cases a *prima facie* justification for urinalysis or blood testing might exist, the same problems of effectiveness persist. How is the knowledge of the drug use attained by urinalysis and/or blood testing supposed to prevent the harm? Only if there is a causal link between the use and the potentially harmful behavior, would such knowledge be relevant. Even if we get the results of the test immediately, there is the necessity to have an established causal link between specific drug use and anticipated harmful personality disorders in specific people.

But it cannot be the task of an employer to determine that a specific drug is causally related to harm-causing personality disorders. Not every controlled substance is equally likely to cause personality changes in every person in every case. The establishment of the causal link between the use of certain drugs and harm-causing personality disorders is not the province of the employer, but the province of experts studying the effects of drugs. The burden of proof is on the employer to establish that the substance being investigated has been independently connected with the relevant psychological impairment and then, predict on that basis that the specific employee's psychological judgment has been or will soon be impaired in such a way as to cause harm.

But even when this link is established, it would seem that less intrusive means could be used to detect the potential problems, rather than relying upon the assumption of a causal link. Psychological tests of judgment, perception and memory, for example, would be a less intrusive and more direct means for acquiring the relevant information which is, after all, the likelihood of causing harm and not the presence of drugs *per se*. In short, drug testing even in these cases doesn't seem to be very effective in preventing harm on the spot.

Still, this does not mean it is not effective at all. Where it is most effective in preventing harm is in its getting people to stop using drugs or in identifying serious drug addiction. Or to put it another way, urinalysis and blood tests for drug use are more effective in preventing potential harm when they serve as a deterrent to drug use *before* it occurs, since it is very difficult to prevent harm by diagnosing drug use *after* it has occurred but before the potentially harmful behavior takes place.

Drug testing can be an effective deterrent when there is regular or random testing of all employees. This will prevent harm by inhibiting (because of the fear of detection) drug use by those who are occasional users and those who do not wish to be detected.

It will probably not inhibit or stop the use by the chronic addicted user, but it will allow an employer to discover the chronic user or addict, assuming that the tests are accurately administered and reliably evaluated. If the chronic user's addiction would probably lead to harmful behavior of others, the harm is prevented by taking that user off the job. Thus regular or random testing will prevent harms done by deterring the occasional user and by detecting the chronic user.

There are six possibilities for such testing:

1. Regularly scheduled testing of all employees
2. Regularly scheduled testing of randomly selected employees
3. Randomly scheduled testing of all employees
4. Randomly scheduled testing of randomly selected employees
5. Regularly scheduled testing of employees selected for probable cause
6. Randomly scheduled testing of employees selected for probable cause

Only the last two seem morally acceptable as well as effective.

Obviously, randomly scheduled testing will be more effective than regularly scheduled testing in detecting the occasional user, because the occasional users can control their use to pass the tests, unless of course tests were given so often (a practice economically unfeasible) that they needed to stop altogether. Regular scheduling probably will detect the habitual or addicted user. Randomly selecting people to test is probably cheaper, as is random scheduling, but it is not nearly as effective as testing all. Besides, the random might miss some of the addicted altogether, and will not deter the risk takers as much as the risk aversive persons. It is, ironically, the former who are probably potentially more harmful.

But these are merely considerations of efficiency. We have said that testing without probable cause is unacceptable. Any type of regular testing of all employees is unaccept-

able. We have argued that testing employees without first establishing probable cause is an unjustifiable violation of employee privacy. Given this, and given the expense of general and regular testing of all employees (especially if this is done by responsible laboratories), it is more likely that random testing will be employed as the means of deterrence. But surely testing of randomly selected innocent employees is as intrusive to those tested as is regular testing. The argument that there will be fewer tests is correct on quantitative grounds, but qualitatively the intrusion and unacceptability are the same. The claim that employers should be allowed to sacrifice the well-being of (some few) innocent employees to deter (some equally few) potentially harmful employees seems, on the face of it, unfair. Just as we do not allow the state randomly to tap the telephones of just any citizen in order to prevent crime, so we ought not allow employers to drug test all employees randomly to prevent harm. To do so is again to treat innocent employees solely as a means to the end of preventing potential harm.

This leaves only the use of regular or random drug-testing as a deterrent in those cases where probable cause exists for believing that a particular employee poses a threat of harm. It would seem that in this case, the drug testing is acceptable. In such cases only the question of effectiveness remains: Are the standard techniques of urinalysis and blood-testing more effective means for preventing harm than alternatives such as dexterity tests? It seems they are effective in different ways. The dexterity tests show immediately if someone is incapable of performing a task, or will perform one in such a way as to cause harm to others. The urinalysis and blood-testing will prevent harm indirectly by getting the occasional user to curtail their use, and by detecting the habitual or addictive user, which will allow the employer to either give treatment to the addictive personality or remove them from the job. Thus we can conclude that drug testing is effective in a limited way, but aside from inhibiting occasional users because of fear of detection, and discovering habitual users, it seems problematic that it does much to prevent harm that couldn't be achieved by other means.

Consider one final issue in the case of the occasional user. They are the drug users who do weigh the risks and benefits and who are physically and psychologically free to decide. The question in their case is not simply "will the likelihood of getting caught by urinalysis or blood-testing deter this individual from using drugs?" Given the benefits of psychological tests and dexterity tests described above, the question is "will the rational user be more deterred by urinalysis or blood testing than by random psychological or dexterity tests?" And, if this is so, is this increase in the effectiveness of a deterrent sufficient to offset the increased expense and time required by drug tests? We see no reason to believe that behavioral or judgment tests are not, or cannot be made to be, as effective in determining what an employer needs to know (i.e., that a particular employee may presently be a potential cause of harm). If the behavioral, dexterity and judgment tests can be as effective in determining a potential for harm, we see no reason to believe that they cannot be as effective a deterrent as drug tests. Finally, even if a case can be made for an increase in deterrent effect of drug testing, we are skeptical that this increased effectiveness will outweigh the increased inefficiencies.

In summary, we have seen that deterrence is effective at times and under certain conditions allows the sacrificing of the privacy rights of innocent employees to the future and speculative good of preventing harms to others. However, there are many ways to deter drug use when that deterrence is legitimate and desirable to prevent harm. But random testing, which seems the only practicable means which has an impact in preventing harm is the one which most offends workers rights to privacy and which is most intrusive of the rights of the innocent. Even when effective, drug testing as a deterrent must be checked by the rights of employees. . . .

DRUG TESTING FOR PROSPECTIVE EMPLOYEES

Let's turn finally to drug testing during a pre-employment interview. Assuming the job description and responsibilities have been made clear, we can say that an employer is entitled to expect from a prospective employee whatever performance is agreed to in the employment contract. Of course, this will always involve risks, since the employer must make a judgment about future performances. To lower this risk, employers have a legitimate claim to some information about the employee. Previous work experience, training, education, and the like are obvious candidates since they indicate the person's ability to do the job. Except in rare circumstances drug use itself is irrelevant for determining an employee's ability to perform. (Besides, most people who are interviewing know enough to get their systems clean if the prospective employer is going to test them.)

We suggest that an employer can claim to have an interest in knowing (a) whether or not the prospective employee *can* do the job and (b) whether there is reason to believe that once hired the employee *will* do the job. The first can be determined in fairly straightforward ways: past work experience, training, education, etc. Presumably past drug use is thought more relevant to the second question. But there are straightforward and less intrusive means than drug testing for resolving this issue. Asking the employee "Is there anything that might prevent you from doing this job?" comes first to mind. Hiring the employee on a probationary period is another way. But to inquire about drug use here is to claim a right to know too much. It is to claim a right to know not only information about what an employee *can* do, but also a right to inquire into whatever background information *might* be (but not necessarily *is*) causally related to what an employee *will* do. But the range of factors that could be relevant here, from medical history to psychological dispositions to family plans, is surely too open-ended for an employer to claim as a *right* to know.

It might be responded that what an employer is entitled to expect is not a certain level of output, but a certain level of effort. The claim here would be that while drug use is only contingently related to what an employee *can* do, it is directly related to an employee's *motivation* to do the job. Drug use then is *de facto* relevant to the personal information that an employee is *entitled* to know.

But this involves an assumption mentioned above. The discussion so far has assumed that drugs will adversely affect job performance. However, some drugs are performance *enhancing* whether they are concerned with actual *output* or *effort*. The widespread use of steroids, pain-killers, and dexadrine among professional athletes are perhaps only the most publicized instances of performance enhancing drugs. (A teacher's use of caffeine before an early-morning class is perhaps a more common example.) More to the point, knowledge of drug use tells little about motivation. There are too many other variables to be considered. Some users are motivated and some are not. Thus the motivational argument is faulty.

We can conclude, then, that whether the relevant consideration for prospective employees is output or effort, knowledge of drug use will be largely irrelevant for predicting. Employers ought to be positivistic in their approach. They should restrict their information gathering

to measurable behavior and valid predictions (What has the prospect done? What can the prospect do? What has the prospect promised to do?) and not speculate about the underlying *causes* of this behavior. With a probationary work period always an option, there are sufficient non-intrusive means for limiting risks available to employers without having to rely on investigations into drug use.

In summary, we believe that drug use is information that is rightfully private and that only in exceptional cases can an employer claim a right to know about such use. Typically, these are cases in which knowledge of drug use could be used to prevent harm. However, even in those cases we believe that there are less intrusive and more effective means available than drug testing for gaining the information that would be necessary to prevent the harm. Thus, we conclude that drug testing of employees is rarely justified, and mostly inefficacious.

NOTES

1. *The New Republic* (March 31, 1986).
2. "A Defense of Employee Rights," Joseph Des-Jardins and John McCall, *Journal of Business Ethics* 4 (1985). We should emphasize that our concern is with the *moral* rights of privacy for employees and not with any specific or prospective *legal* rights. Readers interested in pursuing the legal aspects of employee drug testing should consult: "Workplace Privacy Issues and Employee Screening Policies" by Richard Lehe and David Middlebrooks in *Employee Relations Law Journal* (Vol. 11, no. 3) pp. 407–21; and "Screening Workers for Drugs: A Legal and Ethical Framework," by Mark Rothstein, in *Employee Relations Law Journal* (vol. 11, no. 3) pp. 422–36.
3. "Privacy, Polygraphs, and Work," George Brenkert, *Business and Professional Ethics Journal* 1 (1) (Fall 1981). For a more general discussion of privacy in the workplace see "Privacy in Employment" by Joseph DesJardins, in *Moral Rights in the Workplace* edited by Gertrude

Ezorsky (Albany, NY, SUNY Press, 1987). A good resource for philosophical work on privacy can be found in "Recent Work on the Concept of Privacy," by W. A. Parent, in *American Philosophical Quarterly* 20 (Oct. 1983): 341–56.

4. *U.S. News and World Report* (Aug. 1983): *Newsweek* (May 1983).

5. The philosophical literature on informed consent is often concerned with "informed consent" in a medical context. For an interesting discussion of informed consent in the workplace, see Mary Gibson, *Worker's Rights* (Totowa, NJ, Rowman and Allanheld, 1983), especially pp. 13–14 and 74–75.

6. For a reiteration of this point and a concise argument against drug testing, see Lewis L. Maltby, "Why Drug Testing Is a Bad Idea," *Inc.* (June 1987): 152–53. "But the fundamental flaw with drug testing is that it tests for the wrong thing. A realistic program to detect workers whose condition puts the company or other people at risk would test for the condition that actually creates the danger. The reason drunk or stoned airline pilots and truck drivers are dangerous is their reflexes, coordination, and timing are deficient. This impairment could come from many situations — drugs, alcohol, emotional problems — the list is almost endless. A serious program would recognize that the real problem is workers' impairment, and test for that. Pilots can be tested in flight simulators. People in other jobs can be tested by a trained technician in about 20 minutes — at the job site," p. 152.

Drug Testing and the Right to Privacy: Arguing the Ethics of Workplace Drug Testing

Michael Cranford

Drug testing is becoming an increasingly accepted method for controlling the effects of substance abuse in the workplace. Since drug abuse has been correlated with a decline in corporate profitability and an increase in the occurrence of work-related accidents, employers are justifying drug testing on both legal and ethical grounds. Recent estimates indicate that the costs to employers of employee drug abuse can run as high as $60 billion per year.[1] Motorola, before implementing its drug testing program in 1991, determined that the cost of drug abuse to the company — in lost time, impaired productivity, and health-care and workers compensation claims — amounted to $190 million in 1988, or approximately 40 percent of the company's net profit for that year.[2] As these effects on the workplace are viewed in light of a much larger social problem — one which impacts health care and the criminal justice system, and incites drug-related acts of violence — advocates of drug testing argue that the workplace is an effective arena for engaging these broader concerns. The drug-free workplace is viewed as causally antecedent and even sufficient to the development of drug-free communities.

From Michael Cranford, "Drug Testing and the Right to Privacy." *Journal of Business Ethics*, 17: 1805–1815, 1998. Reprinted with Permission from Kluwer Academic Publishers.

The possibility of using workplace drug interventions to effect social change may obscure the more fundamental question of whether or not drug testing is an ethical means of determining employee drug abuse. While admitting that drug testing could mitigate potential harms, some CEOs have elected not to follow the trend set by Motorola and an estimated 67 percent of large companies,[3] and instead argue that drug testing surpasses the employer's legitimate sphere of control by dictating the behavior of employees on their own time and in the privacy of their own homes.[4] Recent arguments in favor of a more psychologically-sensitive definition of employee privacy place employer intrusions into this intimate sphere of self-disclosure on even less certain ethical grounds.[5] The ethical status of workplace drug testing can be expressed as a question of competing interests, between the employer's right to use testing to reduce drug-related harms and maximize profits, over against the employee's right to privacy, particularly with regard to drug use which occurs outside the workplace.

In this paper I will attempt to bring clarity to this debate and set the practice of workplace drug testing on more certain ethical grounds by advancing an argument which justifies workplace drug testing. I will begin by showing that an employee's right to privacy is violated when personal information is collected or used by the employer in a way which is irrelevant to the contractual relationship which exists between employer and employee. I will then demonstrate that drug testing is justified within the terms of the employment contract, and therefore does not amount to a violation of an employee's right to privacy. After responding to a battery of arguments to the contrary, I will propose that drug testing can be ethically justified under the terms of an employment contract.

PRIVACY AND PERFORMANCE OF CONTRACT

Legal definitions of privacy inevitably rely on the 1890 *Harvard Law Review* article "The Right to Privacy" by Samuel Warren and Louis Brandeis. This article offered an understanding of privacy for which a constitutional basis was not recognized until the 1965 case *Griswold v. Connecticut* (381 U.S. 479). In both instances, privacy was understood as an individual's right "to be let alone," with the Griswold decision according citizens a "zone of privacy" around their persons which cannot be violated by governmental intrusion. This definition, utilized by the Court in numerous decisions since the 1965 ruling, will not be adequate for describing the employee's claim to privacy in an essentially social and cooperative setting like the workplace. In such a condition an absolute right "to be let alone" cannot be sustained, and it may well prove impossible for an employee to maintain a "zone of privacy" when the terms of employment entail certain physical demands. This is not to argue that a right to privacy does not exist in this setting; rather, we must conclude that the aforementioned conditions are not necessary components in such a right.

A more useful definition begins with the idea of a person's right to control information about herself and the situations over which such a right may be legitimately extended. For example, information to the effect that an individual possesses a rare and debilitating disease is generally considered private, but a physician's coming to know that a patient has such a disease is not an invasion of privacy. One might also note that while eavesdropping on a conversation would normally constitute an invasion of privacy, coming to know the same information because the individual inadvertently let it slip in a casual conversation would not. These and other examples demonstrate that the right to privacy is not violated by the mere act of coming to know something private, but is instead contingent on the relationship between the knower and the person about whom the information is known.

George Brenkert formulates this understanding as follows: Privacy involves a relationship between a person A, some information X, and another individual Z. A's right of privacy is violated only when Z comes to possess information X and no relationship exists between A and Z that would justify Z's coming to know X.[6] Brenkert notes that what would justify Z coming to know X is a condition in which knowing X and having a certain access to A will enable Z to execute its role in the particular relationship with A. In such a case, Z is entitled to information X, and A's privacy is in no way violated by the fact that Z knows. Thus, a physician is justified in coming to know of a patient's disease (say, by running certain diagnostic tests), since knowing of the disease will enable her to give the patient medical treatment. One cannot be a physician to another unless one is entitled to certain information and access to that person. Conversely, one can yield one's right to privacy by disclosing information to another that the relationship would not normally mandate. To maintain a right to privacy in a situation where another would normally be entitled to the information to enable them to fulfill the terms of the relationship is, quite simply, to violate the terms of the relationship and make fulfillment of such terms impossible. In the case of our earlier example, to refuse a physician access to the relevant points of one's health status is to make a physician–patient relationship impossible. Similarly, to refuse an employer access to information regarding one's capability of fulfilling the terms of an employment contract is to violate an employer–employee relationship.

The argument advanced at this point is that drug testing involves access to and information about an employee that are justified under the terms of the implicit contractual agreement between employer and employee. An employer is therefore entitled to test employees for drug use. This statement relies on at least two important assumptions. First, a contractual model of employer–employee relations is assumed over against a common law, agent–principal model. It is not the case that employees relinquish all privacy rights in return for employment, as the common law relationship may imply, but rather that the terms of the contract, if it is valid, set reasonable boundaries for employee privacy rights consistent with the terms and expectations of employment. The argument offered here is that drug testing does not violate those boundaries. I am also assuming that drug abuse has a measurable and significant impact on an employee's ability to honor the terms of the employment contract. Employers are entitled to know about employee drug abuse on the grounds that such knowledge is relevant to assessing an employee's capability to perform according to the terms of the agreement. Without arguing for the connection between drug abuse and employee performance at length, the reader's attention is directed to studies which, if not absolutely incontestable in their methodology, are nonetheless reasonably set forth.[7]

In support of this argument, I would first direct attention to other types of information about an employee that an employer is entitled to know, and in coming to know such information does not violate the employee's privacy. Employers are entitled to information about a current or prospective employee's work experience, education, and job skills — in short, information relevant for determining whether or not the employee is capable of fulfilling her part of the contract. More critically, the employer is not only entitled to such information, but is entitled to obtain such information through an investigatory process, both to confirm information the employee has voluntarily yielded about her qualifications, as well as to obtain such relevant information as may be lacking (i.e., inadvertently omitted or, perhaps, intentionally withheld).

Brenkert further adds that an employer is entitled to information which relates to elements of one's social and moral character:

> A person must be able not simply to perform a certain activity, or provide a service, but he must also be able to do it in an acceptable manner — i.e., in a manner which is approximately as efficient as others, in an honest manner, and in a manner compatible with others who seek to provide the services for which they were hired.[8]

Again, the employer is entitled to know, in the case of potential employees, if they are capable of fulfilling their part of the contract, and, in the case of existing employees, if they are adhering to the terms and expectations implicit in the contract. While this latter case can often be confirmed by direct observation of the employee's actions at the work site, on occasion the employer is entitled to information regarding behavior which can be observed at the workplace but originates from outside of it (such as arriving at work late, or consuming large quantities of alcohol prior to arriving). As all of these actions may be in violation of the terms of employment, the employer is entitled to know of them, and in coming to know of them does not violate the employee's privacy.

My point in offering these examples is to suggest that drug testing is a method of coming to know about an employee's ability to fulfill the terms of contract which is analogous to those listed. An exploratory process, in seeking to verify an employee's ability to do a certain job in connection with reasonable expectations for what that job en-

tails, may also validly discover characteristics or tendencies that would keep the employee from performing to reasonable expectations. Drug testing is precisely this sort of process. As a part of the process of reviewing employee performance to determine whether or not they are fulfilling the terms and expectations of employment satisfactorily, drug testing may be validly included among other types of investigatory methods, including interviews with coworkers, skills and proficiency testing, and (in some professions) medical examinations. The fact that an employee may not want to submit to a drug test is entirely beside the point; the employee may just as likely prefer not to include a complete list of personal references, or prefer that the employer not review her relations with other employees. In all these cases, the employer is entitled to know the relevant information, and in coming to know these things does not violate the employee's privacy. The employee may withhold this information from the employer, but this action is tantamount to ending the employer–employee relationship. Such a relationship, under the terms of employment, includes not only each party's commitment to benefit the other in the specific way indicated, but also entitles each to determine if the other is capable of performance according to the terms of contract. In this way, each retains the free ability to terminate the relationship on the grounds of the other's nonperformance.

Of course, not just any purpose of obtaining information relevant to evaluating performance under the terms of contract can automatically be considered reasonable. For instance, an employer cannot spy on a prospective employee in her own home to determine if she will be a capable employee. I offer the following criteria as setting reasonable and ethical limits on obtaining relevant information (though note that the requirement of relevancy is in each case already assumed).

1. *The process whereby an employer comes to know something about an employee (existing or prospective) must not be unnecessarily harmful or intrusive*

The information may not result from investigatory processes which are themselves degrading or humiliating by virtue of their intrusiveness (e.g., strip searches, spying on an employee while they use the bathroom, interviewing a divorced spouse, or searching an employee's locker) or which may prove unhealthy (e.g., excessive use of x-rays, or torture). (Note: Degrading processes of securing information must be distinguished from processes of securing information which is itself degrading. The latter is not necessarily in violation of this or successive criteria).

2. *The process whereby an employer comes to know something about an employee must be efficient and specific*

The information must result from an efficient and specific process — i.e., a process which is the most direct of competing methods (though without compromising point 1 above), and should result in information which corresponds to questions of performance under the terms of the employment contract, and should not result in information that does not so correspond. For example, detailed credit checks may help a bank decide whether a prospective employee is a capable manager of finances, but not directly (only inferentially), and it would also provide a great deal of information that the employer is not entitled to see. Consulting the employee's previous employer, on the other hand, may provide the relevant information directly and specifically.

3. *The process whereby an employer comes to know something about an employee must be accurate, or if not itself precise, then capable of confirmation through further investigation*

The information must result from a dependable source; if a source is not dependable and is incapable of being verified for accuracy, the employer is not justified in pursuing this avenue of discovery. Thus, the polygraph must be excluded, since it is occasionally inaccurate and may in such cases result in information that cannot be verified. In addition, disreputable sources of information, or sources that may have an interest in misrepresenting the information being sought, should not be used.

Having outlined these, I offer my argument in full: Drug testing is not only a method of coming to know about an employee's ability to fulfill the terms of contract which is analogous to those listed earlier, but which also is reasonable under the criteria listed above.

1. *Drug testing is not harmful or intrusive*

In the Supreme Court case *Samuel K. Skinner v. Railway Labor Executives' Association* (489 U.S. 602), the Court determined that both blood and urine tests were minimally intrusive. While the Court acknowledged that the act of passing urine was itself intensely personal, obtaining a urine sample in a medical environment and without the use of direct observation amounted to no more than a minimal intrusion. The Court justified not only testing of urine but also testing of blood by focusing on the procedure of testing (i.e., "experience . . . teaches that the quantity of blood extracted is minimal," and pointing out that since such tests are "commonplace and routine in everyday life," the tests posed "virtually no risk, trauma, or pain." The Court's findings on this case are compelling, and are consistent with my contention that drug testing is not unnecessarily harmful or intrusive. While such testing does amount to an imposition upon an employee (i.e., by requiring her to report to a physician and provide a urine sample) in a way that may not be commonplace for many employees, the Court ruled that since this takes place within an employment context (where limitations of movement are assumed), this interference is justifiable and does not unnecessarily infringe on privacy interests.

2. *Drug testing is both efficient and specific*

In fact, drug testing is the most efficient means of discovering employee drug abuse. In addition to providing direct access to the information in question, the results of drug testing do not include information that is irrelevant. The test targets a specific set of illegal substances. It can be argued (and has been) that drug testing is not efficient because it does not test for impairment — only for drug use. But this point ignores the fact that the test is justified on a correlation between drug abuse and employee productivity more generally; impairment is itself difficult or impossible to measure, since the effects of a given quantity of substance vary from individual to individual and from one incidence of use to another. The fact that impairment is an elusive quantity cannot diminish the validity of testing for drug abuse. This criticism also ignores the fact that the test is an effective means of deterring impairment, providing habitual users a certain expectation that their drug use will be discovered if it is not controlled.

3. *Drug testing can be conducted in a way which guarantees a high degree of precision*

It is well known that the standard (and relatively inexpensive) EMIT test has a measurable chance of falsely indicating drug use, and is also susceptible to cross-reactivity with other legal substances. But confirmatory testing, such as that performed using gas chromatography/mass spectrometry, can provide results at a high level of accuracy. This confirmatory testing, as well as a host of other stringent safeguards, is required of all laboratories certified by the National Institute on Drug Abuse.

In summary, my contention is that an employer is entitled to drug test on the grounds that the information derived is relevant to confirm the employee's capacity to perform according to the terms of employment, and that such testing is a reasonable means of coming to know such information. Other points in favor of drug testing, which are not essential to my preceding argument but congruent with it, include the following two items.

First, drug testing is an opportunity for employer beneficence. Testing permits the employer to diagnose poor employee performance and require such individuals to participate in employer-sponsored counseling and rehabilitative measures. Employers are permitted to recognize that drug abuse is a disease with a broad social impact that is not addressed if employees who perform poorly as a result of drug abuse are merely terminated. Second, a specific diagnosis of drug abuse in the case of poor employee performance might protect the employer from wrongful termination litigation, in the event that an employee refuses to seek help regarding their abuse. The results of drug testing might confirm to the court that the termination was effected on substantive and not arbitrary grounds.

DRUG TESTING AND QUESTIONS OF JUSTIFICATION

A number of arguments have been offered which suggest that drug testing is not justified under terms of contract, or is not a reasonable method by which an employer may come to know of employee drug abuse, and therefore amounts to a violation of employee privacy. These arguments include a rejection of productivity as a justification for testing, charges that testing is coercive, and that it amounts to an abuse of employee privacy by controlling behavior conducted outside the workplace. I will respond to each of these in turn.

First, some have charged that arguing from an employer's right to maximize productivity to a justification for drug testing is problematic. DesJardins and Duska point out that employers have a valid claim on some level of employee performance, such that a failure to perform to this level would give the employer a justification for firing or finding fault with the employee. But it is not clear that an employer has a valid claim on a optimal level of employee performance, and that is what drug testing is directed at achieving. As long as drug abuse does not reduce an employee's performance beyond a reasonable level, an employer cannot claim a right to the highest level of performance of which an employee is capable.[9]

DesJardins and Duska further point out the elusiveness of an optimal level of performance. Some employees perform below the norm in an unimpaired state, and other employees might conceivably perform above the norm in an impaired state. "If the relevant consideration is whether the employee is producing as expected (according to the normal demands of the position and contract) not whether he/she is producing as much as possible, then knowledge of drug use is irrelevant or unnecessary."[10] This is because the issue in question is not drug use *per se*, but employee productivity. Since drug use need not correlate to expectations for a given employee's productivity, testing for drug use is irrelevant. And since it is irrelevant to fulfillment of the employment contract, testing for drugs is unjustified and therefore stands in violation of an employee's privacy.

While I agree that it is problematic to state that an employer has a right to expect an optimal level of performance from an employee, I would argue that the employer does have a right to a workplace free from the deleterious effects of employee drug abuse. Drug testing, properly understood, is not directed at effecting optimal performance, but rather performance which is free from the effects of drug abuse. Since the assessment which justifies drug testing is not based on the impact of drug abuse on a given employee's performance, but is correlated on the effects of drug abuse on workplace productivity more generally, drug testing does measure a relevant quantity.

It is also overly simplistic to state that employers need not test for drugs when they can terminate employees on the mere basis of a failure to perform. Employers are willing to tolerate temporary factors which may detract from employee performance; e.g., a death in the family, sickness, or occasional loss of sleep. But employers have a right to distinguish these self-correcting factors from factors which may be habitual, ongoing, and increasingly detrimental to productivity, such as drug abuse. Such insight might dramatically impact their course of action with regard to how they address the employee's failure to perform. It is therefore not the case, as DesJardins and Duska suggest, that "knowledge of the cause of the failure to perform is irrelevant."[11]. . .

Some argue that any testing which involves coercion is inherently an invasion of employee privacy. Placing employees in a position where they must choose between maintaining their privacy or losing their jobs is fundamentally coercive. For most employees, being given the choice between submitting to a drug test and risking one's job by refusing an employer's request is not much of a decision at all."[12] While Brenkert's arguments against the use of the polygraph are directed at that device's inability to distinguish the reason behind a positive reading (which may not, in many instances, indicate an intentional lie), his argument that the polygraph is coercive is pertinent to the question of drug testing as well.

Brenkert notes that if an employee

> ... did not take the test and cooperate during the test, his application for employment would either not be considered at all or would be considered to have a significant negative aspect to it. This is surely a more subtle form of coercion. And if this be the case, then one cannot say that the person has willingly allowed his reactions to the questions to be monitored. He has consented to do so, but he has consented under coercion. Had he a truly free choice, he would not have done so.[13]

Brenkert's point is surprising, in that his own understanding is that A's privacy is limited by what Z is entitled to know in order to execute its role with respect to A. If Z (here, the corporation) is entitled to know X (whether or not the employee abuses drugs) in order to determine if A (the employee) is capable of performing according to the terms of employment, then the employee has no right to privacy with respect to the information in question. While this does not authorize the corporation to obtain the information in just any manner, the mere fact that the employee would *prefer* that the employer not know cannot be sufficient to constitute a right to privacy in the face of the employer's legitimate entitlement. The employee can freely choose to withhold the information, but this is not so much invoking a right to privacy as it is rejecting the terms of contract.

If Brenkert's criticism of employer testing were valid, then potentially all demands made by the employer on the employee — from providing background information to arriving at work on time — would count as coercive, since in every case where the employee consents to the demand there is a strong possibility that she would not have consented if she was offered a truly free choice. But these demands are reasonable, and the employer is entitled to demand them under the terms of employment, just as the employee is entitled to profit by acceding to such demands. . . .

RESERVATIONS AND POLICY RECOMMENDATIONS

. . . It is the position adopted in this article that a corporation is entitled to drug test its employees to determine employee capacity to perform according to the terms of the employment contract. That drug testing is not, however, in the large majority of cases, directed at maximizing the employee's best interests, suggests that employers should avail themselves of their right to drug test within reasonable limits. In light of this conclusion, the following policy recommendations are directed at employers, with the goal of balancing the employer's right to drug test with a more substantive regard for the dignity and privacy of employees.

1. *Testing should focus on a specifically targeted group of employees*

In the case of employees who are testing without regard for questions of safety, I would strongly urge that testing only be done when probable cause exists to suspect that an employee is using controlled substances. Probable cause might include uncharacteristic behavior, obvious symptoms of impairment, or a significantly diminished capacity to perform their duties. Utilizing probable cause minimizes the intrusive aspect of testing by yielding a higher percentage of test-positives (i.e., requiring probable cause before testing will inherently screen out the large majority of negatives). Even with this stipulation, a drug program may provide a reasonable deterrence factor at the workplace.

It should be noted that this qualification does not apply in cases of job applicants. Employers who insist on testing potential employees will typically do so under a general suspicion of drug use, and may in that cause assume a condition of probable cause.

> 2. *When testing is indicated, it should not be announced ahead of time*

Regularly scheduled testing runs the risk of losing its effectiveness by providing an employee sufficient time to contrive a method of falsifying the sample. Drug testing, if it is to be used at all, should be used in a way which maximizes its effectiveness and accuracy.

> 3. *Employees who test positive for drug abuse should be permitted the opportunity to resolve their abusive tendencies and return to work without penalty or stigma*

Employees should only be terminated for an inability to resolve their abuse, once early detection and substantial warning have been made. Employers can mitigate the dehumanizing aspect of this technology by using it as an opportunity to assist abusive employees with their problems, and permitting them to return to their old positions if they can remedy their habitual tendencies. Toxicological testing should therefore be accompanied by a full range of employee assistance interventions.

NOTES

1. According to SAMHSA (Substance Abuse and Mental Health Services Administration), cited in Ira A. Lipman, "Drug Testing is Vital in the Workplace," *U.S.A. Today Magazine* 123 (January 1995), 81.

2. Dawn Gunsch, "Training Prepares Workers for Drug Testing," *Personnel Journal* 72 (May 1993): 52.

3. According to the U.S. Bureau of Labor Statistics, cited in Rob Brookler, "Industry Standards in Workplace Drug Testing," *Personnel Journal* 71 (April 1992): 128.

4. See Lewis L. Maltby, "Why Drug Testing is a Bad Idea," *Inc.* (June 1987): 152.

5. On this point see Michele Simms, "Defining Privacy in Employee Health Screening Cases: Ethical Ramifications Concerning the Employee/Employer Relationship," *Journal of Business Ethics* 13 (1994): 315–325.

6. George G. Brenkert, "Privacy, Polygraphs, and Work," *Business and Professional Ethics Journal* 1 (1981): 23.

7. See, for example, U.S. Department of Health and Human Services, *Drugs in the Workplace: Research and Evaluation Data*, ed. S. W. Gust and J. M. Walsh (Rockville, MD, National Institute on Drug Abuse Monograph 91, 1989), and National Research Council/Institute of Medicine, *Under the Influence? Drugs and the American Work Force*, ed. J. Normand, R. O. Lempert, and C. P. O'Brien (Washington, DC, Committee on Drug Use in the Workplace, 1994). For example, a prospective study of preemployment drug testing in the U.S. Postal Service showed after 1.3 years of employment that employees who had tested positive for illicit drug use at the time they were hired were 60% more likely to be absent from work than employees who tested negative (*Drugs in the Workplace*, pp. 128–132; *Under the Influence*, p. 134).

8. Brenkert, "Privacy, Polygraphs, and Work," 25.

9. DesJardins and Duska, "Drug Testing in Employment," *Business and Professional Ethics Journal* 6 (1987): 5.

10. Ibid., 6.

11. Ibid.

12. Ibid., 16–17,

13. Brenkert, "Privacy, Polygraphs, and Work," 28–29.

The Ethics of Genetic Screening in the Workplace

Joseph Kupfer

Today we are witnessing the onslaught of "testing" in the workplace. We test for personality, aptitude, competence, "truthfulness," drugs, and now genetic make-up. Clearly, some of this testing may well be warranted, but genetic "screening" as it's called raises some peculiar questions of its own — questions of meaning and questions of morality. In what follows, I shall spell out the nature of genetic screening, its possible purposes or values, and then raise some moral questions about it.

THE ISSUE AND ITS BACKGROUND

Genetic research is one of those areas of science which has clear practical benefits. If we know that we are carrying a gene for an inheritable illness, such as Huntington's disease, we can make a more informed choice about procreation. Knowledge of our genetic disposition toward heart disease or high blood pressure can prompt us to change our patterns of eating and exercise. And once informed of our genetically based vulnerability to lung disease, we are able to avoid threatening work conditions. Indeed, this was the first goal of genetic screening in the workplace: to enable the employee to steer clear of work situations which were liable to call forth a disabling condition or disease (henceforth, simply "disorder").

Obviously, businesses also had an interest in this goal. Fewer disabled workers means reduction in costs caused by illness, absenteeism, health insurance, workers' compensation, and turnover. In addition, the first workplace screening was a response by business to 1970s legislation making business responsible for health in the workplace. DuPont, Dow Chemical, and Johnson and Johnson were among the first companies to implement genetic screening.[1] The tests were voluntary and there was no threat of job loss, rather, "warning" and "relocating" to less hazardous conditions or functions were the procedure. Indeed, DuPont's testing for sickle cell trait was requested by its own black workers! So, at its inception, genetic screening of workers seemed to be a mutually agreed upon practice aimed at mutual benefits — workers and owners cooperating for the good of all.

If this were all there was to genetic screening in the workplace, obviously, there would be little need for moral discussion. But, corporations have an interest in extending the purpose of screening beyond its original scope — to deny people work. What began as a benign program can be modified to serve only the interests of business. After all, relocating workers or modifying existing conditions so that they will be less hazardous takes time, effort, and money. It's just plain cheaper to fire or not hire a worker who is at "genetic risk." The facts of the matter, however, make the whole issue more complicated. They also point to moral difficulties with the use of genetic screening to exclude workers from jobs, what we shall consider "discriminatory genetic screening."

Before investigating the moral issues involved, we must get clear on the scientific ones concerning *how* genetic screening, in fact,

From Joseph Kupfer, "The Ethics of Genetic Screening in the Workplace," *Business Ethics Quarterly* 3:1 (1993). Reprinted with permission.

works. There are serious limitations to what we can learn from genetic screening and they have moral implications. The limitations on the knowledge afforded by genetic screening are of two sorts — technical and causal. Technical limitations are determined by the level of sophistication of our techno-scientific understanding. Causal constraints depend upon how genes actually bring about disorders.

Each kind of limitation itself involves two sets of variables. Technical restrictions on genetic knowledge turn on (1) whether the gene itself has been located or simply correlated with other DNA material, and (2) whether knowledge of other family members is necessary to determine the presence of the affecting gene. Causal restrictions on genetic knowledge involve (1) whether the affecting gene requires other genes to produce the disorder, and (2) whether the gene causes the disorder with inevitability or just creates a vulnerability to it. We shall consider the two sorts of limitations on genetic knowledge by examining in order these sets of variables for their significance for the practice of genetic screening.

TECHNICAL LIMITATIONS

First is the question of whether the gene itself has been located. Hemophilia, Duchenne muscular dystrophy, and cystic fibrosis are among the few exceptions where the genetic test actually identifies the gene in question. What is more typical are DNA "probes" or "markers" which indicate the likelihood of the gene's presence. "Most of today's probes aren't capable of pinpointing a bad gene. They can only detect sequences of healthy genes called markers, that are usually found near a bad one."[2] When "restriction" enzymes are introduced into the chromosome material, DNA fragments are generated: specifically, strips of genetic material called restriction fragment length polymorphisms (RFLPs), whose pat-

terns can be statistically associated with the occurrence of a particular disorder.[3] In the case of Huntington's disease, for example, the probe detects "a piece of DNA that is so close to the as yet unidentified Huntington's gene that it is inherited along with the gene."[4]

This technical limitation — inability to locate the particular gene in question — means that we are usually dealing with statistical correlations. The marker can be inherited without the defective gene; therefore, uncovering the marker must be treated with caution. Conversely, as Marc Lappe warns,[5] failure to turn up the marker does not guarantee the gene's absence!

In order to establish the correlation between the marker and the disorder, collateral data may be needed. One kind, "linkage analysis," points to our second set of variables — whether or not reference to family members is needed. Linkage analysis is comparing a given individual's DNA pattern with both affected and unaffected family members. The marker for Huntington's disease, for example, is useless if there are no living family members *with* the disease. This is because what is needed is to identify the piece of DNA material *as* a marker for Huntington's disease. Its association with the disease must be ascertained by comparison with DNA fragments of surviving relatives.

This is obviously very time consuming and expensive, prohibitively so for workplace application. It also requires the consent of family members who may not be employed by the company (over whom the company can exert little leverage). In contrast, "direct markers" indicate a genetic connection with a disorder without linkage analysis. The marking of the genes for hemophilia, cystic fibrosis, and adult polycystic kidney disease can be ascertained directly. These are more feasible for workplace screening.

Another sort of collateral data that is frequently needed involves the use of "flanking probes" in order to ascertain the presence of "modifier" genes. This leads us to consideration of the causal limitations of the knowledge gleaned from genetic screening.

CAUSAL LIMITATIONS

Our third set of variables concerns how the genetic material generates the disorder: whether the disorder is caused by one or several genes. When a disorder is coded for by more than a single gene, the gene in question must interact with these other genes in order to be expressed (as a disorder). For screening to have predictive value it must indicate the presence (or absence) of these auxiliary, "modifier" genes. For instance, in the case of Gaucher's disease, the gene marked by the DNA probe is associated with three forms of the disease. While one of the varieties of this neurological disorder is severe, the other two are fairly mild.[6] Without corroboration from modifier genes, which form of Gaucher's disease the individual will develop can't be determined.

One interesting combination of variables occurs in Huntington's disease. It is caused by a single gene; however, that gene has not yet been located. Therefore, it is identified by means of other DNA material, *and* correlation of the material with the disease requires linkage analysis. Because it is caused by a single gene, if that gene can be identified, then linkage analysis won't be needed. In addition, it will be known with virtual certainty that the individual will be afflicted. As with adult polycystic kidney disease, all carriers of the gene for Huntington's disease develop the disorder. The causal tie between the gene and the disorder is virtually absolute.

But this is the rare exception. The great majority of genes do not lead inevitably to the disorder. They create a susceptibility or vulnerability, not a certainty of expression. Our last set of variables concerns this — the nature of the gene's causal efficacy. Conditions such as high cholesterol levels and high blood pressure, and diseases such as Alzheimer's disease and diabetes, are determined by "contingency" genes. Certain contingencies must be met before these genes bring about their respective disorders.

One of these contingencies is the presence of other genes, as we have just noted. In addition, the expression of most genetically based disorders requires the influence of biological, social, or psychological factors. It is already common knowledge that diet and exercise (biological and social influences) can affect the onset of coronary artery disease and high blood pressure. The same also holds for diabetes and back arthritis.

What does it *mean* to say that the gene produces a disposition or susceptibility to a disorder? One fourth of the people with the genetic marker for "ankylosing spondylitis" develop this debilitating back arthritis. Put another way, someone with the marker is between forty and one hundred times more likely to develop ankylosing spondylitis than is someone without this genetic material.[7] Even in such "high odds" cases like this one, however, 75 percent of the people with the genetic marker do *not* develop the arthritis. Work and work conditions, for instance, contribute greatly to its onset. For many genetically determined disorders, the individual may have considerable control over whether and how severely the disorder occurs. Knowledge of our genetic constitution can be helpful in making practical decisions rather than simply forecasting our fate.

CONSIDERATIONS OF PRIVACY

We come now to the moral questions of whether and to what extent genetic screening in the workplace is justified. Recall that we are talking about discriminatory screening which is designed to exclude workers from jobs, rather than to "warn and relocate." I shall argue that considerations of privacy and justice mitigate against screening or at least its untrammeled deployment.

Let's begin with considerations of privacy. When information is gathered about us our privacy may be infringed upon in varying degrees. Whether our privacy is violated depends on such things as whether we consent to the gathering of the information, the nature of the information, and what happens as a result of its gathering. What I would like to focus on here is the issue of control and autonomy. Many different sorts of information can be obtained, most of it valuable to the company. Some information concerns such things as credit ratings or religious affiliations, other involves ascertaining physical facts by monitoring drug use. Is genetic screening any different in principle from drug screening, polygraph tests, or surveillance? In at least one regard it seems to be. Although in most cases, we have some control over whether a gene is expressed as a disorder, we cannot control whether we *have* the gene in the first place. Whether we have the disposition, the vulnerability to the disorder, is out of our hands.

We have some say over our work, religion, credit rating, and most of us can choose to use drugs or not. But not so with genes. They are in and of us, forever. This lack of control is especially compounded in the workplace because of related lack of power in this context. First, most workers are not in a position to refuse to cooperate with demands for screening. When this is the case, they have no control over the gathering of information about which they also lack control. This lack of power is magnified by workers' overall status in the workplace. In spite of unionization, most workers have little say over working conditions, product manufacture, wages, promotions, and firing.

We need to see testing in general, and genetic screening in particular, within the context of the employer–employee relationship. Testing workers gives employers and managers still greater control over workers' lives. Screening of all sorts would be different, and experienced differently, in a context in which power were more equitably distributed in the workplace. This seems especially important in the area of testing for genetically based disorders, precisely because we have no control over our genetic makeup.

This sense of powerlessness is critical to the special type of stigmatization associated with genetic defects. When screening uncovers a genetic abnormality, the individual can feel morally defective — cursed or damned. This could and has happened simply from acquiring genetic information under the most benign circumstances. Thus, Madeleine and Lenn Goodman found considerable stigmatization among Jewish people identified as carriers of Tay-Sachs disease even though no obvious disadvantages followed from such identification.[8] But when the information is used prejudicially, as in the workplace discrimination we are here considering, the likelihood and intensity of stigmatization increases. As Thomas Murray notes, diagnosing an illness as genetically caused may *label* the person as *constitutionally* weak, making finding another job difficult.[9]

All of these aspects of the situation help explain why the loss of privacy suffered in genetic screening in the workplace is serious. The screening is for properties over which the worker has no control and is not responsible; it occurs in a context of relative powerlessness; and it is likely to result in stigmatization with profound costs to his or her life-chances. The genetic screening as described here involves loss of privacy, but the stigmatization and its repercussions, as we shall see, are a matter of *injustice*. Loss or forfeiture of privacy is less defendable the less just the situation under which it occurs and the less just the purposes for which it is used.

The invasion of privacy is greater when the genetic screening is "across the board" rather than selective. When businesses screen for *any* potential disease or debilitating condition, it is like having the police come and search your house just to see what they'll turn up. In both cases, there is clearly an "interest" in uncovering the relevant danger. The state and employer reduce their respective risks. But such interests are not overriding, not in a society which claims to value the individual's autonomy and privacy. The employer has no more right to a total genetic profile than he has to information about one's sexual habits, recreational activities, or religious and political beliefs — even though knowledge of these and other details of our lives might well be of use to him.

Testing for job-specific susceptibilities is more warranted since directly connected to the work context and the employer's role in bringing about the disorder. It is more like searching someone's home for specific items, such as guns or counterfeit money. Presumably, there is a good reason for looking in both sorts of case. Since screening for just a *few,* job-related genetic dispositions, less of the self is being "searched." Therefore, there is probably less sense of being violated or stigmatized. The individual is told that she is unfit to do this particular job, for example, heavy lifting because of the disposition to back arthritis. She is not labelled as constitutionally weak due to some general condition, such as vulnerability to heart disease.

Even here, however, another threat looms. It is all too likely that employers will tend to use such information to fire employees rather than improve workplace conditions. It's cheaper. But perhaps it's the employer's responsibility to make the workplace safe, even for those with susceptibilities to environmentally-triggered disorders. People who

have a disposition to lung disease, for example, might be able to work in this particular factory at no increased risk *if* the employer provided better air ventilation and circulation. This issue seems to be a matter of justice: who should bear the burden of workplace danger.

CONSIDERATIONS OF JUSTICE

We turn now directly to considerations of justice. The first sort of consideration focuses on the individual and the nature of genetic causation. The second concerns these individuals as members of a paying public.

In the great majority of cases, genetic markers indicate merely a predisposition for a disorder, not the inevitability of its onset. (Even when inevitable, in many cases the degree of severity remains unpredictable.) It seems unjust to penalize an individual for something that has not yet come to pass and which may well be prevented by him. It is unjust to act as if the individual is already diseased or disabled, especially when he may run a *lower* risk than others without the marker because of healthful life-choices made on the basis of this information.

It is like treating someone as though guilty until proven innocent. In the case of genetically caused susceptibility to a disorder, it is worse because carrying the gene is beyond the person's control. Considerations of justice suggest that there is something wrong in penalizing people for conditions which are beyond their control. Of course, sometimes people are justly denied benefits or privileges on account of uncontrollable conditions. Thus, we don't allow blind people to drive or people who have slow reaction times to be air-traffic controllers. But this is not penalizing someone so much as finding them unqualified for performance of a task. Public safety certainly does and should operate as a constraint on opportunity. However, this kind of consideration is rare in the case of genetically based disorders; moreover, it should come into play only with the onset of the disabling condition, not with the mere discovery of a genetic propensity toward it. In a society proclaiming commitment to egalitarian principles, we shouldn't further handicap people who may become disabled by depriving them of work while they are still able to do the job.

The question of the justness of discriminatory genetic screening can also be posed from the larger, social perspective. It arises from the social nature and purpose of genetic research. Genetic research, including testing individuals and groups, was developed to help people. By diagnosing genetic predispositions, testing could enable people to make beneficial decisions concerning themselves, family members, and potential offspring. When individuals already manifested certain disorders, voluntary genetic counselling was designed to help provide diagnosis, prognosis, and information for vital decisions.

This is analogous to diagnostic reading tests conducted in the public schools. These are designed to help students get remedial help when needed. Instead, imagine a situation where such tests were used to "weed out" the weakest students so that they didn't clutter up the classroom and drain teaching resources. Surely we would find such a policy unjust, if not outrageous! This would be similar to the discriminatory use of genetic screening. Like individuals with contingency markers, slow readers often can *alter* their futures. In both cases, the diagnostic tests can be used to assist the individual to deal with his problem and make life-enhancing choices. On the other hand, the tests can be used to exclude the individual from certain beneficial opportunities: jobs in the case of genetic screening, and instruction to improve reading skills in the case of the reading tests.

Each use of the diagnostic test can be viewed as part of a larger model. The "diagnostic-therapeutic" model takes as primary the interests of the individuals being tested. The "competition" model, however, takes as primary the interests of some other group or institution: the business in the case of genetic testing, the school or superior students in the case of reading diagnosis. On the competition model, the "defective" worker or student is displaced in favor of the competing interests.

My analogy between the school reading test and genetic screening being used against the diagnosed individuals faces the following objection. In the case of the reading test, public education is paid for by public monies; therefore, everybody has an equal right to instruction, including those with reading disabilities. But in the case of genetic screening, the employer is operating privately. She is under no obligation to serve the interests of the employee (or prospective employee). The parallel between people with reading disabilities and those genetically marked for disorders would then break down on the basis of the public/private distinction.

My reply is that genetic research and the procedures employed in genetic screening were developed with public monies. They were carried out by means of government grants and publicly financed facilities such as state universities. Even private universities and research institutes rely greatly on government monies for equipment and salaries, as well as the findings generated by the public institutions. Moreover, these public funds were allocated for the expressed purposes of increasing scientific knowledge and helping society's members. Promotion of these social goods was used to legitimate if not justify investing society's taxes in genetic research. For private businesses to use the knowledge and technology developed through this research in order to deny some of its members employment seems unjust. This is so even if private companies market instruments and procedures for the genetic screening; the technologies *these* private companies are selling could only have been developed on the shoulders of publicly financed (and publicly available) research.

This brings us to the importance of health. Health is unlike most other goods because it is a prerequisite for so many things we value. Without it, we are cut off from the joys of recreation, travel, the arts, work, socializing, sometimes even life itself. Depending on the degree of infirmity, even such simple, apparently available delights as reading, talking, or walking may be denied the individual. The economic benefits of work are usually needed for people to receive adequate long-term health care, so that depriving them of work is likely to be condemning people to lack of health.

Denying a person work on the basis of the *disposition* to develop a disorder may, ironically, increase its likelihood of occurrence. Prevention of its occurrence might require repeated diagnostic tests, treatment, or therapy; it might require the economic wherewithal for a particular health regimen, such as exercise. Even if the lack of work doesn't contribute to the onset of the genetically marked disorder through economic deprivation, it compounds the individual's plight. He not only suffers from the potential to develop this particular disorder, but is now unemployed (and probably uninsured) to boot. He is now economically unprotected against *other* misfortunes and subjected to the psychological stress which could foster other disorders.

What should we conclude from all this? It seems to me that these considerations of privacy and justice argue strongly against general, discriminatory genetic screening in the workplace. Thomas Murray has a list of requirements that a morally defensible exclu-

sion policy must meet. Among them are two that especially turn on considerations of justice.[10] The policy must exclude workers from but a few jobs so that those affected stand a good chance of finding other employment. Otherwise, we'd be treating them unjustly by virtually denying them the opportunity to work at all. In addition, the exclusion shouldn't single out groups that have already been unjustly treated. This is important since genetic dispositions are often inherited along racial and ethnic lines such as the high black incidence of sickle cell anemia and the high Jewish incidence of Tay-Sachs. This, too, is a matter of justice. We shouldn't compound prior injustices with present ones.

I would qualify Murray's conditions with the following restrictions. Corporate screening should be confined to work-specific disorders, rather than probe for a general genetic profile. Moreover, the company should make it a policy to try to relocate the employee to a less hazardous work site or activity, just as the first companies engaged in screening did. This degree of constraint seems minimal in light of the importance of privacy and justice.

NOTES

1. William Pat Patterson, "Genetic Screening: How Much Should We Test Employees?," *Industry Week* (June 1, 1987), pp. 47–48.
2. Kathleen McAuliffe, "Predicting Diseases," *U.S. News and World Report* (May 25, 1987), p. 65.
3. Kathleen Nolan and Sara Swenson, "New Tools, New Dilemmas: Genetic Frontiers," *The Hastings Center Report* (October/November, 1988), p. 65.
4. Gina Kolati, "Genetic Screening Raises Questions For Employers and Insurers," *Research News* (April 18, 1986), p. 317.
5. Marc Lappe, "The Limits of Genetic Inquiry," *The Hastings Center Report* (August, 1987), p. 7.
6. Ibid., p. 8.

7. Marc Lappe, *Genetic Politics* (New York: Simon and Schuster, 1979), p. 61.

8. Madeleine and Lenn Goodman, "The Over-selling of Genetic Anxiety," *The Hastings Center Report* (October, 1982), p. 249. There was, however, fear of loss of marriage eligibility among many of the people tested. The Goodmans also cite a study of sickle cell trait in Greece, where "possession of sickle cell trait had become a socially stigmatized status, introducing new anxieties into this rural community," p. 26.

9. Thomas Murray, "Warning: Screening Workers for Genetic Risk," *The Hastings Center Report* (February, 1983).

10. Ibid., p. 8. Murray also includes the following: sound scientific basis linking anomaly to exposure to disease; risk should be very large and the disease should be severe and irreversible; and that the number of people excluded should be very small. This last stricture doesn't strike me as all that convincing. It isn't the number of people affected that *makes* a policy unjust. Although many suffering an injustice is worse than few suffering it, injustice done even to few is still injustice and weighs against the policy.

The Genetics Revolution, Economics, Ethics, and Insurance

Patrick L. Brockett
E. Susan Tankersley

INTRODUCTION

A revolution is taking place in genetic research by the name of the "Human Genome Project" (HGP). This project, initiated in 1984, is a twenty-year, six-billion-dollar international science project designed to completely map the entire genetic structure of the human species. Basically, the human genetic structure (Genome) consists of 24 different chromosome types made up of only four different amino acids which combine in various sequences (in a double helix shape) to determine the genetic structure of the living entity being examined. These four amino acids (Adenine, Guanine, Cytosine, and Thiamin) can be viewed as the analog of a four-letter alphabet whose permutations and combinations dictate all physical characteristics (and some say certain psycho-logical or social characteristics as well) via their interrelations and ordering. In all, the human genome has on the order of three billion total base pairs, so this cryptographic exercise of "breaking the human genetic code" like a military code is, indeed, a monumental undertaking. Already, tremendous headway has been made, and certain chromosomes have been mapped (e.g., the location and function of the various genetic positions have been flagged, and links have been established with individual characteristics and diseases). Scientists have already mapped most of chromosome 21, and, in fact, over four thousand disorders have now been identified and linked to specific sites on specific chromosomes.

The potential boons to mankind deriving from this research are dramatic — one need only imagine a world without congenital dis-

From Patrick L. Brockett and E. Susan Tankersley, "The Genetics Revolution, Economics, Ethics, and Insurance," *Journal of Business Ethics*, 16: 1661–1676, 1997. Reprinted with permission from Kluwer Academic Publishers.

eases or birth defects. These boons will only materialize, of course, if we are able to cure genetically-based diseases by genetic engineering, for example, by the introduction of genetically altered viruses into defective cells to substitute their DNA structure for that of the invaded cell. These viruses could be used to carry a new "correctly coded" DNA into the diseased cells. Such genetic engineering portends the ability to alter the genetic composition of an individual and actually cure genetically-based diseases. For example, one might have the option of "curing" Down's syndrome or Huntington's disease rather than facing the option of aborting a chromosomally defective fetus. Although this may seem almost like futuristic Jurassic Park science fiction to the lay observer, the time is now. Twenty humans are now living who have been treated for genetically linked diseases using genetic engineering.

While the boons may appear tremendous, the ethical and moral pitfalls are equally monumental, especially as they concern the insurance industry. Over four thousand diseases have now been explicitly identified and linked to specific sites on specific chromosomes, leading the way for potential detection of diseases (or perhaps even the propensity towards a disease) long before symptoms become apparent. However, it may be years, (if ever) before this knowledge can be utilized to find an approach to "cure" the disease. During this interval of time, the knowledge is available, but no control is in sight. Medical ethicists fear an era of "genetic discrimination" which could threaten the very ability of those with identifiable genetic structures to find employment. This scenario is not outlandish. James Gusella, the discoverer of the marker for the dominant Huntington's disease gene, did not make the information available to interested medical geneticists until *four years* after the discovery because he feared the potential impact and emotional ef-

fect the information might have on the inflicted individual and the potential implications for discrimination against those with the condition (*Nature*, 1983).

Would you want to know that you will develop diabetes or some deadly or debilitating disease in twenty years when no cure presently exists? Now throw another variable into the equation. After having tested positive for a disease-related gene sequence (perhaps even tested against your will), insurance companies may deny you health insurance coverage, or employers may deny you employment without your ever having exhibited a single symptom! The majority of workers in the United States are employed by small business, and the extremely high costs of insuring a person with a known genetic risk factor could (and already has in some circumstances) force the cancellation of health insurance, worker's compensation insurance, life insurance, or even employment itself for genetically "tagged" individuals. Because the effects of many genetic abnormalities can be controlled if caught early enough and treated, you may not, in fact, *ever* actually exhibit the characteristic for which your insurance or employment was denied!

On the other hand, the HGP is also a dream come true for insurance companies. From the perspective of insurers, who view themselves as financial intermediaries, the ultimate rationale for using this genetic-based information for classification purposes is economic. They wish to achieve subgroups of policyholders with reasonably homogeneous expectations of loss, each of whom will pay similar premiums in a class. As a group, policyholders then share in any realized losses due to fortuitous adverse experience of the individuals in the group. The insurer merely provides a vehicle for the risk transfer or sharing among the homogeneous policyholders. Using genetic information, insurance companies will be able to better predict the future expected costs of a life of health insurance policy and in so doing develop a more economically efficient classification system for insureds. Most importantly, companies will be able to pick and choose those individuals with low expected future costs relative to the premiums charged.

Possible societal conflict arises at this point, as insurance companies try to insure individuals with low expected future costs (relative to the premiums they are able to charge) and try not to provide coverage to individuals who will develop an expensive disorder, or for which the uncertainty in cost amount is too great. Indeed, it is discrimination (in a reverse sense) if superior knowledge is available concerning future loss costs and the insurer does not use this information. It is obviously not equitable to overcharge a person whose genetic risk profile indicates a low expected loss, any more than it is to overcharge a person whose sex or race is different, but who does not otherwise represent an increased risk to the financial stability of the insurance pool.

This paper discusses these ethical issues as well as the economic issues associated with the gathering of generic information on humans from the perspective of the insurance industry and society. The intent of this paper is not to *solve* the ethical problems posed to the insurance industry by the HGP, but rather to present an unbiased view of the many sides to the issues and propose some possible solutions.

UNFAIR DISCRIMINATION AND INSURANCE CLASSIFICATION SCHEMES: AN ECONOMIC PERSPECTIVE

As noted previously, insurance companies attempt to place insureds, into homogeneous subgroups where each insured pays a premium or price which closely reflects his or her *ex ante* expected losses. Classification is the process by which this is accomplished.

The classification process might be labeled as involving either "fair" or "unfair" discrimination of the insured, depending upon the particular context of the classification scheme being used and the ethical values of the observer. Nevertheless, classification is a form of stratification which is inherently discriminatory which, according to the *Webster's New Collegiate Dictionary* (1973), is "the process by which two stimuli differing in some aspect are responded to differently" or also "the act, practice of instance of discriminating categorically rather than individually." The process of discriminating between risks (using classification) has positive benefits from the perspective of the insurer in that it promotes the equitable distribution of loss costs and helps to make insurance more attractive to all classes of insureds (because the price charged is relatively close to the expected losses of an insured risk).

A fundamental purpose of classification schemes for discriminating among potential insureds is to allow the insurer to charge the insured a premium proportional to the expected cost or the risk that he/she is perceived to bring to the insurer. This concept is logically unchallenged in many lines of insurance (e.g., in fire insurance, it is noncontroversial to charge higher rates for wood frame structures than for brick or stone structures; in life insurance, it is logical to charge higher premiums to smokers than to nonsmokers, etc.) In automobile insurance, as well, there is evidence that the consumers strongly agree with the notion that "people should pay different rates for car insurance based upon the degree of risk they represent to the insurance company." The same argument might logically be applied to the setting of premiums for health insurance and the use of genetic information.

When there *is* suppression of information and the insurers are forced to charge the same rate to insured persons who have different expected costs, then the insurance pricing might not only be viewed as "unfairly discriminatory" to the group of lower expected cost persons, but will also encourage moral hazard and adverse selection against the insurer. The financial effects of these adverse incentives ultimately drive rates upward and may even threaten the solvency of insurers.

Distinguishing between risks as to expected costs allows a reduction in the amount of financial cross subsidization between various groups of insureds in an insurance pool. That is, high-risk (or high-expected-cost) insureds are distinguished from lower-risk (or lower cost) individuals in a pool and charged higher prices than are low-risk insureds. Each insured then pays his or her own fair share of expected future loss costs for the insurance pool, as is normally considered to be equitable. The ignoring of the level of a pertinent variable related significantly to the expected losses can be viewed as a wealth transfer (subsidization) from the lower risk individuals (who are overpaying according to best estimates of their expected losses) to the higher risk individuals (who are underpaying according to best estimates of their expected losses).

Appropriate use of all pertinent information for the purpose of insurance classification also reduces or prevents the occurrence of adverse selection. The adverse incentives associated with charging high- and low-risk insureds the same rates occur because of the incentive for the lower-risk individuals, who are subsidizing the high-risk individuals, to drop out of an insurance pool or find alternative means of pre-loss or post-loss financing. As low-risk insureds drop out of the insurance pool due to being charged a disproportionate share of the pool's expected losses, the only insureds left will be the high-risk ones. In fact, the high-risk individuals (or those who know they are high-risk due to having had genetic tests results which were not

communicated to the insurance company) will disproportionately purchase insurance and will eventually constitute a larger portion of the risk pool. This will then necessitate that even higher premiums be charged, starting the cycle again. This adverse selection of insured individuals can lead, in severe circumstances, to a complete market failure if only high-risk insureds choose to purchase insurance. Thus, using all available information related to the estimation of the prospective losses associated with the risk in the insurance classification helps to maintain the viability of competitive insurance markets as risk transfer and pooling mechanisms. . . .

The "equitable" nature of charging each person according to his or her perceived risk costs sometimes comes into conflict with the social concerns or moral imperatives expressed by society at particular points in time. In these cases, society, through laws or regulation, constrains the open competitive market choice of insurance classification variables. For example, there is actuarial evidence showing statistically significant relationships between losses and race in certain lines of insurance. As a society, however, the United States of America is very concerned with charging higher costs based (even in part) on race. For this reason, anti-discrimination laws have increased the restrictions on classification and underwriting variables, and legislators and regulators have also imposed restrictions on the competitive market determination of rates for certain lines of insurance in various states.

While certain potential classification variables such as race or ethnic or national origin are not legal to use in ratemaking because it has been deemed to be socially unacceptable to use such information, it is debatable as to who gains and who loses in the wealth transfer inherent in a mandated suppression of information. It has simply been deemed to be socially unacceptable to discriminate along these lines, as a matter of public policy. If these restrictions were repealed, for example, then certain racial groups would pay more for life insurance, less for life annuities, more for health insurance, etc. The financial impacts would be differential across races, and economic realignment would ensue. . . .

UNFAIR DISCRIMINATION AND INSURANCE CLASSIFICATION SCHEMES: AN ETHICAL PERSPECTIVE

One could argue that in many cases of unfair discrimination involving race, sex, religion, and disability the discrimination was not justified. For example, a woman can do the same job as a man, but employers just do not have equal pay scales for women and men. With genetic disorders, however, some feel discrimination is justified. Since a sick person presents a much different risk profile to a health insurer than a healthy person, insurance companies should be able to choose which individuals they will insure. Economically and statistically, although this argument for genetic discrimination is valid from an economical and statistical frame of reference, the argument may not hold true when the question of ethics is considered. Is it ethical to deny health insurance to people who possess specific genes when they have no control over their genetic coding? Since most individuals obtain health insurance through employer-sponsored (and often subsidized) group plans, employment discrimination against those with certain genes can follow from high expected prospective health insurance loss costs.

In 1988, to learn about the extent of genetic discrimination, Dr. Paul Billings (medical geneticist and director of Harvard Medical School's Clinic for Inherited Disease) placed an advertisement in journals and magazines requesting information from people who had experienced genetic discrimination.

The study was organized by the Genetics Study Group in Cambridge, Massachusetts. The following are a few of the genetic discrimination cases related in personal communications to Dr. Billings:

- A man with an excellent driving record was unable to renew his automobile insurance when the company found he had Charcot Marie Tooth Disease (CMT), a neurological disorder, even though the disease had been stable and non-progressive for twenty years.
- An eight-year-old who was diagnosed at birth with Phenylketonuria (PKU) was ineligible for insurance under a group plan even though with proper diet she had developed into a normal and healthy child.
- A young man who had been diagnosed as hemochromatotic (excessive iron) but had been stabilized for many years through a regimen of phlebotomie (blood letting) was denied life insurance even though his parents, who had the same affliction, had lived into their 80s.

From these examples, one can see that in a competitive economic insurance market, companies do not necessarily assume a potential insured is healthy until proven sick. In fact, any *hint* of future health problems can become a strike against an individual ever obtaining insurance. As the preceding examples illustrate, underwriting guidelines sometimes use available information to build worst case scenarios even if these scenarios are biased or unlikely predictors of one's health. The previously described case of the man trying to renew his automobile insurance demonstrates how insurance companies can act in an illogical manner. Since the man has been issued a driver's license by his home state and has developed an excellent driving record, one might easily assume the man is able to drive safely. A hyperactive teenager would probably be a greater risk to the insurance company than this man. In the other two cases cited, the insurance companies appear to have only looked at the fact that the individuals had a genetic disorder and seem to have disregarded information concerning stabilized health and good outlooks for the future.

Still other examples of genetic discrimination were given by Blakeslee (1990) and are described as follows:

- A California man was denied health insurance when he changed jobs because he had the *gene* for neurofibromatosis, even though he exhibited no signs of the disease.
- A pregnant Missouri woman underwent a blood screening test which showed that her fetus might have an abnormally formed spinal cord. Although the fetus had a chance of being perfectly normal, her insurance company refused to pay for tests to confirm the findings on the grounds that the fetus had a pre-existing condition.
- A Texas woman was turned down for life and disability insurance because her doctor had noted on records that her mother *might have* died of Huntington's disease. Her mother had never been diagnosed, however.

Because of the possibility of losing their insurance coverage, still other people refuse to be tested for a disease, even though early medical treatment might lessen the effects of the disease.

Even though current practices in the insurance industry seem a bit extreme, they do not compare to possible future discriminatory practices.

The propensity towards dying from many of the leading causes of death in the United States today (heart disease, cancer, diabetes) may be genetically linked, and, when the HGP discovers the implications of more genetic disorders, the potential for discrimination in insurance will dramatically increase. If genetic tests become widely available or required for insurance coverage (or for employment), a large number of people will be tagged as possessing such genes. If insurance companies have access to this information

this discrimination will likely occur since, as has been previously argued, it is economically inefficient to ignore available information which can be efficiently used to better estimate expected losses. People who are unable to obtain health insurance and need health care will be forced to exhaust any money they have and then approach the government as their only hope for survival.

Employers and Genetic Screening

Employers, who are another major provider of health insurance, should also be considered when examining the effect of genetic information on the industry. Of the 250 million Americans with health insurance, 150 million people have health insurance through their employers, about fifteen million people have individual policies, and the rest are covered through Medicare and Medicaid. If only six percent of Americans have individual health insurance policies, one might ask why genetic discrimination in insurance is such a threat to the health care of Americans. Since many people view insurance through employment as almost guaranteed insurance, one might ask why genetic discrimination is such a threat to American health care when only 6 percent of Americans have individual health insurance policies. With 60 percent of Americans relying upon their employers to provide health insurance, any threat to insurance through employment is a threat to the health care of America (Greely, 1992).

Employers pay for health care for their employees through three different methods. In the first method, community rating, the insurer charges each employer an amount per employee that corresponds to the insurer's average costs in that region. The second method, experience rating, differs from the first in that the insurer charges different premiums to different employers depending upon the experience of the employees over the past year or based on the experience of a rolling average of past years. The competitive nature of insurance has lead companies to use experience rating more frequently than community rating. The last method is self-insurance, where the employer takes on the risks instead of the insurer (Greely, 1992).

Although no comprehensive statistics about employment-related health plans exist, evidence from a recent survey shows that self-insurance is the leading method of providing employment-related health coverage. When employers self-insure and select their own employees, they have an incentive to select employees with lower expected health costs. Similarly, employers who pay for health care through experience rating have the same incentive to select employees with lower expected health cost. Since employers are more likely to pay premiums based upon experience rating instead of community rating, most employers are likely to have an incentive to take current and expected future health costs into account in their employment decisions.

For small-sized employers, an employee with large health care costs could make a major difference in operating expenses; thus, these employers would have an especially large incentive to select individuals with lower expected costs. With employers having incentives to genetically discriminate, an even larger problem emerges. Genetically tagged individuals would face unemployment and uninsurability, and the majority of these individuals would therefore be forced to go to the government for help. . . .

SOME RECOMMENDATIONS

After looking at problems regarding the HGP, we can now look at future scenarios in the insurance industry.

One option would be for the industry to continue as usual with the current laws and en-courage insurance companies to use all available information to decide whether or not to accept an individual as a possible risk to write. In this scenario, the number of uninsurable individuals will increase as more genetic tests are developed. If the ADA holds, these individuals will only be able to obtain insurance from their employment or the government (Medicare/Medicaid). If their employers are small, then their coverage could be dropped if the expected costs of the genetic disorders are very large. In this case, an increasing number of individuals will be uninsurable, and the majority will be forced to deplete any savings they have and then seek governmental help as their only option for health care.

The government would have three options. First, the government could refuse to provide health care to these individuals in view of its budgetary and other constraints. This scenario seems unlikely. The second option would be for the government to levy some form of tax, such as an income tax or an employment tax, to pay for health care costs of the "uninsurable" individuals. The main problems with this option are that U.S. citizens will not be happy with more taxes and the cost per covered individual in this program would be very expensive, since the individuals in the pool have higher than average risks. A third option would be for employers to be forced to provide health care to all employees. This would provide coverage to the majority of Americans; however, such a situation would force many small businesses to cease operations because of the large expense of health care.

A second scenario would include the passage of legislation which allows for some type of controlled discrimination but which prohibits insurance companies from discrimination against individuals with specified genetic markers. Such laws already exist in many states with respect to sickle cell disease. Under this plan, adverse selection would be the largest downfall for insurance companies as individuals would know the risks that they face, but the insurance companies would not. Although this legislation would ensure that individuals seeking individual insurance policies could obtain coverage, individuals with group insurance from a small employer would still be in danger of losing their coverage due to the reasons stated previously. To ensure insurance coverage for employees of small firms, the government could develop an insurance pool especially for small employers. The cost of such a program could be fully funded by the small employers using a large risk pooling mechanism (similar to community rating but with larger geographical coverage). No taxes would then need to be imposed upon the general population.

A third option for the insurance industry would be national health care in which the government would insure everyone, and simply allow no discrimination to occur. Although the government's costs for a national health care program would be very large in the beginning, the costs might decrease in the long run if enough preventive care were taken. However, the effect upon the insurance industry would be disastrous. Since only a small number of people would seek individual health policies and since large employers would probably keep their employee health insurance, many insurance companies would be forced into other lines of insurance or into supplementary policy arenas as has happened with the Canadian nationalized health insurance program.

After examining different scenarios, one can see that the future of the U.S. health insurance industry truly lies in the hands of the U.S. government and the HGP. The industry, which has taken a short-term view of the situation, wants to discriminate on the basis of genetic information in order to attain current positive returns; however, in the long run, such discrimination may eventually lead the industry into failure due to the reasons stated previously. The industry's best alternative is to take an active role in the promulgation of rules concerning usage of information from the HGP. Instead of viewing genetic information as another variable to use in discrimination risks, the insurance industry should view genetic information as a better predictor of future costs and use this information to set up more risk pools and calculate reserves more accurately. Accurate rates eliminate moral hazard and adverse selection problems, but may produce affordability problems for insurance for certain individuals. This is where the government can assist certain individuals.

Another important use of genetic information would be preventive care. Insurance companies could develop incentives such as credits for all insureds, and especially those individuals more prone to disease, to take preventive health measures. Insurance companies could give credits for preventive care. For example, people take a defensive driving course to obtain a discount on their automobile insurance and to remove tickets from their records. Although no one likes to take these classes, they do like the discount (or the lack of insurance rate increase in the case of a remaining ticket). A similar situation arises in the health insurance industry as many people only go to the doctor when a problem arises. To reduce long-term costs, insurance companies could require all insureds to have annual physicals and could offer strong financial incentives to encourage those insureds who have genetic disorders to take all measures available to prevent the development of the disorder.

CONCLUSION

The Human Genome Project is an incredible leap forward in scientific technology that is expected to prevent much disease and physical suffering in the world. In the intervening years, however, while researchers work to assume complete accuracy in identifying genetic disorders and develop effective methods to alter defective genes, policies must be established and legislation enacted to protect individuals from a new kind of discrimination as well as invasion of their personal privacy. The information and comments in this paper are meant to provide an overview of the many ramifications of genetic testing as it relates to the insurance industry and to suggest possible solutions.

REFERENCES

1983 (Nov), 'A Polymorphic DNA Marker Genetically Linked to Huntington's Disease', *Nature* **306,** 234.

Billings, Paul: 1988–1989 *Study of the Genetics Study Group* (Cambridge, MA).

Blakeslee, Sandra: (1990, Dec 27), 'Ethicists See Omens of an Era of Genetic Bias', *The New York Times* **B9.**

Greely, Henry T.: 1992, 'Health Insurance, Employment Discrimination, and the Genetics Revolution,' in L. Hood and D. Kevles (eds.), *The Code of Codes: Scientific and Social Issues in The Human Genome Project* (Harvard University Press), pp. 264–280.

Ethical Issues in Electronic Performance Monitoring

G. Stoney Alder

INTRODUCTION

Although it is difficult to identify exactly how many workers are subjected to electronic performance (EPM), there is little doubt that the practice is extensive. Estimates indicate that over 26 million workers are electronically monitored. Between 1990 and 1992 more then 70,000 U.S. companies spent more than $500 million on monitoring software and this figure is expected to exceed $1 billion by 1996. Extensive and growing use of electronic performance monitoring in organizations has resulted in considerable debate between and among politicians, business groups, and employee advocate groups. Advocates of electronic monitoring approach the debate in teleological terms arguing that monitoring benefits organizations, customers, and society. Its critics approach the

issue in deontological terms countering that monitoring is dehumanizing, invades worker privacy, increases stress and worsens health, and decreases work-life quality. In contrast to this win-lose approach, this paper argues that electronic monitoring is inherently value neutral and that an approach which emphasizes communication in the design and implementation of monitoring systems offers a win-win solution that should satisfy both deontological and teleological ethicists. . . .

TELEOLOGICAL ARGUMENTS FOR ELECTRONIC MONITORING

. . . The majority of arguments made in support of electronic performance monitoring have clear utilitarian overtones. The emphasis of such arguments is generally on the

From G. Stoney Alder, "Ethical Issues in Electronic Performance Monitoring: A Consideration of Deontological and Teleological Perspectives." Journal of Business Ethics, 17: 729–743, 1998. Reprinted with permission from Kluwer Academic Publishers.

nonmoral results or benefits of electronic performance monitoring for organizations and society. This is seen clearly in the statements supporters of the Privacy for Consumers and Workers Act made at the Senate hearings concerning the Act.

Richard J. Barry, co-founder/owner of First Security Services Corporation, testified in behalf of Securities Companies Organized for Legislative Action (SCOLA) as follows:

> As it stands now, S. 984 appears to be . . . unnecessarily burdensome especially for small businesses. We agree that protecting consumer and worker privacy in the workplace is wholly important and appropriate. We also believe, however, that those interests must be in balance with the appropriate use of security to protect consumers and workers safety and to safeguard company assets.(Barry, 1993, p. 1)

Michael J. Tamer, president of Teknekron Infoswith Corporation, similarly focuses on the benefits of monitoring. However, he extends his argument to include the positive results that accrue not only to organizations and their employees, but also to society as a whole:

> For these businesses, the ability to evaluate the effectiveness and competitiveness of their call center operations is absolutely critical and this ability is largely dependent upon obtaining reliable quantitative and qualitative data through electronic monitoring . . . U.S. companies have found it increasingly important to perform qualitative and quantitative evaluations in their efforts to compete in a global market place . . . the restrictions [on electronic monitoring] . . . may ultimately preclude initiatives in TQM . . . New job market opportunities . . . have opened up tremendous opportunities for the disabled, the elderly and the working parent. . . . The legislation, if not significantly modified, will adversely affect these job markets. In conclusion, Teknekron Infoswitch believes that when used fairly and ethically, monitoring in the Call Center environment can benefit the employer, the employee, and the customer. (Tamer, 1993, pp. 1–6).

John Gerdelman, Senior Vice President for Consumer Markets of MCI, similarly referred to nonmoral results as justification for electronic performance monitoring. He testified that MCI, "listens in on phone calls to help train operators and ensure the quality of customer service." He further argued that, "Coaching is good, it helps you be a winning team."

Thus, proponents of electronic performance monitoring justify the practice on utilitarian grounds by arguing that it results in the greatest amount of nonmoral good. Considerable empirical and theoretical research support these claims. Effective monitoring has repeatedly been demonstrated to lead to increased productivity, improved quality and service, and decreased costs. MCI, Pacific Bell, and GE have all markedly improved their service through electronic performance monitoring (Gerdelman, 1993). GE, for example, increased its customer satisfaction rate to 96 percent by implementing a telephone surveillance system.

Reduced costs and increased productivity have also been associated with effective electronic performance monitoring. For example, companies that install a call accounting system can expect to reduce phone bills by at least 10 percent and simultaneously increase productivity. After using a call accounting system for one month, a California insurance company realized a productivity increase equivalent to 7.5 man weeks per month which resulted in a 15 percent ($81,000) monthly savings. . . .

DEONTOLOGICAL CONDEMNATION OF EPM

In contrast to business groups, who take a teleological approach to defend the use of technology to monitor worker performance, critics of the practice approach the issue in deontological terms. . . .

Kant articulates a "master" or super ordinate right, the categorical imperative, which dictates how we should always act. . . .

Kant's categorical imperative consists of two primary rules: 1) "Act only on that maxim which you can at the same time will to become a universal law" and 2) "Always act so that you treat humanity, whether in your own person or in another, as an end, and never merely as a means." In essence, humans must never be treated as means to an end but as persons worthy of dignity and respect in themselves.

Kant's perspective heavily influences Werhane (1985) who argues for the consideration of basic human rights which all humans have by virtue of their inherent value. Additionally, these rights are of such importance that they should be respected regardless of other practical interests or benefits. Werhane further contends that consideration of basic rights prevails over teleological concerns with beneficial results by claiming that, "no act of harming another person that reduces his or her freedom can be justified even if it benefits others." . . .

Several deontological arguments in favor of the Privacy for Consumers and Workers Act, and hence against electronic performance monitoring, were voiced to the Senate. An exposition of three testimonials will serve as an example of the flavor of these arguments. First, when introducing the Bill to the Senate, Senator Simon argued that electronic performance monitoring constitutes a serious invasion of privacy:

> As a nation, we have supported laws that protect us from our neighbors and our government spying on us and invading our privacy, everywhere but in the workplace. The United States stands alone with South Africa in failing to protect a worker's rights in this regard . . . it is indeed a sad irony that while the Federal Bureau of Investigation is required by law to obtain a court order to wiretap a conversation, even in cases of national security, employers are permitted to spy at will on their employees and the public (U.S. Senate, Statements on introduced bills and joint resolutions, 1993).

Gwendolyn Johnson, member of the board of directors of the American Nurses Association, similarly referred to privacy concerns as she called for limitations on employers' ability to electronically monitor performance in the name of workers' rights:

> We commend the committee for holding hearings on workplace privacy and applaud Senator Simon's long commitment to protecting the rights of our nation's workers. ANA supports the passage of S. 984. . . . The Bill addresses three factors of particular concern to nurses: 1) the intrusive, invasive nature of electronic monitoring; 2) the growth in technology that will continue to make new forms of monitoring available; and 3) the added stress to employees who are subjected to electronic monitoring . . . This practice is discriminatory, invades privacy, raises sexual harassment concerns and is clearly unacceptable . . . ANA believes that workplace privacy issues must be vigilantly monitored.

In addition to this familiar concern with electronic monitoring, Johnson indicated that the practice may violate workers's basic rights by jeopardizing their health:

> These Orwellian technological advances have given rise to the need for regulations and systems to protect the health and safety of health care workers . . . For nurses, who are working daily under the pressure of providing care in life and death situations, the added stress of wondering who is watching them change clothes, or similar invasions of privacy is unnecessarily burdensome. We believe that those practices should be illegal (Johnson, 1993).

Barbara Easterling, secretary treasurer of the Communications Workers of America, similarly raised concerns for the harm electronic performance monitoring can do to employees by raising anxiety levels:

A typical operator handles more than 1,100 calls in 7½ hour shift . . . The operator is required to complete each call in 30 seconds or less. The emphasis on quantitative measurement places operators in the anxiety producing dilemma of having to choose between performing their duties in a manner that satisfies the needs of the public or attaining the average work time dictated by company computer (Austin, 1993).

Senator Simon likewise called attention to the fact that electronic performance monitoring may violate basic human rights by resulting in health problems:

The stress that these employees experience should not be overlooked . . . workplace stress cost this country an estimated $50 billion dollars per year in health costs and lost productivity . . . In many ways, electronic monitoring acts as an electronic whip that drives the fast pace of today's workplace in the growing service industry. Electronically monitored employees . . . must carry out repetitive duties that require rigorous attention to detail, executed under the stress of constant supervision and the demand for a faster output. Unrestrained surveillance of workers has turned many modern offices into electronic sweatshops (U.S. Senate, Statements on introduced bills and joint resolutions, 1993).

These senate testimonials clearly indicate that opponents of electronic monitoring take a deontological approach to the debate by arguing that the practice causes harm to and violates basic rights of employees. . . .

Opponents of electronic performance monitoring often frame their argument in terms that closely parallel deontological ethics. Specifically, they argue that electronic monitoring violates workers' rights by invading their privacy, increasing their stress levels and worsening their health, dehumanizing them, and decreasing their work-life quality. However, close examination of these arguments and the evidence that supports them reveals that these are, in reality, criticisms of the use of electronic performance monitoring and not of electronic performance monitoring in and of itself. Thus, it would appear that electronic monitoring, like many other management practices, is an inherently neutral tool that may be utilized ethically or unethically. Thus, conversation should focus not on whether monitoring is ethical or unethical but rather on how monitoring technology may be utilized ethically. The next section will highlight how a communicative approach may facilitate organizations' ability to utilize electronic monitoring technology ethically.

COMMUNICATIVE-ETHICAL APPROACH TO EPM

Two major phases should be considered when organizations utilize electronic technology to monitor their workers: design and implementation. Thus, this section argues that the difference between ethical and unethical electronic monitoring is found in the way organizations design and implement the system. Specifically, it is argued that a communicative-ethical approach which emphasizes communication in the design and implementation of monitoring systems offers a solution to the monitoring dilemma that should satisfy both deontological and teleological ethicists. As described below, the communicative-ethical approach to monitoring advanced here requires that organizations emphasize four communication-related processes when designing and implementing monitoring systems. First, employees subjected to monitoring should be permitted to communicate their preferences and give input into the design of the system. Second, organizations should fully communicate monitoring-related practices and inform employees when monitoring occurs. Third, organizations need to supplement electronic feedback with face-to-face human feedback. Finally, steps should be taken to ensure that such feedback is supportive and non-punitive. Each of these four processes will be discussed as they relate to the design or implementation of an electronic monitoring system.

When first conceptualizing an electronic performance monitoring system, management should communicate with, and seek input from, those employees who will be affected by the system. DeTienne and Abbott (1993) argue that electronic monitoring systems are more successful when employees are allowed to provide input into the design of the system because they are more likely to accept and support the system. The Office of Technology Assessment similarly discovered that when workers had the opportunity to participate in the design and implementation of computer monitoring systems, they were more likely to focus on the positive aspects of its use. In addition to leading to greater success, this approach is also more ethical because it values individual input and recognizes that those subject to monitoring have needs and desires. In essence, it recognizes and respects their innate human value rather than objectifying, manipulating, and devaluing them. Although employee input regarding the technical aspects of the system may prove of little value, organizations should seek input regarding the standards to be associated with electronic monitoring as well as the scope of activities to be subject to monitoring.

Monitoring is usually accompanied by performance standards to assess employee performance. When these standards are unrealistically high, increased stress may result. In fact, much of the criticism against electronic performance monitoring is that it is frequently used in connection with unrealistic standards. . . .

In contrast, employee input may enable organizations to establish more realistic performance standards and provide for more ethical monitoring by reducing stress. This is consistent with Nebeker and Tatum's (1993) studies of the effects of monitoring under different levels of performance standards and rewards. These investigations led Nebeker and Tatum to conclude that with a combination of high standards and no rewards or easy standards when rewards are offered, computer monitoring may result in increased productivity, satisfaction, and reduced stress all at the same time.

Employee input should also be sought regarding the scope of activities to be subject to monitoring. As discussed previously, several organizations utilize electronic technology to monitor private, personal activities such as personal phone calls, dressing rooms activities, and the number of trips to the bathroom. It was also argued previously that such monitoring may constitute an invasion of privacy and dehumanize workers. However, DeTienne and Abbott (1993) argue that, "the level of management oversight employee desire differs greatly." Consequently, "an effective electronic monitoring system must be designed with the level of management oversight employees need, and will tolerate, in mind." Based on this assertion, they argue that the first question a systems developer must ask is what type of system is appropriate for the employees who will be subject to it.

Along these lines, it is conceivable that the activities that should be protected from monitoring will differ greatly depending on the particular employee group and environmental context. For example, if an organization's bathrooms and/or locker rooms have been subject to significant amounts of violent crime or theft, it is possible that employees will tolerate, and even desire, monitoring in those locations. Thus, soliciting employee input regarding the scope of activities and locations to be covered by monitoring should enable organizations to implement more ethical monitoring which both respects worker privacy and fulfills their needs.

In addition to soliciting input from employees regarding performance standards and the scope of monitoring, organizations should communicate with employees regarding monitoring. This includes informing potential and current employees that the organization performs electronic monitoring, what is monitored, and how the information obtained from monitoring is used by the firm. This is essential to ethical monitoring because electronic monitoring that is done without the knowledge or consent of workers devalues and marginalizes employees by denying them the right to avoid surveillance. In addition, organizations should inform employees when, in fact, they are being monitored. This is crucial because silent or covert monitoring may violate workers' basic right to privacy. Indeed, critics of covert monitoring claim it is tantamount to spying, creates an atmosphere of mistrust, and intrudes on employee privacy. . . .

Computers may be used to provide workers with performance feedback through computerized messages such as "You are not working as fast as the person next to you" (DeTienne and Abbott, 1993). However, when feedback is provided in this manner, it is dehumanizing and unethical because it eliminates human interaction between employees and supervisors and replaces it with one-way mechanized messages between workers and the computer. However, when supplemented with human interaction and face-to-face communication between workers and supervisors, electronic performance monitoring may be humanizing and ethical. Aiello (1993) found that the monitored workers he investigated experienced increased stress because they felt lonelier. This clearly may occur when monitoring reduces human contact, but when human contact is maintained, this affect could be eliminated or at least minimized.

In addition to supplementing computer feedback with face-to-face supervisory feedback, ethical organizations should ensure

that this communication is supportive and non-threatening. . . .

Senge . . . discusses the importance of dialogue to group and organizational effectiveness. According to Senge, there are two primary types of discourse, dialogue and discussion. Participants in discussion are concerned with, "heaving ideas back and forth in a winner-take-all competition." The purpose of discussion, in essence, is to win by having your point of view prevail. Dialogue, in contrast, is concerned, not with winning, but with "thinking together," moving beyond individual views, and doing things right. Senge indicates that three basic conditions are essential to effective dialogue: 1. all participants must "suspend" their assumptions, literally hold them "as if suspended before us"; 2. all participants must regard one another as colleagues; and 3. there must be a facilitator who "holds the context" for dialogue.

These conceptualizations of dialogue have clear implications regarding both the source and type of feedback provided in connection with electronic monitoring. Feedback consisting of one-way computerized messages is clearly characteristic of both monologue and discussion as it is non-personal, focuses exclusively on the message sent to the employee, and provides no opportunity for the employees to respond to the message. As a result, there is no "thinking together" or moving beyond individual views.

Similarly, punitive feedback resembles monologue as its purpose is to command and coerce. Punitive feedback is also characteristic of discussion because it is driven by supervisor assumptions and violates dialogue's demand for colleagueship. In essence, when electronic technology is used as the sole source of feedback or when monitoring is used in connection with punitive, threatening feedback, it serves to classify, measure, and analyze workers as objects, not as whole people. It is dehumanizing and unethical. In contrast, when electronic monitoring is supplemented with supportive, human interaction and feedback, it is characteristic of the dialogical approach to communication and is ethical because it is supportive, values workers, and demonstrates genuine interest in their development.

Dialogical perspectives, then, indicate that feedback should not come primarily from computers or be punitive or threatening. Instead, feedback should include personal interaction and be supportive. Its primary aim should be to train, coach, and develop workers in order to help them attain their maximum potential. The approach several organizations take to electronic performance monitoring is exemplary in this regard. MCI, for example, utilizes monitoring to help train and coach its customer service representatives and claims that it helps provide immediate feedback essential to effective training (Gerdelman, 1993). General Electric similarly credits much of its 96 percent customer satisfaction rate to its telephone surveillance system which emphasizes communication between "coaches" and employees. Finally, a California insurance company used a telephone accounting system for one month and subsequently communicated the results to its employees. Although the company took no disciplinary action, the system resulted in dramatic cost savings and productivity increases.

Thus, positive communication in both system design and implementation is the key to ethical electronic performance monitoring. When organizations involve those who will be subjected to monitoring in its design, inform them of monitoring, supplement electronic feedback with human interaction, and provide supportive, non-punitive feedback, they overcome many of the deontological objections to electronic performance monitoring without losing the organizational or societal benefits of monitoring. . . .

CONCLUSION

The extensive and growing use of electronic performance monitoring in organizations has resulted in considerable debate. However, several problems inherent to this debate preclude it from generating any solid conclusions. Consequently, the debate is likely to continue for years to come. For example, proponents for both sides of the issue focus almost exclusively on their own agenda and refuse to consider the entire picture. Advocates of electronic monitoring, for example, employ teleological arguments and focus on the benefits of electronic monitoring that accrue to businesses, customers, society, and, to a limited extent, employees. However, in raising these arguments, they almost completely ignore deontological arguments and employee rights. Critics of electronic monitoring, in contrast, use deontological arguments and focus on the potential electronic monitoring has to violate employee rights. Specifically, they argue that electronic monitoring violates workers' rights by invading their privacy, increasing their stress levels and worsening their health, dehumanizing them, and decreasing their work-life quality. However, in raising these arguments, they fail to acknowledge the power electronic monitoring has to result in many positive outcomes for workers, organizations, and society.

In contrast to these approaches, this paper argues that electronic performance monitoring is not inherently ethical or unethical. Monitoring is one of many management tools (such as performance reviews or compensations systems) that, although inherently value neutral, may be used ethically or unethically. Thus, conversation should focus not on whether monitoring is ethical or unethical but rather on how monitoring technology may be utilized ethically. The communicative-ethical approach outlined here indicates that communication in both system design and implementation is the key to ethical electronic performance monitoring and offers four rules for ethical monitoring: 1) involve those who will be subjected to monitoring in the systems design, 2) inform employees of monitoring practices, 3) supplement electronic feedback with human interaction, and 4) make feedback supportive, non-punitive, and non-coercive. Adherence to these four rules for ethical monitoring eliminates many of the deontological objections to electronic performance monitoring while simultaneously preserving the benefits monitoring provides employees, organizations, and society. Thus, a communicative-ethical approach to electronic monitoring considers both deontological and teleological perspectives and offers a solution that is potentially acceptable to both employee advocacy groups and business groups.

REFERENCES

Aiello, J. R.: 1993, Computer-based Work Monitoring: Electronic Surveillance and its Effects', *Journal of Applied Social Psychology* **23**, 499–507.

Austin, J. B.: 1993, 'Simon Bill would Curb Monitoring of Workers', *Chicago Sun Times* (Wednesday, 23 June 1993), (N) 23.

Barry, R. J.: 1993, Statement on behalf of Security Companies Organized for Legislative Action (SCOLA) before the senate labor and human resources subcommittee on employment and productivity, United States Senate, 22 June 1993.

DeTienne, K. B. and N. T. Abbott: 1993, 'Developing an Employee Centered Electronic Monitoring System', *Journal of Systems Management* **44**, 12.

Gerdelman, J.: 1993, Statement before the Subcommittee on Employment and Productivity, Committee on Labor and Human Resources, United States Senate, 22 June 1993.

Johnson, G.: 1993, Testimony of the American Nurses Association before the senate labor and human resources subcommittee on employment and productivity, United States Senate, 22 June 1993.

Nebeker, D. M. and C. B. Tatum: 1993, 'The Effects of Computer Monitoring, Standards, and Rewards on Work Performance, Job Satisfaction, and Stress', *Journal of Applied Social Psychology* **23**, 508–536.

Tamer, M. J.: 1993, Statement Before the Senate Labor and Human Resources Subcommittee on Employment and Productivity, United States Senate, 22 June 1993.

U.S. Senate, Statements on Introduced Bills and Joint Resolutions: 1993, 139 Congressional Record S6121–02.

Werhane, P.: 1985, *Persons, Rights, and Corporations* (Prentice-Hall, Englewood Cliffs, NJ).

WHISTLEBLOWING

Whistleblowing and Employee Loyalty

Ronald Duska

There are proponents on both sides of the issue — those who praise whistleblowers as civic heroes and those who condemn them as "finks." Maxwell Glen and Cody Shearer, who wrote about the whistleblowers at Three Mile Island say, "Without the *courageous* breed of assorted company insiders known as whistle-blowers — workers who often risk their livelihoods to disclose information about construction and design flaws — the Nuclear Regulatory Commission itself would be nearly as idle as Three Mile Island. . . . That whistleblowers deserve both gratitude and protection is beyond disagreement."[1]

Still, while Glen and Shearer praise whistleblowers, others vociferously condemn them. For example, in a now infamous quote, James Roche, the former president of General Motors said:

> Some critics are now busy eroding another support of free enterprise — the loyalty of a management team, with its unifying values and cooperative work. Some of the enemies of business now encourage an employee to be *disloyal* to the enterprise. They want to create suspicion and disharmony, and pry into the proprietary interests of the business. However this is labeled — industrial espionage, whistle blowing, or professional responsibility — it is another tactic for spreading disunity and creating conflict.[2]

From Roche's point of view, not only is whistleblowing not "courageous" and not deserving of "gratitude and protection" as Glen and Shearer would have it, it is corrosive and impermissible.

Discussions of whistleblowing generally revolve around three topics: (1) attempts to define whistleblowing more precisely, (2) debates about whether and when whistleblowing is permissible, and (3) debates about whether and when one has an obligation to blow the whistle.

In this paper I want to focus on the second problem, because I find it somewhat disconcerting that there is a problem at all. When I first looked into the ethics of whistleblowing it seemed to me that whistleblowing was a good thing, and yet I found in the literature claim after claim that it was in need of defense, that there was something wrong with it, namely that it was an act of disloyalty.

If whistleblowing is a disloyal act, it deserves disapproval, and ultimately any action of whistleblowing needs justification. This disturbs me. It is as if the act of a good Samaritan is being condemned as an act of interference, as if the prevention of a suicide needs to be justified.

In his book *Business Ethics*, Norman Bowie claims that "whistleblowing . . . violate(s) a *prima facie* duty of loyalty to one's employer." According to Bowie, there is a duty of loyalty that prohibits one from reporting his employer or company. Bowie, of course, recognizes that this is only a *prima facie* duty, that is, one that can be overridden by a higher duty to the public good. Nevertheless, the axiom that whistleblowing is disloyal is Bowie's starting point.[3]

Bowie is not alone. Sissela Bok sees "whistleblowing" as an instance of disloyalty:

> The whistleblower hopes to stop the game; but since he is neither referee nor coach, and since he blows the whistle on his own team, his act is seen as a *violation of loyalty*. In holding his position, he has assumed certain obligations to his colleagues and clients. He may even have subscribed to a loyalty oath or a promise of confidentiality. . . . Loyalty to colleagues and to clients comes to be pitted against loyalty to the public interest, to those who may be injured unless the revelation is made.[4]

Bowie and Bok end up defending whistleblowing in certain contexts, so I don't necessarily disagree with their conclusions. However, I fail to see how one has an obligation of loyalty to one's company, so I disagree with their perception of the problem and their starting point. I want to argue that one does not have an obligation of loyalty to a company, even a *prima facie* one, because companies are not the kind of things that are properly objects of loyalty. To make them objects of loyalty gives them a moral status they do not deserve and in raising their status, one lowers the status of the individuals who work for the companies. Thus, the difference in perception is important because those who think employees have an obligation of loyalty to a company fail to take into account a relevant moral difference between persons and corporations.

But why aren't companies the kind of things that can be objects of loyalty? To answer that we have to ask what are proper objects of loyalty. John Ladd states the problem this way, "Granted that loyalty is the wholehearted devotion to an object of some kind, what kind of thing is the object? Is it an abstract entity, such as an idea or a collective being? Or is it a person or group of persons?"[5] Philosophers fall into three camps on the question. On one side are the idealists who hold that loyalty is devotion to something more than persons, to some cause or abstract entity. On the other side are what Ladd calls "social atomists," and these include empiricists and utilitarians, who think that at most one can only be loyal to individuals and that loyalty can ultimately be explained away as some other obligation that holds between two people. Finally, there is a moderate position that holds that although idealists go too far in postulating some super-personal entity as an object of loyalty, loyalty is still an important and real relation that holds between people, one that cannot be dismissed by reducing it to some other relation.

There does seem to be a view of loyalty that is not extreme. According to Ladd, "'loyalty' is taken to refer to a relationship between persons — for instance, between a lord and his vassal, between a parent and his children, or between friends. Thus the object of loyalty is ordinarily taken to be a person or a group of persons."[6]

But this raises a problem that Ladd glosses over. There is a difference between a person or a group of persons, and aside from in-

stances of loyalty that relate two people such as lord/vassal, parent/child, or friend/friend, there are instances of loyalty relating a person to a group, such as a person to his family, a person to this team, and a person to his country. Families, countries, and teams are presumably groups of persons. They are certainly ordinarily construed as objects of loyalty.

But to what am I loyal in such a group? In being loyal to the group am I being loyal to the whole group or to its members? It is easy to see the object of loyalty in the case of an individual person. It is simply the individual. But to whom am I loyal in a group? To whom am I loyal in a family? Am I loyal to each and every individual or to something larger, and if to something larger, what is it? We are tempted to think of a group as an entity of its own, an individual in its own right, having an identity of its own.

To avoid the problem of individuals existing for the sake of the group, the atomists insist that a group is nothing more than the individuals who comprise it, nothing other than a mental fiction by which we refer to a group of individuals. It is certainly not a reality or entity over and above the sum of its parts, and consequently is not a proper object of loyalty. Under such a position, of course, no loyalty would be owed to a company because a company is a mere mental fiction, since it is a group. One would have obligations to the individual members of the company, but one could never be justified in overriding those obligations for the sake of the "group" taken collectively. A company has no moral status except in terms of the individual members who comprise it. It is not a proper object of loyalty. But the atomists go too far. Some groups, such as a family, do have a reality of their own, whereas groups of people walking down the street do not. From Ladd's point of view the social atomist is wrong because he fails to recognize the kinds of groups that are held together by "the ties that bind." The atomist tries to reduce these groups to simple sets of individuals bound together by some externally imposed criteria. This seems wrong.

There do seem to be groups in which the relationships and interactions create a new force or entity. A group takes on an identity and a reality of its own that is determined by its purpose, and this purpose defines the various relationships and roles set up within the group. There is a division of labor into roles necessary for the fulfillment of the purposes of the group. The membership, then, is not of individuals who are the same but of individuals who have specific relationships to one another determined by the aim of the group. Thus we get specific relationships like parent/child, coach/player, and so on, that don't occur in other groups. It seems then that an atomist account of loyalty that restricts loyalty merely to individuals and does not include loyalty to groups might be inadequate.

But once I have admitted that we can have loyalty to a group, do I not open myself up to criticism from the proponent of loyalty to the company? Might not the proponent of loyalty to business say: "Very well. I agree with you. The atomists are short-sighted. Groups have some sort of reality and they can be proper objects of loyalty. But companies are groups. Therefore companies are proper objects of loyalty."

The point seems well taken, except for the fact that the kinds of relationships that loyalty requires are just the kind that one does not find in business. As Ladd says, "The ties that bind the persons together provide the basis of loyalty." But all sorts of ties bind people together. I am a member of a group of fans if I go to a ball game. I am a member of a group if I merely walk down the street. What binds people together in a business is not sufficient to require loyalty.

A business or corporation does two things in the free enterprise system: It produces a good or service and it makes a profit. The making of a profit, however, is the primary function of a business as a business, for if the production of the good or service is not profitable, the business would be out of business. Thus nonprofitable goods or services are a means to an end. People bound together in a business are bound together not for mutual fulfillment and support, but to divide labor or make a profit. Thus, while we can jokingly refer to a family as a place where "they have to take you in no matter what," we cannot refer to a company in that way. If a worker does not produce in a company or if cheaper laborers are available, the company — in order to fulfill its purpose — should get rid of the worker. A company feels no obligation of loyalty. The saying "You can't buy loyalty" is true. Loyalty depends on ties that demand self-sacrifice with no expectation of reward. Business functions on the basis of enlightened self-interest. I am devoted to a company not because it is like a parent to me; it is not. Attempts of some companies to create "one big happy family" ought to be looked on with suspicion. I am not devoted to it at all, nor should I be. I work for it because it pays me. I am not in a family to get paid, I am in a company to get paid.

The cold hard truth is that the goal of profit is what gives birth to a company and forms that particular group. Money is what ties the group together. But in such a commercialized venture, with such a goal, there is no loyalty, or at least none need be expected. An employer will release an employee and an employee will walk away from an employer when it is profitable for either one to do so.

Not only is loyalty to a corporation not required, it more than likely is misguided. There is nothing as pathetic as the story of the loyal employee who, having given above and beyond the call of duty, is let go in the restructuring of the company. He feels betrayed because he mistakenly viewed the company as an object of his loyalty. Getting rid of such foolish romanticism and coming to grips with this hard but accurate assessment should ultimately benefit everyone.

To think we owe a company or corporation loyalty requires us to think of that company as a person or as a group with a goal of human fulfillment. If we think of it in this way we can be loyal. But this is the wrong way to think. A company is not a person. A company is an instrument, and an instrument with a specific purpose, the making of profit. To treat an instrument as an end in itself, like a person, may not be as bad as treating an end as an instrument, but it does give the instrument a moral status it does not deserve; and by elevating the instrument we lower the end. All things, instruments and ends, become alike.

Remember that Roche refers to the "management team" and Bok sees the name "whistleblowing" coming from the instance of a referee blowing a whistle in the presence of a foul. What is perceived as bad about whistleblowing in business from this perspective is that one blows the whistle on one's own team, thereby violating team loyalty. If the company can get its employees to view it as a team they belong to, it is easier to demand loyalty. Then the rules governing teamwork and team loyalty will apply. One reason the appeal to a team and team loyalty works so well in business is that businesses are in competition with one another. Effective motivation turns business practices into a game and instills teamwork.

But businesses differ from teams in very important respects, which makes the analogy between business and a team dangerous. Loyalty to a team is loyalty within the context of sport or a competition. Teamwork and team loyalty require that in the circumscribed activity of the game I cooperate with my fellow players, so that pulling all together, we may win. The object of (most) sports is victory. But winning in sports is a social convention, divorced from the usual goings on of society. Such a winning is most times a harmless, morally neutral diversion.

But the fact that this victory in sports, within the rules enforced by a referee (whistleblower), is a socially developed convention taking place within a larger social context makes it quite different from competition in business, which, rather than being defined by a context, permeates the whole of society in its influence. Competition leads not only to victory but to losers. One can lose at sport with precious few consequences. The consequences of losing at business are much larger. Further, the losers in business can be those who are not in the game voluntarily (we are all forced to participate) but who are still affected by business decisions. People cannot choose to participate in business. It permeates everyone's lives.

The team model, then, fits very well with the model of the free market system, because there competition is said to be the name of the game. Rival companies compete and their object is to win. To call a foul on one's own teammate is to jeopardize one's chances of winning and is viewed as disloyalty.

But isn't it time to stop viewing corporate machinations as games? These games are not controlled and are not ended after a specific time. The activities of business affect the lives of everyone, not just the game players. The analogy of the corporation to a team and the consequent appeal to team loyalty, although understandable, is seriously misleading, at least in the moral sphere where competition is not the prevailing virtue.

If my analysis is correct, the issue of the permissibility of whistleblowing is not a real issue since there is no obligation of loyalty to a company. Whistleblowing is not only permissible but expected when a company is harming society. The issue is not one of disloyalty to the company, but of whether the whistleblower has an obligation to society if blowing the whistle will bring him retaliation.

NOTES

1. Maxwell Glen and Cody Shearer, "Going After the Whistle-blowers," *Philadelphia Inquirer*, Tuesday, August 2, 1983, Op-ed page, p. 11A.

2. James M. Roche, "The Competitive System, to Work, to Preserve, and to Protect," *Vital Speeches of the Day* (May 1971): 445.

3. Norman Bowie, *Business Ethics* (Englewood Cliffs, N.J.: Prentice Hall, 1982), pp. 140–143.

4. Sissela Bok, "Whistleblowing and Professional Responsibilities," *New York University Education Quarterly* 2 (1980): 3.

5. John Ladd, "Loyalty," *The Encyclopedia of Philosophy* 5: 97.

6. Ibid.

Whistleblowing and Trust: Some Lessons from the ADM Scandal

Daryl Koehn

The 1980s witnessed a flurry of articles regarding the ethics of whistleblowing. These articles tended to focus on three issues: (1) the definition of whistleblowing; (2) whether and when it was permissible to violate one's obligations of loyalty to colleagues or one's profession/corporation; and (3) whether a threat to the public interest actually obligates someone with knowledge of this threat to make this knowledge public.[1] These same issues have surfaced in recent discussions of the act of whistleblowing by Mark Whitacre at Archer Daniels Midland. While I do not think these three issues are morally irrelevant to a discussion of whistleblowing, I am troubled by the fact that the entire discussion to date has focused on the issue of duty. In this commentary, I want to focus less on the question of duty and more on the question of personal, corporate, and public trust: Does whistleblowing foster or destroy moral trust? What makes whistleblowers and the companies for whom they work worthy of employee and public trust?

I shall use the alleged events at ADM to explore these questions. The reader should keep in mind that I am not writing a case history of whistleblowing at ADM. At the time of this writing, we have yet to hear much of the company's side of the story nor do we know exactly what evidence Whitacre has to support his allegation that the company engaged in price-fixing with their competitors. What matters for my purposes here is not that these events did occur but that they could have occurred and they raise serious and interesting questions for corporate, individual and public behavior.

Reprinted with permission of *The Online Journal of Ethics*, http://www.stthom.edu/cbes.

PART ONE: WHISTLEBLOWING AND ITS EFFECTS ON TRUST

It will be helpful to begin with a working definition of a whistleblower. Following Sisela Bok, I shall define whistleblowers as persons who "sound an alarm from within the very organization in which they work, aiming to spotlight neglect or abuses that threaten the public interest.[2] Several features of this definition are relevant to thinking about trust. First, the whistleblower claims to be acting in the public interest. He or she tries to occupy the moral highground by calling attention to some matter the whistleblower thinks the public will be, or should be, concerned about. I say "concerned about" rather than simply "interested in" because the whislte-blower claims to be more than a mere tattler. If I were to disclose the religious preferences of my boss, we would not think such disclosure constituted whistleblowing because it is hard to see what public interest is involved. Given the very real risks of being fired, demoted, ostracized, or attacked by those the whistleblower is accusing of negligence or abuse, the whistleblowers generally must think of themselves as on something akin to a mission. They try to portray themselves as acting on behalf of an interest higher than their own — the public interest.

I dwell on this point to emphasize that the whistleblower has made some assumptions as to what constitutes the public interest. He may have erred in his assessment of the nature of the public interest. Or he may have misevaluated his "facts." The facts may be unsound, or they may be sound yet irrelevant to the public interest. If we take trust as the trustor's belief that he or she is the recipient of the good will of the trusted party, the whistleblower can be thought of as portraying himself as a trustworthy person who has acted in good will toward the public and who merits the public's trust. Mark Whitacre, for ex-

ample, portrayed himself as the white knight of the consumer, a consumer whom ADM had allegedly declared to be the enemy.[3] However, if Whitacre's accusations result in the demise of ADM and the loss of a major supplier of consumer goods, we may well wonder whether Whitacre has acted in fact in the public's interest. Moreover, Whitacre himself arguably has something of a skewed view of public interest since he seems perfectly willing to engage in predatory, monopolistic pricing.[4] According to his own account, he balked at his company's pricing policy only when his colleagues tried to engage in price-fixing.[5] Given that the customer is hurt by monopolistic pricing as well as price-fixing, his whistleblowing at this late date may be less an attempt to aid the customer and the public than to save his own skin. More generally, if and when a whistleblower's motives are mixed, we have some reason to wonder, on the one hand, whether he is trustworthy and, on the other hand, to perhaps be more sympathetic to a company who charges that the whistleblower has betrayed it and the public as well.

Second, the whistleblower believes that there is a substantial audience who will attend to her disclosures. If an employee calls up the press and discloses that the CEO wears blue shirts to work every day, his announcement is likely to be greeted by the reporter with a stifled yawn, if not a burst of profanity. To say that the whistleblower's disclosure is in the public interest just is to say that it has the makings of a good story. The tale, therefore, will likely attract the press and maybe the regulatory authorities as well. It can quickly become sensationalized as people begin to speculate on the extent and magnitude of the alleged corporate misconduct. Furthermore, the regulatory authorities may begin an elaborate investigation on the theory that any abuse known by one individual may just be the tip of the iceberg. The Federal authorities, for example, are not merely sub-poenaeing many of ADM's records; they have also asked for the records of many of ADM's competitors.[6] There is a very real danger of a witchhunt, for as Bok reminds us, secret police almost always rely on informers and have a history of widening the charges against those accused.[7] Such reflections suggest that it is incumbent upon a whistleblower who truly wants to merit the public's trust to try to explore issues internally before going public with her accusations.

There are, of course, difficulties associated with going public internally. I shall say more about these shortly. My point here is that whistleblowing may harm public trust in our institutions, rather than restore it, if whistle-blowing creates a whirlwind of suspicion and the impression that corruption is everywhere. Fellow employees of whistleblowers may be justifiably irritated at a colleague who makes accusations to the press without ever running these same charges by them or without seeking their interpretation of actions and events within the corporation. It may be unfair for the corporation to try to dismiss a whistle-blower as a troublemaker with few social skills. On the other hand, the whistleblower may very well be someone who is overly suspicious or inclined to make wild accusations without verifying her facts. Moreover, if the whistleblower does not try to work internally first to try to resolve what she perceives as a problem, it is difficult to see how she can claim to be trying to right the problem. It is striking that Whitacre, by his own account, had heard allegations of price-fixing for many years and had simply ignored them,[8] treating them as though they were someone else's problem. But if he really cared for the company and for the public interest, why did he not investigate these charges when he first heard them? Given that he was in line to be president of ADM, he surely should have worried about this problem and taken steps to

address a problem that he was bound to inherit. Conversely, one wonders why he would have wanted to be president of a company that was in his judgment engaged in dastardly deeds. At a minimum, it seems as though he should have interested himself many years ago in the question of whether and why ADM had a history of tolerating price-fixing.

Another way of putting the point is as follows: Whistleblowers are part and parcel of the corporate culture on which they blow the whistle. They are often rather senior because it is those issuing orders who usually have the most control over and the most knowledge about what is occurring within the corporation. At the point of public disclosure, the whistleblower assigns responsibility for the abuse to someone else and thereby distances himself from any responsibility. But matters are rarely so clean. If one has worked many years for a company, taken a salary from them, followed their policies, then one is arguably complicitous in the practices of that corporation. The traditional discussion of whistle-blowing pits the individual's loyalty to the company against his loyalty to himself. But this formulation presupposes that that self is a private self, totally independent of the company. I am saying that the self is a company self as well. And while it may be convenient for the whistleblower to talk as though it is him against the big bad company, such talk is suspect to the extent that the whistleblower has supported the company. Blowing the whistle may not increase public trust to the extent the public is rightly suspicious of the whistleblower's own history within the corporation.

Third, the whistleblower is levelling an accusation of neglect or abuse at particular persons within the corporation. These accusations are not pleasant for the accused whose lives may be permanently disrupted by what may turn out to be false charges. At a minimum, the lives of the accused will be unsettled for a substantial amount of time as the press picks up the story and as investigations run their course. While no one should be above the law, we also should not be insensitive to the need for due process. We should also remember that passions almost always run high around whistleblowers' accusations because the whistleblower's charge applies to present activities of a corporation or profession.[9] No one blows the whistle or shows much interest in past abuses with few present effects or in remote, unlikely future events. The alleged danger is present and a person's emotions are engaged, which is all the more reason for exercising extreme caution in making charges and in evaluating them.

The above observations suggest that corporate employees and leaders rightly are concerned about the effect of whistleblowing not merely on corporate morale but on the ability of employees to work together in relative harmony. This harmony becomes close to impossible when the atmosphere is a highly charged one of mutual suspicion. Note that I am not saying that an employee has an overriding loyalty of duty to the group for which he works. It may well be, as Ronald Duska has argued, that the corporation is not the kind of group to which one can be loyal.[10] In any case, there is no prima facie duty to be loyal to any group. A profession such as medicine is worth serving not because it is a group but because its end — the health of individuals — is a genuine good. The end, not the group per se, commands group members' loyalty. We do not, for example, say that agents have a prima facie duty to the Ku Klux Klan or the mafia. The person who leaves such a group does not override a prima facie duty. Rather, there never was a duty to be a part of a group engaged in unethical behavior.

My point then is not that the employee acts wrongly because whistleblowing is disloyal. The wrongness in the whistleblowing consists instead in acting to destroy work-place atmosphere if and when this destruction could have been avoided by adopting a less accusatory stance or by working within the corporation. Whistleblowing may destroy trust. And trust within a corporation is good when the trust is a reasoned trust, born of open and probing discussions with one's peers regarding matters of joint concern. Whistleblowing should be evaluated in light of its consequences for this reasoned trust not in light of its effects on irrational loyalty or its relation to a non-existent prima facie duty of group loyalty.

PART TWO: RESPONSIBILITIES OF BOTH WHISTLEBLOWER AND CORPORATION

This last comment raises what I take to be the central moral issue connected with whistleblowing: What can both whistleblower and corporation do to foster reasoned trust and to avoid a situation in which employees feel they have to go outside the company to get their concerns addressed?

Given the very real dangers associated with whistleblowing and the all-too-human propensities toward self-righteousness and misinterpretation, it is clear that the would-be whistleblower and corporation alike should make every effort to discuss perceived abuses and negligence before it gets to the point where the whistleblower thinks a public accusation must be made. The corporation thus has a responsibility to provide a regular forum for free and open discussion of possible abuses. Participants should have equal and reciprocal rights to question one another, to bring evidence, etc. They should not be penalized in any way for participation in this forum. It is striking that ADM had no such forum. In fact, communication was so bad within the company that the CEO's own son apparently did not know until after the fact that the father had called in the FBI to help investigate whether production at ADM was being sabotaged.[11]

Conversely, the whistleblower must be willing to come forward and be identified. It is close to impossible for the accused to mount a defense or even seek clarification when the accuser is anonymous. This requirement to publicly participate increases the odds that the would-be whistleblower will doublecheck her facts before going public. Discussion will also tend to dispel employees' perception that corruption is everywhere. In fact, regular discussion should deflate a good deal of the anger and anxiety regarding corporate problems. Employees will come to see that, yes, their corporation has problems and oversights but, yes, their corporation is routinely and professionally addressing these difficulties. Participation in such a forum will require a good deal of courage on the part of employees and a good bit of restraint on the part of a corporate hierarchy tempted to retaliate against any and all perceived threats.

Second, it is incumbent on corporate leadership to examine the tasks they impose on their employees. An employee can only be morally required to do that which is possible. If the employee is placed in an untenable position, than he will feel anxious, trapped, and may be driven to try to escape from this position by taking his predicament public in an effort to gain public sympathy and support. Whitacre, for example, apparently was expected to do cutrate pricing with a view to grabbing a large market share while at the same time showing either minimal losses or a profit.[12] Price-fixing becomes a temptation in a corporate environment with these unreasonable expectations, and reasoned trust is not given much of a chance to flourish. For their part, the employees must critically examine the position they are being asked to assume. It is curious that Whitacre professed unease about recruiting competitors for their expertise when he himself seems to have been recruited from a German competitor precisely for his expertise![13] Uncritical naivete on the part of employees becomes morally culpable to the extent that they fail to raise objections that would promote in-house discussion of possibly unethical practices.

Third, a company that desires the reasoned trust of its employees must grant the employees access to information about the company's practices. When a whistleblower accuses a company of malpractice, all employees of the corporation feel slightly tainted and anxious. They may feel betrayed not just by the whistleblower but also by the company whom they perceive as having hid relevant information from them. Secrecy encourages corporate paranoia. One of the best ways to combat it is to run as open a corporation as possible. The more access employees have, the more the corporation can legitimately hold them accountable for their actions and the more responsibility the employees will feel for actions they have known about and have had a chance to discuss. If there is genuine access to information about corporate practices, employees have a responsibility to seek out and to consider the implications of this information. It becomes less legitimate for them to bury their heads in the sand and then at some late date cry "Foul!" And this is how it should be in a corporation where all parties are genuinely committed to acting well.

Fourth, and finally, all members of the corporation have a responsibility to critically examine their actions, even if they have been taught to perform these acts and rewarded for doing so. A recent study comparing Japanese and American managers' attitudes toward ethics showed that the American managers were far more focussed on marketing than their foreign competitors and tended to think of immorality as occurring largely within marketing. This focus is problematic in several ways. It encourages managers to overlook ways in which they are treating their employees badly (e.g., by imposing unreasonable job requirements upon them). Furthermore, to the extent that American managers see only particular marketing practices as immoral, they fail to consider whether marketing itself may not be in some ways immoral. For example, does the idea of "targeting" specific groups of people for specific products wind up instrumentalizing the customer? If this customer is little more than a means to selling this product, it is not much of a leap to begin to think (as ADM allegedly did) of the customer as an enemy whose demand for low prices is keeping the company from attaining maximal profit.[14] More thought needs to be given to the nature of the core practices of business and less attention devoted to the bribery, price-fixing, etc. which may merely be symptoms of a sick practice. Unless and until these practices are well-scrutinized by the people who are engaged in them and who have the most knowledge about them, we should expect to continue to have a series of nasty abuses springing up and surprising us.

The corporate atmosphere also should be scrutinized. ADM's anti-bureaucratic rhetoric is a case in point. Whitacre mentions it several times and indicates that ADM has historically prided itself on its ability to get things done. However, what gets dismissed as bureaucracy is often the system of checks and balances within the firm. Anti-bureaucratic rhetoric may encourage, at worst, an attitude of lawlessness and at best, a "can-do" approach which may, as in the case of Whitacre, breed enthusiasm but not do much for thoughtfulness.

CONCLUSION

While whistleblowing sometimes may be the only way to call attention to serious abuses by professions or corporations, whistleblowing is not unambiguously ethically good. It is perhaps best seen as an option of last recourse. Rather than concentrating on when whistleblowing is moral, our time would be better spent thinking about how to improve corporate and professional environments so that employees and clients will not be driven to adopt this strategy.

NOTES

1. Ronald Duska, "Whistleblowing and Employee Loyalty," in Tom L. Beauchamp and Norman E. Bowie, *Ethical Theory and Business* (Englewood Cliffs, NJ: Prentice Hall, 1993), pp. 312–316.
2. Sisela Bok, "Whistleblowing and Professional Responsibility," in Beauchamp, op. cit.
3. Mark Whitacre as told to Ronald Henkoff, "My Life as a Corporate Mole for the FBI," in *Fortune* (Sept. 4, 1995), pp. 56–62.
4. Ibid.
5. Ibid. Ronald Henkoff comments that Whitacre's preferred approach to pricing "sounds a lot like predatory pricing," in Henkoff, "So Who Is This Mark Whitacre, and Why Is He Saying These Bad Things about ADM?," in *Fortune* (Sept. 4, 1995), pp. 64–67.
6. See "Suicide Hurts Government's ADM Case," Monday, August 14, 1995 at clari.news.crime.murders on the Worldwide Web.
7. Bok, op. cit.
8. Whitacre, op. cit.
9. Bok also discusses the fact that the charges apply to present wrongdoing. Bok, op. cit.
10. Duska, op. cit.
11. Whitacres, op. cit.
12. Ibid.
13. Ibid.
14. Ibid.

LEGAL PERSPECTIVES

State of New York v. Wal-Mart Stores, Inc.

Supreme Court of New York, Appellate Division

OPINION: Mercure, J. In February 1993, defendant discharged two of its employees for violating its "fraternization" policy, which is codified in defendant's 1989 Associates Handbook and prohibits a "dating relationship" between a married employee and another employee, other than his or her own spouse. In this action, plaintiff seeks reinstatement of the two employees with back pay upon the ground that their discharge violated Labor Law § 201–d (2) (c) which forbids employer discrimination against employees because of their participation in "legal recreational activities" pursued outside of work hours. Defendant moved pursuant to CPLR 3211 (a) (7) to dismiss the complaint. Supreme Court denied the motion with regard to the first cause of action, concluding that "dating" while one is married "may well be 'recreational activities' within the meaning of [Labor Law § 201–d (2)(c)]," but granted the motion with regard to the second cause of action, predicated upon Executive Law § 63 (12), which prohibits repeated or persistent illegality in the transaction of business. The parties cross-appeal.

We are not at all persuaded by Supreme Court's effort to force "a dating relationship" within the definition of "recreational activities" and accordingly reverse so much of its order as denied the motion to dismiss the first cause of action. Labor Law § 201–d (1) (b) defines "recreational activities" as meaning: "any lawful, leisure-time activity, for which the employee receives no compensation and which is generally engaged in for recreational purposes, including but not limited to sports, games, hobbies, exercise, reading and the viewing of television, movies and similar material." In our view, there is no justification for proceeding beyond the fundamental rule of construction that "[w]here words of a statute are free from ambiguity and express plainly, clearly and distinctly the legislative intent, resort may not be had to other means of interpretation." To us, "dating" is entirely distinct from and, in fact, bears little resemblance to "recreational activity." Whether characterized as a relationship or an activity, an indispensable element of "dating," in fact its raison d'etre, is romance, either pursued or realized. For that reason, although a dating couple may go bowling and under the circumstances call that activity a "date," when two individuals lacking amorous interest in one another go bowling or engage in any other kind of "legal recreational activity," they are not "dating."

Moreover, even if Labor Law § 201–d (1) (b) was found to contain some ambiguity, application of the rules of statutory construction does not support Supreme Court's interpretation. We agree with defendant that, to the extent relevant, the voluminous legislative history to the enactment, including memoranda issued in connection with the veto of two earlier more expansive bills, evinces an obvious intent to limit the statutory protection to certain clearly defined categories of leisure-time activities. Further, in view of the specific inclusion of "sports, games, hobbies, exercise, reading and the viewing of television, movies and similar material" within the statutory definition of "recreational activities," application of the doctrine of *noscitur a sociis*[1] compels the conclusion that personal relationships fall outside the scope of legislative intent.

Nor is there any realistic danger that this construction will permit employers to infringe upon the right of employees to engage in protected off-hours pursuits by wrongly characterizing dispassionate recreational activity as dating. To the contrary, recognition of the distinction between "dating" and "recreational activity" imposes upon the employer the enhanced burden of establishing not only joint activity of a recreational nature, but the employees' mutual romantic interest as well. Similarly, this construction in no way diminishes the statutory protection afforded social relationships between unmarried employees or married employees having no romantic interest or involvement with one another.

DISSENT: Yesawich Jr., J. (Dissenting). I respectfully dissent, for I find defendant's central thesis, apparently accepted by the majority, that the employment policy at issue only prohibits romantic entanglements and not other types of social interaction, to be wholly without merit. While the majority encumbers the word "dating" with an "amorous interest" component, there is nothing in defendant's fraternization policy, its application — defendant does not allege that its two former employees manifested an intimate or amatory attitude toward each other — or even in defendant's own definition of a "date," "a social engagement between persons of opposite sex" (*Webster's Ninth New Collegiate Dictionary*, 325 [1988]), that leads to such a conclusion.

More importantly, I do not agree that "dating," whether or not it involves romantic attachment, falls outside the general definition of "recreational activities" found in Labor Law § 201–d (1) (b). The statute, by its terms, appears to encompass social activities, whether or not they have a romantic element, for it includes *any* lawful activity pursued for recreational purposes and undertaken during leisure time. Though no explicit definition of "recreational purposes" is contained in the statute, "recreation" is, in the words of one dictionary, "a means of refreshment or diversion" (*Webster's Ninth New Collegiate Dictionary,* 985 [1985]); social interaction surely qualifies as a "diversion."

Moreover, while the majority assures that the construction it adopts "in no way diminishes the statutory protection afforded social relationships between unmarried employees," I am less sanguine, because the majority's holding implies that the statute affords no protection to any social relationship that might contain a romantic aspect, regardless of the marital status of the participants, or the impact that the relationship has on their capacity to perform their jobs.

In my view, given the fact that the Legislature's primary intent in enacting Labor Law § 201–d was to curtail employers' ability to discriminate on the basis of activities that are pursued outside of work hours, and that have no bearing on one's ability to perform one's job, and concomitantly to guarantee employees a certain degree of freedom to conduct their lives as they please during nonworking hours, the narrow interpretation adopted by the majority is indefensible. Rather, the statute, and the term "recreational activities" in particular, should be construed as broadly as the definitional language allows, to effect its remedial purpose.

And while it is true that, as a general rule of statutory construction, the breadth of an inclusory phrase is to be considered limited by

[1]Noscitur a Sociis, *it is known from its associates.* Under this doctrine, the meaning of questionable or doubtful words or phrases in a statute may be ascertained by reference to the meaning of other words or phrases associated with it.

the specific examples accompanying it, this principle must yield where necessary to carry out the underlying purpose of the enactment. Additionally, it is only applicable when the examples fall into a single, well-defined class, and are not themselves general in nature. Here, the list, which includes vast categories such as "hobbies" and "sports," as well as very different types of activities (e.g., exercise, reading), appears to have been compiled with an eye toward extending the reach of the statute. This, coupled with the explicit directive that the definition is *not* to be limited to the examples given, provides further indication that the term "recreational activities" should be construed expansively. Accordingly, I would affirm Supreme Court's denial of defendant's motion to dismiss the first cause of action. . . .

Pasch v. Katz Media Corporation, Katz Radio Group, and Christal Radio

United States District Court for the Southern District of New York

BACKGROUND

According to the Complaint, Plaintiff, Judy Pasch, was employed by Christal Radio, a division of Katz Media, from November 16, 1981 to June, 1983, at which time she resigned. Plaintiff states that she performed her job as an assistant to the Vice-President/Divisional Manager of Christal Radio and New York/National Sales Coordinator faithfully and diligently during her employment with Defendants and received numerous salary increases and increased responsibilities.

On February 22, 1993, Mark Braunstein, a Vice-President and General Sales Manager of Christal, was discharged by the President of Christal, William Fortenbaugh. Plaintiff and Mr. Braunstein had maintained a "personal relationship" while they were employed by Christal and had been residing together since 1990 with the full knowledge of Defendants.

Plaintiff alleges that on February 24, 1993, on the pretext that Christal was to be reorganized, Mr. Fortenbaugh advised Plaintiff that her position was to be eliminated under the reorganization, and that her services in her present position were no longer required. Plaintiff alleges that in an effort to demean her, she was then demoted to a position which was the same entry level position she had held when first employed by Defendants in 1981.

Plaintiff contends that the aforesaid demotion occurred solely because Plaintiff continued to maintain a personal relationship with Mr. Braunstein and that it occurred in an effort to humiliate her and force her to quit. Plaintiff claims that no reorganization of Christal occurred, and that when Defendant displaced her from her previous position and replaced her with a male employee with fewer qualifications, she was constructively terminated from her employment. Plaintiff left Defendants' employment in June, 1993.

DISCUSSION . . .

II. Co-habitation as a Protected Activity

Count III of the Complaint alleges that Plaintiff's discharge occurred in violation of New York Labor Law § 201–d. New York Labor Law § 201–d (2) (c) provides in pertinent part:

It shall be unlawful for any employer or employment agency . . . to discharge from employment . . . an individual because of an individual's legal recreational activities outside work hours, off of the employer's premises and without use of the employer's equipment or other property.

The statute defines recreational activity as

any lawful, leisure-time activity, for which the employee receives no compensation and which is generally engaged in for recreational purposes, including but not limited to sports, games, hobbies, exercise, reading and the viewing of television, movies and similar material.

The purpose of the statute is to "prohibit employers from discriminating against their employees simply because the employer does not like the activities an employee engages in after work." New York State Assembly 215th Session, Senate Memo at 9 (1992). The statute further provides that

the provisions of subdivision two of this section shall not be deemed to protect activity which creates a material conflict of interest related to the employer's trade secrets, proprietary information or other proprietary or business interest.

Therefore, although an employer ordinarily may not discharge an employee for lawful off-hour recreational activities, an employer may discharge an employee for conduct that is detrimental to the company or that impacts an employee's job performance.

In the case at bar, Plaintiff's "cohabitation" is alleged to have occurred outside work hours, off of the employer's premises and without use of the employer's equipment or other property. Plaintiff therefore argues that her conduct enjoys statutory protection, and that discharge on grounds of such conduct is statutorily prohibited.

Defendants argue that cohabitation should not be considered a recreational activity and

therefore should not be protected by the statute. See *State v. Wal-Mart Stores, Inc.*, 207 A.D.2d 150, 621 N.Y.S.2d 158 (3rd Dept. 1995). In Wal-Mart, the state brought a section 201(d)(2)(c) action seeking the reinstatement of two employees who were discharged for violating the employer's fraternization policy, which prohibited "dating" between a married employee and another employee other than his/her spouse. Id. The Wal-Mart Improper Workplace Conduct policy prohibited "romantic involvements between workers regardless of whether such involvement takes place outside of work hours and off the employer's premises, or whether such involvement constitutes habitually poor performance, incompetence or misconduct, or whether such involvement creates a material conflict of interest related to Wal-Mart's proprietary or business interest." The Wal-Mart majority found that "dating" was not a "recreational activity" and therefore not protected under New York Labor Law.

In the instant case, Plaintiff alleges that she was dismissed for living with an individual who was not a co-employee at the time of the alleged discriminatory employment decision, and not for violating company rules or analogous regulations. The Defendants argue that because there is no relevant distinction between "dating" and maintaining a personal relationship through cohabitation Wal-Mart compels dismissal of Count III. Nevertheless, although the activity involved in Wal-Mart and the present case are similar, this Court reaches a different conclusion regarding the statutory protection afforded by § 201–d.

A federal court faced with a question of state law must look to the rules of decisions as announced by the state court of last resort, and is "not free to reject the state rule merely because it has not received the sanction of the highest state court." Although a federal court is not bound by lower courts decisions, "the decision of an intermediate state court on a question of state law is binding on (a diversity court) unless we find persuasive evidence that the highest state court would reach a different conclusion." In determining how New York's highest court would rule, the settled principles which are applied to New York Law accord particular significance to the legislative history and statutory purpose. Thus, "a federal district court will consider, just as a state court would, the statutory language, pertinent legislative history, the statutory scheme set in historical context, how the statute can be woven into the state law with the least distortion of the total fabric, state decisional law, federal cases which construe the state statute, scholarly works and any other reliable data tending to indicate how the New York Court of Appeals would resolve the questions presented."

The Court believes that the New York Court of Appeals would not construe the statute so narrowly as to exclude "cohabitation" from the class of recreational activities protected by the statute. A careful reading of the statute and its Pocket Bill indicates that "cohabitation" that occurs off the employer's premises, without use of the employer's equipment and not on the employer's time, should be considered a protected activity for which an employer may not discriminate, absent some showing that such activity involves a material conflict of interest with the employer's business interests.

The Wal-Mart majority found in "the voluminous legislative history to the enactment of 201–d, including memoranda issued in connection with the veto of two earlier more expansive bills, an obvious intent to limit the statutory protection to certain clearly defined categories of leisure-time activities." Nevertheless, this Court reads the legislative history as evidencing an intent to include cohabitation as a recreational activity protected by the statute. This conclusion is based on a review of the earlier bills and reasons stated by Governor Cuomo, then Governor of New York, for vetoing the bills. The 1990 Bill stated

> it shall be unlawful discriminatory practice for any person, employer or employment agency to: 1) refuse to hire, employ, license or discriminate against any individual because of such individual's engagement in a legal activity during non-working hours; or 2) bar or discharge from employment an individual or discriminate against such individual in compensation, promotion or terms, conditions or privileges of employment because of such individual's engagement in a legal activity during non-working hours.

The 1990 bill was vetoed because the bill failed to protect an employer's right to consider conduct material to the employment relationship. Specifically, "under the bill, employers would not be allowed to prohibit employees form engaging in outside employment that is in conflict with their job responsibilities. Thus, for example, an employer could moonlight with a supplier, customer, or even a competitor, of a company. To go a step further, this bill would allow an employee of a company to endorse a competitor's product and leave the company with no recourse to terminate or otherwise discipline the employee."

The 1991 Bill stated

> unless provided otherwise by law, it shall be an unlawful practice for any person, employer or employment agency to: A) refuse to hire, employ, license or discriminate against any individual because of such individual's engagement in a legal activity during non-working hours; or B) bar or discharge from employment an individual or discriminate against such individual in compensation, promotion or terms, conditions or privileges of employment because of such individual's engagement in a legal activity during non-working hours. The provisions of subdivision one of this section shall not be deemed to protect legal activity which: A) materially threatens an employer's legitimate conflict of interest policy reasonably designed to protect the employer's trade secrets, proprietary information or other proprietary interests;

The 1991 bill was vetoed because it did not define "key terms, such as 'legal activities' and . . . (because) this bill would establish a wider protection without any recognition of the reasonable needs of employers to maintain some control over activities of their employees which, albeit legal, may have a negative effect on the mission of the employer."

The current statute was then amended to read

> the provision of subdivision one of this section shall not be deemed to protect activity which: A) . . . creates a material conflict of interest related to the employer's trade secrets, proprietary information, or other proprietary or business interest . . .

In addition, the new version substituted "recreational/leisure activity" for "legal activity," thereby clarifying the scope of statutory protection.

As stated by Senator Lack, the bill's sponsor, the current statute is intended to remedy

> instances in which employers are trying to regulate an employee's off duty activities, contending that what employees do off-hours has an impact on the employer. But should an employer have a right to forbid a person from engaging in a legal activity, such as wearing a button for a particular candidate, simply because the employer does not agree with those political sentiments? . . . We have long since passed the days of company towns, where the company told you when to work, where to live and what to buy in their stores. This bill will ensure that employers do not tell us how to think and play on our own time.

Thus, "the bill exempts from its protection employee activities which constitute a material conflict of interest with the employer's business interest, or violate State law or collectively negotiated conflict of interest provisions, and permits employer action related to the employee's actual on-the-job performance."

In sum, legislative history shows that the purpose of the statute is to prohibit employers from discriminating against their employees simply because the employer does not like the activities an employee engages in after work. The legislative history indicates the statute was intended to include social activities, whether or not they have a romantic element, so long as the activity occurs outside work hours, off of the employer's premises and without use of the employer's equipment or other property; and does not create a material conflict of interest related to the employer's trade secrets, proprietary information, or other proprietary or business interest. The Court therefore reaches a conclusion similar to that of Justice Yesawich, the dissenting judge in Wal-Mart, who maintained that "dating" falls within the class of leisure or recreational activities protected by § 201–d. Justice Yesawich stated:

> given the fact that the legislature's primary intent . . . was to curtail employers' ability to discriminate on the basis of activities . . . that have no bearing on one's ability to perform one's job, and concomitantly to guarantee employees a certain degree of freedom to conduct their lives as they please during nonworking hours, the narrow interpretation adopted by the majority is indefensible.

The narrow interpretation urged by Defendants here is likewise indefensible. Dismissal of the Plaintiff's case at this point in the litigation is thus premature. The Plaintiff has alleged sufficient facts to make out a prima facie case under New York Labor Law § 201.d(2)(c).

CONCLUSION

For the reasons discussed above, Defendants' motion for judgment on the pleading is denied.

IT IS SO ORDERED.

Dated: New York, New York

August 7, 1995

Robert P. Patterson, Jr.

U.S.D.J.

Luedtke v. Nabors Alaska Drilling, Inc.

Superior Court of Alaska

This case addresses one aspect of drug testing by employers. A private employer, Nabors Alaska Drilling, Inc. (Nabors), established a drug testing program for its employees. Two Nabors employees, Clarence Luedtke and Paul Luedtke, both of whom worked on drilling rigs on the North Slope, refused to submit to urinalysis screening for drug use as required by Nabors. As a result they were fired by Nabors. The Luedtkes challenge their discharge on the following grounds:

1. Nabors' drug testing program violates the Luedtkes' right to privacy guaranteed by article I, section 22 of the Alaska Constitution;
2. Nabors' demands violate the covenant of good faith and fair dealing implicit in all employment contracts;
3. Nabors' urinalysis requirement violates the public interest in personal privacy, giving the Luedtkes a cause of action for wrongful discharge; and
4. Nabors' actions give rise to a cause of action under the common law tort of invasion of privacy.

Nabors argues that the Luedtkes were "at will" employees whose employment relationship could be terminated at any time for any reason. Alternatively, even if termination had to be based on "just cause," such cause existed because the Luedtkes violated established company policy relating to employee safety by refusing to take the scheduled tests.

This case raises issues of first impression in Alaska law including: whether the constitutional right of privacy applies to private parties; some parameters of the tort of wrongful discharge; and the extent to which certain employee drug testing by private employers can be controlled by courts.

FACTUAL AND PROCEDURAL BACKGROUND

The Luedtkes' cases proceeded separately to judgment. Because they raised common legal issues, on Nabors' motion they were consolidated on appeal.

Paul's Case

Factual Background. Paul began working for Nabors, which operates drilling rigs on Alaska's North Slope, in February 1978. He began as a temporary employee, replacing a permanent employee on vacation for two weeks. During his two weeks of temporary work, a permanent position opened up on the rig on which he was working and he was hired to fill it. Paul began as a "floorman" and was eventually promoted to "driller." A driller oversees the work of an entire drilling crew.

Paul started work with Nabors as a union member, initially being hired from the union hall. During his tenure, however, Nabors "broke" the union. Paul continued to work without a union contract. Paul had no written contract with Nabors at the time of his discharge.

During his employment with Nabors, Paul was accused twice of violating the company's drug and alcohol policies. Once he was suspended for 90 days for taking alcohol to the North Slope. The other incident involved a search of the rig on which Paul worked.

768 P. 2d 1123 (1989). Opinion by Judge Compton.

Aided by dogs trained to sniff out marijuana, the searchers found traces of marijuana on Paul's suitcase. Paul was allowed to continue working on the rig only after assuring his supervisors he did not use marijuana.

In October 1982, Paul scheduled a two-week vacation. Because his normal work schedule was two weeks of work on the North Slope followed by a week off, a two-week vacation amounted to 28 consecutive days away from work. Just prior to his vacation, Paul was instructed to arrange for a physical examination in Anchorage. He arranged for it to take place on October 19, during his vacation. It was at this examination that Nabors first tested Paul's urine for signs of drug use. The purpose of the physical, as understood by Paul, was to enable him to work on off-shore rigs should Nabors receive such contracts. Although Paul was told it would be a comprehensive physical he had no idea that a urinalysis screening test for drug use would be performed. He did voluntarily give a urine sample but assumed it would be tested only for "blood sugar, any kind of kidney failure [and] problems with bleeding." Nabors' policy of testing for drug use was not announced until November 1, 1982, almost two weeks after Paul's examination.

In early November 1982, Paul contacted Nabors regarding his flight to the North Slope to return to work. He was told at that time to report to the Nabors office in Anchorage. On November 5, Paul reported to the office where a Nabors representative informed him that he was suspended for "the use of alcohol or other illicit substances." No other information was forthcoming from Nabors until November 16 when Paul received a letter informing him that his urine had tested positive for cannabinoids. The letter informed him that he would be required to pass two subsequent urinalysis tests, one on November 30 and the other on December 30, before he would be allowed to return to work. In response Paul hand delivered a let-

ter drafted by his attorney to the Manager of Employee Relations for Nabors, explaining why he felt the testing and suspension were unfair. Paul did not take the urinalysis test on November 30 as requested by Nabors. On December 14, Nabors sent Paul a letter informing him he was discharged for refusing to take the November 30 test.

Procedural Background.   Following his discharge, Paul applied for unemployment compensation benefits with the Alaska State Department of Labor (DOL). DOL initially denied Paul benefits for the period of December 12, 1982 through January 22, 1983 on the ground that his refusal to take the urinalysis test was misconduct under AS 23.30.379(a). Paul appealed that decision and on January 27, 1983, the DOL hearing officer concluded that the drug re-test requirement was unreasonable. On that basis, the hearing officer held that Paul's dismissal was not for misconduct. Nabors appealed to the Commissioner of Labor, who sustained the decision of the appeals tribunal.

Paul initiated this civil action in November 1983. He asserted claims for wrongful dismissal, breach of contract, invasion of privacy, and defamation. Nabors moved for and was granted summary judgment on the invasion of privacy claim, on both the constitutional and common law tort theories. Prior to trial Paul voluntarily dismissed his defamation claim. The trial court, in a non-jury trial, held for Nabors on Paul's wrongful dismissal and breach of contract claims.

Paul appeals the trial court's rulings with regard to his wrongful dismissal, breach of contract, and invasion of privacy claims.

Clarence's Case

Factual Background.   Clarence has had seasonal employment with Nabors, working on drilling rigs, since the winter of 1977–78. Prior to beginning his first period of employment, he completed an employment application which provided for a probationary period.

In November 1982 Clarence became subject to the Nabors drug use and testing policy. In mid-November a list of persons scheduled for drug screening was posted at Clarence's rig. His name was on the list. The people listed were required to complete the test during their next "R & R" period. During that next "R & R" period Clarence decided he would not submit to the testing and informed Nabors of his decision.

Nabors offered to allow Clarence time to "clean up" but Clarence refused, insisting that he thought he could pass the test, but was refusing as "a matter of principle." At that point Nabors fired Clarence. The drug test that would have been performed on Clarence was the same as that performed on Paul.

Procedural Background. Following his discharge Clarence also sought unemployment compensation benefits with the DOL. Nabors objected because it believed his refusal to submit to the drug test was misconduct under AS 23.20.379(a). After a factual hearing and two appeals, the Commissioner of Labor found that "Nabors has not shown that there is any connection between off-the-job drug use and on-the-job performance." Thus, there was no showing that Nabors' test policy was related to job misconduct. Furthermore, the Commissioner adopted factual findings that 1) no evidence had been submitted by Nabors linking off-duty drug use with on-the-job accidents, and 2) Nabors was not alleging any drug use by Clarence.

Clarence filed his complaint in this case in November 1984. He alleged invasion of privacy, both at common law and under the Alaska Constitution, wrongful termination, breach of contract, and violation of the implied covenant of good faith and fair dealing. The trial court granted summary judgment in favor of Nabors on all of Clarence's claims. No opinion, findings of fact or conclusions of law were entered.

Clarence appeals the award of summary judgment on all counts.

DISCUSSION

The Right to Privacy

The right to privacy is a recent creation of American law. The inception of this right is generally credited to a law review article published in 1890 by Louis Brandeis and his law partner, Samuel Warren. Brandeis & Warren, *The Right to Privacy,* 4 Harv.L.Rev. 193 (1890). Brandeis and Warren observed that in a modern world with increasing population density and advancing technology, the number and types of matters theretofore easily concealed from public purview were rapidly decreasing. They wrote:

> Recent inventions and business methods call attention to the next step which must be taken for the protection of the person, and for securing to the individual what Judge Cooley calls the right "to be let alone." Instantaneous photographs and newspaper enterprise have invaded the sacred precincts of private and domestic life; and numerous mechanical devices threaten to make good the prediction that "what is whispered in the closet shall be proclaimed from the housetops."

Id. at 195 (footnotes omitted). Discussing the few precedential cases in tort law in which courts had afforded remedies for the publication of private letters or unauthorized photographs, Brandeis and Warren drew a common thread they called "privacy." They defined this right as the principle of "inviolate personality." *Id.* at 205.

While the legal grounds of this right were somewhat tenuous in the 1890s, American jurists found the logic of Brandeis and Warren's arguments compelling. The reporters of the first Restatement of Torts included a tort entitled "Interference with Privacy." By 1960, Professor Prosser could write that "the right of privacy, in one form or another, is declared to exist by the overwhelming majority of the American courts." . . . He cited cases in which private parties had been held liable in tort for eavesdropping on private conversations by means of wiretapping and microphones, or for peering into the windows of homes. In addition, while Brandeis and Warren were mainly concerned with the publication of private facts, Professor Prosser identified four different manifestations of the right to privacy: intrusion upon the plaintiff's seclusion; public disclosure of embarrassing private facts; publicity which places the plaintiff in a false light; and appropriation, for the defendant's pecuniary advantage of the plaintiff's name or likeness. Professor Prosser's categories form the framework of the expanded tort of invasion of privacy found in the Restatement (Second) of Torts.

Eventually the right to privacy attained sufficient recognition to be incorporated in several state constitutions. Alaska (adopted 1972); Cal. (adopted 1972); Haw. (adopted 1978); Mont. (adopted 1972).

Interpreting the Constitution of the United States, the United States Supreme Court in 1965 held that a Connecticut statute banning the use of birth control devices by married couples was "repulsive to the notions of privacy surrounding the marriage relationship." . . . The Supreme Court wrote that "specific guarantees in the Bill of Rights have penumbras, formed by emanations from those guarantees that help give them life and substance. Various guarantees create zones of privacy." . . . Justice Goldberg's concurrence suggested that the right of marital privacy was fundamental to the concept of liberty. . . . Since *Griswold* the Supreme Court has found the federal constitutional right of privacy to apply to a number of other situations. . . .

In this case the plaintiffs seek to fit their cases within at least one of four legal frameworks in which the right to privacy has found expression: constitutional law, contract law, tort law, and the emerging mixture of theories known as the public policy exception to the at-will doctrine of employment law.

The Right to Privacy Under the Alaska Constitution

The Alaska Constitution was amended in 1972 to add the following section:

> *Right of Privacy.* The right of the people to privacy is recognized and shall not be infringed. The legislature shall implement this section.

We observe initially that this provision, powerful as a constitutional statement of citizens' rights, contains no guidelines for its application. Nor does it appear that the legislature has exercised its power to apply the provision; the parties did not bring to our attention any statutes which "implement this section."

The Luedtkes argue that this court has never clearly answered the question of whether article I, section 22 applies only to state action or whether it also governs private action. The Luedtkes urge this court to hold that section 22 governs private action. This question was broached in *Allred v. State*. In *Allred* this court was faced with the question of whether a psychotherapist–patient privilege exists in Alaska. We found the privilege in the common law rather than under the constitutional right to privacy:

Since it is apparent that [the psychotherapist] was not a police agent, we do not perceive any state action that would trigger the constitutional privacy guarantees. . . .

Our dictum in *Allred* comports with traditional constitutional analysis holding that the constitution serves as a check on the power of government: "That all lawful power derives from the people and must be held in check to preserve their freedom is the oldest and most central tenet of American constitutionalism." L. Tribe, *American Constitutional Law.* In the same vein, we have written in regard to Alaska's constitutional right to privacy: "[T]he primary purpose of these constitutional provisions is the protection of 'personal privacy and dignity against unwarranted intrusions by the State.'" . . .

[1] The parties in the case at bar have failed to produce evidence that Alaska's constitutional right to privacy was intended to operate as a bar to private action, here Nabors' drug testing program. Absent a history demonstrating that the amendment was intended to proscribe private action, or a proscription of private action in the language of the amendment itself, we decline to extend the constitutional right to privacy to the actions of private parties.

Wrongful Termination

[2] In *Mitford v. de LaSala,* this court held that at-will employment contracts in Alaska contain an implied covenant of good faith and fair dealing. In *Knight v. American Guard & Alert, Inc.* (Alaska 1986), we acknowledged that violation of a public policy could constitute a breach of that implied covenant. We wrote:

The [plaintiff's] claim, concerning alleged termination in violation of public policy, is in accord with a theory of recovery accepted in many states. We have never rejected the public policy theory. Indeed, it seems that the public policy approach is largely encompassed within the implied covenant of good faith and fair dealing which we accepted in *Mitford.*

We conclude that there is a public policy supporting the protection of employee privacy. Violation of that policy by an employer may rise to the level of a breach of the implied covenant of good faith and fair dealing. However, the competing public concern for employee safety present in the case at bar leads us to hold that Nabors' actions did not breach the implied covenant.

The Luedtkes Were At-Will Employees. [3, 4] First, we address the Luedtkes' arguments that they were not at-will employees, but rather that they could be fired only for good cause. The key difference between these two types of employment is whether the employment contract is for a determinable length of time. Employees hired on an at-will basis can be fired for any reason that does not violate the implied covenant of good faith and fair dealing. However, employees hired for a specific term may not be discharged before the expiration of the term except for good cause. Neither of the Luedtkes had any formal agreements for a specified term, so any such term, if it existed, must be implied.

In *Eales v. Tanana Valley Medical-Surgical Group, Inc.,* 663 P.2d 958 (Alaska 1983), we held that where an employer promised employment that would last until the employee's retirement age, and that age was readily determinable, a contract for a definite duration would be implied. We also held that no additional consideration need be given the employee to create a contract for a definite term.

The Luedtkes' cases are distinguishable from that of the plaintiff in *Eales.* The Luedtkes received benefits, such as medical insurance and participation in a pension or profit sharing plan, which continued as long as they were employed. However, Nabors never gave an indication of a definite duration for their employment, nor a definite endpoint to their employment. Instead, Nabors merely provided benefits consistent with modern employer/employee relations.

There Is a Public Policy Supporting Employee Privacy. The next question we address is whether a public policy exists protecting an employee's right to withhold certain "private" information from his employer. We believe such a policy does exist, and is evidenced in the common law, statutes and constitution of this state. . . .

Alaska law clearly evidences strong support for the public interest in employee privacy. First, state statutes support the policy that there are private sectors of employee's lives not subject to direct scrutiny by their employers. For example, employers may not require employees to take polygraph tests as a condition of employment. AS 23.10.037. In addition, AS 18.80.200(a) provides:

> It is determined and declared as a matter of legislative finding that discrimination against an inhabitant of the state because of race, religion, color, national origin, age, sex, marital status, changes in marital status, pregnancy, or parenthood is a matter of public concern and that this discrimination not only threatens the rights and privileges of the inhabitants of the state but also menaces the institutions of the state and threatens peace, order, health, safety and general welfare of the state and its inhabitants.

This policy is implemented by AS 18.80.220, which makes it unlawful for employers to inquire into such topics in connection with prospective employment. This statute demonstrates that in Alaska certain subjects are placed outside the consideration of employers in their relations with employees. The protections of AS 18.80.220 are extensive. This statute has been construed to be broader than federal anti-discrimination law. . . . We believe it evidences the legislature's intent to liberally protect employee rights.

Second, as previously noted, Alaska's constitution contains a right to privacy clause. While we have held, *supra,* that this clause does not proscribe the private action at issue, it can be viewed by this court as evidence of a public policy supporting privacy. . . .

Third, there exists a common law right to privacy. The Restatement (Second) of Torts § 652B provides:

> *Intrusion upon Seclusion* One who intentionally intrudes, physically or otherwise, upon the solitude or seclusion of another or his private affairs or concerns, is subject to liability to the other for invasion of his privacy, if the intrusion would be highly offensive to a reasonable person.

While we have not expressly considered the application of this tort in Alaska, we have recognized its existence.

Thus, the citizens' right to be protected against unwarranted intrusions into their private lives has been recognized in the law of Alaska. The constitution protects against governmental intrusion, statutes protect against employer intrusion, and the common law protects against intrusions by other private persons. As a result, there is sufficient evidence to support the conclusion that there exists a public policy protecting spheres of employee conduct into which employers may not intrude. The question then becomes whether employer monitoring of employee drug use outside the work place is such a prohibited intrusion.

The Public Policy Supporting Employee Privacy Must Be Balanced Against the Public Policy Supporting Health and Safety. Since the recent advent of inexpensive urine tests for illicit drugs, most litigation regarding the use of these tests in the employment context has concerned government employees. The testing has been challenged under the proscriptions of federal fourth amendment search and seizure law. This body of law regulates only governmental activity, and as a result is of limited value to the case at bar, which involves private activity. However, the reasoning of the federal courts regarding the intrusiveness of urine testing can illuminate this court's consideration of the extent to which personal privacy is violated by these tests.

In *Capua v. City of Plainfield*, 643 F. Supp. city firefighters sued to enjoin random urinalysis tests conducted by the fire department. The court wrote:

> Urine testing involves one of the most private of functions, a function traditionally performed in private, and indeed, usually prohibited in public. The proposed test, in order to ensure its reliability, requires the presence of another when the specimen is created and frequently reveals information about one's health unrelated to the use of drugs. If the tests are positive, it may affect one's employment status and even result in criminal prosecution.
>
> We would be appalled at the spectre of the police spying on employees during their free time and then reporting their activities to their employers. Drug testing is a form of surveillance, albeit a technological one. Nonetheless, it reports on a person's off-duty activities just as surely as someone had been present and watching. It is George Orwell's "Big Brother" Society come to life.

While there is a certain amount of hyperbole in this statement, it does portray the *potential* invasion that the technology of urinalysis makes possible. It is against this potential that the law must guard. Not all courts view urine testing with such skepticism, believing the intrusion justified in contemporary society.

Judge Patrick Higginbotham assumed a more cynical stance in *National Treasury Employees Union v. Von Raab,* observing that there is little difference between the intrusiveness of urine testing and the intrusiveness of other affronts to privacy regularly accepted by individuals today. He wrote:

> The precise privacy interest asserted is elusive, and the plaintiffs are, at best, inexact as to just what that privacy interest is. Finding an objectively reasonable expectation of privacy in urine, a waste product, contains inherent contradictions. The district court found such a right of privacy, but, in fairness, plaintiffs do not rest there. Rather, it appears from the plaintiffs' brief that it is the manner of taking the samples that is said to invade privacy, because outer garments in which a false sample might be hidden must be removed and a person of the same sex remains outside a stall while the applicant urinates. Yet, apart from the partial disrobing (apparently not independently challenged) persons using public toilet facilities experience a similar lack of privacy. The right must then be a perceived indignity in the whole process, a perceived affront to personal identity by the presence in the same room of another while engaging in a private body function.
>
> It is suggested that the testing program rests on a generalized lack of trust and not on a developed suspicion of an individual applicant. Necessarily there is a plain implication that an applicant is part of a group that, given the demands of the job, cannot be trusted to be truthful about drug use. The difficulty is that just such distrust, or equally accurate, care, is behind every background check and every security check; indeed the information gained in tests of urine is not different from that disclosed in medical records, for which consent to examine is a routine part of applications for many sensitive government posts. In short, given the practice of testing and background checks required for so many government jobs, whether any expectations of privacy by these job applicants were objectively reasonable is dubious at best. Certainly, to ride with the cops one ought to expect inquiry, and by the surest means, into whether he is a robber.

. . . As Judge Higginbotham observes, society often tolerates intrusions into an individual's privacy under circumstances similar to those present in urinalysis. We find this persuasive. It appears, then, that it is the reason the urinalyis is conducted, and not the conduct of the test, that deserves analysis.

This court discussed, on the one hand, the reasons society protects privacy, and, on the other hand, the reasons society rightfully intrudes on personal privacy in *Ravin v. State*. *Ravin* addressed the issue of whether the state could prohibit the use of marijuana in the home. We held that it could not. We observed that "the right to privacy amendment to the Alaska Constitution cannot be read so as to make the possession or ingestion of marijuana itself a fundamental right." Rather, we "recognized the distinctive nature of the home as a place where the individual's privacy receives special protection." However, we recognized also that this "fundamental right" was limited to activity which remained in the home. We acknowledged that when an individual leaves his home and interacts with others, competing rights of others collectively and as individuals may take precedence:

> Privacy in the home is a fundamental right, under both the federal and Alaska constitutions. We do not mean by this that a person may do anything at anytime as long as the activity takes place within a person's home. There are two important limitations on this facet of the right to privacy. First, we agree with the Supreme Court of the United States, which has strictly limited the *Stanley* guarantee to possession for purely private, noncommercial use in the home. And secondly, we think this right must yield when it interferes in a serious manner with the health, safety, rights and privileges of others or with the public welfare. No one has an absolute right to do things in the privacy of his own home which will affect himself or others adversely. Indeed, one aspect of a private matter is that it is private, that is, that it does not adversely affect persons beyond the actor, and hence is none of their business. When a matter does affect the public, directly or indirectly, it loses its wholly private character, and

can be made to yield when an appropriate public need is demonstrated.

The *Ravin* analysis is analogous to the analysis that should be followed in cases construing the public policy exception to the at-will employment doctrine. That is, there is a sphere of activity in every person's life that is closed to scrutiny by others. The boundaries of that sphere are determined by balancing a person's right to privacy against other public policies, such as "the health, safety, rights and privileges of others." . . .

The Luedtkes claim that whether or not they use marijuana is information within that protected sphere into which their employer, Nabors, may not intrude. We disagree. As we have previously observed, marijuana can impair a person's ability to function normally:

> The short-term physiological effects are relatively undisputed. An immediate slight increase in the pulse, decrease in salivation, and a slight reddening of the eyes are usually noted. There is also impairment of psychomotor control. . . .

We also observe that work on an oil rig can be very dangerous. We have determined numerous cases involving serious injury or death resulting from accidents on oil drilling rigs. In addition, in Paul's case the trial court expressly considered the dangers of work on oil rigs. It found:

> 13. It is extremely important that the driller be drug free in the performance of his tasks in order to insure the immediate safety of the other personnel on the particular drill rig.
> 14. It is extremely important that the driller be drug free in the performance of his tasks in order to insure the safety and protection of the oil field itself and the oil resource contained within it.

[5] Where the public policy supporting the Luedtkes privacy in off-duty activities conflicts with the public policy supporting the

protection of the health and safety of other workers, and even the Luedtkes themselves, the health and safety concerns are paramount. As a result, Nabors is justified in determining whether the Luedtkes are possibly impaired on the job by drug usage off the job.

We observe, however, that the employer's prerogative does have limitations.

First, the drug test must be conducted at a time reasonably contemporaneous with the employee's work time. The employer's interest is in monitoring drug use that may directly affect employee performance. The employer's interest is not in the broader police function of discovering and controlling the use of illicit drugs in general society. In the context of this case, Nabors could have tested the Luedtkes immediately prior to their departure for the North Slope, or immediately upon their return from the North Slope when the test could be reasonably certain of detecting drugs consumed there. Further, given Nabors' need to control the oil rig community, Nabors could have tested the Luedtkes at any time they were on the North Slope.

Second, an employee must receive notice of the adoption of a drug testing program. By requiring a test, an employer introduces an additional term of employment. An employee should have notice of the additional term so that he may contest it, refuse to accept it and quit, seek to negotiate its conditions, or prepare for the test so that he will not fail it and thereby suffer sanctions.

[6, 7] These considerations do not apply with regard to the tests both Paul and Clarence refused to take. Paul was given notice of the future tests. He did not take the November 30 test. As a result, Nabors was justified in discharging Paul. Clarence had notice and the opportunity to schedule his test at a reasonable time. However, he refused to take any test. As a result, Nabors was justified

in discharging Clarence. Neither discharge violated the implied covenant of good faith and fair dealing. . . .

Common Law Right to Privacy Claims

We recognize that "[t]he [common law] right to be free from harassment and constant intrusion into one's daily affairs is enjoyed by all persons." *Siggelkow v. State,* . . . As previously discussed, that law is delineated in the Restatement (Second) of Torts § 652B, entitled Intrusion upon Seclusion. That section provides: "One who intentionally intrudes . . . upon the solitude or seclusion of another or his private affairs or concerns, is subject to liability . . . if the intrusion would be highly offensive to a reasonable person."

[8, 9] It is true, as the Luedtkes contend, that publication of the facts obtained is not necessary. Instead, the liability is for the offensive intrusion. . . . However, courts have construed "offensive intrusion" to require either an unreasonable manner of intrusion, or intrusion for an unwarranted purpose. . . . Paul has failed to show either that the manner or reason for testing his urine was unreasonable. During his physical, he voluntarily gave a urine sample for the purpose of testing. Therefore, he cannot complain that urine testing is "highly offensive." . . . Paul can only complain about the purpose of the urine test, that is, to detect drug usage. However, we have held, *supra,* that Nabors was entitled to test its employees for drug usage. As a result, the intrusion was not unwarranted. Paul complains additionally that he was not aware his urine would be tested for drug usage. In this regard we observe that Paul was not aware of any of the tests being performed on his urine sample. Nor did he know the ramifications of those tests. But he did know that whatever the results were they would be reported to Nabors. Therefore, his complaint

about a particular test is without merit. We conclude that for these reasons Paul could not maintain an action for invasion of privacy with regard to the urinalysis conducted October 19.

As to the urinalyses Paul and Clarence refused to take, we hold that no cause of action for invasion of privacy arises where the intrusion is prevented from taking place. . . .

Warthen v. Toms River Community Memorial Hospital

Superior Court of New Jersey

Plaintiff Corrine Warthen appeals from a summary judgment of the Law Division dismissing her action against defendant Toms River Community Memorial Hospital (Hospital). Plaintiff sought to recover damages for her allegedly wrongful discharge in violation of public policy following her refusal to dialyze a terminally ill double amputee patient because of her "moral, medical and philosophical objections" to performing the procedure.

The facts giving rise to this appeal are not in dispute and may be summarized as follows. The Hospital, where plaintiff had been employed for eleven years as a registered nurse, terminated plaintiff from its employment on August 6, 1982. For the three years just prior to her discharge, plaintiff had worked in the Hospital's kidney dialysis unit. It is undisputed that plaintiff was an at-will employee.

Plaintiff alleges that during the summer of 1982 her supervisor periodically assigned her to dialyze a double amputee patient who suffered from a number of maladies. On two occasions plaintiff claims that she had to cease treatment because the patient suffered cardiac arrest and severe internal hemorrhaging during the dialysis procedure. During the first week of 1982 plaintiff again was sched-

uled to dialyze this patient. She approached her head nurse and informed her that "she had moral, medical, and philosophical objections" to performing this procedure on the patient because the patient was terminally ill and, she contended, the procedure was causing the patient additional complications. At that time the head nurse granted plaintiff's request for reassignment.

On August 6, 1982, the head nurse again assigned plaintiff to dialyze the same patient. Plaintiff once again objected, apparently stating that she thought she had reached agreement with the head nurse not to be assigned to this particular patient. She also requested the opportunity to meet with the treating physician, Dr. DiBello. Dr. DiBello informed plaintiff that the patient's family wished him kept alive through dialysis and that he would not survive without it. However, plaintiff continued to refuse to dialyze the patient, and the head nurse informed her that if she did not agree to perform the treatment, the Hospital would dismiss her. Plaintiff refused to change her mind, and the Hospital terminated her.

Plaintiff subsequently instituted this action alleging that she was wrongfully discharged by the Hospital without justification and in

---

488 A.2d 299 (1985). Opinion by Judge Michels.

violation of public policy. The Hospital denied liability to plaintiff and alleged, by way of a separate defense, that plaintiff's termination was appropriate because she had the status of an at-will employee. Following completion of pretrial discovery, the Hospital moved for summary judgment, which the trial court denied because it perceived "that there [was] . . . a question of fact as to whether or not there is a public policy as articulated in the nurses' code of ethics that would permit somebody in the nursing profession to refuse to participate in a course of treatment which is against her principles in good faith." However, upon reconsideration, the trial court granted the motion, concluding that "the nurses' code of ethics is a personal moral judgment and permits the nurse to have a personal moral judgment, but it does not rise to a public policy in the face of the general public policies that patients must be cared for in hospitals and patients must be treated basically by doctors and doctors' orders must be carried out." This appeal followed.

Plaintiff contends that the trial court erred in granting summary judgment because her refusal to dialyze the terminally ill patient was justified as a matter of law by her adherence to the *Code for Nurses,* a code of ethics promulgated by the American Nurses Association, and that determining whether adherence to the *Code* "constitutes a public policy question" is a question of fact which should be resolved by a jury, not by the trial court. We disagree. . . .

Plaintiff relies on the "public policy" exception to the "at-will employment" doctrine to justify her claim that defendant wrongfully discharged her. As has often been stated at common law, "in the absence of an employment contract, employers or employees have been free to terminate the employment relationship with or without cause." . . . Recently, in *Pierce v. Ortho Pharmaceutical Corp., supra,* the Supreme Court recognized a developing

exception to the traditional "at-will employment" doctrine, holding that "an employee has a cause of action for wrongful discharge when the discharge is contrary to a clear mandate of public policy." . . .

As a preliminary matter plaintiff contends that identifying the "clear mandate of public policy" constitutes a genuine issue of material fact for the jury rather than, as occurred in the instant case, a threshold question for the trial judge. To support her contention plaintiff cites *Kalman v. Grand Union Co.,* . . . in which we said:

> It is the employee's burden to identify "a specific expression" or "a clear mandate" of public policy which might bar his discharge. [Citation omitted]. What constitutes a qualifying mandate is a fact question. . . .

However, quoting the following explanatory language from *Ortho Pharmaceutical,* we went on to emphasize that "the judiciary must define the cause of action in case-by-case determinations." . . .

In *Ortho Pharmaceutical* plaintiff, a physician and research scientist, was dismissed because of her opposition to continued laboratory research, development and testing of the drug loperamide, which Ortho intended to market for the treatment of diarrhea. The plaintiff was opposed to the drug because it contained saccharin and because she believed that by continuing work on loperamide she would violate her interpretation of the Hippocratic oath. The Court held, *as a matter of law,* that where plaintiff merely contended saccharin was controversial, not dangerous, and the FDA had not yet approved human testing of loperamide, the Hippocratic oath did not contain a clear mandate of public policy preventing the physician from continuing research. Then, not finding any issue of material fact, the Supreme Court remanded the case to the trial court for the entry of summary judgment.

Thus, identifying the mandate of public policy is a question of law, analogous to interpreting a statute or defining a duty in a negligence case. . . . As the Chancery Court said in *Schaffer v. Federal Trust Co.,* . . .

"Public policy has been defined as that principle of law which holds that no person can lawfully do that which has a tendency to be injurious to the public, or against the public good." . . . The term admits of no exact definition. . . . The source of public policy is the statutes enacted by the legislature and in the decisions of the courts; there we find what acts are considered harmful to the public and therefore unlawful.

Public policy is not concerned with minutiae, but with principles. Seldom does a single clause of a statute establish public policy; policy is discovered from study of the whole statute, or even a group of statutes *in pari materia.* . . .

Based on the foregoing, we hold that where a discharged at-will employee asserts wrongful discharge on public policy grounds, the trial court must, as a matter of law, determine whether public policy justified the alleged conduct. Then, assuming the pleadings raise a genuine issue of material fact, it is for the jury to determine the truth of the employee's allegations. Here, therefore, the issue of whether the *Code for Nurses* represented a clear expression of public policy did not present a genuine issue of material fact precluding the entry of summary judgment.

Plaintiff next contends that, as a matter of law, the *Code for Nurses* constitutes an authoritative statement of public policy which justified her conduct and that the trial court therefore improperly granted defendant's motion for summary judgment. In *Ortho Pharmaceutical* the Supreme Court discussed the role of professional codes of ethics as sources of public policy in "at-will employment" cases:

In certain instances, a professional code of ethics may contain an expression of public policy.

However, not all such sources express a clear mandate of public policy. For example, a code of ethics designed to serve only the interests of a profession or an administrative regulation concerned with technical matters probably would not be sufficient. Absent legislation, the judiciary must define the cause of action in case-by-case determinations. An employer's right to discharge an employee at will carries a correlative duty not to discharge an employee who declines to perform an act that would require a violation of a clear mandate of public policy. However, unless an employee at will identifies a specific expression of public policy, he may be discharged with or without cause. . . .

The Court carefully warned against confusing reliance on professional ethics with reliance on personal morals:

Employees who are professionals owe a special duty to abide not only by federal and state law, but also by the recognized codes of ethics of their professions. That duty may oblige them to decline to perform acts required by their employers. However, an employee should not have the right to prevent his or her employer from pursuing its business because the employee perceives that a particular business decision violates the employee's personal morals, as distinguished from the recognized code of ethics of the employee's profession. . . .

The burden is on the professional to identify "a specific expression" or "a clear mandate" of public policy which might bar his or her dismissal. . . .

Here, plaintiff cites the *Code for Nurses* to justify her refusal to dialyze the terminally ill patient. She refers specifically to the following provisions and interpretive statement:

THE NURSE PROVIDES SERVICES WITH RESPECT FOR HUMAN DIGNITY AND THE UNIQUENESS OF THE CLIENT UNRESTRICTED BY CONSIDERATIONS OF SOCIAL OR ECONOMIC STATUS, PERSONAL ATTRIBUTES, OR THE NATURE OF HEALTH PROBLEMS.

1.4 THE NATURE OF HEALTH PROBLEMS

The nurse's concern for human dignity and the provision of quality nursing care is not limited by personal attitudes or beliefs. If personally opposed to the delivery of care in a particular case because of the nature of the health problem or the procedures to be used, the nurse is justified in refusing to participate. Such refusal should be made known in advance and in time for other appropriate arrangements to be made for the client's nursing care. If the nurse must knowingly enter such a case under emergency circumstances or enters unknowingly, the obligation to provide the best possible care is observed. The nurse withdraws from this type of situation only when assured that alternative sources of nursing care are available to the client. If a client requests information or counsel in an area that is legally sanctioned but contrary to the nurse's personal beliefs, the nurse may refuse to provide these services but must advise the client of sources where such service is available. [American Nurses Association, *Code for Nurses with Interpretive Statements.* . . .

Plaintiff contends that these provisions constitute a clear mandate of public policy justifying her conduct. . . .

It is our view that as applied to the circumstances of this case the passage cited by plaintiff defines a standard of conduct beneficial only to the individual nurse and not to the public at large. The overall purpose of the language cited by plaintiff is to preserve human dignity; however, it should not be at the expense of the patient's life or contrary to the family's wishes. The record before us shows that the family had requested that dialysis be continued on the patient, and there is nothing to suggest that the patient had, or would have, indicated otherwise. . . .

Recently, in *In re Conroy, supra,* our Supreme Court confirmed this State's basic interest in the preservation of life, . . . and our recognition, embraced in the right to self-determination, that all patients have a fundamental right to expect that medical treatment will not be terminated against their will. . . . This basic policy mandate clearly outweighs any policy favoring the right of a nurse to refuse to participate in treatments which he or she personally believes threatens human dignity. Indeed, the following passage from the *Code for Nurses* echoes the policy cited by *Conroy* and severely constrains the ethical right of nurses to refuse participation in medical procedures:

1.4 THE NATURE OF HEALTH PROBLEMS

The nurse's respect for the worth and dignity of the individual human being applies irrespective of the nature of the health problem. It is reflected in the care given the person who is disabled as well as the normal; the patient with the long-term illness as well as the one with the acute illness, or the recovering patient as well as the one who is terminally ill or dying. It extends to all who require the services of the nurse for the promotion of health, the prevention of illness, the restoration of health, and the alleviation of suffering. [American Nurses Association, *Code for Nurses with Interpretive Statements.* . . .

The position asserted by plaintiff serves only the individual and the nurses' profession while leaving the public to wonder when and whether they will receive nursing care. . . . Moreover, as the Hospital argues, "[i]t would be a virtual impossibility to administer a hospital if each nurse or member of the administration staff refused to carry out his or her duties based upon a personal private belief concerning the right to live. . . ."

Concededly, plaintiff had to make a difficult decision. Viewing the facts in a light most beneficial to plaintiff, she had dialyzed the particular patient on several occasions in the past, and on two of those occasions plaintiff says the patient had suffered cardiac arrest and severe internal hemorrhaging during the dialysis procedure. The first time plaintiff objected to performing the procedure her head nurse agreed to reassign her, and at that time plaintiff apparently believed she had an agreement with the head nurse not to be assigned to this particular patient. She also believed she had fulfilled her ethical obligation by making her refusal to participate in the procedure "known in advance and in time for other appropriate arrangements to be made for the client's nursing care."

Nonetheless, we conclude as a matter of law that even under the circumstances of this case the ethical considerations cited by plaintiff do not rise to the level of a public policy mandate permitting a registered nursing professional to refuse to provide medical treatment to a terminally ill patient, even where that nursing professional gives his or her superiors advance warning. Beyond this, even if we were to make the dubious assumption that the *Code for Nurses* represents a clear expression of public policy, we have no hesitancy in concluding on this record that plaintiff was

motivated by her own personal morals, precluding application of the "public policy" exception to the "at-will employment" doctrine. Plaintiff alleged that each time she refused to dialyze the patient she told the head nurse that she had "moral, medical and philosophical objections" to performing the procedure. She makes no assertion that she ever referred to her obligations and entitlements pursuant to her code of ethics. In addition, the very basis for plaintiff's reliance on the *Code for Nurses* is that she was personally opposed to the dialysis procedure. By refusing to perform the procedure she may have eased her own conscience, but she neither benefited the society-at-large, the patient, nor the patient's family.

Accordingly, the judgment under review is affirmed.

Potter v. Village Bank of New Jersey

Superior Court of New Jersey

The crucial question raised in this appeal is whether a bank president and chief executive officer who blows the whistle on suspected laundering of Panamanian drug money is protected from retaliatory discharge by the public policy of this State. We answer in the affirmative. We also hold that the retaliatory discharge in this case constituted an intentional tort which exposed defendants to compensatory and punitive damages. We affirm the judgment.

A

Plaintiff Dale G. Potter became the president and chief executive officer of the Village Bank of New Jersey (Village Bank) on November 15,

1982. His employment was terminated in May or June 1984. On June 13, 1984 plaintiff filed a complaint in the Chancery Division against Village Bank alleging that his job had been wrongfully terminated. Plaintiff sought reinstatement to his position as chief executive officer and president of the bank. . . .

After the matter was transferred to the Law Division, plaintiff filed an amended complaint. . . . In the four-count amended complaint plaintiff sought compensatory and punitive damages based on (1) fraudulent inducement, (2) breach of contract, (3) tortious interference with the employment relationship and (4) wrongful termination.

The case was tried to a jury over a four-day period. . . . At the end of plaintiff's case, the

543 A.2d 80 (1985). Opinion by Judge J. H. Coleman.

trial judge granted defendants' motion for involuntary dismissal of plaintiff's claims of fraudulent inducement, breach of contract and wrongful interference with the employment relationship. The only remaining claim was for wrongful discharge. . . .

The claim of wrongful discharge was submitted to the jury as to the remaining defendants, Village Bank and Em Kay. The jury answered the following special interrogatories:

Q1. Did the Defendants wrongfully discharge the plaintiff?

A. Yes.

Q2. Was the plaintiff damaged by such wrongful discharge?

A. Yes.

Q3. What amount of compensatory damages, if any, should the plaintiff be awarded for such wrongful discharge?

A. $50,000.

Q4. What amount of punitive damages, if any, should the plaintiff be awarded for such wrongful discharge?

A. $100,000.

After the trial judge denied defendants' motion for judgment notwithstanding the verdict, final judgment was entered in the sum of $162,575.40, which consisted of $100,000 in punitive damages, $50,000 in compensatory damages plus $12,575.40 in prejudgment interest on the compensatory damages.

Village Bank and Em Kay Holding Corporation have appealed from the entire judgment. Plaintiff has cross-appealed from the involuntary dismissals at the end of plaintiff's evidence.

The pivotal issue presented to the jury was whether plaintiff resigned or was discharged in violation of a clear mandate of public policy. Based on the evidence presented, the jury concluded he was fired contrary to a clear mandate of public policy. The following evidence supports that finding. Em Kay Holding Corporation (Em Kay) owns 93% of the stock of Village Bank. The remaining 7% is distributed among other shareholders. Em Kay is owned by the Em Kay Group which has its headquarters in Panama City, Panama. Em Kay Group is owned by Mory Kraselnick and Moises Kroitoro.

Bart and Kraselnick negotiated with plaintiff for employment at Village Bank. In September 1982 when the president of Village Bank suffered a heart attack, plaintiff was offered and accepted a position with the bank as a "holding company consultant." Plaintiff became president and chief executive officer of Village Bank two months later. Between then and January 1983, Kraselnick frequently telephoned plaintiff to request that Village Bank make large loans to companies that did business with Kraselnick and companies owned by Kraselnick. With few exceptions, plaintiff refused these requests.

After a January 21, 1983 meeting Kraselnick told plaintiff: "[I]f I ever ask you to do anything wrong, I'll stand up in front of you." At the time, plaintiff did not understand the meaning of the statement. Over the next couple of months, however, many cash deposits of between $8,000 and $9,300 were made into the accounts of Kraselnick, Bart, Noel Kinkella (office manager of Em Kay Equities whose president was Bart) and several of the companies in the Em Kay Group.

On March 24, 1983 plaintiff learned that Village Bank was advertising his job in the *Wall Street Journal*. When plaintiff confronted Kraselnick about this, he was told "You're not as outspoken and enthusiastic as I want you to be when you meet me." After plaintiff defended his position, the two temporarily reconciled.

On March 31, 1983 Kinkella went to Village Bank with a shopping bag filled with money. She made seven $9,000 deposits to accounts held by Kraselnick, Bart, Kinkella and four Em Kay related companies. Plaintiff became suspicious that drug money was being laundered so he called the New Jersey Commissioner of Banking and reported the transactions and requested advice. Before plaintiff could meet with the Commissioner, Kinkella deposited another package of about $50,000 in cash. When plaintiff asked Bart about the money, Bart told him that it was for lease payments between two related aeronautical companies in the Em Kay Group. Plaintiff became more suspicious that the large cash deposits were related to laundering of Panamanian drug money. When the Commissioner eventually met with plaintiff, he told plaintiff to maintain anonymity and that a full investigation would be undertaken. The jury was not informed about the details of plaintiff's suspicions.

Audits of the bank were conducted starting around the end of April or the beginning of May 1983. On June 28, 1983 plaintiff advised Village Bank's board of directors of the examination, but not of his meeting with the Commissioner. In July 1983 plaintiff filed currency transaction reports with the Department of the Treasury reporting the cash deposits.

In September 1983 Village Bank's board of directors raised plaintiff's salary from $65,000 to $75,000. Kraselnick also offered plaintiff a $10,000 bonus in cash so he "wouldn't pay income taxes" on it. When plaintiff refused to accept the bonus in cash, the bonus was not paid. In December 1983 the United States Attorney's Office for New Jersey issued subpoenas to the bank for the production of documents "on a list of accounts" related to the Em Kay Group. Plaintiff was also interviewed by representatives from that office.

On January 6, 1984 plaintiff executed his first written employment contract with Village Bank. The term was for one year beginning November 15, 1983. The contract provided for a base salary of $75,000, with a bonus at the discretion of the board of directors.

At some time between July and December 1983, plaintiff told Steven S. Radin, secretary to the Village Bank board of directors, that he "had gone to the Commissioner and reported the [cash] transactions." In January 1984 Radin informed Bart and Kraselnick of what plaintiff had told him. This angered Kraselnick. At the next scheduled board meeting, the directors were informed.

Immediately after the board meeting, Kraselnick asked plaintiff why he went to the Commissioner of Banking. When plaintiff responded "I thought that it was drug money," Kraselnick stated "you're probably right." From that point on, plaintiff contended that he was isolated from running the bank effectively since his subordinates in the bank were ordered not to talk to him. Further, there were several instances where Kraselnick questioned plaintiff's judgment and accused him of doing things incorrectly.

Plaintiff testified that Radin and at least two of Village Bank's directors advised him that he was about to be fired before plaintiff wrote a letter on May 22, 1984. The letter was written to Kraselnick which stated in pertinent part:

> I wanted to be able to communicate directly with you and since my requests for a face to face meeting with you have been rejected, I am using this as my only recourse. At this point in time, I am considering myself "de facto" fired since Allan Bart has told several directors and John Bjerke, among others, that "Potter's gone" and in turn at least one director has communicated the same to several customers who have even discussed it with people in the Bank including myself. Needless to say, the lack of discretion in discussing this situation in this way can only serve to hurt the Bank and the people in it. However, it has been done and the effect of it, in my opinion, has been that I consider myself at this point in time essentially to be terminated only without the pre-requisite action of the Board of Directors.

Shortly after the letter was written, plaintiff told members attending a board meeting that the letter was not intended as a letter of resignation. He reiterated this point in a May 31, 1984 letter to Radin.

By letter dated June 1, 1984, Radin notified plaintiff that

> ...it was the consensus of the Board that the Bank pay you full salary until the termination (November 15, 1984) of your present contract. During that period of time you would have the use of a car, office and secretarial assistance. Also you would receive all ordinary employee benefits. In consideration of these severance terms the Board requested a general release from you for the Bank, its directors and officers. The Board gave you until June 1, 1984 to accept or reject this offer. From May 24, 1984 until June 1, 1984 you were placed on leave of absence with pay.

Plaintiff rejected the proposal made by the board. When plaintiff attempted to attend a June 11 board meeting with his attorney, the board asked him to leave the bank. . . .

B

Subsequent to the trial in this matter Kraselnick, Bart, Bjerke and Village Bank were indicted by a federal grand jury for the District of New Jersey for allegedly conspiring to defraud the United States and making fraudulent statements in violation of 31 *U.S.C.* § 5311 *et seq.,* 31 *C.F.R.* § 103.22 *et seq.,* and 18 *U.S.C.* §§ 371, 1001 and 1002. The alleged criminal violations are based on their failure to report large cash transactions at Village Bank during the time Potter was president and chief executive officer.

31 *U.S.C.* § 5313(a) provides, in pertinent part:

> (a) When a domestic financial institution is involved in a transaction for the . . . receipt . . . of United States coins or currency (or other monetary instruments the Secretary of the Treasury prescribes), in an amount, denomination, or amount and denomination, or under circumstances the Secretary prescribes by regulation, the institution and any other participant in the transaction the Secretary may prescribe shall file a report on the transaction at the time and in the way the Secretary prescribes. A participant acting for another person shall make the report as the agent or bailee of the person and identify the person for whom the transaction is being made.

Pursuant to this authority, the Secretary of the Treasury promulgated regulations which mandate the reporting of transactions in currency of more than $10,000.

Because the deposits in this case were slightly less than $10,000, plaintiff was not required by the strict wording of the statute and regulations to report the cash transactions. However, there is existing authority holding that a bank officer may not structure a single transaction in currency as multiple transactions to avoid the reporting requirements. A financial institution must aggregate all transactions by one customer in one day.

. . . Potter did much more than "protest [] [the] directors' improprieties" relating to a regulatory scheme. He blew the whistle on suspected criminal conduct involving one or more directors. Hence, Potter's termination relates to the public policy designed to encourage citizens to report suspected criminal violations to the proper authorities in order to ensure proper enforcement of both state and federal penal laws. . . . Nowhere in our society is the need for protection greater than in protecting well motivated citizens who blow the whistle on suspected white collar and street level criminal activities. If "no person can lawfully do that which has a tendency to be injurious to the public or against the public good" because of public policy, *Allen v. Commercial Casualty Insurance Co.,* . . . surely whistle blowers of suspected criminal violations must be protected from retaliatory discharge. It stands to reason that few people would cooperate with law enforcement officials if the price they must pay is retaliatory discharge from employment. Clearly, that would have a chilling effect on criminal investigations and law enforcement in general.

Additionally, after the plaintiff's employment was terminated, the Legislature enacted the Conscientious Employee Protection Act, . . . effective September 5, 1986. Under the act, an employee who has been terminated because of reporting suspected criminal violations, has the right to file a retaliatory tort claim in addition to other remedies. We read this legislative enactment as a codification of public policy established through judicial decisions. . . .

We hold that the public policy of the State of New Jersey should protect at will employees — including bank presidents — who in good faith blow the whistle on one or more bank directors suspected of laundering money from illegal activities. . . .

clear mandate of public policy is entitled to recover economic and noneconomic losses. Such an employee may recover (1) the amount he or she would have earned from the time of wrongful discharge for a reasonable time until he or she finds new employment, including bonuses and vacation pay, less any unemployment compensation received in the interim, . . . (2) expenses associated with finding new employment and mental anguish or emotional distress damages proximately related to the retaliatory discharge, . . . and (3) the replacement value of fringe benefits such as an automobile and insurance for a reasonable time until new employment is obtained. . . .

The jury awarded $50,000 in compensatory damages. In addition, the jury awarded $100,000 in punitive damages. We are completely satisfied that both the compensatory and punitive damages awarded are supported by sufficient credible evidence and were consonant with the law. . . .

C

We hold that an at will employee who has sustained a retaliatory discharge in violation of a

CASES

CASE 1. *The Reluctant Security Guard*

David Tuff, 24, is a security guard who has been working for the past 17 months for the Blue Mountain Company in Minneapolis, Minnesota. Blue Mountain manages and operates retail shopping malls in several midwestern states. The company has a security services division that trains and supplies mall security guards, including those for the Village Square Mall where Tuff has been employed.

From Anna Pinedo and Tom L. Beauchamp, "The Reluctant Security Guard." *Case Studies in Business, Society and Ethics*, edited by Tom L. Beauchamp, Prentice Hall, Upper Saddle River, NJ. 1998. Reprinted with permission.

Minnesota state and local laws require that security officers be licensed and approved by the county police department. Security officers are required to obey the police unit's rules. Tuff completed the required training, passed the security guard compulsory examination, and was issued a license. Tuff has consistently carried out his guard duties conscientiously. Previously a four-year military policeman in the U.S. Marine Corps. his commanding officer had praised both his service and his integrity.

Part of his job training at Blue Mountain required that Tuff learn the procedures found in the *Security Officer's Manual,* which uses military regulations as a model. Two sections of this manual are worded as follows:

Section V, subsection D.

Should a serious accident or crime, including all felonies, occur on the premises of the licensee, it shall be the responsibility of the licensee to notify the appropriate police department immediately. Failure to do so is a violation of the provisions of this manual.

Furthermore, the manual permits the following action if the provisions are violated:

Section X1 — disciplinary and deportment
   A. General
   1. The Private Security Coordinator may reprimand a licensee as hereinafter provided. In cases of suspension or revocation, the licensee shall immediately surrender his identification card and badge to the County Police Department. . . .
   B. Cause for Disciplinary Action
   13. Any violation of any regulation or rule found in this manual is cause for disciplinary action.

The reverse side of a security officer's license bears these statements:

Obey The Rules and Regulations Promulgated By The Superintendent Of Police.

We will obey all lawful orders and rules and regulations pertaining to security officers promulgated by the superintendent of police of the county or any officer placed by him over me.

Given this language, Tuff believed that his license could be revoked or suspended for *any* failure to report illegal behavior such as drunk driving and selling narcotics. He had sworn to uphold these regulations at the end of his training and had later signed a statement acknowledging that he knew a police officer could ask for his badge if a conflict should arise.

Fourteen months after Tuff joined the company, Blue Mountain issued new rules of procedure outlining certain assigned duties of its security guards. These rules required security officers "to order and escort intoxicated persons, including persons driving under the influence of alcohol, off its parking lots and onto the public roads." The rules did not instruct security officers to either arrest the drivers or to contact or alert the police.

Tuff immediately, and publicly, opposed the company's new policy. Over the ensuing months, he expressed his dissatisfaction to every company officer he could locate. He complained to his immediate superiors, sometimes several times a day, that he was being asked to set a drunk out on the road who might later kill an innocent person. Tuff described to these supervisors imagined scenarios in which a drunk clearly violated the law, and he then asked them what he would be expected to do in these circumstances under the new rules.

His immediate supervisor, Director of Security Manuel Hernandez, told him that if any such situation arose he should contact the supervisor in charge, who would make the decision. Hernandez noted that most drunks do not weave down the road and hit someone. Tuff was not satisfied and used abusive language in denouncing the rules.

Hernandez became angry and told Tuff that his complaints irritated his supervisors and that they could tolerate only so much of his behavior. Hernandez also cautioned him that he should worry less about his license and more about his paycheck. Neither man put any complaint in writing. Tuff never received a written warning or reprimand from any company official. Tuff maintained that he considered the policy to be illegal, violative of the rules he had sworn to uphold, and dangerous to the maintenance of his license. Neither his supervisor nor the company manager agreed with his interpretation. They encouraged him to continue his job as usual, but under the new rules.

Tuff then contacted a volunteer organization working to prevent drunk driving. At first he simply sought the organization's interpretation of the law, but later, he voiced a specific complaint about the Blue Mountain policy. His supervisors were approached by some representatives of the volunteer organization, who expressed strong opposition to Blue Mountain's policy for security guards and treatment of drunk drivers.

In the following weeks, Tuff discussed the company policy with several other concerned security guards. He met with security officers Fred Grant and Robert Ladd at a restaurant after work. They discussed the company procedure and its conflict with their licensing requirements and sworn commitments. They considered going to the local newspaper with their grievances against the company policy.

Tuff then contacted a local television news station and a local newspaper. He talked to four reporters about several drunk driving incidents at Blue Mountain parking lots. The reporters pursued Tuff's complaint by talking to company officials about the policy. The reporters proved to their editors' satisfaction that Tuff's complaints to the media were not given in reckless disregard of the truth and were, in fact, entirely truthful.

Hernandez called Tuff into his office to discuss these disclosures to the newspaper. Hernandez asked Tuff to sign a document acknowledging that he had spoken with news reporters concerning Blue Mountain company policies, but he refused to sign. Hernandez reminded him of a company policy prohibiting an employee from talking to the media about company policies. This policy is mentioned on a list of company rules distributed to all employees that states that violation of the rules could result in dismissal or in disciplinary procedures. Tuff knew the company rule but did not consider his revelations a violation, because he had not spoken with the press *on company time.*

Hernandez considered Tuff's interpretation of the rule's scope ridiculous. He consulted with the company's Council of Managers that afternoon. Every manger agreed that Tuff's interpretation of the rule showed a blatant disregard for company policy and that Tuff's excuse was an ad hoc rationalization. They also agreed that Tuff had shown himself to be a complainer and a man of poor judgment, qualities that rendered him unsuitable to be a Blue Mountain security guard. The discussion of this problem at the meeting took little more than five minutes. Council members instructed Hernandez to give Tuff a few days' leave to reflect on the situation. Hernandez duly reported this conclusion to Tuff, who then departed for his home. The number of days of leave he should take was not specified, but both men agreed in an amicable though tense setting that they would be in touch.

Three days later an article about the company's policies appeared in the local newspaper, along with a picture of Tuff in the mall, about to report for work. This story prompted an editorial that was critical of the company on a local television station. The story relied entirely on data provided by Tuff, some of which had been copied from his nightly shift reports.

The newspaper had also interviewed Sergeant Shriver of the county police department. He corraborated Tuff's interpretation that any failure by a security guard to report those driving while intoxicated or those under the influence of drugs constituted a violation of the security manual and the specific terms of the officer's license. He also confirmed Tuff's statement that police officers routinely inspect security officers' activities and that the police have instructions to look for failures to comply with license requirements.

After the television editorial, Blue Mountain began to receive phone calls at a rate of approximately 15 per hour, with over 90 percent of the callers expressing opposition to the company's policies. Several callers indicated that they would no longer patronize the malls mentioned in the newspaper story.

The Council of Managers immediately reconvened to consider this escalation of the problem. Its members agreed that Tuff had to be fired for his violation of the company rule against disclosures to the news media. The managers considered Tuff's revelations an unforgivable act of disloyalty. They discussed whether the proper and precise reason for Tuff's dismissal was his disclosure of confidential information or his approaching the media. Their decision on this point required a sharpening of a vaguely worded corporate rule; a careful process of interpretation revealed that approaching the media is grounds for dismissal even if no disclosure of confidential information is made.

Five working days later, Tuff was called into the company manger's office and dismissed. The manager informed him that the reason for this dismissal was his discussions with the press, a violation of company policy.

Tuff then issued a public statement. He explained that his complaints against Blue Mountain Company's procedures had stemmed from his concern to protect the public and other security officers. Tuff had discussed the policy with the company's other security guards, who had all expressed some degree of concern over the policy because it forced them to violate their licensing requirements and subjected them to possible license suspension or revocation. Based on these encounters, Tuff believed that he was acting on their behalf as well as on his own.

Tuff also disclosed a legal argument he wanted to pursue: He contended that his admissions to the media and his complaints about company policy were protected activities. The company interfered with, restrained, and coerced its employees in the exercise of their rights, as protected by the National Labor Relations Act of 1935, by suspending and eventually dismissing Tuff for his disclosures to the press, which violated company policy.

Tuff brought his case to the National Labor Relations Board (NLRB), whose members determined that Blue Mountain was within its legal rights to fire him. The board found that whistleblowers are legally protected only if they engage in "concerted activity" together with their fellow workers, Because Tuff had acted alone for the most part, he was not protected. However, a NLRB spokesperson said the board made no moral judgment on either the employer's or the employee's conduct. The parties' moral behavior, he said, was not at stake in the NLRB decision.

Questions

1. Was the security guard right to take the action he did? Would you have taken the same action? Why or why not?

2. Is this a case of an unjust dismissal?

3. Should there be a law to protect employees from losing their jobs for this kind of activity?

4. Think of some creative ways other than dismissal to handle this situation.

CASE 2. *Probable Cause and Drug Testing*

Global Concern, Inc., is a small import-export company located in Seattle. Beth Sandino is the second shift shipping and receiving supervisor for Global Concern. Over a period of several weeks Beth has noticed a change in the behavior of Steve Osterhaut, one of the second shift inventory clerks. Steve's job is to record all incoming and outgoing shipments in the company's somewhat antiquated computer database. Steve is normally stoical and introverted. Recently, however, he has been more talkative and given to outbreaks of laughter. He has also been more productive and has approached Beth on several occasions with ideas for updating the inventory management system.

Beth has noticed that this change in Steve's behavior is most apparent after Steve has had lunch with Jim Morrison, the new second shift forklift operator. Jim's performance has been consistently satisfactory since the day he began work for Global Concern. As far as Beth can tell, his personal behavior has also been consistent since he began work. One day after lunch Beth noticed an empty package of cigarette papers in Steve's wastebasket. She suspects that Steve and Jim have been smoking marijuana during their lunch break.

Questions

1. Do you think Beth would be justified in having Steve tested for drug use? Would she be justified in having Jim tested for drug use? Explain.
2. Would DesJardins and Duska support the decision to test Steve? To test Jim? Explain.
3. Assume that Beth decided to bring the matter of testing Steve and Jim to senior management. Should senior management initiate a policy of universal drug testing? Explain.
4. In justifying a decision to test or not to test, do you think it would make a difference if Global Concern specialized in the import and export of industrial explosives? Would it make a difference to DesJardins and Duska? Explain.

This case was prepared by D. G. Arnold. Reprinted by permission.

CASE 3. *A Matter of Principle*

Nancy Smith was hired May 1, 1988, as the associate director of Medical Research at a major pharmaceutical company. The terms of Ms. Smith's employment were not fixed by contract, and as a result she is considered to be an "at-will" employee. Two years later Ms. Smith was promoted to Director of Medical Research Therapeutics, a section that studied nonreproductive drugs.

One of the company's research projects involved the development of loperamide — a liquid treatment for acute and chronic diarrhea to be used by infants, children, and older persons who were unable to take solid

This case was prepared by Norman E. Bowie on the basis of the appeal decision in *Pierre v. Ortho Pharmaceutical Corporation*, Superior Court of New Jersey, 1979.

medication. The formula contained saccharin in an amount that was 44 times higher than that the Food and Drug Administration permitted in 12 ounces of an artificially sweetened soft drink. There are, however, no promulgated standards for the use of saccharin in drugs.

The research project team responsible for the development of loperamide unanimously agreed that because of the high saccharin content, the existing formula loperamide was unsuitable for distribution in the United States (apparently the formula was already being distributed in Europe). The team estimated that the development of an alternative formula would take at least three months.

The pharmaceutical's management pressured the team to proceed with the existing formula, and the research project team finally agreed. Nancy Smith maintained her opposition to the high saccharin formula and indicated that the Hippocratic Oath prevented her from giving the formula to old people and children. Nancy Smith was the only medical person on the team, and the grounds for her decision was that saccharin was a possible carcinogen. Therefore Nancy Smith was unable to participate in the clinical testing.

Upon learning that she was unwilling to participate in the clinical testing, the management removed her from the project and gave her a demotion. Her demotion was posted, and she was told that management considered her unpromotable. She was charged specifically with being irresponsible, lacking in good judgment, unproductive, and uncooperative with marketing. Nancy Smith had never been criticized by supervisors before. Nancy Smith resigned because she believed she was being punished for refusing to pursue a task she thought unethical.

Questions

1. Was Nancy Smith terminated, or did she resign voluntarily?
2. Should the pharmaceutical's management have the right to terminate Nancy Smith if she refused to participate in the clinical testing?
3. Under the circumstances of her "resignation," should she have the right to sue for reinstatement to her position as Director of Medical Research Therapeutics?
4. If you were the judge in such a court case, how would you rule and on what grounds?

CASE 4.   *A "State-of-the-Art" Termination*

Monday had been the most humiliating day of Bill Collin's life. Rumors of downsizing had been swirling for months, and every computer analyst in Bill's department knew that the ax would fall on some of them. Bets had even been taken on who would stay and who would go. When the news was finally delivered, Bill was not surprised. He also understood the necessity of reducing the computer support staff in view of the merger that had made many jobs redundant, and he felt confident that he would find a new job fairly quickly. What upset him was the manner in which he had been terminated.

Bill arrived in the office at eight o'clock sharp to find a memo on his desk about a

From *Ethics and the Conduct of Business*, 2nd edition by John R. Boatright, © 1993. Reprinted by permission of Prentice Hall, Inc. Upper Saddle River, NJ.

nine-thirty meeting at a hotel one block away. Since this site was often used for training sessions, he gave the notice little thought. Bill decided to arrive a few minutes early in order to chat with colleagues, but he found himself being ushered quickly into a small conference room where three other people from his department were already seated. His greeting to them was cut short by a fourth person whom Bill had never seen before. The stranger explained that he was a consultant from an outplacement firm that had been engaged to deliver the bad news and to outline the benefits the company was providing for them. Once he started talking, Bill felt relieved: The package of benefits was greater than he had dared hope. All employees would receive full salary for six months plus pay for accrued vacation time; medical insurance and pension contribution would be continued during this period; and the outplacement firm would provide career counseling and a placement service that included secretarial assistance, photocopying and fax service, and office space. The consultant assured the four longtime employees that the company appreciated their years of service and wanted to proceed in a caring manner. It was for this reason that they hired the best consulting firm in the business, one that had a reputation for a "state-of-the-art" termination process.

Bill's relief was jolted by what came next. The consultant informed the four that they were not to return to their office or to set foot inside the corporate office building again; nor were they to attempt to contact anyone still working for the company. (At this point, Bill suddenly realized that he had no idea how many employees might be in other four-person groups being dismissed at the same time.) The contents of their desks would be boxed and delivered to their homes; directories of their computer files would be provided, and requests for any personal material would be honored after a careful review of their contents to make sure that no proprietary information was included. The consultant assured them that all passwords had already been changed, including the password for remote access. Finally, they were instructed not to remain at the hotel but to proceed to a service exit where prepaid taxis were stationed to take them home.

Bill regretted not being able to say good-bye to friends in the office. He would have liked some advance warning in order to finish up several projects that he had initiated and to clear out his own belongings. The manner in which he had been terminated was compassionate up to a point, Bill admitted, but it showed that the company did not trust him. A few days later, Bill understood the company's position better when he read an article in a business magazine that detailed the sabotage that had been committed by terminated employees who had continued access to their employer's computer system. Some disgruntled workers had destroyed files and done other mischief when they were allowed to return to their offices after being informed of their termination. One clever computer expert had previously planted a virtually undetectable virus that remained dormant until he gained access long enough through a co-worker's terminal to activate it. The advice that companies were receiving from consulting firms that specialize in termination was: Be compassionate, but also protect yourself. Good advice, Bill thought, but the humiliation was still fresh in his mind.

Questions

1. Was the termination of Bill Collin legally justified? Morally justified?
2. Leaving aside the morality of the termination itself, did the company treat Bill justly?

3. Was the fear of sabotage adequate justification for not allowing Bill back on company property or to say goodbye to his friends?

4. How could the company handle the termination process better while at the same time taking account of reports of sabotage at other companies?

CASE 5. *Health and Genetic Screening*

During the past decade, biologists have made significant strides in the field of genetics. Media attention has focused on gene splicing, the creation of new forms of life, and the increase in the quality, size, and disease resistance of agricultural products.

However, this new technology is also enabling biologists to delve into complex genetic information. Soon DNA tests will be able to provide full physical and mental profiles of human beings. Apart from the issues that such testing will present for parents-to-be, complexities could develop in the workplace as well.

The Office of Technology Assessment of the House Committee on Science and Technology surveyed the five hundred largest U.S. industrial companies, fifty private utilities, and eleven unions and found that seventeen had used genetic testing to screen employees for the sickle-cell trait or enzyme deficiencies.

Genetic screening also could reveal an individual's tolerance for or susceptibility to chemicals used in the workplace. With health insurance costs increasing exponentially, employers are trying to improve employee health with routine medical screening, creation of smoke-free environments, and drug testing. Genetic profile tests could be used to hire only those individuals who meet certain minimum health requirements and are thus likely to keep health insurance costs down.

Insurers have used AIDS screening as a prerequisite for medical insurance coverage; similarly, genetic tests could predict susceptibility to heart disease and cancer. Genetic tests allow insurers to screen applicants and either deny coverage or create high-risk pools for those in high risk groups.

Scientist Robert Weinberg has stated:

> A belief that each of us is ultimately responsible for our own behavior has woven our social fabric. Yet in the coming years, we will hear more and more from those who write off bad behavior to the inexorable forces of biology and who embrace a new astrology in which alleles rather than stars determine individuals' lives. It is hard to imagine how far this growing abdication of responsibility will carry us.
>
> As a biologist, I find this prospect a bitter pill. The biological revolution of the past decades has proven extraordinarily exciting and endlessly fascinating, and it will, without doubt, spawn enormous benefit. But as with most new technologies, we will pay a price unless we anticipate the human genome project's dark side. We need to craft an ethic that cherishes our human ability to transcend biology, that enshrines our spontaneity, unpredictability, and individual uniqueness. At the moment, I find myself and those around me ill equipped to respond to the challenge.[1]

Starting in 1972, DuPont screened its black employees for sickle-cell anemia, which affects one in every four to six hundred black

Americans. Requested by the Black DuPont Employees Association to perform the genetic screening, DuPont administered the voluntary test not to deny jobs, but to offer employees relocation to chemical-free areas where the disease would not be triggered.

Critics of DuPont said the testing allowed the company to transfer workers rather than clean up its work environment. DuPont's medical director responded,

> This is a very naive view. No one can operate at zero emissions, exposures — zero anything. There has to be an agreed-upon practical, safe limit. But there are some employees who are more susceptible to certain diseases than others. It's only common sense to offer them the opportunity to relocate.[2]

In the 1960s, certain workers at an Israeli dynamite factory became ill with acute hemolytic anemia, which causes the walls of the red blood cells to dissolve, thus decreasing the cells' ability to circulate oxygen throughout the body. The workers were transferred to other parts of the plant, but genetic screening revealed that all of them had a G–6–PD deficiency, which causes hemolytic anemia upon exposure to chemicals. The information allowed the factory to place workers properly and led it to reduce chemical levels in the plant.[3]

Questions

1. What impact does genetic screening have on an employee's privacy?
2. In what ways should employers regard genetic screening as necessary?
3. Is DuPont's sickle-cell anemia screening program justifiable? Explain.
4. Discuss how genetic screening might lead to discrimination.
5. Will genetic screening help employers increase safety in the workplace?
6. What impact might the Americans with Disabilities Act have on genetic screening?

NOTES

1. Robert Weinberg. "Genetic Screening," *Technology Review* (April 1991): 51.
2. William P. Patterson, "Genetic Screening." *Industry Week* (1 June 1987): 48.
3. Thoms H. Murray, "Genetic Testing at Work: How Should It Be Used?" *Personnel Administrator* (September 1985): 90–92.

Suggested Supplementary Readings

ALDERMAN, ELLEN and CAROLINE KENNEDY. *The Right to Privacy.* New York: Alfred A. Knopf, 1995.

ARVEY, RICHARD D., and GARY L. RENZ. "Fairness in the Selection of Employees." *Journal of Business Ethics* 11 (May, 1992): 331–40.

BIRSCH, DOUGLAS, "The Universal Drug Testing of Employees." *Business and Professional Ethics Journal* 14 (1995): 43–60.

BRENKERT, GEORGE. "Freedom, Participation and Corporations: The Issue of Corporate (Economic) Democracy." *Business Ethics Quarterly* 2 (July 1992): 251–69.

BRENKERT, GEORGE. "Privacy, Polygraphs, and Work." *Business and Professional Ethics Journal* 1 (Fall 1981): 19–34.

CASTE, NICHOLAS J. "Drug Testing and Productivity." *Journal of Business Ethics* 11 (April 1992): 301–06.

DALTON, DAN R., and MICHAEL B. METZGER. "'Integrity Testing' for Personnel Selection: An Unsparing Perspective." *Journal of Business Ethics* 12 (February 1993): 147–56.

DANDEKAR, NATALIE. "Can Whistleblowing Be FULLY Legitimated?" *Business and Professional Ethics Journal* 10 (Spring 1991): 89–108.

DECEW, JUDITH WAGNER. *In Pursuit of Privacy* Ithaca: Cornell University Press, 1997.

DE GEORGE, RICHARD. "The Right to Work: Law and Ideology." *Valparaiso University Law Review* 19 (Fall 1984): 15–35.

DESJARDINS, JOSEPH R., and JOHN J. MCCALL. "A Defense of Employee Rights." *Journal of Business Ethics* 4 (October 1985): 367–76.

ETZIONI, AMITAI. *The Limits of Privacy.* New York: Basic Books, 1999.

EWIN, R. E. "Corporate Loyalty: Its Objects and Its Grounds." *Journal of Business Ethics* 12 (May 1993): 387–96.

EWING, DAVID W. *Freedom Inside the Organization: Bringing Civil Liberties to the Workplace.* New York: E. P. Dutton, 1977.

EXTEJT, MARIAN M., and WILLIAM N. BOCKANIC. "Issues Surrounding the Theories of Negligent Hiring and Failure to Fire." *Business and Professional Ethics Journal* 8 (Winter 1989): 21–34.

EZORSKY, GERTRUDE, ed. *Moral Rights in the Workplace.* Albany, N.Y.: State University of New York Press, 1987.

FIELDER, JOHN H. "Organizational Loyalty." *Business and Professional Ethics Journal* 11 (Spring 1992): 71–90.

GLAZER, M. P., and P. M. GLAZER. *The Whistle Blowers: Exposing Corruption in Government and Industry.* New York: Basic Books, 1989.

HANSON, KAREN. "The Demands of Loyalty." *Idealistic Studies* 16 (April 1986): 195–204.

HAUGHEY, JOHN C. "Does Loyalty In the Workplace Have a Future?" *Journal of Business Ethics* 3 (January 1993): 1–16.

HIRSCHMAN, ALBERT. *Exit, Voice and Loyalty.* Cambridge, MA: Harvard University Press, 1970.

HUBBARD, RUTH, and ELIJAH WALD. *Exploding the Gene Myth.* Boston: Beacon Press, 1993.

KEELEY, MICHAEL, and JILL W. GRAHAM. "Exit, Voice and Ethics." *Journal of Business Ethics* 10 (May 1991): 349–55.

KUPFER, JOSEPH. "Privacy, Autonomy, and Self-Concept." *American Philosophical Quarterly* 24 (January 1987): 81–89.

LEE, BARBARA A. "Something Akin to a Property Right: Protections for Job Security." *Business and Professional Ethics Journal* 8 (Fall 1989): 63–81.

LIPPKE, RICHARD L. "Work, Privacy, and Autonomy." *Public Affairs Quarterly* 3 (April 1989): 41–53.

MAITLAND, IAN. "Rights in the Workplace: A Nozickian Argument." *Journal of Business Ethics* 8 (December 1989): 951–54.

MOORE, JENNIFER. "Drug Testing and Corporate Responsibility: The 'Ought Implies Can' Argument." *Journal of Business Ethics* 8 (April 1989): 279–87.

NEAR, JANEY P., and MARCIA P. MICELI. "Whistle-Blowers in Organizations: Dissidents or Reformers?" *Research in Organizational Behavior* 9 (1987): 321–68.

NIXON, JUDY L., and JUDY F. WEST. "The Ethics of Smoking Policies." *Journal of Business Ethics* 8 (December 1989): 409–14.

PETTIT, PHILIP. "The Paradox of Loyalty." *American Philosophical Quarterly* 25 (April 1988): 163–71.

PFEIFFER, RAYMOND S. "Owing Loyalty to One's Employer." *Journal of Business Ethics* 11 (July 1992): 535–43.

PHILLIPS, MICHAEL J. "Should We Let Employees Contract Away Their Rights Against Arbitrary Discharge?" *Journal of Business Ethics* 13 (April 1994): 233–42.

ROTHSTEIN, MARK A. "Drug Testing in the Workplace: The Challenge to Employee Relations and Employment Law." *Chicago-Kent Law Review* 63 (1987).

RUST, MARK. "Drug Testing." *ABA Journal* 1 (November 1986): 51–54.

STIEBER, JACK, and MICHAEL MURRAY. "Protection Against Unjust Discharge: The Need for a Federal Statute." *Journal of Law Review* 16 (Winter 1983): 319–41.

WESTIN, ALAN F., and STEVEN SALISBURY. *Individual Rights in the Corporation: A Reader on Employee Rights.* New York: Pantheon, 1980.

WINSTON, MORTON, E. "Aids, Confidentiality, and the Right to Know." *Public Affairs Quarterly* 2 (April 1988): 91–104.

Chapter Six

Hiring, Firing, and Discriminating

INTRODUCTION

FOR DECADES WOMEN and minorities were barred from some of the most desirable institutions and positions in North America. Even when declared unconstitutional, discrimination persisted in many quarters. This discrimination has led to a widespread demand for effective policies to produce justice for those previously and presently discriminated against. However, policies that establish goals, timetables, and quotas that are intended to ensure more equitable opportunities have provoked controversy. Recent controversy has centered on whether *affirmative action* programs, *reverse discrimination*, and criteria of *comparable worth* are appropriate forms of remedy.

The term *affirmative action* refers to positive steps taken to hire persons from groups previously and presently discriminated against. This term has been used to refer to everything from open advertisement of positions to employment and admission quotas. For over two decades U.S. federal laws have encouraged or required corporations to advertise jobs fairly and to promote the hiring of members of formerly abused groups. As a result, corporate planning has often used employment goals or targeted employment outcomes to eliminate the vestiges of discrimination.

The term *preferential hiring* refers to hiring that gives preference in recruitment and ranking to groups previously and presently affected by discrimination. This preference can be in the form of goals or quotas or in the act of choosing minorities over other candidates having equal credentials. A powerful symbolic difference exists between a *goal* and a *quota*, although both can be expressed in percentages. Goals are mandated or negotiated targets and timetables, whereas quotas have come to symbolize policies that can result in reverse discrimination, primarily against white males.

The Basis of Preferential Policies

Affirmative action programs have affected U.S. businesses in profound ways. Consider, for example, the impact of these policies on the Monsanto Chemical Company. In 1971, Monsanto found itself with few black and few female employees. In that same year, the Department of Labor announced that affirmative action would be enforced. In complying, Monsanto tripled the number of minority employees in the next fourteen years, aggressively promoted women and blacks into middle management positions, and eliminated racial hiring patterns in technical and craft positions. Monsanto reported that it achieved these goals without diluting the quality of its employees. The firm has also said that it has no intention of abandoning its affirmative action programs. The program's focus has, however, shifted from *hiring* minorities to *promoting* them within the company.[1]

Such preferential policies are often said to have their foundations in the principle of compensatory justice, which requires that if an injustice has been committed, just compensation or reparation is owed to the injured person(s). Everyone agrees that if an individual has been injured by past discrimination, he or she should be compensated for past injustice. However, controversy has arisen over whether past discrimination against *groups* such as women and minorities justifies compensation for current group members. Critics of group preferential policies hold that only identifiable discrimination against individuals calls for compensation.

Ronald Reagan was the first U.S. president to oppose preferential hiring. He and his successor, George Bush, campaigned against quotas and then sought to roll them back. The Department of Justice was the administration's vanguard, but other government agencies were intimately involved. In 1985, Chairman of the U.S. Civil Rights Commission, Clarence Pendleton, reported to the president his conviction that the Commission had succeeded in making racial and group quotas a "dead issue." He maintained that public controversy over preferential treatment had been replaced with a vision of a color-blind society that is an "opportunity society" rather than a "preference society."[2]

Although the conclusion that quotas are a dead issue is questionable, given current civil rights law and business practice, Pendleton's comment illustrates the split that now exists between two primary, competing positions in U.S. society: (1) that the only means to the end of a color-blind, sex-blind society is preferential treatment and (2) that a color-blind, sex-blind society can be achieved by guaranteeing equal opportunities to all citizens. According to the second position, employers must never use criteria favoring color, sex, or any such irrelevant consideration when hiring or promoting personnel. The goal is to eradicate discrimination, not to perpetuate it through reverse discrimination. These two competing positions agree that compensation is justified for particular victims of discrimination, but they disagree about whether compensation is owed to individuals as members of groups.

The articles in this chapter by Thomas Nagel and N. Scott Arnold address the fundamental ethical issues that have emerged from congressional, executive, and judicial conclusions about the moral and legal responsibilities of businesses to eradicate discrimination. A major moral issue is whether preferential policies requiring that preference be given to minority candidates over otherwise better qualified white males is a justified instance of compensatory justice or a form of unjust discrimination. The dispute centers on whether such practices of preferential treatment are either (1) just, (2) unjust, or (3) not just, but still permissible.

1. Those who claim that such compensatory measures are just, or are required by justice, argue that past discrimination persists in the present. Blacks who were victims of past discrimination are still handicapped or discriminated against, whereas the families of past slave owners are still being unduly enriched by inheritance laws. Those who have inherited wealth accumulated by iniquitous practices have no more right to their wealth than the sons of slaves, who have some claim to it as a matter of compensation. In the case of women, the argument is that our culture is structured to equip them with a lack of self-confidence, that it prejudicially excludes them from much of the work force, and that it treats them as a low-paid auxiliary labor unit. Consequently, only highly independent women can be expected to compete with males on initially fair terms. A slightly stronger argument is that compensation is fair because it is owed to those who have suffered unjust treatment. For example, if veterans are owed preferential treatment because of their service and sacrifice to country, blacks and women are owed preferential treatment because of their economic sacrifices, systematic incapacitation, and consequent family and group losses.

2. Those who claim that group compensatory measures are unjust argue that no criteria exist for measuring just compensation, that employment discrimination in society is presently minor and controllable, and that those harmed by past discrimination are no longer alive to be compensated. Instead of providing compensation, they argue, strict equality as well as merit hiring and promotion should be enforced, while attacking the roots of discrimination. Also, some now successful but once underprivileged minority groups argue that their long struggle for equality is being jeopardized by programs of "favoritism" to blacks and women. In his contribution, Scott Arnold argues that most of the controversial affirmative actions programs are unjustified. He tries to cut across competing ideologies by using arguments based on management's fiduciary responsibility to its shareholders to act in the firm's best financial interest and the state's responsibilities to its citizens. Arnold presents the striking thesis that "even if the demands of justice require preferential treatment programs, the government is not justified in requiring or encouraging them."

3. The third view is that some compensatory measures are not just because they violate principles of justice, but are still justifiable by moral principles other than justice. Nagel, a proponent of this view, argues that "there is an element of individual unfairness" in strong affirmative action plans, but these plans are justified as a means to the end of eradicating an intolerable social situation. Tom L. Beauchamp argues that even some forms of reverse discrimination can be justified as a means to the end of a nondiscriminatory society. Like Arnold, Beauchamp discusses both the voluntary preferential treatment programs that have been of

special interest to senior management and state-mandated programs. He concludes that both can be justified under certain circumstances.

Since both Beauchamp and Arnold believe their conclusions hold only under certain conditions, it is possible (however unlikely) that they might agree on a broad range of justified and unjustified policies, despite their apparent theoretical differences.

The Problem of Reverse Discrimination

The U.S. Supreme Court has held that federal law permits private employers to create plans that favor groups traditionally discriminated against. The moral justification, if any, for such plans and the acceptability of any reverse discrimination created by the plans, however, remain controversial.

Among writers who support policies even when they permit reverse discrimination, a mainline approach has been to argue that under certain conditions compensation owed for past wrongs justifies present policies that produce reverse discrimination. Beauchamp does not employ this argument that compensation is owed to classes for *past* wrongs; instead, he maintains that reverse discrimination is permissible to eliminate or alleviate *present* discriminatory practices that affect whole classes of persons (especially practices of minority exclusion). He introduces factual evidence for his claim that invidious discrimination is pervasive in society. Because discrimination now prevails, Beauchamp contends that policies that may eventuate in reverse discrimination are unavoidable in reaching the end of eliminating ongoing discrimination.

Opponents of this position argue that reverse discrimination violates fundamental, overriding principles of justice and cannot be justified. As Arnold points out in his essay, there exist quite a variety of arguments in opposition to both affirmative action and reverse discrimination. Arguments that have received widespread attention include the following: (1) Some persons who are not responsible for the past discrimination (for example, qualified young white males) pay the price; preferential treatment is invidiously discriminatory because innocent persons are penalized solely on the basis of their race or sex. (2) Male members of minority groups such as Polish, Irish, Arabic, Chinese, and Italian members of society — who were previously discriminated against — inevitably will bear a heavy and unfair burden of compensating women and other minority groups. (3) Many individual members of any class selected for preferential treatment never have been unjustly treated and therefore do not deserve preferential policies. (4) Compensation can be provided to individuals who were previously treated unfairly without resorting to reverse discrimination.

As the court cases in this chapter indicate, the problems associated with preferential and discriminatory hiring are surprisingly complicated. In three cases decided in the late 1980s, the Supreme Court supported the permissibility of specific numerical goals in affirmative action plans that are intended to combat a manifest imbalance in traditionally segregated job categories (even if the particular workers drawn from minorities were not victims of past discrimination). In *Local 28 v. Equal Employment Opportunity Commission*, otherwise known as *Sheet Metal Workers*, a specific minority hiring goal of 29.23 percent had been established. The Court held that quotas involved in the 29 percent goal are justified when dealing with persistent or egregious discrimination. The Supreme Court held that the history of Local 28 was one of complete "foot-dragging resistance" to the idea of hiring without discrimination in their apprenticeship training programs from minority groups. The Court argued that

> even where the employer or union formally ceases to engage in discrimination, informal mechanisms may obstruct equal employment opportunities. An employer's reputation for discrimination may discourage minorities from seeking available employment. In these circumstances, affirmative race-conscious relief may be the only means available to assure equality of employment opportunities and to eliminate those discriminatory practices and devices which have fostered racially stratified job environments to the disadvantage of minority citizens.

However, in a 1989 opinion included in this chapter, the Supreme Court held in *City of Richmond v. J. A. Croson* that Richmond, Virginia, officials could not require contractors to set aside 30 percent of their budget for subcontractors who owned "minority business enterprises." The Court held that this plan did not exhibit sufficient government interest to justify the plan and that the plan was not written to remedy the effects of prior discrimination. The Court found that this way of fixing a percentage based on race, in the absence of evidence of identified past discrimination, denied citizens an equal opportunity to compete for the subcontracts. Parts of the reasoning in *Croson* were affirmed in the 1995 case of *Adarand Constructors Inc. v. Pena.*

Some writers have interpreted *Croson, Adarand,* and other recent cases as the dismantling of affirmative action, specifically all affirmative action plans that contain specific numerical goals. Other readers of these cases, however, find a continuation of the Supreme Court's long line of vigorous defenses of minority rights and the protection of those rights, including the implementation of the rights in corporate policies. As important as these cases are, no comprehensive criteria have yet been established for legally valid affirmative action plans.

Comparable Worth

The slogan "equal pay for equal work" has been at the center of discussions about workplace discrimination, and the gap between men's and women's pay has been the major issue. *Comparable worth* refers to comparable pay for work of comparable value. This notion is used to refer to several principles that persons should be paid on an identical scale for jobs requiring the same competence, education, effort, stress, and responsibility. Judith M. Hill and Ellen Frankel Paul discuss these principles in this chapter as attempts to grasp the justice and implications of the idea of "comparable pay for comparable worth." They link the issues to gender discrimination, class interests, and liberal and conservative philosophies, with a particular emphasis on whether there is a need to reorganize society to achieve a more equitable wage structure. (See Chapter 9 for issues of social justice and fair wages.)

The term *comparable worth* continues to be unpopular in the corporate environment, because adjusting pay scales to eliminate discrimination undercuts setting pay scales according to free market values. In the corporate world, rating scales and employment practices modeled on the idea of comparable pay are typically referred to as schemes of "pay equity" or "internal equity," rather than comparable worth.

Federal law in the United States holds that workers in the same job cannot be paid differently merely because of race or sex. The Equal Pay Act of 1963 specifies that employers must pay employees the same wages for equal work in jobs requiring equal skill, effort, and responsibility. However, a pay differential may be permissible if based on merit, seniority, or the quality or quantity of production. Few would dispute these premises, but the principle of comparable worth extends beyond the notions of "same job" and "equal work" to "jobs of the same value." For example, San Francisco's Amfac Corp. hired a consultant to ensure that their "french-fry cooker in Portland is paid the same as [their] sugar-cane worker in Hawaii,"[3] under the assumption that their jobs are of the same value to the corporation.

Comparable worth is based on the idea that traditionally male positions, such as miner and truck driver, can be rated comparably to traditionally female positions, such as secretary or nurse. Any unjustified differential in pay can be reduced or eliminated. The goal is to pay women and others who may have been discriminated against according to their responsibilities, experience, contributions, and training. Jobs that are equal in value with respect to these characteristics are to be considered identical in value, despite the fact that women and minorities in these positions have typically been paid less than men. Comparable-worth advocates believe that a system that values such work less is discriminatory.

In the mid-1980s, the U.S. Civil Rights Commission adopted a report that urged federal agencies to reject the principle of comparable worth. The Commission's chairman once called the principle of comparable worth "the looniest idea since 'Looney Tunes' came on the screen." The Commission held that employers should be held accountable for individual discriminatory acts and policies but not be required to combat social attitudes or to alter industry-preferred forms of evaluating the worth of jobs. Two months later the Equal Employment Opportunity Commission unanimously adopted the principle that federal law does not require comparable worth and that factual differences in pay scales are no grounds for asserting discrimination. Shortly thereafter, the Justice Department filed its first "friend-of-the-court" brief in a comparable-worth case and sided with the state of Illinois in a case in which nurses were seeking higher pay on comparable-worth grounds. In this context, the Justice Department argued that the comparable-worth theory made "a mockery of the ideal of pay equity" and would necessarily depend on "subjective evaluations" by those who made judgments of comparability.[4]

Several court cases have confronted problems of comparable worth. Reprinted in this chapter is the case of *American Federation of State, County, and Municipal Employees v. Washington*. In this class-action case, a large number of state employees sued the State of Washington on grounds of sex discrimination. The claim was that the state had unjustly compensated employees in jobs where females predominate at lower rates than comparable positions in which males predominate. The plaintiffs maintained that despite dissimilarities in the positions, studies indicated that the jobs were of "comparable worth." The court finds against the claim that sex discrimination is warranted by this payment structure.

Part of the dispute about comparable worth is *conceptual*. As the authors in this chapter note, different meanings are attached to "comparable worth" and to the principles that implement it. The Reagan administration defined *comparable worth* as requiring that all jobs of the same value to society be paid equally. This interpretation required a wholesale restructuring of wage scales and was therefore judged extremely difficult to implement. However, many who favor comparable worth use a different definition based on the idea of pay equity, as specified in the Equal Pay Act of 1963: All differentials in wages must be justified by nondiscriminatory and relevant considerations such as seniority, merit pay, skills, and stress.

Corporate America has typically taken a negative view of comparable worth in its public statements, as have the *Wall Street Journal*'s editors, the U.S. Chamber of Commerce, and the National Association of Manufacturers, among others. This skepticism may, in part, stem from the conceptual confusion over the definition of *comparable worth*. But there are other problems. Opponents of comparable worth argue that it cannot be implemented because it is beyond the experts' capacity to determine objective values for different jobs. They claim that its enforcement would require massive federal intervention, even if it could be implemented. In addition, comparable worth invites exorbitant contract disputes and unending litigation, disturbs the flexibility and diversity in hiring and promotion that is essential to a free market, and neglects the facts that women have less work experience, less seniority, and a lower rate of unionization.

Proponents of comparable worth believe the principle itself is an essential tool needed to eliminate the systematic undervaluation of women's contributions. Proponents argue that policies of comparable worth are essential to fairness. Policies can be implemented and structured along the lines of models already being used in traditional job-analysis and job-evaluation processes. Proponents point out that corporations have tried to implement "equal value to the company" by using ratings, pay scales, job-evaluation systems, and so forth. Management has furthered this attempt by using market-wage survey techniques. From this perspective, comparable worth expresses the need for a unified system of job evaluation that measures the relative value of all positions in the corporation. It also introduces a broader element of fairness into employment practices and reduces or possibly eliminates institutionalized systems of injustice. Proponents often admit that unfairness cannot be completely eliminated, but they insist that unfairnesses can be carefully monitored.

Implementation of comparable-worth criteria has been controversial. Presumably implementation can proceed by (1) negotiation at the bargaining table, (2) internal development at corporations, and (3) external imposition by governments. All three means are currently under discussion and experiment. The first approach to comparable worth has been heavily promoted by the American Federation of State, County, and Municipal Employees (AFSCME), which won impressive precedential comparable-worth pay adjustments in Chicago, Los Angeles, Iowa, Minnesota, Wisconsin, New York, and Connecticut — despite the decision in the state of Washington. These changes were generally achieved by labor negotiation, rather than court battles.

Some corporations have begun to develop programs of comparable worth. For example, AT&T, BankAmerica, Chase Manhattan, IBM, Motorola, and Tektronix have introduced systems of job comparisons that will allow the cross-job evaluations essential for comparable worth. In these systems, factors that express a job's "worth" — years of education, degree of responsibility, necessary skill, amount of noise in the work environment, and physical labor — are rated on a point scale. Jobs with equal points are to be compensated equally. For example, AT&T worked with its unions to devise a plan in which fourteen measurements were adopted to evaluate by point ratings such factors as keyboard skills, job stress, and abilities to communicate.[5]

A similar set of potentially revolutionary changes that would be externally imposed on corporations are under scrutiny in several state legislatures, but these developments have slowed in recent years. Minnesota was the first to adopt such a plan for state employees. The U.S. federal government has been largely uninterested. Meanwhile, other countries have been more aggressive. Canada enacted a comparable-worth law that covers all workers under federal jurisdiction, and in Great Britain a similar law was imposed on an unwilling Prime Minister.

The Problem of Sexual Harassment

Among the oldest forms of discrimination in the workplace, but one of the newest in business ethics and U.S. courts, is sexual harassment. Statistics on its prevalence are somewhat unreliable, but studies and surveys suggest that between 15 percent and 65 percent of working women encounter some form of sexual harassment, depending on type of job, work force, location, and the like. Studies also indicate an increase of sexual harassment complaints during the past decade. The landmark U.S. Supreme Court case of *Meritor Savings Bank v. Vinson* (reprinted in this chapter) was decided in 1986. This case cited a wide range of activities in the workplace as constituting sexual harassment under Title VII of the Civil Rights Act of 1964. The case has significantly impacted discussions of workplace discrimination and the development of corporate policies to police it.

The most widespread form of sexual harassment now seems to be offensive sexual innuendos that generate embarrassment and anger, rather than coercive threats demanding sexual favors or physical abuse. Some studies suggest that sexual harassment has recently become less overt, but not less commonplace. Forms of sexual harassment that condition a job or promotion on sexual favors have declined, but an increase has occurred in unwanted sexual advances such as propositions, offensive posters, degrading comments, kisses and caresses, improper joking and teasing, and the like.

Men and women often have different views of what constitutes an unwelcome sexual advance, comment, or environment. However, in *Meritor*, the Supreme Court extended protections against sexual harassment beyond circumstances of asking for sexual favors to any form of offensive remark and sexual conduct that creates a hostile working environment. Before *Meritor*, sexual harassment had often been thought to involve attempted coercion: an attempt to present a threat the person approached could not reasonably resist. In the typical case, a person's job or promotion was conditioned on performing a sexual favor. However, after *Meritor*, it has been widely agreed that many forms of sexual harassment do not involve an irresistible threat and are not coercive.

Establishing a precise definition of *sexual harassment* has proved difficult. The centerpiece of many definitions has been how to take account of persistent behavior involving unwelcome sexual remarks, advances, or requests that negatively affects working conditions and put these behaviors in the form of a definition. The conduct need not involve making a sexual favor a condition of employment or promotion, and it need not be imposed on persons who are in no position to resist the conduct. Even someone who is in a strong position to resist the approach can be sexually harassed. Derogatory gestures, offensive touching, and leering can affect workers' performance and create a sense that the workplace is inhospitable, irrespective of their ability to resist. The conduct need not be "sexual" in a narrow sense or even sexually motivated. For example, the conduct can be gender-specific, involving demeaning remarks about, for example, how women underperform in their job assignments.

The notion of causing or allowing a "hostile working environment" has been at the forefront of recent attempts in government and law to define "*sexual harassment*," but it has proved difficult to define both terms so that they are not overly broad. What makes for a hostile or intimidating workplace? Do teasing and denigrating remarks count? What is it to denigrate? Which forms of conduct overstep the bounds of being friendly and humorous? Employees in some corporations have complained that corporate policies are written so that asking someone out for a drink after work or expressing sexual humor can easily be construed as unwelcome conduct that creates a hostile working environment.

Standards of offensive or unwelcome sexual behavior have also been difficult to formulate. The "reasonable person" standard of what counts as offensive or unwelcome has been replaced in some courts with a "reasonable woman" standard that tries to determine whether a male's comments or advances directed toward a woman would be considered offensive by taking the reasonable woman's point of view rather than the reasonable person's point of view. This shift from a gender-neutral standard should make it easier for women to file lawsuits success-fully, because men might not find offensive what a woman would. However, if one takes the view, as many now do, that harassment is largely a matter of how the indi-vidual feels when approached by another person, then the standard of the reason-able woman will be too weak. The standard would have to be whether *this person* finds conduct offensive, not whether *the reasonable woman* so finds it. Although the law is not likely to move in the direction of a subjective standard, ethics literature is increasingly moving in that direction.

In this chapter, Andrew Altman and Vaughana Feary discuss the array of meanings, types, and problems of sexual harassment. They take an especially care-ful look at the complicated questions that surround the problems of defining the term and of limiting its scope so that it is neither too narrow nor too broad. Alt-man begins with legal prohibitions of discrimination and the ways sexual harass-ment is a form of sex discrimination. He tries to explicate, refine, and defend by moral argument the existing law in the United States. Feary's wide-ranging article is critical of corporations for not understanding the nature and objectives of sexual harassment guidelines and for not having adequate programs to eliminate the hos-tile workplaces that foster harassment. She proposes several ways in which the cor-porate world might catch up to the problem.

Efforts to remove sexual harassment from the corporate workplace appear to have increased since the 1986 *Meritor* decision, although there is controversy about how seriously to take the increased interest. Many major corporations now have some form of training and grievance policies. Corporations with sexual harassment policies for all management levels report that unwelcome comments and touching have declined significantly after initiating the policies. One reason for increased corporate interest is that corporations have been held legally liable for the behav-ior of their supervisors, even when corporate officials above the supervisors were unaware of the behavior. Although these lawsuits and corporate policies have made corporations more sensitive to the issues, little evidence exists that top exec-utives have given urgent priority to the improvement and enforcement of sexual harassment policies.

NOTES

1. Aric Press, and others, "The New Rights War." *Newsweek* (December 30, 1985), pp. 66–69.
2. Juan Williams, "Quotas Are a 'Dead Issue,' Rights Panel Chairman Says." *Wash-ington Post* (January 30, 1985), p. A2.
3. "Labor Letter." *Wall Street Journal* (April 16, 1985), p. 1, col. 5.
4. Brief filed with the 7th U.S. Circuit Court of Appeals in Chicago. See Los Angeles Times Service, "U.S. Court Brief Assails 'Comparable Worth' Pay," *International Herald Tribune* (August 19, 1985), p. 3.
5. Cathy Trost, "Pay Equity, Born in Public Sector, Emerges as an Issue in Private Firms." *Wall Street Journal* (July 8, 1985), p. 15.

A Defense of Affirmative Action

Thomas Nagel

The term "affirmative action" has changed in meaning since it was first introduced. Originally it referred only to special efforts to ensure equal opportunity for members of groups that had been subject to discrimination. These efforts included public advertisement of positions to be filled, active recruitment of qualified applicants from the formerly excluded groups, and special training programs to help them meet the standards for admission or appointment. There was also close attention to procedures of appointment, and sometimes to the results, with a view to detecting continued discrimination, conscious or unconscious.

More recently the term has come to refer also to some degree of definite preference for members of these groups in determining access to positions from which they were formerly excluded. Such preference might be allowed to influence decisions only between candidates who are otherwise equally qualified, but usually it involves the selection of women or minority members over other candidates who are better qualified for the position.

Let me call the first sort of policy "weak affirmative action" and the second "strong affirmative action." It is important to distinguish them, because the distinction is sometimes blurred in practice. It is strong affirmative action — the policy of preference — that arouses controversy. Most people would agree that weak or precautionary affirmative action is a good thing, and worth its cost in time and energy. But this does not imply that strong affirmative action is also justified.

I shall claim that in the present state of things it is justified, most clearly with respect to blacks. But I also believe that a defender of the practice must acknowledge that there are serious arguments against it, and that it is defensible only because the arguments for it have great weight. Moral opinion in this country is sharply divided over the issue because significant values are involved on both sides. My own view is that while strong affirmative action is intrinsically undesirable, it is a legitimate and perhaps indispensable method of pursuing a goal so important to the national welfare that it can be justified as a temporary, though not short-term, policy for both public and private institutions. In this respect it is like other policies that impose burdens on some for the public good.

THREE OBJECTIONS

I shall begin with the argument against. There are three objections to strong affirmative action: that it is inefficient; that it is unfair; and that it damages self-esteem.

The degree of inefficiency depends on how strong a role racial or sexual preference plays in the process of selection. Among candidates meeting the basic qualifications for a position, those better qualified will on the average perform better, whether they are

Testimony before the Subcommittee on the Constitution of the Senate Judiciary Committee, June 18, 1981. Reprinted by permission of Professor Nagel.

doctors, policemen, teachers, or electricians. There may be some cases, as in preferential college admissions, where the immediate usefulness of making educational resources available to an individual is thought to be greater because of the use to which the education will be put or because of the internal effects on the institution itself. But by and large, policies of strong affirmative action must reckon with the costs of some lowering in performance level: the stronger the preference, the larger the cost to be justified. Since both the costs and the value of the results will vary from case to case, this suggests that no one policy of affirmative action is likely to be correct in all cases, and that the cost in performance level should be taken into account in the design of a legitimate policy.

The charge of unfairness arouses the deepest disagreements. To be passed over because of membership in a group one was born into, where this has nothing to do with one's individual qualifications for a position, can arouse strong feelings of resentment. It is a departure from the ideal — one of the values finally recognized in our society — that people should be judged so far as possible on the basis of individual characteristics rather than involuntary group membership.

This does not mean that strong affirmative action is morally repugnant in the manner of racial or sexual discrimination. It is nothing like those practices, for though like them it employs race and sex as criteria of selection, it does so for entirely different reasons. Racial and sexual discrimination are based on contempt or even loathing for the excluded group, a feeling that certain contacts with them are degrading to members of the dominant group, that they are fit only for subordinate positions or menial work. Strong affirmative action involves none of this: it is simply a means of increasing the social and economic strength of formerly victimized groups, and does not stigmatize others.

There is an element of individual unfairness here, but it is more like the unfairness of conscription in wartime, or of property condemnation under the right of eminent domain. Those who benefit or lose out because of their race or sex cannot be said to deserve their good or bad fortune.

It might be said on the other side that the beneficiaries of affirmative action deserve it as compensation for past discrimination, and that compensation is rightly exacted from the group that has benefited from discrimination in the past. But this is a bad argument, because as the practice usually works, no effort is made to give preference to those who have suffered most from discrimination, or to prefer them especially to those who have benefited most from it, or been guilty of it. Only candidates who in other qualifications fall on one or other side of the margin of decision will directly benefit or lose from the policy, and these are not necessarily, or even probably, the ones who especially deserve it. Women or blacks who don't have the qualifications even to be considered are likely to have been handicapped more by the effects of discrimination than those who receive preference. And the marginal white male candidate who is turned down can evoke our sympathy if he asks, "Why me?" (A policy of explicitly *compensatory* preference, which took into account each individual's background of poverty and discrimination, would escape some of these objections, and it has its defenders, but it is not the policy I want to defend. Whatever its merits, it will not serve the same purpose as direct affirmative action.)

The third objection concerns self-esteem, and is particularly serious. While strong affirmative action is in effect, and generally known to be so, no one in an affirmative action category who gets a desirable job or is admitted to a selective university can be sure that he or she has not benefited from the policy. Even those who would have made it anyway fall under suspicion, from themselves and from others: it comes to be widely felt that success does not mean the same thing for women and minorities. This painful damage to esteem cannot be avoided. It should make any defender of strong affirmative action want the practice to end as soon as it has achieved its basic purpose.

JUSTIFYING AFFIRMATIVE ACTION

I have examined these three objections and tried to assess their weight, in order to decide how strong a countervailing reason is needed to justify such a policy. In my view, taken together they imply that strong affirmative action involving significant preference should be undertaken only if it will substantially further a social goal of the first importance. While this condition is not met by all programs of affirmative action now in effect, it is met by those which address the most deep-seated, stubborn, and radically unhealthy divisions in the society, divisions whose removal is a condition of basic justice and social cohesion.

The situation of black people in our country is unique in this respect. For almost a century after the abolition of slavery we had a rigid racial caste system of the ugliest kind, and it only began to break up twenty-five years ago. In the South it was enforced by law, and in the North, in a somewhat less severe form, by social convention. Whites were thought to be defiled by social or residential proximity to blacks, intermarriage was taboo, blacks were denied the same level of public goods — education and legal protection — as whites, were restricted to the most menial occupations, and were barred from any positions of authority over whites. The visceral feeling of black inferiority and untouchability that this system expressed were deeply ingrained in the members of both races, and

they continue, not surprisingly, to have their effect. Blacks still form, to a considerable extent, a hereditary social and economic community characterized by widespread poverty, unemployment, and social alienation.

When this society finally got around to moving against the caste system, it might have done no more than to enforce straight equality of opportunity, perhaps with the help of weak affirmative action, and then wait a few hundred years while things gradually got better. Fortunately it decided instead to accelerate the process by both public and private institutional action, because there was wide recognition of the intractable character of the problem posed by this insular minority and its place in the nation's history and collective consciousness. This has not been going on very long, but the results are already impressive, especially in speeding the advancement of blacks into the middle class. Affirmative action has not done much to improve the position of poor and unskilled blacks. That is the most serious part of the problem, and it requires a more direct economic attack. But increased access to higher education and upper-level jobs is an essential part of what must be achieved to break the structure of drastic separation that was left largely undisturbed by the legal abolition of the caste system.

Changes of this kind require a generation or two. My guess is that strong affirmative action for blacks will continue to be justified into the early decades of the next century, but that by then it will have accomplished what it can and will no longer be worth the costs. One point deserves special emphasis. The goal to be pursued is the reduction of a great social injustice, not proportional representation of the races in all institutions and professions. Proportional racial representation is of no value in itself. It is not a legitimate social goal, and it should certainly not be the aim of strong affirmative action, whose drawbacks make it worth adopting only against a serious and intractable social evil.

This implies that the justification for strong affirmative action is much weaker in the case of other racial and ethnic groups, and in the case of women. At least, the practice will be justified in a narrower range of circumstances and for a shorter span of time than it is for blacks. No other group has been treated quite like this, and no other group is in a comparable status. Hispanic-Americans occupy an intermediate position, but it seems to me frankly absurd to include persons of oriental descent as beneficiaries of affirmative action, strong or weak. They are not a severely deprived and excluded minority, and their eligibility serves only to swell the numbers that can be included on affirmative action reports. It also suggests that there is a drift in the policy toward adopting the goal of racial proportional representation for its own sake. This is a foolish mistake, and should be resisted. The only legitimate goal of the policy is to reduce egregious racial stratification.

With respect to women, I believe that except over the short term, and in professions or institutions from which their absence is particularly marked, strong affirmative action is not warranted and weak affirmative action is enough. This is based simply on the expectation that the social and economic situation of women will improve quite rapidly under conditions of full equality of opportunity. Recent progress provides some evidence for this. Women do not form a separate hereditary community, characteristically poor and uneducated, and their position is not likely to be self-perpetuating in the same way as that of an outcast race. The process requires less artificial acceleration, and any need for strong affirmative action for women can be expected to end sooner than it ends for blacks.

I said at the outset that there was a tendency to blur the distinction between weak and strong affirmative action. This occurs especially in the use of numerical quotas, a topic on which I want to comment briefly.

A quota may be a method of either weak or strong affirmative action, depending on the circumstances. It amounts to weak affirmative action — a safeguard against discrimination — if, and only if, there is independent evidence that average qualifications for the positions being filled are no lower in the group to which a minimum quota is being assigned than in the applicant group as a whole. This can be presumed true of unskilled jobs that most people can do, but it becomes less likely, and harder to establish, the greater the skill and education required for the position. At these levels, a quota proportional to population, or even to representation of the group in the applicant pool, is almost certain to amount to strong affirmative action. Moreover it is strong affirmative action of a particularly crude and indiscriminate kind, because it permits no variation in the degree of preference on the basis of costs in efficiency, depending on the qualification gap. For this reason I should defend quotas only where they serve the purpose of weak affirmative action. On the whole, strong affirmative action is better implemented by including group preference as one factor in appointment or admission decisions, and letting the results depend on its interaction with other factors.

I have tried to show that the arguments against strong affirmative action are clearly outweighed at present by the need for exceptional measures to remove the stubborn residues of racial caste. But advocates of the policy should acknowledge the reasons against it, which will ensure its termination when it is no longer necessary. Affirmative action is not an end in itself, but a means of dealing with a social situation that should be intolerable to us all.

Affirmative Action and the Demands of Justice

N. Scott Arnold

This essay is about the moral and political justification of affirmative action programs in the United States. Both legally and politically, many of these programs are under attack, though they remain ubiquitous. The concern of this essay, however, is not with what the law says but with what it should say. The main argument advanced in this essay concludes that most of the controversial affirmative action programs are unjustified. . . .

I. AFFIRMATIVE ACTION PROGRAMS

Affirmative action programs exist in a variety of institutional settings. They can be found as a part of the policies that govern hiring, promotion, and retention (in both the public and private sectors); the awarding of contracts; and admissions to training programs, universities, and professional schools. All such programs can be classified in two broad categories, what can be called "outreach efforts" and "preferential treatment programs." Outreach efforts are intended to broaden the search for the best talent, where "best" is defined by reference to the institution's goals and objectives. One purpose of such programs is to seek to reassure women and minorities that the institution in question does not discriminate on the basis of race, gender, or ethnicity, and that the institution is genuinely concerned to recruit the best talent or award the contract to the most deserving firm. Such programs include advertising in minority-targeted media (e.g., black-owned newspapers), taking extra time and effort to examine the credentials of minority applicants (time and effort that would not be extended to majority applicants with identical records), and setting up or attending special job-fairs or minority-owned business exhibitions to get acquainted with talent that firms and organizations would otherwise not be aware of. Some may complain about these programs on the grounds of unfairness to those not targeted, but such complaints are not widely voiced and are not the subject of the main controversy over affirmative action.

Preferential treatment programs are another matter. These involve taking race, gender, or ethnicity into account as a positive factor in the awarding of contracts, in hiring, or in admissions. It may be a small factor, breaking ties between otherwise equally qualified applicants or contractors, or it may be a rather more important factor, which operates to give preference to the minimally qualified or the less qualified over the more qualified applicants or contractors. Let us consider the various categories of preferential treatment programs in a bit more detail:

1. Minority set-asides. Minority set-aside programs require or encourage government agencies or general contractors who do business with the government to set aside a certain percentage of the total dollar value of a contract for minority-owned (or women-owned) businesses. This may involve an inflexible requirement, or there may be financial incentives for general contractors to do this, or there may even be a form of "bid-rigging" by government agencies to ensure that minority firms are awarded the contract.

2. Preferential hiring. Hiring policies in the public sector or in the private sector sometimes take race into account as a positive factor in hiring decisions. The operation of preferential hiring programs results in the hiring of members of minorities who would not be hired if race were not a non-negligible factor in the decision. Those doing the hiring may have in mind target percentages that they would like to meet for minority hires ("goals," as they are sometimes called), or they may be operating with relatively hard quotas. The line between goals and quotas is never a clear one, however; few quotas are insensitive to (other) qualifications, and few goals are mere aspirations. What makes something a quota is that those doing the hiring will not seriously consider nonminority candidates for a position or a range of positions for an extended period of time while they search for suitable minority candidates. The mind-set is to find the best qualified minority person for the job. A non-minority candidate would be considered only if no minimally qualified minority candidate could be found at a reasonable search cost.

Quotas are of dubious legality in most settings, since Section 703(j) of Title VII of the 1964 Civil Rights Act states:

> [N]othing contained in this subchapter shall be interpreted to require any employer . . . to grant preferential treatment to any individual or to any group because of the race, color, religion, sex, or national origin of such individual or group on account of an imbalance which may exist with respect to the total number or percentage of persons of any race, color, religion, sex, or national origin employed by any employer . . . in comparison with the total number or percentage of persons of such race, color, religion, sex, or national origin in any community. . . . [1]

However, in some settings quotas have been upheld.[2] Indeed, the courts have sometimes ordered hiring by the numbers as a remedy in discrimination suits.[3] In any event, the dubious legality of quotas does not prevent them from being used. If a manager is in part evaluated and rewarded on the basis of his contribution to his organization's affirmative action goals, minority status will be an important factor in his hiring decisions. As historian Herman Belz has written, describing preferential treatment programs developed in the private sector:

> Many corporations used an equal employment opportunity measurement system that offered rewards and penalties intended to change the behavior of managers, showing them how to arrive at an "ideal" number of minorities in the work force. . . . [C]ompany executives increasingly included equal employment opportunity performance along with traditional business indicators as a standard in overall evaluation.[4]

An important subcategory of preferential treatment programs in the private sector are what might be called *defensive preferential hiring programs.* Firms that do business with the U.S. government and have more than fifty employees, or contracts with the government worth more than $50,000, are required to submit elaborate affirmative action plans, complete with minority hiring goals and timetables within which those goals are to be achieved. Failure to meet these goals according to the timetables can result in an investigation by the

[1]42 U.S.C. 2000e-2(j).

[2]Kaiser Aluminum had a training program that used racial preferences for blacks over whites, which was upheld by the Supreme Court in *United Steelworkers of America v. Weber,* 443 U.S. 193 (1979).
[3]See, e.g., *Morrow v. Crisler,* 491 F.2d 1053 (1974), and *NAACP v. Allen,* 493 F.2d 614 (1974).
[4]Herman Belz, *Equality Transformed* (New Brunswick, NJ: Transaction Publishers, 1991), p. 105. See also Theodore V. Purcell, S.J., et al., "What Are the Social Responsibilities of Psychologists in Industry? A Symposium." *Personnel Psychology,* 27 (Autumn 1974): 436.

Office of Federal Contract Compliance Programs (OFCCP). This in turn can mean enormous administrative burdens for the firm, lawsuits, and/or the loss of the contract. To avoid these burdens, risks, and the sheer intrusiveness of the bureaucracy, very often the rational thing for firms to do is to hire by the numbers. This is certainly more efficient than designing and implementing ever more elaborate outreach programs whose prospects for success are uncertain.

Another situation in which defensive preferential hiring programs are used is to avoid what are called "disparate impact lawsuits." Anytime a company with fifteen or more employees (whether or not it is a government contractor) has job requirements, uses tests, or has hiring practices that have a negative "disparate impact" on minorities, it is risking a discrimination lawsuit from disappointed job applicants or from public-spirited lawyers who recruit clients to bring these suits. For example, suppose that 12 percent of the relevant population is African American and the use of a test or job qualification results in hiring only 6 percent African Americans. This test or job qualification is said to have a (negative) disparate impact on African Americans and can serve as a basis for a lawsuit. The company can still use the test or qualification, but it faces certain hurdles. It can argue that the definition of the reference population that serves to define the disparate impact should be restricted to those with certain job-related qualifications or to those who actually applied for the position, or it can contest the definition of the firm's workforce (e.g., does the workforce include other divisions of the firm located elsewhere?). Perhaps most importantly, the company can argue that the test or qualification that produced the disparate impact is job-related and consistent with business necessity. This can defeat a claim of discrimination based on disparate impact. For example, if one is hiring physi-

cians, applicants must be licensed to practice medicine, and if this requirement has a disparate impact on a protected minority population, that would be legally acceptable. Once the business necessity of the challenged practice has been established, it is then open to the plaintiff to argue that there are other selection criteria that would have a less disparate impact which the employer could have used in place of the challenged practice.

The way the law is currently interpreted has had some perverse effects. It is often very difficult or expensive to establish that a test or requirement is in fact a business necessity, at least given the stringent way the courts have interpreted this.[5] Consequently, it is often rational for companies to drop the requirement or practice before it is challenged and hire by the numbers as best they can, so as to ward off a disparate-impact lawsuit. Or they can continue to use the practice that has a disparate impact and bundle it with a more subjective screening device (e.g., an interview) and use the latter to get the numbers to "come out right." Although the government does not mandate these strategies — and indeed specifically prohibits them in Section 703(j), as quoted above — these strategies are clearly encouraged by the way Title VII of the Civil Rights Act has been interpreted to allow hiring practices with disparate impact to serve to get a lawsuit started. . . .

This essay offers a rather different argument against preferential treatment programs. I want to begin by discussing a relatively rare variant of these programs — purely voluntary preferential treatment programs in publicly traded corporations in the private sector. These programs are *not* defensive in nature but are voluntarily instigated by senior management. For example, the Disney

---

[5]See Richard Epstein, *Forbidden Grounds: The Case against Employment Discrimination Laws* (Cambridge, MA: Harvard University Press, 1992), pp. 212–22.

Corporation instituted a set-aside program for minority contractors in the planned expansion of its California facilities. There seems to have been no pressure on the firm to do this from any layer of government, but they decided to set aside $450 million for minority contractors out of a total budget of $3 billion.[6] Similarly, a corporation might have a preferential hiring program that is voluntary in the sense that it would remain in place even if the law were changed so that firms did not need to maintain such programs in order to receive government contracts or to avoid lawsuits. Although there may be few such programs in either hiring or contracting, a discussion of them will prove a useful preliminary to a discussion of the much more common mandated set-asides and defensive preferential hiring programs. More specifically, the next section argues that, subject to some qualifications and exceptions, these voluntary set-asides and hiring programs are wrong; subsequent sections apply the same reasoning to more common types of preferential treatment programs that are mandated or encouraged by the government.

II. THE PROBLEM WITH PURELY VOLUNTARY PREFERENTIAL TREATMENT PROGRAMS

The argument to be advanced in this section is a moral one, not a legal one. The law introduces complications that will be addressed shortly, but the main argument of this section concerns the morality of purely voluntary preferential treatment programs in contracting and hiring. The first premise is that management has a fiduciary responsibility to its shareholders to act in the firm's best financial interests, subject to the constraints im-

posed by the law. There may be exceptions to this general principle, and thus it is a rebuttable presumption, but typically when a board of directors hires a chief executive officer (CEO) or a management team, there is a shared understanding that management will act in the firm's best financial interests. This shared understanding is the basis of the fiduciary responsibility (and thus the moral obligation) of the CEO or management team. Possible exceptions to one side, there is an ambiguity in the concept of what constitutes the firm's best financial interests. Is it maximizing profits in the near term? Increasing market share? Maximizing shareholder value? Or some combination of these? Answers to these questions can be variable and indeterminate, though they may be addressed at the time the board hires the CEO or management team. Nevertheless, as agents for the firm's principals (i.e., the stockholders), management's primary goal and responsibility is to advance the financial interests of the firm. However the ambiguity about the firm's best financial interests is resolved, there is the further difficulty of identifying which policies will actually further that goal. Management's moral responsibility to the shareholders does not require perfection in the choice of policies, but it does require that managers act according to their best judgment about what will advance the financial interests of the firm. One thing this implies is that managers are not permitted to further their own conception of justice by instituting programs such as Disney's, at least when they foresee that this is not financially advantageous to the firm. . . .

Now for the exceptions and complications. Note that this argument does not apply to privately held firms owned and managed by one individual. An owner of such a firm might decide on his own to implement a preferential treatment program; if there is anything morally objectionable about this, it is not because the managers have violated a fiduciary obligation to the

---

[6]Chris Woodyard, "Disney to Boost Minority Builders," *Los Angeles Times* (June 16, 1992), p. D2. Subsequently, the planned expansion was significantly scaled back.

owners. Similarly, the owners of a closely held corporation might jointly agree to order management (which might consist of one or more of their number) to institute a preferential treatment program not required or encouraged by law. Finally, there could be cases in which the owners of a privately held company announce, upon making an initial public offering of stock, that the company will pursue such programs as a matter of company policy, even if it is detrimental to the firm's financial interests. Or they could go before the shareholders at the annual shareholders' meeting and announce their intention to pursue preferential policies that are not in the firm's financial interests, detailing their best estimates of the costs and benefits (both financial and otherwise) of these policies. Under those circumstances, shareholders would have no grounds for complaint. Let us suppose, however, that a firm's management does not do either of these things. Suppose instead that they simply decide, perhaps with the acquiescence of the board of directors, to pursue a social-justice agenda (or an environmental agenda, or a charitable-giving agenda) that foreseeably harms the firm's financial interests. They do not tell the shareholders about it, or if they do, they do so after the fact and mislead them about its costs and benefits. Under such circumstances, they have violated their fiduciary obligations to the shareholders and thus have acted wrongly.

One objection to this argument would be to charge that purely voluntary preferential treatment programs in contracting and hiring really are in a firm's best financial interests. Proponents of affirmative action often claim that a diverse workforce is in the company's best financial interests, and indeed can point to an array of diversity programs that large corporations have instituted and an army of diversity consultants whom companies have hired to run them.

It is difficult to evaluate this objection for the simple reason that it is difficult to determine how many preferential treatment programs in

contracting or hiring are truly voluntary in the sense that they would persist in the absence of any legal pressure to maintain them. The proliferation of diversity programs does not prove very much in this context for at least two reasons. First, and most obviously, antidiscrimination law is extremely far-reaching in its coverage. As I noted above, disparate-impact lawsuits can be brought against any firm with more than fifteen employees. As for set-asides, an estimated 27 million people work for firms that do business with the federal government.... An expensive and elaborate diversity program is part of a well-conceived defensive preferential treatment program for large companies.

Second, diversity programs include much more than preferential programs in hiring and contracting. They often include attempts to achieve a more harmonious and effective workforce by sensitizing workers to cultural and gender differences. They also try to prevent, or at least insulate the company from, other types of lawsuits (e.g., those arising from the Americans with Disabilities Act, sexual harassment lawsuits). For these reasons, the percentage of preferential hiring and contracting programs that would continue to exist in the absence of threats of Title VII litigation or the loss of government contracts is impossible to determine. For the sake of argument, however, let us grant that there could be purely voluntary preferential treatment programs which management reasonably believes are in a firm's best financial interests; the above argument would not apply to such programs, if in fact they do exist....

III. NONVOLUNTARY PREFERENTIAL TREATMENT PROGRAMS: THE PEROTIAN ARGUMENT AND THE DEMANDS OF JUSTICE

The argument of Section II does not address the most common types of preferential treatment programs that are currently in force —

those which the state mandates or encourages. These include minority set-asides and preferential hiring programs involving government contractors, as well as defensive programs in the private sector that are instituted to avoid disparate-impact lawsuits. When people talk about the affirmative action controversy, these are the programs (along with similar programs in higher education) that they are taking about.

It seems that an argument parallel to the one set out above could be mounted against these programs as well. Government bureaus are analogous to firms, with citizens occupying a role analogous to that of shareholders. Because former presidential candidate Ross Perot reminds us that in a democracy the citizens own their government, let us call this "the Perotian Argument."[7] Whether or not citizens literally own their government as Perot maintains, it is clear that they have a legitimate expectation that the government will try to get the best mix of quality and price in the goods and services that it buys from the private sector. They also have a legitimate expectation that the government will not gratuitously impose added costs or reduced quality on goods and services exchanged in purely private business dealings. Of course, the legitimacy of these expectations is purely moral, not epistemic. Only the very naive believe that governments generally meet these expectations. Most citizens are well aware that governments very often do not. But they should. By mandating and encouraging preferential treatment programs, however, the government violates citizens' legitimate expectations about how their government will behave.

There are two premises in this argument: that the citizens of a democracy have a legitimate expectation that the government will not act in such a way as to raise the price and/or reduce the quality of goods and services in both the public and private sectors; and that nonvoluntary preferential treatment programs violate this expectation. The first is hard to argue with, at least as a general proposition. It is simply a demand that government act efficiently in procuring goods and services and in affecting the private sector. There are undoubtedly exceptions to this general proposition, and thus it is a rebuttable presumption; indeed, proponents of preferential treatment programs may insist that in this area an exception should be made because of the demands of justice. This claim will be taken up in due course, but for now it is sufficient to note that those who control the government in a democracy do not own the resources they control. They have a fiduciary relationship with the citizenry that closely parallels the relationship between corporate officers and shareholders; this serves as the basis for the legitimate expectations just mentioned. . . .

Proponents of these programs might agree with all this and yet insist that even though these programs do impose real costs, that is simply the price of justice. Justice, John Rawls asserts, is the first virtue of social institutions.[8] If justice requires preferential treatment programs, so be it. This is essentially the same objection raised against the purely voluntary programs considered in the last section. It is now time to give it full consideration. I shall argue that even if the demands of justice require preferential treatment programs, the government is not justified in requiring or encouraging them. In other words, the argument that follows grants, for

---

[7]Or is it the taxpayers who own the government? Not all citizens are taxpayers and not all taxpayers are citizens, though the two groups substantially overlap. Since I do not wish to claim that anyone literally owns the government, this complication need not be pursued. All that is claimed in what follows is that citizens or taxpayers have a principal-agent relationship with their government analogous to shareholders' relationship to management, at least when it comes to the government's dealings in the economy.

[8]John Rawls, *A Theory of Justice* (Cambridge, MA: The Belknap Press of Harvard University Press, 1971), p. 3.

the sake of discussion, that justice requires preferential treatment programs, and yet concludes that these programs are, all things considered, unjustified.

This argument starts with some suggestive parallels with Locke's observations about the problems of a state of nature. Recall that a state of nature is a pre-political society in which people have various natural rights, including the rights to life, liberty, and property. In addition, they have the right to punish those who violate their other rights. All this gives rise to what Locke calls the "inconveniences of a state of nature." These include the following: Some people cannot enforce their rights. Some people do not correctly apply the natural law, or they tend to be biased when judging in their own cases, or they tend to mispunish, overpunish, etc. They use the demands of justice as a cloak to further their own interests and/or the interests of their friends at the expense of others and at the expense of justice. This worry is a special case of the central worry of Western political philosophy, at least in the liberal tradition: How is government to be limited? Whether or not one believes in Lockean rights, there is no doubt that the state faces a permanent threat — very often realized — of being hijacked to serve private interests. Historically, state power has been used to advance private interests at the expense of the public interest, including the demands of justice, however one understands these concepts. . . .

Two plausible requirements . . . must be met if the power of the state is to be used to further some conception of the demands of (distributive or compensatory) justice:

(i) Proponents of state action must get a political consensus for doing what justice requires. A political consensus does not require unanimity among the people or their elected representatives, but it does require that supporters of government intervention make their case publicly and get an on-the-record vote from the legislature or from the electorate through a referendum. Let us call this the *Public Justification requirement.* . . .

(ii) Proponents of state action must explain how and why their proposal will not permit state power to be systematically abused to further private interests at the expense of those disadvantaged by the policies in question. Very often, proposed legislation will foreseeably but unavoidably help groups and individuals it is not intended to help at the expense of groups and individuals it is not intended to harm; if this is so, that fact has to be made public and a case has to be made that this is a cost worth paying. . . .

IV. MINORITY SET-ASIDE PROGRAMS

The main question this section and the next will address is whether minority set-aside programs and nonvoluntary preferential hiring programs satisfy the two requirements. Let us begin with the former. Minority set asides began in 1968 with the Small Business Administration. The SBA served as prime contractor for other governmental agencies, awarding procurement contracts to small businesses. It interpreted its statutory authority to allow it to set aside a certain percentage of its contracts to businesses owned by "socially and economically disadvantaged" individuals, which was further interpreted to apply primarily to "minority business enterprises" (MBEs). The first set-aside program legislated by Congress was included in the 1977 Public Works Employment Act (PWEA).[9] It required each prime contractor to set aside 10 percent of the dollar value of the contract for MBEs, which were explicitly defined as businesses at least 50 percent owned by members of minority groups; or, if the business

---

[9]Information in this and subsequent paragraphs on the set-aside provision in the PWEA comes from the *Congressional Record,* 95th Congress, 1st session (1977), pp. 5327–30.

was a joint stock company, at least 51 percent of the stock had to be owned by minorities. Targeted minorities included African Americans, Hispanics, Asians, Native Americans, Eskimos, and Aleuts. The PWEA contained a provision to suspend the requirement if there were no available minority firms. In subsequent years, state and local governments instituted their own minority set-aside programs modeled on federal programs. Other set-aside programs at the federal level were introduced piecemeal, either by executive order or as part of other legislation.

Do minority set-aside programs meet the Public Justification requirement? Set-aside programs instituted by the executive branch (such as the SBA's program) were not subject to any public debate and discussion in Congress; they were simply imposed by the executive branch, so they clearly do not meet the requirement. The case of set-asides mandated by Congress is not as simple, since set-aside provisions can be found in many pieces of legislation that Congress passed and that the president signed into law. The crucial issue is the legislative history of a given set-aside provision.

The first of these provisions — the one included in the PWEA — is especially important, since it set the precedent; proponents of subsequent programs appealed to it as conferring presumptive validity on their proposals. One would expect that the first modern attempt to introduce race-conscious programs by legislation would occasion considerable congressional debate and discussion, but in fact that did not happen. There were no committee hearings or reports relating to the minority set-aside provision in the PWEA, probably because the provision was offered as a floor amendment in the House of Representatives. It passed on a voice vote and was accorded similar treatment in the Senate. . . .

V. PREFERENTIAL TREATMENT IN HIRING

Though minority set-asides are an important form of preferential treatment, preferential hiring programs are more significant. They impact many more people and seem to have provoked more passionate debate. The vast majority of preferential hiring programs are mandated or encouraged by the government and would likely not exist but for that pressure. They fall into three categories: (1) those mandated by the courts in response to successful discrimination suits; (2) defensive preferential hiring programs encouraged by the executive branch for contractors doing business with the federal government; and (3) defensive preferential hiring programs undertaken to ward off disparate-impact lawsuits. Let us consider each of these in turn to see if the Public Justification and Anti-Hijacking requirements were satisfied when these programs were instituted.

1. *Court-ordered preferential hiring programs.* Courts occasionally order hiring (or promotions) by the numbers in response to successful lawsuits brought under Title VII of the 1964 Civil Rights Act. Section 706 of Title VII gives a court considerable discretion in ordering remedies for discriminatory practices. In response to a finding of discrimination, Section 706(g)(1) says,

> the court may enjoin the respondent from engaging in such unlawful employment practice and may order such affirmative action as may be appropriate which may include but is not limited to reinstatement or hiring of employees, with or without back pay . . . or any other equitable relief that the court deems appropriate.[10]

Though it is doubtful whether "quota relief" is consistent with Section 703(j) of Title VII,

---

[10]42 U.S.C. 2000e-(g)(1).

the courts have assumed that it is and have on occasion ordered hiring or promotion by the numbers. They have forced employers to hire a certain percentage of minorities against whom no discrimination has been proven or even alleged. Typically, these remedies are imposed on employers who seem particularly racist or sexist in their policies and practices. This remedy fails to satisfy the Public Justification requirement, even if it is legally permissible, since nowhere in the Civil Rights Act is this remedy explicitly mentioned. Congress never debated and sanctioned hiring or promotion by the numbers as a remedy for discrimination, no matter how egregious. The fact, if indeed it is a fact, that Congress somehow left the door open for quota remedies is irrelevant for the purposes of the Public Justification requirement, since this requirement imposes burdens on the legislature. This form of affirmative action is relatively rare, however, in comparison to the next two types to be considered, so perhaps we should not make too much of this failure.

2. *Preferential hiring under various executive orders.* In 1965, President Lyndon Johnson issued Executive Order 11246, which created the Office of Federal Contract Compliance (later renamed the Office of Federal Contract Compliance Programs) and led to the establishment of defensive preferential hiring programs by government contractors. Later, President Richard Nixon extended preferential hiring requirements to cover the civil service in Executive Order 11478. The story of the development of this policy has been told elsewhere. The "goals and timetables" approach to hiring was inaugurated under these executive orders, which remain in effect to this day. The OFCCP has considerable power over firms doing business with the government. Many such firms do business exclusively (or nearly exclusively) with the government and can ill-afford to walk away from

government contracts. Though firms are nominally prohibited from hiring by the numbers, they must submit an affirmative action plan, complete with goals and timetables. The failure of so-called "good faith efforts" to yield the right hiring numbers can bring the OFCCP down on a contractor with a vengeance. This office has much more power than the EEOC, since it can deny contracts without a court finding that a company has been guilty of discrimination. OFCCP officials can simply refuse to certify a company as able to bid on contracts. Although this sanction has seldom been applied, the threat of it is usually sufficient to get compliance. . . .

3. *Other defensive preferential hiring programs.* Defensive preferential hiring programs among firms not doing business with the federal government came into existence in response to judicial interpretation of Title VII of the 1964 Civil Rights Act. In *Griggs v. Duke Power* (1971)[11] and subsequent cases, the Supreme Court ruled that hiring practices and policies having a disparate impact on minorities were prima facie suspect and could be grounds for a Title VII lawsuit. Moreover, the EEOC has made it clear that it will not bring disparate-impact lawsuits against employers who abide by what is called "the 80 percent rule."[12] This rule states that if the percentage of women or minorities a firm hires is at least 80 percent of their percentage in the relevant populations, the firm will not ordinarily be subject to an investigation and a disparate-impact lawsuit. Rational firms have responded to these pressures by instituting preferential hiring programs to reach safe harbor from such lawsuits. In 1989, the Supreme Court pulled back from the standards imposed by *Griggs* and its progeny in

[11]401 U.S. 424 (1971).
[12]Uniform Guidelines on Employee Selection Procedures (1978), 29 C.F.R. Section 1607.4D (1989).

Ward's Cove Packing Co. v. Antonio.[13] It lessened the pressure on businesses to engage in preferential hiring by redistributing the burden of proof in disparate-impact cases. In response to the Court's ruling in *Ward's Cove,* Congress reimposed the *Griggs* standards in the Civil Rights Act of 1991. Were the Public Justification and Anti-Hijacking requirements satisfied for preferential hiring programs anywhere in this series of events? Let us begin with the original legislation: Title VII of the 1964 Civil Rights Act.

If one purpose of Title VII was to foster preferential hiring programs, proponents of the law would have had to make clear that employment practices that have a disparate impact on minorities create a rebuttable presumption of discrimination. Under this construal of Title VII, the intended beneficiaries would be the women and minorities who successfully sued, as well as those who would be hired to avoid such suits, and presumably other women and minorities who might indirectly benefit from preferential hirings and promotions. The intended victims would be the owners of the businesses who, for whatever reason, used employment practices (or hired managers who used such practices) that created a disparate impact. Others in the firm, such as other managers who would have to struggle with affirmative action regulations and other employees who would be negatively affected in a variety of ways, might also count as intended victims of the policy, though that depends on how the argument is framed. The argument would have to be made that the benefits of the law, as so interpreted, outweigh the costs.

What about the unintended beneficiaries and victims? The Anti-Hijacking requirement stipulates that they have to be identified as well. The main unintended victims are, of course, the nonminority candidates who otherwise would have gotten the jobs. Academic defenders of preferential hiring are quick to point out that their being excluded is not a result of stereotyping and does not stigmatize them in the way ordinary racial discrimination would. Moreover, if there were ways to solve the underlying social problems without hurting these people, defenders of preferential hiring programs would probably embrace them. All this makes the victim status of disappointed majority job candidates unintended, however foreseeable their plight is. However, they are still adversely affected, and whatever the demands of justice, the lack of stigmatization is cold comfort to someone who did not get a job or promotion because of his or her race or gender. The unintended beneficiaries of preferential hiring programs are a little harder to identify. Clearly, government bureaucrats and lawyers in the equal employment opportunity/affirmative action industry count as foreseen though unintended beneficiaries. In addition, the private sector has its affirmative action officers, "diversity consultants," and others who profit from attempts to eliminate (perceived) social injustice.

The above identifies the intended and unintended beneficiaries and victims of preferential hiring programs, an identification essential to satisfying the Public Justification and Anti-Hijacking requirements. The main problem for defenders of preferential hiring programs is that legislators supporting Title VII never made this case. . . .

---

[13]490 U.S. 642 (1989). [See the case presentation below in this volume. Ed.]

Goals and Quotas in Hiring and Promotion

Tom L. Beauchamp

Since the 1960s, government and corporate policies that set goals for hiring women and minorities have been sharply criticized. Their opponents maintain that many policies establish indefensible quotas and discriminate in reverse against sometimes more qualified white males. In 1991, President George Bush referred to the word "quota" as the "dreaded q-word." Quotas, he said, had "finally" been eliminated from government policies. Such opposition is understandable. No worker wants to lose a job to a less qualified person, and no employer wants to be restricted in its hiring and promotion by a quota.

Although some policies that set target goals and adopt quotas sometimes violate rules of fair and equal treatment, such policies can be justified. My objective in this paper is to defend policies that set goals and quotas. I argue that goals and quotas, rightly conceived, are congenial to management — not hostile as they are often depicted. Both the long-range interest of corporations and the public interest are served by carefully selected preferential policies.

I. TWO POLAR POSITIONS

In 1965, President Lyndon Johnson issued an executive order that announced a toughened federal initiative requiring goals and timetables for equal employment opportunity.[1] This initiative was the prevailing regulatory approach for many years. But recently two competing schools of thought on the justifia-

bility of preferential programs have come into sharp conflict, one mirroring the views of Bush, and the other mirroring those of Johnson.

The first school, like Bush, stands in opposition to quotas, accepting the view that all persons are entitled to an equal opportunity and to constitutional guarantees of equal protection in a color-blind, nonsexist society. Civil rights laws, in this approach, should offer protection only to individuals who have been victimized by forms of discrimination, not groups. Hiring goals, timetables, and quotas only work to create new victims of discrimination.

The second school, like Johnson, supports strong affirmative action policies. The justification of affirmative action programs is viewed as the correction of discriminatory employment practices, not group compensation for prior injustice. This second school views the first school as construing "equal opportunity" and "civil rights" so narrowly that persons affected by discrimination do not receive adequate aid in overcoming the effects of prejudice. This second school believes that mandated hiring protects minorities and erodes discrimination, whereas the identification of individual victims of discrimination would be, as the editors of *The New York Times* once put it, the "project of a century and [would] leave most victims of discrimination with only empty legal rights."[2]

These two schools may not be as far apart morally as they first appear. If legal enforcement of civil rights law could efficiently and comprehensively identify discriminatory treatment and could protect its victims, both schools would agree that the legal-enforcement strategy is preferable. But there are at least two reasons why this solution will not be accepted by the second school. First, there is the unresolved issue of whether those in contemporary society who have been advantaged by *past* discrimination (for example, wealthy owners of family businesses) deserve their advantages. Second, there is the issue of whether *present*, ongoing discrimination can be successfully, comprehensively, and fairly combatted by identifying and prosecuting violators without resorting to quotas. This second issue is the more pivotal and is closely related to the justification of quotas.

A "quota," as used here, does not mean that fixed numbers of employees should be hired regardless of an individual's qualification for a position. Quotas are simply target employment percentages. In some cases a less qualified person may be hired or promoted; but it has never been a part of affirmative action to hire below the threshold of "basically qualified,"[3] and often significant questions exist in the employment situation about the exact qualifications needed for positions.[4] Quotas, then, are numerically expressible goals that one is obligated to pursue with good faith and due diligence. If it is impossible to hire the basically qualified persons called for by the goals in a given time frame, the schedule can be relaxed, as long as the target goals, the due diligence, and the good faith continue. The word *quota* does not mean "fixed number" in any stronger sense.

II. DATA ON DISCRIMINATION

Discrimination affecting hiring and promotion is not present everywhere in our society, but it is pervasive. An impressive body of statistics constituting prima facie evidence of discrimination has been assembled in recent years. It indicates that: (1) women with identical credentials are promoted at approximately one-half the rate of their male counterparts; (2) 69 percent or more of the white-collar positions in the United States are held by women, but only approximately 10 percent of the management positions are held by women; (3) 87 percent of all professionals in the private business sector are of oriental origin, but they constitute only 1.3 percent of the management positions; (4) in the total U.S. population, 3 out of 7 employees hold white-collar positions, whereas the ratio is only 1 of 7 for blacks; (5) blacks occupy over 50 percent of the nation's jobs as garbage collectors and maids, but only 4 percent of the nation's management positions.[5]

Such statistics are not decisive indicators of discrimination, but additional facts also support the conclusion that racist and sexist biases powerfully influence the marketplace. Consider prevailing biases in real estate rentals and sales. Studies have shown that there is an 85 percent probability that blacks will encounter discrimination in rental housing and a 50 percent probability that blacks will suffer discrimination in purchasing a house and in applying for a mortgage; that blacks suffer more discrimination than other economically comparable minority groups; and that there may be as many as two million instances of discrimination in the U.S. housing market each year in the United States. One study indicates that approximately 80 percent of American residential neighborhoods in the largest 29 metropolitan areas remained entirely segregated from 1960 to 1980. Not socioeconomic status, but race, is the difference in real estate sales and loans.[6]

If we shift from housing to jobs, a similar pattern is found, especially for black males, for whom employment has become steadily more difficult in almost every sector from the mid-1970s through the early 1990s.[7] In 1985 the

Grier Partnership and the Urban League produced independent studies that reveal striking disparities in the employment levels of college-trained blacks and whites in Washington, DC, one of the best markets for blacks. Both studies found that college-trained blacks have much more difficulty than their white counterparts in securing employment. Both cite discrimination as the major underlying factor.[8]

A 1991 study by the Urban Institute is a powerful illustration of the problem. This study examined employment practices in Washington, DC and Chicago. Equally qualified, identically dressed white and black applicants for jobs were used to test for bias in the job market, as presented by newspaper-advertised positions. Whites and blacks were matched identically for speech patterns, age, work experience, personal characteristics, and physical build. Investigators found repeated discrimination against black male applicants. The higher the position, the higher they found the level of discrimination to be. The white men received job offers three times more often than the equally qualified blacks who interviewed for the same position. The authors of the study concluded both that discrimination against black men is "widespread and entrenched" and that fears of reverse discrimination by white males are unfounded because the effects of discrimination more than offset any effects of reverse discrimination.[9]

These statistics help frame the significance of racial discrimination in the United States. Although much is now known about patterns of discrimination, much remains to be discovered, in part because it is hidden and subtle.

III. PROBLEMS OF PROOF AND INTENTION

We typically conceive racism and sexism as an intentional form of favoritism or exclusion, but major problems confronting American business and government arise from *unintended* institutional practices. Employees are frequently hired through a network that, without design, excludes women or minority groups. For example, hiring may occur through personal connections or by word of mouth, and layoffs may be entirely controlled by a seniority system. The actual hiring policies themselves may be racially and sexually neutral. Nonetheless, they can have an adverse effect on the ability of minorities in securing positions. There may be no intention to discriminate against anyone; nonetheless, the system has discriminatory consequences. In some cases, past discrimination that led to unfair hiring practices and an imbalanced work force is perpetuated even when there is no desire to perpetuate them.

In 1985 the U.S. Supreme Court unanimously held that persons may be guilty of discriminating against the handicapped when there is no "invidious animus, but rather [a discriminatory effect] of thoughtlessness and indifference — of benign neglect." The Court held that discrimination would be difficult and perhaps impossible to prevent if *intentional* discrimination alone qualified as discrimination.[10] Discrimination is still invisible to many who discriminate. This, in my judgment, is the main reason quotas are an indispensable government and management tool: They are the only way to break down old patterns of discrimination and thereby change the configuration of the workplace.

Courts in the United States have on a few occasions resorted to quotas because an employer had an intractable history and a bullheaded resistance to change that necessitated strong measures. The Supreme Court has never directly supported quotas using the term "quota,"[11] but it has upheld affirmative action programs that contain numerically expressed hiring formulas that are intended to reverse the patterns of both intentional and unintentional discrimination.[12] At the same time, the Supreme Court has suggested that some programs using these formulas have gone too far.[13] Whether the formulas are excessive depends on the facts in the individual case. From this perspective, there is no inconsistency between *Fullilove v. Klutznick* (1980), which allowed percentage set-asides for minority contractors, and *City of Richmond v. J. A. Croson Co.* (1989), which disallowed certain set-asides. The later case of *Adarand Constructors Inc. v. Pena* (1995) defended a standard requiring that there be a compelling governmental interest for race-based preferences in construction contracts for minority-owned companies; it continued the long line of cases that weigh and balance different interests.

I believe the Supreme Court has consistently adhered to this balancing strategy and that it is the right moral perspective as well as the proper framework for American law.[14] Numerical goals or quotas should be implemented only when necessary to overcome the discriminatory impact of insensitive institutional policies and irrelevant criteria used for employment. Proposed formulas can be excessive here just as they can elsewhere.

Although I have distinguished between intentional practices and unintentional practices that have discriminatory impact, the two often work together. For example, the practices and framework of policies in a corporation may be nondiscriminatory, but those implementing the practices and policies may have discriminatory attitudes. Fair rules can easily be exploited or evaded by both personnel officers and unions, who often use criteria for hiring and promotion such as "self-confidence," "fitting in," "collegiality," and "personal appearance," among other superficial characteristics.[15]

Issues about the breadth and depth of discrimination may divide us as a society more than any other issue about affirmative action. If one believes there is but a narrow slice of surface discrimination, one is likely to agree with what I have called the first school. But if one believes discrimination is deeply, almost invisibly entrenched in our society, one is apt to agree with the second school. I have been arguing for the perspective taken by the second school, but this perspective needs to be specified to prevent it from assuming the same bullheaded insensitivity that it pretends to locate elsewhere. Discriminatory attitudes and practices are likely to be deep-seated in some institutions, while shallow or absent in others. Society is not monolithic in the depth and breadth of discrimination. In some cases affirmative action programs are not needed, in other cases only modest good faith programs are in order, and in still others enforced quotas are necessary to break down discriminatory patterns.

Because we deeply disagree about the depth, breadth, and embeddedness of discrimination, we disagree further over the social policies that will rid us of the problem. Those who believe discrimination is relatively shallow and detectable look for formulas and remedies that center on *equal opportunity*. Those who believe discrimination is deep, camouflaged, and embedded in society look for formulas that center on *measurable outcomes*.[16]

IV. WHY CORPORATIONS SHOULD WELCOME GOALS AND QUOTAS

Little has been said to this point about corporate policy. I shall discuss only so-called *voluntary* programs that use target goals and quotas. They stand in sharp contrast to legally enforced goals and quotas, and there are at least three reasons why it is in the interest of responsible businesses to use aggressive plans that incorporate goals and quotas: (1) an improved work force, (2) maintenance of a bias-free corporate environment, and (3) congeniality to managerial planning.

(1) First, corporations that discriminate will fail to look at the full range of qualified persons in the market and, as a result, will employ a higher percentage of second-best employees. The U.S. work force is projected to be 80 percent women, minorities, and immigrants by the year 2000, and corporations are already reporting both that they are finding fewer qualified workers for available positions and that they have profited from vigorous, internally generated rules of nonracial, nonsexist hiring.[17] Hal Johnson, a senior vice-president at Travelers Cos., noted the benefits in adopting goals and quotas: "In [the 1990s] more of the work force is going to be minorities — Hispanics, blacks — and women. The companies that started building bridges back in the 1970s will be all right. Those that didn't won't."[18]

Goals and quotas that are properly conceived should yield superior, not inferior employees. No one would argue, for example, that baseball has poorer talent for dropping its color barrier. To find the best baseball talent, bridges had to be built that extended, for example, into the population of Puerto Rico. Businesses will be analogously improved if they extend their boundaries and provide proper training and diversity programs. Bill McEwen of the Monsanto Corporation and spokesperson for the National Association of Manufacturers (NAM) notes that this extension has long been happening at NAM companies:

We have been utilizing affirmative action plans for over 20 years. We were brought into it kicking and screaming. But over the past 20 years we've learned that there's a reservoir of talent out there, of minorities and women that we hadn't been using before. We found that [affirmative action] works.[19]

Maintaining a high quality work force is consistent with the management style already implemented in many companies. For example, James R. Houghton, Chairman of Corning Glass, has established voluntary quotas to increase the quality of employees, not merely the number of women and black employees. Corning established the following increased-percentage targets for the total employment population to be met between 1988 and 1991: women professionals to increase from 17.4 percent to 23.2 percent, black professionals to increase from 5.1 percent to 7.4 percent, the number of black senior managers to increase from 1 to 5, and the number of women senior managers to increase from 4 to 10. Corning management interpreted the targets as follows: "Those numbers were not commandments set in stone. We won't hire people just to meet a number. It will be tough to meet some of [our targets]." Corning found that it could successfully recruit in accordance with these targets, but also found severe difficulty in maintaining the desired target numbers in the work force because of an attrition problem. The company continues to take the view that in an age in which the percentage of white males in the employment pool is constantly declining, a "total quality company" must vigorously recruit women and minorities using target goals.[20]

A diverse work force can, additionally, create a more positive employment environment and better serve its customers. An internal U.S. West study found that white males were ten times more likely to be promoted than minority women (black, Hispanic, and Asian). As a result, the company designed a plan to promote its female employees and to prepare employees for more demanding positions. U.S. West adopted the view that a diverse group of employees is better suited to develop new and creative ideas than a homogeneous group that approaches problems from a similar perspective and that racial and sexual patterns of discrimination in hiring have to be combatted by target-driven hiring programs. They therefore targeted "Women of Color" for training and promotion.[21]

Many corporations have found that vigorous affirmative action has economic and not only social benefits. Diversity in the work force produces diversity of ideas, different perspectives on strategic planning, and improved, more open personnel policies. As a result, as the director of personnel at Dow Chemical puts it, "If anything, there is [in the corporate world] a new push on affirmative action plans because of the increasing numbers of women and minorities entering the work force."[22]

(2) Second, pulling the foundations from beneath affirmative-action hiring would open old wounds in many municipalities and corporations that have been developing target goals and quotas through either a consent-decree process with courts or direct negotiations with representatives of minority groups and unions. These programs have, in some cases, been agonizingly difficult to develop and would disintegrate if goals and timetables were ruled impermissible. The P.Q. Corporation, for example, reports that it has invested years of training in breaking down managerial biases and stereotypes while getting managers to hire in accordance with affirmative action guidelines. The corporation is concerned that without the pressure of affirmative action programs, managers will fail to recognize their own biases and use of stereotypes. Removal of voluntary programs might additionally stigmatize a business by signalling to minorities that a return to older patterns of discrimination is permissible. Such stigmatization is a serious blow in today's competitive market.[23]

(3) Third, affirmative action programs involving quotas have been successful for the

corporations that have adopted them, and there is no need to try to fix what is not broken. As the editors of *Business Week* maintained, "Over the years business and regulators have worked out rules and procedures for affirmative action, including numerical yardsticks for sizing up progress, that both sides understand. It has worked and should be left alone."[24] It has worked because of the abovementioned improved work force and because of a businesslike approach typical of managerial planning: Managers set goals and timetables for almost everything — from profits to salary bonuses. From a manager's point of view, setting goals and timetables is simply a basic way of measuring progress.

One survey of 200 major American corporations found that the same approach has often been taken to the management of affirmative action: Over 75 percent of these corporations already use "voluntary internal numerical objectives to assess [equal employment opportunity] performance." Another survey of 300 top corporate executives reported that 72 percent believe that minority hiring improves rather than hampers productivity, while 64 percent said there is a need for the government to help bring women and minorities into the mainstream of the work force. Many corporations have used their records in promotion and recruitment to present a positive image of corporate life in public reports and recruiting brochures. Such reports and brochures have been published, for example, by Schering-Plough, Philip Morris, Exxon, AT&T, IBM, Westinghouse, and Chemical Bank.[25]

Affirmative action has also worked to increase productivity and improved consumer relationships. Corporations in consumer goods and services industries report increased respect and increased sales after achieving affirmative action results. They report that they are able to target some customers they otherwise could not reach, enjoy increased competitiveness, and better understand consumer complaints as a result of a more diverse work force. Corporations with aggressive affirmative action programs have also been shown to outperform their competitors.[26]

V. CONCLUSION

If the social circumstances of discrimination were to be substantially altered, my conclusions in this paper would be modified. I agree with critics that the introduction of preferential treatment on a large scale runs the risk of producing economic advantages to individuals who do not deserve them, protracted court battles, congressional lobbying by power groups, a lowering of admission and work standards, reduced social and economic efficiency, increased racial and minority hostility, and the continued suspicion that well-placed minorities received their positions purely on the basis of quotas. These reasons constitute a strong case against affirmative action policies that use numerical goals and quotas. However, this powerful case is not sufficient to overcome the still stronger counterarguments.

NOTES

1. Executive Order 11,246. C.F.R. 339 (1964-65). This order required all federal contractors to develop affirmative action policies.
2. "Their Right to Remedy, Affirmed," *The New York Times* (July 3, 1986), p. A30.
3. This standard has been recognized at least since *EEOC v. AT&T*, No. 73-149 (E.D. Pa. 1973). See also U.S. Department of Labor, Employment Standards Administration, Office of Federal Contract Compliance Programs, "OFCCP: Making EEO and Affirmative Action Work," January 1987 OFCCP-28.
4. See Laura Purdy, "Why Do We Need Affirmative Action?" *Journal of Social Philosophy* 25 (1994): 133–143.
5. See Bron Taylor, *Affirmative Action at Work: Law, Politics, and Ethics* (Pittsburgh: University of Pittsburgh Press, 1991); National Center for Education Statistics, *Faculty in Higher Education Institutions, 1988, Contractor Survey Report*, compiled Susan H. Russell, et al. (Washington: U.S. Dept. of Education, March 1990), pp. 5–13; Herman Schwartz, "Affirmative Action," *Minority Report*, ed. L. W. Dunbar (New York: Pantheon Books, 1984), pp. 61–62; Betty M. Vetter, ed., *Professional Women and Minorities: A Manpower Data Resource Service*, 8th ed. (Washington: Commission on Science and Technology, 1989); Irene Pave, "A Woman's Place Is at GE, Federal Express, P&G. . . ." *Business Week* (June 23, 1986), pp. 75–76.
6. See *A Common Destiny: Blacks and American Society,* ed. Gerald D. Jaynes and Robin M. Williams, Jr., Committee on the Status of Black Americans, Commission on Behavioral and Social Sciences and Education, National Research Council (Washington, DC: NAS Press, 1989), pp. 12–13, 138–48; Glenn B. Canner and Wayne Passmore, "Home Purchase Lending in Low-Income Neighborhoods and to Low-Income Borrowers," *Federal Reserve Bulletin* 81 (Feb., 1995): 71–103; Yi-Hsin Chang, "Mortgage Denial Rate for Blacks in '93 Was Double the Level for Whites, Asians," July 29, 1994, p. A2; "Business Bulletin," *The Wall Street Journal.* (February 28, 1985), p. 1; Constance L. Hays, "Study Says Prejudice in Suburbs Is Aimed Mostly at Blacks," *The New York Times* (November 23, 1988), p. A16.
7. Paul Burstein, *Discrimination, Jobs, and Politics* (Chicago: University of Chicago Press, 1985). Bureau of Labor Statistics, *Employment and Earnings* (Washington, DC: U.S. Department of Labor, Jan. 1989). *A Common Destiny,* op. cit., pp. 16–18, 84–88.
8. As reported by Rudolf A. Pyatt, Jr., "Significant Job Studies," *The Washington Post* (April 30, 1985), pp. D1–D2.
9. See Margery Austin Turner, Michael Fix, and Raymond Struyk, *Opportunities Denied, Opportunities Diminished: Discrimination in Hiring* (Washington, DC: The Urban Institute, 1991).

10. *Alexander v. Choate,* 469 U.S. 287, at 295.

11. But the Court comes very close in *Local 28 of the Sheet Metal Workers' International Association v. Equal Employment Opportunity Commission,* 106 S.Ct. 3019 — commonly known as *Sheet Metal Workers.*

12. *Fullilove v. Klutznick,* 448 U.S. 448 (1980); *United Steelworkers v. Weber,* 443 U.S. 193 (1979); *United States v. Paradise,* 480 U.S. 149 (1987); *Johnson v. Transportation Agency,* 480 U.S. 616 (1987).

13. *Firefighters v. Stotts,* 467 U.S. 561 (1984); *City of Richmond v. J. A. Croson Co.,* 109 S.Ct. 706 (1989); *Adarand Constructors Inc. v. Federico Pena,* 63 LW 4523 (1995); *Wygant v. Jackson Bd. of Education,* 476 U.S. 267 (1986); *Wards Cove Packing v. Atonio,* 490 U.S. 642.

14. For a very different view, stressing inconsistency, see Yong S. Lee, "Affirmative Action and Judicial Standards of Review: A Search for the Elusive Consensus." *Review of Public Personnel Administration* 12 (Sept.–Dec., 1991): 47–69.

15. See the argument to this effect in Gertrude Ezorsky, *Racism & Justice: The Case for Affirmative Action* (Ithaca, NY: Cornell University Press, 1991), Chap. 1.

16. For a balanced article on this topic, see Robert K. Fullinwider, "Affirmative Action and Fairness." *Report from the Institute for Philosophy & Public Policy* 11 (University of Maryland, Winter 1991), pp. 10–13.

17. See L. Joseph Semien, "Opening the Utility Door for Women and Minorities." *Public Utilities Fortnightly* (July 5, 1990), pp. 29–31; Irene Pave, "A Woman's Place," p. 76.

18. As quoted in Walter Kiechel, "Living with Human Resources." *Fortune* (August 18, 1986), p. 100.

19. As quoted in Peter Perl, "Rulings Provide Hiring Direction: Employers Welcome Move." *The Washington Post* (July 3, 1986), pp. A1, A11.

20. Tim Loughran, "Corning Tries to Break the Glass Ceiling." *Business & Society Review* 76 (Winter, 1991), pp. 52–55.

21. Richard Remington, "Go West, Young Woman!" in *Telephony* 215 (Nov. 1988), pp. 30–32; Diane Feldman, "Women of Color Build a Rainbow of Opportunity," *Management Review* 78 (Aug. 1989), pp. 18–21.

22. Loughran, op. cit., p. 54.

23. See Jeanne C. Poole and E. Theodore Kautz, "An EEO/AA Program that Exceeds Quotas — It Targets Biases." *Personnel Journal* 66 (Jan. 1987): 103–105. Mary Thornton, "Justice Dept. Stance on Hiring Goals Resisted." *The Washington Post* (May 25, 1985), p. A2; Pyatt, "The Basis of Job Bias," p. D2; Linda Williams, "Minorities Find Pacts with Corporations Are Hard to Come By and Enforce." *The Wall Street Journal* (August 23, 1985), p. 13.

24. Editorial, "Don't Scuttle Affirmative Action." *Business Week* (April 5, 1985), p. 174.

25. "Rethinking *Weber:* The Business Response to Affirmative Action." *Harvard Law Review* 102 (Jan. 1989), p. 661, note 18; Robertson, "Why Bosses Like to Be Told," p. 2.

26. See "Rethinking *Weber,*" esp. pp. 668–70; Joseph Michael Pace and Zachary Smith, "Understanding Affirmative Action: From the Practitioner's Perspective," *Public Personnel Management* 24 (Summer 1995): 139–147

PAY EQUITY AND COMPARABLE WORTH

Pay Equity

Judith M. Hill

In 1974, the state of Washington commissioned a study to compare the jobs of state employees. The criteria for comparison were:

Knowledge and skills. How many years of education, training, experience, are required for each job?

Mental demands. How much thought goes into the day to day performance of each job?

Accountability. How free is each worker to take action on his/her own initiative? How great is the impact of each worker's decisions? (How many people are affected? How significantly?)

Working conditions. What degree of hazard, stress, physical discomfort is associated with each job?

Points were assigned for factors in each of these categories, and jobs having roughly equal total scores were considered comparable.

With this system of comparison, it was found that on average, women were paid about 20 percent less than men in comparable jobs.[1] For example, registered nurses (who are predominantly female) scored higher than any other job category; but computer systems analysts (who are predominately male) earned about 56 percent more than RNs. Clerical supervisors (mostly women) scored higher than chemists (mostly men), but chemists earned about 41 percent more. Telephone operators and retail clerks scored higher than truck drivers, but truck drivers earned about 30 percent more.[2]

However, having discovered these inequities, the state did nothing to correct the situation, deeming it too costly. Eventually, the state was sued by the union involved, AFSCME (The American Federation of State, County and Municipal Employees), which claimed that the state discriminated against women, in violation of Title VII of the 1964 Civil Rights Act. Their argument was that since the wage gap between predominantly male and predominately female occupations evidently cannot be accounted for by reference to differences in the difficulty or responsibility of the worked performed, the most plausible explanation of the pay discrepancies is that work identified as "women's work" has been systematically undervalued. . . .

In what follows, I will present the case in favor of pay equity, then raise and discuss what I take to be the major objections that have been brought against it, arguing that none of the reasons for rejecting pay equity is convincing.

I

The argument in defense of pay equity is essentially as follows:

(1) People should be treated equally, except when there is a morally relevant reason for treating them differentially;

(2) The mere fact that employees are doing different kinds of work, as such, is **not** a morally relevant reason for treating them differentially; and

(3) The fact that the people involved have **consented** to differential treatment — e.g., to work for a relatively low salary — is not sufficient reason for differential treatment.

From Judith M. Hill, "Pay Equity," *International Journal of Applied Philosophy*, vol. 3, no. 3, Spring, 1987.

Therefore, employees who are performing jobs which are of comparable worth with respect to such factors as the amount of training required, degree of responsibility involved, supply of trained workers in the field relative to demand, should be paid equally. . . .

Premise (1) is a very weak equality principle. It does not insist on equality, nor even on equal treatment. It only claims that there is a presumption in favor of equal treatment: so that any divergence has to be justified. . . .

The second premise of the argument in defense of pay equity is that the fact that people are doing different kinds of work, as such, is not a morally relevant reason for treating them differentially. In other words, the fact that a computer systems analyst has to have more training than a secretary, or that the systems analyst's job involves a greater degree of responsibility, or harsher working conditions than the secretary's job, certainly would constitute morally relevant reason for treating them differentially. Indeed, most proponents of pay equity would concede that the fact that systems analysts are in greater demand (relative to supply) than secretaries, would be morally relevant reason for differential pay. But the mere fact that secretaries and systems analysts have **different** jobs, as such — the fact that they perform different kinds of tasks — is not morally relevant reason for differential pay.

In defense of this premise, I would begin by pointing out that what counts as a morally relevant reason to do anything depends upon one's normative moral theory, but that there are a limited number of possibilities: (1) considerations to the effect that a certain course of action would promote the greatest good of the greatest number of people, or (2) consideration to the effect that some people have a **right** to take a certain course of action, or to expect others to take a certain course of action. . . .

A third possible line of argument, according to which **an individual employer has a right to treat employees differentially** on grounds that they are doing different kinds of work (or on any other grounds), is less easy to dismiss. Assuming that property rights include the right to dispose of one's property in any way that one sees fit, it might be argued that the owner of a company (or his agent) has a right to offer whatever salaries he deems appropriate to people whose services he utilizes. He has, indeed, a right to pay differential salaries to people performing **identical** jobs, if he so wishes.

In other words, according to this argument, property owners do not have to have any reason for disposing of their property in any way they like. Property owners do not have to justify differential treatment of employees.

This argument might be taken in either of two ways. It could be meant as a claim that moral considerations have no relevance within the context of decisions concerning what to do with one's property, or within a business context. In the absence of any grounds for believing that such an exemption from moral concerns should apply only to property owners in disposing of their property, this argument simply begs the question as to the obligations of employers to employees.

Alternatively, the argument from property rights might be taken as a corollary of a stronger claim: That no one, including employers, is bound by the dictum that like cases should be treated alike. This amounts to a rejection of the whole project of morality. If we do not have to have reasons for our behavior toward others, moral considerations cannot begin to find a foothold. . . .

The third premise of the pay equality argument denies the legitimacy of one last reason sometimes offered as justifying differential pay for comparable jobs: **the fact that all parties concerned have agreed to differential treatment.**

In other words, women choose to be nurses or teachers and secretaries, knowing full well that these jobs pay less than others that might be thought to be of comparable worth. In short, women implicitly consent to the relatively low salaries they receive. According to some opponents of pay equity, it is precisely this consent which justifies those salaries. "If the women with low-paying jobs had an equal opportunity to work at the jobs with higher salaries, but never took advantage of that opportunity, if they never sought the higher-paying jobs, where's the discrimination?"[3]

In assuming that an arrangement which all concerned parties have agreed upon **could not be unjust,** this argument assumes that economic justice is strictly a matter of consent, of noncoercion. It views justice in the distribution of property as simply a procedural matter of behaving honestly and with respect for the rights of others; the **outcome** of this procedure is irrelevant. Thus, justice cannot be achieved by coercively taking honestly acquired wealth from some and giving it to others in order to bring about some **pattern** of distribution, whether this be a pattern of simple equality, or an historical pattern according to which people receive goods in proportion to the difficulty and/or importance of the work they have done. No such patterned principle of distributive justice is acceptable. . . .

II

At least two objections to pay equity have been raised which do not depend on a denial of the essential fairness of the idea that pay should reflect the nature of the work one does, but seek to undermine the force of the principle of pay equity by claiming that it is unworkable, or would have unacceptable consequences.

The first objection I will consider concerns the objectivity of the concept of comparable worth. According to this objection, there is no non-arbitrary way to compare the worth of different jobs, and therefore, no objective basis to the claim that women's work is undervalued. Differential pay for different jobs can always be justified on grounds that the jobs in question are not comparable, because the relative worth of different jobs is a strictly subjective matter. In other words, even if there were total agreement that knowledge and skills, responsibility, and working conditions are the relevant factors in measuring the worth of a job — and this itself is debatable — there could well be disagreement over the relative weight assigned to each of these categories. If any ten people were asked to rank, in order of worth, the jobs performed by (1) fire fighters, (2) coal miners, (3) elementary school teachers, (4) airline pilots, and (5) office managers, they would almost certainly produce ten different orderings.

This objection actually attacks a straw man. There is a perception of pay equity fostered by its opponents to the effect that what is being proposed is that the government generate a single list ranking all of the jobs in all of the companies in the country, and require that the salary attaching to any job reflect its place in this ranking. Obviously such a project would presuppose a single correct system for evaluating and comparing jobs.

But this is not what is being proposed. The charge of undervaluation of women's work does not charge employers with a failure to use "the correct system" of evaluation and comparison, but with a failure to use any consistent system of evaluation. . . .

In other words, most employers already use some scheme for evaluating and comparing employees. The Hay Associates, the consulting firm that performed the comparable worth study for the city of San Jose, performs evaluations for more than 200 members of the Fortune 500, working with each firm to develop a system of criteria that reflects the firm's own sense of the worth of different jobs. Job evaluation systems are not a new idea dreamed up by proponents of pay equity.

However, many organizations are inconsistent in their evaluations. This inconsistency is what proponents of pay equity object to.

Inconsistency in job evaluation schemes may show up in several different ways. One sort of inconsistency is the assignment of different numbers of points for the same factor, depending on whose job it is a part of. For example, AT&T uses separate job evaluation schemes for managerial and non-managerial employees. The managerial evaluation system assigns a high point value for customer contact; but the non-managerial scheme gives almost no points for customer contact. The effect is to justify the low pay that telephone operators receive relative to other non-managerial employees who have less customer contact. AT&T evidently values good customer relations on the part of telephone operators as well as on the part of managerial employees: Telephone operators are monitored for courtesy and attitude in dealing with customers. But only managerial employees receive points for customer relations.[4]

Another sort of inconsistency involves a failure to assign any points at all for aspects of a job that are deemed to be *innate* skills. A certain element of this rationale is probably responsible for the lower valuation of customer relations in predominantly female jobs. Certainly it seems to figure in evaluations of child care jobs. (For example, the U.S. Department of Labor rates dog pound attendants and zoo keepers higher than nursery school teachers.[5]) This sort of reasoning is objectionable because the idea that child care skills and general nurturant behavior are innate to women is based on a sexist stereo-

type. Furthermore, systems that fail to give points for "innate women's skills" usually *do* assign points for skills used in predominantly male jobs even though there is just as much reason to believe that some of these are innate, e.g., mechanical aptitude, aggressive behavior. Thus, this practice tends to betray an internal inconsistency as well as a mistaken assumption.

Finally, some companies do not have any particular system of their own for evaluating different jobs in order to determine salaries, but simply set salaries in accordance with the going market rate. If there is no single correct system of comparing jobs, couldn't this be as good a method of salary determination as any based on a set of criteria of worth developed by some consulting firm? In other words, even if we grant that pay should reflect the relative worth of an employee's contribution, doesn't the market provide the best way to determine relative worth?

The trouble with relying strictly on the market system to determine salaries is that the market does not reflect any consistent view of the worth of jobs. As the studies conducted in the Washington case, and by the National Commission on Pay Equity, have established, the market rate has much more to do with unionization and with employer preference and discrimination, than with the marginal productivity of a job.[6]

In sum, the objection to pay equity based on the assumption that it presupposes an objective standard of value for different jobs, is misguided. Most proponents of pay equity ask only that employers use a **consistent** standard of job evaluation throughout their organization.

A second objection commonly raised against the implementation of a pay equity policy is that it would work against women's interests. Some 85 percent of all women in the labor force are clustered, for one reason or another, in only about 24 (out of 400+)

job categories. Undeniably, these are, for the most part, among the most poorly paid jobs. But, according to this objection, at least part of the reason for the fact that these predominantly female jobs are poorly paid is that there is already an oversupply of people (women) seeking them. **This situation would only be exacerbated by pay equity,** which, by insisting on a higher rate of pay for these jobs, would attract **more** people, male and female, to these fields, and would provide some additional reason for women not to go into non-traditional fields. Thus pay equity would work against one of the major objectives of the women's movement.

This objection is mistaken on two counts. In the first place, the hypothesis that oversupply is responsible for the low pay of women's work flies in the face of a lot of evidence to the contrary. RNs have been in short supply for years, yet nurses are still found to be underpaid by comparable worth studies. A shortage of elementary and secondary school teachers has been developing over the past several years, and is rapidly approaching crisis proportions, but teachers are still notoriously underpaid, by almost anyone's standards. Qualified secretaries are increasingly difficult to find, but a secretary in the Virginia state university system, serving a department of ten members, is paid barely a living wage.

I suppose it might be said that the market moves slowly to respond to shortages. But some of these shortages are so long standing that this argument loses credibility. A more plausible explanation is that the market wage has more to do with unionization and employer discrimination than with supply and demand.

There is another fallacy in this objection concerning the counterproductivity of pay equity. It assumes that women are primarily, or significantly, motivated in their career choice by financial considerations. If this

were not assumed, there would be no ground for the claim that increasing pay for traditionally women's work would discourage women from entering nontraditional fields.

But this assumption is false. If women were primarily influenced by financial considerations in their choice of careers, **there would not be the clustering of women in low-paying fields** that this objection correctly points out. Women are clustered in low-paying fields for a variety of reasons, including the fact that we are still socialized to cast ourselves in supportive, nurturant roles (e.g., teaching, nursing, secretarial work); the fact that these jobs afford the greater flexibility women still need in order to juggle job and family;[7] and the fact that there is still discrimination against women in non-traditional fields.[8] As these reasons for choosing careers in the traditional, low-paying fields are eliminated, there is every reason to expect that women will move in increasing numbers to non-traditional fields looking for greater challenges and opportunities, whether or not the traditional women's fields have begun to offer salaries that reflect the worth of the work performed in them. . . .

In Part I, I offered a defense of the position rejecting these attempts to justify differential pay for jobs of comparable worth. In Part II, I addressed attacks on the practicability of a policy of pay equity.

In the absence of any more compelling reasons for the differential pay received by people performing different but comparable jobs, we may conclude that employees performing comparable jobs should be paid equally.

NOTES

1. *Wall Street Journal* (September 19, 1983), p. 12E.
2. *Wall Street Journal* (January 20, 1984), p. 28E.

3. William Bradford Reynolds, Assistant Attorney General for Civil Rights, in *The New York Times* (January 22, 1984), p. 16L.

4. Ronnie J. Steinberg, "A Want of Harmony: Perspectives on Wage Discrimination and Comparable Worth," in *Comparable Worth and Wage Discrimination,* ed., Helen Remick (Temple University Press, Philadelphia, 1984), p. 22.

5. Mary Witt and Patricia K. Naherny, *Women's Work; Up From 878 — Report on the **Directory of**

*Occupational Titles** Research Project* (Madison: Women's Education Resources, University of Wisconsin-Extension, 1975).

6. NRC/NAS Committee Report, p. 65.

7. Paula England, "Socioeconomic Reasons for Job Segregation," *Comparable Worth and Wage Discrimination.*

8. Herbert Hill, "The Equal Employment Opportunity Commission: Twenty Years Later," *Journal of Intergroup Relations* XI(4) (Winter 1983): 45–72.

Resolving the Debate over Comparable Worth: Some Philosophical Considerations

Ellen Frankel Paul

Both the comparable worth opponents and the judges who have been reluctant to read a comparable worth remedy into Title VII base their opposition to the concept essentially on economic grounds. The critics argue that imposing comparable worth would have these deleterious economic consequences: It would be far too costly; it would cause economic disruption in the form of inflation, unemployment, and an inability to compete on international markets; and, more generally, it would undermine our free-market system.

The case the opponents make against comparable worth is *prima facie* quite persuasive, and the question then becomes: Can the comparable worth advocates surmount that case by rebutting the essential charges? After a careful examination of the arguments of both sides, I conclude that they cannot. While I am sympathetic to the goals that have prompted many people to support comparable worth — women's equality in the work place and a soci-

ety free of invidious discrimination — comparable worth is not the appropriate remedy. . . .

COMPARABLE WORTH AND INTRINSIC VALUE

When the critics charge that comparable worth depends on a notion of intrinsic value that can be measured on an objective scale, they have identified a fundamental misconception that underpins the case for imposing comparable worth. . . .

The classical economists of the nineteenth century, as well as Karl Marx, argued for an objective theory of value, the labor theory. Normally, the classical economists contended, the price of commodities depends upon the amount of labor spent in bringing them to market. Market forces, such as scarcity or a temporary shift in demand, could modify this price, so that the market price would fluctuate around this norm.

From Ellen Frankel Paul, *Equity and Gender: The Comparable Worth Debate,* pp. 109, 111–24, 129–30, © 1989, Transaction Publishers, New Brunswick, New Jersey. Reprinted by permission of Transaction Publishers. All rights reserved.

The theory had numerous, glaring problems. The principal one was that it could not explain everyday market phenomena. For example, why is the price of water negligible while the price of diamonds is substantial? Water has great use value to sustain life, while diamonds have only a frivolous, ornamental function. The labor theory of value fell in the late nineteenth century to a more sophisticated theory, one that did not claim that value was derived from any objective quality, but rather that value depended upon the subjective judgments of people in the marketplace, and the supply of the good in question.

This marginal utility theory of value had several noteworthy advantages over its objective, labor-theory competitor. It solved the water-diamond "paradox." Diamonds are priced higher than water because people are willing to pay more for them. Diamonds are relatively scarce, compared with water, hence the marginal unit of diamonds commands a higher price than the marginal unit of water. If water suddenly became scarce, people would value it more highly and be willing to pay more to acquire it, and its price would rise.

The marginal theory also explained what the labor theory could not; that is, how prices are set for everyday commodities in the market. The new theory could explain why misdirected labor time — that is, time spent producing widgets no one wants — would command no equivalent compensation in the marketplace; it could explain why commodities embodying the same labor time did not appear to trade equally on the market. . . .

Marginal utility theory, thus, overcame another problem inherent in a labor theory of value: that every factor of production — labor, land, entrepreneurship — required a different theory to explain how its price was set.

Now, what bearing does all of this have on comparable worth? Comparable worth shares with the labor theory of value a desire to discover some objective characteristics of worth or value apart from the valuations in the marketplace derived from the choices of actual buyers. For comparable worth, the hours of labor embodied in a thing no longer set its value, but rather, the value of labor itself can be determined by assessing its components: knowledge, skills, mental demands, accountability, working conditions.

What comparable worth's proponents are searching for is some identifiable, objective qualities that are transferable from job to job and that everyone could, at least theoretically, agree upon. But are they not searching in vain? The perpetual squabbles among evaluators performing studies in the states, the instructions of consultants to the evaluation committees that they should go with their gut instincts in assessing points, and the reevaluations that go on once the scores have been assembled are empirical evidence of a problem that really lies on the theoretical level.

If there is no intrinsic value to a job, then it cannot be measured. Let us look at the wage-setting process as it unfolds in the market to see what the price of labor means, if it does not mean a measurement of intrinsic value.

A job has value to someone who creates it and is willing to pay someone to do it. The price of that job is set in the labor market, which is nothing more than an arena for satisfying the demands for labor of various sorts by numerous employers. What an employer is willing to pay for the type of labor he needs depends on his assessment of what that labor can contribute to the ultimate product and what price he thinks those products will command in the market. The labor market is an impersonal process. In most cases, employers and potential employees do not know each other before the process is begun. It is impersonal in another way, also. No individual employer can exercise much influence over the price of labor of the kind he needs. Only in the rarest of cases, where no alternative employers are available to willing workers, will any one employer have much of an impact on the overall job market. Such influence characterizes centrally planned, government-owned economies much more than it does market economies. To the extent that markets are distorted by government-imposed monopolies or cartels, the actual market departs from the theoretical one.

The supporters of comparable worth consider this view of the market naive. Rather, they say, markets are dominated by monopolies that dictate wages to workers who by-and-large have no other options. The problem with this argument is that it is simply not true that the labor market in the United States is largely dominated by monopolies. What has characterized capitalist economies since the Industrial Revolution is precisely the options that workers have, the fluidity of labor markets, and the ever-changing possibilities the market creates. Unlike the Middle Ages, where workers' options were essentially limited to following the paternal occupation and where class status was very nearly immutable, capitalism presents workers with a plethora of options.

Indeed, this kaleidoscopic choice is precisely the aspect of capitalism to which its early opponents, both of the socialist and patriarchal variety, most vehemently objected. Where monopolies do exist, they are usually the result of governmental interference, for example, by grants of monopoly, and not by the action of the marketplace. While temporary monopolies may arise in a free market, they tend not to last, as upstart companies and their new technology eventually upset the staid "monopolists."

To return to our description of the labor market, if an employer, through discriminatory motivation or any other reason, wishes to pay less than the prevailing wage for a certain kind of labor, one of three things will normally happen. He will get no takers. He will get fewer takers than he needs. Or the quality of the applicant pool will be lower than the job requires. Conversely, if he wishes to pay more, he will get many applicants and some of them will be of higher quality than normal in that job classification.

In the former case, the employer jeopardizes his business by presumably making his products less marketable and his operation less efficient; in the latter case, the employer may benefit his business if his more skilled employees produce more products or a better product that the consumers are willing to pay a higher price to acquire. The consumer, however, may not be willing, and then the business would be jeopardized.

Thus, employers are, in the normal case, pretty much tied to paying prevailing market wages. Those employers who discriminate for irrelevant reasons — like race, sex, religion — put themselves at a competitive disadvantage by restricting the pool of labor from which they can select workers. If discrimination against blacks or women, for example, were prevalent in the society, the price of such labor would be lower than for comparable labor provided by members of other groups. Those employers willing to hire the despised will benefit from lower prices for their labor and will enjoy a competitive edge. In the absence of laws enshrined by governments to perpetuate discrimination, the market should correct for it over time by penalizing discriminatory employers and rewarding the others. Eventually, the wages of the discriminated will rise.

If jobs have no intrinsic worth, then the comparable worth position has been severely wounded, for it bases its case on precisely such an assumption. What I have argued is that jobs have no intrinsic value within the context of market economy. Now, that is an important caveat. A competing system, one that sets the prices for all goods, services, and labor by a central planning agency could provide an alternative framework to the market. But would the price of various types of labor be objectively set in such a system? All we could say is that the planners would tell everyone else what each job was worth. Via job evaluations, direct flashes of insight, or whatever methodology they chose, the wages of labor would be set and everyone would abide by those directives. One might call such a system objective in the sense that departures from the assigned wages might be punishable, but using the term in the way we normally do, it seems like rampant subjectivism. . . .

Leaving aside the most radical who embrace socialism or Marxism, most contend that they do not wish to replace the market, only to make it fairer to women. They profess to see nothing radical about their chosen tool, only a natural progression from the equal opportunity laws we already have on the books. But if they do not wish to abandon the market, they must somehow surmount the argument that jobs do not have intrinsic worth or objective value within the market context. They have not done so, because it is impossible to understand the market and to argue for objective value. If they cannot make the argument, they are left with no choice, logically, but to embrace central planning, in which the only form of "objectivity" would be the decrees of those in authority; or, as George Orwell might have said: a world in which objectivity equals subjectivity.

Another problem with this quest for objective value or worth is that it confuses moral language with economic language. Surely, economists talk about value: they mean by the value of a commodity what it will trade for at any particular time in the marketplace. There is nothing mysterious, no essence that lies buried beneath this market value (at least since the labor theory of value was abandoned).

What the comparable worth people mean by value is something essential to any particular type of labor. They are looking for some higher order moral principle that, irrespective of the market, can compare the work of the plumber to the tree-trimmer to the grocer to the secretary to the nurse. Within our society, there is no agreement about higher order moral principles: about what contributes to the good life; what activities are worthy of pursuit in their own right; what kinds of behavior contribute to the welfare of society. How can we expect individuals in society to agree about how particular jobs contribute to ends, when those ends themselves are in dispute?

Wouldn't it be an unpleasant world if people did agree about values, if those values could be objectively measured as they were exemplified in different jobs, and if they were paid accordingly? Then, if Michael Jackson earned a million dollars for each performance while an emergency room nurse received $20 for her work during the same two hours, we would know that he was really worth 50,000 times as much as she; that is, that society valued her contribution so very much less. We would know, simply by the salary paid to each person in such a society, exactly what his social contribution and, presumably, his social status was. But on a market we cannot even infer that a plumber making $10 an hour is worth more or less to his employer than a teacher who earns the same wage is worth to hers. Such comparisons are vacuous. One's worth, in the moral sense, is not measured in the marketplace by one's wage. Price and salary are economic terms, and they depend upon the available supply and the demand for particular kinds of labor. Value and worth are moral terms, as comparable worth's supporters intend them, and they do not equate well at all with price in the marketplace. Thus, even the market cannot equate the worth (in the moral sense) of one job with another; all it shows is that at any particular time secretaries are paid more or less than zoo keepers.

Any attempt to employ "objective" job assessment criteria must be inherently discretionary. That blanket statement stands unrefuted by the comparable worth camp. I believe it is logically impossible for them to surmount this difficulty: for they cannot find objectivity by appealing to the views of experts who, as human beings, bring their prejudices to any assessment; nor can they find it by abandoning the market and embracing central planning, which is nothing more than personal whims enshrined in decrees. . . .

The comparable worth critics are correct: there is no intrinsic value to any job, and, hence, they can neither be measured nor compared.

COMPARABLE WORTH AND THE MARKET

Most proponents of comparable worth argue that it is not an alternative to the market, that it is like other correctives to the market that have been instituted by government in recent years. I contend that this is false. Comparable worth, unlike the Equal Pay Act, Title VII, and affirmative action, cannot be grafted onto the market. Rather, the market and comparable worth emanate from two entirely different normative assumptions about individual action.

The market exemplifies the assumption that individual consumers ought to be sovereign, that their desires ought to rule the economy. Comparable worth assumes that individuals ought not be the final arbiters of economic life. Some individuals, rather, should place their judgments above those of the rest of their countrymen. These "experts" will ensure that wage decisions are made on equitable, nonprejudicial grounds.

The Equal Pay Act said to employers that you cannot pay women less than you pay men for the same job. Title VII said to employers that you cannot discriminate in hiring, promotion, compensation, and so forth between men and women. And affirmative action said to employers that you must try to advance women, as historic victims of discrimination, to positions in which they had been underrepresented. All of these mandates interfered with employers' rights (and employees' rights, too). All limited employers' freedom. Formerly, an employer could hire whomever he liked, pay whatever he liked, and use any criteria for hiring that he wished.[1]

But comparable worth is different. Instead of employers determining their wage scales by evaluating their demand for a certain type of labor and the supply of it on the market, "expert" boards would have to examine the jobs in each firm or government bureau and set wage scales according to the comparability of different jobs. While most comparable worth advocates do not envision one wage board doing this for the entire economy — as the National War Labor Board tried to do during World War II — it is obvious that some national standards would have to evolve or be imposed, either by legislative act, bureaucratic decree, or judicial interpretation. Without such a universal standard, employers would be left in perpetual limbo about how to stay on the right side of the law: they would hang on each turn of the judicial worm.

Even if there were many boards rather than one, this would still prove problematical on several grounds, in addition to the ones previously raised in the discussion of intrinsic worth. The very reason for having "expert" boards to assess jobs rather than the market is to eliminate subjectivity and, thus, prejudice. But can the boards accomplish this?

As Richard Burr graphically illustrated with his comparisons of state comparable worth studies, they cannot. All people have prejudices, and if that is too harsh a term, all have tastes. Consultants in their comparable worth evaluations have proven themselves systematically more sympathetic to white-collar than blue-collar jobs, to credentials over job experience (thus reversing some of the alleged biases in traditional job evaluations). What is to ensure that a board acts impartially? Will we need another board to assess the fairness of the first, and yet another to judge the fairness of the second. Or, more likely, will we witness appeals courts frequently replacing the judgments of district court judges with their own, and then the Supreme Court every once in a while getting in the act. We seem to be caught in an infinite regress problem, with no theoretical end point short of God and no practical end point short of the Supreme Court. . . .

A moderate supporter of comparable worth might respond to such an argument that she only wants to proceed on a firm-by-firm basis, rather than by imposing a sweeping, national reform. But this would be an unstable solution — as I think many of those who advocate it realize — a slippery slope. Companies forced to adopt comparable worth as a result of suits would be at a competitive disadvantage, as their labor costs would rise and there would be little incentive, except to avoid litigation, for other firms to adopt comparable worth, which would likewise disadvantage them. In the end, comparable worth would have to be a national program; piecemeal action simply will not secure the cooperation of all employers in an effort that runs counter to their self-interest.

Thus, the market and comparable worth seem to be mutually exclusive. Either we have market-set wages or we have wages set by administrative boards and courts. The former has decided advantages, since it is both efficient and voluntaristic. The latter has the twin faults that it cannot be put into operation without producing chaos, and that it replaces individual sovereignty with the opinions of "experts."

DISCRIMINATION

Comparable worth proponents believe the market for women's work has been distorted by centuries of discrimination. The market devalues the work of women, and hence it should be supplanted.

The work of June O'Neill and others in demythologizing the wage gap is compelling. It is clear that if women exhibited precisely the same characteristics as men — the same level of education and mix of courses, the same longevity at present employment, the same work force participation levels, and so forth — the "wage gap" would shrink to a "wage pittance" of a few cents, as indeed it has for younger women and single women. The case for massive distortions of the market resulting from discrimination just has not been convincingly made. A gap of 10 percent, which can be putatively accounted for by other intangible factors like motivation, goals, and family commitments, simply cannot carry the case for revolutionizing our market system.

William R. Beer, a sociologist at Brooklyn College, raises an interesting point in trying to assess how important discrimination is in the lives of women (and blacks, too) in the United States. Why not ask the members of the relevant groups how discrimination has affected their lives. Beer cites a study conducted by *The New York Times,* in November 1983, in which they did precisely that. Three questions were posed: "In the place where you work now, do you think you've ever been discriminated against because you're a woman in terms of salary, responsibility, or promotion?" Seventy-seven percent of the women questioned answered "no." "In other places where you have worked, have you ever been discriminated against because you're a woman?" Seventy-three percent said "no." "Has it ever happened to you, that in seeking work, you applied for a job that interested you, only to learn they wanted to hire a man and not a woman?"

Eighty-three percent responded "no." Beer concludes that it is false to suppose that a case can be made for systemic discrimination, although individual instances of such discrimination certainly do arise.[2]

But leaving this aside, there is something else fundamentally flawed about the proponents' line of argument. Comparable worth cannot eliminate discrimination from the labor market, and neither can any other scheme, including the market. The purpose of any hiring process is precisely to discriminate. A personnel director does not only look for skills in hiring an applicant. Such intangibles as personality, looks, motivation, and so forth play a factor. Just as any employer discriminates in hiring, so the consulting firms or wage boards would impose their tastes and value judgments. . . .

Have we fulfilled the liberal ideal of openness and colorblindness that motivated the framers of the Civil Rights Act of 1964, or rather have we moved closer to a genuinely racist society: one that asks employers to keep tallies on the number of preferred minorities they interview for each available job and threatens them with penalties if the "goals" are not met; and one that requires job applicants to fill out forms to identify themselves by race? What would comparable worth do except add another layer of discrimination to the Orwellian attempt to create a discrimination-free society by practicing official discrimination?

Let us discriminate for a time in women's favor until the wage gap disappears, the proponents maintain, and then all will be well and comparable worth can be discarded. If we have learned anything by the experience of the last two and a half decades, it is that one antidiscrimination scheme follows ever closer on the heels of the preceding one. It is a never ending process once favored groups achieve their more-than-equal position, the less favored begin to organize and demand their privileges from the government. In the end, I am afraid, a society emerges that is much more discriminatory, much more con-

scious of racial, sexual, and religious differences than it ever was before the process began. Comparable worth for women today; minorities tomorrow; and everyone the day after tomorrow. Then, the free market is gone, and along with it economic liberty and consumer sovereignty.

If discrimination — meaning tastes — is irremediable, why should we prefer comparable worth and the discrimination of "experts" to the market and the discrimination generated by the free choices of all of us?

EQUALITY OF OPPORTUNITY V. EQUALITY OF RESULTS

The labor market as it currently operates in the United States embodies a conception of equality that political theorists call equality of opportunity. All positions in society ought to be open to everyone, without any artificial barriers of race, religion, nationality, sex, and so forth being placed in anyone's way. Where the actual world departs from this model, government intervenes to guarantee the rights of those who have been discriminated against. While equality of opportunity has its problems — it interferes with personal liberty as adumbrated above — it is preferable to the view of equality embodied in the comparable worth position. Equality of opportunity is the liberal conception enshrined in the Civil Rights Act and its successors.

Equality of results, or some looser variant of it, seems to be the vision embraced by comparable worth's adherents. As I have argued earlier, the attempt to put such a principle into operation (as Nozick argued) is doomed to failure. Life will always intervene to upset the carefully balanced apple cart. Even if this were not so, I do not think equality of results is an appealing moral objective. It is contrary to our tradition, going back to John Locke and the natural law theorists, of treating each person as an individual. Equality of results demands that each person be treated as a component of an organic society; the parts must be rearranged and rewarded so the entire organism will be just.

The comparable worth camp might respond that the foregoing is merely an historical argument about Western traditions and is not in itself compelling. I think it is more than that. It is based upon a realization that individuals are different — they have disparate talents, needs, desires, and tastes. These differences cannot be denied. Any attempt to fit such heterogeneous beings into one scheme to judge "worth" would involve a massive amount of paternalism: much more extensive and intrusive than the protective labor laws of the late nineteenth century that the comparable worth people so rightly condemn. If individuals freely hiring on the market and individuals freely offering their services determine that dog catchers are "worth" more than nurses and the comparable worth board or court thinks otherwise, then the wishes of countless employers and workers will count for nothing.

Equality of opportunity is more appealing than equality of results because at least it gives more respect to the wishes of individuals and it just tries to guarantee that the process of selection is in some sense "fair." It does not require making independent assessments of the value to society or to a firm of the work of baseball players, laundresses, plumbers, or secretaries. It leaves such decisions to the marketplace. . . .

MARKETS ARE JUST

In a market system, everyone is free to produce what he likes, to trade with other willing partners, and to give or bequeath his wealth to anyone he chooses. The system is based on a simple and just principle — that those who produce are entitled to the products of their labor. John Locke, the political philosopher who most influenced our Founding Fathers, understood well that by defending a right to property he was also defending the rights of life and liberty. Very often, he spoke only of property, meaning by it to include the other two rights. Where property rights are insecure, and even more where they are abrogated, liberty will not long survive. We have seen this truism borne out time and again; in fact, too many times for any reasonable person to doubt its veracity. From Russia to China, from Ethiopia to Cuba, from East Germany to Mozambique, deprivation of economic liberty has meant the death of liberty. Despite great differences in culture, state of development, geographical locale, and racial composition between these countries, the result has always been the same.

Another feature of the market system deserves more attention than it has received thus far in the debate over comparable worth. The "market system" is not really a "system" at all, in the sense that a system implies something designed or ordered — like a game, with rules handed down by a creator. Rather, the market — and this is one of Friedrich Hayek's great insights — is a "spontaneous order." It results from not interfering with people and letting them do what they want, what they freely choose to do, in the absence of the initiation of force. Thus, capitalism, rightly understood, is just what people do when you leave them alone to do anything that is peaceful, or, in Lockean terms, anything that does not invade the like rights of others.

Comparable worth, however, would deprive individuals of an important component of this liberty of action by denying them part of their contractual liberty. This liberty, it should be noted, involves no force by one party upon another, and thus comparable worth would breach the spontaneous order by initiating the use of compulsion. To be more specific, comparable worth would deprive employers of the liberty to freely dispose of their property: to decide how much they are willing to spend on a particular type of labor.

One group of women who would be harmed if comparable worth artificially inflated entry-level salaries are women entrepreneurs, especially those in the process of creating new businesses, since these start-up companies are usually quite labor intensive. But even more significantly, comparable worth would deny many workers the liberty to negotiate contracts with potential employers. Just as minimum wage laws prevent unskilled teenagers — particularly those from minority groups — from gaining entry-level working experience by agreeing to work at low wages, comparable worth would price the labor of many women beyond their economic worth to employers. These women would be denied their basic economic liberty to freely negotiate contracts.

Comparable worth supporters would in all likelihood deride this argument: "What value is a liberty that lets women work at wage levels that are so low they are demeaning?" However, to women reentering the labor market after a marriage has broken up, to women just out of high school, to newly arrived immigrants, and to those with little skill, the freedom to take the clerical, factory, and sales jobs is the difference between having a chance to better themselves or being condemned to dependency. Comparable worth, by artificially raising the wages of such jobs, would restrict the number of such positions and make the lot of the poorest and least skilled women that much worse. This is neither just nor expedient.

MARKETS EXPRESS CONSUMER SOVEREIGNTY

Employers are consumers of labor, but they are also intermediaries between the ultimate consumers of their products and their laborers. Employers produce goods by combining various factors of production, and they hope these goods will mesh with what consumers want. They do so as efficiently as their competitors, or else they are soon out of business. Thus, comparable worth is not simply an attempt to replace the decisions of employers with the decisions of "experts," bureaucrats, and judges: Comparable worth seeks ultimately to replace the decisions of consumers themselves about how they wish to spend their money.

To most comparable worth advocates, those who embrace comparable worth because they see it as a means for bettering women's earnings, the tendency of comparable worth to undermine consumer sovereignty ought to be disturbing. Women are consumers, and they ought to value the liberty that has created the abundance we all enjoy. The more radical supporters of comparable worth, however, understand that the concept is a wedge they can use to undermine our free market economy, and I expect that they are not at all disconcerted by the tendency of comparable worth to replace the choice of consumers with the opinions of "experts." These radicals constitute, however, only a small proportion of those who support comparable worth.

NOTES

1. I do not intend to ignore the Wagner Act and minimum wage laws, which had already greatly circumscribed employers' latitude in compensating employees.
2. William R. Beer, "The Wages of Discrimination." *Public Opinion* (July/August 1987).

Making Sense of Sexual Harassment Law

Andrew Altman

I

Over the past two decades, judges and legal theorists have created and developed the legal doctrine of sexual harassment. The United States has been in the forefront of these developments, and my focus in this article will be on U.S. law and American theorists. Yet, it must be noted that the law of other nations also prohibits sexual harassment. For example, Canadian courts have held that sexual harassment violates that nation's antidiscrimination statutes. And courts in the United Kingdom and other European Community states have found sexual harassment to be illegal.

Under current U.S. law, sexual harassment claims may be brought under Title VII of the Civil Rights Act of 1964, state fair employment practice laws, local ordinances, or under a tort claim. My main concern will be with Title VII, although the tort law will be relevant to some of my analysis. Title VII prohibits discrimination on account of race, color, religion, sex, or national origin in the terms, conditions, or privileges of employment. The courts have held that sexual harassment is a form of sex discrimination and thus a violation of Title VII.[1]

---

[1] This understanding of sexual harassment was affirmed by the Supreme Court in *Meritor Savings Bank v. Vinson* 477 U.S. 57 (1986).

Current doctrine distinguishes between two broad types of sexual harassment: quid-pro-quo and hostile environment. In the context of the workplace, quid-pro-quo harassment (QPQH) consists of unwelcome sexual advances, demands, or propositions acceptance of which is made a condition of obtaining some employment-related benefit or avoiding some employment-related harm. Hostile environment harassment (HEH) consists of unwelcome sexual conduct that unreasonably interferes with work performance or creates a sufficiently hostile or offensive work environment.

In this article, I undertake an explication, refinement, and defense of the existing law of sexual harassment. My aim is to show that current law is quite defensible in broad outline but that it needs to be explicated more clearly and systematically and defended more cogently than American courts and theorists have so far managed. . . .

II

HEH is best understood as speech or conduct that (a) is addressed to or oriented toward an employee's sexuality and (b) amounts to a material and unreasonable interference with her job performance. By "sexuality" I mean a person's sexual desires, attitudes, and activities. It is not to be conceptually equated with

---

From Andrew Altman, "Making Sense of Sexual Harassment Law," *Philosophy & Public Affairs*, Winter, 1996, Vol. 25, no. 1. Reprinted by permission of Princeton University Press.

"sex" as used in the phrase "sex discrimination." Persons can be discriminated against on the basis of their sex even if the treatment they receive is not addressed to their sexuality. Conceptually speaking, this is an elementary point, but it is one that is repeatedly misunderstood by courts and commentators.

"Material interference" with job performance should be broadly construed so that it includes cases in which the harassment creates obstacles or burdens that make it more difficult for the victim to maintain her job performance and prospects, even if she is successful in overcoming those difficulties. Moreover, "material interference" should cover harassing actions that harm the victim's occupational prospects by diminishing the regard in which she is held by her coworkers or supervisors.

One key issue to resolve in specifying the meaning of "unreasonable interference" is whether the standard of reasonableness should be gender-neutral or gendered. . . . For now, the point is that the law should include a reasonableness standard of some kind, because employers should not be held liable if an employee's work performance suffers from remarks or conduct that would not have interfered with the work of a reasonable employee. The law justifiably expects employees to be reasonable and denies them legal means to shift to their employer costs they incur as a consequence of their own unreasonableness.

Acts of HEH are typically part of the broader class of social acts I will call "put-downs." Specific kinds of put-down include demeaning, degrading, debasing, and humiliating. There are significant differences here. For instance, humiliating a person is a more brutal put-down than demeaning her in that it can be reasonably expected to cause overwhelming shame. And some kinds of put-down, such as degradation and debasement, carry the implication that the victim is to be treated as less than a full human.

Prototypical put-downs are communicative acts targeting some specific person(s) and having the following features: The acts are reasonably construed as affirming that the target's status is subordinate to that of the agent's and as communicating that affirmation to her, and it is reasonable to expect that the acts will be found objectionable by the targeted person and cause her unwarranted distress or harm.

In a typical case of actionable HEH, the harassing conduct amounts to a put-down addressed in some way to the employee's sexuality, and the interference it creates with the employee's job performance is unreasonable precisely because of its character as a put-down. This is not to say that all workplace put-downs addressed to a person's sexuality should count as actionable HEH. For example, in some instances, an unrepeated and relatively mild sexual put-down would have only a vanishing effect on a reasonable employee's job performance and should not be actionable. To hold otherwise is to take an overly protective view of those who are put down. One can hardly go through life without being at the wrong end of many put-downs, and it is reasonable for the law to expect that people will have developed some "protective hide" to ward them off and get on with their lives.

Yet, actionable HEH usually does involve sexually demeaning or degrading the victim, and perhaps it almost always does when the victim is a woman and the perpetrator a man. That is because male-on-female harassment is reasonably seen as reflecting and reinforcing a demeaning view of women that relegates them to second-class status in the workplace. On that view, it is enough for male workers that they do their job, but when it comes to female workers, they must also serve as the objects of the sexual attentions of the males.

However, it would be going too far to include as part of the very definition of HEH that it is sexually demeaning or involves some other kind of sexual put-down. We should leave conceptual space for cases in which there is a material and unreasonable interference with job performance, even though the victim does not construe (and it is not reasonable to construe) the harassing behavior as a put-down. In such cases, the behavior would be reasonably found to be very annoying and disruptive of work activities without being seen as demeaning.

It might be argued that the requirement of material and unreasonable interference sets too strict a standard for judging HEH lawsuits and that sexual conduct or remarks directed at an employee should be actionable even if they do not rise to that level. The Supreme Court has adopted this position in its most recent sexual harassment ruling, *Harris v. Forklift Systems.*[2] The Court held that if a work environment is sufficiently hostile or abusive, as judged by a reasonable person, then there may be a violation of Title VII's guarantee of workplace equality. Several variables must be taken into account in determining whether an environment is sufficiently hostile: unreasonable interference with job performance (or prospects) is one variable, but others include the frequency and the severity of the discriminatory conduct. The Court says that all variables need to be weighed and that sufficiently severe and frequent harassment violates the law's requirement of equality, even if there is no unreasonable interference with job performance. . . .

Current doctrine requires that acts be "unwelcome" in order to count as actionable HEH. Roughly put, an unwelcome act is one that the targeted person finds objectionable and would have preferred not to have occurred. Courts have sometimes used the un-

welcomeness requirement to put the burden on the plaintiff of establishing that she found objectionable the alleged acts of HEH. But this placement of the burden of proof cannot be justified, in light of the best understanding of HEH. Remarks or actions that interfere with work performance — especially when reasonably construed as demeaning or degrading — should be presumed to be unwelcome by those at whom they are directed. The unstated and unwarranted premise behind judicial judgments to the contrary is that women are generally at work, not simply to do their jobs, but to find mates and are rather indiscriminate in their receptiveness to male advances.

Notwithstanding some court opinions, it should not be necessary for a plaintiff to have expressed to the perpetrator — or to anyone else — her objection to his sexual remarks, if the remarks are, prima facie, reasonably construed as demeaning or degrading. The law should expect persons to understand how others may reasonably construe what they do or say and to adjust their behavior accordingly. In order to avoid liability on the ground that his actions were not unwelcome, an employee who makes remarks to a coworker that are, prima facie, reasonably construed as sexually demeaning should be required to show that he had sufficient reason to think that the coworker would not in fact object to them. In short, along with the presumption of unwelcomeness goes the defendant's burden of showing that he reasonably believed his behavior to be not unwelcome.

Courts have also used the unwelcomeness requirement to license inquiry into the plaintiff's style of dress and workplace demeanor. There are cases in which this kind of inquiry has rested on demeaning and unwarranted assumptions about women. For example, contrary to the Supreme Court's claim, the way a woman dresses is not "obviously relevant" in determining whether she welcomed

---

[2]*Harris v. Forklift Systems* 114 S.Ct. 367 (1993).

sexual behavior directed at her by a boss or coworker.[3] The assumption of its relevance rests on the unwarranted and sexist view that women who dress in ways that men find attractive are likely to be indiscriminately inviting men to direct sexual remarks and behavior toward them.

Some feminist critics of existing doctrine have suggested that the unwelcomeness requirement be jettisoned entirely. For example, Susan Estrich argues that the requirement perpetuates sexist assumptions about women and is "gratuitously punitive" because it allows the defendant to shift the focus of the case from him to the plaintiff and to invoke sexist views in portraying the plaintiff as "unworthy of respect or decency."[4] If the defendant's conduct could be reasonably construed as sexually demeaning or degrading, Estrich claims, then he should not be allowed to escape liability by refocusing the case on the plaintiff. . . .

Estrich's underlying assumption is that, in harassment cases, protecting the right of women to fair employment opportunity should automatically trump the principle of legal fairness. I do not know that she is right about that, but even if she is, it is unlikely that courts will jettison the unwelcomeness requirement: By now it is a firmly entrenched part of doctrine. Accordingly, the best feasible approach may be to argue that the requirement should be folded into the unreasonableness condition as I have suggested, with the appropriate burdens of proof, and to expose and criticize decisions that apply the requirement on the basis of sexist assumptions about women. In that way, any tendency of the unwelcomeness requirement to perpetuate such assumptions might be mitigated, even if it cannot be eliminated.

---

[3] *Meritor Savings Bank v. Vinson* 477 U.S. 57, 69 (1986).
[4] Susan Estrich, "Sex at Work," *Stanford Law Review* 43 (1991): 833.

III

Like HEH, QPQH is addressed to its victim as a sexual being and uses her sexuality against her. But unlike HEH, the perpetrator of QPQH seeks to gain sexual favors from his victim, and he attempts to do so by taking advantage of the authority he has over her in the hierarchy of the workplace. It is commonly held that such efforts by the harasser amount to coercion of the employee and that the coercive character of QPQH shows why statutory prohibitions on it are justified.

The concept of coercion has been subject to much philosophical controversy over the past few decades. Central to the controversy has been the question of whether there is an essential normative element to the concept. It is not necessary to settle that question for the purpose of explicating and defending the law of sexual harassment. However, it is necessary to explain why it should be illegal for a supervisor to say to a subordinate, "Have sex with me and I'll give you a promotion," but not illegal to say, "Land the IBM contract and I'll give you a promotion."

Many people would answer that the difference between the two statements is that the former is coercive and the latter is not. But the answer is incomplete unless it is elaborated in a way that explains how that difference provides grounds for having a legal ban on the one statement but not the other. Such an explanation would necessarily involve a normative claim about what is wrong with a supervisor's making one statement but not the other. For the purposes of the law, it makes no difference whether this normative element is folded into the concept of coercion or treated as separate. Either way, a constructive interpretation of the law needs to explain why we are justified in making it illegal for a supervisor to say "Have sex with me and I'll give you a promotion."

So why are we so justified? My suggestion is this: Such statements violate the employee's right against having employment-related benefits (or burdens) accorded her on the basis of her willingness to perform sexual favors for her supervisor or employer. Such a right can be seen as an aspect of the more general right to fair employment opportunity and . . . an implication of the right to equal consideration. In contrast, fair employment opportunity clearly does not involve any claim against having job benefits or burdens made contingent on success in job-related activities.

Although the rules against HEH and QPQH both protect the right of fair employment opportunity, they do it in somewhat different ways. The ban on HEH protects against sexually oriented remarks or behaviors that unreasonably interfere with job performance. The ban on QPQH protects against efforts of the employer to extend the scope of his authority to include the sexual activities of the employee. There is some overlap, since one way of unreasonably interfering with job performance is by trying to extend one's authority into the domain of the employee's sexual behavior. And courts have recognized this by allowing evidence of such conduct by employers into cases that charge HEH. But demands or requests by an employer for sexual favors in return for employment benefits are not at all necessary for actionable HEH. In fact, the perpetrator in a case of HEH need not even be the employer or anyone with the authority to give or withhold employment benefits: A coworker with no more workplace authority than the victim can be liable for HEH.

As with HEH, current doctrine requires that conduct be "unwelcome" in order to count as QPQH: A plaintiff who did not find a sexual proposition unwelcome at the time it was made was not the victim of actionable harassment. Courts have done little to clarify the meaning of 'unwelcome' in this context

other than to suggest that it involves more than whether or not the employee acceded to the sexual proposition. A woman may accede solely out of fear of losing her job, for example, in which case current doctrine would count the sexual proposition as an unwelcome one. Beyond that, the meaning of the unwelcomeness requirement and its rationale have been left rather unclear.

The requirement should be understood in terms of an employee's waiver of her right against having job benefits or burdens accorded her on the basis of her compliance with the boss's sexual demands or propositions. There should be a strong presumption that employees have not waived that right, and the law should require that, prior to extending a proposition of sex in return for a job benefit, employers have good reason, based on the employee's words and actions, to think that she has waived her right. In cases where the employer does not have such reason, courts should judge the employer's sexual proposition to have been unwelcome, even if the employee acceded to it. On the other hand, in cases where the prior words and actions of the employee made it reasonable for the employer to think that she had waived her right, courts should judge the employer's sexual proposition to have been not unwelcome.

The application of the unwelcomeness requirement in the context of a QPQH case carries with it all of the pitfalls noted previously in connection with HEH cases: Sexist assumptions can easily distort the determination of whether the requirement has been met. And courts have virtually invited the use of such assumptions by ruling, for example, that a woman's style of dress is a relevant consideration. However much these pitfalls may argue for eliminating the unwelcomeness requirement, it is a firmly entrenched part of doctrine. The best feasible approach, then, may be to insist on the strong presumption that employees have not waived their right to keep their sexual activities beyond the scope of their employer's authority and to criticize courts when they permit sexist assumptions to be introduced by defendants in an effort to overcome that presumption.

IV

One of the unsettled areas of law related to sexual harassment doctrine concerns "sexual favoritism," the act of an employer or supervisor in giving a job benefit to an employee in return for her willingness to perform sexual favors for him. Of course, if the initial sexual proposition came from the employer and was unwelcome to the employee, then we have a case of QPQH. But whether or not the proposition was unwelcome or even came from the employer, we can still ask whether other employees who are in competition for that job benefit have had their legal rights violated by the employer's action. The developing doctrine of sexual favoritism addresses that question.

In cases of sexual favoritism, the employer is using sexual criteria for decisions distributing the benefits and burdens of employment. Even though the plaintiff in such a case has not been propositioned by her boss, her opportunities on the job have been determined, in part, by the boss's sexual desire for another employee. The boss has not violated the plaintiff's right against having job benefits and burdens distributed to her according to her compliance with the boss's sexual propositions or demands. But the more general right of fair employment opportunity has been violated in a way that is very similar to cases of QPQH: in both sorts of cases, irrelevant sexual criteria play a role in determining the plaintiff's employment prospects. In the case of QPQH, the criterion is the plaintiff's willingness to accede to the employer's sexual propositions. In the case of favoritism, it is another employee's willingness to accede to his sexual wishes.

Yet, however wrong favoritism is, the question remains whether it makes sense to regard it as a form of sex discrimination under Title VII. In order to answer that question, let us first consider the differential gender-effects of favoritism and then a gender-neutral account of those effects.

At first glance, it may seem that women as a group actually benefit from sexual favoritism. After all, such favoritism gives women a route to advancement that men typically lack. But such a view of the matter does not look seriously enough at the implications of two important premises on which the view rests: (1) Men occupy positions of workplace authority in far greater percentages than do women, and (2) men are much more inclined than women to use their power in the workplace to seek sexual favors from employees of the opposite sex.

These premises explain why women rather than men tend to be the ones at whom sexual favoritism is directed. But once we jettison the sexist assumption that women typically welcome the prospect of trading sex for job benefits, the two premises also point to the conclusion that women as a group suffer greater disadvantage than do men from the existence of sexual favoritism.

First, it is inevitable that in many instances of favoritism the boss's sexual proposition will be unwelcome to the woman, thus amounting to QPQH. And even where bosses would not retaliate against an employee for refusing, it will often be the case that she reasonably fears retaliation and so complies with the unwelcome proposition. Assuming that most women at whom sexual favoritism is directed do not wish to trade sex for job benefits, the female "beneficiaries" of sexual favoritism will typically and reasonably feel themselves forced into sexual relations they would prefer not to have. Finally, sexual favoritism helps to reinforce social beliefs that demean women and perpetuate workplace discrimination against them, such as the belief that women typically "sleep" their way to the top, or that they are generally less competent at their jobs than men are.

It is also possible to describe the systemic effects of sexual favoritism in gender-neutral terms and to justify a prohibition on favoritism on the grounds that it unfairly disadvantages persons on account of an irrelevant characteristic of theirs, *viz.,* their sex. On those grounds, men who are harmed by sexual favoritism should also have a good cause of action. But the gender-neutral justification would be only part of the strongest case for barring favoritism. As with HEH and QPQH, the strongest justification for banning sexual favoritism and regarding it as a form of sex

discrimination would incorporate both the gender-neutral account and the claim that the effect of favoritism is to place women as a group at a systemic disadvantage relative to men in the workplace. . . .

V

The law of sexual harassment is barely two decades old. It is still finding its way toward a clear and persuasive formulation. Judges and theorists have made a reasonable start, and current doctrine is, in broad outline, quite defensible. Yet, confusion remains about certain aspects of the law. It has been the aim of this article to resolve some of that confusion in a way that systematically explicates the legal doctrine and provides the best justification for it.

Sexual Harassment: Why the Corporate World Still Doesn't "Get It"

Vaughana Macy Feary

With the widely publicized charges of sexual harassment brought by neurosurgeon Dr. Frances Conley against Stanford Medical School, the electrifying allegations of Professor Anita Hill against Judge Clarence Thomas, and the sordid Tailhook scandal involving sexual misconduct in the military, the problem of sexual harassment finally exploded into the headlines. As yesterday's silent victims began joining a swelling chorus of protest from today's working women, corporate America suddenly began admitting that sexual harassment is an explosive communication problem. Yet despite all the recent ballyhoo over sexual harassment in the workplace, corporate America still doesn't really "get it," much less understand how to put an end to it.

If sexual harassment in the workplace is to be understood and eliminated, then not only corporate America, but the entire international business community must recognize and discard some old myths about the nature of ethics, and about the relationship between ethics, law and business, as well as some newer myths about sexual harassment, itself. . . .

SEXUAL HARASSMENT AS A WIDESPREAD MORAL PROBLEM

Why has the business community taken so long to admit that sexual harassment in the workplace is a serious problem? The reason seems to be that it still believes Myth Number

One — the tired old joke that business ethics is an oxymoron; business should not really take ethics seriously.

There are numerous statistical studies which show that sexual harassment is an old problem. One of the earliest surveys, conducted by *Redbook* magazine in 1976, found that nine out of ten women responding to the survey had encountered sexual harassment on the job.[1] . . . A *Working Woman* survey published in June, 1992 found that 60 percent of the respondents had been victimized; it attributed this still higher percentage to the fact that the women polled held positions as executives, for "women in managerial and professional positions, as well as those working in male dominated companies are more likely to experience harassment."[2] . . .

One tenth of sexual harassment complaints are now being filed by men.[3] Studies also show that workers may be victimized by supervisors or peers, individuals or groups. . . .

Despite all the evidence indicating that sexual harassment was a major problem in the workplace, the business community remained largely indifferent. . . . A few companies such as Corning, which began its attempts to combat sexual harassment as early as the 1970s, and DuPont, which has long held workshops designed to sensitize managers to the problem, were responsive.[4] Few other companies followed their leadership. It took the Thomas hearings to finally galvanize the business community into recognizing that sexual harassment was rapidly becoming the communication problem of the '90s. . . .

SEXUAL HARASSMENT
IN THE WORKPLACE —
A HISTORICAL OVERVIEW

It was not until *Meritor Savings Bank* v. *Vinson* 447 U.S. 57 (1986), a case in which the plaintiff alleged that she had been harassed, raped,

threatened, and forced to acquiesce to further sexual contacts for fear of losing her job, that the Supreme Court, relying heavily upon the 1980 EEOC guidelines, affirmed that "quid pro quo sexual harassment" AND "environmental harassment" ("unwelcome" sexual conduct that "unreasonably interferes with an individual's job performance" or sustains an "intimidating, hostile or offensive working environment") both constitute violations of Title VII. . . .

Still more legal problems are emerging because now even alleged perpetrators are suing on the grounds of wrongful discharge. Corporations who have faced, or are facing, such suits include: Polaroid, Newsday, General Motors, AT&T, DuPont, Boeing, and Rockwell International.[5] According to the most recent 1992 *Working Woman* survey, it may cost corporate America more than $1 billion over the next five years to settle existing lawsuits. The business community has paid a high price for its allegiance to outworn myths, not only in punitive damages, but also in marred corporate images. Any lessons learned have been learned at too high a cost.

WHY CORPORATIONS
STILL DON'T GET IT

. . . Corporations STILL don't get it, but they are trying. Most corporations have adopted the recommendations of the United States Merit Systems Protections Board, enunciated in 1988. . . . One management consultant in the field estimates that 90 percent of Fortune 500 companies will offer . . . programs within the year — despite the fact that her package can cost as much as $100,000.[6] Ironically, sexual harassment has now become a thriving business.

Unfortunately, it is doubtful that most of the existing types of sexual harassment education currently being offered by human resource consultants are likely to be very effective because such programs overlook the role of power in organizations and the potential for the abuse of organizational power in today's job market. An effective educational program should result in the reduction and eventual elimination of harassing behaviors without inflicting further damage upon the groups most likely to be victimized, but it is doubtful that even where there is a clearly defined corporate policy about sexual harassment, a formal grievance procedure, and strictly enforced sanctions for non-compliance that incidents of sexual harassment will be fully reported or greatly reduced. . . .

It is very difficult for employees in subordinate positions to insist upon their rights. Sexual harassment is often subtle and difficult to prove. Even if victims do prove their case, they have every reason to fear subtle forms of retaliation in their current positions and subtle forms of discrimination if they attempt to secure other positions. Claims about unfair hiring and promotion decisions are difficult to substantiate, especially in a climate where there are too many equally well qualified applicants for the few positions available. . . .

The kinds of sexual harassment education currently being offered in most corporations are not likely to deter potential victimizers because they are still based on old myths . . . — [e.g.] the belief that most moral problems result from ignorance about facts explains why corporations are hiring consultants to deluge employees with facts about sexual harassment. Of course we need to know the facts, but a lot of this information is old news, and educating people about facts is simply not enough. Moral problems occur not only when there is ignorance or disagreement about facts, but also when there is disagreement about values. There is no logical inconsistency between acknowledging legal and statistical facts about sexual harassment and refusing to take a moral stand. Only moral education can bridge the gap by providing reasons for giving up deeply entrenched ideas that, at best, the issue of sexual harassment is "much ado about nothing" or, at worst, a "legal menace" to which many managers may deeply resent being subjected. . . .

THE DEFINITION OF SEXUAL HARASSMENT

Undoubtedly one of the biggest obstacles to "getting" sexual harassment is . . . the belief that the concept of sexual harassment (like most moral concepts) is "murky." Some people worry that there are such deep cultural and gender based differences about the topic that no satisfactory definition can ever be provided. . . . A great deal of this popular wisdom, however, seems to stem from ignorance about the sophistication of EEOC guidelines, or from deliberate attempts on the part of some members of the political, business, or legal communities to prey on such ignorance and to create a backlash. . . .

[Edmund] Wall . . . believes that the mental states of both the perpetrator and the victim are essential defining elements of sexual harassment.[7] He believes that subjective features are essential in defining sexual harassment because, although a range of behaviors can, on occasion, be identified as sexual harassment, almost any of the behaviors, given different mental states of alleged victimizers and victims, may not qualify as sexual harassment at all. Perhaps a quid pro quo offer was only "banter" or perhaps the alleged victim really welcomed the offer as a "career opportunity."[8] Wall seems very concerned with preventing the much popularized innocent man/paranoid woman scenario.[9] Certainly, his inclusion of the perpetrator's mental states differs from EEOC guidelines which focus on the mental states of a victim, or more accurately, a reasonable victimized person. . . .

Some theorists, such as Larry May and John C. Hughes, as well as EEOC guidelines, hold that sexual harassment always constitutes discrimination.[10] . . . Wall disagree[s] because, . . . [he] argues, a bisexual might sexually harass both sexes without the action being discriminatory. This line of argument seems rather silly as an objection to EEOC guidelines and does nothing to establish that sexual harassment is not discriminatory. The whole purpose of Title VII was to prevent invidious discrimination against any employee in the work place, not merely women. . . .

Wall . . . [is] also in agreement that the presence of coercion and/or negative consequences resulting from harassment, are not necessary conditions for the existence of sexual harassment because the victim's personality and values contribute to the effect that a sexual offer will have upon that person. . . . [He is] no doubt correct, but . . . [he] fails to appreciate that the revised EEOC guidelines are compatible with their position. EEOC guidelines do not define sexual harassment in terms of coercion. EEOC guidelines hold that for behavior to constitute sexual harassment, it must be "unwelcome," and decisions about whether a victim found conduct to be unwelcome are to be based upon facts about her conduct. Furthermore, where the victim has submitted to the sexual conduct, the pivotal issue in determining whether the conduct was harassment is whether the conduct was unwelcome; the issue of whether the conduct was voluntary has been ruled to have "no materiality" whatever. . . .

Wall believes that distress on the part of the actual victim is one of the necessary conditions for sexual harassment. Wall simply seems to be wrong here. Women have been conditioned to stoically accept a great deal of sexual behavior which may harm them professionally. Nevertheless, a reasonable person who had not been so conditioned, might be quite justifiably distressed. It is the issue of

whether it would be rational to be distressed, rather than the issue of actual distress which seems central to defining sexual harassment, and this issue is already accommodated within EEOC guidelines.

If we examine the definitions finally proposed by . . . Wall, we will see that neither definition is any improvement over the definition already proposed by the EEOC. . . .

There seem to be a number of difficulties with Wall's definition. The worst difficulty is that it is too narrow. It excludes sexist harassment (e.g., demeaning remarks about women in general) and a great deal of environmental harassment (e.g., the display of objectionable sexual objects, discussions of sexual matters unrelated to work, etc.) which most people would want to include. Certainly excluding those elements requires considerably more argument than the perfunctory claim that "girlie" posters probably are better classified as bad taste rather than sexual harassment.[11] Wall's definition does not seem to accord with our basic intuitions. If indeed Judge Thomas did discuss the kinds of topics (e.g., his sexual endowments and prowess, pornographic movies, and the coke can incident) with Professor Hill that she alleges he did, most people would agree that she was certainly being subjected to a hostile work environment, even if he never said that he had an interest in engaging in sex with her or suggested that anyone else had such an interest. This seems to contradict Wall's belief that the content of what is communicated is immaterial.

There could also be cases of even quid pro quo sexual harassment in which few of the four conditions Wall specifies obtain. Wall simply fails to recognize that, in the case of sexual harassment, communication fails, not merely because the message is not communicated in an appropriate manner, but because, given the inequalities in status and income between employees, many employees (most of them women) do not feel at liberty to communicate honestly; few can afford to pay the price of honest communication.

If . . . Wall's definitions won't do, how should sexual harassment be defined? Don't their difficulties provide still more justification for all the current ballyhoo about the "murkiness" of sexual harassment and the new dangers perfectly well intentioned men and employers may face now that the problem of sexual harassment is being publicly acknowledged? Quite the contrary, defining sexual harassment for the purposes of business ethics is NOT a major philosophical problem. Although, given the difficulty of honest communication, one can hope that the courts will ultimately employ the reasonable person standards in deciding whether conduct is "welcome," the meaning of sexual harassment is reasonably well defined in EEOC guidelines.

Sexual harassment seems to be one of those concepts like the concept "game," to use Wittgenstein's famous example, which form a family. Family members have family resemblances, but there is no shared feature all members of a family necessarily have in common. As a consequence, trying to set out necessary and sufficient conditions for sexual harassment is a thoroughly futile enterprise. The futility of that enterprise, however, does nothing to support the myth that the concept of sexual harassment is hopelessly murky. We are clear enough in paradigm cases about what people mean when they claim they are being sexually harassed. . . .

Of course, in addition to paradigmatic cases of sexual harassment identified by law, there are also borderline cases about which corporations, and in some cases the courts, will have to make decisions. As sexual harassment is a quasi-moral term, legal decisions about borderline cases will almost certainly be based upon whether the questionable behavior is sufficiently morally objectionable to

count as sexual harassment in the legal sense. All of this suggests that, for the purpose of business ethics, corporations would be well advised not only to educate their employees about EEOC guidelines, but also to educate them about the moral reasons which justify the belief that sexual harassment is genuinely immoral and ought to be legally prohibited. . . .

WHY SEXUAL HARASSMENT IN THE WORKPLACE IS MORALLY WRONG AND WHY IT OUGHT TO BE LEGALLY PROHIBITED

. . . What follows is a very brief outline of some good moral reasons for taking the problem of sexual harassment in the workplace seriously, for regarding it as morally objectionable, and for believing that it should be illegal.

First, sexual harassment is morally wrong because it physically and psychologically harms victims, and because environments which permit sexual harassment seem to encourage such harms. Even the most liberal moral theories acknowledge that harm to others is our strongest moral reason for restricting liberty. As the majority of victims in the past have been women, most of the evidence in support of the claim that sexual harassment is harmful is based upon evidence about women, but presumably any group which was habitually so victimized would suffer similar effects.

Some sexual harassment cases associated with "intimidating, hostile, or offensive working environment" involve rape or physical assault. Furthermore, both quid pro quo harassment and environmental harassment can cause sexual harassment trauma syndrome. This syndrome involves both physical and psychological symptoms. . . .

Some sexual touching which qualifies as sexual harassment under EEOC guidelines (even when it is confined to a single severe incident) may not inflict any direct physical harm on women, but permitting unwanted touching may encourage physical violence against women. . . .

EEOC guidelines also hold that nonphysical conduct (e.g., sexual jokes, sexual conversation, the display of pornographic materials, etc.) in cases where it forms a repeated pattern does qualify as sexual harassment. The courts have been divided about this matter.[12] The 1986 Attorney General's Commission on Pornography did conclude that, although there is no general connection between pornography and violence, exposure to sexually degrading and violent materials does contribute to sexual violence against women.[13] The EEOC guidelines can be justified, in part, on the grounds of preventing physical harm to women.

Second, Wall is quite correct in emphasizing that sexual harassment violates privacy rights. Privacy, like pornography, is a controversial subject. . . . Presumably unwanted sexual touching would violate zones of privacy emanating from the Third and Fourth Amendments; if our homes cannot be invaded, presumably our bodies should be doubly sacrosanct. There are also moral rights to specific types of privacy in the workplace.[14] . . . Given that sexual matters are irrelevant in assessing an individual's ability to perform a job, privacy rights seem to preclude any inquiries by managers about the sexual lives of their employees outside of the workplace, and to provide a clear moral justification for discouraging sexual conversations within it.

Third, there are certainly historical and causal correlations between sexual harassment and discrimination. . . . Recent studies verify that women, and especially women of color, are still the group most likely to be victimized by sexual harassment, and that they are usually harassed by men occupying positions of superior authority. Given the complicated connections between discrimination, violence, inequalities in power, and sexual misconduct, corporations have a duty to insist upon sexual propriety in the workplace in order to protect any employee from becoming a victim of further discrimination.

Fourth, sexual harassment violates liberty rights. . . . Sexual harassment restricts liberty. A 1979 Working Women's Institute study found that 24 percent of sexual harassment victims were fired for complaining, while another 42 percent left their jobs. . . . To suggest that women should leave their jobs and deviate from their career tracks when confronted with sexual harassment is only to add injury to injury. Worse yet, it plays into vicious stereotypes that victims of sexual abuse "ask for it."

Fifth, sexual harassment violates rights to fair equality of opportunity. . . . There is a wealth of evidence to suggest that women do not enjoy fair equality in the workplace and that sexual harassment is part of the problem. Sexual harassment stress syndrome, resulting from quid pro quo and environmental harassment, impairs job performance. A hostile work environment undermines respect for women making it difficult for them to exercise authority and command respect. Pornography, sexual conversation, sexual and sexist jokes, girlie posters, and the like, are morally objectionable because they violate women's rights to enjoy fair equality of opportunity. . . .

CONCLUSION

. . . Sexual harassment is a serious moral problem. To get to the root of the problem, the corporate world must begin to reason critically, to relinquish old myths, to take a strong moral stand, and to provide moral education for employees. It must then assess the effectiveness of that education by conducting anonymous surveys of those groups with the least powerful positions or with the most complaints in the past to determine whether there is a reduction of complaints among those respondents. Until then, sexual harassment will be a potentially explosive communication problem.

NOTES

1. Conte, Alba. *Sexual Harassment in the Workplace: Law and Practice* (New York: Wiley Law Publications, John Wiley and Sons, Inc., 1990), p. 2.
2. Sandoff, Ronni. "Sexual Harassment: The Inside Story," (*Working Woman* Survey). *Working Woman* (June 1992).
3. Templin, Neal. "As Women Assume More Power, Charges Filed by Men May Rise," *The Wall Street Journal* (October 18, 1991), p. B3.
4. Segal, Troy and Zachary Schiller. "Six Experts Suggest Ways to Negotiate the Minefield," *BusinessWeek* (October 12, 1991), 33.
5. Lublin, JoAnn. "As Harassment Charges Rise, More Men Fight Back," *The Wall Street Journal* (October 18, 1991), p. B4.
6. Lublin, JoAnn. "Sexual Harassment Is Topping Agenda in Many Executive Education Programs," *The Wall Street Journal* (December 2, 1991), p. B1.
7. Wall, Edmund. "The Definition of Sexual Harassment," *Public Affairs Quarterly* 5 (4) (October 1991): 371–385.
8. Ibid., pp. 380–1.
9. Ibid., pp. 376–378.
10. Hughes, Larry and May, John C, "Is Sexual Harassment Coercive?", in Gertrude Ezorsky, Ed., *Moral Rights in the Workplace* (New York: State of New York Press, 1982), pp. 115–22.
11. Wall, p. 383.
12. Siegel, Larry J. *Criminology*, 4th ed. (St. Paul, MN: West Publishing Co., 1989), pp. 491–493.
13. Siegel, p. 406.
14. Brenkert, George G. "Privacy, Polygraphs and Work," *Contemporary Issues in Business Ethics* ed. Joseph R. DesJardins and John J. McCall. (Belmont, CA: Wadsworth Publishing Co., 1985), pp. 227–237.

LEGAL PERSPECTIVES

Local 28 of the Sheet Metal Workers' International Association v. Equal Employment Opportunity Commission

Supreme Court of the United States

In 1975, petitioners were found guilty of engaging in a pattern and practice of discrimination against black and Hispanic individuals (nonwhites) in violation of Title VII of the Civil Rights Act of 1964, 42 U.S.C. § 2000e *et seq.*, and ordered to end their discriminatory practices, and to admit a certain percentage of nonwhites to union membership by July

106 S.Ct. 3109 (1986).

1981. In 1982 and again in 1983, petitioners were found guilty of civil contempt for disobeying the District Court's earlier orders. They now challenge the District Court's contempt finding, and also the remedies the court ordered both for the Title VII violation and for contempt. Principally, the issue presented is whether the remedial provision of Title VII, see 42 U.S.C. § 2000e-5(g), empowers a district court to order race-conscious relief that may benefit individuals who are not identified victims of unlawful discrimination.

Petitioner Local 28 of the Sheet Metal Workers' International Association (Local 28) represents sheet metal workers employed by contractors in the New York City metropolitan area. Petitioner Local 28 Joint Apprenticeship Committee (JAC) is a management-labor committee which operates a 4-year apprenticeship training program designed to teach sheet metal skills. . . .

Petitioners, joined by the EEOC, argue that the membership goal, the [Employment, Training, Education and Recruitment Fund ("the Fund")] order, and other orders which require petitioners to grant membership preferences to nonwhites are expressly prohibited by § 706(g), 42 U.S.C. § 2000e-5(g), which defines the remedies available under Title VII. Petitioners and the EEOC maintain that § 706(g) authorizes a district court to award preferential relief only to the actual victims of unlawful discrimination. They maintain that the membership goal and the Fund violate this provision, since they require petitioners to admit to membership, and otherwise to extend benefits to, black and Hispanic individuals who are not the identified victims of unlawful discrimination. We reject this argument, and hold that § 706(g) does not prohibit a court from ordering, in appropriate circumstances, affirmative race-conscious relief as a remedy for past discrimination. Specifically, we hold that such relief may be appropriate where an employer or a labor union has engaged in persistent or egregious discrimination, or where necessary to dissipate the lingering effects of pervasive discrimination.

Section 706(g) states: "If the court finds that the respondent has intentionally engaged in or is intentionally engaging in an unlawful employment practice . . . , the court may enjoin the respondent from engaging in such unlawful employment practice, and order such affirmative action as may be appropriate, which may include, but is not limited to, reinstatement or hiring of employees, with or without back pay . . . , or any other equitable relief as the court deems appropriate. . . . No order of the court shall require the admission or reinstatement of an individual as a member of a union, or the hiring, reinstatement, or promotion of an individual as an employee, or the payment to him of any back pay, if such individual was refused admission, suspended, or expelled, or was refused employment or advancement or was suspended or discharged for any reason other than discrimination on account of race, color, religion, sex, or national origin in violation of . . . this title." 78 Stat. 261, as amended and as set forth in 42 U.S.C. § 2000e-5(g).

The language of § 706(g) plainly expresses Congress' intent to vest district courts with broad discretion to award "appropriate" equitable relief to remedy unlawful discrimination. . . . Nevertheless, petitioners and the EEOC argue that the last sentence of § 706(g) prohibits a court from ordering an employer or labor union to take affirmative steps to eliminate discrimination which might incidentally benefit individuals who are not the actual victims of discrimination. This reading twists the plain language of the statute.

The last sentence of § 706(g) prohibits a court from ordering a union to admit an individual who was "refused admission . . . for any reason other than discrimination." It does not, as petitioners and the EEOC suggest, say that a court may order relief only for the actual victims of past discrimination. The sentence on its face addresses only the situation where a plaintiff demonstrates that a union (or an employer) has engaged in unlawful discrimination, but the union can show that a particular individual would have been refused admission even in the absence of discrimination, for example, because that individual was unqualified. In these circumstances, § 706(g) confirms that a court could not order the union to admit the unqualified individual. . . . In this case, neither the membership goal nor the Fund order required petitioners to admit to membership individuals who had been refused admission for reasons unrelated to discrimination. Thus, we do not read § 706(g) to prohibit a court from ordering the kind of affirmative relief the District Court awarded in this case.

The availability of race-conscious affirmative relief under § 706(g) as a remedy for a violation of Title VII also furthers the broad purposes underlying the statute. Congress enacted Title VII based on its determination that racial minorities were subject to pervasive and systematic discrimination in employment. . . . Title VII was designed "to achieve equality of employment opportunities and remove barriers that have operated in the past to favor an identifiable group of white employees over other employees. . . . In order to foster equal employment opportunities, Congress gave the lower courts broad power under § 706(g) to fashion "the most complete relief possible" to remedy past discrimination. . . .

In most cases, the court need only order the employer or union to cease engaging in discriminatory practices, and award make-whole relief to the individuals victimized by those practices. In some instances, however, it may be necessary to require the employer

or union to take affirmative steps to end discrimination effectively to enforce Title VII. Where an employer or union has engaged in particularly longstanding or egregious discrimination, an injunction simply reiterating Title VII's prohibition against discrimination will often prove useless and will only result in endless enforcement litigation. In such cases, requiring recalcitrant employers or unions to hire and to admit qualified minorities roughly in proportion to the number of qualified minorities in the work force may be the only effective way to ensure the full enjoyment of the rights protected by Title VII. . . .

Affirmative race-conscious relief may be the only means available "to assure equality of employment opportunities and to eliminate those discriminatory practices and devices which have fostered racially stratified job environments to the disadvantage of minority citizens." . . .

Finally, a district court may find it necessary to order interim hiring or promotional goals pending the development of nondiscriminatory hiring or promotion procedures. In these cases, the use of numerical goals provides a compromise between two unacceptable alternatives: an outright ban on hiring or promotions, or continued use of a discriminatory selection procedure. . . .

Many opponents of Title VII argued that an employer could be found guilty of discrimination under the statute simply because of a racial imbalance in his work force, and would be compelled to implement racial "quotas" to avoid being charged with liability. *Weber,* 443 U.S., at 205, 99 S.Ct., at 2728. At the same time, supporters of the bill insisted that employers would not violate Title VII simply because of racial imbalance, and emphasized that neither the Commission nor the courts could compel employers to adopt quotas solely to facilitate racial balancing. *Id.,* at 207, n. 7, 99 S.Ct., at 2729, n. 7. The debate concerning what Title VII did and did not require culminated in the adoption of § 703(j), which stated expressly that the statute did not require an employer or labor union to adopt quotas or preferences simply because of a racial imbalance. However, while Congress strongly opposed the use of quotas or preferences merely to maintain racial balance, it gave no intimation as to whether such measures should be acceptable as *remedies* for Title VII violations. . . .

The purpose of affirmative action is not to make identified victims whole, but rather to dismantle prior patterns of employment discrimination and to prevent discrimination in the future. Such relief is provided to the class as a whole rather than to individual members; no individual is entitled to relief, and beneficiaries need not show that they were themselves victims of discrimination. In this case, neither the membership goal nor the Fund order required petitioners to indenture or train particular individuals, and neither required them to admit to membership individuals who were refused admission for reasons unrelated to discrimination. . . .

The court should exercise its discretion with an eye toward Congress' concern that race-conscious affirmative measures not be invoked simply to create a racially balanced work force. In the majority of Title VII cases, the court will not have to impose affirmative action as a remedy for past discrimination, but need only order the employer or union to cease engaging in discriminatory practices and award make-whole relief to the individuals victimized by those practices. However, in some cases, affirmative action may be necessary in order effectively to enforce Title VII. As we noted before, a court may have to resort to race-conscious affirmative action when confronted with an employer or labor union that has engaged in persistent or egregious discrimination. Or such relief may be necessary to dissipate the lingering effects of pervasive discrimination. Whether there might be

other circumstances that justify the use of court-ordered affirmative action is a matter that we need not decide here. We note only that a court should consider whether affirmative action is necessary to remedy past discrimination in a particular case before imposing such measures, and that the court should also take care to tailor its orders to fit the nature of the violation it seeks to correct. In this case, several factors lead us to conclude that the relief ordered by the District Court was proper.

First, both the District Court and the Court of Appeals agreed that the membership goal and Fund order were necessary to remedy petitioners' pervasive and egregious discrimination. The District Court set the original 29 percent membership goal upon observing that "[t]he record in both state and federal courts against [petitioners] is replete with instances of their bad faith attempts to prevent or delay affirmative action." 401 F.Supp., at 488. The court extended the goal after finding petitioners in contempt for refusing to end their discriminatory practices and failing to comply with various provisions of RAAPO. In affirming the revised membership goal, the Court of Appeals observed that "[t]his court has twice recognized Local 28's long continued and egregious racial discrimination . . . and Local 28 has presented no facts to indicate that our earlier observations are no longer apposite." 753 F.2d, at 1186. In light of petitioners' long history of "foot-dragging resistance" to court orders, simply enjoining them from once again engaging in discriminatory practices would clearly have been futile. Rather, the District Court properly determined that affirmative race-conscious measures were necessary to put an end to petitioners' discriminatory ways.

Both the membership goal and Fund order were similarly necessary to combat the lingering effects of past discrimination. In light of the District Court's determination that the union's reputation for discrimination operated to discourage nonwhites from even applying for membership, it is unlikely that an injunction would have been sufficient to extend to nonwhites equal opportunities for employment. Rather, because access to admission, membership, training, and employment in the industry had traditionally been obtained through informal contacts with union members, it was necessary for a substantial number of nonwhite workers to become members of the union in order for the effects of discrimination to cease. The Fund, in particular, was designed to insure that non-whites would receive the kind of assistance that white apprentices and applicants had traditionally received through informal sources. On the facts of this case, the District Court properly determined that affirmative, race-conscious measures were necessary to assure the equal employment opportunities guaranteed by Title VII.

Second, the District Court's flexible application of the membership goal gives strong indication that it is not being used simply to achieve and maintain racial balance, but rather as a benchmark against which the court could gauge petitioners' efforts to remedy past discrimination. The court has twice adjusted the deadline for achieving the goal, and has continually approved of changes in the size of the apprenticeship classes to account for the fact that economic conditions prevented petitioners from meeting their membership targets; there is every reason to believe that both the court and the administrator will continue to accommodate *legitimate* explanations for petitioners' failure to comply with the court's orders. Moreover, the District Court expressly disavowed any reliance on petitioners' failure to meet the goal as a basis for the contempt finding, but instead viewed this failure as symptomatic of petitioners' refusal to comply with various

subsidiary provisions of RAAPO. In sum, the District Court has implemented the membership goal as a means by which it can measure petitioners' compliance with its orders, rather than as a strict racial quota.

Third, both the membership goal and the Fund order are temporary measures. Under AAAPO "[p]referential selection of [union members] will end as soon as the percentage of [minority union members] approximates the percentage of [minorities] in the local labor force." *Weber*, 443 U.S., at 208–209, 99 S.Ct., at 2730; see *United States v. City of Alexandria*, 614 F.2d, at 1366. Similarly, the Fund is scheduled to terminate when petitioners achieve the membership goal, and the court determines that it is no longer needed to remedy past discrimination. The District Court's orders thus operate "as a temporary tool for remedying past discrimination without attempting to 'maintain' a previously achieved balance." *Weber*, 443 U.S., at 216, 99 S.Ct., at 2734 (Blackmun, J., concurring).

Finally, we think it significant that neither the membership goal nor the Fund order "unnecessarily trammel[s] the interests of white employees." *Id.* 443 U.S., at 208, 99 S.Ct., at 2730; *Teamsters*, 431 U.S., at 352–353, 97 S.Ct., at 1863–1864. Petitioners concede that the District Court's orders did not require any member of the union to be laid off, and did not discriminate against existing union members. See *Weber, supra*, 443 U.S., at 208, 99 S.Ct., at 2729–2730; see also 30 St. Louis U.L.J., at 264. While whites seeking admission into the union may be denied benefits extended to their nonwhite counterparts, the court's orders do not stand as an absolute bar to such individuals; indeed, a majority of new union members have been white. See *City of Alexandria, supra*, at 1366. Many provisions of the court's orders are race-neutral (for example, the requirement that the [Joint Apprenticeship Committee (JAC)] assign one apprentice for every four journeyman workers), and petitioners remain free to adopt the provisions of AAAPO and the Fund order for the benefit of white members and applicants.

Petitioners also allege that the membership goal and Fund order contravene the equal protection component of the Due Process Clause of the Fifth Amendment because they deny benefits to white individuals based on race. We have consistently recognized that government bodies constitutionally may adopt racial classifications as a remedy for past discrimination. . . . We conclude that the relief ordered in this case passes even the most rigorous test — it is narrowly tailored to further the Government's compelling interest in remedying past discrimination.

In this case, there is no problem . . . with a proper showing of prior discrimination that would justify the use of remedial racial classifications. Both the District Court and Court of Appeals have repeatedly found petitioners guilty of egregious violations of Title VII, and have determined that affirmative measures were necessary to remedy their racially discriminatory practices. More importantly, the District Court's orders were properly tailored to accomplish this objective. First, the District Court considered the efficacy of alternative remedies, and concluded that, in light of petitioners' long record of resistance to official efforts to end their discriminatory practices, stronger measures were necessary. . . . Again, petitioners concede that the District Court's orders did not disadvantage *existing* union members. While white applicants for union membership may be denied certain benefits available to their nonwhite counterparts, the court's orders do not stand as an absolute bar to the admission of such individuals; again, a majority of those entering the union after entry of the court's orders have been white. We therefore conclude that the District Court's orders do not violate the equal protection safeguards of the Constitution.

Finally, Local 28 challenges the District Court's appointment of an administrator with broad powers to supervise its compliance with the court's orders as an unjustifiable interference with its statutory right to self-governance. See 29 USC § 401(a). Preliminarily, we note that while AAAPO gives the administrator broad powers to oversee petitioners' membership practices, Local 28 retains complete control over its other affairs. Even with respect to membership, the administrator's job is to insure that petitioners comply with the court's orders and admit sufficient numbers of nonwhites; the administrator does not select the particular individuals that will be admitted, that task is left to union officials. In any event, in light of the difficulties inherent in monitoring compliance with the court's orders, and especially petitioners' established record of resistance to prior state and federal court orders designed to end their discriminatory membership practices, appointment of an administrator was well within the District Court's discretion. . . .

To summarize our holding today, six members of the Court agree that a district court may, in appropriate circumstances, order preferential relief benefiting individuals who are not the actual victims of discrimination as a remedy for violations of Title VII, . . . that the District Court did not use incorrect statistical evidence in establishing petitioners' nonwhite membership goal, that the contempt fines and Fund order were proper remedies for civil contempt, and that the District Court properly appointed an administrator to supervise petitioners' compliance with the court's orders. Five members of the Court agree that in this case, the District Court did not err in evaluating petitioners' utilization of the apprenticeship program, and that the membership goal and the Fund order are not violative of either Title VII or the Constitution. The judgment of the Court of Appeals is hereby *Affirmed.* . . .

City of Richmond v. J. A. Croson Company

Supreme Court of the United States

In this case, we confront once again the tension between the Fourteenth Amendment's guarantee of equal treatment to all citizens, and the use of race-based measures to ameliorate the effects of past discrimination on the opportunities enjoyed by members of minority groups in our society. . . .

I

On April 11, 1983, the Richmond City Council adopted the Minority Business Utilization Plan (the Plan). The Plan required prime contractors to whom the city awarded construction contracts to subcontract at least 30 percent of the dollar amount of the contract to one or more Minority Business Enterprises (MBEs). Ordinance No. 83-69-59, codified in Richmond, Va., City Code, § 12-156(a) (1985). The 30 percent set-aside did not apply to city contracts awarded to minority-owned prime contractors. *Ibid.*

The Plan defined an MBE as "[a] business at least fifty-one (51) percent of which is owned and controlled . . . by minority group members." § 12-23, p. 941. "Minority group members" were defined as "[c]itizens of the United States who are Blacks, Spanish-speaking, Orientals, Indians, Eskimos, or Aleuts." *Ibid.* There was no geographic limit to the Plan; an otherwise qualified MBE from anywhere in the United States could avail itself of the 30 percent set-aside. The Plan declared that it was "remedial" in nature, and enacted "for the purpose of promoting wider partici-

pation by minority business enterprises in the construction of public projects." § 12-158(a). The Plan expired on June 30, 1988, and was in effect for approximately five years. *Ibid.*

The Plan authorized the Director of the Department of General Services to promulgate rules which "shall allow waivers in those individual situations where a contractor can prove to the satisfaction of the director that the requirements herein cannot be achieved." § 12-157. To this end, the Director promulgated Contract Clauses, Minority Business Utilization Plan (Contract Clauses). Section D of these rules provided: "No partial or complete waiver of the foregoing [30 percent set-aside] requirement shall be granted by the city other than in exceptional circumstances. To justify a waiver, it must be shown that every feasible attempt has been made to comply, and it must be demonstrated that sufficient, relevant, qualified Minority Business Enterprises . . . are unavailable or unwilling to participate in the contract to enable meeting the 30 percent MBE goal." . . .

The Plan was adopted by the Richmond City Council after a public hearing. App. 9–50. Seven members of the public spoke to the merits of the ordinance: five were in opposition, two in favor. Proponents of the set-aside provision relied on a study which indicated that, while the general population of Richmond was 50 percent black, only .67 percent of the city's prime construction contracts had been awarded to minority businesses in the 5-year period from 1978 to 1983. . . .

109 S.Ct. 706 (1989).

There was no direct evidence of race discrimination on the part of the city in letting contracts or any evidence that the city's prime contractors had discriminated against minority-owned subcontractors. . . .

. . . On September 6, 1983, the city of Richmond issued an invitation to bid on a project for the provision and installation of certain plumbing fixtures at the city jail. On September 30, 1983, Eugene Bonn, the regional manager of J.A. Croson Company (Croson), a mechanical plumbing and heating contractor, received the bid forms. The project involved the installations of stainless steel urinals and water closets in the city jail. Products of either of two manufacturers were specified, Acorn Engineering Company (Acorn) or Bradley Manufacturing Company (Bradley). Bonn determined that to meet the 30 percent set-aside requirement, a minority contractor would have to supply the fixtures. The provision of the fixtures amounted to 75 percent of the total contract price. . . .

Bonn subsequently began a search for potential MBE suppliers. The only potential MBE fixture supplier was Melvin Brown, president of Continental Metal Hose, hereafter referred to as "Continental." However, because of Continental's inability to obtain credit approval, Continental was unable to submit a bid by the due date of October 13, 1983. Shortly thereafter and as a direct result, Croson submitted a request for a waiver of the 30 percent set-aside. Croson's waiver request indicated that Continental was "unqualified" and that the other MBEs contacted had been unresponsive or unable to quote. Upon learning of Croson's waiver request, Brown contacted an agent of Acorn, the other fixture manufacturer specified by the city. Based upon his discussions with Acorn, Brown subsequently submitted a bid on the fixtures to Croson. Continental's bid was $6,183.29 higher than the price Croson had included for the fixtures in its bid to the city.

This constituted a 7 percent increase over the market price for the fixtures. With added bonding and insurance, using Continental would have raised the cost of the project by $7,663.16. On the same day that Brown contacted Acorn, he also called city procurement officials and told them that Continental, an MBE, could supply the fixtures specified in the city jail contract. On November 2, 1983, the city denied Croson's waiver request, indicating that Croson had 10 days to submit an MBE Utilization Commitment Form, and warned that failure to do so could result in its bid being considered unresponsive.

Croson wrote the city on November 8, 1983. In the letter, Bonn indicated that Continental was not an authorized supplier for either Acorn or Bradley fixtures. He also noted that Acorn's quotation to Brown was subject to credit approval and in any case was substantially higher than any other quotation Croson had received. Finally, Bonn noted that Continental's bid had been submitted some 21 days after the prime bids were due. In a second letter, Croson laid out the additional costs that using Continental to supply the fixtures would entail, and asked that it be allowed to raise the overall contract price accordingly. The city denied both Croson's request for a waiver and its suggestion that the contract price be raised. The city informed Croson that it had decided to rebid the project. On December 9, 1983, counsel for Croson wrote the city asking for a review of the waiver denial. The city's attorney responded that the city had elected to rebid the project, and that there is no appeal of such a decision. Shortly thereafter Croson brought this action under 42 U.S.C. § 1983 in the Federal District Court for the Eastern District of Virginia, arguing that the Richmond ordinance was unconstitutional on its face and as applied in this case.

The District Court upheld the Plan in all respects . . . [and held that] the 30 percent figure was "reasonable in light of the undisputed fact that minorities constitute 50 percent of the population of Richmond." *Ibid.*

Croson sought certiorari from this Court. We granted the writ, vacated the opinion of the Court of Appeals, and remanded the case for further consideration in light of our intervening decision in *Wygant v. Jackson Board of Education,* 476 U.S. 267, 106 S.Ct. 1842, 90 L.Ed.2d 260 (1986). . . .

On remand, a divided panel of the Court of Appeals struck down the Richmond set-aside program as violating both prongs of strict scrutiny under the Equal Protection Clause of the Fourteenth Amendment. *J.A. Croson Co. v. Richmond,* 822 F.2d 1355 (CA4 1987) (*Croson II*). . . .

In this case, the debate at the city council meeting "revealed no record of prior discrimination by the city in awarding public contracts. . . ." *Croson II, supra,* at 1358. Moreover, the statistics comparing the minority population of Richmond to the percentage of *prime* contracts awarded to minority firms had little or no probative value in establishing prior discrimination in the relevant market, and actually suggested "more of a political than a remedial basis for the racial preference." 822 F.2d, at 1359. The court concluded that, "[i]f this plan is supported by a compelling governmental interest, so is every other plan that has been enacted in the past or that will be enacted in the future." *Id.,* at 1360.

The Court of Appeals went on to hold that even if the city had demonstrated a compelling interest in the use of a race-based quota, the 30 percent set-aside was not narrowly tailored to accomplish a remedial purpose. The court found that the 30 percent figure was "chosen arbitrarily" and was not tied to the number of minority subcontractors in Richmond or to any other relevant number. *Ibid.* The dissenting judge argued that the majority had "misconstrue[d] and

misapplie[d]" our decision in Wygant. 822 F.2d, at 1362. We noted probable jurisdiction of the city's appeal, . . . and we now affirm the judgment.

II

. . . Congress, unlike any State or political subdivision, has a specific constitutional mandate to enforce the dictates of the Fourteenth Amendment. The power to "enforce" may at times also include the power to define situations which *Congress* determines threaten principles of equality and to adopt prophylactic rules to deal with those situations. . . .

That Congress may identify and redress the effects of society-wide discrimination does not mean that, *a fortiori,* the States and their political subdivisions are free to decide that such remedies are appropriate. Section 1 of the Fourteenth Amendment is an explicit *constraint* on state power, and the States must undertake any remedial efforts in accordance with that provision. To hold otherwise would be to cede control over the content of the Equal Protection Clause to the 50 state legislatures and their myriad political subdivisions. The mere recitation of a benign or compensatory purpose for the use of a racial classification would essentially entitle the States to exercise the full power of Congress under § 5 of the Fourteenth Amendment and insulate any racial classification from judicial scrutiny under § 1. We believe that such a result would be contrary to the intentions of the Framers of the Fourteenth Amendment, who desired to place clear limits on the States' use of race as a criterion for legislative action, and to have the federal courts enforce those limitations. . . .

It would seem equally clear, however, that a state or local subdivision (if delegated the authority from the State) has the authority to eradicate the effects of private discrimination within its own legislative jurisdiction. This authority must, of course, be exercised within the constraints of § 1 of the Fourteenth Amendment. . . . As a matter of state law, the city of Richmond has legislative authority over its procurement policies, and can use its spending powers to remedy private discrimination, if it identifies that discrimination with the particularity required by the Fourteenth Amendment. . . .

Thus, if the city could show that it had essentially become a "passive participant" in a system of racial exclusion practiced by elements of the local construction industry, we think it clear that the city could take affirmative steps to dismantle such a system. It is beyond dispute that any public entity, state or federal, has a compelling interest in assuring that public dollars, drawn from the tax contributions of all citizens, do not serve to finance the evil of private prejudice. . . .

III.A

The Equal Protection Clause of the Fourteenth Amendment provides that "[N]o State shall . . . deny to *any person* within its jurisdiction the equal protection of the laws" (emphasis added). As this Court has noted in the past, the "rights created by the first section of the Fourteenth Amendment are, by its terms, guaranteed to the individual. The rights established are personal rights." *Shelley v. Kraemer,* 334 U.S. 1, 22, 68 S.Ct. 836, 846, 92 L.Ed. 1161 (1948). The Richmond Plan denies certain citizens the opportunity to compete for a fixed percentage of public contracts based solely upon their race. To whatever racial group these citizens belong, their "personal rights" to be treated with equal dignity and respect are implicated by a rigid rule erecting race as the sole criterion in an aspect of public decision making. . . .

Classifications based on race carry a danger of stigmatic harm. Unless they are strictly reserved for remedial settings, they may in fact promote notions of racial inferiority and lead to a politics of racial hostility. . . .

III.B

The District Court found the city council's "findings sufficient to ensure that, in adopting the Plan, it was remedying the present effects of past discrimination in the *construction industry.*" Supp.App. 163 (emphasis added). Like the "role model" theory employed in *Wygant,* a generalized assertion that there has been past discrimination in an entire industry provides no guidance for a legislative body to determine the precise scope of the injury it seeks to remedy. It "has no logical stopping point." *Wygant, supra,* at 275, 106 S.Ct., at 1847 (plurality opinion). "Relief" for such an ill-defined wrong could extend until the percentage of public contracts awarded to MBEs in Richmond mirrored the percentage of minorities in the population as a whole.

Appellant argues that it is attempting to remedy various forms of past discrimination that are alleged to be responsible for the small number of minority businesses in the local contracting industry. Among these the city cites the exclusion of blacks from skilled construction trade unions and training programs. This past discrimination has prevented them "from following the traditional path from laborer to entrepreneur." Brief for Appellant 23–24. The city also lists a host of nonracial factors which would seem to face a member of any racial group attempting to establish a new business enterprise, such as deficiencies in working capital, inability to meet bonding requirements, unfamiliarity with bidding procedures, and disability caused by an inadequate track record. *Id.,* at 25–26, and n. 41.

While there is no doubt that the sorry history of both private and public discrimination in this country has contributed to a lack of opportunities for black entrepreneurs, this observation, standing alone, cannot justify a rigid racial quota in the awarding of public contracts in Richmond, Virginia. Like the claim that discrimination in primary and secondary schooling justifies a rigid racial preference in medical school admissions, an amorphous claim that there has been past discrimination in a particular industry cannot justify the use of an unyielding racial quota.

It is sheer speculation how many minority firms there would be in Richmond absent past societal discrimination, just as it was sheer speculation how many minority medical students would have been admitted to the medical school at Davis absent past discrimination in educational opportunities. Defining these sorts of injuries as "identified discrimination" would give local governments license to create a patchwork of racial preferences based on statistical generalizations about any particular field of endeavor.

These defects are readily apparent in this case. The 30 percent quota cannot in any realistic sense be tied to any injury suffered by anyone. . . .

There is nothing approaching a prima facie case of a constitutional or statutory violation by *anyone* in the Richmond construction industry. . . .

The District Court accorded great weight to the fact that the city council designated the Plan as "remedial." But the mere recitation of a "benign" or legitimate purpose for a racial classification, is entitled to little or no weight. . . . Racial classifications are suspect, and that means that simple legislative assurances of good intention cannot suffice. . . .

In this case, the city does not even know how many MBEs in the relevant market are qualified to undertake prime or subcontracting work in public construction projects. . . . Nor does the city know what percentage of total city construction dollars minority firms now receive as subcontractors on prime contracts let by the city.

To a large extent, the set-aside of subcontracting dollars seems to rest on the unsupported assumption that white prime contractors simply will not hire minority firms. . . . Without any information on minority participation in subcontracting, it is quite simply impossible to evaluate overall minority representation in the city's construction expenditures.

The city and the District Court also relied on evidence that MBE membership in local contractors' associations was extremely low. Again, standing alone this evidence is not probative of any discrimination in the local construction industry. There are numerous explanations for this dearth of minority participation, including past societal discrimination in education and economic opportunities as well as both black and white career and entrepreneurial choices. Blacks may be disproportionately attracted to industries other than construction. . . . The mere fact that black membership in these trade organizations is low, standing alone, cannot establish a prima facie case of discrimination. . . .

While the States and their subdivisions may take remedial action when they possess evidence that their own spending practices are exacerbating a pattern of prior discrimination, they must identify that discrimination, public or private, with some specificity before they may use race-conscious relief. . . .

In sum, none of the evidence presented by the city points to any identified discrimination in the Richmond construction industry. We, therefore, hold that the city has failed to demonstrate a compelling interest in apportioning public contracting opportunities on the basis of race. To accept Richmond's claim that past societal discrimination alone can serve as the basis for rigid racial preferences would be to open the door to competing claims for "remedial relief" for every disadvantaged group. The dream of a Nation of equal citizens in a society where race is irrelevant to personal opportunity and achievement would be lost in a mosaic of shifting preferences based on inherently unmeasurable claims of past wrongs. . . .

convenience. But the interest in avoiding the bureaucratic effort necessary to tailor remedial relief to those who truly have suffered the effects of prior discrimination cannot justify a rigid line drawn on the basis of a suspect classification. . . . Under Richmond's scheme, a successful black, Hispanic, or Oriental entrepreneur from anywhere in the country enjoys an absolute preference over other citizens based solely on their race. We think it obvious that such a program is not narrowly tailored to remedy the effects of prior discrimination.

IV

Since the city must already consider bids and waivers on a case-by-case basis, it is difficult to see the need for a rigid numerical quota. . . .

Given the existence of an individualized procedure, the city's only interest in maintaining a quota system rather than investigating the need for remedial action in particular cases would seem to be simple administrative

V

. . . Because the city of Richmond has failed to identify the need for remedial action in the awarding of its public construction contracts, its treatment of its citizens on a racial basis violates the dictates of the Equal Protection Clause. Accordingly, the judgment of the Court of Appeals for the Fourth Circuit is Affirmed.

American Federation of State, County, and Municipal Employees (AFSCME) v. State of Washington

United States Court of Appeals for the Ninth Circuit

Opinion: KENNEDY, Circuit Judge: In this class action affecting approximately 15,500 of its employees, the State of Washington was sued in the United States District Court for the Western District of Washington. The class comprises state employees who have worked or do work in job categories that are or have

been at least 70 percent female. The action was commenced for the class members by two unions, the American Federation of State, County, and Municipal Employees (AFSCME) and the Washington Federation of State Employees (WFSE). In all of the proceedings to date and in the opinion which follows, the plaintiffs are referred to as AF-SCME. The district court found the State discriminated on the basis of sex in violation of Title VII of the Civil Rights Act of 1964, 42 U.S.C. § § 2000 e-2(a) (1982), by compensating employees in jobs where females predominate at lower rates than employees in jobs where males predominate, if these jobs, though dissimilar, were identified by certain studies to be of comparable worth. The State appeals. We conclude a violation of Title VII was not established here, and we reverse.

The State of Washington has required salaries of state employees to reflect prevailing market rates. . . . Throughout the period in question, comprehensive biennial salary surveys were conducted to assess prevailing market rates. The surveys involved approximately 2,700 employers in the public and private sectors. The results were reported to state personnel boards, which conducted hearings before employee representatives and agencies and made salary recommendations to the State Budget Director. The Director submitted a proposed budget to the Governor, who in turn presented it to the state legislature. Salaries were fixed by enactment of the budget.

In 1974 the State commissioned a study by management consultant Normal Willis to determine whether a wage disparity existed between employees in jobs held predominantly by women and jobs held predominantly by men. The study examined sixty-two classifications in which at least 70 percent of the employees were women, and fifty-nine job classifications in which at least 70 percent of the employees were men. It found a wage disparity of about 20 percent, to the disadvantage of employees in jobs held mostly by women, for jobs considered of comparable worth. Comparable worth was calculated by evaluating jobs under four criteria: knowledge and skills, mental demands, accountability, and working conditions. A maximum number of points was allotted to each category: 280 for

knowledge and skills, 140 for mental demands, 160 for accountability, and 20 for working conditions; and every job was assigned a numerical value under each of the four criteria. The State of Washington conducted similar studies in 1976 and 1980, and in 1983 the State enacted legislation providing for a compensation scheme based on comparable worth. The scheme is to take effect over a ten-year period. . . .

AFSCME filed charges with the Equal Employment Opportunity Commission (EEOC) in 1981, alleging the State's compensation system violated Title VII's prohibition against sex discrimination in employment. The EEOC having taken no action, the United States Department of Justice issued notices of right to sue, expressing no opinion on the merits of the claims. In 1982 AFSCME brought this action in the district court, seeking immediate implementation of a system of compensation based on comparable worth. The district court ruled in favor of AFSCME and ordered injunctive relief and back pay. Its findings of fact, conclusions of law, and opinion are reported. *American Federation of State, County, and Municipal Employees v. State of Washington,* 578 F. Supp. 846 (W.D. Wash. 1983) (*AFSCME I*).

AFSCME alleges sex-based wage discrimination throughout the state system, but its explanation and proof of the violation is, in essence, Washington's failure as early as 1979 to adopt and implement at once a comparable worth compensation program. The trial court adopted this theory as well. *AFSCME I,* 578 F. Supp. at 865-71. The comparable worth theory, as developed in the case before us, postulates that sex-based wage discrimination exists if employees in job classifications occupied primarily by women are paid less than employees in job classifications filled primarily by men, if the jobs are of equal value to the employer, though otherwise dissimilar. . . . We must determine whether comparable worth, as presented in this case, affords AFSCME a basis for recovery under Title VII.

Section 703(a) of Title VII states in pertinent part:

> It shall be an unlawful employment practice for an employer —
>
> (1) . . . to discriminate against any individual with respect to his compensation, terms, conditions or privileges of employment, because of such individual's . . . sex . . . or
>
> (2) to limit, segregate or classify his employees or applicants for employment in any way *which would deprive or tend to deprive any individual of employment opportunities* . . . because of such individual's . . . sex.

The Bennett Amendment to Title VII, designed to relate Title VII to the Equal Pay Act, . . . and eliminate any potential inconsistencies between the two statutes, provides:

> It shall not be an unlawful employment practice under this subchapter for any employer to differentiate upon the basis of sex in determining the amount of the wages or compensation paid or to be paid to employees of such employer if such differentiation is authorized by the provisions of section 206(d) of title 29.

It is evident from the legislative history of the Equal Pay Act that Congress, after explicit consideration, rejected proposals that would have prohibited lower wages for comparable work, as contrasted with equal work. . . . The legislative history of the Civil Rights Act of 1964 and the Bennett Amendment, however, is inconclusive regarding the intended coverage of Title VII's prohibition against sex discrimination, and contains no explicit discussion of compensation for either comparable or equal work. . . .

In the instant case, the district court found a violation of Title VII, premised upon both the disparate impact and the disparate treatment theories of discrimination. *AFSCME I,* 578 F. Supp. at 864. Under the disparate impact theory, discrimination may be established by showing that a facially neutral employment practice, not justified by business necessity, has a disproportionately adverse impact upon members of a group protected under Title VII. . . .

We consider next the allegations of disparate treatment. Under the disparate treatment theory, AFSCME was required to prove a prima facie case of sex discrimination by a preponderance of the evidence. . . . In an appropriate case, the necessary discriminatory animus may be inferred from circumstantial evidence. *Furnco,* 438 U.S. at 579-80 (discriminatory intent may be inferred from the actions of an employer where "experience has proved that in the absence of any other explanation it is more likely than not that those actions were bottomed on impermissible considerations"); *Teamsters,* 431 U.S. at 335 n. 15. Our review of the record, however, indicates failure by AFSCME to establish the requisite element of intent by either circumstantial or direct evidence.

AFSCME contends discriminatory motive may be inferred from the Willis study, which finds the State's practice of setting salaries in reliance on market rates creates a sex-based wage disparity for jobs deemed of comparable worth. AFSCME argues from the study that the market reflects a historical pattern of lower wages to employees in positions staffed predominantly by women; and it contends the State of Washington perpetuates that disparity, in violation of Title VII, by using market rates in the compensation system. The inference of discriminatory motive which AFSCME seeks to draw from the State's participation in the market system fails, as the State did not create the market disparity and has not been shown to have been motivated by impermissible sex-based considerations in setting salaries. . . .

While the Washington legislature may have the discretion to enact a comparable worth plan if it chooses to do so, Title VII does not obligate it to eliminate an economic inequality which it did not create. . . . Title VII was enacted to ensure equal opportunity in employment to covered individuals, and the State of Washington is not charged here with barring access to particular job classifications on the basis of sex.

We have recognized that in certain cases an inference of intent may be drawn from statistical evidence . . . . We have admonished, however, that statistics must be relied on with caution. Though the comparability of wage rates in dissimilar jobs may be relevant to a determination of discriminatory animus . . . job evaluation studies and comparable worth statistics alone are insufficient to establish the requisite inference of discriminatory motive critical to the disparate treatment theory . . . . The weight to be accorded such statistics is determined by the existence of independent corroborative evidence of discrimination. We conclude the independent evidence of discrimination presented by AFSCME is insufficient to support an inference of the requisite discriminatory motive under the disparate treatment theory.

AFSCME offered proof of isolated incidents of sex segregation as evidence of a history of sex-based wage discrimination. The evidence is discussed in *AFSCME I*, 578 F. Supp. at 860, and consists of help wanted advertisements restricting various jobs to members of a particular sex. These advertisements were often placed in separate "help wanted — male" and "help wanted — female" columns in state newspapers between 1960 and 1973, though most were discontinued when Title VII became applicable to the states in 1972. At trial, AFSCME, called expert witnesses to testify that a causal relationship exists between sex segregation practices and sex-based wage discrimination, and that the effects of sex segregation practices may persist even after the practices are discontinued. However, none of the individually named plaintiffs in the action ever testified regarding specific incidents of discrimination. The isolated incidents alleged by AFSCME are insufficient to corroborate the results of the Willis study and do not justify an inference of discriminatory motive by the State in the setting of salaries for its system as a whole. Given the scope of the alleged intentional act, given the attempt to show the core principle of the State's market-based compensation system was adopted or maintained with a discriminatory purpose, more is required to support the finding of liability than these isolated acts, which had only an indirect relation to the compensation principle itself.

We also reject AFSCME's contention that, having commissioned the Willis study, the State of Washington was committed to implement a new system of compensation based on comparable worth as defined by the study. Whether comparable worth is a feasible approach to employee compensation is a matter of debate. . . . Assuming, however, that like other job evaluation studies it may be useful as a diagnostic tool, we reject a rule that would penalize rather than commend employers for their effort and innovation in undertaking such a study. . . . The results of comparable worth studies will vary depending on the number and types of factors measured and the maximum number of points allotted to each factor. A study which indicates a particular wage structure might be more equitable should not categorically bind the employer who commissioned it. The employer should also be able to take into account market conditions, bargaining demands, and the possibility that another study will yield different results. . . .

We hold there was a failure to establish a violation of Title VII under the disparate treatment theory of discrimination, and reverse the district court on this aspect of the case as well. The State of Washington's initial reliance on a free market system in which employees in male-dominated jobs are compensated at a higher rate than employees in dissimilar female-dominated jobs is not in and of itself a violation of Title VII, notwithstanding that the Willis study deemed the positions of comparable worth. Absent a showing of discriminatory motive, which has not been made here, the law does not permit the federal courts to interfere in the market-based system for the compensation of Washington's employees.

Certain procedural errors were committed by the district court, including misallocating the burdens of proof and precluding the State from presenting much of its evidence.

Though these errors complicate our review of the record unnecessarily, they need not be addressed, given our disposition on the merits of the case.

REVERSED.

Meritor Savings Bank, FSB v. Vinson, et al.

Supreme Court of the United States

This case presents important questions concerning claims of workplace "sexual harassment" brought under Title VII of the Civil Rights Act of 1964, 78 Stat. 253, as amended, 42 U.S.C. § 2000e *et seq.*

I

In 1974, respondent Mechelle Vinson . . . started as a teller-trainee, and thereafter was promoted to teller, head teller, and assistant branch manager. She worked at the same branch for four years, and it is undisputed that her advancement there was based on merit alone. In September 1978, respondent notified her supervisor, Sidney Taylor, that she was taking sick leave for an indefinite period. On November 1, 1978, the bank discharged her for excessive use of that leave.

Respondent brought this action against Taylor and the bank, claiming that during her four years at the bank she had "constantly been subjected to sexual harassment" by Taylor in violation of Title VII. She sought injunctive relief, compensatory and punitive damages against Taylor and the bank, and attorney's fees.

At the 11-day bench trial, the parties presented conflicting testimony about Taylor's behavior during respondent's employment.* Respondent testified that during her probationary period as a teller-trainee, Taylor treated her in a fatherly way and made no sexual advances. Shortly thereafter, however, he invited her out to dinner and, during the course of the meal, suggested that they go to a motel to have sexual relations. At first she refused, but out of what she described as fear of losing her job she eventually agreed. According to respondent, Taylor thereafter made repeated demands upon her for sexual favors, usually at the branch, both during and after business hours; she estimated that over the next several years she had intercourse with him some 40 or 50 times. In addition, respondent testified that Taylor fondled her in front of other employees, followed her into the women's restroom when she went there alone, exposed himself to her, and even

---

*Like the Court of Appeals, this Court was not provided a complete transcript of the trial. We therefore rely largely on the District Court's opinion for the summary of the relevant testimony.

forcibly raped her on several occasions. These activities ceased after 1977, respondent stated, when she started going with a steady boyfriend.

Respondent also testified that Taylor touched and fondled other women employees of the bank, and she attempted to call witnesses to support this charge. But while some supporting testimony apparently was admitted without objection, the District Court did not allow her "to present wholesale evidence of a pattern and practice relating to sexual advances to other female employees in her case in chief, but advised her that she might well be able to present such evidence in rebuttal to the defendants' cases." *Vinson v. Taylor*, 22 EPD ¶30, 708, p. 14,693, n. 1, 23 FEP Cases 37, 38–39, n. 1 (DC 1980). Respondent did not offer such evidence in rebuttal. Finally, respondent testified that because she was afraid of Taylor she never reported his harassment to any of his supervisors and never attempted to use the bank's complaint procedure.

Taylor denied respondent's allegations of sexual activity, testifying that he never fondled her, never made suggestive remarks to her, never engaged in sexual intercourse with her, and never asked her to do so. He contended instead that respondent made her accusations in response to a business-related dispute. The bank also denied respondent's allegations and asserted that any sexual harassment by Taylor was unknown to the bank and engaged in without its consent or approval.

The District Court denied relief and . . . ultimately found that respondent "was not the victim of sexual harassment and was not the victim of sexual discrimination" while employed at the bank.

Although it concluded that respondent had not proved a violation of Title VII, the District Court nevertheless went on to address the bank's liability. After noting the bank's express policy against discrimination,

and finding that neither respondent nor any other employee had ever lodged a complaint about sexual harassment by Taylor, the court ultimately concluded that "the bank was without notice and cannot be held liable for the alleged actions of Taylor."

The Court of Appeals for the District of Columbia Circuit reversed. . . . The court stated that a violation of Title VII may be predicated on either of two types of sexual harassment: harassment that involves the conditioning of concrete employment benefits on sexual favors, and harassment that, while not affecting economic benefits, creates a hostile or offensive working environment. . . . Believing that "Vinson's grievance was clearly of the [hostile environment] type," and that the District Court had not considered whether a violation of this type had occurred, the court concluded that a remand was necessary.

The court further concluded that the District Court's findings that any sexual relationship between respondent and Taylor "was a voluntary one" did not obviate the need for a remand. . . .

As to the bank's liability, the Court of Appeals held that an employer is absolutely liable for sexual harassment practiced by supervisory personnel, whether or not the employer knew or should have known about the misconduct. The court relied chiefly on Title VII's definition of "employer" to include "any agent of such a person," 42 U.S.C. §2000e(b), as well as on the EEOC Guidelines. The court held that a supervisor is an "agent" of his employer for Title VII purposes, even if he lacks authority to hire, fire, or promote, since "the mere existence — or even the appearance — of a significant degree of influence in vital job decisions gives any supervisor the opportunity to impose on employees." . . .

In accordance with the foregoing, the Court of Appeals reversed the judgment of the District Court and remanded the case for further proceedings. . . .

II

Title VII of the Civil Rights Act of 1964 makes it "an unlawful employment practice for an employer . . . to discriminate against any individual with respect to his compensation, terms, conditions, or privileges for employment, because of such individual's race, color, religion, sex, or national origin." . . .

Respondent argues, and the Court of Appeals held, that unwelcome sexual advances that create an offensive or hostile working environment violate Title VII. Without question, when a supervisor sexually harasses a subordinate because of the subordinate's sex, that supervisor "discriminate[s]" on the basis of sex. . . .

First, the language of Title VII is not limited to "economic" or "tangible" discrimination. The phrase "terms, conditions, or privileges of employment" evinces a congressional intent "'to strike at the entire spectrum of disparate treatment of men and women'" in employment. . . .

Second, in 1980 the EEOC issued Guidelines specifying that "sexual harassment," as there defined, is a form of sex discrimination prohibited by Title VII. . . .

In defining "sexual harassment," the Guidelines first describe the kinds of workplace conduct that may be actionable under Title VII. These include "[u]nwelcome sexual advances, requests for sexual favors, and other verbal or physical conduct of a sexual nature." 29 CFR § 1604.11(a) (1985). Relevant to the charges at issue in this case, the Guidelines provide that such sexual misconduct constitutes prohibited "sexual harassment," whether or not it is directly linked to the grant or denial of an economic *quid pro quo,* where "such conduct has the purpose or

effect of unreasonably interfering with an individual's work performance or creating an intimidating, hostile, or offensive working environment." . . .

In concluding that so-called "hostile environment" (*i.e.,* non *quid pro quo*) harassment violates Title VII, the EEOC drew upon a substantial body of judicial decisions and EEOC precedent holding that Title VII affords employees the right to work in an environment free from discriminatory intimidation, ridicule, and insult. . . .

Since the Guidelines were issued, courts have uniformly held, and we agree, that a plaintiff may establish a violation of Title VII by proving that discrimination based on sex has created a hostile or abusive work environment. . . .

For sexual harassment to be actionable, it must be sufficiently severe or pervasive "to alter the conditions of [the victim's] employment and create an abusive working environment." *Ibid.* Respondent's allegations in this case — which include not only pervasive harassment but also criminal conduct of the most serious nature — are plainly sufficient to state a claim for "hostile environment" sexual harassment. . . .

The fact that sex-related conduct was "voluntary," in the sense that the complainant was not forced to participate against her will, is not a defense to a sexual harassment suit brought under Title VII. The gravamen of any sexual harassment claim is that the alleged sexual advances were "unwelcome." 29 CFR § 1604.11(a) (1985). While the question whether particular conduct was indeed unwelcome presents difficult problems of proof and turns largely on credibility determinations committed to the trier of fact, the District Court in this case erroneously focused on the "voluntariness" of respondent's participation in the claimed sexual episodes. The correct inquiry is whether respondent by her conduct indicated that the alleged sexual advances were unwelcome, not whether her actual participation in sexual intercourse was voluntary. . . .

III

Although the District Court concluded that respondent had not proved a violation of Title VII, it nevertheless went on to consider the question of the bank's liability. Finding that "the bank was without notice" of Taylor's alleged conduct, and that notice to Taylor was not the equivalent of notice to the bank, the court concluded that the bank therefore could not be held liable for Taylor's alleged actions. The Court of Appeals took the opposite view, holding that an employer is strictly liable for a hostile environment created by a supervisor's sexual advances, even though the employer neither knew nor reasonably could have known of the alleged misconduct. The court held that a supervisor, whether or not he possesses the authority to hire, fire, or promote, is necessarily an "agent" of his employer for all Title VII purposes, since "even the appearance" of such authority may enable him to impose himself on his subordinates. . . .

The EEOC, in its brief as *amicus curiae,* contends that courts formulating employer liability rules should draw from traditional agency principles. Examination of those principles has led the EEOC to the view that where a supervisor exercises the authority actually delegated to him by his employer, by making or threatening to make decisions affecting the employment status of his subordinates, such actions are properly imputed to the employer whose delegation of authority empowered the supervisor to undertake them. . . . Thus, the courts have consistently held employers liable for the discriminatory discharges of employees by supervisory personnel, whether or not the employer knew, should have known, or approved of the supervisor's actions. . . .

The EEOC suggests that when a sexual harassment claim rests exclusively on a "hostile environment" theory, however, the usual basis for a finding of agency will often disappear. In that case, the EEOC believes, agency principles lead to

a rule that asks whether a victim of sexual harassment had reasonably available an avenue of complaint regarding such harassment, and, if available and utilized, whether that procedure was reasonably responsive to the employee's complaint. If the employer has an expressed policy against sexual harassment and has implemented a procedure specifically designed to resolve sexual harassment claims, and if the victim does not take advantage of that procedure, the employer should be shielded from liability absent actual knowledge of the sexually hostile environment (obtained, *e.g.,* by the filing of a charge with the EEOC or a comparable state agency). In all other cases, the employer will be liable if it has actual knowledge of the harassment or if, considering all the facts of the case, the victim in question had no reasonably available avenue for making his or her complaint known to appropriate management officials." Brief for United States and EEOC as *Amici Curiae* 26.

As respondent points out, this suggested rule is in some tension with the EEOC Guidelines, which hold an employer liable for the acts of its agents without regard to notice. 29 CFR § 1604.11(c) (1985). The Guidelines do require, however, an "examin[ation of] the circumstances of the particular employment relationship and the job [f]unctions performed by the individual in determining whether an individual acts in either a supervisory or agency capacity."

We hold that the Court of Appeals erred in concluding that employers are always automatically liable for sexual harassment by their supervisors. For the same reason, absence of notice to an employer does not necessarily insulate that employer from liability. *Ibid.*

Finally, we reject petitioner's view that the mere existence of a grievance procedure and a policy against discrimination, coupled with respondent's failure to invoke that procedure, must insulate petitioner from liability. While those facts are plainly relevant, the situation before us demonstrates why they are not necessarily dispositive. Petitioner's general nondiscrimination policy did not address sexual harassment in particular, and thus did not alert employees to their employer's interest in correcting that form of discrimination. App. 25. Moreover, the bank's grievance procedure apparently required an employee to complain first to her supervisor, in this case Taylor. Since Taylor was the alleged perpetrator, it is not altogether surprising that respondent failed to invoke the procedure and report her grievance to him. Petitioner's contention that respondent's failure should insulate it from liability might be substantially stronger if its procedures were better calculated to encourage victims of harassment to come forward.

IV

In sum, we hold that a claim of "hostile environment" sex discrimination is actionable under Title VII, that the District Court's findings were insufficient to dispose of respondent's hostile environment claim, and that the District Court did not err in admitting testimony about respondent's sexually provocative speech and dress. As to employer liability, we conclude that the Court of Appeals was wrong to entirely disregard agency principles and impose absolute liability on employers for the acts of their supervisors, regardless of the circumstances of a particular case.

Accordingly, the judgment of the Court of Appeals reversing the judgment of the District Court is affirmed, and the case is remanded for further proceedings consistent with this opinion.

CASES

CASE 1.   *"Harassment" at Brademore Electric*

Maura Donovan is a recent graduate of UCLA who now works as a low-level administrative assistant for Keith Sturdivant at the Brademore Electric Corporation, a large Los Angeles electrical contractor. Keith interviewed and hired Maura to work directly under him.

Maura had been employed at Brademore only three weeks when Keith approached her to go out on the weekend. Maura was taken somewhat by surprise and declined, thinking it best not to mix business and pleasure. But two days later Keith persisted, saying that

Maura owed him something in return for his "getting" her the job. Maura was offended by this comment, knowing that she was well qualified for the position, but Keith seemed lonely, almost desperate, and she agreed to go with him to the Annual Renaissance Fair on Saturday afternoon. As it turned out, she did not have an enjoyable time. She liked the fair, but found Keith a bit crude and at times almost uncivil in the way he treated employees at the Fair. She hoped he would not ask her out again.

This case was prepared by Tom L. Beauchamp.

But Monday morning he came back with the idea that they go on an overnight sailboat trip with some of his friends the next weekend. Maura politely declined. But Keith persisted, insisting that she owed her job to him. Maura found herself dreading the times she saw Keith coming down the corridor. What had been a very nice work environment for her had turned into a place of frequent dread. She spent a lot of time working to avoid Keith.

For four straight weeks, Keith came up with a different idea for how they might spend the weekend — always involving an overnight trip. Maura always declined. After the second week, she lied and told him that she was dating a number of other men. She said she was quite interested in two of these men and that she did not see any future with Keith. Keith's reaction was to become even more insistent that they had a future together and to continue to ask her out.

Keith had become quite infatuated with Maura. He watched her every movement, whenever he had the opportunity. Sometimes he openly stared at her as she walked from one office to another. He began to have sexual fantasies about her, which he disclosed to two male supervisors. However, he never mentioned to Maura that he had in mind any form of sexual relationship.

Keith's direct supervisor, Vice President B. K. Singh, became aware of Keith's interest in Maura from two sources. First, he was told about the sexual fantasies by one of Keith's two male friends to whom Keith made the disclosures. Second, Maura had that same day come to his office to complain about what she considered sexual harassment. Mr. Singh became concerned about a possible contaminated work environment, but he did not think that he or Maura could make any form of harassment charge stick. The company had no corporate policy on harassment. Mr. Singh considered the situation to be just another case of one employee asking another out and being overly persistent. Mr. Singh decided not to do anything right away, not even to discuss the problem with Keith. He was worried that if he did take up the matter with Keith at such an early stage, he would himself be creating a hostile work environment. He believed Keith's advances would have to worsen before he should intervene or take the problem to the President.

Questions

1. Is Keith's conduct a case of sexual harassment? Is it a clear case, a borderline case, or no case at all?

2. Is it justifiable for Mr. Singh to adopt a position of nonintervention? Should he speak with Keith? What would you do if you were in his position?

3. Does the fact that Maura agreed once to go out with Keith mean that she has encouraged him to make further requests? If so, was she sufficiently discouraging at a later point?

CASE 2. *Sing's Chinese Restaurant*

The Bali Hai Corporation started as a small Chinese restaurant in Boston, Massachusetts, in 1959. The restaurant was an exact replica of a Chinese pagoda. Over the years, the restaurant, owned and managed by Arnold Sing, became known for its food and atmosphere. Customers were made to feel as if they were actually in China. In the last few years, Sing decided to incorporate and open other similar restaurants throughout the country. Sing, who had come to the United States from China in the early 1940s, was very strict in keeping up his reputation for good food and atmosphere. He had a policy of hiring only waiters of Oriental descent. He felt this added to his customers' dining pleasure and made for a more authentic environment. For kitchen positions, though, Sing hired any qualified applicants.

About a year ago at Sing's Bali Hai in Washington, DC, there was a shortage of waiters. An advertisement was placed in the newspaper for waiters, and the manager of the store was instructed by Sing to hire only Orientals. The manager was also reminded of Bali Hai's commitment to a reputation for good food and atmosphere. Two young men, one black and one white, both with consider-

able restaurant experience, applied for the waiters' jobs. The manager explained the policy of hiring only Orientals to the young men, and he also told them he could get them work in his kitchen. The two men declined the positions and instead went directly to the area Equal Employment Office and filed a complaint. Sing's defense was that the policy was only to preserve the atmosphere of the restaurant. He said the Oriental waiters were needed to make it more authentic. Sing also added that he hired blacks, whites, and other races for his kitchen help.

Questions

1. Is Sing's defense a good one under the law? Why or why not?
2. Is Sing's defense a good one under the standards of morality? Why or why not?
3. Is this a case of "preferential hiring"? Of "reverse discrimination"?

CASE 3.   *Wards Cove Packing Co. v. Atonio*

Two companies operated salmon canneries in remote areas of Alaska, which canneries functioned only during the summer salmon runs. There were two general types of jobs at the canneries: cannery line jobs, which were unskilled positions, and "noncannery" jobs, which were predominantly skilled positions but varied from engineers and bookkeepers to cooks and boat crew members. The cannery workers were predominantly nonwhite, mainly Filipinos, whom the companies hired through a hiring hall agreement with a predominantly Filipino union local in Seattle, and Alaska Natives, hired from villages near the canneries. The noncannery workers were

predominantly white and were hired during the winter through the companies' offices in Washington and Oregon. Virtually all of the noncannery jobs paid more than the cannery jobs, and noncannery workers used dormitory and mess hall facilities that were separate from and allegedly superior to those of the cannery workers. A class of nonwhite cannery workers who were or had been employed at the canneries in question brought an action against the companies in the United States District Court for the Western District of Washington, which action charged the companies with employment discrimination on the basis of race in violation of a provision of

Supreme Court of the United States. 490 U.S. 642; 109 S. Ct. 2115; 1989 U.S. Lexis 2794; 104 L. Ed. 2d 733; 57 U.S.L.W. 4583; 49 Fair Empl. Prac. Cas. (BNA) 1519; 50 Empl. Prac. Dec. (CCH) P39,021.

Title VII of the Civil Rights Act of 1964 (42 USCS 2000e-2(a)). Specifically, it was alleged that the racial stratification of the work force was caused by several of the companies' hiring and promotion practices, including a rehire preference, a lack of objective hiring criteria, the separate hiring channels, and a practice of not promoting from within. . . .

On certiorari, the United States Supreme Court . . . held that (1) racial imbalance in one segment of an employer's work force is not sufficient to establish a prima facie case of disparate impact with respect to the selection of workers for the employer's other positions; (2) in this case, the comparison between the percentage of cannery workers who are nonwhite and the percentage of noncannery workers who are nonwhite did not make out a prima facie disparate-impact case; (3) the plaintiff in such a case bears the burden of isolating and identifying the specific employment practices that are allegedly responsible for any observed statistical disparities; and (4) if the plaintiff establishes a prima facie disparate-impact case, the employer bears the burden of producing evidence of a business justification for its employment practice, but the burden of persuasion on this issue remains with the plaintiff.

Blackmun, J., joined by Brennan and Marshall, JJ., dissented, expressing the view that the opinion of the court took three major strides backwards in the battle against racial discrimination by (1) upsetting the long-standing distribution of burdens of proof in Title VII disparate-impact cases; (2) barring the use of internal work force comparisons in the making of a prima facie case of discrimination, even where the structure of the industry in question rendered any other statistical comparison meaningless; and (3) requiring practice-by-practice statistical proof of causation, even where such proof would be impossible.

Questions

1. Are the canneries' hiring practices discriminatory? If so, what company policies should be adopted?
2. Is there a correlation between the hiring practices for cannery workers and noncannery workers? Should the practices be the same or separate, even though the positions are different?
3. Is it an acceptable practice for the cannery to rehire skilled noncannery workers it has worked with previously? Is it acceptable even if the noncannery workers are predominantly white?

CASE 4. *Weber and the Kaiser Aluminum Steelworkers Plan*

In 1974 the United Steelworkers of America and Kaiser Aluminum & Chemical Corp. established an employment agreement that addressed an overwhelming racial imbalance in employment in Kaiser plants. Of primary concern was the lack of skilled black craftsworkers. This concern arose because of an ongoing exclusion of black craftsworkers. In an attempt to remove the disparity and create a fair employment policy, an affirmative action plan ("the plan") was agreed to, whereby

This case was abstracted from Supreme Court materials by Katie Marshall and Tom L. Beauchamp.

black craft-hiring goals were set for each Kaiser plant equal to the percentage of blacks in the respective local labor forces . . . [and] to enable plants to meet these goals, on-the-job training programs were established to teach unskilled workers — black and white — the skills necessary to become craftsworkers (443 U.S. 198 [1979]).

Under the guidelines of the plan, 50 percent of those selected for the newly instituted training program were to be black employees *until* the goals of the plan were accomplished, after which the 50 percent provision would be discontinued.

Such a plan was instituted at the Gramercy, Louisiana, plant from which the major problems had arisen and where blacks constituted less than 2 percent of the skilled craftsworkers, although they were approximately 39 percent of the Gramercy labor force. Subsequently, thirteen trainees, of which seven were black, were selected in accordance with the guidelines of the plan. The black trainees had less seniority than many white production workers who were denied training status. Brian Weber, one such production worker, argued that he and others had been unduly discriminated against. He thought the plan was a violation of Title VII of the Civil Rights Act of 1964. A District Court and a Court of Appeals held that Title VII had been violated. The U.S. Supreme Court then addressed the issue of whether

employers were forbidden from enacting such affirmative action plans to alleviate racial imbalances.

The Supreme Court held that forbidding such affirmative action plans under Title VII would be in direct contradiction to its purpose, because the statutory words call upon "employers and unions to self-examine and to self-evaluate their employment practices and to endeavor to eliminate, so far as possible, the vast vestiges of an unfortunate and ignominious page in this country's history" (433 U.S. 204 [1978]). The Supreme Court concluded that the Kaiser plan purposes "mirror[ed] those of the statute," because both the plan and the statute "were designed to break down old patterns of racial segregation [and] both were structured to open employment opportunities for Negroes in occupations which have been traditionally closed to them." The Supreme Court reversed the opinions of the lower courts (433 U.S. 208 [1978]).

Questions

1. Are the percentage figures in this case "quotas"? Are they justified under the circumstances?

2. Does Kaiser have a fair employment policy? If not, how should it be revised?

3. Is there reverse discrimination against Weber? If so, is it justified?

CASE 5.　*Firefighters Local Union No. 1784 v. Stotts*

Respondent Carl Stotts, a black member of petitioner Memphis, Tennessee, Fire Department, filed a class action in Federal District Court charging that the Department and certain city officials were engaged in a pattern or practice of making hiring and promotion decisions on the basis of race in violation of, *inter alia,* Title VII of the Civil Rights Act of 1964.

Supreme Court of the United States: 467 U.S. 561; 104 S. Ct. 2576; 1984 U.S. Lexis 108; 81 L. Ed. 2d 483; 52 U.S.L.W. 4767; 34 Fair Empl. Prac. Cas. (BNA) 1702; 34 Empl. Prac. Dec. (CCH) P34,415.

This action was consolidated with an action filed by respondent Fred Jones, also a black member of the Department, who claimed that he had been denied a promotion because of his race. Thereafter, a consent decree was entered with the stated purpose of remedying the Department's hiring and promotion practices with respect to blacks. Subsequently, when the city announced that projected budget deficits required a reduction of city employees, the District Court entered an order preliminarily enjoining the Department from following its seniority system in determining who would be laid off as a result of the budgetary shortfall, since the proposed layoffs would have a racially discriminatory effect and the seniority system was not a bona fide one. A modified layoff plan, aimed at protecting black employees so as to comply with the court's order, was then presented and approved, and layoffs pursuant to this plan were carried out. This resulted in white employees with more seniority than black employees being laid off when the otherwise applicable seniority system would have called for the layoff of black employees with less seniority. The Court of Appeals affirmed, holding that although the District Court was wrong in holding that the seniority system was not bona fide,

it had acted properly in modifying the consent decree. . . .

JUSTICE WHITE delivered the opinion of the Court. Petitioners challenge the Court of Appeals' approval of an order enjoining the City of Memphis from following its seniority system in determining who must be laid off as a result of a budgetary shortfall. Respondents contend that the injunction was necessary to effectuate the terms of a Title VII consent decree in which the City agreed to undertake certain obligations in order to remedy past hiring and promotional practices. Because we conclude that the order cannot be justified, either as an effort to enforce the consent decree or as a valid modification, we reverse.

Questions

1. Is seniority or diversity upheld in this instance? What do each of the courts argue?
2. Is it justifiable for the Department to lay off new minority workers and maintain seniority even if it has a discriminatory effect?
3. Is the Supreme Court decision concerning the Memphis Fire Department applicable to business or is it only relevant to emergency services?

CASE 6.   *Comparable Worth in the Female Section?*

The County of Washington, Oregon, established salary scales for its guards in the county jail during the 1970s. Female guards in the female section were paid one-third to one-eighth less than male guards of the comparable rank and experience in the male section.

The female guards complained that they were paid unequal wages for work substantially

equal to that performed by male guards and that the underlying reason was sex discrimination. The pay scale for males had been determined by the county's survey of outside markets for guards, but the pay scale for females was not similarly set. The survey indicated that the average outside pay standard is that female correctional officials are paid about 95 percent as much as male correctional officials.

This case was prepared by Tom L. Beauchamp.

Nonetheless, the County of Washington decided to pay women only 70 percent of the salary paid to men. The county intentionally scaled down the female guards' work below the outside market level. However, the county had not had difficulty hiring women in the local region at its pay scales.

The county said there were two major differences in the jobs for men and women: The male guards supervised more than ten times as many prisoners per guard as did the female guards, and the females, unlike the males, were required to spend part of their time on clerical jobs (considered less valuable by the county). The county therefore held that the females' jobs were not substantially equal to those of the male guards and merited less than equal pay. The county objected to the idea that any outside authority such as the courts could evaluate its pay scales without placing virtually every employer at risk of scrutiny by the courts for not paying comparable wages.

Questions

1. Is this a "comparable worth" case, a case involving sex discrimination, or a simple case of fair salaries? Is it all of these?
2. Are there relevant differences between the male jobs and the female jobs that would justify a lower scale for women?

Suggested Supplementary Readings

AALBERTS, ROBERT J., AND LORNE H. SEIDMAN. "Sexual Harassment by Clients, Customers, and Suppliers: How Employers Should Handle an Emerging Legal Problem." *Employee Relations Law Journal* 20 (Summer, 1994): 85–100.

BAUGH, S. GAYLE. "On the Persistence of Sexual Harassment in the Workplace." *Journal of Business Ethics* 16 (1997): 899–908.

BEAUCHAMP, TOM L. "In Defense of Affirmative Action." *Journal of Ethics* 2 (1998): 143–158.

BLOCH, FARRELL. *Antidiscrimination Law and Minority Employment: Recruitment Practices and Regulatory Constraints.* Chicago, IL: The University of Chicago Press, 1994.

BLUM, LINDA M. *Between Feminism and Labor: The Significance of the Comparable Worth Movement.* Berkeley, CA: University of California Press, 1991.

BOXILL, BERNARD. *Blacks and Social Justice.* Totowa, NJ: Rowman and Littlefield, 1992.

BROWNE, M. NEIL, and ANDREA M. GIAMPETRO. "The Socially Responsible Firm and Comparable Worth." *American Business Law Journal* 25 (Fall 1987).

COHEN, MARSHALL, THOMAS NAGEL, and THOMAS SCANLON, eds. *Equality and Preferential Treatment.* Princeton, NJ: Princeton University Press, 1977.

CRAIN, KAREN A., and KENNETH A. HEISCHMIDT. "Implementing Business Ethics: Sexual Harassment." *Journal of Business Ethics* 14 (April 1995): 299–308.

CROUCH, MARGARET A. "The 'Social Etymology' of 'Sexual Harassment'." *Journal of Social Philosophy* 29 (1998): 19–40.

DANDEKER, NATALIE. "Contrasting Consequences: Bringing Charges of Sexual Harassment Compared with Other Cases of Whistleblowing." *Journal of Business Ethics* 9 (1990).

EGLER, THERESA DONAHUE. "Five Myths About Sexual Harassment." *HR Magazine* 40 (January 1995): 27–30.

ENGLAND, PAULA. *Comparable Worth: Theories and Evidence.* New York: Aldine De Gruyter, 1992.

ERLER, EDWARD J. "The Future of Civil Rights: Affirmative Action Redivivus." *Notre Dame Journal of Law and Ethics* 11 (1997): 15–65.

EZORSKY, GERTRUDE. *Racism and Justice.* Ithaca, NY: Cornell University Press, 1991.

FICK, BARBARA J. "The Case for Maintaining and Encouraging the Use of Voluntary Affirmative Action in Private Sector Employment." *Notre Dame Journal of Law and Ethics* 11 (1997): 159–170.

FINE, LESLIE M., C. DAVID SHEPHERD, and SUSAN L. JOSEPHS. "Sexual Harassment in the Sales Force: The Customer Is NOT Always Right." *Journal of Personal Selling & Sales Management* 14 (Fall 1994): 15–30.

FISCHEL, DANIEL, and EDWARD LAZEAR. "Comparable Worth and Discrimination in Labor

Markets." *University of Chicago Law Review* 53 (Summer, 1986).

FULLINWIDER, ROBERT K. "The Life and Death of Racial Preferences." *Philosophical Studies* 85 (1997): 163–180.

———. *The Reverse Discrimination Controversy.* Totowa, NJ: Rowman and Allanheld, 1980.

GRIFFITH, STEPHEN. "Sexual Harassment and the Rights of the Accused." *Public Affairs Quarterly* 13 (1999): 43–71.

GUNDERSON, MORLEY. "Pay and Employment Equity in the United States and Canada." *International Journal of Manpower* 15 (1994): 26–43.

HOLMES, ROBERT L. "Sexual Harassment and the University." *Monist* 79 (1996): 499–518.

HORNE, GERALD. *Reversing Discrimination: The Case for Affirmative Action.* New York: International Publishers, 1992.

KALANTARI, BEHROOZ. "Dynamics of Job Evaluation and the Dilemma of Wage Disparity in the United States." *Journal of Business Ethics* 14 (1995): 397–403.

KERSHNAR, STEPHEN. "Uncertain Damages to Racial Minorities and Strong Affirmative Action." *Public Affairs Quarterly* 13 (1999): 83–98.

KEYTON, JOANN, and RHODES, STEVEN C. "Sexual Harassment: A Matter of Individual Ethics, Legal Definitions, or Organizational Policy?" *Journal of Business Ethics* 16 (1997): 129–146.

KILLINGSWORTH, MARK R. *The Economics of Comparable Worth.* Kalamazoo, MI: W.E. Upjohn Institute for Employment Research, 1990.

LADENSON, ROBERT. "Ethics in the American Workplace." *Business and Professional Ethics Journal* 14 (1995): 17–31.

LEAP, TERRY L., and LARRY R. SMELTZER. "Racial Remarks in the Workplace: Humor or Harassment?" *Harvard Business Review* 62 (1984).

LEMONCHECK, LINDA, and HAJDIN, MANE. *Sexual Harassment: A Debate.* Lanham, MD: Rowman & Littlefield, 1997.

MICELI, MARCIA P., and others. "Employers' Pay Practices and Potential Responses to 'Comparable Worth' Litigation." *Journal of Business Ethics* 7 (May, 1988).

MOSLEY, ALBERT G., and CAPALDI, NICHOLAS. *Affirmative Action: Social Justice or Unfair Preference?* Lanham, MD: Rowman & Littlefield, 1996.

MORRIS, CELIA. *Bearing Witness: Sexual Harassment and Beyond — Everywoman's Story.* Boston: Little, Brown & Company, 1994.

ORAZEM, PETER F., and J. PETER MATTILA. "The Implementation Process of Comparable Worth." *Journal of Political Economy* 98 (1990).

PACE, JOSEPH MICHAEL, and ZACHARY SMITH. "Understanding Affirmative Action: From the Practitioner's Perspective." *Public Personnel Management* 24 (1995): 139–147.

PAETZOLD, RAMONA L., and BILL SHAW. "A Postmodern Feminist View of 'Reasonableness' in Hostile Environment Sexual Harassment." *Journal of Business Ethics* 13 (1994): 681–692.

PAUL, ELLEN FRANKEL. *Equity and Gender: The Comparable Worth Debate.* New Brunswick, NJ: Transaction Publishers, 1989.

PETERSEN, DONALD J., and DOUGLAS P. MASSENGILL. "Sexual Harassment Cases Five Years After *Meritor Savings Bank v. Vinson.*" *Employee Relations Law Journal* 18 (1992-93): 489–515.

PHILIPS, MICHAEL. "Preferential Hiring and the Question of Competence." *Journal of Business Ethics* 10 (1991).

PINCUS, LAURA, and BILL SHAW, "Comparable Worth: An Economic and Ethical Analysis." *Journal of Business Ethics* 17 (1998): 455–470.

PLATT, ANTHONY M. "The Rise and Fall of Affirmative Action." *Notre Dame Journal of Law and Ethics* 11 (1997): 67–78.

POJMAN, LOUIS P. "The Case against Affirmative Action." *International Journal of Applied Philosophy* 12 (1998): 97–115.

PURDY, LAURA. "Why Do We Need Affirmative Action?" *Journal of Social Philosophy* 25 (1994): 133–143.

QUINN, JENNIFER M. "Visibility and Value: The Role of Job Evaluation in Assuring Equal Pay for Women." *Law & Policy in International Business* 25 (1994): 1403–1444.

REMICK, HELEN. *Comparable Worth and Wage Discrimination.* Philadelphia: Temple University Press, 1984.

RHOADS, STEVEN F. *Incomparable Worth: Pay Equity Meets the Market.* Cambridge: Cambridge University Press, 1993.

ROSENFELD, MICHEL. *Affirmative Action and Justice: A Philosophical and Constitutional Inquiry.* New Haven, CT: Yale University Press, 1991.

SEGRAVE, KERRY. *The Sexual Harassment of Women in the Workplace, 1600 to 1993.* Jefferson, NC: McFarland & Company, 1994.

SHANEY, MARY JO. "Perceptions of Harm: The Consent Defense in Sexual Harassment Cases." *Iowa Law Review* 71 (1986).

SHRAGE, LAURIE. "Some Implications of Comparable Worth." *Social Theory and Practice* 13 (1987): 77-102.

SINGER, M. S., and A. E. SINGER. "Justice in Preferential Hiring." *Journal of Business Ethics* 10 (1991).

SUNSTEIN, CASS R. "The Limits of Compensatory Justice." *Nomos* 33 (1991): 281–310.

THOMAS, LAURENCE. "On Sexual Offers and Threats." In *Moral Rights in the Workplace*, edited by Gertrude Ezorsky. Albany, NY: State University of New York Press, 1987.

WAGNER, ELLEN J. *Sexual Harassment in the Workplace: How to Prevent, Investigate, and Resolve Problems in Your Organization.* New York: Amacom [American Management Association], 1992.

WALL, EDMUND, ed. *Sexual Harassment: Confrontations and Decisions.* Buffalo, NY: Prometheus Books, 1992.

WALUCHOW, WIL. "Pay Equity: Equal Value to Whom?" *Journal of Business Ethics* 7 (1988): 185–189.

WARNKE, GEORGIA. "Affirmative Action, Neutrality, and Integration." *Journal of Social Philosophy* 29 (1998): 87–103.

WELLS, DEBORAH L., and BEVERLY J. KRACHER. "Justice, Sexual Harassment, and the Reasonable Victim Standard." *Journal of Business Ethics* 12 (1993): 423–431.

YORK, KENNETH M. "Defining Sexual Harassment in Workplaces: A Policy-Capturing Approach." *Academy of Management Journal* 32 (1989).

Chapter Seven

Marketing and Disclosure

INTRODUCTION

Marketing Practices

Marketing ethics explores decision making that emerges at several different levels in corporate life, such as whether to place a new product on the market, how to price a product, how to advertise, and how to conduct sales. Marketing research, pricing, advertising, selling, and international marketing have all come under close ethical scrutiny in recent years. Ethical issues about marketing are centered on obligations to disclose information. Advertising is the most visible way businesses present information to the public, but it is not the only way in which information is communicated, nor even the most important. Sales information, annual reports containing financial audits, public relations presentations, warranties, trade secrets, and public education and public health campaigns are other vital means by which corporations manage, communicate, and limit information.

A classic defense of American business practice is that business provides the public with what it wants; the consumer is king in the free enterprise system, and the market responds to consumer demands. This response is often said to represent the chief strength of a market economy over a collectivist system. Freedom of consumer choice is unaffected by government and corporate controls. But consider the following controversy about freedom of choice. The Federal Trade Commission (FTC) in late 1984 and early 1985 "reconsidered" its rule prohibiting supermarket advertising of items when those items are not in stock. The rule had been enacted in 1971 to combat frustration among shoppers who found empty shelves in place of advertised goods and often wound up substituting more expensive items. FTC officials suggested that the rule may have been unduly burdensome for the supermarket industry and that "market forces" would eliminate or curtail those who dishonestly advertise. Consumer groups argued that relaxing the rule would permit more expensive stores to lure shoppers by advertising low prices, leading many shoppers to spend more overall than they would have spent in a low-budget store. Mark Silbergeld of the Consumers Union argued that the Commission was acting in ignorance of the *real purpose* of supermarket advertising, which is to present a "come-on to get people into their stores."[1]

In the last thirty years it has been widely appreciated that this problem is only one among many that confront marketers of goods and services. Some problems are commonplace — for example, withholding vital information, distortion of data, and bluffing. Other problems of information control are more subtle. These include using information to attract customers, using annual reports as public relations devices, giving calculated "news releases" to the press, avoiding disclosures to workers that directly affect their health and welfare, and industrial spying. Rights of autonomy and free choice are at the center of these discussions. In some forms, withholding information and manipulating advertising messages threaten to undermine the free choice of consumers, clients, stockholders, and even colleagues. Deceptive and misleading statements limit freedom by restricting the range of choice and causing a person to do what he or she otherwise might not do.

Aside from these *autonomy*-based problems, there are *harm*-based problems that may have little to do with making a choice. For example, in a now classic case, the Nestlé corporation was pressured to suspend infant formula advertising and aggressive marketing tactics in developing countries. This controversy focused less on the freedom-based issue of the right to the dissemination of information than on preventing a population from harming itself through inadequate breastfeeding and inadequate appreciation of the risks of the use of infant formula. Such harm-based issues are mentioned in this chapter, but restrictions of free choice by manipulative influence are the central issue.

The inception of the problem is that consumers are frequently unable to evaluate the variety of goods and services available to them without some kind of help. There is generally a large "knowledge gap," as it is now called, between consumer and marketer. The consumer either lacks vital information or lacks the skills to evaluate the good or service. This circumstance leads to a situation in which the consumer must place trust in a service agency, producer, or retailer. Many marketers are well aware of this situation and feel acutely that they must not abuse their position of superior information. Many also engage in marketing *trust* no less than a product or service they are attempting to sell. When the felt or proclaimed trust is breached (whether intentionally or by accident), the marketer–consumer relationship is seriously endangered.

In their contributions to this chapter, Richard DeGeorge and George Brenkert present their views on several of these issues about marketing ethics. DeGeorge presents a general overview of marketing ethics, and Brenkert gives special attention to the strategy of marketing trust.

Advertising

Many critics deplore the values presented in advertising as well as the effects advertising has on consumers. Other critics are more concerned about specific practices such as advertising directed at vulnerable groups like children, the poor, and the elderly; advertising that exploits women or uses fear appeals; advertising that uses subliminal messages; and the advertising of liquor and tobacco products. Although critics have consistently denounced misleading or information-deficient advertising, the moral concepts underlying these denunciations have seldom been carefully examined. What is a deceptive or misleading advertisement? Is it, for example, deceptive or misleading to advertise a heavily sweetened cereal as "nutritious" or as "building strong bodies"? Are such advertisements forms of lying? Are they manipulative, especially when children are the primary targets or people are led to make purchases they do not need and would not have made had they not seen the advertising? If so, does the manipulation derive from some form of deception? For example, if an advertisement that touts a particular mouthwash as germ-killing manipulates listeners into purchasing the mouthwash, does it follow that these consumers have been deceived?

Does such advertising represent a deprivation of free choice, or is it rather an example of how free choice determines market forces? Control over a person is exerted through various kinds of influence, but not all influences actually control. Some forms of influence are desired and accepted by those who are influenced, whereas others are unwelcome. Many influences can easily be resisted by most persons; others can prove irresistible. Human reactions to influences such as corporate-sponsored information and advertising presentations cannot in many cases be determined or easily studied. Frank Dandrea, vice president of marketing for Schiefflin & Co., the importer of Hennessy's Cognac, once said that in their advertisements "The idea is to show a little skin, a little sex appeal, a little tension."[2] This effect is accomplished by showing a scantily clad woman holding a brandy snifter and staring provocatively in response to a man's interested glance. Hennessy tries to use a mixture of sex and humor. Other companies use rebates and coupons. All these methods are attempts to influence, and it is well known that they are at least partially successful. However, the influence of these strategies and the moral acceptability of these influences have been less carefully examined.

There is a continuum of controlling influence in our daily lives, running from coercion, at the controlling end of the continuum, to persuasion and education, both noncontrolling influences. Coercion requires an intentional and successful influence through an irresistible threat of harm. A coercive action negates freedom because it entirely controls the person's action. Persuasion, by contrast, involves a successful appeal to reason in order to convince a person to accept freely what is advocated by the persuader. Like informing, persuading is entirely compatible with free choice.

Manipulation covers the great gray area of influence. It is a catchall category that suggests the act of getting people to do what is advocated without resorting to coercion and without appealing to reasoned argument. In the case of *informational* manipulation, on which several selections in this chapter concentrate, information is managed so that the manipulated person will do what the manipulator intends. Whether such uses of information necessarily compromise or restrict free choice is an unresolved issue. One plausible view is that some manipulations — for instance, the use of rewards such as free trips or lottery coupons in direct mail advertising — are compatible with free choice, whereas others — such as deceptive offers or tantalizing ads aimed at young children — are not compatible with free choice. Beer, wine, and tobacco advertising aimed at teenagers and young adults has been under particularly harsh criticism in recent years, on grounds that sex, youth, fun, and beauty are directly linked in the advertising to dangerous products, with noticeable success. As Tom Beauchamp and Michael Phillips point out in their essays, these issues raise complex questions of both individual moral responsibility and collective moral responsibility in marketing products.

Many problems with advertising fall somewhere between acceptable and unacceptable manipulation. Consider these two examples: Anheuser-Busch ran a television commercial for its Budweiser Beer showing some working men heading for a brew at day's end. The commercial began with a shot of the Statue of Liberty in the background, included close-up shots of a construction crew working to restore the Statue, and ended with the words, "This Bud's for you, you know America takes pride in what you do." This statement may seem innocent, but the Liberty-Ellis Island Foundation accused Anheuser-Busch of a "blatant attempt to dupe [i.e., manipulate] consumers" by implying that Budweiser was among the sponsors helping to repair the Statue. The Foundation was particularly irritated because Anheuser-Busch had refused such a sponsorship when invited by the Foundation, whereas its rival, Stroh Brewing Company, had subsequently accepted an exclusive brewery sponsorship.[3]

A second case comes from Kellogg's advertising for its All-Bran product. The company ran a campaign linking its product to the prevention of cancer, apparently causing an immediate increase in sales of 41 percent for All-Bran. Although many food manufacturers advertise the low-salt, low-fat, low-calorie, or high-fibre content of their products, Kellogg went further, citing a specific product as a way to combat a specific disease. It is illegal to make claims about the health benefits of a specific food product without FDA approval, and Kellogg did not have this approval. Yet officials at both the National Cancer Institute and the FDA were not altogether critical of the ads. On the one hand, officials at these agencies agree that a high-fibre, low-fat diet containing some of the ingredients in All-Bran does help prevent cancer. On the other hand, no direct association exists between eating a given product and preventing cancer, and certainly no single food product can function like a drug as a preventative or remedy for such a disease.

The Kellogg ad strongly suggested that eating All-Bran was everything one needed to do to prevent cancer. Such a claim is potentially misleading in several respects. The ad did not suggest how much fibre people should eat, nor did it note that people can consume too much fibre while neglecting other essential minerals. Further, no direct scientific evidence linked the consumption of this product with the prevention of cancer, and this product could not be expected to affect all types of cancer. Is the Kellogg promise manipulative, or is the ad, as Kellogg claims, basically a truthful, health-promotion campaign? Does it contain elements of both?

One of the court cases in this chapter — *Coca-Cola Co. v. Tropicana Products, Inc.* — focuses on a central question of the ethics of advertising. In this case, the two main competitors for the chilled orange juice market in the United States came into a direct conflict. The Coca-Cola Co., maker of Minute Maid Orange Juice, sued Tropicana Products on grounds of false advertising. Tropicana had claimed in its advertisements that its brand of orange juice is "as it comes from the orange" and the only "brand not made with concentrate and water." Coke asserted that this claim is false and that Tropicana is pasteurized and sometimes frozen prior to packaging. Coke also claimed that it had lost sales of its product as a result of this misrepresentation. The court agrees with Coke both that the company has lost sales and that consumers have been misled by Tropicana's advertising campaign.

These examples illustrate the broad categories on the continuum of controlling influences that are under examination in this chapter. Other forms of influence besides manipulation — such as *indoctrination* and *seduction* — might be mentioned, but, in the end, especially for advertising, the difference between *manipulation* and *persuasion* is the key matter. Of course, the question arises whether unjustifiably manipulative advertising or competition occurs very often, or even at all. In his contribution to this chapter, Phillips addresses this question. He argues that in and around this question there are not only a nest of ethical questions about the acceptability of advertising, but equally difficult empirical questions about the effects advertising actually has on persons.

Sales

Some of these issues about disclosure, deception, and manipulation are as prominent in sales as in advertising. The attractive pricing of products is a first step in sales, and questions have been raised about pricing itself. For example, there have been accusations of price gouging of specific populations, such as those in poor neighborhoods and the elderly. The more common problems, however, concern failures (intentional or not) to disclose pertinent information about a product's function, quality, or price. A simple example is the common practice of selling a product at a low price because it is the previous year's model, although it is not disclosed that the latest models are already out and in stock.

As the marketplace for products has grown more complex and sophisticated, buyers have become more dependent upon salespersons to know their products and to tell the truth about them. The implicit assumption in some sales contexts is that bargaining and deception about a selling price are parts of the game, just as they are in real estate and labor negotiations. Nevertheless, this "flea market" and "horse-trader" model of sales is unsuited to other contemporary markets. The salesperson is expected to have superior knowledge and is treated as an expert on the product, or at least as one who obtains needed information about a product. In this climate, it seems unethical for salespersons to take advantage of a buyer's implicit trust by using deceptive or manipulative techniques. Yet, if it is unethical to disclose too little, does it follow that the ethical salesperson has an obligation to disclose everything that might be of interest to the customer? For example, must the salesperson disclose that his or her company charges more than a competitor? What principles rightly govern the transfer of information during sales?

James M. Ebejer and Michael J. Morden point out in their article in this chapter that some salespersons view their relationship to the customer under the model of *caveat emptor* (let the buyer beware), whereas, at the other extreme, some salespersons see their role as that of paternalistic protector of the customer's interests. These authors argue for a professional sales ethic that they describe as "limited paternalism," which they propose as a regulative standard. Using this standard, a salesperson should be his or her "buyer's keeper" by identifying the needs of customers and disclosing information essential to meeting those needs. The salesperson is obligated to use this approach even if customers do not understand what their best interests are. Ebejer and Morden believe this approach maximizes mutual exchange and mutual advantage, evidently a utilitarian criterion for proper sales disclosures.

In a second article on sales practices, David Holley probes the social role of the salesperson. He concludes that there is a general obligation to disclose all information that a consumer would need to make a reasonable judgment about whether to purchase a product or service. Holley argues that this rule is superior to several alternatives that have been proposed in the literature.

Changes in the climate of sales of the sort proposed in the articles in this chapter could potentially have a massive impact in business. More persons are employed in sales than any other area of marketing, and sales has commonly been critized as the closely monitored area of business activity. Salespersons appear to be more prone to unethical conduct if substantial portions of their income are dependent upon commissions, competition is fierce and unregulated, dubious practices of disclosure have become common, sales managers are removed from actual selling practices, and codes of ethics are widely disregarded in the industry.

Bluffing and Strategic Disclosure

Whether marketing practices can be justified by the "rules of the game" in business is another major question. Some have argued that marketing is analogous to ordinary arms-length transactions in which we all engage — for example, when purchasing a used automobile. In these situations, bluffing, overstatement, and enticement are expected and invite similar countermoves. Although abuse and contempt are not tolerated, deception is tolerated and even encouraged as long as all players know the rules of the game and occupy roughly equal bargaining positions. This model suggests, on the one hand, that deceptive practices and sharp practices can be justifiable. On the other hand, limits must be set to restrict deception, manipulation, and cunning maneuvers that take advantage of a competitor's misfortune.

In raising these questions about deception, it is well to remember that manipulation can take many forms: offering rewards, threatening punishments, instilling fear, and so forth. The principal form discussed in this chapter is the manipulation of information. Here the manipulator modifies a person's sense of options by affecting the person's understanding of the situation. Deception, bluffing, and the like are used by the manipulator to change not the person's *actual* options but only the person's *perception* of the options. The more a person is deprived of a relevant understanding in the circumstances, the greater the effect on the person's free choice.

One does not need extensive experience in business to know that many deceptive practices, like bluffing and slick sales techniques, are widely practiced and widely accepted. It is common knowledge that automobile dealers do not expect people to pay the sticker price for automobiles; but it is a closely guarded secret as to how much can be knocked off that price. A certain amount of quoting of competitors, bargaining, moving "extras" under the basic price, and going to managers for approval is part of the game. A similar situation prevails in real estate transactions, in which the asking price for a house is seldom the anticipated selling price, as well as at bargaining sessions, in which labor leaders overstate wage demands and management understates the wage increases it is willing to grant.

The intent is to manipulate, however gently. In his article "Is Business Bluffing Ethical?" Albert Z. Carr recognizes that such practices are characteristic of business and maintains that they are analogous to the game of poker. According to Carr, just as conscious misstatement, concealment of pertinent facts, exaggeration, and bluffing are morally acceptable in poker, they are acceptable in business. What makes such practices acceptable, Carr says, is that all parties understand the rules of the game. In advertising, for example, exaggeration and bluffing are understood to be part of the selling game. Only an extraordinarily naive person would believe advertisements without casting a skeptical eye on the images and words issuing from a television set.

Yet there are moral limits to the game, even if the rules of the game are grasped by all. Suppose that Pamela is willing to sell her home for $160,000, if that is the best price she can get. She puts the home on the market at $170,000. A potential buyer's initial offer is $160,000. Pamela turns the offer down, telling him that $165,000 is her rock-bottom price. He then purchases the home for $165,000. Many people would characterize her behavior as shrewd bluffing and certainly not an immoral lie. Many people would think more of her, rather than less. However, suppose she manufactured the claim that another party was writing up a contract to buy the house for $165,000 and that she would sell it to him for the same $165,000 price because both she and he were Baptists. In this case, many people would maintain that she had told at least one lie, probably two, but are the lies unjustified or merely part of the game? Would it make any moral difference if she were to have her brother pretend to make her an offer and draw up a fake contract so that the prospective buyer would be pressured to buy?

The sophistication of the audience, standard practice in the business, and intention of the informer all need to be considered to decide whether gilded information is unacceptable. Manipulation and deception can result as much from what is not said as from what is said. For example, true information can be presented out of context and thereby be misleading.

A classic problem about disclosure of information appears in *Backman v. Polaroid Corporation*. In this case, investors alleged that Polaroid had obtained negative information about its product Polavision but had failed to disclose to investors unfavorable facts that were known about the product. In effect, the claim is that Polaroid manipulated investors into purchasing the stock at a higher value than its actual worth. A similar charge led to accusations against Salomon, Inc., in late 1991 for both moral and legal failures to disclose properly to shareholders a stock option plan and cash bonus plan that benefited top corporate executives. Investors charged that the level of compensation diluted the value of the stock. Salomon responded that it had "followed the rules" of disclosure in its mailings to stockholders.[4]

Despite such examples, Carr maintains that it is morally permissible to deceive others in these ways as long as everyone knows that such actions are accepted in the business world as standard practice. Carr would presumably say that neither Polaroid nor Salomon did anything wrong so long as it is accepted that unfavorable facts about a product or compensation scheme do not have to be disclosed. However, this perception raises many problems. For example, bluffing, active deception, and lack of disclosure interfere with the way markets work when good information is available and may also create instability in markets and hurt productivity and stifle competition.

Carr's criteria are either rejected or restated in a more guarded form in the next article by Thomas Carson. Carson argues that people commonly misstate their bargaining positions in the course of business negotiations, but that these misstatements often do not involve lying. He maintains that bluffing and other forms of negotiation are legitimate when one has good reason to believe that the other party understands the rules and is engaging in the same form of activity. However, it is impermissible to misstate one's negotiating or bargaining position whenever one does not have good reason to believe that the other party is engaging in a similar form of misstatement. Thus, by contrast to Carr, Carson argues that bluffing is often immoral when the attempt to lie or bluff is unilateral. To follow out the game metaphor, Carson is insisting not only that the rules of the game be understood but that the game be on a level playing surface for all players.

NOTES

1. Sari Horwitz, "FTC Considers Letting Food Stores Advertise Out-of-Stock Items," *Washington Post* (December 27, 1984), p. E1.

2. As quoted in Amy Dunkin and others, "Liquor Makers Try the Hard Sell in a Softening Market," *Business Week* (May 13, 1985), p. 56.

3. "Anheuser-Busch Sued on Ad Showing Statue of Liberty," *Wall Street Journal* (November 28, 1984), p. 43.

4. Robert J. McCartney, "Investors Hit Salomon on Bonuses," *Washington Post* (October 23, 1991), pp. C1, C5.

MARKETING, TRUTH, AND TRUST

Marketing and Truth

Richard T. DeGeorge

MARKETING

Once a manufacturer produces a certain product, its aim is to sell it. Marketing is the process by which it does so. Marketing techniques seek to solve a variety of problems in order to sell the product or service that a company produces or provides. Marketing research attempts to determine customer demand and the most efficient and profitable means by which this demand can be met. . . . Markets can only rarely be predicted with certainty, and the ability to manipulate markets and market demand is much less than many critics claim. Yet the temptation to try to manipulate markets, to lessen one's chances of failure by illegal or immoral means, is often present. We shall examine just a few of the areas where the temptations to act immorally are significant, and where some practices are morally questionable. These areas are competition, pricing, bidding, and consumer marketing.

Competition

We have already seen that competition is part of the free-enterprise system. Competition tends to produce efficiency in the market and benefits the general consumer by resulting in a variety of goods at the best prices. But the competitive market works to the advantage of the buyer only when the competitive process is fair. Although the government plays a role in trying to keep competition fair, government regulation is not enough. Unless those engaged in the competitive process operate fairly and honestly, the system itself is undermined. Moral standards have a role to play and do play it daily, but the temptations to violate the standards of honesty and fair competition for one's personal benefit or that of one's firm are also constantly present.

One major way of undermining competition is through the creation of monopolies. If a firm is able to create and maintain a monopoly in any area, then it has no competitive restraints on its prices. It may consequently charge what it wants, as long as there is a market willing to purchase its product or service at the price it sets. But how does a firm gain a monopoly? . . . Undercutting the competition might be done in several ways. One way is simply to price one's product lower than that of the competition. If this is possible because a firm is more efficient, is more productive, and is able to operate at lower cost, or is satisfied with lower profit margins, the process is fair. It is part of the competitive system and leads to the efficiency the system promises. But a large producer may undercut a smaller competitor by selling products for less than they cost to produce, absorbing the loss for a short time, with the intent of capturing the market. It thus forces the competitor also to sell at a loss or lose its market share. If the smaller competitor is unable to operate at a loss or to match prices, it will eventually go under. A large corporation can target its areas of competition; it will keep up its profits in one geographical or product area and use these profits to subsidize its loss in another area, where it wishes to drive out the competition. . . .

If we admit that monopolies constitute a restraint on the market, which is detrimental to the general public, and are therefore not morally justifiable, then practices executed with the intent of producing monopolies are also not morally justifiable. In the United States, takeovers by large companies must often be approved by government to preclude the formation of monopolies. Forcing out competition by selling products below cost without taking over the competitors is at least morally questionable, though not illegal.

A second way of controlling competition is for a small group of producers of a product to collude for their common good. They may agree, for instance, not to compete against one another in certain areas, dividing up the market among them. Or they may agree on

the prices to charge — a practice known as *price fixing*. Such collusion is generally illegal because it undermines the competitive system to the detriment of the buyer. It is also immoral. The collusion may be done so subtly that it cannot be proven to be collusion. This may preclude legal prosecution, but it does not change the immorality of the action. . . .

Pricing

Pricing is an important part of the marketing process. A producer wishes to sell its product at a profit and must price its product appropriately in order to do so. The producer must be able to control its costs. But competition, if it is fair, will force the producer to price its product at its true worth. If the price is set too high, the market for it may shrink so that its sales are less than what is required for it to make a profit, or it may not be as attractive to a buyer, who can purchase from a competitor a similar product at a lower price. Unless one is in a monopolistic position, setting prices is in part a result of the market, and one's success depends in part on knowing the market conditions.

We shall deal with only two issues in pricing: overpricing, and markup and markdown.

Overpricing is a special issue in marketing. In general, the competitive system should preclude the possibility of overpricing where this means charging much more than the producer knows the product is worth, thus yielding an excessive profit. There are some who might claim that overpricing is a misnomer because there is no specific limit of justifiable profit. But this claim assumes that prices are competitive, and they are not always competitive. We have already mentioned the possibility that a producer in a monopolistic position can charge more than it would otherwise be able to do. There are other ways, however, that overpricing can take place. In each case they involve either a monopolistic position, force, or ignorance on the part of the buyer. One of the claims made about merchants in poor areas, ghettos, and slums, for instance, is that they overcharge their customers. They are in effect in a monopolistic position; their customers are not mobile enough to go to other parts of the city to buy what they want at competitive prices. They need the goods available at the only source available to them — the local store. The store is thus in a position to charge more than it would otherwise do, to the disadvantage of the consumer. Some store owners in such locations admit that they charge higher prices for goods than stores elsewhere, but they claim that their insurance costs, including rates for fire, robbery, and personal risk, are higher than elsewhere. These factors, they claim, justify their higher prices. Whether this is sufficient justification depends on the relation of these costs to the increase in the price of the goods they sell. . . .

In addition to cases of forced need and no other supplier, ignorance on the part of the buyer often provides the occasion for overpricing. This is possible primarily among poorly educated people, but it is possible even among the well educated. Techniques of overpricing vary. They range from simply charging more for goods than they usually sell for, to charging more than an item is worth, on the assumption that the buyer will think that because it costs more it must be better than a lower-priced competing product. In all these cases, the seller counts on the ignorance of the buyer. To do this is to take advantage of the buyer, and that is not morally justifiable. In the long run, the practice undermines the system, sows distrust of all products and prices, and fails to treat people with the respect they deserve.

Markups are a specific form of pricing. Instead of simply determining the price at which to sell to wholesalers, a manufacturer may calculate all the markups for all the middlemen and the retailer, and set or suggest a retail sales price. This price is a guide to the retailer regarding the price at which the item is to be sold. Unless the item is sold at the same price at all outlets, defenders of the practice maintain, the purchaser will be confused as to the real value of the item. . . . Although calculating and suggesting a retail sales price are not immoral, trying to enforce such a price stifles competition and is not in the best interest of the consumer. The step from these observations to declaring it immoral is a short one.

We have assumed that the various markups were at least justifiable. A clearly immoral practice, because it is deceptive, is setting a price for a product higher than that at which it is ever sold, so that it can always be sold at a discount. This is deceptive, because to sell at a discount implies a discount from its real price, not a discount from an artificially inflated one.

Although it is illegal to prevent discounts, in 1997 the U.S. Supreme Court ruled that a manufacturer may, under conditions to be worked out over time in response to a Federal court case, place a ceiling on the retail price a seller can charge for a product. A car manufacturer, for instance, can prevent a dealer from selling a car for more than the sticker price, even if the model is in short supply and great demand. Whether manufacturers will impose such limits remains to be seen. But if they do, they can stop price gouging on their products by retailers who might attempt to take advantage of short supplies or long waits for the product. The intent of the ruling was to protect the consumer from overpricing.

Bidding

Bidding is a commonly used practice. It is sometimes used by a seller, as at an auction, to get the highest price. More often, it is used by a buyer, to get the lowest price. It is used in construction projects, by government and large firms in seeking supplies purchased in quantity, and by firms in seeking subcontractors and suppliers. Bidding is a morally justifiable procedure, providing it is fair. Keeping it fair is not always easy.

Not all bidding is secret, as the case of an auction illustrates. But much of it is. How does one justify secret bidding? Why should bidding not be an open process? The answer is that secrecy tends to produce fairer bids and lower prices for the purchaser. This happens in two ways. If the process were open, a firm that could make a profit at a price considerably less than the competition would make a bid only just enough less to win the contract. This bid might well be higher than the lowest bid he would offer if he did not know what the competition was and simply operated on his cost plus what he considered an acceptable, competitive profit.

Second, if the competition were open, a firm might start out at a bid low enough to scare off others from bidding, even though the bid is not the lowest he would offer if forced to make a secret bid. Therefore, secrecy per se is not morally unjustifiable. But if the bidding process is to be secret, then in fairness to all parties it must be kept secret. Any violation of secrecy by any of the parties violates the fairness condition of bidding. Often a government or company will not accept bids above a certain amount. If no bids are lower than that amount, it will not proceed, and will restudy its options. But it may hope to get a bid lower than the highest it is willing to pay. Clearly, the figure it is willing to pay must be kept secret if the bidding is to be fair. Any leaks violate the procedure. . . .

Bidding is a morally defensible practice in business, but it is open to many abuses, and it must be carefully controlled if it is to be kept fair.

Consumer Marketing

The opportunities for fraud, deception, and unethical practices are endless, but most such practices are clearly immoral and so raise no ethical problems. Advertising poses special problems, which we shall deal with separately. A few of the issues of current concern, however, include truth-in-lending, unit pricing, and labeling and dating. All of these have become items of consumer concern and the focus of attention by the consumers' movement. The consumers' movement can be seen at least in part as a reaction to marketing practices perceived as unfair or as less fair than they could or should be.

Truth-in-lending concerns the true amount paid by those who purchase items on the installment plan, who get loans to finance purchases, or who buy with credit cards. One sales technique is to state how much an item bought on time or credit will cost in terms of monthly payments. If little or no mention is made of the actual total cost of the purchase, the terms of the loan, or the true annual interest rate, consumers enter into legally binding contracts without full knowledge of what they are agreeing to. Some find out too late that their goods can be repossessed if they miss a payment or that they are actually paying two or three times more than the original price of an item because of interest and other payments.

These practices were not illegal, and a prudent and cautious buyer could have found out the exact nature of the contract into which he or she was entering. But this frequently requires a good deal of investigation and figuring — more than the average consumer is used to. Truth-in-lending therefore became a consumer demand, justified as a means of making transactions fair. The moral demands have been translated into legal obligations as well.

Unit pricing is an attempt to enable buyers to make accurate comparisons based on price. Most consumers would expect, for instance, to pay less per ounce for a soap powder bought in volume than the same brand packaged in a small box. This is not always the case, however. If both the contents of each box and the prices are not stated in round numbers, it is sometimes difficult to know which is the better buy. The same is true regarding competing brands. Yet one of the ways in which competition is supposed to take place in our system is based on price comparison. Pricing techniques that make it difficult to compare prices are not deceptive or immoral, but they do not help the consumer judge on the basis of price. . . .

Labeling and dating are other demands consumers have voiced to make the transactions into which they enter fair. When one buys a garment it is often difficult to know exactly what it is made of, whether it is a synthetic fabric, a natural fiber, or a mixture, or what the proportions are of each fiber. In effect, one buys blindly, unless the information is supplied. Availability of adequate information on both sides is a necessary condition if a transaction is to be fair. Hence, demanding such labeling is morally justifiable.

Unless the ingredients of processed foods are listed, in descending order, according to the quantity of each contained in the package, the purchaser does not know exactly what he or she is buying. In the case of perishable goods, unless a date by which an item must be sold is stamped on the product, there is no way for a buyer to know how fresh the product is and how long it can be kept before it spoils. Consumer demands in all these instances are legitimate; these practices not only prevent deception and misleading marketing techniques, but they also help to keep transactions fair, and so help the free-market system to operate as it should.

ADVERTISING

Although moral issues arise in other aspects of marketing, public and governmental concern has tended to focus on the advertising of consumer products to the general public. Corporations are thought capable of handling their own wants and of being qualified to determine on their own what they need. Although they are legally protected against fraud, they are less likely than the ordinary consumer to be taken in by misleading advertising or to be sold what they do not want.

Once a producer makes a commodity, his object is to sell it. To do so he must inform potential buyers that the product is available, what it does, and why it might be a product they want or need. Advertising provides this information to large numbers of people. A product might be advertised through a direct-mail campaign or through use of the media — newspapers, magazines, TV. Advertising, therefore, is part of the process of selling one's products. Because any sale is a transaction between a buyer and a seller, the transaction is fair if both parties have available adequate, appropriate information about the product, and if they enter into the transaction willingly and without coercion. From a moral point of view, because advertising helps achieve the goal of both seller and buyer, it is morally justifiable and permissible, providing it is not deceptive, misleading, or coercive. Advertising can be abused, but it is not inherently immoral. . . .

We should put aside three morally irrelevant charges brought against advertising. The first charge, that advertising is not necessary in a socialist economic system and that it is an immoral part of capitalism, is vague and for the most part untrue. In every economic system there must be some way of letting potential buyers know of the existence of goods. Any producer must make known that a product is available if people are to know that they can buy it. Displaying an item in a window, so that people can see it, is a form of advertising, as is displaying it on a shelf. In a society of comparative scarcity, where only essentials are available, people may constantly be on the lookout for products they want, spotting them when they arrive on a shelf. They may then, through word of mouth, transmit the information that the product is available. Before long there are lines of people waiting to purchase the item, and soon it is sold out. Those who did not get the item then wait for it to appear again. Or if an item is a staple, and generally available, people know where it can be purchased and simply go to that store when they need it. In such a society, advertising plays a comparatively small role. . . .

A second charge against advertising that we can dismiss from a moral point of view is its frequent poor taste; it is offensive to one's finer sensibilities. The charge can hardly be denied. But poor taste is not immoral. As members of society, we can make known our displeasure at such advertising, either by vocal or written protest, or by not purchasing the item advertised. However, we should distinguish between poor taste and immorality.

A third charge claims that advertising takes advantage of people, either by forcing them to buy what they do not want or, more plausibly, by psychologically manipulating them to buy what they do not need. According to this view, people are not able to resist the lure of the vast resources available to producers for advertising campaigns. Manipulation and coercion through advertising are immoral. . . . But the charge is clearly an overstatement if it asserts that all members of the public are gullible, unsophisticated, and manipulable by media advertising. Advertising would be immoral if it always and necessarily manipulated and coerced people, but it does not. The difficulty is in deciding what is manipulative and what is not; who should be protected from certain kinds of advertising, and who does not need such protection. The notion of protection from advertising is closely linked to government paternalism. To what extent are people to be allowed to make their own decisions, and to what extent should government protect them against themselves because of its superior knowledge of their real needs and wants? The Federal Trade Commission (FTC) and the Food and Drug Administration (FDA) are the two American agencies with major responsibility for policing advertising. The standards they adopt are frequently more restrictive and paternalistic than morality requires. They have sometimes ruled that advertising is misleading if only 5 percent of the population would be misled by it.

Marketing Trust: Barriers and Bridges

George G. Brenkert

INTRODUCTION

The discovery of trust by marketing, and by business more generally, began in the 1960s. Over the past decade, trust has increasingly become the focus of discussion and concern.

Discussions of trust within a marketing context have taken two general directions, giving rise to the intentionally ambiguous title of this paper. On the one hand, there are discussions of the role that trust plays in the various areas of marketing, such as distribution, advertising, retailing, and marketing research. The aim of these discussions has included examining the actual effects trust has on marketing relations and the competitive advantages it poses.

However, trust is also discussed as something that is itself to be marketed. By this I refer to various measures, both explicit and implicit, which firms undertake to arouse or develop trust in customers, clients, suppliers and/or other firms with which they deal. Thus, a firm might explicitly promote itself as trustworthy in order to attract those with whom it wishes to do business. On the other hand, a firm might offer guarantees, warranties, or liberal return policies as a way of implying to its customers that it is trustworthy.

Now it may be granted that these two topics are interrelated. It is because of the role that trust has in the various areas of business that people in marketing have pursued the marketing of trust. Nevertheless, the focus of this paper is on the marketing of trust. In particular, I am concerned with various moral conditions of, barriers to and implications for efforts to cultivate trust in others with whom one has a business relationship. This is a topic which, I believe, deserves additional attention.

MARKETING, TRUST AND MARKETING TRUST

It is not surprising that business firms have become more concerned about the trust — or distrust — which they encounter among employees, customers, other firms and the general public. Increased discussion of trust has occurred at a time when *Fortune* magazine has spoken about "The Trust Gap" that exists between employees and employers (Farnham, 1989). Talk of "lean and mean" has given rise to correspondent actions, such as downsizing and re-engineering, which have undercut the trust and loyalty of employees. Out in the community and amongst customers trust has suffered as well. Apple juice for children turns out to be sugared water. Stock accounts are turned over excessively. Car owners seeking repairs are taken for a ride when excessive repairs are done. Legal suits are filed to silence the public comments of those who protest against corporate actions. Jobs are moved out of the country. Relatives of those who have been the victims of airline or auto crashes have their deceased family members' past life stories attacked in the courtroom. It seems that trust should be placed upon some "Endangered Species" list. . . .

Trust facilitates the relationships sought, while mistrust hinders or undercuts them.

From George G. Brenkert, "Marketing Trust: Barriers and Bridges," *Business and Professional Ethics Journal,* vol. 16, nos. 1–3, pp. 77–81, 83–86, 88–98 (edited), 1997. Reprinted by permission.

Accordingly, marketers (and business more generally) have sought to develop trusting relations with their various constituencies. Sears, for example, encouraged potential customers of its financial services to "Trust Sears to Make It Work for You." The American Automobile Association urges its customers to "Travel with Someone You Trust." Even foreign firms have gotten into the act. For example, the Indian auto firm Maruti claims to be "Building Trust. Worldwide."

It is reasonable, I believe, to refer to the efforts of marketers to instill, develop, foster or bring about trust in them on the parts of their customers, clients, the public or other firms with which they deal as instances of "marketing trust." There is good reason to believe that those with whom they are dealing want to trust those with whom they do business. These firms suppose that their own objectives will be furthered by such trust. They engage in various explicit and implicit activities to fulfill these objectives, as well as those with whom they do business. Accordingly, when marketers seek to develop trusting relations with customers, firms, suppliers, clients, and/or government agencies, we may surely speak of them as "marketing trust."

Now it is striking, but not surprising, that the reasons given above for developing and fostering trusting relations are prudential in nature, i.e., they appeal to the self-interest of the firms involved. Surely this reflects the context within which such trust is sought, viz., the competitive market in which each member is, at the least, seeking self-gain or profit. . . .

In particular, does the marketing of trust lead to paradox? One reason to think that it does is that those who want someone else to trust them have some other motive or reason why they want the other person to trust them. This is because one's trust of someone else is always the trust that they do (or not do) something. Accordingly, if you want me to trust you, there must be something which you want me

to do. And, in a market setting, if that which you want me to do is linked with fulfilling your own interests, then I may well wonder how much in fulfilling your interests I am endangering my own interests. Are you willing to continue this relation if — or when — it goes against your own interests? And when might this occur? Further, if you want me to trust you, are you willing to trust me or is this to be an asymmetrical relation? How may I know that you are trustworthy within the pressures of competitive markets? However, this very questioning which I go about concerning the effect on my own interests and our potential relation would seem to suggest a lack of trust. Consequently, we need to look closely at the conditions of and barriers to marketing trust.

THE NATURE OF TRUST

Whether, how and in which ways trust might be marketed depends, of course, upon what trust is. . . .

First, trust is not necessarily a form of "mutual confidence," as some have maintained, though in relations of mutual trust this is, of course, the case. Still, when Sears, for example, asks its customers to trust them, Sears is not offering to engage in a relation of mutual confidence or reliance. Accordingly, we speak in two different ways about creating trusting relations. On the one hand, we might speak of creating a sense of trust in someone else for one's self. Here the relationship need not be reciprocal. I may have this sense of trust in other persons or institutions, even if they are not aware of my own particular existence. They need simply be aware that there are people with my kinds of vulnerabilities and expectations, and be prepared not to take advantage of us. On the other hand, we might speak of creating a trusting relationship with someone else where the trust runs both ways. Each member of the relation trusts the other member not to take advantage of his or her vulnerabilities. This is a case of mutual trust, in which the relationship is reciprocal.

Second, trust is not a short-term kind of thing. Though trust can be eliminated or destroyed in a moment, what exists for only a moment cannot be trust. Trust requires a period of time to be established for it is during this time that certain dispositions or tendencies to act in various ways towards the one to be trusted are developed. Obviously, this period of time can be longer or shorter. Accordingly, persons or firms cannot market trust in the same manner that they might market some product for which there need be no further relation with the firm. In the case of trust, firms must do various things over time to develop trust, rather than simply present a product which might be wholly evaluated on its own.

Third, trust is always relative to some action or purpose, as well as some context. I may seek to have you trust me so that: You will not feel inhibited from buying products from me; you will enter a joint venture with me to produce a particular product; or, perhaps, you will supply certain products, resources or information to me in some foreign market. As such, trust is a four-place relation: "X trusts Y to do (or not to do) Z within a context C." This implies that I might trust a person in one context, but not in another. Further, since trust is relational, one cannot be trustworthy simply by oneself but always in relation to some other individuals or agents. Accordingly, when I try to instill or bring about trust of another in me, I may address the context, the action, the person/group I want to trust me, or some feature of myself. . . .

MARKETING TRUST

The preceding account of trust not only helps display the complexity of this concept, but also has indicated some initial implications for the marketing of trust. We need now to look more directly at the moral conditions of and the barriers to efforts to market trust. I have indicated above the self-interested context in which trust has been recommended to marketers. What is involved in gaining, fostering or marketing trust in a market setting in which competition and one's self-interests urge one to exploit all advantages and control all variables in one's interactions with others? It would seem that, in such a situation, self-interest may not only provide reasons to trust, but may also pose an important barrier to trust. That is, if trust is something of value to marketers because of the sales it helps promote and the competitive advantages it creates, then some may simply see this as an occasion to realize self-interests. Consider, for example, the following statement which is indicative of the tendency to slide from trust to self-interests:

> One prominent example [of efforts in marketing to develop close relationships with buyers] is 'consultative selling,' by which the salesperson makes recommendations that are in the customer's best long-term interests, even if a competitive offer must be recommended. One of the basic arguments in support of consultative selling is that this approach helps the salesperson gain the customer's trust. Trust is not the only important factor in the customer-salesperson relationship, but it helps determine the ability of a salesperson to influence a prospect (Swan and Nolan, 1985: 39).

This passage suggests that trust is important for salespersons because it increases their ability, not so much to make recommendations in that person's best long-term interests, but to gain an influence over a prospect to purchase one's own products. But, if this is the case, then the "consultative selling" is a cover or dissimulation for what is really going on, viz., an attempt to win influence over a customer so that the salesperson's own interests can be fulfilled. However, unless this is explicitly acknowledged and agreed upon, this would seem to be a corruption of trust, rather than its realization.

Now though the reasons for marketing trust, noted in this preceding passage and at the outset of this paper, are all self-interested, it is clear that marketing trust cannot be subject simply to the conditions of individual self-interest. If marketers were simply to look to self-interest, they would fail in their efforts to engender or foster trust.

There are two reasons for this. First, market relations themselves impose various limitations on self-interest, viz., deception, fraud and coercion are incompatible with such relations. Self-interest, however, might dictate deception, fraud or coercion. It might suggest that an individual deceive other persons or firms into believing that he or she has certain characteristics so as to gain their trust, but to take advantage of their vulnerabilities. The market supposedly rules out such behaviors. Thus, the market operates on the basis of constrained self-interest.

Second, trust also imposes limitations on self-interest in that those who may be trusted are those, we have seen, who will not take advantage of the vulnerabilities of others. Now the vulnerabilities of a person or group are relative to the abilities of others to do them harm. Since the context we are addressing is one of a competitive market situation in which each member is seeking his or her own self-interests, trust requires that the fulfillment of those self-interests is not contingent upon harming those with whom one has a trusting relation. However, trust does not require that another person or agent be wholly altruistic or some kind of saint without self-interests. Trust and self-interest may conflict, but they are not wholly incompatible. The real question focuses on the level and the extent to which they may be compatible. Obviously, trust is compatible with fulfillment of those self-interests which are in accord with

not taking advantage of the vulnerabilities of those with whom one has a trusting relation. However, we can hardly assume that such self-interest is always compatible with the interests of others who trust us. . . .

Trust requires a consistency to one's behavior. Those who act erratically or who may simply act in ways contrary to their other behaviors are poor candidates for trust. Those who do act consistently develop a reputation for steadfastness which may serve to identify them as potential trustworthy agents. In general, the consistency and reputation of persons or organizations we might trust can be known prior to engaging in trusting relations with them.

However, sometimes these characteristics may not accord with a "deeper" reality concerning them. They may be more surface phenomena or more appearance than reality. To learn about the more guarded characteristics of people or organizations, it may be necessary to engage in initial trusting relations with them. Only then may one learn whether more extensive and complete forms of trust are possible. . . .

Further, trust also requires some indication that both members share certain common values or motives. This requirement ensures that the self-interests of each member of the relation are not wholly in conflict and thus liable to lead each member to impinge on the self-interests and vulnerabilities of the other. It is this point that Morgan and Hunt capture when they urge that trust may be developed when firms attend to "maintaining high standards of corporate values and allying oneself with exchange partners having similar values." Firms and individuals who fulfill this condition may more readily refrain from "taking advantage of their exchange partners" (Morgan and Hunt, 1994: 34).

Third, trustworthy agents seek to align the expectations of trustees with their own capabilities and intentions. These expectations may be out of alignment in three different directions: They may be too restrained, too exaggerated, or simply different. Expectations which are too restrained and those which are simply different create barriers to trust; those which are too exaggerated create potential dangers for continuing trust. With regard to restrained expectations, there are a number of studies which show that people generally tend to believe that others are less moral than they are. Hence, we go into many situations believing that those we deal with may not maintain the higher standards that we do. This may well translate into our viewing them as less reliable and less trustworthy. Similarly, expectations that are utterly different than one expects may also create barriers to overcome in establishing trusting relations with others. Trust, in these situations, requires some assurance that prospective trusted agents are who they claim to be and that their standards and expectations are compatible with one's own.

On the contrary, if the expectations of potential trustees are considerably out of line with the abilities and prospects of one's self, then there may be little one can do to retain their trust. Thus, if one is forced to engage in certain actions, e.g. downsizing, it may be that this will destroy any trust if the expectations of others are that this should never happen under any circumstances. Similarly, if a firm's other marketing or advertising efforts greatly trumpet one's abilities and efforts on behalf of customers that are out-of-line with one's actual abilities or efforts, the expectations of potential trustees may also be out of alignment. Trust is the likely casualty. Accordingly, trustworthy agents will seek to avoid leading trustees to have exaggerated expectations regarding the nature of the relationship. . . .

Fourth, those agents who would develop closer forms of reciprocal trust must give some indication of their preparedness to be open to the trustee, i.e. to reveal privileged aspects of one's self that are linked with one's own vulnerabilities. This may involve "communicating valuable information, including expectations, market intelligence, and evaluations of the partner's performance" (Morgan and Hunt, 1994: 34). Similarly, a firm might allow itself to be "open to outside auditing of the exchange relationship" (Barney and Hansen, 1994: 187). In short, one must make very clear and open the nature of what one wants the other to do to the fulfillment of one's own and the other's interests, as well as engage in a similar openness oneself. . . .

Fifth, the trustworthiness of firms is enhanced the greater the extent to which they have engaged in the creation of a corporate structure which fosters trust, and removes structural (or other) impediments to trust, e.g. certain kinds of bonuses and penalties that promote trust violation. Doing this helps ensure that there are no incentives within one member of the relation to violate its trust.

Finally, I have noted earlier that trust in the marketing situation involves an expectation that the trusted agent will do (or not do) certain things. Accordingly, competence is an important part of trust. Thus, if a firm seeks the trust of others, it must be able to demonstrate its competence in the area in which trust is sought. . . .

Now a tension may arise here to the extent that the trusting relation depends upon the trustee's confidence in the competence of the trusted. For example, if a trusted firm reveals certain incompetencies (which may or may not be material to the products it provides to its trustees) it may fear that the confidence (and hence the trust) of its trustees will be undercut. Thus, to maintain or to boost the confidence of its trustees, the firm embellishes on its competencies. Clearly, if the competencies are material to their relationship, the firm is engaging in trust violating behavior. . . .

MAINTAINING TRUST

With regard to maintaining trust, one must continue to act upon (or maintain) all the bases which have been mentioned above for establishing trust. Thus, one must continue to act consistently, sustain common motives, maintain appropriate competencies, and be open with trustees.

However, in addition to these conditions, several others are also relevant. For example, to maintain trust it would seem incumbent on a trusted agent to give warning if difficulties in fulfilling the above conditions begin to arise. This is, in effect, an implication of the condition noted above regarding trusted agents seeking not to raise certain unwarranted beliefs or expectations in trustees. In this instance, it is a question of not allowing previously appropriate beliefs or expectations to become inappropriate or unwarranted due to changing circumstances. . . .

Another barrier to maintaining trusting relations are conflicts of interest. It might seem that there is always a conflict of interest which is embedded in marketing situations. A firm might offer to act in ways which are in the trustee's best long-term, or basic, interests. Nevertheless, surely the firm has its own agenda which may not foster the trustee's interests. Thus, dedicated agents of a mutual fund company who can only sell their own firm's programs may not be able to fulfill their client's trusting expectations if they are that such agents will simply do the best by them that could possibly be done. Such agents can only do best by their clients within the context of their particular firm's offerings. Unless this context is made explicit, self-interested reasons of the agent and the firm may lead to conflicting interests and thereby threaten trust.

However, such preceding conflicts are not examples of conflicts of interests so much as conflicting interests. The danger of conflict-

ing interests for trusting relations lies in their not being acknowledged. That is, one or both of the members of the relation does not understand what the context is within which the trust occurs. Once they are acknowledged, adjustments may be made which preserve trust. Conflicts of interest, on the contrary, are instances in which "it is morally wrong or illegal or illegitimate *to serve both interests*" (Margolis, 1978: 362). Suppose, for example, that Sears and a supplier had a trusting relation. If, then, a major competitor sought out the supplier to do something which revealed confidences which Sears had provided to it within their trusting relation, then the supplier would have a conflict of interest if it proceeded. Such conflicts of interest are not addressed by revealing them, as in the case of conflicting interests, so much as by avoiding them. Only in this way may trusting relations be maintained.

A third concern regarding the maintaining of trust is the danger of becoming too dependent on the trusted. Trusting another agent, especially in the context of market relations, may lead to problems of dependency. This is both a practical and a moral issue. Since trust reduces the complexity of our relations by protecting us from various threats to our interests, particularly rich forms of it can also insulate us from challenge which may itself be valuable in market situations. This can occur not only to individuals but also with firms. . . .

A final set of implications for maintaining trust may be drawn out by considering the situation when trust fails, i.e. something happens which undercuts the trust of the trustee. Thus, one might look to failures of trust in cases such as Sears Auto Shop, Beech-Nut's children's apple juice or Dow Corning's breast implants. In situations such as these, maintenance of trust requires a number of responses which are widely known, though too often not acted upon. Since I cannot here provide a complete account, I would simply note the importance of the following. Individuals and/or firms must engage in an analysis of what happened, why it happened and who was responsible. They must take responsibility for what they did that led to the rupture of trust. The sooner such responsibility is taken the better. They must establish measures to prevent such actions (and similar occurrences) in the future. Involvement of trustees in this process may help the process of reaffirming or reconstituting the trusting relation. Injuries to trustees as a result of the trusted's actions require some form of compensation. In short, firms which seek to market trust had better be prepared not only for success in promoting trust, but also for occasions when that trust is breached or fails. The road back may be a long road, but inept actions can make it even longer.

DISSOLVING TRUST

There are occasions when relations involving particularly significant or rich forms of trust may require dissolution, not necessarily because such trust has been violated, but because both members of the relation can no longer, or no longer wish to, sustain the demands of trust. When it comes to the dissolution of trust, a number of other behaviors are also indicated.

First, if the dissolution is initiated by one of the members of the relation, there should be some warning and justification of one's actions for terminating the relationship. Many times the danger to an individual or firm does not come from the actions of another, but the timing of those actions. Forewarning (and justification) may remove much of the sting of the dissolution of a trusting relation.

Second, what has previously transpired ought not to be used against former trustees. If one firm's trust of another has led it to re-veal various aspects of itself which it keeps otherwise confidential, then those aspects should remain confidential after the trusting relation has ended. Thus, in terminating a trusting relationship one will not use knowledge gained in that relationship to the detriment of the trustee. Accordingly, one would not be justified in using exchanged trade secrets if a new relationship is developed with another marketer.

Third, steps should be taken to minimize harm to trustees through the dissolution. The dissolution of trusting relationships does not license one to begin taking advantage of a former trustee's vulnerabilities which had hitherto been off limits, thereby harming the trustee. Instead, it permits one to avoid taking on such commitments in the future.

Finally, all activities which seek to instill in trustees the kind or level of trust which is being dissolved should be stopped. Otherwise, contradictory messages will be given to former trustees. In short, a firm which does not want to maintain special trusting relations with another firm ought not to continue to engage in activities which encourage that other firm to maintain those special forms of trust.

CONCLUSION

The importance of trust has been increasingly recognized over the past few decades. This has given rise to efforts by business firms to develop trust in them by individual customers as well as by other business firms. These efforts may reasonably be referred to as efforts to market trust. Inasmuch as trust involves various beliefs and dispositions on the part of trustees to act in risky or uncertain situations such that they allow their vulnerabilities to be exposed to the trusted, trust cannot be marketed in the same manner as other goods.

Though trust is generally recommended to marketers and business on the basis of self-interested reasons, it is clear that trust requires the restraint or restriction of action upon self-interests. These restrictions, as well as barriers and bridges to trust, cannot be spelled out simply through various accounts of the role of self-interest. Instead, a variety of behaviors and conditions implicated in trusting require elaboration.

These behaviors are to be identified in the efforts of parties who seek to create trust, maintain trust, and dissolve trust. Their elaboration suggests further barriers and conditions for those who would market trust. Unless these features of trust are closely considered, those who seek to develop trusting relationships may, on the contrary, have the effect of creating greater mistrust regarding themselves and cynicism in those they would have trust them. Only in these ways can the paradox of marketing trust be answered.

REFERENCES

Barney, J. B., and M. H. Hansen. "Trustworthiness as a Source of Competitive Advantage." *Strategic Management Journal* 15 (1994): 175–190.

Farnham, A. "The Trust Gap." *Fortune* 120 (December 4, 1989): 56–58, 62, 68, 74, 78.

Margolis, J. "Conflict of Interest and Conflicting Interests," in Tom L. Beauchamp and Norman E. Bowie (Eds.), *Ethical Theory and Business.* Englewood Cliffs, NJ: Prentice-Hall, 1978, pp. 361–372.

Morgan, R. M., and S. D. Hunt. "The Commitment-Trust Theory of Relationship Marketing." *Journal of Marketing* 58 (July, 1994): 20–38.

Swan, J. E., and J. J. Nolan. "Gaining Customer Trust: A Conceptual Guide for the Salesperson." *Journal of Personal Selling & Sales Management* 5 (November, 1985): 39–48.

ADVERTISING

Manipulative Advertising

Tom L. Beauchamp

Lake Jewelers closed after being in business in Detroit for 36 years. Arthur Lake, president of the local Chamber of Commerce, was not as yet financially imperilled. But he said his business was gradually being ruined by his competitors' misleading advertisements. Lake cited, in particular, "phony discounting," in which retailers present fake percentage markdowns from "suggested retail prices" that are imaginary or artificially inflated. Advertisements depict prices as bargains (50 to 78 percent off), when in fact the prices are comparatively high. Lake said that customers are "duped into thinking" they receive bargains, and that "ethical" merchants find it extremely difficult to compete against such advertisements.[1]

In this paper, I assess a range of criticisms that, like this one, accuse advertisers of manipulating customers into purchases based on incorrect or inconclusive information. I am concerned exclusively with manipulations that limit free action, especially in the food and alcoholic-beverage industries and in advertising by banks, savings and loans, and brokerage houses. I begin with the rudiments of a theory of influence and manipulation, and then return to advertising.

THE CONTINUUM OF INFLUENCES

To determine whether advertising diminishes free choice, we need to examine how external influences affect free choice. The antithesis of being free is being controlled by an alien influence that deprives one of self-direction. I use terms such as "freedom" and "free to act" to refer specifically to the absence of controlling external influences or constraints.

Coercion is a frequently analyzed form of controlling influence, but coercion does not exhaust the forms of controlling influence. It lies at one end of a continuum of influence. It is at the end that eliminates freedom and entirely compromises free choice. At the other end of the continuum are forms of influence such as (rational) persuasion. Other points on the continuum include indoctrination, seduction, and the like. At one end of the continuum are completely *controlling* influences; at the other end, wholly *noncontrolling* influences in no way undermine a person's free choice.

Three broad categories or classes of influence are spread across this continuum: coercion, manipulation, and persuasion. (1) Coercive influences are always controlling influences; (2) manipulative influences are sometimes controlling influences; and (3) persuasive influences are never controlling influences. Many choices are not substantially free, although we commonly think of them as free. These include actions under powerful family and religious influences, purchases made under partial ignorance of the quality of the merchandise, and deference to an authoritative physician's judgment. Many actions fall short of ideal free action because of a lack of understanding or control by another person. But the central question is whether actions are sufficiently or adequately free, not whether they are ideally or wholly free.

FROM COERCION TO PERSUASION

I begin with definitions of coercion, manipulation, and persuasion that express their differences.

First, *coercion* occurs if one party deliberately and successfully uses force or a credible threat of unwanted, avoidable, and serious harm in order to compel a particular response from another person. No matter how attractive or overwhelming an offer, coercion is not involved unless a threatening sanction is presented. Advertisements directed at a starving population that "offer" food and medical attention in return for marketable blood constitutes a threat and not a mere offer, and so are coercive. But such circumstances are extremely rare in advertising, and thus the problem of "coercive advertising" is a contrived issue that we need not address.

Second, *persuasion* is a deliberate and successful attempt by one person to encourage another to freely accept beliefs, attitudes, values, or actions through appeals to reason. The first person offers what he or she believes to be good reasons for accepting the desired perspective. In paradigmatic cases of persuasion, these good reasons are conveyed through structured verbal facts or argument. However, good reasons can also be expressed through nonverbal communication such as visual evidence. "Rational" persuasion is sometimes distinguished from "nonrational" persuasion, but I will consider only rational persuasion. ("Nonrational" persuasion is a form of manipulation, as defined below.)

The Kellogg Co., which has been attacked for its child-oriented advertisements of presweetened, ready-to-eat cereals presents an example of self-proclaimed persuasive advertising. Executive Vice President William E. LaMothe once testified before the Senate Select Committee on Nutrition and Human Needs that Kellogg has adopted the following approach to advertising its products: "Our company is very conscious of the fact that social responsibilities go hand-in-hand with business responsibilities. The steps that we are taking to contribute to the improvement of the understanding of the need for a complete and adequate breakfast reflect this consciousness." Any company acting on the principle that advertising should "contribute to the improvement of the understanding" and using bona fide informational appeals to convince viewers to eat healthier breakfasts is employing a policy of persuasion.[2]

The essence of rational persuasion is inducing change by convincing a person through the merit of the reasons put forward.[3] However, "the merit of the reasons" is a tricky notion. Judgments about the credibility and expertise of a person who advances an argument affect our acceptance of a message no less than the premises and the soundness of the argument used. Does persuasion then occur? Acceding to an argument simply because one likes the person who presents the argument — as in Pepsi's television ads using famous entertainment stars — or finds the person physically attractive — as in typical magazine advertising for Virginia Slims — can be distinguished from accepting an argument because the person is an expert and therefore likely to be correct. The same arguments are often more persuasive if the reasons are presented by a professional rather than by an inexperienced amateur. Authori-

tative judgment often rationally persuades although fully developed persuasive arguments are not presented.

It is sometimes difficult to determine from the description of an attempt to influence whether the influence is a case of persuasion or a case of manipulation. The central question is not what is done, said, or suggested, but how or through what psychological processes the person responded to and was affected by the influence. Advertising can persuade some persons while misleading others who receive the same message. For example, an FTC staff report concerning children's television noted the following about children six years and under:

> (1) They place indiscriminate trust in televised advertising messages; (2) they do not understand the persuasive bias in television advertising; and (3) the techniques, focus and themes used in child-oriented television advertising enhance the appeal of the advertising message and the advertised product. Consequently, young children do not possess the cognitive ability to evaluate adequately child-oriented television advertising.[4]

Although children under six cannot understand the intent of a commercial message, the report argues, children over six often can. Children under six are manipulated, whereas some over six are persuaded. Many questions remain unanswered about the depth and manner of television advertising's influence on both children and adults. For example, there are questions about the effect of television advertising, about the ability of persons to process cognitively the advertising information, about the ability of various persons to discriminate between the content of the program and the commercial, and about the ability of persons to resist appeals even if they understand them to be commercial in nature.

There are also questions about what counts as a good reason, or even a reason at all. Suppose an advertiser believes that the reasons used in an ad are bad reasons, but knows that the persons at whom the advertisement is directed believe they are good reasons. Is this an attempt at persuasion by giving good reasons, or an attempt at manipulation by motivating purchases for bad reasons? Whether anyone except the consumer believes the reason to be a good reason sometimes seems irrelevant. For example, an advertiser may believe it is absurd to buy a soap because it smells good when the wrapper is opened, but if people value the soap for this reason, then the soap's attractive aroma seems to be a good reason to promote the product. Similarly, if a mother believes falsely that a tasty snack food will make her baby healthier, can this be a good reason? As the ads become more deceptive or harmful, we are more likely to abstain from calling them "good reasons." Our criteria of "good reasons" will be governed by a broader conception of legitimate and illegitimate influence.

Consumer protection groups and sometimes government officials focus on the consumers' *response* to advertising and on its human effects, rather than on the *intention* of those who create the advertising. By contrast, those who defend controversial advertising focus more on the intentions of advertising agencies and manufacturers in marketing a product — namely, on the intent to sell a "good product." These different emphases exhibit further complications, because an advertisement created with good intentions nonetheless can be misleading or nonrationally controlling.

MANIPULATION

I move now from coercion and persuasion to the central class of problematic influences. Manipulation is a broad category that includes any successful attempt to elicit a desired response from another person by noncoercively modifying choices available to that person or by nonpersuasively altering another person's perceptions of available choices. A variety of concepts explain this portion of the continuum between coercion and persuasion. Current literature mentions incentives, strong offers, indoctrination, propaganda, emotional pressure, irrational persuasion, temptation, seduction, and deception. I am using the single word *manipulation* to cover all parts of this vast territory.

The major difference between informational manipulation and persuasion is that the former involves deception used to influence a person's choice or action, whereas persuasion is not based on deception. In being influenced by information, persuasion is an attempt to get one to believe what is correct, sound, or backed by good reasons. Manipulation is an attempt to induce one to believe what is not correct, unsound, or not backed by good reasons.

We should, however, be cautious in using words like "misleading" and "deceptive," which have both subjective and objective connotations. People are often misled by their own bizarre inferences or by their lack of concentration. A presentation is not necessarily misleading because it is misunderstood or because it leads persons to believe what is false. The goal of eliminating all misleading subjective interpretation is a noble ideal but too demanding as a standard for public advertising.

MANIPULATION IN ADVERTISING

This account of manipulation and the continuum of influence applies to many forms of advertising. I shall discuss advertising for banks, foods, alcoholic beverages, and cigarettes.

Bank Advertising

Banks regularly advertise for new accounts, but some of these advertisements are manipulative, not persuasive. The advertisements I examine are all for fixed-term deposits that pay more than one rate over the term. Banks advertise a high, short-duration rate of interest in very large type, while a lower rate is noted in far smaller type, as is the fact that the lower rate is effective for a far longer term. Also relegated to the smaller print, if mentioned at all, is any statement of effective annual yield or yield over the course of the account. These advertisements are designed to convey the message to a reader that the significant rate for the thrifty-minded is the one in large type, rather than either the effective annual yield or the underlying, lower rate. The ads also often present the rates as "tax-free" or "tax-exempt," when they are only tax-deferred.

A dramatic form of this kind of advertising occurred when interest rates were higher than they presently are and the competition for Individual Retirement Account (IRA) customers was more intense than it currently is. It became apparent to banks that advertising campaigns were more effective as the rates offered were adjusted to higher levels. The higher advertised rates were purely promotional for short, introductory durations and had little or no benefit on annual yields. For example, the Riggs National Bank in Washington, DC, which advertises itself as "The Most Important Bank in the Most Important City in the World," started out advertising at 14%, but quickly saw the effects of the trends in advertising higher rates and rocketed up to 25% for a short introductory duration, after which the money was locked in at a far lower rate. Standard Federal started out with 15%, then quickly went to 17% and finally to 25% without otherwise

changing its ads. Other banks were not about to lose customers, and they followed suit.

How successfully do these ads work to influence customers to open new accounts? An official of the Riggs Bank interviewed by the *Washington Post* confirmed that the promotional rate brought in a large influx of customers from the start. After Riggs raised the promotional rate from 14% to 25%, three times as many depositors signed up for Riggs IRAs on the days the 25% rate was run than had signed up on the days the 14% rate had been run.[5]

More important than short duration at high rates is the inherent complication and confusion involved in interpreting the split rate in a context in which there are no uniform practices, standardized rates, or conventional expectations. This is not a mere problem of chaos in a shifting industry. It is beyond the powers of many readers to compute average effective annual yields over the life of the deposit, and yet this computation yields the only material information because withdrawals cannot be made from these accounts without loss of *all* interest — promotional as well as long-term. It is beyond the powers of many readers to make significant comparisons across the different banks. The split rate, the method of compounding, and the term of the deposit make for too many complicated calculations, even among those few customers who might figure out how to make the basic computations.

For example, Riggs' 25% promotional, two-month rate was accompanied by an underlying rate of 10.87% for 28 months, while Chevy Chase Savings and Loan's two-month 15% promotional rate was accompanied by an underlying rate of 11.5% for 28 months. The *undisclosed* (unadvertised) data were that Chevy Chase had an average annual effective yield of 12.39%, while for Riggs the average annual effective yield was 12.31%.

Food Advertising

Deceptive disclosure is likewise found in food labeling and marketing. In 1990–91, the FDA criticized Ragu and Procter and Gamble for its "fresh" claims on processed, packaged foods, such as pasta sauces.[6] These two cases set a precedent for government regulation for an extensive network of food labeling, which had become deceptive and often baffling. Use of words such as *fat free, cholesterol free, fresh,* and *low sugar* traded on consumer ignorance and led to a war of subtle misrepresentation.

Several problems are involved in such deceptive labeling and corresponding advertising. A consumer with high cholesterol typically buys products with labels stating "cholesterol free." However, these products often contain additional sugars or fats to maintain the flavor, creating further, often hidden or undisclosed health risks. To cite a typical example, in 1990 the FDA forced CPC International, marketer of Mazola Corn Oil, to discontinue claims that Mazola helped reduce cholesterol levels. The FDA objected to this claim because the label failed to acknowledge that the product had a high fat content.[7] Mazola is a good product that has no cholesterol; in this respect its ads were correct. However, no margarine helps reduce cholesterol levels, although some margarines present a reduced threat to health by comparison to others. All oils are 100% fat, but some have a healthier fat content than others. This was hardly the message communicated by Mazola.

A similar problem occurs in percentage labeling and advertising. An Oscar Mayer turkey product that advertised itself as "98% fat-free" measured this claim about fat content by weight, not by caloric intake. But of the 12 calories in each super-thin slice of this turkey, approximately 9 of the calories are fat. From this perspective, a critical one for those who seek to reduce the fat content in their diet, 98% fat-free is equivalent to 75% fat-caloric content.

These forms of deception mislead consumers into believing in nonexistent health benefits, or at least in misleading claims about them. But these problems are subtle difficulties by comparison to many other advertisements for food products. Health claims in labeling had progressed in late 1991, at the time of the FDA's toughest crackdown, to the point that many manufacturers had reached the conclusion that they had to place some sort of misleading health claim on their label in order to remain competitive. More than one-third of all new food products on the market in 1991 made a claim using some health-related message, without specifying what the message meant. The FDA effectively wrote a new set of standards for food labelling in order to stop this manipulation of consumers. The agency gave standardized meanings to terms such as "light," "reduced," "extra light," "low-fat," and "low in cholesterol" in a circumstance in which they were functioning more as buzzwords to attract customers than as truthful claims.[8]

This FDA decision was praised, not condemned, by leading food manufacturers, such as Kraft General Foods. The reason is that nutritious products that are truthfully labeled make for good advertising and solid sales. These products do better in the market when untruthful claims for inferior products are absent. But the other side of this fact is that manipulation of consumer belief is good for sales of inferior products as long as it goes undetected or unchallenged.

Lifestyle Advertising

A third genre of advertising, often used in cigarette and alcohol advertising, is known as lifestyle advertising. These ad campaigns do not focus on the benefits of a product, but rather on a desirable lifestyle that can be associated with the product. Ads aim either to create the association or psychologically reinforce associations that already exist. A typical example is making a link between alcohol consumption and having a good time at parties, on vacations, and the like.

Manipulation occurs whenever lifestyle advertisements successfully reinforce a certain lifestyle, often in people who cannot legally purchase the product. For example, Brown and Williamson Tobacco Corp. attempted to revitalize their Kool cigarette brand through creating the KOOL PENGUIN. This creature, with a spiked, Vanilla Ice hairdo, attractive dark glasses, and youthful personality, appeared on billboards, in magazines, and in store displays. The penguin did not directly advocate that minors smoke cigarettes, but it did reinforce youthful perceptions that smoking is cool and a bit rebellious. Company spokesperson Patrick Stone claimed that, although the KOOL PENGUIN resembles Saturday morning cartoon characters and child-hero figures, the company made no attempt to sell to minors.[9]

This interpretation is implausible. The Kool figure's appeal is strictly for the young. It invites smoking and entices a group vulnerable to such appeals. Kool's market share had fallen 4.9% just prior to its ad, which appears to have been created to cover lost ground. Because the adult market was at the time still declining, the only place to recover ground was with youths who either do not smoke or do not have a preferred brand. This strategy has long been used in the cigarette industry, and the controversy surrounding the KOOL

PENGUIN is not new. Camel cigarettes, with noticeable success in the underage market, has long used the cartoon camel figure of Joe Camel, whose coolness was expressed through a leather-jacket image. After selectively placing ads in literature read by minors, Camel's brand share among minors escalated from .5% to 32.8%.[10] The ad campaigns appeared to be especially effective in reaching children under 13. The Camel ads led to a suit in 1994–1996 in federal courts for misleading advertising that attempts to lure children (90% of all new smokers) into smoking.[11]

Alcohol advertising presents a similar form of lifestyle advertising that critics claim reinforces underage drinking. Surgeon General Antonia Novella called for all beer and wine advertisers to cease television advertising immediately on grounds of its manipulative effect and health risks. To support this request she cited major breweries' advertising campaigns targeted at audiences under the legal drinking age. The Surgeon General attacked lifestyle advertisements associating alcohol use with beauty, sex, popularity, and good times. Beach scenes, party scenes, and romantic adventures are manipulative in that they reinforce young peoples' perceptions that one needs only to consume a few beers to loosen up, fit in with the crowd, and have a good time.[12]

A similar style of advertising is found in a "fortified dessert wine," Cisco, which has a 20% alcohol content level, although its packaging is noticeably similar to a standard wine cooler — a clear glass container with a wraparound neck label. Most wine coolers have a 4–5% alcohol content. Purchasers, particularly underage drinkers, often do not realize Cisco's potency. Marketed under the slogan "Cisco takes you by surprise," it has been documented that Cisco consumption effects include "combativeness, hallucinations, disorientation, [and] loss of motor control and consciousness."[13] When combined with its "cooler style" packaging, Cisco's marketing success and potency led the Surgeon General to declare Cisco "a dangerous fortified wine, and the ultimate 'wine fooler'."[14]

AN OBJECTION IN DEFENSE OF THE ADVERTISING INDUSTRY

One objection to this analysis of manipulative advertising is that persons of normal maturity, liberty, and resistibility, do make free choices, in which case my criticism of advertising would fail. Can we not expect persons to take care of themselves when hearing an advertisement no less than when shopping in a department store with attractive displays on every counter? Advocates often defend advertising and marketing by a rules-of-the-game model: There are more or less established, well-delineated procedures or moves for marketing a product. The consumer is well acquainted with these rules of the game, and consumers are often in an equal bargaining position.

One can easily become upset about advertising directed at children, and other vulnerable parties, because the ordinary rules of the game are either suspended or violated. The unsuspecting child may be sacrificed to the greed of the toymaker or cookie manufacturer. But is not advertising, placed in a more favorable light, analogous to activities in which we all engage — for example, purchasing a house or bargaining over the price of a rug in an overpriced store?

This defense of advertising overlooks the fact that advertisers manipulate not only the weak and unwary, but persons of normal discernment and resistibility. Advertisers know the art of subtle deception and manipulation. They use attractive rates, enticing images,

and a variety of forms of suggestion to hinder reasoned choice. Advertising should enable or at least not prevent an informed choice about purchase of the product or service. It should be persuasive in presentation, not manipulative.

Rules of acceptable advertising therefore should encompass more than the mere creation of a market. If persons are misled in the attempt to make an intelligent choice or are enticed into the choice by deception, the advertising has an enormous burden of justification — no matter the target population or the implicit rules of the game.

When implicit rules of games are inadequate, as they are at the present time in advertising, external standards are needed to challenge the presuppositions that underlie the rules. If assumptions in the rules permit inessential and less nutritious products to be advertised to children and adults alike as essential or highly nutritious, and when merchants like Arthur Lake, with whom we began, are driven out of business by "competitive" advertising, we know that some assumptions about the rights of advertisers need to be defended by good reasons.

My proposal, then, is that a simple moral rule be adopted: Advertisements should be persuasive and should be judged morally inappropriate and socially unacceptable when they are manipulative.

NOTES

1. Walter B. Smith, "For Lake, Jewelry Has Lost Its Glitter," *The Detroit News* (December 9, 1982), p. 3B.
2. William E. LaMothe, "Testimony," in Part 5 — TV Advertising of Food to Children, Hearings before the Senate Select Committee on Nutrition and Human Needs, 93rd Congress, 1st Session, 1973, p. 258. By contrast, see the later

development in which the state of Texas sued Kellogg for manipulative advertising. See Jennifer Lawrence, "Texas Notches a Win over Kellogg" (regarding Heartwise Cereal), *Advertising Age* 62 (April 8, 1991), p. 6.

3. See Stanley I. Benn, "Freedom and Persuasion," *Australasian Journal of Philosophy* 45 (December 1967): 265.

4. *FTC Final Staff Report and Recommendation in the Matter of Children's Advertising*, 43 Fed. Reg. 17967, TRR No. 215–60, (1981), p. 3.

5. L. Ross, "IRA Jungle Grows More Dense as Tax Time Draws Near," *Washington Post* (March 19, 1984), Business Section, p. 34; Mary W. Walsh, "Banks' Policies on Figuring and Advertising Deposit Interest Make Picking Rates Hard," *Wall Street Journal* (October 8, 1984), Sec. 2, p. 33.

6. Laurie Freeman and Julie Liesse, "FDA Starts Getting Tough on Good Labeling," *Advertising Age* 61 (September 10, 1990), p. 87; "FDA Puts Squeeze on P&G Over Citrus Hill Labeling," *Wall Street Journal* (April 25, 1991), pp. B1, B4.

7. Steven W. Colford and Judann Dagnoli, "FDA Readies Second Strike," *Advertising Age* (May 13, 1991): 1, 46.

8. FDA, "Food Labeling Regulations: Information Sheet," November 6, 1991 (Washington: DHHS, Public Health Service). For a criticism of FDA rules, see John E. Calfee, "Worried about Your Health? FDA Isn't." *Wall Street Journal* (September 12, 1994), p. A16.

9. Paul Farhi, "Kool's Penguin Draws Health Officials' Heat," *The Washington Post* (October 23, 1991), pp. C1, C7.

10. See Chad Rubel, "Research Fuels Debate about Cigarettes, Kids," *Marketing News* 29 (July 17, 1995), p. 10.

11. Paul M. Barrett, "Supreme Court Gives Green Light to Suit Against Tobacco Concern's Cartoon Ads" (on *R. J. Reynolds Tobacco Co. v. Mangini*). *Wall Street Journal* (November 29, 1994), p. A24; Steven W. Colford, "Joe Camel Heads for Showdown in California Court." *Advertising Age* 65 (December 5, 1994), p. 16; Claude R. Martin, "Ethical Advertising Research Standards: Three Case Studies." *Journal of Advertising* 23 (September 1994): 17–29; Gary Levin, "Poll: Camel Ads Are Effective with Kids." *Advertising Age* 63 (April 27, 1992), p. 12.

12. Paul Farhi, "Novello Urges Tough Curbs on Liquor Ads." *The Washington Post* (November 5, 1991), pp. D1, D8.

13. National Council on Alcoholism and Drug Dependence, *NCADD Demands Removal of Cisco from Market*, NCADD press release, September 13, 1990.

14. Public statement of Antonia C. Novello, M.D., M.P.H., U.S. Surgeon General, Press Conference, January 9, 1991.

The Inconclusive Ethical Case
Against Manipulative Advertising

Michael J. Phillips

INTRODUCTION

Back in 1982, the *Business and Society Review* sponsored an exchange on advertising (Colloquy, 1982). The occasion was a statement by Robert Heilbroner in the June 11, 1981 *New York Review of Books:*

> If I were asked to name the deadliest subversive force within capitalism — the single greatest source of its waning morality — I would without hesitation name advertising. How else should one identify a force that debases language, drains thought, and undoes dignity? If the barrage of advertising, unchanged in its stone and texture, were devoted to some other purpose — say the exaltation of the public sector — it would be recognized in a moment for the corrosive element that it is. But as the voice of the private sector it escapes this startled notice. (p. 64)

The colloquy's business and advertising participants made several predictable responses to Heilbroner's statement. Advertising, they said, stimulates technological advance by enabling innovative firms to inform consumers about their products. By thus enhancing competition, it also helps prevent market concentration and the stagnation that frequently accompanies it. Because advertising provides the media with financial support, moreover, it helps keep them free from government control. And since people approach advertising more or less rationally, there are limits on its ability to manipulate consumers.

However, William Winpisinger, then president of the International Association of Machinists and Aerospace Workers, saw things differently.

> I am in wholehearted agreement with Professor Heilbroner's view of advertising as a corrosive element in our society. Its major function and purpose has been to feed already bloated corporate beasts. They've discovered that the only way they can keep their revenues up is by paying exorbitant sums to advertising professionals who combine art and psychology to exploit and manipulate the vast range of human fears and needs. (p. 65)

He concluded his remarks with the ritual demand that corporate influence on public policy be neutralized.

This article explores the ethical implications of Winpisinger's perception that advertisers successfully "exploit and manipulate the vast range of human fears and needs." It begins by defining its sense of the term "manipulative advertising." Then the article asserts for purposes of argument that manipulative advertising actually works. Specifically, I make two controversial assumptions about such advertising: (1) that it plays a major role in increasing the general propensity to consume, and (2) that it powerfully influences individual consumer purchase decisions. With the deck thus stacked against manipulative advertising, the article goes on to inquire whether either assumption justifies its condemnation, by considering four ethical criticisms of manipulative advertising. Ethically, I conclude, manipulative advertising is a most problematic practice. If probabilistic asser-

From Michael J. Phillips, "The Inconclusive Ethical Case Against Manipulative Advertising," *Business and Professional Ethics Journal*, vol. 13, no. 4, pp. 31–34, 46–51, 55, 59–60, 63–64 (edited), 1994. Reprinted by permission.

tions are valid in ethics, that is, the odds strongly favor the conclusion that manipulative advertising is wrong. Nevertheless, there still is room for doubt about its badness. Like the apparently easy kill that continually slips out of the hunter's sights, manipulative advertising evades the clean strike that would justify its condemnation for once and all.

WHAT IS MANIPULATIVE ADVERTISING?

Some ethical evaluations of advertising (e.g., Crisp, 1987, p. 413) use the label "persuasive advertising" to name the phenomenon discussed in this article. However, because there is such a thing as rational persuasion and because such persuasion seems unobjectionable (Benn, 1967, pp. 265–66), this usage is questionable. Thus, following Tom Beauchamp (1984), I employ the term "manipulative advertising." According to Beauchamp, manipulation occupies a position about midway along a continuum of influences ranging from coercion, at one end, to rational persuasion, at the other (pp. 3–6). He defines it as including "any deliberate attempt by a person P to elicit a response desired by P from another person Q by noncoercively altering the structure of actual choices available to Q or by nonpersuasively altering Q's perceptions of those choices" (p. 8). Virtually all of Beauchamp's examples, however, involve what lawyers call deceptive advertising. Deceptive advertising involves false or misleading assertions or omissions that cause reasonable consumers to form erroneous judgments about the nature of a product.

What, then, is manipulative advertising? As used here, the term relates mainly to the "nonpersuasively altering Q's perceptions" portion of Beauchamp's definition. Building on that language, I define "manipulative advertising" as advertising that tries to favorably alter consumers' perceptions of the advertised product by appeals to factors other than the product's physical attributes and functional performance. There is no sharp line between such advertising and advertising that is nonmanipulative; even purely informative ads are unlikely to feature unattractive people and depressing surroundings. Nor is it clear what proportion of American advertising can fairly be classed as manipulative. Suffice it to say that that proportion almost certainly is significant. As we will see, advertising's critics sometimes seem to think that all of it is manipulative.

Perhaps the most common example of manipulative advertising is a technique John Waide (1987, pp. 73–74) calls "associative advertising." Advertisers using this technique try to favorably influence consumer perceptions of a product by associating it with a non-market good (e.g., contentment, sex, vigor, power, status, friendship, or family) that the product ordinarily cannot supply on its own. By purchasing the product, their ads suggest, the consumer somehow will get the nonmarket good. Michael Schudson describes this familiar form of advertising as follows: "The ads say, typically, 'buy me and you will overcome the anxieties I have just reminded you about' or 'buy me and you will enjoy life' or 'buy me and be recognized as a successful person' or 'buy me and everything will be easier for you' or 'come spend a few dollars and share in this society of freedom, choice, novelty, and abundance'" (1986, p. 6). Through such linkages between product and nonmarket good, associative advertising seeks to increase the product's perceived value and thus to induce its purchase. Because these linkages (e.g., the connection between beer and attractive women) generally make little sense, such advertising is far removed from rational persuasion. . . .

AUTONOMY

The Autonomy-Related Objection to Manipulative Advertising

If manipulative advertising has the effects this article assumes, it apparently denies autonomy to the individuals it successfully controls. On this article's assumptions, people become consumers and make product choices precisely through "agencies and causes outside [their] control," and not through "conscious and critical evaluation" or "independent and rational reflection." To Lippke, moreover, advertising also has an "implicit content" that further suppresses autonomy. Among other things, this implicit content causes people to accept emotionalized, superficial, and oversimplified claims; desire ease and gratification rather than austerity and self-restraint; let advertisers dictate the meaning of the good life; defer to their peers; and think that consumer products are a means for acquiring life's nonmaterial goods (1990, pp. 44–47). People so constituted are unlikely to be independent, self-governing agents who subject all social pressures to an internal critique. Nor is it likely that they would have much resistance to manipulative appeals to buy particular products.

Are Consumers Autonomous on Levitt's Assumptions?

On Levitt's assumptions, however, perhaps consumers do act autonomously when they submit to manipulative advertising. If Levitt (1970) is correct: (1) manipulative advertising works much as its critics say that it works; because (2) consumers suspend disbelief in its claims and embrace its illusions; because (3) they want, need, and demand those illusions to cope with human existence; while (4) nonetheless knowing on some level that

those illusions indeed are illusions. In sum, one might say, advertising manipulates consumers because they knowingly and rationally want to be manipulated. That is, they half-consciously sacrifice their autonomy for reasons that make some sense on Levitt's assumptions about human life. In still other words, they more or less autonomously relinquish their autonomy. This might be thought inconsistent with autonomy itself, but on Levitt's bleak assumptions even a "self-directed" person who exercises "independent and rational reflection" (Lukes, 1973, p. 52) might well do the same. Unless autonomy is an inalienable right, it seems difficult to object to such a decision if Levitt's factual argument is sound.

Levitt's argument, however, appears to concern only individual purchase decisions, and not advertising's assumed ability to socialize people to accept consumerism and reject autonomy. But his argument is broad enough to explain this second process. On Levitt's assumptions, people would more or less knowingly embrace consumerism because unfiltered reality is too much to bear, and would reject autonomy in favor of Lippke's "implicit content" because autonomy offers too little payoff at too much cost. If those assumptions are accurate, moreover, people arguably have sound reasons for behaving in these ways.

Arrington's Attempt to Reconcile Manipulation and Autonomy

In the previous section, I argued that Levitt's assumptions at least are plausible. Demonstrating their truth, however, obviously would be a difficult endeavor. For this reason, at least, they are not a decisive objection to the claim that manipulative advertising undermines autonomy. Another way to attack that claim, however, is to adopt a conception of autonomy that is consistent with advertising's manipulations. Robert Arrington attempts just such a reconciliation.

Arrington begins his attempt by asking whether advertising creates desires which are not the consumer's own. His answer is: "Not necessarily, and indeed not often" (1982, p. 7). In reaching this conclusion, Arrington does not deny that advertising frequently manipulates consumers. Instead, he maintains that this manipulation is consistent with autonomous choice. . . .

How can manipulation and autonomy coexist? As I just suggested, the key to their reconciliation is a particular conception of autonomy. Although Arrington does not explicitly define the term "autonomy," he does provide a practical test for distinguishing autonomous and non-autonomous desires. He does so by utilizing a distinction between first-order and second-order desires that apparently originated with Harry Frankfurt (1989).

> To obtain a better understanding of autonomous and non-autonomous desires, let us consider some cases of a desire which a person does not *acknowledge* to be his own even though he *feels* it. The kleptomaniac has a desire to steal which in many instances he repudiates. . . . And if I were suddenly overtaken by a desire to attend an REO concert, I would immediately disown this desire. . . . These are examples of desires which one might have but with which one would not identify. They are experienced as foreign to one's character or personality. Often a person will have . . . a second-order desire . . . *not* to have another desire. In such cases, the first-order desire [the other desire] is thought of as being nonautonomous, imposed on one. When on the contrary a person has a second-order desire to maintain and fulfill a first-order desire, then the first-order desire is truly his own, autonomous, original to him. So there is in fact a distinction between desires which are the agent's own and those which are not, but this is not the same as the distinction between desires which are innate to the agent and those which are externally induced. (p. 7)

Arrington then asserts that because people generally do not disown or repudiate the products they purchase, those purchase decisions usually are autonomous. "[M]ost of the desires induced by advertising I fully accept, and hence most of these desires are autonomous. The most vivid demonstration of this is that I often return to purchase the same product over and over again, without regret or remorse" (p. 7). In fact, Arrington concludes, even purchase decisions induced by subliminally implanted advertising could be autonomous if the consumer's implanted subconscious desires are consistent with her conscious ones (p. 7).

For Arrington, then, the autonomy of one's desires and one's subsequent actions is determined by after-the-fact, second-order reflection on their congruence with one's nature, and not by their genesis inside the individual. Because it allows for external manipulation, autonomy so conceived may be inconsistent with the notions of self-direction, self-governance, and self-rule described earlier. . . .

Lippke attempts to dismiss Arrington's argument by claiming that while it may hold for particular choices consumers make (my second assumption about advertising's powers), Arrington has nothing to say about advertising's general tendency to promote a consumer consciousness (my first assumption). "If advertising induces uncritical acceptance of the consumer lifestyle as a whole, then Arrington's vindication of it with respect to the formation of particular desires or the making of particular choices *within* that lifestyle is hardly comforting" (1990, p. 39). But Arrington's conception of autonomy probably is broad enough to include the adoption of a consumer lifestyle as well as specific product decisions. Just as a person can engage in second-order reflection on her product choices, she also could ask herself whether she identifies with her consumer lifestyle.

But if people have been thoroughly socialized to accept consumerism, can second-order reflection on that fact be genuinely autonomous? Even if such people could step back and ask "Is this consumer-person really me?", would not the answer invariably be "Yes"? The same argument probably applies to individual purchase decisions. If I bought product X because its advertising successfully associated the product with my strong desires for power, status, and sexual conquest, how likely am I to reject it upon second-order reflection?

To deal with such problems, Dworkin has a second criterion for autonomy — one that Arrington's article apparently does not mention. This is the *procedural independence* of the second-order identification process. Procedural independence means that the identification "is not itself influenced in ways which make . . . [it] in some way alien to the individual" — for example, by being "influenced by others in such a fashion that we do not view it as being his own" (Dworkin, 1989, p. 61). For a person's individual purchases and her acceptance of consumerism to be autonomous, therefore, her second-order reflection on each must be uninfluenced in the sense just described. But can this be the case if advertising is as strong a force as its critics claim? On that assumption, how can our consumer be sure that her second-order reflection is sufficiently free from advertising's influence? To be certain, she may have to make a third-level identification with her second-level judgment. But for the reasons just stated, one also can doubt the genuineness of the third-level identification, which means that a fourth level of reflection is necessary. Because the same doubt can be raised about the fourth level, however, we seem to be forced into an infinite regress (e.g., Christman, 1991, pp. 7–8; Thalberg, 1989, p. 130).

To summarize, Arrington's claim that most advertising-induced purchases are au-tonomous apparently can be valid only if: (1) his conception of autonomy is sound, and (2) people actually exhibit procedural independence when they identify with their purchase decisions. Both of these assumptions are questionable. It is difficult not to suspect a conception of autonomy so capacious as to include purchases induced by subliminal advertising. On almost any notion of the self, such purchases are not self-determined at the time they occur; the most that can be said for them is that they meet the approval of some later self. Perhaps for this reason, the "received model" of autonomy has not gone unchallenged. For example, one recent competing account of the concept focuses on the conditions under which desires are formed and actions take place, rather than the actor's after-the-fact identification with a desire or an action (e.g., Christman, 1991, pp. 10–18).

As for the second assumption required by Arrington's account, it seems difficult to determine whether a person's subsequent approval of his consumerist orientation or his individual purchases was genuine, or was wholly or partially produced by the advertising that by hypothesis caused each. The question is the procedural independence of the identification process, and determining this may require an infinite series of identifications with one's previous identification. . . .

Because manipulative advertising encourages advertisers to ignore the well-being of their targets and encourages those targets to neglect the cultivation of nonmarket goods, Waide concludes that it makes us less virtuous persons and therefore is morally objectionable (1987, pp. 74–75). Many other critics of advertising make the same general point. The Heilbroner quotation that opened this article is an example. On another occasion Heilbroner called advertising "perhaps the single most value-destroying activity of a business civilization," due to the "subversive influence of the relentless effort to persuade people to change their lifeways, not out of any knowledge of, or deeply held convictions about the 'good life,' but merely to sell whatever article or service is being pandered" (1976, pp. 113–14). His main specific complaint is that by offering a constant stream of half-truths and deceptions, advertising makes "cynics of us all" (p. 114). . . .

CONCLUDING REMARKS

For all the preceding reasons, it seems that there is no completely definitive basis for condemning manipulative advertising. But this obviously is not to say that the practice is morally unproblematic. . . .

Except perhaps for hard-core utilitarians, . . . manipulative advertising is a morally dubious practice. However, this conclusion may depend heavily on a critical assumption made earlier: that manipulative advertising actually works. Specifically, I assumed that such advertising: (1) socializes people to adopt a consumerist lifestyle, and (2) strongly influences individual purchase decisions. But what happens if, by and large, each assumption is untrue? . . .

If manipulative advertising neither determines people's values nor directs their purchases, it is also hard to see how the practice denies their autonomy. On the same assumption, it likewise seems improbable that manipulative advertising significantly undermines virtues such as moderation, reasonableness, self-control, self-discipline, and self-reliance in its targets. However, because advertisers still would be trying to manipulate consumers, their honesty and benevolence would continue to be compromised by such behavior. This is especially true since by hypothesis they now would be peddling an ineffective marketing technique to the businesses they profess to serve.

REFERENCES

Arrington, R.: 1982, "Advertising and Behavior Control," *Journal of Business Ethics,* 1(1): 3–12.

Beauchamp, T.: 1984, "Manipulative Advertising," *Business and Professional Ethics Journal,* 3(3 & 4): 1–22.

Benn, S.: 1967, "Freedom and Persuasion," *The Australasian Journal of Philosophy,* 45: 259–75.

Christman, J.: 1991, "Autonomy and Personal History," *Canadian Journal of Philosophy,* 21(1): 1–24.

Colloquy: 1982, "Advertising and the Corrupting of America," *Business and Society Review,* 1(41): 64–69.

Crisp, R.: 1987, "Persuasive Advertising, Autonomy, and the Creation of Desire," *Journal of Business Ethics,* 6: 413–18.

Dworkin, G.: 1989, "The Concept of Autonomy," in Christman, J. (ed.), *The Inner Citadel: Essays on Individual Autonomy* (New York: Oxford U.P.), pp. 54–62.

Frankfurt, H.: 1989, "Freedom of the Will and the Concept of a Person," in J. Christman (ed.), *The Inner Citadel: Essays on Individual Autonomy* (New York: Oxford U.P.), pp. 63–76.

Heilbroner, R.: 1976, *Business Civilization in Decline* (New York: W. W. Norton).

Levitt, T.: 1970, "The Morality (?) of Advertising," *Harvard Business Review* (July–August): 84–92.

Lippke, R.: 1990, "Advertising and the Social Conditions of Autonomy," *Business and Professional Ethics Journal,* 8(4): 35–58.

Lukes, S.: 1973, *Individualism* (Oxford: Basil Blackwell).

Schudson, M.: 1986, *Advertising, The Uneasy Persuasion: Its Dubious Impact on American Society* (New York: Basic Books, 2nd ed.).

Thalberg, I.: 1989, "Hierarchical Analyses of Unfree Action," in Christman, J. (ed.), *The Inner Citadel: Essays on Individual Autonomy* (New York: Oxford U.P.), pp. 123–36.

Waide, J.: 1987, "The Making of Self and World in Advertising," *Journal of Business Ethics,* 6(2): 73–79.

SALES

Paternalism in the Marketplace: Should a Salesman Be His Buyer's Keeper?

James M. Ebejer
and Michael J. Morden

The moral relationship between salespersons and their customers can range from *caveat emptor* to paternalism. We propose that between these extremes is a realistic professional ethic for sales that we will refer to as "limited paternalism."

At one extreme is *caveat emptor* — "let the buyer beware." We do not claim there is anything inherently immoral about such a position, only that it is no longer appropriate in our society. Games can be played by various rules, as long as all participants know those rules. When two old horse-traders tried to strike a bargain, it was understood that the seller could be assumed to misrepresent the condition of the animal and the buyer was warned to be on his guard. Perhaps this situation was not unfair since both participants knew the rules, entered into the agreement voluntarily, and had the opportunity to examine the merchandise. However, the contemporary consumer frequently purchases goods or services which he cannot be expected to judge for himself. The workings of an insurance policy are as mysterious to us as those of a VCR. A salesperson, with her superior understanding, is in such a position to exploit our ignorance, that few of us would want to play the game if the rule of the market-place were understood to be strictly "let the buyer beware."

At the other extreme is the practice of paternalism. A standard definition of paternalism is "the interference with a person's liberty of action justified by reasons referring exclusively to the welfare, good, happiness, needs, interests, or values of the person being coerced" (Dworkin, 1971). In other words, paternalism occurs when an individual, presumably in a position of superior knowledge, makes a decision for another person to protect this other from some type of harm. Paternalism implies that the first person deprives the second of liberty of autonomy. This infraction on liberty is thought justified because, in the mind of the first person, it is "for his own good." Recently, a merchant refused to sell tropical fish to a patron because she felt he was not changing the water in his tank often enough. Although the merchant was infringing on the customer's liberty based on her superior knowledge, the interference was for his own good (and presumably the good of the fish). The merchant was being paternalistic.

Most of us expect paternalism in certain situations. If the service we are purchasing is an appendectomy, we typically allow the salesman (in this case the surgeon) a major role in deciding whether we need the service. We rely on the ethics of the profession to protect

Journal of Business Ethics 7 (1988): 337–339. © 1988 by Kluwer Academic Publishers. Reprinted by permission of Kluwer Academic Publishers.

us from the possible exploitation. The old-fashioned physician considered such paternalism part of his role, but modern medicine emphasizes the patient's informed consent. The professionals use their superior knowledge to make the medical diagnosis, but they are expected to explain treatment options available to the patient so the latter can make the moral decision. Thus even in the most paternalistic of contexts we find that professionalism justifies only a limited paternalism.

This limited paternalism, which is typically an element in professionalism, applies when an individual in a position of superior knowledge has an active duty to explain the consequences of a decision. Here the "father-like" individual does not make the decision for the other. The only liberty that is violated is the freedom to be ignorant: the consumer is protected from an uninformed decision that could be detrimental to him.

To claim that a salesperson is professionally required to inform customers fully about a product or service, to disclose fully all relevant information without hiding crucial stipulations in small print, to ascertain that they are aware of their needs and the degree to which the product or service will satisfy them, is to impose upon the salesperson the positive duty of limited paternalism. According to this standard a salesperson is, to a limited degree, "his buyer's keeper."

Consider the following example: A woman takes her car to an auto repair shop and tells the mechanic she needs a new muffler and exhaust pipes because her car makes too much noise. While examining the car, the mechanic concludes that the excessive noise occurs because there is a hole in the tail pipe. The mechanic was told to replace the exhaust pipes and the muffler. He has three options: (1) replace the exhaust pipes and the muffler as requested by the car's owner and collect (say) $90.00; (2) talk to the owner,

refuse to do as requested since all that is needed is a $20.00 tail pipe; (3) talk to the owner, explain the situation, and let her decide for herself if she really wants to spend $70.00 more than is necessary to fix the car.

When confronted with this situation, many repairmen or auto parts salespersons would choose the first option: collect as much money as possible. This is perfectly legal since the car's owner did authorize complete replacement. Some perhaps would act paternalistically by following the second option: replace the tail pipe for $20.00, but refuse to replace the longer exhaust pipe and the muffler because it is not necessary. But now he has infringed on the owner's right to decide for herself. Perhaps the owner wanted to be absolutely certain that her exhaust system was perfect and would not need work again soon. Maybe she is rich and does not mind spending the extra money. In any case, it is her car, her money, and her decision. Option number three is the best ethical choice and the standard required for professional responsibility: the mechanic has a duty to inform the owner of facts of which she might not be aware since she is not the expert. The choice should be left to the owner.

But consider a different situation: a customer in a store that specializes in stereo equipment is consulting a salesperson about the specifications, quality and prices of various amplifiers. The salesperson is considered an expert on all equipment available for sale in the show room. After some deliberation, the customer tentatively decides he would like to own a Super Max amplifier. But before making the purchase, he asks the salesperson one more question: "Is there anything else I should know about this particular model before giving you the cash?" Now, to the best of her knowledge, the salesperson has accurately communicated the advantages of the amplifier, told him the price — $400, and that this particular unit does meet his needs. However, she also knows that the same model is being sold at an appliance store across the street for only $350! Does our standard require that she tell the buyer about this possible savings? Clearly not. Although the salesperson was aware of the competitor's price, she did not withhold information that only an expert would know. Anyone could easily find out how much the amplifier sold for at the other stores. The knowledge was not part of the technical expertise that marks her as a professional and which the buyer was presumably relying upon. However, if she held back information, relevant to the decision, which a non-expert could not be expected to know, then her behavior would be unethical by our standard.

Nearly all "hard sell" techniques are unethical according to this standard. Many salespersons intentionally keep information from potential buyers. They try to sell the most expensive product a customer will buy without regard to the needs of that person. Granted, some revenue may be lost in the short term from telling customers the bad as well as the good about a product or service, but profits will increase in the long run. Once a salesperson earns a reputation for being "honest" — i.e., ethical, interested in mutual exchange to mutual advantage rather than exploitation — he will have more satisfied customers, more referrals, and, eventually, greater income from an overall increase in sales. Even where the policy might not profit the salesperson in a specific case, it is a rule which if generally followed would produce the greatest good for the greatest number. Furthermore, it treats the customer the way we ourselves would want to be treated; it is a rule we would agree to even if we didn't know whether we were going to be the salesperson or the customer; finally, it bases sales ethics on widely accepted standards of professionalism. Clearly it is consistent with our ordinary ethical assumptions.

REFERENCE

Dworkin, Gerald: 1971, "Paternalism," in *Morality and Law,* ed. Richard Wasserstrom. Belmont, CA, p. 108.

Information Disclosure in Sales

David M. Holley

The issue of information disclosure is an important topic for a number of areas of applied ethics. Discussions in medical ethics often deal with the question of how much information should be given to a patient by health care professionals. A central topic of journalistic ethics is what kind of information the public has a right to know. In business ethics, discussions of information disclosure have dealt with areas such as disclosure of health and safety risks to employees, financial information to stockholders, and product safety information to consumers.[1]

One area of business ethics which seems inadequately explored, but holds both theoretical and practical interest, is the question

Journal of Business Ethics **17**: 631–641, 1998. © 1998 Kluwer Academic Publishers. Printed in the Netherlands.

of exactly how much information a salesperson is obligated to give to a potential customer in selling a product. Unlike the field of health care in which roles such as physician or nurse are paradigms of professions which carry with them clearly recognized responsibilities to serve the best interest of the patient, a salesperson is not generally thought to have such a professional responsibility to customers. In fact it is usually expected that the activity of sales will involve a primary pursuit of the interests of the seller. While there are legal obligations to disclose certain types of information, the question of what moral responsibilities a salesperson has is open to dispute.

An attempt to resolve the matter and specify a salesperson's moral responsibilities to disclose information raises two important theoretical questions: (1) To what extent can ethical argument help to define the moral responsibilities of a social role when these are only vaguely defined in a culture? and (2) How is empirical information about common practice relevant to making normative judgments? This paper considers these issues in the context of an examination of ethical responsibilities for information disclosure in sales. . . .

MORAL GUIDELINES AND SOCIAL ROLES

Suppose we imagine the various options with regard to a salesperson's duty to disclose specific information in some situation to lie along a continuum with one end of the continuum representing a requirement for a high level of information disclosure and the other a requirement for a minimal level of information disclosure:

Low level   High level

‒ ‒ ‒ ‒ ‒ ‒ ‒ ‒ ‒ ‒ ‒ ‒ ‒ ‒ ‒ ‒ ‒ ‒

  1   2   3   4   5

If we assume that a salesperson has a responsibility to answer a customer's questions nondeceptively, we could represent various points on the continuum as rules requiring particular levels of additional disclosure such as the following:

1. *Minimal Information Rule:* The buyer is responsible for acquiring information about the product. There is no obligation to give any information the buyer does not specifically ask about.

2. *Modified Minimal Information Rule:* The only additional information the seller is obligated to give is information a buyer might need to avoid risk of injury (safety information).

3. *Fairness Rule:* In addition to safety information, a seller is responsible for giving the buyer any information needed to make a reasonable judgment about whether to purchase the product which the buyer could not reasonably be expected to know about unless informed by the seller.

4. *Mutual Benefit Rule:* In addition to safety information, the seller is responsible for giving the buyer any information needed to make a reasonable judgment about whether to purchase the product which the buyer does not possess.

5. *Maximal Information Rule:* A seller is responsible for giving the buyer any information relevant to deciding whether to purchase the product.

What considerations might move us toward one end of the continuum or the other? One approach is to take the perspective of the buyer. A person attracted by the ideal of the golden rule might ask, "What would I want the salesperson to tell me if I were purchasing the product?" . . .

Trying to get a determinate answer from a moral ideal such as the golden rule also leads to some implausible conclusions. Suppose, for example, that what I would want as a buyer in some situation is an objective analysis of the merits and disadvantages of this product in relation to competing products. Does this automatically imply that the information should be supplied in the desired form by the salesperson? To think so is to disregard the salesperson's role as an advocate of the product. A jury member may need enough information to formulate a reasonable judgment of guilt or innocence, but it would be far-fetched to conclude that this gives the defense attorney a responsibility to provide all the necessary information. To think so overlooks the attorney's role as an advocate (as well as the responsibilities of others in the legal system).

These considerations suggest that deciding how much information a salesperson should provide depends upon an understanding of the nature of the salesperson's role. While there are various types of sales, we can say in general that a salesperson is supposed to act toward achieving a particular goal: getting people to purchase a product. Describing the activity as sales probably also implies that the method of achieving this goal is some type of persuasion rather than coercion. But determining the proper limits of this persuasion calls for some conception of the context of sales activities. If, for example, we viewed selling a product as a kind of game (a metaphor which has been applied to many business activities), then supplying or withholding information might plausibly be viewed as strategies employed to win (make the sale). If the game is like poker, we could even imagine that essentially deceptive strategies (bluffing) could be an accepted part of the game.[2] Someone adopting this picture might argue that a salesperson should disclose information only when it is strategically advantageous to do so.

However, this picture of sales activities is clearly deficient. Part of the problem is that it presupposes relatively equal parties who know that they are involved in a game and what the nature and goals of this game are. Even if this is adequate as an account of some business situations, it hardly seems to apply as

a general picture of the buyer–seller relationship. Furthermore, efficient functioning of the buyer–seller relationship presupposes a higher degree of trust than game metaphors would suggest to be appropriate. Buyers must depend to some extent on information they receive from sellers, and if we imagine that the information is not reliable, we are imagining a situation which, if widespread enough, undermines the ends for which the marketplace exists.

On the other hand, the need of the buyer to depend on the seller is not as great as the need of a patient to rely on the objectivity and good judgment of a physician. In that case it seems necessary to build into the professional role a duty to seek the patient's wellbeing which limits and overrides the physician's activities as a profitseeker. The professional requirement is connected with the extreme vulnerability of patients to the pure pursuit of economic self-interest by physicians.

While buyers are generally less vulnerable than patients, there are cases where the interest involved is significant enough to call for certain limits on self-interest in the pursuit of a sale. For example, suppose that use of a product involves some danger of physical injury which the buyer is unlikely to know about. Withholding the information is in effect subjecting the buyer to a risk of physical injury which she/he does not voluntarily agree to accept. Given the importance of avoiding physical injury and the vulnerability of virtually everyone to hidden dangers, there would be a strong moral reason for modifying the minimal information rule to require that such risks be revealed. The limit here could be stated in terms of applying a general principle of non-injury to sales situations, perhaps something like, "Do not act in ways which are likely to result in injury to another person without the informed and reasonable consent (explicit or implicit) of that person." . . .

REASONABLE EXPECTATIONS AND BUYER KNOWLEDGE

The moral credentials of what I have called the fairness rule rest upon the claim that this rule assures fair treatment of all parties. I shall interpret this to mean that a system utilizing this rule gives all parties to a transaction an adequate opportunity to protect their individual interests. If information is needed but unavailable, it should be revealed; if it is needed and available, the party who needs it can seek it out.

We should notice, however that applying this rule depends upon assessing what the buyer can reasonably be expected to know. How is this assessment to be made? Is the seller to think about what buyers in general can reasonably be expected to know, or about what some subgroup of buyers of which this buyer is a member can reasonably be expected to know, or perhaps about what this individual buyer can be expected to know? Different answers to this question yield different requirements about what information needs to be disclosed.

Suppose I am selling antiques, and I am dealing with a person I know to be a collector and retailer of antiques. It seems plausible to suggest that I would be justified in assuming this person to have a certain level of knowledge about the value of antiques. Suppose it becomes evident to me that this dealer is not aware of a distinction between the item I am selling and a more valuable item with which it might be confused. Do I have an obligation to enlighten him?

According to the mutual benefit rule, the answer would be yes. If we interpret the fairness rule to be relative to the individual person, we would have to determine whether this individual buyer could be expected to know this distinction, and it is unclear how such a determination is to be made. So perhaps the most promising way of applying the fairness rule is to regard "what a person can reasonably be expected to know" as applying relative to some relevant class membership. In this case I might have obligations to reveal to someone acting as an expert only what that person could not be expected to know, even with expertise in the field. Of course, in a particular case I might have good reason for revealing more: say, for example that I have a long-term relationship with this individual which has been mutually beneficial and that she would regard my withholding information I know she does not have negatively, possibly resulting in the disruption of the relationship, but this need not imply that there is a moral obligation to reveal the information.

If we interpret the fairness rule to apply relative to group membership and if we distinguish at least between cases in which the buyer is reasonably regarded as an expert in knowledge of some area from cases in which the buyer should not be regarded as an expert, the rule provides different guidance about what should be revealed to experts as opposed to what should be revealed to non-experts. Should the class of nonexperts be subject to further division? Perhaps the general public could be divided into sophisticated consumers and unsophisticated or naive consumers. Given this distinction, the fairness rule would imply that a salesperson is obligated to reveal more when dealing with an unsophisticated consumer. The main problem with making this distinction is that it would be difficult in practice to determine the type of consumer being dealt with in a particular transaction. I might become aware that I am dealing with a particularly naive consumer, but how much effort must I expend in making such a determination?

From a practical point of view it would probably be more realistic to have some expectations of a level of information to be revealed to the general public which would result in informed and reasonable judgment in the vast majority of cases. Exactly how much information this is would depend on what level of informed judgment is high enough and what percentage of customers making such a judgment is good enough. Assuming that such a determination could be made, the fairness rule on this interpretation would require disclosure of information sufficient for a reasonable judgment by a high percentage of customers falling in the relevant class.

But what if in the course of a sales transaction it becomes evident that a particular buyer has not been given enough information to judge reasonably (e.g., because this buyer is more uninformed or naive than might be expected of the average buyer)? Or what if the buyer is using misinformation which the seller did not cause but could correct? If the fairness rule is to be interpreted to require that information be supplied in such cases, then it is functionally equivalent to the mutual benefit rule in these cases. This would probably be distasteful to most advocates of the fairness rule, since the whole point of a rule less stringent than the mutual benefit rule is to place some responsibility for acquiring information on the buyer rather than the seller. To build in a requirement that misinformation or ignorance must be corrected seems to defeat much of the purpose of the rule.

If the seller could distinguish between those buyers who could have acquired the relevant information with an appropriate level of effort and those who could not because of unavoidable deficiencies or circumstantial difficulties, it would be possible to make allowances for the latter class, but not the former. But except in obvious cases, such a distinction would often be difficult to make. So a decision to act in accordance with the fairness rule probably means deciding to withhold information both from the culpably irresponsible as well as many of the unavoidably ignorant.

VULNERABILITY AND DEPENDENCE

It is relatively easy to think of some cases in which withholding information seems unconscionable. The financial advisor who sells to an elderly widow with very limited resources a risky investment without making the risk clear surely exemplifies substandard ethics. The failure to disclose in such a case takes advantage of one who is in a vulnerable position. Whatever we might say about exchanges in which both parties have adequate opportunity to protect their interests, we must still take into account that some individuals may be relatively defenseless, either permanently or temporarily. A disclosure rule which allows such people to be exploited when their vulnerability is apparent would fail one of the most basic of ethical tests. So if the fairness rule is to be ethically defensible, some restrictions must be built in to limit the pursuit of self-interest at the expense of those who might be persuaded to act in ways which are clearly contrary to their interests.

Some writers have raised the general question of whether a salesperson needs to behave paternalistically.[3] This way of putting the question can be misleading, since paternalistic action involves overriding or limiting another's choice or ability to choose. While a salesperson may occasionally have such a responsibility when dealing with individuals who are incompetent or behaving in clearly irrational ways, there is ordinarily no obligation to refuse to sell a legitimate product because the purchase is judged not to be in the buyer's interest. However, the question of how hard to push a sale when it appears to diverge from a customer's interest can arise fairly often. It is all very well to say that the customer is the one who should decide what is in his/her interest, but if the salesperson is strategically withholding information crucial to making such a judgment, this defense seems hollow.

Consider the case of a person of very limited education, intelligence, and sophistication who lives on a small social security income and needs roof repairs. A salesperson recommends and makes the case for a total reroofing with the finest materials available, a choice which will mean using up a small savings account and acquiring a significant debt. The salesperson makes no attempt to explore cheaper alternatives, and the customer is not sufficiently astute to inquire about them. What seems to make nondisclosure objectionable in this case is the customer's limited capacity to protect his own interests. He relies on the salesperson to provide not only information but a kind of guidance. To follow a policy or revealing only as much as an average customer would need in effect deprives this very vulnerable customer of what he needs to know, but is unable to learn without help.

Examples involving extremely vulnerable consumers suggest that even if the fairness rule were a sufficient guide to disclosure in some cases, there are situations in which the relationship between salesperson and customer involves such an imbalance of power that the customer is not adequately protected. In such cases the buyer is dependent on the seller for information, and failure to provide crucial information becomes more like a betrayal of trust than an admirable competitive move.

While cases involving extremely vulnerable individuals furnish the clearest illustrations of the limits of the fairness rule, we can see problems with this rule even in transactions involving more skillful buyers. Suppose Simon wants to buy a rocker-recliner. Because he has children who have been rough on furniture, Simon tells a salesperson that he is especially concerned about finding a piece that can endure their abuse. Simon notices that a particular manufacturer has advertised a "lifetime warranty" on its chairs. He assumes that this means that anything which goes wrong with the chair is covered. The salesperson knows that the lifetime warranty does not include the kind of damage children are likely to inflict on the chair, but does not mention this, nor does she mention that a cheaper chair of a lesser-known manufacturer with a more limited warranty is actually more likely to provide the kind of durability this customer seeks.

What is apparent from this kind of example is that ordinary customers often interpret the salesperson's role to be not merely an advocate for a particular product, but a kind of consultant who can be relied upon to help the customer satisfy particular needs. Withholding information of relevance to attaining such satisfaction would often be a refusal to accept a role the customer is expecting to be performed.

While we can imagine the marketplace working without salespeople functioning as consultants, the complexity of the modern marketplace often makes it practically necessary, even if not absolutely necessary, to rely on sellers to provide information which could have been attained with enough effort, but is not likely to be possessed by the average consumer because of a variety of limitations, including limitations of time. As a result the salesperson comes to be relied upon to provide the customer with enough infomation to enable him or her to satisfy particular needs.

This kind of dependence of customer on salesperson is avoidable only with great difficulty. It is a dependence brought about by complexities involved in navigating the marketplace under social conditions such as ours. The vulnerabilities brought about by such practical necessities create a need for building into the salesperson's role some degree of responsibility for providing information needed by the customer to judge how to satisfy his or her needs and desires.

Hence, the fairness rule is inadequate as a general account of what a salesperson is obligated to disclose. While there may be certain limited contexts in which such a rule can function, they would primarily involve individuals with significant expertise in a particular area and an implicit willingness to protect their own interests. Under such conditions it might be permissible to disregard the interests of the buyer, but we should not be misled into thinking of these as paradigmatic of the buyer-seller relationship generally.

THE MUTUAL BENEFIT RULE

How far is a salesperson obligated to go in serving the customer's interests through information disclosure? The strongest kind of obligation which could be advocated would claim that a salesperson must seek to produce optimal benefit for the customer. Such a requirement would mean that a salesperson might often have to direct a customer to buy merchandise from a competitor offering superior or equal quality for a lower price. In effect it could virtually deny the salesperson's role as an advocate for her own company's products.

The maximal information rule calls upon the salesperson to provide any information relevant to deciding whether to purchase a product. Presumably this would include objective comparisons of the strengths and weaknesses of various alternatives. It would place on the salesperson the responsibility for supplying customers with the sort of analysis we expect from a *Consumer Reports* product test. While we can imagine such a requirement, it is difficult to see how it could work without undermining the competitive structure of the market.

What seems to be needed is a rule which could still allow the salesperson to function as a product advocate but limit that advocacy in ways conducive to fulfillment of the customer's needs. The mutual benefit rule requires the salesperson to disclose enough information to allow the customer to make a reasonable judgment about whether to purchase the product. How strict a requirement this is depends on how we interpret "reasonable." We need not interpret this term to designate an optimal choice. In most cases there are a range of products and purchases that could satisfy a particular customer's needs. Given varieties of product features, some may be better in some respects and worse in others, but equally satisfactory. Furthermore, there are many equally reasonable ways of evaluating how much money a particular product feature is worth or how much time and effort should be expended in shopping. It can be entirely reasonable to patronize a store with knowledgeable and reliable salespeople even if that occasionally means paying a higher price for comparable merchandise.

Thus, we could loosely interpret the mutual benefit rule to require that the salesperson provide enough information for a customer to make a judgment which is satisfactory, given his or her particular needs, desires, and budget. This need not imply a requirement to make extensive inquiries about the particular customer's situation (though some products such as life insurance or financial investments or home purchases might make such knowledge necessary). In most cases a salesperson could make general assumptions based on what most customers in the market for this kind of product are concerned about. As distinctive concerns or needs become apparent, however, this standard would require them to be taken into account. Hence, for example, in the rocker-recliner case described earlier, the customer's concern about damage children might cause is relevant to what information this customer needs.

The distinction between the mutual benefit rule and the maximal information rule is that the latter requires disclosure of all infomation relevant to a purchase decision while the former requires disclosure only of enough information for a reasonable judgment. Suppose we compare the two with regard to disclosure of price information. All relevant information would probably include clear cost comparisons to products with similar features sold by competitors. But given the above interpretation of "reasonable," the mutual benefit rule would allow disclosure of the price of a product without comparative information as long as the price is not so much out of line that the purchase could not be judged competitive. Requiring that comparative information about price be furnished only when the price is clearly uncompetitive is probably equivalent to a requirement to price one's products competitively, something most merchants would say the market generally requires them to do anyway.

The mutual benefit rule, even with the permissive interpretation I have given it, builds in some protection of customer vulnerabilities. The spirit of this rule of information disclosure would mean a salesperson should not knowingly encourage choices which would be against the interests of someone in the customer's position. Notice that is not the same as saying that the salesperson should always promote the choice he or she would have made in the customer's position. The salesperson is free under this rule, as I have interpreted it, to advocate a range of reasonable choices.

Such a rule would require the disclosure of defects which might significantly diminish the value of the product. Unlike the fairness rule, this requirement would apply regardless of whether the defects could be discovered with a reasonable amount of effort. It would not, however, require disclosure of all details which might be regarded as negative unless they clearly bear on a purchaser's central concerns. Hence, one selling a house ordinarily need not disclose that the next-door neighbors are obnoxious, but would be required to disclose that the city planned to construct a major freeway a hundred yards away or that the foundation has a crack which will soon need repair.

With a relatively loose interpretation of what counts as a reasonable judgment, the mutual benefit rule comes closest to satisfying the important ethical and practical concerns. Hence, there is good reason to regard this rule as our primary norm for information disclosure in sales This conclusion is consistent with the possibility of recognizing specialized contexts in which buyers need fewer protections. So, for example, we might regard the fairness rule as adequate for situations in which buyers are representing themselves as professionals in the relevant field.

CONCLUSION

I have attempted to use ethical argument to render more precise the extent of a salesperson's obligation to disclose information to a customer. The argument takes into account features of the contemporary marketplace which call for locating the disclosure requirement somewhere in the neighborhood of a permissively interpreted mutual benefit rule. Even if my argument is correct, it does not establish precisely what information needs to be revealed in every case since the concept of "reasonableness" used in interpreting the mutual benefit rule can be highly elastic. Nevertheless, it does furnish a guideline for ruling out some clearly unethical conduct as well as some conduct which some people's moral intuitions would allow.

NOTES

1. E.g., Faden, R. and Tom Beauchamp: 1992, "The Right to Risk Information and the Right to Refuse Workplace Hazards," in Tom

Beauchamp and Norman Bowie (eds.), *Ethical Theory and Business,* 4th ed. (Prentice-Hall, Englewood Cliffs, NJ). Frederick, Robert and Michael Hoffman: 1990, "The Individual Investor in Securities Markets: An Ethical Analysis," *Journal of Business Ethics* **9,** 579–589. Stern, Louis: 1967, "Consumer Protection via Increased Information," *Journal of Marketing* **31,** 48–52. DeGeorge, Richard: 1995: *Business Ethics,* 4th ed. "Corporate Disclosure" (Prentice-Hall, Englewood Cliffs, NJ), pp. 284–293.

2. Carr, Albert: 1968, "Is Business Bluffing Ethical?", *Harvard Business Review* **46,** 143–153.

3. Ebejer, James and Michael Morden: 1988, "Paternalism in the Marketplace: Should a Salesman Be His Buyer's Keeper?", *Journal of Business Ethics* **7,** 337–339. Walters, Kerry: 1989, "Limited Paternalism and the Pontius Pilate Plight," *Journal of Business Ethics* **8,** 955–962. Brockway, George: 1993, "Limited Paternalism and the Salesperson: A Reconsideration," *Journal of Business Ethics* **12,** 275–279.

BLUFFING

Is Business Bluffing Ethical?

Albert Z. Carr

A respected businessman with whom I discussed the theme of this article remarked with some heat, "You mean to say you're going to encourage men to bluff? Why, bluffing is nothing more than a form of lying! You're advising them to lie!"

I agreed that the basis of private morality is a respect for truth and that the closer a businessman comes to the truth, the more he deserves respect. At the same time, I suggested that most bluffing in business might be regarded simply as game strategy — much like bluffing in poker, which does not reflect on the morality of the bluffer.

I quoted Henry Taylor, the British statesman who pointed out that "falsehood ceases to be falsehood when it is understood on all sides that the truth is not expected to be spoken" — an exact description of bluffing in poker, diplomacy, and business. I cited the analogy of

the criminal court, where the criminal is not expected to tell the truth when he pleads "not guilty." Everyone from the judge down takes it for granted that the job the of the defendant's attorney is to get his client off, not to reveal the truth; and this is considered ethical practice. I mentioned Representative Omar Burleson, the Democrat from Texas, who was quoted as saying, in regard to the ethics of Congress, "Ethics is a barrel of worms"[1] — a pungent summing up of the problem of deciding who is ethical in politics.

I reminded my friend that millions of businessmen feel constrained every day to say *yes* to their bosses when they secretly believe *no* and that this is generally accepted as permissible strategy when the alternative might be the loss of a job. The essential point, I said, is that the ethics of business are game ethics, different from the ethics of religion.

He remained unconvinced. Referring to the company of which he is president, he declared: "Maybe that's good enough for some businessmen, but I can tell you that we pride ourselves on our ethics. In 30 years not one customer has ever questioned my word or asked to check our figures. We're loyal to our customers and fair to our suppliers. I regard my handshake on a deal as a contract. I've never entered into price-fixing schemes with my competitors. I've never allowed my salesmen to spread injurious rumors about other companies. Our union contract is the best in our industry. And, if I do say so myself, our ethical standards are of the highest!"

He really was saying, without realizing it, that he was living up to the ethical standards of the business game — which are a far cry from those of private life. Like a gentlemanly poker player, he did not play in cahoots with others at the table, try to smear their reputations, or hold back chips he owed them.

But this same fine man, at that very time, was allowing one of his products to be advertised in a way that made it sound a great deal better than it actually was. Another item in his product line was notorious among dealers for its "built-in obsolescence." He was holding back from the market a much-improved product because he did not want to interfere with sales of the inferior item it would have replaced. He had joined with certain of his competitors in hiring a lobbyist to push a state legislature, by methods that he preferred not to know too much about, into amending a bill then being enacted.

In his view these things had nothing to do with ethics; they were merely normal business practice. He himself undoubtedly avoided outright falsehoods — never lied in so many words. But the entire organization that he ruled was deeply involved in numerous strategies of deception.

PRESSURE TO DECEIVE

Most executives from time to time are almost compelled, in the interests of their companies or themselves, to practice some form of deception when negotiating with customers, dealers, labor unions, government officials, or even other departments of their companies. By conscious misstatements, concealment of pertinent facts, or exaggeration — in short, by bluffing — they seek to persuade others to agree with them. I think it is fair to say that if the individual executive refuses to bluff from time to time — if he feels obligated to tell the truth, the whole truth, and nothing but the truth — he is ignoring opportunities permitted under the rules and is at a heavy disadvantage in his business dealings.

But here and there a businessman is unable to reconcile himself to the bluff in which he plays a part. His conscience, perhaps spurred by religious idealism, troubles him. He feels guilty; he may develop an ulcer or a nervous tic. Before any executive can make profitable use of the strategy of the bluff, he needs to make sure that in bluffing he will not lose self-respect or become emotionally disturbed. If he is to reconcile personal integrity and high standards of honesty with the practical requirements of business, he must feel that his bluffs are ethically justified. The justification rests on the fact that business, as practiced by individuals as well as by corporations, has the impersonal character of a game — a game that demands both special strategy and an understanding of its special ethics.

The game is played at all levels of corporate life, from the highest to the lowest. At the very instant that a man decides to enter business, he may be forced into a game situation, as is shown by the recent experience of a Cornell honor graduate who applied for a job with a large company. This applicant was given a psychological test which included the statement, "Of the following magazines, check any that you have read either regularly or from time to time, and double-check those which interest you most. *Reader's Digest, Time, Fortune, Saturday Evening Post, The New Republic, Life, Look, Ramparts, Newsweek, Business Week, U.S. News & World Report, The Nation, Playboy, Esquire, Harper's, Sports Illustrated.*"

His tastes in reading were broad, and at one time or another he had read almost all of these magazines. He was a subscriber to *The New Republic,* an enthusiast for *Ramparts,* and an avid student of the pictures in *Playboy.* He was not sure whether his interest in *Playboy* would be held against him, but he had a shrewd suspicion that if he confessed to an interest in *Ramparts* and *The New Republic,* he would be thought a liberal, a radical, or at least an intellectual, and his chances of getting the job, which he needed, would greatly diminish. He therefore checked five of the more conservative magazines. Apparently it was a sound decision, for he got the job.

He had made a game player's decision, consistent with business ethics.

A similar case is that of a magazine space salesman who, owing to a merger, suddenly found himself out of a job:

> This man was 58, and, in spite of a good record, his chance of getting a job elsewhere in a business where youth is favored in hiring practice was not good. He was a vigorous, healthy man, and only a considerable amount of gray in his hair suggested his age. Before beginning his job search he touched up his hair with a black dye to confine the gray to his temples. He knew that the truth about his age might well come out in time, but he calculated that he could deal with that situation when it arose. He and his wife decided that he could easily pass for 45, and he so stated his age on his résumé.

This was a lie: yet within the accepted rules of the business game, no moral culpability attaches to it.

THE POKER ANALOGY

We can learn a good deal about the nature of business by comparing it with poker. While both have a large element of chance, in the long run the winner is the man who plays with steady skill. In both games ultimate victory requires intimate knowledge of the rules, insight into the psychology of the other players, a bold front, a considerable amount of self-discipline, and the ability to respond swiftly and effectively to opportunities provided by chance.

No one expects poker to be played on the ethical principles preached in churches. In poker it is right and proper to bluff a friend out of the rewards of being dealt a good hand. A player feels no more than a slight twinge of sympathy, if that, when — with nothing better than a single ace in his hand — he strips a heavy loser, who holds a pair, of the rest of his chips. It was up to the other fellow to protect himself. In the words of an excellent poker player, former President Harry Truman, "If you can't stand the heat, stay out of the kitchen." If one shows mercy to a loser in poker, it is a personal gesture, divorced from the rules of the game.

Poker has its special ethics, and here I am not referring to rules against cheating. The man who keeps an ace up his sleeve or who marks the cards is more than unethical; he is a crook, and can be punished as such — kicked out of the game or, in the Old West, shot.

In contrast to the cheat, the unethical poker player is one who, while abiding by the letter of the rules, finds ways to put the other players at an unfair disadvantage. Perhaps he unnerves them with loud talk. Or he tries to get them drunk. Or he plays in cahoots with someone else at the table. Ethical poker players frown on such tactics.

Poker's own brand of ethics is different from the ethical ideals of civilized human relationships. The game calls for distrust of the other fellow. It ignores the claim of friendship. Cunning deception and concealment of one's strength and intentions, not kindness and openheartedness, are vital in poker. No one thinks any the worse of poker on that account. And no one should think any the worse of the game of business because its standards of right and wrong differ from the prevailing traditions of morality in our society. . . .

"WE DON'T MAKE THE LAWS"

Wherever we turn in business, we can perceive the sharp distinction between its ethical standards and those of the churches. Newspapers abound with sensational stories growing out of this distinction:

> We read one day that Senator Philip A. Hart of Michigan has attacked food processors for deceptive packaging of numerous products.[2]
> The next day there is a Congressional to-do over Ralph Nader's book, *Unsafe At Any Speed,* which demonstrates that automobile companies for years have neglected the safety of car-owning families.[3]
> Then another Senator, Lee Metcalf of Montana, and journalist Vic Reinemer show in their book, *Overcharge,* the methods by which utility companies elude regulating government bodies to extract unduly large payments from users of electricity.[4]

These are merely dramatic instances of a prevailing condition; there is hardly a major industry at which a similar attack could not be aimed. Critics of business regard such behavior as unethical, but the companies concerned know that they are merely playing the business game.

Among the most respected of our business institutions are the insurance companies. A group of insurance executives meeting re-

cently in New England was startled when their guest speaker, social critic Daniel Patrick Moynihan, roundly berated them for "unethical" practices. They had been guilty, Moynihan alleged, of using outdated actuarial tables to obtain unfairly high premiums. They habitually delayed the hearings of lawsuits against them in order to tire out the plaintiffs and win cheap settlements. In their employment policies they use ingenious devices to discriminate against certain minority groups.[5]

It was difficult for the audience to deny the validity of these charges. But these men were business game players. Their reaction to Moynihan's attack was much the same as that of the automobile manufacturers to Nader, of the utilities to Senator Metcalf, and of the food processors to Senator Hart. If the laws governing their businesses change, or if public opinion becomes clamorous, they will make the necessary adjustments. But morally they have in their view done nothing wrong. As long as they comply with the letter of the law, they are within their rights to operate their businesses as they see fit.

The small business is in the same position as the great corporation in this respect. For example:

> In 1967 a key manufacturer was accused of providing master keys for automobiles to mail-order customers, although it was obvious that some of the purchasers might be automobile thieves. His defense was plain and straightforward. If there was nothing in the law to prevent him from selling his keys to anyone who ordered them, it was not up to him to inquire as to his customers' motives. Why was it any worse, he insisted, for him to sell car keys by mail, than for mail-order houses to sell guns that might be used for murder? Until the law was changed, the key manufacturer could regard himself as being just as ethical as any other businessman by the rules of the business game.[6]

Violations of the ethical ideals of society are common in business, but they are not necessarily violations of business principles. Each year the Federal Trade Commission orders hundreds of companies, many of them of the first magnitude, to "cease and desist" from practices which, judged by ordinary standards, are of questionable morality but which are stoutly defended by the companies concerned.

In one case, a firm manufacturing a well-known mouthwash was accused of using a cheap form of alcohol possibly deleterious to health. The company's chief executive, after testifying in Washington, made this comment privately:

> "We broke no law. We're in a highly competitive industry. If we're going to stay in business, we have to look for profit wherever the law permits. We don't make the laws. We obey them. Then why do we have to put up with this 'holier than thou' talk about ethics? It's sheer hypocrisy. We're not in business to promote ethics. Look at the cigarette companies, for God's sake! If the ethics aren't embodied in the laws by the men who made them, you can't expect businessmen to fill the lack. Why, a sudden submission to Christian ethics by businessmen would bring about the greatest economic upheaval in history!" It may be noted that the government failed to prove its case against him.

CAST ILLUSIONS ASIDE

Talk about ethics by businessmen is often a thin decorative coating over the hard realities of the game. . . .

The illusion that business can afford to be guided by ethics as conceived in private life is often fostered by speeches and articles containing such phrases as, "It pays to be ethical," or, "Sound ethics is good business." Actually, this is not an ethical position at all; it is a self-serving calculation in disguise. The speaker is really saying that in the long run a company can make more money if it does not antagonize competitors, suppliers, employees, and customers by squeezing them too hard. He is saying that oversharp policies reduce ultimate gains. That is true, but it has nothing to do with ethics. The underlying attitude is much like that in the familiar story of the shopkeeper who finds an extra $20 bill in the cash register, debates with himself the ethical problem — should he tell his partner? — and finally decides to share the money because the gesture will give him an edge over the s.o.b. the next time they quarrel.

I think it is fair to sum up the prevailing attitude of businessmen on ethics as follows:

We live in what is probably the most competitive of the world's civilized societies. Our customs encourage a high degree of aggression in the individual's striving for success. Business is our main area of competition, and it has been ritualized into a game of strategy. The basic rules of the game have been set by the government, which attempts to detect and punish business frauds. But as long as a company does not transgress the rules of the game set by law, it has the legal right to shape its strategy without reference to anything but its profits. If it takes a long-term view of its profits, it will preserve amicable relations, so far as possible, with those with whom it deals. A wise businessman will not seek advantage to the point where he generates dangerous hostility among employees, competitors, customers, government, or the public at large. But decisions in this area are, in the final test, decisions of strategy, not of ethics.

. . . If a man plans to make a seat in the business game, he owes it to himself to master the principles by which the game is played, including its special ethical outlook. He can then hardly fail to recognize that an occasional bluff may well be justified in terms of the game's ethics and warranted in terms of economic necessity. Once he clears his mind on this point, he is in a good position to match his strategy against that of the other players. He can then determine objectively whether a bluff in a given situation has a good chance of succeeding and can decide when and how to bluff, without a feeling of ethical transgression.

To be a winner, a man must play to win. This does not mean that he must be ruthless, cruel, harsh, or treacherous. On the contrary, the better his reputation for integrity, honesty, and decency, the better his chances of victory will be in the long run. But from time to time every businessman, like every poker player, is offered a choice between certain loss or bluffing within the legal rules of the game. If he is not resigned to losing, if he wants to rise in his company and industry, then in such a crisis he will bluff — and bluff hard. . . .

In the last third of the twentieth century even children are aware that if a man has become prosperous in business, he has sometimes departed from the strict truth in order to overcome obstacles or has practiced the more subtle deceptions of the half-truth or the misleading omission. Whatever the form of the bluff, it is an integral part of the game, and the executive who does not master its techniques is not likely to accumulate much money or power.

NOTES

1. *The New York Times*, March 9, 1967.
2. *The New York Times*, November 21, 1966.
3. New York, Grossman Publishers, Inc., 1965.
4. New York, David McKay Company, Inc., 1967.
5. *The New York Times*, January 17, 1967.
6. Cited by Ralph Nader in "Business Crime," *The New Republic*, July 1, 1967, p. 7.

Second Thoughts About Bluffing

Thomas Carson

INTRODUCTION

In the United States it is common, perhaps even a matter of course, for people to misstate their bargaining positions during business negotiations. I have in mind the following kinds of cases, all of which involve deliberate false statements about one's bargaining position, intentions, or preferences in a negotiation: 1) I am selling a house and tell a prospective buyer that $90,000 is absolutely the lowest price that I will accept, when I know that I would be willing to accept as little as $80,000 for the house. 2) A union negotiator says that $13.00 an hour is the very lowest wage that his union is willing to consider when, in fact, he has been authorized by the union to accept a wage as low as $12.00 an hour. 3) I tell a prospective buyer that I am in no hurry to sell my house when, in fact, I am desperate to sell it within a few days.[1] Such statements would seem to constitute lies — they are deliberate false statements made with the intent to deceive others about the nature of one's own bargaining position. 1) and 2) clearly constitute lies according to standard dictionary definitions of lying. The *Oxford English Dictionary* defines the word "lie" as follows: "a false statement made with the intent to deceive." Also see *Webster's International Dictionary of the English Language* (1929), "to utter a falsehood with the intent to deceive."

The cases described above should be contrasted with instances of bluffing which do not involve making false statements. An ex-

© 1993. *Business Ethics Quarterly*, Volume 3, Issue 4.

ample of the latter case would be saying "I want more" in response to an offer which I am willing to accept rather than not reach an agreement at all. This paper will focus on cases of bluffing which involve deliberate false statements about one's bargaining position or one's "settlement preferences."

I will defend the following two theses:

a. Appearances to the contrary, this kind of bluffing typically does not constitute lying. (I will argue that standard dictionary definitions of lying are untenable and defend an alternative definition hinted at, but never clearly formulated, by W. D. Ross. On my definition, deliberate false statements about one's negotiating position usually do not constitute lies *in this society.*)

b. It is usually permissible to misstate one's bargaining position or settlement preferences when one has good reason to think that one's negotiating partner is doing the same and it is usually impermissible to misstate one's negotiating position if one does not have good reason to think that the other party is misstating her position (preferences).

There are significant puzzles and uncertainties involved in applying my definition of lying to cases of misstating one's bargaining position. Because of this, I intend to make my argument for b) independent of my argument for a). My arguments for b) are compatible with (but do not presuppose) the view that misstating one's position is lying and that lying is *prima facie* wrong. I will conclude the paper with a brief examination of other related deceptive stratagems in negotiations.

THE ECONOMIC SIGNIFICANCE OF BLUFFING

In a business negotiation there is typically a range of possible agreements that each party would be willing to accept rather than reach no agreement at all. For instance, I might be willing to sell my home for as little as $80,000. (I would prefer to sell the house for $80,000 *today*, rather than continue to try to sell the house.) My range of acceptable agreements extends upward without limit — I would be willing to accept any price in excess of $80,000 rather than fail to make the sale today. Suppose that a prospective buyer is willing to spend as much as $85,000 for the house. (She prefers to buy the house for $85,000 today rather than not buy it at all today.) The buyer's range of acceptable agreements presumably extends downward without limit — she would be willing to purchase the house for any price below $85,000. In this case the two bargaining positions overlap and an agreement is possible (today). Unless there is some overlap between the minimum bargaining positions of the two parties, no agreement is possible. For example, if the seller's lowest acceptable price is $80,000 and the buyer's highest acceptable price is $70,000 no sale will be possible unless at least one of the parties alters her position.

If there is an overlap between the bargaining positions of the negotiators, then the actual outcome will depend on the negotiations. Consider again our example of the negotiation over the sale of the house. The owner is willing to sell the house for as little as $80,000 and the prospective buyer is willing to pay as much as $85,000. Whether the house sells for $80,000, $85,000, somewhere between $80,000 and $85,000, or even whether it sells at will be determined by the negotiations. In this case, it would be very advantageous for either party to know the other person's minimum acceptable position and disadvantageous for either to reveal her position to the other. For example, if the buyer knows that the lowest price that the seller is willing to accept is $80,000, she can drive him towards the limit of his range of acceptable offers. She knows that he will accept an offer of $80,000 rather than have her break off the negotiations. In negotiations both buyer and seller will ordinarily have reason to keep their own bargaining positions and intentions secret.

It can sometimes be to one's advantage to mislead others about one's own minimum bargaining position. In the present case, it would be to the seller's advantage to cause the buyer to think that $85,000 is the lowest price that he (the seller) will accept. For in this case the buyer would offer $85,000 for the house — the best possible agreement from the seller's point of view. (It would also be easy to imagine cases in which it would be to the buyer's advantage to mislead the seller about her bargaining position.) There are various ways in which the seller might attempt to bluff the buyer in order to mislead her about his position. 1) He might set a very high "asking price," for example, $100,000. 2) He might initially refuse an offer and threaten to cut off the negotiations unless a higher offer is made while at the same time being prepared to accept the offer before the other person breaks off the negotiations. (I have in mind something like the following. The prospective buyer offers $80,000 and the seller replies: "I want more than that. I'm not happy with $80,000. Why don't you think about it and give me a call tomorrow.") 3. He might misrepresent his own bargaining position.

The kind of deception involved in 1) and 2) does not (or need not) involve lying or making false statements. 3) involves a deliberate false statement intended to deceive the other party and thus constitutes lying according to the standard definition of lying.

Attempting to mislead the other person about one's bargaining position can backfire and prevent a negotiation from reaching a mutually acceptable settlement which both parties would have preferred to no agreement at all. For example, suppose that the seller tells the buyer that he won't accept anything less than $95,000 for the house. If the buyer believes him she will break off the negotiations, since, by hypothesis, she is not willing to pay $95,000 for the house. Unless he knows the other person's bargaining position, a person who misrepresents his own position risks losing the opportunity to reach an acceptable agreement. By misstating one's position one also risks angering the other party and thereby causing him to modify his position or even break off the negotiations. (Truthful statements about one's own position might be perceived as lies and thus also risk alienating one's counterpart.)

THE CONCEPT OF LYING

A New Definition of Lying

. . . My definition of lying is inspired by Ross's claim that the duty not to lie is a special case of the duty to keep promises. Ross holds that (at least in ordinary contexts) we make an implicit promise to be truthful when we use language to communicate with others. To lie is to break an implicit promise to be truthful.[2]

Ross's view that making a statement (ordinarily) involves making an implicit promise that what one says is true suggests the following provisional definition of "lying" (Ross himself never attempts to define "lying"):

> A lie is a false statement which the "speaker" does not believe to be true made in a context in which the speaker warrants the truth of what he says.

This definition handles the earlier counter-example. Not only is the implicit warranty of truthfulness in force in the case of the witness's testimony in court, the witness explicitly warrants the truth of what he says by swearing an oath. Another virtue of the present analysis is that it makes sense of the common view that lying involves a violation of trust. To lie, on my view, is to invite trust and encourage others to believe what one says by warranting the truth of what one says and at the same time to betray that trust by making false statements which one does not believe to be true. . . .

Lying and Bluffing

What are the implications of my analysis of lying for the issue of bluffing? Negotiations between experienced and "hardened" negotiators in our society (e.g, horse traders and realtors) are akin to a game of "Risk." It is understood that any statements one makes about one's role or intentions as a player during a game of "Risk" are not warranted to be true. In negotiations between hardened and cynical negotiators statements about one's intentions or settlement preferences are not warranted to be true. But it would be too strong to hold that nothing that one says in negotiations is warranted to be true. Convention dictates that other kinds of statements concerning the transaction being contemplated, e.g., statements to the effect that one has another offer, are warranted as true. So, for example, on my view, it would be a lie if I (the seller) were to falsely claim that someone else has offered me $85,000 for my house.

I am strongly inclined to believe that statements about one's minimum negotiating position are not warranted to be true in negotiations between "hardened negotiators" who recognize each other as such. I cannot here propose general criteria for determining when one may be said to warrant the truth of what one says. Therefore, what follows is somewhat conjectural. A cynical negotiator typically does not expect (predict) that her counterpart will speak truthfully about his minimum negotiating position. This alone is not enough to remove the implicit warranty of truth. A pathological liar who denies his

every misdeed warrants the truth of what he says, even if those he addresses do not *expect* (predict) that what he says is true. The crucial feature of a negotiation which distinguishes it from the foregoing case is that in ordinary negotiations each party *consents* to renouncing the ordinary warranty of truth. There are various ways in which people consent to removing the default warranty of truth. Business negotiations are ritualized activities to which certain unstated rules and expectations (both in the sense of predictions and demands) apply. It is not expected that one will speak truthfully about one's negotiating position. Those who understand this and who enter into negotiations with other parties who are known to share this understanding implicitly consent to the rules and expectations of the negotiating ritual. In so doing, they consent to remove the warranty of truth for statements about one's minimum negotiating position. . . .

Before moving on to other issues, I would again like to stress the following two points: 1) my application of my definition of lying to this case is tentative and conjectural, and 2) my arguments concerning the moral status of bluffing do not depend on the assumption that misstating one's bargaining position or intentions is (typically) not a case of lying (my arguments are compatible with the view that misstating one's position or intentions is lying).

THE MORAL STATUS OF BLUFFING (PRELIMINARY CONSIDERATIONS)

Carr's Defense of Bluffing

In a well-known paper Albert Carr argues that misstating one's negotiating position is morally permissible.[3] Business, he argues, is a game like poker — a game in which special norms apply. The moral norms appropriate to the game of business or a game of poker are different from those appropriate to ordinary contexts.

> No one expects poker to be played on the ethical principles preached in churches. In poker it is right and proper to bluff a friend out of the rewards of being dealt a good hand. . . . Poker's own brand of ethics is different from the ethical ideals of civilized human relationships. The game calls for distrust of the other fellow. It ignores the claim of friendship. Cunning, deception, and concealment of one's strength and intentions, not kindness and openheartedness, are vital in poker. No one thinks any the worse of poker on that account. And no one should think any the worse of business because its standards of right and wrong differ from the prevailing traditions of morality in our society. . . . [4]

Carr claims that just as bluffing is permissible according to the special rules of poker, so it is permissible according to the rules of business.

What are the rules of the business game? How can we determine whether or not a particular rule or practice is part of the business game? Carr's position is confused on this point. At a number of points he suggests that the "rules of the business game" are simply our society's conventional moral standards for business, i.e., those standards which are thought by most people to govern the conduct of businesspeople. Carr defends a number of questionable business practices and argues that they are all morally justifiable, *because* they are standard practice and are regarded as permissible by conventional morality.

> In his view these things had nothing to do with ethics; they were merely normal business practice.[5]
> This was a lie; yet within the accepted rules of the business game, no moral culpability attaches to it.[6]

In other passages Carr seems to assume that the appropriate rules for business are those set by the law.

If the laws governing their business change, or if public opinion becomes clamorous, they will make the necessary adjustments. But morally they have in their view done nothing wrong. As long as they comply with the letter of the law, they are within their rights to operate their businesses as they see fit.[7]

There are three possible ways to interpret the principle to which Carr appeals in trying to justify bluffing and other questionable business practices.

a. Any action or practice engaged in by businesspeople in a given society is morally permissible provided that it is consistent with the ethical rules or principles which are generally accepted in that society.

b. Any action or practice engaged in by businesspeople in a given society is morally permissible provided that it is consistent with the laws of that society.

c. Any action or practice engaged in by businesspeople in a given society is morally permissible provided that it is consistent with *both* i) the society's conventional ethical rules or principles governing those actions and practices, *and* ii) the laws of that society.

On any of these readings, Carr's argument is most implausible. One can't justify an act or practice *simply because* it is consistent with conventional morality. Similarly, the fact that an action or practice is permitted by the law does not suffice to establish its moral permissibility. Conventional morality and the law are not infallible moral guidelines. In the past, many immoral practices, most notably slavery, were condoned by the conventional morality and legal codes of our own and many other societies. . . .

VARIATIONS ON THE EXAMPLE

1) Is *lying worse than mere deception*? Consider the following case. Suppose that I want the other party to hold false beliefs about my

minimum bargaining position. I want him to think that $90,000 is the lowest price that I'm willing to accept for my house when, in fact, I'm willing to sell it for as little as $80,000. However, I am very much averse to lying about this and I believe that misstating my own position would be a lie. I am willing to try to deceive or mislead him about my intentions, but I am not willing to lie about them. Here, as in many cases, it is possible to think of true but equally misleading things to say so as to avoid lying. Suppose that our lowest acceptable selling price is $80,000, but I want you to think that it is actually around $85,000. Instead of lying, I could say "my wife told me to tell you that $85,000 is absolutely the lowest price that we are willing to accept." The trick here would be to have my wife utter the words "tell the buyer that $85,000 is absolutely the lowest price that we will accept." In saying this she would not be stating our minimum position, but rather helping to create the ruse to fool the buyer. It is very doubtful that this is morally preferable to lying. Intuitively, it strikes me as worse. Many people (perhaps most) seem to believe that making true but deceptive statements is preferable to lying. This is demonstrated by the fact that many (most?) of us will, on occasion, go through verbal contortions or give very careful thought to exactly what we say in order to mislead others without lying. In this kind of case lying does not seem to be morally preferable to "mere deception."

Consider another example in which the difference between lying and mere deception does not seem to be morally significant. Suppose that two parents go out of town for the weekend leaving their two adolescent children home alone. The parents give their son strict orders that under no circumstances is he permitted to entertain his girlfriend in the house while they are away. The parents call during the weekend to "check up" on the children. They speak with their daughter.

"What's going on there? What is your brother up to? He doesn't have Nora [his girlfriend] there does he?" The son is entertaining Nora in the house at the time that they call. The daughter does not want to get her brother in trouble, but, on the other hand, she doesn't want to lie. She does not answer the last question directly, but replies with the following true, but misleading, statement. "He's fine; he's watching the ball game with Bob." (Bob is a male friend who *is* there but is about to leave.)

2) *Claiming to have another offer.* On my view, the fact that misstating one's position is a very common practice can often help justify misstating one's own position. Because misstating one's bargaining position is such a widespread practice in our society, one is often justified in assuming that one's negotiating partner is misrepresenting her position. If the other person states a minimum bargaining position, then one is justified in thinking that she is misrepresenting that position, in the absence of reasons for thinking that she is not.

There are other ways of deceiving others about one's bargaining position which are not common practice. The following two cases are among the kinds that I have in mind here:

Case #1. I (the seller) say to a prospective buyer "I have another offer for $80,000, but I'll let you have it if you can beat the offer" when, in fact, I don't have another offer.

Case #2. I (the seller) want you to think that I have another offer. I have my brother come over and in your presence pretend to offer me $80,000 for the condo. (You don't know that he is my brother.) I say to my brother "the other person was here first. I'll have to let him/her see if he/she wants to meet the offer." I turn to the seller and say "It's yours for $80,000."

What I say in the first case is clearly a lie. It is a deliberate false statement which is warranted to be true and is intended to deceive others. My action in this case is *prima facie* very wrong. I am putting extreme pressure on the other person and may panic her into a rash decision. Falsely claiming to have another offer could, in principle, be justified by appeal to SD [the principle of self-defense]. If the buyer was falsely representing the possibility of another comparable deal, then a Rossian theory might conceivably justify me in doing the same. This is very unlikely in the ordinary course of things. This means that it is unlikely that one could defend lying in such a case by appeal to the need to defend one's own interests. My actions in case #2 seem intuitively even worse than those in #1. Case #2 does not involve lying but it does involve an elaborate scheme of deception and is potentially very harmful to the buyer. The same general things that I said about case #1 apply here. My actions in this case are *prima*

facie very wrong. In principle, a Rossian theory could justify those actions, but that is very unlikely. . . .

NOTES

1. This example is taken from "Shrewd Bargaining on the Moral Frontier: Towards a Theory of Morality in Practice," J. Gregory Dees and Peter C. Crampton, *Business Ethics Quarterly*, 1 (2) (April 1991): 143.
2. W. D. Ross, *The Right and the Good* (Oxford, 1930), p. 21.
3. Albert Carr, "Is Business Bluffing Ethical?" in *Ethical Issues in Business*, third edition, Thomas Donaldson and Patricia Werhane, eds. (Englewood Cliffs, NJ: Prentice Hall, 1988).
4. Carr, pp. 72–73; see also pp. 69 and 70.
5. Carr, p. 70.
6. Carr, p. 72.
7. Carr, p. 73; also see p. 75.

LEGAL PERSPECTIVES

Irving A. Backman v. Polaroid Corporation

United States Court of Appeals (First Circuit)

This is a class action brought by Irving A. Backman on behalf of himself and all other persons who purchased shares of stock of defendant Polaroid Corporation on the open market between January 11 and February 22, 1979, allegedly misled by defendant's conduct that violated Section 10(b) of the Securities Exchange Act of 1934 and Rule 10b-5 of the regulations promulgated thereunder. Suit was filed in June 1979. . . . The improprieties asserted, both in

the complaint and in plaintiffs' opening to the jury, as responsible for plaintiffs' purchasing shares before a substantial drop in the market, were defendant's failure to disclose unfavorable facts about its new product, Polavision, an instant movie camera. Following trial on liability, the jury found for plaintiffs. . . . On appeal, a divided panel . . . granted a new trial. On this rehearing en banc we reverse and order judgment for defendant. . . .

910 F. 2d 10 (1st Cir. 1990).

In their amended complaint plaintiffs alleged that defendant failed to disclose that Polavision, introduced in the spring, had been unprofitable throughout 1978, and would continue so, significantly, at least through 1979; that it had been excessively inventoried and had suffered lagging sales; that little, if any, information had been made public; that defendant knew that this undisclosed information was material to investors, and that major investment research firms had publicly projected defendant's earnings based on assumptions defendant knew were contrary to the true facts, all of which nondisclosure was in violation of the securities laws.

Secondly, plaintiffs re-alleged the above, and added that over the years defendant had advertised that it was a growth company, and that, through its successes, the investment community had come to consider it the best of the growth companies, and that its failing to make the above disclosures operated as a fraud and deceit on the investing public, was a "fraud on the market," and constituted an unlawful manipulation thereof. . . .

However, mere market interest is no basis for imposing liability. We said [in a former case] the materiality of the information claimed not to have been disclosed . . . is not enough to make out a sustainable claim of securities fraud. Even if information is material, there is no liability under Rule 10b-5 unless there is a duty to disclose it.

A duty to disclose "does not arise from the mere possession of non-public information." . . .

In a twelve day trial [the plaintiffs] precisely followed their opening, alleging, simply, nondisclosure of material information. As summarized in their final argument,

> Polaroid . . . violated the federal securities laws which require full disclosure so that people who purchase and sell securities do so on a fair playing field; that people have the same information and people can make their investment decisions based on having all of the information and having truthful information. . . . [Y]ou have to find that Polaroid had adverse information, that information was material — i.e., that it was important — and that Polaroid knowingly and deliberately withheld it. *And that's all we're asking you to do here.* (Emphasis supplied.)

The summation was not an inadvertence, but was in accord with plaintiffs's own testimony.

Q. Now, Mr. Backman, in this action you are not claiming, are you, that the financial information put out by Polaroid was in any way false and misleading, are you?
A. I think you'll have to refer to the complaint. I believe the failure to disclose is just as improper as providing false information. And I believe the essence of my suit deals with the failure to disclose. . . . I do claim it was false and misleading because the failure to disclose is just as misleading a (sic) improper disclosure.

This, of course, is not so, "Silence, absent a duty to disclose, is not misleading under Rule 10b-5." . . .

We have gone into this at length, not so much to show the emptiness of plaintiff's first claim — agreed to by the full panel — but to accent our finding that there had been no falsity or misleading by defendant in any respect. In eight years of preparation and twelve days of trial, the words misrepresentation and misleading never crossed plaintiffs' lips. . . .

It appeared that Dr. Edwin H. Land, the founder and at all times president or C.E.O. of Polaroid, had added to his invention of the world-famous instant still camera another exceptional invention — an instant movie camera, Polavision. It appeared throughout the case, however, that Polavision's sales appeal did not correspond with the quality of the invention. Launched in early 1978 with great fanfare, the estimates for fall, to which production had been geared, proved to be substantially excessive. As a result, in late October, Eumig, the Austrian manufacturer, having earlier been told to increase production, was instructed to reduce by 20,000. In mid-November Eumig was told to take out another 90,000 sets, and to halt production. Plaintiffs' panel brief, quoting the fortuitous language of Eumig's cable acknowledgment, "to now finally stop production entirely," gives the impression that the halt was intended to be permanent. Conveniently, from plaintiffs' standpoint, dots in the quotation replace the subsequent sentence, "Steps have been taken to ensure a quick new start-up of production on a reduced scale." This omission aids plaintiffs in their recitation, the regrettable incorrectness of which we will come to, that "management knew that Polavision was a commercial failure." Thereafter, fourth quarter internal figures, not publicly released, confirmed that the original Polavision estimates (also not released) had been substantially excessive.

The next event was a newspaper release published on January 9, 1979, that Rowland Foundation, a charitable trust established by Dr. and Mrs. Land, was to sell 300,000 shares of Polaroid, in part for funds for a new project, and in part to diversify its portfolio. Defendant participated in the preparation of the release, but not in the action itself. It is not claimed that the release was in any way untrue. Plaintiffs' claim is misleading because additional information should then have been given the public. The sale was consummated on January 11. . . .

On February 22, 1979, immediately following the annual meeting, defendant announced further facts about Polavision's lack of success, and the market fell, shortly, by some 20%. . . .

Plaintiffs' brief now finds assisted misrepresentation because "Polaroid featured Polavision on the cover," plaintiffs point out that

after President McCune "announced record worldwide sales and earnings for both the third quarter and the first nine months of 1978, . . . Mr. McCune noted that the Company's worldwide manufacturing facilities continue to operate at close to maximum capacity," whereas, in fact, Polavision's contract supplier, Eumig, was told, shortly before the report, to hold up on 20,000 units. We note, first, that the statement, taken as a whole, was true; it expressly recognized an absence of totality. Of more specific importance, it flagged, on three of its three and half pages of text, that Polavision's effect on earnings was negative. . . . With this emphasized three times, we ask did this report mislead investors to buy stock because Polavision was doing so well?

Plaintiffs quote *Roeder*, 814 F.2d at 26, that even a voluntary disclosure of information that a reasonable investor would consider material must be "complete and accurate." This, however, does not mean that by revealing one fact about a product, one must reveal all others, that, too, would be interesting, market-wise, but means only such others, if any, that are needed so that what was revealed would not be "so incomplete as to mislead." . . . Disclosing that Polavision was being sold below cost was not misleading by reason of not saying how much below. Nor was it misleading not to report the number of sales, or that they were below expectations. . . .

We come, next, to the January 9 Rowland Foundation sale release. There was nothing untrue or misleading in the release itself, but plaintiffs say, with support from the panel opinion, that it should have contained additional information in order to keep the November report from being misleading. . . .

Obviously, if a disclosure is in fact misleading when made, and the speaker thereafter learns of this, there is a duty to correct it. . . . In special circumstances, a statement, correct at the time, may have a forward intent and connotation upon which parties may be expected to rely. If this is a clear meaning, and there is a change, correction, more exactly, further disclosure, may be called for. . . . Fear that statements of historical fact might be claimed to fall within it, could inhibit disclosures altogether. And what is the limit? In the present case if the shoe were on the other foot, and defendant could have, and had, announced continued Polavision profits, for how long would it have been under a duty of disclosure if the tide turned? Plaintiffs' contention that it would be a jury question is scarcely reassuring. . . .

After indicating reluctance to accept plaintiffs' contention that the Third Quarter Report was misleading when made, the panel opinion, in holding that it could be found misleading in light of later developments, said as follows.

> [E]ven if the optimistic Third Quarter Report was not misleading at the time of its issuance, there is sufficient evidence to support a jury's determination that the report's relatively brief mention of Polavision difficulties *became* misleading in light of the subsequent information acquired by Polaroid indicating the seriousness of Polavision's problems. This subsequent information included . . . Polaroid's decision to . . . stop Polavision production by its Austrian manufacturer, Eumig, *and its instruction to its Austrian supplier to keep this production cutback secret*. We feel that a reasonable jury could conclude that this subsequent information rendered the Third Quarter Report's brief mention of Polavision expenses misleading, triggering a duty to disclose on the part of Polaroid. (Emphasis in orig.)

At the time of the Rowland sale, while selling the stock had absolutely nothing to do with Polaroid's financial health. . . . some might find it less than forthcoming for the press release not to have at least mentioned Polavision's difficulties so that the investing public could assess for themselves the reasons behind the sale.

That this was an improper mix was made conspicuous by plaintiffs' oral argument.

> [W]e've cited the specific passages of Mr. Mc-Cune's testimony in our brief, where Mr. Mc-Cune testified that the expression, "continued to reflect substantial expenses" was intended to convey that that condition would continue in the future. . . . What we're saying is that a jury could find that this statement, even if it wasn't misleading when issued, became misleading because of the forward-looking nature.

This is a failure to recognize that what Mr. McCune said was a single, simple, statement, that substantial expenses had made Polavision's earnings negative. Though the panel opinion characterized it as "relatively brief," it was precisely correct, initially. Even if forward-looking, it remained precisely correct thereafter. . . . In arguing that the statement did not "remain true," plaintiffs' brief, unabashedly, points solely to matters outside the scope of the initial disclosure, in no way making it incorrect or misleading, originally, or later.

The shell in plaintiffs' gun at trial . . . are all percussion cap and no powder. . . . Plaintiffs have no case.

Coca-Cola Company v. Tropicana Products, Inc.

United States Court of Appeals for the Second Circuit

A proverb current even in the days of ancient Rome was "seeing is believing." Today, a great deal of what people see flashes before them on their TV sets. This case involves a 30-second television commercial with simultaneous audio and video components. We have no doubt that the byword of Rome is as valid now as it was then. And, if seeing something on TV has a tendency to persuade a viewer to believe, how much greater is the impact on a viewer's credulity when he both sees and hears a message at the same time?

In mid-February of 1982 defendant Tropicana Products, Inc. (Tropicana) began airing a new television commercial for its Premium Pack orange juice. The commercial shows the renowned American Olympic athlete Bruce Jenner squeezing an orange while saying "It's pure, pasteurized juice as it comes from the orange," and then shows Jenner pouring the fresh-squeezed juice into a Tropicana carton while the audio states "It's the only leading brand not made with concentrate and water."

Soon after the advertisement began running, plaintiff Coca-Cola Company (Coke, Coca-Cola), maker of Minute Maid orange juice, brought suit in the United States District Court for the Southern District of New York, 538 F. Supp. 1091, against Tropicana for false advertising in violation of section 43(a) of the Lanham Act. The statute provides that anyone who uses a false description or representation in connection with goods placed in commerce "shall be liable to a civil action by [anyone]. . . . Who believes that he is or is likely to be damaged by the use of. . . . such false description or representation." 15 U.S.C. § 1125(a) (1976). Coke claimed the commercial is false because it incorrectly rep-

resents that Premium Pack contains unprocessed, fresh-squeezed juice when in fact the juice is pasteurized (heated to about 200 degrees Fahrenheit) and sometimes frozen prior to packaging. The court below denied plaintiff's motion for a preliminary injunction to enjoin further broadcast of the advertisement pending the outcome of this litigation. In our view preliminary injunctive relief is appropriate.

Perhaps the most difficult element to demonstrate when seeking an injunction against false advertising is the likelihood that one will suffer irreparable harm if the injunction does not issue. It is virtually impossible to prove that so much of one's sales will be lost or that one's goodwill will be damaged as a direct result of a competitor's advertisement. Too many market variables enter into the advertising-sales equation. Because of these impediments, a Lanham Act plaintiff who can prove actual lost sales may obtain an injunction even if most of his sales decline is attributable to factors other than a competitor's false advertising. In fact, he need not even point to an actual loss or diversion of sales.

The Lanham Act plaintiff must, however, offer something more than a mere subjective belief that he is likely to be injured as a result of the false advertising, Id. at 189; he must submit proof which provides a reasonable basis for that belief. The likelihood of injury and causation will not be presumed, but must be demonstrated in some manner.

Two recent decisions of this Court have examined the type of proof necessary to satisfy this requirement. Relying on the fact that the products involved were in head-to-head competition, the Court in both cases directed the issuance of a preliminary injunction under the Lanham Act. Vidal Sassoon, 661 F.2d at 227; Johnson & Johnson, 631 F.2d at 189-91. In both decisions the Court reasoned that sales of the plaintiffs' products would probably be harmed if the competing products' advertising tended to mislead consumers in the manner alleged. Market studies were used as evidence that some consumers were in fact misled by the advertising in issue. Thus, the market studies supplied the causative link between the advertising and the plaintiffs' potential lost sales, and thereby indicated a likelihood of injury.

Applying the same reasoning to the instant case, if consumers are misled by Tropicana's commercial, Coca-Cola probably would suffer irreparable injury. Tropicana and Coca-Cola are the leading national competitors for the chilled (ready-to-serve) orange juice market. If Tropicana's advertisement misleads consumers into believing that Premium Pack is a more desirable product because it contains only fresh-squeezed, unprocessed juice, then it is likely that Coke will lose a portion of the chilled juice market and thus suffer irreparable injury.

Evidence in the record supports the conclusion that consumers are likely to be misled in this manner. A consumer reaction survey conducted by ASI Market Research, Inc. and a Burke test, measuring recall of the commercial after it was aired on television, were admitted into evidence, though neither one was considered by the district court in reference to irreparable injury. The trial court examined the ASI survey regarding the issue of likelihood of success on the merits, and found that it contained various flaws which made it difficult to determine for certain whether a large number of consumers were misled. We do not disagree with those findings. We note, moreover, that despite these flaws the district court ruled that there were

at least a small number of clearly deceived ASI interviewees. Our examination of the Burke test results leads to the same conclusion, i.e., that a not insubstantial number of consumers were clearly misled by the defendant's ad. Together these tests provide sufficient evidence of a risk of irreparable harm because they demonstrate that a significant number of consumers would be likely to be misled. The trial court should have considered these studies on the issue of irreparable injury . . .

Once the initial requisite showing of irreparable harm has been made, the party seeking a preliminary injunction must satisfy either of the two alternatives regarding the merits of his case. We find that Coca-Cola satisfies the more stringent first alternative because it is likely to succeed on the merits of its false advertising action.

Coke is entitled to relief under the Lanham Act if Tropicana has used a false description or representation in its Jenner commercial. When a merchandising statement or representation is literally or explicitly false, the court may grant relief without reference to the advertisement's impact on the buying public. When the challenged advertisement is implicitly rather than explicitly false, its tendency to violate the Lanham Act by misleading, confusing or deceiving should be tested by public reaction.

In viewing defendant's 30-second commercial at oral argument, we concluded that the trial court's finding that this ad was not facially false is an error of fact. Since the trial judge's finding on this issue was based solely on the inference it drew from reviewing documentary evidence, consisting of the commercial, we are in as good a position as it was to draw an appropriate inference. We find, therefore, that the squeezing-pouring sequence in the Jenner commercial is false on its face. The visual component of the ad makes an explicit representation that

Premium Pack is produced by squeezing oranges and pouring the freshly squeezed juice directly into the carton. This is not a true representation of how the product is prepared. Premium Pack juice is heated and sometimes frozen prior to packaging. Additionally, the simultaneous audio component of the ad states that Premium Pack is "pasteurized juice as it comes from the orange." This statement is blatantly false — pasteurized juice does not come from oranges. Pasteurization entails heating the juice to approximately 200 degrees Fahrenheit to kill certain natural enzymes and microorganisms which cause spoilage. Moreover, even if the addition of the word "pasteurized" somehow made sense and effectively qualified the visual image, Tropicana's commercial nevertheless represented that the juice is only squeezed, heated and packaged when in fact it may actually also be frozen.

Hence, Coke is likely to succeed in arguing that Tropicana's ad is false and that it is entitled to relief under the Lanham Act. The purpose of the Act is to insure truthfulness in advertising and to eliminate misrepresentations with reference to the inherent quality or characteristic of another's product. The claim that Tropicana's Premium Pack contains only fresh-squeezed, unprocessed juice is clearly a misrepresentation as to that product's inherent quality or characteristic. Since the plaintiff has satisfied the first preliminary injunction alternative, we need not decide whether the balance or hardships tips in its favor.

Because Tropicana has made a false representation in its advertising and Coke is likely to suffer irreparable harm as a result, we reverse the district court's denial of plaintiff's application and remand this case for issuance of a preliminary injunction preventing broadcast of the squeezing-pouring sequence in the Jenner commercial.

CASES

CASE 1. *Marketing Malt Liquor*

During the summer of 1991, the surgeon general of the U.S. and advocacy groups led by the Center for Science in the Public Interest (CSPI) launched a campaign to remove G. Heileman Brewing Company's malt liquor PowerMaster from store shelves. The LaCrosse, Wisconsin-based brewer had experienced a series of financial setbacks. In January 1991 the company filed for protection from creditors in a New York bankruptcy court, claiming to be "struggling under a huge debt load." (Alix Freedman, "Heileman Will Be Asked to Change Potent Brew's Name," *The Wall Street Journal,* June 20, 1991, p. B1.) In an attempt to reverse its financial decline, Heileman introduced PowerMaster with a 5.9 percent alcohol content. Most malt liquors (defined by law as beers with alcohol levels above 4 percent) have a 5.5 percent average content, as compared with the typical 3.5 percent alcohol level of standard beers.

PowerMaster came under fire from both anti-alcohol and African American activists. These groups charged that Heileman had created the name and the accompanying advertising campaign, which featured a black male model, with the intent of targeting young black men, who consume roughly one-third of all malt liquors. U.S. Surgeon

General Antonia Novello joined the Heileman critics, calling the PowerMaster marketing campaign insensitive. Citing the economic burden that a legal contest to retain the brand name would entail, the company discontinued the product. However, beer industry executives and members criticized the government's role in the controversy. One newspaper columnist cited race as the critical factor in the campaign to remove PowerMaster, noting that the "It's the power" advertising slogan used in the marketing of Pabst Brewing Co.'s Olde English 800 malt liquor had gone unchallenged. James Sanders, president of the Washington, DC-based Beer Institute, contended that the government focused on the PowerMaster label to avoid having to focus on other factors such as unemployment and poverty, the real problems that the black community confronts.

Questions

1. Would it be deceptive or manipulative advertising to call your beer "PowerMaster" and to use black male models?
2. Is it ethically insensitive for a company to target a specific market identified by race and gender?

CASE 2. *Marketing the Giant Quart*

Your company sells its products only in the state of New Wyoming, where state law does not prohibit marketing your cola in "giant quarts." A quart is a standard measure, so a giant quart is the same size as an ordinary quart. A survey conducted by your firm indicates that 40 percent of cola buyers think that a giant quart is larger than a regular quart.

Questions

1. Would it be deceptive marketing to call your bottle a giant quart?

2. Does it make any difference in the ethics of marketing as to what percentage of cola buyers think that a giant quart is larger than a regular quart?
3. Suppose a firm sold a half gallon of soda for $.99. In ads, the half-gallon size was called the giant size. The firm finds it necessary to increase the price of soda to $1.09. With the new price comes a new name — the giant economy size. Is the use of the new name deceptive?
4. Should there be a standard according to product for large, extra large, giant, and family sizes? Why?

CASE 3. *Advertising Joe Camel*

According to the Centers for Disease Control and Prevention in Atlanta, the cigarette industry is currently losing a half-million customers a year in the United States to lung-cancer and smoking-related deaths. The percentage of adults who smoke has also dropped dramatically. As a result of this declining market, cigarette manufacturers need customers in alternative population segments. They currently favor advertisements that depict an optimum lifestyle, suggesting one could enjoy that lifestyle when smoking certain cigarettes.

Statistics show that almost 50 percent of smokers begin by the age of 15. A few tobacco companies have been criticized for crossing the fine line between general advertising and advertising directed at children. Although companies insist that advertising themes such as the animated "Joe Camel" and his female counterpart "Josephine Camel," introduced in 1994, do nothing more than promote the product to users, these advertisements have been severely criticized. The California Supreme Court in San Francisco decided in 1994 to hear the case brought by a California woman against RJR's "Joe Camel" campaign. The court upheld the lawsuit because "the allegations against R. J. Reynolds were based not on smoking and health, but on a 'more general' duty imposed under state law 'not to engage in unfair competition by advertising illegal conduct,' namely, smoking by minors." (Paul Barrett, "Supreme Court Gives Green Light to Suit Against Tobacco Concern's Cartoon Ads," *The Wall Street Journal,* November 29, 1994, p. A24.)

Opposition to cigarette advertising is not confined to the American market. As of Octo-

ber 1, 1991, all cigarette advertising on television was banned throughout Europe. In addition, each European country began some form of prohibition. For example, the United Kingdom began to require tobacco advertisers to place one of six warning labels on cigarette packages including one that reads "smoking kills." In France, tobacco ads must devote 20 percent of the space to warning labels.

Questions

1. Is there an ethical issue about advertising in this case, or is the only real objection that smoking cigarettes is harmful to health?
2. Should cigarette advertising using the media be banned altogether?
3. Does it make any moral difference whether the advertising a U.S. company does is at home or abroad?

CASE 4. *Green Advertising*

In an environmental study, 83 percent of respondents said they prefer buying environmentally safe products, and 37 percent claimed they would pay up to 15 percent more for environmentally safe packaging. These findings present the marketer with a tangible incentive. The practice of so-called green promotion and advertising is an attempt to use corporate publicity to create a message of corporate initiative in creating a healthier, improved natural environment. In a typical example, Japan's Kirin Beer launched its "Earth Beer" to be marketed worldwide with a picture of the earth on a

green label. Promotionally, Kirin claimed that the product was "earth friendly." However, this beer was not produced or packaged differently from Kirin's original products or the products of other beer manufacturers. Kirin has not been the only company to try to fill the consumer's desire for environmentally friendly products. In 1988 only 2.8 percent of all new products touted an environmental advantage, but this number jumped to 13.0 percent in 1993 and 10.5 percent in 1994.

The rise of green promotion poses this question: Are companies taking action to improve the environment, or is it purely

This case was prepared by Katy Cancro and revised by Jeff Greene, using articles in *Advertising Age* in May, June, and September 1991, a Reuters report in *The Washington Post,* August 28, 1991, and *The Journal of Advertising* Summer 1995, special issue.

publicity? Friends of the Earth President Brent Blackwelder claims that, in many cases, green advertising is not warranted by the conduct of the corporation. For example, he claims that DuPont is not a conscientious protector of the environment, although it uses green advertising. Blackwelder contends that "it's morally reprehensible to portray this type of image [in advertising] when they have this type of track record."

The background of his position on DuPont is as follows. In September 1991, DuPont launched a television ad campaign featuring barking sea lions, jumping dolphins, and other animals enjoying fresh, unpolluted seas. The ad strongly implied that Dupont was making major changes to protect the environment. A Friends of the Earth report, by contrast, claimed that DuPont had the highest ratio of pollution to profit (14 percent) and that the company paid nearly $1 million monthly from 1989 to June 1991 in fines for environmental infractions. The report also noted that after the devastating 1990 Exxon tanker accident, DuPont's oil-marketing subsidiary promoted its plans to build two new double-hulled tankers to prevent oil spills as a unique environmental strategy. However, since one out of every six crude oil tankers was already double hulled, DuPont's "change" was not a new initiative.

In response to these claims, DuPont issued a public statement that said, "It seems to be a rehash of several of DuPont's most serious environmental challenges — all of which we are working diligently to resolve." DuPont also noted that it had begun working on several new projects to benefit the environment. For example, DuPont had begun developing a chemical to reduce ozone-depleting fluorocarbons and had initiated a buyback of fluorocarbon-producing products in an effort to preserve the ozone layer.

The Federal Trade Commission held public hearings in the summer of 1991 to investigate claims of deceptive green advertising. The following year, in July 1992, the commission issued *Guides for the Use of Environmental Marketing Claims*. The publication attempted to prevent some of the bogus claims that companies were making about their products and to assist the consumer in identifying products that really are making a difference in improving the environment.

Questions

1. Is environmental advertising sometimes no more than a new form of *deceptive* advertising? What makes it deceptive, if it is?
2. Does green advertising damage the consumer, or is it a harmless method of developing the reputation of the corporation?
3. To what extent should companies be held responsible for demonstrating a track record of environmental preservation that corresponds to its green advertising?
4. Should green advertising be federally regulated?

CASE 5.   *Food Labels and Artful Sales*

Packaged foods in supermarkets contain a list of the ingredients on the package as well as other information. Much of that information is required by law. However, research has indicated that what is said or not said on the label has an important effect on the sales of the product.

This case was written by Norman E. Bowie and Tom L. Beauchamp.

Market research has shown that some consumers react *positively* to the word *granola* when marketing cereals and snacks. Granola bars saw retail sales grow 290 percent from 1980 through 1985 — the fastest growing segment of the candy bar market at that time. Granola bars were first introduced into the market as health food products, and the ingredients were fashioned for consumers concerned about nutrition. However, many complained that they tasted like cardboard. Manufacturers then changed the products by adding peanut butter, chocolate chips, marshmallows, and sugar. Although the bars gradually became more like candy bars than granola in their nutritional value and sugar content, they are slightly more nutritious than conventional candy bars. They have a higher fiber content, slightly less fat, and a higher percentage of complex carbohydrates. Advertising has continued to present the product with a healthful image, strengthening the public's association of the term *granola* with such concepts as "health food" and "healthy." Quaker Oats, General Mills, and Hershey Foods have emphasized the "wholesomeness" and "goodness" of their granola bars in their advertising. In order to compete, conventional candy bar companies also decided to advertise their products as healthy snacks. This trend of the 1980s continued throughout the 1990s.

The amount of sugar is not the only concern of consumers. Also important is the amount of complex carbohydrates, protein, and vitamins a food contains, as well as its fat content, sodium content, and calories. Although this information is printed on the label, the numbers found there are a function of serving size and are often presented in a way difficult for many persons to interpret. The consumer's information is specified in protein content, calories, and the like *per serving*, but the larger the serving size, the higher the numbers are likely to be. Reducing the serving size lowers the number of calories and the amount of sodium. Companies have therefore begun describing as a "serving" an amount that is much less than most people ordinarily serve themselves.

Questions

1. Are such marketing practices by candy, cereal, and soup companies manipulative? Deceptive?

2. Should companies be permitted to change the name, contents, or serving size without changing the product or the amount of the product?

3. The term *sugar-free* literally means "free of sucrose." Since many people purchase sugar-free foods to assist them with weight loss, should a standard be required so that "sugar-free" means "free of any high-calorie sweetener"?

4. Flexi-labeling permits wording such as "contains one or more of the following." Hence, the statement that a product "contains sunflower oil, coconut oil, and/or palm oil" is legally permitted. However, sunflower seed oil is a polyunsaturated fat, whereas the other two are saturated fats. Since polyunsaturated fats are more healthy, should flexi-labeling be prohibited?

CASE 6.   *Computer Math for Car Loans*

It is not unusual for automobile dealers to offer customers a financing plan to facilitate a new car purchase. These dealers often say that a customer can borrow money at a stated rate of interest, deposit it in a bank at a lower rate, and come out ahead. To sell this idea, dealers are using an Automatic Data Processing (ADP) computer software program that computes the amount of interest the customer will pay on a car loan and the amount the customer will earn on the same sum deposited in a certificate of deposit or savings account for the same length of time. The presentation to the customer is that the interest earned on the deposit will usually exceed the amount paid on the loan, even if the loan rate is considerably higher.

Here is a typical example used in the presentation. A customer borrows $6,469.31 for 36 months at 13 percent interest. He or she will pay $1,417.22 in interest over the three years, a figure based on a declining balance as he or she pays off the loan; the total to be paid is $7,882.52 in both principal and interest. By borrowing the money, the customer is able to leave his or her $6,469.31 in a bank account at 7.5 percent interest. In the account, the customer will earn $1,650.60 in 36 months, for a total balance of $8,119.91. From this presentation, it appears that the customer would save $233.39 by borrowing the money and leaving cash in the bank.

The Federal Trade Commission claims that although this software is mathematically correct, it presents an incomplete and misleading picture to the customer. It is impossible to save money by borrowing at a higher interest rate than that which one earns from an investment. To return to the example, one cannot borrow money at 13 percent interest, earn 7.5 percent on savings, and come out ahead. The ADP software does calculate the correct interest rate, but it calculates these rates with two different methods. It does not take into account repayment of the loan principal with the amount of interest generated from the savings account. As a customer repays the loan in monthly increments, the interest he or she earns on the savings decreases; over 36 months of withdrawals, the actual interest on the remaining balance in the account would be far less than $1,417.22. Therefore, interest on the savings account will be lower than the interest paid to the dealer when the car owner withdraws money to pay off the car.

Studies suggest that the average consumer does not have the ability to identify this discrepancy and to recalculate the actual amount of money he or she will spend on the car, taking into account the decrease in cash in the bank. As a result, consumers may make financially unsound decisions and incur a net financial loss.

For this reason the FTC sought and consummated an agreement with Automatic Data Processing that would alter the software provided to automobile dealers. ADP is prohibited by this agreement from continuing to represent the value of financing as it had; ADP agreed to delete the charts shown on the screen to customers. However, the company refused to admit that the software was actually misleading or defective, and the FTC

This case was prepared by Katy Cancro and Tom L. Beauchamp from interviews with automobile dealers and by reference to "Computer Car-Loan Math Doesn't Add Up," by Albert B. Crenshaw (*Washington Post,* August 31, 1991, p. C1); and "Firm, FTC Settle Charges on Claims in Auto Financing," by Gilbert Fuchsberg (*Wall Street Journal,* August 31, 1991, p. 3).

did not require such an acknowledgment. In response to FTC claims, Arthur Weinbach, senior vice president of ADP, contended that many other software programs on the market "basically do the same thing. It's been a standard industry practice."

Mr. Weinbach appears to be correct. Moreover, automobile dealers were not required by the FTC agreement to stop using their own sales approaches or charts to augment the ADP software. Many automobile dealers have continued to use the same approach even though they lack on-screen charts to show to customers. There is no regulation prohibiting automobile dealers from presenting information in this manner, and it

has become standard practice to do so. As they have done even before the ADP software, dealers continue to lead consumers to believe that they can save money by financing a car.

Questions

1. Has the FTC in any way helped the consumer? Should the consumer be helped?
2. Is ADP merely providing dealers with a more graphic presentation of what they say anyway? Is ADP guilty of consumer deception, or is it a legitimate "buyer beware" situation?

CASE 7. *The Conventions of Lying on Wall Street*

Salomon Brothers is among an elete group authorized to purchase U.S. Treasury notes from the U.S. government for resale to private investors. These notes are sold periodically at Treasury auctions. Before each auction, a firm receives "buy" orders from customers. The firm then tries to buy securities at the lowest possible price. The government places some restrictions on the bidding. First, a firm may purchase no more than 35 percent of the notes offered at a given auction for its portfolio. Second, if a firm holds large orders from an investor, it can buy bonds directly for that customer, and these bonds are *not* included in the 35 percent limit. If a firm is unable to purchase enough securities to fill the orders from its customers, the firm must then buy from competing firms at a higher rate than the auction rate.

In July 1991, Salomon Brothers, Inc., confessed to illegally purchasing U.S. Treasury notes on three separate occasions. They ex-

ploited the system in two ways. First, at the December, February, and May auctions, Salomon used customers' names to submit false bids. That is, they ordered bonds for customers who had *not* placed orders and did not know their names were being used. After the auction, Salomon added these bonds to its own portfolio. On second occasion, Salomon worked with a customer to purchase a large quantity of bonds in the customer's name. Salomon then bought back a portion of the bonds, effectively making a net purchase from the auction greater than 35 percent. Using this strategy, Salomon purchased 46 percent of Treasury notes sold on one occasion and 57 percent of the securities sold on another occasion.

Treasury auctions are also affected by the prevalent practice of sharing information. Current and former traders at several prominent Wall Street investment banks admit they regularly have shared "secrets" about the size

---

This case was prepared by Tom L. Beauchamp and revised by Jeff Greene.

and price of their bids at government auctions. This collusion to create a low bidding strategy results in firms paying less to the federal government. Consequently, the government makes less money to finance debt, causing an increase in taxes and interest rates.

This collusion is further complicated by strategies of deception. Lying has been tolerated and indeed has been expected for many years as part of the competition for trading. "It is part of the playing field. It's ingrained in the way the Street operates," one industry executive says, "I've stood out there on that trading floor and they lie to each other (before the auctions). That's part of the game. It was an exception when traders actually told the truth to each other about their bidding strategy." He adds, "They lie through their teeth to each other. You want to catch the [other] guy in an awkward position and pick him off."

In a report to the U.S. Congress, the Federal Home Mortgage Company claimed that two-thirds of Wall Street firms that it regularly deals with have lied to the agency to increase the chances of buying as many of the agency's securities as possible. Such deceit is so pervasive and routine on Wall Street that it has come to be regarded as the preferred and accepted way of doing business — the "standard of practice," as some put it. The common practice of submitting inflated orders has come under scrutiny from securities firms and the Federal Trade Commission, but the practice is so pervasive that it cannot be easily remedied. A small group of dealers holds purchasing power on the market and has long operated with financial success and with no serious challenges to its mode of operation.

One bond market specialist says, "I'm not condoning it or excusing it or saying it didn't go to an extreme . . . but people forget that the markets which are under the spotlight are part of that kind of distribution activity which for centuries has [been] associated with a fair amount of caveat emptor and puffery." The

traditions of bluffing, deception, and puffery have created an environment in which every player in the "game" expects deception as the condition for playing.

Questions

1. Is Wall Street actually a "game," and can these allegations and expectations be applied equally to every participant?
2. Should the FTC ignore deceit and collusion on Wall Street since it is ingrained in the system? Why or why not?
3. Does Wall Street have a valid standard of practice for disclosing information?

Suggested Supplementary Readings

ALLMON, DEAN E., and JAMES GRANT. "Real Estate Sales Agents and the Code of Ethics." *Journal of Business Ethics* 9 (October 1990).

ATTAS, DANIEL. "What's Wrong with 'Deceptive' Advertising?" *Journal of Business Ethics* 21 (1999): 49–59.

BEAUCHAMP, TOM L. *Case Studies in Business, Society, and Ethics.* 4th ed. Englewood Cliffs, NJ: Prentice-Hall, 1998, Chap 2.

BELLIZZI, JOSEPH, and ROBERT HITE. "Supervising Unethical Salesforce Behavior." *Journal of Marketing* 53 (April 1989).

BOWIE, NORMAN, and RONALD F. DUSKA. "Applying the Moral Presuppositions of Business to Advertising and Hiring." In *Business Ethics,* 2nd ed., Norman E. Bowie and Ronald F. Duska. Englewood Cliffs, NJ: Prentice-Hall, 1990.

BROCKWAY, GEORGE. "Limited Paternalism and the Salesperson: A Reconsideration." *Journal of Business Ethics* 12 (April 1993): 275–80.

Business and Professional Ethics Journal 3 (Spring-Summer 1984). The entire issue is devoted to ethical issues in advertising.

CAMENISCH, PAUL. "Marketing Ethics." *Journal of Business Ethics* 10 (April 1991).

COHEN, WILLIAM, and HELENA CZEPIEC. "The Role of Ethics in Gathering Corporate Intelligence." *Journal of Business Ethics* 7 (March 1988): 199–203.

CRISP, ROGER. "Persuasive Advertising, Autonomy, and the Creation of Desire." *Journal of Business Ethics* 6 (1987): 413–18.

DABHOLKAR, PRATIBHA A., and JAMES J. KELLARIS. "Toward Understanding Marketing Students' Ethical Judgement of Controversial Personal Selling Practices." *Journal of Business Research* 24 (June 1992): 313–29.

DE CONINCK, J. B., and D. J. GOOD. "Perceptual Differences of Sales Practitioners and Students Concerning Ethical Behavior." *Journal of Business Ethics* 8 (September 1989) 667–76.

GREENLAND, LEO. "Advertisers Must Stop Conning Consumers." *Harvard Business Review* (July/Aug. 1974): 18–28, 156.

HARE, R. M. "Commentary on Beauchamp's 'Manipulative Advertising'." *Business Professional Ethics Journal* 3 (Spring–Summer 1984): 23–28.

HITE, ROBERT E., and others. "A Content Analysis of Ethical Policy Statements Regarding Marketing Activities." *Journal of Business Ethics* 7 (October 1988).

HOLLEY, DAVID M. "A Moral Evaluation of Sales Practices." *Business and Professional Ethics Journal* 5 (1986-87): 3–21.

JONES, GARY E. "Lying and Intentions." *Journal of Business Ethics* 5 (August 1986): 347–49.

KAUFMANN, PATRICK J., N. CRAIG SMITH, and GWENDOLYN K. ORTMEYER. "Deception in Retailer High-Low Pricing: A 'Rule of Reason' Approach." *Journal of Retailing* 70 (Summer 1994): 115–38.

KOEHN, DARYL. "Business and Game-Playing: The False Analogy." *Journal of Business Ethics* 16 (1997): 1447–52.

KING, CAROLE. "It's Time to Disclose Commissions." *National Underwriter* 94 (November 19, 1990).

LACZNICK, GENE R. "Marketing Ethics: Onward Toward Greater Expectations." *Journal of Public Policy and Marketing* 12 (1993): 91–96.

LACZNICK, GENE R., and PATRICK E. MURPHY, eds. *Marketing Ethics.* Lexington, MA: Lexington Books, 1985.

LACZNICK, GENE R., and PATRICK E. MURPHY. *Ethical Marketing Decisions: The Higher Road.* Boston: Allyn and Bacon, 1993.

LIPPKE, RICHARD L. "Advertising and the Social Conditions of Autonomy." *Business and Professional Ethics Journal* 8 (1989): 35–58.

MACHAN, TIBOR R. "Advertising: The Whole or Only Some of the Truth?" *Public Affairs Quarterly* 1 (October 1987): 59–71.

MAES, JEANNE D, and others. "The American Association of Advertising Agencies (4As) Standards of Practice: How Far Does this Professional Association's Code of Ethics' Influence Reach?" *Journal of Business Ethics* 17 (1998): 1155–1161.

MURPHY, PATRICK E., and M. D. PRIDGEN, "Ethical and Legal Issues in Marketing," *Advances in Marketing and Public Policy* 2 (1991): 185–244.

OAKES, G. "The Sales Process and the Paradoxes of Trust." *Journal of Business Ethics* 9 (August 1990): 671–79.

PERKINS, ANNE G. "Advertising: The Costs of Deception." *Harvard Business Review* 72 (May–June 1994): 10–11.

PETERSON, ROBIN T. "Physical Environment Television Advertisement Themes." *Journal of Business Ethics* 10 (March 1991).

POLONSKY, MICHAEL JAY, and others. "Communicating Environmental Information: Are Marketing Claims on Packaging Misleading?" *Journal of Business Ethics* 17 (1998): 281–94.

PHILLIPS, BARBARA J. "In Defense of Advertising: A Social Perspective." *Journal of Business Ethics* 16 (1997): 109–118.

PRESCOTT, JOHN E. *Advances in Competitive Intelligence.* Vienna, VA: Society of Competitor Intelligence Professionals, 1989.

QUINN, JOHN F. "Moral Theory and Defective Tobacco Advertising and Warnings." *Journal of Business Ethics* 8 (November 1989).

SMITH, N. CRAIG, and JOHN A. QUELCH. *Ethics in Marketing Management.* Homewood, IL: Irwin, 1992.

SULLIVAN, ROGER J. "A Response to 'Is Business Bluffing Ethical?'" *Business and Professional Ethics Journal* 3 (Winter 1984).

VALLANCE, ELIZABETH. *Business Ethics at Work.* New York: Cambridge University Press, 1995.

VITELL, SCOTT J., and SHELBY D. HUNT. "The General Theory of Marketing Ethics: A Partial Test of the Model." *Research in Marketing Annual* 10 (1990): 237–66.

WILLIAMS, GERALD J. *Ethics in Modern Management.* New York: Quorum Books, 1992.

WONG, KENMAN L. "Tobacco Advertising and Children: The Limits of First Amendment Protection." *Journal of Business Ethics* 15 (1996): 1051–1064.

Chapter Eight

Ethical Issues
in International Business

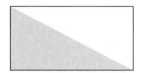

INTRODUCTION

THERE IS NO QUESTION that markets are international and that failure to recognize this fact could be fatal. Most firms realize that competitors for their market share could come from any corner of the globe. Even fairly small regional firms often attempt to market their products internationally. Of course, there is much more to the awareness of international issues than the development of international markets. As people in all parts of the world travel outside their own countries, they discover that countries differ on many matters of right and wrong. In some instances what is considered right or acceptable in one country is considered wrong or unacceptable in another. In addition, many of the problems that affect one country have an impact on other nations. Two excellent examples come to us from two very different problems — maintaining the integrity of financial markets and protecting the world environment. Radioactive material from damaged nuclear power plants has spread well beyond national borders, as witnessed by the disaster at the Russian nuclear power plant at Chernobyl. Ailing nuclear power plants in Russia and elsewhere remain an international threat. Moreover, the phenomenon of global warming is no respecter of national borders. Thus, we are all forced to think internationally whether we want to or not.

And there is plenty to think about. Bribery, extortion, and the issue of facilitating payments remain common problems. When firms try to take advantage of a lower cost structure, whether it be lower wages or lower taxes, they are often accused of exploitation. Consumers in developed countries have become increasingly aware of the alleged sweatshop conditions under which the goods they purchase are manufactured and assembled. And many would argue that the more developed countries and the companies that do business there have an obligation to help resolve the social problems, especially the problem of poverty that affects other parts of the world. However, before we can address these specific issues with much authority, an overarching problem needs to be addressed.

Are Any Universal Moral Norms Applicable to International Business?

There is a wide variety of opinion on what is acceptable conduct in international business, and a general skepticism prevails that questions whether there are any universal norms for ethical business practice. An international company involved in business abroad must face the question, "When in Rome, should it behave as the Romans do?" For purpose of this discussion, the home country of a business firm is where it has its headquarters or where it has its charter of incorporation. A host country is any other country where that firm does business.

When the norms of the home country and the norms of the host country are in conflict, a multinational corporation has four options: (1) Follow the norms of the home country because that is the patriotic thing to do; (2) follow the norms of the host country to show proper respect for the host country's culture; (3) follow whichever norm is most profitable; (4) follow whichever norm is morally best. (The four alternatives are not mutually exclusive.)

To choose option (4) requires, as Norman Bowie points out in his article, an appeal to international moral norms for business practice. Bowie's discussion shows the importance of establishing the existence and content of these international norms. Bowie bases his argument for international norms on three considerations. First, widespread agreement already exists among nations, as illustrated by the large number of signatories to the United Nations Declaration of Human Rights and by the existence of a number of international treaties establishing norms of business practice. Two excellent examples of the latter are the "Guidelines for Multinational Enterprises," adopted by the Organization of Economic Cooperation and Development, and the Caux Roundtable Principles of Business (reproduced in this chapter.) It should also be added that there are a number of industry-wide codes or agreements on the proper conduct of business matters.

Second, Bowie argues that certain moral norms must be endorsed if society is to exist at all. Corporations ought to accept the moral norms that make society and hence business itself possible. This argument is a powerful argument against the view known as ethical relativism. *Ethical relativism* asserts that whatever a country says is right or wrong for a country, *really* is right or wrong for that country. But if there are ethical norms that must be adopted if a country is to exist at all, then obviously the rightness of these norms is not justified by being endorsed in any particular country.

Third, Bowie uses certain Kantian arguments to show that business practice presupposes certain moral norms if it is to exist at all. Bowie refers to these norms as the *morality of the marketplace*. For example, there must be a moral obligation for business to keep its contracts if business is to exist at all. Bowie's argument is not merely theoretical. Russia has had great difficulty in adopting a capitalist economy because businesspersons and business firms have either been unwilling or unable to pay their bills. Without institutions to enforce contracts, business practice is fragile at best. It should also be pointed out that similar arguments could be used by utilitarians. If certain moral rules or traits such as truth telling or honesty give a multinational corporation a competitive advantage, then eventually these moral norms or traits will be adopted by all multinationals because those that do not will not survive.

The claim that there are universal values or moral norms that should be followed by all multinationals whether in Rome or not is not inconsistent with the idea that there is a wide range of situations where variations in conduct are permissible. To use Donaldson and Dunfee's term, there is considerable *moral free space* even in a world where there are universal moral norms. And we in the United States certainly have things to learn about the strengths of business practices in other parts of the world. To focus on Asia, we have included two articles. The article by Daryl Koehn addresses the more general question of what we can learn from Eastern philosophy. Discussions of trust have become important in American and European thinking about business. Koehn shows how our thinking about trust and other important ideas concerning business practice can be enriched by a study of Eastern philosophy.

In his article, Iwao Taka provides the religious and philosophical basis for business ethics in Japan. As a result, certain practices that would be morally questionable in our culture are seen as morally appropriate or even required in Japanese culture. Consider the keiretsu system that is so often criticized in the United States as being anticompetitive and hence unfair. In a keiretsu system the capital for each firm is supplied by the banks in that firm's keiretsu, and the firm uses a limited number of suppliers from that firm's keiretsu. The fact that a supplier outside the keiretsu could provide a product at a cheaper price is not normally a decisive criterion. Since foreign (non-Japanese) firms are not members of any Japanese keiretsu, they have an especially difficult time breaking into the Japanese market. However, as Taka points out, the special treatment given keiretsu members is consistent with what Taka calls the Concentric Circles view of ethical obligations. One's ethical obligations are greatest to those close to you, e.g., family, and are least to those most different from you, e.g., foreigners. As Taka says, this ethical point of view rests in turn on Confucianism, which permits "people to treat others in proportion to the intimacy of their relations."

Understanding Japanese ethics also explains some of the criticisms that the Japanese level against American business practice. They believe that American firms are short-sighted, focusing only on the short term, that American executives are paid too highly, and that American companies lay off workers too quickly.

On the other hand, Taka realizes that Japan's ethical system is also subject to criticism. Japan should take its obligations to non-Japanese more seriously, even if foreigners are in the outermost circle. Japan also has been criticized for discriminating against women and for driving workers too hard so that some literally die from overwork (karoshi).

In her article, Patricia Werhane provides a theoretical framework for the kind of analysis provided by Koehn and Taka. She points out that to some extent our view of the world is constructed from the society in which we live. Werhane refers to these images as mental models and she conclusively shows that we should not impose our mental models about capitalism and business practice on other cultures. Thus the task of the manager of an international firm is to avoid a rigid imposition of his or her views on foreign subsidiaries while at the same time avoiding a relativism that would ensnare the firm in violations of legitimate universal norms.

Finally, this discussion of "When in Rome Should We Do as the Romans Do?" has legal ramifications as well. Do the laws of the United States protect U.S. citizens when they work for U.S. companies abroad? Rulings of the Supreme Court indicate that they do when Congress specifically indicates that they do. Whether Congress actually intended the protection of the Title VII of the Civil Rights Act of 1964 to apply to U.S. citizens working abroad for a U.S. company was the subject in 1991 of U.S. Supreme Court case *Boureslan v. Aramco* (reprinted in part in the Legal Perspectives section of this chapter). When the Court ruled that Congress had not explicitly included citizens working for U.S. companies abroad, Congress was forced quickly to amend the law so that they could be included.

What about the rights of foreigners who are injured abroad by U.S. corporations? Do they have any rights to relief in American courts? Normally, they do not under the doctrine of *forum non conveniens* (it is not the convenient forum). It makes more practical sense for foreigners to seek relief in the country where the injury took place. But, in *Dow Chemical Company and Shell Oil Company v. Domingo Castro Alfaro et al.,* the Supreme Court of Texas disagrees. The reasoning of the Court is presented in the Legal Perspectives section of this chapter.

Bribery

One of the norms that Bowie believes is being adopted internationally is a norm that condemns bribery. Such a norm received legal recognition in the United States with the passage of the Foreign Corrupt Practices Act in 1977. That act, which was amended in 1988, makes it illegal for U.S. companies to pay bribes in order to do business abroad. Spokespersons for American business have long criticized the law on the grounds that it puts American firms at a competitive disadvantage. Other countries operate under no such restrictions. Although the United States did take the lead in this respect, more and more organizations are passing rules outlawing bribery. For example, the European Community has done so. Also, there is no clear evidence that American companies have suffered an appreciable competitive disadvantage in the early years following the passage of the Act. For example, a study by Kate Gillespie showed that U.S. export business in the Middle East has not been lost. Her analysis is based on data showing that the share of U.S. exports of the total exports to the countries of the region from 1970–1982 had not declined.[1] Iran was an exception, but that had nothing to do with the Foreign Corrupt Practices Act; Iran was under an embargo for much of that time due to the seizure of American hostages.

Another criticism of the Foreign Corrupt Practices Act was that it was an example of American moral imperialism — a charge that is often levelled against American regulations. However, in this case, the charge of moral imperialism is false since the FCPA does not force other countries or the multinationals of other countries to follow America's lead. It simply required U.S. companies to follow American moral norms with respect to bribery when doing business abroad.

A third criticism of the FCPA is more telling, however. That criticism is that the Act does not adequately distinguish among gift giving, facilitating payments, bribery, and extortion. The FCPA does allow for facilitating payments and that allowance was expanded when the law was amended in 1988. However, the law does not sufficiently distinguish between bribery and extortion. The chief difference between bribery and extortion is who does the initiating of the act. A corporation pays a bribe when it offers to pay or provide favors to a person or persons of trust to influence the latter's conduct or judgment. A corporation pays extortion money when it yields to a demand for money in order to have accomplished what it has a legal right to have accomplished without the payment. The difference between extortion and a facilitating payment is one of degree. It is also often difficult to distinguish a gift from a bribe. That conceptual issue is the focus of Steidlemeier's article on gift giving in China. Steidlemeier shows that if you fully understand Chinese culture and the importance that the concept of reciprocity plays within it, a manager can successfully give gifts without engaging in bribery. One can conclude from Steidlemeier's analysis that a manager can and should understand and appreciate the culture in which he or she works while at the same time honoring certain universal norms such as the one against bribery. A similar lesson can be drawn from the article by Donaldson and Dunfee. They argue that in many situations an international corporation should respect the moral norms of the country in which it operates, but they also show that the norm against bribery is a universal norm and thus a business is morally obligated not to bribe.

Capitalism and the Third World

One of the more telling criticisms of capitalism is that it has benefited the rich and powerful industrial nations at the expense of the poorer nonindustrial nations, which are somewhat mistakenly called the nations of the third world. Perhaps the issue that is receiving the most attention is the allegations surrounding the use of foreign suppliers for produced goods — especially in the apparel industry. Some of these foreign suppliers to such companies as Nike have been accused of operating sweatshops. The sweatshop issue has become the chief activist cause on college campuses, and there have been calls for universal standards and the monitoring of their implementation. Some calls have already been successful. On October 7, 1999, Nike reversed policy and released the location of forty-two of 365 factories. Then on October 18, 1999 Reebok International, Ltd. released the first independent factory audit of two Indonesian factories undertaken by a human rights group. A few days later Liz Claiborne, Inc. released a critical report of an audit of a Guatemalan factory and Mattel, Inc. will publish a comprehensive review of eight of its plants in four countries.[2]

Monitoring is not limited to individual companies. The Fair Labor Association is made up of industry and human rights representatives. This group was created by a Presidential task force and includes such companies as Adidas, Salomon, Levi Strauss and Co., Nike, Reebok, Liz Claiborne, and Phillips-Van Heusen.[3] The addition of monitoring to the codes of conduct established in the early nineties drives home the point made in Chapter 3, that codes of ethics need to be monitored and enforced if they are to be taken seriously.

Not everyone is so quick to condemn the practices of multinationals in this area. Several prominent economists have spoken out claiming that the wages paid to the workers of foreign suppliers in the third world are hardly immoral "slave wages," but rather represent an increase in the standard of living. These arguments are summarized and defended in the article by Ian Maitland. Moreover, if child labor is the issue, the moral thing to do, economist Gary S. Becker argues, is to pay parents to keep children, especially daughters who are often less valued, in school. That approach is superior to laws that simply remove children from the workplace and derive families of an important source of income.[4]

Finally, we must question the assumption that capitalism cannot be modified to be a cause for good in the third world. Interestingly, some of the most prominent professors of strategy are arguing that there are viable markets among the poor. Michael Porter is serving as a consultant to firms who want to do business in the inner cities of America. Traditionally, few grocery chains have had outlets in the inner city. Now some are reconsidering. Similarly, C. K. Prahalad is arguing that capitalism has a genuine role to play in the development of the poorest economies in Africa and portions of Asia. The selections from the book *The Price of a Dream* discuss one experiment by the Grameen Bank to make capitalists out of the women of Bangladesh by loaning them as little as the equivalent of $15.

NOTES

1. Kate Gillespie, "Middle East Response to the Foreign Corrupt Practices Act." *California Management Review* 29 (1987) 9–30.
2. Aaron Bernstein, "Sweatshops: No More Excuses," *Business Week* (November 7, 1999), pp. 104–06.
3. Ibid.
4. Gary S. Becker, "'Bribe' Third World Parents to Keep Their Kids in School," *Business Week* (November 22, 1999).

WHEN IN ROME, SHOULD YOU DO AS THE ROMANS DO?

Relativism and the Moral Obligations of Multinational Corporations

Norman Bowie

Now that business ethics is a fashionable topic, it is only natural that the behavior of multinational corporations should come under scrutiny. Indeed, in the past few decades multinationals have allegedly violated a number of fundamental moral obligations. Some of these violations have received great attention in the press. . . .

The charges of immoral conduct constitute a startling array of cases where multinationals are alleged to have failed to live up to their moral obligations. However, the charges are of several distinct types. Some have also been brought against purely domestic U.S. firms — for example, issues involving a safe working environment or safe products. Other charges are unique to multinationals — the charge that a multinational values the safety of a foreigner less than the safety of a home country resident. Still others are charges that companies try to justify behavior in other countries that is clearly wrong in the United States, for example, the bribing of government officials.

In this essay, I will focus on the question of whether U.S. multinationals should follow the moral rules of the United States or the moral rules of the host countries (the countries where the U.S. multinationals do business). A popular way of raising this issue is to ask whether U.S. multinationals should follow the advice "When in Rome, do as the Romans do." In discussing that issue I will argue that U.S. multinationals would be morally required to follow that advice if the theory of ethical rela-

tivism were true. On the other hand, if ethical universalism is true, there will be times when the advice would be morally inappropriate. In a later section, I will argue that ethical relativism is morally suspect. Finally, I will argue that the ethics of the market provide some universal moral norms for the conduct of multinationals. Before turning to these questions, however, I will show briefly that many of the traditional topics discussed under the rubric of the obligations of multinationals fall under standard issues of business ethics.

OBLIGATIONS OF MULTINATIONALS THAT APPLY TO ANY BUSINESS

As Milton Friedman and his followers constantly remind us, the purpose of a corporation is to make money for the stockholders — some say to maximize profits for the stockholders. According to this view, multinationals have the same fundamental purpose as national corporations. However, in recent years, Friedman's theory has been severely criticized. On what moral grounds can the interests of the stockholders be given priority over all the other stakeholders?[1] For a variety of reasons, business ethicists are nearly unanimous in saying that no such moral grounds can be given. Hence, business executives have moral obligations to all their

This piece is composed of selections from Norman Bowie, "The Moral Obligations of Multinational Corporations," *Problems of International Justice* (edited by Steven Luper-Foy), 1988 and Norman Bowie "Relativism, Cultural and Moral," *The Blackwell Encyclopedic Dictionary of Business Ethics* (edited by Patricia Werhane and R. Edward Freeman) Blackwell, Cambridge, MA, 1997. Reprinted with permission of the author and Blackwell Publishers.

stakeholders. Assuming that Friedman's critics are correct, what follows concerning the obligations of multinationals?

Can the multinationals pursue profit at the expense of the other corporate stakeholders? No; the multinational firm, just like the national firm, is obligated to consider all its stakeholders. In that respect there is nothing distinctive about the moral obligations of a multinational firm. However, fulfilling its obligations is much more complicated than for a national firm. A multinational usually has many more stakeholders. It has all the classes of stakeholders a U.S. company has but multiplied by the number of countries in which the company operates.[2]

It also may be more difficult for the multinational to take the morally correct action. For example, one of the appealing features of a multinational is that it can move resources from one country to another in order to maximize profits. Resources are moved in order to take advantage of more favorable labor rates, tax laws, or currency rates. Of course, the pursuit of such tactics makes it more difficult to honor the obligation to consider the interests of all stakeholders. Nonetheless, the increased difficulty does not change the nature of the obligation; multinationals, like nationals, are required to consider the interests of all corporate stakeholders.

Should a multinational close a U.S. plant and open a plant in Mexico in order to take advantage of cheap labor? That question is no different in principle from this one: Should a national firm close a plant in Michigan and open a plant in South Carolina in order to take advantage of the more favorable labor climate in South Carolina? The same moral considerations that yield a decision in the latter case yield a similar decision in the former. (Only if the interests of Mexican workers were less morally significant than were the interests of U.S. workers could any differentiation be made.)

These examples can be generalized to apply to any attempt by a multinational to take advantage of discrepancies between the home country and the host country in order to pursue a profit. Any attempt to do so without considering the interests of all the stakeholders is immoral. National firms and multinational firms share the same basic obligations. If I am right here, there is nothing distinctive about the many problems faced by multinationals, and much of the discussion of the obligations of multinationals can be carried on within the framework of traditional business ethics.

DISTINCTIVE OBLIGATIONS

Certain obligations of multinationals do become distinctive where the morality of the host country (any country where the multinational has subsidiaries) differs from or contradicts the morality of the home country (the country where the multinational was legally created). The multinational faces a modern version of the "When in Rome, should you do as the Romans do?" question. That question is the focus of this essay.

On occasion, the "when in Rome" question has an easy answer. In many situations the answer to the question is yes. When in Rome a multinational is obligated to do as the Romans do. Because the circumstances Romans face are different from the circumstances Texans face, it is often appropriate to follow Roman moral judgments because it is entirely possible that Romans and Texans use the same moral principles, but apply those principles differently.

This analysis also works the other way. Just because a certain kind of behavior is right in the United States does not mean that it is right somewhere else. Selling infant formula in the United States is morally permissible in most circumstances, but, I would argue, it is not morally permissible in most circumstances to sell infant formula in Third World countries. U.S. water is safe to drink.

Many moral dilemmas disappear when the factual circumstances that differentiate two cultures are taken into account. It is important to note, however, that this judgment is made because we believe that the divergent practices conform to some general moral principle. The makers of infant formula can sell their product in an advanced country but not in a Third World country because the guiding principle is that we cannot impose avoidable harm on an innocent third party. Selling infant formula in underdeveloped countries would often violate that common fundamental principle; selling the formula in developed countries usually would not.

This situation should be contrasted with cases where the home and the host country have different *moral* principles. Consider different moral principles for the testing of new drugs. Both countries face the following dilemma. If there are fairly lax standards, the drug may have very bad side effects, and if it is introduced too quickly, then many persons who take the drug are likely to be harmed — perhaps fatally. On the other hand, if a country has very strict standards and a long testing period, the number of harmful side effect cases will be less, but a number of people who could have benefited from benign drugs will have perished because they did not survive the long testing period. Where is the trade-off between saving victims of a disease and protecting persons from possible harmful side effects? To bring this problem home, consider a proposed cure for cancer or for AIDS. Two different countries could set different safety standards such that plausible moral arguments could be made for each. In such cases, it is morally permissible to sell a drug abroad that could not yet be sold in the United States.

If all cases were like this one, it would always be morally permissible to do as the Romans do. But alas, all cases are not like this one. Suppose a country totally ignores the problem of side effects and has no safety standards at all. That country "solves" the trade-off problem by ignoring the interests of those who might develop side effects. Wouldn't that country be wrong, and wouldn't a multinational be obligated not to market a drug in that country even if the country permitted it?

If the example seems farfetched, consider countries that are so desperately poor or corrupt that they will permit companies to manufacture and market products that are known to be dangerous. This is precisely the charge that was made against American Vanguard when it exported the pesticide DBCP. Aren't multinationals obligated to stay out even if they are permitted?

That question leads directly to the question of whether multinationals always should do in Rome as the Romans do. To sort through that issue, Figure 1 may be useful. Thus far, I have focused on I and IIA. The remainder of the essay considers the range of ethical problems found in IIB.

In IIB4, the multinational has an obligation to follow the moral principles of the host country because on the issue at hand those of the host country are justified while those of the home country are not. Although Americans may believe that there are few such obligations because their moral principles are far more likely to be justified, it is not hard to think of a contrary case. Suppose it is a moral obligation in a host country that no corporation fire someone without due cause. In other words, in the host country employment at will is morally forbidden. Although I shall not argue for it here, I think the employment-at-will doctrine cannot stand up to moral scrutiny. Hence, in this case, multinationals are obligated to follow the moral principle of the host country. Except for economic reasons (falling demand for one's product), a multinational is morally obligated not to fire an employee without just cause.

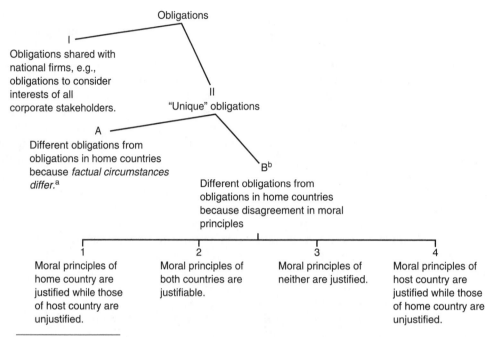

Obligations

I —
Obligations shared with
national firms, e.g.,
obligations to consider
interests of all
corporate stakeholders.

II
"Unique" obligations

A —
Different obligations from
obligations in home countries
because *factual circumstances
differ.*[a]

B[b]
Different obligations from
obligations in home countries
because disagreement in moral
principles

1	2	3	4
Moral principles of home country are justified while those of host country are unjustified.	Moral principles of both countries are justifiable.	Moral principles of neither are justified.	Moral principles of host country are justified while those of home country are unjustified.

[a]In my view, different obligations still conform to universal principles.
[b]It is assumed that the different moral principles referred to here and below refer to the same moral issue. It is also stipulated that "unjustified" in IIB1 and IIB4 means that the unjustified principles are in conflict with the canons of justification in ethics.

FIGURE 1.   Obligations of Multinationals

In IIB3, if the moral principles with respect to a given issue are not justified, then the multinational is under no moral obligation to follow them (except in the weak sense where the multinational is under a legal obligation and hence under a moral obligation to obey the law). Actually, IIB3 can be further subdivided into cases where the moral principles are not justified and where the moral principles cannot be justified. Theocratic states with moral principles based on revelation but not in contradiction with rationally justified moral principles are examples of the former. When the "moral" principles based on revelation are in contradiction with rationally justified moral principles, we have an example of the latter. In this latter case, a multinational is obligated not to follow the moral principles of the host country. In these cases, when in Rome, multinationals are not to do as the Romans do.

In case IIB2, multinationals may do in Rome as the Romans do. In this case, the moral principles of the host country are justified.

Finally, in case IIB1, the multinational is obligated not to follow the moral principles of the host country. In these cases, the principles of the host country are contrary to the canons of ethics.

In summary, then, U.S. multinationals are obligated to do as the Romans do in IIB4, are permitted to do as the Romans do in IIB2 and in IIB3 where the moral principles of the

Romans are consistent with what morality would justify. U.S. multinationals are obligated *not* to do as the Romans do in IIB1 and IIB3 where the moral principles of the Romans are inconsistent with what morality would justify.

Notice, however, that the entire analysis assumes there is some means of justifying ethical principles independent of the fact that a society believes they are justified. Otherwise, for example, I could not say that the moral principles of a home country are not justified while those of the host country are. But who is to say whether the moral principles of a country are justified or when they run counter to universal morality. Besides, perhaps there is no universal morality. What then?

RELATIVISM

Cultural relativism is a descriptive claim that ethical practices differ among cultures; that, as a matter of fact, what is considered right in one culture may be considered wrong in another. Thus truth of falsity of cultural relativism can be determined by examining the world. The work of anthropologists and sociologists is most relevant in determining the truth or falsity of cultural relativism, and there is widespread consensus among social scientists that cultural relativism is true.

Moral relativism is the claim that what is really right or wrong is what the culture says is right or wrong. Moral relativists accept cultural relativism as true, but they claim much more. If a culture sincerely and reflectively adopts a basic moral principle, then it is morally obligatory for members of that culture to act in accordance with that principle.

The implication of moral relativism for conduct is that one ought to abide by the ethical norms of the culture where one is located. . . . Relativists in ethics would say, "One ought to follow the moral norms of the culture." In terms of business practice, consider the question, "Is it morally right to pay a bribe to gain business?" The moral relativist would answer the question by consulting the moral norms of the country where one is doing business. If those norms permit bribery in that country, then the practice of bribery is not wrong in that country. However, if the moral norms of the country do not permit bribery, then offering a bribe to gain business in that country is morally wrong. The justification for that position is the moral relativist's contention that what is really right or wrong is determined by the culture.

Is cultural relativism true? Is moral relativism correct? As noted, many social scientists believe that cultural relativism is true as a matter of fact. But is it?

First, many philosophers claim that the "facts" aren't really what they seem. Early twentieth-century anthropologists cited the fact that in some cultures, after a certain age, parents are put to death. In most cultures such behavior would be murder. Does this difference in behavior prove that the two cultures disagree about fundamental matters of ethics? No, it does not. Suppose the other culture believes that people exist in the afterlife in the same condition that they leave their present life. It would be very cruel to have one's parents exist eternally in an unhealthy state. By killing them when they are relatively active and vigorous, you insure their happiness for all eternity. The *underlying* ethical principle of this culture is that children have duties to their parents, including the duty to be concerned with their parents' happiness as they approach old age. This ethical principle is identical with our own. What looked like a difference in ethics between our culture and another turned out, upon close examination, to be a difference based on what each culture takes to be the facts of the matter. This example does, of course, support the claim that as a matter of fact ethical principles vary according to culture. However, it does not support the stronger conclusion that *underlying* ethical principles vary according to culture.

Cultures differ in physical setting, in economic development, in the state of their science and technology, in their literacy rate, and in many other ways. Even if there were universal moral principles, they would have to be applied in these different cultural contexts. Given the different situations in which cultures exist, it would come as no surprise to find universal principles applied in different ways. Hence we expect to find surface differences in ethical behavior among cultures even though the cultures agree on fundamental universal moral principles. For example, one commonly held universal principle appeals to the public good; it says that social institutions and individual behavior should be ordered so that they lead to the greatest good for the greatest number. Many different forms of social organization and individual behavior are consistent with this principle. The point of these two arguments is to show that differences among cultures on ethical behavior may not reflect genuine disagreement about underlying principles of ethics. Thus it is not so obvious that any strong form of cultural relativism is true.

But are there universal principles that are accepted by all cultures? It seems so; there does seem to be a whole range of behavior, such as torture and murder of the innocent, that every culture agrees is wrong. A nation-state accused of torture does not respond by saying that a condemnation of torture is just a matter of cultural choice. The state's leaders do not respond by saying, "We think torture is right, but you do not." Rather, the standard response is to deny that any torture took place. If the evidence of torture is too strong, a finger will be pointed either at the victim or at the morally outraged country:

"They do it too." In this case the guilt is spread to all. Even the Nazis denied that genocide took place. What is important is that *no* state replies that there is nothing wrong with genocide or torture.

In addition, there are attempts to codify some universal moral principles. The United Nations Universal Declaration of Human Rights has been endorsed by the member states of the UN, and the vast majority of countries in the world are members of the UN. Even in business, there is a growing effort to adopt universal principles of business practice. In a recent study of international codes of ethics, Professors Catherine Langlois and Bodo B. Schlegelmilch[3] found that although there certainly were differences among codes, there was a considerable area of agreement. William Frederick has documented the details of six international compacts on matters of international business ethics. These include the aforementioned UN Universal Declaration of Human Rights, the European Convention on Human Rights, the Helsinki Final Act, the OECD Guidelines for Multinational Enterprises and Social Policy, and the United Nations Conduct on Transnational Corporations (in progress) (Frederick, 1991). The Caux Roundtable, a group of corporate executives from the United States, Europe, and Japan, are seeking worldwide endorsement of a set of principles of business ethics. Thus there are a number of reasons to think that cultural relativism, at least with respect to basic moral principles, is not true, that is, that it does not accurately describe the state of moral agreement that exists. This is consistent with maintaining that cultural relativism is true in the weak form, that is, when applied only to surface ethical principles.

But what if differences in fundamental moral practices among cultures are discovered and seem unreconcilable? That would lead to a discussion about the adequacy of moral relativism. The fact that moral practices do vary widely among countries is cited as evidence for the correctness of moral relativism. Discoveries early in the century by anthropologists, sociologists, and psychologists documented the diversity of moral beliefs. Philosophers, by and large, welcomed corrections of moral imperialist thinking, but recognized that the moral relativist's appeal to the alleged truth of cultural relativism was not enough to establish moral relativism. The mere fact that a culture considers a practice moral does not mean that it is moral. Cultures have sincerely practiced slavery, discrimination, and the torture of animals. Yet each of these practices can be independently criticized on ethical grounds. Thinking something is morally permissible does not make it so.

Another common strategy for criticizing moral relativism is to show that the consequences of taking the perspective of moral relativism are inconsistent with our use of moral language. It is often contended by moral relativists that if two cultures disagree regarding universal moral principles, there is no way for that disagreement to be resolved. Since moral relativism is the view that what is right or wrong is determined by culture, there is no higher appeal beyond the fact that culture endorses the moral principle. But we certainly do not talk that way. When China and the United States argue about the moral rights of human beings, the disputants use language that seems to appeal to universal moral principles. Moreover, the atrocities of the Nazis and the slaughter in Rwanda have met with universal condemnation that seemed based on universal moral principles. So moral relativism is not consistent with our use of moral language.

Relativism is also inconsistent with how we use the term "moral reformer." Suppose, for instance, that a person from one culture moves to another and tries to persuade the other culture to change its view. Suppose

someone moves from a culture where slavery is immoral to one where slavery is morally permitted. Normally, if a person were to try to convince the culture where slavery was permitted that slavery was morally wrong, we would call such a person a moral reformer. Moreover, a moral reformer would almost certainly appeal to universal moral principles to make her argument; she almost certainly would not appeal to a competing cultural standard. But if moral relativism were true, there would be no place for the concept of a moral reformer. Slavery is really right in those cultures that say it is right and really wrong in those cultures that say it is wrong. If the reformer fails to persuade a slaveholding country to change its mind, the reformer's antislavery position was never right. If the reformer is successful in persuading a country to change its mind, the reformer's antislavery views would be wrong — until the country did in fact change its view. Then the reformer's antislavery view would be right. But that is not how we talk about moral reform.

The moral relativist might argue that our language should be reformed. We should talk differently. At one time people used to talk and act as if the world were flat. Now they don't. The relativist could suggest that we can change our ethical language in the same way. But consider how radical the relativists' response is. Since most, if not all, cultures speak and act as if there were universal moral principles, the relativist can be right only if almost everyone else is wrong. How plausible is that?

Although these arguments are powerful ones, they do not deliver a knockout blow to moral relativism. If there are no universal moral principles, moral relativists could argue that moral relativism is the only theory available to help make sense of moral phenomena.

An appropriate response to this relativist argument is to present the case for a set of universal moral principles, principles that are correct for all cultures independent of what a culture thinks about them. This is what adherents of the various ethical traditions try to do. The reader will have to examine these various traditions and determine how persuasive she finds them. In addition, there are several final independent considerations against moral relativism that can be mentioned here.

First, what constitutes a culture? There is a tendency to equate cultures with national boundaries, but that is naive, especially today. With respect to moral issues, what do US cultural norms say regarding right and wrong? That question may be impossible to answer, because in a highly pluralistic country like the United States, there are many cultures. Furthermore, even if one can identify a culture's moral norms, it will have dissidents who do not subscribe to those moral norms. How many dissidents can a culture put up with and still maintain that some basic moral principle is the cultural norm? Moral relativists have had little to say regarding criteria for constituting a culture or how to account for dissidents. Unless moral relativists offer answers to questions like these, their theory is in danger of becoming inapplicable to the real world.

Second, any form of moral relativism must admit that there are some universal moral principles. Suppose a culture does not accept moral relativism, that is, it denies that if an entire culture sincerely and reflectively adopts a basic moral principle, it is obligatory for members of that culture to act in accord with that principle. Fundamentalist Muslim countries would reject moral relativism because it would require them to accept as morally permissible blasphemy in those countries where blasphemy was permitted. If the moral relativist insists that the truth of every moral principle depends on the culture, then she must admit that the truth of moral relativism depends on the culture. Therefore the moral relativist must admit that at least the principle of moral relativism is not relative.

Third, it seems that there is a set of basic moral principles that every culture must adopt. You would not have a culture unless the members of the group adopted these moral principles. Consider an anthropologist who arrives on a populated island: How many tribes are on the island? To answer that question, the anthropologist tries to determine if some people on some parts of the island are permitted to kill, commit acts of violence against, or steal from persons on other parts of the island. If such behavior is not permitted, that counts as a reason for saying that there is only one tribe. The underlying assumption here is that there is a set of moral principles that must be followed if there is to be a culture at all. With respect to those moral principles, adhering to them determines whether there is a culture or not.

But what justifies these principals? A moral relativist would say that a culture justifies them. But you cannot have a culture unless the members of the culture follow the principles. Thus it is reasonable to think that justification lies elsewhere. Many believe that the purpose of morality is to help make social cooperation possible. Moral principles are universally necessary for that endeavor.

THE MORALITY OF THE MARKETPLACE

Given that the norms constituting a moral minimum are likely to be few in number, it can be argued that the argument thus far has achieved something — that is, multinationals are obligated to follow the moral norms required for the existence of a society. But the argument has not achieved very much — that is, most issues surrounding multinationals do not involve alleged violations of these norms. Perhaps a stronger argument can be found by making explicit the morality of the marketplace. That there is an implicit morality of the market is a point that is often ignored by most economists and many businesspersons.

Although economists and businesperons assume that people are basically self-interested, they must also assume that persons involved in business transactions will honor their contracts. In most economic exchanges, the transfer of product for money is not simultaneous. You deliver and I pay or vice versa. As the economist Kenneth Boulding put it: "without an integrative framework, exchange itself cannot develop, because exchange, even in its most primitive forms, involves trust and credibility."[4]

Philosophers would recognize an implicit Kantianism in Boulding's remarks. Kant tried to show that a contemplated action would be immoral if a world in which the contemplated act was universally practiced was self-defeating. For example, lying and cheating would fail Kant's tests. Kant's point is implicitly recognized by the business community when corporate officials despair of the immoral practices of corporations and denounce executives engaging in shady practices as undermining the business enterprise itself.

Consider what John Rawls says about contracts:

> Such ventures are often hard to initiate and to maintain. This is especially evident in the case of covenants, that is, in those instances where one person is to perform before the other. For this person may believe that the second party will not do his part, and therefore the scheme never gets going. . . . Now in these situations there may be no way of assuring the party who is to perform first except by giving him a promise, that is, by putting oneself under an obligation to carry through later. Only in this way can the scheme be made secure so that both can gain from the benefits of their cooperation.[5]

Rawls's remarks apply to all contracts. Hence, if the moral norms of a host country permitted practices that undermined con-

tracts, a multinational ought not to follow them. Business practice based on such norms could not pass Kant's test.

In fact, one can push Kant's analysis and contend that business practice generally requires the adoption of a minimum standard of justice. In the United States, a person who participates in business practice and engages in the practice of giving bribes or kickbacks is behaving unjustly. Why? Because the person is receiving the benefits of the rules against such activities without supporting the rules personally. This is an example of what John Rawls calls freeloading. A freeloader is one who accepts the benefits without paying any of the costs.

> In everyday life an individual, if he is so inclined, can sometimes win even greater benefits for himself by taking advantage of the cooperative efforts of others. Sufficiently many persons may be doing their share so that when special circumstances allow him not to contribute (perhaps his omission will not be found out), he gets the best of both worlds. . . . We cannot preserve a sense of justice and all that this implies while at the same time holding ourselves ready to act unjustly should doing so promise some personal advantage.[6]

This argument does not show that if bribery really is an accepted moral practice in country X, that moral practice is wrong. What it does show is that practices in country X that permit freeloading are wrong and if bribery can be construed as freeloading, then it is wrong. In most countries I think it can be shown that bribery is freeloading, but I shall not make that argument here.

The implications of this analysis for multinationals are broad and important. If activities that are permitted in other countries violate the morality of the marketplace — for example, undermine contracts or involve freeloading on the rules of the market — they nonetheless are morally prohibited to multinationals that operate there. Such multinationals are obligated to follow the moral norms of the market. Contrary behavior is inconsistent and ultimately self-defeating.

Our analysis here has rather startling implications. If the moral norms of a host country are in violation of the moral norms of the marketplace, then the multinational is obligated to follow the norms of the marketplace. Systematic violation of marketplace norms would be self-defeating. Moreover, whenever a multinational establishes businesses in a number of different countries, the multinational provides something approaching a universal morality — the morality of the marketplace itself. If Romans are to do business with the Japanese, then whether in Rome or Tokyo, there is a morality to which members of the business community in both Rome and Tokyo must subscribe — even if the Japanese and Romans differ on other issues of morality.

NOTES

1. For the purpose of this discussion, a stakeholder is a member of a group without whose support the organization would cease to exist. The traditional list of stakeholders includes stockholders, employees, customers, suppliers, lenders, and the local community where plants or facilities are located.

2. Of course, one large U.S. company with 10 plants in 10 different states has more classes of stakeholders than 1 U.S. company with 1 U.S. plant and 1 foreign subsidiary.

3. C. Langlois and B. B. Schlegelmilch, "Do Corporate Codes of Ethics Reflect National Character? Evidence from Europe and the United States," *Journal of International Studies,* 21(a), pp. 519–539.

4. Kenneth E. Boulding, "The Basis of Value Judgments in Economics," in *Human Values and Economic Policy,* Sidney Hook, ed. (New York: New York University Press, 1967), p. 68.

5. John Rawls, *A Theory of Justice* (Cambridge, MA: Harvard University Press, 1971), p. 569.

6. Ibid., p. 497.

What Can Eastern Philosophy Teach Us About Business Ethics?

Daryl Koehn

As Asian markets have grown, there has been a corresponding increase in interest among businesspeople and philosophers in so-called "Asian Values." Knowledge of the values and ethical systems of Asians is touted as necessary if Western businesses are to successfully negotiate the opening of markets in Japan, South Korea and China and to sell their products to the citizens of these countries. *Real politik* has played an important role as well in generating interest in Asian Values. With the increased

wealth of these developing countries has come a greater say in international affairs. Westerners now feel compelled to take note of Asians and to understand them as well as possible. Moreover, as Asian markets have become more lucrative, the power of Southeast Asian governments has increased simply by virtue of the fact that they control which businesses get access to their people and on what terms. The power of voice, coupled with this power to regulate access, has gotten the West's attention.

From Daryl Koehn, "What Can Eastern Philosophy Teach Us about Business Ethics?," *Journal of Business Ethics,* 19: 71–79, 1999. Reprinted by permission from Kluwer Academic Publishers.

However, although it is now fashionable to allude to Asian Values, it is far from clear what this term means. In the first part of this paper, I argue: 1) that it is dubious whether such values exist other than as a rhetorical category; 2) that we need to consider the ethics of using such a term; and 3) that we are better advised to speak of certain strands of ethical thinking articulated by particular thinkers within specific countries (e.g., Japan, South Korea, China, etc.). In the second part, I take up two such strands — the ethical views of the famous Japanese ethicist Watsuji Tetsuro and of Confucius. I argue that many of their ideas have profound implications for the conduct of business and the way in which we evaluate that conduct.

PART ONE: THE RHETORIC OF "ASIAN VALUES"

It is questionable whether Asian Values do exist or ever could do so. The term "Asia" refers to an enormous geographical area. China, Japan, India and the rest of the Southeast and East Asian countries fall under the rubric. The former U.S.S.R., too, historically has been considered part of Asia by Europeans. The same is true of what we now term the Mideast. The Greek historian Herodotus, for example, consistently treats Persia and Phoenicia as Asian empires. As one would expect, given the vastness of Asia, the cultures therein very tremendously, reflecting just about every world religion — Buddhism (in numerous varieties), Shintoism, Confucianism, Islam, Christianity, etc. While we can carve out a certain region of the globe and label it "Asia," it is very hard to ascertain what values all of these different cultures might share.

Identifying a "core" set of Asian Values is not the only problem. Even if there were some widely shared values within this region,

these values would not be static. Asian Values would be just as subject as Western ones to the transforming effect of political and economic factors. The contrast between Western and Asian Values has the unfortunate effect of making it seem as though the two are eternally opposed to each other. For example, one common variant of this distinction opposes Western individualism to Asian collectivism and deference to authority. Yet, as Kawato rightly notes, the West has not always been as committed to individualism as it now is.[1] Europeans in the Middle Ages were much more clannish than they are today. Aristotle argues that the Greek polis evolved out of tribal arrangements in which there was one dominant leader to whom all tribe members deferred.[2] Asia might become more "individualistic" or the West more "tribal" or "group-centered" as the years unfold. No culture is hermetically sealed and, as Midgely argues, to think that a culture is a closed system grossly misunderstands cultures and their evolution, an evolution stimulated and influenced by contact with other cultures.[3] In other words, "Asian Values" might once have been "Western Values" (or vice versa) and could become so again. So, even if there were a core set of distinct Asian Values, it would be simpleminded to treat these values in a completely ahistorical fashion.

Given the exceptionally diverse cultures of that region we in the West name "Asia"; and given the dynamism inherent in cultural values, we have good reason to doubt whether some monolithic static set of Asian Values exists now, ever has, or ever will. That is not to deny that some leaders in some countries in this region routinely invoke Asian Values. But the rhetorical purposes to which this invocation are being put need to be critically evaluated. . . .

The more substantive issue centers on just what the content of these supposedly unique Asian Values are. It is said, for example, that

Asians focus more on responsibilities while Westerners are obsessed with rights. While it is true that neither Buddhism nor Confucianism conceptualizes human rights, the fact that they have not been mentioned in the past by these religions does not mean that the idea of rights in no way resonates with the people living in Asia. Confucius' injunction "Let the government not interfere, so that the people may thrive" sounds like a Western liberal value. Buddhism does not appear especially hostile to rights either. Given this religion's focus on human development, the Buddhist might very well accept that there are human rights but then try to connect them with human potentiality and "feelings and consciousness relative to injustice and inequality." One can get some sense of what such a connection might look like in the context of the Tibetan legal system. This legal system recognizes the individual's "right" to a fair trial, and the court employs procedures designed to insure a fair trial. The system differs from that of most Western countries in the way in which it thinks about punishment. In Tibet, the punishment is not designed to "fit the crime" so much as to suit the particular individual being punished. The punishment should be such as to bring the "criminal" to greater insight and a higher level of awareness. . . .

PART TWO: LEARNING FROM WATSUJI TETSURO AND CONFUCIUS

At one level, then, "Eastern ethics" has nothing to teach us about business ethics since such ethics may not even exist. If we take the expression "Eastern ethics" in a more limited sense, however, and think of it as applying to the ethics of particular individuals living within China or Japan or India, then business can learn something from Eastern ethics. While there may not be a single ethic of the

Japanese or Chinese, individual thinkers such as Confucius and Watsuji Tetsuro have unquestionably both captured and influenced some dimensions of the ways in which their fellow citizens think about what is morally right. In the remainder of this paper, I draw upon these two thinkers to examine three larger themes:

1. The meaning of trust
2. Relations for life
3. Ethics beyond rights

The Meaning of Trust

Since Watsuji speaks at length about trust, I will develop his idea of trust and show how it contrasts with some views dominant within the Anglo-American tradition. For Watsuji, human social relations are not grounded in trust. Rather trust is based in human being or *ningen sonzai*. Society cannot be the result of a voluntary decision by citizens to come together and to agree to show each other mutual good will. Trust exists because we are all always already related to each other in a variety of ways — as parents of children and children of parents; as spouses, clients, employees, supervisors, subordinates, etc. We move within these relations conforming to expectations we did not form. Even to deny these expectations is indirectly to confirm them. Over time such role expectations change as the result of individual rebellion, but they do not disappear. Another set of role expectations emerges to take the place of the prior set.

Trusting others is nothing other than living and acting within this social matrix. Sometimes people betray us, but betrayals do not destroy trust. There is no betrayal where there is no trust; and trust exists wherever there are human beings — i.e., activities in accordance with relations. In fact, most betrayals are parasitic upon trust. To take Watsuji's example: The pickpocket can operate only as long as people are not excessively guarded when shopping, going to movies or, more generally, moving within the public space. A theft does not destroy this trust. It might make the individual more cautious but that individual will still be trusting in most dimensions of his or her life. Our trust is never the result of some cost-benefit calculation. Nor is it something we repose in another on the strength of evidence. Anyone who is human trusts simply by virtue of being human.

Perhaps only among enemies at war has trust completely ceased to exist. When each side desires to exterminate the other, humanity is not present. Or maybe we should say it is present but in a very attenuated form. For even here there is a relation of sorts — the relation of enemy to enemy. To declare someone an enemy is to say he or she is not a friend. That means, though, that friendship is potentially applicable to the enemy in a way that it is not with respect to inanimate things. We do not go around saying of rocks or a bottle of distilled vinegar, "It is my enemy." So enemies have a relation and maybe even a modicum of trust.

This non-voluntaristic, non-contractarian, non-evidentiary notion of trust has several interesting implications for business practice: For example, trust is not something companies can or should market. Companies already have our trust, a point that gets driven home every time we read how easy the unscrupulous find it to con the rest of us. Instead of seeing themselves as winning our trust by compiling a good record of healthy products and safe working conditions, businesses should understand themselves as striving to be true to the trust they enjoy simply by virtue of being a human institution operating within the social matrix. Being true to this trust should be the guiding intention behind every action, not just an idea that comes into play when it is time to roll out a major marketing campaign or to negotiate with workers. There is no single moment when trust is reposed or withheld. It is always present as part of the structure of humanity. The issue is therefore less one of whether others will trust you than one of whether you will be true to human being.

Truth also takes on a different meaning within this scheme. Trust cannot be built up by speaking the truth — i.e., by making one's words and deeds correspond with the fact of the matter. Truth depends upon trust. A "true" friend is not one who gives us the facts. Rather true friends speak in the way our friendship with them merits. Similarly businesses will not earn our trust by pursuing a strategy of "truth in advertising." Instead businesspeople should speak in accordance with a consciousness of what it means to be a businessperson in society, a businessperson who is already trusted by customers, government officials, suppliers, etc. Truth should not emerge as the result of a strategic calculation but out of the businessperson's strong sense of himself or herself as a human being in that role which is but one among many.

Truth and trust have the same structure wherever they exist. Watsuji would thus agree in spirit with the powerful statement of Aaron Feuerstein, the CEO whose family rebuilt Malden Mills after a devastating fire: "God is one. There is no god of the family, god of the marketplace, god of the temple. God is one and is present everywhere." For Feuerstein, there never was a possibility of not rebuilding the family-owned business. He was a human being in a community of people who had built their lives around the mill. He thus spoke as a true CEO when he rejected out of hand suggestions that he rebuilt because doing so was a shrewd way of making money.

Relations Are for Life

Both Watsuji and Confucius reject the radical, atomistic understanding of human beings. To be human is always already to be in relation — or, more precisely, in a matrix of interrelated highly determinate relations (e.g., parent–child: older–younger sibling; teacher–student: superior–subordinate, etc.). These relations are for life. Certain problems which plague Western thought simply do not arise in this alternative worldview. For example, if the person is an individual and if an individual is identified with the capacity for rational thought, then a comatose person suffering extensive brain damage may not be a person at all within this Western framework. This problem does not arise in a Watsujian or Confucian framework. The comatose daughter does not cease to be the daughter of the mother. She is and forever will be that mother's child. Should she die, she remains the mother's "dead daughter." Nor does the next daughter in line become the eldest daughter upon her sister's death. She, too, remains the second daughter for life.

Since relations are for life, the person of *jen* or humanity does not form new relations lightly. Friendships, for example, require both parties to show good will to each other as long as each is alive. The sense of obligation to the friend may extend beyond death. For example, the friend may feel it is necessary to help the child of a dead friend to get a college education. The Chinese were shocked and offended when Nixon declared himself a friend to China because America and China would each get something out of the relation. This attitude of expediency is utterly foreign to the way the person of *jen* or person with a true heart (*makoto*) thinks about friendship. Showing good will, not getting advantage, is the mark of the true friend.

From the Watsujian and Confucian perspectives, commercial relations are longterm as well. An action or choice is not good simply because it has taken into account the interests of stockholders or many stakeholders. It goes without saying that the effect of one's actions on the larger social matrix of rela-

tions must always be considered. It is also necessary for the actor to consider the longterm effect of her actions on relations. Each generation of agents shows such regard; and that accounts for why many commercial relations in Japan and China (Taiwan, Hong Kong, etc.) go back many generations.

Businesses are not, therefore, selling products or marketing their reputation. They are establishing a relation or, in the catchy phrase of one modern author, developing a customer for life. Customers in Japan historically have not been especially price-conscious; they stick with those they know. Habits have changed somewhat as the Japanese travelled abroad and came to see how much more costly some items were in Japan than in America or Europe. Yet customers still expect that those who sell them a product will stand behind that product for years and will prove solicitous in their service to the buyer. Some Japanese realtors will go into a home after the escrow has been closed and get the utilities turned on as part of the after-sales follow-up. They understand the real relationship begins after the house has been purchased. Manufacturers will continue to buy from suppliers with whom they have done business in the past, even if these suppliers charge more than others. In China, too, people feel beholden to those who have helped them in the past. Favors are not accepted lightly because one will have to reciprocate.

There are numerous problems with such a system. It is difficult to dump a distributor or supplier who fails to do a good job. These longterm relations may limit competition. Newcomers cannot simply buy marketshare by offering loss leaders in a system where customers remain exceptionally loyal to brand-names. On the other hand, there is an important lesson here for both businesspeople and business ethicists — namely, that business transactions do not occur in a void or in some separate discrete "economic" sphere completely cut off from the rest of social life. The habits acquired in one sphere carry over into others. If we want our citizenry to know what it means to be a good parent and a true friend, then we need to think about the form and bases of our economic transactions as well. Encouraging people to respond only to price signals may develop a deeply-rooted worldview in which everything is valued using a standard of expediency alone.

Ethics Beyond Rights

A third important strand common to Watsuji and Confucius is their emphasis on what we owe to each other. It is tempting to say that their systems and, for that matter, the Japanese and Chinese cultures are duty-based while Western cultures are rights-based. This distinction, while nice and tidy, simplifies too much. If the ethics of the Japanese and Chinese have no idea of rights, they equally have no idea of duty. Duties are the correlatives of rights. There cannot be one without the other. Both duties and rights are enforceable claims. Citizens have the right to demand that elected officers fulfill their responsibilities — i.e., the duties of their office. If the officers fail to do so, the citizens have a right to impeach them, sue, vote them out of office, etc. But the duties Watsuji and Confucius are describing are not enforceable. Quite the contrary. As the noted Japanese legal theorist Kawashima Takeyoshi has observed, it is ethically "improper for the other party (beneficiary) of an obligation to demand or claim that the obligated person fulfill his obligation. An obligation is considered valueless, if, although it is fulfilled by the obligated person, he does not fulfill it in addition with a special friendliness or favor toward the other party.

In other words, the actual value of social obligations depends upon the good will and favor of the obligated person, and there is no place for the existence of the notion of right. . . ."

So an obligation does not derive ethical value from the fact that a rational being would make this demand and want to enforce it. Whatever ethical worth it has comes from the agent's perception or intuitive understanding of her place in the whole of human relations. This understanding will lead her to act with *makoto* or a true-heartedness or *jen* — i.e., humanity. Acts of *makoto* or *jen* are ethically good. An act which honored another's "rights" but which was not done voluntarily or in the spirit of *jen* would not be ethically (or politically) good.

This point of view subordinates the law to moral considerations. Mere adherence to a statute (or, for that matter, a principle such as the categorical imperative) cannot be ethically good. Simple conformity does not exhibit *makoto* or *jen*. In addition, always obeying the law will lead one into a mechanical life. Laws by definition are general. They are not necessarily suited to the circumstances of the particular case or the specific relation. They may therefore be hostile to our true-hearted efforts to honor the requirements of particular human relations. It is better not to try to legislate too much. What laws do exist should be enforced in a spirit of equity or *jen*.

This more flexible approach can be dangerous. Those who enforce the law are given a tremendous amount of discretion. If the judges are people of *makoto*, then perhaps the decisions will prove just and appropriate. But such people are not always at the helm of the ship of state. If the judge hands down a bad decision, those affected by the decision have traditionally had few, if any, rights to which they can appeal in order to protest the decision.

The approach does have certain strengths, though, that are relevant to business practice. Managers and employees avoid asserting mutually incompatible rights. While there sometimes are strikes in Japan, these strikes usually occur after a settlement has been reached. They last for one day and are intended more as a PR device for making a statement than a mechanism of confrontation designed to force management's hand. (Strikes also occur with some frequency in South Korea, a supposedly Confucian country. This difference may be due to the greater impact the rights-oriented United States has had on the Korean subcontinent where it has maintained a military presence since 1950, a presence on which the South Koreans rely in order to preserve their democracy.)

Parties who are disagreeing are not so likely to get locked into a rigid position. Both sides must consider what it would mean to be true to the employee-manager relation. Doing so will almost certainly involve them in what Richard Nielsen has termed "double-loop" negotiations. In this form of negotiations, each side does not try to win and to enforce its will. Instead, they put their controlling values — the values behind their position — into play along with their demands. Each side has the opportunity to affect and mold the other sides' values. The opportunity does not guarantee that these controlling values will be refined. But it at least opens the door to this possibility.

Finally, this more flexible approach changes what it means for a business to be socially responsible. In the West, we tend to say, "Business has a right to make a profit, but they must do so in a socially responsible way." This formulation makes it hard to assess social responsibility. How much profit does business have a right to make? And might not the largely unfettered pursuit by private institutions of maximum profit lead to the greatest social good? If so, then it would be better to just let business go its own way without interference by the government or any other

social institution. In other words, having granted business the right to make a profit, the problem becomes one of fitting business back into society. The Watsujian and Confucian approaches, by contrast, treat business as just one of many institutions thoroughly embedded within the social matrix. It is not entitled to make absolute claims for itself. The question for the businessperson, as for every human being in the society, is: What is the good of the larger whole and how can I behave in such a way as to contribute to that whole? The first responsibility of an agent is to consider the whole. Only after having done so is the agent able to be true to the specific human relation in which he or she is operating.

On this second view, the business ethicist should be less concerned with whether multinational corporations or their local subsidiaries are honoring workers' rights to a safe environment or a living wage and more concerned with the larger questions of what contributions business is making to China or Japan. As Henry Rosemont, a Sinologist, has put it, we should be asking what a person of good will would wish for the Chinese at this point in their moral development (Rosemont). When we ask that question, we are driven to admit that it is not at all clear that the Chinese will be well-served if American and European countries sell them hundreds of thousands of cars. The Chinese already have severe pollution problems and do not have the road infrastructure to support a huge increase in automobile transportation. The loss of life may be huge just as it was in Nigeria when Western automobiles arrived before eye glasses. Focussing on the rights questions obscures these larger questions, questions which require Westerners to look at their own business practices and controlling values more closely instead of demonizing the Chinese or other developing countries in Asia.

CONCLUSION

Adopting the perspective of Watsuji or Confucius is certainly not a panacea for all that ails the West. However, taking this tradition seriously will help us to identify our own prejudices regarding business practice as well as to learn about some alternative conceptions of key business ideas such as trust. We may not want to accept these ideas but at least we will be in a better position to make an informed argument for why they should be rejected and to understand the criticisms some Chinese or Japanese businesspeople and philosophers may make regarding our own tradition.

NOTES

1. Akio Kawato, "Beyond the Myth of Asian Values," first published in *Chuokoron*, (December, 1995) at http://ifrm.glocom.jp/DOC.

2. Aristotle, *Politics,* 1252b.
3. Mary Midgley, *Can't We Make Moral Judgments?* (New York: St. Martin's Press, 1993), pp. 87–96. Many tend to forget that the United States has played an enormous role in shaping modern Japan. "The differences between Japan before and after 1945 are dramatic. In the years of occupation following the war, the U.S.A. refashioned all of Japan's political and social institutions. During the war, for example, Japan was dominated by the military caste. Afterwards, the U.S. written constitution officially defined Japan as a pacifist state." Daniel Nassim, "Shaming the Japanese," in *Living Marxism* 81 (July/August 1995) at www.junius.co.uk/LM/LM81/LM81_Books.html.

Business Ethics: A Japanese View

Iwao Taka

I. TWO NORMATIVE ENVIRONMENTS — RELIGIOUS DIMENSION

In order to evaluate the traditional ethical standards of the Japanese business community, it is necessary to describe the Japanese cultural context or background. When it comes to cultural or ethical background, we can classify Japanese conscious and unconscious beliefs into a "religious dimension" and a "social dimension," in that Japanese culture cannot be understood well in terms of only one of the two dimensions. While the former is closely combined with a metaphysical concept or an idea of human salvation, the latter is based on how Japanese observe or conceive their social environment. Stated otherwise, while the former is "ideal-oriented," the latter is "real-oriented."

First, the religious dimension. This dimension supplies a variety of concrete norms of behavior to the Japanese in relation to the ultimate reality. As a consequence, I shall call this dimension the "normative environment."

From Iwao Taka, "Business Ethics: A Japanese View," *Business Ethics Quarterly* 4:1, (1994). Used with permission.

By this I mean the environment in which most events and things acquire their own meanings pertaining to something beyond the tangible or secular world. Following this definition, there are mainly two influential normative environments in Japan: the "transcendental normative environment" and the "group normative environment."

1. Transcendental Normative Environment

One of the famous Japanese didactic poems says, "Although there are many paths at the foot of a mountain, they all lead us in the direction of the same moon seen at the top of the mountain." This poem gives us an ontological equivalent of "variety equals one." To put it in another way, though there are innumerable phenomena in this tangible world, each individual phenomenon has its own *numen* (soul, spirit, reason-d'être, or spiritual energy), and its numen is ultimately connected with the unique numen of the universe. In Japanese, this ultimate reality is often called "natural life force," "great life force of the universe," *michi* (path of righteousness), *ri* (justice), *ho* (dharma, laws), and the like.

"Transcendentalism" is the philosophy that every phenomenon is an expression of the great life force and is ultimately connected with the numen of the universe. It follows that the environment where various concrete norms come to exist may be called the "transcendental normative environment." What is more, the set of these norms is simply called "transcendental logic."

In this transcendental environment, everyone has an equal personal numen. This idea has been philosophically supported or strengthened by Confucianism and Buddhism. That is to say, in the case of neo-Confucianism, people are assumed to have a mi-

crocosm within themselves, and are considered condensed expressions of the universe (macrocosm). Their inner universe is expected to be able to connect with the outer universe.

In the case of Buddhism, every living creature is said to have an equal Buddhahood, a Buddhahood which is very similar with the idea of numen and microcosm. Buddhism has long taught, "Although there are differences among living creatures, there is no difference among human beings. What makes human beings different is only their name."

In addition, however, under the transcendental normative environment, not only individuals but also jobs, positions, organizations, rituals, and other events and things incorporate their own "numina." Needless to say, these numina are also expected to be associated with the numen of the universe.

Deities of Shintoism, Buddhism, and the Japanese new religions, which have long been considered objects of worship, are often called the "great life force of the universe," or regarded as expressions of that force. In this respect, the life force can be sacred and religious. On the other hand, however, many Japanese people have unconsciously accepted this way of thinking without belonging to any specific religious sect. In this case, it is rather secular, non-religious, and atheistic. Whether it is holy or secular, the significant feature of Japan is that this transcendental normative environment has been influential and has been shared by Japanese people.

2. Meaning of Work in the Transcendental Environment

Inasmuch as Japanese people live in such a normative environment, the meaning of work for them becomes unique. That is to say, work is understood to be a self-expression of the great life force. Work is believed to have its own numen so that work is one of the ways to reach something beyond the secular world or the ultimate reality. Accordingly, Japanese people unconsciously and sometimes consciously try to unify themselves with the great life force by concentrating on their own work.

This propensity can be found vividly in the Japanese tendency to view seemingly trivial activities — such as arranging flowers, making tea, practicing martial arts, or studying calligraphy — as ideal ways to complete their personality (or the ideal ways to go beyond the tangible world). Becoming an expert in a field is likely to be thought of as reaching the stage of *kami* (a godlike state). Whatever job people take, if they reach the *kami* stage or even if they make a strong effort to reach it, they will be respected by others.

M. Imai has concluded that whereas Western managers place priority on innovation, Japanese managers and workers put emphasis on *Kaizen* (continuous improvement of products, of ways to work, and of decision-making processes). While innovation can be done intermittently only by a mere handful of elites in a society, *Kaizen* can be carried on continuously by almost every person.

> Technological breakthroughs in the West are generally thought to take a Ph.D., but there are only three Ph.D.s on the engineering staff at one of Japan's most successfully innovative companies — Honda Motor. One is founder Soichiro Honda, whose Ph.D. is an honorary degree, and the other two are no longer active within the company. At Honda, technological improvement does not seem to require a Ph.D.[1]

The transcendental normative environment has contributed to the formation of this Japanese propensity to place emphasis on *Kaizen*. Work has been an important path for Japanese people to reach the numen of the universe. Thus, they dislike skimping on their work, and instead love to improve their products, ways of working, or the decision-making processes. These Japanese attitudes are closely linked with the work ethics in the transcendental normative environment. Kyogoku describes this as follows:

> In marked contrast with an occidental behavioral principle of "Pray to God, and work!" at the cloister, in Japan, "Work, that is a prayer!" became a principle. In this context, devotion of one's time and energy to work, concentration on work to such a degree that one is absorbed in the improvement of work without sparing oneself, and perfectionism of "a demon for work," became institutional traditions of Japan.[2]

In this way, the transcendental environment has supplied many hard workers to the Japanese labor market, providing an ethical basis for "diligence." Nonetheless, it has not created extremely individualistic people who pursue only their own short-term interests. Because they have hoped for job security and life security in the secular world, they have subjectively tried to coordinate their behavior so as to keep harmonious relations with others in the group. Within this subjective coordination, and having the long-term perspective in mind, they pursue their own purposes.

3. Group Normative Environment

The second or group normative environment necessarily derives from this transcendental normative environment, insofar as the latter gives special raisons d'être not only to individuals and their work, but also to their groups. As a result of the transcendental environment, every group holds its own numen. The group acquires this *raison d'être*, as long as it guarantees the life of its members and helps them fulfill their potentials.

But once a group acquires its *raison d'être*, it insists upon its survival. An environment in which norms regarding the existence and prosperity of the group appear and affect its members is called the "group normative environment," and the set of the norms in this environment is called "group logic."

In Japan, the typical groups have been: *ie* (family), *mura* (local community), and *kuni* (nation). After World War II, although the influence of *ie* and *kuni* on their members has been radically weakened, one cannot completely ignore their influence. *Mura* has also lost much power over its members, but *kaisha* (business organization) has taken over many functions of *mura,* in addition to some functions of *ie.* These groups are assumed to have their own numen: *ie* holds the souls of one's ancestors, *mura* relates to a *genius loci* (tutelary deity), *kaisha* keeps its corporate tradition (or culture), and *kuni* has Imperial Ancestors' soul. . . .

Groupism and a group-oriented propensity, which have often been pointed out as Japanese characteristics, stem from this group normative environment.

II. THE ETHICAL DILEMMA OF LIVING BETWEEN TWO ENVIRONMENTS

Japanese often face an ethical dilemma arising from the fact that they live simultaneously in the two different influential normative environments. In the transcendental environment, groups and individuals are regarded as equal numina and equal expressions of the great life force. In the group environment, however, a group (and its representatives) is considered to be superior to its ordinary members, mainly because while the group is expected to be able to connect with the numen of the universe in a direct way, the members are not related to the force in the same way. The only way for the members to connect with the life force is through the activities of their group.

Depending on which normative environment is more relevant in a given context, the group stands either above or on an equal footing with its members. Generally speaking, as long as harmonious human relations within a group can be maintained, discretion is allowed to individuals. In this situation, the transcendental logic is dominant.

But once an individual begins asking for much more discretion than the group can allow, or the group starts requiring of individuals much more selfless devotion than they are willing to give, ethical tension arises between the two environments. In most cases, the members are expected to follow the requirements of the group, justified by the group logic. . . .

The assertion or gesture by a group leader to persuade subordinate members to follow, is called *tatemae* (formal rule). *Tatemae* chiefly arises from the need of the group to adapt itself to its external environment. In order to adjust itself, the group asks its members to accept changes necessary for the group's survival. In this moment, the group insists upon *tatemae.* On the other hand, the assertion or gesture by the members to refuse *tatemae,* is called *honne* (real motive). *Honne* mainly comes from a desire to let the subordinates' numen express itself in a free way.

Usually, a serious confrontation between *tatemae* and *honne* is avoided, because both the leader and subordinates dislike face-to-face discussions or antagonistic relations. Stated otherwise, the members (the leader and the subordinates) tend to give great weight to harmonious relations within the group. Because of this, the leader might change his or her expectation toward the subordinates, or the subordinates might refrain from pursuing their direct self-interest. In either case, the final decision maker is unlikely to identify whose assertion was adopted, or who was right in the decision making, since an emphasis on who was correct or right in the group often disturbs its harmony.

Simply described, this ambiguous decision-making is done in the following way. The group lets the subordinates confirm a priority of group-centeredness, and requires their selfless devotion. This requirement is generally accepted without reserve in the group normative environment. But if the subordinate individuals do not really want to follow the group orders, they "make a wry face," "look displeased," "become sulky," or the like, instead of revealing their opinions clearly. These attitudes are fundamentally different from formal decision-making procedures. In this case, taking efficiency and the harmonious relation of the group into consideration, the group "gives up compelling," "relaxes discipline," or "allows *amae*" of the subordinates.

If the failure to follow the norms endangers the survival of the group, the leader repeatedly asks the members to follow the order. In this case, at first, the leader says, "I really understand your feeling," in order to show that he or she truly sympathizes with the members. And then he or she adds, "This is not for the sake of me, but for the sake of our group." Such persuasion tends to be accepted, because almost everybody implicitly believes that the group has its own numen and the group survival will bring benefits to all of them in the long run. . . .

III. ETHICS OF CONCENTRIC CIRCLES — SOCIAL DIMENSION

Due to human bounded cognitive rationality or cultural heritage, Japanese moral agents, whether individuals or corporations, tend to conceptualize the social environment in a centrifugal order similar to a water ring. Although there are many individuals, groups, and organizations which taken together constitute the overall social environment, the Japanese are likely to categorize them into

four concentric circles: family, fellows, Japan, and the world. On the basis of this way of thinking, Japanese people and organizations are likely to attribute different ethics or moral practices to each circle. Let us look at the concentric circles of individuals and of corporations respectively.

* * *

1. The Concentric Circles of Corporations

Just as individuals understand their social environment as concentric circles, so groups such as corporations have a similar tendency to characterize their environment. For the sake of simplicity, I shall classify the corporate environment into four circles: quasi-family, fellows, Japan, and the world.

First, corporations have a quasi-family circle. Of course, though corporations do not have any blood relationships, they might still have closely related business partners. For example, parent, sister, or affiliated companies can be those partners. "Vertical *keiretsu*" (Vertically integrated industrial groups like Toyota, Hitachi, or Matsushita groups) might be a typical example of the quasi-family circle. In this circle we find something similar to the parent–child relationship.

The main corporate members (about 20 to 30 companies in each group) of "horizontal *keiretsu*" (industrial groups such as Mitsubishi, Mitsui, Sumitomo, Dai Ichi Kangyo, Fuyo, and Sanwa groups) might be viewed as quasi-family members. Nonetheless, most of the cross-shareholding corporations in the horizontal *keiretsu* should be placed in the second circle, because their relations are less intimate than commonly understood.

In the second circle, each corporation has its own main bank, fellow traders, distant affiliated firms, employees, steady customers, and the like. If the corporation or its executives belong to some outside associations like *Nihon Jidousha Kogyo Kai* (Japanese Auto Manufacturers Association), *Doyukai* (Japan Association of Corporate Executives), *Keidanren* (Japan Federation of Economic Organizations), etc., the other members of such outside associations might constitute part of the second circle of the corporation. And if the corporation is influential enough to affect Japanese politics or administration, the Japanese governmental agencies or ministries, and political parties might constitute part of this circle.

Recognition within the fellow circle requires that there must be a balance between benefits and debts in the long run. On account of this, if a corporation does not offer enough benefits to counterbalance its debts to others in this circle, the corporation will be expelled from the circle, being criticized for neither understanding nor appreciating the benefits given it by others. On the other hand, if the corporation can successfully balance benefits and debts or keep the balance in the black, it will preferentially receive many favorable opportunities from other companies or interest groups. For these reasons, every corporation worries about the balance sheet of benefits and debts in the fellow circle.

This way of recognizing the business context is closely related to original Confucianism, in that Confucianism allows people to treat others in proportion to the intimacy of their relations. Unlike Christianity, Confucianism does not encourage people to love one another equally. It rather inspires people to love or treat others differentially on the grounds that, if people try to treat everybody equally in a social context, they will often face various conflicts among interests. This does not mean that Confucianism asserts that people should deny love to unacquainted people. The main point of this idea is that, although people have to treat all others as human beings, they should love intensely those with whom they are most intimate; those who cannot love this way cannot love strangers either. I can call this "the differential principle" in Confucianism. Influenced or justified by this differential principle, Japanese corporations also classify their business environment in this way.

In the Japan circle, the fellow circle ethics is substantially replaced by "the principle of free competition." Competitors, unrelated corporations, ordinary stockholders, consumers, (for ordinary corporations, the Japanese government constitutes part of this circle) and so forth, all fall within this circle. Yet almost all corporations in this circle know well that the long-term reciprocal ethics is extremely important in constructing and maintaining their business relations, because of their similar cultural background. This point makes the third circle different from the world circle.

In the fourth or world circle, corporations positively follow "the principle of free competition," subject to the judicial system, with less worrying about their traditional reputations. Roughly speaking, the behavioral imperatives for corporations turn out to be producing or supplying high quality and low price products, dominating much more market share, and using the law to resolve serious contractual problems.

As in the case of the individuals, the world circle is conceived as a relatively chaotic sphere causing corporate attitudes to become contradictory. On the one hand, Japanese corporations tend to exclude foreign counterparts that do not understand the extant Japanese business practices, hoping to maintain the normative order of its own business community. Notwithstanding these closing attitudes, on the other hand, they yearn after foreign technologies, know-how, products, and services which are expected to help corporations to be successful and competitive in the Japanese and world market. In particular, western technologies have long been objects of admiration for Japanese companies. This tendency vividly shows their global attitudes.

2. Dynamics of the Concentric Circles

Now that I have roughly described the static relations among the concentric circles (of individuals and of corporations), I need to show the dynamic relations among these circles, that is to say, how these circles are interrelated. . . . In order to describe these complicated relations in a parsimonious light, I shall limit my discussion to the relations between the members of an "ideal big Japanese corporation" and its business environment. By a "big Japanese corporation," I mean the "idealized very influential organization" in an industry that places priority on the interests of employees, and holds a long-term strategic perspective. By "operation base" in this context, I mean the place where the members can relax, charge their energy, and develop action programs to be applied to the business environment. Whether the corporation can be such a base or not heavily depends on its members' abilities with respect to human relations: their ability to sympathize or understand other members' feelings, their ability to put themselves in the others' position, their ability to internalize other members' expectations toward them, and the like.

It has been said that in Japanese corporations, many people have such abilities. For instance, E. Hamaguchi has called people with these abilities "the contextuals" in contrast with "the individuals."

> An "individual" is not a simple unit or element of a society, but a positive and subjective member. This so-called "individual-centered model of man" is the typical human model of the western society.
>
> This model, however, is clearly different from the Japanese model. The Japanese human model is a "being between people" or an internalized being in its relations. This can be called "the contextual" in contrast with the individual.[3]

To be sure, these abilities have also positively contributed to the performance of Japanese corporations. The corporations have not rigidly divided work into pieces and distributed them to each employee so as to clarify the responsibilities each has to take. The corporations have rather let employees work together so that the contextual members make up for the deficiencies of one another allowing the quality of products and efficiency of performance to be surprisingly improved.

On the contrary, the business environment as a "battlefield" is reckoned to be a strenuous sphere, where "the law of the jungle" is the dominant ethical principle. In the market, the principle of free competition replaces the ethics expected in an operation base (quasi-family and fellow circles). What is more, this principle of free competition is justified by the transcendental logic, because, as I have described earlier, in the transcendental environment, work is one of the most important "ways" or "paths" to reach something sacred or the ultimate reality. In this way, "the principle of free competition" in the battlefield and "the transcendental logic" are coincidentally combined to encourage people to work hard, an encouragement which results in survival and the development of the corporation.

Wealth, power, market share, competitive advantage, or other results acquired in this business context become important scales to measure the degree of the members' efforts to proceed on the "path" to the ultimate stage. And based on these scales, contributors are praised within the operation base, namely in a corporation, in an industrial group, or in Japan.

For example, the Japanese government, administrative agencies, or ministries have so far endorsed the efforts of corporations under the present *Tenno* system (the Emperor System of Japan). The decoration and the Order of Precedence at the Imperial Court have been given to corporate executives who have contributed to the development of the Japanese economy.

Theoretically speaking, it is very hard to compare the performance of various corporations in different industries of a nation, simply because each industry has its own scale or own philosophy to measure performance. In the case of Japan, however, the annual decoration and attendance at the Imperial Court plays the role of a unitary ranking scale, applied to every industry as well as non-business-related fields. Since the Japanese mass media makes the annual decoration and attendance public, the Japanese people know well who or which corporations are praiseworthy winners.

3. The Group Environment and the Concentric Circles

Now that I have explained both the group normative environment and the concentric circles of corporations, I should make clear the relationship between the group normative environment and the concentric circles. According to the group logic, each group has its own numen and has different social status. For example, even if the R&D unit of corporation A has its own numen, the status of the unit is lower than that of A itself. The status of A is also lower than that of the leading company B in the same industry. The status of B is lower than that of the Japanese government. But if I observe their relations from the viewpoint of concentric circles, these groups can be members of the same fellow circle of corporation C. Namely, the R&D

unit of corporation A, company B, and the government can constitute part of the fellow circle of C. Therefore, even if they are in the same fellow circle, it does not mean that all members have equal status in the group normative environment.

For these reasons, reciprocal relations within the fellow circle are varied according to the members' status in the group normative environment. For instance, because, in most cases, the Japanese government is regarded as a powerful agent in the fellow circle of large corporation C, C makes efforts to maintain its good relations with the government and is likely to depend on the government.

The main reason why *gyosei-shido* (administrative guidance) has so far worked well in Japan comes from this dependent trait of the corporation and from the fact that the administrative agencies or ministries have a very important status in the second circle of the large Japanese corporations.

Each Japanese corporation also maintains relations with the business associations such as *Keidanren* and *Doyukai*. Once an authoritative business association declares *tatemae,* the member corporations make efforts to follow the formal rules, even though they might have some doubts about *tatemae,* simply because those associations hold socially or politically higher status in the group normative environment.

IV. JAPANESE RECOGNITION OF THE AMERICAN BUSINESS COMMUNITY

Because Japanese follow the transcendental logic, group logic, and concentric circles' ethics, their way of observing other business societies might appear to be idiosyncratic. And this idiosyncrasy might bring serious misunderstanding to trading partners such as the United States, European industrialized countries, Asian NIEs, and the other developing countries.

Because of this, I would like to clarify how Japanese conceive the American business community: how the American business community is seen in the eyes of the Japanese business people who adopt the two normative logics and the concentric circles' ethics.

1. Job Discrimination and the Transcendental Logic

First, as noted earlier, in the transcendental normative environment, whatever job people take, they are believed to reach the same goal or the same level of human development. Because of this logic, Japanese are unlikely to evaluate others in terms of their "job" (specialty). They would rather evaluate one another in terms of their "attitudes" toward work.

To be concrete, it is not important for Japanese to maintain the principle of the division of labor. Of importance is the process and the result of work. If people cannot attain goals in the existing framework of the division of labor, they are likely to try other alternatives which have not been clearly defined in the existing framework. This kind of positive attitude toward work is highly appreciated in Japan.

On the contrary, a society such as the United States, where jobs are strictly divided, is perceived as not only inefficient but also discriminatory in Japanese eyes. To be sure, this society might hold a belief that the division of labor makes itself efficient or makes it possible for diverse people to utilize their own abilities. The Japanese business community, however, is likely to assume that people's reluctance to help others' work in the same group is based on job discrimination.

In America, in a large retail shop, for instance, often those who sell a heavy consumer product are reluctant to carry it for the customer. They have a specific person, whose job is just to carry goods, do so. If the person is busy with other goods, the salespeople will ask the customer to wait until the person is finished carrying the other goods.

Similarly, those who manage a large shop typically do not clean up the street in front of their shop. They let a janitor do so. Even if they find garbage there, when the janitor has not come yet, they are likely to wait for the janitor. This kind of attitude of salespeople or managers is regarded as inefficient and discriminatory by Japanese.

2. Employees' Interest and the Group Logic

Second, in the group normative environment, the group is believed to hold its own numen and expected to guarantee the members' life. That is to say, a corporation is thought to exist for its employees rather than for its shareholders.

Because of this logic, the Japanese business community ethically questions American general attitudes toward the company where many accept the ideas that 1) a company is owned by its shareholders, 2) executives should lay off the employees whenever the layoff brings benefits to the shareholders, 3) executives should buy other companies and sell part of their own company whenever such a strategy brings benefits to the shareholders, etc.

Of course, even in Japan, shareholders are legal owners of a company so that the shareholders might use their legal power to change the company in a favorable way for themselves. Therefore, many Japanese corporations have invented a legitimate way to exclude the legal rights of shareholders, i.e.

"cross-shareholding." This is the practice in which a corporation allows trusted companies to hold its own shares, and in return the corporation holds their shares. By holding shares of one another and refraining from appealing to the shareholders' rights, they make it possible to manage the companies for the sake of the employees.[4] Because this cross-shareholding is based on mutual acceptance, any attempts to break this corporate consortium from the outside, whether Japanese or foreigners, are often stymied by the consortium of the member corporations.

For example, in April 1989, Boone Company, controlled by T. Boone Pickens, bought a 20 percent stake in Koito Manufacturing, Japanese auto parts maker. In 1990, Pickens increased it to 25 percent, becoming Koito's largest single shareholder.[5] But because Pickens asked for seats on Koito's board for himself as well as three Boone Company associates, and requested an increase in Koito's annual dividend, he was labeled as a "greenmailer" in the Japanese business community. As a result, the other consortium members cooperatively protected Koito from the Pickens' attack.[6] . . .

In addition, the layoff of employees and the high salaries of American executives are also regarded as unethical by the Japanese business community. . . . In Japan, when executives face serious difficulties, they first reduce their own benefits, then dividends and other costs, and, after that, employees' salary or wage. If the situation is extremely hard to overcome with these measures, they sell assets and only as a last resort do they lay off workers. Even in this case, the executives often find and offer new job opportunities for those who are laid off, taking care of their family's life.

Because of this, Japanese executives criticize the American business climate in which only salaries of executives keep rising, even while they lay off employees (especially in the 1980s). This criticism is also based on the Japanese group normative logic.

3. Claims Against the Japanese Market and the Concentric Circles' Ethics

As I have noted above, because of the framework of concentric circles, especially of the ethics of the fellow circle, foreign corporations often face difficulties entering the Japanese market. Although Japanese admit that the market is very hard to enter, a majority of them believe that it is still possible to accomplish entry.

Even if the Japanese market has many business-related practices such as semi-annual gifts, entertainment, cross-shareholding, "triangular relationship" among business, bureaucracy, and the Liberal Democratic Party, the long-term relationship is formed mainly through a series of business transactions.

That is to say, the most important factor in doing business is whether suppliers can respond to the assemblers' requests for quality, cost, the date of delivery, and the like, or on how producers can respond to the retailers' or wholesalers' expectations. . . .

Foreign corporations might claim that because they are located outside Japan, they cannot enter even the Japan circle. On this claim, the Japanese business community is likely to insist that if they understand the "long-term reciprocal ethics," they can enter the Japan circle; and what is more, might be fellows of Japanese influential corporations. As I have described, what makes the Japan circle different from the world circle is that people in the Japan circle know well the importance of this ethics. In fact, successfully enjoying the Japanese market are foreign corporations such as IBM, Johnson & Johnson, McDonald's, Apple, and General Mills which have understood well this ethics.

In this respect, realistically, the Japanese business community interprets the criticism by the American counterpart of the Japanese market as unfair and unethical. To put it differently, Japanese believe that if foreign corporations understand the long-term ethics, they will easily be real members of the Japanese business community.

V. ETHICAL ISSUES OF THE JAPANESE BUSINESS COMMUNITY

I have shown how Japanese people conceive the American business society and its business-related practices from the viewpoint of the two normative environments and the concentric circles. Yet this does not mean that the Japanese business community has no ethical problems. On the contrary, there are many issues it has to solve. What are the ethical issues of the Japanese business community? . . .

1. Discrimination and the Transcendental Logic

I will shed light on the organizational issues (opening the Japanese organizations) from the prime value of transcendental logic. The prime value here is "everybody has an equal microcosm." Whether men or women, Japanese or foreigners, hard workers or non-hard workers, everybody has to be treated equally as a person. When I observe the organizational phenomena from the viewpoint of this value, there are at least the following two discriminatory issues.

First, the transcendental logic has worked favorably only for male society. That is, in this normative environment, Japanese women have been expected to actualize their potentials through their household tasks. Those tasks have been regarded as their path toward the goal. Of course, insofar as women voluntarily agree with this thinking, there seems to be no ethical problem. And in fact, a majority of women have accepted this way of living to date. Nonetheless, now that an increasing number of women work at companies and hope to get beyond such chores as making tea to more challenging jobs, the Japanese corporations have no longer been allowed to treat women unequally.

Second, the transcendental normative logic itself has often been used to accuse cer-tain workers of laziness. As far as a worker voluntarily strives to fulfill his or her own potential according to the transcendental logic, this presents no ethical problems. Nevertheless, once a person begins to apply the logic to others and evaluate them in terms of their performance, the transcendental logic easily becomes the basis for severe accusations against certain workers.

For example, even if a man really wants to change his job or company, his relatives, colleagues, or acquaintances are unlikely to let him do so, because they unconsciously believe that any job or any company can lead him to the same high stage of human development, if he makes efforts to reach it. Put in a different way, it is believed that despite the differences between the jobs or companies, he can attain the same purpose in either. On account of this, many Japanese say, "once you have decided and started something by yourself, you should not give up until reaching your goal." This is likely to end up justifying a teaching that "enough is as good as a feast."

If the person does not follow this teaching, thereby refusing overtime or transfers, he will jeopardize his promotion and be alienated from his colleagues and bosses, since he is not regarded as a praiseworthy diligent worker. Even if he is making efforts to fulfill his potential in work-unrelated fields, he is not highly appreciated, simply because what he is doing is not related to the company's work.

Analyzing those practices from the viewpoint of the prime value (everybody has equal microcosm), I cannot help concluding that the Japanese business community should alter its organizational climate.

2. Employees' Dependency and the Group Logic

In the group normative environment, groups are regarded as having a higher status than their individual members. Because the members are inclined to take this hierarchical order for granted, they come to be dependent on the groups. And their groups also come to be dependent on the next higher groups. This dependency of the agents, whether of individuals or groups, brings the following two problems into the Japanese business community. Because of the dependent trait, 1) the individual members of the group refrain from expressing their opinions about ethical issues, and 2) they tend to obey the organizational orders, even if they disagree with them. The first tendency is related to decision making, while the second affects policy implementation. . . .

One of the typical examples which shows this tendency of members to waive their basic rights is *karoshi* (death caused by overwork). In 1991, the Japanese Labor Ministry awarded 33 claims for *karoshi*. Since it is very hard to prove a direct and quantifiable link between overwork and death, this number is not large enough to clarify the actual working condition, but is certainly large enough to show that there is a possibility of turning the group logic into unconditional obedience.

This corporate climate not only jeopardizes the employees' right to life, but also hampers the healthy human development of the individual members. Because of this, the Japanese business community has to alter this group-centered climate into a democratic ground on which the individuals can express their opinions more frankly than before.

3. Exclusiveness of the Concentric Circles

The Japanese conceptualization of the social environment in a centrifugal framework is closely connected with Confucianism (the differential principle): It allows people to treat others in proportion to the intimacy of their relationships. As I touched upon before, however, the main point of this principle is not that people should deny love to strangers, but rather that those who cannot love their most intimate relatives intensely are surely incapable of loving strangers. Stated otherwise, even if the way to achieve a goal is to love differentially, the goal itself is to love everybody. Therefore, "to love everybody" should be regarded as the prime value of the concentric circles' ethics.

If I look at the Japanese market (opening the Japanese market) from the viewpoint of this prime value, there appear to be at least the following two issues. 1) The Japanese business community has to make an effort to help foreigners understand the concept of long-term reciprocal ethics. This effort will bring moral agents of the world circle into the Japan circle. 2) The Japanese community has to give business opportunities to as many newcomers as possible. This effort will bring the newcomers into the fellow circles.

The first issue is how to transfer foreign corporations from the world circle to the Japan circle. . . . This "fairness" implies that they treat foreign companies the same as they treat other Japanese firms. To put it differently, the concept of "fairness" encourages the Japanese corporations to apply the same ethical standard to all companies.

Although this is a very important point of "fairness," there is a more crucial problem involved in opening the market. That is how to let newcomers know what the rules are and how the Japanese business community applies the rules. As mentioned before, for the purpose of constructing and maintaining business relationships with a Japanese company (a core company), a foreign firm has to be a fellow of the company. In this fellow circle, every fellow makes efforts to balance benefits and debts with the core company in material and spiritual terms in the long run, since making a long-term balance is the most important ethics. Yet balancing them is too complicated to be attained for the foreign corporation, as long as benefits and debts are rather subjective concepts.

For example, in Japan, if company A trusts the executive of company B and helps B, when B is in the midst of serious financial difficulties, then B will give the most preferential trade status to A after overcoming its difficulties. B will rarely change this policy, even if B finishes repaying its monetary debts to A. Moreover, even if A's products are relatively expensive, as long as the price is not extraordinarily unreasonable, B will continue to purchase A's output. If A's products are not sophisticated enough to meet B's standard, B will often help A to improve A's products in various ways.

If A's help is understood only as financial aid, this close relationship between A and B will not appear reasonable. In Japan, in most cases, B is deeply impressed by the fact that A has trusted B (even if B is in serious difficulties) so that B continues to repay its spiritual debts to A as long as possible. Yet if B were to change this policy soon after repaying the borrowed capital to A, and if it began buying the same but cheaper products from company C, not only A but also other corporations which have been aware of this process from the beginning will regard B as an untrustworthy company in their business community.

"Fairness" in a Japanese sense might involve asking foreign companies to follow the former way of doing business. Nonetheless, foreign companies, especially Americans, do not understand "fairness" this way. Their understanding is rather similar to the latter behavior of B: switching from A to C. This difference of understanding "fairness" between Americans and Japanese undoubtedly causes a series of accusations against each other.

The Japanese business community should not let this happen over and over again. If the community takes the prime value seri-

ously, as the first duty, it has to explain the long-term reciprocal ethics to foreign counterparts in an understandable way. This effort will help the foreigners enter the Japan circle.

But even if they can enter the Japan circle successfully, there still remains another problem. That is how those foreigners, which have been already in the Japan circle, enter the fellow circles of influential Japanese corporations. This is related to the second issue of opening the Japanese market.

Even when foreign companies understand and adopt long-term reciprocal ethics, they might not be able to enter those fellow circles, if they rarely have the chance to show their competitive products or services to the influential corporations. On account of this, as an ethical responsibility, the Japanese corporations should have "access channels" through which every newcomer can equally approach.

To be sure, the "mutual trust" found in the fellow circle should not be blamed for everything. But if the trust-based business relation is tightly combined among a few influential corporations, it tends to exclude newcomers. As long as such a relation is not against the Japanese Antimonopoly Law, it is safe to say that efforts to maintain the relationship are not problematic, because most of the corporations do so according to their free will. Despite that, if I look at the exclusive tendency of a fellow circle like that of the Japanese distribution system, I cannot help saying that the trust-based relation is a critical obstacle for newcomers.

If the Japanese business community follows the prime value (to love everybody) of the concentric circles' ethics, it has to make an effort to remove the obstacles to entry. One of the ideal ways to do so is to give newcomers more competitive bids than before. Of course, it is not obligatory for Japanese corporations to accept every bidder as a fel-

low after the tender. If a bidder is not qualified as an ideal business partner in terms of
its products or services, Japanese corporations do not need to start transactions with
the bidder. But as a minimum ethical requirement, Japanese corporations should
have access channels through which every
newcomer can equally approach them. . . .

NOTES

1. M. Imai, *Kaizen* (New York: McGraw-Hill Publishing Company, 1986), p. 34.
2. Kyogoku, *Nihon no Seiji* (Politics of Japan)
   (Tokyo: Tokyo University Press, 1983)
   pp. 182–83.

3. E. Hamaguchi, *"Nihon Rashisa" no Saihakken
   (Rediscovery of Japaneseness)* (Tokyo: Kodansha,
   1988), pp. 66–67.
4. This practice was basically formed for a purpose of defending Japanese industries from
   foreign threats. But at the same time, Japanese people thought this threat might destroy
   the employee-centered management. T. Tsu-
   ruta, *Sengo Nihon no Sangyo Seisaku (Industrial
   Policies of Post-War Japan)* (Tokyo: Nihon
   Keizai Shinbunsha, 1982), pp. 121–30.
5. W. C. Kester, *Japanese Takeovers: The Global
   Contest for Corporate Control* (Cambridge:
   Harvard Business School Press, 1991),
   pp. 258–59.
6. *Mainichi Daily News* (May 15, 1990).

Exporting Mental Models: Global Capitalism in the 21st Century

Patricia H. Werhane

When one is asked to enumerate the most
challenging ethical issues business will face in
the next century, the list is long. Environmental sustainability, international trade,
exploitation, corruption, unemployment,
poverty, technology transfer, cultural diversity (and thus relativism) are a few obvious
candidates. Underlying these and other issues is a more serious global phenomenon:
the exportation of Western capitalism.

There is a mental model of free enterprise,
a model primarily created in the United States,
that is being exported, albeit unconsciously,
as industrialized nations expand commerce
through the globalization of capitalism. This
model is not one of greedy self-interested cow-
boy capitalists eagerly competing to take advantage of resources, low-priced employment,
or offshore regulatory laxity. Rather I am referring to another model, one that has worked
and worked well in most of North America and
Western Europe for some time. This model
contends that industrialized free enterprise in
a free trade global economy, where businesses
and entrepreneurs can pursue their interests
competitively without undue regulations or
labor restrictions, will produce growth and
well-being, i.e., economic good, in every country or community where this phenomenon is
allowed to operate. . . .

From Patricia H. Werhane, "Exporting Mental Models: Global Capitalism in the 21st Century, *Business Ethics Quarterly*, 10(1)(2000), 353–362. Reprinted with permission.

What is wrong with adapting a model for global capitalism out of the highly successful American model for free enterprise? What is wrong with economic growth and improved standards of living, particularly in developing countries? Isn't reduction of poverty a universally desirable outcome? The tempting answer is that there is nothing wrong with this model. In this paper I shall suggest that a more thoughtful reply requires some qualifications.

To begin, let me explain the notion of mental models. Although the term is not always clearly defined, "mental model" connotes the idea that human beings have mental representations, cognitive frames, or mental pictures of their experiences, representations that model the stimuli or data with which they are interacting, and these are frameworks that set up parameters through which experience, or a certain set of experiences, is organized or filtered (Werhane 1991, 1998, 1999).

> Mental models are the mechanisms whereby humans are able to generate descriptions of system purpose and form, explanations of system functioning and observed system states, and predictions of future system states. (Rouse and Morris 1986, p. 351)

Mental models might be hypothetical constructs of the experience in question or scientific theories; they might be schema that frame the experience, through which individuals process information, conduct experiments, and formulate theories; or mental models may simply refer to human knowledge about a particular set of events or a system. Mental models account for our ability to describe, explain, and predict, and may function as protocols to account for human expectations that are often formulated in accordance to these models.

Mental models function as selective mechanisms and filters for dealing with experience. In focusing, framing, organizing, and ordering what we experience, mental models bracket and leave out data, and emotional and motivational foci taint or color experience. Nevertheless, because schema we employ are socially learned and altered through religion, socialization, culture, educational upbringing, and other experiences, they are shared ways of perceiving, organizing, and learning.

Because of the variety and diversity of mental models, none is complete, and "there are multiple possible framings of any given situation" (Johnson 1993, p. 9). By that I mean that each of us can frame any situation, event, or phenomenon in more than one way, and that same phenomenon can also be socially constructed in a variety of ways. It will turn out that the way one frames a situation is critical to its outcome, because "[t]here are ... different moral consequences depending on the way we frame the situation" (Johnson 1993).

Why is the notion of mental models of concern for business, and in particular, for global business? Let me explain by using some illustrations. One of the presuppositions of Western free enterprise, a supposition that fueled and made possible the industrial revolution, is that feudalism, at least as it is exhibited through most forms of serfdom, is humiliating, it demeans laborers, and worse, it does not allow serfs, in particular, to create or experience any sense of what it would mean to be free, free to live and work where one pleases (or to be lazy), to own property, and choose how one lives. Adam Smith even argued that feudalism is inefficient as well. It is commonly, although not universally, argued that individual property ownership is a social good. In agriculturally based economies, in particular, owning one's own farm land is considered a necessary step toward freedom and self-reliance. The industrial revolution, coupled with free commerce, wage labor, and property ownership, changes the feudal mental model, and, it is commonly argued, improves the lives of serfs, farm workers, and tenant farmers, in particular.

However, as Akiro Takahashi points out in a recent article in *Business Ethics Quarterly*, even 20th-century feudal arrangements are complex social institutions. One cannot simply free the serfs or sharecroppers, engage in redistributive land reform, and hope that a new economic arrangement will work out. Takahashi's example is from a 1960s rice-growing community in Luzon in the Philippines. From as long as anyone can remember until land reforms in the 1970s the village had operated as a fiefdom. There were a few landholders and the rest of the villagers were tenant farmers. In order to work the land, each year the tenant farmers paid rents equal to half the net production of their farms. But because the tenant farmers were always in debt to the landlords, they usually owed all the net production to the landlords. The tenant farmers in fact never paid their debts, but because of high interest rates, as much as 200 percent, their debt increased each year so that they really could never leave the property. Since in fact what was owed the landlord was the *net* produce, each sharecropper was allowed to hire workers to farm the land they rented. So tenant farmers hired workers from other landlords or from other communities to till and harvest. Each sharecropper, in turn, went to work for another landlord's sharecropper. In addition, it was common practice for the harvesters not to do a perfect job, leaving often as much as 20 to 25 percent of the rice unharvested. Gleaning was not allowed by tenant farmers or their families on the land they rented. But the wives of the farm workers and rest of the community "gleaned" the rest of the rice for themselves. In this way the poor were supported by the landlord and tenant farmers got some rice. The landlords pretended none of this occurred, still demanding the net

product from each of its tenant farmers (Takahaski 1997, pp. 39–40).

The value of private ownership (as linked to personal freedom) is a perfectly fine idea in principle. But abstracting that idea and universalizing it as a mental model for all reform has severe negative moral consequences, as the following example illustrates.

> Seven years ago, the prayers of 39 families were answered when the government [of Mexico] gave them this 1,000-acre communal farm in southern Mexico to raise livestock. Today the exhausted pastures are a moonscape of dust and rock. Cattle here don't graze quietly; they root like pigs as they yank rare blades of grass from the parched earth. . . . All arable land has been split into five-acre patches of corn per family. To stay alive, the men earn 21 cents an hour cutting sugar cane in nearby fields.
>
> Farms like this one, known as ejidos, have helped the government win political support in the countryside by answering peasant demands for "land and liberty" that date back to the revolution of 1910. Unfortunately, this continuing land-redistribution plan has done a better job of carving farmland into small, barren plots than it has of growing food or providing a decent living for farmers.
>
> . . . Farmers tend to split their parcels among their sons, and with two-thirds of farms already smaller than 12.5 acres, there isn't any room in the countryside for the next generations. (Frazier 1984, pp. 1, 18)

Another example: the Neem tree is a wild scraggly tree that grows well throughout India. For thousands of years, in hundreds of villages throughout that country the Neem tree has had a special place in the community. The tree has special religious meaning in some Hindu sects. Its leaves are used as pesticides, spread on plants to protect them from insects. Various herbal medicines are made from Neem leaves and bark, its products are used as contraceptives and for skin ailments, and many Indians brush their teeth with small Neem branches. Because of its effectiveness as a pesticide, recently the W. R.

Grace Company began studying the tree, and in 1992 they developed a pesticide, Neemix. Neemix works as effectively as Neem leaves and has a long shelf life, thus making it more desirable as a pesticide than the leaves. Following the guidelines of the Indian government regarding patenting, Grace patented Neemix, opened a plant in India, and manufactured the product.

However, there have been mass protests against this patenting, both from Indians and from the Foundation on Economic Trends, a biotechnology watchdog organization. The argument is that Grace committed "biopiracy" because the Neem tree belongs to Indians, and products from the tree cannot be patented. Moreover, such patenting and manufacture of Neemix and other products drives up prices of Neem such that the indigenous poor, to whom the tree belongs, can no longer have access to the trees (Severence et al. 1999; Vijayalakshmi, Radha, and Shiva, 1995).

A fourth illustration: SELF, the Solar Electric Light Fund, a United States-based NGO, for some time has been developing a project aimed at electrifying rural communities in China. SELF has promoted a small photovoltaic (PV) solar unit that produces about 20 to 60 watts of energy. SELF has a policy of not giving away its photovoltaic units. This is because, it argues, if people have to pay something, even a small amount, for this service, they will value it more. So SELF has set up complex long-term lending schemes so that some poor rural people in China can afford electricity and own their own units as well (Sonenshein et al. 1997a).

SELF has been highly successful in some rural communities in China, so it decided to export that project to South Africa, concentrating on small Zulu villages. Working with village leaders in one community, SELF tried a pilot project, with the aim of providing electricity for 75 homes in a small village of Maphephethe. Six units were installed and were well received, and those receiving the units were delighted to have reliable power. However, one serious problem developed. Previous to the introduction of PV technology all the villagers lived modest but similar lives in a fairly egalitarian community. Now, those who have PV units are able to improve their social and economic status by operating manual sewing machines at night. The distribution of PV technology has upset a very delicate social balance by creating social stratification within this community (Sonenshein et al. 1997b).

What do these examples tell us? They tell us something very simple, something we should have learned years ago from the Nestle infant formula cases. American (or in Nestle's case, Western European) mental models of property and free enterprise cannot be exported uniformly to every part of the world without sometimes producing untoward consequences. This is because the notion of what is good or a social good is a socially constructed idea that is contextually and culturally relative. Abstract ideas such as autonomy, equality, private property, ownership, and community create mental models that take on different meanings depending on the social and situational context. Differing notions of community, ownership, intellectual property, exchange, competition, equality, and fairness, what Walzer calls social goods, create cultural anomalies that cannot be overcome simply by globalizing private free enterprise and operating in the same way everywhere (see Walzer 1983, Chapter One).

Land reform based on the notion of private ownership will not be successful in every community without making drastic social changes that alter communal relationships, family traditions, and ancient practices. This does not mean that land reform is wrongheaded; it suggests that it must be reconceived in each situation, so that what falls under the rubric of "reform" is contextually relevant such that change does not destroy the cultural fabric underlying what is to be changed.

It is tempting to argue that what is needed in remote communities or in some developing countries is a rule of law, similar to Anglo-Saxon law, that respects rights and property ownership, enforces contracts, protects equal opportunity, etc., along with adequate mechanisms for enforcement. Indeed, it has been argued, I think with some merit, that one of the difficulties in Russia today is inadequate commercial laws or means to enforce them. But this argument, too, needs qualification. For example, intellectual property rights, already under siege with the electronic revolution, cannot merely be spelled out in every instance using a Western notion of ownership without infringing on some deeply rooted traditions and customs. An Anglo-Saxon model of patent protection, adapted in Indian law, may not be appropriate in many parts of rural India.

Do these examples, and there are thousands of others, point to the conclusion that because of the relativity of custom and culture, we should either abandon the ideal of global economic well-being, or, alternately, simply continue to convert the world into versions of Dallas? Is the aim a television in every village? Or is John Gray correct when he declares in his recent book that "the global economy system [based on Western *laissez-faire* free enterprise] is immoral, inequitable, unworkable, and unstable" (Zakaria 1999, p. 16)?

These two alternatives, as I have crudely stated them, present us with unnecessary dilemmas as if there were only two sorts of responses to problems of globalizing free enterprise. I want to suggest that there are other ways to deal with these issues.

The existence of widespread complex cultural, social, community, and even religious differences along with differing social goods does not imply that we can neither operate in those settings if they are alien to our own nor merely export Western versions of capitalism. To appeal again to Michael Walzer, despite the plurality and incommensurability of cross-cultural social goods, there is a thin thread of agreement, across cultures and religious difference, about the "bads," what cannot be tolerated or should not be permitted in any community. Walzer also calls these thin threads of agreement "moral minimums" (Walzer 1994). Human suffering, abject poverty, preventable disease, high mortality, and violence are abhorred wherever they occur. We are uncertain about the constitution of the "good life," but there is widespread agreement about deficient or despicable living conditions, indecencies, violations of human rights, mistreatment, and other harms.

Given that perspective, almost everyone will agree that poverty, however contextually defined, disease, high infant mortality, and violence are bads. Alleviating suffering of these sorts is surely a good. Improving economic conditions, in most cases, alleviates poverty and human suffering, if not violence. Then, is not economic value added in the form economic growth the proper solution to those evils?

We must cautiously reach that conclusion. Economic growth is not a "bad." Indeed, in most cultures it is considered a social good. But the notion cannot be identified without qualification with a Western idea of free enterprise. The model of economic growth in each context has to be framed in terms of each particular culture and its social goods. Free enterprise and private ownership, as practiced in most industrialized nations, can be, in many contexts, viable options, but only if they are modified so as not to destroy the fabric of a particular set of social goods, or replace that fabric with a new "good" that destroys, without replacing, all the elements of that culture. For example, land reform and the redistribution of property, apparently worthwhile projects to free tenant farmers from feudal bonds, will be successful only if the new landholders have means to function as economically viable farmers and in ways that do not threaten age-old traditions. As the Philippines example demonstrates, the fragile distributive system in the feudal community cannot be dismantled merely for the sake of independence and private ownership without harming complex communal relationships that maintained this system for centuries.

As purveyors of free enterprise, when moving into new communities and alien cultures corporate managers need to test their business mental models, *especially* if a particular system, service, or product has been successful in a number of markets. One needs to examine one's own mental models and try to fathom which models are operating in the community in which a company is planning to operate. In particular, it is important to find out what the operative social structures and community relationships are, what it is that this community values as its social goods, and try to imagine how those might be different given the introduction of a new kind of economic system. Because it is *not* just "the economy, stupid." What matters are social relationships; family, religious, and community traditions; and values — deeply held values about what is important and treasured — that is, those social goods a community cannot give up without sacrificing more than its lack of material well-being. If endemic poverty is an evil, we must create new ways to engage in free enterprise that takes into account, and even celebrates, cultural difference. . . .

In a new article in the *Harvard Business Review,* Stuart Hart and C. K. Prahalad make a different kind of argument for this same point. Hart and Prahalad contend that it happens to be in the long-term self-interest of global multinational companies to tread cautiously and with respect in alien cultural contexts. This is because, in brief, developing countries represent 80 percent of the population of the world and thus are an as yet untapped source of growth and development. If that growth is done carefully through working within indigenous constraints, the result could be the creation of exciting new products and services that enhance rather than destroy communities while at the same time benefiting the companies in question (Hart and Prahalad 1999).

The challenge is to create new mental models for global business that achieve the aims Hart and Prahalad propose. There is at least one such attempt by a large transnational corporation to do exactly this. Unilever is a multibillion-dollar global company with over 300,000 employees operating in almost 100 countries. Its main products are foods, fish, chemicals, and household products. Because it was founded in the Netherlands, a country one-third of which is reclaimed from the seas, Unilever has always been concerned with questions of environmental sustainability. In addition, the more recent expansion of its agricultural and fishing operations in remote communities has made Unilever increasingly aware of cultural difference. Beginning in 1993, Unilever began a process that resulted in a corporate-wide initiative that they call The Triple Bottom Line (Vis 1997). The rationale for this initiative is that if Unilever is going to continue to be successful in the next century, its success depends on its worldwide financial, ecological, and social assets. So Unilever changed the definition of "economic value added" to an expanded triple bottom line that measures economic, ecological, and community assets, liabilities, profits (or benefits), and losses. According to Unilever in its statement of corporate purpose and practice, each of these assets is of equal importance, and its aim is to be able to quantify the corporate contributions to each of these three areas. This may sound Pollyannaish, but Unilever's defense of this initiative could have been written by Milton Friedman.

> Each type of asset represents a source of value to the company and its shareholders. The sustained development of each of these sources of value ensures that the overall value accruing to shareholders is built up sustainably over the long term. This is in essence the significance of sustainable development to a company that aims at sustainable profit growth and long-term value creation for its shareholders, [customers], and employees. (Vis 1997, p. 3)

As part of this Triple Bottom Line initiative, Unilever is currently engaged in a series of small enterprises in a few small villages in India to develop new products aimed at the rural poor. These are microdevelopment projects, because the products they are supporting require little capital, they are locally produced, and of only indigenous interest. Unilever's goal, however, is to make those villages and their inhabitants economically viable managers, entrepreneurs, and customers as those notions are defined and make sense within a particular village culture and in ways that are not environmentally threatening. Whether this example will be a success story remains to be seen. There is to date no outcomes data, since the case events are still unfolding, and it will be some years before one can determine whether these projects are successes.

Is this stretching the limits of what we should expect from global corporations? Not according to Unilever. It argues that human flourishing in diverse settings creates needs for a diversity of products and services, products and services that Unilever will be able to provide. At the same time human well-being creates long-term economic value added, both for Unilever and for the cultures and communities in which it operates.

BIBLIOGRAPHY

Frazier, Steve. 1984. "Peasant Politics: Mexican Farmers Get Grants of Small Plots, But Output is Meager." *Wall Street Journal,* June 4, pp. 1, 18.

Hart, Stuart and Prahalad, C. K. 1999. "Strategies for the Bottom of the Pyramid: Creating Sustainable Development." *Harvard Business Review,* November-December.

Johnson, Mark. 1993. *Moral Imagination.* Chicago: University of Chicago Press.

Rouse, William B. and Morris, Nancy M. 1986. "On Looking Into the Black Box: Prospects and Limits in the Search for Mental Models." *Psychological Bulletin* 100: 349–363.

Severence, Kristi; Spiro, Lisa; and Werhane, Patricia H. 1999. "W. R. Grace Co. and the Neemix Patent." *Darden Case Bibliography:* UVA-E-0157. Charlottesville: University of Virginia Press.

Sonenshein, Scott; Gorman, Michael E.; and Werhane, Patricia H. 1997a. "SELF." *Darden Case Bibliography:* UVA-E-0112. Charlottesville: University of Virginia Press.

———. 1997b. "Solar Energy in South Africa." *Darden Case Bibliography:* UVA-E-0145. Charlottesville: University of Virginia Press.

Takahashi, Akiro, "Ethics in Developing Economies of Asia." *Business Ethics Quarterly* 7: 33–45.

Vijayalakshmi, K.; Radha, K. S.; and Shiva, Vandana. 1996. *Neem: A User's Manual.* Madras: Centre for Indian Knowledge Systems.

Vis, Jan-Kees. 1997. *Unilever: Putting Corporate Purpose Into Action.* Unilever Publication.

Walzer, Michael. 1983. *Spheres of Justice.* New York: Basic Books.

———. 1994. *Thick and Thin.* Notre Dame: Notre Dame University Press.

Werhane, Patricia H. 1991. "Engineers and Management: The Challenge of the Challenger Incident." *Journal of Business Ethics* 1: 605–616.

———. 1998. "Moral Imagination and Management Decision Making." *Business Ethics Quarterly* Special Issue No. 1: 75–98.

———. 1999. *Moral Imagination and Management Decision Making.* New York: Oxford University Press.

Zakaria, Fareed. 1999. "Passing the Bucks [a review of Gray's *False Dawn*]." *New York Times Book Review,* April 25, pp. 16, 18.

BRIBERY

Gift Giving, Bribery, and Corruption: Ethical Management of Business Relationships in China

P. Steidlmeier

Gift giving is a prevalent social custom in China in all areas of life: in family and in significant relationships *(guanxi)*, as well as in dealing with political authorities, social institutions and business people. For all that, from an ethical perspective, it is very difficult to know when it is proper to give or receive a gift, what sort of gift is appropriate, or what social obligations gift giving imposes.

Anyone who has lived in a foreign culture knows how difficult it is to successfully adapt to the local way of doing things. One can spend many months learning how to behave, only to find it all too easy to still commit tremendous *faux pas*. For foreigners, the cultural logic and social practices of gift giving present one of the most difficult lessons in learning how to "do business right" in China. Not surprisingly, many Westerners unfamiliar with Chinese culture often make the easy identification of gifts with bribes and allege that the Chinese are promiscuously corrupt in their business practices *(Economist, 1995a, 1995b)*. Such an easy identification is, however, incorrect. The Chinese themselves are well aware of the differences. There is hardly an issue that has so preoccupied the Chinese media and incited debate over the past years as bribery and corruption. Within Chinese culture itself, there are, indeed, moral parameters to distinguish morally proper gift giving from bribery and corruption.

In this paper I assess the cultural and moral differences between gift giving, bribery and corruption and set forth guidelines for managing business relations in China. I begin with a cultural framework of analysis and then proceed to analyze transactions based upon reciprocity in terms of 1) the action itself and 2) the moral intention of the agents. I conclude with moral guidelines for ethical management.

DEVELOPING A CULTURAL FRAMEWORK FOR RECIPROCITY

John Noonan (1984, p. 3) observes: "Reciprocity is in any society a rule of life, and in some societies at least it is *the* rule of life." China is one of those societies where reciprocity is a foundational pillar of social intercourse. To approach another and bring nothing is unusual, to say the least. To accept a gift and not reciprocate is perceived as morally wrong.

A social custom such as gift giving expresses deeper socially embraced behavioral ideals and norms of mutuality and "right relationships" between people. Practices of gift giving in China include visual behavioral patterns *(organizational artifacts)*, which are enshrined in *rites (li)* of proper conduct. Such

From P. Steidlmeier, "Gift Giving, Bribery, and Corruption: Ethical Management of Business Relationships in China," *Journal of Business Ethics,* 20, 121–132, 1999. Reprinted with permission from Kluwer Academic Publishers. The original article has been edited and most references deleted.

rites themselves are rooted in normative and prescriptive canons of righteousness (*yi*) and benevolence (*ren*), which express why such actions are culturally meaningful or logical. In general terms, *cultural logic* underscores the numerous socio-cultural values and beliefs that are embedded within organizations and function as a sort of internal gyroscope, which governs the social behavior of people. It is, nonetheless, difficult to discern when it is proper to give a gift, what its nature should be and to whom it should be given. Such discernment is ultimately a matter of *social knowledge*. Proper social knowledge represents the ability to align behavioral patterns with cultural logic.

In the area of business, a manager needs to gather and correlate such cultural information and its supporting ethical data in ways that make sense and render it usable. The three principal aspects of the cultural data base — artifacts, social knowledge and cultural logic — are summarized in Table I. In daily practice companies require a concrete understanding of acceptable business behavior patterns and an appreciation of why people do things in a certain way. To be suc-cessful business practices must be grounded in an accurate reading of these three levels of social meaning.

While cultural logic represents the transcendental values and worldview that underlie a culture, such as harmony, justice and right relations, artifacts represent the empirically observed behavior of people as they interact with one another, such as exchanging gifts, taking a certain place at table, or greeting a visitor at the airport. Social knowledge mediates between these two levels in determining what is appropriate. For example, if a visitor is coming from abroad, who is the proper person to meet him or her at the airport and what type of gift would be correct.

While the underlying traditional Chinese cultural logic provides the fundamental ethos of business practices, social knowledge provides a clearer map of "the rules of the game," through the mechanisms of routinely expected behavior patterns. The "rules of the game" reflect what people collectively, through social consensus and organizational will, find desirable. They provide specific ways of doing things within the overall structure of normative ethical parameters. Gift giving, for example, is ex-

TABLE I.   Cultural Databases

Artifacts	Artifacts represent those things that can be seen or heard, e.g. what gifts are given to whom and under what circumstances; artifacts also include such things as how offices are laid out, how people run meetings, how honorifics are used in situations of interaction and so forth. This level of the data base includes the "who-what-where-when" part of the story.
Social knowledge	Social knowledge includes the social processes and values that people can offer as reasons when questioned, e.g. why and how people should act as they do. It provides the reason why it is proper to give a particular person a particular gift at a particular time, as well as the contrary. In this section of the data base the "how" and "why" of gift giving is covered.
Cultural logic	Cultural logic provides the worldview which grounds social behavior and knowledge. This part of the data base provides the ideals, values and principles which serve as society's internal gyroscope. It provides a vision of the most fundamental relationships people have to others, to their environment, to truth and reality, to understanding human nature, to time.

pected behavior, which shows respect to another person and strengthens relationships. The practice is also bounded by rules of moral legitimacy, which may in the end lead to defining some gifts as illegitimate forms of corruption. Chinese sources themselves are well aware of this (He, 1994; Liu and Xiong, 1994).

In China, gift giving forms part of a larger picture: belonging to a network of personal relationships (*guanxi*). That these relationships be "right" is a matter of utmost moral and practical concern. Gift giving is one of the ways of nurturing such relationships and strengthening the trust, caring, reciprocity and commitment between the parties. In practical terms, the quality of such relationships emerges as a universal primary reference point in judging what one ought to do. In day to day business, these realities lead to patterns of choice and the determination of priorities that are expressed in concrete deeds, such as favoring in commercial deals those people with whom one has close relationships of *guanxi*.

INTERACTING WITH OTHERS IN CHINA

Chinese culture exhibits a very nuanced social philosophy of *relationships*. These embody both the *respect* one person owes another in terms of face (*myan dz*) as well as obligations of mutual rights and duties (*quanli yu yiwu*), which bind people together. The predominant social structures of Chinese society are found in the web of significant relationships (*guanxi*), based upon family, geographic origin, school mates and so forth. A person's *guanxi* outlines who matters and how much they matter and provides the primary basis of moral claims for one person upon another.

Such relationships in China are not unidimensional. In fact, they embrace many different levels of intensity. Most generally, they are ranked in order of importance as follows: family, friends or fellows (school mates, colleagues, distant relatives, friends of friends), other Chinese, and the outside world. This ordering is also reflected within a business enterprise: the business itself is a quasi-family and evokes primary loyalties, followed by ties with the enterprises's principal alliances (with banks, suppliers, traders, customers), other Chinese businesses and economic agents, and then the outside world. The principal challenge for a foreign corporation is to insert itself as closely as possible within the inner circles.

In dealing with the Chinese, it is very important to be aware of such things as practices of gift giving and receiving, the proper role for host organizations and guests, correct ways to handle introductions, etiquette in eating and drinking, proper decorum with superiors, peers and inferiors in the workplace, how to handle and express disagreements, proper dress and so forth.

Chinese social behavior has traditionally been quite prescriptive in terms of rites (*li*) and forms of courtesy, manners, politeness, and correct decorum (*li mao*). "*Li*" is highly ritualistic and expresses the proper public manner of relating to a superior, an equal or inferior in extending greetings, speaking, taking a seat, drinking or any expression of self towards another. As pointed out in the previous section, "*Li*" rests upon a broader normative ethic of "right relations," which, for instance, express the heart of ethical concerns in the Confucian tradition. In China, position within the group, rather than over the group or in distinction to it, is far more important than independence from the group. Likewise, respect for others ("face") is of paramount importance and is manifested through gift giving, deference, not publicly disagreeing, public honors within a group, and so forth. Both relationship networks (*guanxi*) and the social stature of face (*myan dz*) are enshrouded in public rituals (*li*), which express status, respect and bonding in formal terms.

Attention must first be paid to instrumental organizational dynamics of structure, control, incentives and time. Chinese organizations tend to emphasize high-status definition and follow the rules of *guanxi* and familial structures. U.S. organizations are more low-status and more rule-based, closely following formal rules and regulations rather than "following relationships." Control mechanisms in the former tend to be more cooperative and based on personal trust, and incentives take forms that emphasize loyalty and security. In the West, control is often more conflictive and regulatory, with incentives based upon individual achievement and merit. In the West, time is a precious commodity as the slogan "time is money" suggests; in China time is put to the service of relationships.

Further, one must consider a central dynamic of personal organizational interaction that stands out: individualism versus group identity. In the West people often define themselves as standing out from the group, emphasizing individual creativity, achievement, reward and status. In China people are more at pains to define their place within a group. This becomes more evident when applying the cultural process to doing business in China.

According to William de Bary (1991, pp. 3–4):

> Reciprocity, then becomes the basis of self-cultivation. One defines ones "self" in relation to others and to the Way which unites them. Thus is constructed the web of reciprocal obligations or moral relations in which one finds oneself, defines oneself. Apart from these one can have no real identity. And yet these relations alone, it is equally important to recognize, do not define one totally.
> . . . for Confucius the individual exists in a delicate balance with his social environment, reconciling his own self respect with respect for others, his inner freedom with the limiting circumstances of his own situation in life.

For Chinese, gift giving is a natural dynamic of any relationship: It shows a relationship is valued and is a means of expressing respect and honor for the other person. Gifts express good will and gratitude and, in many ways, can be considered a dynamic form of "social contracting." The difficult aspects of gift giving have more to do with assessing the proper proportionality between persons and the implied sense of obligation or reciprocity that is entailed in giving or receiving a particular gift. For example, in dealing with a Chinese delegation, the leader should receive a better gift than subordinates. One often must proceed by trial and error; however, exchanging equivalent gifts is not a bad rule of thumb: a meal for a meal, a pen for a pen. To avoid bribery, it is important to focus upon whether, through the gift, one is asking one party or other to engage in behavior that is not an integral or legitimate part of the set of transactions at hand, which form the backdrop for meeting in the first place. For example, depositing 1% of a multi-million dollar transaction's value in a Swiss bank account in order to get an official to sign off on a deal could not be construed as a gift. . . .

MORAL ANALYSIS OF RECIPROCITY

How is reciprocity, as a general type of moral action, to be analyzed? To call what is empirically a transfer of resources between parties 1) giving a gratuity or 2) bribery, or 3) a commission involves interpreting the meaning of the empirically observed event. Such interpretation draws upon core human values, respect for local traditions, and an appreciation of context.

To label it "bribery" is already to make a moral judgment. For in ordinary English (or Chinese) the word bribery itself (*huilu*) connotes a wrongful transfer of resources between parties. Wrongful because the gift giver and receiver apparently strike a deal, which puts their own interests above other parties, who have legitimate prior claims in the transaction and on whose behalf the agents are acting. It not only breaks down trust between people and their agents, but also undermines the legitimacy of social institutions.

It is just this action which I wish to scrutinize before we characterize it with a label. In Table II I outline the elements of analysis of reciprocity in resource transfers. The moral analysis of such a resource transfer can be exceedingly difficult to carry out. The resource transfer itself can be termed the "empirical part" of the action. It is empirically descriptive of what takes place and, in this sense, is morally neutral. Moral judgment about the action, however, is not neutral.

Analysis of Reciprocity as a "Type of Moral Action"

In objective categories moral understanding of an existential kind of action demands clarification of values as well as concrete knowledge of ends, means and consequences. Moral judgment then seeks to decide:

1) whether as a type of action "X" is right or wrong
2) whether as a specific instance a particular action "x" is good or bad, and
3) whether the parties (agents) involved are to be praised or blamed

The paying of a commission is ostensibly the least troublesome resource transfer. Morally, it is embedded in a freely undertaken and fair contract framework and represents remuneration in a transaction of mutually beneficial exchange. As a type of action the ends sought, means taken and consequences which ensue are usually justified in terms of instrumental values (efficiency, utility) and self-interest. Such an action is only morally correct if it is consistent with fundamental values of justice and basic moral virtues. Furthermore, the intentions of the parties must be honorable and neither their consciences nor freedom are impaired. However, all of this can be

TABLE II. Moral Analysis of Reciprocity

	Bribery	*Gratuity*	*Commission*
A. As a type of moral action			
Social purpose (end)	Gain acquiescence	Express gratitude	Pay for services
Values	Utilitarian	Utilitarian and/or altruistic	Mutual benefit and reciprocal fairness
Means	To give something the other would appreciate	To give something the other would appreciate	To give what was agreed upon
Consequences	Double-effect	Helps the others and build rapport	Fair mutual benefit
B. From the perspective of moral agents			
Individual intention	Success of transaction	Gratitude and future good will	Fairness in contract
Degree of freedom	Condition of success	Voluntary, but there may be social pressure (tip)	Free contractual obligation
Conscience	No one hurt; lesser of two evils	Those with abundance should be generous	Honesty and promise keeping

easily suborned. Values of self-interest can be transformed into raw selfishness and expediency replace justice. Some would argue that commissions have become the favorite form of bribery in the United States, because they offer the cloak of legality.

Giving a gratuity, such as a tip, is a bit more difficult to analyze. If it altruistically expresses gratitude — a bonus for a job well done and performance exceeding expectations — it is a sign of generosity and esteem for the other. But if the tippee somehow indirectly communicates that such remuneration is a precondition for good service, then it becomes coercive and a form of extortion. The problem is not with a 15% service charge announced as a matter of policy, but with coercive behavior. Such coercive behavior, in fact, is a partial breach of the contract which is implied when one buys a meal, takes a cab, or gets a haircut: the service promised for a certain price will not, in fact be delivered for that rate. In giving gratuities, people may respond immediately that there is both a commonly known socio-cultural expectation and approval of tipping in general. The "gratuity portion" of the tip is then reserved to the rate: whether 12% or 20%. In fact, tipping is usually considered part of the tippee's ordinary income. In that sense it represents a suitable means to a good end with beneficial consequences. It may be considered both a "right" type of action as well as a "good" action in the context of a particular tip.

The latter judgment could be altered, however, depending upon the subjective intentions of those involved and the degree of coercion. Tipping may, in fact, mask either bribery or extortion. In coercive tipping, the tipee extorts extra payments for a service. In bribery, the tipper may seek special consideration — the best table without having to either make reservations or wait. In the end, the overall analytical framework of *values-end-means-consequences* remains ambiguous. As

with commissions, the phenomenon of giving gratuities can either be morally uplifting or an expression of corruption.

Bribery itself emerges as extremely complex. Defined as a *type of action* it is clearly wrong. However, as noted above, to say bribery is wrong is to utter a tautology. That is, bribery (*huilu*) defines a wrongful type of action. To use an example from Kant, we describe a type of action and its conditions (end, means, values, consequences), name it bribery, and then ask: would one want to make this action universal? The answer is "no." The previous discussion of epistemology and worldview are very important here. For if we asked the question in terms of Mill's utilitarianism (does it produce the greatest happiness for the greatest number?) the answer may well be quite different, whether considering bribery as an individual act or as a rule of behavior. To say that bribery is always wrong can only be established in the context of a specific worldview and a specific value set that one takes as universal and absolute. Subjectively, it is necessarily relative.

Analysis of Reciprocity in Terms of Moral Agents

It is important to move from the analysis of bribery as a *type of action* to a concrete situation. When one asks whether a particular instance of bribery may be good or bad or whether the parties involved may be praiseworthy or blameworthy, the analysis becomes considerably more nuanced because of the complexity of the concrete situation. In this context, the analyst must be particularly careful of ethnocentrism. To the point, to what degree does what appears to be bribery fulfill the conditions set forth in the abstract definition of bribery as a *type of action?*

This is further complicated when, in addition to grasping all the details of a situation, one tries to understand the moral agent him/herself: subjective factors of conscience, intention and degrees of freedom are factored in. In actions of reciprocity, where resources are exchanged between parties, the level of development of each party's conscience may enter in to mitigate circumstances. Bribery in the face of intractably corrupt officials and the certain closing of a plant due to a lost contract, differs from bribery to enrich oneself so as to build a third villa estate. Indeed, officials involved in the Lockheed case, argued the former case and that, in the end, they chose the lesser of two evils. In such cases one may arrive at different judgments of the agents being praiseworthy or blameworthy.

Attention must be paid to the social situation and context. I am not at this point arguing a situational ethics where a *type of action* is right or wrong according to the particular circumstances. Rather, the very concrete definition of the action taking place (i.e. of what is actually happening) derives from the sociohistorical context in the first place. That is, the question is not whether "bribery" is all right in Shanghai but not in Kansas City. Rather, is this manner of reciprocity and resource transfer in Shanghai a bribe? This point is crucial to understanding the social purpose and consequences of the transaction and to judging whether this instance is good or bad and whether and to what degree the agents are morally blameworthy or praiseworthy. In many parts of the developing world what a Western observer would call a bribe is, in fact, closer to a tip or the socially expected form of the tippee's remuneration. That does not mean that "anything goes." . . .

Even if the *end* or purpose of the transaction is good — the firm is engaged in selling a product very good for the people — the analyst must also ask whether the *means* adopted are suitable and whether the *intentions* of the parties are honorable. Phenomenologically,

it is difficult to distinguish a bribe from a tip or a commission or consulting fee. In the end, moral judgment depends upon the social understanding of the meaning of the action as derived from analysis of ends and means, consequences and intentions.

Provided the end or purpose is good, the key difference seems to reside not in the phenomenology of the transaction itself in terms of *means* and *consequences,* but in the *intention* of those who are involved, conditioned by *conscience* and *effective freedom.* The essence of bribery is conflict of interest between self and one's publicly accepted fiduciary duties. Secondly, it affects the *means* a person employs to fulfill his or her fiduciary duty. The appropriateness of the resource transfer in a particular case and the praiseworthiness or blameworthiness of the parties depends upon the overall social consequences of the action and the intentions of the agents. What if the intentions of the briber are actually good with reference to the project and fulfilling his or her fiduciary duties but those of the bribee are greed? Even then, the action may not be completely bad. Enter the *principle of double effect:* One may make the judgment that the success of the project is impossible without the bribe *and* the good consequences of the project clearly outweigh the evils of the bribe.

SOME GUIDELINES FOR "DOING BUSINESS RIGHT" IN CHINA

The guidelines I suggest below are based upon two sets of beliefs: 1) the moral ambiguity one experiences in differentiating bribes from gratuities and commissions and 2) the present situation in China with respect to political and business corruption.

From the above sections, it is clear that it is impossible to clearly distinguish gratuities, bribes and commissions on an empirical basis. Bribes can easily be dressed in the garb of "legitimate commissions" or gratuitous expressions of esteem. Furthermore, in analyzing whether a transaction is morally right or wrong and whether the agents are praiseworthy or blameworthy pivotal elements such as conscience, effective freedom, the determinative dynamics of the situation, and cumulative consequences are often beyond measurement. In the end, these facts attest to the reality that moral probity is ever a matter of discernment of what, in the Socratic tradition, is called wisdom: figuring out how to be excellent at being human.

From Chinese voices themselves, we know the following:

1) Corruption is endemic, especially since the reforms of the last decades.
2) Corruption reaches the highest levels of the ruling elite.
3) Corruption flies in the face of Chinese (as well as Marxist) tenets and traditions of public morality and the moral dimensions of a public official's responsibility.
4) The "corruption debate" among the Chinese also functions as cover for a power struggle or, perhaps more accurately, for multiple power struggles between factions in the post–Deng Xiaoping era.
5) Chinese "rules of the game" lack transparency as well as universality across both a) regions and b) factions — leaving local officials with tremendous discretionary power.

If the above observations regarding both ethical judgments in general, and the Chinese social milieu, in particular, are substantially correct, what is a company doing business in China to do? In part, the answer depends upon the company's intentions: Does it wish to behave ethically? or merely legally? or to do "whatever it takes" to make money without getting caught?

The answer to the last of the above questions is simply try to implement "applied Machiavellianism," realizing, however, that the Chinese have developed traditions that in many ways outdo *The Prince!* At present, the

atmosphere is ambiguous and opportunistic situations abound.

Simply aiming for legal compliance can be more difficult but, still it is not too formidable. For a U.S. multinational, the rules of the game from the American side are fairly clear, as expressed in numerous regulations, ranging from the FCPA in 1977, the Omnibus Trade and Competitiveness Act of 1988, government agency directives and legal rulings. At the same time, strategies to circumvent them through third parties and holding companies have been developing at a rapid rate. The main problem for foreign multinationals is found on the Chinese side, where, they claim, there is no real *transparency* in the applicable laws and regulations. Regulations vary across ministries and are interpreted differently in different regions. People can be caught and held liable without even knowing their transgressions. As a simple example, it is very dangerous to pay a "commission" to someone whose power base is eroding and who is about to be deposed. The main strategy a foreign company should adopt in order to achieve simple legal and regulatory compliance is to be sure to have the right set of Chinese patrons on one's side at all levels and regions and to have them, as partners, become the guarantors of legitimacy. There are, indeed, such a sufficient number of official Chinese denouncements of corruption that they provide a foreign company with cover. The foreign company should use this material as part of a stated policy to be a "worthy guest" in China, while shifting the burden of assuring that they are in full compliance to their Chinese partner. Frequently, foreign companies are at a disadvantage because they are ignorant of the many powerful official Chinese statements regarding their history of international dealings and their policies regarding corruption. I know only of Chinese policies condemning corruption, not advocating it. It makes strategic sense to use this material as the motivating force for avoiding corruption in China, rather than simply appealing to the FCPA as the motivation for one's actions.

For those companies truly desiring to be ethical, the problem is more complex, not the least is being "closed out" of deals, which are then snapped up by competitors willing to play the game.

As a general rule of thumb, a U.S. intelligence consultant, Kroll Associates (Asia) have suggested the following guidelines in choosing a local partner:

1) Investigate the backgrounds of local executives you place in charge of company matters. Did they do a good job for their previous company? Or did they leave after two years, taking the entire team with them? A common occurrence.

2) Ensure no one individual has total control over company matters.

3) Treat remarks such as "China is different" and "You shouldn't get involved" as a red light.

4) Establish regular and detailed auditing systems to ensure transparency.

To which I would add:

5) Be aware of the political standing of your counterparts and do not get caught in the cross fire of Chinese power struggles.

6) Explain your difficulties to the Chinese side (deriving from the U.S. government, stockholders, competitors, . . .) and offer alternatives that are legitimate — especially something that addresses key Chinese policy objectives (e.g. technology transfer), the attainment of which will give leverage.

7) As much as possible use Chinese sources themselves as the basis for your unwillingness to do corrupt deals.

8) Rather than becoming entangled in a specific minor bribe, place the whole matter in a broader context of negotiation. Rather than reactively saying "yes" or "no" to a specific bribe, proactively build up negotiating lever-

age and a viable set of alternatives at the outset.

This last point of building negotiating leverage is highly important. I conclude this article with a sketch of its basic elements. In the end, if one's objective is to attain "A", he/she should a) devise simultaneous and multiple means of doing so as well as b) build up negotiating leverage. This not only allows one's Chinese counterpart to save face by having a menu to consider, it secures effective freedom in negotiations. . . .

Negotiation is an important part of strategy. Few things are "take it or leave it" and it is important to build and maintain latitude for creative imagination. Some important considerations are:

1) Let the other side know your constraints (for example, an American company threatened by FCPA) and indicate what your "feasibility area" is.

2) Offer alternatives that have a "legitimate business reason" (for example, explain that you cannot give cash but can provide training).

3) Indicate that you are actively pursuing various partners; the competition within China between different companies, government ministries, and geographic regions is intense; let them know you have alternatives so as not to become boxed in or dependent.

4) Let them know you are aware of their own official regulations and hint that exposure would be embarrassing for everyone — everyone fears their own potential enemies.

There are no hard and fast rules for such negotiations. However, it is clear that companies that have a product, technology or service critical to China have far more leverage than those companies for whom China can find easy substitutes. Further, a company that has other viable partners and alternatives also gains negotiating leverage. Overall, it makes sense for a company to primarily attend to three things: First, to diversify its Chinese partners as well as Asia Pacific partners so that it does not become boxed in by a single deal. Regionally, China is very diverse and it is possible to have a number of partners. At the same time it is important to form partnerships from the outside. In this way a particular deal becomes part of a China strategy but not the only viable option.

Second, it is important to offer one's Chinese counterparts alternatives that are both legitimate and that address important needs in Chinese development. Rather than simply paying a bribe, one can offer a local official help in marketing local products or special training (as Japanese trading companies are prone to do) and other consulting services.

Third, a company can gain leverage by presenting its approach in China's own terms. It should become familiar with China's internal documentation and processes regarding corruption and economic development. Rather than preaching from a Western pulpit — which Chinese find easy to counter — they should arm themselves with the ideals and procedures embedded in China's own development policies. China ardently desires to be an integral part of world commerce. The case should be made that standard international fair business practices are in its own economic interests.

Negotiating is not to be a frontal attack, but rather a strategy of creative imagination.

Diversification of both partners and alternative courses of action brings (moral) freedom and reduces risk. Such a diversified negotiating context will set the stage for more creative solutions that are both morally right and strategically sound. In many ways the most difficult part of ethics is not denouncing what is wrong but the creative imagination and courage to craft something new. Diversified negotiation helps create the effective freedom to do just that.

REFERENCES

de Bary, William Theodore: 1991, *Learning for One's Self: Essay on the Individual in Confucian Thought* (Columbia University Press, Lincolnwood, IL).

Economist, 1995a, "Business Ethics: Hard Graft in Asia" (May 27), p. 61.

Economist, 1995b, "The Politics of Corruption" (May 20), p. 33.

He, Shougang: 1994, "Warning: Misplacement of Moral Concepts in Contemporary China," *Shehui (Society)* 110 (March), 93–94; JPRS-CAR-94-036, June 10, 49–50.

Liu, Luoying and Xiong Guochang: 1994, "'Red-Envelope' Phenomenon Analyzed in Context of Market Competition," *Faxue (Jurisprudence)* 151 (June 10), 7–10; JPRS-CAR-94-048, pp. 74–75.

Noonan, John T., Jr.: 1984, *Bribes* (Macmillan and Co., New York, NY).

When Ethics Travel: The Promise and Peril of Global Business Ethics

Thomas Donaldson and Thomas W. Dunfee

Global managers often must navigate the perplexing gray zone that arises when two cultures — and two sets of ethics — meet. Suppose:

You are a manager of Ben & Jerry's in Russia. One day you discover that the most senior officer of your company's Russian joint venture has been "borrowing" equipment from the company and using it in his other business ventures. When you confront him, the Russian partner defends his actions. After all, as a part owner of both companies, isn't he entitled to share in the equipment?

Or, competing for a bid in a foreign country, you are introduced to a "consultant" who offers to help you in your client contacts. A brief conversation makes it clear that this person is well connected in local government and business circles and knows your customer extremely well. The consultant will help you prepare and submit your bid and negotiate with the customer . . . for a substantial fee. Your peers tell you that such arrangements are normal in this country — and that a large part of the consulting fee will go directly to staff people working for your customer. Those who have rejected such help in the past have seen contracts go to their less-fussy competitors (Anonymous case study).

What should you do in such cases? Should you straighten out your Russian partner? How should you deal with the problem of bribery? Bribery is just like tipping, some people say. Whether you tip for service at dinner or bribe for the benefit of getting goods through customs, you pay for a service rendered. But while many of us balk at a conclusion that puts bribery on a par with tipping, we have difficulty articulating why. . . .

THE INTEGRATED SOCIAL CONTRACT THEORY (ISCT) GLOBAL VALUES MAP

In the face of conflicting and confusing advice, the application of categories to global problems is helpful. The broadest categories for sorting authentic global norms through ISCT may be displayed in a diagram (see Figure 8–1).

The concentric circles represent core norms held by particular corporations, industries, or economic cultures. Particular values of a corporation, as expressed through its actions and policies, may be plotted as points within the circles.

- *Hypernorms:* These include, for example, fundamental human rights or basic prescriptions common to most major religions. The values they represent are by definition acceptable to all cultures and all organizations.
- *Consistent norms:* These values are more culturally specific than those at the center, but are *consistent both with hypernorms and other legitimate norms,* including those of other economic cultures. Most corporations' ethical codes and vision-value statements would fall within this circle. Johnson & Johnson's famous "Credo" and AT&T's "Our Common Bond" are examples.
- *Moral Free Space:* As one moves away from the center of the circle to the circle signifying moral free space, one finds norms that are inconsistent with at least some other legitimate norms

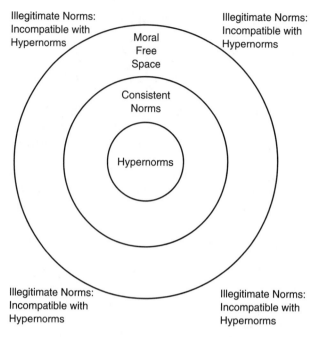

FIGURE 8–1.   Categories of Authentic Global Norms under ISCT

existing in other economic cultures. Such norms can be in mild tension with hypernorms, even as they are compatible with them. They often express unique, but strongly held, cultural beliefs.

- *Illegitimate Norms:* These are norms that are incompatible with hypernorms. When values or practices reach a point where they transgress permissible limits (as specified, say, by fundamental human rights), they fall outside the circle and into the "incompatible" zone. Exposing workers to unreasonable levels of carcinogens (asbestos), for example, is an expression of a value falling outside the circle.

NAVIGATING USING THE ISCT MAP: THE CASE OF BRIBERY AND SENSITIVE PAYMENTS

To gain an understanding of the implications of ISCT for international business, it helps to apply it to a single, concrete instance. Ac-

cordingly, we shall probe the issue of corruption — in particular, the question of bribery or "sensitive payments." Although a single example, it is one with ringing significance for contemporary global business. It is widely known that sensitive payments flourish in many parts of the globe. Once this illustrative application is complete, we will draw — later in the chapter — implications of ISCT for a much broader array of international cases.

Consider two typical instances of sensitive payments. First, there is the practice of low-level bribery of public officials in some developing nations. In some developing countries, for example, it is difficult for any company, foreign or national, to move goods through customs without paying low-level officials a few dollars. The payments are relatively small, uniformly assessed, and accepted as standard practice. But the salaries of such officials are sufficiently low that the officials require the additional income. One suspects the salary levels are set with the prevalence of bribery in mind.

Or consider a second kind of instance where a company is competing for a bid in a foreign country, and where in order to win the competition a payment must be made not to a government official, but to the employee of a private company. Nonetheless, it is clear that the employee, instead of passing on the money to the company, will pocket the payment. In a modified version of this scenario, the bribe may even appear one level deeper. For example, a company competing for a bid may be introduced to a "consultant" who offers to help to facilitate client contacts.

It is not obvious where the norms and issues that arise from such cases should be situated on the ISCT map, if indeed they belong there at all. Are practices involving such payments examples of authentic norms, thus qualifying them to be located on the map? Are payments invariably direct violations of hypernorms and hence located outside the circles in the "illegitimate" arena? Or, instead, do some practices tolerating payments qualify as expressions of moral free space?

As we saw earlier in this chapter, ethical views about business vary around the globe. Bribery is no exception. Not only does the incidence of bribery vary, so does its perception as being unethical. . . .

From the vantage point of ISCT, then, are there ethical problems with bribery? The answer is "yes," as the following list clarifies:

1. *From the standpoint of the bribe recipient, the acceptance usually violates a microsocial contract specifying the duties of the agent, i.e., the bribe recipient, to the principal, i.e., the employing body, such as the government, a private company, etc.*

Perhaps the most obvious problem with bribery is that it typically involves the violation of a duty by the person accepting the bribe to the principal for whom he acts as an

agent. Note that in both the illustrative cases above, the bribe recipient performs an action at odds with the policies established by his employer. In the case of the customs official, he accepts money for a service that he was supposed to provide anyway. In the case of the company competing for a bid, the employee pockets money in violation of company policy, and the company is short-changed. In other words, if the money belongs to anyone, it belongs to the customer's company, not the individual employee. Such policies may or may not be written down. Often they are explicit, but even where they are not, they usually reflect well-understood, implicit agreements binding the employee as agent to the interests of his employer (the principal). In short, even when not formally specified, such duties flow from well-understood microsocial contracts existing within the relevant economic community.

But while this rationale shows one ethical problem with bribery, it is inconclusive. To begin with, it shows an ethical objection to accepting a bribe, but says nothing about offering a bribe. Has the person making the payment also committed an ethical error? Second, although violating a duty to an employer is one reason for considering an act unethical, it remains uncertain whether this reason could not be overridden by other, more pressing reasons. Perhaps other microsocial contracts in the culture firmly endorse the ethical correctness of bribe giving and bribe taking. Perhaps these microsocial contracts, along with an employee's legitimate interest in supporting his family, etc., override the prima facie obligation of the employee to follow the policies of his employer. It makes sense to explore the further implications of ISCT.

2. *Bribery is typically not an authentic norm.*

The mythology is that bribery is accepted wherever it flourishes. This image is badly distorted. Despite the data mentioned earlier that shows variance in the degree to which various people regard bribery as unethical in comparison with other unethical activity, there is a surprising amount of fundamental agreement that bribery is unethical.

All countries have laws against the practice. This is a striking fact often overlooked by individuals who have something to gain by the practice. "There is not a country in the world," writes Fritz Heimann, "where bribery is either legally or morally acceptable." That bribes have to be paid secretly everywhere, and that officials have to resign in disgrace if the bribe is disclosed, makes it clear that bribery violates the moral standards of the South and the East, just as it does in the West" (Heimann, 1994, p. 7).

Some countries, even ones where the practice has flourished, not only outlaw it, but prescribe draconian penalties. "In Malaysia, which is significantly influenced by the Moslem prescriptions against bribery, execution of executives for the offense of bribery is legal." In China in 1994, the President of the Great Wall Machinery and Electronics High-Technology Industrial Group Corp., Mr. Shen Haifu, was executed by a bullet to the back of his neck for bribery and embezzlement offenses.

Many broad efforts are currently being made against bribery. The OECD is among the leading organizations mounting such efforts, in part due to U.S. pressure resulting from a provision in the amendment of the Foreign Corrupt Practices Act, which requires the President to take steps to bring about a level playing field of global competition. At a symposium held in Paris, France, in March 1994, the OECD launched a campaign aimed at reducing the incidence of bribery in trade transactions, especially in international contracts. And in 1996 an OECD committee, with support from an international nongovernmental organization (NGO) dedicated to eradicating

bribery, Transparency International, passed a resolution requiring that all member countries pass laws prohibiting the tax-deductibility of bribery in foreign transactions undertaken by their domestic firms. The outcome of this last effort is unclear at the time of this writing; but the OECD is clearly ramping up its battle against bribery. Reflecting this same spirit, some academics have suggested (Laczniak, 1990) the implementation of a worldwide code against bribery and the use of ethical impact statements by corporations. Many leading accounting firms, among them Arthur Andersen, KPMG, and Coopers & Lybrand, now offer services that enhance the ability of internal auditing functions to control the payment of bribes.

When one of the authors of this book (Donaldson) interviewed CEOs in India in 1993, he discovered that they were willing to acknowledge that their companies constantly engaged in bribery and payoffs. (They justify their actions on grounds of extortion — the practice began with the Indian government, and they were forced to bribe.) More surprising, however, was their disgust for the practice. They had no illusions about the propriety of bribery, and were aware that its most pernicious aspect was its effect on efficiency. Under ISCT this implies that even among a community of bribe payers, bribery cannot necessarily be established as an authentic norm.

Philip Nichols (1997) cites specific references from each of the world's major religions condemning bribery. "Corruption is condemned and proscribed," he writes, "by each of the major religious and moral schools of thought. Buddhism, Christianity, Confucianism, Hinduism, Islam, Judaism, Sikhism, and Taoism each proscribe corruption. Adam Smith and David Ricardo condemned corruption, as did Karl Marx and Mao Tse Tung" (Nichols, 1997, pp. 321–322).

In short, in many if not most instances, the necessary condition imposed by ISCT that the norm be authentic — i.e., that it is both acted upon and believed to be ethically correct by a substantial majority of the members of a community — cannot be met. To the extent that this is true, most instances of bribery would fail the ISCT test.

3. *Bribery may violate the hypernorm supporting political participation as well as the efficiency hypernorm.*

Even this last consideration, however, leaves a nagging doubt behind. In particular, is bribery only wrong because most people dislike it? Is there nothing more fundamentally wrong with bribery? Suppose, hypothetically, that the world came to change its mind about bribery over the next thirty years. Suppose that in some future state, a majority of people finds bribery morally acceptable. If so, would bribery be ethically correct? In such a world, would reformers who spoke out against bribery be speaking illogical nonsense?

The answer to this question turns on the further question of whether a hypernorm disallowing bribery exists. For if such a hypernorm existed, then no legitimate microsocial norm could support bribery, and, in turn, it would deserve moral condemnation even in a world whose majority opinion endorsed it.

At least two hypernorms may be invoked in seeking a more fundamental condemnation of bribery. The first is rather obvious. To the extent that one places a positive, transnational value on the right to political participation, large bribes of publicly elected officials damage that value. For example, when Prime Minister Tanaka of Japan bought planes from the American aircraft manufacturer Lockheed in the 1970s, after accepting tens of millions of dollars in bribes, people questioned whether he was discharging his duties as a public official correctly. In addition to the fact that his actions violated the law, the

Japanese citizenry was justified in wondering whether their interests, or Tanaka's personal political interest, drove the decision. Implicit in much of the political philosophy written in the Western world in the last three hundred years — in the writings of Rousseau, Mill, Locke, Jefferson, Kant, and Rawls — is the notion that some transcultural norm supports a public claim for the citizenry of a nation-state to participate in some way in the direction of political affairs. Many (see, e.g., Shue, 1980; Donaldson, 1989; and Universal Declaration of Human Rights, 1948) have discussed and articulated the implications of this right in current contexts. If such a right exists, then it entails obligations on the part of politicians and prospective bribe givers to not violate it. In turn, large-scale bribery of high government officials of the sort that the Lockheed Corporation engaged in during the 1970s would be enjoined through the application of a hypernorm. It would thus be wrong regardless of whether a majority of the members of an economic community, or even the majority of the world's citizens, endorsed it.

This, then, is the first hypernorm that may affect an ISCT interpretation of bribery. But notice that it, too, leaves nagging questions unanswered. Suppose it is true that large-scale payoffs to public officials in democratic or quasi-democratic countries are proscribed by considerations of people's right to political participation. In such countries, bribery may defeat meaningful political rights. But many countries in which bribery is prevalent are not democratic. Bribery in countries such as Zaire, Nigeria, and China may not have a noticeable effect on political participation by ordinary citizens, since that participation is directly repressed by authoritarian governments.

Many other troubling questions may be raised. What about much smaller payoffs to public officials? And what about bribes not to public officials, but to employees of corporations? It seems difficult to argue that small, uniformly structured bribes to customs officials, or that bribes to purchasing agents of companies in host countries, seriously undermine people's right to political participation. These questions prompt the search for yet another hypernorm relevant to the issue of bribery.

The second hypernorm that appears relevant to the present context is the efficiency hypernorm. That hypernorm, again, requires that economic agents efficiently utilize resources in which their society has a stake. As explained earlier, the hypernorm arises because all societies have an interest in husbanding public resources, developing strategies to promote aggregate economic welfare (Efficiency Strategies), and, in turn, developing economizing parameters to do so. Indeed, nations and NGOs that oppose bribery most commonly couch their opposition in terms of the damage bribery does to the economic efficiency of the nation-state.

Is bribery inefficient? It certainly appears to be. As the economist Kenneth Arrow noted years ago, "a great deal of economic life depends for its viability on a certain limited degree of ethical commitment" (Arrow, 1973, p. 313). To the extent that market participants bribe, they interfere with the market mechanism's rational allocation of resources, and their actions impose significant social costs. When people buy or sell on the basis of price and quality, with reasonable knowledge about all relevant factors, the market allocates resources efficiently. The best products relative to price, and, in turn, the best production mechanisms, are encouraged to develop. But when people buy or sell not on the basis of price and quality, but on the basis of how much money goes into their own pockets, the entire market mechanism is distorted. By misallocating resources, bribery damages economic efficiency. As economists

Bliss and Di Tella (1997) note, "Corrupt agents exact money from firms." Corruption affects, they observe, the number of firms in a free-entry equilibrium, and in turn increases costs relative to profits. In contrast, "the degree of deep competition in the economy increases with lower overhead costs relative to profits; and with a tendency towards similar cost structures" (Bliss & Di Tella, 1997, p. 1). Corruption can even be shown to take a toll on social efforts to improve economic welfare, including industrial policy initiatives (Ades & Di Tella, 1997), and on predictability in economic arrangements.

A striking example of the effect of corruption on predictability occurred recently in Brazil. When a large U.S. company's crates were unloaded on the docks of Rio de Janeiro, handlers regularly pilfered them. The handlers would take about 10 percent of the contents of the crates. Not only did the company lose this portion of the contents, it also never knew which 10 percent would be taken. Finally, in desperation, the company began sending two crates for every one sent in the past. The first crate contained 90 percent of the merchandise normally sent; the second contained 10 percent. The handlers learned to take the second crate and to leave the first untouched. The company viewed this as an improvement. It still suffered a 10 percent loss — but it now knew which 10 percent it would lose (Donaldson, 1996)!

Interviews with Indian CEOs in 1993 revealed that they were well aware that inefficiency metastasizes as decisions are made not on the basis of price and quality, but on the basis of how much money people are getting under the table. This they acknowledged as their principal reason for concern about the widespread phenomenon of Indian bribery. Again, the market is a remarkably efficient tool for allocating resources, but it only works if people buy based on price and quality — not clandestine payoffs. A trip to the streets of Calcutta in 1993 would have brought home the bitter fruits of corruption. The Indian economy in 1993 was one so inefficient that even dramatic redistribution of wealth would leave most of its inhabitants in dire poverty. The poverty is so stark that social activists have given up their attempt to enforce child labor laws, and have turned instead to advocating better working conditions for children — better conditions, for example, for eight-year-old children in match factories. Most of the Indian executives interviewed believed that a great deal of India's economic inefficiency was driven by the presence of massive corruption.

NGOs and government bodies usually cite the negative impact of bribery on efficiency as their principal rationale for attempting to eliminate it. From 1993 to 1997, the OECD targeted bribery as one of its key concerns. Its rationale has focused almost exclusively on the way corrupt practices hamper development of international trade by "distorting competition, raising the cost of transactions and restricting the operation of free markets" (Yannaca-Small, 1995).

As David Vogel notes, the conviction that bribery harms efficiency is especially pronounced in the United States, the only country to pass a comprehensive act against bribery that prohibits bribes to officials of non-U.S. countries, i.e., the Foreign Corrupt Practices Act. He writes, "The U.S. view that not only bribery but other forms of corruption are regarded as inefficient . . . [helps] account for the fact that during the fifteen year period from 1977 to 1992, the United States fined or imprisoned more corporate officers and prominent businessmen than all other capitalist countries combined (Vogel, 1992).

The rejection of bribery through ISCT, using an appeal to hypernorms, refutes the claim often heard that bribery is inevitably the product of primitive, nonuniversalistic

perspectives. For example, the philosopher David Fisher once commented:

> Bribery, as a practice, belongs to a pre-modern world in which inequality of persons is assumed, and in which moral obligation is based on (1) birth into gender and class, (2) birth order, and (3) personal relationships that define duties. The theoretical perspectives of modern ethics, such as those of Kant or Mill, have little to offer those who inhabit such worlds, because they construe moral identity in ways that deny the universalism implied by all forms of modern ethics (Fisher, 1996).

This seems wrong-headed. Developing countries possess at least as many universalistic conceptions as developed ones. To think otherwise is to indulge in the kind of moral imperialism that brought well-educated scientists in the nineteenth century to regard all primitive people as "savages." Recent studies of the moral development of people in Belize, for example, found that they scored higher on Kohlberg-style moral development tests than did people in the United States. A comparative field study evaluated the moral reasoning used by U.S. and Belize business students in resolving business-related moral dilemmas. The Belize business students, inhabitants of a less-developed country, though with a Western heritage, resolved the dilemmas using higher stages of moral judgment than did the U.S. business students (Worrell et al., 1995).

Nonetheless, at the level most individual managers confront it, bribery has no satisfactory solution. Refusing to bribe is very often tantamount to losing business. Often sales and profits are lost to more unscrupulous companies, with the consequence that both the ethical company and the ethical individual are penalized. (Of course, companies help employees caught in the bribery trap by having clear policies and giving support to employees who follow them.) The answer, then, lies not at the level where individuals face bribery, but at the level of the host country's background institutions. A solution involves a broadly based combination of business pressure, legal enforcement, and political will. Companies, in turn, should make a point not only of speaking out against bribery, but of doing so in cooperation with other companies.

REFERENCES

Ades, A. & Di Tella, A. 1997. National champions and corruption: Some unpleasant interventionist arithmetic. Paper presented at the University of Pennsylvania, Philadelphia.

Arrow, K. J. 1973. Social responsibility and economic efficiency. *Public Policy,* 3(21): 300–317.

Bliss, C., & Di Tella, R. 1997. Does competition kill corruption? Paper presented at the University of Pennsylvania, Philadelphia.

Donaldson, T. 1996. Values in tension: Ethics away from home. *Harvard Business Review,* 74(5): 48–56.

Donaldson, T. 1989. The ethics of international business. New York: Oxford University Press.

Fisher, D. 1996. A comment on bribery. E-mail communication, April 16, in IABS Listserver.

Heimann, F. F. 1994. Should foreign bribery be a crime? Cited in Nichols, P. M. 1997. Outlawing transnational bribery through the World Trade Organizational. *Law and Policy in International Business,* 28(2): 305–386 (footnote 73).

Laczniak, G. R. 1990. International marketing ethics. *Bridges,* 155–177.

Nichols, P. M. 1997. Outlawing transnational bribery through the World Trade Organization. *Law and Policy in International Business,* 28(2): 305–386.

Shue, H. 1980. *Basic rights: Subsistence, affluence, and U.S. foreign policy.* Princeton, NJ: Princeton University Press.

Universal declaration of human rights. 1948. Reprinted in T. Donaldson & P. Werhane (Eds.). 1979. *Ethical issues in business:* 252–255. Englewood Cliffs, NJ: Prentice Hall.

Vogel, D. 1992. The globalization of business ethics: Why America remains distinctive. *California Management Review,* 35(1): 30–49.

Worrell, D., Walters, B. & Coalter, T. 1995. Moral judgement and values in a developed and a developing nation: A comparative analysis. *Academy of Management Best Paper Proceedings:* 401–405.

Yannaca-Small, C. 1995. Battling international bribery: The globalization of the economy. *OECD Observer:* 16–18.

CAPITALISM IN THE THIRD WORLD

The Campus Anti-Sweatshop Movement

Richard Appelbaum
and Peter Dreier

Each year of the past five, the annual survey of national freshman attitudes conducted by the University of California at Los Angeles has hit a new record low with students who say it is important to keep up with political affairs. At 26 percent this year, it was down from 58 percent when the survey was first done in 1966.

— *Boston Globe,* February 15, 1999

From Richard Appelbaum and Peter Dreier, The Campus Anti-Sweatshop Movement, *The American Prospect* 46 (Sept.–Oct.) 71–78, 1999. Reprinted with permission.

From: Arne David Ekstrom <ekstrom@NSMA.Arizona.EDU>
To: usas@listbot.com [United Students Against Sweatshops listserve]
Date: Thursday, April 29, 1999
Subject: U of Arizona STUDENTS AGAINST SWEATSHOPS SIT-IN CONTINUES

For those of you who are wondering, the University of Arizona sit-in is STILL GOING ON! We have reached a USAS record of 200 hours and still counting. Negotiations are still going slowly although progress is being made. We could still most definitely use your support in the form of emails, phone calls, and letters. Morale tends to go up and down but support ALWAYS keeps it high!

our cell phone: (520) 400-1066 (somewhat unreliable)
our email: akolers@u.arizona.edu (avery),
lsnow@u.arizona.edu (laura)
our President's email: President Likins at
plikins@lan.admin.arizona.edu
our President's phone: (520) 621-5511

If University of Arizona activist Arne Ekstrom was aware of today's widely reported student apathy, he certainly was not deterred when he helped lead his campus anti-sweatshop sit-in. Nor, for that matter, were any of the other thousands of students across the United States who participated in anti-sweatshop activities during the past academic year, coordinating their activities on the United Students Against Sweatshops (USAS) listserv (a listserv is an online mailing list for the purpose of group discussion) and Web site.

Last year's student anti-sweatshop movement gained momentum as it swept westward, eventually encompassing more than 100 campuses across the country. Sparked by a sit-in at Duke University, students organized teach-ins, led demonstrations, and occupied buildings — first at Georgetown, then northeast to the Ivy League, then west to the Big Ten. After militant actions at Notre Dame, Wisconsin, and Michigan made the *New York Times, Business Week, Time,* National Public Radio, and almost every major daily newspaper, the growing student movement reached California, where schools from tiny Occidental College to the giant ten-campus University of California system agreed to limit the use of their names and logos to sweatshop-free apparel. Now the practical challenge is to devise a regime of monitoring and compliance.

The anti-sweatshop movement is the largest wave of student activism to hit campuses since students rallied to free Nelson Mandela by calling for a halt to university investments in South Africa more than a decade ago. This time around, the movement is electronically connected. Student activists bring their laptops and cell phones with them when they occupy administration buildings, sharing ideas and strategies with fellow activists from Boston to Berkeley. On the USAS listserv, victorious students from Wisconsin counsel neophytes from Arizona and Kentucky, and professors at Berkeley and Harvard explain how to calculate a living wage and guarantee independent monitoring in Honduras.

The target of this renewed activism is the $2.5 billion collegiate licensing industry — led by major companies like Nike, Gear, Champion, and Fruit of the Loom — which pays colleges and universities sizable royalties in exchange for the right to use the campus logo on caps, sweatshirts, jackets, and other items. Students are demanding that the workers who make these goods be paid a living wage, no matter where in the world industry operates. Students are also calling for an end to discrimination against women workers, public disclosure of the names and addresses of all factories involved in production, and independent monitoring in order to verify compliance.

These demands are opposed by the apparel industry, the White House, and most universities. Yet so far students have made significant progress in putting the industry on the defensive. A growing number of colleges and clothing companies have adopted "codes of conduct" — something unthinkable a decade ago — although student activists consider many of these standards inadequate.

In a world economy increasingly dominated by giant retailers and manufacturers who control global networks of independently owned factories, organizing consumers may prove to be a precondition for organizing production workers. And students are a potent group of consumers. If students next year succeed in building on this year's momentum, the collegiate licensing industry will be forced to change the way it does business. These changes, in turn, could affect the organization of the world's most globalized and exploitative industry — apparel manufacturing — along with the growing number of industries that, like apparel, outsource production in order to lower labor costs and blunt worker organizing.

THE GLOBAL SWEATSHOP

In the apparel industry, so-called manufacturers — in reality, design and marketing firms — outsource the fabrication of clothing to independent contractors around the world. In this labor-intensive industry where capital requirements are minimal, it is relatively easy to open a clothing factory. This has contributed to a global race to the bottom, in which there is always someplace, somewhere, where clothing can be made still more cheaply. Low wages reflect not low productivity, but low bargaining power. A recent analysis in *Business Week* found that although Mexican apparel workers are 70 percent as productive as U.S. workers, they earn only 11 percent as much as their U.S. counterparts; Indonesian workers, who are 50 percent as productive, earn less than 2 percent as much.

The explosion of imports has proven devastating to once well-paid, unionized U.S. garment workers. The number of American garment workers has declined from peak levels of 1.4 million in the early 1970s to 800,000 today. The one exception to these trends is the expansion of garment employment, largely among immigrant and undocumented workers, in Los Angeles, which has more than 160,000 sweatshop workers. Recent U.S. Department of Labor surveys found that more than nine out of ten such firms violate legal health and safety standards, with more than half troubled by serious violations that could lead to severe injuries or death. Working conditions in New York City, the other major domestic garment center, are similar.

The very word "sweatshop" comes from the apparel industry, where profits were "sweated" out of workers by forcing them to work longer and faster at their sewing machines. Although significant advances have been made in such aspects of production as computer-assisted design, computerized marking, and computerized cutting, the industry still remains low-tech in its core production process, the sewing of garments. The basic unit of production continues to be a worker, usually a woman, sitting or standing at a sewing machine and sewing together pieces of limp cloth.

The structure of the garment industry fosters sweatshop production. During the past decade, retailing in the United States has become increasingly concentrated. Today, the four largest U.S. retailers — Wal-Mart, Kmart, Sears, and Dayton Hudson (owner of Target and Mervyns) — account for nearly two-thirds of U.S. retail sales. Retailers squeeze manufacturers, who in turn squeeze the contractors who actually make their products. Retailers and manufacturers preserve the fiction of being completely separate from contractors because they do not want to be held legally responsible for workplace violations of labor, health, and safety laws. Retailers and manufacturers alike insist that what happens in contractor factories is not their responsibility — even though their production managers and quality control officers are constantly checking up on the sewing shops that make their clothing.

The contracting system also allows retailers and manufacturers to eliminate much uncertainty and risk. When business is slow, the contract is simply not renewed; manufacturers need not worry about paying unemployment benefits or dealing with idle workers who might go on strike or otherwise make trouble. If a particular contractor becomes a problem, there are countless others to be found who will be only too happy to get their business. Workers, however, experience the flip side of the enormous flexibility enjoyed by retailers and manufacturers. They become contingent labor, employed and paid only when their work is needed.

Since profits are taken out at each level of the supply chain, labor costs are reduced to a tiny fraction of the retail price. Consider the economics of a dress that is sewn in Los Angeles and retails for $100. Half goes to the department store and half to the manufacturer, who keeps $12.50 to cover expenses and profit, spends $22.50 on textiles, and pays $15 to the contractor. The contractor keeps $9 to cover expenses and profits. That leaves just $6 of the $100 retail price for the workers who actually make the dress. Even if the cost of direct production labor were to increase by half, the dress would still only cost $103 — a small increment that would make a world of difference to the seamstress in Los Angeles, whose $7,000 to $8,000 in annual wages are roughly two-thirds of the poverty level. A garment worker in Mexico would be lucky to earn $1,000 during a year of 48 to 60 hour workweeks; in China, $500.

At the other end of the apparel production chain, the heads of the 60 publicly traded U.S. apparel retailers earn an average

$1.5 million a year. The heads of the 35 publicly traded apparel manufacturers average $2 million. In 1997, according to the *Los Angeles Business Journal*, five of the six highest-paid apparel executives in Los Angeles all came from a single firm: Guess?, Inc. They took home nearly $12.6 million — enough to double the yearly wages of 1,700 L.A. apparel workers.

Organizing workers at the point of production, the century-old strategy that built the power of labor in Europe and North America, is best suited to production processes where most of the work goes on in-house. In industries whose production can easily be shifted almost anywhere on the planet, organizing is extremely difficult. Someday, perhaps, a truly international labor movement will confront global manufacturers. But in the meantime, organized consumers may well be labor's best ally. Consumers, after all, are not as readily moved as factories. And among American consumers, college students represent an especially potent force.

KATHIE LEE AND ROBERT REICH

During the early 1990s, American human rights and labor groups protested the proliferation of sweatshops at home and abroad — with major campaigns focusing on Nike and Gap. These efforts largely fizzled. But then two exposés of sweatshop conditions captured public attention. In August 1995, state and federal officials raided a garment factory in El Monte, California — a Los Angeles suburb — where 71 Thai immigrants had been held for several years in virtual slavery in an apartment complex ringed with barbed wire and spiked fences. They worked an average of 84 hours a week for $1.60 an hour, living eight to ten persons in a room. The garments they sewed ended up in major retail chains, including Macy's, Filene's and Robinsons-May, and for brand-name labels like B.U.M., Tomato, and High Sierra. Major daily papers and TV networks picked up on the story, leading to a flood of outraged editorials and columns calling for a clamp-down on domestic sweatshops. Then in April 1996, TV celebrity Kathie Lee Gifford tearfully acknowledged on national television that the Wal-Mart line of clothing that bore her name was made by children in Honduran sweatshops, even though tags on the garments promised that part of the profits would go to help children. Embarrassed by the publicity, Gifford soon became a crusader against sweatshop abuses.

For several years, then-Labor Secretary Robert Reich (now the *Prospect's* senior editor) had been trying to inject the sweatshop issue onto the nation's agenda. The mounting publicity surrounding the El Monte and Kathie Lee scandals gave Reich new leverage. After all, what the apparel industry primarily sells is image, and the image of some of its major labels was getting a drubbing. He began pressing apparel executives, threatening to issue a report card on firms' behavior unless they agreed to help establish industry-wide standards.

In August 1996, the Clinton administration brought together representatives from the garment industry, labor unions, and consumer and human rights groups to grapple with sweatshops. The members of what they called the White House Apparel Industry Partnership (AIP) included apparel firms (Liz Claiborne, Reebok, L.L. Bean, Nike, Patagonia, Phillips-Van Heusen, Wal-Mart's Kathie Lee Gifford brand, and Nicole Miller), several nonprofit organizations (including the National Consumers League, Interfaith Center on Corporate Responsibility, International Labor Rights Fund, Lawyers Committee for Human Rights, Robert F. Kennedy Memorial Center for Human

Rights, and Business for Social Responsibility), as well as the Union of Needletrades, Industrial and Textile Employees (UNITE), the Retail, Wholesale, and Department Store Union, and the AFL-CIO.

After intense negotiations, the Department of Labor issued an interim AIP report in April 1997 and the White House released the final 40-page report in November 1998, which included a proposed workplace code of conduct and a set of monitoring guidelines. By then, Reich had left the Clinton administration, replaced by Alexis Herman. The two labor representatives on the AIP, as well as the Interfaith Center on Corporate Responsibility, quit the group to protest the feeble recommendations, which had been crafted primarily by the garment industry delegates and which called, essentially, for the industry to police itself. This maneuvering would not have generated much attention except that a new factor — college activism — had been added to the equation.

A "SWEAT-FREE" CAMPUS

The campus movement began in the fall of 1997 at Duke when a group called Students Against Sweatshops persuaded the university to require manufacturers of items with the Duke label to sign a pledge that they would not use sweatshop labor. Duke has 700 licensees (including Nike and other major labels) that make apparel at hundreds of plants in the U.S. and in more than 10 other countries, generating almost $25 million annually in sales. Following months of negotiations, in March 1998 Duke President Nannerl Keohane and the student activists jointly announced a detailed "code of conduct" that bars Duke licensees from using child labor, requires them to maintain safe workplaces, to pay the minimum wage, to recognize the right of workers to unionize, to disclose the locations of all factories making products with Duke's name, and to allow visits by independent monitors to inspect the factories.

The Duke victory quickly inspired students on other campuses. The level of activity on campuses accelerated, with students finding creative ways to dramatize the issue. At Yale, student activists staged a "knit-in" to draw attention to sweatshop abuses. At Holy Cross and the University of California at Santa Barbara, students sponsored mock fashion shows where they discussed the working conditions under which the garments were manufactured. Duke students published a coloring book explaining how (and where) the campus mascot, the Blue Devil, is stitched onto clothing by workers in sweatshops. Activists at the University of Wisconsin infiltrated a homecoming parade and, dressed like sweatshop workers in Indonesia, carried a giant Reebok shoe. They also held a press conference in front of the chancellor's office and presented him with an oversized check for 16 cents — the hourly wage paid to workers in China making Nike athletic shoes. At Georgetown, Wisconsin, Michigan, Arizona, and Duke, students occupied administration buildings to pressure their institutions to adopt (or, in Duke's case, strengthen) anti-sweatshop codes.

In the summer of 1998, disparate campus groups formed United Students Against Sweatshops (USAS). The USAS has weekly conference calls to discuss their negotiations with Nike, the Department of Labor, and others. It has sponsored training sessions for student leaders and conferences at several campuses where the sweatshop issue is only part of an agenda that also includes helping to build the labor movement, NAFTA, the World Trade Organization, women's rights, and other issues. . . .

Indeed, the anti-sweatshop movement has been able to mobilize wide support because it strikes several nerves among today's college students, including women's rights (most sweatshop workers are women and some factories have required women to use birth control pills as a condition of employment), immigrant rights, environmental concerns, and human rights. After University of Wisconsin administrators brushed aside anti-sweatshop protestors, claiming they didn't represent student opinion, the activists ran a slate of candidates for student government. Eric Brakken, a sociology major and anti-sweatshop leader, was elected student body president and last year used the organization's substantial resources to promote the activists' agenda. And Duke's student government unanimously passed a resolution supporting the anti-sweatshop group, calling for full public disclosure of the locations of companies that manufacture Duke clothing. . . .

THE INDUSTRY'S NEW CLOTHES

Last November, the White House-initiated Apparel Industry Partnership created a monitoring arm, the Fair Labor Association (FLA), and a few months later invited universities to join. Colleges, however, have just one seat on FLA's 14-member board. Under the group's bylaws the garment firms control the board's decisionmaking. The bylaws require a "supermajority" to approve all key questions, thus any three companies can veto a proposal they don't like.

At this writing, FLA member companies agree to ban child and prison labor, to prohibit physical abuse by supervisors, and to allow workers the freedom to organize unions in their foreign factories, though independent enforcement has not yet been specified. FLA wants to assign this monitoring task to corporate accounting firms like PricewaterhouseCoopers and Ernst & Young, to allow companies to select which facilities will be inspected, and to keep factory locations and the monitoring reports secret. Student activists want human rights and labor groups to do the monitoring.

This is only a bare beginning, but it establishes the crucial moral precedent of companies taking responsibility for labor conditions beyond their shores. Seeing this foot in the door, several companies have bowed out because they consider these standards too tough. The FLA expects that by 2001, after its monitoring program has been in place for a year, participating firms will be able to use the FLA log on their labels and advertising as evidence of their ethical corporate practices. [See Richard Rothstein, "The Starbucks Solution: Can Voluntary Codes Raise Global Living Standards?" *TAP*, July-August 1996.]

The original list of 17 FLA-affiliated universities grew to more than 100 by mid-summer of this year. And yet, some campus groups have dissuaded college administrations (including the Universities of Michigan, Minnesota, Oregon, Toronto, and California, as well as Oberlin, Bucknell, and Earlham Colleges) from joining FLA, while others have persuaded their institutions (including Brown, Wisconsin, North Carolina, and Georgetown) to join only if the FLA adopts stronger standards. While FLA members are supposed to abide by each country's minimum-wage standards, these are typically far below the poverty level. In fact, no company has made a commitment to pay a living wage.

The campus movement has succeeded in raising awareness (both on campus and among the general public) about sweatshops as well as the global economy. It has contributed to industry acceptance of extraterritorial labor standards, something hitherto considered utopian. It has also given thousands of students experience in the nuts and bolts of social activism, many of whom are likely to carry their idealism and organizing experiences with them into jobs with unions, community and environmental groups, and other public interest crusades.

So far, however, the movement has had only minimal impact on the daily lives of sweatshop workers at home and abroad. Nike and Reebok, largely because of student protests, have raised wages and benefits in their Indonesian footwear factories — which employ more than 100,000 workers — to 43 percent above the minimum wage. But this translates to only 20 cents an hour in U.S. dollars, far below a "living wage" to raise a family and even below the 27 cents Nike paid before Indonesia's currency devaluation. Last spring Nike announced its willingness to disclose the location of its overseas plants that produce clothing for universities. This created an important split in industry ranks, since industry leaders have argued that disclosure would undermine each firm's competitive position. But Nike has opened itself up to the charge of having a double standard, since it still refuses to disclose the location of its non-university production sites.

Within a year, when FLA's monitoring system is fully operational, students at several large schools with major licensing contracts — including Duke, Wisconsin, Michigan, North Carolina, and Georgetown — will have lists of factories in the U.S. and overseas that produce university clothing and equipment. This information will be very useful to civic and labor organizations at home and abroad, providing more opportunities to expose working conditions. Student activists at each university will be able to visit these sites — bringing media and public officials with them — to expose working conditions (and, if necessary, challenge the findings of the FLA's own monitors) and support organizing efforts by local unions and women's groups.

If the student activists can help force a small but visible "ethical" niche of the apparel industry to adopt higher standards, it will divide the industry and give unions and consumer groups more leverage to challenge the sweatshop practices of the rest of the industry. The campus anti-sweatshop crusade is part of what might be called a "conscience constituency" among consumers who are willing to incorporate ethical principles into their buying habits, even if it means slightly higher prices. Environmentalists have done the same thing with the "buy green" campaign, as have various "socially responsible" investment firms. . . .

Thanks to the student movement, public opinion may be changing. And last spring, speaking both to the International Labor Organization in Geneva and at the commencement ceremonies at the University of Chicago (an institution founded by John D.

Rockefeller and a stronghold of free market economics, but also a center of student anti-sweatshop activism), President Clinton called for an international campaign against child labor, including restrictions on government purchases of goods made by children.

A shift of much apparel production to developing countries may well be inevitable in a global economy. But when companies do move their production abroad, student activists are warning "you can run but you can't hide," demanding that they be held responsible for conditions in contractor factories no matter where they are. Students can't accomplish this on their own, but in a very short period of time they have made many Americans aware that they don't have to leave their consciences at home when they shop for clothes.

The Great Non-Debate Over International Sweatshops

Ian Maitland

In recent years, there has been a dramatic growth in the contracting out of production by companies in the industrialized countries to suppliers in developing countries. This globalization of production has led to an emerging international division of labor in footwear and apparel in which companies like Nike and Reebok concentrate on product design and marketing but rely on a network of contractors in Indonesia, China, Central America, etc., to build shoes or sew shirts according to exact specifications and deliver a high quality good according to precise delivery schedules. As Nike's vice president for

Asia has put it, "We don't know the first thing about manufacturing. We are marketers and designers."

The contracting arrangements have drawn intense fire from critics — usually labor and human rights activists. These "critics" (as I will refer to them) have charged that the companies are (by proxy) exploiting workers in the plants (which I will call "international sweatshops") of their suppliers. Specifically the companies stand accused of chasing cheap labor around the globe, failing to pay their workers living wages, using child labor, turning a blind eye to abuses of human

From Ian Maitland, "The great non-debate over international sweatshops," *British Academy of Management Annual Conference Proceedings*, September, pp. 240–265, 1997. Reprinted with permission.

rights, being complicit with repressive regimes in denying workers the right to join unions and failing to enforce minimum labor standards in the workplace, and so on.

The campaign against international sweatshops has largely unfolded on television and, to a lesser extent, in the print media. What seems like no more than a handful of critics has mounted an aggressive, media-savvy campaign which has put the publicity-shy retail giants on the defensive. The critics have orchestrated a series of sensational "disclosures" on prime time television exposing the terrible pay and working conditions in factories making jeans for Levi's or sneakers for Nike or Pocahontas shirts for Disney. One of the principal scourges of the companies has been Charles Kernaghan who runs the National Labor Coalition (NLC), a labor human rights group involving 25 unions. It was Kernaghan who, in 1996, broke the news before a Congressional committee that Kathie Lee Gifford's clothing line was being made by 13- and 14-year-olds working 20-hour days in factories in Honduras. Kernaghan also arranged for teenage workers from sweatshops in Central America to testify before Congressional committees about abusive labor practices. At one of these hearings, one of the workers held up a Liz Claiborne cotton sweater identical to ones she had sewn since she was a 13-year-old working 12 hours days. According to a news report, "[t]his image, accusations of oppressive conditions at the factory and the Claiborne logo played well on that evening's network news." The result has been a circus-like atmosphere — as in Roman circus where Christians were thrown to lions.

Kernaghan has shrewdly targeted the companies' carefully cultivated public images. He has explained: "Their image is everything. They live and die by their image. That gives you a certain power over them." As a result, he says, "these companies are sitting ducks. They have no leg to stand on. That's why it's possible for a tiny group like us to take on a giant like Wal-Mart. You can't defend paying someone 31 cents an hour in Honduras. . . ."[1] Apparently most of the companies agree with Kernaghan. Not a single company has tried to mount a serious defense of its contracting practices. They have judged that they cannot win a war of soundbites with the critics. Instead of making a fight of it, the companies have sued for peace in order to protect their principal asset — their image.

Major U.S. retailers have responded by adopting codes of conduct on human and labor rights in their international operations. Levi-Strauss, Nike, Sears, JCPenney, Wal-Mart, Home Depot, and Philips Van-Heusen now have such codes. As Lance Compa notes, such codes are the result of a blend of humanitarian and pragmatic impulses: "Often the altruistic motive coincides with "bottom line" considerations related to brand name, company image, and other intangibles that make for core value to the firm."[2] Peter Jacobi, President of Global Sourcing for Levi-Strauss has advised: "If your company owns a popular brand, protect this priceless asset at all costs. Highly visible companies have any number of reasons to conduct their business not just responsibly but also in ways that cannot be portrayed as unfair, illegal, or unethical. This sets an extremely high standard since it must be applied to both company-owned businesses and contractors. . . ."[3] And according to another Levi-Strauss spokesman, "In many respects, we're protecting our single largest asset: our brand image and corporate reputation."[4] Nike recently published the results of a generally favorable review of its international operations conducted by former American U.N. Ambassador Andrew Young.

Recently a truce of sorts between the critics and the companies was announced on the White House lawn with President Clinton and Kathie Lee Gifford in attendance. A presidential task force, including representatives of labor unions, human rights groups and apparel companies like L.L. Bean and Nike, has come up with a set of voluntary standards which, it hopes, will be embraced by the entire industry. Companies that comply with the code will be entitled to use a "No Sweat" label.

OBJECTIVE OF THIS PAPER

In this confrontation between the companies and their critics, neither side seems to have judged it to be in its interest to seriously engage the issue at the heart of this controversy, namely: What are appropriate wages and labor standards in international sweatshops? As we have seen, the companies have treated the charges about sweatshops as a public relations problem to be managed so as to minimize harm to their public images. The critics have apparently judged that the best way to keep public indignation at boiling point is to oversimplify the issue and treat it as a morality play featuring heartless exploiters and victimized third world workers. The result has been a great non-debate over international sweatshops. Paradoxically, if peace breaks out between the two sides, the chances that the debate will be seriously joined may recede still further. Indeed, there exists a real risk (I will argue) that any such truce may be a collusive one that will come at the expense of the very third world workers it is supposed to help.

This paper takes up the issue of what are appropriate wages and labor standards in international sweatshops. Critics charge that the present arrangements are exploitative. I proceed by examining the specific charges of exploitation from the standpoints of both (a) their factual and (b) their ethical sufficiency. However, in the absence of any well-established consensus among business

ethicists (or other thoughtful observers), I simultaneously use the investigation of sweatshops as a setting for trying to adjudicate between competing views about what those standards should be. My examination will pay particular attention to (but will not be limited to) labor conditions at the plants of Nike's suppliers in Indonesia. I have not personally visited any international sweatshops, and so my conclusions are based entirely on secondary analysis of the voluminous published record on the topic.

WHAT ARE ETHICALLY APPROPRIATE LABOR STANDARDS IN INTERNATIONAL SWEATSHOPS?

What are ethically acceptable or appropriate levels of wages and labor standards in international sweatshops? The following four possibilities just about run the gamut of standards or principles that have been seriously proposed to regulate such policies.

(1) *Home-country standards:* It might be argued (and in rare cases has been) that international corporations have an ethical duty to pay the same wages and provide the same labor standards regardless of where they operate. However, the view that home-country standards should apply in host-countries is rejected by most business ethicists and (officially at least) by the critics of international sweatshops. Thus Thomas Donaldson argues that "[b]y arbitrarily establishing U.S. wage levels as the benchmark for fairness one eliminates the role of the international market in establishing salary levels, and this in turn eliminates the incentive U.S. corporations have to hire foreign workers."[5] Richard DeGeorge makes much the same argument: If there were a rule that said that "that American MNCs [multinational corporations] that wish to be ethical must pay the same wages abroad as they do at home, . . . [then] MNCs would have little incentive to move their manufacturing abroad; and if they did move

abroad they would disrupt the local labor market with artificially high wages that bore no relation to the local standard or cost of living."[6]

(2) *"Living wage" standard:* It has been proposed that an international corporation should, at a minimum, pay a "living wage." Thus DeGeorge says that corporations should pay a living wage "even when this is not paid by local firms."[7] However, it is hard to pin down what this means operationally. According to DeGeorge, a living wage should "allow the worker to live in dignity as a human being." In order to respect the human rights of its workers, he says, a corporation must pay "at least subsistence wages and as much above that as workers and their dependents need to live with reasonable dignity, given the general state of development of the society."[8] As we shall see, the living wage standard has become a rallying cry of the critics of international sweatshops. Apparently, DeGeorge believes that it is preferable for a corporation to provide no job at all than to offer one that pays less than a living wage. . . .

(3) *Classical liberal standard:* Finally, there is what I will call the classical liberal standard. According to this standard a practice (wage or labor practice) is ethically acceptable if it is freely chosen by informed workers. For example, in a recent report the World Bank invoked this standard in connection with workplace safety. It said: "The appropriate level is therefore that at which the costs are commensurate with the value that informed workers place on improved working conditions and reduced risk."[9] Most business ethicists reject this standard on the grounds that there is some sort of market failure or the "background conditions" are lacking for markets to work effectively. Thus for Donaldson full (or near-full) employment is a prerequisite if workers are to make sound choices regarding workplace safety: "The average level of unemployment in the developing countries today exceeds 40 percent, a figure that has frustrated the application of neoclassical economic principles to the international economy on a score of issues. With full employment, and all other things being equal, market forces will encourage workers to make trade-offs between job opportunities using safety as a variable. But with massive unemployment, market forces in developing countries drive the unemployed

to the jobs they are lucky enough to land, regardless of the safety."[10] Apparently there are other forces, like Islamic fundamentalism and the global debt "bomb," that rule out reliance on market solutions, but Donaldson does not explain their relevance.[11] DeGeorge, too, believes that the necessary conditions are lacking for market forces to operate benignly. Without what he calls "background institutions" to protect the workers and the resources of the developing country (e.g., enforceable minimum wages) and/or greater equality of bargaining power exploitation is the most likely result.[12] "If American MNCs pay workers very low wages . . . they clearly have the opportunity to make significant profits."[13] DeGeorge goes on to make the interesting observation that "competition has developed among multinationals themselves, so that the profit margin has been driven down" and developing countries "can play one company against another."[14] But apparently that is not enough to rehabilitate market forces in his eyes.

THE CASE AGAINST INTERNATIONAL SWEATSHOPS

To many of their critics, international sweatshops exemplify the way in which the greater openness of the world economy is hurting workers. . . . Globalization means a transition from (more or less) regulated domestic economies to an unregulated world economy. The superior mobility of capital, and the essentially fixed, immobile nature of world labor, means a fundamental shift in bargaining power in favor of large international corporations. Their global reach permits them to shift production almost costlessly from one location to another. As a consequence, instead of being able to exercise some degree of control over companies operating within their borders, governments are now locked in a bidding war with one another to attract and retain the business of large multinational companies.

The critics allege that international companies are using the threat of withdrawal or withholding of investment to pressure governments and workers to grant concessions. "Today [multinational companies] choose between workers in developing countries that compete against each other to depress wages to attract foreign investment." The result is a race for the bottom — a "destructive downward bidding spiral of the labor conditions and wages of workers throughout the world. . . ."[15] . . . Thus, critics charge that in Indonesia wages are deliberately held below the poverty level or subsistence in order to make the country a desirable location. The results of this competitive dismantling of worker protections, living standards and worker rights are predictable: deteriorating work conditions, declining real incomes for workers, and a widening gap between rich and poor in developing countries. I turn next to the specific charges made by the critics of international sweatshops.

Unconscionable Wages

Critics charge that the companies, by their proxies, are paying "starvation wages" and "slave wages." They are far from clear about what wage level they consider to be appropriate. But they generally demand that companies pay a "living wage." Kernaghan has said that workers should be paid enough to support their families and they should get a "living wage" and "be treated like human beings."[16] . . . According to Tim Smith, wage levels should be "fair, decent or a living wage for an employee and his or her family." He has said that wages in the maquiladoras of Mexico averaged $35 to $55 a week (in or near 1993) which he calls a "shockingly substandard wage," apparently on the grounds that it "clearly does not allow an employee to feed and care for a family adequately."[17] In

1992, Nike came in for harsh criticism when a magazine published the pay stub of a worker at one of its Indonesian suppliers. It showed that the worker was paid at the rage of $1.03 per day which was reportedly less than the Indonesian government's figure for "minimum physical need."[18]

Immiserization Thesis

Former Labor Secretary Robert Reich has proposed as a test of the fairness of development policies that "Low-wage workers should become better off, not worse off, as trade and investment boost national income." He has written that "[i]f a country pursues policies that . . . limit to a narrow elite the benefits of trade, the promise of open commerce is perverted and drained of its rationale."[19] A key claim of the activists is that companies actually impoverish or immiserize developing country workers. They experience an absolute decline in living standards. This thesis follows from the claim that the bidding war among developing countries is depressing wages. . . .

Widening Gap Between Rich and Poor

A related charge is that international sweatshops are contributing to the increasing gap between rich and poor. Not only are the poor being absolutely impoverished, but trade is generating greater inequality within developing countries. Another test that Reich has proposed to establish the fairness of international trade is that "the gap between rich and poor should tend to narrow with development, not widen."[20] Critics charge that international sweatshops flunk that test. They say that the increasing GNPs of some developing countries simply mask a widening gap between rich and poor. "Across the world, both local and foreign elites are getting richer from the exploitation of the most vulnerable."[21] And, "The major adverse consequence of quickening global economic integration has been widening income disparity within almost all nations. . . ."[22] There appears to be a tacit alliance between the elites of both first and third worlds to exploit the most vulnerable, to regiment and control and conscript them so that they can create the material conditions for the elites' extravagant lifestyles.

Collusion with Repressive Regimes

Critics charge that, in their zeal to make their countries safe for foreign investment, Third World regimes, notably China and Indonesia, have stepped up their repression. Not only have these countries failed to enforce even the minimal labor rules on the books, but they have also used their military and police to break strikes and repress independent unions. They have stifled political dissent, both to retain their hold on political power and to avoid any instability that might scare off foreign investors. Consequently, critics charge, companies like Nike are profiting from political repression. "As unions spread in [Korea and Taiwan], Nike shifted its suppliers primarily to Indonesia, China and Thailand, where they could depend on governments to suppress independent union-organizing efforts."[23]

EVALUATION OF THE CHARGES AGAINST INTERNATIONAL SWEATSHOPS

The critics' charges are undoubtedly accurate on a number of points: (1) There is no doubt that international companies are chasing cheap labor. (2) The wages paid by the international sweatshops are — by American standards — shockingly low. (3) Some developing country governments have tightly controlled or repressed organized labor in order to prevent it from disturbing the flow of foreign investment. Thus, in Indonesia, independent unions have been suppressed. (4) It is not unusual in developing countries for minimum wage levels to be lower than the official poverty level. (5) Developing country governments have winked at violations of minimum wage laws and labor rules. However, most jobs are in the informal sector and so largely outside the scope of government supervision. (6) Some suppliers have employed children or have subcontracted work to other producers who have done so. (7) Some developing country governments deny their people basic political rights. China is the obvious example; Indonesia's record is pretty horrible but had shown steady improvement until the last two years. But on many of the other counts, the critics' charges appear to be seriously inaccurate. And, even where the charges are accurate, it is not self-evident that the practices in question are improper or unethical, as we see next.

Wages and Conditions

Even the critics of international sweatshops do not dispute that the wages they pay are generally higher than — or at least equal to — comparable wages in the labor markets where they operate. According to the International Labor Organization (ILO), multinational companies often apply standards relating to wages, benefits, conditions of work, and occupational safety and health, which both exceed statutory requirements and those practiced by local firms."[24] The ILO also says that wages and working conditions in so-called Export Processing Zones (EPZs) are often equal to or higher than jobs outside. The World Bank says that the poorest workers in developing countries work in the informal sector where they often earn less than half what a formal sector employee earns. Moreover, "informal and rural workers often must work under more hazardous and insecure conditions than their formal sector counterparts.[25]

The same appears to hold true for the international sweatshops. In 1996, young women working in the plant of a Nike supplier in Serang, Indonesia were earning the Indonesian legal minimum wage of 5,200 rupiahs or about $2.28 each day. As a report in the *Washington Post* pointed out, just earning the minimum wage put these workers among higher-paid Indonesians: "In Indonesia, less than half the working population earns the minimum wage, since about half of all adults here are in farming, and the typical farmer would make only about 2,000 rupiahs each day."[26] The workers in the Serang plant reported that they save about three-quarters of their pay. A 17-year-old woman said: "I came here one year ago from central Java. I'm making more money than my father makes." This woman also said that she sent about 75 percent of her earnings back to her family on the farm.[27] Also in 1996, a Nike spokeswoman estimated that an entry-level factory worker in the plant of a Nike supplier made five times what a farmer makes.[28] Nike's chairman, Phil Knight, likes to teasingly remind critics that the average worker in one of Nike's Chinese factories is paid more than a professor at Beijing University.[29] There is also plentiful anecdotal evidence from non-Nike sources. A worker at the Taiwanese-owned King Star Garment Assembly plant in Honduras told a reporter that he was earning seven times what he earned in the countryside.[30] In Bangladesh, the country's fledgling garment industry was paying women who had never worked before between $40 and $55 a month in 1991. That compared with a national per capita income of about $200 and

the approximately $1 a day earned by many of these women's husbands as day laborers or rickshaw drivers.[31]

The same news reports also shed some light on the working conditions in sweatshops. According to the *Washington Post,* in 1994 the Indonesian office of the international accounting firm Ernst & Young surveyed Nike workers concerning worker pay, safety conditions and attitudes toward the job. The auditors pulled workers off the assembly line at random and asked them questions that the workers answered anonymously. The survey of 25 workers at Nike's Serang plant found that 23 thought the hours and overtime worked were fair, and two thought the overtime hours too high. None of the workers reported that they had been discriminated against. Thirteen said the working environment was the key reason they worked at the Serang plant while eight cited salary and benefits.[32] The *Post* report also noted that the Serang plant closes for about ten days each year for Muslim holidays. It quoted Nike officials and the plant's Taiwanese owners as saying that 94 percent of the workers had returned to the plant following the most recent break. . . .

There is also the mute testimony of the lines of job applicants outside the sweatshops in Guatemala and Honduras. According to Lucy Martinez-Mont, in Guatemala the sweatshops are conspicuous for the long lines of young people waiting to be interviewed for a job.[33] Outside the gates of the industrial park in Honduras that Rohter visited "anxious onlookers are always waiting, hoping for a chance at least to fill out a job application [for employment at one of the apparel plants]."[34]

The critics of sweatshops acknowledge that workers have voluntarily taken their jobs, consider themselves lucky to have them, and want to keep them. . . . But they go on to discount the workers' views as the product of confusion or ignorance, and/or they just argue that the workers' views are beside the point. Thus, while "it is undoubtedly true" that Nike has given jobs to thousands of people who wouldn't be working otherwise, they say that "neatly skirts the fundamental human-rights issue raised by these production arrangements that are now spreading all across the world."[35] Similarly the NLC's Kernaghan says that "[w]hether workers think they are better off in the assembly plants than elsewhere is not the real issue."[36] Kernaghan, and Jeff Ballinger of the AFL-CIO, concede that the workers desperately need these jobs. But "[t]hey say they're not asking that U.S. companies stop operating in these countries. They're asking that workers be paid a living wage and treated like human beings."[37] Apparently these workers are victims of what Marx called false consciousness, or else they would grasp that they are being exploited. According to Barnet and Cavanagh, "For many workers . . . exploitation is not a concept easily comprehended because the alternative prospects for earning a living are so bleak."[38]

Immiserization and Inequality

The critics' claim that the countries that host international sweatshops are marked by growing poverty and inequality is flatly contradicted by the record. In fact, many of those countries have experienced sharp increases in living standards — for all strata of society. In trying to attract investment in simple manufacturing, Malaysia and Indonesia and, now, Vietnam and China, are retracing the industrialization path already successfully taken by East Asian countries like Taiwan, Korea, Singapore and Hong Kong. These four countries got their start by producing labor-intensive manufactured goods (often electrical and electronic components, shoes, and garments) for export markets. Over time they

graduated to the export of higher value-added items that are skill-intensive and require a relatively developed industrial base.[39]

As is well known, these East Asian countries achieved growth rates exceeding eight percent for a quarter century. . . . The workers in these economies were not impoverished by growth. The benefits of growth were widely diffused: These economies achieved essentially full employment in the 1960s. Real wages rose by as much as a factor of four. Absolute poverty fell. And income inequality remained at low to moderate levels. It is true that in the initial stages the rapid growth generated only moderate increases in wages. But once essentially full employment was reached, and what economists call the Fei-Ranis turning point was reached, the increased demand for labor resulted in the bidding up of wages as firms competed for a scarce labor supply.

Interestingly, given its historic mission as a watchdog for international labor standards, the ILO has embraced this development model. It recently noted that the most successful developing economies, in terms of output and employment growth, have been "those who best exploited emerging opportunities in the global economy."[40] An "export-oriented policy is vital in countries that are starting on the industrialization path and have large surpluses of cheap labour." Countries which have succeeded in attracting foreign direct investment (FDI) have experienced rapid growth in manufacturing output and exports. The successful attraction of foreign investment in plant and equipment "can be a powerful spur to rapid industrialization and employment creation." "At low levels of industrialization, FDI in garments and shoes and some types of consumer electronics can be very useful for creating employment and opening the economy to international markets; there may be some entrepreneurial skills created in simple activities like garments (as has happened in Bangladesh). More-over, in some cases, such as Malaysia, the in-vestors may strike deeper roots and invest in more capital-intensive technologies as wages rise."

According to the World Bank, the rapidly growing Asian economies (including Indone-sia) "have also been unusually successful at sharing the fruits of their growth."[41] In fact, while inequality in the West has been grow-ing, it has been shrinking in the Asian economies. They are the only economies in the world to have experienced high growth *and* declining inequality, and they also show shrinking gender gaps in education. . . .

Profiting from Repression?

What about the charge that international sweatshops are profiting from repression? It is undeniable that there is repression in many of the countries where sweatshops are lo-cated. But economic development appears to be relaxing that repression rather than strengthening its grip. The companies are supposed to benefit from government poli-cies (e.g., repression of unions) that hold down labor costs. However, as we have seen, the wages paid by the international sweat-shops already match or exceed the prevailing local wages. Not only that, but incomes in the East Asian economies, and in Indonesia, have risen rapidly. . . .

The critics, however, are right in saying that the Indonesian government has opposed in-dependent unions in the sweatshops out of fear they would lead to higher wages and labor unrest. But the government's fear clearly is that unions might drive wages in the modern industrial sector *above* market-clearing lev-els — or, more exactly, further above market. It is ironic that critics like Barnet and Ca-vanagh would use the Marxian term "reserve army of the unemployed." According to Marx, capitalists deliberately maintain high levels of unemployment in order to control the work-ing class. But the Indonesian government's policies (e.g., suppression of unions, resis-tance to a higher minimum wage and lax en-forcement of labor rules) have been directed at achieving exactly the opposite result. The government appears to have calculated that high unemployment is a greater threat to its hold on power. I think we can safely take at face value its claims that its policies are gen-uinely intended to help the economy create jobs to absorb the massive numbers of unem-ployed and underemployed.[42]

LABOR STANDARDS IN INTERNATIONAL SWEATSHOPS: PAINFUL TRADE-OFFS

Who but the grinch could grudge paying a few additional pennies to some of the world's poorest workers? There is no doubt that the rhetorical force of the critics' case against international sweatshops rests on this ap-parently self-evident proposition. However, higher wages and improved labor standards are not free. After all, the critics themselves attack companies for chasing cheap labor. It follows that, if labor in developing countries is made more expensive (say, as the result of pressure by the critics), then those countries will receive less foreign investment, and fewer jobs will be created there. Imposing higher wages may deprive these countries of the one comparative advantage they enjoy, namely low-cost labor.

We have seen that workers in most "inter-national sweatshops" are already relatively well paid. Workers in the urban, formal sec-tors of developing countries commonly earn more than twice what informal and rural workers get. Simply earning the minimum wage put the young women making Nike shoes in Serang in the top half of the income distribution in Indonesia. Accordingly, the critics are in effect calling for a *widening* of the economic disparity that already greatly favors sweatshop workers.

By itself that may or may not be ethically objectionable. But these higher wages come at the expense of the incomes and the job opportunities of much poorer workers. As economists explain, higher wages in the formal sector reduce employment there and (by increasing the supply of labor) depress incomes in the informal sector. The case against requiring above-market wages for international sweatshop workers is essentially the same as the case against other measures that artificially raise labor costs, like the minimum wage. In Jagdish Bhagwati's words: "Requiring a minimum wage in an overpopulated, developing country, as is done in a developed country, may actually be morally wicked. A minimum wage might help the unionized, industrial proletariat, while limiting the ability to save and invest rapidly which is necessary to draw more of the unemployed and nonunionized rural poor into gainful employment and income."[43] The World Bank makes the same point: "Minimum wages may help the most poverty-stricken workers in industrial countries, but they clearly do not in developing nations. . . . The workers whom minimum wage legislation tries to protect — urban formal workers — already earn much more than the less favored majority. . . . And inasmuch as minimum wage and other regulations discourage formal employment by increasing wage and nonwage costs, they hurt the poor who aspire to formal employment."[44]

The story is no different when it comes to labor standards other than wages. If standards are set too high they will hurt investment and employment. The World Bank report points out that "[r]educing hazards in the workplace is costly, and typically the greater the reduction the more it costs. Moreover, the costs of compliance often fall largely on employees through lower wages or reduced employment. As a result, setting standards too high can actually lower workers' welfare. . . ."[45] Perversely, if the higher standards advocated by critics retard the growth of formal sector jobs, then that will trap more informal and rural workers in jobs which are far more hazardous and insecure than those of their formal sector counterparts.

The critics consistently advocate policies that will benefit better-off workers at the expense of worse-off ones. If it were within their power, it appears that they would reinvent the labor markets of much of Latin America. Alejandro Portes' description seems to be on the mark: "In Mexico, Brazil, Peru, and other Third World countries, [unlike East Asia], there are powerful independent unions representing the protected sector of the working class. Although their rhetoric is populist and even radical, the fact is that they tend to represent the better-paid and more stable fraction of the working class. Alongside, there toils a vast, unprotected proletariat, employed by informal enterprises and linked, in ways hidden from public view, with modern sector firms." . . .

Of course, it might be objected that trading off workers' rights for more jobs is unethical. But, so far as I can determine, the critics have not made this argument. Although they sometimes implicitly accept the existence of the trade-off (we saw that they attack Nike for chasing cheap labor), their public statements are silent on the lost or forgone jobs from higher wages and better labor standards. At other times, they imply or claim that improvements in workers' wages and conditions are essentially free. . . .

In summary, the result of the ostensibly humanitarian changes urged by critics are likely to be (1) reduced employment in the formal or modern sector of the economy, (2) lower incomes in the informal sector,

(3) less investment and so slower economic growth, (4) reduced exports, (5) greater inequality and poverty.

CONCLUSION: THE CASE FOR NOT EXCEEDING MARKET STANDARDS

It is part of the job description of business ethicists to exhort companies to treat their workers better (otherwise what purpose do they serve?). So it will have come as no surprise that both the business ethicists whose views I summarized at the beginning of this paper — Thomas Donaldson and Richard DeGeorge — objected to letting the market alone determine wages and labor standards in multinational companies. Both of them proposed criteria for setting wages that might occasionally "improve" on the outcomes of the market.

Their reasons for rejecting market determination of wages were similar. They both cited conditions that allegedly prevent international markets from generating ethically acceptable results. Donaldson argued that neoclassical economic principles are not applicable to international business because of high unemployment rates in developing countries. And DeGeorge argued that, in an unregulated international market, the gross inequality of bargaining power between workers and companies would lead to exploitation.

But this paper has shown that attempts to improve on market outcomes may have unforeseen tragic consequences. We saw how raising the wages of workers in international sweatshops might wind up penalizing the most vulnerable workers (those in the informal sectors of developing countries) by depressing their wages and reducing their job opportunities in the formal sector. Donaldson and DeGeorge cited high unemployment and unequal bargaining power as conditions

that made it necessary to bypass or override the market determination of wages. However, in both cases, bypassing the market in order to prevent exploitation may aggravate these conditions. As we have seen, above-market wages paid to sweatshop workers may discourage further investment and so perpetuate high unemployment. In turn, the higher unemployment may weaken the bargaining power of workers vis-à-vis employers. Thus such market imperfections seem to call for more reliance on market forces rather than less. Likewise, the experience of the newly industrialized East Asian economies suggests that the best cure for the ills of sweatshops is more sweatshops. But most of the well-intentioned policies that improve on market outcomes are likely to have the opposite effect.

Where does this leave the international manager? If the preceding analysis is correct, then it follows that it is ethically acceptable to pay market wage rates in developing countries (and to provide employment conditions appropriate for the level of development). That holds true even if the wages pay less than so-called living wages or subsistence or even (conceivably) the local minimum wage. The appropriate test is not whether the wage reaches some predetermined standard but whether it is freely accepted by (reasonably) informed workers. The workers themselves are in the best position to judge whether the wages offered are superior to their next-best alternatives. (The same logic applies *mutatis mutandis* to workplace labor standards).

Indeed, not only is it ethically acceptable for a company to pay market wages, but it may be ethically unacceptable for it to pay wages that exceed market levels. That will be the case if the company's above-market wages set precedents for other international companies which raise labor costs to the point of discouraging foreign investment. Furthermore, companies may have a social responsibility to transcend their own narrow preoccupation with protecting their brand image and to publicly defend a system which has greatly improved the lot of millions of workers in developing countries.

NOTES

1. Steven Greenhouse, "A Crusader Makes Celebrities Tremble." *New York Times* (June 18, 1996), p. B4.

2. Lance A. Compa and Tashia Hinchliffe Darricarrere, "Enforcement Through Corporate Codes of Conduct," in Compa and Stephen F. Diamond, *Human Rights, Labor Rights, and International Trade* (Philadelphia: University of Pennsylvania Press, 1996) p. 193.

3. Peter Jacobi in Martha Nichols, "Third-World Families at Work: Child Labor or Child Care." *Harvard Business Review* (Jan.-Feb., 1993).

4. David Sampson in Robin G. Givhan, "A Stain on Fashion; The Garment Industry Profits from Cheap Labor." *Washington Post* (September 12, 1995), p. B1.

5. Thomas Donaldson, *Ethics of International Business,* (New York: Oxford University Press, 1989), p. 98.

6. Richard DeGeorge, *Competing with Integrity in International Business* (New York: Oxford University Press, 1993) p. 79.

7. Ibid., pp. 356–7.

8. Ibid., p. 78.

9. World Bank, *World Development Report 1995, "Workers in an Integrating World Economy"* (Oxford University Press, 1995) p. 77.

10. Donaldson, *Ethics of International Business,* p. 115.

11. *Ibid.,* p. 150.

12. DeGeorge, *Competing with Integrity,* p. 48.

13. *Ibid.,* p. 358.

14. *Ibid.*

15. Terry Collingsworth, J. William Goold, Pharis J. Harvey, "Time for a Global New Deal," *Foreign Affairs* (Jan–Feb, 1994), p. 8.

16. William B. Falk, "Dirty Little Secrets," *Newsday* (June 16, 1996).

17. Tim Smith, "The Power of Business for Human Rights." *Business & Society Review* (January 1994), p. 36.

18. Jeffrey Ballinger, "The New Free Trade Heel." *Harper's Magazine* (August, 1992), pp. 46–7. "As in many developing countries, Indonesia's minimum wage, . . . , is less than poverty level." Nina Baker, "The Hidden Hands of Nike," *Oregonian* (August 9, 1992).

19. Robert B. Reich, "Escape from the Global Sweatshop; Capitalism's Stake in Uniting the Workers of the World." *Washington Post* (May 22, 1994). Reich's test is intended to apply in developing countries "where democratic institutions are weak or absent."

20. *Ibid.*

21. Kenneth P. Hutchinson, "Third World Growth." *Harvard Business Review* (Nov.–Dec., 1994).

22. Robin Broad and John Cavanaugh, "Don't Neglect the Impoverished South." *Foreign Affairs* (December 22, 1995).

23. John Cavanagh & Robin Broad, "Global Reach; Workers Fight the Multinationals." *The Nation,* (March 18, 1996), p. 21. See also Bob Herbert, "Nike's Bad Neighborhood." *New York Times* (June 14, 1996).

24. International Labor Organization, *World Employment 1995* (Geneva: ILO, 1995) p. 73.

25. World Bank, *Workers in an Integrating World Economy,* p. 5.

26. Keith B. Richburg, Anne Swardson, "U.S. Industry Overseas: Sweatshop or Job Source?: Indonesians Praise Work at Nike Factory." *Washington Post* (July 28, 1996).

27. Richburg and Swardson, "Sweatshop or Job Source?" The 17 year-old was interviewed in the presence of managers. For other reports that workers remit home large parts of their earnings see Seth Mydans, "Tangerang Journal; For Indonesian Workers at Nike Plant: Just Do It." *New York Times* (August 9, 1996), and Nina Baker, "The Hidden Hands of Nike."

28. Donna Gibbs, Nike spokeswoman on ABC's *World News Tonight,* June 6, 1996.

29. Mark Clifford, "Trading in Social Issues; Labor Policy and International Trade Regulation," *World Press Review* (June 1994), p. 36.

30. Larry Rohter, "To U.S. Critics, a Sweatshop; for Hondurans, a Better Life." *New York Times* (July 18, 1996).

31. Marcus Brauchli, "Garment Industry Booms in Bangladesh." *Wall Street Journal* (August 6, 1991).

32. Richburg and Swardson, "Sweatshop or Job Source?"

33. Lucy Martinez-Mont, "Sweatshops Are Better Than No Shops." *Wall Street Journal* (June 25, 1996).

34. Rohter, "To U.S. Critics a Sweatshop."

35. Barnet & Cavanagh, *Global Dreams*, p. 326.

36. Rohter, "To U.S. Critics a Sweatshop."

37. William B. Falk, "Dirty Little Secrets," *Newsday* (June 16, 1996).

38. Barnet and Cavanagh, "Just Undo It: Nike's Exploited Workers." *New York Times* (February 13, 1994).

39. Sarosh Kuruvilla, "Linkages Between Industrialization Strategies and Industrial Relations/Human Resources Policies: Singapore, Malaysia, The Philippines, and India." *Industrial & Labor Relations Review* (July, 1996), p. 637.

40. The ILO's Constitution (of 1919) mentions that: ". . . the failure of any nation to adopt humane conditions of labour is an obstacle in the way of other nations which desire to improve the conditions in their own countries." ILO, *World Employment 1995,* p. 74.

41. World Bank, *The East Asian Miracle* (New York: Oxford University Press, 1993) p. 2.

42. Gideon Rachman, "Wealth in Its Grasp, a Survey of Indonesia." *Economist* (April 17, 1993), pp. 14–15.

43. Jagdish Bhagwati & Robert E. Hudec, eds. *Fair Trade and Harmonization* (Cambridge: MIT Press, 1996), vol. 1, p. 2.

44. World Bank, *Workers in an Integrating World Economy,* p. 75.

45. *Ibid.,* p. 77. As I have noted, the report proposes that the "appropriate level is therefore that at which the costs are commensurate with the value that informed workers place on improved working conditions and reduced risk. . . ." (p. 77).

The Price of a Dream

David Bornstein

The director of the Krishi Bank, A. M. Anisuzzaman, was having a bad day when Yunus walked into his office. And as soon as he sat down, the banker seized the opportunity to vent his frustrations about intellectuals and "academicians" and all of Yunus's colleagues who were continually complaining about the terrible job he was doing. What were they contributing to Bangladesh? "They talk, they don't do any work," he said. "They complain about everything that we do. Nobody helps me to get this bank cleaned up but everybody complains about all the inefficiency and the malpractice."

It was a sunny afternoon in 1994 when Yunus related the story to me in his office. He sat behind a desk piled high with files. He appeared stylish in a well-pressed, short-sleeve shirt, trousers, and sandals. His dark wavy hair was combed back and to the side. His hands moved lightly in the air as he spoke. He had long, graceful fingers. I had seen a few of his drawings — colorful village scenes — painted on cards that he had sent to branches to commemorate the end of Ramadan.

A representative of the Ford Foundation interviewed on *60 Minutes,* in 1990, had compared Yunus to Gandhi, J.F.K., and Martin Luther King, Jr. My friend who had worked on the documentary film about the Grameen Bank had mentioned that when she first met Yunus she said to him, "So you *are* mortal," and he replied, "Don't be too sure." And months before I left for Bangladesh, a Canadian aid official had told me: "Yunus has a real presence, and it is the presence of a *president*." (Indeed, rumors were circulating in late 1995 to the effect that due to political unrest, Yunus might soon be appointed Bangladesh's caretaker prime minister until an election could be held.)

Now I understood what they meant. I could feel his magnetism. His face was marvelously expressive. He laughed heartily and generously. When he smiled, he squinted, his cheeks grew round and his shoulders dropped. But when his emotion or indignation took hold, his face grew commanding, even leonine. His eyes pressed out as in a caricature; at times they seemed about to bulge out of their sockets.

Shortly into the interview I forgot that I was in the presence of an economist. The man before me would have been bored silly by calculus or statistics or staple theory. He certainly was not the same person who authored the Vanderbilt University Ph.D. dissertation entitled: "Optimal Allocation of Multi-purpose Reservoir Water: A Dynamic Programming Model."

No, this man was a storyteller, and like one who is practiced in the art of telling children's tales, he was acutely aware of his listener's limitations. Nothing he said was the least bit complicated; everything was kept simple, at times deceptively simple. He came off as surprisingly accessible for someone running an organization with more than 12,000 employees. Many people more influential than I had interviewed Yunus; nevertheless, he granted my first request for an interview the same day. He never asked, nor did he seem to care a whit, about my credentials. I had come to Bangladesh to write about his bank; that was my qualification.

And yet, although I felt disarmed by Yunus, I did not feel at ease in his presence.

He spoke humorously of human absurdity, but beneath the surface it was clear that he was dead serious and quite adamant about his ideas. Einstein's words on Gandhi seemed to fit: "[A] man of wisdom and humility, armed with resolve and inflexible consistency."

Yunus's central theme was that a great many people suffered terribly and unnecessarily because of human inaction and folly. So, of course, it couldn't really be called folly; in truth, it was gross negligence. And here he demanded, *insisted* on full attention. I found it difficult to pull my eyes away from his when he spoke, even just to jot down a note or check my tape recorder. And although I felt pulled in, I was conscious of being somehow pushed away. Perhaps I anticipated this. I had been told that very few people got close to Yunus. In a culture that is compulsively social, not even his most intimate colleagues felt free to drop by his apartment or invite him to a dinner party. As head of the Grameen Bank, Yunus welcomed visitors from around the world and made himself available for their questions. But if he had the power to charm, he also had the power, and it seemed the desire, to remain distant. As an individual apart from the Grameen Bank, he seemed unapproachable.

The office window was open. Outside, the air was filled with clanking sounds — construction workers putting the finishing touches on Grameen's new office building.

"So he loves talking," Yunus said. "And he kept on talking for hours. So when I get a chance, I try to say a few words, but he brushes me off and goes on.

"So finally I said, 'Look, would you please stop and listen to what I have to say.'

"He says, 'Go on, say it.'

"I say, 'I cannot clean up your whole mess — it's too much. But this is what I'm doing in Chittagong through the Janata Bank. Why don't you give me a branch of the

Krishi Bank in Jobra and give the responsibility of running that branch to me? I'll make the rules. And I'll demonstrate what can be done. And give me one year's time and one million takas that I can use as loans. And after one year if you don't like it, throw me out. It can't be any worse than what's going on in the rest of the country. But something good might come out of it. And if something good comes out of it and you like it, and you don't like the other parts, just pick up that one good piece and use it in other ways. Forget about the rest of it. And if you'd like me to continue, give me another year. I'll continue. If you don't like it, throw me out.'"

Anisuzzaman immediately accepted Yunus's proposal. "It will be done," he said. "You will have a branch. Do you need anything more?"

"Now that I have become the managing director of one branch," Yunus replied, "I don't need anything more. Whatever I need, I can solve myself."

Anisuzzaman called his regional director in Chittagong and told him: "Doctor Yunus will be coming back to Chittagong tomorrow" — and he asked Yunus his flight time and continued over the telephone — "you be at his house in the campus before he arrives, and from then on you take orders from him so far as the project that he is talking about is concerned."

"This is the kind of guy he is," explained Yunus. "He just said I could do it. I thought everything was resolved. So when I went back, sure enough the poor guy is waiting for me. Because after all the big guy told him to."

"What is it that I'm supposed to do?" the banker asked.

"I'm not sure myself," Yunus replied. "Why don't we sit down and I'll tell you what I told him and you tell me how to get it done."

"I explained that there will be a branch in Jobra and that branch will be run by me."

"That cannot be done," the man replied.

"But he said it could be done."

"The first thing is that you have to submit a proposal for a project, write out the details, give the budget, and so on. And I will offer my opinion on this project and it will be sent to my immediate boss; he will give his comments and it will go up the ladder to the managing director — because I cannot write to the managing director myself. And then he will decide which way to go.

"Even the managing director cannot give away his authority just like that," the banker explained. "He has to take it to the board and the board has to decide. And there are certain things even the board cannot change, because they have to do with fundamental principles of the bank. So you have to go back to the Parliament or whoever made the law for that. And your suggestion involves that kind of change."

"Well, I don't know anything about *that*," said Yunus. "He didn't say anything about a proposal. But if you need a proposal, why don't you ask me questions and I'll answer them, and we'll put it down and that will be my proposal?"

"So this fellow became very scared," he recalled. "He said, 'I better not ask you questions. Why don't I come back on another convenient day and bring my colleagues so that we can all write it down together and try to develop a project proposal.'"

"Good enough," Yunus said.

A date was arranged. When the bankers finished the first draft, Yunus rewrote it, giving himself more autonomy. The bankers objected.

"This is what I want," declared Yunus. "You cannot change it."

"It cannot be done," replied the bankers.

"So a compromise was made," Yunus recalled. "It became not quite a branch; it became a booth, a window. I named it the Experimental Grameen Branch. It didn't say that I took it over. It said there would be some experimental things going on but the manager is still the final authority — with the understanding that he would allow me to do certain things."

The Experimental Grameen Branch opened the following spring in a thatch hut with bamboo walls and a tin roof. On its first day in business, it disbursed 52,000 takas to twenty-four villagers. That summer, it signed up another 341 customers. By September, the bank had spread to three villages and disbursed more than a half million takas — about $15,000 — to four hundred villagers, one quarter of whom were women. The default rate was less than one percent.

With the increased workload, Yunus took a closer look at procedures. At the rate things were growing, even a small oversight could develop into a crisis. One problem the students discovered was that grouping by activity made little sense, because it failed to ensure that group members shared close personal ties, and in any event, people often switched businesses. If the group was to be the basis of loan security, it had to be a stable unit. So the students decided to form groups of villagers who knew each other well.

Then there was the issue of group size. If the group was too large, those with weaker personalities would get lost in the crowd, while everybody's sense of accountability would be diminished. If it was too small, it wouldn't allow for a range of pursuits and opinions. After trial and error, Yunus settled on the number five. Part of this was intuitive: A working hand has five fingers; there are five pillars of faith in Islam, and each day, five calls to prayer.

Each group elected a "chairman" and "secretary," positions that rotated annually; and two new funds were introduced: the Group Fund and the Emergency Fund. The Group Fund was a collective savings from which villagers could borrow when they needed a short-term loan. Initially, each borrower was to deposit one taka per week into this fund,

but as it became clear how critical the Group Fund was to long-term security, Yunus introduced a 5 percent "group tax" to be levied on each loan.

The Emergency Fund was a reserve into which borrowers had to contribute a fee at the end of the year. In case of default, accident, or theft, the group could make use of this money however it saw fit. All appropriations from the Group and Emergency Funds required the consent of all five members. (In later years, the Emergency Fund would evolve into a form of life insurance. When a Grameen borrower dies, her beneficiary today receives a payment of up to 5,000 takas — about one year's income for a poor villager.)

To appreciate the importance of these two funds, one has to look closely at the roots of poverty in Bangladesh. Most foreign observers see Bangladesh's troubles as a combination of ignorance and bad luck — often with the legacy of colonialism thrown in as an afterthought. When Bangladesh declared independence, its wealth had been largely depleted, its cotton and textile industries long destroyed, and international observers looked at this tiny country with its tens of millions of villagers, with its floods and droughts and cyclones, with a literacy rate of 25 percent, and they shook their heads gravely. Bangladesh, the diplomats agreed, would be an "international basket case."

Who could argue with them? And yet the way Yunus saw it, he didn't have to worry about Bangladesh's problems; he only had to worry about the problems of a few hundred villagers. He had little use for the diplomats' pronouncements. Such views of national poverty were counterproductive, he felt. They only obscured the reality of individual poverty, and individual poverty was the result of social processes that could be readily understood and addressed.

Shortly after his arrival at Chittagong University, Yunus had directed his students to survey the landless of Jobra and record each family's history, focusing on their changes in fortune over three generations. He was particularly interested in land, by far the most important asset to a villager. The rise in landlessness was well documented in Bangladesh: Since World War II, the proportion of landless had jumped from 20 percent to more than 50 percent of the population. Of the landless villagers surveyed, Yunus discovered that 252 had lost their land in their own lifetimes, 89 in their fathers', and 18 in their grandfathers'.

The population surge in recent decades, due in part to improvements in sanitation and the spread of medical services and immunization programs, was often cited as the prime reason for the increase in landlessness, and some even argued that medical advances had exacerbated the situation in Bangladesh. Yunus was not interested in debating whether technological advancements made matters better or worse. Technology wasn't going away. For him the more relevant question was, With so much land changing hands, which villagers lost and which ones gained? And why?

The pattern was fairly predictable, as he discovered. A family with some land would start to fall behind for any of a number of reasons: illness, a poor crop, theft, dowry, the death of a father, or a natural disaster, such as a flood. Until they could recover, they would have to borrow money for food, perhaps for a few months, perhaps only for a few weeks. There is perhaps no country in the world in which the "time value" of money is as great as in Bangladesh, with its cycles of dearth and plenty. A family whose food stocks are depleted, say, six weeks before harvest can borrow forty kilograms of rice on the condition that they repay eighty kilograms two months later — an effective annual interest rate of 600 percent. If a villager needs a fast loan to purchase medicine, his only recourse may be to mortgage or sell his land, doing so in the vain hope that he might one day recover it.

In the end, wealth flows in one direction: steadily and inexorably, from poor to rich. Despite Bangladesh's problems with floods and cyclones and droughts, its most oppressive poverty is not the result of natural disasters but of social processes; and in Jobra, Yunus discovered that the first step is often the establishment of a credit relationship with a moneylender.

The Group Fund was designed to bring this process to a halt by providing a pool of short-term, inexpensive credit so that villagers would not have to resort to moneylenders or dig into their productive capital each time they encountered difficulties. Withdrawals were not permitted from this fund. If a member needed money, the group had to sanction a loan; the other four dictated the terms. (Usually, villagers grant interest-free loans to one another.) When explaining the rationale for the group tax, the students would compare it to a women's tradition in Bangladesh of setting aside a handful of rice before each meal. "You don't miss it but soon you accumulate a sizable amount," they would say.

Some villagers protested but Yunus retained the tax because he believed that the only hope poor people had of gaining control over their lives was through saving and asset accumulation.

Two other changes were introduced: The definition of a "landless" person was expanded to include villagers whose families were "functionally landless," which meant they did not own enough land to live off for most of the year. (A local unit of measurement, one *kani*, equal to .4 acres, was initially set as the upper limit.)

An organizational hierarchy was established. Up to six groups formed a center — with men and women kept separate. Each center elected a center chief and deputy center chief. All loans were to be collected at weekly center meetings.

The system seemed capable of managing a growing clientele, so after the new procedures were finalized, Yunus encoded them in a set of bylaws and statements of principle called the *Bidhimala:* the constitution. Dipal served as his amanuensis. "I had the best handwriting," he explained.

Section 1.0 read: "The objective of the Grameen Bank Project is to introduce and institutionalize a non-traditional banking system in rural areas which would provide credit facilities under special terms and conditions. This project attempts to serve those rural people who are not covered by the traditional banking system. The success of this project entirely depends on the sincere efforts to follow the rules and regulations prescribed below."

The *Bidhimala* covered the formation of groups and centers; the duties of group chairmen and secretaries, center chiefs and deputy center chiefs; the procedures for disbursements and collections; the administration of the group and emergency funds; the protocol for forming and dissolving groups; and provisions for amendments to the constitution.

Because half the population fit into Grameen's target market, managers were supposed to be selective when establishing a new branch. Ideally, the first members admitted should come from the poorest families; next, slightly better off villagers; and last, those at the upper limit of the bank's eligibility criterion. In reality, many branch managers diverge from this ideal because they find it easier to work with the less poor. The same applies to villagers: both Aleya (rich) and Aleya (poor) told me, in identical words: "We don't take the absolutely landless. They *eat* the money." Poorer women are free to form their own groups, but they generally have little influence over other villagers. And they are often reluctant to speak up for themselves. To overcome this, bank workers must actively seek out the poorest villagers and help them into groups.

Many do. Idealism remains an important lubricant in the mechanism of the bank. A few older managers even described themselves to me as "freedom fighters." Having fought against Pakistani soldiers in 1971, they now feel that by slowly building national capacity, they are weaning Bangladesh from its reliance on foreign aid. A number of managers I met had forgone soft jobs in towns, only to be stationed in remote areas away from their families. But even with their best efforts, there is resistance at all levels to taking on the most difficult cases: the bottom poor.

There is no easy solution to this problem, and, indeed, some bank managers feel that it cannot be solved, only controlled. Ultimately, it stems from the bank's fundamental contradiction: trying to achieve financial viability while serving the "poorest of the poor."

"We keep on reminding ourselves, but we don't succeed all the time," Yunus told me. "There are a lot of people within our areas who would have been the first priority of the Grameen Bank but still they're not members."

Branch manages are evaluated on a series of subjective and objective criteria, of which, in theory, financial performance is only one consideration. In practice, just as university admissions offices tend to give more weight to SAT scores than free-form essays, Grameen managers tend to place more emphasis on hard data than qualitative measures. Loan performance is paramount. If a branch manager tries to penetrate the very bottom poor, he will naturally have a tougher time covering his costs. This manager can explain the reasons for his low disbursements in a narrative report, but his area manager, who supervises ten branches, and who is also evaluated on financial performance, may not be interested in the story behind the numbers.

This imperfect evaluation system can lead to inconsistencies and policy contradictions, especially in the hands of less idealistic, more expedient managers. "Encouragement is given officially to take in the poorest," a branch manager told me. "But, informally, some managers give hints that it's better to avoid the very poorest people. They won't say it directly but they'll let you know."

"The people we're talking about have no permanent residence," he added. "They're floaters. One day they're here, one day they're there. Where would we find them?" I recalled what Yunus used to tell his staff in Tangail when they said the same thing: "If you create a condition that will make them want to stay, they will stay."

Today, the pressure on the bank to demonstrate financial viability is stronger than ever and the question of how well the bank is reaching the lowest segment of its target market continues to be debated within the head office. Without a doubt, loans go to the poorest half of the population and, within that subdivision, Grameen certainly reaches a great many extremely poor villagers. But among the staff, some now question whether they are capable of reaching the "poorest of the poor" in large numbers, or whether reaching the poorest "economically active" villagers — say, above the bottom 10 percent — is the most that Grameen, or any bank, can realistically strive for. "Now that we

are stabilizing our growth, we'll be making a special drive to reach these people," Muzammel told me in 1992. "We may put in columns on reports: How many widows do you have as borrowers? How many women who have been deserted? Now we think we are in a comfortable position to see whether what is considered 'nonviable poor' can be brought in, in large numbers."

Two years later the debate was still raging. Meanwhile, rumors were circulating in the head office about villagers in Tangail who fell above the eligibility threshold being admitted to the bank. This was strictly prohibited in the *Bidhimala*. Nurjahan had already dispatched spies to the zone. "The situation is unclear right now," she told me in a matter-of-fact tone. "But one thing is *very clear:* If the staff have accepted people above the limit, they will be punished."

Elsewhere, she was experimenting with special loans-in-kind programs targeted at the hard-core poor. "We have to take it upon ourselves to recruit these hard-to-reach people since the members are reluctant to take them. We are trying to bring in those who have absolutely no hope in life."

While the head office investigated Tangail, Yunus had forbidden new groups to be formed in the zone. "We get very concerned when we hear this," he told me. "We want to see the people at the bottom come in, but the tendency for the staff is to look up. I keep arguing, if that's the logic, then you'll be looking for the richest guy in the village. Because the logical conclusion is that you end up as a commercial bank."

LEGAL PERSPECTIVES

Ali Boureslan v. Arabian American Oil Company and Aramco Services Company

Supreme Court of the United States

These cases present the issue whether Title VII applies extraterritorially to regulate the employment practices of United States employers who employ United States citizens abroad. The United States Court of Appeals for the Fifth Circuit held that it does not, and we agree with that conclusion.

Petitioner Boureslan is a naturalized United States citizen who was born in Lebanon. The respondents are two Delaware corporations, Arabian American Oil Company (Aramco), and its subsidiary, Aramco Service Company (ASC). Aramco's principal place of business is Dhahran, Saudia Arabia, and it is licensed to do business in Texas. ASC's principal place of business is Houston, Texas.

In 1979, Boureslan was hired by ASC as a cost engineer in Houston. A year later he was transferred, at his request, to work for Aramco in Saudi Arabia. Boureslan remained with Aramco in Saudi Arabia until he was discharged in 1984. After filing a charge of discrimination with the Equal Employment Opportunity Commission (EEOC), he instituted this suit in the United States District Court for the Southern District of Texas against Aramco and ASC. He sought relief under both state law and Title VII of the Civil Rights Act of 1964, on the ground that he was harassed and ultimately discharged by respondents on account of his race, religion, and national origin.

Respondents filed a motion for summary judgment on the ground that the District Court lacked subject matter jurisdiction over Boureslan's claim because the protections of Title VII do not extend to United States citizens employed abroad by American employers. The District Court agreed, and dismissed Boureslan's Title VII claim; it also dismissed his state-law claims for lack of pendent jurisdiction, and entered final judgment in favor of respondents. A panel for the Fifth Circuit affirmed. After vacating the panel's decision and rehearing the case en banc, the court affirmed the District Court's dismissal of Boureslan's complaint. Both Boureslan and the EEOC petitioned for certiorari. We granted both petitions for certiorari to resolve this important issue of statutory interpretation.

Both parties concede, as they must, that Congress has the authority to enforce its laws beyond the territorial boundaries of the United States. Whether Congress has in fact exercised that authority in this case is a matter of statutory construction. It is our task to determine whether Congress intended the protections of Title VII to apply to United States citizens employed by American employers outside of the United States.

It is a long-standing principle of American law "that legislation of Congress, unless a contrary intent appears, is meant to apply only within the territorial jurisdiction of the

---

Majority opinion by Chief Justice Rehnquist decided March 26, 1991. Reprinted with permission from *The United States Law Week* Vol. 59, pp. 4226–29 (March 26, 1991). Published by The Bureau of National Affairs, Inc. (800–372–1033).

United States." This "canon of construction . . . is a valid approach whereby unexpressed congressional intent may be ascertained." It serves to protect against unintended clashes between our laws and those of other nations which could result in international discord.

In applying this rule of construction, we look to see whether "language in the [relevant act] gives any indication of a congressional purpose to extend its coverage beyond places over which the United States has sovereignty or has some measure of legislative control." We assume that Congress legislates against the backdrop of the presumption against extraterritoriality. Therefore, unless there is "the affirmative intention of the Congress clearly expressed," we must presume it "is primarily concerned with domestic conditions."

Boureslan and the EEOC contend that the language of Title VII evinces a clearly expressed intent on behalf of Congress to legislate extraterritorially. They rely principally on two provisions of the statute. First, petitioners argue that the statute's definitions of the jurisdictional terms "employer" and "commerce" are sufficiently broad to include U.S. firms that employ American citizens overseas. Second, they maintain that the statute's "alien exemption" clause necessarily implies that Congress intended to protect American citizens from employment discrimination abroad. Petitioners also contend that we should defer to the EEOC's consistently held position that Title VII applies abroad. We conclude that petitioners' evidence, while not totally lacking in probative value, falls short of demonstrating the affirmative congressional intent required to extend the protections of the Title VII beyond our territorial borders.

Title VII prohibits various discriminatory employment practices based on an individual's race, color, religion, sex, or national origin. An employer is subject to Title VII if it has employed 15 or more employees for a specified period and is "engaged in an industry affecting commerce." An industry affecting commerce is "any activity, business, or industry in commerce or in which a labor dispute would hinder or obstruct commerce or the free flow of commerce and includes any activity or industry 'affecting commerce' within the meaning of the Labor-Management Reporting and Disclosure Act of 1959. "Commerce," in turn, is defined as "trade, traffic, commerce, transportation, transmission, or communication among the several States; or between a State and any place outside thereof; or within the District of Columbia, or a possession of the United States; or between points in the same State but through a point outside thereof."

Petitioners argue that by its plain language, Title VII's "broad jurisdictional language" reveals Congress's intent to extend the statute's protections to employment discrimination anywhere in the world by a U.S. employer who affects trade "between a State and any place outside thereof." More precisely, they assert that since Title VII defines "States" to include States, the District of Columbia, and specified territories, the clause "between a State and any place outside thereof" must be referring to areas beyond the territorial limit of the United States.

Respondents offer several alternative explanations for the statute's expansive language. They contend that the "or between a State and any place outside thereof" clause "provide[s] the jurisdictional nexus required to regulate commerce that is not wholly within a single state, presumably as it affects both interstate and foreign commerce" but not to "regulate conduct exclusively *within* a foreign country." They also argue that since the definitions of the terms "employer," "commerce," and "industry affecting commerce," make no mention of "commerce with foreign nations," Congress cannot be said to have intended that the statute apply overseas. In support of this argument, petitioners point to Title II of the Civil Rights Act of 1964, governing public accommodation, which specifically defines commerce as it applies to foreign nations. Finally, respondents argue that while language present in the first bill considered by the House of Representatives contained the terms "foreign commerce" and "foreign nations," those terms were deleted by the Senate before the Civil Rights Act of 1964 was passed. They conclude that these deletions "[are] inconsistent with the notion of a clearly expressed congressional intent to apply Title VII extraterritorially."

We need not choose between these competing interpretations as we would be required to do in the absence of the presumption against extraterritorial applications discussed above. Each is plausible, but no more persuasive than that. The language relied upon by petitioners — and it is they who must make the affirmative showing — is ambiguous, and does not speak directly to the question presented here. The intent of Congress as to the extraterritorial application of this statute must be deduced by inference from boilerplate language which can be found in any number of congressional acts, none of which have ever been held to apply overseas. *See, e.g.,* Consumer Product Safety Act; Federal Food, Drug, and Cosmetic Act; Transportation Safety Act of 1974; Labor-Management Reporting and Disclosure Act, of 1959; Americans with Disabilities Act of 1990.

Petitioners' reliance on Title VII's jurisdictional provisions also finds no support in our case law; we have repeatedly held that even statutes that contain broad language in their definitions of "commerce" that expressly refer to "*foreign* commerce," do not apply abroad. For example, in *New York Central R. Co.* v. *Chisholm* (1925), we addressed the extraterritorial application of the Federal Employers Liability Act (FELA). FELA provides that com-

mon carriers by railroad while engaging in "interstate or foreign commerce" or commerce between "any of the States or territories and any foreign nation or nations" shall be liable in damages to its employees who suffer injuries resulting from their employment. Despite this broad jurisdictional language, we found that the Act "contains no words which definitely disclose an intention to give it extraterritorial effect" and therefore there was no jurisdiction under FELA for a damages action by a U.S. citizen employed on a U.S. railroad who suffered fatal injuries at a point 30 miles north of the U.S. border into Canada.

Similarly, in *McCulloch* v. *Sociedad Nacional de Marineros de Honduras* (1963), we addressed whether Congress intended the National Labor Relations Act to apply overseas. Even though the NLRA contained broad language that referred by its terms to foreign commerce, this Court refused to find a congressional intent to apply the statute abroad because there was not "any specific language" in the Act reflecting congressional intent to do so.

The EEOC places great weight on an assertedly similar "broad jurisdictional grant in the Lanham Act" that this Court held applied extraterritorially in *Steele* v. *Bulova Watch Co.* (1952). In *Steele,* we addressed whether the Lanham Act, designed to prevent deceptive and misleading use of trademarks, applied to acts of a U.S. citizen consummated in Mexico. The Act defined commerce as "all commerce which may lawfully be regulated by Congress." The stated intent of the statute was "to regulate commerce within the control of Congress by making actionable the deceptive and misleading use of marks in such commerce." While recognizing that "the legislation of Congress will not extend beyond the boundaries of the United States unless a contrary legislative intent appears," the Court concluded that in light of the fact that the allegedly unlawful conduct had some effects within the United States, coupled with the Act's "broad jurisdictional grant" and its "sweeping reach into 'all commerce which may lawfully be regulated by Congress,'" the statute was properly interpreted as applying abroad.

The EEOC's attempt to analogize this case to *Steele* is unpersuasive. The Lanham Act by terms applies to "all commerce which may lawfully be regulated by Congress." The Constitution gives Congress the power "[t]o regulate Commerce with foreign Nations, and among the several States, and with the Indian Tribes." Since the Act expressly stated that it applied to the extent of Congress's power over commerce, the Court in *Steele* concluded that Congress intended that the statute apply abroad. By contrast, Title VII's more limited, boilerplate "commerce" language does not support such an expansive construction of congressional intent. Moreover, unlike the language in the Lanham Act, Title VII's definition of "commerce" was derived expressly from the LMRDA, a statute that this Court had held, prior to the enactment of Title VII, did not apply abroad.

Thus petitioner's argument based on the jurisdictional language of Title VII fails both as a matter of statutory language and of our previous case law. Many acts of Congress are based on the authority of that body to regulate commerce among the several States, and the parts of these acts setting forth the basis for legislative jurisdiction will obviously refer to such commerce in one way or another. If we were to permit possible, or even plausible interpretations of language such as that involved here to override the presumption against extraterritorial application, there would be little left of the presumption.

Petitioners argue that Title VII's "alien exemption provision," "clearly manifests an intention" by Congress to protect U.S. citizens with respect to their employment outside of the United States. The alien exemption provision says that the statute "shall not apply to an employer with respect to the employment of aliens outside any State." Petitioners contend that from this language a negative inference should be drawn that Congress intended Title VII to cover United States *citizens* working abroad for United States employers. There is "[no] other plausible explanation [that] the alien exemption exists," they argue, because "[i]f Congress believed that the statute did not apply extraterritorially, it would have had no reason to include an exemption for a certain category of individuals employed outside the United States." Since "[t]he statute's jurisdictional provisions cannot possibly be read to confer coverage only upon aliens employed outside the United States," petitioners conclude that "Congress could not rationally have enacted an exemption for the employment of aliens abroad if it intended to foreclose *all* potential extraterritorial applications of the statute."

Respondents resist petitioners' interpretation of the alien-exemption provision and assert two alternative *raisons d'etre* for that language. First, they contend that since aliens are included in the statute's definition of employee, and the definition of commerce includes possessions as well as "States," the purpose of the exemption is to provide that employers of aliens in the possessions of the United States are not covered by the statute. Thus, the "outside any State" clause means outside any State, but within the control of the United States. Respondents argue that "[t]his reading of the alien exemption provision is consistent with and supported by the historical development of the provision" because Congress's inclusion of the provision was a direct response to this Court's interpretation of the term "possessions" in the Fair Labor Standards Act in *Vermilya-Brown Co.* v. *Connell* (1948), to include leased bases in foreign nations that were within the control of the United States. They conclude that the alien exemption provision was included "to limit the impact of *Vermilya-Brown* by excluding from coverage employers of aliens in areas under U.S. control that" were not encompassed within Title VII's definition of the term "State."

Second, respondents assert that by negative implication, the exemption "confirm[s] the coverage of aliens in the United States." They contend that this interpretation is consistent with our conclusion in *Espinoza* v. *Farah Mfg. Co.* (1973), that aliens within the United States are protected from discrimination both because Title VII uses the term "individual" rather than "citizen," and because of the alien-exemption provision.

If petitioners are correct that the alien-exemption clause means that the statute applies to employers overseas, we see no way of distinguishing in its application between United States employers and foreign employers. Thus, a French employer of a United States citizen in France would be subject to Title VII — a result at which even petitioners balk. The EEOC assures us that in its view the term "employer" means only "American employer," but there is no such distinction in this statute, and no indication that EEOC in the normal course of its administration had produced a reasoned basis for such a distinction. Without clearer evidence of congressional intent to do so than is contained in the alien-exemption clause, we are unwilling to ascribe to that body a policy which would raise difficult issues of international law by imposing this country's employment-discrimination regime upon foreign corporations operating in foreign commerce. . . .

Similarly, Congress failed to provide any mechanisms for overseas enforcement of Title VII. For instance, the statute's venue provisions, § 2000e–5(f)(3), are ill-suited for extraterritorial application as they provide for venue only in a judicial district in the state where certain matters related to the em-

ployer occurred or were located. And the limited investigative authority provided for the EEOC, permitting the Commission only to issue subpoenas for witnesses and documents from "anyplace in the United States or any Territory or possession thereof," § 2000e–9, suggests that Congress did not intend for the statute to apply abroad.

It is also reasonable to conclude that had Congress intended Title VII to apply overseas, it would have addressed the subject of conflicts with foreign laws and procedures. In amending the Age Discrimination in Employment Act of 1967 (ADEA), to apply abroad, Congress specifically addressed potential conflicts with foreign law by providing that it is not unlawful for an employer to take any action prohibited by the ADEA "where such practices involve an employee in a workplace in a foreign country, and compliance with [the ADEA] would cause such employer . . . to violate the laws of the country in which such workplace is located." Title VII, by contrast, fails to address conflicts with the laws of other nations.

Finally, the EEOC, as one of the two federal agencies with primary responsibility for enforcing Title VII, argues that we should defer to its "consistent" construction of Title VII, first formally expressed in a statement issued after oral argument but before the Fifth Circuit's initial decision in this case (Apr. 1989), "to apply to discrimination against American citizens outside the United States." Citing a 1975 letter from the EEOC's General Counsel, 1983 testimony by its Chairman, and a 1985 decision by the Commission, it argues that its consistent administrative interpretations "reinforce" the conclusion that Congress intended Title VII to apply abroad.

In *General Electric Co.* v. *Gilbert* (1976), we addressed the proper deference to be afforded the EEOC's guidelines. Recognizing that "Congress, in enacting Title VII, did not confer upon the EEOC authority to promulgate rules or regulations," we held that the level of deference afforded "will depend upon the thoroughness evident in its consideration, the validity of its reasoning, its consistency with earlier and later pronouncements, and all those factors which give it power to persuade, if lacking power to control.'"

The EEOC's interpretation does not fare well under these standards. As an initial matter, the position taken by the Commission "contradicts the position which [it] had enunciated at an earlier date, closer to the enactment of the governing statute." The Commission's early pronouncements on the issue supported the conclusion that the statute was limited to domestic application. ("Title VII . . . protects all individuals, both citizen and noncitizens, domiciled or residing in the United States, against discrimination on the basis of race, color, religion, sex, or national origin.") While the Commission later intimated that the statute applied abroad, this position was not expressly reflected in its policy guidelines until some 24 years after the passage of the statute. The EEOC offers no basis in its experience for the change. The EEOC's interpretation of the statute here thus has been neither contemporaneous with its enactment nor consistent since the statute came into law. As discussed above, it also lacks support in the plain language of the statute. While we do not wholly discount the weight to be given to the 1988 guideline, its persuasive value is limited when judged by the standards set forth in *Skidmore*. We are of the view that, even when considered in combination with petitioners' other arguments, the EEOC's interpretation is insufficiently weighty to overcome the presumption against extraterritorial application.

Our conclusion today is buttressed by the fact that "[w]hen it desires to do so, Congress knows how to place the high seas within the jurisdictional reach of a statute." *Argentine Republic* v. *Amerada Hess Shipping Corp.* (1989). Congress's awareness of the need to make a clear statement that a statute applies overseas is amply demonstrated by the numerous occasions on which it has expressly legislated the extraterritorial application of a statute. . . .

Petitioners have failed to present sufficient affirmative evidence that Congress intended Title VII to apply abroad. Accordingly, the judgment of the Court of Appeals is *Affirmed*.

Dow Chemical Company and Shell Oil Company v. Domingo Castro Alfaro et al.

Supreme Court of Texas

Because its analysis and reasoning are correct I join in the majority opinion without reservation. I write separately, however, to respond to the dissenters who mask their inability to agree among themselves with competing rhetoric. In their zeal to implement their own preferred social policy that Texas corporations not be held responsible at home for harm caused abroad, these dissenters refuse to be restrained by either express statutory language or the compelling precedent, previously approved by this very court, holding

786 S.W. 2d 674 (Tex. 1990). Concurring opinion by Judge Doggett.

that forum non conveniens does not apply in Texas. To accomplish the desired social engineering, they must invoke yet another legal fiction with a fancy name to shield alleged wrongdoers, the so-called doctrine of *forum non conveniens*. The refusal of a Texas corporation to confront a Texas judge and jury is to be labelled "inconvenient" when what is really involved is not convenience but connivance to avoid corporate accountability.

The dissenters are insistent that a jury of Texans be denied the opportunity to evaluate the conduct of a Texas corporation concerning decisions it made in Texas because the only ones allegedly hurt are foreigners. Fortunately Texans are not so provincial and narrow-minded as these dissenters presume. Our citizenry recognizes that a wrong does not fade away because its immediate consequences are first felt far away rather than close to home. Never have we been required to forfeit our membership in the human race in order to maintain our proud heritage as citizens of Texas.

The dissenters argue that it is *inconvenient* and *unfair* for farmworkers allegedly suffering permanent physical and mental injuries, including irreversible sterility, to seek redress by suing a multinational corporation in a court three blocks away from its world headquarters and another corporation, which operates in Texas this country's largest chemical plant. Because the "doctrine" they advocate has nothing to do with fairness and convenience and everything to do with immunizing multinational corporations from accountability for their alleged torts causing injury abroad, I write separately.

THE FACTS

Respondents claim that while working on a banana plantation in Costa Rica for Standard Fruit Company, an American subsidiary of Dole Fresh Fruit Company, headquartered in Boca Raton, Florida, they were required to handle dibromochloropropane ["DBCP"], a pesticide allegedly manufactured and furnished to Standard Fruit by Shell Oil Company ["Shell"] and Dow Chemical Company ["Dow"]. The Environmental Protection Agency issued a notice of intent to cancel all food uses of DBCP on September 22, 1977. 42 Fed. Reg. 48026 (1977). It followed with an order suspending registrations of pesticides containing DBCP on November 3, 1977. 42 Fed. Reg. 57543 (1977). Before and after the E.P.A.'s ban of DBCP in the United States, Shell and Dow apparently shipped several hundred thousand gallons of the pesticide to Costa Rica for use by Standard Fruit. The Respondents, Domingo Castro Alfaro and other plantation workers, filed suit in a state district court in Houston, Texas, alleging that their handling of DBCP caused them serious personal injuries for which Shell and Dow were liable under the theories of products liability, strict liability and breach of warranty.

Rejecting an initial contest to its authority by Shell and Dow, the trial court found that it had jurisdiction under Tex. Civ. Prac. & Rem. Code Ann. § 71.031 (Vernon 1986), but dismissed the cause on the grounds of forum non conveniens. The court of appeals reversed and remanded, holding that Section 71.031 provides a foreign plaintiff with an absolute right to maintain a death or personal injury cause of action in Texas without being subject to forum non conveniens dismissal. 751 S.W.2d 208. Shell and Dow have asked this court to reverse the judgment of the court of appeals and affirm the trial court's dismissal.

Shell Oil Company is a multinational corporation with its world headquarters in Houston, Texas. Dow Chemical Company, though headquartered in Midland, Michigan, conducts extensive operations from its Dow Chemical USA building located in Houston. Dow operates this country's largest chemical manufacturing plant within 60 miles of Houston in Freeport, Texas. The district court where this lawsuit was filed is three blocks away from Shell's world headquarters, One Shell Plaza in downtown Houston.

Shell has stipulated that all of its more than 100,000 documents relating to DBCP are located or will be produced in Houston. Shell's medical and scientific witnesses are in Houston. The majority of Dow's documents and witnesses are located in Michigan, which is far closer to Houston (both in terms of geography and communications linkages) than to Costa Rica. The respondents have agreed to be available in Houston for independent medical examinations, for depositions and for trial. Most of the respondents' treating doctors and co-workers have agreed to testify in Houston. Conversely, Shell and Dow have purportedly refused to make their witnesses available in Costa Rica.

The banana plantation workers allegedly injured by DBCP were employed by an American company on American-owned land and grew Dole bananas for export soley to American tables. The chemical allegedly rendering the workers sterile was researched, formulated, tested, manufactured, labeled and shipped by an American company in the United States to another American company. The decision to manufacture DBCP for distribution and use in the third world was made by these two American companies in their corporate offices in the United States. Yet now Shell and Dow argue that the one part of this equation that should not be American is the legal consequences of their actions.

FORUM NON CONVENIENS — "A COMMON LAW DOCTRINE OUT OF CONTROL"

As a reading of Tex. Civ. Prac. & Rem. Code Ann. § 71.031 (Vernon 1986) makes clear, the doctrine of forum non conveniens has been statutorily abolished in Texas. The decision in *Allen* v. *Bass,* . . . approved by this court, clearly holds that, upon a showing of personal jurisdiction over a defendant, article

4678, now section 71.031 of the Texas Civil Practice & Remedies Code, "opens the courts of this state to citizens of a neighboring state and gives them an absolute right to maintain a transitory action of the present nature and to try their cases in the courts of this state."

Displeased that *Allen* stands in the way of immunizing multinational corporations from suits seeking redress for their torts causing injury abroad, the dissenters doggedly attempt to circumvent this precedent. Unsuccessful with arguments based upon Texas law, they criticize the court for not justifying its result on public policy grounds.

Using the "Doctrine" to Kill the Litigation Altogether

Both as a matter of law and of public policy, the doctrine of forum non conveniens is without justification. The proffered foundations for it are "considerations of fundamental fairness and sensible and effective judicial administration." . . . In fact, the doctrine is favored by multinational defendants because a forum non conveniens dismissal is often outcome-determinative, effectively defeating the claim and denying the plaintiff recovery. . . .

Empirical data available demonstrate that less than four percent of cases dismissed under the doctrine of forum non conveniens ever reach trial in foreign court.[1] A forum non conveniens dismissal usually will end the litigation altogether, effectively excusing any liability of the defendant. The plaintiffs leave the courtroom without having had their case resolved on the merits.

The *Gulf Oil* Factors — Balanced Toward the Defendant

Courts today usually apply forum non conveniens by use of the factors set forth at length in *Gulf Oil Corp. v. Gilbert* . . . Briefly summarized, those factors are (i) the private interests of the litigants (ease and cost of access to documents and witnesses); and (ii) the public interest factors (the interest of the forum state, the burden on the courts, and notions of judicial comity). In the forty-three years in which the courts have grappled with the *Gulf Oil* factors, it has become increasingly apparent that their application fails to promote fairness and convenience. Instead, these factors have been used by defendants to achieve objectives violative of public policy. . . .

The Public Interest Factors. The three public interest factors asserted by Justice Gonzalez may be summarized as (1) whether the interests of the jurisdiction are sufficient to justify entertaining the lawsuit; (2) the potential for docket backlog; and (3) judicial comity. . . .

The next justification offered by the dissenters for invoking the legal fiction of "inconvenience" is that judges will be overworked. Not only will foreigners take our jobs, as we are told in the popular press; now they will have our courts. The xenophobic suggestion that foreigners will take over our courts "forcing our residents to wait in the corridors of our courthouses while foreign causes of action are tried," Gonzalez dissent, 786 S.W.2d at 690, is both misleading and false.

It is the height of deception to suggest that docket backlogs in our state's urban centers are caused by so-called "foreign litigation." This assertion is unsubstantiated empirically both in Texas and in other jurisdictions rejecting forum non conveniens.[2] Ten states, including Texas, have not recognized the doctrine. Within these states, there is no evidence that the docket congestion predicted by the dissenters has actually occurred. The best evidence, of course, comes from Texas itself. Although foreign citizens have enjoyed the statutory right to sue defendants living or doing business here since the 1913 enactment of the predecessor to Section 71.031 of the Texas Civil Practice and Remedies Code,

reaffirmed in the 1932 decision in *Allen,* Texas has not been flooded by foreign causes of action.

Moreover, the United States Supreme Court has indicated that docket congestion "is a wholly inappropriate consideration in virtually every other context." . . . If we begin to refuse to hear lawsuits properly filed in Texas because they are sure to require time, we set a precedent that can be employed to deny Texans access to these same courts.

Nor does forum non conveniens afford a panacea for eradicating congestion:

> Making the place of trial turn on a largely imponderable exercise of judicial discretion is extremely costly. Even the strongest proponents of the most suitable forum approach concede that it is inappropriately time-consuming and wasteful for the parties to have to "litigate in order to determine where they shall litigate." If forum non conveniens outcomes are not predictable, such litigation is bound to occur. . . . In terms of delay, expense, uncertainty, and a fundamental loss of judicial accountability, the most suitable forum version of forum non conveniens clearly costs more than it is worth.

Robertson, *supra,* 103 L.Q.Rev. at 414, 426.

Comity — deference shown to the interests of the foreign forum — is a consideration best achieved by rejecting forum non conveniens. Comity is not achieved when the United States allows its multinational corporations to adhere to a double standard when operating abroad and subsequently refuses to hold them accountable for those actions. As S. Jacob Scherr, Senior Project Attorney for the Natural Resources Defense Counsel, has noted

> There is a sense of outrage on the part of many poor countries where citizens are the most vulnerable to exports of hazardous drugs, pesticides and food products. At the 1977 meeting of the UNEP Governing Council, Dr. J.C. Kiano, the Kenyan minister for water development, warned that developing nations will no

longer tolerate being used as dumping grounds for products that had not been adequately tested "and that their peoples should not be used as guinea pigs for determining the safety of chemicals."

Comment, *U.S. Exports Banned For Domestic Use, But Exported to Third World Countries,* 6 Int'l Tr.L.J. 95, 98 (1980–81) [hereinafter *"U.S. Exports Banned"*].

Comity is best achieved by "avoiding the possibility of 'incurring the wrath and distrust of the Third World as it increasingly recognizes that it is being used as the industrial world's garbage can.'" Note, *Hazardous Exports from a Human Rights Perspective,* 14 Sw.U.L. Rev. 81, 101 (1983) [hereinafter *"Hazardous Exports"*] (quoting Hon. Michael D. Barnes (Representative in Congress representing Maryland)).[3] . . .

PUBLIC POLICY AND THE TORT LIABILITY OF MULTINATIONAL CORPORATIONS IN UNITED STATES COURTS

The abolition of forum non conveniens will further important public policy considerations by providing a check on the conduct of multinational corporations (MNCs). *See Economic Approach,* 22 Geo.Wash.J. Int'l L. & Econ. at 241. The misconduct of even a few multinational corporations can affect untold millions around the world.[4] For example, after the United States imposed a domestic ban on the sale of cancer-producing TRIS-treated children's sleepwear, American companies exported approximately 2.4 million pieces to Africa, Asia and South America. A similar pattern occurred when a ban was proposed for baby pacifiers that had been linked to choking deaths in infants. *Hazardous Exports, supra,* 14 Sw.U.L.Rev. at 82. These examples of indifference by some corporations towards children abroad are not unusual.[5]

The allegations against Shell and Dow, if proven true, would not be unique, since production of many chemicals banned for domestic use has thereafter continued for foreign marketing.[6] Professor Thomas McGarity, a respected authority in the field of environmental law, explained:

During the mid-1970s, the United States Environmental Protection Agency (EPA) began to restrict the use of some pesticides because of their environmental effects, and the Occupational Safety and Health Administration (OSHA) established workplace exposure standards for toxic and hazardous substances in the manufacture of pesticides. . . . [I]t is clear that many pesticides that have been severely restricted in the United States are used without restriction in many Third World countries, with resulting harm to fieldworkers and the global environment.

McGarity, *Bhopal and the Export of Hazardous Technologies,* 20 Tex.Int'l L.J. 333, 334 (1985) (citations omitted). By 1976, "29 percent, or 161 million pounds of all the pesticides exported by the United States were either unregistered or banned for domestic use." McWilliams, *Tom Sawyer's Apology: A Reevaluation of United States Pesticide Export Policy,* 8 Hastings Int'l & Comp.L.Rev. 61, 61 & n. 4 (1984). It is estimated that these pesticides poison 750,000 people in developing countries each year, of which 22,500 die. *Id.* at 62. Some estimates place the death toll from the "improper marketing of pesticides at 400,000 lives a year." *Id.* at 62 n. 7.

Some United States multinational corporations will undoubtedly continue to endanger human life and the environment with such activities until the economic consequences of these actions are such that it becomes unprofitable to operate in this manner. At present, the tort laws of many third world countries are not yet developed. *An Economic Approach, supra,* 22 Geo. Wash.J.Int'l L. & Econ. at 222–23. Industrialization "is occurring faster than the development of domestic infrastructures necessary to deal with the problems associated with industry." *Exporting Hazardous Industries, supra,* 20 Int'l L. & Pol. at 791. When a court dismisses a case against a United States multinational corporation, it often removes the most effective restraint on corporate misconduct. *See An Economic Approach, supra,* 22 Geo.Wash. J.Int'l L. & Econ. at 241.

The doctrine of forum non conveniens is obsolete in a world in which markets are global and in which ecologists have documented the delicate balance of all life on this planet. The parochial perspective embodied in the doctrine of forum non conveniens enables corporations to evade legal control merely because they are transnational. This perspective ignores the reality that actions of our corporations affecting those abroad will also affect Texans. Although DBCP is banned from use within the United States, it and other similarly banned chemicals have been consumed by Texans eating foods imported from Costa Rica and elsewhere. *See* D. Weir & M. Schapiro, *Circle of Poison* 28–30, 77, 82–83 (1981). In the absence of meaningful tort liability in the United States for their actions, some multinational corporations will continue to operate without adequate regard for the human and environmental costs of their actions. This result cannot be allowed to repeat itself for decades to come.

As a matter of law and of public policy, the doctrine of forum non conveniens should be abolished. Accordingly, I concur. . . .

NOTES

1. Professor David Robertson of the University of Texas School of Law attempted to discover the subsequent history of each reported transnational case dismissed under forum non conveniens from *Gulf Oil v. Gilbert,* 330 U.S. 501, 67 S.Ct. 839, 91 L.Ed. 1055 (1947) to the end of 1984. Data was received on 55 personal injury cases and 30 commercial cases. Of the 55 personal injury cases, only one was actually tried in a foreign court. Only two of the 30 commercial cases reached trial. *See* Robertson, *supra,* at 419.

2. Evidence from the most recent and largest national study ever performed regarding the pace of litigation in urban trial courts suggests that there is no empirical basis for the dissenters' argument that Texas dockets will become clogged without forum non conveniens. The state of Massachusetts recognizes forum non conveniens. *See Minnis v. Peebles,* 24 Mass.App. 467, 510 N.E.2d 289 (1987). Conversely, the state of Louisiana has explicitly not recognized forum non conveniens since 1967. . . . Nevertheless, the study revealed the median filing-to-disposition time for tort cases in Boston to be 953 days; in New Orleans, with no forum non conveniens, the median time for the disposition of tort cases was only 405 days. The study revealed the median disposition time for contract cases in Boston to be 1580 days, as opposed to a mere 271 days in New Orleans where forum non conveniens is not used. J. Goerdt, C. Lomvardias, G. Gallas & B. Mahoney, Examining Court Delay — The Pace of Litigation in 26 Urban Trial Courts, 1987 20, 22 (1989).

3. A senior vice-president of a United States multinational corporation acknowledged that "[t]he realization at corporate headquarters that liability for any [industrial] disaster would be decided in the U.S. courts, more than pressure from Third World governments, has forced companies to tighten safety procedures, upgrade plants, supervise maintenance more closely and educate workers and communities." Wall St. J., Nov. 26, 1985, at 22, col. 4 (quoting Harold Corbett, senior vice-president for environmental affairs at Monsanto Co.).

4. As one commentator observed, U.S. multinational corporations "adhere to a double standard when operating abroad. The lack of stringent environmental regulations and worker safety standards abroad and the relaxed enforcement of such laws in industries using hazardous processes provide little incentive for [multinational corporations] to protect the safety of workers, to obtain liabil-

ity insurance to guard against the hazard of product defects or toxic tort exposure, or to take precautions to minimize pollution to the environment. *This double standard has caused catastrophic damages to the environment and to human lives.*"

Note, *Exporting Hazardous Industries: Should American Standards Apply?*, 20 Int'l L. & Pol. 777, 780–81 (1988) (emphasis added) (footnotes omitted) [hereinafter *"Exporting Hazardous Industries"*]. *See also* Diamond, *The Path of Progress Racks the Third World*, *New York Times*, Dec. 12, 1984, at B1, col. 1.

5. A subsidiary of Sterling Drug Company advertised Winstrol, a synthetic male hormone severely restricted in the United States since it is associated with a number of side effects that the F.D.A. has called "virtually irreversible," in a Brazilian medical journal, picturing a healthy boy and recommending the drug to combat poor appetite, fatigue and weight loss. *U.S. Exports Banned, supra*, 6 Int'l Tr.L.J. at 96. The same company is said to have marketed Dipyrone, a painkiller causing a fatal blood disease and characterized by the American Medical Association as for use only as "a last resort," as "Novaldin" in the Dominican Re-

public. "Novaldin" was advertised in the Dominican Republic with pictures of a child smiling about its agreeable taste. *Id.* at 97. "In 1975, thirteen children in Brazil died after coming into contact with a toxic pesticide whose use had been severely restricted in this country." *Hazardous Exports, supra*, 14 Sw.U.L. Rev. at 82.

6. Regarding Leptophos, a powerful and hazardous pesticide that was domestically banned, S. Jacob Scherr stated that "In 1975 alone, Velsicol, a Texas-based corporation exported 3,092,842 pounds of Leptophos to thirty countries. Over half of that was shipped to Egypt, a country with no procedures for pesticide regulation or tolerance setting. In December 1976, the *Washington Post* reported that Leptophos use in Egypt resulted in the death of a number of farmers and illness in rural communities. . . . But despite the accumulation of data on Leptophos' severe neurotoxicity, Velsicol continued to market the product abroad for use on grain and vegetable crops while proclaiming the product's safety."

U.S. Exports Banned, 6 Int'l Tr.L. J. at 96.

Caux Round Table, Principles for Business

INTRODUCTION

The Caux Round Table believes that the world business community should play an important role in improving economic and social conditions. As a statement of aspirations, this document aims to express a world standard against which business behavior can be measured. We seek to begin a process that identifies shared values, reconciles differing values, and thereby develops a shared perspective on business behavior acceptable to and honored by all.

These principles are rooted in two basic ethical ideals: *kyosei* and human dignity. The Japanese concept of *kyosei* means living and working together for the common good — enabling cooperation and mutual prosperity to coexist with healthy and fair competition. "Human dignity" refers to the sacredness or value of each person as an end, not simply as a means to the fulfillment of others' purposes or even majority prescription.

The General Principles in Section 2 seek to clarify the spirit of *kyosei* and "human dignity," while the specific Stakeholder Principles in Section 3 are concerned with their practical application.

In its language and form, the document owes a substantial debt to *The Minnesota Principles,* a statement of business behavior developed by the Minnesota Center for Corporate Responsibility. The Center hosted and chaired the drafting committee, which included Japanese, European, and U.S. representatives.

Business behavior can affect relationships among nations and the prosperity and well-being of us all. Business is often the first contact between nations and, by the way in which it causes social and economic changes, has a significant impact on the level of fear or confidence felt by people worldwide. Members of the Caux Round Table place their first emphasis on putting one's own house in order, and on seeking to establish what is right rather than who is right.

SECTION 1. PREAMBLE

The mobility of employment, capital, products and technology is making business increasingly global in its transactions and its effects.

Laws and market forces are necessary but insufficient guides for conduct.

Responsibility for the policies and actions of business and respect for the dignity and interests of its stakeholders are fundamental.

Shared values, including a commitment to shared prosperity, are as important for a global community as for communities of smaller scale.

For these reasons, and because business can be a powerful agent of positive social change, we offer the following principles as a foundation for dialogue and action by business leaders in search of business responsibility. In so doing, we affirm the necessity for moral values in business decision making.

Without them, stable business relationships and a sustainable world community are impossible.

SECTION 2. GENERAL PRINCIPLES

Principle 1. The Responsibilities of Businesses: Beyond Shareholders Toward Stakeholders

The value of a business to society is the wealth and employment it creates and the marketable products and services it provides to consumers at a reasonable price commensurate with quality. To create such value, a business must maintain its own economic health and viability, but survival is not a sufficient goal.

Businesses have a role to play in improving the lives of all their customers, employees, and shareholders by sharing with them the wealth they have created. Suppliers and competitors as well should expect businesses to honor their obligations in a spirit of honesty and fairness. As responsible citizens of the local, national, regional and global communities in which they operate, businesses share a part in shaping the future of those communities.

Principle 2. The Economic and Social Impact of Business: Toward Innovation, Justice and World Community

Businesses established in foreign countries to develop, produce or sell should also contribute to the social advancement of those countries by creating productive employment and helping to raise the purchasing power of their citizens. Businesses also should contribute to human rights, education, welfare, and vitalization of the countries in which they operate.

Businesses should contribute to economic and social development not only in the countries in which they operate, but also in the world community at large, through effective and prudent use of resources, free and fair competition, and emphasis upon innovation in technology, production methods, marketing and communications.

Principle 3. Business Behavior: Beyond the Letter of Law Toward a Spirit of Trust

While accepting the legitimacy of trade secrets, businesses should recognize that sincerity, candor, truthfulness, the keeping of promises, and transparency contribute not only to their own credibility and stability but also to the smoothness and efficiency of business transactions, particularly on the international level.

Principle 4. Respect for Rules

To avoid trade frictions and to promote freer trade, equal conditions for competition, and fair and equitable treatment for all participants, businesses should respect international and domestic rules. In addition, they should recognize that some behavior, although legal, may still have adverse consequences.

Principle 5. Support for Multilateral Trade

Businesses should support the multilateral trade systems of the GATT/World Trade Organization and similar international agreements. They should cooperate in efforts to promote the progressive and judicious liberalization of trade and to relax those domestic measures that unreasonably hinder global commerce, while giving due respect to national policy objectives.

Principle 6. Respect for the Environment

A business should protect and, where possible, improve the environment, promote sustainable development, and prevent the wasteful use of natural resources.

Principle 7. Avoidance of Illicit Operations

A business should not participate in or condone bribery, money laundering, or other corrupt practices: indeed, it should seek cooperation with others to eliminate them. It should not trade in arms or other materials used for terrorist activities, drug traffic or other organized crime.

SECTION 3. STAKEHOLDER PRINCIPLES

Customers

We believe in treating all customers with dignity, irrespective of whether they purchase our products and services directly from us or otherwise acquire them in the market. We therefore have a responsibility to:

- provide our customers with the highest quality products and services consistent with their requirements;
- treat our customers fairly in all aspects of our business transactions, including a high level of service and remedies for their dissatisfaction;
- make every effort to ensure that the health and safety of our customers, as well as the quality of their environment, will be sustained or enhanced by our products and services;
- assure respect for human dignity in products offered, marketing, and advertising; and
- respect the integrity of the culture of our customers.

Employees

We believe in the dignity of every employee and in taking employee interests seriously. We therefore have a responsibility to:

- provide jobs and compensation that improve workers' living conditions;
- provide working conditions that respect each employee's health and dignity;
- be honest in communications with employees and open in sharing information, limited only by legal and competitive constraints;
- listen to and, where possible, act on employee suggestions, ideas, requests and complaints;
- engage in good faith negotiations when conflict arises;
- avoid discriminatory practices and guarantee equal treatment and opportunity in areas such as gender, age, race and religion;
- promote in the business itself the employment of differently abled people in places of work where they can be genuinely useful;
- protect employees from avoidable injury and illness in the workplace;
- encourage and assist employees in developing relevant and transferable skills and knowledge; and
- be sensitive to the serious unemployment problems frequently associated with business decisions, and work with governments, employee groups, other agencies and each other in addressing these dislocations.

Owners/Investors

We believe in honoring the trust our investors place in us. We therefore have a responsibility to:

- apply professional and diligent management in order to secure a fair and competitive return on our owners' investment;
- disclose relevant information to owners/investors subject only to legal requirements and competitive constraints;
- conserve, protect and increase the owners/investors' assets; and

- respect owners/investors' requests, suggestions, complaints, and formal resolutions.

Suppliers

Our relationship with suppliers and subcontractors must be based on mutual respect. We therefore have a responsibility to:

- seek fairness and truthfulness in all our activities, including pricing, licensing, and rights to sell;
- ensure that our business activities are free from coercion and unnecessary litigation;
- foster long-term stability in the supplier relationship in return for value, quality, competitiveness and reliability;
- share information with suppliers and integrate them into our planning processes;
- pay suppliers on time and in accordance with agreed terms of trade; and
- seek, encourage and prefer suppliers and subcontractors whose employment practices respect human dignity.

Competitors

We believe that fair economic competition is one of the basic requirements for increasing the wealth of nations and ultimately for making possible the just distribution of goods and services. We therefore have a responsibility to:

- foster open markets for trade and investment;
- promote competitive behavior that is socially and environmentally beneficial and demonstrates mutual respect among competitors;
- refrain from either seeking or participating in questionable payments or favors to secure competitive advantages;
- respect both tangible and intellectual property rights; and
- refuse to acquire commercial information by dishonest or unethical means, such as industrial espionage.

Communities

We believe that as global corporate citizens we can contribute to such forces of reform and human rights as are at work in the communities in which we operate. We therefore have a responsibility in those communities to:

- respect human rights and democratic institutions, and promote them wherever practicable;
- recognize government's legitimate obligation to the society at large and support public policies and practices that promote human development through harmonious relations between business and other segments of society;

- collaborate with those forces in the community dedicated to raising standards of health, education, workplace safety and economic well-being;
- promote and stimulate sustainable development and play a leading role in preserving and enhancing the physical environment and conserving the earth's resources;
- support peace, security, diversity and social integration;
- respect the integrity of local cultures; and
- be a good corporate citizen through charitable donations, educational and cultural contributions, and employee participation in community and civic affairs.

CASES

CASE 1. *Foreign Assignment*

Sara Strong graduated with an MBA from UCLA four years ago. She immediately took a job in the correspondent bank section of the Security Bank of the American Continent. Sara was assigned to work on issues pertaining to relationships with correspondent banks in Latin America. She rose rapidly in the section and received three good promotions in three years. She consistently got high ratings from her superiors, and she received particularly high marks for her professional demeanor.

In her initial position with the bank, Sara was required to travel to Mexico on several occasions. She was always accompanied by a male colleague even though she generally handled similar business by herself on trips within the United States. During her trips to Mexico she observed that Mexican bankers seemed more aware of her being a woman and were personally solicitous to her, but she didn't discern any major problems. The final

decisions on the work that she did were handled by male representatives of the bank stationed in Mexico.

A successful foreign assignment was an important step for those on the "fast track" at the bank. Sara applied for a position in Central or South America and was delighted when she was assigned to the bank's office in Mexico City. The office had about twenty bank employees and was headed by William Vitam. The Mexico City office was seen as a preferred assignment by young executives at the bank.

After a month, Sara began to encounter problems. She found it difficult to be effective in dealing with Mexican bankers — the clients. They appeared reluctant to accept her authority, and they would often bypass her in important matters. The problem was exacerbated by Vitam's compliance in her being bypassed. When she asked that the clients be referred back to her, Vitam

This case was prepared by Thomas Dunfee and Diana Robertson, The Wharton School.

replied, "Of course, that isn't really practical." Vitam made matters worse by patronizing her in front of clients and by referring to her as "my cute assistant" and "our lady banker." Vitam never did this when only Americans were present and in fact treated her professionally and with respect in internal situations.

Sara finally complained to Vitam that he was undermining her authority and effectiveness; she asked him in as positive a manner as possible to help her. Vitam listened carefully to Sara's complaints, then replied, "I'm glad that you brought this up, because I've been meaning to sit down and talk to you about my little game playing in front of the clients. Let me be frank with you. Our clients think you're great, but they just don't understand a woman in authority, and you and I aren't going to be able to change their attitudes overnight. As long as the clients see you as my assistant and deferring to me, they can do business with you. I'm willing to give you as much responsibility as they can handle your having. I *know* you can handle it. But we just have to tread carefully. You and I know that my remarks in front of clients don't mean anything. They're just a way of playing the game Latin style. I know it's frustrating for you, but I really need you to support me on this. It's not going to affect your promotions. You just have to act like it's my responsibility." Sara replied that she would try to cooperate, but that basically she found her role demeaning.

As time went on, Sara found that the patronizing actions in front of clients bothered her more and more. She spoke to Vitam again, but he was firm in his position and urged her to try to be a little more flexible, even a little more "feminine."

Sara also had a problem with Vitam over policy. The Mexico City office had five younger women who worked as receptionists and secretaries. They were all situated at work stations at the entrance of the office. They were required to wear standard uniforms that were colorful and slightly sexy. Sara protested the requirement that uniforms be worn because (1) they were inconsistent to the image of the banking business and (2) they were demeaning to the women who had to wear them. Vitam just curtly replied that he had received a lot of favorable comments about the uniforms from clients of the bank.

Several months later, Sara had what she thought would be a good opportunity to deal with the problem. Tom Fried, an executive vice president who had been a mentor for her since she arrived at the bank, was coming to Mexico City; she arranged a private conference with him. She described her problems and explained that she was not able to be effective in this environment and that she worried that it would have a negative effect on her chance of promotion within the bank. Fried was very careful in his response. He spoke of certain "realities" that the bank had to respect, and he urged her to "see it through" even though he could understand how she would feel that things weren't fair.

Sara found herself becoming more aggressive and defensive in her meetings with Vitam and her clients. Several clients asked that other bank personnel handle their transactions. Sara has just received an Average rating, which noted "the beginnings of a negative attitude about the bank and its policies."

Questions

1. What obligations does an international company have to ensure that its employees are not harmed, for instance, by having their chances for advancement limited by the social customs of a host country?

2. What international moral code, if any, is being violated by Security Bank of the American Continent?

3. Has the bank made the correct decision by opting to follow the norms of the host country?

4. What steps can be taken on the part of the internationals and their employees to avoid or resolve situations in which em-

ployees are offended or harmed by host country practices?

5. In this situation does morality require respect for Mexican practices, or does it require respect for Sara Strong? Are these incompatible?

CASE 2.   *The Nestlé Corporation*

Nestlé Corporation, a large international conglomerate, was attacked by many individuals and groups who claimed that the rising infant mortality rate in third-world nations was due to the aggressive sales promotions of the infant formula companies, which influenced women to switch from traditional breast-feeding methods to the more "modern" idea of bottle feeding. Their primary target was the Nestlé Company of Switzerland, which accounted for 50 percent of third world sales of infant formula.

The declining birthrate in industrialized countries, which began in the 1960s, caused all the infant formula companies concern. They had seen the popularity of formula feeding expand their sales tremendously during and after World War II, but in the 1960s their sales began to diminish as the market became saturated. They viewed the developing and underdeveloped countries as potential sources of new markets to restore declining sales.

As reports began to appear about women in the third world who were abandoning breast feeding, many health professionals became alarmed because of the widespread lack of basic nutritional knowledge and adequate sanitation in the third world, two conditions that were necessary for using infant formula safely. It was estimated that only 29 percent of the rural areas and 72 percent of the

urban areas in the third world had potable water for mixing formula or for sanitizing feeding equipment. The lack of sanitation facilities and the absence of clean water would only be remedied with further development. The lack of education in underdeveloped countries often meant that people did not properly mix formulas or did not follow correct sanitary procedures. Sometimes a poor family would also stretch the formula by adding extra water.

Despite these problems, the infant formula companies mounted aggressive marketing and promotional campaigns in third-world countries. These marketing and promotional practices included extensive mass media advertising, large quantities of free promotional samples to doctors and maternity wards, gifts of equipment, trips and conferences for medical personnel, and the use of company representatives called "milk nurses" whose jobs entailed promoting and explaining formula feeding to new mothers. Billboards and posters prominently displayed pictures of fat, rosy-cheeked babies, subtly suggesting that the healthiest babies were those fed formula.

By 1977, an organization called the Infant Formula Action Coalition (INFACT) had been formed in Minneapolis to address the problem. This organization attempted to create public awareness and economic pressure

This case was written by Eugene Buchholz, Loyola University of New Orleans, and is reprinted from *Business Environment and Public Policy* with permission.

through a nationwide boycott of all Nestlé products. Nestlé was chosen because it had the largest share of the world market and also because it was based in Switzerland and could not be pressured through shareholder resolutions in the United States. The boycott, which had the support of the National Council of Churches, had little effect on Nestlé's business, but the antiformula movement did get the attention of some very powerful groups.

Despite Nestlé's initial reluctance to go along with an International Code of Breast Feeding and Infant Formula Marketing adopted by the World Health Organization in 1981, in March 1982 the company announced that it would observe the code. In a further step, Nestlé set up the Infant Formula Audit Commission, composed of doctors, scientists, and churchpeople under the direction of former Secretary of State Edmund Muskie, to monitor its own conduct.

In general, the industry, responding to recommendations from the International Council of Infant Food Industries (ICIFI) and the World Health Organization, started to demarket its products. *Demarketing* means that efforts to sell a product are reduced or stopped completely because of risks to health or safety and is usually initiated because of management decisions, public pressure, or government regulation. Demarketing is ordinarily carried out in declining markets or markets in which a company can no longer compete successfully, but in the developing countries, demarketing decisions were made for growing markets and contrary to usual business practice.

Questions

1. Should Nestlé have avoided marketing its products in lesser developed countries?
2. Is the Nestlé Corporation morally responsible for the malnutrition that resulted when the formula "was stretched" by adding extra water?
3. Did INFACT act morally in putting economic pressure on Nestlé?
4. Was the development of a voluntary code a good way to resolve the problem? Would another type of code have been a better solution?

CASE 3.   *Facilitation or Bribery: Cultural and Ethical Disparities*

Geletex, Inc., is a U.S. telecommunications corporation attempting to expand its operations worldwide. As Geletex begins its operations in other countries, it has discovered cultural, governmental, and ethical standards that differ significantly from country to country and from those in the United States. Geletex has had a code of ethics for its U.S. operations since 1975. The company's director of compliance, Jed Richardson, provides ongoing training for employees, runs a hotline through which employees can report problems and is well known and respected throughout the company for his high standards and trustworthiness. As Geletex's international operations grow, Jed is becoming increasingly uncomfortable with what appear to be double standards for the company's U.S. operations and its operations in other countries. Jed, who has been traveling to each of the Geletex international offices, has found the following situations, which since have been causing him some sleepless nights:

- In the Lima, Peru, office, Jed, in reviewing financial records, discovered that the commissions expense for the branch is unusually high. Geletex pays its salespeople commissions for each commercial customer they recruit for cellular or long-distance services. Jed knows from experience that some companies pay unusually high sales commissions to disguise the fact that salespeople are paying kickbacks in exchange for contracts. In the United States, such payments would be commercial bribery and a violation of Geletex's code of ethics. When Jed confronted the Lima, Peru, district manager and questioned him about the high commissions, he responded, "Look, things are different down here. We've got a job to do. If the company wants results, we've got to get things moving any way we can."

- In the Stockholm, Sweden, office, Jed noted a number of college-age student employees who seemed to have little work to do. Again, Jed questioned the district manager, who responded, "Sure, Magnus is the son of a telecommunications regulator. Caryl is the daughter of a judge who handles regulatory appeals in utilities. Andre is a nephew of the head of the governing party. They're bright kids, and the contacts don't hurt us. In the Scandanavian culture, giving jobs to children is part of doing business."

- In the Bombay, India, office, Jed noted that many different payments had been made to both the Indian government and government officials. When Jed voiced his concern, the district manager responded, "I can explain every payment. On this one, we needed the utilities [water and electricity] for our offices turned on. We could have waited our turn and had no services for ninety days, or we could pay to get moved to the top of the list and have our utilities turned on in forty-eight hours. On the check for licensing, again, we could have waited six months to get licensed or pay to expedite it and be licensed."

Jed is an expert on the Foreign Corrupt Practices Act (FCPA). The act permits "facilitation" or "grease" payments but prohibits bribes. Facilitation opens doors or expedites processes; it does not purport to influence outcomes. Jed is unsure about Geletex's international operations and compliance with the law. He is very unsure about Geletex having an international code of ethics.

Questions

1. Do any of the offices' actions violate the FCPA?

2. Must a business adopt the ethical standards of a host culture in order to succeed?

3. Are all of the actions in the various offices ethical?

4. If you were Jed, what ethical standards would you develop for international operations?

5. Does Jed's firm create any internal problems by allowing different conduct in different countries and cultures?

6. The American Bar Association reports that there have been only 16 bribery prosecutions under the FCPA since 1977. However, thousands of others have settled voluntarily rather than go to trial. Is the FCPA necessary for international business operations? Does it impede U.S. businesses' success in other countries?

CASE 4. *The Gap*

On Monday July 24, 1995, Stanley Raggio, senior vice president for international sourcing and logistics for The Gap, Inc., opened a copy of *The New York Times* and found the article on The Gap. There, in a story by Bob Herbert, he saw his boss, Donald G. Fisher, being castigated for sourcing practices that he, Stan Raggio, was charged with managing.

> The hundreds of thousands of young (and mostly female) factory workers in Central America who earn next to nothing and often live in squalor have been an absolute boon to American clothing company executives like Donald G. Fisher, the chief executive of the Gap and Banana Republic empire, who lives in splendor and paid himself more than $2 million last year.
>
> Judith Viera is an 18-year-old who worked at a maquiladora plant in El Salvador that made clothing for The Gap and other companies. She was paid a pathetic 56 cents an hour.
>
> Donald Fisher should meet Judith Viera, spend some time with her, listen to her as she describes in a still-childish voice her most innocent of dreams. She would like to earn enough money to buy a little more food for her mother and two sisters. She would like to go to high school. But Donald Fisher is a busy man. It takes a great deal of time to oversee an empire balanced on the backs of youngsters like Ms. Viera (and her counterparts in Asia).[1]

The article in *The New York Times* was one of hundreds that were to appear in newspapers across the United States during the next few months describing human rights violations and subsistence-level wages at suppliers in Central America from which The Gap and other clothing retailers sourced their apparel.

The Gap, Inc. is a chain of retail stores that sell casual apparel, shoes, and accessories for men, women, and children. Headquartered in San Francisco, the stores operate under a variety of names including: Gap, Banana Republic, Old Navy Clothing Company, GapKids, and babyGap. All merchandise sold by the chain is private label.[2]

The Gap was founded in 1969 when Donald Fisher and his wife, Doris, opened a small clothing store near San Francisco State University. By 1971 they were operating six Gap stores. In 1983 Fisher enticed Millard Drexler, former president of Ann Taylor, into taking over as the new president of The Gap, while Fisher became Chief Executive Officer and Chairman of the company. Drexler transformed the company by replacing the drab lines of clothing the store had been stocking with new brightly colored lines of rugged high quality cotton clothes.

In 1995 Fisher retired as CEO and Drexler, now aged 50, took over the title. By now The Gap had 1348 well-located stores in the U.S. and Puerto Rico, 72 in Canada, 49 in the United Kingdom, and 3 in France. Competition was intense and earlier R. H. Macy and Federated stores had been forced to file chapter 11 bankruptcy. The Gap, however, had been doing very well, with 1994 profits of $258 million on sales of $3.723 billion.[3]

Apparel stores like The Gap purchased their clothes from manufacturers in the United States and around the world. Some 20,000 contractors in the United States, most employing 5 to 50 workers, sewed clothes for companies like The Gap. The apparel manufacturing industry in the United States was

From *Business Ethics: Concepts and Cases* 4th edition by Manuel Velasquez, © 1993. Reprinted by permission of Prentice Hall, Inc., Upper Saddle River, NJ.

under intense pressure from imports since the work was so labor-intensive, and labor was less regulated and much cheaper in many developing countries, depressing both wages and working conditions in the United States. For example, it is estimated that in China, wage rates in the apparel industry are approximately one-twentieth of U.S. rates. Since 1990 the United States had lost more than a half a million textile and apparel jobs, and companies struggling to survive in the United States often had working conditions as bad as anything to be found in developing countries. A 1989 study by the General Accounting Office discovered that two-thirds of the 7000 garment shops in New York City were sweatshops.[4] A spot check by the Labor Department in Southern California had found that 93 percent of the shops checked had health and safety violations.

The Gap contracted with over 500 manufacturers around the world who made the Company's private-label apparel according to Gap's specifications. Gap Inc. purchased about 30 percent of its clothes from manufacturers located in the United States and 70 percent from vendors located in 46 foreign countries. No single supplier provided more than 5 percent of its merchandise.

On May 10, 1993, a toy-factory fire in Thailand killed over two hundred workers and injured five hundred. The top factory was owned by Kader Industries, which made toys at the plant for some of the largest toy companies in the United States including, Toys R Us, Fisher-Price and Tyco. U.S. Customs Service documents revealed that during the first three months of 1993, U.S. companies had imported more than 270 tons of toys from the Thai factory. The accident drew attention not only to the responsibilities of the toy industry, but to the responsibilities of all U.S. industries and consumers in ensuring that products are made under safe and humane working conditions regardless of where they are produced.

In the wake of concern over third world working conditions, The Gap had also adopted a set of "Sourcing Principles and Guidelines." These provided standards that vendors had to meet including: engage in no form of discrimination, use no forced or prison labor, employ no children under 14 years of age, provide a safe working environment for employees, pay the legal minimum wage or the local industry standard — whichever is greater, meet all applicable local environmental regulations and comply with The Gap's own more stringent environmental standards, neither threaten nor penalize employees for their efforts to organize or bargain collectively, uphold all local customs laws. To ensure compliance with its standards The Gap sent a "Gap Field Representative" to conduct an "in-depth interview" with a prospective supplier prior to the initiation of a business relationship.

Among the suppliers from whom The Gap sourced its clothes was one in El Salvador run by Mandarin International, a Taiwanese-owned company that operated apparel assembly plants around the world. The Gap had begun contracting with the Mandarin plant in El Salvador about 1992. A worker there was paid approximately 12 cents for assembling a Gap three-quarter sleeve T-shirt or turtleneck which retailed at about $20 in the United States. Wages at the Mandarin plant averaged 56 cents an hour, a level that was claimed to provide only 18 percent of the amount needed to support a family of four but which was consistent with the industry standard for the region.[5]

El Salvador is now a constitutional democracy.[6] In 1992 the country finally had ended a 12-year civil war that had torn the country apart with massacres and death squad killings and that had left 70,000 people dead. In spite of dramatic declines, the level of violence in El Salvador remained high, particularly murder, assaults, and robberies, including crimes against women and children. About 40 percent of the population was living below the poverty level. In spite of increases in the average monthly wage, inflation had brought about a decline in real wages. This in turn had encouraged foreign apparel makers to set up apparel factories there.

The government maintained six "free trade zones" where foreign countries are allowed to import and export goods for assembly within the country without paying tariffs. Foreign companies operating within the free trade zones are called "maquiladoras" and they often paid better than companies outside the zones. Although the law prohibits employers from firing or harrassing employees who are trying to start a union, government authorities sometimes do not enforce this requirement. The Labor Code also prohibits minors between 14 and 18 years of age from being worked more than 6 hours a day, and the maximum normal workweek for adults is set at 44 hours unless overtime rates are paid. However, these rules are also not always enforced.

Troubles erupted at the Mandarin plant — which was located in one of the free trade zones — in early February 1995 when workers notified the company of their intent to form a union, a right authorized by the Salvadoran labor code.[7] The Ministry of Labor granted the union legal status, the first union to be recognized in a free trade zone in El Salvador.

The Mandarin company was notified of the legal status of the union on February 7. It responded by closing down the plant on February 8. Workers spent that day and night camped out in front of the factory. The next morning company security guards attacked and beat some of the female workers.[8] An emergency commission met, and the evening of February 9, the company agreed to end the lock-out, to recognize the union, and to comply with the Salvadoran Labor Code. A few days later, however, Mandarin fired over 150 union members and supporters.[9]

In late March 1995 managers at The Gap became aware of claims that the management of the Mandarin factory was resisting union efforts to organize, in violation of Gap guidelines. Events at the plant were starting to receive publicity in the media, particularly with legislation now pending in Congress that would affect imports from the area. A Gap executive, Stan Raggio, went to El Salvador to investigate the situation.[10] While there he interviewed a number of workers regarding conditions at the factory. At the conclusion of his visit he reported that he had found no human rights abuses or other violations of the company's corporate sourcing policies. The company would, however, continue to monitor the situation at Mandarin. In April The Gap suspended placement of new orders at the Mandarin plant and announced it would not place more orders until it had determined whether the allegations were well-founded.[11]

On Monday May 15, the workers' union called a work stoppage to protest the continued firings of union people. Company guards are said to have physically attacked and beat union leaders when they stood up to announce the work stoppage.[12] Mandarin again closed the plant and fired all of the union leadership. An emergency commission was again convened and it again reached an agreement with the company, and the next morning the company reopened its doors. The company, however, refused to hire back the union leaders the next day. In May The Gap's Stanley P. Raggio again went to El Salvador to investigate the situation, and was again unable to get clear testimony from workers interviewed at the plant that their union rights were being violated.

American unions, such as the International Ladies' Garment Workers Union, had long been concerned by conditions in off-shore apparel sweatshops like the Mandarin plant with which American apparel manufacturers had to compete. Until the conditions of apparel workers in those countries improved, the plight of apparel workers in the United States would probably also remain unchanged since American companies could not afford worker amenities when they were competing against foreign companies that provided their workers with the barest minimum. Union leadership, therefore, had turned increasing attention to improving the conditions of labor in countries outside the United States with whom U.S. workers were now competing.

The National Labor Relation Committee, a coalition of 25 labor unions, now made plans to launch a national campaign early in the summer of 1995 protesting harsh conditions faced by workers in Caribbean and Central American apparel contracting plants. The union decided to focus attention on workers' attempts to unionize the Mandarin plant, on the subsistence wages prevalent in the area, and on the sweatshop conditions at the plant.

During the summer of 1995, the National Labor Committee, arranged to have two young maquiladora workers — Judith Viera, an 18-year-old former employee at Mandarin, and Claudia Molina, a 17-year-old former employee at Orion Apparel, a Korean-owned maquiladora in Choloma, Honduras — spend 59 days crisscrossing the United States and Canada, visiting over 20 cities to criticize The Gap and other companies at press conferences and public meetings arranged by the National Labor Committee. At press conferences, the two women and representatives of the National Labor Committee accused The Gap of a "cover-up" of the situation at Mandarin, and described in detail long hours of work for 56 cents an hour; violence against union supporters, sexual harassment from supervisors, lack of clean drinking water, not being allowed to use rest rooms, and being forced to sweep the factory grounds under a torrid sun as a pun-

ishment. The publicity focused enormous attention on The Gap and its vendor in El Salvador. Major articles based on interviews with the two employees appeared in all major newspapers in the country.[13] The National Labor Relations Committee urged consumers to boycott The Gap and to telephone or write to Gap executives voicing their displeasure about conditions at their vendor's factory. Union officials demanded that The Gap undertake a joint investigation, with the National Labor Relations Committee, of the situation at Mandarin, should pressure Mandarin to reinstate the fired union workers, and should commit itself to third party, independent monitoring of contractors' compliance with the GAP code of conduct. The union noted plans to begin a "broader range of coordinated actions at GAP stores across the United States and Canada — leafleting consumers, etc." starting the day after Thanksgiving, when the critical Christmas buying season began.[14]

The week of August 27, Stanley Raggio once again visited El Salvador and met with U.S. and El Salvadoran government officials as well as several current and former factory workers in an attempt to objectively assess conditions at the factory. In a public statement issued after the visitation the company stated that "Despite this intensive effort our investigation has not uncovered any significant evidence supporting the allegations or indicating that there has been any serious violations of our sourcing guidelines. Based on our investigation, we have determined with confidence that the Mandarin factory treats its workers well and meets our standards of fairness and decency."[15] The National Labor Relations Committee responded with news releases stating that several "human rights organizations" had verified its accusations and that workers had not spoken with The Gap out of fear.

On the evening of Wednesday, August 2, Stanley Raggio met with Charles Kernaghan, executive director of the National Labor Committee to discuss the charges against the plant that the National Labor Committee was making in its summer campaign. Earlier that same day the NLC had held a demonstration at The Gap's distribution center in San Francisco. Both sides felt the discussions were productive but there were no immediate changes.[16]

Two months later, Bob Herbert, writer for the *New York Times,* visited El Salvador to investigate the situation for himself. On October 9 and on October 13 the *New York Times* published articles by him that were harshly critical of The Gap for continuing to claim that there was no evidence to corroborate the charges of the National Labor Committee.[17] Herbert claimed to have interviewed over 30 women in El Salvador who had been fired for being union members. He had interviewed the president of the Mandarin plant who had confirmed that the women had worked at the plant but had "left" in late June. Interviews with local church groups and with the Government's Office for the Defense of Human Rights, he said, had also confirmed the mass firing of union workers.

The question that now faced Stan Raggio and his fellow managers was: what to do?

Questions

1. What course of action would you recommend to Stanley Raggio? Should The Gap give in to the Union's demand that The Gap "undertake a joint investigation, with the National Labor Relations Committee, of the situation at Mandarin, should pressure Mandarin to reinstate the fired union workers, and should commit itself to third party, independent monitoring of contractors' compliance with the GAP code of conduct?"

2. Should companies like The Gap attempt to get their suppliers to pay more than the local industry standard when it is insufficient to live on? Should they pay wages in the Third World that are equivalent to U.S. wages? Should they provide the same levels of medical benefits that are provided in the United States? The same levels of workplace safety?

3. Is a company like The Gap morally responsible for the way its suppliers treat their workers? Explain your answer.

NOTES

1. Bob Herbert, "Sweatshop Beneficiaries," *New York Times* (July 24, 1995).
2. Patrick J. Spain and James R. Talbot, eds., *Hoover's Handbook of American Companies, 1996* (Austin, TX: The Reference Press, 1996), p. 394.
3. The Gap, *Annual Report,* 1995.
4. "Look Who's Sweating Now: How Robert Reich Is Turning Up the Heat on Retailers." *Business Week* (16 October 1995).
5. Letter of Charles Kernaghan, Executive Director, National Labor Committee Education Fund In Support of Worker and Human Rights in Central America, 15 Union Square, New York, NY 10003; dated May 18, 1995.
6. Information in this and the following paragraphs is drawn from: U.S. Department of State's *Country Reports on Human Rights Practices for 1994* (Washington: U.S. Government Printing Office, 1995).
7. Richard Rothstein, "USAID Teaching El Salvador How to Suppress Labor," *The Sacramento Bee,* (Final Edition), 8 June 1995.
8. National Labor Committee, News Release, 28 June 1995.
9. "Free Trade Zone Organizers Told 'Blood Will Flow,'" *LaborLink,* June–August, 1995, no. 4.
10. The Gap, Press Release, reported in *Business Wire Information Services,* 28 July 1995.
11. Joyce Barrett, "Caribbean Rights Group Heading for Gap Offices," *Women's Wear Daily,* 2 August, 1995.
12. *Ibid.*
13. Articles appeared in: the *New York Times* (July 21, 24), the *Washington Post* (July 24), the *Los*

Angeles Times (July, date unknown), The *Miami Herald* (July 1), The *Toronto Star* (August 16), The Toronto *Globe and Mail* (August 16), the Twin Cities' *Star Tribune* (July 7), the *Hartford Journal* (July 12), the *Toledo Blade* (July 31), the *San Francisco Examiner* (August 2), the *San Francisco Chronicle* (August 1), the *Sacramento Bee* (June 8, August 1), the New York *Newsday* (June 27), the New York *Daily News*, the *Women's Wear Daily* (August 2, 4, 9, 11), and dozens of other major metropolitan newspapers around the United States.

14. Letter entitled "Outline/Proposal, The GAP Campaign, A Strategy to Win" from National Labor Committee Education Fund in Support of Worker and Human Rights in Central America, 15 Union Square, New York, NY 10003, dated October 18, 1995.

15. Letter of Dotti Hatcher, Director, Sourcing & Trade Compliance, The Gap, dated September 11, 1995.

16. "Gap Meets Right Grapon Salvador," *Women's Wear Daily*, (4 August 1995).

17. Bob Herbert, "Not a living wage." (Op-Ed) *New York Times,* (9 October, 1995) and "In Deep Denial" (Op-Ed), *New York Times* (13 October 1995).

CASE 5. *Texaco in the Ecuadorean Amazon*

Ecuador is a small nation on the northwest coast of South America. During its 170-year history, Ecuador has been one of the least politically stable South American nations. In 1830 Ecuador achieved its independence from Spain. Ecuadorean history since that time has been characterized by cycles of republican government and military intervention and rule. The period from 1960–1972 was marked by instability and military dominance of political institutions. From 1972–1979 Ecuador was governed by military regimes. In 1979 a popularly elected president took office, but the military demanded and was granted important governing powers. The democratic institutional framework of Ecuador remains weak. Decreases in public sector spending, increasing unemployment, and rising inflation have hit the Ecuadorean poor especially hard. World Bank estimates indicate that in 1994 35 percent of the Ecuadorean population lived in poverty, and an additional 17 percent were vulnerable to poverty. In January 2000 Ecuador was again shaken by economic and political turmoil — a military coup d'état toppled the elected president and replaced him with his vice president, whom the military supports.

The Ecuadorean Amazon is one of the most biologically diverse forests in the world. It is home to cicadas, scarlet macaws, squirrel monkeys, freshwater pink dolphins, and thousands of other species. Many of these species have small populations, making them extremely sensitive to disturbance. Indigenous Indian populations have lived in harmony with these species for centuries. They have fished and hunted in and around the rivers and lakes. And they have raised crops of cacao, coffee, fruits, nuts, and tropical woods in chakras, models of sustainable agroforestry.

Ten thousand feet beneath the Amazon floor lies one of Ecuador's most important

This case was prepared by Denis G. Arnold and is based on James Brooke, "New Effort Would Test Possible Coexistence of Oil and Rain Forest," *The New York Times,* February 26, 1991; Dennis M. Hanratty, ed., *Ecuador: A Country Study,* 3rd ed. (Washington D.C.: Library of Congress, 1991); Anita Isaacs, *Military Rule and Transition in Ecuador, 1972–92* (Pittsburgh: University of Pittsburgh Press, 1993); *Ecuador Poverty Report* (Washington D.C.: The World Bank, 1996); Joe Kane, *Savages* (New York: Vintage Books, 1996); Eyal Press, "Texaco on Trial," *The Nation,* May 31, 1999; and "Texaco and Ecuador," *Texaco: Health, Safety & the Environment,* 27 September 1999, <www.texaco.com/she/index.html> (16 December 1999).

resources: rich deposits of heavy grade crude oil. The Ecuadorean government regards the oil as the best way to keep up with the country's payments on its $12 billion foreign debt obligations. For twenty years American oil companies, lead by Texaco, extracted oil from beneath the Ecuadorean Amazon in partnership with the government of Ecuador. (The United States is the primary importer of Ecuadorean oil.) They constructed 400 drill sites and hundreds of miles of roads and pipelines, including a primary pipeline that extends for 280 miles across the Andes. Large tracts of forest were clear cut to make way for these facilities. Indian lands, including chakras, were taken and bulldozed, often without compensation. In the village of Pacayacu the central square is occupied by a drilling platform.

Officials estimate that the primary pipeline alone has spilled more than 16.8 million gallons of oil into the Amazon over an eighteen-year period. Spills from secondary pipelines have never been estimated or recorded; however, smaller tertiary pipelines dump 10,000 gallons of petroleum per week into the Amazon, and production pits dump approximately 4.3 million gallons of toxic production wastes and treatment chemicals into the forest's rivers, streams, and groundwater each day. (By comparison, the Exxon Valdez spilled 10.8 million gallons of oil into Alaska's Prince William Sound.)

Texaco ignored prevailing oil industry standards that call for the reinjection of waste deep into the ground. Rivers and lakes were contaminated by oil and petroleum; heavy metals such as arsenic, cadmium, cyanide, lead, and mercury; poisonous industrial solvents; and lethal concentrations of chloride salt and other highly toxic chemicals. The only treatment these chemicals received occurred when the oil company burned waste pits to reduce petroleum content. Villagers report that the chemicals return as black

rain, polluting what little fresh water remains. What is not burned off seeps through the unlined walls of the pits into the groundwater. Cattle are found with their stomachs rotted out, crops are destroyed, animals are gone from the forest, and fish disappear from the lakes and rivers. Health officials and community leaders report adults and children with deformities, skin rashes, abscesses, headaches, dysentery, infections, respiratory ailments, and disproportionately high rates of cancer. In 1972 Texaco signed a contract requiring it to turn over all of its operations to Ecuador's national oil company, Petroecuador, by 1992. Petroecuador inherited antiquated equipment, rusting pipelines, and uncounted toxic waste sites. Independent estimates place the cost of cleaning up the production pits alone at $600 million. From 1995–1998 Texaco spent $40 million on cleanup operations in Ecuador. In exchange for these efforts the government of Ecuador relinquished future claims against the company.

Numerous international accords — including the 1972 Stockholm Declaration on the Human Environment signed by over one hundred countries, including the United States and Ecuador — identify the right to a clean and healthy environment as a fundamental human right and prohibit both state and private actors from endangering the needs of present and future generations. A group of 30,000 Ecuadoreans, including several indigenous tribes, have filed a billion-dollar class-action lawsuit against Texaco in U.S. court under the Alien Tort Claims Act. Enacted in 1789, the law was designed to provide noncitizens access to U.S. courts in cases involving a breach of international law, including accords. Texaco maintains that the case should be tried in Ecuador. However, Ecuador's judicial system does not recognize the concept of a class action suit and has no history of environmental litigation.

Furthermore, Ecuador's judicial system is notoriously corrupt (a recent poll by George Washington University found that only 16 percent of Ecuadoreans have confidence in their judicial system) and lacks the infrastructure necessary to handle the case (e.g., the city in which the case would be tried lacks a courthouse). Texaco has defended its actions by arguing that it is in full compliance with Ecuadorean law and that it had full approval of the Ecuadorean government.

Questions

1. Given the fact that Texaco operated with the approval of the Ecuadorean government, is Texaco's activity in the Amazon ethically justifiable? Explain.

2. Does Texaco have a moral obligation to provide additional funds and technical expertise to clean up areas of the Amazon it is responsible for polluting? Does it have a moral obligation to provide medical care for the residents of the Amazon region who are suffering from the effects of the pollution? Explain.

3. Does the fact that the military plays a dominant role in Ecuadorean political life undermine Texaco's claim that its environmental practices are justified because they were permitted by the government of Ecuador? Explain.

4. Does the example of Texaco's conduct in Ecuador indicate a need for enforceable regulations governing transnational corporate activity? Explain.

Suggested Supplementary Readings

ABENG, TANRI. "Business Ethics in Islamic Context: Perspectives of a Muslim Business Leader." *Business Ethics Quarterly* 7 (1997): 47–54

AVIVA, GEVA, "Moral Problems of Employing Foreign Workers." *Business Ethics Quarterly* 9 (1999): 381–403.

BRENKERT, GEORGE C. "Can We Afford International Human Rights?" *Journal of Business Ethics* 11 (July 1992): 515–21.

BRENNAN, BARTLEY A. "The Foreign Corrupt Practices Act Amendments of 1988: The Death of a Law." *North Carolina Journal of International Law & Commerce Regulation* 15 (1990): 229–47.

CARSON, THOMAS L. "Bribery, Extortion, and 'The Foreign Corrupt Practices Act.'" *Philosophy and Public Affairs* 14 (Winter 1985): 66–90.

DEGEORGE, RICHARD. *Competing with Integrity in International Business.* New York: Oxford University Press, 1993.

———. "International Business Ethics: Russia and Eastern Europe." *Social Responsibility: Business, Journalism, Law and Medicine* 19 (1993): 5–23.

DOLLINGER, MARC J. "Confucian Ethics and Japanese Management Practices." *Journal of Business Ethics* 7 (August 1988): 575–83.

DONALDSON, THOMAS. *The Ethics of International Business.* New York: Oxford University Press, 1989.

———. "The Language of International Corporate Ethics," *Business Ethics Quarterly* 2 (July 1992): 271–81.

———. "Values in Tension: Ethics Away from Home," *Harvard Business Review* (September/October 1996): 48–62.

FILATOTCHEV, IGOR, KEN STARKEY, and MIKE WRIGHT. "The Ethical Challenge of Management Buy-outs as a form of Privatization in Central and Eastern Europe." *Journal of Business Ethics* 13 (July 1994): 523–32.

FREDERICK, WILLIAM C. "The Moral Authority of Transnational Corporate Codes." *Journal of Business Ethics* 10 (1991): 165–177.

GETZ, KATHLEEN. "International Codes of Conduct: An Analysis of Ethical Reasoning." *Journal of Business Ethics* 9 (1990): 567–77.

GILLESPIE, KATE. "Middle East Response to the Foreign Corrupt Practices Act." *California Management Review* 29 (Summer, 1987): 9–30.

HART, STUART, and C.K. PRAHALAD, "Strategies for the Bottom of the Pyramid: Creating Sustainable Development." *Harvard Business Review,* November-December, 1999.

HAZERA, ALEJANDRO. "A Comparison of Japanese and U.S. Corporate Financial Accountability." *Business Ethics Quarterly* 5 (July, 1995): 479–97.

HINDMAN, HUGH D., and CHARLES G. SMITH. "Cross-Cultural Ethics and the Child Labor

Problem." *Journal of Business Ethics* 19 (March, 1999): 21–33.

HOFFMAN, W. MICHAEL, and Others, eds. *Ethics and the Multinational Enterprise.* Washington, DC: University Press of America, 1985.

HUSTED, BRYAN W. "Honor Among Thieves: A Transaction-Cost Interpretation of Corruption in Third World Countries." *Business Ethics Quarterly* 4 (January 1994): 17–27.

LANE, HENRY W., and DONALD G. SIMPSON. "Bribery in International Business: Whose Problem Is It?" *Journal of Business Ethics* 3 (February, 1984): 35–42.

LANGLOIS, CATHERINE C., and BODO B. SCHLEGELMILCH. "Do Corporate Codes of Ethics Reflect National Character? Evidence from Europe and the United States." *Journal of International Business Studies* 21 (Fall 1990): 519–39.

LEVY, ANNE C. "Putting the 'O' Back in EEO: Why Congress Had to Act So Swiftly After the Supreme Court Decision in *Bourselan.*" *Columbia Business Law Review* (1991): 239–68.

NOONAN, JOHN T. JR. *Bribes.* New York: Macmillan and Co., 1984.

PASTIN, MARK, and MICHAEL HOOKER. "Ethics and the Foreign Corrupt Practices Act." *Business Horizons* 23 (December 1980): 43–47.

PRATT, CORNELIUS B. "Multinational Corporate Social Policy Process for Ethical Responsibility in Sub-Saharan Africa." *Journal of Business Ethics* 10 (July, 1991): 527–41.

SEN, AMRTYA. "Human Rights and Asian Values." New York: Carnegie Council on Ethics and International Affairs, 1997.

STEIDLMEIER, PAUL. "The Moral Legitimacy of Intellectual Property Claims: American Business and Developing Country Perspectives." *Journal of Business Ethics* 12 (February, 1993): 157–64.

TUBBS, WALTER. "Karoushi: Stress-death and the Meaning of Work." *Journal of Business Ethics* 12 (November, 1993): 869–77.

VELASQUEZ, MANUEL. "International Business, Morality, and the Common Good." *Business Ethics Quarterly* 2 (January 1992): 26–40.

WINDSOR, DUANE, and LEE E. PRESTON. "Corporate Governance, Social Policy and Social Performance in the Multinational Corporation." *Research in Corporate Social Performance and Policy* 10 (1988).

WOKUTCH, RICHARD E., and JON M. SHEPARD. "The Maturing of the Japanese Economy: Corporate Social Responsibility Implications." *Business Ethics Quarterly* 9 (1999): 541–558.

Chapter Nine

Social and Economic Justice

INTRODUCTION

ECONOMIC DISPARITIES AMONG individuals and nations have generated heated controversy over systems for distributing and taxing income and wealth. Sustained political conflicts in the United States concern the justification of taxes, corporate profits, plant closings, international debt relief, and executive salaries and bonuses.

Several well-reasoned and systematic answers to these and related questions have been grounded in theories of justice — that is, theories of how social and economic benefits, services, and burdens should be distributed. In Chapter One we briefly analyzed some problems of ethical theory and justice. In the present chapter, the major distinctions, principles, and methods of moral argument in theories of justice are treated. The first four articles address the question, "Which general system of social and economic organization is most just?" The later articles address the justice of particular policies and forms of behavior.

Theories of Distributive Justice

What a person deserves or is entitled to is often decided by specific rules and laws, such as those governing state lotteries, food stamp allocation, health care coverage, admission procedures for universities, and the like. These rules may be evaluated, criticized, and revised by reference to moral principles such as equality of persons, nondiscriminatory treatment, property ownership, protection from harm, compensatory justice, retributive justice, and so forth. The word *justice* is used broadly to cover both these principles and specific rules derived from the same principles, but developed for specific situations.

Economists have sometimes complained about philosophers' approaches to justice, on grounds that a "fair price" or "fair trade" is not a matter of moral fairness: Prices may be low or high, affordable or not affordable, but not fair or unfair. It is simply unfortunate, not unfair, if one cannot afford to pay for something or if another person is paid forty times what you are paid. The basis of this exclusion of price as a consideration of justice is the market-established nature of prices and salaries. To speak of "unfair" prices, trade, or salaries is to express a negative opinion, of course; but these economists reason that from a market perspective any price is fair. Salaries must be treated in the same way.

However, the economist may be missing the philosopher's point. The philosopher is asking whether the market itself is a fair arrangement. If so, what makes it fair? If coercion is used in the market to set prices, is this maneuver unfair, or does it render the market not a free market? If health care and education are distributed nationally or internationally with vast inequality, can high prices on essential items such as health care goods and university tuition be fair? If a multinational company has a monopoly on an essential foodstuff, is there no such thing as a price that is too high? These questions of fairness fall under the topic of distributive justice.

The term *distributive justice* refers to the proper distribution of social benefits and burdens. A theory of distributive justice attempts to establish a connection between the properties or characteristics of persons and the morally correct distribution of benefits and burdens in society. *Egalitarian* theories emphasize equal access to primary goods (see John Rawls's article); *communitarian* theories emphasize group goals, collective control, and participation in communal life, by contrast to liberal political systems that emphasize individual welfare and rights (see Michael Walzer's article); *libertarian* theories emphasize rights to social and economic liberty and deemphasize collective control (see Robert Nozick's essay); and *utilitarian* theories emphasize a mixed use of such criteria resulting in the maximization of both public and individual interests (see Peter Singer's article).

Systematic theories of justice attempt to elaborate how people should be compared and what it means to give people what is due them. Philosophers attempt to achieve the needed precision by developing material principles of justice, so called because they put material content into a theory of justice. Each material principle of justice identifies a relevant property on the basis of which burdens and benefits should be distributed. The following list includes the major candidates for the position of principles of distributive justice.

1. To each person an equal share
2. To each person according to individual need
3. To each person according to that person's rights
4. To each person according to individual effort
5. To each person according to societal contribution
6. To each person according to merit

A theory of justice might accept more than one of these principles. Some theories accept all six as legitimate. Many societies use several, in the belief that different rules are appropriate to different situations.

In the utilitarian theory, problems of justice are viewed as one part of the larger problem of how to maximize value, and it is easy to see how a utilitarian might use all of these material principles to this end. The ideal distribution of benefits and burdens is simply the one having this maximizing effect. According to utilitarian Peter Singer in his essay in this chapter, a heavy element of political planning and economic redistribution is required to ensure that justice is done. Because utilitarianism was treated in Chapter One, detailed considerations will be given in this introduction only to egalitarian, libertarian, and communitarian theories.

Egalitarian Theory

Equality in the distribution of social benefits and burdens has a central place in many influential ethical theories. For example, in utilitarianism different people are equal in the value accorded their wants, preferences, and happiness, and in Kantian theories all persons are considered equally worthy and deserving of respect as ends in themselves. Egalitarian theory treats the question of how people should be considered equal in some respects (for example, in their basic political and moral rights and obligations), yet unequal in others (for example, in wealth and social burdens such as taxation).

Radical and Qualified Egalitarianism. In its radical form, egalitarian theory proposes that individual differences are always morally insignificant. Distributions of burdens and benefits in a society are just to the extent that they are equal, and deviations from absolute equality in distribution are unjust. For example, the fact that in the United States more than 35 percent of the wealth is owned by less than one-half percent of the population makes U.S. society unjust, according to this theory, no matter how relatively "deserving" the people at both extremes might be. The radical egalitarian would view these figures as evidence that American society is unjust.

However, most egalitarian accounts are guardedly formulated, so that persons are not entitled to equal shares of all social benefits and so that individual merit justifies some differences in distribution. Egalitarianism, so qualified, is concerned only with basic equalities among individuals. For example, egalitarians prefer *progressive* tax rates (higher incomes taxed more heavily than lower) rather than *proportional* rates (each unit taxed the same). This preference may seem odd since a proportional rate treats everyone equally. However, qualified egalitarians reason that progressive rates tax the wealthy more and thereby distribute wealth more evenly.

John Rawls's Theory. In recent years a qualified egalitarian theory in the Kantian tradition has enjoyed wide discussion. John Rawls's *A Theory of Justice* maintains that all economic goods and services should be distributed equally except when an unequal distribution would work to everyone's advantage (or at least to the advantage of the worst off in society). Rawls presents this egalitarian theory as a direct challenge to utilitarianism. He argues that social distributions produced by maximizing utility permit violations of basic individual liberties and rights. Being indifferent to the distribution of satisfactions among individuals, utilitarianism permits the infringement of people's rights and liberties in order to produce a proportionately greater utility for all concerned.

Rawls defends a hypothetical social contract procedure that is strongly indebted to what he calls the "Kantian conception of equality." Valid principles of justice are those to which all persons would agree if they could freely and impartially consider the social situation. Impartiality is guaranteed by a conceptual device Rawls calls the "veil of ignorance." Here each person is imagined to be ignorant of all his or her particular characteristics, for example, the person's sex, race, IQ, family background, and special talents or handicaps. Theoretically, this veil of ignorance would prevent the adoption of principles biased toward particular groups of persons.

Rawls argues that under these conditions people would unanimously agree on two fundamental principles of justice. The first requires that each person be permitted the maximum amount of basic liberty compatible with a similar liberty for others. The second stipulates that once this equal basic liberty is assured, inequalities in social primary goods (for example, income, rights, and opportunities) are to be allowed only if they benefit everyone. Rawls considers social institutions to be just if and only if they conform to these principles of the social contract. He rejects radical egalitarianism, arguing that inequalities that render everyone better off by comparison to being equal are desirable.

Rawls formulates what is called the *difference principle:* Inequalities are justifiable only if they maximally enhance the position of the "representative least advantaged" person, that is, a hypothetical individual particularly unfortunate in the distribution of fortuitous characteristics or social advantages. Rawls is unclear about who might qualify under this category, but a worker incapacitated from exposure to asbestos and living in poverty clearly would qualify. Formulated in this way, the difference principle could allow, for instance, extraordinary economic rewards to business entrepreneurs, venture capitalists, and corporate takeover artists if the resulting economic situation were to produce improved job opportunities and working conditions for the least advantaged members of society, or possibly greater benefits for pension funds holding stock for the working class.

The difference principle rests on the moral viewpoint that because inequalities of birth, historical circumstance, and natural endowment are undeserved, persons in a cooperative society should make more equal the unequal situation of its naturally disadvantaged members. This and other Rawlsian ideas are defended in this chapter in the international context by Thomas Donaldson, who argues that it is unjust to allow the economically least well off in developing countries to be harmed as a result of conditions imposed as part of international loan arrangements. In the preceding article, Richard De George explains how justice and fairness are central to the ethics of international business. He is concerned more with bilateral negotiation than the Rawlsian framework, but De George too insists that it is unjust for wealthy nations to impose a sense of justice on relatively undeveloped countries. "Reciprocity," he maintains, "is the procedural key to justice."

Libertarian Theory

What makes a libertarian theory *libertarian* is the priority given to distinctive procedures or mechanisms for ensuring that liberty rights are recognized in social and economic practice, typically the rules and procedures governing economic acquisition and exchange in capitalist or free-market systems.

Role of Individual Freedom. The libertarian contends that it is a basic violation of justice to ensure equal economic returns in a society. In particular, individuals are seen as having a fundamental right to own and dispense with the products of their labor as they choose, even if the exercise of this right leads to large inequalities of wealth in society. Equality and utility principles, from this perspective, sacrifice basic liberty rights to the larger public interest by exploiting one set of individuals for the benefit of another. The most apparent example is the coercive extraction of financial resources through taxation.

Robert Nozick's Theory. Libertarian theory is defended in this chapter by Robert Nozick, who refers to his social philosophy as an "entitlement theory" of justice. Nozick argues that a theory of justice should work to protect individual rights and should not propound a thesis intended to "pattern" society through arrangements such as those in socialist and (impure) capitalist countries in which governments take pronounced steps to redistribute the wealth.

Nozick's libertarian position rejects all distributional patterns imposed by material principles of justice. He is thus committed to a form of *procedural* justice. That is, for Nozick there is no pattern of just distribution independent of fair procedures of acquisition, transfer, and rectification. This claim has been at the center of controversy over the libertarian account, and competing theories of justice are often reactions to an uncompromising commitment to pure procedural justice. For example, Donaldson's Rawlsian convictions and De George's proposals about mutual negotiation may be interpreted as a response to the libertarian tradition.

Communitarian Theory

Moral and political theories that advocate individual responsibility, free-market exchanges, and limited community control are often called *liberal* theories. "Liberalism," which places the individual at the center of moral and political life, views the state as properly limited in the event of a conflict with individual rights such as freedom of association, expression, and religion. The state's proper role is to protect and enforce basic moral and political rights, often called *civil rights*.

Rising up against liberalism in recent years has been a tide of communitarian theories. Although a diverse lot, communitarian theories share many ideas. They see typical liberal theories such as those of Rawls and Nozick (and even Mill and

Singer) as subverting communal life and the obligations and commitments that grow out of that perspective on life. These theorists see persons as *constituted* by communal values and thus as best suited to achieve their good through communal life, not state protections or individual moral and political rights.

Communitarians object to the way Rawlsian liberalism has made justice the first virtue of social institutions and then has patterned those institutions to protect the individual against society. The communitarian believes that justice is a less central virtue of social life, one needed only when communal values have broken down into conflicts of the sort litigated in court. Rather than conceptualizing the state's role as that of enforcer of rights allowing individuals to pursue any course they wish, the communitarian takes the view that the community may rightly be expected to impose on individuals certain conceptions of virtue and the good life.

The sole representative of communitarian theories in this chapter is Michael Walzer, a moderate communitarian not as opposed to liberalism as hard-line communitarians. For him notions of justice are not based on some "rational" or "natural" foundation external to the society. Rather, standards of justice are developed internally as the community evolves. Something has to be "given-as-basic" in every ethical theory, and the communitarian sees everything as deriving from communal values and historical practices. Conventions, traditions, and loyalties therefore play a more prominent role in communitarian theories than they do in the other theories we encounter in this chapter.

Communitarians recognize that people sometimes have good reason to challenge and even reject values accepted by the community. To this end, Walzer argues that a community ethic must be particularly vigilant to avoid "oppressing" minorities. Although an individual has a right to challenge community values, a communitarian will not accept an individual's personal values as either moral or respectable when those values depart from the central, defining moral values of the community.

A somewhat communitarian perspective (*res communis*) is found in the article by Thomas Franck on the law of the sea. He emphasizes that the idea that the seas and coastal shelves should be shared by all nations as a matter of distributive justice is a very recent and still somewhat underdeveloped idea — and one that has broadened our ideas of "shareholders" and "resources" held in common. This idea, he maintains, has deeply affected the fishing industry and will continue to produce changes that will affect international business.

Visions of Justice Beyond the Free Market

Many philosophers argue that a conception of fundamental individual rights more inclusive than Nozick's must be recognized in any adequate theory of justice. Even in strictly economic terms, these writers maintain, Nozick's conception of individual rights is excessively restricted. They challenge the proponents of libertarianism to answer the following questions: Why should we assume that people's economic rights extend only to the acquisition and dispensation of private property according to the free-market rules? Is it not equally plausible to posit more substantive moral rights in the economic sphere — say, rights to health care, decent levels of education, and decent standards of living?

Nozick's ideal is generally agreed to be plausible for free transactions among informed and consenting parties who start as equals in the bargaining process. However, this ideal is rarely the case beyond circumstances of contractual bargaining among equals. Contracts, voting privileges, individuals investing in the stock market, and family relationships may involve bluffing, differentials of power and wealth, manipulation, and the like. These factors work systematically to disadvantage vulnerable individuals. Imagine, for example, that over the course of time one group in society gains immense wealth and political influence compared with another group. Even if the *transactions* leading to this imbalance may have been legitimate, the *outcome* is not acceptable. If an individual's bargaining position has been deeply eroded, does he or she have a right to protection from social inequalities that have emerged? If he or she is destined to poverty as a result, is there a legitimate claim of justice, as Rawls proposes?

If people have a right to a minimal level of material means, their rights are violated whenever economic distributions leave some with less than that minimal level. A commitment to individual rights, then, may result in a theory of justice that requires a more activist role for government, even if one starts with free-market or libertarian assumptions. Many philosophers agree with Nozick that economic freedom is a value deserving of respect and protection. They disagree, however, with the claim that the principles and procedures that libertarians advocate protect this basic value.

The Principle of Need. In reaction to these problems, some reject the pure procedural commitments of the libertarian theory and replace them with a principle specifying human need as the relevant respect in which people are to be compared for purposes of determining social and economic justice. Donaldson seems to be a prime example of this approach.

Much turns on how the notion of need is defined and implemented. For purposes of justice, a principle of need would be least controversial if it were restricted to fundamental needs. If malnutrition, bodily injury, and the withholding of certain information involve fundamental harms, we have a fundamental need for nutrition, health care facilities, and education. According to theories based on this material principle, justice places the satisfaction of fundamental human needs above the protection of economic freedoms or rights.

This construal of the principle of need has provided alternatives to libertarian justice. Yet there may be some room for reconciliation between the principle of need and libertarianism. Many advanced industrial countries have the capacity to produce more than is strictly necessary to meet their citizens' fundamental needs. One might argue that *after* everyone's fundamental needs have been satisfied, *then* justice requires no particular pattern of distribution. For example, some current discussions of the right to health care and the right to a job are rooted in the idea of meeting basic medical and economic needs, but only basic needs. In this way, a single unified theory of justice might require the maintenance of certain patterns in the distribution of basic goods (for example, a decent minimum level of income, education, and health care), while allowing the market to determine distributions of goods beyond those that satisfy fundamental needs.

This approach accepts a two-tiered system of access to goods and services: (1) social coverage for basic and catastrophic needs, and (2) private purchase of other goods and services. On the first tier, distribution is based on need, and everyone's basic needs are met by the government. Better services may be made available for purchase in an economic system on the second tier. This proposal seems to present an attractive point of convergence and negotiation for libertarians, communitarians, utilitarians, and egalitarians. It provides a premise of equal access to basic goods, while allowing additional rights to economic freedom. Theories such as utilitarianism and communitarianism may also find the compromise particularly attractive because it serves to minimize public dissatisfaction and to maximize community welfare. The egalitarian finds an opportunity to use an equal access principle, and the libertarian retains free-market production and distribution. However, the system clearly does involve compromise by all parties.

Conclusion

Rawls, Nozick, and their utilitarian and communitarian opponents all capture some intuitive convictions about justice, and each theory exhibits strengths as a theory of justice. Rawls's difference principle, for example, describes a widely shared belief about justified inequalities. Nozick's theory makes a strong appeal in the domains of property rights and liberties. Utilitarianism is widely used in the Western nations in the development of public policy, and communitarian theories in some form supply the prevailing model of justice in many nations.

Perhaps, then, there are several equally valid, or at least equally defensible, theories of justice. There could, on this analysis, be libertarian societies, egalitarian societies, utilitarian societies, and communitarian societies, as well as societies based on mixed theories or derivative theories of taxation and redistribution. However, this possibility raises other problems in ethical theory discussed in Chapter One, in particular, relativism and moral disagreement, and before this conclusion is accepted, the details of the arguments in the selections in this chapter should be carefully assessed.

THEORIES OF SOCIAL JUSTICE

An Egalitarian Theory of Justice

John Rawls

THE ROLE OF JUSTICE

Justice is the first virtue of social institutions, as truth is of systems of thought. A theory however elegant and economical must be rejected or revised if it is untrue; likewise laws and institutions no matter how efficient and well-arranged must be reformed or abolished if they are unjust. Each person possesses an inviolability founded on justice that even the welfare of society as a whole cannot override. For this reason justice denies that the loss of freedom for some is made right by a greater good shared by others. It does not allow that the sacrifices imposed on a few are outweighed by the larger sum of advantages enjoyed by many. Therefore in a just society the liberties of equal citizenship are taken as settled; the rights secured by justice are not subject to political bargaining or to the calculus of social interests. The only thing that permits us to acquiesce in an erroneous theory is the lack of a better one; analogously, an injustice is tolerable only when it is necessary to avoid an even greater injustice. Being first virtues of human activities, truth and justice are uncompromising.

These propositions seem to express our intuitive conviction of the primary of justice. No doubt they are expressed too strongly. In any event I wish to inquire whether these contentions or others similar to them are sound, and if so how they can be accounted for. To this end it is necessary to work out a theory of justice in the light of which these assertions can be interpreted and assessed. I shall begin by considering the role of the principles of justice. Let us assume, to fix ideas, that a society is a more or less self-sufficient association of persons who in their relations to one another recognize certain rules of conduct as binding and who for the most part act in accordance with them. Suppose further that these rules specify a system of cooperation designed to advance the good of those taking part in it. Then, although a society is a cooperative venture for mutual advantage, it is typically marked by a conflict as well as by an identity of interests. There is an identity of interests since social cooperation makes possible a better life for all than any would have if each were to live solely by his own efforts. There is a conflict of interests since persons are not indifferent as to how the greater benefits produced by their collaboration are distributed, for in order to pursue their ends they each prefer a larger to a lesser share. A set of principles is required for choosing among the various social arrangements which determine this division of advantages and for underwriting an agreement on the proper distributive shares. These principles are the principles of social justice: they provide a way of assigning rights and duties in the basic institutions of society and they define the appropriate distribution of the benefits and burdens of social cooperation. . . .

Excerpted from John Rawls, *A Theory of Justice* (Cambridge, Mass.: Harvard University Press, 1971), pp. 3–4, 11–15, 18–19, 60–62, 64–65, 100–104, 274–277. Reprinted by permission of Oxford University Press and The Belknap Press of Harvard University Press, © 1971 by The President and Fellows of Harvard College.

THE MAIN IDEA OF THE THEORY OF JUSTICE

My aim is to present a conception of justice which generalizes and carries to a higher level of abstraction the familiar theory of the social contract as found, say, in Locke, Rousseau, and Kant. In order to do this we are not to think of the original contract as one to enter a particular society or to set up a particular form of government. Rather, the guiding idea is that the principles of justice for the basic structure of society are the object of the original agreement. They are the principles that free and rational persons concerned to further their own interests would accept in an initial position of equality as defining the fundamental terms of their association. These principles are to regulate all further agreements; they specify the kinds of social cooperation that can be entered into and the forms of government that can be established. This way of regarding the principles of justice I shall call justice as fairness.

Thus we are to imagine that those who engage in social cooperation choose together, in one joint act, the principles which are to assign basic rights and duties and to determine the division of social benefits. Men are to decide in advance how they are to regulate their claims against one another and what is to be the foundation charter of their society. Just as each person must decide by rational reflection what constitutes his good, that is, the system of ends which it is rational for him to pursue, so a group of persons must decide once and for all what is to count among them as just and unjust. The choice which rational men would make in this hypothetical situation of equal liberty, assuming for the present that this choice problem has a solution, determines the principles of justice.

In justice as fairness the original position of equality corresponds to the state of nature in the traditional theory of the social contract. This original position is not, of course, thought of as an actual historical state of affairs, much less as a primitive condition of culture. It is understood as a purely hypothetical situation characterized so as to lead to a certain conception of justice. Among the essential features of this situation is that no one knows his place in society, his class position or social status, nor does any one know his fortune in the distribution of natural assets and abilities, his intelligence, strength, and the like. I shall even assume that the parties do not know their conceptions of the good or their special psychological propensities. The principles of justice are chosen behind a veil of ignorance. This ensures that no one is advantaged or disadvantaged in the choice of principles by the outcome of natural chance or the contingency of social circumstances. Since all are similarly situated and no one is able to design principles to favor his particular condition, the principles of justice are the result of a fair agreement or bargain. For given the circumstances of the original position, the symmetry of everyone's relations to each other, this initial situation is fair between individuals as moral persons, that is, as rational beings with their own ends and capable, I shall assume, of a sense of justice. The original position is, one might say, the appropriate initial status quo, and thus the fundamental agreements reached in it are fair. This explains the propriety of the name "justice as fairness": it conveys the idea that the principles of justice are agreed to in an initial situation that is fair. The name does not mean that the concepts of justice and fairness are the same, any more than the phrase "poetry as metaphor" means that the concepts of poetry and metaphor are the same.

Justice as fairness begins, as I have said, with one of the most general of all choices which persons might make together, namely, with the choice of the first principles of a conception of justice which is to regulate all subsequent criticism and reform of institutions. Then, having chosen a conception of justice, we can suppose that they are to choose a constitution and a legislature to enact laws, and so on, all in accordance with the principles of justice initially agreed upon. Our social situation is just if it is such that by this sequence of hypothetical agreements we would have contracted into the general system of rules which defines it.

. . . It may be observed, however, that once the principles of justice are thought of as arising from an original agreement in a situation of equality, it is an open question whether the principle of utility would be acknowledged. Offhand it hardly seems likely that persons who view themselves as equals, entitled to press their claims upon one another, would agree to a principle which may require lesser life prospects for some simply for the sake of a greater sum of advantages enjoyed by others. Since each desires to protect his interests, his capacity to advance his conception of the good, no one has a reason to acquiesce in an enduring loss for himself in order to bring about a greater net balance of satisfaction. In the absence of strong and lasting benevolent impulses, a rational man would not accept a basic structure merely because it maximized the algebraic sum of advantages irrespective of its permanent effects on his own basic rights and interests. Thus it seems that the principle of utility is incompatible with the conception of social cooperation among equals for mutual advantage. It appears to be inconsistent with the idea of reciprocity implicit in the notion of a well-ordered society. Or, at any rate, so I shall argue.

I shall maintain instead that the persons in the initial situation would choose two rather different principles: the first requires equality in the assignment of basic rights and duties, while the second holds that social and economic inequalities, for example inequalities

of wealth and authority, are just only if they result in compensating benefits for everyone, and in particular for the least advantaged members of society. These principles rule out justifying institutions on the grounds that the hardships of some are offset by a greater good in the aggregate. It may be expedient but it is not just that some should have less in order that others may prosper. But there is no injustice in the greater benefits earned by a few provided that the situation of persons not so fortunate is thereby improved. The intuitive idea is that since everyone's well-being depends upon a scheme of cooperation without which no one could have a satisfactory life, the division of advantages should be such as to draw forth the willing cooperation of everyone taking part in it, including those less well situated. Yet this can be expected only if reasonable terms are proposed. The two principles mentioned seem to be a fair agreement on the basis of which those better endowed, or more fortunate in their social position, neither of which we can be said to deserve, could expect the willing cooperation of others when some workable scheme is a necessary condition of the welfare of all. Once we decide to look for a conception of justice that nullifies the accidents of natural endowment and the contingencies of social circumstance as counters in quest for political and economic advantage, we are led to these principles. They express the result of leaving aside those aspects of the social world that seem arbitrary from a moral point of view. . . .

THE ORIGINAL POSITION AND JUSTIFICATION

. . . The idea here is simply to make vivid to ourselves the restrictions that it seems reasonable to impose on arguments for principles of justice, and therefore on these principles themselves. Thus it seems reasonable and generally acceptable that no one should be advantaged or disadvantaged by natural fortune or social circumstances in the choice of principles. It also seems widely agreed that it should be impossible to tailor principles to the circumstances of one's own case. We should insure further that particular inclinations and aspirations, and persons' conceptions of their good, do not affect the principles adopted. The aim is to rule out those principles that it would be rational to propose for acceptance, however little the chance of success, only if one knew certain things that are irrelevant from the standpoint of justice. For example, if a man knew that he was wealthy, he might find it rational to advance the principle that various taxes for welfare measures be counted unjust; if he knew that he was poor, he would most likely propose the contrary principle. To represent the desired restrictions one imagines a situation in which everyone is deprived of this sort of information. One excludes the knowledge of those contingencies which sets men at odds and allows them to be guided by their prejudices. In this manner the veil of ignorance is arrived at in a natural way. . . .

TWO PRINCIPLES OF JUSTICE

I shall now state in a provisional form the two principles of justice that I believe would be chosen in the original position. . . .

The first statement of the two principles reads as follows.

> **First:** each person is to have an equal right to the most extensive basic liberty compatible with a similar liberty for others.
>
> **Second:** social and economic inequalities are to be arranged so that they are both (a) reasonably expected to be to everyone's advantage, and (b) attached to positions and offices open to all. . . . [The Difference Principle]

By way of general comment, these principles primarily apply, as I have said, to the basic structure of society. They are to govern the assignment of rights and duties and to regulate the distribution of social and economic advantages. As their formulation suggests, these principles presuppose that the social structure can be divided into two more or less distinct parts, the first principle applying to the one, the second to the other. They distinguish between those aspects of the social system that define and secure the equal liberties of citizenship and those that specify and establish social and economic inequalities. The basic liberties of citizens are, roughly speaking, political liberty (the right to vote and to be eligible for public office) together with freedom of speech and assembly; liberty of conscience and freedom of thought; freedom of the person along with the right to hold (personal) property; and freedom from arbitrary arrest and seizure as defined by the concept of the rule of law. These liberties are all required to be equal by the first principle, since citizens of a just society are to have the same basic rights.

The second principle applies, in the first approximation, to the distribution of income and wealth and to the design of organizations that make use of differences in authority and responsibility, or chains of command. While the distribution of wealth and income need not be equal, it must be to everyone's advantage, and at the same time, positions of authority and offices of command must be accessible to all. One applies the second principle by holding positions open, and then, subject to this constraint, arranges social and economic inequalities so that everyone benefits.

These principles are to be arranged in a serial order with the first principle prior to the second. This ordering means that a departure from the institutions of equal liberty required by the first principle cannot be justified, or compensated for, by greater social and economic advantages. The distribution of wealth and income, and the hierarchies of authority must be consistent with both the liberties of equal citizenship and equality of opportunity.

It is clear that these principles are rather specific in their content, and their acceptance rests on certain assumptions that I must eventually try to explain and justify. A theory of justice depends upon a theory of society in ways that will become evident as we proceed. For the present, it should be observed that the two principles (and this holds for all formulations) are a special case of a more general conception of justice that can be expressed as follows.

> All social values — liberty and opportunity, income and wealth, and the bases of self-respect — are to be distributed equally unless an unequal distribution of any, or all, of these values is to everyone's advantage.

Injustice, then, is simply inequalities that are not to the benefit of all. Of course, this conception is extremely vague and requires interpretation.

As a first step, suppose that the basic structure of society distributes certain primary goods, that is, things that every rational man is presumed to want. These goods normally have a use whatever a person's rational plan of life. For simplicity, assume that the chief primary goods at the disposition of society are rights and liberties, powers and opportunities, income and wealth. These are the social primary goods. Other primary goods such as health and vigor, intelligence and imagination, are natural goods; although their possession is influenced by the basic structure, they are not so directly under its control. Imagine, then, a hypothetical initial arrangement in which all the social primary goods are equally distributed: everyone has similar rights and duties, and income and wealth are evenly shared. This state of affairs provides a benchmark for judging improvements. If certain inequalities of wealth and organizational powers would make everyone better off than in this hypothetical starting situation, then they accord with the general conception.

Now it is possible, at least theoretically, that by giving up some of their fundamental liberties men are sufficiently compensated by the resulting social and economic gains. The general conception of justice imposes no restrictions on what sort of inequalities are permissible; it only requires that everyone's position be improved. . . .

Now the second principle insists that each person benefit from permissible inequalities in the basic structure. This means that it must be reasonable for each relevant representative man defined by this structure, when he views it as a going concern, to prefer his prospects with the inequality to his prospects without it. One is not allowed to justify differences in income or organizational powers on the ground that the disadvantages of those in one position are outweighed by the greater advantages of those in another. Much less can infringements of liberty be counterbalanced in this way. Applied to the basic structure, the principle of utility would have us maximize the sum of expectations of representative men (weighted by the number of persons they represent, on the classical view); and this would permit us to compensate for the losses of some by the gains of others. Instead, the two principles require that everyone benefit from economic and social inequalities. . . .

THE TENDENCY TO EQUALITY

I wish to conclude this discussion of the two principles by explaining the sense in which they express an egalitarian conception of justice. Also I should like to forestall the objection to the principle of fair opportunity that it leads to a callous meritocratic society. In order to prepare the way for doing this, I note several aspects of the conception of justice that I have set out.

First we may observe that the difference principle gives some weight to the considerations singled out by the principle of redress. This is the principle that undeserved inequalities call for redress; and since inequalities of birth and natural endowment are undeserved, these inequalities are to be somehow compensated for. Thus the principle holds that in order to treat all persons equally, to provide genuine equality of opportunity, society must give more attention to those with fewer native assets and to those born into the less favorable social positions. The idea is to redress the bias of contingencies in the direction of equality. In pursuit of this principle greater resources might be spent on the education of the less rather than the more intelligent, at least over a certain time of life, say the earlier years of school.

Now the principle of redress has not to my knowledge been proposed as the sole criterion of justice, as the single aim of the social order. It is plausible as most such principles are only as a prima facie principle, one that is to be weighed in the balance with others. For example, we are to weigh it against the principle to improve the average standard of life, or to advance the common good. But whatever other principles we hold, the claims of redress are to be taken into account. It is thought to represent one of the elements in our conception of justice. Now the difference principle is not of course the principle of redress. It does not require society to try to even out handicaps as if all were expected to compete on a fair basis in the same race. But the difference principle would allocate resources in education, say, so as to improve the long-term expectation of the least fa-

vored. If this end is attained by giving more attention to the better endowed, it is permissible; otherwise not. And in making this decision, the value of education should not be assessed only in terms of economic efficiency and social welfare. Equally if not more important is the role of education in enabling a person to enjoy the culture of his society and to take part in its affairs, and in this way to provide for each individual a secure sense of his own worth.

Thus although the difference principle is not the same as that of redress, it does achieve some of the intent of the latter principle. It transforms the aims of the basic structure so that the total scheme of institutions no longer emphasizes social efficiency and technocratic values. . . .

. . . The natural distribution is neither just nor unjust; nor is it unjust that men are born into society at some particular position. These are simply natural facts. What is just and unjust is the way that institutions deal with these facts. Aristocratic and caste societies are unjust because they make these contingencies the ascriptive basis for belonging to more or less enclosed and privileged social classes. The basic structure of these societies incorporates the arbitrariness found in nature. But there is no necessity for men to resign themselves to these contingencies. The social system is not an unchangeable order beyond human control but a pattern of human action. In justice as fairness men agree to share one another's fate. In designing institutions they undertake to avail themselves of the accidents of nature and social circumstance only when doing so is for the common benefit. The two principles are a fair way of meeting the arbitrariness of fortune; and while no doubt imperfect in other ways, the institutions which satisfy these principles are just. . . .

There is a natural inclination to object that those better situated deserve their greater advantages whether or not they are to the benefit of others. At this point it is necessary to be clear about the notion of desert. It is perfectly true that given a just system of cooperation as a scheme of public rules and the expectations set up by it, those who, with the prospect of improving their condition, have done what the system announces that it will reward are entitled to their advantages. In this sense the more fortunate have a claim to their better situation; their claims are legitimate expectations established by social institutions, and the community is obligated to meet them. But this sense of desert presupposes the existence of the cooperative scheme; it is irrelevant to the question whether in the first place the scheme is to be designed in accordance with the difference principle or some other criterion.

Perhaps some will think that the person with greater natural endowments deserves those assets and the superior character that made their development possible. Because he is more worthy in this sense, he deserves the greater advantages that he could achieve with them. This view, however, is surely incorrect. It seems to be one of the fixed points of our considered judgments that no one deserves his place in the distribution of native endowments, any more than one deserves one's initial starting place in society. The assertion that a man deserves the superior character that enables him to make the effort to cultivate his abilities is equally problematic, for his character depends in large part upon fortunate family and social circumstances for which he can claim no credit. The notion of desert seems not to apply to these cases. Thus the more advantaged representative man cannot say that he deserves and therefore has a right to a scheme of cooperation in which he is permitted to acquire benefits in ways that do not contribute to the welfare of others. There is no basis for his making this claim. From the standpoint of common sense, then, the difference

principle appears to be acceptable both to the more advantaged and to the less advantaged individual. . . .

BACKGROUND INSTITUTIONS FOR DISTRIBUTIVE JUSTICE

The main problem of distributive justice is the choice of a social system. The principles of justice apply to the basic structure and regulate how its major institutions are combined into one scheme. Now, as we have seen, the idea of justice as fairness is to use the notion of pure procedural justice to handle the contingencies of particular situations. The social system is to be designed so that the resulting distribution is just however things turn out. To achieve this end it is necessary to get the social and economic process within the surroundings of suitable political and legal institutions. Without an appropriate scheme of these background institutions the outcome of the distributive process will not be just. Background fairness is lacking. I shall give a brief description of these supporting institutions as they might exist in a properly organized democratic state that allows private ownership of capital and natural resources. . . .

In establishing these background institutions the government may be thought of as divided into four branches.[1] Each branch consists of various agencies, or activities thereof, charged with preserving certain social and economic conditions. These divisions do not overlap with the usual organization of government but are to be understood as different functions. The allocation branch, for example, is to keep the price system workably competitive and to prevent the formation of unreasonable market power. Such power does not exist as long as markets cannot be made more competitive consistent with the requirements of efficiency and the facts of geography and the preferences of households. The allocation branch is also charged with identifying and correcting, say by suitable taxes and subsidies and by changes in the definition of property rights, the more obvious departures from efficiency caused by the failure of prices to measure accurately social benefits and costs. To this end suitable taxes and subsidies may be used, or the scope and definition of property rights may be revised. The stabilization branch, on the other hand, strives to bring about reasonably full employment in the sense that those who want work can find it and the free choice of occupation and the deployment of finance are supported by strong effective demand. These two branches together are to maintain the efficiency of the market economy generally.

The social minimum is the responsibility of the transfer branch. . . . The essential idea is that the workings of this branch take needs into account and assign them an appropriate weight with respect to other claims. A competitive price system gives no consideration to needs and therefore it cannot be the sole device of distribution. There must be a division of labor between the parts of the social system in answering to the common sense precepts of justice. Different institutions meet different claims. Competitive markets properly regulated secure free choice of occupation and lead to an efficient use of resources and allocation of commodities to households. They set a weight on the conventional precepts associated with wages and earnings, whereas a transfer branch guarantees a certain level of well-being and honors the claims of need. . . .

It is clear that the justice of distributive shares depends on the background institutions and how they allocate total income, wages and other income plus transfers. There is with reason strong objection to the competitive determination of total income, since this ignores the claims of need and an appropriate standard of life. From the standpoint of the legislative stage it is rational to insure oneself and one's descendants against these contingencies of the market. Indeed, the difference principle presumably requires this. But once a suitable minimum is provided by transfers, it may be perfectly fair that the rest of total income be settled by the price system, assuming that it is moderately efficient and free from monopolistic restrictions, and unreasonable externalities have been eliminated. Moreover, this way of dealing with the claims of need would appear to be more effective than trying to regulate income by minimum wage standards, and the like. It is better to assign to each branch only such tasks as are compatible with one another. Since the market is not suited to answer the claims of need, these should be met by a separate arrangement. Whether the principles of justice are satisfied, then, turns on whether the total income of the least advantaged (wages plus transfers) is such as to maximize their long-run expectations (consistent with the constraints of equal liberty and fair equality of opportunity).

Finally, there is a distribution branch. Its task is to preserve an approximate justice in distributive shares by means of taxation and the necessary adjustments in the rights of property. Two aspects of this branch may be distinguished. First of all, it imposes a number of inheritance and gift taxes, and sets restrictions on the rights of bequest. The purpose of these levies and regulations is not to raise revenue (release resources to government) but gradually and continually to correct the distribution of wealth and to prevent concentrations of power detrimental to the fair value of political liberty and fair equality of opportunity. For example, the progressive principle might be applied at the beneficiary's end.[2] Doing this would encourage the wide dispersal of property which is a necessary condition, it seems, if the fair value of the equal liberties is to be maintained.

NOTES

1. For the idea of branches of government, see R. A. Musgrave, *The Theory of Public Finance* (New York: McGraw-Hill, 1959), Ch. 1.

2. See Meade, *Efficiency, Equality and the Ownership of Property,* pp. 56f.

The Entitlement Theory

Robert Nozick

The term "distributive justice" is not a neutral one. Hearing the term "distribution," most people presume that some thing or mechanism uses some principle or criterion to give out a supply of things. Into this process of distributing shares some error may have crept. So it is an open question, at least, whether *re*distribution should take place; whether we should do again what has already been done once, though poorly. However, we are not in the position of children who have been given portions of pie by someone who now makes last minute adjustments to rectify careless cutting. There is no *central* distribution, no person or group entitled to control all the resources, jointly deciding how they are to be doled out. What each person gets, he gets from others who give to him in exchange for something, or as a gift. In a free society, diverse persons control different resources, and new holdings arise out of the voluntary exchanges and actions of persons. . . .

The subject of justice in holdings consists of three major topics. The first is the *original acquisition of holdings,* the appropriation of unheld things. This includes the issues of how unheld things may come to be held,

the process, or processes, by which unheld things may come to be held, the things that may come to be held by these processes, the extent of what comes to be held by a particular person, and so on. We shall refer to the complicated truth about this topic, which we shall not formulate here, as the principle of justice in acquisition. The second topic concerns the *transfer of holdings* from one person to another. By what processes may a person transfer holdings to another? How may a person acquire a holding from another who holds it? Under this topic come general descriptions of voluntary exchange, and gift and (on the other hand) fraud, as well as reference to particular conventional details fixed upon in a given society. The complicated truth about this subject (with placeholders for conventional details) we shall call the principle of justice in transfer. (And we shall suppose it also includes principles governing how a person may divest himself of a holding, passing it into an unheld state.)

If the world were wholly just, the following inductive definition would exhaustively cover the subject of justice in holdings.

1. A person who acquires a holding in accordance with the principle of justice in acquisition is entitled to that holding.
2. A person who acquires a holding in accordance with the principle of justice in transfer, from someone else entitled to the holding, is entitled to the holding.
3. No one is entitled to a holding except by (repeated) applications of 1 and 2.

The complete principle of distributive justice would say simply that a distribution is just if everyone is entitled to the holdings they possess under the distribution. . . .

Not all actual situations are generated in accordance with the two principles of justice in holdings: the principle of justice in acquisition and the principle of justice in transfer. Some people steal from others, or defraud them, or enslave them, seizing their product and preventing them from living as they choose, or forcibly exclude others from competing in exchanges. None of these are permissible modes of transition from one situation to another. And some persons acquire holdings by means not sanctioned by the principle of justice in acquisition. The existence of past injustice (previous violations of the first two principles of justice in holdings) raises the third major topic under justice in holdings: the rectification of injustice in holdings. If past injustice has shaped present holdings in various ways, some identifiable and some not, what now, if anything, ought to be done to rectify these injustices? . . .

HISTORICAL PRINCIPLES AND END-RESULT PRINCIPLES

The general outlines of the entitlement theory illuminate the nature and defects of other conceptions of distributive justice. The entitlement theory of justice in distribution is *historical*; whether a distribution is just depends upon how it came about. In contrast, *current time-slice principles* of justice hold that the justice of a distribution is determined by how things are distributed (who has what) as judged by some *structural* principle(s) of just distribution. A utilitarian who judges between any two distributions by seeing which has the greater sum of utility and, if the sums tie, applies some fixed equality criterion to choose the more equal distribution, would hold a current time-slice principle of justice. As would someone who had a fixed schedule of trade-offs between the sum of happiness and equality. According to a current time-slice principle, all that needs to be looked at, in judging the justice of a distribution, is who ends up with what; in comparing any two distributions one need look only at the matrix presenting the distributions. No further information need be fed into a principle of justice. It is a consequence of such principles of justice that any two structurally identical distributions are equally just. . . .

Most persons do not accept current time-slice principles as constituting the whole story about distributive shares. They think it relevant in assessing the justice of a situation to consider not only the distribution it embodies, but also how that distribution came about. If some persons are in prison for murder or war crimes, we do not say that to assess the justice of the distribution in the society we must look only at what this person has, and that person has, and that person has, . . . at the current time. We think it relevant to ask whether someone did something so that he deserved to be punished, *deserved* to have a lower share. . . .

PATTERNING

. . . Almost every suggested principle of distributive justice is patterned: to each according to his moral merit, or needs, or marginal product, or how hard he tries, or the weighted sum of the foregoing, and so on. The principle of entitlement we have sketched is *not* patterned. There is no one natural dimension or weighted sum or combination of a small number of natural dimensions that yields the distributions generated in accordance with the principle of entitlement. The set of holdings that results when some persons receive their marginal products, others win at gambling, others receive a share of their mate's income, others receive gifts from foundations, others receive interest on loans, others receive gifts from admirers, others receive returns on investment, others make for themselves much of what they have, others find things, and so on, will not be patterned. . . .

To think that the task of a theory of distributive justice is to fill in the blank in "to each according to his _____" is to be predisposed to search for a pattern; and the separate treatment of "from each according to his _____" treats production and distribution as two separate and independent issues. On an entitlement view these are *not* two separate questions. Whoever makes something, having bought or contracted for all other held resources used in the process (transferring some of his holdings for these cooperating factors), is entitled to it. . . .

So entrenched are maxims of the usual form that perhaps we should present the entitlement conception as a competitor. Ignoring acquisition and rectification, we might say:

> From each according to what he chooses to do, to each according to what he makes for himself (perhaps with the contracted aid of others) and what others choose to do for him and choose to give him of what they've been given previously (under this maxim) and haven't yet expended or transferred.

This, the discerning reader will have noticed, has its defects as a slogan. So as a summary and great simplification (and not as a maxim with any independent meaning) we have:

> *From each as they choose, to each as they are chosen.*

HOW LIBERTY UPSETS PATTERNS

It is not clear how those holding alternative conceptions of distributive justice can reject the entitlement conception of justice in holdings. For suppose a distribution favored by one of these non-entitlement conceptions is realized. Let us suppose it is your favorite one and let us call this distribution D_1; perhaps everyone has an equal share, perhaps shares vary in accordance with some dimension you treasure. Now suppose that Wilt Chamberlain is greatly in demand by basketball teams, being a great gate attraction. (Also suppose contracts run only for a year, with players being free agents). He signs the following sort of contract with a team: In each home game, twenty-five cents from the price of each ticket of admission goes to him. (We ignore the question of whether he is "gouging" the owners, letting them look out for themselves.) The season starts, and people cheerfully attend his team's games; they buy their tickets, each time dropping a separate twenty-five cents of their admission price into a special box with Chamberlain's name on it. They are excited about seeing him play; it is worth the total admission price to them. Let us suppose that in one season one million persons attend his home games, and Wilt Chamberlain winds up with $250,000, a much larger sum than the average income and larger even than anyone else has. Is he entitled to this income? Is this new distribution D_2, unjust? If so, why? There is *no* question about whether each of the people was entitled to the control over the resources they held in D_1; because that was the distribution (your favorite) that (for the purposes of argument) we assumed was acceptable. Each of these persons *chose* to give twenty-five cents of their money to Chamberlain. They could have spent it on going to the movies, or on candy bars, or on copies of *Dissent* magazine, or of *Monthly Review*. But they all, at least one million of them, converged on giving it to Wilt Chamberlain in exchange for watching him play basketball. If D_1 was a just distribution, and people voluntarily moved from it to D_2, transferring parts of their shares they were given under D_1 (what was it for if not to do something with?), isn't D_2 also just? If the people were entitled to dispose of the resources to which they were entitled (under D_1) didn't this include their being entitled to give it to, or exchange it with, Wilt Chamberlain? Can anyone else complain on grounds of justice? Each other person already has his legitimate share under D_1. Under D_1, there is nothing that anyone has that anyone else has a claim of justice against. After someone transfers something to Wilt Chamberlain, third parties *still* have their legitimate shares; *their* shares are not changed. By what process could such a transfer among two persons give a rise to a legitimate claim of distributive justice on a portion of what was transferred, by a third party who had no claim of justice on any holding of the others *before* the transfer? To cut off objections irrelevant here, we might imagine the exchanges occurring in a socialist society, after hours. After playing whatever basketball he does in his daily work, or doing whatever other daily work he does, Wilt Chamberlain decides to put in *overtime* to earn additional money. (First his work quota is set; he works time over that.) Or imagine it is a skilled juggler people like to see, who puts on shows after hours. . . .

The general point illustrated by the Wilt Chamberlain example is that no end-state principle or distributional patterned principle of justice can be continuously realized without continuous interference with

people's lives. Any favored pattern would be transformed into one unfavored by the principle, by people choosing to act in various ways; for example, by people exchanging goods and services with other people, or giving things to other people, things the transferrers are entitled to under the favored distributional pattern. To maintain a pattern one must either continually interfere to stop people from transferring resources as they wish to, or continually (or periodically) interfere to take from some person's resources that others for some reason chose to transfer to them. . . .

Patterned principles of distributive justice necessitate *re*distributive activities. The likelihood is small that any actual freely-arrived-at set of holdings fits a given pattern; and the likelihood is nil that it will continue to fit the pattern as people exchange and give. From the point of view of an entitlement theory, redistribution is a serious matter indeed, involving, as it does, the violation of people's rights. (An exception is those takings that fall under the principle of the rectification of injustices.) . . .

LOCKE'S THEORY OF ACQUISITION

. . . [Let us] introduce an additional bit of complexity into the structure of the entitlement theory. This is best approached by considering Locke's attempt to specify a principle of justice in acquisition. Locke views property rights in an unowned object as originating through someone's mixing his labor with it. This gives rise to many questions. What are the boundaries of what labor is mixed with? If a private astronaut clears a place on Mars, has he mixed his labor with (so that he comes to own) the whole planet, the whole uninhabited universe, or just a particular plot? Which plot does an act bring under ownership? . . .

Locke's proviso that there be "enough and as good left in common for others" is meant to ensure that the situation of others is not worsened. . . .

. . . I assume that any adequate theory of justice in acquisition will contain a proviso similar to [Locke's]. . . .

I believe that the free operation of a market system will not actually run afoul of the Lockean proviso. . . . If this is correct, the proviso will not . . . provide a significant opportunity for future state action.

Rich and Poor

Peter Singer

One way of making sense of the non-consequentialist view of responsibility is by basing it on a theory of rights of the kind proposed by John Locke or, more recently, Robert Nozick. If everyone has a right to life, and this right is a right *against* others who might threaten my life, but not a right *to* assistance from others when my life is in danger, then we can understand the feeling that we are responsible for acting to kill but not for omitting to save. The former violates the rights of others, the latter does not.

Should we accept such a theory of rights? If we build up our theory of rights by imagining, as Locke and Nozick do, individuals living independently from each other in a 'state of nature', it may seem natural to adopt a conception of rights in which as long as each leaves the other alone, no rights are violated. I might, on this view, quite properly have maintained my independent existence if I had wished to do so. So if I do not make you any worse off than you would have been if I had had nothing at all to do with you, how can I have violated your rights? But why start from such an unhistorical, abstract and ultimately inexplicable idea as an independent individual? We now know that our ancestors were social beings long before they were

human beings, and could not have developed the abilities and capacities of human beings if they had not been social beings first. In any case we are not, now, isolated individuals. If we consider people living together in a community, it is less easy to assume that rights must be restricted to rights against interference. We might, instead, adopt the view that taking rights to life seriously is incompatible with standing by and watching people die when one could easily save them. . . .

THE OBLIGATION TO ASSIST

The Argument for an Obligation to Assist

The path from the library at my university to the Humanities lecture theatre passes a shallow ornamental pond. Suppose that on my way to give a lecture I notice that a small child has fallen in and is in danger of drowning. Would anyone deny that I ought to wade in and pull the child out? This will mean getting my clothes muddy, and either cancelling my lecture or delaying it until I can find something dry to change into; but compared with the avoidable death of a child this is insignificant.

From Peter Singer, "Rich and Poor," in *Practical Ethics* (New York: Cambridge University Press, 1979), pp. 166, 168–179. Reprinted with permission of the publisher.

A plausible principle that would support the judgment that I ought to pull the child out is this: if it is in our power to prevent something very bad happening, without thereby sacrificing anything of comparable moral significance, we ought to do it. This principle seems uncontroversial. It will obviously win the assent of consequentialists; but non-consequentialists should accept it too, because the injunction to prevent what is bad applies only when nothing comparably significant is at stake. Thus the principle cannot lead to the kinds of actions of which non-consequentialists strongly disapprove — serious violations of individual rights, injustice, broken promises, and so on. If a non-consequentialist regards any of these as comparable in moral significance to the bad thing that is to be prevented, he will automatically regard the principle as not applying in those cases in which the bad thing can only be prevented by violating rights, doing injustice, breaking promises, or whatever else is at stake. Most non-consequentialists hold that we ought to prevent what is bad and promote what is good. Their dispute with consequentialists lies in their insistence that this is not the sole ultimate ethical principle: that it is *an* ethical principle is not denied by any plausible ethical theory.

Nevertheless the uncontroversial appearance of the principle that we ought to prevent what is bad when we can do so without sacrificing anything of comparable moral significance is deceptive. If it were taken seriously and acted upon, our lives and our world would be fundamentally changed. For the principle applies, not just to rare situations in which one can save a child from a pond, but to the everyday situations in which we can assist those living in absolute poverty. In saying this I assume that absolute poverty, with its hunger and malnutrition, lack of shelter, illiteracy, disease, high infant mortality and low life expectancy, is a bad thing. And I assume that it is within the power of the affluent to reduce absolute poverty, without sacrificing anything of comparable moral significance. If these two assumptions and the principle we have been discussing are correct, we have an obligation to help those in absolute poverty which is no less strong than our obligation to rescue a drowning child from a pond. Not to help would be wrong, whether or not it is intrinsically equivalent to killing. Helping is not, as conventionally thought, a charitable act which it is praiseworthy to do, but not wrong to omit; it is something that everyone ought to do.

This is the argument for an obligation to assist. Set out more formally, it would look like this.

First premise: If we can prevent something bad without sacrificing anything of comparable significance, we ought to do it.

Second premise: Absolute poverty is bad.

Third premise: There is some absolute poverty we can prevent without sacrificing anything of comparable moral significance.

Conclusion: We ought to prevent some absolute poverty.

The first premise is the substantive moral premise on which the argument rests, and I have tried to show that it can be accepted by people who hold a variety of ethical positions.

The second premise is unlikely to be challenged. Absolute poverty is, as [Robert] McNamara put in, "beneath any reasonable definition of human decency" and it would be hard to find a plausible ethical view which did not regard it as a bad thing.

The third premise is more controversial, even though it is cautiously framed. It claims only that some absolute poverty can be prevented without the sacrifice of anything of comparable moral significance. It thus avoids the objection that any aid I can give is just 'drops in the ocean' for the point is not whether my personal contribution will make any noticeable impression on world poverty as a whole (of course it won't) but whether it will prevent some poverty. This is all the argument needs to sustain its conclusion, since the second premise says that any absolute poverty is bad, and not merely the total amount of absolute poverty. If without sacrificing anything of comparable moral significance we can provide just one family with the means to raise itself out of absolute poverty, the third premise is vindicated.

I have left the notion of moral significance unexamined in order to show that the argument does not depend on any specific values or ethical principles. I think the third premise is true for most people living in industrialized nations, on any defensible view of what is morally significant. Our affluence means that we have income we can dispose of without giving up the basic necessities of life, and we can use this income to reduce absolute poverty. Just how much we will think ourselves obliged to give up will depend on what we consider to be of comparable moral significance to the poverty we could prevent: colour television, stylish clothes, expensive dinners, a sophisticated stereo system, overseas holidays, a (second?) car, a larger house, private schools for our children. . . . For a utilitarian, none of these is likely to be of comparable significance to the reduction of absolute poverty; and those who are not utilitarians surely must, if they subscribe to the principle of universalizability, accept that at least *some* of these things are of far less moral significance than the absolute poverty that could be prevented by the money they cost. So the third premise seems to be true on any plausible ethical view — although the precise amount of absolute poverty that can be prevented before anything of moral significance is sacrificed will vary according to the ethical view one accepts.

Objections to the Argument

Taking Care of Our Own. Anyone who has worked to increase overseas aid will have come across the argument that we should look after those near us, our families and then the poor in our own country, before we think about poverty in distant places.

No doubt we do instinctively prefer to help those who are close to us. Few could stand by and watch a child drown; many can ignore a famine in Africa. But the question is not what we usually do, but what we ought to do, and it is difficult to see any sound moral justification for the view that distance, or community membership, makes a crucial difference to our obligations.

Consider, for instance, racial affinities. Should whites help poor whites before helping poor blacks? Most of us would reject such a suggestion out of hand, [by appeal to] the principle of equal consideration of interests: people's needs for food has nothing to do with their race, and if blacks need food more than whites, it would be a violation of the principle of equal consideration to give preference to whites.

The same point applies to citizenship or nationhood. Every affluent nation has some relatively poor citizens, but absolute poverty is limited largely to the poor nations. Those living on the streets of Calcutta, or in a drought-stricken region of the Sahel, are experiencing poverty unknown in the West. Under these circumstances it would be wrong to decide that only those fortunate enough to be citizens of our own community will share our abundance.

We feel obligations of kinship more strongly than those of citizenship. Which parents could give away their last bowl of rice if their own children were starving? To do so would seem unnatural, contrary to our nature as biologically evolved beings — although whether it would be wrong is another question altogether. In any case, we are not faced with that situation, but with one in which our own children are well-fed, well-clothed, well-educated, and would now like new bikes, a stereo set, or their own car. In these circumstances any special obligations we might have to our children have been fulfilled, and the needs of strangers make a stronger claim upon us.

The element of truth in the view that we should first take care of our own, lies in the advantage of a recognized system of responsibilities. When families and local communities look after their own poorer members, ties of affection and personal relationships achieve ends that would otherwise require a large, impersonal bureaucracy. Hence it would be absurd to propose that from now on we all regard ourselves as equally responsible for the welfare of everyone in the world; but the argument for an obligation to assist does not propose that. It applies only when some are in absolute poverty, and others can help without sacrificing anything of comparable moral significance. To allow one's own kin to sink into absolute poverty would be to sacrifice something of comparable significance; and before that point had been reached, the breakdown of the system of family and community responsibility would be a factor to weigh the balance in favour of a small degree of preference for family and community. This small degree of preference is, however, decisively outweighed by existing discrepancies in wealth and property.

Property Rights. Do people have a right to private property, a right which contradicts the view that they are under an obligation to give some of their wealth away to those in absolute poverty? According to some theories of rights (for instance, Robert Nozick's) provided one has acquired one's property without the use of unjust means like force and fraud, one may be entitled to enormous

wealth while others starve. This individualistic conception of rights is in contrast to other views, like the early Christian doctrine to be found in the works of Thomas Aquinas, which holds that since property exists for the satisfaction of human needs, "whatever a man has in superabundance is owed, of natural right, to the poor for their sustenance." A socialist would also, of course, see wealth as belonging to the community rather than the individual, while utilitarians, whether socialist or not, would be prepared to override property rights to prevent great evils.

Does the argument for an obligation to assist others therefore presuppose one of these other theories of property rights, and not an individualistic theory like Nozick's? Not necessarily. A theory of property rights can insist on our *right* to retain wealth without pronouncing on whether the rich *ought* to give to the poor. Nozick, for example, rejects the use of compulsory means like taxation to redistribute income, but suggests that we can achieve the ends we deem morally desirable by voluntary means. So Nozick would reject the claim that rich people have an "obligation" to give to the poor, in so far as this implies that the poor have a right to our aid, but might accept that giving is something we ought to do and failure to give, though within one's rights, is wrong — for rights is not all there is to ethics.

The argument for an obligation to assist can survive, with only minor modifications, even if we accept an individualistic theory of property rights. In any case, however, I do not think we should accept such a theory. It leaves too much to chance to be an acceptable ethical view. For instance, those whose forefathers happened to inhabit some sandy wastes around the Persian Gulf are now fabulously wealthy, because oil lay under those sands; while those whose forefathers settled on better land south of the Sahara live in absolute poverty, because of drought and bad harvests. Can this distribution be acceptable from an impartial point of view? If we imagine ourselves about to begin life as a citizen of either Kuwait or Chad — but we do not know which — would we accept the principle that citizens of Kuwait are under no obligation to assist people living in Chad?

Population and the Ethics of Triage. Perhaps the most serious objection to the argument that we have an obligation to assist is that since the major cause of absolute poverty is overpopulation, helping those now in poverty will only ensure that yet more people are born to live in poverty in the future.

In its most extreme form, this objection is taken to show that we should adopt a policy of "triage." The term comes from medical policies adopted in wartime. With too few doctors to cope with all the casualties, the wounded were divided into three categories: those who would probably survive without medical assistance, those who might survive if they received assistance, but otherwise probably would not, and those who even with medical assistance probably would not survive. Only those in the middle category were given medical assistance. The idea, of course, was to use limited medical resources as effectively as possible. For those in the first category, medical treatment was not strictly necessary; for those in the third category, it was likely to be useless. It has been suggested that we should apply the same policies to countries, according to their prospects of becoming self-sustaining. We would not aid countries which even without our help will soon be able to feed their populations. We would not aid countries which, even with our help, will not be able to limit their population to a level they can feed. We would aid those countries where our help might make the difference between success and failure in bringing food and population into balance.

Advocates of this theory are understandably reluctant to give a complete list of the countries they would place into the 'hopeless' category; but Bangladesh is often cited as an example. Adopting the policy of triage would, then, mean cutting off assistance to Bangladesh and allowing famine, disease and natural disasters to reduce the population of that country (now around 80 million) to the level at which it can provide adequately for all.

In support of this view Garrett Hardin has offered a metaphor: we in the rich nations are like the occupants of a crowded lifeboat adrift in a sea full of drowning people. If we try to save the drowning by bringing them aboard our boat will be overloaded and we shall all drown. Since it is better that some survive than none, we should leave the others to drown. In the world today, according to Hardin, "lifeboat ethics" apply. The rich should leave the poor to starve, for otherwise the poor will drag the rich down with them. . . .

Anyone whose initial reaction to triage was not one of repugnance would be an unpleasant sort of person. Yet initial reactions based on strong feelings are not always reliable guides. Advocates of triage are rightly concerned with the long-term consequences of our actions. They say that helping the poor and starving now merely ensures more poor and starving in the future. When our capacity to help is finally unable to cope — as one day it must be — the suffering will be greater than it would be if we stopped helping now. If this is correct, there is nothing we can do to prevent absolute starvation and poverty, in the long run, and so we have no obligation to assist. Nor does it seem reasonable to hold that under these circumstances people have a right to our assistance. If we do accept such a right, irrespective of the consequences, we are saying that, in Hardin's metaphor, we would continue to haul the drowning into our lifeboat until the boat sank and we all drowned.

If triage is to be rejected it must be tackled on its own ground, within the framework of consequentialist ethics. Here it is vulnerable. Any consequentialist ethics must take probability of outcome into account. A course of action that will certainly produce some benefit is to be preferred to an alternative course that may lead to a slightly larger benefit, but is equally likely to result in no benefit at all. Only if the greater magnitude of the uncertain benefit outweighs its uncertainty should we choose it. Better one certain unit of benefit than a 10 percent chance of 5 units; but better a 50 percent chance of 3 units than a single certain unit. The same principle applies when are we trying to avoid evils.

The policy of triage involves a certain, very great evil: population control by famine and disease. Tens of millions would die slowly. Hundreds of millions would continue to live in absolute poverty, at the very margin of existence. Against this prospect, advocates of the policy place a possible evil which is greater still: the same process of famine and disease, taking place in, say, fifty years time, when the world's population may be three times its present level, and the number who will die from famine, or struggle on in absolute poverty, will be that much greater. The question is: how probable is this forecast that continued assistance now will lead to greater disasters in the future?

Forecasts of population growth are notoriously fallible, and theories about the factors which affect it remain speculative. One theory, at least as plausible as any other, is that countries pass through a "demographic transition" as their standard of living rises. When people are very poor and have no access to modern medicine their fertility is high, but population is kept in check by high death rates. The introduction of sanitation, modern medical techniques and other improvements reduces the death rate, but initially has little effect on the birth rate. Then population grows rapidly. Most poor countries are now in this phase. If standards of living continue to rise, however, couples begin to realize that to have the same number of children surviving to maturity as in the past, they do not need to give birth to as many children as their parents did. The need for children to provide economic support in old age diminishes. Improved education and the emancipation and employment of women also reduce the birthrate, and so population growth begins to level off. Most rich nations have reached this stage, and their populations are growing only very slowly.

If this theory is right, there is an alternative to the disasters accepted as inevitable by supports of triage. We can assist poor countries to raise the living standards of the poorest members of their population. We can encourage the governments of these countries to enact land reform measures, improve education, and liberate women from a purely child-bearing role. We can also help other countries to make contraception and sterilization widely available. There is a fair chance that these measures will hasten the onset of the demographic transition and bring population growth down to a manageable level. Success cannot be guaranteed; but the evidence that improved economic security and education reduce population growth is strong enough to make triage ethically unacceptable. We cannot allow millions to die from starvation and disease when there is a reasonable probability that population can be brought under control without such horrors.

Population growth is therefore not a reason against giving overseas aid, although it should make us think about the kind of aid to give. Instead of food handouts, it may be better to give aid that hastens the demographic transition. This may mean agricultural assistance for the rural poor, or assistance with education, or the provision of contraceptive services. Whatever kind of aid proves most effective in specific circumstances, the obligation to assist is not reduced.

One awkward question remains. What should we do about a poor and already over-populated country which, for religious or nationalistic reasons, restricts the use of contraceptives and refuses to slow its population growth? Should we nevertheless offer development assistance? Or should we make our offer conditional on effective steps being taken to reduce the birthrate? To the latter course, some would object that putting conditions on aid is an attempt to impose our own ideas on independent sovereign nations.

So it is — but is this imposition unjustifiable? If the argument for an obligation to assist is sound, we have an obligation to reduce absolute poverty; but we have no obligation to make sacrifices that, to the best of our knowledge, have no prospect of reducing poverty in the long run. Hence we have no obligation to assist countries whose governments have policies which will make our aid ineffective. This could be very harsh on poor citizens of these countries — for they may have no say in the government's policies — but we will help more people in the long run by using our resources where they are most effective.

Spheres of Justice

Michael Walzer

COMPLEX EQUALITY AND PLURALISM

Distributive justice is a large idea. It draws the entire world of goods within the reach of philosophical reflection. Nothing can be omitted; no feature of our common life can escape scrutiny. Human society is a distributive community. That's not all it is, but it is importantly that: we come together to share, divide, and exchange. We also come together to make the things that are shared, divided, and exchanged; but that very making — work itself — is distributed among us in a division of labor. My place in the economy, my standing in the political order, my reputation among my fellows, my material holdings: all these come to me from other men and women. It can be said that I have what I have rightly or wrongly, justly or unjustly; but given the range of distributions and the number of participants, such judgments are never easy.

The idea of distributive justice has as much to do with being and doing as with having, as much to do with production as with consumption, as much to do with identity and status as with land, capital, or personal possessions. Different political arrangements enforce, and different ideologies justify, different distributions of membership, power, honor, ritual eminence, divine grace, kinship and love, knowledge, wealth, physical security, work and leisure, rewards and punishments, and a host of goods more narrowly and materially conceived — food, shelter, clothing, transportation, medical care, commodities of every sort, and all the odd things (paintings, rare books, postage stamps) that human beings collect. And this multiplicity of goods is matched by a multiplicity of distributive procedures, agents, and criteria. There are such things as simple distributive systems — slave galleys, monasteries, insane asylums, kindergartens (though each of these, looked at closely, might show unexpected complexities); but no full-fledged human society has ever avoided the multiplicity. We must study it all, the goods and the distributions, in many different times and places.

There is, however, no single point of access to this world of distributive arrangements and ideologies. There has never been a universal medium of exchange. Since the decline of the barter economy, money has been the most common medium. But the old maxim according to which there are some things that money can't buy is not only normatively but also factually true. What should and should not be up for sale is something men and women always have to decide and have decided in many different ways. Throughout history, the market has been one of the most important mechanisms for the distribution of social goods; but it has never been, it nowhere is today, a complete distributive system.

Similarly, there has never been either a single decision point from which all distributions are controlled or a single set of agents making decisions. No state power has ever been so pervasive as to regulate all the patterns of sharing, dividing, and exchanging out of which a society takes shape. Things slip away from the state's grasp; new patterns are worked out — familial networks, black markets, bureaucratic alliances, clandestine political and religious organizations. State officials can tax, conscript, allocate, regulate, appoint, reward, punish, but they cannot capture the full range of goods or substitute themselves for every other agent of distribution. Nor can anyone else do that: there are market coups and cornerings, but there has never been a fully successful distributive conspiracy.

And finally, there has never been a single criterion, or a single set of interconnected criteria, for all distributions. Desert, qualification, birth and blood, friendship, need, free exchange, political loyalty, democratic decision: each has had its place, along with many others, uneasily coexisting, invoked by competing groups, confused with one another.

In the matter of distributive justice, history displays a great variety of arrangements and ideologies. But the first impulse of the philosopher is to resist the displays of history, the world of appearances, and to search for some underlying unity: a short list of basic goods, quickly abstracted to a single good; a single distributive criterion or an interconnected set; and the philosopher himself standing, symbolically at least, at a single decision point. I shall argue that to search for unity is to misunderstand the subject matter of distributive justice. Nevertheless, in some sense the philosophical impulse is unavoidable. Even if we choose pluralism, as I shall do, that choice still requires a coherent defense. There must be principles that justify the choice and set limits to it, for pluralism does not require us to endorse every proposed distributive criterion or to accept every would-be agent. Conceivably, there is a single principle and a single legitimate kind of pluralism. But this would still be a pluralism that encompassed a wide range of distributions. By contrast, the deepest assumption of most of the philosophers who have written about justice, from Plato onward, is that there is one, and only one, distributive system that philosophy can rightly encompass.

Today this system is commonly described as the one that ideally rational men and women would choose if they were forced to choose impartially, knowing nothing of their own situation, barred from making particularist claims, confronting an abstract set of goods.[1] If these constraints on knowing and claiming are suitably shaped, and if the goods are suitably defined, it is probably true that a singular conclusion can be produced. Rational men and women, constrained this way or that, will choose one, and only one, distributive system. But the force of that singular conclusion is not easy to measure. It is surely doubtful that those same men and women, if they were transformed into ordinary people, with a firm sense of their own identity, with their own goods in their hands, caught up in everyday troubles, would reiterate their hypothetical choice or even recognize it as their own. The problem is not, most importantly, with the particularism of interest, which philosophers have always assumed they could safely — that is, uncontroversially — set aside. Ordinary people can do that too, for the sake, say, of the public interest. The greater problem is with the particularism of history, culture, and membership. Even if they are committed to impartiality, the question most likely to arise in the minds of the members of a political community is not, What would rational individuals choose under universalizing conditions of such-and-such a sort? But rather, What would individuals like us choose, who are situated as we are, who share a culture and are determined to go on sharing it? And this is a question that is readily transformed into, What choices have we already made in the course of our common life? What understandings do we (really) share?

Justice is a human construction, and it is doubtful that it can be made in only one way. At any rate, I shall begin by doubting, and more than doubting, this standard philosophical assumption. The questions posed by the theory of distributive justice admit of a range of answers, and there is room within the range for cultural diversity and political choice. It's not only a matter of implementing some singular principle or set of principles in different historical settings. No one would deny that there is a range of morally permissible implementations. I want to argue for more than this: that the principles of justice are themselves pluralistic in form; that different social goods ought to be distributed for different reasons, in accordance with different procedures, by different agents; and that all these differences derive from different understandings of the social goods themselves — the inevitable product of historical and cultural particularism. . . .

MEMBERSHIP AND JUSTICE

The distribution of membership is not pervasively subject to the constraints of justice. Across a considerable range of the decisions that are made, states are simply free to take in strangers (or not) — much as they are free, leaving aside the claims of the needy, to share their wealth with foreign friends, to honor the achievements of foreign artists, scholars, and scientists, to choose their trading partners, and to enter into collective security arrangements with foreign states. But the right to choose an admissions policy is more basic than any of these, for it is not merely a matter of acting in the world, exercising sovereignty, and pursuing national interests. At stake here is the shape of the community that acts in the world, exercises sovereignty, and so on. Admission and exclusion are at the core of communal independence. They suggest the deepest meaning of self-determination. Without them, there could not be *communities of character,* historically stable, ongoing associations of men and women with some special commitment to one another and some special sense of their common life.[2]

But self-determination in the sphere of membership is not absolute. It is a right exercised, most often, by national clubs or families, but it is held in principle by territorial states. Hence it is subject both to internal decisions by the members themselves (*all* the members, including those who hold membership simply by right of place) and to the external principle of mutual aid. Immigration, then, is both a matter of political choice and moral constraint. Naturalization, by contrast, is entirely constrained: Every new immigrant, every refugee taken in, every resident and worker must be offered the opportunities of citizenship. If the community is so radically divided that a single citizenship is impossible, then its territory must be divided, too, before the rights of admission and exclusion can be exercised. For these rights are to be exercised only by the community as a whole (even if, in practice, some national majority dominates the decision making) and only with regard to foreigners, not by some members with regard to others. No community can be half-metic, half-citizen and claim that its admissions policies are acts of self-determination or that its politics is democratic.

The determination of aliens and guests by an exclusive band of citizens (or of slaves by masters, or women by men, or blacks by whites, or conquered peoples by their conquerors) is not communal freedom but oppression. The citizens are free, of course, to set up a club, make membership as exclusive as they like, write a constitution, and govern one another. But they can't claim territorial jurisdiction and rule over the people with whom they share the territory. To do this is to act outside their sphere, beyond their rights. It is a form of tyranny. Indeed, the rule of citizens over non-citizens, of members over strangers, is probably the most common form of tyranny in human history. . . .

FREE EXCHANGE

Free exchange is obviously open-ended; it guarantees no particular distributive outcome. At no point in any exchange process

plausibly called "free" will it be possible to predict the particular division of social goods that will obtain at some later point.[3] (It may be possible, however, to predict the general structure of the division.) In theory at least, free exchange creates a market within which all goods are convertible into all other goods through the neutral medium of money. There are no dominant goods and no monopolies. Hence the successive divisions that obtain will directly reflect the social meanings of the goods that are divided. For each bargain, trade, sale, and purchase will have been agreed to voluntarily by men and women who know what that meaning is, who are indeed its makers. Every exchange is a revelation of social meaning. By definition, then, no *x* will ever fall into the hands of someone who possesses *y*, merely because he possesses *y* and without regard to what *x* actually means to some other member of society. The market is radically pluralistic in its operations and its outcomes, infinitely sensitive to the meanings that individuals attach to goods. What possible restraints can be imposed on free exchange, then, in the name of pluralism?

But everyday life in the market, the actual experience of free exchange, is very different from what the theory suggests. Money, supposedly the neutral medium, is in practice a dominant good, and it is monopolized by people who possess a special talent for bargaining and trading — the green thumb of bourgeois society. Then other people demand a redistribution of money and the establishment of the regime of simple equality, and the search begins for some way to sustain that regime. But even if we focus on the first untroubled moment of simple equality — free exchange on the basis of equal shares — we will still need to set limits on what can be exchanged for what. For free exchange leaves distributions entirely in the hands of individuals, and social meanings are not subject, or are not always subject, to the interpretative decisions of individual men and women.

Consider an easy example, the case of political power. We can conceive of political power as a set of goods of varying value, votes, influence, offices, and so on. Any of these can be traded on the market and accumulated by individuals willing to sacrifice other goods. Even if the sacrifices are real, however, the result is a form of tyranny — petty tyranny, given the conditions of simple equality. Because I am willing to do without my hat, I shall vote twice; and you who value the vote less than you value my hat, will not vote at all. I suspect that the result is tyrannical even with regard to the two of us, who have reached a voluntary agreement. . . .

Free exchange is not a general criterion, but we will be able to specify the boundaries within which it operates only through a careful analysis of particular social goods. . . .

THE MARKETPLACE

There is a stronger argument about the sphere of money, the common argument of the defenders of capitalism: that market outcomes matter a great deal because the market, if it is free, gives to each person exactly what he deserves. The market rewards us all in accordance with the contributions we make to one another's well-being.[4] The goods and services we provide are valued by potential consumers in such-and-such a way, and these values are aggregated by the market, which determines the price we receive. And that price is our desert, for it expresses the only worth our goods and services can have, the worth they actually have for other people. But this is to misunderstand the meaning of desert. Unless there are standards of worth independent of what people want (and are willing to buy) at this or that moment in time, there can be no deserving-

ness at all. We would never know what a person deserved until we saw what he had gotten. And that can't be right.

Imagine a novelist who writes what he hopes will be a best seller. He studies his potential audience, designs his book to meet the current fashion. Perhaps he had to violate the canons of his art in order to do that, and perhaps he is a novelist for whom the violation was painful. He has stooped to conquer. Does he now deserve the fruits of his conquest? Does he deserve a conquest that bears fruit? His novel appears, let's say, during a depression when no one has money for books, and very few copies are sold; his reward is small. Has he gotten less than he deserves? (His fellow writers smile at his disappointment; perhaps that's what he deserves.) Years later, in better times, the book is reissued and does well. Has its author become more deserving? Surely desert can't hang on the state of the economy. There is too much luck involved here; talk of desert makes little sense. We would do better to say simply that the writer is entitled to his royalties, large or small.[5] He is like any other entrepreneur; he has bet on the market. It's a chancy business, but he knew that when he made the bet. He has a right to what he gets — after he has paid the costs of communal provision (he lives not only in the market but also in the city). But he can't claim that he has gotten less than he deserves, and it doesn't matter if the rest of us think that he has gotten more. The market doesn't recognize desert. Initiative, enterprise, innovation, hard work, ruthless dealing, reckless gambling, the prostitution of talent: All these are sometimes rewarded, sometimes not.

But the rewards that the market provides, when it provides them, are appropriate to these sorts of effort. The man or woman who builds a better mousetrap, or opens a restaurant and sells delicious blintzes, or does a little teaching on the side, is looking to earn money. And why not? No one would want to feed blintzes to strangers, day after day, merely to win their gratitude. Here in the world of the petty bourgeoisie, it seems only right that an entrepreneur, able to provide timely goods and services, should reap the rewards he had in mind when he went to work.

This is, indeed, a kind of "rightness" that the community may see fit to enclose and restrain. The morality of the bazaar belongs in the bazaar. The market is a zone of the city, not the whole of the city. But it is a great mistake, I think, when people worried about the tyranny of the market seek its entire abolition. It is one thing to clear the Temple of traders, quite another to clear the streets. The latter move would require a radical shift in our understanding of what material things are for and of how we relate to them and to other people through them. But the shift is not accomplished by the abolition; commodity exchange is merely driven underground; or it takes place in state stores, as in parts of Eastern Europe today, drearily and inefficiently.

The liveliness of the open market reflects our sense of the great variety of desirable things; and so long as that is our sense, we have no reason not to relish the liveliness. . . .

THE RELATIVITY AND THE NON-RELATIVITY OF JUSTICE

Justice is relative to social meanings. Indeed, the relativity of justice follows from the classic non-relative definition, giving each person his due, as much as it does from my own proposal, distributing goods for "internal" reasons. These are formal definitions that require, as I have tried to show, historical completion. We cannot say what is due to this person or that one until we know how these people relate to one another through the things they make and distribute. There cannot be a just society until there is a society; and the adjective *just* doesn't determine, it only modifies, the substantive life of the societies it describes. There are an infinite number of possible lives, shaped by an infinite number of possible cultures, religions, political arrangements, geographical conditions, and so on. A given society is just if its substantive life is lived in a certain way — that is, in a way faithful to the shared understandings of the members. . . .

We are (all of us) culture-producing creatures; we make and inhabit meaningful worlds. Since there is no way to rank and order these worlds with regard to their understanding of social goods, we do justice to actual men and women by respecting their particular creations. And they claim justice, and resist tyranny, by insisting on the meaning of social goods among themselves. Justice is rooted in the distinct understandings of places, honors, jobs, things of all sorts, that constitute a shared way of life. To override those understandings is (always) to act unjustly.

Just as one can describe a caste system that meets (internal) standards of justice, so one can describe a capitalist system that does the same thing. But now the description will have to be a great deal more complex, for social meanings are no longer integrated in the same way. It may be the case, as Marx says in the first volume of *Capital*, that the creation and appropriation of surplus value "is peculiar good fortune for the buyer [of labor power], but no injustice at all to the seller."[6] But this is by no means the whole story of justice and injustice in capitalist society. It will also be crucially important whether this surplus value is convertible, whether it purchases special privileges, in the law courts, or in the educational system, or in the spheres of office and politics. Since capitalism develops along with and actually sponsors a considerable differentiation of social goods, no account of buying and selling, no description of free exchange, can possibly settle the question of justice. We will need to learn a great deal about other distributive processes and about their relative autonomy from or integration into the market. The dominance of capital outside the market makes capitalism unjust.

The theory of justice is alert to differences, sensitive to boundaries. It doesn't follow from the theory, however, that societies are more just if they are more differentiated. Justice simply has more scope in such societies, because there are more distinct goods, more distributive principles, more agents, more procedures. And the more scope justice has, the more certain it is that complex equality will be the form that justice takes. Tyranny also has more scope. Viewed from the outside, from our own perspective, the Indian Brahmins look very much like tyrants — and so they will come to be if the understandings on which their high position is based cease to be shared. From the inside, however, things come to them naturally, as it were, by virtue of their ritual purity. They don't need to turn themselves into tyrants in order to enjoy the full range of social goods. Or, when they do turn themselves into tyrants, they merely exploit the advantages they already possess. But when goods are distinct and distributive spheres autonomous, that same enjoyment requires exertion, intrigue, and violence. This is the crucial sign of tyranny: a continual grabbing of things that don't come naturally, an unrelenting struggle to rule outside one's own company. . . .

JUSTICE IN THE TWENTIETH CENTURY

. . . Contemporary forms of egalitarian politics have their origin in the struggle against capitalism and the particular tyranny of money. And surely in the United States today it is the tyranny of money that most clearly invites resistance: property/power rather than power itself. But it is a common argument that without property/power, power itself is too dangerous. State officials will be tyrants, we are told, whenever their power is not balanced by the power of money. It follows, then, that capitalists will be tyrants whenever wealth is not balanced by a strong government. Or, in the alternative metaphor of American political science, political power and wealth must check one another: since armies of ambitious men and women push forward from one side of the boundary, what we require are similar armies pushing forward from the other side. John Kenneth Galbraith developed this metaphor into a theory of "countervailing powers."[7] There is also a competing argument according to which freedom is served only if the armies of capitalism are always and everywhere unopposed. But that argument can't be right, for it isn't only equality but freedom, too, that we defend when we block a large number of (the larger number of) possible exchanges. . . .

Money can buy power and influence, as it can buy office, education, honor, and so on, without radically coordinating the various distributive spheres and without eliminating alternative processes and agents. It corrupts distributions without transforming them; and then corrupt distributions coexist with legitimate ones, like prostitution alongside married love. But this is tyranny still, and it can make for harsh forms of domination. And if resistance is less heroic than in totalitarian states, it is hardly less important. . . .

The appropriate arrangements in our own society are those, I think, of a decentralized democratic socialism; a strong welfare state run, in part at least, by local and amateur officials; a constrained market; an open and demystified civil service; independent public schools; the sharing of hard work and free time; the protection of religious and familial life; a system of public honoring and dishonoring free from all considerations of rank or class; workers' control of companies and factories; a politics of parties, movements, meetings, and public debate. But institutions of this sort are of little use unless they are inhabited by men and women who feel at home within them and are prepared to defend them. It may be an argument against complex equality that it requires a strenuous defense — and a defense that begins while equality is still in the making. But this is also an argument against liberty. Eternal vigilance is the price of both.

EQUALITY AND SOCIAL CHANGE

Complex equality might look more secure if we could describe it in terms of the harmony, rather than the autonomy, of spheres. But social meanings and distributions are harmonious only in this respect: that when we see why one good has a certain form and is distributed in a certain way, we also see why another must be different. Precisely because of these differences, however, boundary conflict is endemic. The principles appropriate to the different spheres are not harmonious with one another; nor are the patterns of conduct and feeling they generate. Welfare systems and markets, offices and families, schools and states are run on different principles: so they should be. The principles must somehow fit together within a single culture; they must be comprehensible across the different companies of men and women. But this doesn't rule out deep strains and odd juxtapositions. Ancient China was ruled by a hereditary divineright emperor and a meritocratic bureaucracy. One has to tell a complex story to explain that sort of coexistence. A community's culture is the story its members tell so as to make sense of all the different pieces of their social life — and justice is the doctrine that distinguishes the pieces. In any differentiated society, justice will make for harmony only if it first makes for separation. Good fences make just societies.

We never know exactly where to put the fences; they have no natural location. The goods they distinguish are artifacts; as they were made, so they can be remade. Boundaries, then, are vulnerable to shifts in social meaning, and we have no choice but to live with the continual probes and incursions through which these shifts are worked out. Commonly, the shifts are like sea changes, very slow. . . . But the actual boundary revision, when it comes, is likely to come suddenly, as in the creation of a national health service in Britain after the Second World War: one year, doctors were professionals and entrepreneurs; and the next year, they were professionals and public servants. We can map a program of such revisions, based on our current understanding of social goods. We can set ourselves in opposition, as I have done, to the prevailing forms of dominance. But we can't anticipate the deeper changes in consciousness, not in our own community and certainly not in any other. The social world will one day look different from the way it does today, and distributive justice will take on a different character than it has for us. Eternal vigilance is no guarantee of eternity. . . .

NOTES

1. See John Rawls, *A Theory of Justice* (Cambridge, MA: 1971): Jürgen Habermas, *Legitimation Crisis,* trans. Thomas McCarthy (Boston: 1975), esp. p. 113; Bruce Ackerman, *Social Justice in the Liberal State* (New Haven, 1980).

2. I have taken the term "communities of character" from Otto Bauer (see *Austro-Marxism* [13], p. 107).

3. Cf. Nozick on "patterning," *Anarchy, State, and Utopia,* pp. 155 ff [this text, Chap 9].

4. See Louis O. Kelso and Mortimer J. Adler, *The Capitalist Manifesto* (New York: 1958), pp. 67–77, for an argument that makes the distribution of wealth on the basis of contribution analogous to the distribution of office on the basis of merit. Economists like Milton Friedman are more cautious, but this is surely the popular ideology of capitalism: success is a deserved reward for "intelligence, resolution, hard work, and a willingness to take risks" (George Gilder, *Wealth and Poverty* [New York: 1981], p. 101).

5. See Robert Nozick's distinction between entitlement and desert, *Anarchy, State, and Utopia* (New York: 1974), pp. 155–60.

6. Karl Marx, *Capital,* ed. Frederick Engels (New York, 1967), p. 194; I have followed the translation and interpretation of Allen W. Wood, "The Marxian Critique of Justice," *Philosophy and Public Affairs* 1 (1972): 263ff.

7. John Kenneth Galbraith, *American Capitalism* (Boston: 1956), chap. 9.

INTERNATIONAL ECONOMIC JUSTICE

Negotiating Justice

Richard T. DeGeorge

Basic to the ethics of international business is the task of determining what constitutes fair trade and fair practices. Rules, laws, agreements, and codes are needed, but what should these contain? In a global context that lacks adequate background institutions, what sense can be made of talk about justice? Just as one might ask "Whose ethics?" one might ask "Whose justice?" And although the answer "One's own" is a starting point, it cannot be the ending point: there are two sides to every transaction, and both should agree that the transaction is just.

Consider the denuding the Brazilian Amazon rain forest. That action affects not only Brazil but every other nation of the world, since all will be affected (and many adversely) by the resulting changes in climate. Should the decision to cut its forests be made only by the government of Brazil, only by the logging companies, only by the firms that purchase the lumber, only by the local farmers whose land can no longer support crops, or only by homesteaders who need wood for their houses? The decision is certainly a matter of interest to all of them. And unrestricted free enterprise imposes no limits on what companies might do in such a situation. Brazil — or at least some Brazilians — tends to see further deforestation as being in its economic interest, and it balks at being told that it cannot do with its own lands what the developed countries have already done with theirs. Yet other countries that are significantly affected clearly have a legitimate interest in this matter. Some have argued that, if other countries think that the forests are so important, they should buy them up and

From, *Competing with Integrity in International Business* Richard T. DeGeorge, (New York: Oxford University Press, 1993).

preserve them as parks, or they should otherwise provide Brazil with an attractive alternative to continued clear-cutting. If the free market cannot resolve the problem, negotiation is the only feasible approach — and one that may be aided by the action of intermediary organizations.

Neither the United States nor American multinational corporations are in a position to dictate what constitutes fairness in this and other international transactions. No country or group can or should dictate the rules of international commerce. Claims are often made about the dependence of the South on the North or of developing on developed countries. The demands raised a number of years ago for a New International Economic Order were considered unrealistic by most Northern countries, and consequently these demands have been largely ignored.

Yet if justice and fairness are central to the ethics of international business, then one country cannot decide unilaterally what practices and background institutions are fair or just. All interested parties must be allowed to have a say. Justice and fairness in international business relations are not the result of imposing a preconceived set of structures or ideals on the world. Rather, they are arrived at by negotiation in such a way that all interested and affected parties are represented and have a voice in deciding the rules that will govern the international business game. The dominant position enjoyed by the developed countries financially, technologically, and historically does not give them the right to set the rules. But neither does the relatively undeveloped condition of poor countries give them the right to dictate the terms of trade or loans or aid. Mutual negotiations are necessary. International structures that all parties perceive as fair must be worked out; they cannot be imposed by philosophers or businesspeople or government bureaucrats. Nations, industries, and corporations should

all have an opportunity for input and a voice in hammering out the new structures. It is as unfair to force policies on American multinational businesses as it is to force policies on poor countries or their local businesses. However, each must be willing to give up something. And in this regard U.S. businesses (and the U.S. government acting in business's behalf) have often been less flexible and more recalcitrant than is appropriate in a good-faith negotiation.

Ideally each transaction or case should be resolved in such a way that all affected groups and individuals believe that the resolution is just. Such a conclusion need not involve agreement by the participants on any particular notion of justice. Pluralism of principles, as we have seen, is compatible with agreement on practices, and it is the practices that produce the concrete results. Yet in order to resolve cases and to believe that justice has been done, each of the parties must have a conception of justice with which to assess the proposals under discussion. What is essential is to negotiate and compromise on issues of particular behavior in such a way that the results do not compromise one's principles or integrity.

In American society my beliefs about justice do not automatically justify my interfering with lawful practices that I happen to consider unjust. Many kinds of interaction are properly handled only through political institutions and procedures — that is, through a variety of background institutions. On the international or global level, issues of justice are even more complex. A first difficulty is that adequate background institutions, which normally provide touchstones for assessing what is fair or just in various negotiations or contracts, as well as the means for appeal in adjudicating disputes, are lacking. A second difficulty is that justice is always constituted within a system: it is a function of the accepted values and beliefs of the society in which it is found. In this sense, capitalist society has its own particular notion of justice, according to which (among other things) private property is justifiable. Justice within this system presupposes agreement on a background of accepted law, values, and beliefs. In a capitalist system disputes over property are adjudicated in an attempt to arrive at just results within the system. In a socialist society, the notion of justice rests on a different background of accepted law, values, and beliefs, yielding a socialist conception of justice. If this system establishes that private ownership of the means of production is unjust and illegal, the adjudication of competing claims about property in it will clearly differ from the adjudication of property claims in a capitalist society. Moreover, certain claims will be made in each of these systems that will not arise in the other. How to reconcile claims about property justly when the two systems interact — or when a country such as Poland switches from one system to the other — is a serious problem.

If we divide the world not according to their social structures but according to their level of development, we find certain aspects of justice common to industrially developed countries, and a different perspective on justice taken by developing countries.

From any given point of view, certain other systems and their practices might logically be condemned as unjust. If a socialist system of justice views private property as unjust, that claim does not carry much weight with people who live within the capitalist system — unless they can be persuaded that the socialist conception of justice is superior to the capitalist one. Because each theory of justice is substantively related to a set of practices, convincing others of the correctness of one's point of view most often involves prevailing on those persons to change some of their other beliefs and values. This is no easy task. Fortunately such conversions are not required for interactions between nations or between firms from different nations.

Protest and condemnation of what one believes to be another country's unjust internal policies are appropriate, and they may influence the views and beliefs of people living in that country. If a nation believes that the violation of justice is serious enough, it can move beyond issuing condemnations and forbear from dealing with the nation in question altogether. Thus, the United States, most European countries, and most African countries — which had long condemned South Africa for its apartheid policy — eventually imposed various economic sanctions on that country. If enough nations act likewise, they can ostracize an offending nation from the community of nations. Yet the doctrine of national sovereignty, if respected, limits the extent to which any nation can intervene in the internal affairs of another nation.

The need to have a mechanism for resolving disputes arises once interaction occurs. Since international justice involves equitable transactions between different nations and national firms, it assumes some common basis for the interaction. Nations interact commercially for their mutual benefit; each expects to gain by the transaction.

Given this complex situation of differing conceptions and systems of justice, how may firms achieve justice in their interactions? A fair assessment of existing conditions must serve as the starting point. Although vested interests dictate initial positions in any interaction in the international arena, reciprocity is the procedural key to justice.

Justice as reciprocity means that each of those subject to the contract, practice, institution, or system agrees to the justice of the contract, practice, institution, or system. The agreement of the parties here is not about what in theory constitutes justice but about the justness by their own standards of the contract or practice or institution. From a practical point of view, a contract is just if everyone who is party to it, armed with all the relevant information, agrees that it is just. Similarly, an institution is just if all representatives of the various groups that have a stake in the matter accept it as just. On the international level, reciprocity requires that all nations affected by a practice or involved in a transaction agree to its justness, whatever conception of justice they hold. This suggests that a program that aims at developing just practices and just international and global social structures has the best chance of success if it can elicit reciprocal agreement in support of its endeavors.

Two background conditions for achieving justice on the international level can be identified: true participative reciprocity, and acknowledgment of the formal equality of states in the context of international relations and international law. The additional background already developed by tradition, custom, and law forms a limited basis for speaking of international justice and for determining just and unjust behavior with respect to states. To the extent that nations accept these background conditions, the conditions form a cross-cultural basis for developing additional just international structures. Many Latin American states claim that the international economic system is unjust because it favors developed nations and makes less developed nations dependent on them and subordinate to them. Yet these less developed nations willingly acknowledge the justice of many individual transactions that they and their firms negotiate with other countries and their firms.

Exchange and trade are dominant forms of interaction among nations, and commutative justice governs such activities.[15] Whatever substantive differences may exist among the parties, based on their concepts of justice, commutative justice requires that equal be exchanged for equal and that those who enter into a transaction do so freely, with each seeking to secure its own good. If transactions are forced or take place at forced prices, they are unjust according to most theories of justice. Forced transactions are a form of exploitation, and if one state exploits another or if a multinational exploits a people or the resources of a state, claims for compensatory justice can be raised.

The component of reciprocity is essential in negotiating just commutative transactions. If two agents with different conceptions of justice wish to trade, and if their differing conceptions lead to different evaluations of the terms of the exchange, both must be willing to accept some accommodation of their positions, some agreement on terms, or some third position between the opposing positions. Otherwise, the transaction either will not take place or will be forced and so will be unjust.

Fortunately, moral pluralism seldom involves two countries' or traditions' holding opposite and nondiscretionary views of the morality of a particular action. Rarely does one side hold that an action is prohibited while the other holds that the very same action is obligatory. Most often what one side considers morally forbidden the other side considers morally permissible but not obligatory. In such cases, moral negotiation usually involves the latter country's accepting a restraint on its freedom to act in a way that it considers morally permissible. Thus, again, if an American firm wishes to operate in Saudi Arabia, it may have to enforce a ban on alcohol consumption by its employees. It (and they) may thus agree to a limitation of their freedom that their own morality does not require. Still, agreeing to abide by such a ban does not violate their principles. Similarly, suppose that an American company wishes to do business with a chemicals firm that tolerates a toxicity level at its plant that is harmful to the health of its employees. The American company may be willing to pay enough for the product so that the firm can bring its toxicity level down to an acceptably low level, and it may negotiate such conditions. Since it is extremely unlikely that the chemicals firm considers itself morally required to expose its workers to harmful conditions, such negotiations in no way violate the principles of the chemicals firm. On the contrary, they may enable the firm to do what it would have preferred but was financially unable to do.

Integrity requires fidelity to a personal sense of justice. This means that one cannot impose on others what one believes is unjust, even if they agree to the imposition, and that one cannot accept for oneself conditions that violate one's principles of justice. But neither of these criteria precludes accepting less than one thinks one deserves in absolute terms. Negotiation frequently consists precisely in each side's accepting less than each thinks it would receive in a perfect world, but not less than it thinks is fair under existing conditions. Just as this is true in national labor negotiations, so it is also true in international negotiations.

On the international level, their reasonably equal bargaining power prevents major states from forcing their terms on one another. This rough equality also provides the necessary background condition for arriving at a transaction that the parties agree is just, even if they make their judgments from different conceptions and theories of justice. The unanimous desire to avoid a nuclear war serves as a deterrent to any international act that would be perceived as so grossly unjust that it might provoke a nuclear confrontation. The mutual need for peace is the strongest incentive for cooperation in seeking what all sides consider a just solution to problems. Such state-to-state negotiations provide a framework within which individual commercial transactions can be worked out.

Cross-cultural divisions on the international scale include not only socialist versus capitalist, but rich versus poor, producer versus consumer, lender versus borrower, and more developed versus less developed. Countries lacking resources often make claims that are rejected by the developed countries, which feel that they have the right to their wealth, their resources, and the goods they produce. Chad had no greater claim to the oil produced in the Soviet Union than it had to the oil produced in the United States — even if Chad needed oil for its development. Any proprietary claim it might have made to American or Soviet resources would have met with the countervailing claims of these resource-rich countries that they had the right to use what they produced as they wished and to sell these products at prices they set. Similarly, less developed countries frequently claim that the conditions of trade worked out with more developed countries do not reflect true reciprocity.

What justice involves in trade, aid, defense, or other interactions between rich and poor countries is not a unilateral issue, even though unilateral judgments can be and are made. Differences in the judgments of parties cannot properly be resolved by expecting either side to adopt a different conception or theory of justice or by expecting the poor country to subordinate itself politically in service to one of the developed countries. Rather, a resolution should come about from negotiation on the terms of the transaction.

The pressure of argument, the appeal to moral values other than justice, the pressure of protest, the development of public and of world opinion, and the use of diplomatic, political, and economic pressure are all legitimate means of promoting negotiation between competing views. Negotiation over justice does not mean accommodation to injustice, as one sees injustice. It means widening one's perspective to recognize other claims to justice made from a conflicting perspective. On issues of internal national policy, no accommodation by other countries may be necessary, and an accepted modus vivendi may be mutually tolerated. Some issues, such as slavery, allow no accommodation by those who hold that slavery is unjust. On other issues, such as giving up some of the wealth that one claims to possess by right, or establishing institutions to foster global redistribution of wealth, accommodation does not involve acceding to injustice. The result of accommodation in appropriate cases comes close to an encompassing ideal of justice, mediated by actual conditions and less-than-ideal states of affairs.

International systems of justice can begin with negotiations between two states or among groups of states. Some of these, based on regional alliances, already exist. As these systems in turn interact, the net becomes broader. At its broadest the resulting single system would be truly global, comprising all states. But regardless of how many are involved, reciprocity requires that all affected states or parties agree to the justice of the terms.

This suggests that a just solution to the case of the Brazilian rainforest can only be achieved through negotiation and compromise by all parties whose interests are seriously affected. Those outside Brazil cannot expect Brazilians to forgo development and give up their right to manage their own resources. Brazilians cannot expect their actions — if they adversely affect others — to be simply ignored. A just solution will require imagination as well as negotiation. But only a settlement that all parties consider just will have any hope of permanently resolving the issue.

The Ethics of Conditionality in International Debt

Thomas Donaldson

Increasingly, international financial agencies such as the International Monetary Fund (IMF) and the World Bank lend money to developing countries under conditions that aim at economic reforms, a practice dubbed "conditionality." The standard characteristics of conditionality include restrictions on credit from the domestic banking system, currency devaluation, an agreement to liberalize the economy by removing trade restraints and internal economic controls, and the reduction of government deficits.

Let us begin by noting an oddity about such lending. If, as creditor institutions claim, the austerity typically associated with such conditionality is in the interest of the borrowing country, why then does the borrower so often object to it? One would expect a debtor to pay for good advice, not have to be enticed to accept it. This oddity not only draws attention to the fact that lenders and borrowers often disagree about the wisdom of given structural reform programs, but implies that global lenders who structure conditions are responsible for the shape and fairness of those conditions. The conditions imposed are, in the most important sense, *their* conditions. Being fair, in turn, requires a

From Thomas Donaldson, "The Ethics of Conditionality in International Debt," *Millennium: Journal of International Studies* 20, 2, 1991.

recognition of the distinction between the interests of those who contract for loans and those who suffer or succeed under their conditions, and while the very poor of a Third World country stand to be harmed or helped dramatically by austerity programs, their interests are seldom material factors in the loan approval process.

I will argue that:

> The economically least well off in a developing country ought not be made worse off, even in the short-to-medium term, as a result of conditions imposed as a part of an international loan arrangement made by an intergovernmental loan agency.

I mean by this that the economically least well off ought not be made worse off as a result of the conditions of the loan relative to the level of welfare they would have achieved without the loan. I shall defend the proposition in two ways: first, by appealing to the moral concept of justice, including Rawlsian constructions of distributive justice and the rights-respecting obligations entailed by the concept of justice; and, second, by appealing to the criterion of consistency in moral analysis. . . .

THE HISTORY OF THE PROBLEM

. . . The IMF has moved from a situation immediately following WW II when its mission was narrowly construed as one of encouraging liberal trade relations and making short term loans to handle balance of payments problems, as its formal charter prescribes, to one where issues of development are taken seriously. Indeed, the IMF has undergone a dramatic shift in its debtor portfolio, and is now frequently the lender of last resort for the developing world.

The reason for the shift lies primarily in the diminished sources of alternative funds. The shift to a floating currency market in the 1970s and other economic forces spawned credit and balance of payments problems precisely at a time when development funds of the World Bank were becoming scarcer.[1] Into the breach stepped the private banks, who, flush with oil money from the Arab states, by 1980 accounted for 80 percent of all loans to developing countries, in contrast to only 40 percent in 1970.[2]

When in 1982 Brazil and Mexico lost their creditworthiness, they and private banks turned to the IMF. The nations did so to obtain desperately needed funds; the banks to establish conditions that would help guarantee repayment of their loans. A global train of national defaults in the 1980s were followed by the imposition of new, creditor-imposed austerity measures. Real interest rates (i.e., interest rates adjusted for inflation) for much of Latin America exceeded 30 percent during the 1980s, rates at which most economists agree make growth difficult or impossible.[3] Debt repayments, constrained by increasing interest rates as well as austerity, loan-related conditions and worsening terms of trade (especially the lowering commodity prices for a developing country's exports), combined in the 1980s to give Latin America a dismal decade. . . .

Critics complain that because it is easier to cut the prerogatives of the politically weak, austerity programs in Latin America and elsewhere have a disproportionate and negative impact upon the poor.[4] Demand control policies are subject to the obvious objection that when demand is curtailed, the rich and middle class can give up inessentials, while the poor are left to their own resources. There is no doubt that debt puts enormous pressure on governments to cut welfare programs, and when governments fail to meet IMF specified criteria, the Fund is capable of responding quickly.

Criticism of structural adjustment occurs in a context of adjustment programs' growing adherence to free market development strategy. A Fund sponsored study of nine IMF adjustment programs in seven countries[5] revealed that most of the programs contained: "fiscal policies designed to reduce government deficits; monetary and credit policies to restrain domestic credit expansion . . . ; exchange rate policies, combined with domestic pricing policies . . . ; and labor market policies to restrain real wages in the organized sector, and increase the flexibility of wages and labor markets."[6] Structural reform is encouraged through the IMF's Extended Fund Facility. It augments the Fund's old standby arrangements, and allows repayment schedules to be extended to as long as six years (in contrast to the six months-to-a-year format of the standby arrangements) and thus accommodates medium-term, structural reform programs.

During the 1980s the tone of the IMF's response to criticism of austerity programs shifted. In the early 1980s the Fund insisted that issues of distribution were improper objects of its concern, since it dealt with sovereign countries, who were formally responsible for such matters. But recent IMF publications indicate a willingness at least to study distributive issues and to provide the results of its findings to prospective loan recipients. Nevertheless, the Fund has not backed away from its insistence that distributive concerns are ultimately the sole business of the nation state.

The Fund's literature tends to justify austerity programs' impact on the economically least well off in two ways: first, by noting that even short term negative results for the economically least well off, in the context of reasonable economic restructuring, may well bring long-term benefits; and, second, by denying that the short term negative impacts are as severe as critics have claimed. Yet even Fund believers who insist that adjust-

ment programs play a positive role in protecting the long-term interests of the poor, grant that in the short run the poor frequently suffer — and the short term can be devastating.[7]

Let us grant the IMF's denial that short term impact upon the economically least well off is invariably negative. In some countries, for example, small farmers dominate the agricultural scene and are helped by the expanded opportunities brought by either devaluation (in foreign markets) or the removal of price controls. . . . [But] in claiming that the economically least well off of a third world country ought not to suffer, even in the short term as a result of conditions imposed as a part of an international loan arrangement, it is important to specify that this means they ought not be made worse off as a result of the conditions of the loan *relative to the level of welfare they would have achieved without the loan.*

MORAL THEORY

One way of criticizing debt programs is by pointing to their politically destabilizing effects. But this misses the more fundamental moral issue confronting major lending organizations, namely, how do we frame such obligations regardless of political vicissitudes? Also, interestingly enough, recent analysis suggests that the political case against austerity conditions may be overstated. In recent research, Scott Sidell argues that there is no compelling evidence to assert that political instability on average increases in the face of mounting debt and debt conditionality.[8]

Instead, we can find support for the proposition under consideration by appealing to two uniquely moral concepts, namely, that of justice, including distributive justice, and moral consistency.

GENERAL JUSTICE CONSIDERATIONS

We may presume that, at a minimum, any theory of justice will also be a theory which entails that bona fide rights be respected. . . .

Let us use [a] list of fundamental international rights for which I have recently argued, namely:[9]

1. The right to freedom of physical movement
2. The right to ownership of property
3. The right to freedom from torture
4. The right to a fair trial
5. The right to non-discriminatory treatment (i.e., freedom from discrimination on the basis of such characteristics as race or sex.)
6. The right to physical security
7. The right to freedom of speech and association
8. The right to minimal education
9. The right to political participation
10. The right to subsistence

. . . Every right entails a duty, that is, every right entails that other persons and institutions not violate the right. But correlative duties involve more than failing to actively deprive people of the enjoyment of their rights. Shue, for example, notes that three types of correlative duties are possible for any right, namely duties to 1) avoid depriving; 2) help protect from deprivation; and 3) aid the deprived.[10] While it is obvious that the honoring of rights clearly imposes duties of the first kinds, i.e., to avoid depriving directly, it is less obvious, but frequently true, that honoring them involves acts or omissions that help prevent the deprivation of rights. As I have argued elsewhere, multinational corporations have obligations primarily of the first and second kind, while governments have obligations of all three kinds. For example, a multinational corporation has an obligation not to bribe a high government official because it

has an obligation to help protect the right to political participation; and it has an obligation to refrain from hiring eight year old children for permanent, full time labor because it has an obligation to help protect the right to a minimal education. In both instances, the corporation's possible direct denial of the rights to political participation and minimal education is not at issue. What is at issue, rather, is the organization's correlative obligation to protect the rights from deprivation.

Similarly, governmental organizations have a moral obligation frequently to aid the deprived, i.e., the third category of obligation. If citizens are starving to death, most would agree that the local national government is obliged to step in and provide food, at least insofar as it is capable. And if citizens are denied even a minimal education, the government must similarly do what it can to provide one.

The very moral status of an international organization such as the World Bank or the IMF is ambiguous. One might argue that its functions resemble that of private banks to a point where its responsibilities should mirror those of private, not government, institutions. Yet surely this view neglects the obvious fact that these organizations are composed entirely of member nation-states that are themselves government bodies. Hence, in at least one important sense, both bodies are governmental organizations. Space prevents us from undertaking a thoroughgoing discussion of the issue of the moral status of international lending agencies, and, instead, I propose to nuance it by noting that for purposes of assigning moral status, such agencies are partially, but perhaps not wholly, to be understood as government entities. This means that they are at least responsible for shouldering the correlative obligations attaching to rights that are appropriate for private banks (of the first and second kind), and are also responsible for shouldering *some* correlative obligations appropriate to government agencies (of the third kind), although we shall leave unspecified for present purposes what those duties are.

It follows that the IMF and the World Bank have obligations to refrain from directly depriving people of their rights, as well as, in some instances, to help protect such rights from deprivation. In turn, it follows that any loan arrangement which has the effect of depriving or of failing adequately to protect the economically least well off of a given country of their right to subsistence, or their right to a minimal education, is an arrangement that is unjust, and which ought not be undertaken. I follow Henry Shue in defining the right to subsistence as a right to "minimal economic security," entailing, in turn, a right to, e.g., "unpolluted air, unpolluted water, adequate food, adequate clothing, adequate shelter, and minimal preventative public health care."[11] While what counts as a "minimally sufficient" education may be debated, and while it seems likely, moreover, that the specification of the right to a certain level of education will depend at least in part upon the level of economic resources available in a given country, it is reasonable to assume that any action by a corporation which has the effect of, say, blocking the development of a child's ability to read or write will be morally proscribed on the basis of rights.

Hence, we can say that at a minimum the IMF should refuse to engage in an arrangement that will result in conditions in which the economically least well off are unable to possess adequate food, adequate clothing, minimal education, and minimal preventative public health care. This is a simple requirement of justice, and has obvious application to international lending policies. For in many of the poor debtor countries, the economically least well off, if made still worse off, will fall or stay below levels of adequate education and subsistence.

DISTRIBUTIVE JUSTICE CONSIDERATION

The issue of distributive justice is trickier than that of general justice. Distributive justice, a concept which refers to justice in the distribution of goods, may appear to be irrelevant in international contexts. Indeed, it is not uncommon to hear that while justice in the distribution of key goods such as wealth, food, or health care, is an appropriate topic for national contexts, it is not for international contexts. The recent and monumental analysis of distributive justice undertaken by John Rawls[12] explicitly exempts international considerations from the reach of his famous two principles, i.e., (1) that everyone is entitled to maximal liberty, and (2) that inequalities in the distribution of primary goods are unjust unless everyone, including the average person in the worst affected group, stands to benefit. Rawls's reasons for nationalizing distributive justice are tied to his belief that distributive claims can be evaluated meaningfully only against a background scheme of cooperation that yields goods subject to distribution. Since nation-states are customarily the agents that provide the mechanisms necessary for facilitating cooperative arrangements and for pooling and distributing the fruits of such arrangements, and since such mechanisms are conspicuously not provided on the international scale, it seems both idealistic and implausible to speak seriously of distributive justice on an international scale.

Rawls's underlying reasons stem from the notion of the "circumstances of justice" articulated by the English philosopher, David Hume. . . . Hume argued that people usually find themselves in circumstances manifesting four general characteristics which limit the possibility of justice: dependence, moderate scarcity, restrained benevolence, and individual vulnerability. Rawls refers to the circumstances of justice as "the normal conditions under which human cooperation is both possible and necessary," and gives special attention to the condition of dependence and of moderate scarcity, the latter of which he defines as the existence of natural resources "not so abundant that schemes of cooperation become superfluous," nor "conditions so harsh that fruitful ventures must inevitably break down."[13] He explicitly denies that the former characterizes international relations in a way to make the two principles generally relevant, and he may wish to deny in the instance of some third world nations that the latter is applicable.

In the end, however, it seems clear that considerations of distributive justice do apply to international transactions such as lending to poor countries. To begin with, Rawls may be wrong about the scope of his own theory. As Brian Barry often notes, no scheme of cooperation need exist in order to demonstrate the unjustness of allowing toxic air pollution, generated in one country for the benefit of that country, to waft over into the unpolluted atmosphere of a second country.[14]. . .

Hence, one is brought to wonder whether the so-called circumstances of justice are, in truth, necessary either for the meaningful application of such terms as "just" and "unjust," or for the existence of just institutions. For example, it seems at first glance that if people have either an extravagant abundance of material goods, or an extreme scarcity, then issues of justice will not arise. But first impressions may be misleading. Suppose an extravagant abundance of material goods exists; might not questions of justice nonetheless arise over, say, the bestowing of awards in public contests, or in structuring systems of seniority and status? Or, alternatively, suppose that a dramatic scarcity of goods exists. Might not questions of justice arise in determining, say, who should be utterly deprived in order for others to survive?

Yet, even if Rawls were correct in limiting the *general* application of the two principles in the international realm on the grounds of insufficient interdependence, two considerations show that distributive justice is applicable in the specific instance of international loan arrangements. First, the important distribution issues affecting developing countries do not depend on *inter*-national distributive comparisons (distributions *among* nations), but on intra-national comparisons (distributions *within* a nation). Hence Rawls's principles have important application, even when inter-national distributive comparisons are excluded. In saying that the economically least well off of a third world country ought not suffer as a result of a loan arrangement, we are not making a claim about the distribution of resources among all nations of the world, but only about the distribution of a single country's resources.

Second, the mere existence of an international loan arrangement is not only testimony to a cooperative endeavor, but representative of an underlying economic association in which at least the developed and probably also the developing countries benefit. For the developed world to be left without benefit of the commodities and markets provided by the developing countries would certainly be an economic blow. While the relationship may not be one of absolute dependence, extreme dependence is not required by the concept of the conditions of justice. And certainly no representative of the IMF has ever suggested that the IMF's activities qualify as *pure* charity, that is, charity of a kind such that the developed nations expect no benefits from virtue of their association. This, in turn, implies a satisfaction of the first condition of justice and the relevance of the concept of distributive justice.

It follows that at least insofar as one accepts Rawls's claim that distributive justice entails the principle that no inequality promoting policy is just if it has the effect of failing to aid the worst off class of person, i.e., the "second principle," then no policy affecting a developing country can be labeled just that makes the economically least well off worse off. Hence, any loan arrangement entered into by the World Bank, the IMF, or any other intergovernmental lending agency which has the effect of increasing the poverty of the very poor in a third world country would fail to satisfy the Rawlsian test of distributive justice.

MORAL CONSISTENCY

The final consideration supporting the proposition under consideration invokes the notion of moral consistency. In particular, I am concerned with the tendency of the international lending agencies to insist on the absolute sovereignty of nation states, especially with respect to the issue of the distributive impact of loan arrangements, and the way such an insistence relates to other accepted policies.

Consider, for example, the widely shared conviction among representatives of global lending agencies that the absence of a European or U.S. style government, including even the absence of a truly democratic government, is insufficient to prohibit such loans and moral grounds. That is, almost every international lending agency agrees that a nation ought not be blacklisted from lending simply for reason of nondemocratic practice. The rationale, sometimes explicit, sometimes implicit, turns on the obvious prospect of benefiting those subject to non-democratic rule even through an arrangement with the rulers themselves. The ruled may benefit even though they did not voluntarily engage in the agreement. . . . The justification of lending to non-democratic regimes presumes that lending agencies can fathom the differ-

ence between the interests of the rulers and the ruled, and act accordingly. If so, then there is no reason why they cannot act accordingly also with respect to the issue of distributive justice.

This brings us again to the irony presented at the beginning of the article, namely, why if, as creditor institutions claim, the austerity typically associated with such conditionality is in the interest of the borrowing country, why then does the borrower so often object to it? Again, one would expect a debtor to pay for good advice, not to be enticed to accept it. The answer here, as above, lies in noting that the politicians who contract for loans are not the same persons as those who must suffer or succeed under the loans' conditions, and, as already noted, this distinction is inconsistent with a full reliance on the rationality of decisions made by national governments.

Indeed, the argument that concerns of justice are the exclusive territory of debtor country governments is inconsistent at a still deeper level. Even if we regard international lending arrangements as purely voluntary transactions between consenting parties and leave aside the issue of the contracting rights of governments in contrast to the people they govern, the stipulation of a condition by one party in a proposed voluntary agreement is never regarded as an invasion of the freedom or sovereignty of the other party — since, of course, the other party can voluntarily reject the condition and refuse to engage in the transaction. This is precisely why the loan conditions that are so commonly inserted in international arrangements, i.e., of reducing price controls and inducing monetary restraint, are *not* regarded as a violation of sovereignty. Ordinarily, fiscal policy is regarded as the proper and exclusive province of a sovereign government. The reason why we may not regard the fiscal policy conditions of IMF adjustment agreements to be in violation of national sovereignty is that such conditions are the features of a voluntary statement of reciprocal intent between two sovereign, free agents. But clearly it would be inconsistent to proceed to argue that restrictions on the distributive impact of a given loan arrangement, when set as a condition by an international lending agency to a loan arrangement, violates the national sovereignty of the borrowing country. One cannot have matters both ways.

CONCLUSION

It may be argued that the proposition under consideration *would* be acceptable were it not for the phrase "even in the short to medium term." If the economically least well off must suffer today in order to benefit tomorrow, then how can justice and moral consistency condemn the requisite "medicine"? But this rhetorical question, which poses a hypothetical state of affairs, is misleading, and truth in this instance does not accommodate our hypotheses. First, there is insufficient reason to believe that the economically least well off *must* suffer now in order to achieve their own long term improvement. A social cushion for the poor in austerity programs is an acceptable, much analyzed option. Nor is there any reason to believe that preventing the very poor in the short to medium term from suffering more than they would have in the absence of a loan agreement will shipwreck the future prospects of an adjustment program.

Short term injustice would be more tempting — though even then not justified — if optimistic economic predictions were certain and incorrigible. If we knew for certain that the economically least well off could *only* benefit in the long-term by suffering in the short term, and that the policies that caused them to suffer would *without question* bring long term benefits, our welfare calculations would be different. Yet, even modern economic theory has not reached the point where it allows epistemological certainty about such propositions in individual cases. We cannot predict with absolute certainty that adjustment programs of a certain kind, whether free market or other, will in a given instance deliver the desired result.

For example, it is doubtful that pricist extremists are right when they say that if only prices could be left to market forces, everything would be fine, and that, in turn, no independent public sector action would be necessary. As Paul Streeten notes, even if prices were allowed to rise to a "natural" level in Tanzania, farmers would not benefit by producing more. In Tanzania, roads are so inadequate that even if farmers produced more in response to higher prices, the crops could not be transported.[15] The problem is one of infrastructure, not prices, and the cooperation of the public authority is essential. . . .

It is also well to remember that justice is not a concept admitting of short-term or long-term qualifications. The logic of the concept of justice does not allow one to trade off justice here for justice there, or to trade off justice now for justice later. If an act or policy is unjust, it must not be undertaken. And it must not be undertaken either now or in the future. . . .

NOTES

1. Irving S. Friedman, "The International Monetary Fund: A Founder's Evaluation," in *The Political Morality of the International Monetary Fund. Ethics and Foreign Policy* (New York: Transaction Books) ed., Robert J. Myers, Vol. 3 (1987), pp. 21–22.

2. Henry B. Schechter, "IMF Conditionality and the International Economy: A U.S. Labor Perspective," in *The Political Morality of the International Monetary Fund. Ethics and Foreign Policy* (New York: Transaction Books) ed., Robert J. Myers, Vol. 3 (1987), p. 5.

3. John Williamson, "Reforming the IMF: Different or Better?" in *The Political Morality of the International Monetary Fund. Ethics and Foreign Policy* (New York: Transaction Books) ed., Robert J. Myers, Vol. 3 (1987).

4. Special concern for the poor is evident in the U.S. Catholic Conference Administrative Board in its "Statement on Relieving Third World Debt," *Origins* (October 12, 1989), Vol. 19, 1, 307–314.

5. Chile, the Dominican Republic, Bhana, Kenya, the Philippines, Sri Lanka, and Thailand.

6. Peter Heller, "Fund-Supported Adjustment Programs and the Poor." *Finance & Development* (Washington: The World Bank, December, 1988), pp. 2–5. See also the original study, i.e., Peter S. Heller, A. Lans Bovenberg, Thanos Catsambas, *et al.*, "The Implications of Fund-Supported Adjustment Programs for Poverty: Experiences in Selected Countries" (Washington: International Monetary Fund, May, 1988).

7. Heller, Bovenberg, Catsambas, *et al.,* p. 32.

8. Scott R. Sidell, *The IMF and Third-World Political Instability. Is There a Connection?* (London: The MacMillan Press Ltd., 1988).

9. See especially Thomas Donaldson, *The Ethics of International Business* (New York: Oxford University Press, 1989), chapter 5.

10. Henry Shue, *Basic Rights: Subsistence, Affluence, and U.S. Foreign Policy* (Princeton, NJ: Princeton University Press, 1980), p. 57.

11. Shue, pp. 20–23.

12. John Rawls, *A Theory of Justice* (Cambridge, MA: Harvard University Press, 1971).

13. *Ibid.,* pp. 126–28.

14. Brian Barry, "The Case for a New International Economic Order," in J. Roland Pennock and John W. Chapman, eds., *Ethics, Economics, and the Law: Nomos Vol. XXIV* (New York: New York University Press, 1982).

15. Paul Streeten, "Structural Adjustment: A Survey of the Issues and Options." *World Development* (Boston University) 15 (12) (Pergamon Journals Ltd., 1987), p. 1474.

LEGAL PERSPECTIVES

Law of the Sea and the Common Heritage Principle

Thomas M. Franck

The resources of the seas and seabed have long obsessed humanity and ideas of distributive justice have always featured in discourse about those resources. At various times "justice as fairness" has been expressed in terms of "first come, first served;" in terms of allocational sharing based on technology, proximity, need, or a mixture of all three; in terms of property (the sea as a prolongation of land); and most recently on the "common heritage principle" (CHP) which treats a resource as exploitable in common, or preserved in perpetuity for all. Such terms as *res nostrum, res nullius,* and *res communis* mark differences in notions of fairness deployed at various times to justify distributive systems.

The claim that seas, like territory, could be subject to national sovereignty — *mare nostrum* — was widely accepted in the fifteenth century. A Papal Bull permitted the two

From Thomas M. Franck, *Fairness in International Law and Institutions* (Oxford: Clarendon Press, 1995).

then-dominant Iberian naval powers to divide the seas between them. This territorial-sovereignty approach was challenged by the newer (and predominantly non-Catholic) naval aspirants — Britain and Holland — and, most persuasively, by the young Hugo Grotius, who as lawyer for the Dutch East India Company published his advocacy of *Mare Liberum*. . . . The Grotian principle of *res nullius* prevailed. This meant that for 300 years a general maritime acquiescence developed in the idea that the seas and its fisheries were equally accessible to all nations capable of sailing and fishing, and in that sense fish and seas were a "common" resource, at least beyond the relatively narrow band — normally three miles wide, the proverbial "canon-ball trajectory" — of coastal jurisdiction. In this historic ascendancy of *mare liberum* over *mare nostrum*, however, no thought was given to the resources of the ocean floor and subsoil which were still beyond the dreams of even the most acquisitive imagination.

By the end of World War II, however, thinking began to change radically, in part because of technological development and also because, after the demonstration of recently perfected naval and submarine warfare, states perceived their security to depend on assured access to resources available in adjacent seas. Chile, responding to its wartime shortage of fats and oils, established an aggressive whaling industry and proclaimed an exclusive 200-mile whaling zone off its coast, thereby barring the traditional harvesters of Norway and Japan. This precedent was soon followed by Peru and Ecuador which extended it to fisheries in general. Iceland, asserting its special dependence and historic usage, waged a "cod war" against British fishing fleets in what had traditionally been international waters. The issue eventually came before the International Court. Most important, perhaps, was the attempt by the United States between 1945 and 1946 to claim an ex-

clusive right to exploit resources (primarily petroleum) of the sea bed of its continental shelf. The "Truman Proclamation" claimed the shelf was an extension of the land-mass, and argued that it was therefore "reasonable and just" that the coastal state should have the same exclusive rights of exploitation as on its own sovereign land-mass, albeit without actually asserting any change in the *mare liberum* status of superadjacent waters. When other states failed to object and began to follow suit, sensing the importance of their own shelves, the area of *res nullius* — and, particularly, of exploitable *res nullius* — began to shrink dramatically, a shrinkage soon recognized by customary and conventional law.

Against this background of creeping seaclaims, challenging *res nullius'* long predominance over *res nostrum*, a reaction was inevitable. The only surprise is that this did not take the form of a counter-attack in favor of Grotius' *mare liberum*, but rather consisted of an entirely new fairness claim, one better suited than *res nullius* to express the aspirations of those states (whose numbers were increased by decolonization) with little or no coastline, or lacking significant coastal shelves, and without navigational and technological means to engage in long-distance fishing and deep-sea mining.

The new fairness-based notion of *res communis* was first advanced in 1967 by Malta's Foreign Minister, Dr. Arvid Pardo, who proposed a new item for consideration by the UN General Assembly entitled: "Declaration and Treaty Concerning the Reservation Exclusively for Peaceful Purposes of the Sea-bed and of the Ocean Floor, Underlying the Seas beyond the Limits of Present National Jurisdiction, and the Uses of Their Resources in the Interests of Mankind." That initiative ushered in an entirely new fairness discourse.

In what sense is the concept of *res communis* a manifestation of global fairness? Indirectly, the concept endorses the value of fairness by advancing the sense of community which, as we have noted, is a *sine qua non* of all useful fairness discourse. It does this by proposing both a notion of common title (CHP) and a legitimate institutional regime for allocating or preserving the property held in common.

It also advanced notions of distributive justice. The notion of *res communis* does not of itself determine distributional outcomes, the allocation of goods. But CHP does increase the 'shareholders' in the resource and thereby broadens participation in the process of governance by which distributive and conservational decisions about the resource are made. Even states which lack the technology, finances, or other indicators of capability to explore and exploit the communal resource and which are not geographically situated to extend their land jurisdiction seaward, are shareholders in the *res communis*. The CHP thus promotes the possibility of genuine fairness discourse by increasing the number of parties entitled to participate in it.

Three years after the General Assembly's Declaration based on Dr. Pardo's initiative, just before the beginning of the decade-long negotiations for a new, comprehensive law of the sea treaty, the General Assembly unanimously proposed a new concept in global re-

alty law. It declared that the "sea-bed and ocean floor, and the subsoil thereof, beyond the limits of national jurisdiction . . . as well as the resources of the area, are the common heritage of mankind."[1] Moreover, it was declared, that the area and its resources "shall not be subject to appropriation by any means by States or persons"[2] except in accordance with an "international regime to be established."[3] This regime was to ensure that "exploration of the area and . . . its resources shall be carried out for the benefit of mankind as a whole, irrespective of the geographical location of States, whether landlocked or coastal, and taking into particular consideration the interests and needs of the developing countries."[4] With that, an altogether new fairness discourse was launched in which all states could participate, advancing claims and values, incorporating notions of equal entitlement modified by distributive justice.

NOTES

1. GA Res. 2749 (XXV), Dec. 17, 1970, Art. 1.
2. Ibid., Art. 2.
3. Ibid., Art. 3.
4. Ibid., Art. 7.

CASES

CASE 1. *Baseball Economics*

In December 1981, the Baltimore Orioles Hall-of-Fame pitcher Jim Palmer gave a newspaper interview in Portland, Oregon. He was highly critical of the system of economic incentives operative in baseball. He argued that

money controlled almost all decisions by management and players alike. Many players, he said, "make a lot more money than they should." He argued that the salaries are often determined through "panic" on the part of

This case was prepared by Tom L. Beauchamp and Jeff Greene, using articles from numerous newspapers and journals.

management, which plans at all cost against a situation in which star players leave and join other teams at increased salary levels. He noted that players make $300,000 to $400,000 in their second year and sign multi-year contracts. This kind of security, he said, leads players to relax and to lose their concentration on skilled performance.

On the same day Palmer gave his interview in Portland, Baseball Commissioner Bowie Kuhn was testifying before a Congressional subcommittee on issues surrounding the costs of cable television. Kuhn described the possible introduction of massive cable television broadcasts of baseball as economically intolerable for the sport. Both gate receipts and network television revenues would decline, he held, and this would be a disaster for a sport already "treading on financial quicksand." Kuhn supported this judgment with figures to show that only nine of baseball's twenty-six teams had made a profit in the previous year. He argued that the aggregate loss was $25 million. He further contended that cable television would bring competing sporting events into a city without the consent or agreement of anyone in baseball management.

Ted Turner, who owns both Turner Broadcasting System (cable) and the Atlanta Braves baseball team, also testified at the same hearing as Kuhn. "If baseball is in trouble," he said, "it is because they are paying the [superstar] baseball players a million and half dollars a year. . . . There isn't one single example of a proven economic harm from cable television."

Salaries have continued to rise dramatically. A survey of New York Mets' baseball fans in 1992 indicted that most thought the salary figures outrageous and that the money should be more evenly spread across the players. In 1995, fourteen years after Palmer's interview and this testimony before Congress, players' salaries had escalated beyond what

Palmer, Kuhn, or Turner could have then imagined. The New York Yankees led the league with a record-breaking payroll of $58.1 million. For the 1995 season, the average player's salary was over $1.2 million. Frank Thomas of the Chicago White Sox and Ken Griffey, Jr of the Seattle Mariners were both making over $7 million dollars for the season. The Toronto Blue Jays not only were giving $8 million dollars to David Cone, but also were paying Joe Carter $7.5 million for his services. Finally, the Detroit Tigers were paying slugger Cecil Fielder a whopping $9.2 million to lead a team low in the standings and in gate receipts.

With the explosion of salaries it has become harder and harder for the small market teams to compete, because the big players consistently go for big money. However, in 1994 the Montreal Expos proved, at least for that season, that in some cases more than just money matters. Their $18.6 million payroll was the second lowest in the league, yet when the season ended (because of a strike), they were six games ahead of everyone in the National League, including the Atlanta Braves. However, their dream season would be short-lived because they needed approximately $30 million merely to keep the team together, according to fair market value. Since the club could not even come close to the $30 million figure, it was inevitable that it would lose many of its best players; and it did. "I think that the world realizes that our market cannot support that sort of payroll," said Bill Stoneman, Expos' vice president of baseball operations. "We'd like to re-sign all of our players, but we'd like to be in business a year from now."

Montreal's problem is not unique. Pittsburgh had to break up one of the National League's best teams in the 1990s, and San Diego had to dump its best talent just as the club seemed poised to become a serious contender. It now seems clear that if some sort of revenue sharing does not come into effect, the small market teams will not be able to compete on equal terms.

Questions

1. Does a team like the New York Yankees have an obligation to share some of their revenues with other teams that have a weaker economic base?

2. Do Bowie Kuhn's comments reflect a libertarian or a utilitarian theory of justice?

3. If Peter Singer's proposals (in this chapter) were followed, what would be the obligations of major league baseball players to help the poor both within and outside their own country?

CASE 2.   *Enron and Dabhol Power*

Shortage of electric power is a chronic problem in India. As a consequence, the state government of Maharashtra eventually gave permission to Enron Corporation to build Dabhol Power plant, south of Mumbai, in a joint venture with General Electric, Bechtel Corporation, and the Maharashtra State Electric Board. The United States government actively lobbied for and helped to finance Dabhol Power, which will be the world's largest electricity plant.

In 1997, residents of villages near the construction site of Dabhol Power plant began to protest. The National Alliance of People's Movements has alleged that the state government seized land without compensation. Moreover, activists believe that Dabhol Power will cause serious damage to the environment.

Enron Corporation paid state police to provide security for Dabhol Power. In response to peaceful acts of civil disobedience,

the state police have beaten protesters (especially women), arbitrarily arrested them, and have violated their right of *habeas corpus*. According to Justice Daud, a retired judge of the Mumbai High Court, "In the name of maintaining law and order, they have . . . prevented all forms of peaceful and democratic protest, used force and violence while dealing with all forms of nonviolent protest, and resorted to a number of other subtle means of harassment of agitators."

Questions

1. What arguments about justice can support Enron's construction of Dabhol Power? What arguments can argue against the construction of Dabhol Power?

2. What moral rights of protesters were violated? Who bears moral responsibility for violating those rights?

This case was prepared by Padma Shah based on *Enron Corporation: Corporate Complicity in Human Rights Violations* (Human Rights Watch, 1999); "Enron Enrages Indians" by Amitabh Pal, *Progressive* (November 1997); "Enron's Abuse of Power" by Nityanand Jayaraman, *Multinational Monitor* (September 1997).

CASE 3:   *South Africa and Pharmaceutical Companies*

In 1997, South Africa passed a law designed to allow South Africa's estimated six million HIV-positive patients affordable access to chemotherapeutic agents such as zidovudine. The legislation permitted two trade practices. First, it allowed importing of drugs from the international Agray market. That is, drugs could be imported from the cheapest available source, even if a source was not licensed by the holder of a drug's patent. Second, the law allowed compulsory licensing of drugs. Under this provision, the South African government was permitted to render manufacturing licenses to domestic pharmaceutical companies without the approval of a drug's patent holder.

This form of importing and compulsory licensing are permitted by the World Trade Organization (WTO) under certain conditions. However, more than forty major pharmaceutical companies based in the United States, South Africa, and Europe vehemently objected to the new legislation. The companies claimed that the law would violate their intellectual property rights. Consequently, drug manufacturers filed a lawsuit against the South African government, and, thereby, temporarily blocked implementation of the law. Additionally, they lobbied the United

States Congress and the White House to pressure South Africa to repeal the drug legislation.

The pharmaceutical companies eventually suspended their legal action against South Africa and sought a negotiated settlement. South Africa and the United States reached an understanding that South Africa would adhere to WTO rules that regulate parallel importing and compulsory licensing. In exchange, the United States would drop its demands that the two trade practices be eased.

Questions

1. What theoretical principles of justice would support South Africa's trade legislation? What principles would support the objections of pharmaceutical manufacturers?

2. How would DeGeorge critique the process whereby the United States and the pharamaceutical companies reached, or sought to reach, an agreement with South Africa?

3. Are trade rules crafted by the nonelected World Trade Organization just or unjust?

This case was prepared by Padma Shah based on articles in the *New York Times* (September 10, 1999), A3; (September 18, 1999), A8; *Wall Street Journal* (September 20, 1999), B6; and *Washington Post* (September 18, 1999), A11.

CASE 4.   *Cocaine at the Fortune-500 Level*

Roberto, a pure libertarian in moral and political philosophy, is deeply impressed by his reading of Robert Nozick's account of justice. He lives in Los Angeles and teaches philosophy at a local university. Roberto is also a frequent user of cocaine, which he enjoys immensely and provides to friends at parties. Neither he nor any of his close friends is addicted. Over the years Roberto has become tired of teaching philosophy and now has an opportunity, through old friends who live in Peru, to become a middleman in the cocaine business. Although he is disturbed about the effects cocaine has on some persons, he has never witnessed these effects firsthand. He is giving his friends' business offer serious consideration.

Roberto's research has told him the following: Selling cocaine is a $29 billion plus industry. Although he is interested primarily in a Peruvian connection, his research has shown conclusively that the Colombian cartel alone is large enough to place it among the Fortune 500 corporations. Between 0.75 and 1.1 million jobs in Colombia, Bolivia, and Peru combined are in the cocaine industry — over 5 percent of the entire work force in these countries. These figures are roughly comparable to the dollar and work force figures for the diamond industry throughout the world.

Peruvian President Alan Garcia once described cocaine as Latin America's "only successful multinational." It can be and has been analyzed in traditional business categories, with its own entrepreneurs, chemists, laboratories, employment agencies, small organizations, distribution systems, market giants, growth phases, and so forth. Cocaine's profit margins have narrowed in some markets, while expanding in others. It often seeks new markets in order to expand its product line. For example, in the mid-1980s "crack" — a potent form of smoked cocaine — was moved heavily into new markets in Europe. Between the mid-1960s and the 1990s the demand for cocaine grew dramatically because of successful supply and marketing. Middlemen in Miami and Los Angeles were established to increase already abundant profits. Heavy investments were made in airplanes, efficient modes of production, training managers, and regular schedules of distribution. In the late 1980s there was a downturn in cocaine consumption after the deaths of two prominent athletes. In the early 1990s the market recovered slightly before again slipping in the mid-1990s. However, cocaine remains an enormously powerful industry in many countries.

Roberto sees the cocaine industry as not being subject to taxes, tariffs, or government regulations other than those pertaining to its illegality. It is a pure form of the free market in which supply and demand control transactions. This fact about the business appeals to Roberto, as it seems perfectly suited to his libertarian views. He is well aware that there are severe problems of coercion and violence in some parts of the industry, but he is certain that the wealthy clientele whom he would supply in Los Angeles would neither abuse the drug nor redistribute it to others who might be harmed. Roberto is confident that his Peruvian associates are honorable and that he can escape problems of violence, coercion, and abusive marketing. However, he has just read a newspaper story that cocaine-use emergencies — especially those involving

---

This case was prepared by Tom L. Beauchamp and updated by Jeff Greene, based on accounts in *The Wall Street Journal* and *The Economist*.

cocaine-induced heart attacks — have tripled in the last five years. It is only this fact that has given him pause before deciding to enter the cocaine business. He views these health emergencies as unfortunate but not unfair outcomes of the business. Therefore, it is his humanity and not his theory of justice that gives him pause.

Questions

1. Would a libertarian — as Roberto thinks — say that the cocaine business is not unfair so long as no coercion is involved and the system is a pure function of supply and demand?

2. Does justice demand that cocaine be outlawed, or is this not a matter of justice at all? Are questions of justice even meaningful when the activity is beyond the boundaries of law?

3. Is the distinction Roberto draws between what is unfortunate and what is unfair relevant to a decision about whether an activity is just?

CASE 5.   *Covering the Costs of Health Care*

Medicare and Medicaid were passed into law in the United States to provide coverage for health care costs in populations that could not afford adequate coverage, especially the elderly, poor, and disabled. Then, as now, health care technology produced by major corporations was rapidly being developed and costs were skyrocketing. In 1994, $140 billion was spent on Medicare. Current trends show little letup in this explosion of costs. In 1994 Medicare and Medicaid comprised 16.4% of the total federal budget. By the year 2003 this figure is expected to balloon to approximately 26.4%. Total national expenditures on health care costs in the United States for 1994 were 14% of the Gross Domestic Product. For U.S. corporations and individuals, health care has become a burdensome expense.

With over 37.4 million Americans uninsured, health care costs have been under intense study by many politicians and agencies. In an effort to limit future increases in physician costs, the Omnibus Budget Reconcilia-

tion Act of 1989 created a Medicare Fee Schedule that affected 34.7 million U.S. citizens. This schedule attempts to redistribute payments across specialties in medicine and geographic areas of the country. The legislation called for this restructuring to be phased in over a five-year period from 1992 to 1996. In passing the legislation, members of Congress agreed that Medicare's former payment policies fueled unacceptable increases in expenditure for health care services. Neither the old legislation nor the new covers the kind of catastrophic illness that can wipe out a family's assets and put a family in lifetime debt.

It has been demonstrated that there is substantial variation across the United States in payment rates for services. Urban, specialist, and in-patient services are typically much higher than rural, generalist, and ambulatory services. Surgeons make more money than those in other specialties. It has been widely agreed that these differentials are independent of quality of services, depending more

---

This case was prepared by Tom L. Beauchamp and Jeff Greene.

on urban location, the high costs of specialists, and the like. A large supply of physicians in a single location does not stimulate competition and drive prices down; instead, higher fees for physician services tend to be the norm. Social scientists who have studied the changes made in the Omnibus Budget Reconciliation Act of 1989 predict that large redistributions of Medicare payments among specialties will occur, thus changing long-standing patterns in physicians' salaries.

When Bill Clinton came into office, he promised major reforms in the health care system. The Clinton plan, headed by first lady Hillary Clinton, attempted to steer the nation towards serious health care reform. The idea was to eliminate waste and inflated prices, and to give health care access to all — so-called universal access. However, with many of the economic consequences falling on the business community, the Clinton plan met strong criticism. Private interests spent over $300 million and Republicans fought hard to kill the bill, and they succeeded.

Many believed that the Clinton plan did not adequately handle the primary reason for continued increases in health care costs, namely advances in technology that push the growth of costs in the health care industry much higher than costs in the rest of the economy. Consider a typical case, involving a man named Toney Kincard. For ten years he was tortured by over six hundred seizures a week. Kincard was unable to carry on a conversation, eat dinner with his family, or even shower unsupervised. Despite thousands of dollars spent in drug therapy, he lost both his job and his driver's license. In 1989 he became the second person to try a new product, the Vogus Nerve Stimulator. Since his $50,000 outlay to receive this product, he has been seizure-free and says, "The stimulator was the best thing that happened to my life. It was worth everything it cost."

There is little doubt that such expensive technology is invaluable for improving the lives of many people. However, these products will continue to drive up the price of health care for everyone. If antibiotics had never been discovered, many people would die of pneumonia; now they receive antibiotics and then will die later of a costlier disease. Another example is the discovery in 1980 of the drug cyclosporine, which prevents the body's immune system from rejecting organ transplants. In 1980 the number of liver transplants totalled 15; however, with the help of cyclosporine, this figure jumped to 3,056 in 1992, at a minimum price of $200,000 per transplant. Experts believe that advances in molecular biology and genetic therapy, among many other technologies, will continue to propel the cost of health care in the future. Unless access to high-cost, life-extending technology is rationed, health care costs will continue to increase rapidly.

Questions

1. Is a nation obligated to provide quality health care for the elderly who otherwise could not afford care? Is the obligation unrelated to the ability to pay?

2. Should health care be distributed purely on a free-market basis? Should everyone have access to even the highest priced procedures?

3. Is Medicare justifiable on either utilitarian or egalitarian premises of justice?

4. Would a communitarian approve of Medicare even if he or she did not think the system comprehensive enough? Are libertarians and communitarians necessarily in opposition on the question of state-supported systems of health care coverage?

5. Is it better to extend one person's life a few months at the cost of $200,000 or to spend the money on preventive health care measures such as immunization shots?

Suggested Supplementary Readings

Concepts and Principles of Justice

BEAUCHAMP, TOM L. *Philosophical Ethics.* 3rd ed. New York: McGraw-Hill, 2001. Chaps. 8–9.

CAMPBELL, TOM. *Justice.* London: Macmillan, 1988.

DEGEORGE, RICHARD T. "International Business Ethics." *Business Ethics Quarterly* 4 (1994): 1–9.

FEINBERG, JOEL. "Justice and Personal Desert." In *Nomos 6: Justice,* edited by Carl J. Friedrich and John W. Chapman. New York: Atherton Press, 1963.

JOHNSTON, DAVID. "Is the Idea of Social Justice Meaningful?" *Critical Revue* 11 (1997): 607–14.

KIPNIS, KENNETH, and DIANA T. MEYERS. *Economic Justice.* Totowa, NJ: Rowman and Allanheld, 1985.

KYMLICKA, WILL, ed. *Justice in Political Philosophy: Schools of Thought in Politics.* (2 vols.) Brookfield, VT: Ashgate, 1992.

MILLER, RICHARD. *Moral Differences: Truth, Justice, and Conscience in a World of Conflict.* Princeton: Princeton University Press, 1992.

NAGEL, THOMAS. *Equality and Partiality.* New York: Oxford University Press, 1991.

SEN, AMARTYA. "Economics, Business Principles and Moral Sentiments." *Business Ethics Quarterly* 7 (1997): 5–15.

SOLOMON, ROBERT C., ed. *What Is Justice? Classic and Contemporary Readings.* New York: Oxford University Press, 1990.

STERBA, JAMES P. *Justice for Here and Now.* New York: Cambridge University Press, 1998.

STEWART, ROBERT M., ed. *Readings in Social and Political Philosophy.* New York: Oxford University Press, 1996.

Egalitarian Theories

BARRY, BRIAN. *Theories of Justice.* Berkeley: University of California Press, 1989.

CHRISTMAN, JOHN P. *The Myth of Property: Toward an Egalitarian Theory of Ownership.* New York: Oxford University Press, 1994.

COHEN, G. A. "Where the Action Is: On the Site of Distributive Justice." *Philosophy and Public Affairs* 26 (1997): 3–30.

DANIELS, NORMAN, ed. *Reading Rawls: Critical Studies of a Theory of Justice.* New York: Basic Books, 1975.

KANE, JOHN. "Justice, Impartiality, and Equality: Why the Concept of Justice Does Not Presume Equality." *Political Theory* 24 (1996): 375–93.

NAGEL, THOMAS. "Equality." In *Mortal Questions.* Cambridge, England: Cambridge University Press, 1979.

OKIN, SUSAN. *Justice, Gender, and the Family.* New York: Basic Books, 1989.

POGGE, THOMAS W. "An Egalitarian Law of Peoples." *Philosophy and Public Affairs* 23 (Summer 1994): 195–224.

POGGE, THOMAS W. *Realizing Rawls.* Ithaca, NY: Cornell University Press, 1991.

POJMAN, LOUIS, and ROBERT WESTMORELAND, eds. *Equality: Selected Readings.* New York: Oxford University Press, 1997.

RAWLS, JOHN. "Reply to Alexander and Musgrave." *Quarterly Journal of Economics* 88 (1974): 633–55.

ROEMER, JOHN E. *Theories of Distributive Justice.* Cambridge, MA: Harvard University Press, 1996.

SEN, AMARTYA. *On Economic Inequality.* Oxford: Clarendon Press, 1997.

Libertarian Theories

BOAZ, DAVID. *The Libertarian Reader: Classic and Contemporary Readings.* New York: The Free Press, 1997.

ENGELHARDT, H. TRISTRAM JR. *The Foundations of Bioethics.* 2nd ed. New York: Oxford University Press, 1996.

FRIED, BARBARA. "Wilt Chamberlain Revisited: Nozick's 'Justice in Transfer' and the Problem of Market-Based Distribution." *Philosophy and Public Affairs* 24 (1995): 226–45.

FRIEDMAN, MILTON. *Capitalism and Freedom.* Chicago: University of Chicago Press, 1962.

HAYEK, FRIEDRICH. *Individualism and Economic Order.* Chicago: University of Chicago Press, 1948.

————. *The Mirage of Social Justice.* Vol. 2, *Law, Legislation, and Liberty.* Chicago: University of Chicago Press, 1976.

MACK, ERIC. "Liberty and Justice." In *Justice and Economic Distribution,* edited by John Arthur and William Shaw. Englewood Cliffs, NJ: Prentice Hall, 1978.

MACHAN, TIBOR R., and DOUGLAS B. RASMUSSEN, eds. *Liberty for the Twenty-First Century: Contemporary Libertarian Thought.* Lanham, MD: Rowman and Littlefield, 1995.

PAUL, JEFFREY, ed. *Reading Nozick.* Totowa, NJ: Rowman and Littlefield, 1981.

PERRY, STEPHEN R. "Libertarianism, Entitlement, and Responsibility." *Philosophy and Public Affairs* 26 (1997): 351–396.

Utilitarian Theories

ALLISON, LINCOLN, ed. *The Utilitarian Response: Essays on the Contemporary Viability of Utilitarian Political Philosophy.* London: Sage, 1990.

ARNESON, RICHARD J. "Liberalism, Distributive Subjectivism, and Equal Opportunity for Welfare." *Philosophy and Public Affairs* 19 (1990): 158–94.

FREY, R. G., ed. *Utility and Rights.* Minneapolis: University of Minnesota Press, 1984.

GOLDMAN, ALAN H. "Business Ethics: Profits, Utilities, and Moral Rights." *Philosophy and Public Affairs* 9 (1980): 260–86.

GRIFFIN, JAMES. *Well-Being: Its Meaning, Measurement, and Importance.* Oxford, England: Clarendon Press, 1986.

HARDIN, RUSSELL. *Morality within the Limits of Reason.* Chicago: University of Chicago Press, 1988.

HARSANYI, JOHN C. "Equality, Responsibility, and Justice as Seen from a Utilitarian Perspective." *Theory and Decision* 31 (1991): 141–58.

———. "Rule Utilitarianism, Equality, and Justice." *Social Philosophy and Policy* 2 (1985): 115–27.

POSNER, RICHARD A. *The Economics of Justice.* 2nd ed. Cambridge, MA: Harvard University Press, 1983.

SEN, AMARTYA, and BERNARD WILLIAMS, eds. *Utilitarianism and Beyond.* Cambridge, England: Cambridge University Press, 1982.

Communitarian Theories

AVINERI, SHLOMO, and AVNER DE-SHALIT, eds. *Communitarianism and Individualism.* Oxford, England: Oxford University Press, 1992.

BELL, DANIEL A. *Communitarianism and Its Critics.* Oxford, England: Clarendon Press, 1993.

BUCHANAN, ALLEN. "Assessing the Communitarian Critique of Liberalism." *Ethics* 99 (1989).

FREEDEN, MICHAEL. "Human Rights and Welfare: A Communitarian View." *Ethics* 100 (1990).

GUTMANN, AMY. "Communitarian Critics of Liberalism." *Philosophy and Public Affairs* 14 (1985).

KYMLICKA, WILL. *Liberalism, Community, and Culture.* Oxford, England: Clarendon Press, 1989.

MACINTYRE, ALASDAIR. *Whose Justice? Which Rationality?* Notre Dame, IN: Notre Dame University Press, 1988.

RASMUSSEN, DAVID, ed. *Universalism vs. Communitarianism: Contemporary Debates in Ethics.* Cambridge, MA: MIT Press, 1990.

ROSENBLUM, NANCY L., ed. *Liberalism and the Moral Life.* Cambridge, MA: Harvard University Press, 1989.

SANDEL, MICHAEL J. *Democracy's Discontent: America in Search of a Public Philosophy.* Cambridge, MA: Harvard University Press, 1996.

———. "Democrats and Community." *The New Republic* (February 22, 1988).

WALZER, MICHAEL. "The Communitarian Critique of Liberalism." *Political Theory* 18 (1990).

Issues in International Markets and Social Policy

ATTFIELD, ROBIN, and BARRY WILKINS, eds. *International Justice and the Third World.* New York: Routledge, 1992.

BOWIE, NORMAN. "Fair Markets." *Journal of Business Ethics* 7 (1988).

BUCHANAN, ALLEN. *Ethics, Efficiency and the Market.* Totowa, NJ: Rowman and Allanheld, 1985.

COPP, DAVID. "The Right to an Adequate Standard of Living: Justice, Autonomy, and the Basic Needs." *Social Philosophy and Policy* 9 (Winter 1992): 231–61.

EHRENBERG, RONALD G., and GEORGE H. JAKUBSON. "Why Warn? Plant Closing Legislation." *Regulation* 13 (Summer 1990).

"Note: Resurrecting Economic Rights: The Doctrine of Economic Due Process Reconsidered." *Harvard Law Review* 103 (1990).

JACKSON, KEVIN T. "Global Distributive Justice and the Corporate Duty to Aid." *Journal of Business Ethics* 12 (1993): 547–52.

KINIKI, ANGELO, and Others. "Socially Responsible Plant Closings." *Personnel Administrator* 32 (1987).

KOVACH, KENNETH A., and PETER E. MILLSPAUGH. "Plant Closings." *Business Horizons* 30 (March–April 1987).

LIPPKE, RICHARD L. "Justice and Insider Trading." *Journal of Applied Philosophy* 10 (1993): 215–26.

LUPER-FOY, STEVEN. "Justice and Natural Resources." *Environmental Values* 1 (Spring 1992): 47–64.

——— . *Problems of International Justice.* Boulder, CO: Westview Press, 1988.

MILLSPAUGH, PETER E. "Plant Closing Ethics Root in American Law." *Journal of Business Ethics* 9 (August 1990).

NOWLIN, WILLIAM A., and GEORGE M. SULLIVAN. "The Plant Closing Law: Worker Protection or Government Interference?" *Industrial Management* 31 (November–December 1989).

PRATT, CORNELIUS B. "Multinational Corporate Social Policy Process for Ethical Responsibility in Sub-Saharan Africa." *Journal of Business Ethics* 10 (July 1991): 527–41.

SPINELLO, RICHARD A. "Ethics, Pricing and the Pharmaceutical Industry." *Journal of Business Ethics* 11 (August 1992): 617–26.

STEINER, HILLEL. "Three Just Taxes." In *Arguing for Basic Income,* edited by Philippe Van Parijs. New York: Verso, 1992.